Martin Powalla
55 St-Sylvestre #307
Longueuil
J4H 2W1
# 442-0252

# INVESTMENTS

First Canadian Edition

# INVESTMENTS

## First Canadian Edition

### William F. Sharpe
Stanford University and Sharpe-Tint, Inc.

### Gordon J. Alexander
University of Minnesota

### David J. Fowler
York University

Prentice Hall Canada Inc.

Scarborough, Ontario

**Canadian Cataloguing in Publication Data**

Sharpe, William F.
　Investments
1st Canadian ed.

ISBN 0–13–012915–1

1. Investments–Canada.　2. Investments–Canada–
Problems, exercises, etc.　3. Investment analysis.
I. Alexander, Gordon J., 1947- .　II. Fowler,
David John, 1930- .　III. Title.

HG4521.S48　1993　　332.6' 0971　　C92–095274-7

Prentice-Hall, Inc., Englewood Cliffs, New Jersey
Prentice-Hall International, Inc., London
Prentice-Hall of Australia, Pty., Ltd., Sydney
Prentice-Hall of India Pvt., Ltd., New Delhi
Prentice-Hall of Japan, Inc., Tokyo
Prentice-Hall of Southeast Asia (Pte.) Ltd., Singapore
Editora Prentice-Hall do Brasil Ltda., Rio de Janeiro
Prentice-Hall Hispanoamericana, S.A., Mexico

ISBN: 0–13–012915–1

Acquisitions Editor: Jacqueline Wood
Developmental Editor: Linda Gorman
Copy Editor: Heather McClune
Production Editor: Dawn du Quesnay
Production Coordinator: Theresa Thomas
Cover Design: Julian Cleva
Page Layout: Pronk&Associates

1　2　3　4　5　–RRD–　97　96　95　94　93

Printed and bound in the United States.

*To Kathy*
*WFS*

*To my parents*
*GJA*

*To Lesley*
*DJF*

# BRIEF CONTENTS

# CONTENTS

# 7 PORTFOLIO ANALYSIS   144

# 8 THE CAPITAL ASSET PRICING MODEL   183

# 23 PORTFOLIO PERFORMANCE EVALUATION  717

# PREFACE TO CANADIAN EDITION

When asked by Prentice Hall if I would prepare a Canadian adaptation of *Investments* by Bill Sharpe and Gordon Alexander, I readily agreed. Only later did I realize the magnitude of the task. Despite the need to burn the midnight oil on a number of occasions in order to meet the inexorable deadlines, I have enjoyed this intellectually rewarding undertaking.

Adapting a US text for the Canadian market turned out to be highly instructive. I am now much more aware of the similarities and differences between Canadian and US financial institutions and practices and the way these affect investment decisions. To cut or not to cut — that is the overriding question facing the adapter. The natural temptation, which must be resisted, is to keep all of the original and to add the relevant Canadian material. In general, descriptions of US institutional arrangements were replaced by relevant Canadian material, and the results of US empirical studies were augmented by the corresponding Canadian results where these were available.

Specifically, the four chapters that deal with institutional factors, Chapters 1, Introduction, 2, Securities and Markets, 10, Taxes, and 12, Fixed Income Securities, were extensively rewritten to reflect the Canadian situation. The chapters that deal with the development of investment theory, Chapters 3, Investment Value and Market Price, through 9, Factor Models and Arbitrage Pricing Theory, were substantively changed only where Canadian tests of the Capital Asset Pricing Model and the Arbitrage Pricing Theory could be inserted. The chapters describing financial analysis, investment management, and performance evaluation, Chapters 16, The Valuation of Common Shares, 17, Earnings, and 21, Financial Analysis, through 23 Portfolio Performance Evaluation, are also largely unchanged except for the addition of descriptions of relevant Canadian studies.

Sections of all the remaining chapters were amended in varying degrees to reflect differing institutional arrangements and to report the results of Canadian empirical research.

The US text takes an original approach to the Efficient Markets Hypothesis that I have elected to retain. Rather than concentrate the theory and tests in a single chapter, the theory is described in Chapter 3 and details of the empirical tests are reported in subsequent chapters. Thus, for example, insider trading is discussed in Chapter 15 and earnings and dividend announcements are found in Chapter 17. This approach, I feel, helps to make the students aware of the fact that market efficiency underlies much of both our valuation models and the investment process.

One of the fears I had when starting this project was the possibility that there would not be sufficient Canadian material to justify an adaptation. Although some lacunae exist, it soon became evident that Canadian academics and some practitioners have been diligent researchers of the Canadian scene. Particular mention should be made of the *Canadian Investment Review* as a source of information about the application of theory. The *Review* has been instrumental in making academic research accessible to practitioners and in making the latter's work known to academics. Keith Ambachtsheer, the founder and, until recently, the publisher, is to be congratulated for having had the courage to start such a venture. May the *Review* continue to prosper under its new owners.

Many others have provided assistance in the preparation of this book. My thanks go to my colleagues at the Faculty of Administrative Studies, York University, who provided key references on request. This was particularly true of those in Finance — Elizabeth Maynes, Eli Prisman, Chris Robinson, and Savita Verma. I would also like to thank Phil Anisman, Tim Baikie, Pierre Brodeur, Marcus Dancer, Suzanne Firth, John Friedlan, Larry Gould, Roy Hill, Susan Wolberg Jenah, Vijay Jog, Daniel Kelly, Don Lato, Willie MacKenzie, Melanie Moore, Teng Qiang, Wendy Rudd, Carl Searle, Will Scoffield, Scott Snelgrove, and Mary Webb. I especially appreciated Carl Belle's help in reading and commenting on several chapters and Andy Aziz' contribution to the Instructor's Manual. It has been a pleasure to work with the following people from Prentice Hall: Acquisitions Editor, Jacqueline Wood; Developmental Editor, Linda Gorman; Production Editor, Dawn du Quesnay; and freelance editor, Heather Scott McClune.

When a manuscript finally goes to press, every author is aware that there may still be undetected errors or omissions. Any corrections and/or constructive comments will, therefore, be gratefully received.

David Fowler
October 1992

# ABOUT THE AUTHORS

## WILLIAM F. SHARPE

William F. Sharpe is currently Timken Professor of Finance at the Stanford University Graduate School of Business. Dr. Sharpe has published articles in a number of professional journals, including *Management Science, Journal of Business, Journal of Finance, Journal of Financial Economics, Journal of Financial and Quantitative Analysis*, and the *Journal of Portfolio Management*. Dr. Sharpe is a past President of the American Finance Association, and founder of Sharpe-Tint, Inc., an investment management firm specializing in asset allocation. He received his A.B., M.A., and Ph.D. degrees in Economics from the University of California at Los Angeles.

## GORDON J. ALEXANDER

Gordon J. Alexander is presently the IDS Professor of Finance at the University of Minnesota. Dr. Alexander has published articles in the *Journal of Finance, Journal of Financial Economics, Journal of Financial and Quantitative Analysis, Journal of Banking and Finance, Financial Management*, and the *Journal of Portfolio Management*. In addition, he is currently an Associate Editor for the *Journal of Financial and Quantitative Analysis*, as well as the Book Review Editor of the *Journal of Finance*. Dr. Alexander received his Ph.D. in Finance, M.A. in Mathematics, and M.B.A. from the University of Michigan, and his B.S. in Business Administration from the State University of New York at Buffalo.

## DAVID J. FOWLER

David J. Fowler is an Associate Professor at the Faculty of Administrative Studies at York University in Toronto. Dr. Fowler has published two books, *The Drug Industry: A Case Study in Foreign Control*, and *Endowed Charitable Foundations In Canada: A Study of Spending and Investment Strategies Under Revenue Canada Regulations*, as well as numerous articles in professional publications such as *Journal of Business Finance and Accounting, Journal of Finance, Journal of Financial Economics*, and *Journal of Financial Research*. Dr. Fowler received his B.Sc.(Eng) from the Imperial College of Science & Technology at the University of London, and his M.B.A. and Ph.D. at the University of Toronto.

# Chapter 1

# INTRODUCTION

This book is about investing in marketable securities. Accordingly, it focuses on the investment environment and process. The *investment environment* encompasses the kinds of marketable securities that exist and where and how they are bought and sold. The investment process is concerned with how an investor should proceed in making decisions about marketable securities in which to invest, how extensive the investments should be, and when the investments should be made. Before discussing the investment environment and process in more detail, the term *investment* will be described.

Investment, in its broadest sense, means the sacrifice of certain present value for (possibly uncertain) future value. Two different attributes are generally involved: time and risk. The sacrifice takes place in the present and is certain. The reward comes later, if at all, and the magnitude is generally uncertain. In some cases time predominates (for example, government bonds). In other cases risk is the dominant attribute (for example, call options on common shares). In yet others, both time and risk are important (for example, shares of common stock).

A distinction is often made between investment and *savings*. Savings is defined as foregone consumption; investment is restricted to "real" investment of the sort that increases national output in the future. Although this definition is useful in other contexts, it is not especially helpful here. The distinction between real and financial investments, however, is important.

*Real investments* generally involve some kind of tangible asset, such as land, machinery, or factories. *Financial investments* involve contracts written on pieces of paper, such as shares and bonds. In primitive economies most investment is of the real variety. However, in a modern economy, much investment is of the financial variety. Highly developed institutions for financial investment greatly facilitate real investment. By and large, the two forms of investment are complementary, not competitive.

The financing of an apartment house provides a good example. Apartments are sufficiently tangible ("bricks and mortar") to be considered real investment. Where are the resources required to pay for the land and the construction of the apartments obtained? Some may come from direct investment — for example, a wealthy doctor who wants to build an apartment house may use some of his or her money to finance the project. The rest of the resources may be provided by a mortgage. In essence, someone the doctor loans money, with repayment promised in fixed amounts on a specified schedule over many years. In the typical case the "someone" is not a person but an institution acting as a financial intermediary. Thus, the doctor has made a real investment in the apartment house, and the institution has made a financial investment in the doctor.

As a second example, consider what happens when Canadian Pacific (CP) finds itself in need of money to pay for plant construction. This real investment may be financed by the sale of new common stock in the *primary market* for securities. The common stock itself represents a financial investment to the purchasers, who may subsequently trade these shares in the *secondary market* (for example, on the Toronto Stock Exchange (TSE)). Although transactions in the secondary market do not generate money for CP, the fact that such a market exists makes the common stock more attractive and thus facilitates real investment. Investors would pay less for new shares of common stock if there were no way to sell them quickly and inexpensively later.

These examples have introduced the three main elements of the investment environment — *securities* (also known as financial investments or financial assets), *security markets* (also known as financial markets), and *financial intermediaries* (also known as financial institutions). They are discussed in more detail next.

## 1.1 THE INVESTMENT ENVIRONMENT

### ☐ 1.1.1 Securities

When someone borrows money from a pawnbroker, he or she must leave some item of value as *security*. Failure to repay the loan (plus interest) means that the pawnbroker can sell the pawned item to recover the amount of the loan (plus interest) and perhaps make a profit. The terms of the agreement are recorded via pawn tickets. When a college student borrows money to buy a car, the lender usually holds formal title to the car until the loan is repaid. In the event of default, the lender can repossess the car and attempt to sell it to recover his or her costs. In this case the official certificate of title, issued by the province, serves as the security for the loan.

When someone borrows money for a vacation, he or she may simply sign a piece of paper promising repayment with interest. The loan is unsecured in the sense that there is no collateral, meaning no specific asset has been promised to the lender in the event of default. In such a situation, the lender would have to take the borrower to court to try to recover the amount of the loan. Only a piece of paper, called a *promissory note*, stands as evidence of such a loan.

When a firm borrows money, it may or may not offer collateral. For example, some loans may be secured (backed) by specific assets (buildings, equipment, and so on). Such loans are registered as mortgage bonds, which indicate the terms of repayment and the particular assets pledged to the lender in the event of default. However, it is much more common for a corporation simply to pledge all its assets, perhaps with some provision for the manner in which the division will take place in the event of default. Such a promise is known as a *debenture bond*.

Finally, a firm may promise a right to share in the firm's profits in return for an investor's funds. Nothing is pledged, and no irrevocable promises are made. The firm simply pays whatever its directors deem reasonable from time to time. However, to protect against serious malfeasance, the investor is given the right to participate in the determination of who will be members of the board of directors. His or her property right is represented by a share of common stock, which can be sold to someone else who will then be able to exercise that right. The holder of common shares is said to be an owner of the corporation and can, in theory, exercise control over its operation through the board of directors.

In general, only a piece of paper represents the investor's rights to certain prospects or property and the conditions under which he or she may exercise those rights. This piece of paper, serving as evidence of property rights, is called a *security*. It and with it, all its rights and conditions, may be transferred to another investor. Thus, everything from a pawn ticket to a share of CP common stock is a security. Hereafter the term *security* will be used to refer to *a legal representation of the right to receive prospective future benefits under stated conditions*. One of the objectives of *security analysis* is to identify mispriced securities by determining their prospective future benefits, the conditions under which they will be received, and the likelihood of their occurring.

By and large the focus here is on securities that may be easily and efficiently transferred from one owner to another. Thus, the concern is with shares and bonds rather than with pawn tickets, although much of the material in this book applies to all three types of instruments.

## ☐ 1.1.2  Calculation of Returns

Figure 1.1 and Table 1.1 show the year-by-year results obtained from investing in four types of securities over the 42-year period from 1950 through 1991. In each case the percentage change in a hypothetical investor's wealth from the beginning to the end of the year is shown. This amount, known as the *rate of return* (or simply the return), is calculated as follows:

$$\text{Return} = \frac{\text{end-of-period wealth} - \text{beginning-of-period wealth}}{\text{beginning-of-period wealth}} \quad (1.1)$$

In calculating the return on a security, it is assumed that the investor purchases one unit (for example, one bond or one share of common stock) of the security at the beginning of the period. The cost of this investment is the amount entered in the denominator of equation (1.1). The value in the numerator is the answer to a simple question — how much better (or worse) off is the investor at the end of the period if this investment had been made at the beginning of the period?

For example, assume that Widget Corporation's common stock was selling for $40 per share at the beginning of 1991 and for $45 at the end of 1991 and paid dividends of $3 per share during the year. The 1991 return on Widget would then be calculated as $[(\$45 + \$3) - \$40]/\$40 = .20$, or 20%.[1]

---

[1] Generally, any cash received during the period is treated as if it were received at the end of the period. However, this assumption typically results in an understatement of the actual return. For example, if the dividends on Widget were received at midyear, the investor could have put them in a bank savings account and earned, for example, 4% interest for the rest of the year. This interest then would have amounted to $.04 \times \$3.00 = \$.12$, resulting in the annual return being equal to $[(\$45 + \$3 + \$.12) - \$40]/\$40 = .203$, or 20.3%.

**FIGURE 1-1**
Annual returns, 1950–1991.

*SOURCE:* Reprinted, with permission, from James E. Hatch and Robert W. White, *Canadian Stocks, Bonds, Bills, and Inflation: 1950–1987*, Copyright 1988, The Research Foundation of The Institute of Chartered Financial Analysts, Charlottesville, Va.; Melanie Moore, *ScotiaMcLeod's Handbook of Canadian Debt Market Indices: 1947–1990* (Toronto:ScotiaMcLeod Inc.), 1991 and Melanie Moore, *Debt Market Indices*, December 1991, ScotiaMcleod Inc.

**TABLE 1.1**

Annual Returns: Stocks, Bonds, and Treasury Bills and Changes in the Consumer Price Index (CPI).

| | | Total Returns | | | |
|---|---|---|---|---|---|
| Year | Treasury Bills | Long Canada Bonds | Long Corporate Bonds | Equities | C.P.I |
| 1950 | 0.51 | −0.11 | 2.68 | 27.91 | 6.10 |
| 1951 | 0.71 | −3.01 | −6.44 | 25.50 | 10.73 |
| 1952 | 0.95 | 2.05 | 4.49 | 1.17 | −1.73 |
| 1953 | 1.54 | 3.76 | 3.99 | −8.28 | 0.00 |
| 1954 | 1.53 | 9.78 | 10.34 | 43.61 | 0.35 |
| 1955 | 1.36 | −0.43 | 2.18 | 24.11 | 0.35 |
| 1956 | 2.75 | −3.54 | −7.58 | 8.81 | 3.15 |
| 1957 | 3.83 | 6.60 | 7.58 | −20.58 | 2.03 |
| 1958 | 2.51 | −5.82 | 2.99 | 31.25 | 2.66 |
| 1959 | 4.62 | −4.44 | −4.28 | 4.59 | 1.29 |
| 1960 | 3.31 | 6.88 | 11.94 | 1.78 | 1.28 |
| 1961 | 2.89 | 9.75 | 8.91 | 32.75 | 0.32 |
| 1962 | 4.22 | 3.16 | 4.95 | −7.09 | 1.57 |
| 1963 | 3.63 | 4.59 | 5.38 | 15.60 | 1.86 |
| 1964 | 3.79 | 6.74 | 4.71 | 25.43 | 1.82 |
| 1965 | 3.92 | 1.04 | −0.58 | 6.68 | 2.98 |
| 1966 | 5.03 | 1.72 | −1.53 | −7.07 | 3.48 |
| 1967 | 4.59 | −2.27 | −0.34 | 18.09 | 4.20 |
| 1968 | 6.44 | −0.62 | 2.43 | 22.45 | 4.03 |
| 1969 | 7.09 | −2.36 | −1.04 | −0.81 | 4.65 |
| 1970 | 6.70 | 22.70 | 13.97 | −3.57 | 1.48 |
| 1971 | 3.81 | 11.79 | 14.48 | 8.01 | 4.87 |
| 1972 | 3.55 | 1.59 | 9.51 | 27.38 | 5.10 |
| 1973 | 5.11 | 1.96 | 2.40 | 0.27 | 9.27 |
| 1974 | 7.85 | −0.98 | −5.86 | −25.93 | 12.32 |
| 1975 | 7.41 | 2.74 | 8.35 | 18.48 | 9.53 |
| 1976 | 9.27 | 19.65 | 23.32 | 11.02 | 5.91 |
| 1977 | 7.66 | 4.68 | 10.34 | 10.76 | 9.46 |
| 1978 | 8.34 | 2.76 | 5.00 | 29.66 | 8.36 |
| 1979 | 11.41 | −3.30 | −1.77 | 44.77 | 9.80 |
| 1980 | 14.97 | 3.23 | 1.41 | 30.13 | 11.19 |
| 1981 | 18.41 | −3.26 | −1.96 | −10.25 | 12.10 |
| 1982 | 15.42 | 47.39 | 44.33 | 5.54 | 9.26 |
| 1983 | 9.62 | 8.58 | 12.75 | 35.49 | 4.55 |
| 1984 | 11.59 | 15.85 | 17.87 | −2.39 | 3.76 |
| 1985 | 9.88 | 27.24 | 25.74 | 25.07 | 4.35 |
| 1986 | 9.33 | 18.60 | 13.05 | 8.95 | 4.17 |
| 1987 | 8.48 | 1.26 | 3.37 | 5.88 | 4.15 |
| 1988 | 9.41 | 10.65 | 11.77 | 11.08 | 3.96 |
| 1989 | 12.36 | 15.39 | 14.13 | 21.37 | 5.17 |

**TABLE 1.1**
*(Continued)*

| | | Total Returns | | | |
|---|---|---|---|---|---|
| Year | Treasury Bills | Long Canada Bonds | Long Corporate Bonds | Equities | C.P.I |
| 1990 | 13.48 | 4.64 | 4.53 | −14.80 | 5.00 |
| 1991 | 9.83 | 24.52 | 26.16 | 12.02 | 3.78 |
| Ar. Mean | 6.65 | 6.46 | 7.23 | 11.78 | 4.73 |
| Std. Dev. | 4.32 | 10.31 | 9.85 | 16.58 | 3.53 |

SOURCE: Reprinted, with permission, from James E. Hatch and Robert W. White, *Canadian Stocks, Bonds, Bills, and Inflation: 1950–1987*, Copyright 1988, The Research Foundation of The Institute of Chartered Financial Analysts, Charlottesville, Va.; Melanie Moore, *ScotiaMcLeod's Handbook of Canadian Debt Market Indices: 1947–1990* (Toronto: ScotiaMcLeod Inc.), 1991 and Melanie Moore, *Debt Market Indices*, December 1991, ScotiaMcleod Inc.

## ☐ 1.1.3 Types of Securities

### Treasury Bills

The first type of security listed in Figure 1.1 involves loaning money on a short-term basis (three months to one year) to the Canadian Government.[2] Such a loan carries little (if any) risk that payment will not be made as promised. Moreover, while the rate of return varies from period to period, at the beginning of any single period it is known with certainty. The return on these investments, known as Treasury bills, ranged from a high of 19.09% per year (in 1981) to a low of 0.51% per year (in 1950), with an average value of 5.98% during the entire 38-year period.

### Long-Term Bonds

The second and third types of securities shown in Figure 1.1 involve the purchase of bonds and thus also involve loaning money. Each type of bond represents a long-term commitment on the part of the issuer (that is, the borrower) to the investor (that is, the lender). This commitment is to make cash payments each year (the coupon payment) up to some point in time (the maturity date), when a single final cash payment (the principal) will also be made. The prices at which these bonds can be bought and sold prior to maturity vary from time to time. Thus, while coupon payments are easily predicted, the end-of-period selling price of the security before maturity is uncertain at the beginning of the period, thereby making the return difficult to predict in advance.

The second type of security in Figure 1.1 (Government of Canada bonds, also known as Long Canada bonds) involves loans with a maturity of 10 years or more to the Canadian Government.

The third type of security in Figure 1.1 (industrial bonds, otherwise known as corporate bonds), involves long-term loans to Canadian industrial corporations. This data series is based on a small sample of bonds that are not controlled as to maturity.

---

[2] For more details on the securities described in this section see Chapters 12 and 15.

These two kinds of bonds had their highest annual return in 1982, reaching 47.39% for government bonds and 44.33% for industrial bonds. The lowest annual return, however, was reached in different years. For government bonds, the lowest return occurred in 1958 ($-5.82\%$) whereas for industrial bonds the minimum was reached in 1956 ($-7.58\%$). Government bonds had a lower average return than Treasury bills ($6.46\% < 6.65\%$) while industrial bonds had a higher average return (7.23%) than either government bonds or Treasury bills. As will be discussed later, these relationships are unusual.

## Common Shares

The fourth and final type of security in Figure 1.1 involves the purchase of a group of common stocks, each of which represents a commitment on the part of a corporation to pay periodically whatever its earnings permit and its board of directors deems appropriate as a cash dividend. Although the amount of cash dividends to be paid in a year is subject to some uncertainty, it is relatively predictable. However, the amount for which a share can be bought or sold varies considerably from time to time, making the annual return highly unpredictable. Figure 1.1 shows the return from a portfolio of stocks that approximately replicates the TSE300 Composite Index from 1950 to 1991. Returns ranged from an exciting 44.77% in 1979 to a depressing $-25.93\%$ in 1974 and averaged 11.78% per year over the entire period. Such investments can provide substantial returns, which are larger, on average, than the returns provided by corporate bonds. However, these returns also have substantial variability, being more volatile than those of either type of long-term bond.

Table 1.1 provides year-by-year returns for the four types of securities shown in Figure 1.1. The table also includes the annual percentage change in the Consumer Price Index (CPI) as an indicator of changes in the cost of living. Average annual returns are shown at the bottom of the table. Below these values are the values of the standard deviations of annual returns, which serve as measures of the variability of the returns on the respective securities.[3]

Table 1.2 compares the rates of return on comparable securities in Canada and the US over the period 1950 to 1986. This table shows that average rates of return and standard deviations of returns in the two countries were quite similar which should not be surprising given the degree to which Canada's economy is related to that of the US.

The historical record revealed in Figure 1.1 , Table 1.1, and Table 1.2 illustrates a general principle: *When sensible investment strategies are compared with one another, risk and return tend to go together.* That is, securities that have higher average returns tend to have greater amounts of risk. The fact that Treasury bills outperformed long-term bonds both in Canada and the US can be attributed to their performance in the 1979 to 1981 period when macro-economic policy was successfully designed to drastically reduce inflation. During this period, Treasury bills dramatically outperformed all other fixed income securities by providing an annualized return of 14.05% over the three years compared with $-0.80\%$ for long Canada bonds.

---

[3] Standard deviation was calculated as being equal to the square root of $\sum_{t=1}^{42}(r_t - \bar{r})^2/41$, where $r_t$ is the return for year $t$ ($t = 1$ corresponds to 1950, $t = 2$ to 1951, and so on) and $\bar{r}$ is the average return over the 42-year period. A larger standard deviation means a greater amount of dispersion in the 42 returns and, as discussed in Chapter 6, indicates more risk.

**TABLE 1.2**

A Comparison of Average Annual Returns on Stocks, Bonds, and Treasury Bills and Changes in the CPI in Canada and the US over the Period 1950 to 1986.

| | Canada | | US | |
| | Return | Standard Deviation | Return | Standard Deviation |
|---|---|---|---|---|
| Treasury Bills | 5.92% | 4.20% | 5.85% | 5.32% |
| Long-Term Government Bonds | 5.78 | 10.27 | 5.74 | 12.01 |
| Long Corporate Bonds | 6.63 | 9.82 | 6.38 | 12.27 |
| Equities | 12.92 | 17.87 | 14.20 | 17.89 |
| Changes in the CPI | 4.77 | 3.81 | 5.01 | 5.02 |

SOURCE: Reprinted, with permission, from James E. Hatch and Robert W. White, *Canadian Stocks, Bonds, Bills, and Inflation: 1950–1987*, Copyright 1988, The Research Foundation of The Institute of Chartered Financial Analysts, Charlottesville, Va.

It is important to note that historical variability is not necessarily an indication of future risk. The pattern of returns on Treasury bills provides one example. Although the values have varied from period to period, in any given period the amount to be earned is known in advance and is thus riskless. On the other hand, the annual return on a common stock is very difficult to predict. For such an investment, past variability may provide a fairly good measure of the uncertainty surrounding the future return.

To see how difficult it is to predict common stock returns, cover the portion on Table 1.1 from 1965 on and then try to guess the return in 1965. Having done this, uncover the value for 1965 and try to guess the return for 1966. Proceed in this manner a year at a time, keeping track of your overall predictive accuracy. Unless you are very clever or very lucky, you will conclude that the past pattern of stock returns provides little help in predicting next year's return. It will be seen that this is a characteristic of an *efficient market* — that is, a market where security prices reflect information immediately. At this stage, it is enough to indicate that the past variability of stock returns can be taken as a rough approximation of future risk.

Is one of these four types of securities obviously "the best"? No. To oversimplify, the right security or combination of securities depends on the investor's situation and preferences for return relative to his or her distaste for risk. There may be right or wrong securities for a particular person or purpose. But it would be surprising indeed to find a security that is clearly wrong for everyone and every purpose. Such situations are simply not present in an efficient market.

## ☐ 1.1.4   Security Markets

Security markets exist in order to bring together buyers and sellers of securities, meaning they are mechanisms that exist in order to facilitate the exchange of financial assets. There are many ways in which they can be categorized. One way has already been mentioned — primary and secondary financial markets. Here the key distinction was whether or not the securities were being offered for sale by the issuer. Interestingly, the primary market itself can be subdivided into seasoned and unseasoned new issues. A *seasoned* new issue refers to the offering of an additional amount of an already existing security, whereas an *unseasoned* new issue involves the initial offering of a security to the public. Unseasoned new issues are often referred to as initial public offerings, or ipo's.

Another way of distinguishing security markets involves the life span of financial assets. *Money markets* typically involve financial assets that have a maturity of one year or less, whereas *capital markets* typically involve financial assets that have a maturity greater than one year. Thus, Treasury bills are traded in a money market, and long-term bonds are traded in a capital market.

## ☐ 1.1.5   Financial Intermediaries

Financial intermediaries, also known as financial institutions, are organizations that issue financial claims against themselves (meaning that they sell financial assets representing claims on themselves in return for cash) and use the proceeds from these issues to purchase primarily the financial assets of others. Financial claims against an organization simply represent the right-hand side of its balance sheet, the key distinction between financial intermediaries and other types of organizations involves the items on the left-hand side of the balance sheet.

For example, a chartered bank issues financial claims against itself in the form of debt (for example, chequing and savings accounts) and equity, but then again so does a typical manufacturing firm. However, looking at the assets held by a chartered bank reveals that most of the bank's money is invested in loans to individuals and corporations as well as in government securities such as Treasury bills, whereas the typical manufacturing firm has its money invested mostly in land, buildings, machinery, and inventory. Thus, the bank has invested primarily in financial assets, whereas the manufacturing firm has invested primarily in real assets. Accordingly, banks are classified as financial intermediaries and manufacturing firms are not. Other types of Canadian financial intermediaries include trust companies, caisse populaires, credit unions, life insurance companies, mutual funds, and pension funds.

Having made this introduction to the investment environment, the investment process is introduced next.

## 1.2   THE INVESTMENT PROCESS

As previously mentioned, the investment process describes how an investor should go about making decisions about marketable securities in which to invest, how extensive the investment should be, and when the investment should be made. A five-step procedure for making these decisions forms the basis of the investment process:

1. Set investment objectives and policy.
2. Perform security analysis.
3. Construct a portfolio.
4. Evaluate the performance of the portfolio.
5. Revise the portfolio.

## □ 1.2.1    Investment Objectives and Policy

The first step, setting *investment policy*, involves first determining the investor's objectives and the amount of his or her investable wealth. Since there is a positive relationship between risk and return for sensible investment strategies, it is not appropriate for an investor to say that his or her objective is to make a lot of money. What is appropriate for an investor in this situation is to state that the objective is to attempt to make a lot of money while recognizing there is some chance that large losses may be incurred. Thus, investment objectives should be stated in terms of both risk and return.[4]

This first step of the investment process concludes with identification of the potential categories of financial assets for consideration in the ultimate portfolio. This identification will be based on, among other things, the investment objectives, amount of investable wealth, and tax status of the investor. For example, as shall be seen later, it does not usually make sense for individual investors in high tax brackets to purchase preferred shares or for tax-exempt investors (such as pension funds) to invest in securities that provide significant tax deferral opportunities.

## □ 1.2.2    Security Analysis

The second step of the investment process, performing *security analysis*, involves examining a number of individual securities (or groups of securities) within the broad categories of financial assets previously identified. The principal objectives of security analysis are to identify the expected return and risk characteristics of different securities; to identify securities that fit an investor's tax and liquidity needs and to identify mispriced securities. There are a wide variety of approaches to security analysis. However, most of these approaches fall into one of two classifications. The first classification is known as *technical analysis* (performed by technical analysts). The second is known as *fundamental analysis* (performed by fundamental analysts). In discussing these two approaches to security analysis, the primary focus is on common stocks. The analysis of other financial assets is discussed later.

In its simplest form, technical analysis involves the study of historical stock market prices in an attempt to predict future price movements for the common stock of a particular firm. Initially, past prices are examined in order to identify recurring trends or patterns in price movements. Then, more recent stock prices are analyzed in order to identify emerging trends or patterns that are similar to past ones. This matching of emerging trends or patterns with past ones is done in the belief that these trends or patterns repeat themselves; thus, by identifying an emerging trend or pattern, the analyst will (allegedly) be able to predict future price movements for that particular stock.

When fundamental analysis is used to identify mispriced securities, the starting point is the assumption that the "true" (or "intrinsic") value of any financial asset is

---

[4] In practice investors may have a wide variety of investment objectives, for example, some individuals may look for "good" returns with preservation of capital while others may seek income or capital growth. It will be shown in Chapter 6 that a rational objective can be stated either as "maximize expected return for a given level of risk" or "achieve a target expected return at minimum risk."

equal to the present value of all cash flows that the owner of the asset expects to receive. Accordingly, the fundamental stock analyst will attempt to forecast the timing and size of these cash flows and then will convert them to their equivalent present value by using an appropriate discount factor. What this means is that the analyst must attempt to forecast the stream of dividends that a particular stock will provide in the future, which is equivalent to forecasting the firm's earnings per share and payout ratios. Once the true value of the common stock of a particular firm has been determined, it is compared to the current market price of the common stock in order to see if the stock is fairly priced or not. Stocks that have a true value less than their current market price are known as *overvalued*, or *overpriced*, stocks, whereas those that have a true value greater than their current market price are known as *undervalued*, or *underpriced*, stocks. The magnitude of the difference between the true value and current market price is also important information, since the strength of the analyst's conviction that a given stock is mispriced will depend, in part, on it. Fundamental analysts believe that notable cases of mispricing will be corrected by the market in the future, meaning that prices of undervalued stocks will show unusual appreciation and prices of overvalued stocks will show unusual depreciation.

## ☐ 1.2.3   Portfolio Construction

The third step of the investment process, *portfolio construction*, involves identifying those specific assets in which to invest as well as determining the proportions of the investor's wealth to put in each one. Here the issues of selectivity, timing, and diversification need to be addressed by the investor. *Selectivity*, also known as microforecasting, refers to security analysis and thus focuses on either forecasting price movements of individual securities or on their risk and return characteristics. *Timing*, also known as macroforecasting, involves the forecasting of price movements of common stocks in general relative to fixed-income securities, such as corporate bonds. *Diversification* involves constructing the investor's portfolio in a manner such that risk is minimized, subject to certain restrictions.

## ☐ 1.2.4   Portfolio Performance Evaluation

The fourth step of the investment process, *portfolio performance evaluation*, involves periodically determining how the portfolio performed in terms not only of the return earned but also the risk experienced by the investor. Thus, appropriate measures of return and risk as well as relevant standards (or *benchmarks*) are needed. The results obtained from this step may indicate whether or not portfolio revision is in order.

## ☐ 1.2.5 Portfolio Revision

The fifth step of the investment process, *portfolio revision*, concerns the periodic repetition of the previous four steps. That is, over time the investor may change his or her investment objectives, which, in turn, means that the currently held portfolio may no longer be optimal. Instead, perhaps a new portfolio should be formed by selling some securities currently held and purchasing new ones. Another motivation for revising a given portfolio is that over time the prices of securities change, so that some securities initially considered unattractive may become attractive and others that were attractive may no longer be so. Thus, the investor may want to add the former to his or her portfolio while simultaneously deleting the latter. Such a decision will depend upon, among other things, the size of the transactions costs incurred in making these changes as well as the magnitude of the perceived improvement in the investment outlook for the revised portfolio.

## 1.3 ASSET OWNERSHIP

According to the Toronto Stock Exchange survey carried out in 1989, over 4 million Canadian residents directly and through mutual funds owned preferred and common shares. Table 1.3 shows the percent of the adult population that owned these shares in 1983, 1986, and 1989. However, many more residents had indirect ownership of stocks through other financial intermediaries such as pension plans. There has been a continuous increase in the level of shareownership since these surveys started in 1983. Table 1.4 provides some demographics of shareholders from the 1989 TSE survey. It suggests that the typical shareholder had an above-average income, at least some college education, and was a white-collar worker.

**TABLE 1.3**
Shareowners of Public Corporations, 1983–1989.

| | Shareholders as a Percent of the Adult Population | | |
|---|---|---|---|
| Year | Direct Owners | Mutual Fund Owners | Total [a] |
| 1983 | 9% | 6% | 13% |
| 1986 | 15 | 6 | 18 |
| 1989 | 16 | 11 | 23 |

[a] The total is not the sum of the other two columns because some investors fall into both ownership categories.

SOURCE: The Toronto Stock Exchange, *CANADIAN SHAREOWNERS: Their Profiles and Attitudes*, (Toronto, Ont.), December 1989.

**TABLE 1.4**

Demographics of Shareowners of Public Corporations, 1989.

| Age: | (% of adult population in each age group) |
|---|---|
| 18 to 24 years | 10%[a] |
| 25 to 34 years | 25 |
| 35 to 44 years | 30 |
| 45 to 54 years | 23 |
| 55 years and older | 19 |

| Household income: | (% of adult population in each income class) |
|---|---|
| Under $15,000 | 5% |
| $15,000 to $ 34,999 | 14 |
| $35,000 to $49,999 | 26 |
| $50,000 to $74,999 | 43 |
| $75,000 and over | 55 |

| Education: | (% of adult population in each education class) |
|---|---|
| Less than high school | 10% |
| Completed high school | 18 |
| College/Some University | 26 |
| University Graduate | 42 |

| Occupation: | (% of adult population in each occupation class) |
|---|---|
| Professional and technical | 22.5% |
| Managers and proprietors | 19.5 |
| Clerical and sales | 14.6 |
| Craftsmen and foremen | 6.5 |
| Operatives and laborers | 5.4 |
| Service workers | 3.2 |
| Farmers and farm laborers | .9 |
| Homemakers, retired persons, and nonemployed adults | 27.4 |

[a] This indicates that 10% of all individuals in the 18 to 24 age group own shares.

SOURCE: Toronto Stock Exchange, *CANADIAN SHAREOWNERS: Their Profile and Attitudes*, (Toronto, Ont.), December 1989, pp. 10–14.

Table 1.5 shows the financial assets and liabilities of Canadian households expressed in percentage terms, the figures are from a survey carried out in 1984 and not repeated since. Note that the three largest assets in terms of value are the home, equity in a business, and bank deposits. Stocks are well down the list in terms of percentage of assets owned. The largest liability involves home mortgages. Although some mortgages are held as assets by other individuals (miscellaneous financial assets in the table), most are held by banks and trust companies, who obtain them by lending money provided by individuals (reflected in the table by the first asset listed). The difference between assets and liabilities is large, reflecting the fact that total liabilities are quite small.

**TABLE 1.5**

Financial Assets and Liabilities of Canadian Households, 1984.

| Category | Incidence — %[a] | Composition — %[b] |
|---|---|---|
| *Assets:* | | |
| Bank deposits and currency | 88.5% | 10.2% |
| Canada Savings Bonds | 28.2 | 2.6 |
| All other bonds | 3.4 | 0.5 |
| Stock holdings | 23.7 | 2.2 |
| Registered savings plans | 30.2 | 4.0 |
| Miscellaneous financial assets | 10.4 | 2.4 |
| Total financial assets | 97.2 | 22.0 |
| Market value of home | 58.5 | 42.9 |
| Market value of vacation home | 7.0 | 2.4 |
| Equity in other real estate | 13.1 | 5.8 |
| Market value of cars and trucks | 75.6 | 4.8 |
| Market value of other vehicles | 20.7 | 0.9 |
| Equity in business | 21.3 | 14.1 |
| Total assets | 98.6 | 100.0 |
| *Liabilities:* | | |
| Charge accounts and instalment debt | 43.7 | 0.4 |
| Selected bank loans | 23.5 | 1.9 |
| Loans from other intermediaries | 9.5 | 0.6 |
| Other personal debt | 14.1 | 0.9 |
| Home mortgage | 28.4 | 8.5 |
| Vacation home mortgage | 1.0 | 0.2 |
| Total liabilities | 66.2 | 12.5 |
| *Financial assets less liabilities* | 98.8 | 87.5 |

[a] percent of number of persons surveyed.
[b] percent of total assets.

SOURCE: Statistics Canada, *The Distribution of Wealth in Canada, 1984*, (Ottawa, Ont.), Tables 28 and 29.

## 1.4 THE INVESTMENT INDUSTRY

Table 1.6 shows the number of people employed in the Finance, Insurance, and Real Estate industry in Canada in recent years. As can be seen, the absolute and relative size of the industry has been increasing. In 1990, approximately 1 out of every 17 nonagricultural workers dealt with investments, broadly defined. Some provide advice (known as *investment advisors*), some are in sales, some arrange transfers of property or securities from one investor to another, others manage investors' funds (known as *professional money managers*), and still others handle the record keeping in this most abstract and paper-oriented of industries.

TABLE 1.6
Number of Employees: Finance, Insurance, and Real Estate.

| Employer | Number of Employees (thousands) | | | |
|---|---|---|---|---|
| | 1971 | 1981 | 1986 | 1990 [a] |
| Deposit accepting intermediaries | 133.3 | 261.4 | 287.9 | 331.2 |
| Consumer and business financing | 17.3 | 20.3 | 15.1 | 15.9 |
| Investment intermediaries | 20.3 | 21.6 | 28.2 | 25.9 |
| Insurance carriers | 70.8 | 104.6 | 131.4 | 143.4 |
| Other financial intermediaries | 14.3 | 22.6 | 29.2 | 31.1 |
| Real estate operators | 31.8 | 86.8 | 89.0 | 78.5 |
| Insurance and real estate agents | 70.2 | 118.9 | 156.4 | 222.8 |
| Total | 358.0 | 636.2 | 737.2 | 848.8 |
| Employees in this industry as a percent of total employees in nonagricultural industries | 4.15% | 5.28% | 5.32% | 5.74% |

[a] Estimated

SOURCE: Statistics Canada, *Census of Population*, (Ottawa, Ont.), various years; Statistics Canada, *Employment, Hours and Earnings*, (Ottawa,Ont.),December 1990.

## 1.5 SUMMARY

Because this book is about investing, it focuses on the investment environment and process. In particular, elements of the investment environment, such as securities, markets, and financial intermediaries, are defined and examples are presented. One important concept introduced in this chapter is the notion of an efficient market, defined as a market where security prices immediately reflect new information. In a market that is efficient, securities will be fairly priced, implying that security analysis will not enable investors to make abnormally high returns.

The investment process can be thought of as the method an investor uses to make decisions about marketable securities in which to invest, how extensive the investments should be, and when the investment should be made. A five-step procedure for conducting this process was presented. One method of performing all five steps that is discussed in later chapters involves the use of modern portfolio theory (MPT).

Although the investment industry is of relatively modest importance relative to total employment figures, this part of the economy has a profound impact on virtually everyone's life. A clear understanding of the investment environment and process is valuable not only for the 1 in 17 who work in the industry but also for the 16 who do not. Although most people obtain the majority of their income in the form of salary and wages, income from investments is important to nearly everyone, particularly those who have retired. Accordingly, this book is intended to provide an understanding of the investment environment and process for people with either a professional or a personal interest.

1. Why don't secondary security markets generate capital for the issuers of securities traded in those markets?

2. At the end of 1988, Ray Fisher decided to take $30,000 in savings out of the bank and invest it in a portfolio of stocks and bonds; $10,000 was placed into common stocks and $20,000 into corporate bonds. A year later, at the end of 1989, Ray's stock and bond holdings were worth $13,000 and $16,000, respectively. During 1989, $500 in cash dividends was received on the stocks and $2000 in coupon interest payments was received on the bonds. (This stock and bond income was not reinvested in his portfolio.)
   a. What was the return on Ray's stock portfolio during 1989?
   b. What was the return on Ray's bond portfolio during 1989?
   c. What was the return on Ray's total portfolio during 1989?

3. Does it seem reasonable that higher return securities historically have generally exhibited higher risk? Why?

4. Examining Table 1.1, one can find several years in which Treasury bills produced returns greater than common stocks. How can you reconcile this fact with the statements made in the text citing a positive relationship between risk and return?

5. Again referring to Table 1.1, in terms of total returns, what were the two worst calendar years for common stock investors? Compare these two years in terms of return in "constant dollars" (that is, purchasing power). Does this comparison show that the earlier stock market slump was more or less disastrous than the later one? Explain.

6. Describe how life insurance companies, mutual funds, and pension plans each act as financial intermediaries.

7. Why does it not make sense to establish an investment objective of "making a lot of money"?

8. Distinguish between technical and fundamental security analysis.

## SUGGESTED READINGS

James E. Hatch and Robert W. White, *Canadian Stocks, Bonds, Bills, and Inflation: 1950–1987* (Charlottesville, Va.: The Research Foundation of The Institute of Chartered Financial Analysts, 1988) provides a detailed analysis of historical returns and a useful description of the securities examined.

Melanie Moore, *ScotiaMcleod's Handbook of Canadian Debt Market Indices: 1947–1990* (Toronto, Ont.: ScotiaMcleod Inc., 1991) contains more up-to-date information on both debt and equity returns and is updated annually. ScotiaMcleod also publishes a monthly bulletin entitled *Debt Market Indices*.

*Canadian Shareowners—Their Profile and Attitudes, 1989* is prepared and released by the Strategic Research and Planning Division of The Toronto Stock Exchange and contains the results of their tri-annual survey of Canadian investors.

# Chapter 2

## SECURITIES AND MARKETS

When a security is sold, many people are likely to be involved. Although it is possible for two investors to trade with each other directly, the usual transaction employs the services provided by brokers, dealers, and markets.

A *broker* acts as an agent for an investor and is compensated via commission. Many individual investors deal with brokers in large retail houses — firms with many offices that are connected by private wires with their own headquarters and, through the headquarters, with major markets. The people in these brokerage firms with prime responsibility for individual investors are termed *account executives*, or *registered representatives*.

Institutional investors, such as chartered banks, pension funds, and other financial institutions, deal with these large retail brokerage firms and with smaller *boutiques* that specialize in institutional business. Two other types of brokerage firms are *regional brokerage firms* and *discount brokers*. The former concentrate on transactions within a geographic area, meaning the securities being traded have a special following in that area of the country. This may be because the issuers of the securities are located in that area. Discount brokers provide "bare-bones" services at low cost, meaning they provide fewer services than do *full-service brokerage firms* such as CIBC Wood Gundy or RBC Dominion Securities. Investors who simply want to have their orders executed and do not seek investment advice can save more than half of the commission by using a discount broker.

An account executive's compensation is typically determined, in large part, by the *commissions* paid by his or her customers — an amount that is directly related to the amount of turnover (that is, trading) in an investor's account. This provides some temptation to recommend frequent changes in investors' holdings. Furthermore, since the commission rates on various types of investments differ, there is some temptation to recommend changes in those types of investments with the highest rates. In the long run, however, account executives who encourage excessive turnover (or "churning") will often lose customers and may even be subjected to lawsuits. Nonetheless, such behavior may be advantageous for them in the short run.

It is a simple matter to open an account with a brokerage firm: simply appear at (or call) the local office. A registered representative is assigned to you and helps you to fill out a New Client Application Form. After this form has been signed, everything else can be done by mail or telephone. Transactions are posted to your account as they are to a bank account. For example, you can deposit money, purchase securities using money from the account, and add the proceeds from security sales to the account. Brokers exist (and charge fees) to make security transactions as simple as possible. All that the investor has to do is to provide the broker with what is referred to here as *order specifications*.

In discussing order specifications, it will be assumed that the investor's order involves common stock. In this situation the investor must specify

1. the name of the firm,
2. whether the order is to buy or sell shares,
3. the size of the order,
4. how long the order is to be outstanding, and
5. what type of order is to be used.

The last three specifications are discussed next in more detail.

## 2.1  ORDER SIZE

In buying or selling common stock, the investor places an order involving either a board lot, an odd lot, or both. The size of a board lot on Canadian stock exchanges varies with the price of the stock as shown in Table 2.1.

**TABLE 2.1**
Trading Lot Sizes at Four Canadian Exchanges.

| | Board Lot | | |
| Share Price | ME/TSE | ASE | VSE |
| --- | --- | --- | --- |
| under $0.10 | 1000 | 1000 | 500 |
| at $0.10 to $0.99 | 500 | 500 | 500 |
| at $1.00 to $100.00 | 100 | 100 | 100 |
| over $100.00 | 100 | 10 | 100 |

SOURCE: Canadian Securities Institute, *The Canadian Securities Course*, (Toronto, Ont.), 1989

Any order less than a board lot is referred to as an odd lot. Orders that are for more than 100 shares but are not multiples of 100 are viewed as a mixture of round and odd lots. Thus an order for 259 shares is viewed as an order for two round lots and an odd lot of 59 shares.[1]

---

[1] Occasionally, as on the Alberta Stock Exchange, a round lot is for less than 100 shares. When this happens, it is usually for stocks that are either high-priced or traded infrequently.

# TIME LIMIT

The investor must specify a time limit on his or her order, meaning the time within which the broker should attempt to fill the order. For *day orders*, the broker will attempt to fill the order only during the day in which it was entered. If the order is not filled by the end of the trading session, then it expires. If a time limit is not specified by the investor, the broker will treat an order as a day order. *Good through orders* are valid for a specified number of days and automatically expire if they have not been executed by the expiry date.

*Open orders*, also known as *good-till-canceled*, or GTC, orders, remain in effect until they are either filled or canceled by the investor. However, during the time period before the order has been filled, the broker may periodically ask the investor to confirm the order. In contrast to GTC orders are *fill-or-kill orders*, also known as FOK orders. These are orders stipulating that if the order can only be partially completed, then any portion unfilled will be canceled. *All or none orders*, or AON, requires the trader to execute the total number of shares specified before it will be accepted. Such an order must specify the minimum number of shares required.

*Discretionary orders* allow the broker to set the specifications for the order. The broker may have virtually complete discretion, in which case he or she decides on all the order specifications, or limited discretion, in which case he or she decides only on the price and timing of the order.

# TYPES OF ORDERS

## ☐ 2.3.1   At the Market Orders

The most common type of order is the *at the market order*. Orders that do not specify a price are treated as at the market orders. Here the broker is instructed to buy or sell a stated number of shares immediately. In this situation the broker is obliged to act on a "best-efforts" basis to get the best possible price (as low as possible for a purchase order, as high as possible for a sell order) at the time the order is placed. Consequently, when placing a market order the investor can be fairly certain that the order will be executed but is uncertain of the price. However, there is generally fairly good information available beforehand concerning the likely price at which such an order will be executed. Not surprisingly, market orders are day orders.

## ☐ 2.3.2   Limit Orders

A second type of order is a *limit order*. Here, a *limit price* is specified by the investor when the order is placed with the broker. If the order is to purchase shares, then the broker is to execute the order only at a price that is less than or equal to the limit price. If the order is to sell shares, then the broker is to execute the order only at a price that is greater than or equal to the limit price. Thus, for limit orders to purchase shares the investor specifies a ceiling on the price, and for limit orders to sell shares the investor specifies a floor on the price. In contrast to a market order, an investor using a limit order may not be certain that the order will be executed.

For example, assume that the common stock of the ABC Corporation is currently selling for $25 a share. An investor placing a limit order to sell 100 shares of ABC with a limit price of $30 per share and a time limit of one day is not likely to have his or her order executed, since this price is significantly above the current price of $25. Only if today's price becomes much more favorable (meaning in this case that the stock price rises by at least $5 per share) will the limit order be executed.

## ☐ 2.3.3 Stop Orders

Two special kinds of orders are stop orders (also known as stop-loss orders) and limit stop orders. For a *stop order* the investor must specify what is known as a *stop price*. If it is a sell order, the stop price must be below the market price at the time the order is placed; conversely, if it is a buy order, the stop price must be above the market price at the time the order is placed. If someone else later trades the stock at a price that reaches or passes the stop price, then the stop order becomes, in effect, a market order. Hence, a stop order can be viewed as a conditional market order.

Continuing with the ABC Corporation example, a stop-sell order at $20 would not be executed until a trade involving others had taken place at a price of $20 or lower. Conversely, a stop-buy order at $30 would not be executed until a trade involving others had taken place at a price of $30 or more. If the price did not fall to $20, then the stop-sell order would not be executed. Similarly, if the price did not rise to $30, the stop-buy order would not be executed. In contrast, a limit order to sell at $20 or a limit order to buy at $30 would be executed immediately, since the current market price is $25.

One potential use of stop orders is to "lock in" paper profits. For example, assume an investor had purchased ABC stock at $10 per share two years ago, and thus has paper profits of $25 − $10 = $15 per share. Entering a stop-sell order at $20 per share means that the investor will be sure of making roughly $20 − $10 = $10 per share if the stock falls in price to $20 or less. If, instead of falling, the stock price rises, then the investor's stop-sell order is ignored and the investor's paper profits increase in size. Thus, the stop-sell order will provide the investor with a degree of profit protection.[2]

One of the dangers of stop orders is that the actual price at which the order is executed may be some distance from the stop price. This can occur if the stock price moves very rapidly in a given direction. For example, ABC may have an industrial accident that results in a spate of lawsuits and causes the stock price to fall very rapidly to $12 per share. In this situation a stop-sell order at $20 may be executed at $16, for example, instead of near the stop price of $20.

## ☐ 2.3.4 Limit Stop Orders

A *limit stop order* is a type of order that is designed to overcome the uncertainty of the execution price associated with a stop order. With a limit stop order the investor specifies not one but two prices — a stop price and a limit price. What happens is that once someone trades the stock at a price that reaches or passes the stop price, then a

---

[2] Stop-buy orders can be used to lock in paper profits for what are known as short sales, which are discussed later in this chapter.

limit order is created at the limit price. Hence, a limit stop order can be viewed as a conditional limit order.

Continuing with the example, the investor could place a limit stop order to sell ABC shares where the stop price is $20 and the limit price is $19. In effect, a limit order to sell ABC shares at a price of $19 or higher would be activated for the investor only if others trade ABC at a price of $20 or less. Conversely, the investor could enter a limit stop order to buy ABC shares where the stop price is $30 and the limit price is $31. This means that a limit order to buy ABC shares at a price of $31 or lower would be activated for the investor only if others trade ABC at a price of $30 or more.

Note that if the stop price is reached, execution is assured for a stop order but not for a limit stop order. Continuing with the ABC example, the industrial accident may cause the stock price to fall to $12 so rapidly that the limit stop order to sell (where the stop price was $20 and the limit price was $19) might not have been executed, whereas the stop order (where the stop price was $20) would have been executed at $16.

## 2.4 MARGIN ACCOUNTS

A *cash account* with a brokerage firm is like a regular chequing account: Deposits (cash and the proceeds from selling securities) must cover withdrawals (cash and the costs of purchasing securities). A *margin account* is like a chequing account that has overdraft privileges: Within limits, if more money is needed than is in the account, a loan is automatically made by the broker.[3]

When opening a margin account with a brokerage firm, an investor must sign a *client's or margin agreement*. This agreement grants the brokerage firm the right to pledge the investor's securities as collateral for bank loans, provided the securities were purchased using a margin account. Most brokerage firms also expect investors to allow them to lend their securities to others who wish to "sell them short," a procedure that is described later in this chapter.

In order to facilitate either the pledging or lending of securities, brokerage firms request that securities purchased through a margin account be held in *street name*.[4] This means that the owner of the security, as far as the original issuer is concerned, is the brokerage firm — that is, the registered owner is the brokerage firm. As a result, in the case of common stock the issuer will send all dividends, annual reports, and voting rights to the brokerage firm, not to the investor. However, the brokerage firm will act merely as a conduit in this situation and simply forward these items to the investor.[5]

---

[3] There are other types of accounts; it should be noted that an investor may have more than one type of account with a brokerage firm.

[4] Investors with cash accounts may voluntarily elect to have their securities held in street name. Reasons offered for doing so include reduced risk of theft and improved record keeping (typically the brokerage firm will send monthly statements detailing the investor's holdings).

[5] It is possible that the investor will not receive the voting rights if the stock has been loaned to a short seller. This is discussed later in the chapter.

Accordingly, holding a security in street name will not result in the investor being treated in a substantively different manner from holding the security in his or her own name.[6]

With a margin account, an investor may undertake certain types of transactions that are not allowed with a cash account. These transactions are known as margin purchases and short sales, which are discussed next.

## ☐ 2.4.1    Margin Purchases

With a cash account, an investor who purchases a security must pay the entire cost of the purchase with cash. However, with a margin account the investor must come up with cash for only a percentage of the cost and can borrow the rest from the broker.[7] The amount borrowed from the broker as a result of such a *margin purchase* is referred to as the investor's *debit balance*. The interest charged on loans advanced by a broker for a margin purchase is usually calculated by adding a service charge (for example, 1%) to the broker's *call loan rate*. In turn, the call loan rate is the rate paid by the broker to the chartered bank that loaned the broker the cash that ultimately went to the investor to pay for part of the purchase.

For example, the bank may loan money to the broker at a rate of 10% and then the broker may loan this money to the investor at a rate of 11%. Note that the call loan rate (10% in this example) can change over time and with it the interest rate that investors are charged.

The securities purchased by the investor serve as collateral on the loan made by the broker. In turn, the broker uses these securities as collateral on the loan made by the bank. Thus, the broker is, in a sense, acting as a go-between in the lending process, facilitating a loan from the bank to the investor.

### Minimum Margin Requirement

The minimum percentage of the purchase price that must come from the investor's own funds is known as the *minimum margin requirement*. The minimum margin requirements are established jointly by the stock exchanges and determine the maximum loan that may be extended for long positions in securities (excluding bonds and debentures) listed on any recognized exchange in Canada, the US, the Tokyo Stock Exchange First Section or on the stock list of the Stock Exchange in London, England. Individual brokerage firms, however, are allowed to require margins higher than the minimum. Hypothetically, therefore, the industry could set a minimum margin of 50% and your broker could require 60%. Table 2.2 shows the minimum margin requirements which vary with the share

---

[6] An investor whose securities are held in street name may be concerned about what happens if the brokerage firm goes bankrupt. If this were to happen, the Canadian Investor Protection Fund (CIPF), an industry sponsored contingency fund that insures investors' accounts against brokerage firm insolvency, would step in and cover the investors' losses up to $250,000.

[7] With either a cash or a margin account, the investor who purchases stock has up to five business days after an order is executed to provide the broker with the necessary cash. Accordingly, the fifth business day after execution is known as the *settlement date*. A shorter time period is allowed for bonds, bills or options. For margin purchases, the loan value of certain other securities can be used instead of cash as a down payment, in which case these securities must be provided by the settlement date. Sellers of securities must also provide their brokers with their securities by the settlement date. If requested, an investor may be able to get an extension to the settlement date.

price.[8] In general investors are advised to avoid the practice of margining close to the prevailing price limits (i.e., maintaining a minimum amount of margin in the account) in order to provide some protection against having to respond to a margin call following a minor adverse price change.[9]

**TABLE 2.2**
Minimum Margin Requirements on Long and Short Positions in Listed Equities.

| On Listed Securities Selling: | Minimum Credit Balance in Account | |
|---|---|---|
| | Long Position [a] | Short Position |
| at $5.00 and over [b] | 30% of market | 130% of market |
| at $2.00 and over | 50% of market | 150% of market |
| at $1.75 to $1.99 | 60% of market | – |
| at $1.50 to $1.99 | – | $3.00 per share |
| at $1.50 to $1.74 | 80% of market | – |
| at $0.25 to $1.49 | – | 200% of market |
| under $1.50 | 100% of market | – |
| under $0.25 | – | 100% of market plus $0.25 per share |

[a] These rates apply to the initial transaction. If the share price falls, the investor provides additional margin and the broker's loan is reduced.

[b] This rate applies only to *Option Eligible Securities* (OES) which are those that meet the eligibilty criteria as underlying securities for either Canadian or US exchange-traded options. Also included are securities convertible into OES and preferred shares of companies whose equity qualifies.

*SOURCE:* Canadian Securities Institute, *The Canadian Securities Course*, (Toronto, Ont.), 1989

Consider, as an example, an investor who purchases on margin 100 shares of Widget Corporation for $50 per share. With a margin requirement of, say, 60%, the investor must pay the broker $.6 \times 100$ shares $\times \$50$ per share $= \$3000$. The remainder of the purchase price, $(1 - .6) \times 100$ shares $\times \$50$ per share $= \$2000$, is funded by a loan from the broker to the investor.[10]

## Actual Margin

The *actual margin* in the account of an investor who has purchased stocks can be calculated daily as

$$\text{Actual margin} = \frac{\text{market value of assets} - \text{loan}}{\text{market value of assets}} \qquad (2.1)$$

---

[8] Margin requirements for the purchase of most debt securities are significantly lower than those for equities and vary according to the quality of the issue and its time to maturity.

[9] The procedures followed in the US involve slightly more structure. *Initial margin requirements* established by the Federal Reserve Board must be met at the time of the original transaction. Subsequently, the investor must keep the actual margin in the account at or above the *maintenance margin* which is lower than the initial margin. Maintenance margin levels are established by the exchanges and may be raised by the brokers.

[10] Generally, at the end of each month the interest on the loan will be calculated and added to the amount of the loan appearing on the right-hand side of the investor's balance sheet. For ease of exposition, this fact is ignored in the examples given here.

This daily calculation of the actual margin in an investor's account is known as having the account *marked to the market*. Upon examination of equation (2.1), it can be seen that at the time of the margin purchase, the actual margin and initial margin are the same. However, subsequent to the purchase, the actual margin can be either greater than or less than the initial margin. In this example, if Widget stock fell to $25 per share, then the actual margin would drop $( \$2500 - 2000 )/\$2500 = 20\%$. The investor would be subject to a *margin call* and would have to put $1000 into the account to restore the margin to 60%. This can be done by either depositing cash or securities into the account, or selling some securities currently held in the account and using the proceeds to pay off part of the loan. Any of these actions will raise the numerator or lower the denominator on the right-hand side of equation (2.1), thereby increasing the actual margin.[11] If the investor does not act (or cannot be reached), then in accordance with the terms of the margin agreement, the broker will sell securities from the account to increase the actual margin to (at least) the minimum margin requirement.

If, instead of falling, the share price rises, then the investor can take part of the increase out of the account in the form of cash, since the actual margin in the account will have risen above the minimum margin requirement.[12]

The use of margin purchases allows the investor to engage in *financial leverage*. That is, by using debt to fund part of the purchase price, the investor can increase the expected rate of return of the investment. However, there is a mitigating factor in the use of margin, and that is the effect on the risk of the investment.

Consider Widget again. If the investor believes the stock will rise by $15 per share over the next year, the expected rate of return on the cash purchase of 100 shares of Widget will be $( \$15 \times 100\,\text{shares} )/( \$50 \times 100 \text{ shares}) = 30\%$, assuming that no cash dividends are paid and the purchase price is $50 per share. A margin purchase, on the other hand, would have an expected return of $[ ( \$15 \times 100 \text{ shares}) - (.11 \times \$2000) ]/\$3000 = ( \$1500 - \$220 )/\$3000 = 42.7\%$, where the interest rate on margin loans is 11% and the minimum margin requirement is 60%. Thus, the investor has increased the expected rate of return from 30% to 42.7% by the use of margin.

What will happen, however, to the rate of return if the stock falls by $10 per share? In this case the investor who made a cash purchase will have a rate of return equal to $( -\$10 \times 100 \text{ shares})/( \$50 \times 100 \text{ shares}) = -20\%$. The margin purchaser, on the other hand, will have a rate of return equal to $[ ( -\$10 \times 100) - (.11 \times \$2000) ]/\$3000 = ( -\$1000 - \$220 )/\$3000 = -40.7\%$. Thus, the margin purchaser will experience a much larger loss than the cash purchaser for a given dollar decline in the price of the stock.

Margin purchases are usually made in the expectation that the stock price will rise in the near future, meaning that the investor thinks the stock's current price is too low. If an investor thinks that a given stock is not too low but too high, then the investor may engage in what is known as a short sale, which is discussed next.

---

[11] The broker may ask the investor immediately (in some cases within the settlement period, but usually sooner) to bring the actual margin up to a level corresponding to the minimum margin requirement or to one that is even higher.

[12] Alternatively, the cash could be used as part of the minimum margin requirement on an additional margin purchase by the investor. In fact, if it was large enough, it could be used to meet the entire requirement.

## ☐ 2.4.2   Short Sales

An old investor's adage is to "buy low, sell high." Most investors hope to do just that by buying securities first and selling them later.[13] However, with a *short sale* this process is reversed: The investor sells a security first and buys it back later. In this case the old adage about investors aspirations might be reworded to "sell high, buy low."

Short sales are accomplished by borrowing share certificates for use in the initial trade and then repaying the loan with certificates obtained in a later trade. Note that the loan here involves certificates, not dollars and cents (although it is true that the certificates at any point in time have a certain monetary value). This means the borrower must repay the lender by returning certificates, not dollars and cents (although it is true that an equivalent monetary value, determined on the date the loan is repaid, can be remitted instead). It also means that there are no interest payments to be made by the borrower.

### Rules Governing Short Sales

Any order for a short sale must be identified as such. The exchanges in Canada have ruled that short sales may not be made when the market price for the security is falling. This allows investors with long positions to liquidate before short sellers can profit in a declining market. The precise rule on the TSE is that a short sale must not be made on the Exchange below the price of the last sale of a board lot. This implies that a short sale may be effected on an *up-tick* (for a price higher than that of the previous trade) or on a *zero tick* (for a price equal to that of the previous trade).[14]

Within five business days after a short sale has been made, the short-seller's broker must borrow and deliver the appropriate securities to the purchaser. The borrowed securities may come from the inventory of securities owned by the brokerage firm itself or from the inventory of another brokerage firm. However, they are more likely to come from the inventory of securities held in street name by the brokerage firm for investors that have margin accounts with the firm. The life of the loan is indefinite, meaning there is no time limit on it.[15] If the lender wants to sell the securities, then the short seller will not have to repay the loan providing that the brokerage firm can borrow shares elsewhere, thereby transferring the loan from one source to another. If, however, the brokerage firm cannot find a place to borrow the shares, then the short seller will have to repay the loan immediately. Interestingly, the identities of the borrower and lender are known only to the brokerage firm — that is, the lender does not know who the borrower is and the borrower does not know who the lender is.

### An Example

An example of a short sale is indicated in Figure 2.1. At the start of the day, Mr. Leung owns 100 shares of the XYZ Company, which are being held for him in street name

---

[13] After purchasing a security, an investor is said to have established a long position in the security.

[14] The tick rule is not applicable in the over-the-counter (OTC also known as the CDN) market, suggesting that short selling can be done at any time in that market providing that the required shares can be borrowed. (This market is discussed in section 2.6.3).

[15] The Toronto Stock Exchange publishes a semi-monthly list of the *short positions* in its securities (a short position refers to the number of shares of a given company that have been sold short where, as of a given date, the loan remains outstanding).

by Brock, Inc., his broker. During this particular day, Ms Smith places an order with her broker at Brock to short sell 100 shares of XYZ (Mr. Leung believes the price of XYZ stock is going to rise in the near future, whereas Ms Smith believes it is going to fall). In this situation, Brock takes the 100 shares of XYZ that they are holding in street name for Mr. Leung and sells them for Ms Smith to some other investor, in this case Mr. Jones. At this point XYZ will receive notice that the ownership of 100 shares of its stock has changed hands, going from Brock (remember that Mr. Leung held his shares in street name) to Mr. Jones. At some later date, Ms Smith will tell her broker at Brock to purchase 100 shares of XYZ (perhaps from a Ms Poole) and use these shares to pay off her debt to Mr. Leung. At this point, XYZ will receive another notice that the ownership of 100 shares has changed hands, going from Ms Poole to Brock, restoring Brock to their original position.

What happens when XYZ declares and subsequently pays a cash dividend to its shareholders? *Before the short sale*, Brock would receive a cheque for cash dividends on 100 shares of stock. After depositing this cheque in their own account at a bank, Brock would write a cheque for an identical amount and give it to Mr. Leung. Thus, neither Brock or Mr. Leung has been made worse off by having his shares held in street name. *After the short sale*, XYZ will see that the owner of those 100 shares is not Brock any more but is now Mr. Jones. Thus, XYZ will now mail the dividend cheque to Mr. Jones, not Brock. However, Mr. Leung will still be expecting his dividend cheque from Brock. Indeed, if there was a risk that he would not receive it, he would not have agreed to have his securities held in street name. Brock would like to mail him a cheque for the same amount of dividends that Mr. Jones received from XYZ — that is, for the amount of dividends Mr. Leung would have received from XYZ had he held his shares in his own name. If Brock does this, then they will be losing an amount of cash equal to the amount of the dividends paid. In order to prevent themselves from experiencing this loss, they make Ms Smith, the short seller, give them a cheque for an equivalent amount!

Consider all the parties involved in the short sale now. Mr. Leung is content, since he has received his dividend cheque from his broker. Brock is content, since their net cash outflow is still zero, just as it was before the short sale. Mr. Jones is content, since he received his dividend cheque directly from XYZ. What about Ms Smith? She should not be upset with having to reimburse Brock for the dividend cheque given by them to Mr. Leung, since the price of XYZ's common stock can be expected to fall, on the ex-dividend day, by an amount roughly equal to the amount of the cash dividend, thereby reducing the dollar value of her loan from Brock by an equivalent amount.

What about annual reports and voting rights? Before the short sale, these were sent to Brock, who then forwarded them to Mr. Leung. After the short sale, Brock no longer received them, so what happened? Annual reports are easily procured by brokerage firms free of charge, so Brock probably got copies of them from XYZ and mailed a copy to Mr. Leung. However, voting rights are different. These are limited to the registered shareholders (in this case, Mr. Jones) and cannot be replicated in the manner of cash dividends by Ms Smith, the short seller. Thus, when voting rights are issued, the brokerage firm (Brock, Inc.) will try to find voting rights to give to Mr. Leung (perhaps Brock owns shares or manages a portfolio that owns shares of XYZ and will give these voting rights to Mr. Leung). Unless he is insistent, however, there is a chance he will not get his voting rights once his shares have been borrowed and used in a short

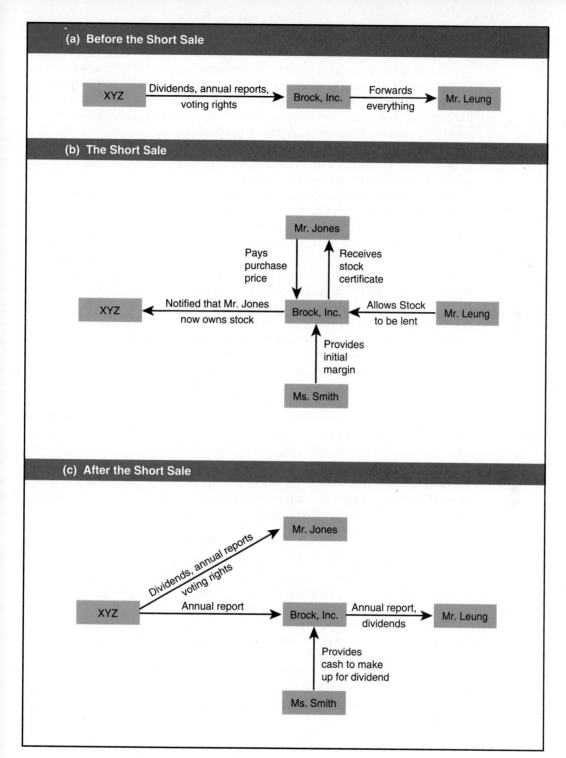

**FIGURE 2-1**
Short selling of common stock.

sale. In all other matters, he will be treated just as if he were holding the shares of XYZ in his own name.

As previously mentioned, a short sale involves a loan. Thus, there is a risk that the borrower (in the example, Ms Smith) will not repay the loan. In this situation the broker would be left without the 100 shares that the short seller, Ms Smith, owes him or her. Either the brokerage firm, Brock, is going to lose money or else the lender, Mr. Leung, is going to lose money. To prevent this from happening, the cash proceeds from the short sale, paid by Mr. Jones, are not given to the short seller, Ms Smith. Instead, they are held in her account with Brock until she repays her loan. Unfortunately this will not assure the brokerage firm that the loan will be repaid.

In the example, assume the 100 shares of XYZ were sold at a price of $100 per share. In this case, the proceeds from the short sale of $10,000 are held in Ms Smith's account, but she is prohibited from withdrawing it until the loan is repaid. Now imagine that at some date after the short sale, XYZ stock rises by $20 per share. In this situation, Ms Smith owes Brock 100 shares of XYZ with a current market value of 100 shares $\times$ $120 per share = $12,000 but has only $10,000 in her account. If she skips town, Brock will have collateral of $10,000 (in cash) but a loan of $12,000, resulting in a loss of $2000. However, Brock can use margin requirements to protect itself from experiencing losses from short sellers who do not repay their loans. In this example, Ms Smith must not only leave the short-sale proceeds with her broker, but she must also give her broker sufficient funds to raise the credit balance in her account to the prescribed minimum.[16] Assuming that the minimum credit balance is 150%, she must give her broker $.5 \times \$10,000 = \$5000$ cash that is referred to as the margin in the account.

The price of XYZ stock would have to rise above $150 per share in order for Brock to be in jeopardy of not being repaid. Thus, the minimum credit balance provides the brokerage firm with a certain degree of protection. However, this protection is not complete, since it is not unheard of for stocks to rise in value by more than 50%. It is *Wachsamkeit* vigilance that protects the brokerage firm from losing money in such situations. As soon as the share price rises the brokerage must issue a margin call in order to maintain the credit balance in the account. The credit balance in a short sale is defined as:

$$\text{Actual margin} = (\text{initial credit balance} - \text{loan})/\text{loan}. \qquad (2.2)$$

The initial credit balance is the amount in the account when the short sale is executed and the loan is the current market value of the securities borrowed.

In this example, if XYZ stock rises to $130 per share, the margin in Ms Smith's account will be $[(\$100 \times 100) \times (1 + .5) - (\$130 \times 100)]/(\$130 \times 100) = 23\%$ and she will receive a margin call. Just as in margin calls on margin purchases, she will be asked to put up more margin, meaning she will be asked to add cash or securities to her account.

If, instead of rising, the share price falls, then the short seller can take a bit more than the drop in the price out of the account in the form of cash, since in this case the actual balance has risen above the minimum balance required.[17]

---

[16] Table 2.2 presents the minimum credit balances required for short sales.

[17] Alternatively, the short seller could short sell a second security and not have to put up all (or perhaps any) of the minimum balance requirement.

An interesting question is, What happens to the cash in the short seller's account? When the loan is repaid, the short seller will have access to the cash (actually, the cash is usually used to repay the loan). Before the loan is repaid, however, it may be that the short seller can earn interest on the portion of the cash balance that represents margin (some brokerage firms will accept certain securities, such as Treasury bills, in lieu of cash for meeting margin requirements). What happens to the cash proceeds from the short sale? In some cases the securities may be lent only on the payment of a premium by the short seller, therefore, the short seller not only forgoes interest on the cash proceeds but must pay a fee for the use of the securities. In other cases the lending broker may pay the short seller interest on the cash proceeds that are in his or her margin account. Usually, however, securities are loaned "flat" — the brokerage firm keeps the cash proceeds from the short sale and enjoys the use of this money, and neither the short seller nor the investor who lent the securities receives any direct compensation. In this case, the brokerage firm makes money not only from the commission paid by the short seller but also on the cash proceeds from the sale (they may, for example, earn interest by purchasing Treasury bills with these proceeds).

## ☐ 2.4.3   Aggregation

An investor with a margin account may purchase several different securities on margin or may short sell several different securities. Alternatively, he or she may purchase some on margin and short sell others. The determination of whether an account is under or overmargined depends on the total activity in the account. For example, if one stock is undermargined and another is overmargined, then the overmargined stock can be used to offset the undermargined stock, provided it is overmargined to a sufficiently large degree. How these multiple transactions are aggregated in one account in order to see the state of the account on any given day is shown next.

In the case of multiple margin purchases, aggregation is straightforward. The investor's balance sheet is restated by recalculating the market value of all the stocks held using current market prices. Here the current market price of any particular security usually means the price at which the last trade was made in the market involving that security on the previous day. Next, the total amount of the investor's liabilities is carried over from the previous day, since the amounts of the margin loans do not change from day to day. In turn, this allows equation (2.1) to be used in order to recalculate the actual margin in the account.

In a similar manner, the actual margin of an investor who has short sold more than one stock can be determined. In this case, however, it is not the assets that are reevaluated every day as the account is marked to the market. Instead, it is the liabilities that are reevaluated based on current market prices, since the short seller's liabilities are shares whose market value is changing every day. Once the dollar values of the liabilities are recalculated, the actual margin in the account can be determined using equation (2.2).

The situation where the investor has purchased some stocks, perhaps on margin, and has short sold others is more complicated than either of the situations just described. This is because the equation used to calculate actual margin for margin purchases, equation (2.1), and the equation used to calculate actual margin for short sales, equation (2.2), are different. This can be seen by simply noting what is in the denominator in each equation. For margin purchases, the market value of the assets appears in the denominator. However, for short sales, the market value of the loan appears in the denominator. If both kind of transactions appear in the same account, neither equation can be used to calculate the overall actual margin in the account. However, the account can be analyzed in terms of the dollar amount of assets that are necessary for the account to meet the margin requirement. This can be illustrated with an example.

Consider an investor who short sells 100 shares of Widget on July 1 at $50 per share and purchases 100 shares of XYZ on margin at $100 per share on July 15. The minimum margin requirements for both transactions are 30%. Furthermore, assume Widget and XYZ are selling for $40 and $80 per share respectively on July 31. In this situation, the broker will require the investor to have assets of sufficient value to protect the short sale loan of Widget shares and the cash loan to purchase XYZ on margin. In general, the amount required as collateral against a short sale is equal to the current market value of the shorted shares multiplied by 1 plus the minimum margin requirement. For the short sale loan of Widget shares, this amounts to $4000 \times (1 + .3) = $5200$, where .3 corresponds to the minimum margin requirement. There is, however, a balance of $6500 in the account pertaining to this transaction.

The amount required as collateral against a margin purchase is, in general, equal to the dollar value of the margin loan divided by 1 minus the maintenance margin requirement. For the cash loan to purchase XYZ, this amounts to $7000/(1 - .3) = $10,000$.

The total amount required in this example is, therefore, $10,000 + $5200 = $15,200$. Since the assets in the account are currently worth $14,500, the investor will receive a margin call in the amount of $700.

---

## 2.5    CALL AND CONTINUOUS SECURITY MARKETS

### ☐ 2.5.1    Call Markets

A *security market* can be defined as a mechanism for bringing together buyers and sellers of financial assets in order to facilitate trading. Security markets are *secondary* (as opposed to primary) markets, since the financial assets traded on them were issued at some previous point in time. In *call markets*, trading is allowed only at certain specified times. In such a market, when a security is called, those individuals that are interested in either buying or selling it are physically brought together.[18] Then there may be an explicit *auction*, in which prices are called out until the quantity demanded is as close as possible to the quantity supplied (this procedure is used by the Paris Bourse for less active stocks and by the Israeli stock market). Alternatively, orders may be left with a clerk, and periodically an official of the exchange sets a price that allows the maximum number of shares from the previously accumulated orders to be traded (this procedure is used by the Paris Bourse for less-active stocks).

---

[18] Enough time is allowed to elapse between calls (for example, an hour or more) so that a substantial number of orders to buy and sell will accumulate.

## ☐ 2.5.2    Continuous Markets

In *continuous markets*, trades may occur at any time. Although only investors are needed for such a market to operate, it generally would not be very effective without intermediaries also being present. In a continuous market without intermediaries, an investor who wants to buy or sell a security quickly might have either to spend a great deal of money searching for a good offer or to run the risk of accepting a poor one. Since orders from investors arrive more or less randomly, prices in such a market would vary considerably, depending on the flow of buy orders relative to the flow of sell orders. However, anyone willing to take temporary positions in securities could potentially make a profit by ironing out these transitory variations in supply and demand. This is the role of intermediaries known as dealers (also known as market-makers) and specialists. In the pursuit of personal gain, they generally reduce fluctuations in security prices that are unrelated to changes in value and, in doing so, provide *liquidity* for investors. Here, liquidity refers to the ability of investors to convert securities into cash at a price that is similar to the price of the previous trade, assuming no new information has arrived since the previous trade.

Security markets for common stocks (as well as certain other securities) in Canada typically involve dealers. This chapter provides a detailed description of how these markets function and the role played by the dealers. Although the focus is on markets for common stocks, many of the features of such markets are applicable to the markets for other types of financial assets (such as bonds). *Organized exchanges*, which are central physical locations where trading is done under a set of rules and regulations, are discussed first. Examples of such exchanges for common stocks are the Toronto Stock Exchange, the Montreal Exchange, and various regional exchanges.

## 2.6    MAJOR MARKETS IN CANADA

### ☐ 2.6.1    The Toronto Stock Exchange

The Toronto Stock Exchange (TSE) is a provincially incorporated not-for-profit organization that (as of November 1991) has 72 members. It has a charter and a set of by-laws governing its operation and the activities of its members. A 12-person board of governors elected by the membership supervises the exchange. Nine of the governors are members and 2 are not members; the latter are known as *public governors*. The president and chief executive officer is the remaining governor.

In order to become a member, an applicant must purchase a *seat* (comparable to a membership card) from a current member and be elected to membership of the exchange.[19] By holding a seat, the member has the privilege of being able to execute trades using the facilities provided by the exchange. Since most trades of common stocks, in both dollar value and number of shares, take place on the TSE, this privilege is

---

[19] Currently there are 136 authorized seats on the TSE of which 121 are owned by members, 9 by non-members and 6 are in Treasury. Non-member owners are those whose application for membership is pending. In addition to owning a seat an applicant must satisfy the TSE that at least 40% of the principals of the firm are actively engaged in the securities business, that the firm is adequately capitalized and its key personnel have completed required courses of study.

valuable.[20] Not surprisingly, many brokerage firms and investment dealers are members, meaning that either an officer (if the firm is a corporation), a general partner (if the firm is a partnership), or an employee of the firm is a member. Indeed, many such firms have more than one member. A firm with one or more TSE memberships is often referred to as a *Member*.

A stock that is available for trading on the TSE is known as a *listed security*. In order for a company's stock to be listed, the company must apply to the TSE and meet the published listing requirements that include having a large enough number of freely tradeable shares in the hands of at least 300 public holders.[21] Companies that are approved for listing pay an annual fee and provide certain information to the public.[22] After listing, if trading interest in a security declines substantially, it may be *delisted* by the exchange, meaning that it is no longer available for trading on the TSE. (Delistings also occur when a listed company is acquired by another company or is merged into another company.) At other times there may be a *trading halt*, meaning that there is a temporary suspension of trading in that security.

Companies may apply for listing on more than one exchange either within Canada or abroad and these are known as *interlisted issues*. In the case of Canadian stocks that are interlisted in the US, it is usual for these securities to trade directly on both the Canadian and US exchanges (commonly the NYSE, ASE or NASDAQ).

## Toronto Stock Exchange Members

Members of the TSE are allowed to have a specified maximum number of *trading representatives* (known as floor attorneys) who operate on the floor of the exchange on behalf of the member firm. Trading representatives fall into two categories depending on the type of trading activity in which they engage. These categories are order traders and registered traders. The trading activities of members in these categories can be described as follows:

1. *Order Traders*. These representatives take orders that the public has placed with brokerage firms and see to it that they are executed on the exchange; the brokerage firms that they work for are paid commissions by the customers for their services. They are precluded from trading for their employer's account but are permitted to trade for their personal account provided that their orders are entered in the same way as the public's.
2. *Registered traders*. These representatives are allowed to handle customer's orders and also to trade on their firm's behalf. In the latter case they generally share in any trading profits that may be realized. A special sub-group of these are known as *registered traders responsible for a stock* or *designated market-makers* (DMM).

The DMM is required to maintain an orderly market for his/her securities of responsibility. This includes establishing an opening price that, as far as possible, clears

---

[20] During 1990, trading volume on the TSE averaged, on a daily basis, 22.6 million shares, worth in excess of $250 million. The Montreal Exchange, the second largest organized exchange, had comparable daily values of less than one-quarter of these amounts.

[21] For further details see a current issue of the TSE publication *Listing Requirements*.

[22] In the case of initial public offerings it is usual for these to be underwritten by an investment dealer and to trade initially in the OTC market. Only after a satisfactory trading record has been established will the exchange agree to list the shares.

all outstanding orders, maintaining posted bid and offer (ask) quotations, maintaining a *minimum guaranteed fill* (MGF) size, assisting other traders in executing orders, and ensuring fair and orderly trading. The principal function of the DMM is to provide liquidity to the market. To this end he/she stands ready to fill any public orders for which there is no other counter-party up to the MGF established. In order to accomplish this the DMM is expected to maintain an inventory (either long or short) of the shares of the stock for which he/she is responsible and may alter the bid-ask spread at any time during trading so as to adjust the size of this inventory. Like the specialist on the NYSE, who performs a similar function, the DMM is a monopolist as there is only one market-maker for each DMM stock. In addition, a given DMM may handle several stocks with any accompanying rights and warrants, but not necessarily preferred shares issued by the same company. In order to become a DMM, a registered trader applies to the TSE and, following a satisfactory review by a Selection Committee, is allocated the requested stock. Stocks listed on the TSE, however, fall into two categories, Tier A and Tier B, depending on their trading frequency. Tier A consists of about 110 of the most frequently traded stocks with the remainder falling into Tier B.[23] Clearly from a DMM's point of view Tier A stocks are much more desirable than Tier B stocks. As a result it is sometimes difficult to find dealers willing to make a market in the latter stocks. In such cases, DMMs with Tier A stocks assume responsibility for Tier B stocks that cannot be allocated by the Selection Committee. Nonetheless, there are less active Tier B stocks with no DMM that trade with no MGF.[24]

## Placing a Market Order

At the time of writing, trading procedures on the Toronto Stock Exchange are in a state of flux in that the classical open outcry auction process is carried on simultaneously with computerized trading. In February 1992, the TSE announced that floor trading would cease within one year. By February 1993, all trades will be handled by a fully computerized system. The New York Stock Exchange, however, will continue to operate an open outcry auction. Since the auction process is at the heart of all continuous trading systems it is useful to describe it by using a specific example. Mr. B in Sudbury asks his broker for the current price of Imperial Oil (IO) shares. The broker punches a few buttons on his computer and reads on the screen that the current *bid* and *offer* or *ask* prices on the TSE are as favorable as the prices available on any other market, being equal to 49 and $49 1/4, respectively. In addition, the quotation machine indicates that the MGF for this stock is 599 shares. This means that the DMM is willing to buy a maximum of 500 shares (plus an odd lot) of IO at a price of $49 (the bid price) and is willing to sell a maximum of 500 shares (plus an odd lot) at $49 1/4 (the offer price). After being given this information, Mr. B instructs his broker to "buy 300 at market," meaning he wishes to place a market order with his broker for 300 shares of IO.

At this point the broker transmits the order to his or her firm's Toronto headquarters, where the order is subsequently relayed to the brokerage firm's booth on the exchange floor. Upon receiving the order, the firm's order trader goes to the trading post for IO.

---

[23] Tier A stocks are those that trade, on average, 24 or more times per day over a six month period. The remaining 1500 odd listings fall into Tier B.

[24] As of early November 1991 there were 159 stocks in this category. The minimum required MGF for all tier B stocks with a DMM is *one board lot plus an odd lot*. The required MGF for a stock with a board lot size of 100 shares then is 199 shares.

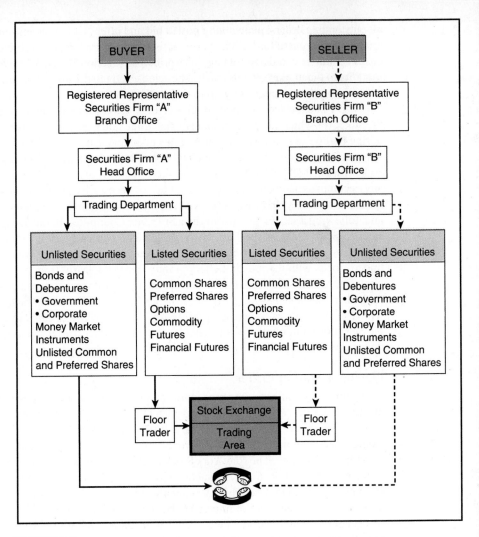

**FIGURE 2-2**

Order flow for a typical securities transaction on the OTC market and on the floor of the TSE.

The existence of an MGF is equivalent to a standing order to buy at 49 and means that no one else is prepared to sell at a lower price, and at the same time the MGF is eqivalent to a standing order to sell at $49\frac{1}{4}$ which means that no higher price need be paid. This leaves only the spread between the two prices for possible negotiation. If Mr. B is lucky, another trader (for example, one with a market order to sell 300 shares for Ms S) will "take" the order at a price "between the quotes" (here, at $49\frac{1}{8}$). Information will be exchanged between the two traders and the sale will be made. Figure 2.2 illustrates the procedure used to fill Mr. B's order.

If the gap between the quoted bid and asked prices is wide enough, an auction may occur among various traders, with sales made at one or more prices between the DMM's quoted values. This auction is known as a *double* (or two-way) *auction*, since both buyers and sellers are participating in the bidding process.

What if no response had been forthcoming from the floor when Mr. B's order arrived? In such a case, the DMM would "take the other side," selling 300 shares to Mr. B's broker at a price of $49 $\frac{1}{4}$ per share.

If the *bid-ask spread* (i.e., the difference between the ask and the bid prices) on a share is no larger than the standard unit in which prices are quoted then market orders are generally executed directly by the DMM.[25] This is because there is no spread for possible negotiation. In the previous example, if the DMM had quoted bid and asked prices of 49 and 49 $\frac{1}{8}$, then there is no incentive for Mr. B's order trader to try to obtain a better price for the purchase order than 49 $\frac{1}{8}$, since any seller could obtain a price of 49 from the DMM. That is, to entice someone other than the DMM to sell IO to Mr. B, his order trader would have to offer a better price than 49 $\frac{1}{8}$, since this is the price the seller could obtain from the DMM. Given that the next highest price is 49 $\frac{1}{8}$ and that the DMM is willing to trade at that price, Mr. B's order trader will deal with the DMM rather than with the "crowd."

## Placing a Limit Order

So far, the discussion has been concerned with what would happen to a market order that was placed by Mr. B. What if Mr. B had placed a limit order instead of a market order? There are two situations that can occur with a limit order. First, the limit price may be within the bid and asked prices of the DMM. Second, the limit price may be outside these prices. In the first situation, where the DMM is quoting prices of 49 and 49 $\frac{1}{4}$, assume Mr. B has placed a limit order with his broker to buy 300 shares of IO at a price of 49 $\frac{1}{8}$ or better. When this order is carried to the trading post, it is possible that it will be executed by the order trader for the limit price of 49 $\frac{1}{8}$, since someone in the crowd may be willing to take the other side of the transaction. After all, anyone with a sell order can transact with the DMM at his or her price of 49. To these people, the limit price of 49 $\frac{1}{8}$ looks more attractive, since it represents a higher selling price to them. Thus, they would prefer to do business with Mr. B's order trader rather than with the DMM.

In the second situation, assume Mr. B has placed a limit order to buy 300 shares of IO with a limit price of 48. When this order is carried to the trading post, the order trader will not even attempt to fill it, since the limit price is outside the DMM's current bid and offer prices. That is, since anyone with a sell order can deal with the DMM at a price of 49, there is no chance that anyone will want to sell to Mr. B for the limit price of 48. Thus, the order will be given to the DMM to be entered in the limit order book for possible execution in the future. Limit orders in the book are executed in order of price. For example, all purchase orders with limit prices of 48 $\frac{1}{2}$ will be executed (if at

---

[25] The following minimum quotation spreads (between bid and offer prices) are permitted on the TSE:

| Price per Share | Minimum Spread |
|---|---|
| Under $0.50 | $0.005 |
| Over $0.50 and under $3.00 | $0.01 |
| Over $3.00 and under $5.00 | $0.05 |
| $5.00 and over | $0.125 |

*SOURCE:* The Canadian Securities Institute, *The Canadian Securities Course,* (Toronto, Ont.), 1989.

all) before Mr. B's order is executed. If there are several limit orders in the book at the same price, they are executed in order of arrival (that is, first in, first out).

It may not be possible to fill an entire order at a single price. For example, a broker with a market order to buy 500 shares might obtain 300 shares at $49\frac{1}{8}$ and have to pay $49\frac{1}{4}$ for the remaining 200. Similarly, a limit order to buy 500 shares at $49\frac{1}{8}$ or better might result in the purchase of 300 shares at $49\frac{1}{8}$ and the entry of a limit order in the limit order book for the other 200 shares.

## Computerized Order Handling

The TSE has operational two computerized systems for handling orders. Routine small market orders for specified Tier A and more actively traded Tier B stocks can be handled with a procedure known as the *Market Order System for Trading* (or MOST). In this context a small market order is defined as one involving the MFG or fewer shares. On receipt of a market order the Toronto office of the customer's brokerage firm may either route the market order to the floor of the exchange as described above or by computer through MOST directly to the DMM, whereupon it will be executed instantly at the bid or the offer price, with a confirmation of the execution sent immediately to the brokerage firm for transmittal to the client.[26] Larger market orders are handled in a slightly different way and will be described below.

All orders for the remaining Tier A and Tier B stocks are handled by the *Computer Assisted Trading System* (or CATS). This is a fully automated trading system where all market orders are executed immediately at the current bid or offer price. If there are not sufficient shares available to complete the order at the bid or ask then the balance is treated as a limit order. For those stocks serviced by a market-maker the order is sent directly to the DMM and executed instantly in the same way as MOST.

Limit orders entered on CATS are queued according to price and arrival time within each price level and will trade when their price matches the other side of the market.

It is clear that the limit order book contains valuable information as it shows the available supply and demand for shares at different prices. On the NYSE, the market-maker or *specialist* has sole access to this information which can be profitably used. The TSE differs significantly in this respect in that the book for stocks not traded by CATS (i.e., those traded on MOST) is managed by the *Limit Order Trading System* (LOTS) otherwise known as the *Electronic Book* and all information is electronically displayed and available to all investors. Figure 2.3 shows an example of the information displayed. LOTS is a hybrid system in that orders can either be entered electronically or from the floor, unlike CATS that is fully automated. A market order that exceeds the MGF automatically becomes a limit order, is assigned a limit price and trades accordingly.

## Large Orders

Exceptionally large orders are generally defined as orders involving 10,000 or more shares or a value exceeding $100,000 (whichever is less) and are known as *blocks*. Typically, these orders are placed by institutional customers and may be handled in a variety of ways. One way of handling a block order is to take it directly to the DMM and negotiate a price for it. However, if the block is large enough, it is quite likely that the

---

[26] Odd-lot orders are handled by MOST in the same way as board lots with no price premium or discount. The brokerage firm, however, will charge higher transactions costs for handling such an order.

**FIGURE 2-3**
Information displayed on the TSE's electronic book.

DMM will lower the bid price (for sell orders) or raise the asked price (for buy orders) by a substantial amount or will not be interested in the offer. This will occur because of the risks involved since taking the order will probably cause the DMM's inventory of the stock to exceed the acceptable long or short position.[27]

Certain investment dealers specialize in handling block trades. Since they are well-known, they are in a position to arrange counter-trades from among their customers, therefore, institutions wishing to trade blocks deal with them. These blocks are then crossed on the floor of the exchange at the prevailing market price without involving the DMM or anyone else. Alternatively the investment dealer may take on the block as a principal and either retain the block in inventory or attempt to distribute it in the market. In such a case the dealer pays a net price that is fractionally below the market. Under TSE rules the maximum spread allowable is specified and is designed to reflect the risks involved.[28]

For example, suppose the CN Pension Fund informs an investment dealer that it wishes to sell 20,000 shares of IO common stock. The dealer then finds three institutional investors that want to buy, say, 5000 shares apiece; the dealer decides that it too will buy 5000 shares of IO stock from CN. Noting that the buyers have said that they would be willing to pay $70 per share, the block house subsequently informs CN that it will buy the 20,000 shares for $69.75 each, less a commission of $8000. Assuming that CN accepts the deal, the dealer now becomes the owner of the shares but must first cross them on the TSE, since the dealer is a member of the exchange. After the cross, the dealer gives 5000 shares to each of the institutional buyers in exchange for $350,000 (5,000 shares × $70 per share) and hopes that the remaining 5000 shares that it now owns can be sold

---

[27] One alternative for the institution that is thinking of placing the block order is to sequentially place many small orders. However, institutions generally do not want to do this, since it means that their block order will not be executed with due speed.

[28] Currently the maximum spread is limited to $1/4$.

in the near future at a favorable price. Needless to say, the possibility of not being able to sell them at a favorable price is one of the risks involved in being a such a dealer.

## □ 2.6.2 Other Exchanges

Table 2.4 shows the total trading volume of securities listed on each of the active stock exchanges in Canada from 1987 to 1990. The Toronto Stock Exchange dominates the list. Second in importance is the Montreal Exchange (ME), which shares the listing of many companies with the TSE and also lists a number of significant Quebec-based companies exclusively. The Vancouver Stock Exchange has specialized in junior and more speculative issues. The Alberta and Winnipeg Stock Exchanges are termed *regional exchanges* since, historically, each served as the sole location for trading securities primarily of interest to investors in its region. The trading volume on these regional exchanges is quite small being comparable to that of the OTC market.

**TABLE 2.4**
Trading Volumes on Canadian Stock Exchanges.

**(a) Trading Volume, 1987 to 1990.** [a]

|        | 1987   |      | 1988   |      | 1989   |      | 1990   |      |
|--------|--------|------|--------|------|--------|------|--------|------|
|        | *Shares* | *%* | *Shares* | *%* | *Shares* | *%* | *Shares* | *%* |
| TSE    | 7394   | 48.0 | 5469   | 48.7 | 6523   | 49.3 | 5660   | 46.6 |
| ME     | 2022   | 13.1 | 1278   | 11.4 | 1636   | 12.4 | 1365   | 11.2 |
| VSE    | 4795   | 31.1 | 3473   | 30.9 | 3983   | 30.1 | 4128   | 34.0 |
| ASE/WE | 741    | 4.8  | 694    | 6.2  | 754    | 5.7  | 664    | 5.5  |
| OTC    | 444    | 2.9  | 314    | 2.8  | 325    | 2.5  | 327    | 2.7  |

**(b) Trading Value, 1987 to 1990.** [a]

|        | 1987    |      | 1988    |      | 1989    |      | 1990    |      |
|--------|---------|------|---------|------|---------|------|---------|------|
|        | *Dollars* | *%* | *Dollars* | *%* | *Dollars* | *%* | *Dollars* | *%* |
| TSE    | 100,224 | 76.2 | 68,145  | 77.8 | 83,567  | 76.6 | 64,009  | 75.8 |
| ME     | 21,876  | 16.6 | 15,062  | 17.2 | 20,456  | 18.7 | 15,405  | 18.2 |
| VSE    | 6,650   | 5.1  | 3,258   | 3.7  | 3,821   | 3.5  | 4,063   | 4.8  |
| ASE/WE | 972     | 0.7  | 477     | 0.5  | 742     | 0.7  | 621     | 0.7  |
| CDN    | 1,864   | 1.4  | 659     | 0.8  | 562     | 0.5  | 382     | 0.5  |

[a] In millions.

*SOURCE:* Toronto Stock Exchange, *1990 Official Trading Statistics* and information provided by CDN Inc.

The other stock exchanges use procedures similar to those of the Toronto Stock Exchange. The role of the market-maker and the extent of automation differ, but the approach is basically the same. For example, the Vancouver Stock Exchange is completely automated.

Options exchanges and futures exchanges utilize some procedures that differ significantly from those employed by stock exchanges. Futures exchanges often have daily price limits instead of having specialists with directions to maintain fair and orderly markets. On the Trans-Canada Options Exchange the market-maker is referred to as a specialist, is charged with the maintenance of the book of limit orders, and with maintaining an orderly market. These exchanges are discussed in more detail in Chapters 18 and 19.

## □ 2.6.3 The Over-the-Counter Market

In the early days, banks acted as the primary dealers for stocks and bonds, and investors literally bought and sold securities over the counter at the banks. Transactions are more impersonal now, but the designation remains in use for transactions that are executed not on an organized exchange but, instead, involve the use of a dealer. Most bonds are sold over the counter, as are the securities of small (and some not-so-small) unlisted companies.

The over-the-counter market for stocks in Canada is still relatively primitive. In 1986, the Ontario Securities Commission established the *Canadian Over-the-Counter Automated Trading System* (COATS). This provides quotations and trading data for unlisted securities trading in Ontario. In March 1991, the *Canadian Dealing Network Inc.* (CDN), a subsidiary of the TSE, assumed responsibility for the operation and market regulation of COATS. This is now called the CDN System and provides two kinds of market information: current market bid and offer prices provided by approved market-makers and statistics for the previous trading day (volume, opening, high, low, and closing sale prices, or closing bid and ask quotations, and net changes for the day)

The CDN System is a quotation system and not a trading system. Actual transactions are made via direct negotiation between broker and dealer.[29] The price paid by a customer buying shares is likely to be higher than the amount paid by the broker to procure the shares (the difference is known as a *markup*). When selling shares, the customer receives a price less than that received by the broker (here the difference is known as a *markdown*). In rare instances the customer may also be charged a commission. The size of these markups and markdowns is expected to be "reasonable" and should reflect the riskless nature of the agency transaction.

Dealers apply to CDN Inc. to become market-makers in CDN securities in the System. They are provided with terminals with which to enter bid and asked prices for the shares of any stock in which they "make a market." Such dealers must be prepared to execute trades for at least one normal trading unit (board lot) at the prices quoted. Table 2.5 shows the size of a board lot that depends on the security's price. As soon as a bid or asked price is entered for a security, it is placed in a central computer file and may be seen by other subscribers (including other dealers) on their own terminals. When new quotations are entered, they replace the dealer's former prices. Market-makers are required to provide uninterrupted bid and ask quotations from 9:30 a.m. to 5:00 p.m.

---

[29] Generally the order will be a market order, since there is no limit order book in the over-the-counter market. Limit orders will be handled (if at all) in an informal manner by the broker, who will periodically check to see if the order can be executed without violating the limit price; stop and stop limit orders are not allowed in the OTC market. 100% margin is required on all OTC transactions.

on every day that the CDN System is open for business. There may be more than one market-maker for any given security.

**TABLE 2.5**
Size of a Board Lot on the CDN System.

| Price Range | Number of Shares |
| --- | --- |
| < $0.10 | 1000 |
| $0.10 to $0.99 | 500 |
| $1.00 to $99.875 | 100 |
| $100 to $199.875 | 10 |
| $200 or more | 1 |

To have quotations displayed on the CDN System, a security must have at least one registered market-maker (that is, one dealer), the firm must meet the OSC reporting requirements and the application to quote must be approved by the Board of Directors of CDN Inc. Other securities that do not meet these requirements simply have their trading statistics reported daily. Currently (as of November 1,1991) there are about 500 securities that have quotations displayed. Brokers with orders to buy or sell securities for which there are no quotations use less formal communication networks to obtain "best execution" for their clients.

## ☐ 2.6.4 The Third and Fourth Markets

These are markets in which securities trade off an organized exchange. Unlike the situation in the United States, the third and fourth markets should not exist in Canada. Under the regulations accompanying the *Ontario Securities Act*, stocks listed on an organized exchange are prohibited from trading in the OTC market. These markets are, however, perfectly viable options for large traders wishing to buy or sell inter-listed Canadian securities, therefore, a brief description of the US situation may be useful.

The term *third market* refers to the trading of any exchange-listed security in the OTC market. The viability of such a market is enhanced today by the fact that their trading hours are not fixed (unlike exchanges) and that they can continue to trade securities even when trading is halted on an exchange.

Many institutions have dispensed with brokers and exchanges altogether for transactions in exchange-listed stocks and other securities. Trades of this type, where the buyer and seller deal directly with each other, are sometimes said to take place in the *fourth market*. In the United States, some of these transactions are facilitated by an automated computer-communications system called *Instinet* which automatically provides quotations and execution.[30] A subscriber can enter a limit order in the computerized "book," where it can be seen by other subscribers, who can, in turn, signal

---

[30] The use of an intermediary such as a computer system makes it difficult to categorize such trades. Some people refer to the market where trades involving a "matchmaker" take place as the 3.5 market. The term fourth market is then used only when referring to the market where no matchmaker is involved.

their desire to take it. Whenever two orders are matched, the system automatically records the transaction and sets up the paperwork for its completion. Subscribers can also use the system to find likely partners for a trade and then conduct negotiations by telephone. A similar system, called Ariel, is used in the United Kingdom.

## 2.7 INFORMATION-MOTIVATED AND LIQUIDITY-MOTIVATED TRADERS

There are two major reasons for security transactions. An investor may believe that a security has become mispriced — meaning that its value is outside the current bid and asked prices. One who feels this way believes that he or she has information not known to (or understood by) the market in general and may be termed an *information-motivated* trader. On the other hand, an investor may simply want to sell some securities to buy a new car, or buy some securities with recently inherited money, or the like. Such a person may be called *liquidity-motivated*: in making security transactions, he or she does not presume that others in the market have evaluated the prospects for the security incorrectly.

Dealers can make money by trading with liquidity-motivated traders or with inept information-motivated traders. But, on the average, they can only lose money by trading with clever information-motivated traders. The larger a dealer's bid-ask spread, the less business he or she will do; but whatever the spread, when a clever information-motivated investor makes a trade, the dealer may expect to lose. In the absence of unwise investors, the very existence of a dealer depends on investors' desires for liquidity. A dealer must select a bid-ask spread wide enough to limit the number of trades with customers possessing superior information, but narrow enough to attract an adequate number of liquidity-motivated transactions.

A dealer can take either a passive or an active role. For example, a bid-ask spread can be established and a tentative price set. As orders come in and are filled, the dealer's inventory (position) will vary and may even become negative when promises to deliver securities exceed promises to accept delivery. But any clear trend suggests that the price should be altered. In effect, a *passive dealer* lets the market indicate the appropriate price.

An *active dealer* tries to get as much information as possible and to alter bid and ask prices in advance to keep the flow of orders more in balance. The better a dealer's information, the smaller the bid-ask spread required to make a profit.

When there is competition among dealers, those who are not well informed either price themselves out of the market by requiring too high a bid-ask spread or go out of business after incurring heavy losses. In general, the interests of investors are best served by a market in which dealers with unlimited access to all sources of information compete with one another.

The usual description of a market assumes that every trader wishes to purchase or sell a known quantity at each possible price. All the traders come together, and in one way or another a price is found that clears the market — that is, makes the quantity demanded as close as possible to the quantity supplied.

This may or may not be an adequate description of the markets for consumer goods, but it is clearly inadequate when describing security markets. The value of any capital asset depends on its future prospects that are almost always uncertain. Any information that bears on such prospects may lead to a revised estimate of value. The fact that a knowledgeable trader is willing to buy or sell some quantity of a security at a particular price is likely to be information of just this sort. Offers to trade may thus affect other offers. Prices may, therefore, both clear markets and convey information.

The dual role of prices has a number of implications. For example, it behooves the liquidity-motivated trader to publicize his or her motives and thereby avoid an adverse effect on the market. Thus an institution purchasing securities for a pension fund that intends simply to hold a representative cross section of securities should make it clear that it does not consider the securities underpriced. On the other hand, any firm trying to buy or sell a large number of shares that it considers mispriced should try to conceal either its motives, its identity, or both (and many try). Such attempts may be ineffective, however, as those asked to take the other side of such trades try to find out exactly what is going on (and many do).

Since offers may affect other offers, the way in which a market functions can affect the prices at which trades are made. And different markets function in different ways. For example, the New York Stock Exchange specialist's "books" contain information on both the prices and the quantities specified in standing orders, but only the lowest ask price and the highest bid price and the quantities associated with each are revealed to the general market. On the TSE, in contrast, the complete contents of the books are public knowledge. In the over-the-counter market, dealers publicly announce bid and ask prices that are firm for small quantities, but they negotiate prices for larger quantities.

The extent to which standing orders are made public may thus affect (1) the prices at which such orders are executed, (2) the extent to which investors will place them with brokers, and (3) the extent to which brokers will place them in a central "book," where they can be seen by others.

Some investors depend almost entirely on price for information about value. This raises the possibility that a clever trader could make money by placing orders to trigger foolish responses from such investors. While this may occur in isolated instances, it is limited by the presence of informed traders who use external information sources to assess value. Given a large-enough number of people who study fundamental aspects, it is possible for most investors to assume that market price reflects value.

# CLEARING PROCEDURES

Most securities are sold the standard way, which requires delivery of certificates within the settlement period. On rare occasions, a sale may be made as a cash transaction, requiring delivery the same day, or as a seller's option, giving the seller the choice of any delivery day within a specified period (typically, no more than 60 days). On other occasions, such as new issues, extensions to the settlement period are granted.

It would be extremely inefficient if every security transaction had to end with a physical transfer of share certificates from the seller to the buyer. A brokerage firm might sell 500 shares of BCE Inc. stock for one client, Mr. S, and later that day buy 500 shares for Ms B, another client. Mr. S's 500 shares could be delivered to his buyer, and Ms B's shares could be obtained by accepting delivery from her seller. However, it would be much easier to transfer Mr. S's shares to Ms B and instruct B's seller to deliver 500 shares directly to S's buyer. This would be especially helpful if the brokerage firm's clients, Mr. S and Ms B, held their securities in street name. Then, the 500 shares they traded would not have to be physically moved and their ownership would not have to be changed on the books of BCE.

## ☐ 2.9.1  Clearing Corporations

The process can be facilitated even more by a *clearing corporation*, the owners of which are brokerage firms, banks, and other financial institutions. Records of transactions made by members during a day are sent there. At the end of the day, both sides of the trades are verified for consistency; then all transactions are netted out. Each member receives a list of the net amounts of securities to be delivered or received along with the net amount of money to be paid or collected. Every day, each member settles with the clearing corporation instead of with various other firms.

In Canada there are two clearing corporations: the *Canadian Depository for Securities Limited* (CDS), to handle trades made on the Montreal Exchange, the Toronto Stock Exchange and in the OTC market and the *West Canada Clearing Corporation* (WCCC) for Alberta and Vancouver Stock Exchange members. Non-participating financial institutions may use CDS or WCCC services as clients of direct participants. Some banks belong simply to facilitate delivery of securities which, for example, may serve as collateral for secured demand loans.

By holding securities in street name and using clearing corporations, brokers can reduce the costs of transfer operations. But even more can be done with book based systems — certificates can be immobilized almost completely. The WCCC together with the *West Canada Depository Trust Company* (WCDTC) accomplishes this by maintaining computerized records of the securities "owned" by its member firms (brokers, banks, and so on). Members' share certificates are credited to their accounts at the WCDTC, but the certificates are transferred to the WCDTC on the books of the issuing corporation and remain registered in its name unless a member subsequently withdraws them. Whenever possible, one member will "deliver" securities to another by initiating a simple bookkeeping entry in which one account is credited and the other debited for the shares involved. Dividends paid on securities held by the WCDTC are simply credited to members' accounts based on their holdings and may be subsequently withdrawn in cash.

**INSURANCE**

When a brokerage firm fails, its clients may discover for the first time that securities and cash balances in their accounts are no longer physically available. This could lead to erosion of investor confidence, therefore, the Toronto, Montreal, Vancouver, and Alberta Stock Exchanges and the Investment Dealers Association of Canada have jointly established the *Canadian Investor Protection Fund* (CIPF) to protect the investing public against losses due to the financial failure of a member of one of the sponsoring organizations. When an investor becomes a customer of a member of any one of the sponsors that customer's accounts are covered by the CIPF. Each account is insured up to a stated amount ($250,000 per account in 1990).[31] The cost of the insurance is borne by the member firms through regular annual fees and periodic special assessments. Should this be insufficient to settle all claims, the CIPF can borrow through a line of credit provided by two Canadian chartered banks.

**2.11**  **COMMISSIONS**

☐ **2.11.1  Fixed Commissions**

Until 1975, the New York Stock Exchange required its member brokers to charge fixed minimum commissions for stocks, with no "rebates, returns, discounts or allowances in 'any shape or manner,' direct or indirect."[32] Fixed commissions were also charged on the TSE and remained in force till 1983.

In the era of fixed commissions, brokerage firms did not compete with one another over commissions. However, those brokerage firms that belonged to the Toronto Stock Exchange competed with one another in a different manner — namely, by offering a panoply of ancillary services to customers. Large institutions were provided with security analysis, performance measurement services, and the like in return for *soft dollars* — brokerage commissions ostensibly paid for having a brokerage firm execute their trades and indirectly designated as payment for services rendered. The US experience indicates that for every $3 in commissions received on large trades, brokerage firms were willing to spend up to approximately $2 to provide ancillary services to the customers. Thus, it follows that it cost brokerage firms roughly $1 per $3 of commission received just to execute a large trade for a customer. Apparently, up to two-thirds of the fixed commission rate ($2 out of $3) on such large orders was pure (marginal) profit.

The existence of fixed commissions has been attributed to the natural monopoly arising from economies of scale in bringing together many people (either physically or via modern communication technology) to trade with one another. The potential profits from such a monopoly are limited by the advantages it confers. The increasing institutionalization of security holdings and progress in communications and computer technology have diminished the advantages associated with a centralized physical exchange. Thus, the removal of legal protection for this particular type of price fixing

---

[31] A given client may have more than one type of account and may, therefore, be able to claim more than the limit shown.

[32] See Wilford J. Eiteman, Charles A. Dice, and David K. Eiteman, *The Stock Market* (New York: McGraw-Hill, 1969), 138.

that occured in 1975 in New York and 1983 in Toronto may only have been another example of a response to technological change.

## ☐ 2.11.2 Competitive Commissions

The system of fixed commissions in the US was finally terminated by the *Securities Act Amendments* of 1975 (but only after repeated challenges by the NYSE). Since May 1, 1975 (known in the trade as *May Day*), brokers have been free to set commissions at any desired rate or to negotiate with customers concerning the fees charged for particular trades. The former procedure is more commonly employed in "retail" trades executed for small investors, whereas the latter is used more often when handling large trades involving institutional investors and others.

Prior to May Day, commission rates in Canada were generally higher than those in the US. Following the introduction of negotiated rates in the US, trading in inter-listed securities tended to migrate to US exchanges where transactions costs were lower. This forced Canadian dealers to match US commission rates on large trades in order to protect their business. On April 1, 1983 Canada moved to negotiated commission rates.[33]

After April 1983, rates for large trades in Canada fell substantially. So did those charged for small trades by firms offering only bare-bones brokerage services. On the other hand, broad-line firms that provided extensive services to small investors for no additional fee continued to charge commissions similar to those specified in the earlier fixed schedules. In succeeding years, as costs have risen, charges for smaller transactions have increased, whereas those for large trades have not.

Increased competition among brokerage firms has resulted in a wide range of alternatives for investors. Following April 1983, some firms *unbundled* — meaning they priced their services separately from their pricing of order execution. Other firms *went discount* meaning they dropped almost all ancillary services and cut commissions accordingly. Still others bundled new services into comprehensive packages. Some of these approaches have not stood the test of time, but just as mail-order firms, discount houses, department stores, and expensive boutiques coexist in retail trade, many different combinations are viable in the brokerage industry.

Figure 2.4 shows typical commission rates charged by retail brokerage firms for small to medium-sized trades. These rates are representative of those charged by full-line retail brokers that provide offices with quotation boards, research reports, account executives available for advice and information, and the like. The rates also apply to trades made by customers whose volume of business is small. Discount firms with little but execution capability typically charge 30% to 70% less.

---

[33] Even before this date commissions were negotiable for trades in excess of $500,000.

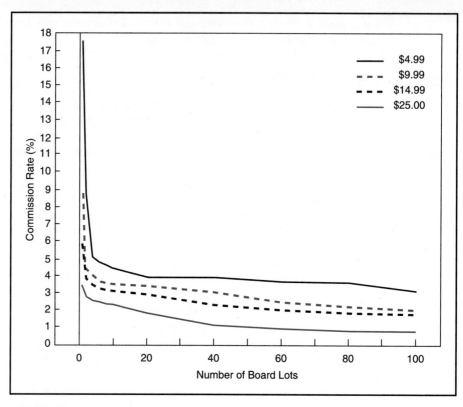

**FIGURE 2-4**
Typical commission rates for selected transactions; dollar commissions as a percentage of the value of the order.

## 2.12  TRANSACTION COSTS

### ☐ 2.12.1  The Bid-Ask Spread

Commission costs are only a portion of the total cost associated with buying or selling a security. Consider a "round-trip" transaction, in which shares are purchased and then sold during a period in which no new information causes investors collectively to reassess the value of the shares (more concretely, the bid and asked prices quoted by dealers do not change). The shares will typically be purchased at the dealers' asked price and sold at the bid price, which is lower. The *bid-ask spread* thus constitutes a portion of the round-trip transaction costs.

According to one study covering US markets, the spread between the bid and asked prices for a typical stock is approximately $.30 per share for the securities of large, actively traded companies. This amounts to less than 1% of the price per share for most stocks of this type—a reasonably small amount to pay for the ability to buy or sell in a hurry.

However, not all securities enjoy this type of liquidity. Shares of smaller firms tend to sell at lower prices but at similar bid-ask spreads. As a result, the percentage transaction cost is considerably larger. This is shown in part (a) of Table 2.6. Stocks were assigned to sectors based on each firm's *market capitalization*, which is equal to the market value of the firm's outstanding equity. For example, if the total market value of the common stock of a company was less than $10 million, it was considered to be in sector 1 (the smallest capitalization sector), and if the market value was greater than $1.5 billion, the company was included in sector 9 (the largest capitalization sector). As the table shows, the larger the capitalization, the greater was the average price per share. Note also that the average spread in dollars was actually greater for the smallest capitalization stocks than for the largest. Most importantly, however, the ratio of the average spread to the average price fell continuously from 6.55% for the smallest sector to .52% for the largest sector. This means that the larger the capitalization of the firm, the greater the liquidity of its shares.

It is possible to draw some tentative conclusions about the Canadian situation. The majority of the stocks traded on the TSE tend to fall into the lower market capitalization deciles shown in Table 2.6 and, therefore, it is likely that transactions costs are generally higher in Canada than in the US. This conclusion is borne out by a study carried out by Tinic and West in the early 1970s in which they compared bid-ask spreads on TSE listed stocks with those on the NYSE and the OTC.[34] Even after controlling for daily trading volume, average stock price, price volatility, trading frequency, and the number of markets in which the security is listed (but not market capitalization) they found that bid-ask spreads on the TSE are larger than those on either of the US markets. As a result they concluded that the price of liquidity was higher on the TSE and the marketability of TSE listed stocks was inferior. They attributed this inferior performance to the lack of a well-developed dealer market in Canada. Whereas the specialist on the NYSE and the dealers on the OTC were committed to filling board lot orders thereby maintaining an active and continuous market, the Registered Traders on the TSE were only required to provide bid and offer quotations and to fill odd-lot orders (at a premium or a discount). Both the market-making function on the TSE and the capitalization of member firms have changed significantly in the past 20 years, therefore, these conclusions require updating and confirmation.

---

[34] Seha M. Tinic and Richard R. West, "Marketability of Common Stocks in Canada and the USA.: A Comparison of Agent Versus Dealer Dominated Markets," *Journal of Finance* 29, no. 3 (June 1974):729–46. Schulman presents evidence that spreads in December 1988 on the TSE 35 stocks were, on average, higher than on the NYSE as shown below:

| | Bid/ask spread | |
|---|---|---|
| | *TSE 35* | *NYSE* |
| High | 1.80% | 1.31% |
| Median | 0.65% | 0.38% |
| Low | 0.22% | 0.08% |

SOURCE: E.Schulman, "The 'Global Village' Securities Market: Will Canada be a Participant...or a Bystander?" *Canadian Investment Review*, II, no. 2 (Fall 1989):61–6. For a difference of opinion on the significance of the spread differential, see K.Cachia and E.Schulman, "Comparison of Bid-Offer Spreads on NYSE and TSE: Comment and Response," *Canadian Investment Review*, III, no. 1 (Spring 1990): 31.

**TABLE 2.6**

Bid-Ask Spreads and Round-Trip Transaction Costs.

### (a) Common Stock Bid-Ask Spreads: Small Orders.

| | | | Capitalization | | | | |
|---|---|---|---|---|---|---|---|
| Sector | From (millions) | To (millions) | Number of Issues | Percent of US Market | Average Price | Average Spread | Spread Price |
| 1 (small) | $   0 | $   10 | 1,009 | .36% | $  4.58 | $.30 | 6.55% |
| 2 | 10 | 25 | 754 | .89 | 10.30 | .42 | 4.07 |
| 3 | 25 | 50 | 613 | 1.59 | 15.16 | .46 | 3.03 |
| 4 | 50 | 75 | 362 | 1.60 | 18.27 | .34 | 1.86 |
| 5 | 75 | 100 | 202 | 1.27 | 21.85 | .32 | 1.46 |
| 6 | 100 | 500 | 956 | 15.65 | 28.31 | .32 | 1.13 |
| 7 | 500 | 1,000 | 238 | 12.29 | 35.43 | .27 | .76 |
| 8 | 1,000 | 1,500 | 102 | 8.87 | 44.34 | .29 | .65 |
| 9 (large) | 1,500 | 99,999 | 180 | 57.48 | 52.40 | .27 | .52 |

### (b) Percentage Round Trip Transaction Costs, Common Stock.

| | Capitalization | | | | | | | | |
|---|---|---|---|---|---|---|---|---|---|
| | Dollar Value of Block ($ thousands) | | | | | | | | |
| Sector | 5 | 25 | 250 | 500 | 1,000 | 2,500 | 5,000 | 10,000 | 20,000 |
| 1 (small) | 17.3% | 27.3% | 43.8% | | | | | | |
| 2 | 8.9 | 12.0 | 23.8 | 34.4% | | | | | |
| 3 | 5.0 | 7.6 | 18.8 | 25.9 | 30.0% | | | | |
| 4 | 4.3 | 5.8 | 9.6 | 16.9 | 25.4 | 31.5% | | | |
| 5 | 2.8 | 3.9 | 5.9 | 8.1 | 11.5 | 15.7 | 25.7% | | |
| 6 | 1.8 | 2.1 | 3.2 | 4.4 | 5.6 | 7.9 | 11.0 | 16.2% | |
| 7 | 1.9 | 2.0 | 3.1 | 4.0 | 5.6 | 7.7 | 10.4 | 14.3 | 20.2% |
| 8 | 1.9 | 1.9 | 2.7 | 3.3 | 4.6 | 6.2 | 8.9 | 13.6 | 18.1 |
| 9 (large) | 1.1 | 1.2 | 1.3 | 1.7 | 2.1 | 2.8 | 4.1 | 5.9 | 8.0 |

*SOURCE:* Thomas F. Loeb, "Trading Cost: The Critical Link Between Investment Information and Results," *Financial Analysis Journal* 39, no. 3 (May/June 1983):41–2.

## ☐ 2.12.2 Price Impact

Brokerage commissions and bid-ask spreads represent transaction costs for small orders (typically 100 shares). For larger-sized orders, the possibility of *price impacts or slippage* must be considered. Consider purchase orders. Due to the law of supply and demand, the larger the size of the order, the more likely the investor's purchase price will be higher. Furthermore, the more rapidly the order is to be completed and the more knowledgeable the individual or organization placing the order, the higher is the purchase price charged by the dealer.

Part (b) of Table 2.6 provides estimates of average costs for transactions in the "upstairs dealer" market. All three sources of costs are included: bid-ask spreads, brokerage commissions, and price impacts. The figures refer to the total cost for a round-trip — a purchase followed by a sale — and reveal that for any capitalization sector, larger block sizes are associated with larger percentage transaction costs. The figures also reveal that for any given dollar-size block, larger capitalization sectors are associated with smaller percentage transaction costs (a similar observation can be made upon examination of panel (a)).

Part (a) of Figure 2.5 plots the percentage transaction costs for blocks of $25,000 each, which corresponds to the values in the third column from the left in part (b) of Table 2.6. Values range from over 27% (for small capitalization stocks) to 1.2% (for large capitalization stocks).

Part (b) of Figure 2.5 shows the relationship between order size and transaction cost for each of the three largest capitalization sectors, which correspond to the last three rows of part (b) of Table 2.6. The figure shows that the impact of a very large order on price can be substantial, and the impact is greater for smaller capitalizations.

## 2.13    PRIMARY DISTRIBUTIONS

The discussion so far has focused on secondary markets for securities, where securities that were initially issued at some previous point in time are subsequently traded. The focus now shifts to the *primary market* for securities, which is the name given to the markets where the initial issuance itself takes place. Some issuers deal directly with purchasers in this market, but many rely on *investment dealers* who act as *underwriters* by serving as intermediaries between issuers and the ultimate purchasers of their securities.[35]

In some instances, only a few large institutional investors are solicited, and the entire issue is sold to one or more of them. Such *private placements* are frequently used for bond issues with the dealer acting as an agent for the issuing corporation. As long as the minimum cash value of the issue is greater than $150,000 and relatively few potential buyers are contacted (say, less than 25), requirements for detailed disclosure, public notice, and so on may be waived, thereby considerably reducing the cost of floating an issue. Such placements are often announced after the fact, via advertisements in the financial press.

When a public sale is contemplated, much more must be done. Many dealers and brokers may serve as intermediaries in the process. One, acting as the "lead" underwriter, will put together a *banking group* and a *selling group*. The banking group includes firms that purchase the securities from the issuing corporation and thus *underwrite* part of the offering. The selling group includes firms that contact potential buyers and do the actual selling, usually on a commission basis.

---

[35] Outside Canada underwriters are generally referred to as *investment bankers*. For more on investment banking, see Chapter 19 of Paul Halpern, J. Fred Weston and Eugene F. Brigham, *Canadian Managerial Finance* (Toronto, Ont.: Holt Rinehart and Winston of Canada, Limited), 1989, Chapter 15 of Richard A. Brealey, Stewart C. Myers, Gordon Sick and Robert Whalley, *Principles of Corporate Finance* (Toronto: McGraw-Hill, 1988), for the US situation see the January/February 1986 issue of the *Journal of Financial Economics*, which contains papers presented at a symposium on investment banking.

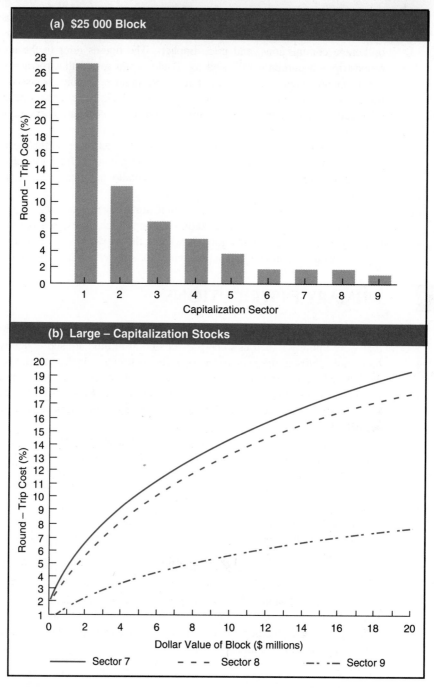

**FIGURE 2-5**
Round-trip transaction costs.

The process begins with discussions between the issuing corporation and one or more investment dealers. Some issuers utilize *competitive bidding* and then select the investment dealer offering the best overall terms. This procedure is used for many government bond issues. Many corporations, however, maintain a continuing relationship with a single underwriter and negotiate the terms of each new offering with that firm. The underwriter is usually heavily involved in the planning of an offering, the terms involved, the amount to be offered, and so on, serving, in effect, as a financial consultant to the corporation.

Once the basic characteristics of an offering have been established, a preliminary *prospectus* disclosing material relevant to the prospective buyer is filed with the provincial securities commission in provinces where these are required. (This prospectus is often referred to as a *red herring*, since it has a disclaimer printed in red ink across the first page that informs the reader that it is not an offer to sell). The actual price of the security is not usually included in the preliminary prospectus, and no final sales may be made until the registration has been approved and a final prospectus issued, indicating the offer price at which the shares will be sold. The final prospectus may be issued about three weeks after all *deficiencies* regarding adequate disclosure have been resolved to the satisfaction of the securities commission. The securities commission, however, does not take a position regarding the investment merits of an offering or the reasonableness of the price.

A security issue may be completely underwritten by an investment dealer and the other members of the syndicate. If it is, the issuing corporation receives the public offering price less a stated percentage spread (although underwriters will occasionally be compensated with some combination of shares and warrants, perhaps in addition to a smaller spread). The underwriters, in turn, sell the securities at the public offering price (or less) and may take some of the securities themselves. Underwriters who provide this sort of *firm commitment* bear all the risk, since the public may not be willing to buy the entire issue.

Not all agreements are of this type. In the case of a *rights offering* (where the current shareholders are given the opportunity to buy the new shares first), an underwriter may agree to purchase, at a fixed price, all securities not taken by current shareholders. This is termed a *standby agreement*. In the case of a nonrights offering (where the shares are offered to the general public first), members of a selling group may serve as agents instead of dealers, agreeing only to handle an offering on a *best-efforts* basis.

During the period when new securities remain unsold, the investment banker is allowed to attempt to "stabilize" the price of the security in the secondary market by standing ready to make purchases at a particular price. Such *pegging* may continue for up to ten days after the official offering date. There is a limit to the amount that can be purchased in this manner, usually stated in the agreement under which the underwriting syndicate is formed, since the members typically share the cost of such transactions. If there is to be any pegging, a statement to that effect must be included in the prospectus.

In any security transaction, there may be explicit and implicit costs. In a primary distribution, the explicit cost is the underwriting spread and the implicit cost is any difference between the public offering price and the price that might have been obtained otherwise. The spread provides the underwriter with compensation for selling the issue and bearing the risk that the issue may not be completely sold to the public, thereby leaving them with ownership of the unsold shares. The lower the public offering price, the smaller the risk that the issue will not be sold quickly at that price. If an issue is substantially underpriced, the selling group can be assured that the securities will sell rapidly, requiring little or no support in the secondary market. Since many corporations deal with only one underwriter and since the larger investment dealers rely on one another for inclusion in syndicates, it has been alleged that issuers pay too much in spreads, given the prices at which their securities are offered. In other words, the returns to underwriting are alleged to be overly large relative to the risks involved, owing to ignorance on the part of issuers or the existence of an informal cartel among investment dealers.

## ☐ 2.13.1   Underpricing of Ipo's

Whether or not returns to underwriting are overly large, a number of *initial public offerings* (ipo's) appear to have been underpriced. Ipo's are the first offerings of shares of a company to the public and are sometimes referred to as *unseasoned offerings*. The abnormal returns for a sample of ipo's in the US are shown in Figure 2.6. Each one of the first 60 months after the initial offering is shown on the horizontal axis, and the corresponding average abnormal return, meaning the average return over and above that of stocks of equal risk, is shown on the vertical axis. The leftmost point indicates the average abnormal return obtained by an investor who purchased such a stock at its offering price and sold it for the bid price at the end of the month during which it was offered. The average abnormal return was substantial: 11.4%. The remaining points show the average abnormal returns that could have been obtained by an investor who purchased the security in the secondary market at the beginning of the month indicated and then sold it in the secondary market at the end of that particular month. Some of these post-offering abnormal returns were positive, but only one was significantly different from zero. Moreover, none was large enough to overcome the transaction costs associated with trades on the secondary market.

On the average, offerings of these unseasoned securities appear to have been underpriced. Investors able to purchase a cross-section of such shares at their offering prices might thus expect better performance than those holding other securities of equal risk. It is not surprising that such offerings are often rationed by the members of the selling group to "favored" customers. It is "not uncommon for underwriters to receive, prior to the effective date, 'public indication of interest' for five times the number of shares available."[36] Unfavored customers are presumably allowed to buy only the new issues that are not substantially underpriced. Since costs may be incurred in becoming a favored customer, it is not clear that even such an investor obtains abnormally large returns overall.

Whereas the return obtained by the purchaser of a new issue may be substantial on average, the amount may be very good or very bad in any particular instance, as Figure 2.7 shows. Although the odds may be in the purchaser's favor, a single investment of this type is far from a sure bet.

A Canadian study examined 115 ipo's in the period 1971 to 1983. The average *first trading day* return was 11.6% with a standard deviation of 40.2%. The minimum first day return was −81.7% and the maximum 196.7%. This duplicates the US finding that

---

[36] Securities and Exchange Commission, *Report of Special Study on Security Markets*, 1973.

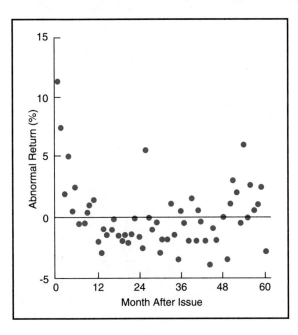

**FIGURE 2-6**

Average abnormal returns: 112 common stock initial public offerings, 1960–1969.

*SOURCE:* Roger G. Ibbotson, "Price performance of Common Stock New Issues," *Journal of Financial Economics* 2, no. 3 (September 1975): 252.

ipo's are, on average, significantly underpriced but no single investment of this type is a certain winner. The range of first day returns recorded, however, is surprisingly large.[37]

## □ 2.13.2  Seasoned Offerings

Interestingly, the announcement of a seasoned US stock offering seems to result in a decline of roughly 2% to 4% in the firm's stock price. This could be because managers tend to issue stock when they think it is overpriced in the marketplace. Thus, the announcement of the offering causes investors to revise downward their assessment of the value of the stock, leading to a price decline. A Canadian study that examined seasoned offerings found that the issuing firm's share price declined, on average, by about 1%, but reported finding little support for the theoretical assymetric information models of Myers and Majluf and Lucas and McDonald.[38]

---

[37] I. Krinsky and W. Rotenberg, "The Valuation of Initial Public Offerings," *Contemporary Accounting Research* 5, no. 2 (Spring, 1989):500–514. See also V.Jog and A. Riding, "Underpricing in Canadian IPOs," *Financial Analysts Journal*, November/December 1987 who reported similar results for a sample of 100 firms.

[38] See Stewart C. Myers and Nicholas S. Majluf, "Corporate Financing and Investment Decisions When Firms have Information That Investors Do Not Have," *Journal of Financial Economics* 13, no. 2 (June 1984):187-221; Wayne H. Mikkelson and M. Megan Partch, "Valuation Effects of Security Offerings and the Issuance Process," *Journal of Financial Economics* 15, no. 1/2 (January/February 1986):31-60; D.Lucas and R.McDonald, "Equity Issues and Stock Price Dynamics," *Journal of Finance*, 1990; and V.Jog and H. Schaller, "Share Price Behavior around the Announcement of New Equity Issues: A New test of the Assymetric Information Models," Carleton University Working Paper, 1991.

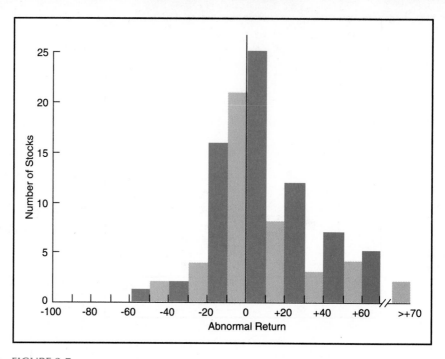

FIGURE 2-7

Average abnormal returns from offering price to bid price at the end of the offering month: 112 common stock initial public offerings, 1960–1969.

*SOURCE:* Roger G. Ibbotson, "Price performance of Common Stock New Issues," *Journal of Financial Economics* 2, no. 3 (September 1975): 248.

### □ 2.13.3 Shelf Registration

A recent change in Canadian regulations has made it possible for corporations to foster greater competition among underwriters. In May 1991, National Policy 44 came into force to allow firms to register securities in advance of issuance. With such a *shelf registration*, securities may be sold up to two years later. With securities "on the shelf," the corporation can request competitive bids from investment bankers and refuse to sell shares if acceptable bids are not forthcoming. It is too early to tell what effect this change has had in Canada. However, shelf registration has been allowed in the US since 1982 and the evidence there seems to suggest that issuing costs have been reduced.[39]

---

[39] See Sanjai Bhagat, M. Wayne Marr, and G. Rodney Thompson, "The Rule 415 Experiment: Equity Markets," *Journal of Finance* 40, no. 5 (December 1985):1385–1401.

**FIGURE 2-8**
Prices for 345 secondary distributions, 1961-1965.

*SOURCE:* Myron S. Scholes, "The Market for Securities: Substitution versus Price Pressure and the Effects of Information on the Share Prices," *Journal of Business* 45, no. 2 (April 1972): 193.

## 2.14   SECONDARY DISTRIBUTIONS

As mentioned earlier, an individual or institution wishing to sell a large block of stock can do so through a secondary distribution. An investment banking group buys the block from the seller and then offers the shares to the public through an organized exchange.

All the Securities Commissions in Canada (except Quebec) require that the sale of securities from a *control position* be accompanied by a prospectus and an underwriter. A control position is one in which the person offering the shares owns a sufficient number as to materially affect control of the company. In most provinces a 20 percent holding is deemed to represent control although there are circumstances under which a smaller holding may be ruled to be a control position. The distribution then proceeds in the same way as a primary distribution.

The impact of the sale of a large block on the market price of the shares provides information on the resiliency of the capital market. The results of a US study are described below. Figure 2.8 shows the average price (adjusted for market changes) for 345 secondary distributions, with the price 25 days prior to the distribution taken as 1.0. On the average, a secondary distribution leads to a 2% to 3% decline in price. Since there is no evidence of a subsequent price rebound, this decline is most likely due to the information contained in the fact that someone has decided to sell. Additional analysis of these results, as shown in Table 2.7, supports the assertion. The size of the decline was related to the identity of the seller — being the greatest for sellers likely to be information-motivated and smallest for sellers likely to be liquidity-motivated.[40]

---

[40] A more recent study has confirmed these findings; see Wayne H. Mikkelson and M. Megan Partch, "Stock Price Effects and Costs of Secondary Distributions," *Journal of Financial Economics* 14, no. 2 (June 1985):165–94.

**TABLE 2.7**

Average Price Decline Versus Type of Seller: 345 Secondary Distributions, 1961-1965.

| Type of Seller | Percentage Change in Adjusted Price From Ten Days Before The Distribution to Ten Days After the Distribution |
|---|---|
| Corporations and officers | 2.9% |
| Investment companies and mutual funds | 2.5 |
| Individuals | 1.1 |
| Estates | .7 |
| Banks and insurance companies | .3 |

*SOURCE:* Myron S. Scholes, "The Market for Securities: Substitution Versus Price Pressure and the Effects of Information on Share Prices," *Journal of Business* 45, no. 2 (April 1972): 202.

## 2.15  REGULATION OF SECURITY MARKETS

Securities regulation in Canada is a provincial responsibility. The first such legislation was enacted in Manitoba in 1912. Other provinces followed suit and for a considerable period legislation in this country resembled a patchwork quilt. Interprovincial cooperation has increased significantly following recognition of the fact that the Canadian market is national and increasingly becoming international in scope. In 1965, the *Report of the Attorney-General's Committee on Securities Legislation in Canada* (the *Kimber Report*) recommended significant revisions to Ontario's securities laws modelled on the US *Securities Act* of 1933 (sometimes called the *truth-in-securities* law) and the *Securities Exchange Act* of 1934. The resulting *Ontario Securities Act, 1966* required registration of new issues, disclosure of relevant information by the issuer, and prohibits misrepresentation and fraud in security sales. It also covers secondary markets by requiring national exchanges, brokers, and dealers to be registered, as well as those who counsel or advise investors and specifying reporting requirements for insider trades. Many of these provisions have been included in securities legislation enacted by other provinces. Subsequent amendments to the *Ontario Securities Act* have included the extension of corporate reporting requirements and the introduction of regulations governing take-over bids. An example of interprovincial cooperation in this area is the adoption of a number of *National Policies* by all the securities commissions in the country. In this way uniformity of regulation across the country has increased.

The organization of the *Ontario Securities Commission* (OSC) is typical of most provincial commissions. There are ten Commissioners consisting of a Chairman, two Vice-Chairmen and seven members, plus a Director who oversees day-to-day operations. Other commissions vary as to the number of members appointed by the provincial governments. The OSC differs from the Securities Commissions in other provinces in having a larger enforcement branch and a department dealing with derivative securities.

Securities legislation relies heavily on the principle of *self-regulation*. The Securities Commissions in general delegate part of their authority over trading practices for listed securities to the organized exchanges within their jurisdiction and maintains a watching brief over their activities. Trading in over-the counter securities has been delegated to the Canadian Dealing Network Inc. (CDN) and the Investment Dealers Association (IDA).

Canadian stocks interlisted on US exchanges fall under the joint jurisdiction of the appropriate provincial body and the US Securities and Exchange Commission (SEC). The SEC imposes more stringent reporting requirements and more extensive information disclosure in prospectuses than is generally required in Canada. On the other hand, the SEC has less strict takeover rules than the OSC, therefore, interlisting may provide a way of avoiding some types of regulatory constraint. In recent years there has been increased cooperation between the SEC and the larger provincial securities commissions in such matters as insider trading, improper trading activity, fraud and incomplete disclosure.

## 2.16 SUMMARY

This chapter has been devoted to describing the mechanics of buying and selling securities along with the operations of security markets. Although the primary focus has been on common shares, most of the material is also applicable to other securities, such as corporate bonds, treasury securities, and preferred shares. Investors face a large number of decisions when buying or selling a security, even if they know which issue they are going to trade. These decisions have been called order specifications here, and they concern such things as how big the order should be, how long the order is to be outstanding, and what type of order to place.

Investors may open up a cash account or a margin account with a brokerage firm. With the former, all transactions involve the use of cash. With the latter, loans will be involved if the investor makes either margin purchases or short sales. In the case of margin purchases, part of the purchase price is paid for by a loan of cash; in the case of short sales, a loan of securities is made. In both of these situations the investor is hoping to buy low, sell high. In the case of the margin purchase the buy occurs first, and the sell occurs second. With a short sale, the order is reversed in that the sell occurs first and the buy occurs second. Financial leverage is involved in both types of transaction in that a given percentage move in the price of the security involved will result in a percentage move of even greater magnitude in the position of the investor. Thus, margin purchases and short sales not only increase an investor's expected return but also increase the investor's risk in regard to the particular security involved.

The major secondary markets for trading common stocks in Canada include organized exchanges such as the Toronto Stock Exchange and the Montreal Exchange. In the TSE, trading is centered around the activities of Designated Market Makers. These individuals are given the responsibility for maintaining a fair and orderly market in certain assigned stocks. In carrying out their responsibilities, DMMs act both as brokers, executing orders, and dealers, quoting bid and asked prices at which they are willing to buy or sell their assigned stocks.

Another kind of secondary market is the over-the-counter market, where individuals act as dealers in a manner similar to a DMM. Both DMMs and OTC dealers face competition from others who are dealers in the same stocks. Under the *Ontario Securities Act* trading in listed securities may not take place outside an organized exchange. Off-exchange trading does, however, occur in the US. When such trading takes place in the OTC market, the trade is often said to have been executed in the third market.

Alternatively, when such trading involves direct contact between the buyer and seller, it is said to take place in the fourth market.

The primary market for securities was also discussed in this chapter. This market involves the initial issuance of securities. Although some issuers deal directly with purchasers, most issuers hire investment bankers to assist them in the sale of the securities.

Regulation of the security markets in Canada involves provincial law. The most prominent regulator is the Ontario Securities Commission, a provincial agency that is run by ten commissioners. The OSC has delegated to the TSE, IDA, and CDN the power to control trading practices that involve their facilities. However, the OSC retains the power to alter or supplement any of the resulting rules and regulations. This method of regulation is often known as *self-regulation*. Whether it is the best method is an issue that is open to much debate.

## QUESTIONS AND PROBLEMS

1. Discuss the advantages and disadvantages to the investor of the following:
   a. Market order
   b. Limit order
   c. Stop order

2. Buck Ewing opened a margin account at a local brokerage firm. Buck's initial investment was to purchase 100 shares of Dover Corporation on margin at $40 per share. Buck borrowed $2000 from a broker to complete the purchase.
   a. At the time of the purchase, what was the actual margin in Buck's account?
   b. If Dover stock subsequently rises in price to $60 per share, what is the actual margin in Buck's account?
   c. If Dover stock subsequently falls in price to $35 per share, what is the actual margin in Buck's account?

3. Helena Company's stock is currently selling for $15 per share. The initial margin requirement is 55% and Roger Anson buys 100 shares of Helena stock with a loan of $600 from his broker. To what price must the shares fall for Roger to receive a margin call?

4. Liz Arlington has deposited $15,000 in a margin account with a brokerage firm. If the margin requirement is 60%, what is the maximum dollar amount of stock that Liz can purchase on margin?

5. Ed Delahanty purchased 500 shares of Niagara Corporation stock on margin at the end of 1988 for $30 per share. The margin requirement was 55%. Ed paid 13% interest on the margin loan and never faced a margin call. Niagara paid dividends of $1.00 per share during 1989.
   a. At the end of 1989, if Ed sold the Niagara stock for $35 per share, what would his rate of return be for the year?
   b. At the end of 1989, if Ed sold the Niagara stock for $25 per share, what would his rate of return be for the year?
   c. Recalculate your answers to parts (a) and (b) assuming that Ed made the Niagara stock purchase for cash instead of on margin.

6. Through a margin account, Cindy Cummings sells short 200 shares of Melville Inc. stock for $50 per share. The margin requirement is 45%.

a. If Melville stock subsequently rises to $60 per share, what is the actual margin in Cindy's account?

b. If Melville stock subsequently falls to $40 per share, what is the actual margin in Cindy's account?

7. Avalon Corporation stock currently sells for $60 per share. The initial margin requirement is 50% and the maintenance margin requirement is 40%. If Willie Keeler sells short 300 shares of Avalon stock, and the price of the stock rises to $65. How much money must Willie provide in response to a margin call?

8. Eddie Gifford is an inveterate short seller. Is it true that Eddie's potential losses are infinite? Why? Conversely, is it true that the maximum return that Eddie can earn on his investment is 100%? Why?

9. On May 1, Ivy Olson sold short 100 shares of Thompson Associates stock at $25 per share and bought on margin 200 shares of Coppermine Company stock for $40 per share. The initial margin requirement was 50%. In June 30, Thompson stock sold for $36 per share and Coppermine stock sold for $45 per share.

a. Prepare a balance sheet showing the aggregate financial position in Ivy's margin account as of June 30.

b. Determine whether Ivy's account is subject to a margin call as of June 30.

10. Differentiate between the roles of a DMM on the TSE and a dealer on the OTC market.

11. Olympia Company is listed on the TSE. George Hartnett, the DMM handling Olympia stock, is currently bidding $25\frac{3}{8}$ and asking $25\frac{5}{8}$. What would be the likely outcomes of the following trading orders?

a. Through a broker, Eva Rooney places a market order to buy 100 shares of Olympia stock. No other broker from the crowd takes the order.

b. Through a broker, Eva places a limit order to sell 100 shares of Olympia stock at 26.

c. Through a broker, Eva places a limit order to buy 100 shares of Olympia stock at $25\frac{1}{2}$. Another broker offers to sell 100 shares at $25\frac{1}{2}$.

12. Because DMMs such as Chuck Goodwin are charged with maintaining a "fair and orderly" market, at times they will be required to sell when others are buying and buy when others are selling. How can Chuck earn a profit when required to act in such a manner?

13. Transaction costs can be thought of as being derived from three sources. Identify and describe those sources.

14. Why are liquid and continuous secondary security markets important to the effective functioning of primary security markets?

## SUGGESTED READINGS

*The Canadian Securities Course* (Toronto, Ont.: The Canadian Securities Institute, 1989). Chapters 3, 15, 16, and 21 cover some of the material in this chapter.

The annual *Official Trading Statistics* compiled by the Publications and Information Services Division of the Toronto Stock Exchange contains a wealth of information about TSE trading activity.

Eric A. Kirzner, "The Toronto Stock Exchange's New Electronic World," *Canadian Investment Review* V, no. 1, Spring 1992 reviews the recent changes proposed by the TSE.

Jeffrey G. MacIntosh and Ronald J. Daniels, "Capital Markets and the Law: The Peculiar Case of Canada," *Canadian Investment Review* III, no. 2 (Fall 1990):77–86 describes the unusual problems faced by Canadian regulators.

# Chapter 3

# INVESTMENT VALUE
# AND MARKET PRICE

Payments provided by securities may differ in both timing and riskiness. Thus, a security analyst must estimate when and under what conditions payments will be received (and, of course, the size of such payments). This typically requires detailed analysis of the firm involved, the industry or industries in which the firm operates, and the economy as a whole.

Once such estimates have been made, the overall investment value of the security must be determined. This generally requires conversion of uncertain future values to certain present values. The current prices of other securities can often be utilized in this process. If it is possible to obtain a similar set of payments in some other way, the market price of doing so provides a benchmark for the investment value of the security being analyzed, since an investor would neither want to pay more than this for the security nor sell it for less. In some cases, however, equivalent alternatives may not exist, or the mere act of buying or selling the security in question in the quantities being considered might substantially affect the price. Under these conditions, the preferences of the investor may have to be utilized explicitly in the process of estimating the security's investment value.

Later chapters discuss in detail the manner in which estimated future payments can be used to determine investment value. Methods for estimating the payments and finding equivalent alternatives will be discussed after the characteristics of the securities have been introduced. In this chapter, some general principles of investment value are presented, leaving procedures designed for specific types of securities for later.

## 3.1   SECURITY PRICE DETERMINATION

Although there are over 300 million shares of the Royal Bank of Canada common stock outstanding, on an average day less than 350 thousand shares will be traded, despite being one of the most actively traded stocks on the TSE. What determines the prices at which such trades take place? A simple (and correct) answer is demand and supply. A more fundamental (and also correct) answer is investors' estimates of the Royal Bank's future earnings and dividends, since such estimates greatly influence demand and supply. Before dealing with such influences, it is useful to examine the role of demand and supply in the determination of security prices.

As shown in the preceding chapter, securities are traded by many people in many different ways. Whereas the forces that determine prices are similar in all markets, they are slightly more obvious in markets using periodic "calls"; one such market, mentioned in Chapter 2, is the Paris Bourse.

## ☐ 3.1.1 The Demand-to-Buy Schedule

At a designated time, all brokers holding orders to buy or sell shares of a given stock for customers gather at a specified location on the floor of the exchange. Some of the orders are market orders. For example, Mr. A may have instructed his broker to buy 100 shares of Michelin at the lowest possible price, whatever it is. His personal *demand-to-buy schedule* at that time is shown in Figure 3.1(a): He wishes to buy 100 shares no matter what the price. Although this schedule captures the contractual nature of Mr. A's market order at a specific point in time, Mr. A undoubtedly has a good idea that his ultimate purchase price will be near the price for which orders were executed just before he placed his order. Thus, his true demand schedule might be sloping downward from the upper-left portion to the lower-right portion of the graph. This is shown by the dashed line in the figure. It indicates his desire to buy more shares if the price is lower. However, to simplify his own tasks as well as his broker's tasks, he has estimated that the price for which his order will be ultimately executed will be in the range at which he would choose to hold 100 shares. In the example shown here, this price is 945 francs per share.

Other customers may place limit orders with their brokers. Thus, Ms B may have instructed her broker to buy 200 shares of Michelin at the lowest possible price if and only if that price is less than or equal to 940 francs per share. Her demand schedule is shown in Figure 3.1(b).

Some customers may give their broker two or more orders for the same security. Thus, Mr. C may wish to buy 100 shares of Michelin at a price of 955 or less, plus an additional 100 shares if the price is at or below 945. To do this, Mr. C places a limit order for 100 shares at 955 and a second limit order for 100 shares at 945. Figure 3.1(c) portrays his demand schedule.

If one could look at all the brokers' books and aggregate all the orders to buy Michelin (both market and limit orders), it would be possible to determine how many shares would be bought at every possible price. Assuming that only Mr. A, Ms B, and Mr. C have placed buy orders, the resulting aggregate demand-to-buy schedule would look like line *DD* in Figure 3.1(d). Note that at lower prices more shares would be demanded.

## ☐ 3.1.2 The Supply-to-Sell Schedule

Brokers will also hold market orders to sell shares of Michelin. For example, Ms X may have placed a market order to sell 100 shares of Michelin at the highest possible price. Figure 3.2(a) displays her *supply-to-sell schedule*. As with market orders to buy, customers generally place such orders on the supposition that the actual price will be in the range in which their true desire to sell the stated number of shares would lie. Thus, Ms X's actual supply schedule might appear more like the dashed line in Figure 3.2(a), indicating her willingness to sell more shares at higher prices.

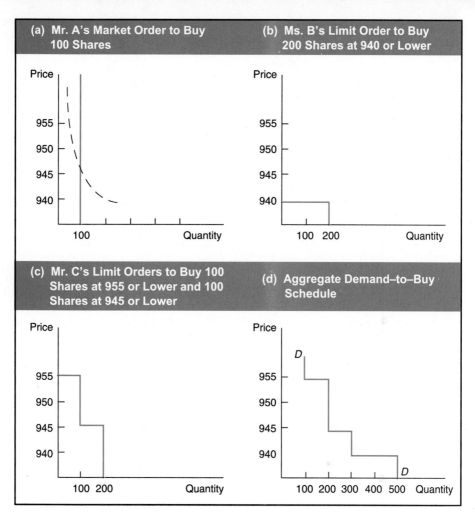

FIGURE 3-1
Individual investors' demand-to-buy schedules.

Customers may also place limit orders to sell shares of Michelin. For example, Mr. Y may have placed a limit order to sell 100 shares at a price of 940 or higher, and Ms Z may have placed a limit order to sell 100 shares at a price of 945 or higher. Panels (b) and (c) of Figure 3.2 illustrate these two supply-to-sell schedules.

As with the buy orders, if one could look at all the brokers' books and aggregate all the orders to sell Michelin (both market and limit orders), it would be possible to determine how many shares would be sold at every possible price. Assuming that only Ms X, Mr. Y, and Ms Z have placed sell orders, the resulting aggregate supply-to-sell schedule would look like line *SS* in Figure 3.2(d). Note that at higher prices more shares would be supplied.

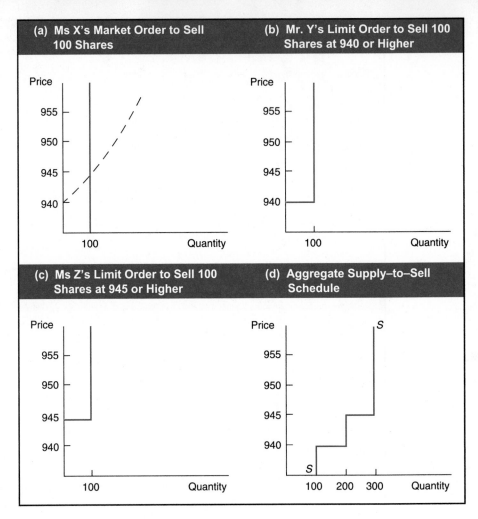

**FIGURE 3-2**
Individual investors' supply-to-sell schedules.

## ☐ 3.1.3 Interaction of the Schedules

The aggregate demand and supply schedules are shown on one graph in Figure 3.3. Generally, no one would have enough information to draw the actual schedules. However, this in no way diminishes the usefulness of the schedules as representations of the underlying forces that are interacting to determine the market-clearing price of Michelin.

What actually happens when all the brokers gather together with their order books in hand? A clerk of the exchange "calls out" a price — for example, 940 francs per share. The brokers then try to complete transactions with one another at that price. Those with orders to buy at that price signify the number of shares they wish to buy. Those with orders to sell do likewise. Some tentative deals will be made, but as Figure 3.3 shows, more shares will be demanded at 940 than will be supplied. In particular, 300 shares will

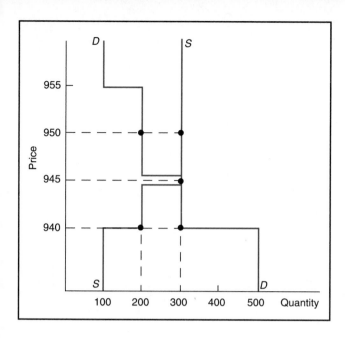

**FIGURE 3-3**
Determining a security's price by the interaction of the demand-to-buy and supply-to-sell schedules.

be demanded, but only 200 shares will be supplied. When trading is completed (meaning all possible tentative deals have been made), there will be a number of brokers calling "buy" but nobody will stand ready to sell to them. The price of 940 is too low.

Seeing this, the clerk will cry out a different price — for example, 950. Since the previous trades are all canceled at this point, the brokers will consult their orders books once again and signify the extent to which they are willing to buy or sell shares at this new price. In this case, as Figure 3.3 shows, when trading is completed, there will be a number of brokers calling "sell," but nobody will stand ready to buy from them. In particular, 300 shares will be supplied but there will be a demand for only 200 shares. The price of 950 is too high.

Undaunted, the clerk will try again, and again, if necessary. Only when there are relatively few unsatisfied brokers will the price (and the associated tentative deals) be declared final. As Figure 3.3 shows, 945 is such a price. At 945, customers collectively wish to sell 300 shares. Furthermore, there is a collective demand for 300 shares at this price. Thus, quantity demanded equals quantity supplied. The price is "just right."

Another way to view this process is to focus on the quantity that would actually be traded at any given price. For any particular price, this is the smaller of (1) the quantity people are willing to buy and (2) the quantity others are willing to sell, as shown in Figure 3.4. At the price where the quantity that would be traded is maximized, demand will equal supply. As can be seen in the figure, this occurs at a price of 945.

Trading procedures employed in security markets vary from auction markets to dealer markets and from call markets to continuous markets. However, the similarities are more important than the differences. In Canada, for example, Designated Market-Makers at the Toronto Stock Exchange and dealers in the over-the-counter market provide some of the functions of the clerk at the Paris Bourse, and trades can take place at

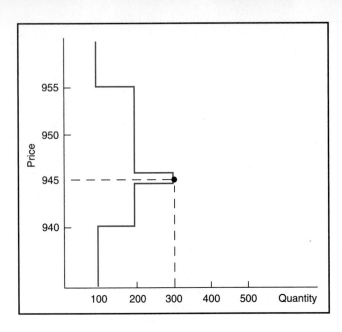

**FIGURE 3-4**
Aggregate quantity traded.

any time. Nevertheless, the basic principles of security price determination still operate. In general, market price equates quantity demanded with quantity supplied.

## 3.2 DEMAND-TO-HOLD SECURITIES

For some purposes it is useful to ignore moment-to-moment changes in customers' orders and focus instead on the fundamental forces at work. Instead of asking how many shares an investor wishes to buy or sell at a given price, the number of shares the investor wishes to hold at that price can be determined. There is, of course, a close relationship between the two quantities. If an investor wishes to hold more shares than are currently held, the difference is the investor's demand-to-buy schedule. Conversely, if an investor wishes to hold fewer shares than are currently held, the difference is the investor's supply-to-sell schedule.

### ☐ 3.2.1 The Demand-to-Hold Schedule

In Figure 3.5 one investor's *demand-to-hold schedule* for a security is shown by curve *dd*. This simply plots the number of shares that the investor wishes to hold at each possible price. In general, lower prices are associated with larger numbers of shares. Of course, the entire schedule is predicated on the investor's current feelings about the security's future prospects. If something makes the investor more optimistic about the security, he or she will generally wish to hold more shares at any given price. In that case, the entire schedule may shift to the right, as shown by curve *d'd'*. Alternatively, if something makes the investor more pessimistic about the security, the entire curve may shift to the left, as shown by curve *d''d''*.

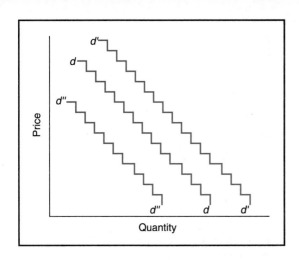

FIGURE 3-5

An individual investors' demand-to-hold schedule.

A factor that complicates an analysis of this type is the tendency for some investors to regard sudden and substantial price changes in a security as indicators of changes in the future prospects of the issuer. In the absence of further information, an investor may interpret such a change as an indication that "someone knows something that I don't know." While exploring the situation, the investor may at least temporarily revise his or her own assessment of the issuer's prospects and, in doing so, may alter the demand-to-hold schedule. For this reason, few investors place limit orders at prices substantially different from the current price, for fear that such orders would be executed only if prospects changed significantly, giving recognition to the idea that a careful reevaluation would be in order before buying or selling shares under such conditions.

Despite this complication, it is possible to construct an aggregate schedule indicating the total number of shares of a given firm that investors will wish to hold at various prices, assuming no change in their views of the relative prospects of the firm. This overall demand-to-hold schedule, obtained by adding the individual investors' demand-to-hold schedules, would look like curve $DD$ in Figure 3.6. In the short run, at least, the available number of shares is fixed — for example, at $Q$ in the figure. Only one price will equate the aggregate demand-to-hold with the available number of shares. In Figure 3.6, it is $P$. At any higher price, current holders of the security will collectively wish to hold fewer shares than are outstanding. In their attempts to sell such shares, they will drive the price down until they or others are willing to hold all the shares. Conversely, if the price is below $P$, investors will collectively wish to hold more shares than are available. In their attempts to buy shares, they will drive the price up until they no longer want additional shares. Ultimately, the price will settle at $P$, where the aggregate demand equals the available quantity.

## □ 3.2.2 Elasticity of the Schedule

How elastic (that is, flat) will the aggregate demand-to-hold schedule for a security be? The answer depends in part on the extent to which the security is regarded as "unique." Securities are considered more unique when they have few close substitutes. Securities are considered less unique when they have more close substitutes. This means

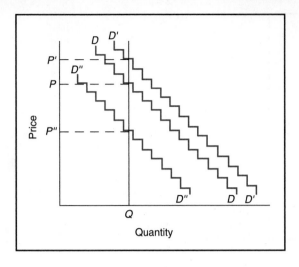

**FIGURE 3-6**

Aggregate demand-to-hold and available quantity schedules.

that the aggregate demand schedule will be more elastic (that is, more flat) for less unique securities. Equivalently, the less unique a security is, the greater the increase in the quantity demanded will be for a given fall in price. This is because these shares will produce a smaller increase in the typical portfolio's risk when substituted for other shares.

## ☐ 3.2.3 Shifts of the Schedule

If one investor becomes more optimistic about the prospects for a security, while at the same time another investor becomes more pessimistic about the same security, they may very likely trade with one another with no effect on the aggregate demand-to-hold schedule. In this situation there will be no change in the market price for the security. However, if more investors become optimistic rather than pessimistic, the schedule will shift to the right (for example, to $D'D'$ in Figure 3.6), causing an increase in price (to $P'$). Correspondingly, if more investors become pessimistic than optimistic, the schedule will shift to the left (for example, to $D''D''$ in Figure 3.6), causing a decrease in price (to $P''$).

---

**3.3**     **THE EFFECTS OF PROCEDURES FOR SHORT SALES**

Thus far, the individual investor's demand-to-hold schedule has been drawn only in the region of positive quantities. But there is more to it: The higher the price, the smaller the quantity the investor will wish to hold. At some price, the desired amount is zero, and at higher prices, the investor may consider short selling the security.

If short sellers received the proceeds from such sales, an individual investor's demand-to-hold schedule for a given security would look like the curve in Figure 3.7(a). This curve can be thought of in either of two ways: as a demand curve (that is, at price A, the investor wishes to hold quantity B) or as a marginal value curve (that is, if quantity B is held, the marginal value of one share more or less will be the amount A).

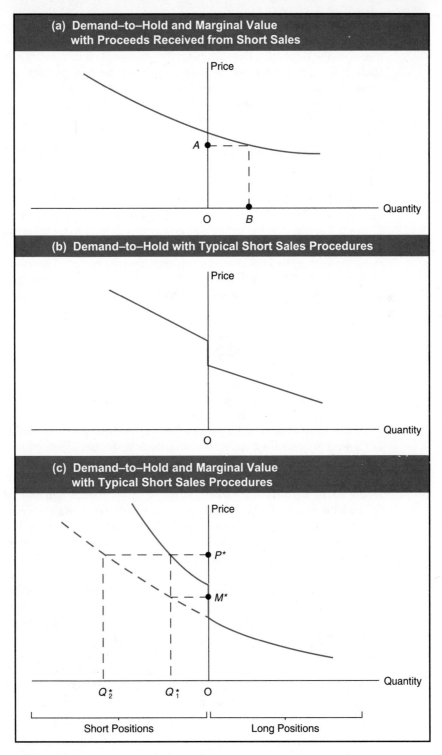

**FIGURE 3-7**
Demand-to-hold curves.

In fact, however, short sellers do not receive the proceeds of such sales. Instead, these proceeds are held by the short seller's brokerage firm as collateral. In most instances, the short seller does not even receive interest on this money and, furthermore, short sellers must meet margin requirements on the face amount of the short-sale proceeds. This changes the situation from that shown in Figure 3.7(a). Selling a security one owns generates cash that can be used for other purposes, but selling a security that one does not own requires an investment of cash. Thus, the decision to go short requires a higher price than it would if the short seller got the full use of the proceeds.[1] The effective demand-to-hold schedule would look like the curve in Figure 3.7(b). To the right of the vertical axis the curve is the same as in Figure 3.7(a), but to the left the curve is higher.

The effect of this is shown in Figure 3.7(c). The solid curve is the effective demand-to-hold schedule. The dashed curve is the portion of the original demand curve in Figure 3.7(a) that is to the left of the vertical axis. If the current price of the security is $P^*$, this investor will go short only $Q_1^*$ shares, not $Q_2^*$ shares. Thus, his or her pessimism about the security will not have as much impact on the market as it would if short sellers got the full use of the short-sale proceeds. In a sense, the person chooses a holding ($Q_1^*$) at which he or she considers the marginal value ($M^*$) to be less than the current market price ($P^*$).

## 3.4 PRICE AS A CONSENSUS

However one chooses to analyze security price determination, it is important to remember that a free market price for a security reflects a kind of consensus. This can be seen in Figure 3.8. Assume that the current market price for this particular security is $P^*$. Some individuals hold the security. For each of them, the situation is like that shown in Figure 3.8(a), where it can be seen that the investor has adjusted his or her portfolio so that the marginal value of a share ($M^*$) equals its market price.

A few investors may be short sellers. Their situation is like that shown in Figure 3.8(b). Because of the short-sale rule, each short seller will have taken a position at which the marginal value of a share is less than the price. Many investors will choose to hold no shares, and thus their position is neither long nor short. Their situation is shown in Figure 3.8(c). For each of them, the marginal value is equal to or, as in the case shown here, somewhat below the market price.

Were it not for short-selling rules, every investor would adjust his or her portfolio holdings until the marginal value of a security equaled its current market price. Since the market price is the same for everyone, so the marginal value would be the same for all investors (assuming all investors pay attention to the market). Price would clearly represent a consensus of investor opinion about value.

Short-selling rules change this situation, but only slightly. Since some investors (primarily pessimists) might choose holdings at which marginal value is below the market price, this market price could be slightly higher than an average of investors' marginal values. Accordingly, securities may be slightly "overpriced."

---

[1] For an argument that this causes securities to be "overpriced," see Edward M. Miller, "Risk, Uncertainty, and Divergence of Opinion," *Journal of Finance* 32, no. 4 (September 1977):1151–68.

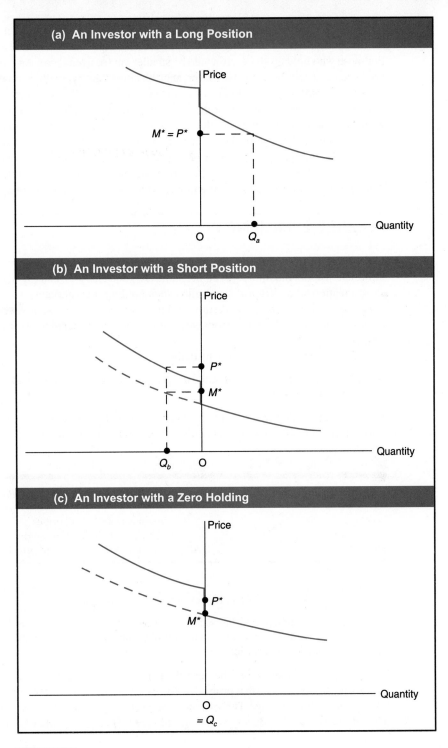

**FIGURE 3-8**
Price of a security as a consensus.

However, short-sale rules are likely to have a small impact on market prices. Even for the short seller, the disparity between market price and marginal value may be small. For those who hold no shares, it would be smaller yet (or even zero). And, for those who hold shares, it will be zero. Moreover, short positions are typically a small fraction of long positions. For practical purposes, price can be reasonably considered to be equal to a consensus opinion of investors concerning marginal value. For it to be seriously in error as an estimate of that value, many investors must be either poorly informed or poor analysts. Moreover, there must be either (1) a preponderance of such investors with overly optimistic forecasts or (2) a preponderance of such investors with overly pessimistic forecasts. Otherwise, the actions of such investors will offset each other, making price a good estimate of the present value of the security's future prospects.

## 3.5 MARKET EFFICIENCY

Imagine a world in which (1) all investors have costless access to currently available information about the future; (2) all investors are good analysts; and (3) all investors pay close attention to market prices and adjust their holdings appropriately. In such a market, a security's price will be a good estimate of its *investment value*, where investment value is the present value of the security's future prospects as estimated by well-informed and capable analysts.

An *efficient market* can now be defined:

A (perfectly) efficient market is one in which every security's price equals its investment value at all times.

In an efficient market, a set of information is fully and immediately reflected in market prices. But what information? A popular definition is the following:[2]

| Form of Efficiency | Set of Information Reflected in Security Prices |
|---|---|
| Weak | Previous prices of securities |
| Semistrong | All publicly available information |
| Strong | All information, both public and private |

An equivalent definition of an efficient market is the following:

A market is efficient with respect to a particular set of information if it is impossible to, on the average, make abnormal profits by using this set of information to formulate buying and selling decisions.

For example, a market would be described as having *weak-form efficiency* if it were impossible to make abnormal profits by using past prices to make decisions about when to buy and sell securities. The evidence suggests that major security markets in the United States and Canada are weak-form efficient. However, neither US nor Canadian

---

[2] Eugene F. Fama, "Efficient Capital Markets: A Review of Theory and Empirical Work," *Journal of Finance* 25, no. 5 (May 1970):383–417.

markets conform quite as well to the definition of *semistrong-form efficiency* (although the lack of a precise meaning for "publicly available" makes this form of efficiency somewhat ambiguous). They conform even less well to the definition of *strong-form efficiency*.[3]

In an efficient market, any new information would be immediately and fully reflected in prices. New information is just that: new, meaning a surprise (anything that is not a surprise is predictable and should have been predicted before the fact). Since happy surprises are about as likely as unhappy ones, price changes in an efficient market are about as likely to be positive as negative. Whereas a security's price might be expected to move upward by an amount that provides a reasonable return on capital (when considered in conjunction with dividend payments), anything above or below this would, in such a market, be unpredictable. In a perfectly efficient market, price changes would be random.[4]

Now consider a crazy market, in which prices never bear any particular relationship to investment value. In such a world, price changes might also appear to be random. However, major security markets in Canada and the United States are certainly not irrational. They may not attain perfect efficiency, but they are certainly much closer to it than to irrationality. To understand financial markets, it is important to understand perfectly efficient markets.

As mentioned earlier, in an efficient market, a security's price will be a good estimate of its investment value, where investment value is the present value of the security's future prospects as estimated by well-informed and capable analysts. Any substantial disparity between price and value would reflect market inefficiency. In a well-developed and free market, major inefficiencies are rare. The reason is not hard to find. Major disparities between price and investment value will be noted by alert analysts, who will seek to take advantage of their discoveries. Securities priced below value (known as underpriced or undervalued securities) will be purchased, creating pressure for price increases due to the increased demand to buy. Securities priced above value (known as overpriced or overvalued securities) will be sold, creating pressure for price decreases due to the increased supply to sell. As investors seek to take advantage of opportunities created by temporary inefficiencies, they will cause the inefficiencies to be reduced, denying the less alert and the less informed a chance to obtain large abnormal profits.

In Canada and the United States there are thousands of professional security analysts and even more amateurs. Not surprisingly, due to their actions the major US and Canadian security markets appear to be much closer to efficiency than to irrationality.

---

[3] For an extensive discussion of efficient markets and related evidence, see Chapters 9 and 11 in George Foster, *Financial Statement Analysis* (Englewood Cliffs, N.J.: Prentice Hall, 1986). Unfortunately there is no comparable summary of Canadian evidence despite the fact that many studies examining the efficiency of Canadian markets have been carried out.

[4] In this situation, security prices are said to follow a *random walk*, meaning that security price changes (say, from one day to the next) are independently and identically distributed. That is, the price change from day $t$ to day $t + 1$ is not influenced by the price change from day $t - 1$ to daty $t$, and the size of the price change from one day to the next can be viewed as being determined by the spin of a roulette wheel (with the same roulette wheel being used every day).

# SUMMARY

This chapter has discussed how the forces of supply and demand interact in determining a security's market price. This price can be thought of as representing a consensus opinion about the future prospects for the security. Furthermore, in an efficient market, a security's market price will fully reflect all available information that is relevant to the security at that time. This can be attributed to the actions of thousands of security analysts, who — upon identifying mispriced securities — place orders that tend to remove the mispricing.

## QUESTIONS AND PROBLEMS

1. What is the difference between call security markets and continuous security markets?
2. How is an investor's demand-to-buy or supply-to-sell schedule for a particular security related to the investor's demand-to-hold schedule for that same security?
3. Using an aggregate demand-to-hold schedule and associated demand-to-buy or supply-to-sell schedules, explain and illustrate the effect of the following events on the equilibrium price and quantity traded of Albany Corporation's common shares.
   a. Albany officials announce that next year's earnings are expected to be significantly higher than analysts had previously forecast.
   b. A wealthy shareholder initiates a large secondary offering of Albany shares.
   c. Another company, quite similar to Albany in all respects except for being privately held, decides to offer its outstanding shares for sale to the public.
4. Short sellers do not receive the proceeds from their short sales, must put up initial margin, and often do not receive interest on these sums held by their brokers. How does this affect the aggregate demand-to-hold schedules for securities?
5. We all know that investors have widely diverse opinions about the future course of the economy and earnings forecasts for various industries and companies. How then is it possible for all these investors to arrive at an equilibrium price for any particular security?
6. Distinguish between the three forms of market efficiency.
7. Is it true that in a perfectly efficient market no investor would consistently be able to earn a profit?
8. While security markets may not be perfectly efficient, what is the rationale for expecting them to be highly efficient?
9. When a corporation announces its earnings for a period, the volume of transactions in its stock may increase, but frequently that increase is not associated with significant moves in the price of its shares. How can this be explained?
10. What are the implications of the three forms of market efficiency for technical and fundamental analysis (discussed in Chapter 1)?
11. The years 1986 and 1987 will probably be long remembered for the insider trading scandals that were exposed in the United States.
    a. Is successful insider trading consistent with the three forms of market efficiency? Explain.
    b. Play the role of devil's advocate and present a case outlining the benefits to financial markets of insider trading.

# SUGGESTED READINGS

Eugene F. Fama, "Efficient Capital Markets: A Review of Theory and Empirical Work," *Journal of Finance* 25, no. 5 (May 1970):383–417 is still the best description of the Efficient Markets Hypothesis.

George Foster, *Financial Statement Analysis* (Englewood Cliffs, N.J.: Prentice Hall, 1986). Chapters 9 and 11 provide a summary of more up-to-date US evidence.

Rui M.C. Guimarães, Brian G. Kingsman and Stephen J. Taylor, eds., *A Reappraisal of the Efficiency of Financial Markets* (New York, NY: Springer-Verlag, 1989) and

Elroy Dimson, *Stock Market Anomalies* (Cambridge, U.K.: Cambridge University Press, 1988) reports evidence from various US and international markets including Canada.

# Chapter 4

# THE VALUATION
# OF RISKLESS SECURITIES

A useful first step in understanding security valuation is to consider those fixed-income securities that are certain of making their promised payments in full and on time. The obvious candidates are the securities representing the debt of the Canadian government. Since the government can print money whenever it chooses, the promised payments for such securities are virtually certain to be made on schedule. However, there is a degree of uncertainty as to the purchasing power of the promised payments. While Government of Canada bonds may be riskless in terms of their nominal payments, they may be quite risky in terms of their real (or inflation-adjusted) payments.

Despite this concern with inflation risk, it will be assumed hereafter that there are fixed-income securities whose nominal and real payments are certain. Specifically, to the extent that inflation exists, it will be assumed that its magnitude can be accurately predicted. Such an assumption makes it possible to focus on the impact of time on security valuation. Having accomplished this, the influence of other attributes on security valuation can be considered.

## 4.1 INVESTMENT

### ☐ 4.1.1 Deciding How Much to Invest

To begin with the simplest possible case, the plight of Robinson Crusoe will be analyzed. Crusoe has just been shipwrecked on an uninhabited island with little more than 20 bushels of corn. His knowledge of shipping routes leads him to expect to be saved in two years. In the meantime, he must decide how much corn to eat this year and how much to plant (that is, to invest) in order to obtain corn to eat next year. In keeping with the goals of this chapter, it will be assumed that the island is not subject to the uncertainties of nature that plague most farmers; Crusoe can be certain of the results of whatever planting he undertakes.

After carefully surveying the island, Crusoe decides that there are 20 plots of arable land, each capable of taking one bushel of corn. The plots differ in exposure, soil quality, and so on. This is shown in Table 4.1, in which the plots are listed in decreasing order of yield. The best plot offers a return of 36% on an investment (that is, a planting) of 1 bushel of corn, whereas the worst plot offers a return of −2%.

**TABLE 4.1**
Productivity of Crusoe's Land.

| Plot Number | Bushels of Corn Planted This Year on Plot | Yield in Bushels of Corn Harvested Next Year on Plot | Return Investment on Plot | Cumulative Yield From This PLus All Previous Plots |
|---|---|---|---|---|
| 1 | 1 | 1.36 | 36% | 1.36 |
| 2 | 1 | 1.34 | 34 | 2.70 |
| 3 | 1 | 1.32 | 32 | 4.02 |
| 4 | 1 | 1.30 | 30 | 5.32 |
| 5 | 1 | 1.28 | 28 | 6.60 |
| 6 | 1 | 1.26 | 26 | 7.86 |
| 7 | 1 | 1.24 | 24 | 9.10 |
| 8 | 1 | 1.22 | 22 | 10.32 |
| 9 | 1 | 1.20 | 20 | 11.52 |
| 10 | 1 | 1.18 | 18 | 12.70 |
| 11 | 1 | 1.16 | 16 | 13.86 |
| 12 | 1 | 1.14 | 14 | 15.00 |
| 13 | 1 | 1.12 | 12 | 16.12 |
| 14 | 1 | 1.10 | 10 | 17.22 |
| 15 | 1 | 1.08 | 8 | 18.30 |
| 16 | 1 | 1.06 | 6 | 19.36 |
| 17 | 1 | 1.04 | 4 | 20.40 |
| 18 | 1 | 1.02 | 2 | 21.42 |
| 19 | 1 | 1.00 | 0 | 22.42 |
| 20 | 1 | .98 | −2 | 23.40 |

The shaded region in Figure 4.1 shows Crusoe's alternatives. He could, of course, eat all 20 bushels of corn this year, leaving him nothing to eat next year; this strategy is plotted at point A in the figure. If Crusoe chooses instead to invest one of his bushels of corn, reducing the amount eaten to 19 bushels, he can look forward to eating 1.36 bushels next year, since he will use the best plot of land.

If, instead, Crusoe chooses to invest 2 bushels of corn, the incremental investment of one additional bushel of corn today yields only 1.34 bushels of corn next year. Why? Because poorer land must be used. This is simply a special case of the more general *principle of diminishing returns*, where the more invested, the smaller the likely return of each additional unit of investment.

The shaded region in the figure portrays all the investment opportunities shown in Table 4.1 for Crusoe's simple economy. Moving from the origin to the right on the horizontal axis represents increasing the amount of current consumption and decreasing the amount of investment. Consequently, the curved boundary to the investment opportunity set slopes down and to the right, indicating that more consumption now will lead to less investment and, thus, less consumption next year.

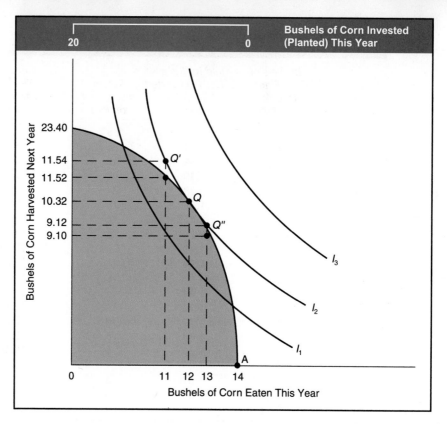

**FIGURE 4-1**
Making the consumption-investment decision.

## ☐ 4.1.2   Using Indifference Curves

How much corn will Crusoe decide to consume now? The answer depends on his feelings about present versus future consumption. These feelings can be shown graphically by a series of indifference curves, each of which displays combinations of current and future consumption that Crusoe finds equally desirable.[1] For example, he considers any combination on curve $I_1$ to be as desirable as any other on that curve. Similarly, he considers any combination of curve $I_2$ to be as desirable as any other on that curve. Furthermore, he would prefer a combination on $I_2$ over one on $I_1$, since the combinations on $I_2$ are "northeast" of those on $I_1$ and, thus, represent a higher level of aggregate consumption. Similarly, Crusoe would prefer a combination on $I_3$ over one on either $I_2$ or $I_1$. To keep from cluttering up the figure, only three of Crusoe's indifference curves have been drawn.

What will Crusoe do? From all his available investment opportunities, he will pick the one that is most desirable. Graphically, this is the investment opportunity

---

[1] These indifference curves should not be confused with the ones presented in Chapter 6, where the decision facing the individual is between risk and return, not current and future consumption.

corresponding to the point where an indifference curve is just tangent to the investment opportunity curve. In the figure, this is shown by point $Q$: From his initial stock of 20 bushels of corn, Crusoe will choose to eat 12 bushels this year and to invest the remaining 8 bushels. As a result of this investment, he will look forward to harvesting 10.32 bushels, all of which he will eat next year while waiting for his ship to come in.

What is the return on Crusoe's investment when he plants 8 bushels of corn now and harvests 10.32 bushels a year later? The rate of return is $(10.32 - 8)/8 = 29\%$. This is the *average return on investment* in the economy as a whole. His *marginal return on investment* is the return he earned on the last bushel planted, which in this case is the eighth bushel. Looking at Table 4.1, it can be seen that this corresponds to the yield on plot number 8, which is 22%.

---

## 4.2    INVESTMENT AND INTEREST

Moving a step closer to reality, assume that Crusoe is not alone. In particular, assume he has been preceded by Friday, who owns all the land on the island outright. However, Crusoe owns all the corn. If no one else were to intrude, the final outcome could depend on some form of cheating or violence. To avoid such an unpleasantry, assume that one of the clerks from the Paris Bourse is scheduled to drop by and "call out" a loan rate at which Crusoe will lend Friday corn today in return for Friday promising to repay a certain amount of corn one year later.

### ☐ 4.2.1   Demand and Supply of Capital

Given a rate at which Friday can borrow corn, how much will he take? Assume that Crusoe will provide corn now if he is paid an interest rate (in corn, not dollars) of 31%. In other words, for every bushel Friday takes, he must pay back 1.31 bushels next year. Referring to Table 4.1, borrowing 1 bushel clearly makes sense. This is because Friday can take the bushel, plant it in plot 1, and have a yield of 1.36 bushels a year later. Then Friday can pay back Crusoe 1.31 bushels, leaving himself a profit of .05 bushels $(1.36 - 1.31)$. Similarly, borrowing a second bushel will add .03 bushels $(1.34 - 1.31)$ to Friday's profit, and borrowing a third bushel will add .01 bushels $(1.32 - 1.31)$ to his profit. However, any more borrowing would be unprofitable for Friday. At an interest rate of 31%, Friday will take 3 bushels of corn. Figure 4.2 shows this, as well as the amount he will borrow at other interest rates, with the step function labeled *demand for capital* (sometimes referred to as the marginal efficiency of capital). Note that the lower the interest rate, the greater will be the quantity of capital (that is, corn) demanded. Not surprisingly, this is simply the information from Table 4.1, plotted in a different form.

How much capital (that is, corn) will Crusoe offer at various interest rates? The answer depends on the initial amount he owns and his attitudes toward present versus future consumption. However, the *supply of capital* shown in Figure 4.2 is typical: the higher the interest rate, the greater the amount of present consumption people are willing to forgo in favor of future consumption.

As in Paris, the visiting clerk wants to maximize the amount invested. Since this will be the smaller of (1) the amount Friday will want to borrow and (2) the amount Crusoe will want to lend, the appropriate interest rate, as shown in Figure 4.2, is about 19%. At this rate Crusoe will want to lend 9 bushels of corn in return for 10.71 bushels

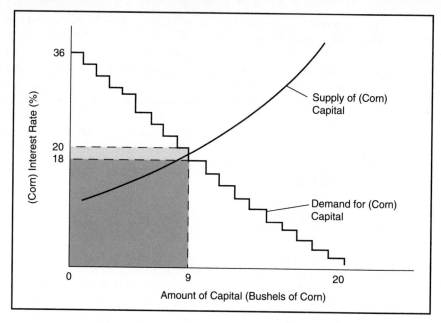

**FIGURE 4-2**
Demand and supply of capital.

[9 + (.19 × 9)] next year. Moreover, at this rate, Friday will want to borrow just 9 bushels, knowing he will obtain a total yield of 11.52 bushels, leaving .81 bushels (11.52 − 10.71) in profit for his undertaking.

In the real world, *interest rates will adjust until the total amount of capital demanded by producers equals the amount that owners of capital are willing to supply.* Fundamentally, demand depends on investment opportunities, whereas supply depends on preferences for present versus future consumption and on the ownership of wealth. Together, they determine the interest rate.

This is often difficult to see, since the day-to-day forces affecting interest rates appear to relate more to government policy, flotations of new securities by corporations, and so on. Although such activities do have an impact on interest rates, they are usually only ripples on the surface; the underlying forces of investment opportunities and preferences for present versus future consumption are the major determinants.

## 4.3    YIELD-TO-MATURITY

Robinson Crusoe was faced with a one-time investment decision, since he knew a ship was coming to rescue him after two years on the island. However, most people consider investments that will pay off not only next year but also the following year, and the year after that, and so on. Since interest rates are associated with investments and investments differ in longevity, there are many interest rates, not just one. Furthermore, there are many ways that interest rates can be calculated. One such method results in an interest rate that is known as the yield-to-maturity; another results in an interest rate known as the spot rate, which is discussed in the next section.

In describing yields-to-maturity and spot rates, three hypothetical riskless securities that are free from default risk, (meaning that investors have no doubts about being paid fully and on time) are assumed to be available. By considering these securities, the impact of differing degrees of default risk on yields-to-maturity and spot rates has been removed. These three securities are referred to as bonds A, B, and C. Bond A matures in one year, at which time the investor will receive $1000. Similarly, bond B matures in two years, at which time the investor will receive $1000. Bond C is a coupon bond that pays the investor $50 one year from now and matures two years from now, paying the investor $1050 at that time. The prices at which these bonds are currently being sold in the market are:

Bond A (the one-year pure-discount bond): $934.58
Bond B (the two-year pure-discount bond): $857.34
Bond C (the two-year coupon bond)　　: $946.93

The *yield-to-maturity* on any fixed-income security is the single interest rate (with interest compounded at some specified interval) that, if paid by a bank on the amount invested, would enable the investor to obtain all the payments made by the security in question. It is a simple matter to determine the yield-to-maturity on the one-year security, bond A. Since an investment of $934.58 will pay $1000 one year later, the yield-to-maturity on this bond is the rate $r_A$ that a bank would have to pay on a deposit of $934.58 in order for the account to have a balance of $1000 after one year. Thus, the yield-to-maturity on bond A is the rate $r_A$ that is the solution to the following equation:

$$(1 + r_A) \times \$934.58 = \$1000 \tag{4.1}$$

which is 7%.

In the case of bond B, assuming annual compounding at a rate $r_B$, an account with $857.34 invested initially (the cost of B) would grow to $(1 + r_B) \times \$857.34$ in one year. Leaving this total intact, the account would grow to $(1 + r_B) \times [(1 + r_B) \times \$857.34]$ by the end of the second year. The yield-to-maturity is the rate $r_B$ that makes this amount equal to $1000. In other words, the yield-to-maturity on bond B is the rate $r_B$ that is the solution to the following equation:

$$(1 + r_B) \times [(1 + r_B) \times \$857.34] = \$1000 \tag{4.2}$$

which is 8%.

For bond C, consider investing $946.93 in an account. At the end of one year, the account would grow in value to $(1 + r_C) \times \$946.93$. Then the investor would remove $50, leaving a balance of $[(1 + r_C) \times \$946.94] - \$50$. At the end of the second year this balance would have grown to an amount equal to $(1 + r_C) \times [(1 + r_C) \times \$946.93] - \$50$. The yield-to-maturity on bond C is the rate $r_C$ that makes this amount equal to $1050:

$$(1 + r_C) \times \{[(1 + r_C) \times \$946.93] - \$50\} = \$1050 \tag{4.3}$$

which is 7.975%.

Equivalently, yield-to-maturity is the discount rate that makes the present value of the promised future cash flows equal to the current market price of the bond.[2] When

---

[2] This calculation assumes that the bond will not be called prior to maturity. If it is assumed that the bond will be called as soon as possible, then the discount rate that makes the present value of the corresponding cash flows equal to the current market price of the bond is known as the bond's *yield-to-call*.

viewed in this manner, yield-to-maturity is analogous to internal rate of return, a concept used for making capital budgeting decisions that is often described in introductory finance textbooks. This can be seen for bond A by dividing both sides of equation (4.1) by $(1 + r_A)$, resulting in:

$$\$934.58 = \frac{\$1000}{(1 + r_A)}. \tag{4.4}$$

Similarly, for bond B both sides of equation (4.2) can be divided by $(1 + r_B)^2$, resulting in:

$$\$857.34 = \frac{\$1000}{(1 + r_B)^2} \tag{4.5}$$

whereas for bond C both sides of equation (4.3) can be divided by $(1 + r_C)^2$:

$$\$946.93 - \frac{\$50}{(1 + r_C)} = \frac{\$1050}{(1 + r_C)^2}$$

or

$$\$946.93 = \frac{\$50}{(1 + r_C)} + \frac{\$1050}{(1 + r_C)^2}. \tag{4.6}$$

Since equations (4.4), (4.5), and (4.6) are equivalent to equations (4.1), (4.2), and (4.3), respectively, the solutions must be the same as before, with $r_A = 7\%$, $r_B = 8\%$, and $r_C = 7.975\%$.

For coupon-bearing bonds, the procedure for determining yield-to-maturity involves trial and error. In the case of bond C, a discount rate of 10% could be tried initially, resulting in a value of $913.22 for the right-hand side of equation (4.6), a value that is too low. This indicates that the number in the denominator is too high, so a lower discount rate, such as 6%, is used next. In this case, the value on the right-hand side is $981.67, which is too high and indicates that 6% is too low. This means the solution is between 6% and 10%, and the search could continue until the answer, 7.975%, is found.

Fortunately, computers are good at trial-and-error calculations. One can describe a very complex series of cash flows to a computer and get an answer concerning yield-to-maturity in short order. In fact, some hand-held calculators come with built-in programs to find yield-to-maturity, where one simply enters the number of days to maturity, the annual coupon payments, and the current market price and then presses the key that indicates yield-to-maturity. The lights blink as the calculator engages in its trial-and-error procedure; then in a few seconds the answer appears.

Yield-to-maturity is the most commonly used measure of a bond's "interest rate," or "return." It can be computed for any bond and it facilitates comparisons among different investments. However, it has some serious drawbacks. In order to understand these drawbacks, the concept of spot rates must be introduced.

# SPOT RATES

A *spot rate* is measured at a given time as the yield-to-maturity on a pure-discount security and can be thought of as the interest rate associated with a spot contract. Such a contract, when signed, involves the immediate loaning of money from one party to another. The loan, along with interest, is to be repaid in its entirety at a specific time in the future. The interest rate that is specified in the contract is the spot rate.

Bonds A and B in the previous example were pure-discount securities, meaning an investor who purchased either one would expect to receive only one cash payment from the issuer. Accordingly, in this example the one-year spot rate is 7% and the two-year spot rate is 8%. In general, the t-year spot rate $s_t$ is the solution to the following equation:

$$P_t = \frac{M_t}{(1 + s_t)^t} \qquad (4.7)$$

where $P_t$ is the current market price of a pure-discount bond that matures in $t$ years and has a maturity value of $M_t$. For example, the values of $P_t$ and $M_t$ for bond B would be $857.34 and $1000, respectively, with $t = 2$.

Spot rates can also be determined in another manner if only coupon-bearing bonds are available for longer maturities. Generally the one-year spot rate ($s_1$) will be known, since there frequently will be a one-year pure-discount Treasury bill available for making this calculation. However, it may be that no two-year pure-discount security exists. Instead, only a two-year coupon-bearing bond may be available for investment, having a current market price of $P_2$, a maturity value of $M_2$, and a coupon payment one year from now equal to $C_1$. In this situation, the two-year spot rate ($s_2$) is the solution to the following equation:

$$P_2 = \frac{C_1}{(1 + s_1)^1} + \frac{M_2}{(1 + s_2)^2}. \qquad (4.8)$$

For example, assume that only bonds A and C exist. In this situation it is known that the one-year spot rate, $s_1$, is 7%. Now, equation (4.8) can be used to determine the two-year spot rate, $s_2$, where $P_2 = \$946.93$, $C_1 = \$50$, and $M_2 = \$1050$:

$$\$946.93 = \frac{\$50}{(1 + .07)^1} + \frac{\$1050}{(1 + s_2)^2}.$$

The solution to this equation is $s_2 = .08 = 8\%$. Thus, the two-year spot rate is determined to be the same in this example regardless of whether it is determined directly by analyzing pure-discount bond B or indirectly by analyzing coupon-bearing bond C in conjunction with bond A. Although this will not always be the case, often the differences are insignificant.

# DISCOUNT FACTORS

Having determined a set of spot rates, it is a straightforward matter to determine the corresponding set of *discount factors*. A discount factor $d_t$ is equivalent to the present value of $1 to be received $t$ years in the future from a government security and is equal to:

$$d_t = \frac{1}{(1 + s_t)^t}. \qquad (4.9)$$

The set of these factors is sometimes referred to as the *market discount function* and changes day to day as spot rates change. In the example, $d_1 = 1/(1 + .07)^1 = .9346$ and $d_2 = 1/(1 + .08)^2 = .8573$.

Once the market discount function has been determined, it is fairly straightforward to find the present value of any default-free security. Let $C_t$ denote the cash payment to be made to the investor at year $t$ on the security being evaluated. The multiplication of $C_t$ by $d_t$ is termed *discounting*: converting the given future value into an equivalent present value. The latter is equivalent in the sense that $P$ present dollars can be converted into $C_t$ dollars in year $t$ via available investment instruments, given the currently prevailing spot rates. An investment paying $C_t$ dollars in year $t$ with certainty should sell for $P = d_t C_t$ dollars today. If it sells for more, it is overpriced; if it sells for less, it is underpriced. These statements rest solely on comparisons with equivalent opportunities in the marketplace. Valuation of default-free investments thus requires no assessment of individual preferences, only careful analysis of available opportunities in the marketplace.

The simplest and, in a sense, most fundamental characterization of the structure of the market for default-free bonds is given by the current set of discount factors, referred to earlier as the market discount function. With this set of factors, it is a simple matter to evaluate a default-free bond that provides more than one payment, for it is, in effect, a package of bonds, each of which provides only one payment. Each amount is simply multiplied by the appropriate discount factor, and the resultant present values are summed.

For example, assume that the government is preparing to offer for sale a two-year coupon-bearing security that will pay $70 in one year and $1070 in two years. What is a fair price for such a security? It is simply the present value of $70 and $1070. This can be determined by multiplying $70 and $1070 by the one-year and two-year discount factors, respectively. Doing so results in ( $70 \times .9346) + ($1070 \times .8573)$, which equals $982.73.

No matter how complex the pattern of payments, this procedure can be used to determine the value of any default-free bond of this type. The general formula for the bond's present value ($PV$) is:

$$PV = \sum_{t=1}^{n} d_t C_t \qquad (4.10)$$

where the bond has promised cash payments $C_t$ for each year $t$ through year $n$.

At this point, it has been shown how spot rates and, in turn, discount factors can be calculated. However, no link between different spot rates (or different discount factors) has been established. For example, it has yet to be shown how the one-year spot rate of 7% is related to the two-year spot rate of 8%. The concept of forward rates makes the link.

In the example, the one-year spot rate was determined to be 7%. This means that the market has determined that the present value of $1 to be paid by the government in one year is $1/1.07, or $.9346. That is, the relevant discount rate for converting a cash flow one year from now to its present value is 7%. Since it was also noted that the two-year spot rate was 8%, the present value of $1 to be paid by the Treasury Department in two years is $1/1.08^2$, or $.8573.

An alternative view of $1 to be paid in two years is that it can be discounted in two steps. The first step determines its equivalent one-year value. That is, $1 to be received in two years is equivalent to $1/(1 + f_{1,2})$ to be received in one year. The second step determines the present value of this equivalent one-year amount by discounting it at the one-year spot rate of 7%. Thus, its current value is

$$\frac{\$1/(1 + f_{1,2})}{(1 + .07)}.$$

However, this value must be equal to $.8573, since it was mentioned earlier that according to the two-year spot rate, $.8573 is the present value of $1 to be paid in two years. That is,

$$\frac{\$1/(1 + f_{1,2})}{(1 + .07)} = \$.8573 \tag{4.11}$$

which has a solution for $f_{1,2}$ of 9.01%.

The discount rate $f_{1,2}$ is known as the *forward rate* from year 1 to year 2. That is, it is the discount rate for determining the equivalent value of a dollar one year from now if it is to be received two years from now. In the example, $1 to be received two years from now is equivalent in value to $1/(1.0901) = \$.9174$ to be received one year from now (in turn, note that the present value of $.9174 is $.9174/1.07 = \$.8573$).

Symbolically, the link between the one-year spot rate, two-year spot rate, and one-year forward rate is:

$$\frac{\$1/(1 + f_{1,2})}{(1 + s_1)} = \frac{\$1}{(1 + s_2)^2} \tag{4.12}$$

which can be rewritten as:

$$(1 + f_{1,2}) = \frac{(1 + s_2)^2}{(1 + s_1)} \tag{4.13}$$

or

$$(1 + s_1)(1 + f_{1,2}) = (1 + s_2)(1 + s_2). \tag{4.14}$$

More generally, for year $t - 1$ and year $t$ spot rates, the link to the forward rate between years $t - 1$ and $t$ is:

$$(1 + f_{t-1,t}) = \frac{(1 + s_t)^t}{(1 + s_{t-1})^{t-1}}, \tag{4.15}$$

or

$$(1 + s_{t-1})^{t-1} \times (1 + f_{t-1,t}) = (1 + s_t)^t. \tag{4.16}$$

There is another interpretation that can be given to forward rates. Consider a contract made now, in which money will be loaned a year from now and paid back two years from now. Such a contract is known as a *forward contract*; the interest rate on the one-year loan that is specified in it (note that the interest will be paid when the loan matures in two years) is known as the forward rate.

It is important to distinguish this rate from the rate for one-year loans that will prevail for deals made a year from now (the spot rate at that time). A forward rate applies to contracts made now but relating to a period "forward" in time. By the nature of the contract, the terms are certain now, even though the actual transaction will occur later. If instead one were to wait until next year and sign a contract to borrow money in the spot market at that time, the terms might turn out to be better or worse than today's forward rate, since the future spot rate is not perfectly predictable.

In the example, the marketplace has priced these securities such that a representative investor making a two-year loan to the government would demand an interest rate equal to the two-year spot rate, 8%. Equivalently, the investor would be willing simultaneously to (1) make a one-year loan to the government at an interest rate equal to the one-year spot rate, 7%, and (2) sign a forward contract with the government to loan the government money one year from now, being repaid two years from now, where the interest rate to be paid is the forward rate, 9.01%.

When viewed in this manner, forward contracts are implicit. However, forward contracts are sometimes made explicitly. For example, a contractor might obtain a commitment from a bank for a one-year construction loan a year hence at a fixed rate of interest. Financial futures markets (discussed in Chapter 19) provide standardized forward contracts of this type. For example, in April 1987 one could contract to pay $984.70 in September 1987 to purchase a 91-day Treasury bill that would pay $1000 in December 1987.

## 4.7   FORWARD RATES AND DISCOUNT FACTORS

In equation (4.9) it was shown that a discount factor for $t$ years could be calculated by adding 1 to the spot rate for $t$ years, raising this sum to the power t, and then taking the reciprocal of the result. For example, it was shown that the two-year discount factor associated with the two-year spot rate of 8% was equal to $1/(1 + .08)^2 = .8573$.

Equation (4.14) suggests an equivalent method for calculating discount factors. In the case of the two-year factor, this method involves multiplying the one-year spot rate by the forward rate and taking the reciprocal of the result:

$$d_2 = \frac{1}{(1 + s_1) \times (1 + f_{1,2})} \quad\quad (4.17)$$

which in the example is

$$d_2 = \frac{1}{(1 + .07) \times (1 + .0901)} = .8573.$$

More generally, the discount factor for year $t$ that is shown in equation (4.9) can be restated as follows:

$$d_t = \frac{1}{(1 + s_{t-1})^{t-1} \times (1 + f_{t-1,t})}. \quad\quad (4.18)$$

Thus, given a set of spot rates, it is possible to determine the market discount function in either of two ways, both of which will provide the same figures. First, the spot rates can be used in equation (4.9) to arrive at a set of discount factors. Alternatively, the spot rates can be used to determine a set of forward rates and then the spot rates and forward rates can be used in equation (4.18) to arrive at a set of discount factors.

## 4.8 DURATION

Most bonds provide periodic coupon payments ("interest" payments) in addition to a final ("par") payment at maturity. Depending on the relative magnitudes of these payments, a bond may be more or less like others with the same maturity date. A measure of the average time prior to the receipt of payment is obtained by calculating the bond's *duration*. This is simply a weighted average of the lengths of time prior to the payments, using the relative present values of the payments as weights.

The two-year coupon bond analyzed earlier provides an illustration. Recall that this bond had a payment of $70 one year hence and that the present value of this payment was $70 × .9346 = $65.42. Its final payment of $1070, to be made two years hence, had a present value of $1070 × .8573 = $917.31. In total, the present value of the bond was $65.42 + $917.31 = $982.73. As shown in Table 4.2, this bond had a duration of 1.9334 years.

**TABLE 4.2**
Calculating the Duration of a Bond.

| Time Until Receipt of Payment (1) | Present Value of Payment (2) | Present Value of Payment as a Proportion of the Present Value of the Bond (3) | (1) × (3) = (4) |
|---|---|---|---|
| 1 | $ 65.42 | $ 65.42/$982.73 = .0666 | .0666 |
| 2 | 917.31 | $917.31/$982.73 = .9334 | 1.8668 |
| | $982.73 | 1.0000 | 1.9334 |

Bonds of similar duration are more likely to react in similar ways to changes in interest rates than are bonds of similar term-to-maturity but different durations. This should not be surprising. Term-to-maturity measures only the time until the last payment is due; it takes no account of the pattern of any intervening payments. Duration takes both factors into account and thus measures a bond's payment characteristics more accurately.[3]

---

[3] Duration is discussed more extensively in Chapter 14.

# COMPOUNDING

Thus far, the discussion has concentrated on annual interest rates by assuming that cash flows are compounded (or discounted) annually. This is often appropriate, but for more precise calculations a shorter period may be more desirable. Moreover, some lenders explicitly compound funds more often than once each year.

*Compounding* is the payment of interest on interest. At the end of each compounding interval, interest is computed and added to principal. This sum becomes the principal on which interest is computed at the end of the next interval. The process continues until the end of the final compounding interval is reached.

No problem is involved in adapting the previously stated formulas to compounding intervals other than a year. The simplest procedure is to count in units of the chosen interval. For example, yield-to-maturity can be calculated using any chosen compounding interval. If payment of $P$ dollars now will result in the receipt of $F$ dollars ten years from now, the yield-to-maturity can be calculated using annual compounding by finding a value $r_a$ that satisfies the equation

$$P(1 + r_a)^{10} = F, \tag{4.19}$$

since $F$ will be received ten annual periods from now. The result, $r_a$, is expressed as an annual rate with annual compounding.

Alternatively, yield-to-maturity can be calculated using semiannual compounding by finding a value $r_s$ that satisfies the equation

$$P(1 + r_s)^{20} = F \tag{4.20}$$

since $F$ will be received 20 semiannual periods from now. The result, $r_s$, is expressed as a semiannual rate with semiannual compounding. It can be doubled to give an annual rate with semiannual compounding; alternatively, the annual rate with annual compounding can be computed for a given value of $r_s$ by using the following equation:

$$1 + r_a = (1 + r_s)^2. \tag{4.21}$$

For example, consider an investment costing $2315.97 that will pay $5000 10 years later. Applying equations (4.19) and (4.20) to this security results in

$$\$2315.97(1 + r_a)^{10} = \$5000$$

and

$$\$2315.97(1 + r_s)^{20} = \$5000$$

respectively, where the solutions are $r_a = 8\%$ and $r_s = 3.923\%$. Thus, this security can be described as having an annual rate with annual compounding of 8%, a semiannual rate with semiannual compounding of 3.923%, and an annual rate with semiannual compounding of $2 \times 3.923\% = 7.846\%$.[4]

To reduce the confusion caused by the many different methods that can be used to express interest rates, the US Federal *Truth-in-Lending Act* requires every lender to compute and disclose the *annual percentage rate* (APR) implied by the terms of a loan.

-----------

[4] Note how, using equation (4.21), $r_a = (1.03923)^2 - 1 = 8\%$, a solution that is the same as the one provided by equation (4.19).

This is simply the yield-to-maturity, computed using the most frequent time between payments on the loan as the compounding interval. Although some complications arise when payments are required at irregular intervals, the use of APRs clearly simplifies the task of comparing lenders' terms. Canadian consumers could benefit from some standardization of reported interest rates.

Semiannual compounding is commonly used to determine the yield-to-maturity for bonds, since coupon payments are usually made twice a year. Most preprogrammed calculators and computers use this approach.

## 4.10 THE BANK DISCOUNT METHOD

One time-honored procedure for reporting interest rates is the *bank discount method*. If someone "borrows" $100 from a bank, to be repaid a year later, the bank will discount the interest of, for instance, 8% and give the borrower $92. According to the bank discount method, this is an interest rate of 8%. The borrower only receives $92, for which he or she must pay $8 in interest after one year. The "true" interest rate (APR) must be based on the money the borrower actually gets to use. In this case, the rate is 8.70%, since $8 / $92 = .0870.

It is a simple matter to convert an interest rate quoted on the bank discount method to a true interest rate. If the bank discount rate is BDR, then the true rate is simply BDR/(1 − BDR). The previous example provides an illustration: $.08 / (1 − .08) = .0870$.

## 4.11 CONTINUOUS COMPOUNDING

When computing an investment's return, the compounding interval can make a difference. For example, regulations may limit a savings institution to paying a fixed rate of interest but make no specifications about the compounding interval. This was the situation in early 1975, when the legal limit on interest paid by savings and loan companies on deposits committed from six to ten years was 7.75% per year. Initially, most savings and loans paid simple interest — thus, $1 deposited at the beginning of the year would grow to $1.0775 by the end of the year. Later, in an attempt to attract depositors, some enterprising savings and loans announced that they would pay 7.75% per year, compounded semiannually at a rate of $7.75\% / 2 = 3.3875\%$. This meant that $1 deposited at the beginning of the year would grow to $1.03875 at the end of six months, and this total would then grow to $1.03875 \times 1.03875 = \$1.079$ by the end of the year, for an effective annual interest rate of 7.9%. This procedure was considered within the letter, if not the spirit, of the law.

Before long, other competitors offered 7.75% per year compounded quarterly (that is, $7.75\% / 4 = 1.938\%$ per quarter), giving an effective annual interest rate of 7.978%. Then others offered to compound the 7.75% rate on a monthly basis (at $7.75\% / 12 = .646\%$ per month), for an effective annual interest rate of 8.031%. The end was reached when one company offered continuous compounding of the 7.75% annual rate. This rather abstract procedure represents the limit as interest is compounded more and more frequently. If $r$ represents the annual rate of interest (in this case, 7.75%) and $n$ is the number of times compounding takes place per year, the effective rate, $r_e$, is given by:

$$\left(1 + \frac{r}{n}\right)^n = 1 + r_e. \tag{4.22}$$

Thus, with semiannual compounding of 7.75%,

$$\left(1 + \frac{.0775}{2}\right)^2 = (1 + .03875)^2 = 1.079,$$

and with quarterly compounding,

$$\left(1 + \frac{.0775}{4}\right)^2 = (1 + .01938)^4 = 1.07978,$$

and so on. As the compounding interval grows shorter, the number of times compounding takes place ($n$) grows larger, as does the effective interest rate, $r_e$.

Mathematicians can prove that as $n$ grows larger, the quantity $[1+(r/n)]^n$ becomes increasingly close to $e^r$, where $e$ stands for the number 2.71828 (rounded to five-place accuracy). In this case, $e^{.0775} = 1.0806$, indicating an effective annual rate of 8.06%.[5]

A more general formula for continuous compounding can also be derived. At an annual rate of r, with continuous compounding, $P$ dollars will grow to $F_t$ dollars $t$ years from now, where the relationship between $P$, $r$, and $F_t$ is:

$$Pe^{rt} = F_t. \tag{4.23}$$

Similarly, the present value of $F_t$ dollars received $t$ years later at an annual rate of $r$ that is continuously compounded will be

$$P = \frac{F_t}{e^{rt}}. \tag{4.24}$$

Thus, if spot rates are expressed as annual rates with continuous compounding, then the discount factors can be calculated as:

$$d_t = \frac{1}{e^{rt}}.$$

These last three formulas can be used for any value of t, including fractional amounts (for example, if $F_t$ is to be received in $2\frac{1}{2}$ years, then $t = 2.5$.)

_____

[5] Tables of natural logarithms may be used for such calculations. The natural logarithm of 1.0806 is .0775, and the antilogarithm of .0775 is 1.0806.

# YIELD CURVES

At any time, fixed income securities will be priced approximately in accord with the existing set of spot rates and their associated discount factors. Although there have been times when all the spot rates were roughly equal in size, generally they have different values. Often the one-year spot rate is less than the two-year spot rate, which in turn is less than the three-year spot rate, and so on (that is, $s_t$ increases as $t$ increases). At other times, the one-year spot rate is greater than the two-year spot rate, which in turn is greater than the three-year spot rate, and so on (that is, $s_t$ decreases as $t$ increases). It is wise for the security analyst to know which case currently prevails, as this is a useful starting point in valuing fixed-income securities.

Unfortunately, this is easier said than done. Only government bonds are clearly free from default risk. However, the features of such bonds may differ from issue to issue. Despite these problems, a summary of the approximate relationship between yields-to-maturity on Government of Canada securities of various terms-to-maturity is presented in the form of a graph illustrating the current yield curve.

A *yield curve* is a graph that shows the yields-to-maturity (on the vertical axis) for government securities of various maturities (on the horizontal axis) as of a particular date. Figure 4.3 provides an example that shows the relationship that existed on three different dates in 1991. This provides an estimate of the current *term structure* of interest rates and changes daily as prices and, hence, yields-to-maturity change. Current yield curves can be obtained from investment dealers and investment cousellors (for a fee). Many institutional investors produce their own on a regular basis.

Generally the relationship between yields and maturities is less than perfect. That is, not all the securities lie exactly on the yield curve. This is largely due to the fact that the yield-to-maturity on a coupon-bearing security is not clearly linked to the set of spot rates currently in existence. Since the set of spot rates is a fundamental determinant of the price of any government security, there is no reason to expect yields to lie exactly on the curve. Indeed, a more meaningful graph would be one where spot rates are measured on the vertical axis instead of yields-to-maturity. With this in mind, an interesting question to ponder is, why are the spot rates of different magnitudes? And why do the differences in these rates change over time, where sometimes long-term spot rates are greater than short-term spot rates and sometimes the opposite occurs? Attempts to answer such questions can be found in various term structure theories.

# TERM STRUCTURE THEORIES

Three theories have been generally used to explain the term structure of interest rates.[6] The focus of the discussion is on the term structure of spot rates, since it is these rates and not yields-to-maturity that are critically important in determining the price of any Treasury security.

---

[6] For a thorough review of these theories and the associated empirical evidence, see Chapter 19 of John H. Wood and Norma L. Wood, *Financial Markets* (San Diego, Calif.: Harcourt Brace Jovanovich, 1985) and Chapter 5 of James C. Van Horne, *Financial Market Rates and Flows* (Englewood Cliffs, N.J.: Prentice Hall, 1984).

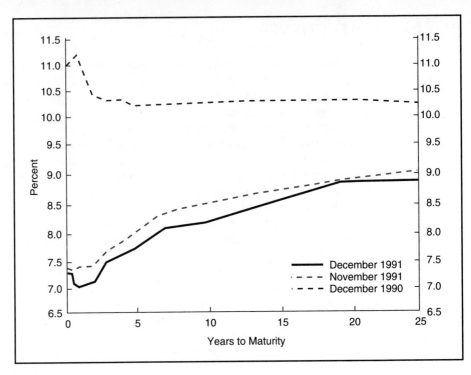

**FIGURE 4-3**
Yield curves of Government of Canada securities, December, 1990, November and December, 1991.

*SOURCE:* ScotiaMcLeod Inc., *Debt Market Indices*, December 31, 1991.

## ☐ 4.13.1 The Unbiased Expectations Theory

The *unbiased expectations theory* holds that the forward rate represents the average opinion of the expected future spot rate for the period in question. Thus, a set of spot rates that is rising can be explained by arguing that the marketplace (that is, the general opinion of investors) believes that spot rates will be rising in the future. Conversely, a set of decreasing spot rates is explained by arguing that the marketplace expects spot rates to be falling in the future.[7]

The marketplace expects spot rates to change because either the real rate or the inflation rate is expected to change. For example, the reason the spot rates are expected to rise could be due to a perception in the marketplace that inflation is going to accelerate in the future. Conversely, spot rates might be expected to decline because of a perception that inflation is going to slow down in the future.

---

[7] Recently a "modern" expectations theory has been developed that is economically more logical than the "unbiased" expectations theory. However, it provides approximately the same empirical implications and explanations of the term structure as those given by the unbiased expectations theory. Thus, given the similarities of the two theories, only the unbiased expectations theory is presented. For more on the modern expectations theory, see Wood and Wood, *Financial Markets*, pp. 645–51.

In order to understand this theory more fully, consider the earlier example where the one-year spot rate was 7% and the two-year spot rate was 8%. The basic question is, Why are these two spot rates different? Equivalently, why is the term structure upward-sloping?

Consider an investor with $1 to invest for two years (for ease of exposition, it will be assumed that any amount of money can be invested at the prevailing spot rates). This investor could follow a *maturity strategy*, investing the money now for the full two years at the two-year spot rate of 8%. With this strategy, at the end of two years the dollar will have grown in value to $1(1.08)(1.08) = $1.1664$. Alternatively, the investor could invest the dollar now for one year at the one-year spot rate of 7%, so that the investor knows that one year from now he or she will have $1(1.07) = $1.07$ to reinvest for one more year.

Although the investor does not know what the one-year spot rate will be one year from now, the investor has an *expectation* about what it will be (this expected future spot rate will hereafter be denoted by $es_{1,2}$). If the investor thinks it will be 10%, then his or her $1 has an expected value two years from now of $1(1.07)(1.10) = $1.177$. In this case, the investor would choose a *rollover strategy*, meaning the investor would choose to invest in a one-year security at 7% rather than in the two-year security, since he or she would expect to have more money at the end of two years by doing so (note that $1.177 > $1.1664$).

However, an expected future spot rate of 10% cannot represent the general view in the marketplace. If it did, people would not be willing to invest money at the two-year spot rate, since a higher return would be expected from investing money at the one-year rate and using the rollover strategy. Thus, the two-year spot rate would quickly rise, since the supply of funds for two-year loans at 8% would be less than the demand. Conversely, the supply of funds for one year at 7% would be more than the demand, causing the one-year rate to fall quickly. Thus, a one-year spot rate of 7%, a two-year spot rate of 8%, and an expected future spot rate of 10% cannot represent an equilibrium situation.

What if the expected future spot rate is 6% instead of 10%? In this case, according to the rollover strategy, the investor would expect $1 to be worth $1(1.07)(1.06) = $1.1342$ at the end of two years. Since this is less than the value the dollar will have if the maturity strategy is followed ($1.1342 < $1.1664$), the investor would choose the maturity strategy. Again, however, an expected future spot rate of 6% cannot represent the general view in the marketplace because if it did, people would not be willing to invest money at the one-year spot rate.

Earlier, it was shown that the forward rate in this example was 9.01%. What if the expected future spot rate was of this magnitude? At the end of two years the value of $1 with the rollover strategy would be $1(1.07)(1.0901) = $1.1664$, the same as the value of $1 with the maturity strategy. In this case, equilibrium would exist in the marketplace because the general view would be that both strategies have the same expected return. Accordingly, investors with a two-year holding period would not have an incentive to choose one strategy over the other.

Note that an investor with a one-year holding period could follow a maturity strategy by investing $1 in the one-year security and receiving $1.07 after one year. Alternatively, a *naive strategy* could be followed, where a two-year security could be purchased now and sold after one year. If so, the expected selling price would be $1.1664/1.0901 = $1.07$, for a return of 7% (the security would have a maturity value of $1.1664 = $1(1.08)(1.08)$, but since the spot rate is expected to be 9.01% in a year, its expected selling price is just the discounted value of its maturity value). Since the maturity and naive strategies have the same expected return, investors with a one-year holding period would not have an incentive to choose one strategy over the other.

Thus, the unbiased expectations theory asserts that the expected future spot rate is equal in magnitude to the forward rate. In the example, the current one-year spot rate is 7% and, according to this theory, the general opinion is that it will rise to a rate of 9.01% in one year. It is this expected rise in the one-year spot rate that is the reason behind the upward-sloping term structure when the two-year spot rate (8%) is greater than the one-year spot rate (7%).

In equation format, the unbiased expectations theory states that the expected future spot rate is equal to the forward rate:

$$es_{1,2} = f_{1,2}. \tag{4.26}$$

Thus, equation (4.14) can be restated with $es_{1,2}$ substituted for $f_{1,2}$, as follows:

$$(1 + s_2)(1 + s_2) = (1 + s_1)(1 + es_{1,2}) \tag{4.27}$$

which can be conveniently interpreted to mean that the expected return from a maturity strategy must equal the expected return on a rollover strategy.[8]

The previous example dealt with an upward-sloping term structure, where the longer the term, the higher the spot rate. It is a straightforward matter to deal with a downward-sloping term structure, where the longer the term, the lower the spot rate. While the explanation for an upward-sloping term structure was that investors expect spot rates to rise in the future, the reason for the downward-sloping curve is that investors expect spot rates to fall in the future.

An interesting followup question is, Why do investors expect spot rates to change, either rising or falling, in the future? A possible answer to this question can be found by noting that the spot rates that are observed in the marketplace are nominal rates. That is, they are a reflection of the underlying real rate and the expected inflation rate.[9] If either (or both) of these rates is expected to change in the future, then the spot rate will be expected to change.

For example, assume a constant real rate of 3%. Since the current one-year spot rate is 7%, this means that the general opinion in the marketplace is that the expected rate of inflation over the next year is approximately 4% (the nominal rate is approximately equal to the sum of the real rate and expected inflation rate). Now, according to the unbiased expectations theory, the expected future spot rate is 9.01%, an increase of 2.01% from the current one-year spot rate of 7%. The spot rate is expected to rise by 2.01% because the inflation rate is expected to rise by 2.01%. That is, the expected inflation rate over the next 12 months is approximately 4%, and over the following 12 months it is expected to be higher, at approximately 6.01%.

To recapitulate, the two-year spot rate (8%) is greater than the one-year spot rate (7%) because investors expect the future one-year spot rate to be greater than the current

---

[8] Equation (4.26) can be expressed more generally as $es_{t-1,t} = f_{t-1,t}$. Thus, using equation (4.16), the unbiased expectations theory states that, in general, $(1 + s_t)^t = (1 + s_{t-1})^{t-1} \times (1 + es_{t-1,t})$.

[9] See Chapter 11 for a discussion of the nature of the relationship between nominal rates, real rates, and expected inflation rates.

one-year spot rate. They expect it to be greater because of an anticipated rise in the expected rate of inflation, from approximately 4% to approximately 6.01%.

In general, when current economic conditions make short-term spot rates abnormally high (owing, say, to a relatively high current rate of inflation), according to the unbiased expectations theory, the term structure should be downward-sloping. This is because inflation would be expected to abate in the future. Conversely, when current conditions make short-term rates abnormally low (owing say, to a relatively low current rate of inflation), the term structure should be upward-sloping, since inflation would be expected to rise in the future. Examination of historical term structures suggest that this is what has actually happened, since the structure has been upward-sloping in periods of lower interest rates and downward-sloping in periods of higher interest rates.

However, examining historical term structures uncovers a problem. In particular, with this theory, it is logical to expect that over time there will be roughly as many occurrences of upward-sloping term structures as downward-sloping term structures. In reality, upward-sloping structures tend to be more frequent. The liquidity preference theory provides an explanation for this observation.

## ☐ 4.13.2 The Liquidity Preference Theory

The *liquidity preference theory* (also known as the liquidity premium theory) starts with the notion that investors are primarily interested in purchasing short-term securities. That is, even though some investors may have longer holding periods, there is a tendency for them to prefer short-term securities. This is because these investors realize that they may need their funds earlier than anticipated and recognize that they face less "price risk" (that is, interest rate risk) if they invest in shorter-term securities.

For example, an investor with a two-year holding period would tend to prefer the rollover strategy, since he or she would be certain of having a given amount of cash at the end of one year, when it may be needed. If a maturity strategy had been followed, then the investor would have to sell the two-year security after one year if cash was needed. However, it is not known now what price the investor would get if he or she were to sell the two-year security in one year. Thus, there is an extra element of risk associated with the maturity strategy that is absent from the rollover strategy.[10]

The upshot is that investors with a two-year holding period will not choose the maturity strategy if it has the same expected return as the rollover strategy, since it is riskier. The only way investors will follow the maturity strategy and buy the two-year securities is if its expected return is higher. That is, borrowers are going to have to pay the investors a risk premium in the form of a greater expected return in order to get them to purchase two-year securities.

Will borrowers be inclined to pay such a premium when issuing two-year securities? Yes, they will be so inclined. First, frequent refinancing may be costly in terms of registration, advertising, paperwork, and so on. These costs can be lessened by issuing

---

[10] Unfortunately, this risk is often referred to as *liquidity risk*, when it more appropriately should be called *price risk*, since it is the price volatility associated with longer-term securities that is of concern to investors. Partially offsetting this price risk is a risk that is present in the rollover strategy and absent from the maturity strategy — namely, the risk associated with having an uncertain reinvestment rate at the end of the first year when the rollover strategy is chosen. The liquidity preference theory assumes that this risk is of relatively little concern to investors.

relatively long-term securities. Second, some borrowers will realize that relatively long-term bonds are a less risky source of funds than relatively short-term bonds, since they will not have to be as concerned about the possibility of refinancing in the future at higher interest rates. Thus, borrowers may be willing to pay more (via higher expected interest costs) for relatively long-term funds.

In the example, the one-year spot rate was 7% and the two-year spot rate was 8%. As mentioned earlier, according to the liquidity preference theory, the only way investors will agree to follow a maturity strategy is if the expected return from doing so is higher than the expected return from following the rollover strategy. This means that the expected future spot rate must be something *less* than the forward rate of 9.01% — perhaps it is 8.6%. If so, then the value of a $1 investment in two years is expected to be $1(1.07)(1.086) = $1.1620$, given the rollover strategy is followed. Since the value of a $1 investment with the maturity strategy is $1(1.08)(1.08) = $1.1664$, it can be seen that the rollover strategy has a lower expected return for the two-year period, which can be attributed to its smaller degree of price risk.

The difference between the forward rate and the expected future spot rate is known as the *liquidity premium*. It is the "extra" return given investors in order to entice them to purchase the more risky two-year security. In the example, it is equal to $9.01\% - 8.6\% = .41\%$. More generally,

$$f_{1,2} = es_{1,2} + L_{1,2} \qquad (4.28)$$

where $L_{1,2}$ is the liquidity premium for the period commencing one year from now and ending two years from now.[11]

How does the liquidity preference theory explain the slope of the term structure? In order to answer this question, note that with the rollover strategy, the expected value of a dollar at the end of two years is $1(1 + s_1)(1 + es_{1,2})$. Alternatively, with the maturity strategy the expected value of a dollar at the end of two years is $1(1 + s_2)(1 + s_2)$. As mentioned earlier, according to the liquidity preference theory there is more risk with the maturity strategy, which in turn means that it must have a higher expected return. That is, the following inequality must hold:

$$\$1(1 + s_2)(1 + s_2) > \$1(1 + s_1)(1 + es_{1,2}) \qquad (4.29)$$

or

$$(1 + s_2)(1 + s_2) > (1 + s_1)(1 + es_{1,2}).$$

This inequality is the key to understanding how the liquidity preference theory explains the term structure.[12]

Consider the downward-sloping case first, where $s_1 > s_2$. The preceding inequality will hold in this situation only if the expected future spot rate ($es_{1,2}$) is substantially

---

[11] It should be noted that while the forward rate can be determined, neither the expected future spot rate nor the liquidity premium can be observed. All that can be done is estimate their respective values.

[12] Equation (4.28) can be expressed more generally as $f_{t-1,t} = es_{t-1,t} + L_{t-1,t}$. Thus, using equation (4.14), the liquidity preference theory states that

$$(1 + s_t)^t = (1 + s_{t-1})^{t-1} \times (1 + es_{t-1,t} + L_{t-1,t}).$$

Since $L_{t-1,t} > 0$, it follows that, in general,

$$(1 + s_t)^t > (1 + s_{t-1})^{t-1} \times (1 + es_{t-1,t}).$$

smaller than the current one-year spot rate ($s_1$).[13] Thus, a downward-sloping term structure will be observed only when the marketplace believes that interest rates are going to decline substantially.

As an example, assume that the one-year spot rate ($s_1$) is 7% and the two-year spot rate ($s_2$) is 6%. Since 7% is greater than 6%, this is a situation where the term structure is downward-sloping. Now, according to the previously given inequality,

$$(1 + .06)(1 + .06) > (1 + .07)(1 + es_{1,2})$$

which can hold only if the expected future spot rate ($es_{1,2}$) is substantially less than 7%. Given the one-year and two-year spot rates, the forward rate ($f_{1,2}$) is equal to 5.01%. Assuming the liquidity premium ($L_{1,2}$) is .41%, then according to equation (4.28), $es_{1,2}$ must be $5.01\% - .41\% = 4.6\%$. Thus, the term structure is downward-sloping because the current one-year spot rate of 7% is expected to decline to 4.6% in the future.

In comparison, the unbiased expectations theory would also explain the term structure by saying that the reason it was downward-sloping was because the one-year spot rate was expected to decline in the future. However, the unbiased expectations theory would expect the spot rate to decline only to 5.01%, not 4.6%.

Consider next the case of a flat term structure, where $s_1 = s_2$. The preceding inequality will hold in this situation only if $es_{1,2}$ is less than $s_1$. Thus, a flat term structure will occur only when the marketplace expects interest rates are going to decline. Indeed, if $s_1 = s_2 = 7\%$ and $L_{1,2} = .41\%$, then $f_{1,2} = 7\%$ and, according to equation (4.28), the expected future spot rate is $7\% - .41\% = 6.59\%$, a decline from the current one-year spot rate of 7%. This is in contrast to the unbiased expectations theory, where a flat term structure would be interpreted to mean that the marketplace expected interest rates to remain at the same level.

The last case of an upward-sloping yield curve is one where $s_1 < s_2$. If it is slightly upward-sloping, this can be consistent with an expectation that interest rates are going to decline in the future. For example, if $s_1 = 7\%$ and $s_2 = 7.1\%$, then the forward rate is 7.2%. In turn, if the liquidity premium is .41%, then the expected future spot rate is $6.79\% = 7.2\% - .41\%$, a decline from the current one-year spot rate of 7%. Thus, the reason for the slight upward slope to the term structure is that the marketplace expects only a slight decline in the spot rate. In contrast, the unbiased expectations theory would argue that the reason for the slight upward slope was the expectation of a slight increase in the spot rate.

If the term structure is more steeply sloped, then it is more likely that the marketplace expects interest rates to rise in the future. For example, if $s_1 = 7\%$ and $s_2 = 7.3\%$, then the forward rate is 7.6%. Continuing to assume a liquidity premium of .41%, equation (4.28) indicates that the marketplace expects the one-year spot rate to rise from 7% to $7.6\% - .41\% = 7.19\%$. The unbiased expectations theory would also explain this steep slope by saying that the spot rate was expected to rise in the future but by a larger amount. In particular, the unbiased expectations theory would state that the spot rate was expected to rise to 7.6%, not 7.19%.

In summary, with the liquidity preference theory, downward-sloping term structures are indicative of an expected decline in the spot rate, whereas upward-sloping term

---

[13] If $es_{1,2}$ were equal to or greater than $s_1$, then the inequality would not hold in the correct direction, since it was assumed that $s_1 > s_2$.

structures may indicate either an expected rise or decline, depending on how steep the slope is. Generally, the steeper the slope, the more likely it is that the marketplace expects spot rates to rise. If roughly half the time investors expect spot rates will rise and half the time investors expect spot rates will decline, then the liquidity preference theory suggests that there should be more occurrences of upward-sloping term structures than downward-sloping ones. As mentioned earlier, this is indeed what has happened.

### ☐ 4.13.3 The Market Segmentation Theory

A third explanation for the determination of the term structure rests on the assumption that there is *market segmentation*: Various investors and borrowers are asserted to be restricted by law, preference, or custom to certain maturities. Perhaps there is a market for short-term securities, another for intermediate-term securities, and a third for long-term securities. According to the market segmentation theory, spot rates are determined by supply and demand conditions in each market. Furthermore, in its most restrictive form, investors and borrowers will not leave their market and enter a different one when the current rates suggest to them that there is a substantially higher expected return available by making such a move.

With this theory, an upward-sloping term structure exists when the intersection of the supply and demand curves for shorter-term funds is at a lower interest rate than the intersection for longer-term funds. Conversely, a downward-sloping term structure would exist when the intersection for shorter-term funds was at a higher interest rate than the intersection for longer-term funds.

### ☐ 4.13.4 Empirical Evidence on the Theories

Empirical evidence based on US data provides some insight into the determinants of the term structure, but it is difficult to assess the relative importance of these three theories with a high degree of precision.

The market segmentation theory receives relatively slight empirical validation. This is understandable when it is realized that the theory will not hold if there are some investors and borrowers who are flexible enough to be willing to move into whatever segment has the highest expected return. By their actions, these investors and borrowers will give the term structure a continuity that is linked to expectations of future interest rates.

There does appear to be some evidence that the term structure conveys information about expected future spot rates, as hypothesized by both the unbiased expectations and liquidity preference theories. However, the evidence tends to favor the latter theory, since liquidity premiums also appear to exist.[14] In particular, there appear to be liquidity premiums of increasing size associated with US Treasury securities of up to roughly one-year in maturity. However, there do not appear to be any additional premiums

---

[14] The empirical evidence is not without dispute. Fama has argued that the evidence is inconsistent with both the unbiased expectations and liquidity preference theories, but McCulloch refutes Fama's findings and argues in favor of the latter theory. See Eugene F. Fama, "Term Premiums in Bond Returns," *Journal of Financial Economics* 13, no. 4 (December 1984):529–46 and J. Huston McCulloch, "The Monotonicity of the Term Premium: A Closer Look," *Journal of Financial Economics* 18, no. 1 (March 1987):185–92 and "An Estimate of the Liquidity Premium, *Journal of Political Economy* 83, no. 1 (February 1975):95–119. See also the sources in footnote 6.

beyond one-year maturities. That is, investors seem to demand a premium in order to get them to purchase a one-year security instead of, say, a one-month security. However, no additional premiums are needed in order to get them to purchase two-year securities (even though the two-year security has more price risk than a one-year security).

Two tests of term structure theories show that Canadian data are consistent with the expectations plus liquidity preference theory in the intermediate maturity range but the existence of some market segmentation in the long end of the market could not be rejected.[15]

In summary, it appears that expectations about future spot rates are important determinants of the term structure. Liquidity premiums appear to exist but do not increase in size beyond roughly a year, meaning that investment strategies involving securities with maturities of one year or more will have roughly the same expected return.

Examining the term structure of interest rates is important for determining the current set of spot rates, which can be used as a basis for valuing any fixed-income security. Such an examination is also important because it provides some information about what the marketplace expects regarding the level of future interest rates.

## 4.14    SUMMARY

In order to understand how bonds are valued in the marketplace, it is convenient initially to examine those fixed-income securities that are free from default risk. The only securities meeting this requirement are those issued by governments; thus, the focus of this chapter has been on those securities and their interest rates.

In periods of changing prices the nominal interest rate may prove a poor guide to the real return obtained by the investor. Although there is no completely satisfactory way to summarize the many price changes that take place in such periods, most governments attempt to do so by measuring the rate of change in a cost-of-living index. For quick calculation, the real interest rate can be estimated by simply subtracting the rate of change in this index from the nominal interest rate.

Often a bond is described and compared to others in terms of its yield-to-maturity, which is the discount rate that makes the present value of all of the bond's promised future cash flows equal to its current market price. A special kind of yield-to-maturity known as a spot rate is useful for security valuation. It is special in that it is the yield-to-maturity on a pure-discount security — that is, a security that has only one promised future cash flow associated with it. Once several related spot rates (each one associated with a different maturity) have been calculated, they can be used to value coupon-bearing government securities, for example.

A forward rate can be thought of as the interest rate that will be paid on money that is borrowed at some specific time in the future and is to be repaid at an even more distant time in the future. The contract that specifies this rate (and all the other terms of the loan) is known as a forward contract. Such a contract differs from a spot contract in

---

[15] J.S.McCallum, "The Expected Holding Period Return, Uncertainty and the Term Structure of Interest Rates," *Journal of Finance* 30, no. 2 (May 1975):307–323 and Maureen E. Howe and John S. McCallum, "The Term Structure of Interest Rates in Canada: The Empirical Evidence," *Journal of Business Administration* 12, no. 1 (Fall 1980):137–146.

that both contracts can be signed at the same time, but the spot contract loan will take place immediately after the signing, whereas the forward contract loan will take place at a later date.

Most bonds provide periodic coupon payments (interest) in addition to a final (par) payment at maturity. Depending on the relative magnitudes of these payments, a bond may be more or less like others with the same maturity date. A measure of the average time prior to the receipt of payment is obtained by calculating the bond's duration. Bonds of similar duration are more likely to react in similar ways to changes in interest rates than are bonds of similar term-to-maturity but different durations.

At any point in time, government securities will be priced approximately in accord with the existing set of spot rates. Although there have been times when all the spot rates are roughly equal in size, generally they have different values. It is wise for the security analyst to know what the yield curve for government securities currently looks like, as this is a useful starting point in valuing fixed-income securities. This curve provides an estimate of the current term structure of interest rates and will change daily as yields-to-maturity change.

Forward rates play an important role in two term structure theories, which are theories that offer explanations for why the yield curve is not flat. That is, these theories offer explanations for why current spot rates associated with different maturities are of different sizes. The unbiased expectations theory states that forward rates represent the consensus opinion about what spot rates will be in the future. In comparison, the liquidity preference theory states that forward rates overstate the consensus opinion about what spot rates will be in the future. Both theories agree that changes in people's expectations about the future level of spot rates (perhaps because of a change in the expected rate of inflation) will cause a change in the term structure.

In contrast to these two theories, the market segmentation theory states that different spot rates have different sizes due to the interaction of supply and demand for funds in markets that are separated from each other by maturity.

Which theory seems to be correct? Although a definitive answer has yet to be provided, the evidence seems to favor the liquidity preference theory when explaining why spot rates of one year or less are of different sizes. However, longer-term spot rates seem to be in accord with the unbiased expectations theory. Thus, examining the term structure of interest rates is important because it provides some information about what the marketplace expects regarding the level of interest rates in the future.

## QUESTIONS AND PROBLEMS

1. At the end of 1974, Eric Biles held a portfolio of long-term government bonds valued at $14,000. At the end of 1981, Eric's portfolio was worth $16,932. Referring to Table 1.1, calculate the annualized real rate of return on Eric's bond portfolio over this seven-year period.

2. Consider two bonds, each with a $1,000 face value and each with three years remaining to maturity.
   a. The first bond is a pure-discount bond that currently sells for $804.96. What is its yield-to-maturity?

b. The second bond currently sells for $775.40 and makes annual coupon payments at a rate of 6% (that is, it pays $60 in interest per year). The first interest payment is due one year from today. What is this bond's yield-to-maturity?

3. Distinguish between spot rates and forward rates.

4. Assume that the current one-year spot rate is 6% and the forward rates for one year hence and two years hence, are, respectively:

$$f_{1,2} = 7\%$$
$$f_{2,3} = 8\%.$$

What should be the market price of a 6% coupon bond, with a $1,000 face value, maturing three years from today? The first interest payment is due one year from today. Interest is payable annually.

5. Assume the government has issued three bonds. The first, which pays $1,000 one year from today, is now selling for $909.09. The second, which pays $100 one year from today and $1,100 one year later, is now selling for $991.81. The third, which pays $1000 one year from today, $1000 one year later, and $1,100 one year after that, is now selling for $977.18.
   a. What are the current discount factors for dollars paid one, two, and three years from today?
   b. What are the forward rates?
   c. Helen Wagner, a friend, offers to pay you $500 one year from today, $600 two years from today, and $700 three years from today in return for a loan today. Assuming that Helen will not default on the loan, how much should you be willing to loan?

6. La Banque Nationale offers a passbook savings account that pays interest at a stated annual rate of 6%. Calculate the effective annual interest rate paid by Banque Nationale if it compounds interest:
   a. Semiannually
   b. Daily (365 days in a year)
   c. Continuously

7. Marty McDonald is considering placing $30,000 in a three-year, default-free fixed-income investment which promises to provide interest at the rate of 8% during the first year, 10% in the second year, and 12% in the third year.
   a. Assuming semiannual compounding, to what value is Marty's investment expected to grow after three years?
   b. Recalculate your answer to part (a) assuming continuous compounding.
   c. What will be Marty's average annual continuously compounded rate of return over the three years?

8. Using *The Globe and Mail: Report on Business* as a data source, turn to the table entitled "Canadian Bonds." Find the yield-to-maturity for as many Government of Canada securities as are listed maturing in three months, six months, nine months, one year, three years, five years, seven years, ten years, and twenty years. With this information, construct the yield curve as of the paper's publication date.

9. Is it true that an observed downward-sloping yield curve is inconsistent with the liquidity preference theory of the term structure of interest rates? Explain.

10. Assume that the current structure of forward interest rates is upward sloping. Which will have a lower yield-to-maturity:

a. A 15-year zero-coupon bond or a 10-year zero-coupon bond?

b. A 10-year 5% coupon bond or a 10-year 6% coupon bond?

11. How would your answers to question 10 change if the forward interest rate structure were downward sloping?

12. Three theories explaining the term structure of interest rates are described in the chapter. Which theory do you believe best explains the relationship between spot rates and term-to-maturity? Provide supporting arguments for your answer.

## SUGGESTED READINGS

Irving Fisher, *The Theory of Interest: As Determined by Impatience to Spend and Opportunity to Invest It* (New York, NY: Augustus M. Kelley, 1965) is the classical analysis of consumption-investment decisions and their effect on the level of interest rates.

John H. Wood and Norma L. Wood, *Financial Markets* (San Diego, Cal.: Harcourt Brace Jovanovich, 1985) Chapter 19 and

James C. Van Horne, *Financial Market Rates and Flows* (Englewood Cliffs, NJ: Prentice Hall, 1984) Chapter 5 contains thorough reviews of term structure theories and the US evidence.

Maureen E. Howe and John S. McCallum, "The Term Structure of interest Rates in Canada: The Empirical Evidence," *Journal of Business Administration* 12, no. 1 (Fall 1980): 137–46 reports one of the few tests of term structure theories using Canadian data.

# Chapter 5

# THE VALUATION OF RISKY SECURITIES

Payments received from riskless securities can be accurately predicted: Neither their amounts nor their timing is uncertain. But many securities do not meet such high standards. Some or all of their payments are *contingent* on events with respect to amount, timing, or both. A bankrupt corporation may not make its promised bond payments in full or on time. A worker who is laid off may pay his or her bills late (or not at all). A corporation may reduce or eliminate its dividend if its business becomes unprofitable, and so on.

The security analyst must try to evaluate these circumstances affecting a risky investment's payments and enumerate the key events upon which such payments are contingent. For example, an aircraft manufacturer's fortunes may depend on whether or not the firm is awarded a major contract by the government, whether or not its recently introduced commercial aircraft is accepted by the airlines, whether or not there is an upturn in the economy with a concomitant increase in demand for airline travel, and so on. To properly value the stock of such a company the analyst must consider each of these contingencies and estimate the corresponding effect on the firm and its stock.

The identification of important influences and the evaluation of the impact of each one is exceedingly difficult. Among other things, the appropriate level of detail must be determined. The number of potentially relevant events is almost always very large, and the analyst must attempt to focus on the relatively few that appear to be most important. In some cases it may be best to differentiate only a few alternatives (for example, whether the economy will turn up, turn down, or stay the same). In some cases, finer distinctions may be needed (for example, whether the gross national product will be up 1%, 2%, 3%, and so on).

The process of identifying and evaluating key influences is central to security analysis. The *use* of such estimates is of concern in this chapter. After the contingencies have been identified and the corresponding payments estimated, how can the value of the security be determined?

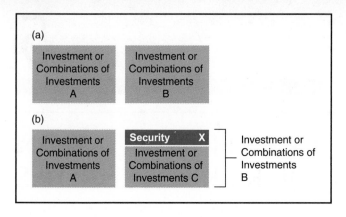

**FIGURE 5-1**
Comparing combinations of investments.

## 5.1    MARKET VERSUS PERSONAL VALUATION

One approach to the valuation of risky securities focuses on the investor's personal attitudes and circumstances. Given his or her assessment of the likelihood of various contingencies, and feelings about the corresponding risks involved in an investment, an investor might determine the amount he or she would be willing to pay, by some sort of introspection. This would be a "personal" valuation of the security.

Such an approach would be appropriate if there were only one investment in the world. But such is not the case. A security need not and should not be valued without considering available alternatives. Current market values of other securities provide important information, since a security is seldom so unique that nothing else is even comparable. Security valuation should not be done in a vacuum; it should instead be performed in a market context.

Key to this approach is the comparison of one investment or combination of investments with others having comparable characteristics. For example, assume that A and B in Figure 5.1(a) are similar in this respect; then the two should be equal in value.

Now imagine that alternative B includes a security that an investor wishes to value—call it X. Moreover, assume that all other securities included in A and B are regularly traded and that their market values (prices) are widely reported and easily determined. Combination B can be thought to have two components: security X and the rest, which will be represented by C, as in Figure 5.1(b). Combination C might include many securities, only one, or, as a very special case, none at all.

If people are willing to purchase combination A for a present value of $PV_A$, they should be willing to purchase combination B for the same amount, since the two provide comparable prospects. Thus,

$$PV_A = PV_B.$$

The present value of B will, however, be simply the sum of the present values of its components:

$$PV_B = PV_X + PV_C.$$

This implies that the present value of security X can be determined solely by reference to market values placed on the securities comprising combinations A and C. Since

$$PV_A = PV_X + PV_C$$

then

$$PV_X = PV_A - PV_C.$$

## 5.2  APPROACHES TO SECURITY VALUATION

It is reasonable enough to say that market prices of "comparable investments" should be used to determine the value of a security. But when are two investments truly comparable?

An obvious case arises when investments provide identical payments in every possible contingency. If an investment's outcome is affected by relatively few events, it may be possible to purchase a set of other investments, each of which pays off in only one of the relevant contingencies. A properly selected mix of such investments may thus be completely comparable to the one to be valued. The next section illustrates this approach with an example drawn from the field of insurance.

A much more common approach to valuation is less detailed but more useful. Two alternatives are considered comparable if they offer similar expected returns and contribute equally to portfolio risk. Central to this view is the need to assess the probabilities of various contingencies. The remainder of this chapter and the next four chapters are devoted to this more widely used *risk-return approach*.

## 5.3  EXPLICIT VALUATION OF CONTINGENT PAYMENTS

### ☐ 5.3.1  Insurance

Insurance policies are highly explicit examples of contingent payments. One can buy a $100,000 one-year "term" life insurance policy on a reasonably healthy 60-year-old for about $2300. This, of course, can be viewed as an investment (albeit a morbid one): The sum of $100,000 will be paid by the insurance company if the insured dies within a year; otherwise nothing at all will be paid. Involved is the sacrifice of a present certain value ($2300) for a future uncertain value. The only relevant event is the possible death of the insured, and the relationship between that event and the amount to be paid is crystal clear.

Now imagine that a reasonably healthy 60-year-old executive asks you for a one-year loan. The executive would like as much as possible now; in return he or she promises to pay you $100,000 at the end of the year. Your problem is to determine the present value of that promise — that is, how much to advance now. Put somewhat differently, you must determine an appropriate interest rate for the loan.

To keep the example simple, assume that the only source of uncertainty is the borrower's ability to remain in this position and thus earn the requisite money, and that this depends only on his or her continued presence among the living. In other words, if the borrower lives, the $100,000 will be repaid in full and on time; otherwise, you will receive nothing.

The piece of paper representing the executive's promise to pay $100,000 is your security X. What is it worth? The answer clearly depends in an important way on the available alternatives. A crucial factor is the current rate of interest.

Assume that the going rate for riskless one-year loans is 8%. If there were no doubt whatever that the executive would repay the loan, it would be reasonable to advance $92,592.59 (since $100,000/$92,592.59 = 1.08$). However, the uncertainty connected with the loan makes this inadvisable. The appropriate amount is obviously less. But how much less?

In this case an answer can easily be determined. It would be entirely reasonable to advance at most $90,292.59, making the *promised* interest rate on the loan approximately 10.75% (since $100,000/90,292.59 = 1.1075$). The basis for this calculation is quite simple. It relies on the fact that an investor can insure against the relevant risk, obtaining an overall position that is completely riskless.

Table 5.1 provides the details. The relevant event is whether or not the executive survives the year. The loan is thus a risky investment, paying $100,000 only if the executive lives. The life insurance policy is also a risky investment, paying $100,000 only if the executive dies. But a *portfolio* that includes both investments is totally riskless: Its owner will receive $100,000, no matter what happens! By paying $90,292.59 for the loan and $2300 for the insurance policy, an investor could give up $92,592.59 now for a certain payment of $100,000 a year hence — obtaining a riskless return of 8%, which is the going rate on other riskless ventures.

**TABLE 5.1**
Costs and Payments for a Loan and an Insurance Policy.

| Item | Event | | |
| --- | --- | --- | --- |
| | Executive Dies | Executive Lives | Cost |
| Loan | 0 | $100,000 | $90,292.59 |
| Insurance policy | $100,000 | 0 | 2,300.00 |
| Total | $100,000 | $100,000 | $92,592.59 |

This is, of course, an application of the general procedure described in the previous section. Figure 5.2 summarizes the details in the format used earlier, for purposes of comparison.

## ☐ 5.3.2  Valuation in a Complete Market

Assume, for the present, that market values can be used to estimate the present value of any contingent payment. A market in which such detailed quotations are available is termed *complete*. While no real market conforms to this specification, it is useful to see how valuation would be done in such circumstances.

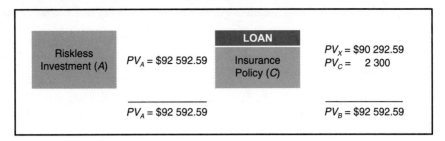

**FIGURE 5-2**
Comparing two riskless investments.

First, a way to represent the present value of a guaranteed commitment to pay \$1 at a specified time if (and only if ) a specified event or "state of the world" occurs is needed. The following will suffice:

$$PV(\$1, t, e)$$

where
  $t$ = the time at which the dollar is to be paid
  $e$ = the event that must occur if the dollar is to be paid.

Armed with this notation, any risky investment can now be analyzed. Every possible contingency could, in theory, be considered separately, giving a (probably very lengthy) list of contingent payments of the following form:

| Time of Payment | Event on Which Payment Is Contingent | Amount of Payment |
|---|---|---|
| $t_1$ | $e_1$ | $D_1$ |
| $t_2$ | $e_2$ | $D_2$ |
| $\vdots$ | $\vdots$ | $\vdots$ |

Of course, some of the events might be the same, as might some of the times and amounts.

To find the present value of the investment, the present value of each of its contingent payments must be found and then added.

| (1) Time of Payment | (2) Event on Which Payment Is Contingent | (3) Amount of Payment | (4) Discount Factor | (5) = (3) × (4) Present Value |
|---|---|---|---|---|
| $t_1$ | $e_1$ | $D_1$ | $PV(\$1, t_1, e_1)$ | $D_1 \times PV(\$1, t_1, e_1)$ |
| $t_2$ | $e_2$ | $D_2$ | $PV(\$1, t_2, e_2)$ | $D_2 \times PV(\$1, t_2, e_2)$ |
| $\vdots$ | $\vdots$ | $\vdots$ | $\vdots$ | $\vdots$ |

Total value = _____

This method of valuation is commonly termed the *state-preference* approach, since it begins with the assumption that people's preferences are for *state-contingent claims* and concludes that securities will be valued on the basis of their payoffs in different "states of the world."

## ☐ 5.3.3   The Limitations of Insurance

Some believe that Lloyd's of London will insure almost anything. If so, this could ease the security analyst's task considerably. He or she would only (!) have to determine the payments ($D_1, D_2, \ldots$) associated with an investment, the times at which they could be made ($t_1, t_2, \ldots$), and the events on which they were contingent ($e_1, e_2, \ldots$). The analyst could then use the premiums specified for the relevant insurance policies as estimates of appropriate discount factors [$PV(\$1, t_1, e_1), (PV(\$1, t_2, e_2), \ldots$], and perform the required calculations.

But even if Lloyd's will insure anything, the premiums charged for many policies might attract no takers. There are a number of interrelated reasons for this. As a case in point, imagine an aerospace company, the future profits of which depend heavily on whether or not the firm will be awarded a major government contract. Why not buy an appropriate insurance policy from Lloyd's, guaranteed to pay off if the firm loses the contract? Then only Lloyd's and the other firms in the industry would care about the outcome.

The idea is obviously whimsical. If Lloyd's were even willing to issue such a policy, the cost would be more than anyone would be likely to pay. But why?

First, because of differences in *information*. Those familiar with the company or the government or both have better information about the likely outcome and can better assess the likelihood of various alternatives. Lloyd's operates at least partly in the dark. To protect itself, it will charge more than otherwise.

Second, there is the likelihood of *adverse selection*. If a policy of this sort is offered at a price low enough to attract anyone at all, the insurer can expect the firms that are least likely to win the contract to buy insurance, whereas those most likely to get the contract will take their chances. This occurs frequently with life insurance. The less healthy an individual, the more likely he or she is to buy a policy; for this reason, the insured is usually required to pass a medical examination as a condition of sale. An examination of the health of a company's bid to win a government award might be much more difficult or expensive, so an insurance company must set its fees for such a policy on the assumption that it would end up insuring the riskiest client or clients.

Another factor is the thoroughly modern phenomenon described by the term *moral hazard*. The purchase of insurance may affect the likelihood of the event in question. If the manager of a firm is insured against the loss of the contract, he or she may well put less effort into the attempt to win it, increasing the likelihood of its loss and the insurance company's obligation to pay off. This explains the reluctance of an insurance company to insure a house or car for more than its replacement value and the desire of many shareholders to have a corporation's officers own some of the firm's stock and none of its competitors' issues. Here again, the insurance company will account for this effect when setting prices.

Finally, there is the simple matter of *overhead*. Insurance people like to eat, as do investors who provide the capital that insurance companies need. The costs of doing business will, over the long pull, be reflected in the prices charged for that business. No financial service is free, and insurance is no exception.

For all these reasons securities markets do not conform to the specifications of the complete-market state-preference model. Although the approach is helpful for addressing certain theoretical issues, it is less useful for investment purposes than the risk-return (or "mean-variance") approach, to which the discussion now turns.

## 5.4  PROBABILISTIC FORECASTING

### ☐ 5.4.1  Assessing Probabilities

Lacking a plethora of widely available and low-cost insurance policies, it is not possible to value an investment without explicitly considering the likelihood of various outcomes. Instead, the analyst must attempt to assess directly the likelihood of each major event that can affect an investment. In short, he or she must engage in *probabilistic forecasting*.

The idea is simple enough, although its implementation is exceedingly difficult. The analyst expresses his or her assessment of the likelihood of every relevant event as a *probability*. If he or she feels that the chances of an event's taking place are 50-50, a probability of .50 is attached to the event. If the chances seem to be 3 out of 4, the probability is $3/4$, or .75 (another way of expressing this is to say that the *odds* are 3 to 1 that the event will take place). If the analyst considers an event to be absolutely *certain*, a probability of 1.0 should be assigned. If he or she feels an event is completely impossible, its probability of occurrence is zero.

It is important, of course, to be consistent in one's estimates. For example, if the events on a list are *mutually exclusive* and *exhaustive* (that is, one of them, but only one, will take place), the probabilities should sum to one.

Probability is, basically, a *subjective* concept. Even simple cases fall under this heading. For example, a gambler may assess the probability of a coin's coming up heads at .5, based on knowledge of coins and observations of the coin in question over the past. But the estimate is still subjective, involving the implicit assumption that the coin really is "fair" and that the past is an appropriate guide to the future. Similar cases arise frequently in security analysis. Relative *frequencies* of various returns in the past are sometimes used as estimates of the *probabilities* of such returns in the future. Clearly this procedure relies on assumptions that require subjective judgment and may in some circumstances be totally inappropriate. Forecasts based on the extrapolation of past relationships are neither wholly objective nor necessarily to be preferred over predictions obtained in more subtle ways.

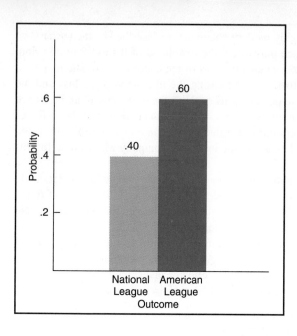

FIGURE 5-3
Probabilities of a National or American League team winning the world series.

Probabilistic forecasting entails a decision to confront uncertainty head on, acknowledge its existence, and try to measure its extent. Instead of attempting to answer a question such as "What will Imperial Oil earn next year?" the analyst explicitly considers some of the more likely alternatives and the likelihood of each one. This brings the analysis out in the open, allowing both the estimator and the user or users of such estimates to assess the reasonableness of the values. Insistence on a single number for each estimate, with no measure of associated uncertainty, would suggest naiveté or insecurity on the part of the producer or the consumer of such predictions.

In some organizations analysts engage in explicit probabilistic forecasting, passing on all their detailed assessments to others charged with bringing together the estimates made within the group. In other organizations the analysts make explicit probabilistic forecasts but summarize their evaluations in a relatively few key estimates, sending only the latter to others. In still other organizations analysts do not engage in explicit probabilistic forecasting; instead, they produce estimates that summarize their implicit beliefs about the probabilities of various events. As always, it is not the form but the substance that matters.

## ☐ 5.4.2   Probability Distributions

It is often convenient to portray probabilistic forecasts graphically. The possible outcomes are represented on the horizontal axis and the associated probabilities on the vertical axis. Figure 5.3 provides an example.

In this case the outcomes are qualitatively different in nature and can be listed only on the horizontal axis; the ordering and spacing are arbitrary.

Figure 5.4 shows a somewhat different case. Here the alternative outcomes differ quantitatively and with regard to only one variable: earnings per share next year. In this instance the analyst has chosen to group together all possibilities from $.90 to $.99,

**FIGURE 5-4**
Probabilities of next year's earnings per share (using wide ranges).

assess the probability that the actual amount will fall within that range, and then repeat the process for the range from $1.00 to $1.09, the range from $1.10 to $1.19, and so on.

The analysis could, of course, have been conducted at a more detailed level, with probabilities estimated for outcomes in the ranges from $.90 to $.94, $.95 to $.99, and so on.

An even more detailed analysis would assign a probability to every possible outcome. In this case the bars would be numerous, and each would be very thin, as shown in Figure 5.5. Note that the more numerous the number of bars, the smaller the sizes of associated probabilities.

The ultimate in a detailed prediction is represented by a *continuous probability distribution*. Such a curve represents, in effect, the tops of many thin bars. (Technically, the curve represents what happens when there is an infinite number of such bars.) Three examples of curves of this type are shown in Figure 5.6; note that the vertical axis now measures probability density (instead of probability).

If continuous probability distributions are to be used, the analyst can forgo explicitly assessing particular individual outcomes. Instead, the analyst must draw a curve that seems to represent the situation as he or she sees it. The relative likelihood of any single outcome (such as earnings per share of $1.035) is zero. However, the relative likelihood of any range of earnings is found by simply finding the size of the area under the curve but above the horizontal axis. Thus, the likelihood of earnings being between $1.03 and $1.04 could be found by measuring the area under the curve between $1.03 and $1.04, which in this case is approximately .07 (that is, there is a chance of 7 out of 100 that earnings will be between $1.03 and $1.04 next year). With a discrete probability distribution such as those shown in Figures 5.4 and 5.5, it was noted that the sum of the probabilities had to be 1. Now, with a continuous probability distribution, the total area under the curve must sum to 1.

**FIGURE 5-5**
Probabilities of next year's earnings per share (using narrow ranges).

## □ 5.4.3 Event Trees

When events follow one another over time or are in any sense dependent on one another, it is often useful to describe the alternative sequences with a tree diagram. Figure 5.7 provides an example.

A borrower has promised to pay $15 one year hence and $8 two years hence, if possible. The analyst feels the odds are only 40-60 that the first payment will in fact be made in full. Otherwise, the analyst feels the borrower will be able to pay only $10 one year hence.

As far as the second year is concerned, the likely situation depends, in this analyst's judgment, on the outcome in the first year. If the borrower manages to pay the full $15 in the first year, the analyst feels the odds are only 1 to 9 that the borrower will be able to meet the $8 commitment at the end of two years. Otherwise, the borrower will pay less: $6. On the other hand, if the borrower pays out $10 in the first year, although there appears to be no chance of recovering the $5 shortfall, the analyst feels the odds are about even that the promised $8 will be paid in the second year. If this does not happen, the analyst feels that $4 will be paid instead.

Figure 5.7 also shows the probability of each of the four possible sequences, or paths, through the tree. For example, the probability that both payments will be made in full is only .04, since there are only 40 chances out of 100 that the first payment will be made, and of those, only 1 out of 10 is expected to be followed by payment in full of the final obligation. This gives 4 out of 100 chances for the sequence: a probability of .04.

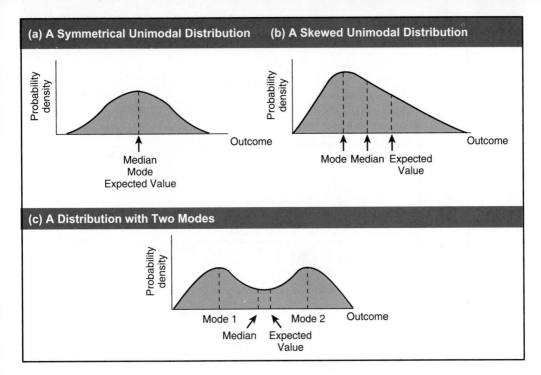

**FIGURE 5-6**
Continuous probability distributions.

## ☐ 5.4.4    Expected Value

Often an analyst is uncertain about an outcome but wishes (or is required) to summarize the situation with one or two numbers — one indicating the *central tendency* of the distribution of outcomes and one measuring *relevant risk*. Both return and risk are discussed in subsequent chapters; the remainder of this chapter concentrates on the former.

How might a single number intended to summarize a set of possible outcomes be obtained? Obviously no satisfactory way can be found if the alternative outcomes differ qualitatively (for example, the National League versus the American League in winning the World Series). But if the outcomes differ quantitatively, and especially if they differ in only one dimension, a number of possibilities present themselves.

Perhaps the most common procedure is to adopt the *most likely* value. This is known as the *mode* of the probability distribution (for a continuous probability distribution, the mode is the outcome with the highest probability density). Figure 5.6 shows the mode of each of the distributions. Note that in Figure 5.6(c) there are two modes: In this case, no single number can be used to answer the question in this manner.

Another alternative is to provide a "50-50" number — a value that is as likely to be too low as to be too high. This is called the *median* of the probability distribution. As shown in Figure 5.6, it may differ significantly from the mode(s).

A third alternative is to use an *expected value* (also known as the mean value), a weighted average of all the possible outcomes, using the associated probabilities as

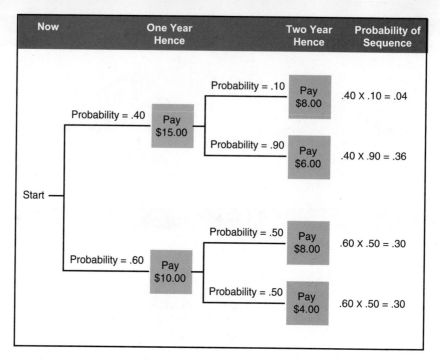

| Now | One Year Hence | Two Year Hence | Probability of Sequence |
|---|---|---|---|
| | Probability = .10 | Pay $8.00 | .40 X .10 = .04 |
| Probability = .40 — Pay $15.00 | Probability = .90 | Pay $6.00 | .40 X .90 = .36 |
| Start | Probability = .50 | Pay $8.00 | .60 X .50 = .30 |
| Probability = .60 — Pay $10.00 | Probability = .50 | Pay $4.00 | .60 X .50 = .30 |

**FIGURE 5-7**
An event tree.

weights. It takes into account all the information expressed in the distribution, both the *magnitude* and the *probability* of occurrence of each possible outcome. Almost any change in an investment's prospects or probabilities will affect the expected value of its outcomes (as it should).

In many instances there are no differences between these three measures. If the distribution is symmetric (each half is a mirror image of the other) and unimodal (there is one most likely value), then the median, mode, and expected value coincide, as in the case shown in Figure 5.6(a). Thus an analyst may choose to think in terms of, say, a 50-50 (median) value, even though the number wanted is the expected value. Only if the underlying probability distribution is highly skewed might this procedure lead to difficulties.

In those cases in which the values do differ, there are good reasons to prefer the expected value. As stated earlier, it takes all the estimates into account. But it has another advantage. Estimates about the prospects for securities serve as inputs for the process of portfolio construction or revision. The expected value of the return for a portfolio is related in a straightforward way to the expected values of the returns for its securities, but neither the median nor the mode for a portfolio can, in general, be determined from comparable values for its securities.

Table 5.2 provides an example of the computation of expected values. An analyst is trying to predict the impact on the prices of two securities of a surprise television address scheduled by the president of the US. The analyst has delineated a number of possible announcements, ranging from changes in the situation in the Middle East through a decision concerning the federal deficit. The alternatives represented in the table have been defined to be mutually exclusive and exhaustive (that is, every possible combination is shown in a different row). After much thought and with some trepidation, the analyst has also estimated the probability of each announcement and the resultant effect on the prices of the two securities. Finally, the analyst has computed the associated values of a portfolio containing one share of each stock.

**TABLE 5.2**
Analysis of Effects of Announcements on Two Securities and a Portfolio of Both Securities.

| Announcement | Probability | Predicted Price of Security A | Predicted Price of Security B | Predicted Value of A Portfolio of A and B |
|---|---|---|---|---|
| a | .10 | $40.00 | $62.00 | $102.00 |
| b | .20 | 42.00 | 65.00 | 107.00 |
| c | .10 | 40.50 | 60.00 | 100.50 |
| d | .25 | 41.00 | 61.00 | 102.00 |
| e | .15 | 38.00 | 65.00 | 103.00 |
| f | .10 | 40.50 | 59.00 | 99.50 |
| g | .05 | 45.00 | 58.00 | 103.00 |
| h | .05 | 40.50 | 58.00 | 98.50 |
| | Expected Values: | $40.73 | $61.90 | $102.63 |

The expected values are shown at the bottom of the table. Each is obtained by multiplying the probability of every announcement by the associated price, then summing. For example, the expected price of security A is determined by computing $[(.10 \times \$40.00) + (.20 \times \$42.00) + \cdots]$; that of security B by computing $[(.10 \times \$62.00) + (.20 \times \$65.00) + \cdots]$; and that of the portfolio by computing $[(.10 \times \$102.00) + (.20 \times \$107.00) + \cdots]$ Not surprisingly, the expected value of the portfolio equals the sum of the expected values of its component securities. When the expected values for the securities are added together, one is, in effect, adding $(.10 \times \$40.00 + \cdots)$ to $(.10 \times \$62.00 + \cdots)$. Clearly this will give the expected value of the portfolio, which is $.10 \times (\$40.00 + \$62.00) + \cdots$.

## ☐ 5.4.5 Expected Versus Promised Yield-to-Maturity

If payments from a bond are certain, there is no difference between the expected yield-to-maturity and the promised amount. However, many bonds fail to meet these standards. Two types of risk may be involved. First, the issuer may defer some payments. A dollar received farther in the future is, of course, worth less than a dollar received on schedule; thus the present value of a bond will be smaller, the greater the likelihood that this might happen. The second type of risk is potentially more serious. The borrower may default, in whole or in part, on some of the interest payments or on the principal at maturity. A firm becomes bankrupt when it is clearly unable to meet such obligations; the courts then divide the remaining assets between the various creditors in accordance with provisions agreed upon when the debts were issued.

To estimate the expected yield-to-maturity for a risky debt instrument, all possible outcomes and the probability of each should be considered. The simple example shown in Figure 5.7 can be used to illustrate the procedure. Assume the security in question costs $15; that is, the borrower wants $15 now in return for a commitment to pay $15 one year hence and $8 two years hence. The promised yield-to-maturity is the interest rate that makes the present value of these payments equal $15. In this case it is 38.51% per year, a substantial figure indeed.

But the analyst feels that the probability of actually receiving this yield-to-maturity is only .04. Table 5.3 shows the possible sequences (paths in the event tree), as well as the probability and the yield-to-maturity for each one. The expected yield-to-maturity is simply the weighted average of these values, using the probabilities as weights (for example, $(.04 \times 38.51\%) + (.36 \times 30.62\%) + (.30 \times 13.61\%) + (.30 \times -5.20\%) =$ 15.09%).

**TABLE 5.3**
Promised Versus Expected Yield-to-Maturity.

| Payment One Year Hence | Payment Two Years Hence | Probability | Yield-to-Maturity |
|---|---|---|---|
| $15 | $8 | .04 | 38.51% |
| 15 | 6 | .36 | 30.62 |
| 10 | 8 | .30 | 13.61 |
| 10 | 4 | .30 | −5.20 |
| | | Expected yield-to-maturity = | 15.09% |

The expected yield-to-maturity is considerably less than the promised amount: 15.09% as opposed to 38.51%. And the former is clearly the more relevant figure for investment analysis.

This is an important point. The yield-to-maturity, as normally calculated, is based on promised payments, made at the promised times. If there is any risk that the borrower's commitments will not be paid fully and on time, the expected yield-to-maturity is less than this figure; and the greater the risk, the greater the disparity. This is illustrated in Table 5.4, which shows the (promised) yield-to-maturity values for four groups of bonds classified by Canadian Bond Rating Service, Inc., a major rating service, as having different degrees of risk. Although the *levels* of all four yields reflect general interest rates at the time, the *differences* between them are primarily due to differences in risk. If promised yields of all bonds were the same, the expected yields of high-risk bonds would be less than those of low-risk ones — an unlikely situation indeed. Instead, riskier bonds promise higher yields so that their expected yields can be at least as large as those of less risky ones.

**TABLE 5.4**

Canadian Bond Rating Service Bond Yields.

| Rating | Yield-to-Maturity |
| --- | --- |
| Canadas | 8.80% |
| AAA | 9.57% |
| AA | 9.68% |
| A | 9.97% |
| BBB | 11.27% |

*SOURCE:* Melanie Moore, *Debt Market Indices, ScotiaMcLeod Inc.,* December 1991.

The nature of most debt obligations would be more obvious if contracts were written somewhat differently. At present, a standard bond with no extra features "guarantees" that the borrower will pay the lender, say, $90 per year for 20 years, then $1000 twenty years hence. A more appropriate statement would indicate that the borrower gurantees to pay *no more than* $90 per year for 20 years, and $1000 twenty years hence.

## 5.5 EXPECTED HOLDING-PERIOD RETURN

### ☐ 5.5.1 Calculating Holding-Period Return

Yield-to-maturity calculations do not take into account any changes in the market value of a security prior to maturity. This might be interpreted as implying that the owner has no interest in selling the instrument prior to maturity, no matter what happens to its price or his or her situation. The calculation also fails to treat intermediate payments in a fully satisfactory way. If the owner does not wish to spend interest payments, he or she might choose to buy more of these securities. But the number that can be bought at any time depends on the price at that time, and yield-to-maturity calculations fail to take this into account.

While few dispute the value of yield-to-maturity as at least an indicator of bond's overall return, it should be recognized as no more than this. For some purposes other measures may prove more useful. Moreover, for other types of securities there is no maturity: Common shares provide the most important example.

A measure that can be used for any investment is *holding-period return.* The idea is to specify a holding period of major interest, and then assume that any payments received during the period are reinvested. Although assumptions may differ from case to case, the usual procedure assumes that any payment received from a security (for example, a dividend from a share, a coupon payment from a bond) is used to purchase more units of that security at the then current market price. Using this procedure, the performance of a security can be measured by comparing the value obtained in this manner at the end of the holding period with the value at the beginning. This *value-relative* can be converted to a holding-period return by subtracting 1 from it:

$$r_{hp} = \frac{\text{value at the end of the holding period}}{\text{value at the beginning of the holding period}} - 1.$$

Put another way: the *holding-period return is the holding-period value-relative minus 1.*

Holding-period return can be converted to an equivalent return per period. Allowing for the effect of compounding, the appropriate procedure would be to find the value that satisfies the relationship

$$(1 + r_g)^N = 1 + r_{hp}$$

or

$$r_g = (\sqrt[N]{1 + r_{hp}}) - 1$$

where:

$N$ = the number of periods in the holding period,

$r_{hp}$ = the holding-period return,

$r_g$ = the equivalent return per period, compounded every period.

Suppose that a stock sold for $46 per share at the beginning of one year, paid dividends of $1.50 during that year, sold for $50 at the end of the year, paid dividends of $2 during the next year, and sold for $56 at the end of that year. What was the return over the two-year holding period?

To simplify the calculations, assume that all dividend payments are received at year-end. Then the $1.50 received during the first year could have bought $1.50/$50, or .03, shares of the stock at the end of the first year. In practice, of course, this would be feasible only if the money were pooled with other funds similarly invested — for example, in a mutual fund or simply in an investor's own portfolio (for example, the dividends from 100 shares could have been used to buy three additional shares). In any event, for each share originally held, the investor would have obtained $1.03 \times \$2$, or $2.06, in dividends in the second year, and have had shares with a value of $1.03 \times \$56$, or $57.68 at the end of the second year. The ending value would thus have been $57.68 + $2.06, giving a value-relative of:

$$\frac{\$59.74}{\$46.00} = 1.2987.$$

The holding-period return was thus 29.87% per two years. This is equivalent to $\sqrt{1.2987} - 1 = .1396$, or 13.96% per year.

An alternative method of computation treats the overall value-relative as the product of value-relatives for the individual periods. For example, if $V_0$ is the value at the beginning, $V_1$ the value at the end of the first year, and $V_2$ the value at the end of the second year:

$$\frac{V_2}{V_0} = \frac{V_2}{V_1} \times \frac{V_1}{V_0}.$$

Moreover, there is no need to carry the expansion in number of shares from period to period, since the factor (1.03 in the example) will simply cancel out in the subsequent periods' value-relatives. Each period can be analyzed in isolation, an appropriate value-relative calculated, and the set of such value-relatives multiplied together.

In our example, during the first year, ownership of shares with an initial value of $46 led to shares and cash with a value of $50 + $1.50 at the end of the year. Thus,

$$\frac{V_1}{V_0} = \frac{\$51.50}{\$46.00} = 1.1196.$$

During the second year, ownership of shares with an initial value of $50 led to shares and cash with a value of $56 + $2 at year-end. Thus:

$$\frac{V_2}{V_1} = \frac{\$58}{\$50} = 1.16.$$

The two-year holding-period value-relative was therefore:

$$1.1196 \times 1.16 = 1.2987$$

which is exactly equal to the value obtained earlier.

The value-relative for each period can be viewed as 1 plus the return for that period. Thus the return on the stock being analyzed was 11.96% in the first year and 16% in the second. The holding-period value-relative is the product of 1 plus each return. If $N$ periods are involved,

$$\frac{V_N}{V_0} = (1 + r_1)(1 + r_2) \cdots (1 + r_N).$$

To convert the result to a holding-period return stated as an amount per period, with compounding, one can take the *geometric mean* of the periodic returns:

$$1 + r_g = \sqrt[N]{(1 + r_1)(1 + r_2) \cdots (1 + r_N)}.$$

More sophisticated calculations may be employed within this overall framework. Each dividend payment can be used to purchase shares immediately upon receipt, or, alternatively, allowed to earn interest in a savings account until year-end. Brokerage and other costs associated with reinvestment of dividends can also be taken into account, although the magnitude of such costs will undoubtedly depend on the overall size of the holdings in question. The appropriate degree of complexity will, as always, be a function of the use for which the values are obtained.

Unhappily, the most appropriate holding period is often at least as uncertain as the return over any given holding period. Neither an investor's situation nor his or her preferences can usually be predicted with certainty. Moreover, from a strategic view, an investment manager would like to hold a given security only as long as it outperforms available alternatives. Attempts to identify such periods in advance are seldom completely successful, but managers quite naturally continue to try to discover them.

Holding-period return, like yield-to-maturity, provides a useful device for simplifying the complex reality of investment analysis. While no panacea, it allows an analyst to focus on the most relevant horizon in a given instance and offers a good measure of performance over such a period.

## □ 5.5.2 Estimating Expected Holding-Period Return

It is a relatively straightforward matter to calculate holding-period return after the fact. It is quite another thing to estimate it in advance. Any uncertainty surrounding payments by the issuer of a security during the period must be taken into account, but this is usually much simpler than the task of estimating the end-of-period market values, which often constitute a large portion of overall return. For example, it might seem a simple matter to estimate the return over the next year for a share of Alcan stock. Dividends to be paid are relatively easy to predict. But the price at year-end will depend on investors' attitudes toward the company and its stock at that time. To predict even a one-year holding-period return one must consider a much longer period and assess not only the company's future but also investors' future attitudes about that future — a formidable task indeed.

Quite clearly, estimation of holding-period return must account in some way for uncertainty. If a single estimate is required, it should conform to the principles stated earlier. Explicitly or implicitly, an *expected value* should be provided. The various possibilities should be considered along with their probabilities.

Expected holding-period return is a weighted average of possible holding-period returns, using probabilities as weights.[1]

## □ 5.5.3    Estimating a Bond's Expected Holding-Period Return

Once the importance of market values is recognized, the presence of a new kind of risk becomes obvious. And the idea of a truly riskless investment becomes a relative matter.

Assume that an investor is interested in a holding period of five years. What sort of investment would be riskless for these purposes? Obviously, one with no default risk, which promises a payment at the end of five years and at no other time. Any other investment will involve some risk. The five-year holding-period return from a bond that provides semiannual coupon payments will depend on the prices at which such payments can be used to purchase additional units of the bond (or some other instrument). The return on a bond with a maturity in excess of five years will depend on the price at which it can be sold at the end of the fifth year. The return on a shorter-maturity bond will depend on the instruments that are available when the proceeds must be reinvested, and their prices at those times.

Since bond prices depend in large part on interest rates, this source of uncertainty is sometimes termed *interest-rate risk* (or price risk). In many cases it is far more important than default risk. Moreover, it makes even Canadian government debt risky, unless there is a perfect correspondence between the investor's desire for cash and the payments promised by the bond in question.

Interest-rate risk should be incorporated in any analysis of expected holding-period return. For Canadian government securities this requires estimates of possible future interest rates and their associated probabilities. For other securities the likely future differentials for various levels of risk must also be taken into account.

## 5.6    EXPECTED RETURN AND SECURITY VALUATION

There is a very simple relationship between expected holding-period return, expected end-of-period value, and current value:

$$\text{Expected holding-period return} = \frac{\text{expected end-of-period value}}{\text{current value}} - 1.$$

---

[1] Expected return is also the *mean* of the probability distribution of holding-period returns — hence the "mean" in the term *mean-variance approach*, which is the cornerstone of modern portfolio theory.

Thus,

$$\text{Current value} = \frac{\text{expected end-of-period value}}{1 + \text{expected holding-period return}}.$$

In words: To value a security, one needs to estimate the expected value at the end of a holding period and the expected return for the holding period that is appropriate for such a security.

The final phase is crucial. What is the "appropriate" expected return, and on what does it depend? Therein lies the remainder of the theory of valuation.

## 5.7    SUMMARY

This chapter has discussed methods of valuing securities whose payments to investors are, to varying degrees, uncertain. One method involves valuing investments that provide identical payments in every possible contingency. However, the risk-return approach is more common and useful. With this approach, two securities are viewed as being comparable if they have similar expected returns and contribute similar amounts of risk to a portfolio.

With the risk-return approach, it might seem appropriate to value a security by using the expected return on an investment that is riskless over the period in question. However desirable such a relatively simple procedure might seem, it is clearly inconsistent with the general behavior of investors.

By and large, investors are risk-averse. Other things equal, they prefer less risk to more. However, other things equal, they also prefer more expected return to less. Not surprisingly, this implies that in the process of valuation one should require a higher expected return on a security, the greater the relevant risk involved.

Risk is not a simple concept: It thus requires extended discussion. The next four chapters provide such discussions.

## QUESTIONS AND PROBLEMS

1. In March of 1987, a major bookmaker in Las Vegas accepted bets on the baseball teams that would eventually go to the World Series. For example, one could pay $10 at the time to bet that the Minnesota Twins would represent the American League in the World Series. The payoff on such a bet was set at $1,500 if the Twins did go to the World Series, and zero otherwise. Payoffs for bets on all teams in the American League West were:

| Team | Payoff per $1 Bet |
| --- | --- |
| California Angels | $ 90 |
| Chicago White Sox | 180 |
| Kansas City Royals | 60 |
| Minnesota Twins | 150 |
| Oakland Athletics | 130 |
| Seattle Mariners | 250 |
| Texas Rangers | 210 |

a. What was the present value of $1 contingent on the event (state of the world) "The Twins go to the World Series"?

b. What was the present value of $1 contingent on the event "The Mariners go to the World Series"?

c. Why did the answers for (a) and (b) differ?

d. If someone had offered to pay you $1 if any team in the American League West went to the World Series, how much would you have paid for this bet ("security")? If you had been virtually certain that one of these teams would go to the World Series, would your answer differ? Why?

2. The probability distribution in Figure 5.6(b) is "skewed to the right." Explain why the distribution's expected value is greater than the median, which in turn is greater than the mode.

3. Calculate the expected return, mode, and median for a stock having the following probability distribution:

| Return | Probability of Occurrence |
|--------|---------------------------|
| −40%   | .03 |
| −10    | .07 |
| 0      | .30 |
| 15     | .10 |
| 30     | .05 |
| 40     | .20 |
| 50     | .25 |

4. Consider Springfield Company, whose stock currently sells for $10 per share. Diane Paskert, a financial analyst, has estimated the stock's potential year-end prices and associated probabilities over the next two years:

   Year 1   The stock has a 30% chance of rising to $20. It has a 60% chance of rising to $12. It has a 10% chance of falling to $8.

   Year 2   If the stock rises to $20 in Year 1, it has a 50% chance of rising to $25 and a 50% chance of falling to $15. If the stock rises to $12 in Year 1, it has a 70% chance of rising to $15 and a 30% chance of falling to $10. If it falls to $8 in Year 1, it has a 40% chance of falling to $4 and a 60% chance of rising to $12.

   a. Draw an event tree for Springfield Company stock.

   b. Based on this event tree, calculate the stock's expected price at the end of year 2.

5. Paul Perritt purchased 100 shares of Montgomery Inc. and held the stock for four years. Paul's holding-period returns over these four years were:

| Year | Return |
|------|--------|
| 1    | +20%   |
| 2    | +30    |
| 3    | +50    |
| 4    | -90    |

a. What was the value-relative of Paul's investment over the four-year period?

b. What was Paul's geometric mean return for the four-year period?

6. Distinguish between expected holding-period return and yield-to-maturity.

7. What are the advantages and disadvantages of using past investment results to assess the probabilities of future investment outcomes?

8. The average annualized return on an index of all TSE common stocks from 1950 through 1987 was 11.78%. If, on January 1, 1988 you had been required to provide an estimate of the expected return on the TSE 300 over the coming year, would you have chosen 11.78%? Why or why not?

## SUGGESTED READINGS

Peter Tryfos, *Business Statistics* (Toronto, Ont.: McGraw-Hill Ryerson, 1989) and

Thomas H. Wonnacott and Ronald J. Wonnacott, *Introductory Statistics for Business and Economics* (New York, N.Y.: John Wiley and Sons, 1984) are good statistics texts with business applications.

# Chapter 6

# THE PORTFOLIO SELECTION PROBLEM

In 1952, Harry M. Markowitz published a landmark paper that is generally viewed as the origin of the "modern portfolio theory" approach to investing.[1] Markowitz's approach to investing begins by assuming that an investor has a given sum of money to invest at the present time. This money will be invested for a particular length of time, known as the investor's *holding period*. At the end of the holding period, the investor will sell the securities that were purchased at the beginning of the period and then either spend the proceeds on consumption or reinvest the proceeds in various securities (or do some of both). Thus, Markowitz's approach can be viewed as a single-period approach, where the beginning of the period is denoted by $t = 0$ and the end of the period is denoted by $t = 1$. At $t = 0$, the investor must make a decision on what particular securities to purchase and hold until $t = 1$.[2] Since a portfolio is a collection of securities, this decision is equivalent to selecting an optimal portfolio from a set of possible portfolios and is thus often referred to as the "portfolio selection problem."

In making this decision at $t = 0$, the investor should recognize that security returns (and thus portfolio returns) over the forthcoming holding period are unknown. Nevertheless, the investor could estimate the *expected returns* (or mean returns) on the various securities under consideration and then invest in the one with the highest expected return. (Methods for estimating expected returns are discussed in Chapter 16.) Markowitz notes that this would generally be an unwise decision because the typical investor, while wanting returns to be high, also wants returns to be as certain as possible. This means that the investor, in seeking both to maximize expected return and minimize uncertainty (that is, *risk* ), has two conflicting objectives that must be balanced against each other when making the purchase decision at $t = 0$. The Markowitz approach for how the investor should go about making this decision gives full consideration to both these objectives.

---

[1] Harry M. Markowitz, "Portfolio Selection," *Journal of Finance* 7, no. 1 (March 1952):77–91. See also his book entitled *Portfolio Selection*, (New Haven, Conn.: Yale University Press, 1959).

[2] Markowitz recognized in Chapter 13 of *Portfolio Selection* that investing was generally a multiperiod activity, where at the end of each period, part of the investor's wealth was consumed and part was reinvested. Nevertheless, his one-period approach can be shown to be optimal under a variety of reasonable circumstances. See Edwin J. Elton and Martin J. Gruber, *Finance as a Dynamic Process*, (Englewood Cliffs, N.J.: Prentice Hall, 1975), particularly Chapter 5.

One interesting consequence of having these two conflicting objectives is that the investor should diversify by purchasing not just one security but several. The ensuing discussion of Markowitz's approach to investing begins by defining more specifically what is meant by initial and terminal wealth.

---

## 6.1 INITIAL AND TERMINAL WEALTH

In equation (1.1) of Chapter 1 it was noted that the one-period rate of return on a security could be calculated as

$$\text{Return} = \frac{\text{end-of-period wealth} - \text{beginning-of-period wealth}}{\text{beginning-of-period wealth}} \tag{1.1}$$

where beginning-of-period wealth is the purchase price of one unit of the security at $t = 0$ (for example, one share of a firm's common stock), and end-of-period wealth is the market value of the unit at $t = 1$, along with the value of any cash (and cash equivalents) paid to the owner of the security between $t = 0$ and $t = 1$.

### ☐ 6.1.1 Determining the Rate of Return on a Portfolio

Since a portfolio is a collection of securities, its return $r_p$ can be calculated in a similar manner:

$$r_p = \frac{W_1 - W_0}{W_0}. \tag{6.1}$$

$W_0$ denotes the aggregate purchase price at $t = 0$ of the securities contained in the portfolio. $W_1$ denotes the aggregate market value of these securities at $t = 1$ as well as the aggregate cash (and cash equivalents) received between $t = 0$ and $t = 1$ from owning these securities. Equation (6.1) can be manipulated algebraically, resulting in

$$W_0(1 + r_p) = W_1. \tag{6.2}$$

From equation (6.2) it can be seen that *initial wealth* (as $W_0$ is sometimes called), when multiplied by 1 plus the rate of return on the portfolio, is equal to *terminal wealth* (as $W_1$ is sometimes called).

Earlier, it was noted that the investor must make a decision on which portfolio to purchase at $t = 0$. In doing so, the investor does not know what the value of $W_1$ will be for most of the various alternative portfolios under consideration, since the investor does not know what the rate of return will be for most of these portfolios.[3] Thus, according to Markowitz, the investor should view the rate of return associated with any one of these portfolios to be what is known in statistics as a *random variable*. Now, it is known from

---

[3] One portfolio that would not have an uncertain rate of return would involve the investor putting all of his or her initial wealth in a government security that matures at $t = 1$. Alternatively, the investor's initial wealth could be put into a term deposit at a bank. However, for almost all other portfolios the rate of return would be uncertain.

## TABLE 6.1

A Comparison of Terminal Wealth Levels for Two Hypothetical Portfolios.

| Level of Terminal Wealth | Percent Chance of Being Below This Level of Terminal Wealth | |
|---|---|---|
| | Portfolio A [a] | Portfolio B [b] |
| $ 70,000 | 0% | 2% |
| $ 80,000 | 0% | 5% |
| $ 90,000 | 4% | 14% |
| $100,000 | 21% | 27% |
| $110,000 | 57% | 46% |
| $120,000 | 88% | 66% |
| $130,000 | 99% | 82% |

[a] The expected return and standard deviation of A are 8% and 10%, respectively.

[b] The expected return and standard deviation of B are 12% and 20%, respectively.
Initial wealth is assumed to be $100,000, and both portfolios are assumed to have normally distributed returns.

statistics that a random variable can be "described" by what are known as its *moments*, two of which are its *expected value* (or mean) and *standard deviation*.[4]

Markowitz's approach to investing asserts that the investor, in making a decision on which portfolio to purchase, should evaluate these portfolios on the basis of their expected returns and standard deviations. That is, the investor should estimate the expected return and standard deviation of each portfolio and then choose the "best" one based on the relative magnitudes of these two parameters. The intuition behind this is actually quite straightforward. Expected return can be viewed as a measure of the potential reward associated with any portfolio, and standard deviation can be viewed as a measure of the risk associated with any portfolio. Thus, once each portfolio has been examined in terms of its potential rewards and risks, the investor is in a position to identify the one portfolio that appears most desirable to him or her.

## An Example

As an example, consider the two alternative portfolios denoted by A and B, shown in Table 6.1. Portfolio A has an expected annual return of 8% and portfolio B has an expected annual return of 12%. Assuming the investor has initial wealth of $100,000 and a one-year holding period, this means that the expected levels of terminal wealth associated with A and B are $108,000 and $112,000, respectively. It would appear, then, that B is the more desirable portfolio. However, A and B have annual standard deviations of 10% and 20%, respectively. Table 6.1 shows that this means there is a 2% chance that the investor will end up with terminal wealth of $70,000 or less if he or she purchases B, whereas there is virtually no chance that the investor's terminal wealth will be less

---

[4] A random variable's expected value is, in a sense, its "average" value. Thus, the expected value for the return of a portfolio can be thought of as its expected, or average, return. The standard deviation of a random variable is a measure of the dispersion (or spread) of possible values the random variable can take on. Accordingly, the standard deviation of a portfolio is a measure of the dispersion of possible returns that could be earned on the portfolio. Sometimes *variance* is used as a measure of the dispersion instead of standard deviation. However, since the variance of a random variable is simply the squared value of the standard deviation of the random variable, this distinction is not of importance here. Later these concepts are discussed in more detail.

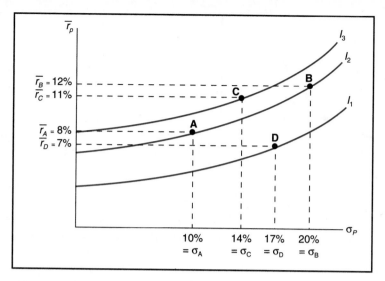

**FIGURE 6-1**
Map of indifference curves for a risk-averse investor.

than $70,000 if A is purchased. Similarly, B has a 5% chance of being worth less than $80,000, whereas A again has no chance. Continuing, B has a 14% chance of being worth less than $90,000, whereas A has only a 4% chance. Going on, B has a 27% chance of being worth less than $100,000, whereas A has only a 21% chance. Since the investor has initial wealth of $100,000, this last observation means there is a greater probability of having a negative return if B (27%) is purchased instead of A (21%). Overall, it can be seen from Table 6.1 that A is less risky than B, meaning that on this dimension A would be more desirable. The ultimate decision in regard to whether to purchase A or B will depend on this particular investor's attitudes toward risk and return, as is shown next.

## 6.2   INDIFFERENCE CURVES

The method that should be used in selecting the most desirable portfolio involves the use of *indifference curves*. These curves represent an investor's preferences for risk and return and thus can be drawn on a two-dimensional figure, where the horizontal axis indicates risk as measured by standard deviation (denoted by $\sigma_p$) and the vertical axis indicates reward as measured by expected return (denoted by $\bar{r}_p$).

Figure 6.1 illustrates a "map" of indifference curves that a hypothetical investor might possess. Each curved line indicates one indifference curve for the investor and represents all combinations of portfolios that the investor would find equally desirable. For example, the investor with the indifference curves in Figure 6.1 would find portfolios A and B (the same two portfolios that were shown in Table 6.1) equally desirable, even though they have different expected returns and standard deviations, since they both lie on the same indifference curve, $I_2$. Portfolio B has a higher standard deviation (20%) than portfolio A (10%) and is therefore less desirable on that dimension. However,

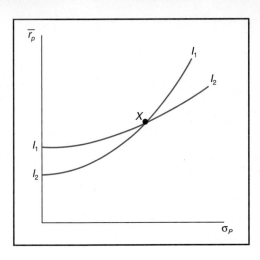

**FIGURE 6-2**
Intersecting indifference curves.

exactly offsetting this loss in desirability is the gain in desirability provided by the higher expected return of B (12%) relative to A (8%). This example leads to the first important feature of indifference curves: *All portfolios that lie on a given indifference curve are equally desirable to the investor.*

An implication of this feature is that *indifference curves cannot intersect.* Consider the two intersecting curves that are shown in Figure 6.2. Here the point of intersection is represented by $X$. Remember that all the portfolios on $I_1$ are equally desirable. This means they are all as desirable as X, since $X$ is on $I_1$. Similarly, all the portfolios on $I_2$ are equally desirable and are as desirable as $X$, since $X$ is also on $I_2$. Given $X$ is on both indifference curves, all the portfolios on $I_1$ must be as desirable as those on $I_2$. But this presents a contradiction, since $I_1$ and $I_2$ are two curves that are supposed to represent different levels of desirability. Thus, in order for there to be no contradiction, these curves cannot intersect.

Although the investor represented in Figure 6.1 would find portfolios A and B equally desirable, he or she would find portfolio C, with an expected return of 11% and a standard deviation of 14%, to be preferable to both of them. This is because portfolio C happens to be on an indifference curve, $I_3$, that is located to the northwest of $I_2$. Now, C has a sufficiently larger expected return relative to A to more than offset its higher standard deviation and, on balance, make it more desirable than A. Equivalently, C has a sufficiently smaller standard deviation than B to more than offset its smaller expected return and, on balance, make it more desirable than B. This leads to the second important feature of indifference curves: *An investor will find any portfolio that is lying on an indifference curve that is "further northwest" to be more desirable than any portfolio lying on an indifference curve that is "less northwest."*

Lastly, it should be noted that *an investor has an infinite number of indifference curves.* This simply means that whenever there are two indifference curves that have been plotted on a graph, it is possible to plot a third indifference curve that lies between them. As can be seen in Figure 6.3, given indifference curves $I_1$ and $I_2$, it is possible to graph a third curve $I^*$ lying between them.

A good question to ask at this point is, How does an investor determine what his or her indifference curves look like? After all, each investor has a map of indifference

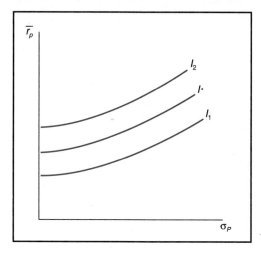

**FIGURE 6-3**
Plotting a third indifference curve between two others.

curves that, while having the previously noted features, is nevertheless unique to that individual. It turns out that one method of explicitly determining the shape and location of an investor's indifference curves involves asking that investor a set of questions about gambles.[5]

For example, an investor might be asked which one of two alternatives he or she would find more desirable. The first alternative would simply involve receiving a certain cash payoff of $5000. The second alternative involves the flip of a coin where heads means a payoff of $4000 and tails means a payoff of $10,000. If the investor states that he or she would prefer the coin flip, then the size of the certain payoff is increased to $5500, for example, and the question is repeated. However, if the certain payoff is preferred, then its payoff is lowered to $4500, for example, and the question is repeated. This procedure of changing the size of the certain payoff and repeating the question is continued until a payoff is reached where the investor finds both alternatives equally desirable. At this juncture it is possible to tell something about the investor's attitudes towards risk and return. Once the investor is asked about other different-sized gambles, it will be possible to estimate the shape and location of his or her indifference curves.

A second method, shown in Chapter 22, involves presenting the investor with a set of hypothetical portfolios, along with their expected returns and standard deviations. Then he or she is asked to choose the most desirable one. Given the choice that is made, the shape and location of the investor's indifference curves can be estimated. This is because it is presumed that the investor would have acted as if he or she has indifference curves in making this choice, even though indifference curves would not have been explicitly used.

In summary, every investor has an indifference map representing his or her preferences for expected returns and standard deviations.[6] This means the investor

---

[5] For an example of how this procedure can be utilized, see Ralph O. Swalm, "Utility Theory—Insights into Risk Taking," *Harvard Business Review* 44, no. 6 (November-December 1966):123–36. Also see footnote 6.

[6] At some point the reader may wonder why an investor's preferences are based only on expected returns and standard deviations. For example, it may seem logical that the investor's preferences should be based on

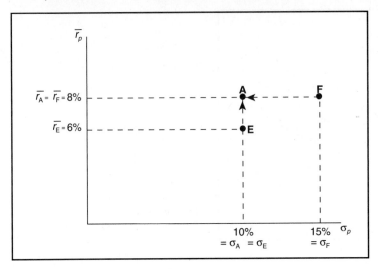

**FIGURE 6-4**
Nonsatiation, risk aversion, and portfolio choice.

should determine the expected return and standard deviation for each potential portfolio, plot them on a graph such as Figure 6.1, and then select the one portfolio that lies on the indifference curve that is furthest northwest. As shown in this example, from the set of the four potential portfolios — A, B, C, and D — the investor should select C.

## 6.3 NONSATIATION AND RISK AVERSION

### ☐ 6.3.1 Nonsatiation

Two assumptions are implicit in this discussion of indifference curves. First, it is assumed that investors, when given a choice between two otherwise identical portfolios, will choose the one with the higher level of expected return. More fundamentally, an assumption of *nonsatiation* is made in utilizing the Markowitz approach, meaning that investors are assumed always to prefer higher levels of terminal wealth to lower levels of terminal wealth. This is because higher levels of terminal wealth allow the investor to spend more on consumption at $t = 1$ (or in the more distant future). Thus, given two portfolios with the same standard deviation such as A and E in Figure 6.4, the investor will choose the portfolio with the higher expected return. In this case, it is portfolio A.

---

expected returns, standard deviations, and the probability that a portfolio will lose money. Two reasons are often stated for why an investor's preferences are based on just expected returns and standard deviations. First, if security returns have normal probability distributions, then portfolio returns are completely described by expected returns and standard deviations. Second, if investors have quadratic utility functions, then they will look only at expected returns and standard deviations in evaluating portfolios. See Gordon J. Alexander and Jack Clark Francis, *Portfolio Analysis*, (Englewood Cliffs, N.J.: Prentice Hall, 1986), particularly Chapters 2 and 3, for more details. It should be noted that there is some dispute about the validity of using utility theory to describe people's behavior. The people holding the opposing viewpoints are typically economists and psychologists, and they are often referred to as rationalists and behaviorists, respectively. For a discussion of their views, see the entire second part of the October 1986 issue of the *Journal of Business*.

However, it is not quite so obvious what the investor will do when having to choose between two portfolios having the same level of expected return but different levels of standard deviation, such as A and F. This is where the second assumption enters the discussion.

## ☐ 6.3.2   Risk Aversion

Generally, it is assumed that investors are *risk-averse*, which means that the investor will choose the portfolio with the smaller standard deviation, A.[7] What does it mean to say that an investor is risk-averse? It means that the investor, when given the choice, will not want to take fair gambles, where a fair gamble is defined to be one that has an expected payoff of zero with an equal chance of winning or losing. For example, imagine flipping a coin where heads means you win $5 and tails means you lose $5. Since the coin has a 50-50 chance of being heads or tails, the expected payoff is $0((.5 × $5) + (.5 × −$5)). Accordingly, the risk-averse investor will choose to avoid this gamble. Intuitively, the investor avoids the gamble because the potential loss represents an amount of "displeasure" that is greater than the amount of "pleasure" associated with the potential gain.

The two assumptions of nonsatiation and risk-aversion are what lead to indifference curves having positive slopes and being convex (convexity means that the slope increases when moving from left to right along the curve).[8] Although it is assumed that all investors are risk-averse, it is not assumed that they have identical degrees of risk aversion. Some investors may be highly risk-averse, and some might be only slightly so. This means that different investors will have different maps of indifference curves. Panels (a), (b), and (c) of Figure 6.5 display maps for investors that are highly risk-averse, moderately risk-averse, and slightly risk-averse, respectively. As can be seen in these figures, a more risk-averse investor has more steeply sloped indifference curves.

## 6.4   CALCULATING EXPECTED RETURNS AND STANDARD DEVIATIONS FOR PORTFOLIOS

The previous section introduced the portfolio-selection problem that every investor faces. It also introduced the investment approach of Harry Markowitz as a method of solving that problem. With this approach, an investor should evaluate alternative portfolios on the basis of their expected returns and standard deviations by using indifference curves. In the case of a risk-averse investor, the portfolio with the indifference curve that is the furthest northwest would be the one selected for investment.

However, at this point certain questions have been left unanswered. In particular, how does the investor calculate the expected return and standard deviation for a portfolio?

---

[7] Investors that are *risk-seeking* would choose F, and investors that are *risk-neutral* would find A and F to be equally desirable. The appendix to this chapter discusses both risk-neutral and risk-seeking investors.

[8] That is, imagine drawing a straight line connecting any two points on an indifference curve. The curve is convex if the straight line lies entirely above the curve. The underlying rationale for convexity lies in utility theory; see footnote 6.

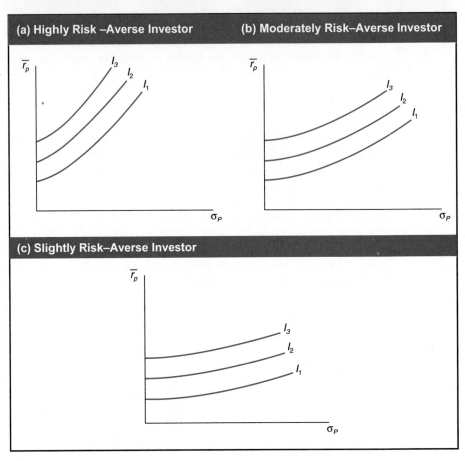

**FIGURE 6-5**
Indifference curves for different types of risk-averse investors.

## ☐ 6.4.1 Expected Returns

With the Markowitz approach to investing, the focus of the investor is on terminal (or end-of-period) wealth, $W_1$. That is, in deciding which portfolio to purchase with his or her initial (or beginning-of-period) wealth, $W_0$, the investor should focus on the effect the various portfolios have on $W_1$. This effect can be measured by the expected return and standard deviation of each portfolio.

As mentioned previously, a portfolio is a collection of securities. Thus, it seems logical that the expected return and standard deviation of a portfolio should depend on the expected return and standard deviation of each security contained in the portfolio. It also seems logical that the amount invested in each security should be important. Indeed, this is the case.

In order to show how the expected return of a portfolio depends on both the expected return of the individual securities and the amount invested in these securities, consider the three-security portfolio shown in Table 6.2(a). Assume that the investor has a one-year holding period and that for this period he or she has estimated the expected returns on Able, Baker, and Charlie shares to be 16.2%, 24.6%, and 22.8%, respectively. This is equivalent to stating that the investor has estimated the expected end-of-period per share values of these three stocks to be, respectively, $46.48 [since ($46.48 − $40)/$40 = 16.2%], $43.61 [since ($43.61 − $35)/$35 = 24.6%], and $76.14 [since ($76.14 − $62)/$62 = 22.8%].[9] Furthermore, assume that this investor has initial wealth of $17,200.

**TABLE 6.2**
Calculating the Expected Return for a Portfolio.

**(a) Security and Portfolio Values.**

| Security Name | Number of Shares in Portfolio (1) | Initial Market Price per Share (2) | Total Investment (3) = (1 × 2) | Proportion of Initial Market Value of Portfolio (4) = (3)/$W_0$ |
|---|---|---|---|---|
| Able Co. | 100 | $40 | $4,000 | $4,000/$17,200 = .2325 |
| Baker Co. | 200 | 35 | 7,000 | 7,000/ 17,200 = .4070 |
| Charlie Co. | 100 | 62 | 6,200 | 6,200/ 17,200 = .3605 |

Sum of proportions = 1.0000

**(b) Calculating the Expected Return for a Portfolio Using End-of-Period Value.**

| Security Name | Number of Shares in Portfolio (1) | Expected End-of-Period Value per Share (2) | Aggregate Expected End-of-Period Value (3) = (1) × (2) |
|---|---|---|---|
| Able Co. | 100 | $46.48 | $46.48 × 100 = $4648 |
| Baker Co. | 200 | 43.61 | 43.61 × 200 = 8722 |
| Charlie Co. | 100 | 76.14 | 76.14 × 100 = 7614 |

$$\text{Expected end-of-period value of portfolio} = \overline{W}_1 = \$20,984$$
$$\text{Portfolio expected return} = \bar{r}_p = \frac{\$20,984 - \$17,200}{\$17,200} =$$

22.00%

*(Continued)*

---

[9] The figures given for the expected end-of-period values include both the expected prices and the expected dividends for the period. For example, Able has an expected end-of-period value of $46.48, which could consist of a hypothetical expected cash dividend of $2 and share price of $44.48. These expected returns and values are estimated by use of security analysis, which is discussed in Chapter 16.

**(c) Calculating the Expected Return for a Portfolio Using Security Expected Returns.**

| Security Name | Proportion of Initial Market Value of Portfolio (1) | Security Expected Returns (2) | Contribution to Portfolio Expected Return (3) = (1) × (2) |
|---|---|---|---|
| Able Co. | .2325 | 16.2% | .2325 × 16.2% = .77% |
| Baker Co. | .4070 | 24.6 | .4070 × 24.6 = 10.01 |
| Charlie Co. | .3605 | 22.8 | .3605 × 22.8 = 8.22 |

Portfolio expected return = $\bar{r}_p$ = 22.00%

## Using End-of-Period Values

The expected return on this portfolio can be calculated in several ways, all of which give the same answer. Consider the method shown in Table 6.2(b). This method involves calculating the expected end-of-period value of the portfolio and then using the formula for calculating rate of return shown in Chapter 1. That is, first the initial portfolio value ($W_0$) is subtracted from the expected end-of-period value of the portfolio ($W_1$), and then this difference is divided by the initial portfolio value ($W_0$), the result of which is the portfolio's expected return. Although the example shown in Table 6.2(b) involves three securities, the procedure can be generalized to any number of securities.

## Using Security Expected Returns

An alternative method for calculating the expected return on this portfolio is shown in Table 6.2(c). This procedure involves calculating the expected return of a portfolio as the weighted average of the expected returns of its component securities. The relative market values of the securities in the portfolio are used as weights. In symbols, the general rule for calculating the expected return of a portfolio consisting of $N$ securities is

$$\bar{r}_p = \sum_{i=1}^{N} X_i \bar{r}_i \qquad\qquad (6.3a)$$

$$= X_1 \bar{r}_1 + X_2 \bar{r}_2 + \cdots + X_N \bar{r}_N \qquad\qquad (6.3b)$$

where:
$\bar{r}_p$ = the expected return of the portfolio,
$X_i$ = the proportion of the portfolio's initial value invested in security $i$,
$\bar{r}_i$ = the expected return of security $i$,
$N$ = the number of securities in the portfolio.

Thus, an *expected return vector* can be used to calculate the expected return for any portfolio formed from the $N$ securities. This vector consists of one column of numbers, where the entry in row $i$ contains the expected return of security i. In the previous example, the expected return vector was estimated by the investor to be

$$\begin{matrix} \text{Row 1} \\ \text{Row 2} \\ \text{Row 3} \end{matrix} \begin{bmatrix} 16.2\% \\ 24.6\% \\ 22.8\% \end{bmatrix}$$

where the entries in rows 1, 2, and 3 denote the expected returns for securities 1, 2, and 3, respectively.

Since the portfolio's expected return is a weighted average of the expected returns of its securities, *the contribution of each security to the portfolio's expected return depends on its expected return and its proportionate share of the initial portfolio's market value.* Nothing else is relevant. It follows from equation (6.3a) that an investor who simply wants the greatest possible expected return should hold one security: the one he or she considers to have the greatest expected return. Very few investors do this, and very few investment advisers would counsel such an extreme policy. Instead, investors should diversify, meaning that their portfolios should include more than one security. This is because diversification can reduce risk, as measured by the standard deviation.

## ☐ 6.4.2  Standard Deviations

A useful measure of risk should somehow take into account both the probabilities of various possible "bad" outcomes and their associated magnitudes. Instead of measuring the probability of a number of different possible outcomes, the measure of risk should somehow estimate the extent to which the actual outcome is likely to diverge from the expected outcome. Standard deviation is a measure that does this, since it is an estimate of the likely divergence of an *actual* return from an *expected* return.

It may seem that any single measure of risk would provide at best a very crude summary of the "bad" possibilities. But in the more common situation where a portfolio's prospects are being assessed, standard deviation may prove to be a very good measure of the degree of uncertainty. The clearest example arises when the *probability distribution* for a portfolio's returns can be approximated by the familiar bell-shaped curve known as a *normal probability distribution*. This is often considered a plausible assumption for analyzing returns on diversified portfolios when the holding period being studied is relatively short (say a quarter or less).

A question with standard deviation as a measure of risk is, Why count "happy" surprises (those above the expected return) at all in a measure of risk? Why not just consider the deviations *below* the expected return? Measures that do so have merit, but if a distribution is symmetric, such as the normal distribution, the results will be the same. Why? Because the left side of a symmetric distribution is a mirror image of the right side. Thus, a list of portfolios ordered on the basis of "downside risk" will not differ from one ordered on the basis of standard deviation if returns are normally distributed.[10]

---

[10] If returns are not normally distributed, the use of standard deviation can still be justified in an approximate sense provided there are small probabilities of extremely high and low returns. See H. Levy and H. M. Markowitz, "Approximating Expected Utility by a Function of Mean and Variance," *American Economic Review* 69, no. 3 (June 1979):308–17; and Yoram Kroll, Haim Levy, and Harry M. Markowitz, "Mean-Variance versus Direct Utility Maximization," *Journal of Finance* 39, no. 1 (March 1984):47–61.

## Formula for Standard Deviation

For the three-security portfolio consisting of Able, Baker, and Charlie, the formula for the standard deviation is

$$\sigma_p = \left[ \sum_{i=1}^{3} \sum_{j=1}^{3} X_i X_j \sigma_{ij} \right]^{1/2} \tag{6.4}$$

where $\sigma_{ij}$ denotes the *covariance* of the returns between security $i$ and security $j$. Covariance is a statistical measure of the relationship between two random variables. That is, it is a measure of how two random variables such as the returns on securities $i$ and $j$ "move together." A positive value for covariance indicates that the securities' returns tend to go together — for example, a better-than-expected return for one is likely to occur along with a better-than-expected return for the other. A negative covariance indicates a tendency for the returns to offset one another — for example, a better-than-expected return for one security is likely to occur along with a worse-than-expected return for the other. A relatively small or zero value for the covariance indicates that there is little or no relationship between the returns for the two securities.

Closely related to covariance is the statistical measure known as correlation, since it is known that the covariance between two random variables is equal to the correlation between the two random variables times the product of their standard deviations:

$$\sigma_{ij} = \rho_{ij} \sigma_i \sigma_j \tag{6.5}$$

where $\rho_{ij}$ (the Greek letter rho) denotes the *correlation coefficient* between the return on security $i$ and the return on security $j$. The correlation coefficient rescales the covariance to facilitate comparison with corresponding values for other pairs of random variables. Correlation coefficients always lie between $-1$ and $+1$. A value of $-1$ represents perfect negative correlation, and a value of $+1$ represents perfect positive correlation. Most cases lie between these two extreme values.

Figure 6.6(a) presents a scatter diagram for the returns on hypothetical securities A and B when the correlation between these two securities is perfectly positive. Note how all the points lie precisely on a straight upward-sloping line. This means that when one of the two securities has a relatively high return, then so will the other. Similarly, when one of the two securities has a relatively low return, then so will the other.

Alternatively, the returns on the two securities will have a perfectly negative correlation when the scatter diagram indicates that the points lie precisely on a straight downward-sloping line, as shown in Figure 6.6(b). In such a case the returns on the two securities can be seen to move opposite each other. That is, when one security has a relatively high return, then the other will have a relatively low return.

A case of special importance arises when the scatter diagram of security returns shows a pattern that cannot be represented even approximately by an upward-sloping or downward-sloping line. In such an instance, the returns are uncorrelated, meaning the correlation coefficient is zero. Figure 6.6(c) provides an example. In this situation, when one security has a relatively high return, then the other can have either a relatively high, low, or average return.

Given an understanding of covariance and correlation, it is important to understand how the double summation indicated in equation (6.4) is performed. Although there are many ways of performing double summation, all of which lead to the same answer, one

**FIGURE 6-6**
Returns on two securities.

way is perhaps more intuitive than the others. It starts with the first summation and sets $i$ at its initial value of 1. Then the second summation is performed for $j$ going from 1 to 3. At this point, $i$ in the first summation is increased by 1, so that now $i = 2$. Again the second summation is performed by letting $j$ go from 1 to 3, except that now $i = 2$. Continuing, $i$ in the first summation is again increased by 1, so that $i = 3$. Then the second summation is again performed by letting $j$ go from 1 to 3. At this point, note that $i = 3$ and $j = 3$, which are the upper limits for both the first and second summations. This means it is time to stop, as the double summation has been finished. This process can be shown algebraically as follows:

$$\sigma_p = \left[ \sum_{j=1}^{3} X_1 X_j \sigma_{1j} + \sum_{j=1}^{3} X_2 X_j \sigma_{2j} + \sum_{j=1}^{3} X_3 X_j \sigma_{3j} \right]^{1/2} \quad (6.6a)$$

$$= [X_1 X_1 \sigma_{11} + X_1 X_2 \sigma_{12} + X_1 X_3 \sigma_{13}$$
$$+ X_2 X_1 \sigma_{21} + X_2 X_2 \sigma_{22} + X_2 X_3 \sigma_{23}$$
$$+ X_3 X_1 \sigma_{31} + X_3 X_2 \sigma_{32} + X_3 X_3 \sigma_{33}]^{1/2} \quad (6.6b)$$

Each term in the double sum involves the product of the weights for two securities, $X_i$ and $X_j$, and the covariance between these two securities. Note how there are nine terms to be added together in order to calculate the standard deviation of a portfolio consisting of three securities. It is no coincidence that the number of terms to be added together (9) equals the number of securities squared ($3^2$).

In general, calculating the standard deviation for a portfolio consisting of $N$ securities involves performing the double sum indicated in equation (6.4) over $N$ securities, thereby involving the addition of $N^2$ terms:

$$\sigma_p = \left[ \sum_{i=1}^{N} \sum_{j=1}^{N} X_i X_j \sigma_{ij} \right]^{1/2}. \quad (6.7)$$

An interesting feature of the double sum occurs when the subscripts $i$ and $j$ refer to the same security. In equation (6.6b) this occurs in the first ($X_1 X_1 \sigma_{11}$), fifth ($X_2 X_2 \sigma_{22}$), and ninth ($X_3 X_3 \sigma_{33}$) terms. What does it mean to have the subscripts for covariance refer to the same security? For example, consider security one (Able) so that $i = j = 1$. Since $\sigma_{11}$ denotes the covariance of security 1 (Able) with security 1 (Able), equation (6.5) indicates that

$$\sigma_{11} = \rho_{11}\sigma_1\sigma_1. \tag{6.8}$$

Now the correlation of any security with itself, in this case $\rho_{11}$, can be shown to be equal to $+1$.[11] This means that equation (6.8) reduces to

$$\sigma_{11} = +1 \times \sigma_1 \times \sigma_1$$
$$= \sigma_1^2 \tag{6.9}$$

which is just the square of the standard deviation of security 1, known as the *variance* of security 1. Thus, the double sum involves both variance and covariance terms.

As an example, consider the following *variance-covariance matrix* for the stocks of Able, Baker, and Charlie:

|  | Column 1 | Column 2 | Column 3 |
|---|---|---|---|
| Row 1 | 146 | 187 | 145 |
| Row 2 | 187 | 854 | 104 |
| Row 3 | 145 | 104 | 289 |

The entry in cell ($i, j$) denotes the covariance between security $i$ and security $j$. For example, the entry in ($1, 3$) denotes the covariance between the first and third securities, which in this case is 145. Also, the entry in cell ($i, i$) denotes the variance of security $i$. For example, the variance of security 2 appears in cell ($2, 2$), and is equal to 854. Using this variance-covariance matrix along with the formula given in equation (6.6b), the standard deviation of the previously mentioned portfolio that had $X_1 = .2325$, $X_2 = .4070$, and $X_3 = .3605$ can now be calculated:

$$
\begin{aligned}
\sigma_p = [&X_1 X_1 \sigma_{11} + X_1 X_2 \sigma_{12} + X_1 X_3 \sigma_{13} \\
+ &X_2 X_1 \sigma_{21} + X_2 X_2 \sigma_{22} + X_2 X_3 \sigma_{23} \\
+ &X_3 X_1 \sigma_{31} + X_3 X_2 \sigma_{32} + X_3 X_3 \sigma_{33}]^{1/2} \\
= [&(.2325 \times .2325 \times 146) + (.2325 \times .4070 \times 187) + (.2325 \times .3605 \times 145) \\
+ &(.4070 \times .2325 \times 187) + (.4070 \times .4070 \times 854) + (.4070 \times .3605 \times 104) \\
+ &(.3605 \times .2325 \times 145) + (.3605 \times .4070 \times 104) + (.3605 \times .3605 \times 289)]^{1/2} \\
= [&277.13]^{1/2} \\
= &16.65\%.
\end{aligned}
$$

There are several interesting features about variance-covariance matrices that deserve mention. First, such matrices are square, meaning that the number of columns equals the number of rows and that the total number of cells for $N$ securities equals $N^2$.

---

[11] Remember that correlation refers to how two random variables move together. If the two random variables are the same, then they must move exactly together with each other. This can be visualized by graphing the values of the same random variable on both the $X$-axis and $Y$-axis. In such a graph, all points would lie on a straight $45°$ line passing through the origin, thereby implying a correlation of $+1$.

Second, the variances of the securities appear on the diagonal of the matrix, which are the cells that lie on a line going from the upper left-hand corner to the lower right-hand corner of the matrix. In the previous example, the variance of security 1 (146) appears in row 1 of column 1. Similarly, the variances of securities 2 and 3 appear in row 2 of column 2 (854) and row 3 of column 3 (289), respectively.

Third, the matrix is symmetric, meaning the number appearing in row $i$ of column $j$ also appears in row $j$ of column $i$. That is, the elements in the cells above the diagonal also appear in the corresponding cells below the diagonal. In the previous example, note that 187 appears in row 1 of column 2, and also in row 2 of column 1. Similarly, 145 appears in both row 1 of column 3 and row 3 of column 1, and 104 appears in both row 2 of column 3 and row 3 of column 2. The reason for this feature is quite simple — the covariance between two securities does not depend on the order in which the two securities are specified. This means that, for example, the covariance between the first and second securities is the same as the covariance between the second and first securities.

## 6.5 SUMMARY

Markowitz's approach to investing is based on statistics, inasmuch as it begins with the premise that security returns are random variables. As with random variables, securities (and, in turn, portfolios) can be compared by examining their moments. Markowitz has suggested that the investor should look at two such moments — expected return and standard deviation. That is, when faced with a set of portfolios, the investor should first determine the expected return (also known as the mean return) and standard deviation of return associated with each portfolio. Having done so, the investor is then in the position of making a fully informed decision about which one to purchase. This decision should hinge on the investor's attitudes toward risk and return as exemplified by his or her indifference curves. In particular, the investor should choose the portfolio that lies on the indifference curve that is furthest northwest.

Having said this, it is logical next to consider two questions: How can the investor make a choice on the basis of expected return and standard deviation when facing an infinite number of possible portfolios? And what happens when one of the securities has a certain return and borrowing is allowed? Chapter 7 provides the answers to these questions.

## APPENDIX A

### Risk-Neutral And Risk-Seeking Investors

Earlier it was mentioned that the Markowitz approach assumes investors are risk-averse. Although this is a reasonable assumption to make, it is not necessary to do so. Alternatively, it can be assumed that investors are either risk-neutral or risk-seeking.

Consider the risk-seeking investor first. This investor, when faced with a fair gamble, will want to take the gamble. Furthermore, larger gambles are more desirable than smaller gambles. This is because the pleasure derived from winning is greater than the displeasure derived from losing. Since there is an equal chance of winning or losing, on balance the risk-seeking investor will want to take the gamble. What this means is that

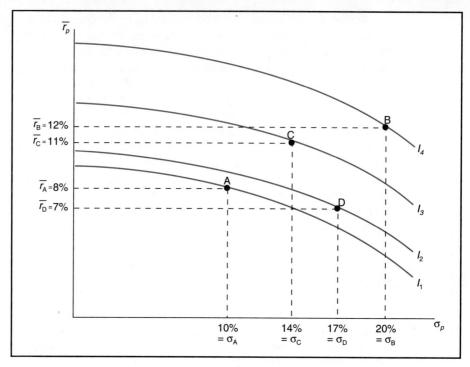

**FIGURE 6-7**
Map of indifference curves for a risk-seeking investor.

when faced with two portfolios that have the same expected return, this type of investor will choose the one with the higher standard deviation.

For example, in choosing between A and F in Figure 6.4, the risk-seeking investor will choose F. This suggests that the risk-seeking investor will have negatively sloped indifference curves.[12] In addition, risk-seeking investors will prefer to be on the indifference curve that is furthest northeast. Figure 6.7 illustrates a map of the indifference curves for a hypothetical risk-seeking investor. As shown in the figure, when choosing among A, B, C, and D (the same four portfolios shown in Figure 6.1), this investor will choose B.

The risk-neutral case lies between the risk-seeking and risk-averse cases. Whereas the risk-averse investor *does not want* to take fair gambles, and the risk-seeking investor *does want* to take such gambles, the risk-neutral investor *does not care* whether or not the gamble is taken. This means that risk, or, more specifically, standard deviation, is unimportant to the risk-neutral investor in evaluating portfolios. Accordingly, the indifference curves for such investors are horizontal lines as shown in Figure 6.8. These investors prefer to be on the indifference curve that is furthest north. When faced with

---

[12] It can also be shown that for a risk-seeking investor, these indifference curves will be concave, meaning their slopes decrease when moving from left to right along any particular one. The underlying rationale for concavity lies in utility theory; see footnotes 6 and 8.

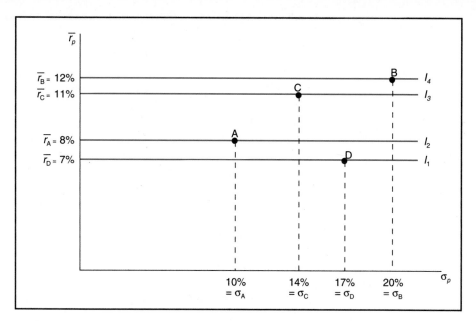

**FIGURE 6-8**
Map of indifference curves for a risk-neutral investor.

the choice of A, B, C, and D, such an investor will choose B, since it has the highest expected return.

Although investors can be either risk-seeking or risk-neutral, there is evidence to suggest that they are more accurately characterized as being, in general, risk-averse. One piece of evidence is the observation that riskier securities have historically had higher average returns, suggesting investors have had to be induced with higher rewards in order to get them to make riskier purchases. If investors were not risk-averse, they would not have had to be induced in this manner.

## QUESTIONS AND PROBLEMS

1. Listed below are a number of portfolios and expected returns, standard deviation of returns, and the amount of satisfaction (measured in utils) they provide Archie Vaughn. Given this information, graph Archie's identifiable indifference curves.

| Portfolio | Expected Return | Standard Deviation | Utility |
|---|---|---|---|
| 1 | 5% | 0% | 10 utils |
| 2 | 6 | 10 | 10 |
| 3 | 9 | 20 | 10 |
| 4 | 14 | 30 | 10 |
| 5 | 10 | 0 | 20 |
| 6 | 11 | 10 | 20 |
| 7 | 14 | 20 | 20 |
| 8 | 19 | 30 | 20 |
| 9 | 15 | 0 | 30 |
| 10 | 16 | 10 | 30 |
| 11 | 19 | 20 | 30 |
| 12 | 24 | 30 | 30 |

2. Why are the indifference curves of typical investors assumed to slope upward to the right?

3. Why are typical investors assumed to prefer portfolios on indifference curves lying to the northwest?

4. What is meant by the statement that "risk-averse investors exhibit diminishing marginal utility"? Why does diminishing marginal utility cause an investor to refuse to accept a "fair bet"?

5. Why are the indifference curves of more risk-averse investors more steeply sloped than those of investors with less risk aversion?

6. Consider the following two sets of indifference curves for investors Hank Wilson and Kate Cuyler. Determine whether Hank or Kate:
   a. Is more risk averse,
   b. Prefers investment A to investment B,
   c. Prefers investment C to investment D.
   Explain the reasons for your answers.

7. Given the following information about four stocks comprising a portfolio, calculate each stock's expected return. Then, using these individual security expected returns, calculate the portfolio's expected return.

| Stock | Initial Investment Value | Expected End-of-Period Investment Value | Proportion of Portfolio Initial Market Value |
|---|---|---|---|
| A | $ 500 | $ 700 | 19.2% |
| B | 200 | 250 | 7.7 |
| C | 1,000 | 1,100 | 38.5 |
| D | 900 | 1,350 | 34.6 |

8. Both the covariance and the correlation coefficient measure the extent to which the returns on securities move together. What is the relationship between the two statistical measures? Why is the correlation coefficient a more convenient measure?

9. Given the following variance-covariance matrix for three securities, as well as the percentage of the portfolio that each security comprises, calculate the portfolio's standard deviation.

|  | Security A | Security B | Security C |
|---|---|---|---|
| Security A | 459 | −211 | 112 |
| Security B | −211 | 312 | 215 |
| Security C | 112 | 215 | 179 |
|  | $X_A = .30$ | $X_B = .50$ | $X_C = .20$ |

10. Listed here are estimates of the standard deviations and correlation coefficients for three stocks.

| Stock | Standard Deviation | Correlation with Stock: A | B | C |
|---|---|---|---|---|
| A | 12% | 1.00 | −1.00 | 0.20 |
| B | 15 | −1.00 | 1.00 | 0.60 |
| C | 10 | 0.20 | 0.60 | 1.00 |

a. If a portfolio is composed of 30% of stock A and 70% of stock C, what is the portfolio's standard deviation?

b. If a portfolio is composed of 30% of stock A, 30% of stock B, and 40% of stock C, what is the portfolio's standard deviation?

c. If you were asked to design a portfolio using stocks A and B, what percentage investment in each stock would produce a zero standard deviation? [*Hint*: Some algebra is necessary to solve this problem. Remember that $X_B = (1 - X_A)$.]

## SUGGESTED READINGS

Kenneth Arrow, *Essays in the Theory of Risk Bearing* (Amsterdam: North Holland Publishing, 1971) and

Harry M. Markowitz, "Portfolio Selection," *Journal of Finance* 7, no. 1 (March 1952):77–91 are both classic works, the former on risk and risk aversion and the latter on security selection.

Gordon J. Alexander and Jack Clark Francis, *Portfolio Analysis* (Englewood Cliffs, NJ: Prentice Hall, 1986). Chapters 2 and 3 contain a discussion on the validity of mean-variance analysis.

# Chapter 7

# PORTFOLIO ANALYSIS

The previous chapter introduced the portfolio selection problem that every investor faces. It also introduced the investment approach of Harry Markowitz as a method of solving that problem. With this approach, an investor should evaluate alternative portfolios on the basis of their expected returns and standard deviations by using indifference curves. In the case of a risk-averse investor, the portfolio with the indifference curve that is the "furthest northwest" would be the one selected for investment.

However, the previous chapter left certain questions unanswered. In particular, how can Markowitz's approach be used once it is recognized that there are an infinite number of portfolios available for investment? What happens when the investor considers investing in a set of securities, one of which is riskless? What happens when the investor is allowed to buy securities on margin? This chapter will provide the answers to these questions, beginning with the first one.

## 7.1 THE EFFICIENT SET THEOREM

As mentioned earlier, an infinite number of portfolios can be formed from a set of $N$ securities. Consider the situation with Able, Baker, and Charlie companies where $N$ is equal to 3. The investor could purchase just shares of Able or just shares of Baker. Alternatively, the investor could purchase a combination of shares of Able and Baker. For example, the investor could put 50% of his or her money in each company, or 25% in one company and 75% in the other, or 33% in one and 67% in the other, or any percent (between 0% and 100%) in one company with the rest going into the other company. Without even considering investing in Charlie, there are already an infinite number of possible portfolios in which to invest.[1]

Does the investor need to evaluate all these portfolios? Fortunately, the answer to this question is no. The key to why the investor needs to look at only a subset of the available portfolios lies in the *efficient set theorem*, which states that:

---

[1] This can be seen by noting that there are an infinite number of points on the real number line between 0 and 100. If these numbers are thought of as representing the percentage of the investor's funds going into shares of Able, with 100 minus this number going into Baker, it can be seen that there are an infinite number of portfolios that could be formed from just two different securities. In making this assertion, however, it has been assumed that an investor can buy a fraction of a share if he or she so desires. For example, the investor can buy not only one or two or three shares of Able but also 1.1 or 1.01 or 1.001 shares.

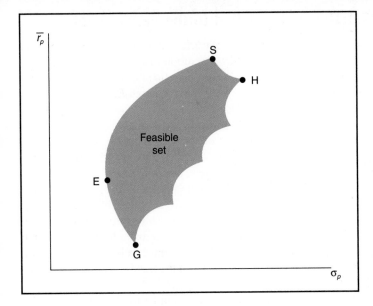

**FIGURE 7-1**
Feasible and efficient sets.

An investor will choose his or her optimal portfolio from the set of portfolios that:

1. Offer maximum expected return for varying levels of risk, and
2. Offer minimum risk for varying levels of expected return.

The set of portfolios meeting these two conditions is known as the *efficient set*, or *efficient frontier*.

## ☐ 7.1.1   The Feasible Set

Figure 7.1 provides an illustration of the location of the *feasible set*, also known as the opportunity set, from which the efficient set can be located. The feasible set simply represents the set of all portfolios that could be formed from a group of $N$ securities. That is, all possible portfolios that could be formed from the $N$ securities lie either on or within the boundary of the feasible set (the points denoted by $G$, $E$, $S$, and $H$ in the figure are examples of such portfolios). In general, this set will have an umbrella-type shape similar to the one shown by the figure. Depending on the particular securities involved, it may be more to the right or left, higher or lower, or fatter or skinnier than indicated here. The point is that its shape will, except in perverse circumstances, look similar to what appears here.[2]

---

[2] The shape of the feasible set shown in Figure 7–1 with the finite frontier GES is the result of a prohibition on short selling of securities. If unlimited short selling is allowed the frontier continues to infinity in both north-easterly and south-easterly directions.

## □ 7.1.2 The Efficient Set Theorem Applied to the Feasible Set

The efficient set can now be located by applying the efficient set theorem to this feasible set. First, the set of portfolios that meet the first condition of the efficient set theorem must be identified. Looking at Figure 7.1, there is no portfolio offering less risk than that of portfolio $E$. This is because if a vertical line were drawn through $E$, there would be no point in the feasible set to the left of the line. Also, there is no portfolio offering more risk than that of portfolio $H$. This is because if a vertical line were drawn through $H$, there would be no point in the feasible set to the right of the line. Thus, the set of portfolios offering maximum expected return for varying levels of risk is the set of portfolios lying on the "northern" boundary of the feasible set between points $E$ and $H$.

Considering the second condition next, there is no portfolio offering an expected return greater than portfolio $S$, since no point in the feasible set lies above a horizontal line going through $S$. Similarly, there is no portfolio offering a lower expected return than portfolio $G$, since no point in the feasible set lies below a horizontal line going through $G$. Thus, the set of portfolios offering minimum risk for varying levels of expected return is the set of portfolios lying on the "western" boundary of the feasible set between points $G$ and $S$.

Remembering that both conditions have to be met in order to identify the efficient set, it can be seen that only those portfolios lying on the "northwest" boundary between points $E$ and $S$ do so. Accordingly, these portfolios form the efficient set, and it is from this set of *efficient portfolios* that the investor will find his or her optimal one. All other portfolios are "inefficient" and can be safely ignored.

## □ 7.1.3 Selection of the Optimal Portfolio

How will the investor select an *optimal portfolio*? As shown in Figure 7.2, the investor should plot his or her indifference curves on the same figure as the efficient set and then choose the portfolio that is on the indifference curve that is furthest northwest. This portfolio will correspond to the point where an indifference curve is just tangent to the efficient set.[3] As can be seen in the figure, this is portfolio $O^*$ on indifference curve $I_2$. Although the investor would prefer a portfolio on $I_3$, no such portfolio exists, and so wanting to be on this indifference curve is just wishful thinking. In regard to $I_1$, there are several portfolios that the investor could choose (for example, $O$). However, the figure shows that portfolio $O^*$ dominates these portfolios, since it is on an indifference curve that is further northwest. Figure 7.3 shows how the highly risk-averse investor will choose a portfolio close to E. Figure 7.4 shows that the investor who is only slightly risk-averse will choose a portfolio close to $S$.[4]

Upon reflection, the efficient set theorem is quite rational. In Chapter 6, it was shown that the investor should select the portfolio that put him or her on the indifference curve furthest northwest. The efficient set theorem, stating that the investor need not be concerned with portfolios that do not lie on the northwest boundary of the feasible set, is a logical consequence.

---

[3] Appendix A discusses some of the principles involved in determining the location of Markowitz's efficient set and the composition of the investor's optimal portfolio.

[4] The risk-neutral investor will choose portfolio $S$, whereas the risk-seeking investor will choose either $S$ or $H$.

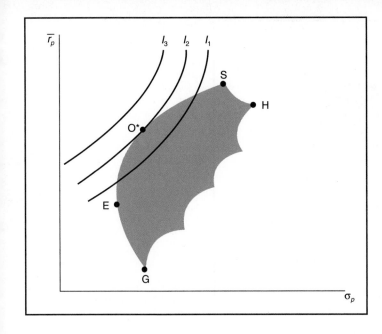

**FIGURE 7-2**
Selecting an optimal portfolio.

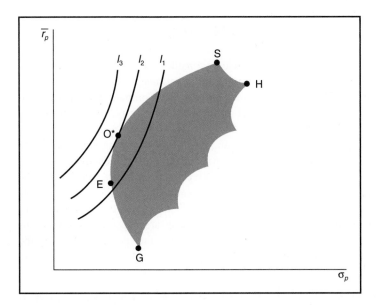

**FIGURE 7-3**
Portfolio selection for a highly risk-averse investor.

Indifference curves for the risk-averse investor were shown to be positively sloped and convex in Chapter 6. Now it will be shown that the efficient set is generally concave, meaning that if a straight line is drawn between any two points on the efficient set, the straight line will lie below the efficient set. This feature of the efficient set is important because it means that there will be only one tangency point between the investor's indifference curves and the efficient set.

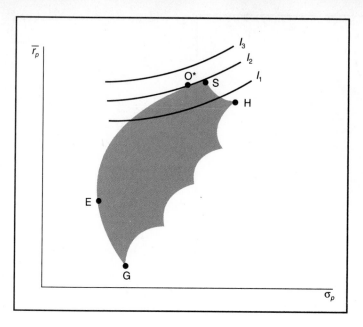

**FIGURE 7-4**
Portfolio selection for a slightly risk-averse investor.

## CONCAVITY OF THE EFFICIENT SET

In order to see why the efficient set is concave, consider the following two-security example. Security 1, the Ark Shipping Company, has an estimated expected return of 5% and standard deviation of 20%. Security 2, the Gold Jewelry Company, has an estimated expected return of 15% and standard deviation of 40%. Their respective locations are indicated by the letters $A$ and $G$ in Figure 7.5.

Now consider all possible portfolios that an investor could purchase by combining these two securities. Let $X_1$ denote the proportion of the investor's funds invested in Ark Shipping and $X_2 = 1 - X_1$ denote the proportion invested in Gold Jewelry. Thus, if the investor purchased just Ark Shipping, then $X_1 = 1$ and $X_2 = 0$. Alternatively, if the investor purchased just Gold Jewelry, then $X_1 = 0$ and $X_2 = 1$. A combination of .17 in Ark Shipping and .83 in Gold Jewelry is also possible, as are respective combinations of .33 and .67, and .50 and .50. Although there are many other possibilities, only the following seven portfolios will be considered:

|       | Portfolio A | Portfolio B | Portfolio C | Portfolio D | Portfolio E | Portfolio F | Portfolio G |
|-------|-------------|-------------|-------------|-------------|-------------|-------------|-------------|
| $X_1$ | 1.00        | .83         | .67         | .50         | .33         | .17         | .00         |
| $X_2$ | .00         | .17         | .33         | .50         | .67         | .83         | 1.00        |

In order to consider these seven portfolios for possible investment, their expected returns and standard deviations must be calculated. All the necessary information to calculate

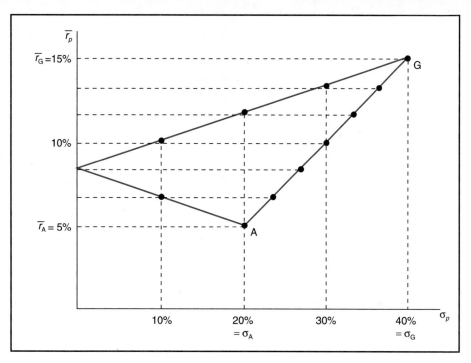

**FIGURE 7-5**
Upper and lower bounds to combinations of securities $A$ and $G$.

the expected returns for these portfolios is at hand. In doing so, equation (6.3a) must be utilized:

$$\bar{r}_p = \sum_{i=1}^{N} X_i \bar{r}_i$$

$$= \sum_{i=1}^{2} X_i \bar{r}_i \qquad\qquad (6.3a)$$

$$= X_1 \bar{r}_1 + X_2 \bar{r}_2$$

$$= (X_1 \times 5\%) + (X_2 \times 15\%).$$

For portfolios $A$ and $G$, this calculation is trivial, since the investor is purchasing shares of just one company. Thus, their expected returns are 5% and 15%, respectively. For portfolios $B, C, D, E,$ and $F$, the expected returns are, respectively:

$$\bar{r}_B = (.83 \times 5\%) + (.17 \times 15\%)$$
$$= 6.70\%$$
$$\bar{r}_C = (.67 \times 5\%) + (.33 \times 15\%)$$
$$= 8.30\%$$
$$\bar{r}_D = (.50 \times 5\%) + (.50 \times 15\%)$$
$$= 10\%$$
$$\bar{r}_E = (.33 \times 5\%) + (.67 \times 15\%)$$
$$= 11.70\%$$
$$\bar{r}_F = (.17 \times 5\%) + (.83 \times 15\%)$$
$$= 13.30\%.$$

In calculating the standard deviation of these seven portfolios, equation (6.7) must be utilized:

$$\sigma_p = \left[ \sum_{i=1}^{N} \sum_{j=1}^{N} X_i X_j \sigma_{ij} \right]^{1/2}$$

$$= \left[ \sum_{i=1}^{2} \sum_{j=1}^{2} X_i X_j \sigma_{ij} \right]^{1/2} \tag{6.7}$$

$$= [X_1 X_1 \sigma_{11} + X_1 X_2 \sigma_{12} + X_2 X_1 \sigma_{21} + X_2 X_2 \sigma_{22}]^{1/2}$$
$$= [X_1^2 \sigma_1^2 + X_2^2 \sigma_2^2 + 2 X_1 X_2 \sigma_{12}]^{1/2}$$
$$= [(X_1^2 \times 20\%^2) + (X_2^2 \times 40\%^2) + 2 X_1 X_2 \sigma_{12}]^{1/2}$$

For portfolios $A$ and $G$, this calculation is trivial, since the investor is purchasing shares of just one company. Thus, their standard deviations are just 20% and 40%, respectively.

For portfolios $B$, $C$, $D$, $E$, and $F$, application of equation (6.7) indicates that the standard deviations depend on the magnitude of the covariance between the two securities. As shown in equation (6.5), this covariance term is equal to the correlation between the two securities multiplied by the product of their standard deviations:

$$\sigma_{12} = \rho_{12} \times \sigma_1 \times \sigma_2$$
$$= \rho_{12} \times 20\% \times 40\%$$
$$= 800 \rho_{12}.$$

This means that the standard deviation of any portfolio consisting of Ark Shipping and Gold Jewelry can be expressed as:

$$\sigma_p = [(X_1^2 \times 20\%^2) + (X_2^2 \times 40\%^2) + (2 X_1 X_2 \times 800 \rho_{12})]^{1/2} \tag{7.1}$$
$$= [400 X_1^2 + 1600 X_2^2 + 1600\% X_1 X_2 \rho_{12}]^{1/2}.$$

Consider portfolio $D$ first. The standard deviation of this portfolio will be somewhere between 10% and 30%, the exact value depending upon the size of the correlation coefficient. How were these bounds of 10% and 30% determined? First, note that for portfolio D, equation (7.1) reduces to:

$$\sigma_D = [(400 \times .25) + (1600 \times .25) + (1600 \times .5 \times .5 \times \rho_{12})]^{1/2} \quad (7.1)$$
$$= [500 + 400\,\rho_{12}]^{1/2}.$$

Inspection of equation (7.2) indicates that $\sigma_D$ will be at a minimum when the correlation coefficient, $\rho_{12}$, is at a minimum. Now, remembering that the minimum value for any correlation coefficient is $-1$, it can be seen that the lower bound on $\sigma_D$ is:

$$\sigma_D = [500 + (400 \times -1)]^{1/2}$$
$$= [500 - 400]^{1/2}$$
$$= [100]^{1/2}$$
$$= 10\%.$$

Similarly, inspection of equation (7.2) indicates that $\sigma_D$ will be at a maximum when the correlation coefficient is at a maximum, which is $+1$. Thus, the upper bound on $\sigma_D$ is:

$$\sigma_D = [500 + (400 \times 1)]^{1/2}$$
$$= (500 + 400)^{1/2}$$
$$= (900)^{1/2}$$
$$= 30\%.$$

In general, it can be seen from equation (7.1) that for any given set of weights $X_1$ and $X_2$, the lower and upper bounds will occur when the correlations between the two securities are $-1$ and $+1$, respectively. Applying the same analysis to the other portfolios reveals that their lower and upper bounds are as follows.

| | Standard Deviation of Portfolio | |
|---|---|---|
| Portfolio | Lower Bound | Upper Bound |
| A | 20% | 20.00% |
| B | 10 | 23.33 |
| C | 00 | 26.67 |
| D | 10 | 30.00 |
| E | 20 | 33.33 |
| F | 30 | 36.67 |
| G | 40 | 40.00 |

These values are shown in Figure 7.5.

Interestingly, the upper bounds all lie on a straight line connecting points $A$ and $G$. This means that any portfolio consisting of these two securities cannot have a standard deviation that plots to the right of a straight line connecting the two securities. Instead, the standard deviation must lie on or to the left of the straight line. This observation suggests a motivation for diversifying a portfolio. Namely, *diversification generally leads to risk reduction*, since the standard deviation of a portfolio will generally be less than a weighted average of the standard deviations of the securities in the portfolio.

Also interesting is the observation that the lower bounds all lie on one of two line segments that go from point $A$ to a point on the vertical axis corresponding to 8.30% and then to point $G$. This means that any portfolio consisting of these two securities cannot have a standard deviation that plots to the left of either of these two line segments. For example, portfolio $B$ must lie on the horizontal line going through the vertical axis at 6.70% but bounded at the values of 10% and 23.33%.

In sum, any portfolio consisting of these two securities will lie within the triangle shown in Figure 7.5, with its actual location depending on the magnitude of the correlation coefficient between the two securities.

What if the correlation were zero? In this case, equation (7.1) reduces to:

$$\sigma_p = [(400\,X_1^2) \times +(1600\,X_2^2) + (1600\,X_1 X_2 \times 0)]^{1/2}$$
$$= [400\,X_1^2 + 1600\,X_2^2]^{1/2}.$$

Applying the appropriate weights for $X_1$ and $X_2$, the standard deviation for portfolios $B, C, D, E$, and $F$ can therefore be calculated as follows:

$$\sigma_B = [(400 \times .83^2) + (1600 \times .17^2)]^{1/2}$$
$$= 17.94\%$$

$$\sigma_C = [(400 \times .67^2) + (1600 \times .33^2)]^{1/2}$$
$$= 18.81\%$$

$$\sigma_D = [(400 \times .50^2) + (1600 \times .50^2)]^{1/2}$$
$$= 22.36\%$$

$$\sigma_E = [(400 \times .33^2) + (1600 \times .67^2)]^{1/2}$$
$$= 27.60\%$$

$$\sigma_F = [(400 \times .17^2) + (1600 \times .83^2)]^{1/2}$$
$$= 33.37\%.$$

Figure 7.6 indicates the location of these portfolios along with the upper and lower bounds that were shown in Figure 7.5. As can be seen, these portfolios — as well as all other possible portfolios consisting of Ark Shipping and Gold Jewelry — lie on a line that is curved or bowed to the left. Although not shown here, if the correlation were less than zero, the line would curve more to the left. If the correlation were greater than zero, it would not curve quite as much to the left. The important point of this figure is that as long as the correlation is less than +1 and greater than −1, the line representing the set of portfolios consisting of various combinations of the two securities will have some degree of curvature to the left. Furthermore, the northwest portion will be concave.

Although the previous example used two individual securities, Ark Shipping and Gold Jewelry, and considered all possible portfolios that could be formed by combining them, it is important to recognize that the same principle holds if two portfolios are combined into a third portfolio. That is, point $A$ in Figure 7.6 could represent a portfolio of securities with an expected return of 5% and a standard deviation of 20%, and point $G$ could represent another portfolio of securities with an expected return of 15% and a standard deviation of 40%. Combining these two portfolios will result in a third portfolio

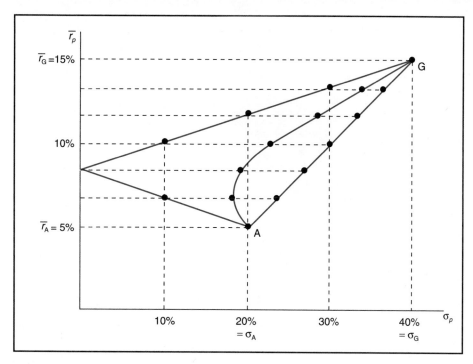

**FIGURE 7-6**
Portfolios formed by combining securities $A$ and $G$.

that has an expected return and standard deviation dependent upon the proportion invested in $A$ and $G$. Assuming the correlation between $A$ and $G$ is zero, the location of the third portfolio will lie on the curved line connecting $A$ and $G$.

Recognizing this, it can now be shown why the efficient set is concave.[5] One way to do this is to show that it cannot have any other shape. Consider the efficient set shown in Figure 7.7. Note that there is a "dent" in it between points $U$ and $V$. That is, there is a region on it where it is not concave. This cannot be a truly efficient set, since an investor could put part of his or her funds in the portfolio located at $U$ and the rest of his or her funds in the portfolio located at $V$. The resulting portfolio, a combination of $U$ and $V$, would have to lie to the left of the alleged efficient set. Thus, the new portfolio would be "more efficient" than a portfolio with the same expected return that was on the alleged efficient set between $U$ and $V$.

For example, consider the portfolio on the alleged efficient set that lies halfway between $U$ and $V$; it is indicated as point $W$ in Figure 7.8. If it truly is an efficient portfolio, then it would be impossible to form a portfolio with the same expected return as $W$ but with a lower standard deviation. However, by putting 50% of his or her funds in $U$ and 50% in $V$, the investor would have a portfolio that dominates $W$, since it would have the same expected return but a lower standard deviation. This lower standard deviation

---

[5] This "curvature property" can also be used to explain why the right-hand side of the feasible set has the scalloped shape noted in Figure 7.1.

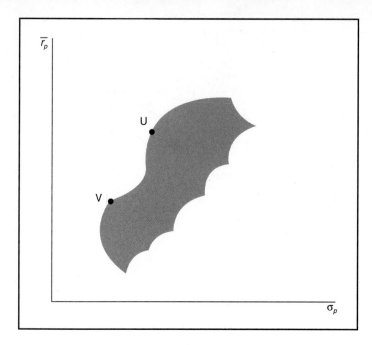

**FIGURE 7-7**
Concavity of the efficient set.

can be explained as follows: If the correlation between $U$ and $V$ were +1, this portfolio would lie on the straight line connecting $U$ and $V$ and would thus have a lower standard deviation than W. In Figure 7.8, $Z$ denotes this point. Since the actual correlation is less than +1, it would have a standard deviation even lower than $Z$'s standard deviation. This means that the alleged efficient set was constructed in error, since it is easy to find "more efficient" portfolios in the region where it is not concave.

With the Markowitz approach, it is assumed that the assets being considered for investment are individually risky. That is, each one of the $N$ risky assets has an uncertain return over the investor's holding period. Since none of the assets has a perfectly negative correlation with any other asset, all the portfolios also have uncertain returns over the investor's holding period and thus are risky. Furthermore, with the Markowitz approach the investor is not allowed to use borrowed money along with his or her initial wealth to purchase a portfolio of assets. This means that the investor is not allowed to use financial leverage, which in Chapter 2 was referred to as margin.

Next, the Markowitz approach to investing is expanded by first allowing the investor to consider investing in not only risky assets but also in a risk-free asset. That is, there will now be $N$ assets available for purchase, consisting of $N - 1$ risky assets and one risk-free asset. Second, the investor will be allowed to borrow money but will have to pay a given rate of interest on the loan.[6] The next section considers the effect of adding a risk-free asset to the set of risky assets.

---

[6] Credit for extending Markowitz's model to include risk-free borrowing and investing belongs to James Tobin in "Liquidity Preference as Behavior Towards Risk," *Review of Economic Studies* 26, no. 1 (February 1958):65–86; and "The Theory of Portfolio Selection," in *The Theory of Interest Rates*, ed. F. H. Hahn and F. P. R. Brechling (London: Macmillan, 1965).

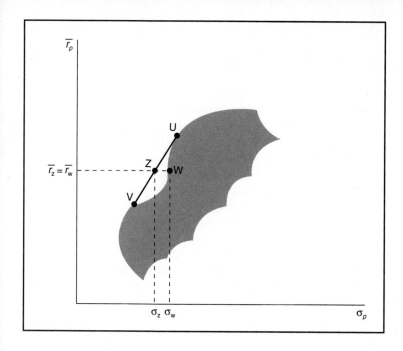

**FIGURE 7-8**
Removing a "dent" from the efficient set.

ALLOWING FOR RISK-FREE INVESTING

## ☐ 7.3.1 Defining the Risk-free Asset

What exactly is a *risk-free asset* in the context of Markowitz's approach? Since this approach involves investing for a single holding period, it means that the return on the risk-free asset is certain. That is, if the investor purchases this asset at the beginning of the holding period, then he or she knows exactly what the value of the asset will be at the end of the holding period. Since there is no uncertainty about the terminal value of the risk-free asset, the standard deviation of the risk-free asset is, by definition, zero.

In turn, this means that the covariance between the rate of return on the risk-free asset and the rate of return on any risky asset is zero. This can be seen by remembering that the covariance between the returns on any two assets $i$ and $j$ is equal to the product of the correlation coefficient between the assets and the standard deviations of the two assets: $\sigma_{ij} = \rho_{ij}\sigma_i\sigma_j$. Given that $\sigma_i = 0$ if $i$ is the risk-free asset, it follows that $\sigma_{ij} = 0$.

Since a risk-free asset has, by definition, a certain return, this type of asset must be some kind of fixed-income security with no possibility of default. Since all corporate securities have some chance of default, the risk-free asset cannot be issued by a corporation. Instead, it must be a security issued by the federal government. However, not just any security issued by the Canadian government qualifies as a risk-free security.

Consider an investor with a three-month holding period who purchases a long Canada Bond maturing in 20 years. Such a security is risky, since the investor does not know what this security will be worth at the end of his or her holding period. That is, interest rates very likely will have changed in an unpredictable manner during the investor's holding period, meaning that the market price of the security will have changed in an unpredictable manner. Since the presence of such *interest-rate risk* makes the value of the bond uncertain, it cannot qualify as a risk-free asset. Indeed, any bond with a maturity date greater than the investor's holding period cannot qualify as a risk-free asset, regardless of whether it matures one day or $19\frac{3}{4}$ years after the end of the investor's holding period.

Next, consider a bond that matures before the end of the investor's holding period, such as a 30-day Treasury bill in the case of an investor with the three-month holding period. In this situation, the investor does not know at the beginning of the holding period what interest rates will be in 30 days. This means that the investor does not know the interest rate at which the proceeds from the maturing Treasury bill can be reinvested (that is, "rolled over") for the remainder of the holding period. The presence of such *reinvestment-rate risk* in all government securities of shorter maturity than the investor's holding period means that these securities do not qualify as a risk-free asset.

This leaves only one type of government security to qualify as a risk-free asset — one with a maturity that matches the length of the investor's holding period. For example, the investor with a three-month holding period would find that a Treasury bill with a three-month maturity date had a riskless return. Since this security matures at the end of the investor's holding period, it provides the investor with an amount of money at the end of the holding period that is known for certain at the beginning of the holding period when an investment decision has to be made.[7]

Investing in the risk-free asset is often referred to as *risk-free lending*, since such an investment involves the purchase of Treasury bills, and thus involves a loan by the investor to the federal government.

With the introduction of a risk-free asset, the investor is now able to put part of his or her money in this asset and the remainder in any of the risky portfolios that are in Markowitz's feasible set. Adding these new opportunities expands the feasible set significantly and, more importantly, changes the location of part of Markowitz's efficient set. The nature of these changes needs to be analyzed, since investors are concerned with selecting a portfolio from the efficient set. In doing so, consideration is given initially to determining the expected return and standard deviation for a portfolio that consists of combining an investment in the risk-free asset with an investment in a single risky security.

## ☐ 7.3.2   Investing in Both the Risk-free Asset and a Risky Asset

In Chapter 6, the companies of Able, Baker, and Charlie were assumed to have expected returns, variances, and covariances as indicated in the following expected return vector and variance-covariance matrix:

$$ER = \begin{bmatrix} 16.2 \\ 24.6 \\ 22.8 \end{bmatrix} \qquad VC = \begin{bmatrix} 146 & 187 & 145 \\ 187 & 854 & 104 \\ 145 & 104 & 289 \end{bmatrix}.$$

---

[7] To be truly risk-free, the security must not provide the investor with any coupon payments during the holding period. Instead, it must provide the investor with only one cash inflow, and that inflow must occur at the end of the investor's holding period. Any intervening coupon payments would subject the investor to reinvestment-rate risk, since he or she would not know the rate at which the coupon payments could be invested for the remainder of the holding period. It should also be noted that the discussion has focused on an asset that is risk-free in nominal terms, since the presence of inflation means that virtually all government securities are risky in real terms.

Defining the risk-free asset as security number 4, consider all portfolios that involve investing in both the common shares of Able and the risk-free asset. Let $X_1$ denote the proportion of the investor's funds invested in Able, and $X_4 = 1 - X_1$ denote the proportion invested in the risk-free asset. If the investor put all his or her money in the risk-free asset, then $X_1 = 0$ and $X_4 = 1$. Alternatively, the investor could put all his or her money in just Able, in which case $X_1 = 1$ and $X_4 = 0$. A combination of .25 in Able and .75 in the risk-free asset is also possible, as are respective combinations of .50 and .50, and .75 and .25. Although there are other possibilities, the focus here will be on these five portfolios:

|  | Portfolio A | Portfolio B | Portfolio C | Portfolio D | Portfolio E |
|---|---|---|---|---|---|
| $X_1$ | .00 | .25 | .50 | .75 | 1.00 |
| $X_4$ | 1.00 | .75 | .50 | .25 | .00 |

Assuming that the risk-free asset has a rate of return (often denoted by $r_f$) of 4%, all the necessary information for calculating the expected returns and standard deviations for these five portfolios is at hand. Equation (6.3a) can be used to calculate the expected returns for these portfolios:

$$\bar{r}_P = \sum_{i=1}^{N} X_i \bar{r}_i \qquad (6.3a)$$

$$= \sum_{i=1}^{4} X_i \bar{r}_i.$$

Now, portfolios $A$, $B$, $C$, $D$, and $E$ do not involve investing in the second and third securities (that is, Baker and Charlie companies), meaning that $X_2 = 0$ and $X_3 = 0$ in these portfolios. Thus, the previous equation reduces to:

$$\bar{r}_p = X_1 \bar{r}_1 + X_4 \bar{r}_4$$
$$= (X_1 \times 16.2\%) + (X_4 \times 4\%)$$

where the risk-free rate is now denoted $\bar{r}_4$.

For portfolios $A$ and $E$ this calculation is trivial, since all the investor's funds are being placed in just one security. Thus, their expected returns are just 4% and 16.2%, respectively. For portfolios $B$, $C$, and $D$, the expected returns are, respectively,

$$\bar{r}_B = (.25 \times 16.2\%) + (.75 \times 4\%)$$
$$= 7.05\%$$
$$\bar{r}_C = (.50 \times 16.2\%) + (.50 \times 4\%)$$
$$= 10.10\%$$
$$\bar{r}_D = (.75 \times 16.2\%) + (.25 \times 4\%)$$
$$= 13.15\%.$$

The standard deviations of portfolios $A$ and $E$ are simply the standard deviations of the risk-free asset and Able, respectively. Thus, $\sigma_A = .00$ and $\sigma_E = 12.08\%$. In calculating the standard deviations of portfolios $B$, $C$, and $D$, equation (6.7) must be utilized:

$$\sigma_p = \left[ \sum_{i=1}^{N} \sum_{j=1}^{N} X_i X_j \sigma_{ij} \right]^{1/2} \tag{6.7}$$

$$= \left[ \sum_{i=1}^{4} \sum_{j=1}^{4} X_i X_j \sigma_{ij} \right]^{1/2} .$$

Remembering that $X_2 = 0$ and $X_3 = 0$ in these portfolios, this equation reduces to

$$\sigma_p = [X_1 X_1 \sigma_{11} + X_1 X_4 \sigma_{14} + X_4 X_1 \sigma_{41} + X_4 X_4 \sigma_{44}]^{1/2}$$
$$= [X_1^2 \sigma_1^2 + X_4^2 \sigma_4^2 + 2 X_1 X_4 \sigma_{14}]^{1/2} .$$

This equation can be reduced even further, since security 4 is the risk-free security that, by definition, has $\sigma_4 = 0$ and $\sigma_{14} = 0$. Accordingly, it reduces to:

$$\sigma_p = [X_1^2 \sigma_1^2]^{1/2}$$
$$= [X_1^2 \times 146]^{1/2}$$
$$= X_1 \times 12.08\% .$$

Thus, the standard deviations of portfolios B, C, and $D$ are:

$$\sigma_B = .25 \times 12.08\%$$
$$= 3.02\%$$
$$\sigma_C = .50 \times 12.08\%$$
$$= 6.04\%$$
$$\sigma_D = .75 \times 12.08\%$$
$$= 9.06\%$$

In summary, the five portfolios have the following expected returns and standard deviations:

| Portfolio | $X_1$ | $X_4$ | Expected Return | Standard Deviation |
|-----------|-------|-------|-----------------|--------------------|
| A | .00 | 1.00 | 4.00% | 0.00% |
| B | .25 | .75 | 7.05 | 3.02 |
| C | .50 | .50 | 10.10 | 6.04 |
| D | .75 | .25 | 13.15 | 9.06 |
| E | 1.00 | .00 | 16.20 | 12.08 |

These portfolios are plotted in Figure 7.9. In this figure, it can be seen that the portfolios lie on a straight line connecting the points representing the location of the risk-free asset

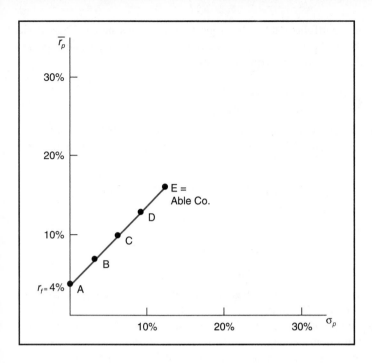

**FIGURE 7-9**
Combining risk-free investing
with investing in a risky asset.

and Able. Although only five particular combinations of the risk-free asset and Able have been examined here, it can be shown that any combination of the risk-free asset and Able will lie somewhere on the straight line connecting them; the exact location will depend on the relative proportions invested in these two assets. Furthermore, this observation can be generalized to combinations of the risk-free asset and any risky asset. That is, any portfolio that consists of a combination of the risk-free asset and a risky asset will have an expected return and standard deviation such that it plots on a straight line connecting them.

## □ 7.3.3  Investing in Both the Risk-free Asset and a Risky Portfolio

Next, consider what happens when a portfolio consisting of more than just one risky security is combined with the risk-free asset. For example, consider the risky portfolio that consists of Able and Charlie in proportions of .80 and .20, respectively. Its expected return (denoted by $\bar{r}_{PAC}$) and standard deviation (denoted by $\sigma_{PAC}$) are equal to:

$$\bar{r}_{PAC} = (.80 \times 16.2\%) + (.20 \times 22.8\%)$$
$$= 17.52\%$$

$$\sigma_{PAC} = [(.80 \times .80 \times 146) + (.20 \times .20 \times 289) + (2 \times .80 \times .20 \times 145)]^{1/2}$$
$$= 12.30\%.$$

Any portfolio that consists of an investment in both $PAC$ and the risk-free asset will have an expected return and standard deviation that can be calculated in a manner identical to what was previously shown for combinations of an individual asset and the risk-free asset. That is, a portfolio that has the proportion $X_{PAC}$ invested in the portfolio $PAC$, and the proportion $X_4 = 1 - X_{PAC}$ in the risk-free asset will have an expected return and standard deviation that are equal to, respectively,

$$\bar{r}_p = (X_{PAC} \times 17.52\%) + (X_4 \times 4\%)$$
$$\sigma_p = X_{PAC} \times 12.30\%.$$

For example, consider investing in a portfolio that consists of $PAC$ and the risk-free asset in proportions of .25 and .75, respectively.[8] This portfolio will have an expected return of

$$\bar{r}_p = (.25 \times 17.52\%) + (.75 \times 4\%)$$
$$= 7.38\%$$

and a standard deviation of

$$\sigma_p = (.25 \times 12.30\%)$$
$$= 3.08\%.$$

Figure 7.10 shows that this portfolio lies on a straight line connecting the risk-free asset and $PAC$. In particular, it is indicated by the point $P$ on this line. Other portfolios consisting of various combinations of $PAC$ and the risk-free asset will also lie on this line, with their exact locations depending on the relative proportions invested in $PAC$ and the risk-free asset. For example, a portfolio that involves investing a proportion of .50 in the risk-free asset and a proportion of .50 in $PAC$ lies on this line exactly halfway between the two end points.

In summary, combining the risk-free asset with any risky portfolio can be viewed as being no different from combining the risk-free asset with an individual risky security. In both cases, the resulting portfolio has an expected return and standard deviation such that it lies on a straight line connecting the two endpoints.

## ☐ 7.3.4  The Effect of Risk-free Investing on the Efficient Set

As mentioned earlier, the feasible set is changed significantly as a result of the introduction of risk-free investing. Figure 7.11 shows how it changes the feasible set for the example at hand. Here, all risky assets and portfolios, not just Able and $PAC$, are considered in all possible combinations with the risk-free asset. In particular, note that there are two boundaries that are straight lines emanating from the risk-free asset. The bottom line connects the risk-free asset with Baker. Thus, it represents portfolios formed by combining Baker and the risk-free asset.

The other straight line emanating from the risk-free asset represents combinations of the risk-free asset and a particular risky portfolio on the efficient set of the Markowitz model. It is a line that is just tangent to the efficient set of the Markowitz model, with the tangency point being denoted by $T$. This tangency point represents a risky portfolio consisting of Able, Baker, and Charlie in proportions equal to, respectively, .12, .19,

---

[8] Note that investing the proportion .25 in portfolio $PAC$ is equivalent to investing the proportion .20(.25 × .80) in Able and the proportion .05(.25 × .20) in Charlie.

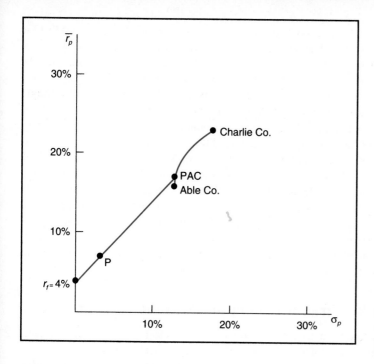

**FIGURE 7-10**
Combining risk-free investing with investing in a risky portfolio.

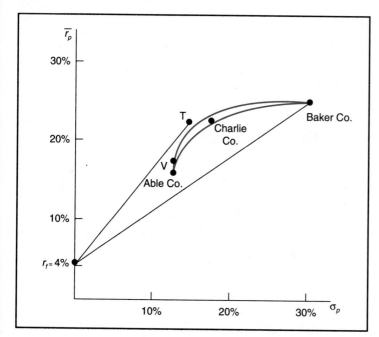

**FIGURE 7-11**
Feasible and efficient sets when risk-free investing is introduced.

and .69.[9] Substituting these proportions into equations (6.3a) and (6.7) indicates that the expected return and standard deviation of $T$ are 22.4% and 15.2%, respectively.

Whereas other risky efficient portfolios from the Markowitz model can also be combined with the risk-free asset, portfolio $T$ deserves special attention because there is no other portfolio consisting purely of risky assets that, when connected by a straight line to the risk-free asset, lies northwest of it. In other words, of all the lines that can be drawn emanating from the risk-free asset and connecting with either a risky asset or risky portfolio, none has a greater slope than the line that goes to $T$.

This is important, since part of the efficient set of the Markowitz model is dominated by this line. In particular, the portfolios on the Markowitz model efficient set going from the minimum risk portfolio, denoted by $V$, to $T$ are no longer efficient when a risk-free asset is made available for investment. Instead, the efficient set now consists of a straight-line segment and a curved segment. The straight-line segment is the straight line going from the risk-free asset to $T$ and thus consists of portfolios made up of various combinations of the risk-free asset and $T$. The curved segment consists of those portfolios to the northwest of $T$ on the Markowitz model efficient set.

## ☐ 7.3.5    The Effect of Risk-free Investing on Portfolio Selection

Figure 7.12 shows how an investor would go about selecting an optimal efficient portfolio when there is a risk-free asset available for investment in addition to a number of risky assets. If the investor's indifference curves look like those shown in panel (a), then the investor's optimal portfolio $O^*$ will involve investing part of his or her initial wealth in the risk-free asset and the rest in $T$ because $O^*$ lies on the straight-line segment of the efficient set.[10] Alternatively, if the investor is less risk-averse and has indifference curves that look like those shown in part (b), then the investor's optimal portfolio $O^*$ will not involve any risk-free investing because $O^*$ lies on the curved segment of the efficient set that lies to the northeast of $T$.

## 7.4    ALLOWING FOR RISK-FREE BORROWING

The analysis presented in the previous section can be expanded by allowing the investor to borrow money. This means that the investor is no longer restricted to his or her initial wealth when it comes time to decide how much money to invest in risky assets.[11] However, if the investor borrows money, then interest must be paid on the loan. Since the interest rate is known and there is no uncertainty about repaying the loan, it is often referred to as *risk-free borrowing*.

---

[9] Just how these weights are determined is shown in Appendix A.

[10] A more risk-averse investor (meaning an investor whose indifference curves have greater slopes) would choose an optimal portfolio that is closer to the risk-free asset on the line that connects the risk-free asset to $T$. Ultimately, if the investor is infinitely risk-averse, the optimal portfolio will consist of an investment in just the risk-free asset.

[11] Allowing for borrowing can be viewed as giving the investor the opportunity to engage in margin purchases if he or she so desires. That is, with borrowing the investor is allowed to use financial leverage.

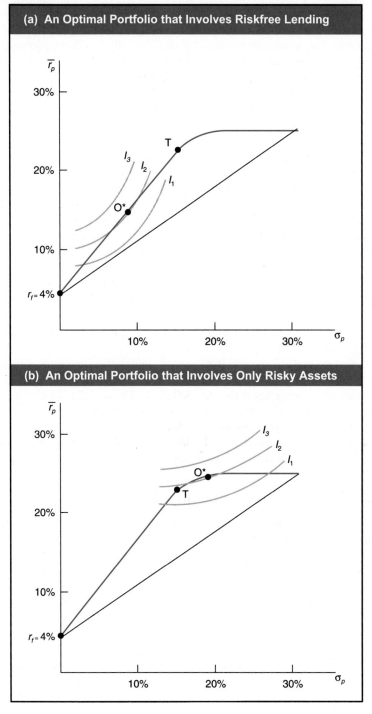

**FIGURE 7-12**
Portfolio selection with risk-free investing.

It will be assumed that the rate of interest charged on the loan is equal to the rate of interest that could be earned from investing in the risk-free asset.[12] Using the earlier example, this means that the investor now not only has the opportunity to invest in a risk-free asset that earns a rate of return of 4% but also may borrow money, for which the investor must pay a rate of interest equal to 4%.

The effect that the introduction of risk-free borrowing has on the location and shape of the efficient set is as significant as the effect that the introduction of risk-free investing had on it. However, it should be recognized that no investor would want simultaneously to invest in the risk-free asset and incur risk-free borrowing. Doing so would mean that the investor was engaged in two activities when an identical position could have been established with only one activity.

For example, an investor who is considering investing $5000 in the risk-free asset in order to earn 4% while at the same time paying interest at a rate of 4% in order to borrow $9300 could equally well borrow $4300 = $9300 − $5000. Accordingly, the investor can be allowed to invest or borrow at the risk-free rate, but not do both, without any loss of generality in the analysis.

Earlier, the proportion invested in the risk-free asset was denoted by $X_4$, and this proportion was constrained to be a nonnegative number between 0 and 1. Now, with the opportunity to borrow at the same rate, $X_4$ will no longer be so constrained. In the earlier example, the investor had initial wealth of $17,200. If the investor borrows money, then he or she will have in excess of $17,200 to invest in the risky securities of Able, Baker, and Charlie.

For example, if the investor borrows $4300, then he or she will have a total of $17,200 + $4300 = $21,500 to invest in these securities. In this situation, $X_4$ can be viewed as being equal to $−\$4,300/\$17,200 = −.25$. However, the sum of the proportions must still equal 1. This means that if the investor has borrowed money, the sum of the proportions invested in risky assets would be greater than 1. For example, borrowing $4300 and investing $21,500 in Able means that the proportion in Able, $X_1$, is $\$21,500/\$17,200 = 1.25$. Note how in this case $X_1 + X_4 = 1.25 + (−.25) = 1$.

## ☐ 7.4.1 Borrowing and Investing in a Risky Security

In order to evaluate the effect that the introduction of risk-free borrowing has on the efficient set, the example presented in the previous section will be expanded. In particular, consider portfolios F, G, H, and I, where the investor borrows a proportion of his or her initial wealth equal to .25, .50, .75, and 1.00, respectively. In all four portfolios, the investor will invest all the borrowed funds as well as his or her own funds in Able. Thus, the proportions for these portfolios can be summarized as follows:

---

[12] Appendix B discusses what happens to the efficient set when the investor is able to borrow but at a rate that is greater than the rate that can be earned by investing in the risk-free asset. Other models based on a variety of different assumptions are presented in Chapter 4 of *Portfolio Analysis* by Gordon J. Alexander and Jack Clark Francis (Englewood Cliffs, N.J.: Prentice Hall, 1986).

| | Portfolio F | Portfolio G | Portfolio H | Portfolio I |
|---|---|---|---|---|
| $X_1$ | 1.25 | 1.50 | 1.75 | 2.00 |
| $X_4$ | −.25 | −.50 | −.75 | −1.00 |

The expected returns of these portfolios are calculated in the same manner shown in the previous section. That is, equation (6.3a) is still used:

$$
\begin{aligned}
\bar{r}_p &= \sum_{i=1}^{N} X_i \bar{r}_i \\
&= \sum_{i=1}^{4} X_i \bar{r}_i \\
&= X_1 \bar{r}_1 + X_4 \bar{r}_4 \\
&= (X_1 \times 16.2\%) + (X_4 \times 4\%).
\end{aligned}
\tag{6.3a}
$$

Thus, portfolios $F, G, H$, and $I$ have the following expected returns:

$$
\begin{aligned}
\bar{r}_F &= (1.25 \times 16.2\%) + (-.25 \times 4\%) \\
&= 19.25\% \\
\bar{r}_G &= (1.50 \times 16.2\%) + (-.50 \times 4\%) \\
&= 22.30\% \\
\bar{r}_H &= (1.75 \times 16.2\%) + (-.75 \times 4\%) \\
&= 25.35\% \\
\bar{r}_I &= (2.00 \times 16.2\%) + (-1.00 \times 4\%) \\
&= 28.40\%.
\end{aligned}
$$

Similarly, the standard deviations of these portfolios are calculated by using equation (6.7), as in the previous section:

$$
\begin{aligned}
\sigma_p &= \left[ \sum_{i=1}^{N} \sum_{j=1}^{N} X_i X_j \sigma_{ij} \right]^{1/2} \\
&= \left[ \sum_{i=1}^{4} \sum_{j=1}^{4} X_i X_j \sigma_{ij} \right]^{1/2}
\end{aligned}
\tag{6.7}
$$

which was shown to reduce to

$$
\sigma_p = X_1 \times 12.08\%.
$$

Thus, the standard deviations of the four portfolios are

$$\sigma_F = 1.25 \times 12.08\%$$
$$= 15.10\%$$
$$\sigma_G = 1.50 \times 12.08\%$$
$$= 18.12\%$$
$$\sigma_H = 1.75 \times 12.08\%$$
$$= 21.14\%$$
$$\sigma_I = 2.00 \times 12.08\%$$
$$= 24.16\%.$$

In summary, these four portfolios, as well as the five portfolios that involve risk-free investing, have the following expected returns and standard deviations:

| Portfolio | $X_1$ | $X_4$ | Expected Return | Standard Deviation |
|---|---|---|---|---|
| A | .00 | 1.00 | 4.00% | 0.00% |
| B | .25 | .75 | 7.05 | 3.02 |
| C | .50 | .50 | 10.10 | 6.04 |
| D | .75 | .25 | 13.15 | 9.06 |
| E | 1.00 | .00 | 16.20 | 12.08 |
| F | 1.25 | − .25 | 19.25 | 15.10 |
| G | 1.50 | − .50 | 22.30 | 18.12 |
| H | 1.75 | − .75 | 25.35 | 21.14 |
| I | 2.00 | −1.00 | 28.40 | 24.16 |

In Figure 7.13, it can be seen that the four portfolios that involve risk-free borrowing ($F$, $G$, $H$, and $I$ ) all lie in the same straight line that goes through the five portfolios that involve risk-free investing ($A$, $B$, $C$, $D$, and $E$ ). Furthermore, the larger the amount of borrowing, the further out on the line the portfolio lies (equivalently, the smaller the value of $X_4$, the further out on the line the portfolio lies).

While only four particular combinations of borrowing and investing in Able have been examined here, it can be shown any combination of borrowing and investing in Able will lie somewhere on this line, with the exact location depending on the amount of borrowing. Furthermore, this observation can be generalized to combinations of risk-free borrowing and an investment in any particular risky asset. That is, borrowing at the risk-free rate and investing all the borrowed money and the investor's own money in a risky asset results in a portfolio that has an expected return and standard deviation that lie on the extension of the straight line connecting the risk-free rate and the risky asset.

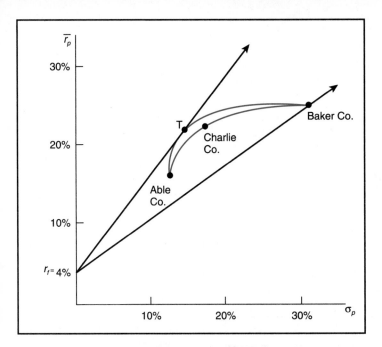

FIGURE 7-13
Combining risk-free borrowing
and investing with investing in
a risky asset.

## ☐ 7.4.2    Borrowing and Investing in a Risky Portfolio

Next, consider what happens when a portfolio of more than one risky asset is purchased
with both the investor's own funds and borrowed funds. Earlier it was shown that
the portfolio having proportions invested in Able and Charlie equal to .80 and .20,
respectively, had an expected return of 17.52% and a standard deviation of 12.30%.
This portfolio was referred to as $PAC$. Any portfolio that involves borrowing money at
the risk-free rate and then investing these funds and the investor's own funds in $PAC$
will have an expected return and standard deviation that can be calculated in a manner
identical to the one previously shown when borrowing was incurred and Able was
purchased. That is, a portfolio that involves borrowing the proportion $X_4$ and investing
these funds and all the investor's own funds in $PAC$ will have an expected return and
standard deviation that are equal to, respectively,

$$\bar{r}_p = (X_{PAC} \times 17.52\%) + (X_4 \times 4\%)$$
$$\sigma_p = X_{PAC} \times 12.30\%.$$

For example, consider borrowing an amount of money equal to 25% of the investor's
initial wealth and then investing all the investor's own funds and these borrowed funds
in $PAC$. Thus, $X_{PAC} = 1 - X_4 = 1 - (-.25) = 1.25$.[13] This portfolio will have an
expected return of

---

[13] Note that investing the proportion 1.25 in portfolio $PAC$ is equivalent to investing the proportion
$1.00(1.25 \times .80)$ in Able and the proportion $.25(1.25 \times .20)$ in Charlie.

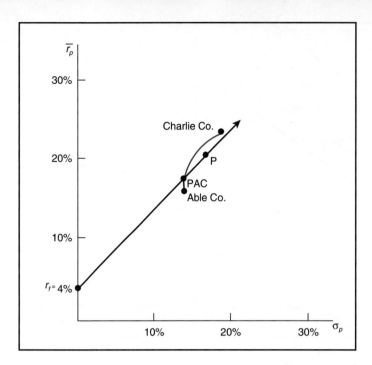

**FIGURE 7-14**
Combining risk-free borrowing and investing with investing in a risky portfolio.

$$\bar{r}_p = (1.25 \times 17.52\%) + (-.25 \times 4\%)$$
$$= 20.90\%$$

and a standard deviation of

$$\sigma_p = (1.25 \times 12.30\%)$$
$$= 15.38\%.$$

In Figure 7.14, it can be seen that this portfolio (denoted by P) lies on the extension of the line that connects the risk-free rate with $PAC$. Other portfolios consisting of $PAC$ and borrowing at the risk-free rate will also lie on this extension, with their exact locations depending on the amount of the borrowing. Thus, borrowing in order to purchase a risky portfolio is no different than borrowing in order to purchase an individual risky asset. In both cases, the resulting portfolio lies on an extension of the line connecting the risk-free rate with the risky investment.

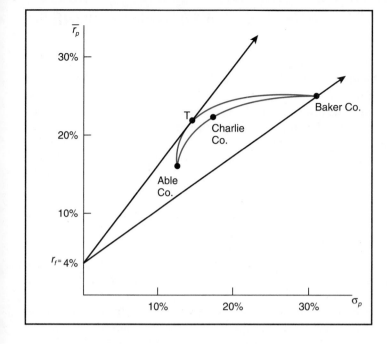

**FIGURE 7-15**
Feasible and efficient sets
when risk-free borrowing and
investing are introduced.

## ALLOWING FOR BOTH RISK-FREE INVESTING AND BORROWING

### ☐ 7.5.1 The Effect of Risk-free Investing and Borrowing on the Efficient Set

Figure 7.15 shows how the feasible set is changed when both risk-free investing and borrowing at the risk-free rate are allowed. Here, all risky assets and portfolios, not just Able and $PAC$, are considered. The feasible set is the entire area between the two lines emanating from the risk-free rate that go through the location of Baker and the portfolio denoted by $T$. These two lines extend indefinitely to the right if it is assumed that there is no limit to the amount of borrowing that the investor can incur.

The straight line that goes through the portfolio $T$ is of special importance, since it represents the efficient set. That is, it represents the set of portfolios that offer the investor the best opportunities, since it represents the set of feasible portfolios lying furthest northwest. Portfolio $T$, as was mentioned earlier, consists of investments in Able, Baker, and Charlie in proportions of .12, .19, and .69, respectively.

As before, the line going through $T$ is just tangent to the Markowitz model efficient set. None of the portfolios, except for $T$, that were on the Markowitz model efficient set are efficient when risk-free investing and borrowing are introduced. This can be seen by noting that every portfolio (except $T$) that lies on the Markowitz model efficient set is dominated by a portfolio on this straight line having the same standard deviation along with a higher expected return.

## ☐ 7.5.2   The Effect of Risk-free Investing and Borrowing on Portfolio Selection

Given the opportunity to either invest or borrow at the risk-free rate, an investor would identify the optimal portfolio by plotting his or her indifference curves on this graph and noting where one of them is tangent to the linear efficient set. Figure 7.16 shows two alternative situations. If the investor's indifference curves look like the ones in panel (a), then the investor's optimal portfolio $O^*$ will consist of an investment in the risk-free asset as well as in $T$. Alternatively, if the investor is less risk-averse and has indifference curves that look like those in part (b), then the investor's optimal portfolio $O^*$ will consist of borrowing at the risk-free rate and investing these funds as well as his or her own funds in $T$.[14]

---

## 7.6   SUMMARY

At this point, the essentials of the Markowitz approach to investing have been presented. There are four stages to this approach. In the first stage the investor, seeking the optimal portfolio to purchase, begins by specifying a set of securities for consideration.

In the second stage, analysis of the prospects of these securities, traditionally known as security analysis, is conducted. This means that the expected returns, variances, and covariances must be estimated for all the securities being considered.

In the third stage, the efficient set is determined. This involves using the previously estimated expected returns, variances, and covariances to determine the composition and location of the efficient portfolios that form the efficient set. If only risky securities are being considered for possible investment, the efficient set will be a curved line that is upward sloping and concave. With the addition of risk-free opportunities, the efficient set becomes a straight line lying to the northwest of the previous curved efficient set. All the portfolios on this straight line involve combining one portfolio consisting of just risky assets with either risk-free investing or risk-free borrowing. Indeed, this portfolio consisting of just risky assets is the only portfolio that the curved efficient set and the straight-line efficient set have in common.

The fourth and final stage is to identify the investor's optimal portfolio. This involves noting the portfolio corresponding to the point where one of the investor's indifference curves is tangent to the efficient set.

In implementing the Markowitz approach, these four stages of portfolio selection may be performed by different people. One or more security analysts may be responsible for stage 2, a portfolio manager for stage 3, and an investment counselor (or adviser), plus the investor, for stages 1 and 4.[15] Some investors may perform some (or all) of these functions themselves. Even in organizations with large staffs, there may be some

---

[14] The less risk-averse the investor is, the smaller the proportion in the risk-free rate ($X_f$) and the larger the proportion in $T(X_T)$.

[15] Regarding stage 4, in some situations, a professional adviser could present the investor with at least a rough assessment of the risk-return trade-offs depicted on the efficient set and then ask the investor to choose a preferred portfolio. In other situations, the adviser could attempt to assess the investor's circumstances and attitudes and then make the choice for the investor. In yet other situations, a money-management organization could describe a set of risk-return attitudes that it plans to assume in its management of a portfolio and then invite those individuals with similar attitudes to purchase shares that represent partial ownership of the portfolio.

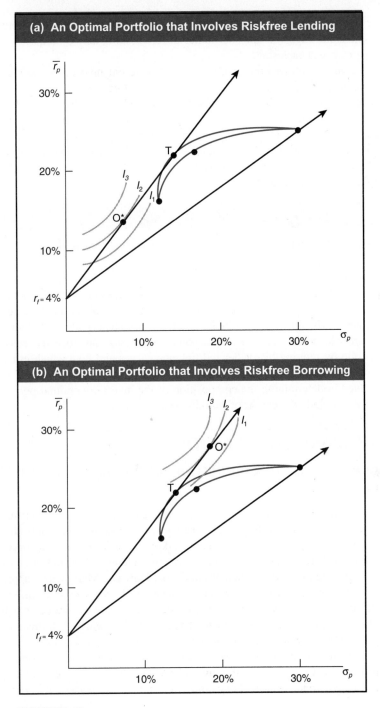

**FIGURE 7-16**
Portfolio selection with risk-free borrowing and investing.

overlap in functions. In summary, it is important to recognize that conceptually different functions are involved and that rather different skills may be required for successful performance at each stage.

Chapter 8 utilizes the model presented here but involves a significant change in focus. So far, the discussion has focused on what economists would call a normative model for investing. That is, a prescriptive model, in which people are told how they should make their investment decisions, has been presented. The realm of positive economics is entered next, wherein the implications that arise if everyone follows this approach to investing is examined. In this examination, it is seen that a descriptive model of how assets are priced can be derived. Logically, this model has been referred to as the capital asset pricing model.

## APPENDIX A

# Determining the Investor's Optimal Portfolio

If the investor is to consider all possible efficient portfolios that can be formed from $N$ securities, there needs to be some way to determine the composition (that is, the security weights) of each one of these portfolios. After this is done, the expected returns and standard deviations of these efficient portfolios can be calculated and then the efficient set can be located on a graph. At this point, the investor can proceed to select the optimal portfolio by plotting his or her indifference curves and note which efficient portfolio corresponds to the tangency point. This appendix describes some of the principles involved in determining the composition of the investor's optimal portfolio. It begins with the curved efficient set of Markowitz.

## A.1    THE MARKOWITZ MODEL

### ☐ A.1.1   Determining the Composition and Location of the Efficient Set

Previously, it was noted that there are an infinite number of possible portfolios available to the investor, but that the investor needs to be concerned with only those portfolios that are on the efficient set. However, Markowitz's efficient set is a curved line, which means that there are an infinite number of points along it. This, in turn, means that there are an infinite number of efficient portfolios! How can Markowitz's approach be used if an investor needs to identify the composition of each one of an infinite number of portfolios? Fortunately, there is no need to despair. Markowitz saw this potential problem and, in a major contribution, presented a method for solving it.[16] It involves the use of a quadratic programming algorithm known as the *critical-line method*.

Although the algorithm is beyond the scope of this book, it is important to recognize what it does. To begin with, the investor must estimate the expected return vector and variance-covariance matrix. For example, consider the three-security example presented

---

[16] See Harry Markowitz, "The Optimization of a Quadratic Function Subject to Linear Constraints," *Naval Research Logistics Quarterly* 3, nos. 1–2 (March-June 1956):111–33.

earlier in the chapter.[17] The expected return vector, denoted by $ER$, and the variance-covariance matrix, denoted by $VC$, were estimated to be

$$ER = \begin{bmatrix} 16.2 \\ 24.6 \\ 22.8 \end{bmatrix} \quad VC = \begin{bmatrix} 146 & 187 & 145 \\ 187 & 854 & 104 \\ 145 & 104 & 289 \end{bmatrix}.$$

The algorithm then identifies a number of *corner portfolios* that are associated with these securities and completely describe the efficient set. A corner portfolio is an efficient portfolio with the following property: Any combination of two adjacent corner portfolios will result in a portfolio that lies on the efficient set between the two corner portfolios. Just what this means is illustrated in the example.

The algorithm begins by identifying the portfolio with the highest expected return. This portfolio corresponds to point $S$ in Figure 7.1 and is an efficient portfolio. It is composed of just one security — the security with the highest expected return. That is, if the investor wanted to purchase that portfolio, all he or she would have to do is to purchase shares of the company whose stock has the highest expected return. Any other portfolio would have a lower expected return, since at least part of the investor's funds would be placed in shares of other companies that have an expected return lower than $S$, thereby causing the portfolio to have an expected return lower than $S$.

In the example, the company whose shares have the highest expected return is the second one, Baker Company. The corresponding efficient portfolio is the first of several corner portfolios that the algorithm will identify. Its composition is given by the following weight vector, denoted by $X(1)$:

$$X(1) = \begin{bmatrix} .00 \\ 1.00 \\ .00 \end{bmatrix}.$$

Its expected return and standard deviation correspond to the expected return and standard deviation of Baker, which are equal to 24.6% and $(854)^{1/2} = 29.22\%$, respectively. In Figure 7.17, this corner portfolio is denoted by $C(1)$.

The algorithm then identifies the second corner portfolio. This portfolio is on the efficient set below the first corner portfolio and has a composition given by the following weight vector, denoted by $X(2)$:

$$X(2) = \begin{bmatrix} .00 \\ .22 \\ .78 \end{bmatrix}.$$

That is, the second corner portfolio is a portfolio where the investor puts 22% of his or her funds into Baker common stock and the remainder, 78%, into Charlie common stock. Applying these weights to equations (6.3a) and (6.7), the expected return and standard deviation of this corner portfolio can be calculated; they are equal to 23.20% and 15.90%, respectively. In Figure 7.17, this corner portfolio is denoted by $C(2)$.

What is important about the first and second corner portfolios is that they are *adjacent* efficient portfolios, and any efficient portfolio lying on the efficient set between

---

[17] This example is based on one from Markowitz's book entitled *Portfolio Selection* (New Haven, Conn.: Yale University Press, 1959): 176–85.

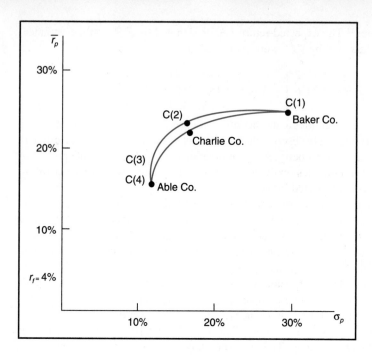

FIGURE 7-17
Corner portfolios.

them has a composition that is just a combination of their compositions. For example, the efficient portfolio lying halfway between them has the following composition:

$$[.5 \times X(1)] + [.5 \times X(2)] = .5 \times \begin{bmatrix} .00 \\ 1.00 \\ .00 \end{bmatrix} + .5 \times \begin{bmatrix} .00 \\ .22 \\ .78 \end{bmatrix} = \begin{bmatrix} .00 \\ .61 \\ .39 \end{bmatrix}.$$

That is, the portfolio has weights of .61 in Baker stock and .39 in Charlie stock. Using equations (6.3a) and (6.7), the expected return and standard deviation of this portfolio turn out to be 23.9% and 20.28%, respectively.

Having identified the second corner portfolio, the algorithm then identifies the third one. Its composition is:

$$X(3) = \begin{bmatrix} .84 \\ .00 \\ .16 \end{bmatrix}.$$

These weights can now be used to calculate the expected return and standard deviation of this portfolio, which are 17.26% and 12.22%, respectively. As was noted for the previous two corner portfolios, this corner portfolio is an efficient portfolio and is denoted by $C(3)$ in Figure 7.17.

Since they are adjacent, combinations of the second and third corner portfolios result in efficient portfolios that lie on the efficient set between them. For example, if the investor puts 33% of his or her money in the second corner portfolio and 67% in the third corner portfolio, then the resulting efficient portfolio has the following composition:

$$[.33 \times X(2)] + [.67 \times X(3)] = .33 \times \begin{bmatrix} .00 \\ .22 \\ .78 \end{bmatrix} + .67 \times \begin{bmatrix} .84 \\ .00 \\ .16 \end{bmatrix} = \begin{bmatrix} .56 \\ .07 \\ .36 \end{bmatrix}.$$

Using equations (6.3a) and (6.7), this portfolio can be shown to have an expected return of 19.10% and a standard deviation of 12.88%.

Earlier it was mentioned that only combinations of *adjacent* corner portfolios will be efficient. This means that portfolios formed by combining *nonadjacent* corner portfolios will not lie on the efficient set. For example, the first and third corner portfolios are nonadjacent, which means that any portfolio formed by combining them will not be efficient. For example, if the investor put 50% of his or her funds in the first corner portfolio and 50% in the third corner portfolio, the resulting portfolio would have the following compositions:

$$[.5 \times X(1)] + [.5 \times X(3)] = .5 \times \begin{bmatrix} .00 \\ 1.00 \\ .00 \end{bmatrix} + .5 \times \begin{bmatrix} .84 \\ .00 \\ .16 \end{bmatrix} = \begin{bmatrix} .42 \\ .50 \\ .08 \end{bmatrix}.$$

With these weights, the expected return and standard deviation of this portfolio can be shown to be equal to 20.93% and 18.38%, respectively. However, this is an inefficient portfolio. Since its expected return (20.93%) lies between the expected return of the second (23.20%) and third (17.26%) corner portfolios, by combining these two adjacent corner portfolios the investor will be able to form an efficient portfolio that has the same expected return but lower standard deviation.[18]

Continuing, the algorithm now identifies the composition of the fourth corner portfolio:

$$X(4) = \begin{bmatrix} .99 \\ .00 \\ .01 \end{bmatrix}.$$

Its expected return and standard deviation can be calculated to be 16.27% and 12.08%, respectively. Having identified this portfolio as the one corresponding to point $E$ in Figure 7.1 (and $C(4)$ in Figure 7.17), meaning it is the portfolio that has the least standard deviation of all feasible portfolios, the algorithm stops. The four corner portfolios, summarized in Table 7.1, completely describe the efficient set associated with the stocks of Able, Baker, and Charlie.

It is a simple matter for the computer, using its capability for graphics, now to draw the graph of the efficient set. Perhaps it will find the composition, and in turn the expected return and standard deviation, for each of 20 efficient portfolios that are evenly spaced between the first and second corner portfolios. Then it will "connect the dots," tracing a straight line between each of the twenty successive portfolios. This will give the graph the appearance of a curved line, as shown in Figure 7.17, since these portfolios

---

[18] In this example, the efficient portfolio having an expected return of 20.93% can be determined by solving the following equation for $Y$: $(23.20\% \times Y) + [17.26\% \times (1-Y)] = 20.93\%$. Since this is a linear equation with one unknown, it can easily be solved. The solution, $Y = .62$, indicates that by putting .62 of his or her funds in the second corner portfolio and $.38(1.00 - .62)$ in the third corner portfolio, the investor will have an efficient portfolio with the same expected return but lower standard deviation (specifically, 14.09%) than the portfolio involving a 50-50 combination of the first and third corner portfolios.

**TABLE 7.1**

Corner Portfolios for a Three Security Example.

| Corner Portfolio | Weights | | | Corner Portfolio | |
|---|---|---|---|---|---|
| | Able Co. | Baker Co. | Charlie Co. | Expected Return | Standard Deviation |
| $C(1)$ | .00 | 1.00 | .00 | 24.60% | 29.22% |
| $C(2)$ | .00 | .22 | .78 | 23.20 | 15.90 |
| $C(3)$ | .84 | .00 | .16 | 17.26 | 12.22 |
| $C(4)$ | .99 | .00 | .01 | 16.27 | 12.08 |

are located close to each other. Proceeding in a similar fashion, 20 efficient portfolios between the second and third corner portfolios will be located and the corresponding segment of the efficient set traced. Then the same procedure will be followed for the region between the third and fourth corner portfolios, at which point the graph has been completely drawn.

## ☐ A.1.2 Determining the Composition of the Optimal Portfolio

Once the location and composition of Markowitz's efficient set have been determined, the composition of the investor's optimal portfolio can be determined. This portfolio, indicated by $O^*$ in Figure 7.2, corresponds to the tangency point between the efficient set and one of the investor's indifference curves. The procedure for determining its composition starts by the investor noting graphically the level of its expected return. That is, from the graph the investor can note where $O^*$ is located and then calibrate its expected return simply by using a ruler and extending a line from it to the vertical axis (with computers, more precise ways exist for doing this).

Having done so, the investor can now identify the two corner portfolios having expected returns "surrounding" this level. That is, the investor can identify the corner portfolio with the expected return nearest but greater than this level (the surrounding corner portfolio that is "above" $O^*$) and the corner portfolio with the expected return nearest but less than this level (the surrounding corner portfolio that is "below" $O^*$).

If the expected return of the optimal portfolio is denoted by $\bar{r}^*$ and the expected returns of these two surrounding portfolios are denoted by $\bar{r}^a$ and $\bar{r}^b$, respectively, then the composition of the optimal portfolio can be determined by solving the following equation for $Y$ :

$$\bar{r}^* = (\bar{r}_a \times Y) + [\bar{r}_b \times (1 - Y)]. \tag{7.3}$$

The optimal portfolio will consist of a proportion $Y$ of the "above" surrounding corner portfolio and a proportion $1 - Y$ of the "below" surrounding corner portfolio.

In the example, if the optimal portfolio had an expected return of 20%, then it can be noted that the second and third corner portfolios are the above and below surrounding corner portfolios, since they have expected returns of 23.20% and 17.26%, respectively. Equation (7.3) thus looks like:

$$20\% = (23.20\% \times Y) + [17.26\% \times (1 - Y)].$$

Solving this equation for $Y$ results in $Y = .46$, meaning that the optimal portfolio consists of a proportion of .46 in the second corner portfolio and .54 in the third corner portfolio. In terms of the amount of investment in the securities of Able, Baker, and Charlie companies, this translates to:

$$[.46 \times X(2)] + [.54 \times X(3)] = .46 \times \begin{bmatrix} .00 \\ .22 \\ .78 \end{bmatrix} + .54 \times \begin{bmatrix} .84 \\ .00 \\ .16 \end{bmatrix} = \begin{bmatrix} .45 \\ .10 \\ .45 \end{bmatrix}.$$

Thus, the investor should put 45%, 10%, and 45% of his or her funds in shares of Able, Baker, and Charlie, respectively.

More generally, if the weight vectors of the above and below surrounding corner portfolios are denoted by $X^a$ and $X^b$, respectively, then the weights for the individual securities comprising the optimal portfolio will be equal to $(Y \times X^a) + [(1 - Y) \times X^b]$.

## A.2  INTRODUCING RISK-FREE OPPORTUNITIES

### ☐ A.2.1  Determining the Composition and Location of the Efficient Set

When risk-free opportunities are added to the Markowitz model, the efficient set is a straight line going through the portfolio $T$. This portfolio is known as the tangency portfolio, since it lies at the point on the curved efficient set of Markowitz that is tangent to a straight line emanating from the risk-free rate.

Determining the composition and location of $T$ involves the same procedures that were presented earlier in this appendix. In the example, portfolio $T$ lies on the curved efficient set of the Markowitz model in Figure 7.15 between the second and third corner portfolios that are shown in Figure 7.17, where they are denoted $C(2)$ and $C(3)$, respectively. Since $T$ lies between these two corner portfolios, its composition is a weighted average of the compositions of $C(2)$ and $C(3)$ that are shown in Table 7.1. These weights (.86 in $C(2)$ and .14 in $C(3)$) can be determined graphically by noting $T$'s expected return. Specifically, a horizontal line can be drawn from $T$ to the vertical axis, where the expected return of $T$ can be measured.

In this case, the expected return is 22.4%. Since $T$ lies between $C(2)$ and $C(3)$, its expected return must be a weighted average of the expected returns of $C(2)$, the above surrounding corner portfolio, and $C(3)$, the below surrounding corner portfolio. Thus, its composition, in terms of $C(2)$ and $C(3)$, can be determined by using equation (7.3) with $\bar{r}^* = 22.4\%$, $\bar{r}^a = 23.20\%$, and $\bar{r}^b = 17.26\%$:

$$22.4\% = (23.20\% \times Y) + [17.26\% \times (1 - Y)].$$

The solution to this equation is $Y = .86$. Thus, $T$ consists of $C(2)$ and $C(3)$ in the proportions of .86 and .14, respectively.

In terms of the amount of investment in Able, Baker, and Charlie, this translates to:

$$[.86 \times X(2)] + [.14 \times X(3)] = .86 \times \begin{bmatrix} .00 \\ .22 \\ .78 \end{bmatrix} + .14 \times \begin{bmatrix} .84 \\ .00 \\ .16 \end{bmatrix} = \begin{bmatrix} .12 \\ .19 \\ .69 \end{bmatrix}.$$

That is, $T$ consists of an investment of 12% in Able, 19% in Baker, and 69% in Charlie.

## ☐ A.2.2 Determining the Composition of the Optimal Portfolio

Once the location and composition of the tangency portfolio have been determined, the straight-line efficient set can be located. Then the composition of the investor's optimal portfolio can be determined. This portfolio, indicated by $O*$ in Figure 7.16, corresponds to the tangency point between the efficient set and one of the investor's indifference curves. The procedure for determining its composition is similar to that described earlier in this appendix for the Markowitz model. It starts by the investor noting graphically the level of its expected return. That is, from the graph the investor can note where $O*$ is located and then calibrate its expected return by simply using a ruler and extending a line from $O*$ to the vertical axis.

If the expected return of the optimal portfolio is denoted by $\bar{r}*$ and the risk-free rate and the expected return of the tangency portfolio are $r_f$ and $\bar{r}_T$, respectively, then the composition of the optimal portfolio can be determined by first solving the following equation for $Y$:

$$\bar{r}* = (\bar{r}_T \times Y) + [r_f \times (1 - Y)]. \tag{7.4}$$

The optimal portfolio will consist of a proportion $Y$ of the tangency portfolio and a proportion $1 - Y$ of the risk-free rate. Thus, the proportions to be invested in each risky security can be calculated by taking their proportion in $T$ and multiplying them by $Y$.

In the example, if the optimal portfolio of the investor corresponds to the one shown in part (a) of Figure 7.16, then $\bar{r}* = 14\%$. Thus, equation (7.4) would be:

$$14\% = (22.4\% \times Y) + [4\% \times (1 - Y)] \tag{7.5}$$

since $\bar{r}_T = 22.4\%$ and $r_f = 4\%$. The solution to equation (7.5) is $Y = .54$, meaning that the optimal portfolio consists of a proportion of .54 in the tangency portfolio and .46 in the risk-free asset. In terms of the amount of investment in the securities of Able, Baker, and Charlie companies, this translates to:

$$[.54 \times X(T)] = .54 \times \begin{bmatrix} .12 \\ .19 \\ .69 \end{bmatrix} = \begin{bmatrix} .07 \\ .10 \\ .37 \end{bmatrix}.$$

Thus, the investor should invest an amount of money that is equal to 7%, 10%, and 37% of his or her initial wealth in shares of Able, Baker, and Charlie, respectively. Furthermore, 46% of the investor's initial wealth should be used to buy Treasury bills, the risk-free asset.

Alternatively, if the optimal portfolio of the investor corresponds to the one shown in part (b) of Figure 7.16, then $\bar{r}* = 27\%$. Thus, equation (7.4) would be:

$$27\% = (22.4\% \times Y) + [4\% \times (1 - Y)] \tag{7.6}$$

and the solution would be $Y = 1.25$, meaning that the optimal portfolio consists of borrowing an amount of money equal to 25% of the investor's initial wealth and then investing the borrowed money and the initial wealth in T. In terms of the amount of investment in the securities of Able, Baker, and Charlie companies, this translates to:

$$[1.25 \times X(T)] = 1.25 \times \begin{bmatrix} .12 \\ .19 \\ .69 \end{bmatrix} = \begin{bmatrix} .15 \\ .24 \\ .86 \end{bmatrix}.$$

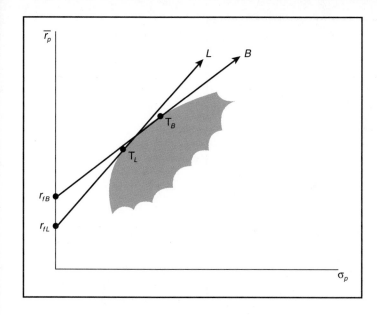

**FIGURE 7-18**
Evaluating different risk-free rates.

Thus, the investor should invest an amount of money that is equal to 15%, 24%, and 86% of his or her initial wealth in shares of Able, Baker, and Charlie, respectively.

## ALLOWING FOR DIFFERENT BORROWING AND LENDING RATES

In this chapter, it was assumed that the investor could borrow funds at the same rate that could be earned on an investment in the risk-free asset. As a result, the feasible set became the area bounded by two straight lines emanating from the risk-free rate. The upper line represented the efficient set and had one portfolio in common with the curved efficient set of the Markowitz model. This portfolio was located where the straight line from the risk-free rate was tangent to the curved efficient set. Now the concern will be with what happens if it is assumed that the investor can borrow but at a rate that is greater than the rate that can be earned by an investment in the risk-free asset. The rate on the risk-free asset will be denoted by $r_{fL}$, where $L$ indicates lending, since, as was mentioned earlier, an investment in the risk-free asset is equivalent to lending money to the government. Also, the rate at which the investor can borrow money will be denoted by $r_{fB}$ and is of a magnitude such that $r_{fB} > r_{fL}$.

One way to understand the effect on the efficient set of assuming that these two rates are different is as follows. First, consider what the efficient set would look like if risk-free borrowing and lending were possible at the same rate, $r_{fL}$. The resulting efficient set would be the straight line shown in Figure 7.18 that goes through the points $r_{fL}$ and $T_L$.

Second, consider what the efficient set would look like if risk-free borrowing and lending were possible at the higher rate, $r_{fB}$. The resulting efficient set would be the

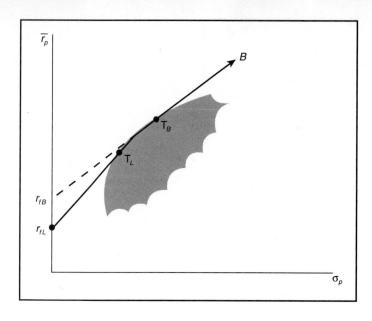

**FIGURE 7-19**
Efficient set when the risk-free rates are different.

straight line shown in Figure 7.18 that goes through the points $r_{fB}$ and $T_B$. Note that the portfolio $T_B$ lies on Markowitz's efficient set above the portfolio $T_L$, since it corresponds to a tangency point associated with a higher risk-free rate.

Third, since the investor cannot borrow at $r_{fL}$, that part of the line emanating from $r_{fL}$ that extends past $T_L$ is not available to the investor and can thus be removed from consideration.

Fourth, since the investor cannot lend at the risk-free rate $r_{fB}$, that part of the line emanating from $r_{fB}$ and going through $T_B$ but lying to the left of $T_B$ is not available to the investor and can thus be removed from consideration. The northwest boundary of what is left, shown in Figure 7.19, is the resulting efficient set.

This efficient set consists of three distinct but connected segments. The first segment is the straight line going from $r_{fL}$ to $T_L$; it represents various amounts of risk-free lending combined with investing in the portfolio of risky assets denoted $T_L$. The second segment is the curved line going from $T_L$ to $T_B$, which represents various risky portfolios that were also on Markowitz's curved efficient set. The third segment is the straight line extending outward from $T_B$; it represents various amounts of borrowing combined with an investment in the risky portfolio denoted by $T_B$.

The optimal portfolio for an investor will be, as before, the portfolio that corresponds to the point where an indifference curve is tangent to the efficient set. Depending on the investor's indifference curves, this tangency point could be on any one of the three segments that comprise the efficient set.

1. When is the standard deviation of a portfolio equal to the weighted average of the standard deviations of the component securities? Show this mathematically for a two-security portfolio. (*Hint*: Some algebra is necessary to solve this problem. Remember that $\sigma_{ij} = \rho_{ij}\sigma_i\sigma_j$. Try different values of $\rho_{ij}$.)

2. In terms of the Markowitz model without risk-free borrowing and lending, explain how an investor goes about identifying his or her optimal portfolio. Use words and graphs. What specific information does the investor need to identify this portfolio?

3. Discuss why the concepts of covariance and diversification are closely related.

4. Briefly explain why the efficient set must be concave.

5. Why is a pure discount government security with no risk of default still risky to an investor whose holding period does not coincide with the maturity date of the security?

6. The covariance between a risk-free asset and a risky asset is zero. Explain why this is the case and demonstrate it mathematically.

7. Why does the efficient set, with the Markowitz model extended to include risk-free borrowing and lending, have only one point in common with the efficient set of the Markowitz model without risk-free borrowing and lending? Why are the other points on the "old" efficient set no longer desirable? Explain with words and graphs.

8. How does the feasible set change when risk-free borrowing and lending are introduced into the Markowitz model? Explain with words and graphs.

9. Given the following expected return vector and variance-covariance matrix for three assets:

$$ER = \begin{bmatrix} 10.1 \\ 7.8 \\ 6.0 \end{bmatrix} \qquad VC = \begin{bmatrix} 210 & 140 & 0 \\ 140 & 90 & 0 \\ 0 & 0 & 0 \end{bmatrix}.$$

and given the fact that Pete Traynor's risky portfolio is split 50-50 between the two risky assets:

   a. Which security of the three must be the risk-free asset? Why?

   b. Calculate the expected return and standard deviation of Pete's portfolio.

   c. If the risk-free asset makes up 25% of Pete's total portfolio, what is the total portfolio's expected return and standard deviation?

10. What will be the effect on total portfolio expected return and risk if you borrow money at the risk-free rate and invest in the optimal risky portfolio.

11. Suppose your level of risk aversion changed as you grew older (and richer) and that you became less risk-averse. In a world of risk-free borrowing and lending, how would your optimal portfolio change? Would the types of risky securities you hold change? Explain with words and graphs.

12. (Appendix Question) What is a corner portfolio? Why are corner portfolios important for identifying the composition of the efficient set?

13. (Appendix Question) How does the efficient set change when the condition of borrowing and lending at the same risk-free rate is changed to borrowing at a rate greater than the rate at which risk-free lending can be conducted? Explain with words and graphs.

# SUGGESTED READINGS

Harry M. Markowitz, *Portfolio Selection* (New Haven, Conn.: Yale University Press, 1959) and

James Tobin, "Liquidity Preference as Behavior Towards Risk," *Review of Economic Studies* 26, no. 1 (February 1958):65–86 extends the original Markowitz model to include riskless borrowing and lending.

Gordon J. Alexander and Jack Clark Francis, *Portfolio Analysis* (Englewood Cliffs, NJ: Prentice Hall, 1986). Chapter 4 describes other extensions of the Markowitz model.

# Chapter 8

# THE CAPITAL
# ASSET PRICING MODEL

Chapters 6 and 7 presented a method for identifying an investor's optimal portfolio. With this method, the investor needs to estimate the expected returns and variances for all securities under consideration. Furthermore, all the covariances among these securities need to be estimated and the risk-free rate needs to be determined. Once this is done, the investor can find out the composition of the tangency portfolio as well as its expected return and standard deviation. At this juncture the investor can identify the optimal portfolio by noting where one of his or her indifference curves touch but do not intersect the efficient set. This portfolio will involve investing in the tangency portfolio, along with a certain amount of either risk-free borrowing or lending, since the efficient set is linear (that is, a straight line).

Such an approach to investing can be viewed as an exercise in *normative economics*, where investors are told what they should do. Thus, the approach is prescriptive in nature. In this chapter the realm of *positive economics* is entered, where a descriptive model of how assets are priced is presented. The model assumes, among other things, that all investors use the approach to investing given in Chapters 6 and 7. The major implication of the model is that the expected return of an asset will be related to a measure of risk for the asset that is known as beta. The exact manner in which expected return and beta are related is specified by the *capital asset pricing model* (CAPM).[1]

This model provides the intellectual basis for a number of the current practices in the investment industry. Although many of these practices are actually based on various extensions and modifications of the CAPM, a sound understanding of the original

---

[1] Credit for the initial development of the CAPM is usually given to William F. Sharpe, "Capital Asset Prices: A Theory of Market Equilibrium under Conditions of Risk," *Journal of Finance* 19, no. 3 (September 1964):425–42; John Lintner, "The Valuation of Risk Assets and the Selection of Risky Investments in Stock Portfolios and Capital Budgets," *Review of Economics and Statistics* 47, no. 1 (February 1965):13–37 and "Security Prices, Risk, and Maximal Gains from Diversification," *Journal of Finance* 20, no. 4 (December 1965):587–615; and Jan Mossin, "Equilibrium in a Capital Asset Market," *Econometrica* 34, no. 4 (October 1966):768–83. A major contribution was also made by Eugene F. Fama in "Risk, Return, and Equilibrium: Some Clarifying Comments," *Journal of Finance* 23, no. 1 (March 1968):29–40, where the Sharpe and Lintner papers were reconciled.

version is necessary in order to understand them. Accordingly, this chapter presents the original version of the CAPM.[2]

---

## 8.1    ASSUMPTIONS

In order to see how assets are priced, a model (that is, a theory) must be constructed. This requires simplification in that the model builder must abstract from the full complexity of the situation and focus only on the most important elements. The way this is achieved is by making certain *assumptions* about the environment. These assumptions need to be simplistic in order to provide the degree of abstraction that allows for some success in building the model. The "reasonableness" of the assumptions (or lack thereof) is of little concern. Instead, the test of a model is in its ability to help one understand and predict the process being modeled. As Milton Friedman, recipient of the 1976 Nobel Memorial Prize in Economics, has stated in a famous essay:

> [T]he relevant question to ask about the "assumptions" of a theory is not whether they are descriptively "realistic," for they never are, but whether they are sufficiently good approximations for the purpose in hand. And this question can be answered only by seeing whether the theory works, which means whether it yields sufficiently accurate predictions.[3]

Some of the assumptions behind the CAPM are also behind the normative approach to investing that was described in the previous two chapters. These assumptions are as follows:

1. Investors evaluate portfolios by looking at the expected returns and standard deviations of the portfolios over a one-period horizon.
2. Investors are never satiated, so when given a choice between two otherwise identical portfolios, they will choose the one with the higher expected return.
3. Investors are risk-averse, so when given a choice between two otherwise identical portfolios, they will choose the one with the lower standard deviation.
4. Individual assets are infinitely divisible, meaning that an investor can buy a fraction of a share if he or she so desires.
5. There is a risk-free rate at which an investor may either lend (that is, invest) or borrow money.
6. Taxes and transactions costs are irrelevant.

To these assumptions the following are added:

7. All investors have the same one-period horizon.
8. The risk-free rate is the same for all investors.
9. Information is freely and instantly available to all investors.
10. Investors have *homogeneous expectations*, meaning that they have the same perceptions in regard to the expected returns, standard deviations, and covariances of securities.

---

[2] Some extended versions of the CAPM are discussed in Appendix A. For a more extensive treatment, see Chapter 8 of Gordon J. Alexander and Jack Clark Francis, *Portfolio Analysis* (Englewood Cliffs, N.J.: Prentice-Hall, 1986).

[3] Milton Friedman, *Essays in the Theory of Positive Economics* (Chicago: The University of Chicago Press, 1953), 15.

As can be seen by examining these assumptions, the CAPM reduces the situation to an extreme case. Everyone has the same information and agrees about the future prospects for securities. Implicitly, this means that investors analyze and process information in the same way. The markets for securities are *perfect*, meaning there are no "frictions" to impede investing; potential impediments such as finite divisibility, taxes, transactions costs, and different risk-free borrowing and lending rates have been assumed away. This allows the focus to be changed from how an individual should invest to what would happen to security prices if everyone invested in a similar manner. By examining the collective behavior of all investors in the marketplace, the nature of the resulting equilibrium relationship between each security's risk and return can be developed.

## 8.2 THE CAPITAL MARKET LINE

### ☐ 8.2.1 The Separation Theorem

Having made these ten assumptions, the resulting implications can now be examined. First, investors would analyze securities and determine the composition of the tangency portfolio. In doing so, *everyone would obtain the same tangency portfolio*. However, this is not surprising, since there is complete agreement among investors on the estimates of the securities' expected returns, variances, and covariances as well as on the size of the risk-free rate. This also means that the linear efficient set (described in Chapter 7) is the same for all investors because it simply involves combinations of the agreed-upon tangency portfolio and risk-free rate.

Since all investors face the same efficient set, the only reason they will choose different portfolios is because they have different indifference curves. Thus, different investors will choose different portfolios from the same efficient set because they have different preferences toward risk and return. For example, as was shown in Figure 7.16, the investor in part (a) will choose a different portfolio than the investor in part (b). However, while the chosen portfolios will be different, *each investor will choose the same combination of risky securities*, denoted by $T$ in Figure 7.16. That is, each investor would spread his or her funds among risky securities in the same relative proportions, adding risk-free borrowing or lending in order to achieve a personally preferred overall combination of risk and return. This feature of the CAPM is often referred to as the *separation theorem*:

> The optimal combination of risky assets for an investor can be determined without any knowledge about the investor's preferences toward risk and return.

In other words, the determination of the optimal combination of risky assets can be made separately from the determination of the shape of an investor's indifference curves.

The reasoning behind the separation theorem involves a property of the linear efficient set that was introduced in Chapter 7. There it was shown that all portfolios located on the linear efficient set involved an investment in a tangency portfolio combined with varying degrees of risk-free borrowing or lending. With the CAPM, each person faces the same linear efficient set, meaning that each person will be investing in the same tangency portfolio (combined with a certain amount of either risk-free borrowing or lending that depends upon that person's indifference curves). It therefore follows that the risky portion of each person's portfolio will be the same.

In the example from Chapter 7, three securities were considered, corresponding to the shares of Able, Baker, and Charlie companies. With a risk-free rate of return of 4%, the tangency portfolio $T$ was shown to consist of investments in Able, Baker, and Charlie in proportions equal to .12, .19, and .69, respectively. If the ten assumptions of the CAPM are made, then the investor shown in part (a) of Figure 7.16 would invest approximately half of his or her money in the risk-free asset and the remainder in $T$. The investor shown in part (b), on the other hand, would borrow an amount of money equal to approximately half of the value of his or her initial wealth and proceed to invest these borrowed funds as well as his or her own funds in $T$.[4] Thus, the proportions invested in the three stocks for the investors of parts (a) and (b) would equal:[5]

$$( .5) \times \begin{bmatrix} .12 \\ .19 \\ .69 \end{bmatrix} = \begin{bmatrix} .060 \\ .095 \\ .345 \end{bmatrix} \quad \text{for the investor in part (a),}$$

$$( 1.5) \times \begin{bmatrix} .12 \\ .19 \\ .69 \end{bmatrix} = \begin{bmatrix} .180 \\ .285 \\ 1.035 \end{bmatrix} \quad \text{for the investor in part (b),}$$

While the proportions to be invested in each of these three risky securities for the panel (a) investor .060, .095, .345) can be seen to be different in size from their values for the panel (b) investor ( .180, .285, 1.035), the relative proportions are the same, being equal to .12, .19, and .69, respectively.

## ☐ 8.2.2  The Market Portfolio

Another important feature of the CAPM is that in equilibrium, each security must have a nonzero proportion in the composition of the tangency portfolio. That is, no security could, in equilibrium, have a proportion in $T$ that was zero. The reasoning behind this feature lies in the previously mentioned separation theorem in which it was asserted that the risky portion of every investor's portfolio would be independent of the investor's risk-return preferences. The justification for the theorem was that the risky portion of each investor's portfolio would simply be an investment in the tangency portfolio. If every investor is purchasing $T$ and $T$ does not involve an investment in each security, then nobody is investing in those securities with zero proportions in $T$. This means that the prices of these zero-proportion securities must *fall*, thereby causing the expected returns of these securities to *rise* until the resulting tangency portfolio has a nonzero proportion associated with them.

In the previous example, Charlie had a current price of $62 and an expected end-of-period price of $76.14. This meant that the expected return for Charlie was ( $76.14 − $62)/$62 = 22.8%. Now imagine that the current price of Charlie is $72, not $62, meaning that its expected return is ( $76.14 − $72)/$72 = 5.8%. If this were the case, the tangency portfolio associated with a risk-free rate of 4% would involve

---

[4] If the investor had initial wealth of $40000, this means that he or she would borrow $20,000 and then invest $60,000 ($40,000 + $20,000) in $T$.

[5] Note how the proportions in these three stocks sum to .5 for the panel (a) investor and 1.5 for the panel (b) investor. Since the respective proportions for the risk-free rate are .5 and −.5, the aggregate proportions for the stocks and risk-free rate sum to 1.0 for each investor.

just Able and Baker in proportions of .90 and .10, respectively.[6] Since Charlie has a proportion of zero, nobody would want to hold shares of Charlie. Consequently, orders to sell would be received in substantial quantities, with virtually no offsetting orders to buy being received. As a result, Charlie's price would fall, as brokers would try to find someone to buy the shares. However, as Charlie's price falls, its expected return would rise, since the same end-of-period price of $76.14 is forecast for Charlie as before and it would now cost less to buy one share. Eventually, as the price falls, investors would change their minds and want to buy shares of Charlie. Ultimately, at a price of $62, investors will want to hold shares of Charlie so that, in aggregate, the number of shares demanded will equal the number of shares outstanding. Thus, in equilibrium, Charlie will have a nonzero proportion in the tangency portfolio.

Another interesting situation could also arise. What if each investor concludes that the tangency portfolio should involve a proportionate investment in the stock of Baker equal to .40, but at the current price of Baker there are not enough shares outstanding to meet the demand? In this situation orders to buy Baker will flood in, and brokers will raise the price in search of sellers. This will cause the expected return of Baker to fall, making it less attractive and thereby reducing its proportion in the tangency portfolio to a level where the number of shares demanded equals the number of shares outstanding.

Ultimately, everything will balance out. When all the price adjusting stops, the market will have been brought into equilibrium. First, each investor will want to hold a certain amount of each risky security. Second, the current market price of each security will be at a level where the number of shares that are demanded equals the number of shares that are outstanding.[7] Third, the risk-free rate will be at a level where the total amount of money borrowed equals the total amount of money lent. As a result, the proportions of the tangency portfolio will correspond to the proportions of what is known as the *market portfolio*, defined as follows:

> The market portfolio is a portfolio consisting of an investment in all securities where the proportion to be invested in each security corresponds to its relative market value. The relative market value of a security is simply equal to the aggregate market value of the security divided by the sum of the aggregate market values of all securities.[8]

The reason the market portfolio plays a central role in the CAPM is because the efficient set consists of an investment in the market portfolio, coupled with a desired amount of either risk-free borrowing or lending. Thus, it is common practice to refer to the tangency portfolio as the market portfolio and to denote it as $M$ instead of $T$. In theory, $M$ consists of not only common stocks but also such other kinds of investments as bonds, preferred shares, and real estate. However, in practice many people restrict $M$ just to common stocks.

While the performance of the market portfolio is not reported in the daily press, indices measuring the performance of some of its major components are available. One

---

[6] Although the expected return of Charlie has been changed, all the variances and covariances as well as the expected returns for Able and Baker are assumed to have the same values that were given in Chapter 7. The singular change in the expected return of Charlie alters not only the composition of the tangency portfolio but, more generally, the location and shape of the efficient set.

[7] In this situation the market for the security is said to have *cleared*.

[8] The aggregate market value for the common stock of a company is equal to the current market price of the shares times the number of shares outstanding.

of the most widely known is Standard & Poor's 500 Stock Price Index (generally referred to as the S&P 500), a value-weighted average of the market prices of 500 large stocks. Since each stock's share price is weighted by the relative market value of its outstanding shares and since primarily stocks with large market values are included, this index represents the performance obtained in the stock market segment of the market portfolio reasonably well.

Complete coverage of the stocks listed on the New York Stock Exchange is provided by the NYSE Composite Index, which is like the S&P 500 in that it is a value-weighted index of share prices but is broader in that it considers more stocks. The American Stock Exchange computes a similar index for the stocks it lists, and the National Association of Security Dealers provides a value-weighted index of the prices of over-the-counter stocks traded on the NASDAQ system. The Wilshire 5000-stock index is the most comprehensive index of common stock prices that is published regularly in the United States and is thus closer than the others to representing the overall performance of American common stocks.[9]

In Canada there are two widely quoted indices — the TSE300 and the Toronto 35 — both based on TSE traded securities. The former is a broadly based index of 300 of the more representative stocks listed on the exchange. It is a unique value-weighted index in that the weights are based on the total number of shares outstanding minus the number of shares in any control blocks. The weights, therefore, are representative of the trading float. There are 35 of Canada's larger publically listed companies in the Toronto 35 Index, which was developed primarily for the trading of derivative securities. This is a modified value-weighted index, although the weights are based on the number of shares outstanding no one stock is permitted to represent more than 10% of the index. The Toronto 35 is also designed to track the TSE300, therefore, all industry groups except Real Estate and Construction are included. The composition of both these indices is altered periodically to reflect changing economic conditions and fluctuating company fortunes.

Without question the most widely quoted market index is the Dow Jones Industrial Average (DJIA). Although based on the performance of only 30 stocks listed on the New York Stock Exchange and utilizing a less satisfactory averaging procedure, the DJIA provides at least a fair idea of what is happening to stock values.[10]

---

[9] There are a variety of other indices of common stock prices that are commonly reported in the daily press. Many of these are components of the major indices. For example, *The Wall Street Journal* reports on a daily basis not only the level of the S&P 500 but also the levels of the Standard & Poor's Industrials, Transportations, Utilities, and Financials. These last four indices reflect the performance of particular sectors of the stock market. Their components, 500 stocks in total, make up the S&P 500. See Chapters 21 and 24 for a more thorough discussion of stock market indices.

[10] Charles Dow started this index in 1884 by simply adding the prices of 11 companies and then dividing the sum by 11. In 1928, securities were added to bring the total number up to 30, and since then the composition of these 30 has been changed periodically. Due to things like stock dividends and splits, the divisor is no longer simply equal to the number of stocks in the index.

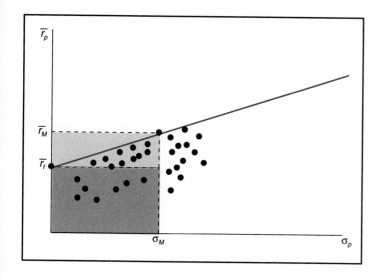

FIGURE 8-1
The capital market line.

## ☐ 8.2.3   The Efficient Set

In the world of the CAPM, it is a simple matter to determine the relationship between risk and return for efficient portfolios. Figure 8.1 portrays it graphically. Point $M$ represents the market portfolio and $r_f$ represents the risk-free rate of return. Efficient portfolios plot along the line starting at $r_f$ and going through $M$ and consist of alternative combinations of risk and return obtainable by combining the market portfolio with risk-free borrowing or lending. This linear efficient set of the CAPM is known as the *capital market line* (CML). All portfolios other than those employing the market portfolio and risk-free borrowing or lending would lie below the CML, although some might plot very close to it.

The slope of the CML is equal to the difference between expected return of the market portfolio and that of the riskless security, $\bar{r}_M - r_f$, divided by the difference in their risks, $\sigma_M - 0$, or $(\bar{r}_M - r_f)/\sigma_M$.[11] Since the vertical intercept of the CML is $r_f$, the straight line characterizing the CML has the following equation:

$$\bar{r}_p = r_f + \left[\frac{\bar{r}_M - r_f}{\sigma_M}\right]\sigma_p \tag{8.1}$$

where $\bar{r}_p$ and $\sigma_p$ refer to the expected return and standard deviation of an efficient portfolio.[12] In the previous example, the market portfolio associated with a risk-free rate of 4% consisted of Able, Baker, and Charlie in the proportions of .12, .19, and .69, respectively. Since it was shown in Chapter 7 that the expected return and standard

---

[11] The slope of a straight line can be determined if the location of two points on the line are known. It is determined by rise over run, meaning it is determined by dividing the vertical distance between the two points by the horizontal distance between the two points. In the case of the CML, two points are known, corresponding to the risk-free rate and the market portfolio, so its slope can be determined in this manner.

[12] The equation of a straight line is of the form $y = a + bx$, where $a$ is the vertical intercept and $b$ is the slope. Since the vertical intercept and slope of the CML are known, its equation can be written as shown here by making the appropriate substitutions for $a$ and $b$.

deviation for a portfolio with these proportions was 22.4% and 15.2%, respectively, the equation for the resulting CML is:

$$\bar{r}_p = 4 + \left[\frac{22.4 - 4}{15.2}\right]\sigma_p$$

$$= 4 + 1.21\sigma_p.$$

Equilibrium in the security market can be characterized by two key numbers. The first is the vertical intercept of the CML (that is, the risk-free rate), which is often referred to as the reward for waiting. The second is the slope of the CML, which is often referred to as the reward per unit of risk borne. In essence, the security market provides a place where time and risk can be traded with their prices determined by the forces of supply and demand. Thus, the intercept and slope of the CML can be thought of as the "price of time" and the "price of risk," respectively. In the example, they are equal to 4% and 1.21, respectively.

## 8.3 THE SECURITY MARKET LINE

### ☐ 8.3.1 Implications for Individual Risky Assets

The CML represents the equilibrium relationship between the expected return and standard deviation for efficient portfolios. Individual risky securities will always plot below the line, since a single risky security, when held by itself, is an inefficient portfolio. The CAPM does not imply any particular relationship between the expected return and the standard deviation (that is, total risk) of an individual security. To say more about the expected return of an individual security, deeper analysis is necessary.

In Chapter 6 the following equation was given for calculating the standard deviation of any portfolio:

$$\sigma_p = \left[\sum_{i=1}^{N}\sum_{j=1}^{N}X_iX_j\sigma_{ij}\right]^{1/2} \tag{6.7}$$

where $X_i$ and $X_j$ denoted the proportions invested in securities $i$ and $j$, respectively, and $\sigma_{ij}$ denoted the covariance of returns between security $i$ and $j$. Now consider using this equation to calculate the standard deviation of the market portfolio:

$$\sigma_M = \left[\sum_{i=1}^{N}\sum_{j=1}^{N}X_{iM}X_{jM}\sigma_{ij}\right]^{1/2} \tag{8.2}$$

where $X_{iM}$ and $X_{jM}$ denote the proportions invested in securities $i$ and $j$ in the market portfolio, respectively. It can be shown that another way to write equation (8.2) is as follows:

$$\sigma_M = \left[X_{1M}\sum_{j=1}^{N}X_{jM}\sigma_{1j} + X_{2M}\sum_{j=1}^{N}X_{jM}\sigma_{2j} + X_{3M}\sum_{j=1}^{N}X_{jM}\sigma_{3j}\right.$$

$$\left. + \cdots + X_{NM}\sum_{j=1}^{N}X_{jM}\sigma_{Nj}\right]^{1/2} \tag{8.3}$$

At this point a property of covariance can be used: The covariance of security $i$ with the market portfolio ($\sigma_{iM}$) can be expressed as:

$$\sum_{j=1}^{N} X_{jM}\sigma_{ij} = \sigma_{iM}.$$  (8.4)

This property, as applied to each one of the $N$ risky securities in the market portfolio, results in the following;

$$\sigma_M = [X_{1M}\sigma_{1M} + X_{2M}\sigma_{2M} + X_{3M}\sigma_{3M} + \cdots + X_{NM}\sigma_{NM}]^{1/2}$$  (8.5)

where $\sigma_{1M}$ denotes the covariance of security 1 with the market portfolio, $\sigma_{2M}$ denotes the covariance of security 2 with the market portfolio, and so on. Thus, the standard deviation of the market portfolio is equal to the square root of a weighted average of the covariances of all the securities with it, where the weights are equal to the proportions of the respective securities in the market portfolio.

At this juncture an important point can be observed. Under the CAPM each investor holds the market portfolio and is concerned with its standard deviation, since that will influence the magnitude of his or her investment in the market portfolio. The contribution of each security to the standard deviation of the market portfolio can be seen in equation (8.5) to depend on the size of its covariance with the market portfolio. Accordingly, each investor will note that *the relevant measure of risk for a security is its covariance with the market portfolio*, $\sigma_{iM}$. This means that securities with larger values of $\sigma_{iM}$ will be viewed by investors as contributing more to the risk of the market portfolio. It also means that securities with larger standard deviations should not be viewed as being riskier than those securities with smaller standard deviations.

From this analysis it follows that securities with larger values for $\sigma_{iM}$ will have to provide proportionately larger expected returns in order for investors to be interested in purchasing them. In order to see why, consider what would happen if such securities did not provide investors with proportionately larger levels of expected return. In this situation these securities would contribute to the risk of the market portfolio while not contributing proportionately to the expected return of the market portfolio. This means that deleting such securities from the market portfolio would cause the expected return of the market portfolio, relative to its standard deviation, to rise. Since investors would view this as a favorable change, the market portfolio would no longer be the optimal risky portfolio to hold. Thus, security prices would be out of equilibrium.

The exact form of the equilibrium relationship between risk and return can be written as follows:

$$\bar{r}_i = r_f + \left[\frac{\bar{r}_M - r_f}{\sigma_M^2}\right]\sigma_{iM}.$$  (8.6)

As can be seen in part (a) of Figure 8.2, equation (8.6) represents a line having a vertical intercept of $r_f$ and a slope of $[(\bar{r}_M - r_f)/\sigma_M^2]$. Since the slope is positive, the equation indicates that securities with larger covariances ($\sigma_{iM}$) will be priced so as to

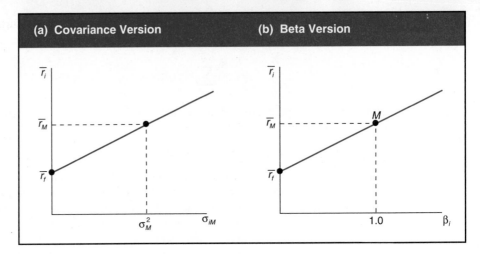

**FIGURE 8-2**
The security market line.

have larger expected returns ($\bar{r}_i$). This relationship between covariance and expected return is known as the *security market line* (SML).[13]

Interestingly, a risky security with $\sigma_{iM} = 0$ will have an expected return equal to the rate on the risk-free security, $r_f$. Intuitively, the reason for this is that the risky security, just like the risk-free security, does not contribute to the risk of the market portfolio. This is so even though the risky security has a positive standard deviation, whereas the risk-free security has a standard deviation of zero.[14]

Also of interest is the observation that a risky security with $\sigma_{iM} = \sigma_M^2$ will have an expected return equal to the expected return on the market portfolio, $\bar{r}_M$. This is because such a security contributes an average amount of risk to the market portfolio.

Another way of expressing the SML is as follows:

$$\bar{r}_i = r_f + (\bar{r}_M - r_f)\beta_i \qquad (8.7)$$

where the term $\beta_i$ is defined as

$$\beta_i = \frac{\sigma_{iM}}{\sigma_M^2}. \qquad (8.8)$$

The term $\beta_i$ is known as the *beta coefficient* (or simply the beta) for security i, and is an alternative way of representing the covariance risk of a security. Equation (8.7) is a different version of the SML, as can be seen in part (b) of Figure 8.2. While having the same intercept as the earlier version shown in equation (8.6), $r_f$, it has a different slope. The slope of this version is $\bar{r}_M - r_f$, whereas the slope of the earlier version was $(\bar{r}_M - r_f)/\sigma_M^2$.

---

[13] A more rigorous derivation of the SML is provided in Appendix B.

[14] It is even possible for some risky securities (meaning securities with positive standard deviations) to have expected returns less than the risk-free rate. According to the CAPM, this will occur if they have $\sigma_{iM} < 0$, thereby contributing a negative amount of risk to the market portfolio (meaning they cause the risk of the market portfolio to be lower than it would be in their absence).

One property of beta is that *the beta of a portfolio is simply a weighted average of the betas of its component securities, where the proportions invested in the securities are the respective weights.* That is, the beta of a portfolio can be calculated as

$$\beta_p = \sum_{i=1}^{N} X_i \beta_i. \tag{8.9}$$

Earlier it was shown that the expected return of a portfolio is a weighted average of the expected returns of its component securities, where the proportions invested in the securities are the weights. This means that since every security plots on the SML, so will every portfolio. More broadly:

> Not only every security but also every portfolio must plot on an upward-sloping straight line in a diagram with expected return on the vertical axis and beta on the horizontal axis.

This means that efficient portfolios plot on both the CML and the SML, whereas inefficient portfolios plot only on the SML.

Also of interest is that the SML must go through the point representing the market portfolio itself. Its beta is 1, and its expected return is $\bar{r}_M$, so its coordinates are $(1, \bar{r}_M)$. Since risk-free securities have beta values of 0, the SML will also go through a point with an expected return of $r_f$ and with coordinates of $(0, r_f)$. This means that the SML will have a vertical intercept equal to $r_f$ and a slope equal to the vertical distance between these two points, $\bar{r}_M - r_f$, divided by the horizontal distance between these two points, $1 - 0$, or $(\bar{r}_M - r_f)/(1 - 0) = \bar{r}_M - r_f$. Thus, these two points suffice to fix the location of the SML, indicating the "appropriate" expected returns for securities and portfolios with different beta values.

The equilibrium relationship shown by the SML comes to exist through the combined effects of investors' adjustments in holdings and the resulting pressures on security prices (as shown in Chapter 3). Given a set of security prices, investors calculate expected returns and covariances and then determine their optimal portfolios. If the number of shares of a security collectively desired differs from the number available, there will be upward or downward pressure on its price. Given a new set of prices, investors will reassess their desires for the various securities. The process will continue until the number of shares collectively desired for each security equals the number available.

For the individual investor, security prices and prospects are fixed, whereas the quantities held can be altered. For the market as a whole, however, these quantities are fixed (at least in the short run) and prices are variable. As in any competitive market, equilibrium requires the adjustment of each security's price until there is consistency between the quantity desired and the quantity available.

It may seem logical to examine historical returns on securities in order to determine whether or not securities have been priced in equilibrium as suggested by the CAPM. However, the issue of whether or not such testing of the CAPM can be done in a meaningful manner is controversial. In addition, Markowitz has suggested that affirmative test results are not necessary in order to make practical use of the CPM.[15]

## ☐ 8.3.2　An Example

In the example that was used earlier, Able, Baker, and Charlie were shown to form the market portfolio in proportions equal to .12, .19, and .69, respectively. Given these proportions, the market portfolio was shown to have an expected return of 22.4% and a standard deviation of 15.2%. The risk-free rate in the example was 4%. Thus, for this example the SML as indicated in equation (8.6) is:

$$\bar{r}_i = r_f + \left[ \frac{\bar{r}_M - r_f}{\sigma_M^2} \right] \sigma_{iM} \tag{8.6}$$

$$= 4 + \left[ \frac{22.4 - 4}{(15.2)^2} \right] \sigma_{iM}$$

$$= 4 + .08\, \sigma_{iM}. \tag{8.10}$$

The following expected return vector and variance-covariance matrix were used in the examples shown in Chapters 6 and 7, and are also used here:

$$ER = \begin{bmatrix} 16.2 \\ 24.6 \\ 22.8 \end{bmatrix} \quad VC = \begin{bmatrix} 146 & 187 & 145 \\ 187 & 854 & 104 \\ 145 & 104 & 289 \end{bmatrix}.$$

At this point, the covariances of each security with the market portfolio can be calculated by using equation (8.4). More specifically, the covariances for the market portfolio for Able, Baker, and Charlie are equal to:

$$\sigma_{1M} = \sum_{j=1}^{3} X_{jM}\sigma_{1j}$$

$$= (.12 \times 146) + (.19 \times 187) + (.69 \times 145)$$

$$= 153$$

$$\sigma_{2M} = \sum_{j=1}^{3} X_{jM}\sigma_{2j}$$

$$= (.12 \times 187) + (.19 \times 854) + (.69 \times 104)$$

$$= 257$$

$$\sigma_{3M} = \sum_{j=1}^{3} X_{jM}\sigma_{3j}$$

$$= (.12 \times 145) + (.19 \times 104) + (.69 \times 289)$$

$$= 236.$$

---

[15] See Chapter 10 of Alexander and Francis, *Portfolio Analysis*; and Harry M. Markowitz, "Nonnegative of Not Nonnegative: A Question About CAPMs," *Journal of Finance* 38, no. 2 (May 1983):283–95.

Note how the SML as given in equation (8.10) states that the expected return for Able should be equal to $4 + (.08 \times 153) = 16.2\%$. Similarly, the expected return for Baker should be $4 + (.08 \times 257) = 24.6\%$ and the expected return for Charlie should be $4 + (.08 \times 236) = 22.8\%$. Each one of these expected returns corresponds to the respective value given in the expected return vector.

Alternatively, equation (8.8) can be used to calculate the betas for the three companies. More specifically, the betas for Able, Baker, and Charlie are equal to:

$$\beta_1 = \frac{\sigma_{1M}}{\sigma_M^2}$$
$$= \frac{153}{(15.2)^2}$$
$$= .66$$
$$\beta_2 = \frac{\sigma_{2M}}{\sigma_M^2}$$
$$= \frac{257}{(15.2)^2}$$
$$= 1.11$$
$$\beta_3 = \frac{\sigma_{3M}}{\sigma_M^2}$$
$$= \frac{236}{(15.2)^2}$$
$$= 1.02.$$

Now equation (8.7) indicated that the SML could be expressed in a form where the measure of risk for an asset was its beta. For the example under consideration, this reduces to:

$$\bar{r}_i = r_f + (\bar{r}_M - r_f)\beta_i$$
$$= 4 + (22.4 - 4)\beta_i \qquad (8.11)$$
$$= 4 + 18.4\beta_i.$$

Note how the SML as given in this equation states that the expected return for Able should be equal to $4 + (18.4 \times .66) = 16.2\%$. Similarly, the expected return for Baker should be $4 + (18.4 \times 1.11) = 24.6\%$ and the expected return for Charlie should be $4 + (18.4 \times 1.02) = 22.8\%$. Each one of these expected returns corresponds to the respective value given in the expected return vector.

It is important to realize that if any other portfolio is assumed to be the market portfolio, meaning that if any set of proportions other than .12, .19, and .69 is used, then such an equilibrium relationship between expected returns and betas (or covariances) will not hold. Consider a hypothetical market portfolio with equal proportions (that is, .333) invested in Able, Baker, and Charlie. Since this portfolio has an expected return of 21.2% and a standard deviation of 15.5%, the hypothetical SML would be as follows:

$$\bar{r}_i = r_f + \left[ \frac{\bar{r}_M - r_f}{\sigma_M^2} \right] \sigma_{iM}$$

$$= 4 + \left[ \frac{21.2 - 4}{(15.5)^2} \right] \sigma_{iM}$$

$$= 4 + .07\,\sigma_{iM}.$$

Able has a covariance with this portfolio of

$$\sigma_{1M} = \sum_{j=1}^{3} X_{jM}\sigma_{1j}$$

$$= (.333 \times 146) + (.333 \times 187) + (.333 \times 145)$$

$$= 159,$$

which means that Able's expected return according to the hypothetical SML should be equal to $4 + (.07 \times 159) = 15.1\%$. However, since this does not correspond to the 16.2% figure that appears in the expected return vector, a portfolio with equal proportions invested in Able, Baker, and Charlie cannot be the market portfolio.[16]

---

## 8.4   MARKET AND UNIQUE RISK

Since beta (or covariance) is the relevant measure of risk for a security according to the CAPM, it is only appropriate to explore the relationship between it and the *total risk* of the security. This relationship is of the following form:

$$\sigma_i = [\beta_i^2 \sigma_M^2 + \sigma_{\epsilon i}^2]^{1/2}. \tag{8.12}$$

Here the total risk of security $i$, measured by its standard deviation and denoted by $\sigma_i$, is shown to be broken down into two components. The first component is the portion related to moves of the market portfolio. It is equal to the product of the square of the beta of the firm and the variance of the market portfolio and is often referred to as the *market* (or systematic) *risk* of the security. The second component is the portion not related to moves of the market portfolio. It is denoted by $\sigma_{\epsilon i}^2$ and is often referred to as the *unique* (or nonmarket or unsystematic) *risk* of the security.

From the earlier example, the betas of Able, Baker, and Charlie were calculated to be .66, 1.11, and 1.02, respectively. Since the standard deviation of the market portfolio was equal to 15.2%, this means that the market risks of the three firms are equal to $(.66^2 \times 15.2^2) = 100$, $(1.11^2 \times 15.2^2) = 285$, and $(1.02^2 \times 15.2^2) = 240$, respectively.

The unique risk of any security can be calculated by squaring both sides of equation (8.12),

$$\sigma_i^2 = \beta_i^2 \sigma_M^2 + \sigma_{\epsilon i}^2 \tag{8.13}$$

---

[16] Baker and Charlie have covariances of 382 and 179, respectively, which means that their expected returns should be equal to $30.74\% = 4 + (.07 \times 382)$ and $16.53\% = 4 + (.07 \times 179)$. However, these figures do not correspond to the respective figures (24.6% and 22.8%) appearing in the expected return vector, indicating there are discrepancies for all three securities. While this example has used the covariance version of the SML, the analysis is similar for the beta version of SML shown in equation (8.7).

and then solving for $\sigma_{\epsilon i}^2$:

$$\sigma_i^2 - \beta_i^2 \sigma_M^2 = \sigma_{\epsilon i}^2. \tag{8.14}$$

Thus, equation (8.14) can be used to calculate the unique risk of Able, Baker, and Charlie, respectively:

$$\sigma\sigma_{\epsilon 1}^2 = 146 - 100$$
$$= 46$$
$$\sigma_{\epsilon 2}^2 = 854 - 285$$
$$= 569$$
$$\sigma_{\epsilon 3}^2 = 289 - 240$$
$$= 49.$$

Unique risk is usually expressed as a standard deviation. This is calculated by taking the square root of $\sigma_{\epsilon i}^2$ and equals $\sqrt{46} = 6.8\%$ for Able, $\sqrt{569} = 23.9\%$ for Baker, and $\sqrt{49} = 7\%$ for Charlie.

At this point one may wonder, Why break total risk into two parts? For the investor, it would seem that risk is risk — whatever its source. The answer lies in the domain of expected returns.

Market risk is related to the risk of the market portfolio and to the beta of the security (or portfolio) in question. Securities (or portfolios) with larger betas will have larger amounts of market risk. In the world of the CAPM, securities (or portfolios) with larger betas will have larger expected returns. These two relationships together imply that securities (or portfolios) with larger market risks should have larger expected returns.

Unique risk is not related to beta. This means that there is no reason why securities (or portfolios) with larger amounts of unique risks should have larger expected returns. Thus, according to the CAPM, market risk is rewarded, whereas unique risk is not.

## 8.5 EXPECTED VERSUS ACTUAL VALUES

Forecasting a security's return is analogous to forecasting tomorrow's high temperature. The meteorologist has some model for estimating what the *expected* high temperature will be. For example, the model may have two components where the expected high is equal to the sum of (1) .9 times the expected low temperature tonight and (2) 14°.

Based on this model, the actual high temperature that subsequently occurs can be thought of as having three components. Specifically, the actual high temperature can be thought of as being equal to the sum of (1) .9 times the actual low tonight, (2) 14°, and (3) a random error term. This random error term can be thought of as representing the outcome from a spin of a roulette wheel, where the expected outcome from spinning the wheel is zero (perhaps the wheel has degrees from $-5°$ to $+5°$ evenly spaced on it).

Note that there are two related models involved here — one for the *expected* high temperature and one for the *actual* high temperature. The analogy with security returns is that there are again two such models involved — one for expected returns (the SML, which has two components) and one for actual returns (the characteristic line, which has three components). The discussion begins with expected returns.

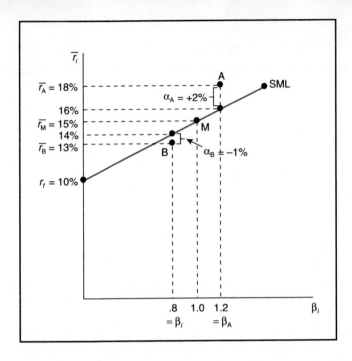

FIGURE 8-3
Equilibrium expected returns for securities.

## EQUILIBRIUM EXPECTED RETURNS

According to the CAPM, asset prices will adjust until equilibrium occurs whereby each and every security plots on the SML. Equivalently, in equilibrium the expected return on security $i$ over the forthcoming holding period will be given by

$$\bar{r}_i^e = r_f + (\bar{r}_M - r_f)\beta_i \qquad (8.15)$$

where:

$\bar{r}_i^e$ denotes the *equilibrium* expected return on security $i$,
$\bar{r}_f$ denotes the risk-free rate,
$\bar{r}_M$ denotes the expected return on the market portfolio, and
$\beta_i$ denotes the beta coefficient for security $i$.

For example, assume the expected return on the market portfolio is 15% and the risk-free rate is 10%. Furthermore, assume securities $A$ and $B$ have betas of 1.2 and .8, respectively. In this situation, the equilibrium expected return on security $A$ is equal to $16\% = 10\% + [(15\% - 10\%) \times 1.2]$. Similarly, the equilibrium expected return on security $B$ is $10\% + [(15\% - 10\%) \times .8] = 14\%$.

Figure 8.3 provides a graphic representation of this example. Since it has been assumed that the expected return on the market portfolio is 15% and the risk-free rate is 10%, the location of the SML has been fixed. This is because it must pass through these two points. As mentioned earlier, the SML indicates that any security with a beta of 1.2 will have an equilibrium expected return of 16%. Similarly, any security with a beta of .8 will have an equilibrium expected return of 14%.

# RETURN-GENERATING PROCESSES

## The Characteristic Line

Equation (8.15) can be rewritten as

$$\bar{r}_i^e - r_f = (\bar{r}_M - r_f)\beta_i \tag{8.16}$$

thereby showing that the equilibrium expected *excess return* for a security over the forthcoming holding period is equal to the product of the expected excess return on the market portfolio and the beta of the security.

However, equation (8.16) is not a model for what the actual excess return on a security will be over the forthcoming holding period. For this purpose, a *return-generating process* is used. The *characteristic line* is a type of return-generating process that is based on equation (8.16):

$$r_i - r_f = (r_M - r_f)\beta_i + \epsilon_i \tag{8.17}$$

where $r_i$ is the actual return on security $i$ that will occur over the forthcoming holding period, $r_f$ is the risk-free rate for this period, and $r_M$ is the actual return on the market portfolio for this period. The term $\beta_i$ is the beta for security $i$ for this period, whereas the last term, $\epsilon_i$, is known as the security's *random error term*.[17]

The random error term for a security is a random variable with an expected value of zero and a standard deviation denoted by $\sigma_{\epsilon i}$. It can be thought of as the outcome that will occur when a roulette wheel is spun. One feature of such a random error term is that its expected outcome is zero.

For example, security $A$ may be thought of as having a random error term corresponding to a roulette wheel with integer values on it that range from $-10\%$ to $+10\%$, with the values evenly spaced.[18] This means that there are 21 possible outcomes, each of which has an equal probability of occurring. Given the range of numbers, it also means that the expected outcome of the random error term is zero:

$$[-10 \times \frac{1}{21}] + [-9 \times \frac{1}{21}] + \cdots + [9 \times \frac{1}{21}] + [10 \times \frac{1}{21}] = 0.$$

As can be seen, this calculation involves multiplying each outcome by its probability of occurring and then summing up the resulting products. The standard deviation of this random error term can now be shown to be equal to 6.06%:

$$[(-10 - 0)^2 \times \frac{1}{21}] + [(-9 - 0)^2 \times \frac{1}{21}] + \cdots$$

$$+ [(9 - 0)^2 \times \frac{1}{21}] + [(10 - 0)^2 \times \frac{1}{21}]^{1/2} = 6.06\%.$$

---

[17] It is also common practice to use the following equation as the return-generating process for a security: $r_i = a_i + r_M\beta_i + e_i$, where $a_i$ is a constant and $e_i$ is a random error term. This equation is also often referred to as the *market model*.

[18] Since the range refers to the possible outcomes and the spacing refers to the probabilities of the various outcomes occurring, it can be seen that the roulette wheel is just a convenient way of referring to the random error term's probability distribution. Typically, it is assumed that the random error term has a normal probability distribution.

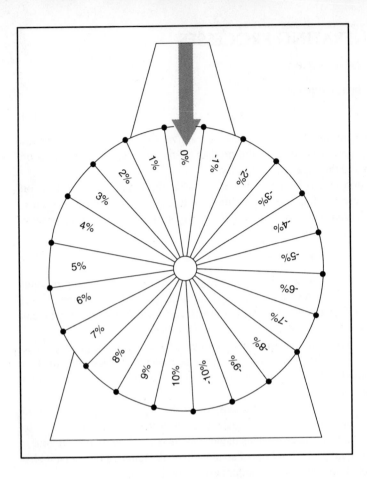

**FIGURE 8-4**
Security A's random error term.

This calculation involves subtracting the expected outcome from each possible outcome, then squaring each one of these differences, multiplying each square by the probability of the corresponding outcome occurring, adding the products, and finally taking the square root of the resulting sum.

Figure 8.4 illustrates the roulette wheel corresponding to this random error term. In general, securities will have random error terms whose corresponding roulette wheels have different ranges and different forms of uneven spacing. Although all will have an expected value of zero, they will typically have different standard deviations. For example, security $B$ may have a random error term whose expected value and standard deviation are equal to 0 and 4.76%, respectively.[19]

---

[19] This would be the case if security $B$ had a random error term whose roulette wheel had integers from $-9\%$ to $+9\%$ on it, but the spacing for each integer between $-5\%$ and $+5\%$ was twice as large as the spacing for each integer from $-9\%$ to $-6\%$ and $+6\%$ to $+9\%$. This means that the probability of any specific integer between $-5\%$ and $+5\%$ occurring is equal to $2/30$, whereas the probability of any specific integer from $-9\%$ to $-6\%$ and $+6\%$ to $+9\%$ occurring is equal to $2/30$.

## ☐ 8.7.2    Actual Excess Returns

The characteristic line for security $i$ given in equation (8.17) suggests that the actual excess return for this particular security can be thought of as having two components. The first component is equal to the actual excess return on the market portfolio, multiplied by the security's beta coefficient. The second component is equal to the outcome from a spin of the roulette wheel for the security.

The characteristic line for security $A$ would look like

$$r_A - r_f = [(r_M - r_f) \times 1.2] + \epsilon_A \qquad (8.18)$$

since the security's beta was determined to be 1.2. Thus, the actual excess return of security $A$ will consist of an excess return on the market portfolio multiplied by 1.2, and a random error term.

Similarly, the characteristic line for security $B$ would look like:

$$r_B - r_f = [(r_M - r_f) \times .8] + \epsilon_B \qquad (8.19)$$

since the security's beta was determined to be equal to .8.

The solid line in part (a) of Figure 8.5 provides a graph of the characteristic line for security $A$. This line corresponds to the characteristic line given by equation (8.18) but without the random error term. Accordingly, the graph for the characteristic line of security $A$ corresponds to the following equation:

$$r_A - r_f = [(r_M - r_f) \times 1.2].$$

Here the vertical axis measures the excess return on security $A$, $r_A - r_f$, whereas the horizontal axis measures the excess return on the market portfolio, $r_M - r_f$. The line goes through two points. First, the line goes through the origin, since the intercept is zero. Second, the line goes through the point corresponding to the equilibrium expected excess return on the security ( $16\% - 10\% = 6\%$ ) and on the market portfolio ( $15\% - 10\% = 5\%$ ). It should be noted that this line will have a slope equal to the beta of the security, 1.2.[20]

Part (b) of Figure 8.5 presents the graph of the characteristic line for security $B$:

$$r_B - r_f = [(r_M - r_f) \times .8].$$

This line also goes through the origin and a point corresponding to the equilibrium expected excess return on the security ( $14\% - 10\% = 4\%$ ) and on the market portfolio ( $15\% - 10\% = 5\%$ ). Note that its slope is equal to the beta of the security, .8.

At this point it can be seen that since the slope of a security's characteristic line is equal to the security's beta, a security's beta measures the sensitivity of the security's returns to the market portfolio's returns. Both lines in Figure 8.5 have positive slopes, indicating that the higher the returns on the market portfolio, the higher the returns on the two securities. However, the two securities have different slopes; hence they have different sensitivities to returns on the market portfolio. Specifically, security $A$ has a higher beta than security $B$; thus, the characteristic line of $A$ has a greater slope than

---

[20]This can be seen by remembering that the slope of a line connecting two points is equal to the vertical distance between the two points divided by the horizontal distance between the two points. In this example, such a calculation results in ( $6\% - 0\%$ )/( $5\% - 0\%$ ) = 1.2, the beta of security $A$.

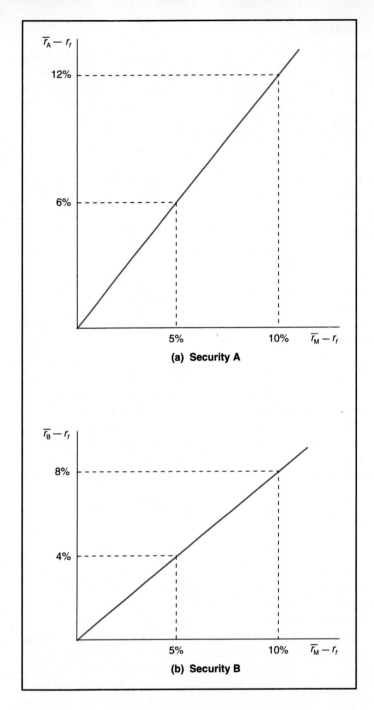

**FIGURE 8-5**
Characteristic lines.

the characteristic line of $B$, indicating that the returns on $A$ are more sensitive than the returns on $B$ to the returns on the market portfolio.

For example, if the market portfolio has a return that is 20%, it will have returned 5% more than expected (its expected return was 15%) and 10% more than the riskfree rate. Part (a) of Figure 8.5 indicates that security $A$ should have an excess return that is 12%, which is 6% ($[(20\% - 10\%) \times 1.2] - 6\%$) more than initially expected in this situation. Similarly, part (b) indicates that security $B$ should have an excess return that is 8%, which is 4% ($[(20\% - 10\%) \times .8] - 4\%$) more than initially expected in this situation. The reason for the 2%(6% − 4%) difference is because security $A$ has a higher beta than security B — that is, $A$ is more sensitive than $B$ to returns on the market portfolio.

The random error term suggests that for a given return on the market portfolio, the actual return on a security will lie off the line shown by its graph.[21] If the actual excess returns on securities $A$ and $B$ subsequently turn out to be 9% and 11%, respectively, and the market portfolio's actual excess return turns out to be 10%, then the actual excess return on $A$ and $B$ could be viewed as having the following two components:

|  | Security A | Security B |
|---|---|---|
| Actual excess return on the market portfolio × beta | 12% = 10% × 1.2 | 8% = 10% × .8 |
| Random error outcome | −3% = 9% − 12% | 3% = 11% − 8% |
| Actual excess return | 9% | 11% |

In this case, the roulette wheels for $A$ and $B$ can be thought of as having been "spun," resulting in values (that is, random error outcomes) of −3% for $A$ and +3% for $B$. These values can be viewed as being equal to the distance by which each security's actual return ended up being above or below its characteristic line.

## 8.8 DIVERSIFICATION

In equation (8.12) the total risk of any security i, measured by its standard deviation and denoted by $\sigma_i$, was shown to consist of two parts: (1) market (or systematic) risk, denoted by $\beta_i^2 \sigma_M^2$, and (2) unique (or nonmarket or unsystematic) risk, denoted by $\sigma_{\epsilon i}^2$.

The characteristic line provides a convenient interpretation for the term $\sigma_{\epsilon i}^2$ in this equation. This term is the variance of the random error term $\epsilon_i$ appearing in equation (8.17).

---

[21] To be completely accurate, if the random error term takes on a value of zero, then the security will lie *on* the line. However, the probability of this occurring is very small for most securities.

## ☐ 8.8.1 Portfolio Total Risk

When the return on every risky *security* is related to the return on the market portfolio as specified in equation (8.17), what can be said about the total risk of a *portfolio*? If the proportion of funds invested in security $i$ for a given portfolio $p$ is denoted by $X_i$, then the actual excess return on this portfolio will be:

$$r_p - r_f = \left( \sum_{i=1}^{N} X_i r_i \right) - r_f$$

$$= \sum_{i=1}^{N} X_i (r_i - r_f). \tag{8.20}$$

Substituting the right-hand side of equation (8.17) for $r_i - r_f$ in equation (8.20) results in the following characteristic line for the portfolio:

$$r_p - r_f = \sum_{i=1}^{N} X_i [(r_M - r_f)\beta_i + \epsilon_i]$$

$$= \left( \sum_{i=1}^{N} X_i \beta_i \right) (r_M - r_f) + \sum_{i=1}^{N} X_i \epsilon_i \tag{8.21}$$

$$= (r_M - r_f)\beta_p + \epsilon_p$$

where

$$\beta_p = \sum_{i=1}^{N} X_i \beta_i \tag{8.22a}$$

$$\epsilon_p = \sum_{i=1}^{N} X_i \epsilon_i. \tag{8.22b}$$

In equation (8.22a) the portfolio's beta ($\beta_p$) is shown to be a weighted average of the betas of the securities ($\beta_i$), using their relative proportions in the portfolio as weights. Similarly, in equation (8.22b) the portfolio's random error term ($\epsilon_p$) is a weighted average of the random error terms of the securities, again using their respective proportions in the portfolio as weights. Thus, the portfolio's characteristic line is a straightforward extension of the characteristic line for individual securities given in equation (8.17).

From equation (8.21), it follows that the total risk of a portfolio, measured by the standard deviation of the portfolio's returns and denoted by $\sigma_p$, will be

$$\sigma_p = [\beta_p^2 \sigma_M^2 + \sigma_{\epsilon p}^2]^{1/2} \tag{8.23}$$

where

$$\beta_p^2 = \left( \sum_{i=1}^{N} X_i \beta_i \right)^2 \tag{8.24a}$$

and, assuming the random error components of security returns are uncorrelated,

$$\sigma_{\epsilon p}^2 = \sum_{i=1}^{N} X_i^2 \sigma_{\epsilon i}^2. \tag{8.24b}$$

Equation (8.23) shows that the total risk of any portfolio can be viewed as having two components similar to the two components of the total risk of an individual security. These components are again referred to as market risk ($\beta_p^2 \sigma_M^2$) and unique risk ($\sigma_{\epsilon p}^2$).

Next, it will be shown that increased *diversification* can lead to the reduction of a portfolio's total risk. This will occur due to a reduction in the size of the portfolio's unique risk, whereas the portfolio's market risk will remain approximately the same size.

## ☐ 8.8.2  Portfolio Market Risk

Generally, the more diversified a portfolio (that is, the larger the number of securities in the portfolio), the smaller each proportion $X_i$ will be. This will not cause $\beta_p$ to either decrease or increase significantly unless a deliberate attempt is made to do so by adding either low or high beta securities, respectively, to the portfolio. That is, since a portfolio's beta is an average of the betas of its securities, there is no reason to suspect that increasing the amount of diversification will cause the portfolio beta, and thus the market risk of the portfolio, to change in a particular direction. Accordingly,

> Diversification leads to *averaging* of market risk.

This makes sense because when prospects for the economy turn sour (or rosy), most securities will fall (or rise) in price. Regardless of the amount of diversification, portfolio returns will always be susceptible to such market-wide influences.

## ☐ 8.8.3  Portfolio Unique Risk

The situation is entirely different for unique risk. In a portfolio, some securities will go up as a result of unexpected good news specific to the company that issued the securities (such as an unexpected discovery of a new drug by a pharmaceutical company). Other securities will go down as a result of unexpected company-specific bad news (such as an industrial accident by a chemical company). Looking forward, approximately as many companies can be expected to have good news as bad news, leading to little anticipated net impact on the return of a "well-diversified" portfolio. This means that as a portfolio becomes more diversified, the smaller its unique risk, and, in turn, its total risk, will be.

This can be quantified precisely if the random error components of returns are assumed to be uncorrelated, as was done when equation (8.24b) was written. Consider the following situation. If the amount invested in each security is equal, then the proportion $X_i$ will equal $1/N$ and the level of unique risk, as shown in equation (8.24b), will be equal to:

$$\sigma_{\epsilon p}^2 = \sum_{i=1}^{N} \left[ \frac{1}{N} \right]^2 \sigma_{\epsilon i}^2$$

$$= \frac{1}{N} \left[ \frac{\sigma_{\epsilon 1}^2 + \sigma_{\epsilon 2}^2 + \cdots + \sigma_{\epsilon N}^2}{N} \right]. \tag{8.25}$$

The value inside the square brackets in equation (8.25) is simply the average unique risk for the component securities. But the portfolio's unique risk is only $1/N$ as large as this, since the term ($1/N$) appears outside the square brackets. Now as the portfolio becomes more diversified, the number of securities in it (that is, $N$) becomes larger. In turn, this means that $1/N$ becomes smaller, resulting in the portfolio having less unique risk.[22] That is,

Diversification can substantially *reduce* unique risk.

Roughly speaking, a portfolio that has 20 or more securities in it will have a negligible amount of unique risk. This means that its total risk will be approximately equal to the amount of market risk that is present.[23] Thus, such portfolios are "well diversified."

## ☐ 8.8.4   An Example

Consider the two securities, $A$ and $B$, that were referred to earlier. These two securities had betas of 1.2 and .8, respectively, and the standard deviations of their random error terms were, respectively, 6.06% and 4.76%. Thus, given that $\sigma_{\epsilon A} = 6.06\%$ and $\sigma_{\epsilon B} = 4.76\%$, it follows that $\sigma_{\epsilon A}^2 = .0606^2 = .0037$ and $\sigma_{\epsilon B}^2 = .0476^2 = .0023$. Now, assume that the standard deviation of the market portfolio, $\sigma_M$, is 8%, which implies that the variance of the market portfolio is $.08^2 = .0064$. Using equation (8.12), this means that the standard deviation of securities $A$ and $B$ are, respectively, as follows:

$$\sigma_A = [(1.2^2 \times .0064) + .0037]^{1/2}$$
$$= (.0129)^{1/2}$$
$$= 11.36\%$$
$$\sigma_B = [(.8^2 \times .0064) + .0023]^{1/2}$$
$$= (.0064)^{1/2}$$
$$= 8.00\%.$$

### A Two-Security Portfolio

Consider combining securities $A$ and $B$ into a portfolio, with an equal amount of the investor's money going into each security. That is, consider a portfolio that has $X_A = .5$ and $X_B = .5$. Since $\beta_A = 1.2$ and $\beta_B = .8$, the beta of this portfolio can be calculated using equation (8.22a):

$$\beta_p = X_A\beta_A + X_B\beta_B$$
$$= (1.5 \times 1.2) + (.5 \times .8)$$
$$= 1.0.$$

Using equation (8.24b), the variance of the portfolio's random error term, $\sigma_{\epsilon p}^2$, will be equal to

$$\sigma_{\epsilon p} = (.5^2 \times .0037) + (.5^2 \times .0023)$$
$$= .0015.$$

---

[22] Actually, all that is necessary for this reduction in unique risk to occur is for the maximum amount invested in any one security to continually decrease as $N$ increases.

[23] See John L. Evans and Stephen Archer, "Diversification and the Reduction of Dispersion: An Empirical Analysis," *Journal of Finance* 23, no. 5 (December 1968):761–67.

In turn, this indicates that the standard deviation of the portfolio's random error term, $\sigma_{\epsilon p}$, is equal to:

$$\sigma_{\epsilon p} = \sqrt{.0015}$$
$$= 3.87\%.$$

From equation (8.23), it can be seen that this portfolio will have the following standard deviation:

$$\sigma_p = [(1.0^2 \times .0064) + .0015]^{1/2}$$
$$= [.0079]^{1/2}$$
$$= 8.89\%.$$

This represents the total risk of the two-security portfolio.

## A Three-Security Portfolio

Consider what would happen if a third security ($C$) was combined with the other two to form a three-security portfolio having $X_A = X_B = X_C = .33$. This third security has a beta of 1.0 and a random error term whose standard deviation ($\sigma_{\epsilon C}$) is 5.50%. Thus, the variance of the random error term is $\sigma_{\epsilon C}^2 = .055^2 = .0030$, and the security's standard deviation is

$$\sigma_C = [(1.0^2 \times .0064) + .0030]^{1/2}$$
$$= [.0094]^{1/2}$$
$$= 9.70\%.$$

First of all, note that the three-security portfolio has the same amount of market risk as the two-security portfolio, since both portfolios have a beta of 1.0:

$$\beta_p = X_A\beta_A + X_B\beta_B + X_C\beta_C$$
$$= (.33 \times 1.2) + (.33 \times .8) + (.33 \times 1.0)$$
$$= 1.0.$$

Thus, increased diversification has not lead to a change in the level of market risk. Instead, it has led to an averaging of market risk.

Using equation (8.24b), the variance of the portfolio's random error term will be equal to

$$\sigma_{\epsilon p}^2 = (.33^2 \times .0037) + (.33^2 \times .0023) + (.33^2 \times .0030)$$
$$= .0010.$$

In turn, this indicates that the standard deviation of the portfolio's random error term is equal to

$$\sigma_{\epsilon p}^2 = \sqrt{.0010}$$
$$= 3.13\%.$$

Note that the standard deviation of this three-security portfolio's random error term is less than the standard deviation of the two-security portfolio's random error term (that is, $3.13\% < 3.87\%$). In turn, the standard deviation of the two-security portfolio's random error term is less than the standard deviation of either one of the securities' random error terms (that is, $3.87\% < 6.06\%$ and $3.87\% < 4.76\%$). Thus, in this example increased diversification has indeed reduced unique risk.

From equation (8.23), it can be seen that this three-security portfolio will have the following standard deviation:

$$\sigma_p = [(1.0^2 \times .0064) + .0010]^{1/2}$$
$$= [.0074]^{1/2}$$
$$= 8.60\%.$$

This represents the total risk of the portfolio and is less than the total risk of the two-security portfolio ($8.60\% < 8.89\%$). Thus, diversification has led to a reduction in total risk.

---

## 8.9     DISEQUILIBRIUM

Many investors spend a great deal of time searching for securities that appear to be *mispriced*. There are two types of mispriced securities:

A security is *underpriced* (or undervalued) if its expected return is greater than the appropriate expected return for securities with comparable relevant attributes.

A security is *overpriced* (or overvalued) if its expected return is less than the appropriate expected return for securities with comparable relevant attributes.

What attributes are relevant? And what is the appropriate expected return for a given set of attributes? The answer depends on which equilibrium theory of asset pricing is used. For the CAPM, only one attribute is relevant (beta), and the appropriate expected return is that shown by the SML, as given in equation (8.15).

Security prices and expected returns either conform to a given equilibrium theory of asset pricing or they do not. If at least some securities do not conform to this theory, then according to that theory there is disequilibrium in their prices and expected returns. However, it is more likely that this particular theory is not valid and some other (perhaps unknown) equilibrium theory is valid. Instead of attempting to discover this theory, an incredibly difficult if not impossible task, many investors assume that most securities are priced to give equilibrium expected returns according to some theory, with certain other ones being mispriced and in disequilibrium.

It is important to note that investors will typically disagree on which securities are mispriced. Some investors may feel that a given security is underpriced, others may feel it is overpriced, and still others may feel it is priced correctly. One implication is that a security may not be mispriced when an investor believes it is mispriced. Keep in mind that the discussion that follows is from the perspective of one investor whose opinions may not be shared by anyone else.

## ☐ 8.9.1  Alpha

The extent to which an investor believes a security is mispriced can be measured by its *alpha*. The idea here is to compare the expected return on a security, denoted by $\bar{r}_i$, with the *equilibrium expected return* for the security, denoted by $\bar{r}_i^e$ in equation (8.15). The equilibrium expected return for a security is what the expected return "should be" if the security were priced correctly.

Specifically, a security's alpha is the *difference between its expected return and an appropriate (equilibrium) expected return*:

$$\alpha_i = \bar{r}_i - \bar{r}_i^e. \tag{8.26}$$

Thus, a security will be mispriced and in disequilibrium if, in the opinion of the investor, it has a nonzero alpha, since then its expected return $\bar{r}_i$ will not be equal to its equilibrium expected return $\bar{r}_i^e$. (How an investor can go about estimating a security's alpha is discussed in Chapter 16).

Equation (8.15) gives the value of the equilibrium expected return for any security based on the CAPM. Thus, equation (8.26) can be rewritten by substituting the right-hand side of equation (8.17) for $\bar{r}_i^e$ in equation (8.26), resulting in

$$\alpha_i = \bar{r}_i - [r_f + (\bar{r}_M - r_f)\beta_i]. \tag{8.27}$$

Equation (8.27) shows that an investor will view a security as being mispriced relative to the CAPM if he or she believes it has a nonzero alpha. This situation will occur if the investor has estimated the security's expected return $\bar{r}_i$ and found it to be different from $r_f + (\bar{r}_M - r_f)\beta_i$.

Continuing with the earlier example, imagine a certain investor has examined the two securities that were referred to as $A$ and $B$ and, as before, estimates their betas to be equal to 1.2 and .8, respectively. However, this investor has estimated the expected return for security $A$ over the forthcoming holding period to be equal to 18%. According to equation (8.27), he or she believes the security is mispriced, since it has a nonzero alpha equal to +2% = 18% − 16%. (Remember that earlier it was shown that any security with a beta of 1.2 has an equilibrium expected return of 16%).

In regard to security $B$, this investor has estimated its expected return to be equal to 13%. Noting it has a nonzero alpha of −1% = 13% − 14%, he or she believes that security $B$ is also mispriced.

Figure 8.6 provides a graphical illustration of this example. Since the expected return on the market portfolio has been assumed to be 15% and the risk-free rate has been assumed to be 10%, the location of the SML is the same as in Figure 8.3. As mentioned earlier, the SML indicates that any security with a beta of 1.2 that is priced correctly will have an expected return of 16%. Similarly, any security with a beta of .8 that is priced correctly will have an expected return of 14%.

It can be seen in Figure 8.6 that with the CAPM, a security's alpha is equal to the vertical distance by which it lies above or below the SML. Thus, a security with a positive estimated alpha (such as $A$) will lie above the SML and be viewed as underpriced. A security with a negative estimated alpha (such as $B$) will lie below the SML and be viewed as overpriced. Securities that are felt to be priced correctly will have estimated alphas of zero and lie on the SML.

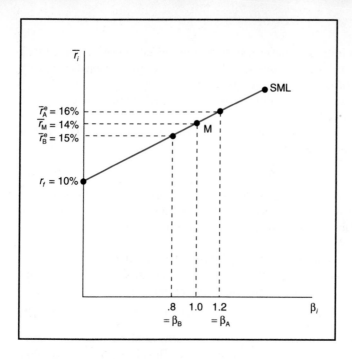

FIGURE 8-6
Alphas for securities.

## ☐ 8.9.2   The Return-Generating Process

Equation (8.27) can be rewritten as

$$\bar{r}_i - r_f = \alpha_i + (\bar{r}_M - r_f)\beta_i \tag{8.28}$$

thereby showing that the expected excess return for a security over the forthcoming holding period has two components, being equal to the sum of (1) the alpha of the security and (2) the product of the expected excess return on the market portfolio and the beta of the security.

However, equation (8.28) is not a model for what the actual excess return on a security will be over the forthcoming holding period. For this purpose a return-generating process that is based on equation (8.28) is used:

$$r_i - r_f = \alpha_i + (r_M - r_f)\beta_i + \epsilon_i. \tag{8.29}$$

It can be seen that, with the exception of alpha ($\alpha_i$), this return-generating process is identical to the one in equation (8.17). Thus, in cases where alpha is zero, the two are identical. Accordingly, equation (8.29) is known as the *characteristic line* for a security, with the one given in equation (8.17) being a special case where alpha is zero.

The characteristic line for security $i$ that is given in equation (8.29) suggests that the actual excess return for this particular security can be thought of as having three components. The first component is equal to the alpha of the security. The second component is equal to the actual excess return on the market portfolio, multiplied by the security's beta coefficient. The third component is equal to the random error term's outcome.

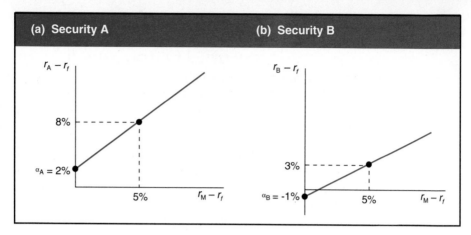

**FIGURE 8-7**
Characteristic lines (with disequilibrium).

In the case of the investor who has estimated security $A$'s alpha and beta to be equal to 2% and 1.2, respectively, the characteristic line for this security would look like:

$$r_A - r_f = 2\% + [(r_M - r_f) \times 1.2] + \epsilon_A. \qquad (8.30\,a)$$

Thus, the actual excess return of security $A$ will consist of an alpha of 2%, the excess return on the market portfolio multiplied by 1.2, and a random error term.

Similarly, the characteristic line for security $B$ would look like

$$r_B - r_f = -1\% + [(r_M - r_f) \times .8] + \epsilon_B \qquad (8.30\,b)$$

since its alpha and beta were estimated to be equal to $-1\%$ and .8, respectively.

## ☐ 8.9.3   Graphing Characteristic Lines

The solid line in panel (a) of Figure 8.7 provides a graph of the characteristic line for security $A$. This line corresponds to the return-generating process given in equation (8.30a) but without the random error term. Accordingly, the graph of the characteristic line for security $A$ corresponds to the following equation:

$$r_A - r_f = 2\% + [(r_M - r_f) \times 1.2].$$

Here the vertical axis measures the expected excess return on the particular security $(r_A - r_f)$, and the horizontal axis measures the expected excess return on the market portfolio $(r_M - r_f)$. The line goes through two points. First, the line goes through the point on the vertical axis corresponding to the value of alpha, which in this case is 2%. Second, the line goes through the point corresponding to the forecasted expected excess return on the security ( 18% − 10% = 8%) and on the market portfolio ( 15% − 10% = 5%). It should be noted that this line will have a slope equal to the beta of the security, which is 1.2 in this example.[24]

---

[24] The slope is equal to ( 8% − 2%)/( 5% − 0%) = 1.2, which is the beta of security $A$.

Part (b) of Figure 8.7 presents the graph of the characteristic line for security $B$:

$$r_B - r_f = -1\% + [(r_M - r_f) \times .8].$$

This line goes through the point on the vertical axis corresponding to the value of security's $B$ alpha, $-1\%$. It also goes through the point corresponding to the forecasted expected excess return on the security ( $13\% - 10\% = 3\%$) and on the market portfolio ( $15\% - 10\% = 5\%$) and has a slope equal to the beta of security $B$, which is .8 in this example.

These two characteristic lines are similar to those shown earlier in Figure 8.5. Both sets of characteristic lines have the same respective slopes, since these slopes correspond to the securities' betas, and these betas are the same regardless of whether or not the securities are mispriced. The only difference in the characteristic lines is in the location of the vertical intercepts. In Figure 8.5, both securities were assumed to be fairly priced and thus had alphas of zero. This resulted in the lines passing through the origin. However, if the securities are believed to be mispriced, then they will have nonzero alphas and their characteristic lines will have a nonzero vertical intercept that corresponds to their alphas as shown in Figure 8.7. Thus, the characteristic lines in Figure 8.7 are parallel to those shown in Figure 8.5.

As in Figure 8.5, the random error term indicates that for a given return on the market portfolio, the actual return on a security will lie off its characteristic line. For example, imagine as before that the actual excess returns on securities $A$ and $B$ subsequently turn out to be 9% and 11%, while the market portfolio's actual excess return turns out to be 10%. In this situation the actual excess returns on $A$ and $B$ would have the following three components, according to the investor who felt these two securities were initially mispriced:

|  | Security A | Security B |
| --- | --- | --- |
| Alpha | 2% | −1% |
| Actual excess return on the market portfolio times beta | 12% = 10% × 1.2 | 8% = 10% × .8 |
| Random error outcome | −5% = 9% − (2% + 12%) | 4% = 11% − (−1% + 8%) |
| Actual excess return | 9% | 11% |

In this case, the roulette wheels for $A$ and $B$ can be thought of as having been spun, resulting in values (that is, random error outcomes) of $-5\%$ for $A$ and $+4\%$ for $B$. These values can be viewed as being equal to the distance each security's actual return ended up being above or below its characteristic line after the holding period had elapsed. Note how these random error outcomes differ from those shown earlier for an investor who felt the securities were fairly priced. Specifically, they differ by the amount of alpha, since fairly priced securities have zero alphas.

# DETERMINING THE EFFICIENT SET

In Chapter 7, the tangency portfolio was shown to correspond to the point where a ray originating from the risk-free rate was tangent to the curved efficient set of risky securities. However, in order to determine the location and composition of the tangency portfolio, the investor must estimate the expected returns for all the securities under consideration as well as all the variances and pairwise covariances. This will enable the investor to construct the curved efficient set of Markowitz. Adding the risk-free rate will subsequently allow the tangency portfolio to be identified, thereby allowing the construction of the linear (that is, straight-line) efficient set. At this point, the optimal portfolio can be identified by noting where one of the investor's indifference curves is tangent to the linear efficient set.

Considerable effort is needed to construct this linear efficient set. First, the expected return for each security must be estimated. Given there are $N$ risky securities, this means that $N$ parameters must be estimated. Second, the variance for each one of these securities must be estimated. Again, since there are $N$ risky securities, this means that another $N$ parameters must be estimated. Third, the covariance between each pair of risky securities must be estimated. There are $(N^2 - N)/2$ of these parameters to be estimated.[25] Lastly, the risk-free rate must be determined. This means that in total the number of parameters that need to be estimated is equal to $(N^2 + 3N + 2)/2$, determined as follows:

| | |
|---|---|
| Expected returns | $N$ |
| Variances | $N$ |
| Covariances | $\dfrac{N^2 - N}{2}$ |
| Risk-free rate | $1$ |
| Total | $\dfrac{N^2 + 3N + 2}{2}$ |

For example, if there were 100 risky securities under consideration, then $[100^2 + (3 \times 100) + 2]/2 = 5151$ parameters would need to be estimated, consisting of 100 expected returns, 100 variances, 4950 covariances, and the risk-free rate. These parameters can be estimated one by one, a task that will be quite time-consuming if not, practically speaking, impossible. Alternatively, an approximate approach based on the characteristic line can be used.[26]

---

[25] This number was arrived at in the following manner. The variance-covariance matrix has $N$ rows and $N$ columns, meaning that there are $N^2$ cells in it whose corresponding parameters need to be estimated. The cells on the diagonal contain the $N$ variances mentioned earlier, leaving $(N^2 - N)$ parameters to be estimated. Since the variance-covariance matrix is symmetric, only those covariances below the diagonal need be estimated (this is because they also appear in corresponding locations above the diagonal), leaving a total of $(N^2 - N)/2$ parameters to be estimated.

[26] It is an approximate approach because it makes a number of assumptions, some of which are questionable. For example, this approach assumes that the random error terms for any two securities are uncorrelated (an assumption that was needed in deriving equation (8.24b)). This means that the outcome from a spin of the

With the "characteristic line approach," the risk-free rate and expected return on the market portfolio must be estimated initially. Then the alpha and beta for each security must be estimated. At this point, $(2 + 2N)$ parameters have been estimated (2 for $r_f$ and $\bar{r}_M$; $2N$ for the alpha and beta for each of $N$ risky securities). In turn, these figures can be used to estimate the expected return for each security using equation (8.28), restated as follows:

$$\bar{r}_i = \alpha_i + [r_f + (\bar{r}_M - r_f)\beta_i]. \qquad (8.31)$$

Earlier, the risk-free rate was determined to be 10% and the expected return on the market portfolio was estimated to be 15%. Given these figures, the expected return for security $A$ was estimated to be 18%, since the alpha and beta of this security were estimated to be 2% and 1.2, respectively:

$$\bar{r}_A = 2\% + 10\% + [(15\% - 10\%) \times 1.2]$$
$$= 18\%.$$

Similarly, the expected return for security $B$ was estimated to be 13%, since its alpha and beta were estimated to be -1% and .8%, respectively:

$$r_B = -1\% + 10\% + [(15\% - 10\%) \times .8]$$
$$= 13\%.$$

Using the characteristic line approach, the variance for any security $i$ can be estimated by multiplying the squared value of the security's beta by the variance of the market portfolio and then adding the variance of the random error term to the product. The equation for doing this is as follows:

$$\sigma_i^2 = \beta_i^2 \sigma_M^2 + \sigma_{\epsilon i}^2 \qquad (8.32)$$

where $\sigma_M^2$ denotes the variance on the market portfolio and $\sigma_{\epsilon i}^2$ denotes the variance of the random error term for security $i$.

Assuming the variance on the market portfolio is 49, the variances of security $A$ and $B$ can be estimated as follows:

$$\sigma_A^2 = (1.2^2 \times 49) + 6.06^2$$
$$= 107.28$$
$$\sigma_B^2 = (.8^2 \times 49) + 4.76^2$$
$$= 54.02$$

respectively. This means that the standard deviations of these securities are estimated to be equal to $10.38\% = \sqrt{107.28}$ and $7.35\% = \sqrt{54.02}$, respectively.

Lastly, the covariance between any two securities $i$ and $j$ can be estimated by the product of three numbers: the beta of security $i$, the beta of security $j$, and the variance of the market portfolio. That is, the following formula can be used:

$$\sigma_{ij} = \beta_i \beta_j \sigma_M^2. \qquad (8.33)$$

---

roulette wheel for one security (such as Mobil) has no bearing on the outcome from a spin of the roulette wheel of any other security (such as Exxon). It can be argued that this is not true for securities within certain industries. See Benjamin F. King, "Market and Industry Factors in Stock Price Behavior," *Journal of Business* 39, no. 1 (January 1966):139–70; and James L. Farrell, Jr., "Analyzing Covariation of Returns to Determine Homogeneous Stock Groupings," *Journal of Business* 47, no. 2 (April 1974):186–207.

Thus, for securities $A$ and $B$, their estimated covariance would be:

$$\sigma_{AB} = 1.2 \times .8 \times 49$$
$$= 47.04.$$

In summary, if the characteristic line approach is used to estimate expected returns, variances, and covariances, then the following parameters must first be estimated:

| | |
|---|---|
| Risk-free rate | 1 |
| Expected return on the market portfolio | 1 |
| Variance of the market portfolio | 1 |
| Alpha for each security | $N$ |
| Beta for each security | $N$ |
| Variance of random error term for each security | $N$ |
| Total | $3N + 3$ |

Thus, for 100 risky securities, $(3 \times 100) + 3 = 303$ parameters need to be estimated when the characteristic line approach is used to determine the efficient set and tangency portfolio. With this approach, once these 303 parameters have been estimated, then it is a simple matter to use equations (8.31), (8.32), and (8.33) to estimate the expected returns, variances, and covariances, in turn, for the risky securities. Alternatively, the expected returns, variances, and covariances could have been estimated one by one, as noted earlier, in which case 5151 parameters would need to be estimated. As can be seen with this example, the characteristic line approach results in a notable reduction in the number of parameters that need to be estimated.

With the characteristic line approach (or the one-by-one approach), after the expected returns, variances, and covariances have been estimated, a computer can be given these values along with the risk-free rate. Then, using a "quadratic programming algorithm" (such as the one described in Appendix A to Chapter 7), the computer can identify the composition and location of the tangency portfolio. Once this is done, the location of the linear efficient set can be determined by simply drawing a line between the risk-free rate and the tangency portfolio. At this juncture, the investor's optimal portfolio can be determined by noting where one of the indifference curves touches (but does not intersect) the linear efficient set.

## 8.11  SUMMARY

The capital asset pricing model is an economic model that describes how securities are priced in the marketplace. It has its roots in the normative mean-variance approach to investing that was first developed by Markowitz. That is, if certain assumptions are made, one of which is that all investors follow Markowitz's approach, then it can be shown that the expected return on a security will be positively and linearly related to the level of its beta. Simply put, the higher a security's beta, the higher its expected return. The beta of a security is, therefore, the relevant measure of the security's risk.

Conversely, the standard deviation (or variance) of a security is not the relevant measure of the security's risk.

The intuitive reasoning behind the CAPM is that each investor is concerned with the standard deviation of the portfolio that he or she holds. Since each investor holds the market portfolio, usually in conjunction with either borrowing or lending at the risk-free rate, this means that investors are concerned with the standard deviation of the market portfolio. Accordingly, individual securities are evaluated in terms of their contribution to the standard deviation of this portfolio. Since this contribution can be measured by the beta of the security, it follows that the relevant measure of the risk of a security is its beta.

This means that investors will consider holding a security with a higher beta only if it has a higher expected return. In a sense, investors have to be enticed to hold riskier securities, and the enticement that they demand is to have such securities carry higher levels of expected return.

An analogy can be made between forecasting the return on a given security and forecasting tomorrow's high temperature at a given location. In order to make the temperature forecast, the meteorologist needs some model for estimating what the expected high temperature will be. Similarly, the investor needs a model for estimating what a security's expected return will be. The version of the SML given in equation (8.28) is such a model. Here the term alpha was introduced as a measure of the amount of a security's mispricing. Positive alphas are indications of underpricing; negative alphas are indications of overpricing. In equilibrium, all securities will be fairly priced and will thus have alphas equal to zero.

A model for the actual high temperature that will occur tomorrow can be thought of as being similar to the expected high temperature model except that it involves actual outcomes and a random error term. A return-generating process known as the characteristic line, given in equation (8.29), provides a similar way of thinking about the actual return that will occur for a given security over the forthcoming holding period. Thus, there are two models for both the meteorologist and the investor. For the meteorologist, there is one for the expected high temperature and one for the actual high temperature. For the investor, there is one for expected returns (such as a version of the SML) and one for actual returns (such as the characteristic line).

Assuming the characteristic line is a reasonably accurate return-generating process for securities, it can be shown that the total risk of a portfolio has two components — market risk and unique risk. Increased diversification will typically lead to a reduction in the total risk of a portfolio until the portfolio contains roughly 20 securities. This can be attributed to a reduction in the amount of unique risk present in the portfolio, since increased diversification leads to an averaging of market risk. However, once the portfolio has roughly 20 securities in it, most of the unique risk will have disappeared, and further diversification will not have a noticeable impact on the total risk of the portfolio.

If securities are priced according to the CAPM, then the investor's optimal portfolio consists of purchasing the market portfolio and engaging in either risk-free lending or risk-free borrowing. If disequilibrium is introduced where an investor believes some securities have nonzero alphas, then the identification of the investor's optimal portfolio becomes more complicated. As shown in this chapter, one approach that is based on the CAPM involves the use of the concept of the characteristic line. This approach simplifies what needs to be forecast in order to determine the composition and location of the tangency portfolio, a portfolio that should be purchased (at least in part) by the investor.

# APPENDIX A

## SOME EXTENDED VERSIONS OF THE CAPM

The original capital asset pricing model makes strong assumptions and gives strong implications. In the years since it was developed, more complex models have been proposed. These models generally involve relaxing some of the assumptions associated with the original CAPM, and are often referred to as *extended versions of the CAPM* (or extended capital asset pricing models). Some of them are described in this appendix, and others are described in Chapter 9.

## A.1 EFFICIENT INVESTMENT POLICIES WHEN BORROWING IS RESTRICTED OR EXPENSIVE

### ☐ A.1.1 The Capital Market Line

The original CAPM assumes that investors can lend or borrow at the same risk-free rate of interest. In reality, such borrowing is likely to be either unavailable or restricted in amount. What impact might the relaxation of this risk-free borrowing assumption have on the CAPM?

A useful way to answer the question makes the following alternative assumptions: (1) investors can lend money risklessly — that is, they can purchase assets that provide a risk-free return of $r_{fL}$; or (2) investors can borrow money without limit at a higher rate of interest, $r_{fB}$. These risk-free rates are shown on the vertical axis of Figure 8.8; the "umbrella area" represents risk-return combinations available from investment solely in risky assets.[27]

If there are no opportunities to borrow or lend at the risk-free rate, the efficient set would be the curve $WT_LT_BY$, and many combinations of risky securities would be efficient. However, the availability of risk-free lending at the rate $r_{fL}$ makes the risky portfolios between $W$ and $T_L$ inefficient, since combinations of risk-free lending and the portfolio plotting at $T_L$ provide more return for the same risk.

Similarly, the ability to borrow money at rate $r_{fB}$ makes another portfolio, denoted by $T_B$, of special interest. Risky portfolios between $T_B$ and $Y$ are now inefficient, since levered holdings of $T_B$ dominate them by providing more return for the same risk.

Investors with attitudes toward risk that suggest neither borrowing nor lending should hold efficient combinations of risky securities plotting along curve $T_LT_B$. Accordingly, their holdings should be tailored to be consistent with differences in their degrees of aversion to risk.

In this situation the CML is now two lines and a curve, corresponding to the line going from $r_{fL}$ to $T_L$, then the curve from $T_L$ to $T_B$, and then the line from $T_B$ on out to the northeast in Figure 8.8.

---

[27] A more rigorous development of this figure is presented in Appendix B of Chapter 7.

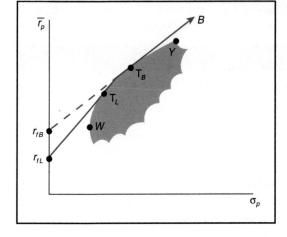

**FIGURE 8-8**

Efficient set when the risk-free rates are different.

## ☐ A.1.2 The Security Market Line

What becomes of the Security Market Line when the risk-free borrowing rate exceeds the risk-free lending rate? The answer depends on whether or not the market portfolio is in fact one of the efficient combinations of risky securities along the boundary between $T_L$ and $T_B$ in Figure 8.8.[28] If it is not, little more can be said. If it is, a great deal can be said.

Figure 8.9 shows a case in which the market portfolio (shown by point $M$) is efficient. In part (a) a line has been drawn that is tangent to the efficient set at point $M$. When this line is extended to the vertical axis, the resulting intercept is denoted $\bar{r}_z$. In part (b) only this tangency line is shown.

A striking characteristic of Figure 8.9(b) is this: It is precisely the same picture that would be produced in a market in which investors could borrow and lend without limit at a hypothetical risk-free rate equal in value to $\bar{r}_z$. Whereas only point $M$ along the line emanating from $\bar{r}_z$ would be attainable, the expected returns of risky securities would be the same as they would be in a hypothetical market with borrowing and lending at $\bar{r}_z$. That is, all risky securities (and portfolios consisting of these securities) would plot along an SML going through point $\bar{r}_z$, as shown in Figure 8.10.

The vertical intercept of the SML indicates the expected return on a security or portfolio with a beta of zero. Accordingly, this extension of the CAPM is termed the *zero-beta capital asset pricing model*. This version of the CAPM implies that the SML will be flatter than implied by the original version, since $\bar{r}_z$ will be above $r_{fL}$. As a practical matter, it means that $\bar{r}_z$ must be inferred from the prices of risky securities, since it cannot simply be found in the quotations of current prices on, for example, Treasury bills. Many organizations both in Canada and the United States that estimate the SML generally find that it conforms more to the zero-beta CAPM than to the original CAPM.

Cases in which borrowing is either impossible or costs more as one borrows larger amounts lead to only minor modifications in the conclusions. As long as the market

---

[28] If investors could obtain the proceeds from short sales and there were no restrictions on such sales, then the maket portfolio would definitely plot on the efficient set between $T_L$ and $T_B$.

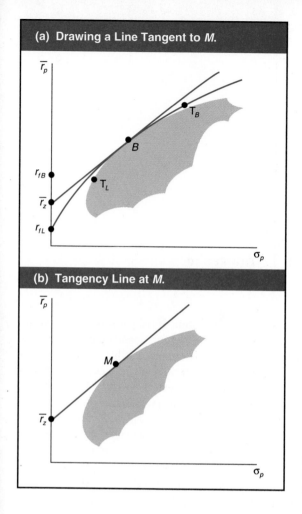

**(a) Drawing a Line Tangent to M.**

**(b) Tangency Line at M.**

FIGURE 8-9
Risk and return when the market portfolio is efficient.

portfolio is efficient, all securities will plot along an SML, but the "zero-beta return" will exceed the risk-free rate at which funds can be invested.

## A.2  HETEROGENEOUS EXPECTATIONS

A number of researchers have examined the implications of assuming that different investors have different perceptions about expected returns, standard deviations, and covariances. More specifically, the assumption of homogeneous expectations has been replaced by these researchers with an assumption of *heterogeneous expectations*.

In one such study, it was noted that each investor would face an efficient set that was unique to him or her.[29] This means that the tangency portfolio (denoted by $T$ in Chapter 7)

---

[29] John Lintner, "The Aggregation of Investor's Diverse Judgements and Preferences in Purely Competitive Security Markets," *Journal of Financial and Quantitative Analysis* 4, no. 4 (December 1969):347–400. For a discussion of the work of other researchers in this area (as well as other extensions of the CAPM), see Chapter 8 of Alexander and Francis, *Portfolio Analysis*.

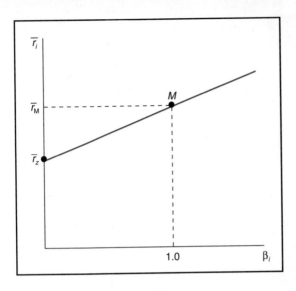

FIGURE 8-10
The "zero-beta" security market line.

is unique to each investor, since the optimal combination of risky assets for an investor depends on that investor's perceptions about expected returns, standard deviations, and covariances. Furthermore, an investor will likely determine that his or her tangency portfolio does not involve an investment in some securities (that is, certain securities may have zero proportions in the tangency portfolio). Nevertheless, the SML will still exist. This was shown by aggregating the holdings of all investors, and remembering that in equilibrium each security's price has to be at a level where the amount of the security demanded equals the supply of the security. Now, however, the equilibrium expected return for each security will be a complex weighted average of all investors' perceptions of its expected return. That is, from the viewpoint of a representative, or average, investor, each security will be priced fairly, so its expected return (as perceived by this investor) will be linearly and positively related to its beta.

## A.3    LIQUIDITY

The original CAPM assumes that investors are concerned only with risk and return. However, other characteristics may also be important to investors. For example, *liquidity* may be important. Here, liquidity refers to the cost of selling or buying a security "in a hurry." For example, a house is regarded as a relatively illiquid investment, since usually a "fair" price for it cannot be obtained quickly. In terms of securities, liquidity may be measured by the size of the spread between the bid and ask prices, with smaller spreads suggesting greater liquidity. Furthermore, it is reasonable to assume that many investors would find more liquid portfolios to be more attractive, keeping everything else the same. However, investors undoubtedly differ in their attitudes toward liquidity. For some it is very important; for others, somewhat important; and for yet others, of little importance.

Under these conditions, security prices would adjust until, overall, investors would be content to hold the outstanding securities. The expected return of a security would be based on two characteristics of the security:

1. The marginal contribution of the security to the risk of an efficient portfolio. This would be measured by the familiar beta $(\beta_i)$ of the security.
2. The marginal contribution of the security to the liquidity of an efficient portfolio. This would be measured by the liquidity $(L_i)$ of the security.

Now, other things equal, investors dislike large values of $\beta_i$ but like large values of $L_i$. This means that two securities with the same beta but different liquidities would not have the same level of expected return. To understand why they would have different levels of expected return, consider what would happen if they had the same level of expected return. In such a situation investors would buy the security with the greater liquidity and sell the one with the lesser liquidity. This would push the price of the first security up and the second one down. Ultimately, in equilibrium the quantity demanded would equal the quantity supplied and the security with the greater liquidity would have a relatively lower expected return. Similarly, two securities with the same liquidity but different betas would not have the same level of expected return. Instead, the security with the higher beta would have a higher expected return.

Figure 8.11 shows the equilibrium relationship one might expect among $\bar{r}_i$, $\beta_i$, and $L_i$. For a given level of $\beta_i$, more liquid securities have lower expected returns. And for a given level of $L_i$, more risky securities have higher expected returns as in the original CAPM. Lastly, there are securities with various levels of $\beta_i$ and $L_i$ that provide the same level of $\bar{r}_i$. The figure is three-dimensional, since now expected returns are related to two characteristics of securities. Accordingly, it is sometimes referred to as a *Security Market Plane*.[30]

If expected returns are based on beta, liquidity, and a third characteristic, then a four-dimensional CAPM would be necessary to describe the corresponding equilibrium.[31] Although a diagram cannot be drawn for this type of extended CAPM, an equation can be written for it. Such an equation, by analogy to the three-dimensional plane, is termed a *hyperplane*.

Whether or not liquidity is an important characteristic of securities has not been demonstrated in a Canadian context. Taxes, however, have been shown to affect before-tax returns on Canadian stocks in a similar way to that found in the United States.[32]

> In equilibrium, all securities will plot on a *Security Market Hyperplane*, where each axis measures the contribution of a security to a characteristic of efficient portfolios that matter (on average) to investors.

---

[30] The term Security Market Plane is a trademark of Wells Fargo Bank. For more on the relationship between liquidity and stock returns, see Yakov Amihud and Haim Mendelson, "Liquidity and Stock Returns," *Financial Analysts Journal* 42, no. 3 (May/June 1986):43–48, and "Asset Pricing and the Bid-Ask Spread," *Journal of Financial Economics* 17, no. 2 (December 1986):223–49.

[31] In the United States taxes were thought to be such a characteristic before the *Tax Reform Act* of 1986, when the tax rate on income from capital gains was less than the tax rate on dividend income. In considering such taxes, one study found that the before-tax expected return of a security was a positive linear function of its beta and its dividend yield. That is, the higher a security's beta or dividend yield, the higher its before-tax expected return. The reason securities with higher dividend yields would have had higher before-tax expected returns was because they would be taxed more heavily. See M. J. Brennan. "Taxes, Market Valuation and Corporate Financial Policy," *National Tax Journal* 23, no. 4 (December 1970):417–27. The issue of whether or not dividends influence before-tax expected returns has been contentious; it is discussed in Chapters 15 and 16 of Thomas E. Copeland and J. Fred Weston, *Financial Theory and Corporate Policy*, (Reading, Mass.: Addison-Wesley, 1988).

[32] See I.G. Morgan, "Dividends and Stock Price Behavior in Canada," *Journal of Business Administration* 12 (Fall 1980):91–106.

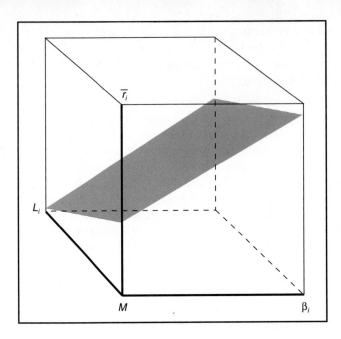

**FIGURE 8-11**
Security market plane.

The relationship between the expected return of a security and its contribution to a particular characteristic of efficient portfolios depends on the attitudes of investors to the characteristic:

> If, on the average, a characteristic (such as liquidity) is liked by investors, then those securities that contribute more to that characteristic will, other things equal, offer lower expected returns. Conversely, if a characteristic (such as beta) is disliked by investors, then those securities that contribute more to that characteristic will offer higher expected returns.

In a capital market with many relevant characteristics, the task of tailoring a portfolio for a specific investor is more complicated, since only an investor with average attitudes and circumstances should hold the market portfolio. In general:

> If an investor likes a characteristic more (or dislikes it less) than the average investor, he or she should generally hold a portfolio with relatively more of that characteristic than is provided by holding the market portfolio. Conversely, if an investor likes a characteristic less (or dislikes it more) than the average investor, he or she should generally hold a portfolio with relatively less of that characteristic than is provided by holding the market portfolio.

For example, consider an investor who likes having a relatively liquid portfolio. Such an investor should hold a portfolio consisting of relatively liquid securities. Conversely, an investor who has relatively little need for liquidity should hold a portfolio of relatively illiquid securities.

The right combination of "tilt" away from market proportions will depend on the extent of the differences between the investor's attitudes and those of the average investor and on the added risk involved in such a strategy. A complex capital market requires all the tools of modern portfolio theory for managing the money of any investor

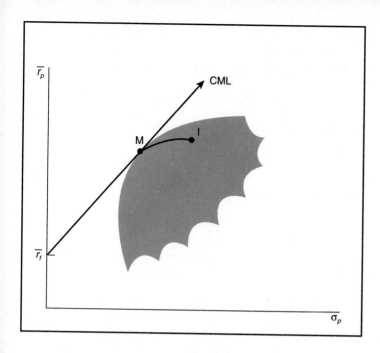

**FIGURE 8-12**
Deriving the security market line.

who is significantly different from the "average investor." On the other hand, in such a world, investment management should be relatively passive: After the selection of an initial portfolio, there should be minor and infrequent changes.

## APPENDIX B

## A DERIVATION OF THE SECURITY MARKET LINE

Figure 8.12 shows the location of the feasible set of the Markowitz model, along with the risk-free rate and the associated efficient set that represents the capital market line. Within the feasible set of the Markowitz model lies every individual risky security. An arbitrarily chosen risky security, denoted by i, has been selected for analysis and is shown on the figure.

Consider any portfolio, denoted by p, that consists of the proportion $X_i$ invested in security $i$ and the proportion $1 - X_i$ invested in the market portfolio $M$. Such a portfolio will have an expected return equal to

$$\bar{r}_p = X_i\bar{r}_i + (1 - X_i)\bar{r}_M \tag{8.34}$$

and a standard deviation equal to

$$\sigma_p = [X_i^2\sigma_i^2 + (1 - X_i)^2\sigma_M^2 + 2X_i(1 - X_i)\sigma_{iM}]^{1/2}. \tag{8.35}$$

All such portfolios will lie on a curved line connecting $i$ and $M$, such as the one shown in Figure 8.12.

Of concern is the slope of this curved line. Since it is a curved line, its slope is not a constant. However, its slope can be determined with the use of calculus. First, using equation (8.34), the derivative of $\bar{r}_p$ with respect to $X_i$ is taken:

$$\frac{d\bar{r}_p}{dX_i} = \bar{r}_i - \bar{r}_M.$$  (8.36)

Second, using equation (8.35), the derivative of $\sigma_p$ with respect to $X_i$ is taken:

$$\frac{d\sigma_p}{dX_i} = \frac{X_i\sigma_i^2 - \sigma_M^2 + X_i\sigma_M^2 + \sigma_{iM} - 2X_i\sigma_{iM}}{[X_i^2\sigma_i^2 + (1 - X_i)^2\sigma_M^2 + 2X_i(1 - X_i)\sigma_{iM}]^{1/2}}.$$  (8.37)

Third, it can be noted the slope of the curved line $iM$, $d\bar{r}_p/d\sigma_p$, can be written as:

$$\frac{d\bar{r}_p}{d\sigma_p} = \frac{d\bar{r}_p/dX_i}{d\sigma_p/dX_i}$$  (8.38)

Finally, the slope of $iM$ can be calculated by substituting equations (8.36) and (8.37) into the numerator and denominator of equation (8.38), respectively:

$$\frac{d\bar{r}_p}{d\sigma_p} = \frac{[\bar{r}_i - \bar{r}_M][X_i^2\sigma_i^2 + (1 - X_i)^2\sigma_M^2 + 2X_i(1 - X_i)\sigma_{iM}]^{1/2}}{X_i\sigma_i^2 - \sigma_M^2 + X_i\sigma_M^2 + \sigma_{iM} - 2X_i\sigma_{iM}}.$$  (8.39)

Of interest is the slope of the curved line $iM$ at the endpoint $M$. Since the proportion $X_i$ is zero at this point, the slope of $iM$ can be calculated by substituting zero for $X_i$ in equation (8.39). After doing so, many terms drop out, leaving:

$$\frac{d\bar{r}_p}{d\sigma_p} = \frac{[\bar{r}_i - \bar{r}_M][\sigma_M]}{\sigma_{iM} - \sigma_M^2}.$$  (8.40)

At $M$ the slope of the CML, $(\bar{r}_M - r_f)/\sigma_M$, must equal the slope of the curved line $iM$. This is because the slope of the curved line $iM$ increases when moving from the endpoint $i$, converging to the slope of the CML at the endpoint $M$. Accordingly, the slope of the curve $iM$ at $M$, as shown on the right-hand side of equation (8.40), is set equal to the slope of the CML:

$$\frac{[\bar{r}_i - \bar{r}_M][\sigma_M]}{\sigma_{iM} - \sigma_M^2} = \frac{\bar{r}_M - r_f}{\sigma_M}.$$  (8.41)

Solving equation (8.41) for $r_i$ results in the covariance version of the SML:

$$\bar{r}_i = r_f + \left[\frac{\bar{r}_M - r_f}{\sigma_M^2}\right]\sigma_{iM}.$$  (8.6)

The beta version of the SML is derived by substituting $\beta_i$ for $\sigma_{iM}/\sigma_M^2$ in equation (8.6).

1. Will an investor who owns the market portfolio have to buy and sell units of the component securities every time the relative prices of those securities change? Why?

2. Explain the significance of the slope of the SML. How might the slope of the SML change over time?

3. The risk of an efficient portfolio to an investor is measured by the standard deviation of the portfolio's returns. Why shouldn't the risk of an individual security be calculated in the same manner?

4. It is true that a security with a high standard deviation of returns is not necessarily highly risky to an investor. Why might you suspect that securities with above-average standard deviations of returns tend to have above-average betas?

5. You are given the following information on two securities, the market portfolio, and the risk-free rate:

| | Expected Return | Correlation with Market Portfolio | Standard Deviation |
|---|---|---|---|
| Security 1 | 15.5% | 0.90 | 20.0% |
| Security 2 | 9.2 | 0.80 | 9.0 |
| Market Portfolio | 12.0 | 1.00 | 12.0 |
| Risk-free Rate | 5.0 | 0.00 | 0.0 |

    a. Draw the SML.
    b. What are the betas of the two securities?
    c. Plot the two securities on the SML.

6. Is an investor who owns any portfolio of risky assets other than the market portfolio exposed to some unique risk?

7. Consider the following information:

| Security | Beta | Equilibrium Expected Return | Expected Return |
|---|---|---|---|
| A | 1.75 | 21.0% | 16.7% |
| B | 1.20 | 16.6 | 24.0 |
| C | 1.30 | 17.4 | 17.4 |
| D | 0.75 | 13.0 | 16.0 |

The risk-free interest rate is 7% and the market portfolio's expected return is 15%.
    a. Calculate the securities' expected alphas.
    b. Plot the SML and the securities' expected returns and equilibrium expected returns.
    c. What should be your investment action with respect to each of these securities?

8. With respect to the return-generating process, how is the standard deviation of the random error term related to the characteristic line?

9. In the following table you are presented with ten years of excess return data for Hartford Inc. and the market portfolio. Plot these excess returns on a graph, with the market portfolio's excess returns on the horizontal axis and Hartford's excess returns on the vertical axis. Draw your best guess of the characteristic line through these points. From this graph only, compute an estimate of the beta of Hartford's stock.

| Year | Hartford Inc. | Market Portfolio |
|------|---------------|------------------|
| 1 | 8.1% | 8.0% |
| 2 | 3.0 | 0.0 |
| 3 | 5.3 | 14.9 |
| 4 | 1.0 | 5.0 |
| 5 | −3.1 | −4.1 |
| 6 | −3.0 | −8.9 |
| 7 | 5.0 | 10.1 |
| 8 | 3.2 | 5.0 |
| 9 | 1.2 | 1.5 |
| 10 | 1.3 | 2.4 |

10. Consider the stocks of two companies, Aurora Ltd. and Burlington Associates.
    a. If you are told that the slope of Aurora Ltd.'s characteristic line is 1.20 and the slope of Burlington Associates' characteristic line is 1.00, which stock is more risky? Why?
    b. If you are now also told that the standard deviation of the random error term for Aurora stock is 10.0%, while it is 21.5% for Burlington stock, how is your answer changed? Explain.

11. You are given the following information on three stocks that make up your portfolio. In addition, you know that the market portfolio has an expected return of 13% and a standard deviation of 18%. The risk-free rate is 5%.

| Stock | Beta | Standard Deviation of Random Error Term | Weight in Portfolio |
|-------|------|------------------------------------------|---------------------|
| A | 1.10 | 7.0% | 29% |
| B | 0.80 | 2.3 | 50 |
| C | 1.00 | 1.0 | 30 |

    a. What is the portfolio's equilibrium expected return?
    b. What is the portfolio's standard deviation?

12. Why is the characteristic line approach a considerably more practical technique than the original Markowitz approach for constructing the efficient set?

# SUGGESTED READINGS

William F. Sharpe, "Capital Asset Prices: A Theory of Market Equilibrium," *Journal of Finance* 19, no. 3 (September 1964):425–42,

John Lintner, "The Valuation of Risk Assets and the Selection of Risky Investments in Stock Portfolios and Capital Budgets," *Review of Economics and Statistics* 47, no. 1 (February 1966):13–37,

Jan Mossin, "Equilibrium in a Capital Asset Market," *Econometrica*, 34, no. 4 (October 1966):768–83, and

Jack Treynor, "Towards a Theory of Market Value of Risky Assets," unpublished manuscript, 1961, all developed the CAPM in a different manner.

Burton G. Malkiel, *A Random Walk Down Wall Street*, (New York, NY: W.W. Norton and Company, 1985) provides a good intuitive explanation of the CAPM.

Fischer Black, "Capital Market Equilibrium with Restricted Borrowing," *Journal of Business* 45, no. 3 (July 1972):444–55 first developed the zero-beta version of the CAPM.

Gordon J. Alexander and Jack Clark Francis, *Portfolio Analysis* (Englewood Cliffs, NJ: Prentice Hall, 1986). Chapter 8 describes other extensions of the CAPM.

# Chapter 9

## FACTOR MODELS AND ARBITRAGE PRICING THEORY

The objective of modern portfolio theory is to provide a means by which the investor can identify his or her optimal portfolio when there are an infinite number of possibilities. Using a framework involving expected returns and standard deviations, it was shown that the investor needs to estimate the expected return and standard deviation for each security under consideration for inclusion in the portfolio, along with all the covariances. With these estimates, the investor can derive the curved efficient set of Markowitz. Then, for a given risk-free rate, the investor can identify the tangency portfolio and determine the location of the linear efficient set. Finally, the investor can invest in the tangency portfolio and borrow or lend at the risk-free rate, with the amount of borrowing or lending depending on the investor's risk-return preferences.

Chapter 8 presented a type of return-generating process known as the characteristic line. However, there are many other types of return-generating processes for securities. These types of processes are often called *factor models* (or index models) because they assert that the return on a security is sensitive to the movements of various *factors* (or indices). In attempting to accurately estimate expected returns, variances, and covariances for securities, these models are potentially more useful than the characteristic line. They have this potential because it appears that actual security returns are sensitive to more than movements in the market portfolio.[1] That is, within the economy there seems to be more than one pervasive factor that affects security returns. Given the belief that there is more than one factor, a goal of security analysis is to identify these factors in the economy and the sensitivities of security returns to movements in these factors. A formal statement of such a relationship is termed a *factor model of security returns*. The discussion begins with the simplest form of such a model, a *single-factor model*.

---

[1] For example, see William F. Sharpe, "Factors in NYSE Security Returns, 1931–1979," *Journal of Portfolio Management* 8, no. 4 (Summer 1982):5–19. Other studies are cited in William F. Sharpe, "Factor Models, CAPMs, and the ABT (sic)," *Journal of Portfolio Management* 11, no. 1 (Fall 1984):21–25.

# SINGLE-FACTOR MODELS

Some investors argue that the return-generating process for securities involves a single factor. Some examples of such a single factor include the growth rate in gross national product (GNP) and the growth rate in industrial production. In general, a single-factor model can be represented in equation form as follows:

$$r_i = a_i + b_i F + e_i \qquad (9.1)$$

where $F$ is the value of the factor and $b_i$ is the *sensitivity* of security $i$ to this factor (sometimes $b_i$ is referred to as the factor loading or attribute of the security). If the value of the factor were zero, the return on the security would equal $a_i + e_i$. Here $e_i$ is a random error term just like the random error term that was discussed in Chapter 8. That is, it is a random variable with an expected value of zero and a given standard deviation $\sigma_{ei}$, and it can be thought of as the outcome occurring from a spin of a roulette wheel. This means that the expected return on security $i$, according to the single-factor model, can be written as:

$$\bar{r}_i = a_i + b_i \bar{F}. \qquad (9.2)$$

Thus, the term $a_i$ can be seen to represent the expected return on security $i$ if the expected value of the factor was zero.

With the single-factor model, it can also be shown that the variance of any security $i$ is equal to

$$\sigma_i^2 = b_i^2 \sigma_F^2 + \sigma_{ei}^2 \qquad (9.3)$$

where $\sigma_F^2$ is the variance of the factor $F$ and $\sigma_{ei}^2$ is the variance of the random error term $e_i$. Furthermore, the covariance between any two securities $i$ and $j$ can be shown to equal

$$\sigma_{ij} = b_i b_j \sigma_F^2. \qquad (9.4)$$

Equations (9.3) and (9.4) are based on two critical assumptions. The first assumption is that the random error term and the factor are uncorrelated, meaning that the outcome of the factor has no bearing on the outcome of the random error term. The second assumption is that the random error terms of any two securities are uncorrelated, meaning that the outcome of the random error term of one security has no bearing on the outcome of the random error term of any other security. In other words, the returns of two securities will be correlated (that is, move together) only through common reactions to the factor. If either of these two assumptions is invalid, then the model is an approximation and a different factor model (perhaps one with more factors) will theoretically be a more accurate model of the return-generating process.

The characteristic line can now be shown to be an example of a single-factor model where the factor is the return on the market portfolio. In Chapter 8, the characteristic line appeared as

$$r_i - r_f = \alpha_i + (r_M - r_f)\beta_i + \epsilon_i \qquad (8.29)$$

where $\alpha_i$ and $\beta_i$ are the alpha and beta of the security, respectively, and $\epsilon_i$ is a random error term with an expected value of zero and a standard deviation of $\sigma_{\epsilon i}$. However, this equation can be rewritten as:

$$
\begin{aligned}
r_i &= r_f + \alpha_i + (r_M - r_f)\beta_i + \epsilon_i \\
&= [\alpha_i + r_f(1 - \beta_i)] + \beta_i r_M + \epsilon_i. \qquad (9.5)
\end{aligned}
$$

Comparing equation (9.5) with the general form of the single-factor model given in equation (9.1), it can be seen that the characteristic line is an example of a single-factor model where the factor is the return on the market portfolio (that is, $F = r_M$). Furthermore, the terms $a_i$ and $b_i$ of the single-factor model can be interpreted to be equal to $[\alpha_i + r_f(1 - \beta_i)]$ and $\beta_i$, respectively.

As an illustration, assume security $i$ has $\alpha_i = +3\%$ and $\beta_i = .9$. Given a risk-free rate of 10%, the characteristic line of this security is

$$r_i - 10\% = 3\% + [(r_M - 10\%) \times .9] + \epsilon_i \qquad (9.6)$$

which can be rewritten as follows:

$$r_i = 10\% + 3\% + [(r_M - 10\%) \times .9)] + \epsilon_i$$
$$= 4\% + .9\, r_M + \epsilon_i. \qquad (9.7)$$

Note how the characteristic line for security $i$, when rewritten as in equation (9.7), is similar to the single-factor model of equation (9.1), where the factor is the return on the market portfolio (that is, $F = r_M$) and $a_i = 4\%$, $b_i = .9$, and $e_i = \epsilon_i$.

However, as mentioned earlier, there are other examples of single-factor models. An investor may believe that it is more accurate to view security returns as being related to one common factor such as the growth rate in GNP. For this investor, $F$ is the growth rate in GNP, $b_i$ is the sensitivity of security $i$ to the growth rate in GNP, and $a_i$ is the expected return of security $i$ if there is zero growth in GNP.

## ☐ 9.1.1 Two Important Features of Single-Factor Models

There are two features of single-factor models that are of interest. First, in order to determine the composition of the tangency portfolio, the investor needs to estimate all the expected returns, variances, and covariances. This can be done with a single-factor model by estimating $a_i$, $b_i$, and $\sigma_{ei}$ for each of the $N$ risky securities. Also needed are the expected value of the factor, $F$, and its standard deviation, $\sigma_F$. With these estimates, equations (9.2), (9.3), and (9.4) can subsequently be used to calculate the expected returns, variances, and covariances for the securities. Using these values, the curved efficient set of Markowitz can then be derived, from which the tangency portfolio can be determined for a given risk-free rate.[2]

The second interesting feature of single-factor models has to do with diversification. Earlier it was shown that diversification leads to averaging of market risk and a reduction in unique risk. This feature is also true for any single-factor model, except now instead of market and unique risk, the words factor and nonfactor risk are used. That is, in equation (9.3) the first term on the right-hand side is known as the *factor risk* of the security, and the second term is known as the *nonfactor* (or idiosyncratic) *risk* of the security.

---

[2] In the case of the characteristic line, this means that the investor needs to estimate $\alpha_i$, $\beta_i$, and $\sigma_{ei}$ for each of the $N$ risky securities; also needed are the expected return on the market portfolio, $\bar{r}_M$, and its standard deviation, $\sigma_M$ along with the risk-free rate, $r_f$. See Chapter 8 for more details.

With a single-factor model, the standard deviation of a portfolio is equal to

$$\sigma_p = \left[ \left( \sum_{i=1}^{N} X_i b_i \right)^2 \sigma_F^2 + \sum_{i=1}^{N} X_i^2 \sigma_{ei}^2 \right]^{1/2}$$

$$= (b_p^2 \sigma_F^2 + \sigma_{ep}^2)^{1/2} \tag{9.8a}$$

where:

$$b_p = \sum_{i=1}^{N} X_i b_i \tag{9.8b}$$

$$\sigma_{ep}^2 = \sum_{i=1}^{N} X_i^2 \sigma_{ei}^2. \tag{9.8c}$$

Equation (9.8a) shows that the total risk of any portfolio can be viewed as having two components similar to the two components of the total risk of an individual security shown in equation (9.3). In particular, the first and second terms on the right-hand side of equation (9.8a) are the factor risk and nonfactor risk of the portfolio, respectively.

As a portfolio becomes more diversified, meaning the number of securities in it becomes larger, each proportion $X_i$ will become smaller. However, this will not cause $b_p$ either to decrease or to increase significantly unless a deliberate attempt is made to do so by having securities with values of $b_i$ that are either low or high, respectively. This is because, as equation (9.8b) shows, $b_p$ is simply a weighted average of the sensitivities of the securities, $b_i$, with the values of $X_i$ serving as weights. Thus, *diversification leads to an averaging of factor risk.*

However, it can be shown that as a portfolio becomes more diversified, there is reason to expect $\sigma_{ep}^2$, the nonfactor risk, to decrease. This can be shown by examining equation (9.8c). Assuming the amount invested in each security is equal, then this equation can be rewritten by substituting $1/N$ for $X_i$:

$$\sigma_{ep}^2 = \sum_{i=1}^{N} \left[ \frac{1}{N} \right]^2 \sigma_{ei}^2$$

$$= \frac{1}{N} \left[ \frac{(\sigma_{e1}^2 + \sigma_{e2}^2 + \cdots + \sigma_{eN}^2)}{N} \right].$$

The value inside the brackets is the average nonfactor risk for the component securities. But the portfolio's nonfactor risk is only $1/N$ as large as this, since the term $1/N$ also appears outside the brackets. Thus, as the portfolio becomes more diversified, the number of securities $N$ in it becomes larger. This means that $1/N$ becomes smaller, which in turn reduces the nonfactor risk of the portfolio. Simply stated, *diversification reduces nonfactor risk.*[3]

---

[3] Actually, all that is necessary for this reduction in nonfactor risk to occur is for the maximum amount invested in any one security to continually decrease as $N$ increases.

# MULTIPLE-FACTOR MODELS

The health of the economy affects most firms, and thus changes in expectations concerning the future of the economy can be expected to have profound effects on the returns of most securities. However, the economy is not a simple, monolithic entity. Several common influences with pervasive effects might be identified:

1. Expectations about the growth rate of real GNP
2. Expectations about real interest rates
3. Expectations about levels of inflation
4. Expectations about future oil prices

Instead of a single-factor model, a multiple-factor model for security returns that considers these various influences may be more accurate. As an example of a multiple-factor model, consider a two-factor model. That is, assume the return-generating process contains two factors.

## ☐ 9.2.1   Two-Factor Models

In equation form, the two-factor model is as follows:

$$r_i = a_i + b_{i1} F_1 + b_{i2} F_2 + e_i \qquad (9.9)$$

where $F_1$ and $F_2$ are the two factors that are pervasive influences on security returns (for example, $F_1$ could be the growth rate in GNP and $F_2$ could be the rate of inflation); and $b_{i1}$ and $b_{i2}$ are the sensitivities of security $i$ to these two factors. As with the single-factor model, $e_i$ is a random error term and $a_i$ is the expected return on security $i$ if each factor has a value of zero.

Four parameters need to be estimated for each security with the two-factor model. They are $a_i$, $b_{i1}$, $b_{i2}$, and the standard deviation of the random error term, denoted by $\sigma_{ei}$. For each of the factors, two parameters need to be estimated. These parameters are the expected value of each factor ($\overline{F}_1$ and $\overline{F}_2$) and the standard deviation of each factor ($\sigma_{F1}$ and $\sigma_{F2}$).

With these estimates, the expected return for any security $i$ can be determined by using the following formula:

$$\bar{r}_i = a_i + b_{i1} \overline{F}_1 + b_{i2} \overline{F}_2. \qquad (9.10)$$

If the factors are uncorrelated, then the variance for any security $i$ will be

$$\sigma_i^2 = b_{i1}^2 \sigma_{F1}^2 + b_{i2}^2 \sigma_{F2}^2 + \sigma_{ei}^2 \qquad (9.11)$$

and the covariance between any two securities $i$ and $j$ can be determined by

$$\sigma_{ij} = b_{i1} b_{j1} \sigma_{F1}^2 + b_{i2} b_{j2} \sigma_{F2}^2. \qquad (9.12)$$

If the factors are correlated, then more complex equations are needed to determine variances and covariances.[4]

---

[4] If the factors are correlated, then equation (9.11) would need to have the term $2 b_{i1} b_{i2} \text{COV}(F_1, F_2)$ added to its right-hand side, and equation (9.12) would need to have the term $(b_{i1} b_{j2} + b_{i2} b_{j1}) \text{COV}(F_1, F_2)$ added to its right-hand side. Here $\text{COV}(F_1, F_2)$ denotes the covariance between the two factors and is equal to the correlation between them times the product of their standard deviations, $\sigma_{F1}$ and $\sigma_{F2}$. Other assumptions are also necessary; for example, the random error terms must be uncorrelated with each other and with each factor.

As with the single-factor model, once the expected returns, variances, and covariances have been determined using these equations, the investor can derive the curved efficient set of Markowitz. Then, for a given risk-free rate, the tangency portfolio can be identified, after which the investor can determine his or her optimal portfolio.

Everything said earlier regarding single-factor models and the effects of diversification apply here as well:

1. Diversification leads to averaging of factor risk.
2. Diversification can substantially reduce nonfactor risk.
3. For a "well-diversified portfolio," nonfactor risk will be insignificant.

As with a single-factor model, the sensitivity of a portfolio to a particular factor in a multiple-factor model is a weighted average of the sensitivities of the securities, where the weights are equal to the proportion invested in each security. This can be seen by noting that the return on a portfolio is a weighted average of the returns of its component securities:

$$r_p = \sum_{i=1}^{N} X_i r_i. \tag{9.13}$$

Substituting the right-hand side of equation (9.9) for $r_i$ on the right-hand side of equation (9.13) results in

$$r_p = \sum_{i=1}^{N} X_i (a_i + b_{i1} F_1 + b_{i2} F_2 + e_i)$$

$$= \left( \sum_{i=1}^{N} X_i a_i \right) + \left( \sum_{i=1}^{N} X_i b_{i1} F_1 \right) + \left( \sum_{i=1}^{N} X_i b_{i2} F_2 \right) + \left( \sum_{i=1}^{N} X_i e_i \right) \tag{9.14}$$

$$= a_p + b_{p1} F_1 + b_{p2} F_2 + e_p$$

where:

$$a_p = \sum_{i=1}^{N} X_i a_i$$

$$b_{p1} = \sum_{i=1}^{N} X_i b_{i1}$$

$$b_{p2} = \sum_{i=1}^{N} X_i b_{i2}$$

$$e_p = \sum_{i=1}^{N} X_i e_i.$$

Note how the portfolio sensitivities, $b_{p1}$ and $b_{p2}$, are weighted averages of the respective individual security sensitivities, $b_{i1}$ and $b_{i2}$.

## □ 9.2.2 Sector-Factor Models

Securities in the same industry or "economic sector" often move together, responding similarly to changes in prospects for that sector. Some investors acknowledge this by using a special kind of multiple-factor model referred to as a *sector-factor model*. In order to use a sector-factor model, each security must be classified as belonging to a sector. For a two-sector-factor model, each security must be classified as belonging to one of two economic sectors.

For example, let sector 1 consist of all industrial companies and sector 2 consist of all nonindustrial companies (such as utility, transportation, and financial companies). It should be kept in mind, however, that both the number of sectors and what each sector consists of is an open matter that is left to the investor to decide.

With this two-sector-factor model, the return-generating process for securities is of the same general form as the two-factor model given in equation (9.9). However, with the two-sector-factor model, $F_1$ and $F_2$ now denote sector-factor 1 and 2, respectively. Furthermore, any particular security belongs to either sector-factor 1 or 2 but not both. By definition this means that, depending on the sector-factor to which the security belongs, the value of either $b_{i1}$ or $b_{i2}$ equals 1; the other one will correspond to the sector-factor to which the security does not belong and will be set equal to 0.

As an illustration, consider Alcan (AL) and Pacific Western Airlines (PWA). The two-sector-factor model for AL would be:

$$r_{AL} = a_{AL} + b_{AL1} F_1 + b_{AL2} F_2 + e_{AL}. \qquad (9.15)$$

However, since AL belongs to sector-factor 1 (the industrial sector), the coefficients $b_{AL1}$ and $b_{AL2}$ are assigned values of 1 and 0, respectively. Having made this assignment, equation (9.15) reduces to:

$$r_{AL} = a_{AL} + F_1 + e_{AL}. \qquad (9.16)$$

Thus, only the values of $a_{AL}$ and $\sigma_{eAL}$ need to be estimated for AL with the two-sector-factor model, whereas with a two-factor model the values of $a_{AL}, b_{AL1}, b_{AL2}$, and $\sigma_{eAL}$ need to be estimated.

Similarly, since PWA belongs to the nonindustrial sector, it would have the following two-sector-factor model:

$$r_{PWA} = a_{PWA} + b_{PWA1} F_1 + b_{PWA2} F_2 + e_{PWA} \qquad (9.17)$$

which would reduce to:

$$r_{PWA} = a_{PWA} + F_2 + e_{PWA} \qquad (9.18)$$

since $b_{PWA1}$ and $b_{PWA2}$ would be assigned values of 0 and 1, respectively. Thus, only the values of $a_{PWA}$ and $\sigma_{ePWA}$ need to be estimated for PWA with the two-sector-factor model.

In general, whereas four parameters need to be estimated for each security with the two-factor model ($a_i, b_{i1}, b_{i2}$, and $\sigma_{ei}$), only two parameters need to be estimated with the two-sector-factor model ($a_i$ and $\sigma_{ei}$), since two parameters have been assigned values of either zero or one. With these estimates of the individual security parameters, along with estimates of $F_1, F_2, \sigma_{F1}^2$, and $\sigma_{F2}^2$, the investor can use equations (9.10), (9.11), and (9.12) to calculate expected returns, variances, and covariances, respectively. This will then enable the investor to derive the curved efficient set of Markowitz, from which the tangency portfolio can be determined for a given risk-free rate.

## □ 9.2.3　General Factor Models

As mentioned earlier, factor models are sometimes called index models. A number of investment firms have used single-index (that is, single-factor) models for portfolio management. Increasingly, however, multiple-index (that is, multiple-factor) models are being employed. Frequently, these models contain both *common factors* that affect all securities to a greater or lesser extent (for example, the growth rate in GNP) and *sector factors* that affect only particular subgroup of securities (for example, industries).[5]

In an important sense, a major task of investment analysis is to determine an appropriate factor model. This means determining how many factors there are and what they represent. Such a task is not easy, and definitive proof that a correct answer has been obtained is extremely unlikely. Differences of opinion concerning the relative usefulness of alternative factor models will persist, providing the investor with a wide range of choice. Once this choice is made, the investor can focus on estimating the appropriate parameters, thereby allowing expected returns, variances, and covariances to be calculated. With these as inputs, the curved efficient set of Markowitz can be derived. From this set the tangency portfolio associated with a given risk-free rate can be determined. At this point, the investor will be able to identify his or her optimal portfolio by finding the combination of the tangency portfolio and risk-free rate that provides the most desirable trade-off of risk and return.

## □ 9.2.4　Factor Models and Equilibrium

It should be kept in mind that a factor model is *not* an equilibrium model of asset pricing. However, if equilibrium exists, then there will be certain relationships between the parameters of the factor model and those of the equilibrium asset pricing model.

For example, if actual returns can be viewed as being generated by a single-factor model where the factor is $r_M$, then according to equation (9.2), expected returns will be equal to $a_i + b_i \bar{r}_M$, since $\overline{F} = \bar{r}_M$. But if equilibrium exists according to the CAPM, then equation (8.7) can be used to show that expected returns will also be equal to $r_f + (\bar{r}_M - r_f)\beta_i$, which can be rewritten as:

$$\begin{aligned}
\bar{r}_i &= r_f + (\bar{r}_M - r_f)\beta_i \\
&= r_f - r_f\beta_i + \bar{r}_M\beta_i \\
&= (1 - \beta_i)r_f + \bar{r}_M\beta_i.
\end{aligned} \qquad (8.7)$$

This means that the parameters of the single-factor model and CAPM must have the following relationships:

$$a_i = (1 - \beta_i)r_f$$
$$b_i = \beta_i.$$

---

[5] See Sharpe, "Factors in NYSE Security Returns." The factor model discussed in this article is subsequently used in Blake R. Grossman and William F. Sharpe, "Financial Implications of South African Divestment," *Financial Analysts Journal* 42, no. 4 (July/August 1986):15–29. To see how factor models can be used to evaluate the performance of portfolio managers, see the Appendix to Chapter 23. For more on multiple-index models, see Gordon J. Alexander and Jack Clark Francis, *Portfolio Analysis* (Englewood Cliffs, N.J.: Prentice Hall, 1986), 83–92.

That is, if expected returns are determined according to the CAPM and actual returns are generated by a single-factor model, then $a_i$ and $b_i$ must be equal to $(1 - \beta_i)r_f$ and $\beta_i$, respectively.

## 9.3     ARBITRAGE PRICING THEORY

*Arbitrage pricing theory* (APT), like the CAPM, is an equilibrium model of asset pricing.[6] Unlike the CAPM, APT assumes that returns are generated by a factor model. Furthermore, although the CAPM made certain strong assumptions about investor preferences (for example, investors were assumed to be risk-averse), APT makes no such strong assumptions. That is, APT is not based on the idea that investors look at portfolios in terms of expected returns and standard deviations. Instead, APT requires only that investors prefer higher levels of wealth to lower levels of wealth.

## ☐ 9.3.1    Factor Portfolios

As mentioned previously, APT assumes returns are generated by a factor model. It does not specify how many factors there are or what they represent. For ease of exposition, assume there are two factors, $F_1$ and $F_2$, which means that security returns are generated according to equation (9.9). It is also necessary to assume that there are "very many" securities and that the sensitivities to the two factors differ substantially among securities.[7]

In such a world, a number of investment strategies exist. Particularly interesting is the strategy involving portfolios that represent *pure factor plays*. Given enough securities with different characteristics, it should be possible to construct a portfolio that has unit sensitivity (that is, a sensitivity of size 1) to one factor, no sensitivity to the other factor, and zero nonfactor risk. The trick in forming such a portfolio is to combine positions in the securities to "hedge out" (that is, remove) the sensitivity of the portfolio to all but one factor. Furthermore, a large number of securities should be held so that the number of securities that will experience "good" nonfactor returns can be expected to be roughly the same as the number of securities that will experience "bad" nonfactor returns. This will result in the portfolio having nearly zero nonfactor risk.

For example, assume that securities $A$, $B$, and $C$ have the following sensitivities:

---

[6] For the initial development of APT, see Stephen A. Ross, "The Arbitrage Theory of Capital Asset Pricing," *Journal of Economic Theory* 13, no. 3 (December 1976):341–60; and "Risk, Return, and Arbitrage," sec. 9 in *Risk and Return in Finance*, vol. I, ed. Irwin Friend and James L. Bicksler (Cambridge, Mass.: Ballinger Publishing Company, 1977).

[7] For a discussion of these assumptions and why the resulting asset pricing equation is not exact but approximate, see Philip H. Dybvig, "An Explicit Bound on Individual Assets' Deviations from APT Pricing in a Finite Economy," *Journal of Financial Economics* 12, no. 4 (December 1983):483–96; and Mark Grinblatt and Sheridan Titman, "Factor Pricing in a Finite Economy," *Journal of Financial Economics* 12, no. 4 (December 1983):497–507. Since the approximation errors are arguably small, the presentation that follows ignores them.

| Security | $b_{i1}$ | $b_{i2}$ |
|----------|----------|----------|
| A | −.40 | 1.75 |
| B | 1.60 | −.75 |
| C | .67 | −.25 |

If an investor has $1000 to invest and puts $300 in security $A$, $700 in security $B$, and nothing in security $C$, then the proportions invested will be $X_A = .3$, $X_B = .7$, and $X_C = .0$. The sensitivity of this portfolio to factors 1 and 2 will be 1 and 0, respectively:

$$b_{p1} = (-.40 \times .3) + (1.60 \times .7) + (.67 \times .0)$$
$$= -.12 + 1.12 + 0$$
$$= 1.0$$
$$b_{p2} = (1.75 \times .3) + (-.75 \times .7) + (-.25 \times .0)$$
$$= .525 - .525 - .000$$
$$= 0.$$

If it were possible to invest in a great many securities like these, it would be possible to create a portfolio with very little nonfactor risk, meaning that $e_p = 0$. Thus, by choosing the proportions appropriately, the investor could create a portfolio (call it pI) that is sensitive only to factor 1:

$$r_{pI} = a_{pI} + F_1 \tag{9.19}$$

Since $b_{pI1} = 1$, $b_{pI2} = 0$, and $e_{pI} = 0$. This would be a *pure factor* 1 portfolio. By design, its return moves with the first factor on a one-for-one basis.

An alternative strategy could create a *pure factor* 2 portfolio. If the investor with $1000 decided to invest $625 in securities like $A$ and $375 in securities like $C$, the sensitivities of the resulting portfolio would be:

$$b_{p1} = (-.40 \times .625) + (1.60 \times .0) + (.67 \times .375)$$
$$= -.25 + .00 + .25$$
$$= .00$$
$$b_{p2} = (1.75 \times .625) + (-.75 \times .0) + (-.25 \times .375)$$
$$= 1.09 + .00 - .09$$
$$= 1.00.$$

If this could be done over many securities, then it would have very little nonfactor risk; the result would be a portfolio (call it pII) sensitive only to factor 2:

$$r_{pII} = a_{pII} + F_2. \tag{9.20}$$

In a market with many securities of diverse characteristics, it would be theoretically possible to create "pure factor" portfolios that are sensitive to only one factor and have insignificant nonfactor risk. In practice, the required conditions are not met completely, meaning it is only possible to create "impure factor" portfolios that are sensitive primarily (but not exclusively) to one factor with relatively little nonfactor risk. Although APT assumes that pure factor portfolios can be created, it should be kept in mind that the reasonableness of the assumption is not of concern. Instead, it is the accuracy of the predictions of APT that are of importance.

## ☐ 9.3.2 Expected Returns on Factor Portfolios

The expected return from a pure factor portfolio will depend on the expected value of the relevant factor. It is convenient to break this expected return into two parts: (1) the risk-free rate of interest and (2) the rest, which is typically indicated by the Greek letter *lambda*, $\lambda$, and may be regarded as the *expected return premium per unit of sensitivity to the factor*. Thus, the expected return on a pure factor 1 portfolio is:

$$\bar{r}_{pI} = r_f + \lambda_1. \tag{9.21}$$

Similarly, the expected return on a pure factor 2 portfolio is:

$$\bar{r}_{pII} = r_f + \lambda_2. \tag{9.22}$$

As an example, if the risk-free rate is 7% and $\bar{r}_{pI}$ is 16.6%, then $\lambda_1$ will be $16.6\% - 7\% = 9.6\%$. And if $\bar{r}_{pII}$ is 13.4%, then $\lambda_2$ will be $13.4\% - 7\% = 6.4\%$. This means that the expected return premiums per unit of sensitivity to factors 1 and 2 are 9.6% and 6.4%, respectively.

It is possible that many alternative combinations of securities could be used to construct a pure factor 1 portfolio. Will each such combination have the same expected return? Under the theory, yes. Whereas pure factor portfolios may not be unique in their composition, their expected returns should be.

Imagine a situation in which two pure factor 1 portfolios had different expected returns. This could only be due to differences in their $a$-values ($a_{pI}$ in equation (9.19)). Now, consider selling short the portfolio with the lower expected return and purchasing the portfolio with the greater expected return. In this situation, the investor stands to make an abnormal return *no matter what happens to factor* 1. This clearly will not persist, because two identical assets (in this case, the two pure factor 1 portfolios) must, in equilibrium, be priced to provide the same expected return.

Opportunities where they are not so priced will cause certain investors, known as *arbitrageurs*, to spring into action. They will purchase the securities in the portfolio with the higher expected return and sell those in the portfolio with the lower expected return. In turn, this will drive up the prices of the former, driving down the expected return of the corresponding portfolio. It will also drive down the prices of the latter, driving up the expected return of the corresponding portfolio. This would continue until the two portfolios have the same expected return.

As a result of prices moving in this fashion, the investor would make an abnormal return and, before long, such an opportunity to get "something for nothing" would have disappeared. That is, *arbitrage* will ensure that all pure factor 1 portfolios will have the same expected return, $r_f + \lambda_1$.[8]

The presence of a risk-free rate is a natural part of APT. With a great many diverse securities, it will be possible to construct a portfolio that has zero sensitivity to every

---

[8] In general, arbitrage takes place when the same security sells for two different prices in two different markets. It involves the purchase of the security in the market where the lower price exists and the near simultaneous sale of the same security in the market with the higher price. One result of doing this is the riskless earning of abnormal profits; another result is that the price discrepancy will disappear quickly.

factor and is sufficiently diversified to have insignificant nonfactor risk. Its expected return, which will be virtually risk-free, can be used as a base from which other expected returns are measured.

## ☐ 9.3.3  Expected Returns on Securities

By splitting funds among (1) a risk-free portfolio and (2) pure factor portfolios, it is possible for the investor to form a portfolio with almost any sensitivity to each factor. Moreover, such portfolios can be constructed to have insignificant nonfactor risks.

For example, assume that the return on security $k$ is related to factors 1 and 2 as follows:

$$r_k = a_k + .8\,F_1 + 1.5\,F_2 + e_k. \tag{9.23a}$$

Thus, if an investor had $1000 to invest, he or she could put it all in security $k$ and have an expected return of

$$\bar{r}_k = a_k + .8\,F_1 + 1.5\,F_2. \tag{9.23b}$$

Now, consider an alternative strategy in which $1300 is borrowed at the risk-free rate to supplement the investor's $1000. This means that the proportion invested in the risk-free asset is $(-\$1300/\$1000) = -1.3 = X_f$. Of the resulting $2300, $800 is invested in a pure factor 1 portfolio and the remaining $1500 is invested in a pure factor 2 portfolio. This means that the proportions invested in these two portfolios are $(\$800/\$1000) = .8 = X_I$ and $(\$1500/\$1000) = 1.5 = X_{II}$, respectively. The expected return on the resulting portfolio, denoted by $K$, can be calculated as a weighted average of its three components:

$$
\begin{aligned}
\bar{r}_K &= (X_f \times r_f) + (X_I \times \bar{r}_{pI}) + (X_{II} \times \bar{r}_{pII}) \\
&= (-1.3 \times r_f) + (.8 \times \bar{r}_{pI}) + (1.5 \times \bar{r}_{pII}) \\
&= (-1.3 \times r_f) + [.8 \times (r_f + \lambda_1)] + [1.5 \times (r_f + \lambda_2)] \qquad (9.24) \\
&= -1.3 r_f + .8 r_f + .8\lambda_1 + 1.5 r_f + 1.5\lambda_2 \\
&= r_f + .8\lambda_1 + 1.5\lambda_2.
\end{aligned}
$$

Note how the expected return of the two pure factor portfolios given in equations (9.21) and (9.22) have been substituted for $\bar{r}_{pI}$ and $\bar{r}_{pII}$, respectively, in equation (9.24).

Now, compare portfolio $K$ with security $k$. Each has a sensitivity of .8 to factor 1 and a sensitivity of 1.5 to factor 2. Security $k$ is subject to additional risk due to uncertainty about its nonfactor return, $e_k$. Portfolio $K$ has virtually no risk of this type. What if the expected return from security $k$ were less than that of portfolio $K$? Clearly, the portfolio would dominate the security, since the portfolio would provide a greater expected return with less risk than the security. A clever arbitrageur could sell security $k$ short and purchase portfolio $K$, expecting to profit from the difference in their expected returns. The situation would not be totally riskless, since the nonfactor return of security $k$ could swamp the difference in expected returns. However, if there were many securities like $k$, this source of risk could be removed through diversification.

What if the expected return from security $k$ were more than that of portfolio $K$? In this case, there is no obvious dominance. However, a clever arbitrageur could sell the portfolio short and purchase the security, expecting to profit from the difference in expected returns. Here too, the situation would not be totally riskless, since the nonfactor return could swamp the difference in expected returns. However, if there were many securities like $k$, this source of risk could be removed through diversification.

The conclusion is that the expected return of security $k$ would be equal to the expected return of portfolio $K$ in equilibrium. That is, arbitrage would ensure that the expected return of security $k$ would be

$$\bar{r}_k = r_f + .8\lambda_1 + 1.5\lambda_2. \tag{9.25}$$

More generally, for any security $i$:

$$\bar{r}_i = r_f + b_{i1}\lambda_1 + b_{i2}\lambda_2. \tag{9.26}$$

Equation (9.26) is the asset pricing equation of APT.[9] In words, it states that:

> The expected return of a security will be related to its sensitivity to each pervasive factor. Moreover, the relationship will be linear, with a common intercept term that is equal to the risk-free rate.

Like the equation obtained from the CAPM, APT equation (9.26) asserts that there is a linear relationship between (1) expected returns and (2) the various relevant attributes of securities. In the case of the CAPM, the relevant security attribute was beta ($\beta_i$), whereas in the case of APT, the relevant security attributes are sensitivities to major factors ($b_{i1}$ and $b_{i2}$). However, as mentioned earlier, APT is silent about how many of these factors exist and what they represent. In turn, this means that APT is silent about the lambda values, such as $\lambda_1$ and $\lambda_2$ in equation (9.26). They can be positive, negative, or zero. Identification of the factors and the associated lambda values involves both empirical work and judgment.

Equation (9.26) refers to equilibrium expected returns for securities. However, disequilibrium can be represented with this equation in a manner similar to the CAPM. In particular, an alpha term can be added to the right-hand side of the equation to indicate the amount of mispricing. An overpriced security would have a negative alpha. This would mean that its expected return would be less than its equilibrium expected return of $r_f + b_{i1}\lambda_1 + b_{i2}\lambda_2$. In turn, this suggests that the security is not an attractive one to purchase (or to hold onto if it is already owned). Similarly, an underpriced security would have a positive alpha, meaning its expected return would be greater than its equilibrium return and that it is an attractive security to purchase.

## 9.4  A SYNTHESIS OF APT AND THE CAPM

Unlike APT, the CAPM does not assume that returns are generated by a factor model. However, this does not mean that the CAPM is inconsistent with a world in which returns are generated by a factor model. Indeed, it is possible to have a world where returns are generated by a factor model, where the remaining assumptions of APT hold and where all the assumptions of the CAPM hold. This situation will now be examined.

---

[9] Equation (9.26) is based on there being two factors in the economy. If there are more factors, the equation is extended in a straightforward manner. For example, if there were three factors, then equation (9.26) would have the term $b_{i3}\lambda_3$ added onto the right-hand side.

## ☐ 9.4.1  Beta Coefficients and Factor Sensitivities

If security returns are generated by a factor model, it is possible to relate the beta coefficient of any particular security to its sensitivities to the factors. Assuming returns are generated by a two-factor model, it can be shown that the covariance of the return on security $i$ with the return of the market portfolio $M$ will be:

$$\text{COV}(r_i, r_M) = [\text{COV}(F_1, r_M) \times b_{i1}] \tag{9.27}$$
$$+ [\text{COV}(F_2, r_M) \times b_{i2}] + \text{COV}(e_i, r_M)$$

where COV denotes covariance of the two variables inside the following parentheses.

In Chapter 8, it was shown that the beta coefficient for a security could be obtained by dividing $\text{COV}(r_i, r_M)$ by the variance of the market portfolio, $\sigma_M^2$:[10]

$$\beta_i = \frac{\text{COV}(r_i, r_M)}{\sigma_M^2}. \tag{9.28}$$

Thus, when both sides of equation (9.27) are divided by $\sigma_M^2$, the result is:

$$\beta_i = \left[\frac{\text{COV}(F_1, r_M)}{\sigma_M^2} \times b_{i1}\right] + \left[\frac{\text{COV}(F_2, r_M)}{\sigma_M^2} \times b_{i2}\right] + \frac{\text{COV}(e_i, r_M)}{\sigma_M^2}. \tag{9.29}$$

As a practical matter, the term $\text{COV}(e_i, r_M)/\sigma_M^2$ will be very small, so little is lost by ignoring it. Each of the other two terms involves the ratio of a factor's covariance with the market portfolio to the variance of the market portfolio. These ratios can be viewed as the *factor betas*. This is because each ratio is identical to the right-hand side of equation (9.28) except that the value of the factor appears in the place of the return on the security:

$$\beta_{F1} = \frac{\text{COV}(F_1, r_M)}{\sigma_M^2} \tag{9.30}$$

$$\beta_{F2} = \frac{\text{COV}(F_2, r_M)}{\sigma_M^2}. \tag{9.31}$$

This leads to the conclusion that

$$\beta_i = \beta_{F1} b_{i1} + \beta_{F2} b_{i2}. \tag{9.32}$$

Since $\beta_{F1}$ and $\beta_{F2}$ are constants and do not vary from one security to another, equation (9.32) shows that the beta coefficient of a security is a function of its sensitivities to the pervasive factors. Accordingly, the reason securities have different betas is because they have different sensitivities.

As an example, assume that the factor beta for GNP, $\beta_{F1}$, is equal to 1.2, and that the factor beta for inflation, $\beta_{F2}$, is .8. Given the sensitivities of securities $A$, $B$, and $C$ that were shown earlier, equation (9.32) can be used to determine their beta coefficients:

$$\beta_A = (1.2 \times -.40) + (.8 \times 1.75) = .92$$
$$\beta_B = (1.2 \times 1.60) + (.8 \times -.75) = 1.32$$
$$\beta_C = (1.2 \times .67) + (.8 \times -.25) = .60.$$

---

[10] See equation (8.6), where $\sigma_{iM}$ was used instead of $\text{COV}(r_i, r_M)$ to denote the covariance of the return on security $i$ with the return of the market portfolio $M$.

## □ 9.4.2 Expected Returns, Factor Betas, and Security Sensitivities

As a result of making the assumptions necessary for the CAPM, the expected return of security $i$ was shown in Chapter 8 to be related to its beta coefficient:

$$\bar{r}_i = r_f + [(\bar{r}_M - r_f)\beta_i]. \tag{8.7}$$

If returns are generated by a two-factor model, the beta coefficient of a security will be related to its sensitivities to the factors and the factor betas, as shown in equation (9.32). Substituting the right-hand side of equation (9.32) for $\beta_i$ in equation (8.7) results in

$$\bar{r}_i = r_f + [(\bar{r}_M - r_f) \times (\beta_{F1} b_{i1} + \beta_{F2} b_{i2})]$$
$$= r_f + [(\bar{r}_M - r_f)\beta_{F1}]b_{i1} + [(\bar{r}_M - r_f)\beta_{F2}]b_{i2}. \tag{9.33}$$

Comparing equation (9.33) to APT asset pricing equation (9.26), it can be seen that if the assumptions of both APT and the CAPM hold, then the lambda terms must have the following values:

$$\lambda_1 = (\bar{r}_M - r_f)\beta_{F1} \tag{9.34}$$
$$\lambda_2 = (\bar{r}_M - r_f)\beta_{F2}. \tag{9.35}$$

Substituting the right-hand side of these two equations into the right-hand side of equation (9.33) results in

$$\bar{r}_i = r_f + \lambda_1 b_{i1} + \lambda_2 b_{i2}. \tag{9.36}$$

By itself, APT says nothing about the sizes or the magnitudes of the factor expected return premiums, $\lambda_1$ and $\lambda_2$. However, if the CAPM also holds, it can provide some guidance. This guidance is given in equations (9.34) and (9.35), which have been shown to exist if the assumptions of both APT and the CAPM hold.

Imagine that factor 1 moves with the market portfolio, meaning that it is positively correlated with the market portfolio and that $COV(F_1, r_M)$ is positive.[11] In turn, $\beta_{F1}$ must be positive because it equals $COV(F_1, r_M)$, a positive number, divided by $\sigma_M^2$, another positive number. Since $\bar{r}_M$ is greater than $r_f$, $(\bar{r}_M - r_f)$ will be positive, and thus $(\bar{r}_M - r_f)\beta_{F1}$ will be positive. It follows from equation (9.34) that $\lambda_1$ will be positive.[12] Furthermore, since $\lambda_1$ is positive, it can be seen in equation (9.36) that the higher the value of $b_{i1}$, the higher will be the expected return of the security. To generalize, if a factor is positively correlated with the market portfolio, then a security's expected return will be a positive linear function of the security's sensitivity to that factor.

With a similar kind of argument, it can be shown that if factor 2 moves against the market portfolio, meaning $F_2$ is negatively correlated with $r_M$, then (1) $\beta_{F2}$ will be negative; (2) $(\bar{r}_M - r_f)\beta_{F2}$ will be negative; and (3) $\lambda_2$ will be negative. Thus, from equation (9.36), it follows that the higher the value of $b_{i2}$, the lower will be the expected return of the security. Again generalizing, if a factor is negatively correlated with the

---

[11] $COV(F_1, r_M)$ will be positive if the correlation is positive, since it is equal to the product of the correlation and the standard deviations of $F_1$ and $r_M$.

[12] The greater the extent to which factor 1 moves with the market portfolio, meaning the higher the correlation between $F_1$ and $r_M$, the greater will be the associated expected return premium, $\lambda_1$. For a discussion of the implications of factor 1 being the market portfolio, see K. C. John Wei, "An Asset-Pricing Theory Unifying the CAPM and APT," *Journal of Finance* 43, no. 4 (September 1988):881–92; and Stephen A. Ross and Randolph W. Westerfield, *Corporate Finance* (St. Louis, Mo.: Times Mirror, 1988), 181–95.

market portfolio, then a security's expected return will be a negative linear function of the security's sensitivity to that factor.

Using the earlier example, where $\beta_{F1} = 1.2$ and $\beta_{F2} = .8$, and assuming that $r_f = 7\%$ and $\bar{r}_M = 15\%$, equation (9.33) will be as follows:

$$\bar{r}_i = r_f + [(\bar{r}_M - r_f)\beta_{F1}]b_{i1} + [(\bar{r}_M - r_f)\beta_{F2}]b_{i2}$$
$$= 7 + [(15 - 7) \times 1.2]b_{i1} + [(15 - 7) \times .8]b_{i2}$$
$$= 7 + 9.6\,b_{i1} + 6.4\,b_{i2}.$$

Note that both $\lambda_1$ and $\lambda_2$ are positive, being equal to 9.6 and 6.4, respectively. Thus, the larger $b_{i1}$ is, the larger $\bar{r}_i$ will be. Furthermore, the larger $b_{i2}$ is, the larger $\bar{r}_i$ will be.

If $\beta_{F2}$ had been equal to $-.8$ instead of $+.8$, then $\lambda_2 = (15 - 7) \times -.8 = -6.4$, and the preceding equation would have been

$$r_i = 7 + 9.6\,b_{i1} - 6.4\,b_{i2}.$$

Thus, a negative value for $\beta_{F2}$ would have led to a negative value for $\lambda_2$. In such a situation, the larger $b_{i2}$ is, the smaller $\bar{r}_i$ will be. Accordingly, the sign of each lambda determines whether a security's expected return is a positive or negative function of its sensitivity to that lambda.

## 9.5 SUMMARY

It seems reasonable to assume that a set of factors generates security returns. It is also reasonable to assume that most investors like higher levels of expected return and dislike higher levels of risk. Thus, it is not unreasonable to argue that the conditions necessary for both APT and the CAPM to hold are in existence.

In such a setting, it can be argued that the two theories combined are more powerful (that is, make stronger predictions) than either one alone and can therefore provide considerably more guidance for investment decisions. While it is interesting to wonder if historical data support either theory (or both), Markowitz has noted that affirmative test results are not necessary in order to make sensible practical use of these asset pricing models.[13] Since one of the more contentious issues currently being debated in finance is whether or not either asset pricing model can be meaningfully tested with historical data, there would appear to be wide latitude for the practical use of such models.[14]

Due to their complex statistical nature, actual usage of these models has generally been confined to professional money managers. These investors have the resources necessary to implement such models in the management of multimillion dollar portfolios. While there are many variations on how these models have been used, undoubtedly more variations will appear in the future as investors gain more experience

---

[13] Harry M. Markowitz, "Nonnegative or Not Nonnegative: A Question About CAPMs," *Journal of Finance* 38, no. 2 (May 1983):283–95.

[14] For an argument that the CAPM cannot be tested, see Richard Roll, "A Critique of the Asset Pricing Theory's Tests; Part I. On Past and Potential Testability of the Theory," *Journal of Financial Economics* 4, no. 2 (March 1977):129–76. For an argument that APT cannot be tested, see Jay Shanken, "The Arbitrage Pricing Theory: Is It Testable?" *Journal of Finance* 37, no. 5 (December 1982):1129–40. A discussion of certain tests of the CAPM and APT, along with Roll and Shanken's arguments, is presented in the appendix. For a more extensive discussion, see Chapters 10 and 14 of Alexander and Francis, *Portfolio Analysis*.

with the models.[15] Nevertheless, it is unlikely that any one model will ever be shown conclusively to be superior to any other, since the models involve "unobservables" such as expected returns, betas, and sensitivities. These unobservables can only be estimated, which means that substantial errors can occur in doing so. As a result, investors will have to decide for themselves what models they favor and how they will use them. Ultimately, the value of any model to the investor will depend on the accuracy of its predictions.

# APPENDIX A

## TESTING EQUILIBRIUM THEORIES OF ASSET PRICING

Equilibrium theories such as the capital asset pricing model and arbitrage pricing theory imply that in the consensus opinion of well-informed investors, securities with certain attributes will, other things being equal, have large expected returns, whereas those with other attributes will have small expected returns. Such concepts are based on opinions held *ex ante* (Latin for "before the fact") about possible returns and their relative probabilities. *Ex post* (Latin for "after the fact"), only one outcome will be recorded for each stock. Investors will then form new and possibly different opinions, another set of stock returns will subsequently be recorded, and so on.

This makes it extremely difficult to test whether security attributes and expected returns do in fact go together in the manner implied by either the CAPM or APT. Moreover, such theories are relatively silent concerning simple ways in which a security's future attributes and expected return might be estimated by processing historical data.

To bridge this gap, a number of investigators have used historical security returns as surrogates for expected returns. This requires an assumption that relevant predictions do not change from period to period and that sufficient information is available to determine what such expectations actually were. Thus, average historical returns are used as estimates of expected returns. Two obvious objections may be made. First, expectations almost certainly change from time to time (nothing in theory suggests this cannot happen). Second, even if expectations did not change over time, an extremely long historical record might be required to obtain reasonably accurate estimates of their magnitudes. Despite these and other problems, it is potentially worthwhile examining historical data.

Any test of an equilibrium theory based on historical data is a joint test of (1) certain assumptions such as the one just mentioned concerning the stability of predictions and (2) a particular theory of equilibrium. If such a test fails, it may indicate that the equilibrium theory is in error. Alternatively, one or more of the other assumptions may be inappropriate. As a practical matter, such tests cannot reject an equilibrium theory. They can, however, provide suggestive evidence.

---

[15] As an example, consider Wells Fargo. In managing common stock portfolios, they have used at one time or another variations of the CAPM that include a liquidity adjustment and a dividend yield adjustment. For a description of how they were used, see George Foster, *Financial Statement Analysis* (Englewood Cliffs, N.J.: Prentice Hall, 1986), 428–30.

# TESTS OF THE CAPITAL ASSET PRICING MODEL

## ☐ A.1.1 Tests Based on US Data

Both the original and extended versions of the capital asset pricing model suggest that, other things being equal, securities with relatively large ex ante betas will have relatively large expected returns. This does not mean that they will necessarily have, ex post, larger actual returns. If the market goes up substantially, actual returns can be expected to be higher for high-beta securities. However, these are expectations, and ignore the unsystematic element of a security's return, which can cause a security with a relatively large beta to have a relatively small return when the market goes up substantially. Thus, even if the CAPM is valid, actual returns may bear little if any relationship to expectations and, hence, to ex ante betas.

An additional problem concerns the measurement of beta. Beta should measure a security's sensitivity to a widely diversified market portfolio that includes all types of stocks, bonds, real estate, and so on. Many empirical studies have instead used a broad-based index of widely traded stocks, since adequate data on other types of securities has been difficult or impossible to obtain. Clearly, a security's beta measured relative to, say, a market portfolio consisting of all stocks listed on the New York Stock Exchange could differ significantly from one measured relative to a market portfolio consisting of all stocks in the United States, let alone a market portfolio consisting of all stocks in the world.

Despite all these problems it is instructive to see how well common stocks with different historical betas have done over time.

### Risk-Return Classes

The development of a computerized file of monthly returns for all stocks listed on the NYSE from 1926 to the present has facilitated extensive investigation of risk and return for such securities.[16] Using this file, the relationship between risk and return can be examined by measuring each security's beta relative to an index of the returns on all NYSE stocks over some historical period (such as five years).[17] Once this has been done, portfolios can be formed that are designed to include many stocks but also to differ as much as possible in regard to the size of their betas. For example, on January 1, 1931, all securities could be listed in order of the size of their historical betas. Then equal dollar amounts of the top 10% of all securities might be placed hypothetically in one portfolio, equal dollar amounts of the next 10% in another portfolio, and so on. On January 1, 1932, the process was repeated by using updated estimates of each security's beta and rebalancing each portfolio to again contain equal dollar proportions of the stocks in the appropriate part of the listing. Thus, the approach is based on one-year holding periods. It defines several *risk-return classes* of stocks with similar historical betas and thus, it is hoped, similar future betas and expected returns.

---

[16] Performed at the Center for Research in Security Prices (CRSP) at the University of Chicago, and sponsored by Merrill Lynch, Pierce, Fenner and Smith, Inc. Currently, a computerized file with daily returns is also available.

[17] Individual security betas can be estimated by using a statistical procedure known as simple regression or ordinary least squares (OLS); for a discussion, see Chapter 15.

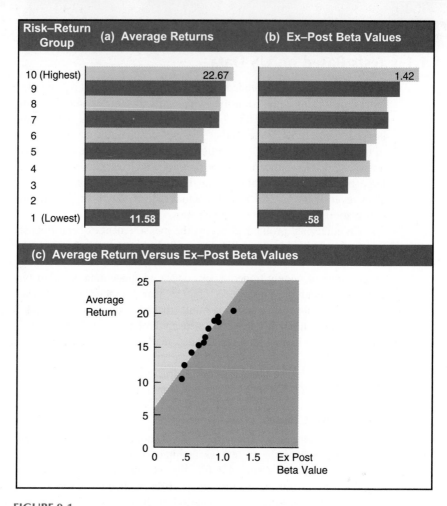

**FIGURE 9-1**

Performance of ten risk-return classes for one-year holding periods, 1931-1967.

*SOURCE:* William F. Sharpe and Guy M. Cooper, "Risk-Return Classes of New York Stock Exchange Common Stocks, 1931–1967," *Financial Analysis Journal* 28, no. 2 (March-April 1972): 51.

Figure 9.1 shows some of the results. In part (a), each bar indicates the arithmetic average annual return from 1931 through 1967 for a risk-return class. Part (b) shows the ex post beta values, and part (c) provides a plot of the average returns and ex post beta values for all ten classes, along with the best-fit regression line.[18] Despite the potential problems with such analyses, the results are substantially consistent with the theoretical CAPM relationship between expected returns and beta values.

Figure 9.2 shows the results from a study concerned with longer holding periods. In this case, eight five-year nonoverlapping periods from mid-1928 through mid-1968 were

---

[18] The equation of the line is $ar_p = 5.54 + 12.75 \beta_p$, where $ar_p$ and $\beta_p$ denote the average return and ex post beta for portfolio $p$; the correlation between $ar_p$ and $\beta_p$ is .97.

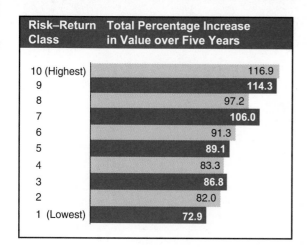

| Risk–Return Class | Total Percentage Increase in Value over Five Years |
|---|---|
| 10 (Highest) | 116.9 |
| 9 | 114.3 |
| 8 | 97.2 |
| 7 | 106.0 |
| 6 | 91.3 |
| 5 | 89.1 |
| 4 | 83.3 |
| 3 | 86.8 |
| 2 | 82.0 |
| 1 (Lowest) | 72.9 |

**FIGURE 9-2**

Average performance of ten risk-return classes over eight five-year holding periods, 1928–1968.

*SOURCE:* Marshall E. Blume and Irwin Friend, "Risk, Investment Strategy and the Long-run Rates of Return," *Review of Economics and Statistics* 56, no. 3 (August 1974): 263.

analyzed and the percentage change in value determined for an account that remained fully invested during each period (all dividends received during the five years were reinvested; portfolios were rebalanced monthly). The results are roughly consistent with a positive relationship between beta values and medium-term returns.

Historic beta values cannot be counted on to predict returns precisely, even relative to market moves, over every period. Figure 9.3 plots the average monthly returns over four different 105-month periods for ten risk-return classes based on historical beta values. In each case, the market return (indicated by a square) exceeded the risk-free rate of interest. Three of the lines of best fit are upward-sloping as expected, but one is not.

### Historical Beta Factor

Many factor models include a security's historical beta as an attribute. The corresponding *historical beta factor* provides a measure of the difference in returns between high-historical beta stocks and low-historical beta stocks, keeping other attributes equal. If historical betas are useful for predicting future betas, the beta factor should be positive in most periods when the return on stocks exceeds the risk-free rate of interest and negative in most periods when the return on stocks is less than the risk-free rate.

Figure 9.4 shows that this has in fact been the case. In months in which the excess return on the New York Stock Exchange (that is, the market return minus the Treasury bill rate) was positive, the beta factor was generally positive — stocks with high-historical betas tended to outperform those with low-historical betas. In months in which the excess return on stocks was negative, the beta factor was generally negative — stocks with high-historical betas tended to underperform those with low-historical betas. The relationship is highly significant statistically (for example, the $t$-statistic of 41.7 is significant at the 99% confidence level).

Although most of the points in Figure 9.4 are in the upper-right and lower-left quadrants, some are not. In such cases the actual relationship between return and beta differed from what might be expected according to the CAPM.

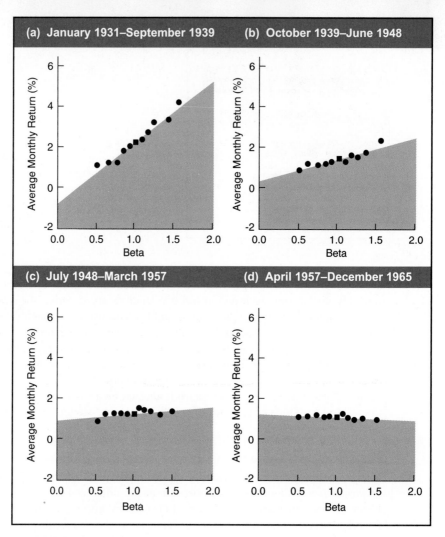

**FIGURE 9-3**

Performance of ten risk-return classes, four 105-month periods, 1931-1965.

*SOURCE:* Fischer Black, Michael C. Jensen, and Myron Scholes, "The Capital Asset Pricing Model: Some Empirical Tests," in Michael C. Jensen (ed.), *Studies in the Theory of Capital Markets* (New York: Praeger Publishers, Inc. 1972): 105–6.

## Tests of the Zero-Beta CAPM

In a detailed test of the original and zero-beta CAPM, portfolio classes were used to examine the relationship between average returns and historical betas. The classes were also tested to see if average returns were related in a nonlinear manner to betas and if average returns were related to unique risks.

Figure 9.5 contrasts the actual relationship for the period from 1938 through mid-1968 with the original CAPM. The vertical intercept, which corresponds to the zero-beta return, is .61% per month (equivalent to approximately 7.32% per year), while the

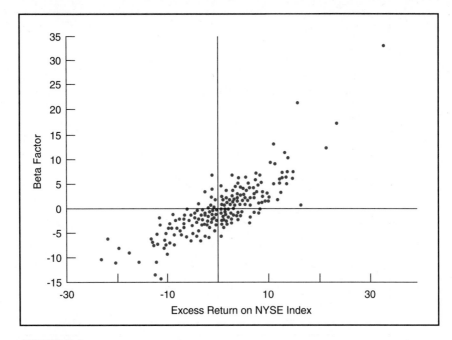

**FIGURE 9-4**

Beta factor values and NYSE returns, 1928-1982.

*SOURCE:* Blake Grossman and William F. Sharpe, "Factors in Security Returns," paper presented at the Center for the Study of Banking and Financial Markets, University of Washington, March 1984.

average Treasury bill return, which corresponds to the risk-free rate of interest, was only .13% per month (equivalent to approximately 1.56% per year). The difference was substantial and statistically significant. Assuming that betas measured relative to a stock index are adequate surrogates for "true" betas measured relative to the overall market portfolio, such results provide more support for the zero-beta version of the CAPM than for the original version.

Similar tests have been performed using returns from securities in other countries, with mixed but not dissimilar results.[19]

## ☐ A.1.2   Tests Based on Canadian Data

Tests of the CAPM using Canadian data have yielded results that can, at best, be described as inconsistent. The first direct test of the CAPM carried out using Canadian data included an examination of both the traditional and the zero-beta versions of the model.[20] The market risk-return relationship was estimated over a 15 year full period

---

[19] For a comprehensive summary of studies using European data, see Gabriel Hawawini, European Equity Markets: Price Behavior and Efficiency, Monograph Series in Finance and Economics 1984–4/5, Salomon Brothers Center for the Study of Financial Institutions, Graduate School of Business Administration, New York University.

[20] Roger Morin, "Market Line Theory and the Canadian Equity Market," *Journal of Business Administration* 12, no. 1 (Fall 1980):57–76.

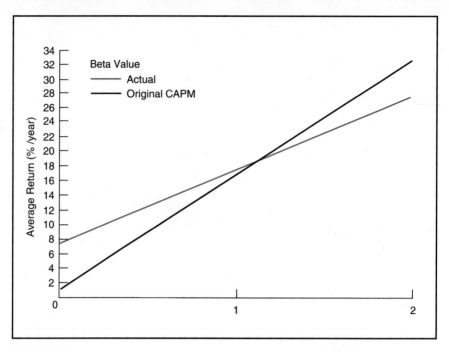

**FIGURE 9-5**

Average return and beta.

*SOURCE:* Adapted from Eugene F. Fama and James D. MacBeth, "Risk, Return and Equilibrium: Empirical Tests," *Journal of Political Economy* 81, no. 3 (May 1973): 622.

and three non-overlapping five year sub-periods from 1957 to 1971 for fifteen risk-return classes following the procedure developed by Black *et al.* described above. In two of the three sub-periods and in the full period, the coefficient of beta is positive (as predicted by the theory) but not statistically significant. In all cases the intercept is larger than the estimated risk free rate and the slope coefficient is smaller than the average excess market return. Furthermore, the slope coefficients varied substantially between sub-periods. These results are similar to those found in the US tests, a finding that is not altogether surprising given the relatively high degree of integration of the Canadian and US financial markets and the significant number of interlisted stocks that were included in the Canadian sample. Unlike the US tests, however, unsystematic risk showed a strongly significant relationship to return — a result that is not consistent with either version of the CAPM.

A second test that used data from 1963 to 1980 also examined both the traditional and zero-beta versions.[21] This study, recognizing the biases introduced into the beta estimates by thin trading, used Dimson's correction procedure (see Chapter 15 for a discussion of these problems). The results were consistent with the traditional version of the theory.

---

[21] M.J.Brennan and E.S.Schwartz, "Canadian Estimates of the Capital Asset Pricing Model," Corporate Finance Division, Department of Finance, Ottawa, July 1982.

Jobson and Korkie tested the CAPM using both US and Canadian data and rejected both versions in four out of five periods with US data and in three out of three periods with Canadian data.[22]

An extensive study by Calvet and Lefoll used a variety of methodologies and reached the following conclusions: 1. systematic risk and return appear to be linearly related although the estimated annual risk premiums depend on the methodology used. Furthermore, the traditional version could not be rejected (in contrast to the US test results); 2. when securities are ranked using both beta and residual risk as joint criteria then both residual risk and non-linearity become significant; 3. the portfolio ranking procedure appears to have a significant effect on the results; 4. skewness is not a significant determinant of security prices.[23]

## A.2 TESTS OF THE ARBITRAGE PRICING THEORY

### A.2.1 Tests Based on US Data

Since the arbitrage pricing theory assumes a factor model of security returns, any test of its predictions must incorporate such a factor model and be, in effect, a joint test of the equilibrium theory and the appropriateness of the selected factor model. Moreover, the APT makes relatively weak predictions. It does imply that when all pervasive factors are taken into account, the remaining portion of return on a typical security should be expected to equal the risk-free interest rate. Testing this implication is possible in principle but difficult in practice. For example, when a model such as that shown in equation (9.9) is fitted to data for stock returns, the "zero factor" will include elements of a "stock factor." Analyses using both bonds and stocks can include corresponding factors explicitly, reducing the possibility that the zero factor does, in fact, include elements of pervasive sources of risk. However, it may never be possible to find a set of securities so diverse that consistency of the zero factor with risk-free interest rates can be used as a test of the APT.

A more promising test concerns the prediction that security expected returns will be related only to sensitivities to pervasive factors. In particular, there should be no relationship between expected returns and securities' nonfactor risks. Since the total risk of a security includes nonfactor risk as well as factor risk, its inclusion in an analysis of expected returns should not help explain differences in expected returns.

One study used data from 1962 through 1972, computing average returns, sensitivities to each of five factors (obtained via factor analysis), and the total standard deviation of returns for 1260 securities.[24] Given the computational demands of the factor analysis method utilized, much of the analysis had to be perfomed on groups of 30 stocks

---

[22] J.D.Jobson and Bob Korkie, "Some Tests of Linear Asset Pricing with Multivariate Normality," *Canadian Journal of Administrative Sciences* 2, no. 1 (June 1985):114–38.

[23] A.L.Calvet and J.Lefoll, "Risk and Return in Canadian Capital Markets," *Canadian Journal of Administrative Sciences* 5, no. 1 (March 1988):1–12.

[24] Richard Roll and Stephen A. Ross, "An Empirical Investigation of the Arbitrage Pricing Theory," *Journal of Finance* 35, no. 5 (December, 1980):1073–1103. For two recent empirical papers that suggest the APT prices most securities with little error and is better than the CAPM, see Bruce N. Lehmann and David M. Modest, "The Empirical Foundations of the Arbitrage Pricing Theory," *Journal of Financial Economics* 21, no. 2 (September 1988):213–54; and Gregory Connor and Robert A. Korajczyk, "Risk and Return in an Equilibrium APT: Application of a New Test Methodology," *Journal of Financial Economics* 21, no. 2 (September 1988):255–89.

rather than on the full set of securities. For each of the resulting 42 groups, regression analysis was performed with average return as the dependent variable and sensitivities to the five factors and total standard deviation as independent variables. In the majority of groups there was a statistically significant relationship between average return and sensitivity to at least one factor; it was also determined that it is unlikely that there are more than five important factors. Furthermore, average returns in the majority of groups were not significantly related to total standard deviation. The results, while not definitive, are consistent with the theory.

A later study found that four macro-economic factors, corresponding to (1) expected and unexpected inflation, (2) industrial production, (3) the yield spread between high-grade and low-grade corporate bonds, and (4) the yield spread between long-term and short-term government bond returns provided a good explanation of expected security returns.[25]

## ☐ A.2.2   Tests Based on Canadian Data

Three tests have been performed using Canadian data.[26] In one study utilizing factor analysis only one significant factor (presumably a proxy for the market portfolio) was identified. In a second, also using factor analysis, only four of twelve factors identified were significant. The analysis included a cross-sectional examination of the intercept to determine first, if it was intertemporally constant and second, if it equalled the risk-free rate. The positive results obtained for both tests support the theory. The third test (or rather series of tests) investigated which macro-economic factors best explain security returns. Two distinct models with different explanatory variables were developed. The first used the same four factors described in the US study above plus a value-weighted market index while the second used the yield spread ((3) above), the value-weighted market index, the rate of growth of unemployment, and the Canada/US exchange rate. The empirical tests showed that, for the sample of securities considered and the time period employed, both models performed equally well. It would appear that the APT is a useful model, but additional testing and analysis is required before it can be applied in practical portfolio applications.

## QUESTIONS AND PROBLEMS

1. In what significant ways does APT differ from the CAPM?
2. Is it true that if one believes APT is a correct theory of asset pricing, then the risk-return relationship derived from the CAPM is necessarily incorrect? Why?

---

[25] See Nai-Fu Chen, Richard Roll, and Stephen A. Ross, "Economic Forces and the Stock Market," *Journal of Business* 59, no. 3 (July 1986):383–403.

[26] L. Kryzanowski and M. C. To,"General Factor Models and the Structure of Security Returns", *Journal of Financial and Quantitative Analysis* 18, no. 1 (March 1983):31–52; Patricia J. Hughes, "A Test of the Arbitrage Pricing Theory", *Canadian Journal of Administrative Sciences* 1, no. 2 (December 1984):195–214; Eben Otuteye, "On the Specification of the Arbitrage Pricing Theory", *Proceedings*, Administrative Sciences Association of Canada Conference, 1991.

3. If security returns are generated by a multiple-factor model and the CAPM does not exist, is the basic process of constructing the efficient set and determining the investor's optimal portfolio materially altered? Explain.

4. Included among the factors that might be expected to be pervasive are growth in real GNP, real interest rates, unexpected inflation, and oil prices. For each factor, provide an example of an industry that is expected to have a high (either positive or negative) sensitivity to the factor.

5. What is meant by the term "arbitrage profit?"

6. Assume that returns on securities are generated by three factors according to the following relationship:

$$r_i = r_f + b_{i1} F_1 + b_{i2} F_2 + b_{i3} F_3 + e_i.$$

Given two securities, $X$ and $Y$, if:

$$r_f = 4\% \quad b_{X1} = 0.07 \quad \sigma_{F1} = 12\%$$
$$F_1 = 5\% \quad b_{X2} = 1.30 \quad \sigma_{F2} = 14\%$$
$$F_2 = 7\% \quad b_{X3} = 1.10 \quad \sigma_{F3} = 8\%$$
$$F_3 = 8\% \quad b_{Y1} = 0.80 \quad \sigma_{eX} = 20\%$$
$$b_{Y2} = 0.90 \quad \sigma_{eY} = 30\%$$
$$b_{Y3} = 1.20$$

a. What is the expected return for stocks $X$ and $Y$?

b. What is the standard deviation of stocks $X$ and $Y$?

7. What is a "pure factor" portfolio? How are such portfolios constructed?

8. Assume that security returns are generated by a factor model in which two factors are pervasive. The sensitivities of two securities and of the risk-free asset to each of the two factors is shown below, along with the expected return on each security.

| Security | $b_{i1}$ | $b_{i2}$ | Expected Return |
|----------|-------|-------|-----------------|
| $A$ | 0.50 | 0.80 | 16.2% |
| $B$ | 1.50 | 1.40 | 21.6 |
| $r_f$ | 0.00 | 0.00 | 10.0 |

a. If Anne Miller has $100 to invest and sells short $50 of security $B$ and purchases $150 of security $A$, what is the sensitivity of Anne's portfolio to the two factors? (Ignore margin requirements.)

b. If Anne now borrows $100 at the risk-free rate and invests the proceeds of the loan along with the original $100 in securities $A$ and $B$ in the same proportions as described in part (a), what is the sensitivity of this portfolio to the two factors?

c. What is the expected return on the portfolio created in part (b)?

d. What is the expected return premium of factor 2?

9. Assume that the CAPM holds and that returns on securities are generated by the following factor model:

$$r_i = r_f + b_{i1} F_1 + b_{i2} F_2 + e_i.$$

You are also given the following information:

$$\sigma_M^2 = 324 \quad b_{A1} = 0.80 \quad b_{B1} = 1.00$$
$$\text{COV}(F_1, r_M) = 156 \quad b_{A2} = 1.10 \quad b_{B2} = 0.70$$
$$\text{COV}(F_2, r_M) = 500$$

    a. Calculate the beta coefficients of securities $A$ and $B$.

    b. If the risk-free rate is 6% and the expected return on the market portfolio is 12%, what is the expected return on securities $A$ and $B$?

10. Benny Kauff has asserted that, "The CAPM does not *assume* that returns are generated by a factor model. However, it does *imply* that returns are generated by a factor model." Explain what Benny means.

11. (Appendix Question) Some people have argued that the market portfolio can never be measured and that the CAPM, therefore, is untestable. Others have argued that the APT specifies neither the number of factors nor their identity and, hence, is also untestable. If these views are correct, does this mean the theories are of no value? Explain.

# SUGGESTED READINGS

Nai-Fu Chen, Richard Roll and Stephen Ross, "Economic Forces and the Stock Market," *Journal of Business* 59, no. 3 (July 1986):383–403 and

William F. Sharpe, "Factors in New York Stock Exchange Security Returns, 1931–1979," *Journal of Portfolio Management* 8, no. 4 (Summer 1982):5–19 explore the factors that may influence security returns.

Stephen Ross, "The Arbitrage Theory of Capital Asset Pricing," *Journal of Economic Theory* 13, no. 3 (December 1976):341–60 and

Stephen Ross, " Risk Return and Arbitrage," sec. 9 of *Risk and Return in Finance*, vol. 1, ed. Irwin Friend and James L. Bicksler (Cambridge, Mass.: Ballinger Publishing Co., 1977) show the development of the APT.

Richard Roll, "A Critique of the Asset Pricing Theory's Tests: Part I. On Past and Potential Testability of the Theory," *Journal of Financial Economics* 4, no. 2, (March 1977):129–76,

Jay Shanken, "The Arbitrage Pricing Theory: Is it Testable?" *Journal of Finance* 37, no. 5 (December 1982):1129–40 and

Gordon J. Alexander and Jack Clark Francis, *Portfolio Analysis* (Englewood Cliffs, N.J.: Prentice Hall, 1986) Chapters 10 and 14, all deal with the issue of testability of asset pricing models.

Patricia J. Hughes, "A Test of the Arbitrage Pricing Theory," *Canadian Journal of Administrative Sciences* 1, no. 2 (December 1984):195–214 and

Eben Otutye, "How Economic Forces Explain Canadian Stock Returns," *Canadian Investment Review* IV, no. 1 (Spring 1991):93–9 both provide a Canadian perspective on the APT.

# Chapter 10

# TAXES

A well-worn saying holds that nothing is certain but death and taxes. Unfortunately, governments are sometimes responsible for the former, and they are virtually always the source of the latter. Governmental activities, moreover, normally play a central role in determining changes in the overall price level of an economy. Occasionally, such changes are in the downward direction — that is, there is deflation. The more common experience, however, is that of rising prices — inflation.

Neither taxation nor inflation should be regarded as an unmitigated evil. Each provides benefits to some individuals that may outweigh the associated costs that others have to bear. Regardless of whether or not the benefits outweigh the costs, both taxes and inflation have an impact on investment decisions and investment results and they are sufficiently important in present-day societies to warrant considerable discussion. While the next chapter deals with inflation, this chapter provides an overview of some of the more important aspects of taxation from the viewpoint of the investor.

Federal and provincial tax laws play a major role in the way securities are priced in the marketplace, since, understandably, investors are concerned with after-tax returns, rather than before-tax returns. Accordingly, the investor should determine the tax rate applicable to him or her before making any investment decision. This tax rate is not the same for all securities for a given individual investor, when both federal and provincial taxes are considered it can be as low as 6.8% in the case of certain stocks and in excess of 50% for corporate bonds. After determining the applicable tax rate, the investor can estimate a security's expected after-tax return and risk. Upon doing so, an investment decision can be made wisely.

## 10.1 TAXES IN CANADA

In Canada, personal and corporate taxes are levied by the federal, the ten provincial, and two territorial governments. In the case of personal income taxes, in all provinces except Quebec, the federal government acts as a collection agency, therefore, individuals file a single tax return with the federal government which then distributes the appropriate amount to the provinces. Residents of Quebec must file two separate tax returns, one with Revenue Canada and one with the Quebec Ministry of Finance.

Many of the specific tax rates and provisions cited in this chapter are contained in the amendments to the *Income Tax Act* that were passed in September 1988. Changes do occur from year to year, and current regulations should, of course, be consulted when preparing tax returns or considering major investment decisions. However, the material given here can be considered broadly representative of current taxation in the Canada.

Generally speaking, the most important taxes for investment decision making are personal and corporate income taxes. The essential elements of each will be described, and the manner in which they influence the pricing of securities will be considered.

## 10.2  CORPORATE INCOME TAXES

There are three forms of business organizations in Canada and in many other countries — corporations, partnerships, and single proprietorships. The corporate form of organization is the largest in terms of the dollar value of assets owned, even though there are more firms organized as partnerships or single proprietorships. Legally, a corporation is regarded as a separate entity, whereas a proprietorship or partnership is considered an extension of its owner or owners. Income earned by proprietorships and partnerships is taxed primarily through the personal income tax levied on their owners. Income earned by a corporation may be taxed twice — once when it is earned, via the corporate income tax, and again when it is received as dividends by holders of the firm's securities, via the personal income tax.[1]

This double taxation of corporate income may at first seem inefficient, if not unfair. It also raises questions about the efficiency of the corporate form of organization. Suffice it to say that limited liability and the ability to subdivide ownership and to transfer shares of that ownership appear to be of sufficient value to more than offset the tax law disadvantages. Moreover, without the corporate income tax, personal tax rates would have to be increased if the level of government expenditures were to remain constant without increasing the national debt.

## ☐ 10.2.1  Corporate Tax Rates (Federal and Provincial)

The corporate income tax is relatively simple in one respect. There are only a few basic rates applicable to all taxable income. The rates vary depending on the size of the corporation and the nature of its operations. Table 10.1 shows the federal and provincial tax rates that came into effect on July 1, 1991.

The federal and provincial rates are additive, thus a Manitoba non-manufacturing large corporation pays 45.8% of all its reported income in combined taxes. As demonstrated in Table 10.1 the tax system favors firms in the manufacturing sector. This is intended to stimulate employment. The system of tax rates is also simple in the sense that the *marginal tax rates* and *average tax rates* are equal because there is a single rate applicable to a given corporation. The marginal tax rate is the tax rate it would pay on an additional dollar of income. The average tax rate is equal to the total amount of taxes paid divided by the total income subject to tax. The average rate measures the overall impact of taxes, but the marginal rate is more relevant for most decisions.

---

[1] The *Income Tax Act* attempts to minimize the effects of double taxation on dividends — an issue to be discussed in more detail later.

**TABLE 10.1**

Federal and Provincial Corporate Tax Rates, 1991.

| Jurisdiction | Small Canadian-Controlled Corporation [a] | | Other Cdn. Corporations | |
|---|---|---|---|---|
| | Mfg. | Non-mfg. | Mfg. | Non-mfg. |
| Federal [b] | 12.8% | 12.8% | 23.8% | 28.8% |
| Provincial: | | | | |
| Alberta | 6.0 | 6.0 | 15.5 | 15.5 |
| British Columbia | 9.0 | 9.0 | 15.0 | 15.0 |
| Manitoba | 10.0 | 10.0 | 17.0 | 17.0 |
| New Brunswick | 9.0 | 9.0 | 17.0 | 17.0 |
| Newfoundland | 10.0 | 10.0 | 17.0 | 17.0 |
| Northwest Terr. | 5.0 | 5.0 | 12.0 | 12.0 |
| Nova Scotia | 10.0 | 10.0 | 16.0 | 16.0 |
| Ontario | 10.0 | 10.0 | 14.5 | 15.5 |
| Quebec | 3.5 | 3.5 | 6.3 | 6.3 |
| Prince Edward I. | 10.0 | 10.0 | 15.0 | 15.0 |
| Saskatchewan | 10.0 | 10.0 | 15.0 | 15.0 |
| Yukon Terr. | 2.5 | 5.0 | 7.5 | 10.0 |

[a] Certain Canadian controled private corporations are eligible for these rates.
[b] Includes the 3% surtax.

SOURCE: KPMG, Peat, Marwick, Thorne, *Tax Facts, 1991*, (Toronto, 1991), p. 27.

## ☐ 10.2.2 Defining Income

Corporate income is partly a philosophic concept, partly an artifact of legal requirements, partly a result of accounting conventions, partly an indication of the hopes of the firm's management, and sometimes only incidentally related to underlying economic factors.

For tax purposes, corporate income is defined as revenues minus expenses. However, a problem arises in measuring these two elements. Simply put, this problem involves determining when to recognize revenues and expenses as having occurred. If a company sells an airplane this year but payment is to be made in instalments over the next 5 years, when is the sales price to be considered taxable revenue? If a new plant is to be built and paid for this year but is to be used to produce goods for the next 20 years, when is the outlay to be considered as an expense? Accountants have a set of procedures, known as generally accepted accounting principles (GAAP), that can be utilized to handle these and many more subtle cases. However, there is extremely wide latitude within these principles.

The government has prescribed certain limits on the procedures that can be used to calculate income when determining a corporation's income tax liability. In some cases, the firm is required to use the same procedures when reporting its income to its shareholders; in other cases it can (and often does) use different procedures, sometimes resulting in a noticeably different income figure.[2]

---

[2] Differences of this sort are usually described in the firm's annual report.

# □ 10.2.3 Depreciation

The determination of the annual amount of depreciation of an asset that is used in a business provides a dramatic example of the effect that alternative accounting procedures can have on income. If a corporation buys a computer for $1 million, it is entitled to charge off this cost as a deductible expense when computing taxable income. Each dollar deducted will reduce taxable income by a dollar and, hence, taxes paid by $0.40, assuming the marginal corporate income tax rate is 40%. Thus, the $1 million outlay will produce tax savings of $400,000. However, the present value of these tax savings depends on the years in which they are obtained. The sooner the cost can be written off, the greater the benefit to the firm. In the best of all possible worlds the corporation and its owners could deduct the entire cost of the computer as an expense in the year in which it is incurred. Barring this, the firm would like to allocate the cost against income as soon as possible.

Revenue Canada (and the provincial authorities), in administering the tax laws, looks at the situation in a different way. Whereas the taxpayer would like to maximize the present value of tax savings, the tax collector would like to minimize it. Thus, the regulations set limits on the manner in which outlays for fixed assets may be deducted as expenses. For example, the cost of land may not be deducted at all, since it is not normally considered to be a depreciating asset, although the cost of improvements to land (for example, sidewalks and buildings) can generally be deducted over a period of years. The cost of fixed assets that are regarded as having a limited useful life may also be deducted over a period of years.

For purposes of reporting corporate income to shareholders, a manager might want to allocate the cost of a fixed asset over the period during which it is expected to contribute to revenue. This is usually called the asset's *estimated useful life*. For tax purposes, as long as the firm is profitable, it is generally advantageous to underestimate the useful life in order to write off the cost as rapidly as possible. To control this urge, the legislation prescribes a standard set of procedures for allocating the costs of fixed assets to years subsequent to their purchase.

When reporting to shareholders, many firms depreciate the costs of fixed assets using the *straight-line method*. With this method, the same proportion of the cost of a particular asset is written off in each year of the asset's useful life. However, the *Income Tax Act* allows a potentially more advantageous procedure to be used for calculating taxable income. The *capital cost allowance* (CCA) system prescribes specific methods of depreciation for various types of assets. For this purpose, assets are divided into 41 broad classes based on the type of asset, its estimated useful life, and the way it is used. For most assets the *declining-balance method (DBM)* is used to calculate CCA claims. The *Act* prescribes specific methods for computing CCA claims for the other assets. Table 10.2 lists some typical examples of the CCA classes with a brief description of the most common assets included in each class, together with the allowable method of calculation. Where declining balance is the approved method, the appropriate rate is shown in column 2 of the table. The method is best described by an illustration. Suppose that a company acquires an asset worth $100,000 in year 1 that falls into class 8. Under the regulations, a 20% declining balance rate is applicable, but only 10% may be claimed in the first year. The table below shows the calculation of the CCA claims for the first five years:

| Year | Undepreciated Balance at Start of Year | CCA Claim | Undepreciated Balance at Year End |
|---|---|---|---|
| 1 | $100,000 | $10,000 | $90,000 |
| 2 | 90,000 | 18,000 | 78,000 |
| 3 | 78,000 | 15,600 | 62,400 |
| 4 | 62,400 | 12,480 | 49,920 |
| 5 | 49,920 | 9,984 | 39,936 |

In theory, at least, the asset is never completely depreciated for tax purposes even though it may no longer exist. A humorist has suggested that this amounts to depreciating the asset's ghost.[3]

Although ultimately the total amount written off will be the same under both the straight-line and declining-balance methods, its present value will generally be greater (and thus, the present value of taxes paid will be smaller) if the latter method is used. With straight-line depreciation, equal percentages of the cost of the property can be deducted each year, whereas with DBM, the larger percentages which can be deducted in the earlier years are offset by smaller percentages in the later years. Accordingly, a firm using DBM will pay lower income taxes in the earlier years and higher income taxes in the later years . Since the total amount of taxes paid over an extended period of time is the same with both methods and since postponing taxes is beneficial due to the time value of money, DBM is usually advantageous.

A notable feature of the CCA system is that the values of assets in the same class may be aggregated in a *pool* and the CCA claim calculated as though it were a single asset. At the end of each year the value of the pool is reduced by the amount of the CCA claimed in that year. Assets in the pool lose their individual identity and there is no need to maintain detailed records for each. The value of any new assets is simply added to the pool and the salvage value (or selling price) of those disposed of subtracted. For example, suppose that a firm had $10,000,000 in the Class 8 pool at the beginning of 1990. During the year it acquired assets worth $1,000,000 and retired none. The CCA claim for 1990 would then be:

$$\$10,000,000 \times 0.2 + \$1,000,000 \times 0.1 = \$2,100,000$$

The normal rate of 20% is applied to the pool, but only half that rate (10%) can be used for the new asset. The value of the pool at the beginning of 1991 then becomes:

$$\$11,000,000 - \$2,100,000 = \$8,900,000$$

During 1991, the firm acquires no new assets but sells surplus assets for $750,000. The CCA claim for 1991 will then be:

$$(\$8,900,000 - \$750,000) \times 0.2 = \$1,630,000$$

---

[3] The DBM is also known as the diminishing-balance or double-declining balance method. For more details on the computation of CCA claims see Paul Halpern, J. Fred Weston and Eugene F. Brigham, *Canadian Managerial Finance*, (Toronto, Ont., Holt, Rinehart and Winston of Canada, Limited), 1989.

**TABLE 10.2**

Short Description of Some Typical Capital Cost Allowance Asset Classes.

| Class Number | CCA Rate [a] | Examples of Types of Assets [b] |
|---|---|---|
| 1 | 4% | Public utility and other similar property; and building or other structure including component parts. |
| 4 | 6% | trolley bus system. |
| 7 | 15% | boat or vessel other than drillship and offshore platform included in Class 41. |
| 8 | 20% | machinery, equipment, furniture and other tangible property not specifically included in any other class; outdoor advertising sign used to earn rental outcome. |
| 9 | 25% | aircraft. |
| 10 | 30% | automotive; computer; film; certain logging equipment; certain resource property; telecommunication spacecraft acquired after 1987. |
| 12 | 100% | tool costing less than $200; certain film; computer software; mine shaft. |
| 15 | | wood assets — cost is written off on the basis of the volume of wood removed. |
| 16 | 40% | taxicab; automobile acquired and leased on a short-term basis; coin-operated video game or pinball machine. |
| 17 | 8% | surface construction such as a road or parking lot. |
| 24 | | equipment designed for water pollution control — 25% in the first year, 50% in the second year and 25% in the third year. |
| 26 | 5% | catalyst; heavy water. |
| 33 | 15% | timber resource property. |
| 35 | 7% | railway car. |
| 37 | 15% | amusement park. |
| 38 | (note 1) | earth moving equipment acquired after 1987. |

Note 1: 40% for 1988, 35% for 1989, 30% thereafter, with daily prorating for non-calendar taxation years.
[a] Only half of the CCA rate may be used in the year in which an asset is acquired.
[b] The alternative method of depreciation to be used is given if the DBM is not prescribed.

and the value of the pool becomes:

$$\$8,900,000 - \$750,000 - \$1,630,000 = \$6,520,000$$

that is carried over to 1992. The rates shown in Table 10.2 are the maximum that may be claimed in any year. If, for any reason, a firm claims less than the maximum then a smaller amount is deducted from the pool and a larger amount is carried over to the next year.

This system significantly simplifies the accounting requirements, but complications arise when either an asset is sold for more than its original purchase price or the last asset in a pool is disposed of. The treatment of these cases goes beyond the scope of this discussion.

There are many reasons why corporate income reported to shareholders may differ from that used for tax purposes, but different depreciation assumptions are often a major factor. If the tax paid by a large, profitable, non-manufacturing corporation in British Columbia diverges significantly from 43.8% (the applicable rate) of its apparent taxable income, as reported to shareholders, examination of the depreciation procedure may prove illuminating.

## □ 10.2.4  Inventory Valuation

Another vexing problem associated with the measurement of corporate income concerns the cost of inventory sold during the year. This problem arises when prices are changing and a firm holds inventory for long periods. Consider the fairly simple case of a retailer of sailboats. At the start of the year the retailer has 100 boats in stock, all purchased for $10,000 each. During the year the retailer takes delivery of 100 more but must pay $11,000 each. During the year 110 boats are sold, which means the retailer ends the year with 90 in stock. What was the cost of the 110 boats that were sold during the year?

The retailer may have sold all the 100 "old" boats first and then sold 10 of the "new" boats, or the retailer may have sold all the 100 new boats first and then sold 10 of the old boats. Alternatively, some other mixture of old and new boats might have been sold. However, specific identification of the boats sold is rarely taken into account in the calculation of revenue. An accountant may assume any of the above combinations, without regard for the actual facts of the situation.

If all the old boats are assumed to have been sold first — this is the *first-in, first-out* (FIFO) method. If all the new boats are assumed to have been sold first — this is the *last-in, first-out* (LIFO) method. If equal numbers of both old and new boats are assumed to have been sold — this is the *average-cost* method.

Revenue Canada has specific rules about inventory valuation which reduce the available choices. Specifically the *Income Tax Act* regulations provide three alternative methods of valuing inventory:

(a) valuation at the lower of cost or fair market value for each item (or class of items if specific items are not readily distinguishable) in the inventory;
(b) valuation of the entire inventory at cost;
(c) valuation of the entire inventory at fair market value.

Once a specific method has been selected it must be used consistently in subsequent years. The costs referred to above may be determined in one of three ways: individual costs associated with specific items in inventory, average cost as described earlier, or FIFO. Unlike other jurisdictions, notably the United States, LIFO is not an acceptable method in Canada.[4]

The effect of the different assumptions on reported income is significant as shown in Table 10.3.

---

[4]For further details about acceptable inventory valuation methods see Revenue Canada Interpretation Bulletin IT-473, *Inventory Valuation*, Ottawa, Ont., March 17,1981, revised December 5, 1986.

**TABLE 10.3**

The Impact of Different Inventory Valuation Methods.

Revenue: *110 Boats at $15,000 = $1,650,000*

| Cost by FIFO Method | Cost by LIFO Method | Cost by Average-Cost Method |
|---|---|---|
| 100 at $10,000 = $1,000,000 | 100 at $11,000 = $1,100,000 | 55 at $10,000 = $ 550,000 |
| 10 at 11,000 = 110,000 | 10 at 10,000 = 100,000 | 55 at 11,000 = 605,000 |
| $1,110,000 | $1,200,000 | $1,155,000 |
| Income $ 540,000 | $ 450,000 | $ 495,000 |
| Tax −183,600 | −153,000 | −168,300 |
| Income after tax $ 356,400 | $ 297,000 | $ 326,700 |
| Cost of remaining | | 45 at $10,000 + |
| inventory: | | |
| 90 at $11,000 = $ 990,000 | 90 at $10,000 = $ 900,000 | 45 at $11,000 = $ 945,000 |

When prices have been rising, the LIFO method will permit a corporation to charge a larger amount to cost of goods sold now, with a smaller amount being charged in the future. This will lower current taxes and raise them in the future. The net result is a fall in the present value of taxes paid, which is beneficial to the owners of the firm. Since rising prices have been prevalent for the past 30 years, one would expect firms to adopt the LIFO method for tax purposes, just as one would expect firms to prefer accelerated depreciation. In the US, before 1970, many firms used FIFO, suggesting that in times of moderate inflation, many managers were willing to sacrifice some real benefits to improve the appearance of their firm's financial statements. However, as the pace of inflation increased, usage of LIFO became much more common. In Canada from the late 1970s to 1988, firms were allowed to deduct 3% of the value of inventories when determining taxable income. This deduction mitigated some of the effects of inflation.

## ☐ 10.2.5 Amortization and Depletion

Allocation of the cost of a fixed asset over its estimated useful life is termed depreciation. A comparable procedure applied to a natural resource, such as a mineral deposit or an oil reserve, is known as *depletion*. When applied to certain intangible assets, such as patent rights, trademarks or goodwill, it is known as *amortization*. Amortization is handled with a procedure similar to that used for the depreciation of tangible assets. For any given business, intangible assets are grouped into one pool. Three-quarters of the cost or value of each asset may be included in the pool and amortized at a 7% declining balance rate.

Depletion is another matter. Depletion is utilized to allocate the cost of finding, developing, or purchasing a so-called wasting asset as an expense against income over a number of years. Revenue Canada treats expenses associated with mineral deposits differently from those associated with oil exploration and development. Specified mineral exploration and development expenses may be aggregated and included in the firm's *earned depletion base*. The firm may then deduct the lesser of either 25% of its resource-derived profits or the balance in its earned depletion base in arriving at its taxable income. Oil and gas exploration and development expenses are pooled and amortized at a 10% declining balance rate in the same way as tangible assets. In both case, these expenses must be related directly to resource development in Canada.

## □ 10.2.6 Deductibility of Interest Payments

In Canada interest is regarded as a business expense and can, therefore, be deducted from revenue when calculating taxable income. For example, consider two firms, each with revenues of $25,000 and noninterest expenses of $15,000. Firm A is financed by both debt and equity and pays $5000 in interest to its creditors. As shown in Table 10.4, its net income after taxes is $4250, which is available to be paid as dividends, if desired. Thus, a total amount of $9250 ($5,000 + $4,250) can be paid to those who provided the firm's capital.

**TABLE 10.4**

The Effect of Deducting Interest Payments.

|  | Firm A | Firm B |
|---|---|---|
| Revenue | $25,000 | $25,000 |
| Cost of goods sold | 15,000 | 15,000 |
| Revenue minus expense | 10,000 | 10,000 |
| Interest paid | 5,000 | 0 |
| Taxable income | 5,000 | 10,000 |
| Tax (at 15%) | 750 | 1,500 |
| Available for dividends | $ 4,250 | $ 8,500 |

The other part of the table shows the results for firm B, which differs only with respect to financing. All its capital was provided by common stock financing. Thus, the entire $10,000 of income is subject to tax, leaving only $8500 for distribution to those who provided the firm's capital.

The deductibility of interest payments provides an apparent tax advantage for the use of debt over equity funds. For this reason, it may seem surprising that firms do not choose to obtain more of their capital by issuing bonds. Indeed, the dramatic difference in tax treatment raises substantial questions about the definition of debt and interest, on the one hand, and stocks and dividend payments, on the other. Revenue Canada pays considerable attention to any arrangement designed to provide the tax characteristics of debt with the financial characteristics of equity. To qualify as debt, there must be a definite lender, a definite borrower, a definite ascertainable obligation (a specific amount), and a time of maturity (date when the debt must be repaid). That is, debt should be represented by an instrument (a legal document such as a contract) that contains an unconditional legal obligation to pay a certain sum either on demand or on a specific date, with interest. Payments made under any other arrangement are not likely to be deductible for purposes of income taxation.

Failure to make interest payments may have serious consequences for the firm and its management. In many cases bankruptcy results, with mandatory and costly corporate reorganization. The greater the magnitude of interest payments in relation to dividend payments, the greater the probability of this type of unfortunate event. This risk of bankruptcy, along with the associated costs of bankruptcy, provides a constraint on the use of debt financing, despite its obvious tax advantage.

## ☐ 10.2.7 Corporate Income from Dividends, Interest, and Capital Gains

The full amount of the dividends *received* by a corporation can be excluded from income when calculating the corporation's income tax liability. The recipient corporation is regarded as a *conduit* between the issuing corporation and individual investors. This special treatment of dividends avoids the partial triple taxation of income. Consider how dividends would be taxed if this exclusion did not exist. Corporation A is taxed on its income and then pays dividends to one of its shareholders, corporation B. Corporation B then pays taxes on its income, which includes the dividends received from A. Finally, the shareholders of B pay income taxes on the dividends received from B. Thus, a dollar of income earned by A would be taxed three times (a tax on A, then a tax on B, then a tax on the shareholders of B) if the dividend exclusion did not exist. With the dividend exclusion, a dollar of income earned by A is taxed, for all practical purposes, only twice. Despite the existence of the dividend tax credit that applies to dividends received by individual investors in Canada some degree of double taxation still exists.

No deduction is allowed for interest received by a corporation; it is simply added to income and taxed at the regular rate. This means that the effective tax rate on interest received from bonds is substantially greater than the rate on common and preferred shares. This differential tax treatment has an effect on the relative prices that corporate investors are willing to pay for these securities, since their concern is with relative after-tax yields. That is, since preferred shares are generally viewed as being riskier than bonds, the after-tax yield on preferred shares needs to be higher in order for investors to be interested in purchasing them. Given the favorable tax treatment on preferred shares for corporate investors, it is possible for preferred shares to have a lower before-tax yield than bonds while still enabling the corporate investor who buys the more risky preferred shares to be rewarded by earning, relative to bonds, a higher after-tax yield.

## ☐ 10.2.8 Tax-Exempt Organizations

Many organizations are wholly or partly exempt from federal income taxes. Nonprofit religious, charitable, or educational foundations generally qualify. Such foundations are required to pay out to their beneficiaries a minimum percentage of the value of their assets (3.5% in 1991). Failure to do so can result in a punitive and confiscatory tax.

Investment companies, often called mutual funds, may elect to be treated as regulated investment companies for tax purposes. This privilege is granted if certain conditions are met. For example, the funds of the investment company must be invested primarily in securities, without undue concentration in any one. Thus, its income takes the form of dividends and interest received on its investments, as well as capital gains from price appreciation realized when investments are sold at a price that is higher than their purchase price. A regulated investment company pays income tax only on income and capital gains not distributed to its shareholders. As a result of this tax treatment, such companies distribute substantially all income and gains and, in doing so, end up not having to pay any taxes.

Employee pension, profit-sharing, and share-ownership plans may also qualify for tax-exempt status. Such a plan may entrust its assets, which are usually securities, to a *fiduciary* (for example, a trust company). The fiduciary receives new contributions, makes required payments, and manages the investments owned by the plan. A fiduciary under a qualified plan (that is, a plan that meets all the requirements of applicable legislation) pays no taxes on either income or capital gains.

Another example of a tax-exempt entity is the personal trust. Here, funds are provided for the benefit of one or more individuals by another individual or individuals with a fiduciary serving as a trustee. Some trusts are created by wills, others by a contract among living persons. Whatever the origin, trusts generally pay taxes only on income that is not distributed to the designated beneficiaries. It is important, however, to have adequate legal and tax advice when establishing these trusts to avoid Revenue Canada's *income attribution rules* which will be discussed later in this chapter.

Income and capital gains earned by investment companies, pension funds, and personal trusts do not go untaxed forever. Payments made to investment company shareholders, pension fund beneficiaries, and the beneficiaries of personal trusts are subject to applicable personal income tax rules. The exemptions apply only to taxes that might otherwise be levied at the previous stage.

## 10.3 PERSONAL INCOME TAXES

Although the corporate income tax is an important feature of the investment scene, its impact on most individuals is indirect. This is not so for the personal income tax. Few investors can avoid dealing with it in detail, at both an economic and an emotional level. Its provisions have major and direct effects on investment behavior.

## ☐ 10.3.1 Personal Tax Rates (Federal)

Taxes must be paid on an individual's world-wide income as defined in the *Income Tax Act*.[5] Capital gains were not included in income for tax purposes until the *Income Tax Act* of 1972 came into force. Certain items may be deducted from income before computing the tax due and capital gains and losses are subject to special procedures which are described in a later section. Deductions of special importance for investment purposes are described in this section as well as in later sections.

Three definitions are relevant for tax purposes. *Total Income* is the sum of income received from all sources including self-employment (reported as gross income less expenses). *Net Income* is total income less certain allowable expenses (for example, contributions to certain retirement funds, union and/or professional dues, alimony payments). *Taxable Income* is net income less other specified deductions.

Despite the 1988 changes to the *Income Tax Act*, many people are still of the opinion that little is simple about personal income taxes in Canada. Table 10.5 shows the federal tax rates in effect in 1991.

---

[5] For more details see Macdonald and Cronkwright, *Income Taxation in Canada*, (Toronto, Ont., Prentice-Hall Canada Inc.), 1989.

**TABLE 10.5**

Personal Federal Income Tax Rates, 1991.

| Taxable Income | Tax Rate |
|----------------|----------|
| $28,784 or less | $0 + 15% on next $28,784 |
| 28,785 to 57,567 | 4,893 + 26% on next $28,784 |
| 57,568 or more | 12,377 + 29% on remainder |

These figures are used to calculate the *gross federal tax*. Each taxpayer is entitled to a non-refundable tax credit which is subtracted directly from the gross federal tax to obtain the *basic federal tax*. Finally the following surtaxes must be added to arrive at the *total federal tax payable:*

> 5% of the basic federal tax on the first $ 12,500,
> plus 10% on any amount over $ 12,500.

## ☐ 10.3.2 Provincial and Territorial Income Taxes

All provinces levy personal income taxes which, except for those in Quebec, are calculated as a percentage of the basic federal tax. These rates vary from 44% in the Northwest Territories to 62% in Newfoundland. Ontario's rate of 53% falls between these two extremes and will be used in subsequent examples. In addition, six provinces (Alberta, Manitoba, Nova Scotia, Ontario, Prince Edward Island, and Saskatchewan) also levy provincial surtaxes on high income taxpayers and four provinces (Alberta, Manitoba, Ontario, and Saskatchewan) allow low income residents a tax reduction.

In any investment decision, the important figure to know is the total federal plus provincial tax payable. Table 10.6 shows the detailed tax calculation for an unmarried resident of Ontario (or a married resident with a spouse earning more than $5757 per year and no children) with a taxable income of $90,000 derived from employment and interest bearing securities and with a non-refundable tax credit of $1100.[6]

Some taxpayers may be able, in addition, to claim a marriage allowance of $ 5233 and other amounts for such items as dependant children, disability allowance, tuition fees, etc. The non-refundable tax credit is 17% of the sum of all these allowances. It is referred to as non-refundable because it can be used to reduce the tax bill to zero but not to generate a refund.

The combined federal and Ontario provincial tax rates are plotted in Figure 10.1. The top line shows the marginal tax (i.e., the tax rate payable on any additional dollar earned).[7] The lower line shows the average tax rate, which is the ratio of total tax paid to total taxable income.

As can be seen in Figure 10.1, the average rate, a measurement of the overall impact of taxes, is below the marginal rate. The latter, however, is more relevant for most

---

[6] Dividends are subject to a different tax treatment from interest payments as described in a later section. In 1991, *all* taxpayers are allowed to claim a basic personal allowance of $6280 in order to calculate their non-refundable tax credit.

[7] The marginal rate shown in Figure 10.1 is a step-function except for taxable incomes between $6471 and $9251 where the Ontario tax reduction is in effect.

**TABLE 10.6**

Detailed Tax Calculation for an Ontario Resident.

| | | |
|---|---|---|
| Taxable Income | $90,000 | |
| On the first | $57,568 tax is | $12,377.00 |
| On the remaining | $32,432 tax at 29% is | 9,405.28 |
| Gross federal tax | | 21,782.28 |
| Less non-refundable tax credit | | 1,100.00 |
| Basic federal tax | | 20,682.28 |
| Federal surcharge: | | |
| on first $12,500 of basic tax (5%) | | 625.00 |
| on the remaining $8,182.28 (10%) | | 818.23 |
| Total federal tax payable | | 22,125.51 |
| | | |
| Provincial tax calculation: | | |
| Basic tax − 53% of basic federal tax | | 10,961.67 |
| Surcharge − 12% of basic tax in excess of $10,000 | | 115.40 |
| Total provincial tax payable | | 11,077.07 |
| | | |
| Total tax collected | | $33,202.58 |
| Marginal tax rate | | 49.11% |
| Average tax rate | | 36.89% |

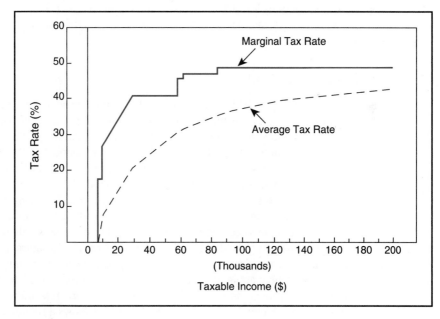

**FIGURE 10-1**

Marginal and average personal tax rates on employment income, 1991.

investment decisions. The larger an investor's taxable income, the closer the average tax rate comes to the marginal tax rate. Consider an investor with a taxable income of

$90,000 who is evaluating an investment opportunity that is expected to increase his or her taxable income by $3000. Using the figures for the combined federal and provincial tax rates, this opportunity will have the following effect on the taxes payable:

|  | Before Increase | After Increase | Difference |
| --- | --- | --- | --- |
| Taxable income | $90,000 | $93,000 | $3000 |
| Tax | 33,203 | 34,676 | 1,473 |
| Spendable income | $56,797 | $58,324 | $1527 |

Marginal tax rate = ($34,676 − $33,203)/$3000 = $1,473/$3000 = 49.1%

As shown in this table, the increase of $3000 in taxable income will result in an increase of $1473 in taxes, leaving a net increase in spendable income of $1527. The calculations for this particular example are simple because the change in taxable income left the taxpayer in the same bracket. Thus, 49.1% of the additional income will be taxed away, leaving 50.9% to be spent. The fact that the average tax rate is 36.89% ($33,203/$90,000) before the increase and 37.28% ($34,676/$93,000) after the increase is irrelevant to this individual in deciding whether or not to make the investment.

When a decision moves income into a higher bracket (a situation that generally applies to taxpayers in lower tax brackets) the computations are more complex. The effective marginal tax rate on such an investment is a weighted average of the two (or more) applicable rates.

## ☐ 10.3.3 Dividend Tax Credit

The *Dividend Tax Credit* (DTC) has a long and honorable history in Canadian tax law. This is a device designed to mitigate the effects of double taxation (corporate plus personal) on dividend income from taxable Canadian corporations.[8] Prior to the 1972 tax reforms, application of the DTC was simple. The full amount of the dividend was included in taxable income and the gross tax payable computed accordingly. The net tax was then the gross tax less twenty percent of the dividend.

Since 1972 the system has been more complicated. The following steps must be followed: first, the dividend is *grossed up* by a factor, $g$; second, the grossed up dividend is included in taxable income and the gross federal tax payable is calculated; third, a factor, $q$, of the grossed up dividend is allowed as a tax credit and subtracted from gross tax to arrive at the basic federal tax; fourth and fifth, the federal surtax and provincial tax (including surtax, where applicable) is then computed as a fraction of the basic federal tax. The fractions, $g$ and $q$, are prescribed in the *Income Tax Act* and its amendments and, therefore, may change from year to year. Table 10.7 shows a sample calculation of the DTC for an Ontario investor in the highest tax bracket of 49.11% who receives a dividend of $1000. For 1991, $g$ is 0.25 and $q$ is 0.1333.

---

[8] Investors who receive dividends from foreign corporations are generally permitted to deduct any foreign tax paid from their Canadian tax payable but may not claim the DTC. These provisions do not mitigate any double taxation that may occur in the source country.

**TABLE 10.7**

Sample Calculation of the Dividend Tax Credit.

| | |
|---|---|
| Dividend received | $1,000.00 |
| Grossed-up dividend | 1,250.00 |
| Gross federal tax payable @ 29% | 362.50 |
| Less: DTC—0.133333 of $1250 | 166.63 |
| Basic federal tax | 195.87 |
| Federal surtax—10% of basic tax | 19.59 |
| Provincial tax and surtax—59.4% of basic tax | 116.27 |
| Extra tax payable on the dividend | 331.73 |
| Marginal tax rate on dividend income | 33.17% |

The DTC system can be expressed algebraically as follows:

$$T = (1 + g)(t_f - q)(1 + t_p + t_s) \tag{10.1}$$

where:

$T$ is the total tax payable per dollar of dividend,

$g$ is the gross-up factor,

$t_f$ is the marginal federal tax rate net of surtax,

$q$ is the DTC factor,

$t_p$ is the provincial tax rate (including any surtax) as a fraction of the basic federal tax and,

$t_s$ is the federal surtax rate.

Substituting the figures used in the table into equation (10.1) results in a tax payable of $0.3317 per dollar of dividend that agrees with the marginal tax rate on dividend income of 33.17% obtained above in Table 10.7. This marginal tax rate is substantially smaller than the rate that the same investor would pay on interest income (49.11%). It is clear, therefore, that, in the absence of any risk considerations, a dividend yield of 7.615% provides the above investor with the same after-tax return as an interest payment of 10%. The relationship between dividend yield and interest payment, however, varies according to the investor's tax bracket.

When both corporate and individual taxes are considered it becomes evident that the DTC offers only a partial mitigation of the double taxation problem. A large corporation in Ontario need earn only $100 in order to provide our investor with a before-tax interest payment of $100 but must earn $123.42 if it is in manufacturing and $136.71 if it is a non-manufacturing concern in order to provide the same investor with a dividend payment of $76.15. In the absence of the DTC even more would have to be earned namely, $162.07. The situation is different for a small Canadian-controlled corporation which needs to earn only $98.64 in order to provide the investor with the same after tax return as an interest payment of $100. In this case there is a slight over-compensation for double taxation.

Stock dividends are treated in the same way as cash dividends. The cash equivalent of the shares received is grossed-up, added to taxable income and the tax calculation completed as before even though the investor has received no cash. This procedure is followed in order to prevent stock dividends from escaping taxation completely because of the lifetime capital gains exemption to be discussed below.

## ☐ 10.3.4 Capital Gains and Losses

Prior to the 1972 tax reform the situation was simple — capital gains were not taxed and capital losses were not deductible.

The provisions of the personal income tax laws, introduced in 1972, dealing with the treatment of capital gains and losses have had a great impact on investor behavior. The taxation of capital gains is now an extremely complex topic. For this reason only the basic elements of these tax provisions will be described here.

### Realization

A change in the market value of a capital asset is not relevant for tax purposes until it is *realized* as a capital gain (or loss) by sale or exchange. If a security purchased for $50 appreciates to a value of $100 in a year, no tax is due on the *unrealized capital gain*. But if it is sold for $120 two years after purchase, the difference of $70 must be declared as a capital gain realized at the time of sale and tax must be paid at the applicable rate.

This rule makes the end of the year an interesting time for stockbrokers. Depending on their situations, their taxpayer-clients may be either anxious or reluctant to realize capital gains or losses before a new tax year begins.

Consider, for example, a taxpayer who earlier in the year sold 1000 shares of stock A for $50 per share, having purchased them three years previously for $20 per share. This investor is liable for taxes on a capital gain of $30,000( 1,000 × ( $50 − $20)). In December the investor considers the 1000 shares of stock B, purchased four years ago for $95 per share, now selling for $65 per share. The investor has an unrealized loss of $30,000( 1,000 × ( $65 − $95)) on the investment in B. The investor believes that stock B will rebound in the near future and, therefore, wants to continue owning it. It might seem that the investor should sell B on December 31 and then buy it back January 1, thereby establishing a capital loss of $30,000 on B to offset the capital gain on A. This would remove the tax liability while essentially maintaining his or her position in B. The tax laws, however, preclude a deduction associated with a *superficial loss* on a *wash sale* where a security is sold and a "substantially identical" one is bought within 30 days.

Brokerage firms publish lists pairing similar stocks for those investors who wish to sell a particular stock for tax purposes; by selling a stock and simultaneously purchasing the matching stock, the investor will continually be able to maintain a portfolio with similar investment characteristics. In the previous example, a brokerage firm may have stocks B and C matched together. These two stocks have different issuers but may be in the same industry and, in the opinion of the brokerage firm, be poised for a similar rebound next year. Accordingly, the investor might sell B and purchase C.

End-of-year sales and purchases motivated by tax considerations are fairly common. At this time, securities that experienced substantial price changes during the year tend to have large numbers of trades as holders sell to realize gains or losses. If buyers recognize that the sellers are motivated by knowledge of the tax laws and not some previously unrecognized bad news affecting the company in question, such "selling pressure" should not seriously depress the company's stock price.

*Capital gains and losses* are those realized on *capital property*, but the *Income Tax Act* has a specific definition of capital property. For tax purposes four different kinds of assets are included in capital property: the taxpayer's *principal residence, personal use property, listed personal property*, and *investment and fixed assets in a business*. Gains or losses on current assets that are an integral part of a taxpayer's business (for example, inventories) are considered regular income. The tax treatment of the four kinds of assets is described below.

The capital gain or loss realized when an asset is sold or exchanged is the difference between the value received and the asset's *adjusted cost base* (ACB). For an asset purchased outright, the (initial) ACB is equal to the actual cost of the asset plus any costs or commissions incurred in making the acquisition. Any costs associated with the disposal of the asset simply reduce the size of the capital gain. The treatment of assets received as a gift or inheritance is described below.

While an asset is held, improvements may be made and their costs added to the ACB. On the other hand, any return of capital must be deducted from the ACB, as must depreciation. The accounting required can become complicated. When identical properties such as common shares are purchased at different times and at different prices these must be pooled in order to determine the ACB. For example, if an investor buys 100 shares at $40 each, then buys another 100 at $50, and later sells 100 shares at $60, what is the realized capital gain? As an adequate identification of the lots is not possible the ACB used is the average acqusition cost of the shares — $45 — and the gain is $15 per share.

The ability to control the realization of capital gains and losses has obvious advantages. Most important, tax can be paid at the most opportune time. The clearest case involves the realization of capital gains around the time of retirement. Shortly before retirement is usually a time when the taxpayer's income is relatively high, which in turn means that the taxpayer's marginal tax rate is relatively high. After retirement the taxpayer's income and, in turn, marginal tax rate are usually substantially lower. Accordingly, it is generally advantageous for the taxpayer who is near retirement to wait until after retirement to realize any capital gains.

## Treatment

The tax treatment on disposal of each of the four types of assets included in capital property will be discussed next.

## Principal Residence

This is nothing more than the taxpayer's family home and is not subject to capital gains tax during the owner's lifetime. Unmarried individuals may own a family home that is tax exempt, but married couples are entitled to only one principal residence per family unit. A vacation home (unless it is the only property the family owns) is, therefore, not exempted from capital gains tax and is treated as *personal use property*.

## Personal Use Property

This is any asset that is primarily for the personal use or enjoyment of the taxpayer and would not normally be considered an investment asset. If the ACB of personal use property is less than $1000 then, for tax purposes, it is deemed to be $1000. If the selling price of the asset is less than $1000 then no tax is payable. If, on the other hand, the selling price exceeds $1000 then three-quarters of the difference between that price and the ACB must be included in taxable income. Losses may not be claimed on the disposal of personal use property.

## Listed Personal Property

This consists predominantly of *collectibles* (works of art, rare books, jewelry, etc.). Capital gains realized on the disposal of listed personal property are treated in the same manner as gains on investment assets. Capital losses may only be used to offset gains realized from the sale of other listed personal property.

## Investment and Fixed Assets in a Non-incorporated Business

All capital gains and losses are brought together to obtain a net capital gain or net capital loss figure. If there are net gains three-quarters of these are included in taxable income whereas three-quarters of net losses (referred to as allowable capital losses) may be used to reduce capital gains in the three immediately preceeding years.[9] As a net result capital gains are taxed at a preferential rate. In the case of an investor in the maximum marginal tax bracket of 49.11%, the capital gains are taxed at an effective rate of 36.84%. Capital losses may be used to offset capital gains.

All individual taxpayers are entitled to a *Lifetime Capital Gains Exemption* of $100,000 on gains from investment assets and a further $400,000 on gains from qualified small businesses and farms. These exemptions refer to the total capital gain not the taxable portion.

## Reporting on Capital or Income Account

The gain or loss on the disposition of an investment asset can be taxed either as a gain or loss of income, or a capital gain or loss at the taxpayer's option. In other words, the taxpayer must choose whether any gains or losses incurred will receive "income or capital treatment." Once the decision has been made then all current and subsequent gains and losses must receive the treatment selected. Certain taxpayers, (security dealers, professional traders, and financial institutions) can only report on their income account. The regulations further specify that certain security transactions *must* receive income treatment regardless of the taxpayer's election. Most of these are specialized transactions, however, two of them are noteworthy:

1. The appreciation of a fixed-income security issued at a significant discount (for example, a 91-day Treasury bill) is considered to be income, it is more akin to interest than to a capital gain.
2. The gain or loss on the short sale of a security is considered to be income.

If Revenue Canada rules that a taxpayer's actions are such that he or she could be considered to be "in the business" of trading securities then all transactions must be reported on the income account. Table 10.8 shows a list of some of the factors that Revenue Canada considers in determining whether or not a taxpayer should be deemed to be carrying on such a business.

---

[9] If any allowable losses are left after extinguishing all prior capital gains then the residue may be carried forward indefinitely.

**TABLE 10.8**

Factors Used by Revenue Canada to Determine a Taxpayer's Status.

(a) frequency of transactions — a history of extensive buying and selling of securities or of a quick turnover of properties.

(b) period of ownership — securities are usually owned only for a short period of time.

(c) knowledge of securities markets — the taxpayer has some knowledge or experience in the securities market.

(d) security transactions form a part of a taxpayer's ordinary business.

(e) time spent — a substantial part of a taxpayer's time is spent studying the securities markets and investigating potential purchases.

(f) financing — security purchases are financed primarily on margin or by some other form of debt.

(g) advertising — the taxpayer has advertised or otherwise made it known that he is willing to purchase securities, and

(h) in the case of shares, their nature — normally speculative in nature or of a non-dividend type.

SOURCE: Revenue Canada, *Interpretation Bulletin IT-479R, Transactions in Securities*, Ottawa, February 24, 1984, revised February 21, 1985.

Investors who undertake frequent transactions or who regularly trade in "exotic" securities should recognize that the proceeds of their trading activities may receive income treatment.

## ☐ 10.3.5  Deductible Expenses

Certain interest payments may be deducted from an individual's income to determine taxable income. As a general rule, interest paid on funds borrowed in order to earn business or investment income is tax deductible. This deduction significantly lowers the effective cost of financing an investment by borrowing. In order to claim this deduction, the investment does not have to be profitable, but it must have a reasonable expectation of generating a profit. Borrowing money at 10% in order to buy Canada Savings Bonds paying 7.5% has no reasonable expectation of producing a profit and, therefore, a portion of the interest payment will be disallowed as a deduction. The 1988 tax amendments also introduced *Cumulative Net Investment Losses* (CNIL) that can reduce the lifetime capital gains exemption discussed earlier. The CNIL account consists of the amount by which *cumulative* investment expenses (generally interest expense and certain tax shelter losses) exceed *cumulative* interest and dividend income. In any given year the investor's lifetime capital gains exemption will be reduced by the amount in the CNIL account. This has the effect of requiring the investor to pay capital gains tax in that year and also of reducing the amount in the CNIL account by the size of the capital gain. Other expenses associated with investing may be deducted from income if they are ordinary and necessary, and in line with reasonable expectations of a profitable return. Thus, fees paid for investment advice or safekeeping of securities (e.g., a safety deposit box) may be deducted.

Investments that habitually produce financial losses but nonfinancial pleasure may be considered hobbies by Revenue Canada who may, therefore, deny some or all of the associated deductions. This possibility should concern the racehorse owner, for example, but not the serious investor.

## ☐ 10.3.6 Alternative Minimum Tax

There has long been a suspicion that certain wealthy individuals are able to use tax shelters and other legitimate deductions to pay out only a small fraction of their income in taxes. An *Alternative Minimum Tax* (AMT) has, therefore, been introduced. The calculation of AMT is complicated. As a rule of thumb, a taxpayer may be liable for the AMT if the following condition holds:

$$\text{Tax Payable} < 0.17 \times (\text{Total Income} - \$40,000)$$

One tax advisor has put forward the following advice for those in the top tax bracket: One, if you are pleased with the small amount of tax that you calculate this year, you may have an AMT problem. Two, if you think you may be subject to the AMT, then get professional advice.[10]

## 10.4  TAX REDUCTION TECHNIQUES

Tax avoidance is a legitimate activity whereas tax evasion is illegal. Legal procedures for reducing immediate taxes fall into the following classifications: tax deferrals and tax shelters. As the name implies, the former are methods for delaying the payment of taxes to a time when the taxpayer expects to face a lower marginal tax rate. The latter, on the other hand, purportedly provide methods for shielding income from taxation.

## ☐ 10.4.1 Tax Deferrals

The two principally used forms of tax deferral will be described here.

The best known and most popular tax deferral technique in Canada is the *Registered Retirement Savings Plan* (RRSP). In any year, taxpayers are permitted to contribute a specified fraction (18% in 1991) of *earned income* (to a specified maximum, $11,500 in 1991) to an RRSP established at a financial institution and to deduct the amount from that year's taxable income.[11] Furthermore, the investment returns can accumulate within the plan tax-free. Withdrawals from the plan are permitted at any time but the amount withdrawn must be added to that year's taxable income.

Full withdrawal, usually on retirement, must occur by age 71 and can receive different tax treatment. The retiree may remove the full amount from the RRSP and purchase an *annuity* that pays the proceeds out over a number of years. Only the annual annuity payment need be included in taxable income. This procedure significantly reduces the overall tax burden on retirement.

---

[10] Richard Birch, *The Canadian Price Waterhouse Personal Tax Advisor, 1990*, (McClelland-Bantam, Inc.), 1989.

[11] Earned income is defined to include employment income, business income, rental income, and some others. The upper contribution limit is expected to increase each year until 1995 when the maximum will be $15,500. The upper limit is less for taxpayers whose employer provides a pension plan. This reduction is consistent with the stated objectives of an RRSP which is to provide retirement income.

An RRSP is a vehicle for accumulating investment returns at a before-tax rate. Suppose that an individual, in the highest tax bracket of 49.11%, wishes to put aside $1200 per year for the next 30 years in an investment that will earn 9% per year. In the absence of an RRSP the investment returns will be taxed each year so that the effective rate of interest will be 4.6071%. At the end of 30 years the individual will have $74,553 on which no further tax is payable. By utilizing an RRSP, the individual can contribute $2344.15 each year to the plan and maintain the same annual disposable income. After 30 years the amount in the plan is $319,525. If this is withdrawn as a lump sum and full tax paid, the net receipt is $163,569 a gain of almost 120%. It is not surprising, therefore, that many Canadians have established RRSPs.

A similar device is a *Deferred Profit Sharing Plan*. This is essentially the same as an RRSP except that the employer makes the contributions directly into the employee's plan. The upper contribution limit of $6250 in 1991 will rise to $7750 in 1994 and be indexed to inflation thereafter. The employer's contribution reduces the amount that the employee can contribute to an RRSP.

## ☐ 10.4.2  Tax Shelters

Income splitting between spouses is an effective way to shelter a portion of investment income and thereby reduce the family's aggregate tax payments. The idea is simple and consists of transferring ownership of income-producing assets from the higher tax bracket family member to the lower tax bracket member or members. Revenue Canada has, however, established a number of rules which must be observed if the income is not to be *attributed* back to the original owner thereby negating the purpose of the exercise. It pays to read the regulations carefully if income splitting is contemplated. One relatively straightforward way to split income is to establish a *Spousal RRSP*. The higher tax bracket family member makes the contributions to the plan in the normal way, but ownership of the plan is vested in the lower tax bracket family member. The benefits of such a plan will be evident at retirement providing that the plan owner is then in a lower tax bracket than the contributor.

Other tax shelters provide more questionable benefits. Many advertisements exhort high tax-bracket investors to put their money in frontier oil and gas exploration, multiple unit real estate, films and videos produced in Canada, and other investments with purportedly attractive tax characteristics. Such "tax shelters" are devised to take advantage of tax provisions allowing large deductions to create a "tax loss" in the present, to be followed by a subsequent profit, generally in the form of a capital gain. Since their attractiveness is greater, the higher the taxpayer's marginal tax rate, presumably only those in the highest brackets should find such investments interesting. These enterprises are generally formed as limited partnerships. A promoter, or general partner, puts together the operation, with individual investors as limited partners. The hoped-for results are tidy profits for the promoter and the investors, at the expense of the tax collector.

A little thought should call into question the likely results for such an investment. First of all, many of the key provisions of tax law have been changed recently, and it is not unrealistic to expect more changes in the future. Second, even if loopholes remain unplugged, economic forces may diminish any opportunities for abnormally high profits. If large gains can be made, why should the promoter share them to any major extent with the investors? But one can go even further. If large profits remain for promoters, why won't more promoters enter the business? The answer is that they will, potentially until the risk and return available from promoting tax shelters is competitive with that in other occupations. Anomalies in the tax laws are more likely to bring abnormally large amounts of investment into film-making programs, oil drilling, and so on, than to provide well-lighted roads to untold riches for high tax-bracket investors.

This is not to deny that advantages can be gained from the early discovery of some scheme for tax-sheltered investment. Often investors in such deals reduce their taxes, as advertised, but only by taking real and permanent losses. Occasionally, the arrangements appear more like con games in which the professional swindler profits at the expense of the amateur investor, leaving the tax collector unscathed.

---

## 10.5 ESTATE AND GIFT TAXES

As of December 1991, there are neither explicit federal nor provincial estate or gift taxes in Canada. Some gifts and estate bequests are taxed as capital gains and losses.

A gift of cash or securities to a spouse incurs no tax liability at the time of transfer, the recipient assumes the asset at the donor's ACB. If the spouse disposes of the asset while the donor is still alive then any capital gain or loss must be reported by the donor in the year of its disposal. For example, in 1987 an investor purchases 500 shares at a price of $6.25 per share plus commissions of $0.25 per share making a total ACB of $6.50 per share. In 1991, she makes a gift of these shares, currently priced at $12.00 per share, to her husband. In 1992, he sells the shares at $15.00 per share realizing a capital gain of $500 \times (15 - 6.5) = \$4250$ that his wife must report in her 1992 tax return. If instead he waits until 1994 (after his wife's demise) to sell the shares for $15.00 per share then he must report the capital gain of $4250.

Gifts to other people, including children, are deemed to have taken place at the fair market value at the time of transfer. The donor, therefore, must report, in the year in which the gift is made, the difference between the fair market value and the ACB, and the recipient must use the fair market value as his or her ACB. If, in the example above, the investor had given the shares to her daughter instead of to her husband she would report an immediate capital gain of $500 \times (12 - 6.5) = \$2750$ in 1991 and the daughter would report a capital gain of $500 \times (15 - 12) = \$1500$ in the year in which she sells them.

On the death of a taxpayer he or she is deemed to have sold all assets immediately prior to decease. Capital gains give rise to a tax liability against the estate except in the case of assets willed to the spouse, which carry the original ACB and, therefore, attract no immediate tax.

The estate must file an income tax return for a deceased taxpayer. This will be a terminal settlement of all unpaid taxes.

# SUMMARY

In spite of the attempts of various elected governmental officials to provide "tax simplification," the federal government has established a set of tax laws that are not only intricate but also change frequently. Further complicating the situation is the existence of provincial tax laws. This chapter has attempted to provide a brief overview of the major provisions of Canadian income tax laws, since they have a major impact on the pricing of securities in the marketplace and a direct bearing on what securities different investors should purchase.

## QUESTIONS AND PROBLEMS

1. Why is the marginal tax rate more relevant to investment decision-making than the average tax rate?
2. Given the following income tax schedule, draw a graph illustrating the marginal and average tax rates as a function of income level.

| Income | Tax Rate |
| --- | --- |
| $    0 – $10,000 | 10% |
| $10,001 – $20,000 | 13 |
| $20,001 – $30,000 | 15 |
| $30,001 – $50,000 | 20 |
| $50,001 and above | 25 |

3. Why would a corporation report one annual income figure to their shareholders and another to the tax authorities?
4. Why do declining-balance depreciation methods offer tax advantages over the straight-line method to those corporations that can use them?
5. Given that interest payments are tax deductible for a corporation while dividend payments are not, why don't corporations finance all of their operations with debt?
6. Preferred shares have several fixed-income characteristics, yet generally provide lower after-tax yields to individual investors than do straight-debt securities. However, corporations seem to find preferred share investments particularly attractive. Why?
7. Heinz Groh expects consumer prices to rise at a 7% rate next year, and has negotiated a 9.5% pay increase. Given a 35% marginal income tax bracket, will this pay increase cause Heinz's real income (that is, purchasing power) to grow? Explain.
8. Is the following statement true or false? Dividends from taxable Canadian corporations are subject to the dividend tax credit, therefore, shares of these corporations are more attractive investments for inclusion in an RRSP than the bonds of the same corporations. Explain your answer.
9. A corporate bond is selling for $950. It matures in a year, at which time the holder will receive $1000. In addition, the bond will pay $50 in interest during the year. What would be the after-tax return on the bond to an investor in the 50% marginal income

tax bracket if capital gains do not receive preferential tax treatment? Recalculate the return assuming that only 75% of any capital gain is taxable.

10. Consider a stock in a taxable Canadian corporation that provides a dividend yield of 6%. To an investor in the following marginal tax brackets, what is the equivalent before-tax yield on a taxable bond? Use the values for $g$ and $q$ given in the text.
    a. 17%
    b. 26%
    c. 34%

11. What is a wash sale? Why does Revenue Canada prohibit such transactions for tax calculation purposes?

12. Jean Lalonde lives in a province where the tax payable is 60% of the basic federal rate. Jean's marginal basic federal tax rate is 26%. There is a federal surtax of 5% but none provincially.
    a. What is Jean's effective provincial marginal tax rate?
    b. What is Jean's effective federal marginal tax rate?
    c. What is Jean's effective combined marginal tax rate?

## SUGGESTED READINGS

The *Income Tax Act* with the accompanying *Interpretation Bulletins* are the authoritative sources of information about matters of taxation. Unfortunately these are generally unreadable and close to incomprehensible to non-specialists. The major chartered accounting firms in Canada produce useful and (generally) readable guides for lay people on an annual basis. See for example, S.Brian Fisher and Paul B. Hickey, eds., KPMG Peat Marwick Thorne, *The Canadian Personal Tax Planning Guide: 1992 Edition* (Scarborough, Ont.: Thomson Professional Publishing Company Canada) 1991 and *Tax Facts: 1991* (Toronto, Ont.: KPMG Peat Marwick Thorne, 1991).

*The Canadian Securities Course* (Toronto, Ont.: The Canadian Securities Institute, 1989). Chapter 17 provides a summary of the taxation of investment income.

# Chapter 11

# INFLATION

The story is told of the modern-day Rip Van Winkle, who awoke in the year 2010 and immediately called his broker. (Fortunately, pay phones at the time permitted a call of up to three minutes without charge.) He first asked what had happened to the $10,000 he had instructed the broker to put in short-term Treasury bills, continually reinvesting the proceeds. The broker promptly informed him that due to high interest rates and the power of compounding, his initial $10,000 investment had grown to be worth over $1 million. Stunned, Mr. Van Winkle inquired about his stocks, which were also worth about $10,000 when he dozed off. The broker told him that he was in for an even more pleasant surprise: They were now worth $2.5 million. "In short, Mr. Van Winkle," said the broker, "you are a millionaire 3.5 times over."

At this point an operator cut in: "Your three minutes are over, please deposit $100 for an additional three minutes." While this clearly overstates the case, there is no doubt that inflation is a major concern for investors. By and large, people have come to fear significant inflation, particularly when it is unpredictable.

This chapter discusses the benefits and costs of inflation, along with who gains and who loses when it is present. The impact that inflation has on investment decisions and results is also discussed.

## 11.1 INFLATION IN CANADA

### ☐ 11.1.1 Measuring Inflation

There is no completely satisfactory way to summarize the price changes that have occurred over a given time period for the large number of goods and services available in Canada. Nevertheless, Statistics Canada has attempted to do so by measuring the cost of a specific mix of major items (a "basket of goods") at various points in time. The "overall" price level computed for this representative combination of items is termed a *cost-of-living index*. The percentage change in this index over a given time period can then be viewed as a measure of the inflation (or deflation) that took place from the beginning of the period to the end of the period.

Whether or not this measure of inflation is relevant for a given individual depends to a major extent on the similarity of his or her purchases to the mix of items used to construct the index. Even if an individual finds the mix to be appropriate at the beginning of a period, the rate of increase in the mix over the time period is likely to overstate the increase in the cost of living for the individual. There are two reasons for this. First, improvements in the quality of the items in the mix are seldom taken adequately into account. This means the end-of-period price for a good is not comparable to the beginning-of-period price, since the good is different. For example, a new Toyota may have a 5% higher sticker price than a similar model had the previous year, but the newer model may have better tires on it than the older model. Hence, it would be inaccurate to conclude that the price of this particular model rose by 5% over the year.

Second and perhaps more important, little or no adjustment is made in the mix as relative prices change. The rational customer can reduce the cost of attaining a given standard of living as prices change by substituting relatively less expensive goods for those that have become relatively more expensive. For example, if the price of beef rises 20% over a given year while the price of chicken rises only 10% over the same year, then the customer may start to eat more chicken and less beef. Failure to take into account this change in the mix will result in an overstatement in the rate of inflation. Despite these two drawbacks, cost-of-living indices provide at least rough estimates of changes in prices.

In Chapter 1, Table 1.1 provided some historical perspective on the rate of inflation in Canada. It showed the annual rate of increase in the *Consumer Price Index* (CPI) from 1950 through 1987.[1] As an aid to interpretation, these rates are plotted on a graph shown in Figure 11.1(a). As can be seen in the figure, the CPI did not grow at a constant rate over the period of 1950 to 1987, however, prices increased in almost every year. Generally speaking, there were four subperiods with different rates of inflation: high inflation in 1950 and 1951, mild inflation from 1952 to 1966, fairly rapid (but uneven) inflation from 1967 to 1982, followed by moderate inflation for 1983 to 1987.

Table 11.1 shows the average annual rate of growth of the CPI for each of these subperiods, measured by what is known as the *geometric mean* growth rate of the CPI. This growth rate, when compounded over the subperiod and applied to the beginning index value, results in the ending index value. For example, at the end of 1977, the CPI was 53.3 and at the end of 1991, it was at 126.4 ( the CPI was adjusted so that its average monthly value in 1986 was 100). Thus, the geometric mean growth rate was 6.36%, since 53.3, when compounded at this rate over 14 years, equals 126.4:

$$126.4 = 53.3 \times (1 + .0636)^{14}.$$

**TABLE 11.1**
Growth Rates of the Canadian Consumer Price Index.

| From | To | Rate of Growth % Per Year |
|------|------|------|
| 1950 | 1951 | 8.3 |
| 1952 | 1965 | 1.3 |
| 1966 | 1982 | 7.3 |
| 1983 | 1991 | 4.3 |

---

[1] The Consumer Price Index is based on the retail prices for a basket of some 540 different goods and services. It is calculated monthly by Statistics Canada.

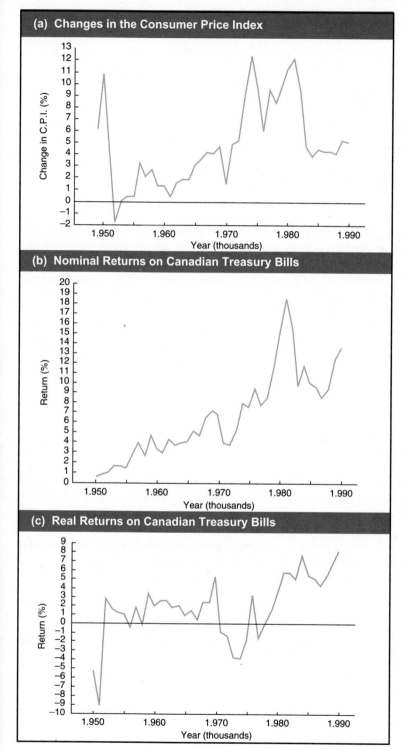

**(a) Changes in the Consumer Price Index**

Change in C.P.I. (%)

Year (thousands)

**(b) Nominal Returns on Canadian Treasury Bills**

Return (%)

Year (thousands)

**(c) Real Returns on Canadian Treasury Bills**

Return (%)

Year (thousands)

**FIGURE 11-1**

Inflation, nominal, and real returns on short-term default-free investments, 12-month periods ending December 1950– December 1991.

*SOURCE:* Reprinted, with permission, from James E. Hatch and Robert W. White, *Canadian Stocks, Bonds, Bills, and Inflation: 1950–1987.* Copyright 1988, The Research Foundation of The Institute of Chartered Financial Analysts, Charlottesville, Va.; Melanie Moore, *ScotiaMcLeod's Handbook of Canadian Debt Market Indices: 1947 - 1990* (Toronto: ScotiaMcLeod Inc.), 1991, and Melanie Moore, Debt Market Indices, December 1991, ScotiaMcleod Inc.

More generally, the geometric mean ($g$) can be calculated by solving the following equation for $g$:

$$C_e = C_b(1 + g)^y \tag{11.1}$$

which results in

$$g = \left(\frac{C_e}{C_b}\right)^{1/y} - 1 \tag{11.2}$$

where $y$ denotes the number of years and $C_e$ and $C_b$ denote the ending and beginning CPI values, respectively.

---

## 11.2 PRICE INDICES

As mentioned earlier, no price index can prove totally satisfactory as an indicator of the cost of living for all consumers. Most indices are likely to overstate the extent to which the cost of attaining a given level of satisfaction actually increases during any inflationary period, even for the people whose purchases the index was intended to reflect. Although this is fairly well understood and most governments compute a number of alternative indices to provide a wider choice for analysis, many people tend to focus on one index as an indicator of the price level.

In Canada, the CPI often fills this role, despite attempts to discourage its widespread use.[2] Recognizing its importance, the composition of the market basket of goods used to make up the CPI has been changed from time to time in order to provide a more representative basket of goods. Furthermore, the process by which the relevant data are gathered and verified has periodically been improved.

---

## 11.3 NOMINAL AND REAL RETURNS

### ☐ 11.3.1 Nominal Returns

Modern economies gain much of their efficiency through the use of money — a generally agreed-upon medium of exchange. Instead of trading corn for a stereo to be delivered in one year, as in a barter economy, the citizen of a modern economy can trade his or her corn for money and then trade this "current" money for "future" money by investing it. Later, the "future" money can be used to buy a stereo. The rate at which the citizen can trade current money for future money depends on the investment he or she makes and is known as the *nominal return* (also known as the nominal rate).

---

[2] A number of authorities prefer "deflators" derived from gross national product figures, but such indices have not received the publicity accorded the CPI.

## □ 11.3.2 Real Returns

In times of changing prices, the nominal return on an investment may be a poor indicator of the *real return* (also known as the real rate) obtained by the investor.[3] This is because part of the additional dollars received from the investment may be needed to recoup the citizen's lost purchasing power due to inflation that has occurred over the investment period. As a result, adjustments to the nominal return are needed to remove the effect of inflation in order to determine the real return. Frequently, the CPI is used for this purpose.

For example, assume that at the start of a given year the CPI is at a level of 121 and that at the end of the year it is at a level of 124. This means that it costs $124 at the end of the year to buy the same amount of the CPI market basket of goods that at the start of the year could have been purchased for $121. Assuming the nominal return is 8% for this year, the citizen who started the year with $121 and invested it would have $121 × 1.08 = $130.68 at year-end. At this point, the citizen could purchase ($130.68/$124) − 1 = .0539 = 5.39% more of the CPI market basket of goods than at the beginning of the year. Thus, the real return for this investment was 5.39%, after allowing for inflation.

These calculations can be summarized in the following formula:

$$\left( C_0 \times \frac{1 + NR}{C_1} \right) - 1 = RR \qquad (11.3)$$

where:
  $C_0$ = CPI at the beginning of the year,
  $C_1$ = CPI at the end of the year,
  NR = the nominal return,
  RR = the real return.

Alternatively, the citizen could note that an increase in the CPI from 121 to 124 can be translated into an inflation rate of (124/121) − 1 = .0248, or 2.48%. Denoting this inflation rate as I, the real return can be calculated using the following formula:

$$\left( \frac{1 + NR}{1 + I} \right) - 1 = RR. \qquad (11.4)$$

Note that for the example, RR = (1.08/1.0248) − 1 = .0539, or 5.39%.

For quick calculation, the real return can be estimated by simply subtracting the inflation rate from the nominal return:

$$NR - I \cong RR \qquad (11.5)$$

where $\cong$ means "is approximately equal to." In this example, the quick method results in an estimate of the real return of 08 − .0248 = .0552, or 5.52%. Thus, the error resulting from use of this method is .0552 − .0539 = .0013, or .13%.[4]

---

[3] Here, real return refers to the increase in purchasing power that the citizen has received as a result of making a particular investment.

[4] This error will be larger for higher rates of inflation. Thus, in those countries with "hyperinflation," the quick method will have a substantial amount of error associated with it. For example, if the nominal return is 110% and the inflation rate is 100%, then the true real return is 5%, but the quick method will indicate it is twice as large, 10%.

### ☐ 11.3.3 The Effect of Investor Expectations

The simplest view of investors' attitudes toward inflation is that they are concerned with real returns, not nominal returns, and that a single price index is adequate to characterize the difference. Looking to the future, investors do not know what the rate of inflation will be, nor do they know what the nominal return on an investment will be. However, in both cases they have expectations about what these figures will be, which are denoted as EI (expected rate of inflation) and ENR (expected nominal return), respectively. Thus, the expected real return on an investment can be approximated by:

$$ERR = ENR - EI. \tag{11.6}$$

If a security is to provide a given expected real return, the expected nominal return must be larger by the expected rate of inflation for the relevant holding period. This can be seen by rearranging equation (11.6):

$$ENR = ERR + EI. \tag{11.7}$$

For example, if the expected rate of inflation is 4% and a given security is to provide investors with an expected real return of 6%, then the security must be priced in the marketplace so that its expected nominal return is 10%. In summary, if investors are concerned with real returns, all securities will be priced by the actions of the marketplace so that expected nominal returns incorporate the expected rate of inflation.

---

## 11.4 INTEREST RATES AND INFLATION

At the start of a given investment holding period, nominal interest rates for securities having no risk of default should cover both a requisite expected real return and the expected rate of inflation for the period in question. At the end of the period, the real return actually received will be the difference between the nominal return and the rate of inflation actually experienced. Only when actual inflation equals expected inflation will the actual real return equal the expected real return on such securities.

As mentioned earlier, Figure 11.1(a) indicates the annual rate of inflation, as measured by changes in the CPI, over the 38-year period 1950–1987. Part (b) shows how short-term nominal interest rates varied over this time period; Treasury bill rates, taken from Table 1.1, are used for this purpose. Part (c), obtained by subtracting part (a) from part (b), represents real returns.

One cannot help being struck by the fact that those who invested in short-term securities over this period frequently ended up with less purchasing power than they started with, since the real return was negative in 11 of the 38 years. Perhaps even more surprising, the average real return over the period 1950 to 1979 was close to zero. Although expected real returns may vary from year to year, the variation is relatively small. Otherwise investors may not have been willing to invest in short-term highly liquid securities even though they expected to earn close to nothing in real terms. If they are currently willing to do so, such securities will be priced to give an expected real return of approximately zero.[5]

---

[5] However, there apparently are periods of time when such securities have an expected real return that is positive. For example, in the 1980–1987 period, Treasury bill returns actually exceeded the rate of change in

If this assumption is made, the "market's" predicted rate of inflation over the near future can be estimated by simply looking at the nominal interest rate (also known as the yield) on short-term government securities, namely, Treasury bills. In a sense, this Treasury bill rate represents a consensus prediction of inflation—a prediction that an "average" investor in this market would make and one that is likely to be more accurate than the predictions of any single forecaster.

11.5

## THE EFFECT OF INFLATION ON BORROWERS AND LENDERS

Although deviations of actual inflation from expected inflation may have relatively little effect on the real return on investments in general, they may have a significant effect on specific investments. In fact, one would expect a direct impact on the real returns associated with investments whose payments are fixed in terms of dollars to be received.

A simple example will illustrate the relationship. Assume that everyone currently expects the rate of inflation to be 5% over the next year and that a lender has agreed to make loans at a nominal rate of 5% (that is, the lender is content with having an expected real return of zero). Thus, one can borrow $100 now and, one year later, pay back $100 \times 1.05 = $105 for a one-year loan. That is, if actual inflation equals expected inflation, a one-year loan would require a payment equivalent to $100 in constant (current) dollars a year hence. In this case, the real rate of interest would turn out to be zero.

Now, imagine that an individual takes advantage of the lender's offer, borrowing $100 for one year. How will the borrower and lender be affected if actual rate of inflation differs from the expected rate of inflation?

Assume that in the first year, prices rise by 9% instead of the expected 5%, meaning that unexpected inflation is 4% = 9% − 5%. In this situation, the short-term borrower gains at the expense of the lender because the borrower still must repay $105, but this is only $105/1.09 = $96.33 in constant dollars terms, less than the amount of the loan. As a result, the lender receives a real rate of interest of ($96.33 − $100)/$100 = −3.67%, instead of the anticipated rate of 0%.

What if first-year prices had risen by only 3%, meaning that unexpected inflation is −2% = 3% − 5%? In this situation, the short-term lender gains at the expense of the borrower. Although the borrower must repay $105, in constant dollars terms this amounts to $105/1.03 = $101.94, greater than the amount of the loan. As a result, the lender receives a real rate of interest of ($101.94 − $100)/$100 = 1.94% instead of the anticipated rate of 0%.

These results can be generalized: When the actual rate of inflation exceeds the expected rate of inflation, those with commitments to make payments that are fixed in nominal terms (debtors) gain in real terms at the expense of those to whom payments are to be made (creditors). Conversely, when actual inflation is less than expected inflation, creditors gain and debtors lose.[6] This uncertainty in the real return on fixed-income

---

the CPI by over 5%. This suggests that investors probably expected a positive real return over the latter part of the period.

[6]More specifically, it can be shown that long-term borrowers are likely to gain somewhat more than short-term borrowers when actual inflation exceeds expected inflation and lose somewhat more when actual

securities that is due to uncertain inflation is frequently referred to as *purchasing power risk*.

---

# INDEXATION

The previous section suggests that in a world of uncertain inflation, even default-free bonds are subject to purchasing power risk. Contractual nominal interest rates can cover expected inflation, but the subsequent real return from any investment with fixed nominal payments will depend on the actual amount of inflation. As long as the two differ, the expected real return will be uncertain. However, there is a way to design a bond so that its expected real return is certain. This involves the use of *indexation*.

If a specified price index can adequately measure purchasing power, there is no reason why a contract cannot be written with specified real payments instead of specified nominal payments. Thus, if the CPI currently stands at $C_0$ and will be $C_1$ one year later, $C_2$ two years later, and so on, in return for a ten-year loan of $100 a borrower might promise to pay $10 \times C_1$ one year later, $10 \times C_2$ two years later, ..., and $110 \times C_{10}$ ten years later. To convert these payments to constant real dollars, each one must be divided by the corresponding price level:

| Time | Amount in Nominal Dollars | Price Level (CPI) | Amount in Real Dollars |
|------|---------------------------|-------------------|------------------------|
| 1 | $10 \times C_1$ | $C_1$ | 10 |
| 2 | $10 \times C_2$ | $C_2$ | 10 |
| ⋮ | ⋮ | ⋮ | ⋮ |
| 10 | $110 \times C_{10}$ | $C_{10}$ | 110 |

The real value of each payment is the amount shown in the final column, regardless of what happens to prices (that is, regardless of the actual values of $C_1$, $C_2$, and so on). Thus, the loan is said to be fully indexed, since all amounts are tied to a stated price index on a one-for-one basis. This means that when the price index goes up by 10%, for example, all the subsequent payments go up by 10%.

In some countries, a great many contracts are tied to standard price indices (two notable examples are Israel and Brazil). Government bonds, returns on savings accounts, wage contracts, pension plans, insurance contracts — all have been indexed at various times and places. In Canada, Canada Pension Plan benefits are indexed, as are the pension plans of civil servants, MPs, and some employees. Some of these are fully indexed, while others are only partially indexed, meaning that payments might be increased by, for example, 75% of the price index increases. Since the mid-1970s personal income tax brackets have been indexed to the CPI of the preceeding year. In

---

inflation falls below expectations. Similarly, long-term lenders are likely to lose somewhat more than short-term lenders when actual inflation exceeds expectations and gain somewhat more when actual inflation falls below expectations.

December 1991, the Canadian government introduced its first indexed bonds, known as Real Return Bonds. They are described in some detail in the next chapter.

The key advantage of indexation is its role in reducing or eliminating purchasing power risk. Typically, higher expected inflation is accompanied by increased uncertainty about the actual rate of inflation. This increased uncertainty means that the potential gains and losses to both nonindexed borrowers and nonindexed lenders are larger. Since both borrowers and lenders dislike the prospect of losses more than they like the prospect of gains, there will be increased pressure for indexation by both borrowers and lenders when a country moves into periods of high inflationary expectations.

Thus, when uncertainty about inflation is substantial, one would expect indexation to become widespread. However, laws regulating interest rates frequently prevent the issuance of fully indexed debt, since these laws usually place a ceiling on the nominal rate but not the real rate. This leads to predictable inefficiencies when expected inflation increases, since rationing of credit that is subject to such ceilings would be required. Rationing would be necessary because a ceiling on the nominal rate means that the real rate declines as inflationary expectations increase, which in turn makes this type of credit attractive to borrowers.[7]

A notable example occurred in Canada in the 1960s. At that time, ceilings placed on nominal rates paid by banks, coupled with increased inflationary expectations, caused a substantial outflow of funds from such companies and a corresponding reduction in the amount of money made available by them for home mortgages. On the other side were those issuers of securities that were not subject to rate ceilings and who offered an appropriate nominal rate and, thus, had little difficulty in attracting funds. The term *disintermediation* was invented to describe this pattern of funds' flow.

Since inflation is generally harder to predict for longer time periods relative to shorter time periods, uncertainty about inflation often leads to a reduction in the average term-to-maturity of newly issued fixed-income securities. Here term-to-maturity refers to the length of time from the date of issue of the security until the date that last payment is to be made. For example, the average term-to-maturity of fixed-coupon debt issued in periods of great inflationary uncertainty is usually shorter than in more stable times.

Alternatively, debt with long maturities can be written with *variable rates* (also known as floating rates) of interest. Such instruments provide long-term debt at short-term rates. Interest payments are allowed to vary, with each one determined by adding a fixed number of percentage points (say, 2%) to a specified base rate that changes periodically. Two base rates frequently used are the prime rate and the yield on 91-day Treasury bills. If short-term interest rates anticipate inflation reasonably well, such a variable rate security is a kind of substitute for a fully indexed bond.

---

[7] Actually, rationing might not occur, since lenders may simply refuse to make those kinds of loans that are subject to ceilings when inflationary expectations are high.

# REPLACEMENT COST ACCOUNTING

One definition of earnings (that is, profits) holds that if a firm paid out the entire amount of earnings each year, it would neither increase nor decrease in size, measured by the real value of its productive capacity. This notion is often summarized by the term *sustainable earnings*. A firm that pays out more than the total amount of such earnings can be expected to decline, whereas one that pays out less can be expected to grow.

Although there may be some objections to the principle of this definition of earnings, there are more problems associated with its implementation. And, these problems are seriously aggravated in an inflationary environment.

Consider a firm that purchases ten units of some semifinished good at the beginning of each year, hires labor to work on it, and then sells the finished product at the end of the year. For simplicity, assume that labor is paid from the proceeds of sales. In the absence of inflation, the firm's operations might be summarized as follows:

| | | |
|---|---:|---:|
| Receipt from sales (10 units at $200 each) | | $2000 |
| Less cost of goods sold: | | |
| Purchase of semifinished goods (10 units at $100 each) | $1000 | |
| Labor wages | 800 | |
| Total cost | | 1800 |
| Net earnings | | $ 200 |
| Net cash received at year-end ($2000 − $800) | | 1200 |

Thus, the firm invests $1000 at the beginning of the year to purchase semifinished goods in order to obtain $1200 a year later, giving the firm a rate of return of 20%. Viewed somewhat differently, after an initial investment of $1000, earnings of $200 can be paid out each year, assuming no inflation. This $200 is the magnitude of sustainable earnings.

Now, assume that after purchasing the semifinished goods, all prices and wages increase by 10%. The results would then be as follows.

| | | |
|---|---:|---:|
| Receipt from sales (10 units at $220 each) | | $2200 |
| Less cost of goods sold: | | |
| Purchase of semifinished goods (10 units at $100 each) | $1000 | |
| Labor wages | 880 | |
| Total cost | | 1800 |
| Net earnings | | $ 320 |
| Net cash received at year-end ($2200 − $880) | | 1320 |

Thus, an investment of $1000 produces a net cash inflow of $1320 one year later, for a return of 32% and earnings of $320. However, this is not the amount of sustainable earnings. Assuming no further inflation, $1100 will be required to replace the inventory of 10 units at the beginning of the next year. This means that only $1320 − $1100 = $220 can be paid out if the firm is to avoid a decline in real productive capacity. Put somewhat differently, the total "earnings" of $320 resulted from an increase in the value of the firm's inventory of $100 plus "adjusted" earnings from normal operations of $220.

To make this distinction, a number of authorities recommend *replacement cost accounting*. In essence, this involves the use of estimated replacement costs (future costs) instead of historic costs (past costs) when calculating profits. In this case such a procedure would give:

| | | |
|---|---:|---:|
| Receipt from sales (10 units at $220 each) | | $2200 |
| Less cost of goods sold: | | |
|   Purchase of semifinished goods (10 units at $110 each) | $1100 | |
|   Labor wages | 880 | |
|     Total cost | | 1980 |
| Net earnings | | $ 220 |
| Net cash received at year-end ($2200 − $880) | | 1320 |

An equivalent procedure would be to subtract an *inventory valuation adjustment* from reported profit. This adjustment would represent the excess of replacement cost over the reported cost:

| | | |
|---|---:|---:|
| Receipt from sales (10 units at $220 each) | | $2200 |
| Less cost of goods sold: | | |
|   Purchase of semifinished goods (10 units at $100 each) | $1000 | |
|   Labor wages | 880 | |
|     Total cost | | 1880 |
| Net earnings | | $ 320 |
| Less inventory valuation adjustment: | | |
|   Replacement cost (10 units at $110 each) | $1100 | |
|   Reported cost (10 units at $100 each) | 1000 | |
|     Amount of adjustment | | 100 |
| Net adjusted earnings | | $ 220 |

Even after the adjustment, profit is stated in current (that is, year-end) dollars. To compare this amount with that of a previous year, the value must be adjusted for price-level changes. In this case, the amount in current dollars is $220, whereas the amount in constant dollars is $220/1.10 = $200 (which is the amount that would have been earned in the absence of inflation).

The size of the appropriate inventory valuation adjustment depends on the length of time inventory is held, the extent of the rise in its replacement cost, and the method used to account for such costs when calculating reported earnings. As discussed in Chapter 10, the LIFO method comes closest to replacement costs, and the FIFO method lies at the other end of the spectrum.

A similar situation arises with capital assets. Using various depreciation formulas, their historic costs are charged to operations over their assumed productive lives. As discussed in Chapter 10, accelerated depreciation is generally used for tax purposes, but other methods may be used for reporting earnings to shareholders. However, assets "used up" in the production process are generally valued at historic, not replacement, costs. Other things being equal, this will cause an understatement of cost and an overstatement of sustainable earnings.

At the beginning of each year, a firm will own certain capital assets. During the year the replacement costs of these assets may change, resulting in associated gains or losses, although such changes may not be realized at that time. The portion of these assets used up in production (and thus depreciated) should be valued at replacement cost in order to estimate sustainable earnings from operations. If historic costs are used instead, the resulting amount should be adjusted to account for the difference between replacement and historic costs.

In September 1979, the Financial Accounting Standards Board issued *Statement of Accounting Standards Number 33* (SFAS 33) requiring public companies with either total assets of more than $1 billion or with inventories, property, plant, and equipment with a gross value of more than $125 million to provide supplementary inflation-adjusted financial statements to their shareholders. This is intended to allow shareholders to estimate more accurately the level of the firm's sustainable earnings. This statement, however, did not provide any clear direction as to which method of price adjustment should be used. Subsequent Accounting Standards were issued that tended to dilute the requirements and in December 1986 SFAS 89 essentially terminated the experiment on the grounds that as inflation had been reduced adjustments were no longer necessary.

In Canada the situation was only slightly better. In December 1982, the Canadian Institute of Chartered Accountants issued *CICA Handbook Section 4510* that requires public companies with (net) total assets of $350 million or inventories plus (gross) fixed assets of $50 million to provide supplementary inflation-adjusted financial statements as in the US. Prescribed methods for carrying out the adjustments were provided, but as the statements are supplementary rather than mandatory they are not subject to audit. As a result, compliance has been poor — about 23 percent of firms provided such information in fiscal 1983 falling to about 4 percent in 1986.[8]

---

**11.8    TAXATION, INFLATION, AND THE RETURN ON CAPITAL**

Certain general features of the Canadian tax system lead to movements of wealth from the private sector to the federal government that increase with the rate of inflation. Thus, one of the potential beneficiaries of inflation is the federal government.[9]

---

[8] For more detailed information on inflation-adjustment see Thomas H. Beechy, *Accounting for Changing Prices* (Toronto: Allyn and Bacon, 1989).

[9] The federal government also benefits from unexpected inflation because it is the largest borrower of funds in the economy and, as shown earlier, borrowers in general benefit when inflation turns out to be higher than expected. The federal government has attempted to mitigate some of the effects of inflation by indexing the levels at which personal tax brackets change.

Consider a one-year security with an expected real pretax return of 7% that is held by someone in a 30% marginal tax bracket. In the absence of inflation, the investor would expect to receive a real return of $(1 - .3) \times 7\% = 4.9\%$. Now, assume that expected rate of inflation is 2%, so that the expected pretax nominal return on the security is $[(1.07 \times 1.02) - 1] = 9.14\%$. In this case, the investor's expected after-tax nominal return is $(1 - .3) \times 9.14\% = 6.40\%$, but in real terms this is $[(1.0640/1.02) - 1] = 4.31\%$. Similarly, if expected inflation is 4%, then the expected pretax nominal return will be 11.28%, the investor's expected after-tax nominal return will be 7.90%, and his or her expected after-tax real return will be 3.75%.

Since it is reasonable to assume that, over time, actual inflation rates will approximately equal expected inflation rates, it can be seen that the higher the actual inflation rate, the lower the actual real after-tax return. In this example, the after-tax real return decreased from 4.9% with no inflation to 4.31% with 2% inflation and to 3.75% with 4% inflation. Thus, taxation of interest income can be viewed as being equivalent to having an effective tax rate on real returns that increases with inflation; that is, the higher the inflation rate, the larger the portion of the real pretax return that is being allocated to the government. This phenomenon could be avoided by levying taxes on real returns instead of nominal returns.

For the expected after-tax real return of a fixed-income security to be the same with a high expected rate of inflation as with a low expected rate of inflation, its current price must be sufficiently lower with the high inflation rate. This will result in the expected pretax nominal return being sufficiently higher in order to compensate for both the higher inflation rate and the larger effective tax rate. In the previous example, the expected pretax nominal return would have to rise to 10.0% if the expected rate of inflation were 2% and to 13.0% if it were 4%. If this asset were a bond that pays the investor $1000 one year later, its current price would have to be $934.58 with no expected inflation, $909.09 with 2% expected inflation, and $884.96 with 4% expected inflation:

| | | | |
|---|---|---|---|
| Expected rate of inflation | 0.0% | 2.0% | 4.0% |
| Expected pretax nominal rate of return | 7.0% | 10.0% | 13.0% |
| Expected after-tax nominal return = | | | |
| (1 − .3) × pretax nominal return | 4.9% | 7.0% | 9.1% |
| Expected after-tax real return = | | | |
| [(1+ after-tax nominal return) ÷ | | | |
| (1+ rate of inflation)] −1 | 4.9% | 4.9% | 4.9% |
| Current price of a bond paying $1000 | | | |
| in one year = $1000/(1+ expected | | | |
| pretax nominal rate of return) | $934.58 | $909.09 | $884.96 |

Unfortunately, this is not the way bond prices and expected pretax nominal returns react to changes in the expected rate of inflation, as is shown next.

It is reasonable to assume that investors are more concerned with real returns than with nominal returns, since real returns reflect how much better off they are after adjusting for inflation. Accordingly, securities that provide a hedge against inflation should be considered more attractive, other things being equal, than those that do not. But what does it mean to say that a security is a "hedge" against inflation? And what does empirical research suggest about the abilities of various types of investments to act as such hedges?

For a tax-exempt investor, a security would be a perfect inflation hedge if its actual nominal rate of return moved one-for-one with the actual rate of inflation, since its real return would then be the same no matter what the rate of inflation. However, as shown in the previous section, for a tax-paying investor, the relationship would have to be more than one-for-one in order for the security to be a perfect hedge against inflation.

### Determining a Security's Sensitivity to Inflation

The ability of a security to hedge against inflation is indicated by the term $h_i$ in the following equation:

$$NR_{it} = a_i + h_i AI_t + w_{it} \qquad (11.8)$$

where:

$NR_{it}$ = the actual nominal return on security $i$ in period $t$,

$a_i$ = a constant,

$h_i$ = a constant representing the sensitivity of security $i$'s return to the rate of inflation,

$AI_t$ = the actual rate of inflation in period $t$, and

$w_{it}$ = the uncertain portion of the nominal return of security $i$ that is not related to the rate of inflation in period $t$.

Now, remember from earlier that the actual rate of inflation in any period can be viewed as having two components:

$$AI_t = EI_t + UI_t \qquad (11.9)$$

where:

$EI_t$ = the expected rate of inflation for period $t$, and

$UI_t$ = the unexpected rate of inflation for period $t$.

Thus, if at the beginning of the period the expected rate of inflation is 5%, but it subsequently turns out actually to be 6%, then the unexpected rate of inflation for the period is +1%.

Equation (11.8) omits the separation in the actual rate of inflation that is shown in equation (11.9). However, such a separation should be made, since a security might serve as a hedge against expected inflation and not against unexpected inflation, or vice versa. Thus, to consider these two components of inflation separately, equation (11.8) can be modified as follows:

$$NR_{it} = a_i + h_i^e EI_t + h_i^u UI_t + w_{it} \qquad (11.10)$$

where:

$h_i^e$ = a constant representing the sensitivity of security $i$'s nominal return to the expected rate of inflation,

$h_i^u$ = a constant representing the sensitivity of security $i$'s nominal return to the unexpected rate of inflation.

The other terms are as defined earlier. Note that at the beginning of period $t$, both $\mathrm{UI}_t$ and $w_{it}$ are uncertain and are as likely to end up being positive as negative at the end of the period. Note also that a security with $h_i^e = 1$ would be regarded as being a perfect hedge against expected inflation, a security with $h_i^u = 1$ would be regarded as being a perfect hedge against unexpected inflation, and a security with both $h_i^e$ and $h_i^u$ equal to 1 would be regarded as being a perfect hedge against actual inflation.

As indicated earlier, a rough estimate of the expected rate of inflation over a short-term period is provided by the return on Treasury bills that mature at the end of the period and are bought at the beginning of the period. For example, the return available today on six-month Treasury bills can be viewed as a consensus estimate of inflation over the forthcoming six months and is therefore representative of the *expected rate of inflation* ($\mathrm{EI}_t$). Once the six months have passed, the actual rate of inflation ($\mathrm{AI}_t$) will be known. At that time, equation (11.9) can be used to estimate the *unexpected rate of inflation* ($\mathrm{UI}_t$) by calculating the difference between the actual rate of inflation and the Treasury bill return.

To determine the sensitivity of any particular security to both expected and unexpected inflation, more than one six-month time period needs to be used. In one US study, 24 six-month time periods — from July 1959 through July 1971 — were used.[10] This means that 24 estimates of both expected and unexpected inflation were calculated. Furthermore, the actual rates of return were calculated for the same 24 six-month periods for a number of different securities. Then, by comparing the returns on these various securities with the estimates of expected and unexpected inflation over a number of periods, the historical sensitivities of the securities ($h_i^e$ and $h_i^u$) were estimated.[11]

Table 11.2 provides the estimates derived in this manner for several types of securities. US government bonds appear to have provided hedges against expected inflation on approximately a one-for-one basis, since their sensitivities to expected inflation are all in the vicinity of a value of 1. However, since all these bonds had negative values of $h_i^u$, they all failed to serve as hedges against unexpected inflation.[12] Furthermore, the values of $h_i^u$ were more negative when the life of the bond was longer. This relationship is not surprising in light of the way investors revise expectations based on recent experience, as shown in the following example.

A study that covered the period 1953 to 1985 found that the situation is not very different in Canada in that a one percent rise in unanticipated inflation resulted in a reduction in the real return on T-bills of 0.8 per cent, on long-term Canada bonds of 3.1 per cent, and in equities of 4.2 per cent.[13]

---

[10] Eugene F. Fama and G. William Schwert, "Asset Returns and Inflation," *Journal of Financial Economics* 5, no. 2 (November 1977):115–46.

[11] The procedure used to estimate these sensitivities is known as multiple regression.

[12] This was also observed for long-term corporate bonds in a later study. See Kenneth R. French, Richard S. Ruback, and G. William Schwert, "Effects of Nominal Contracting on Stock Returns," *Journal of Political Economy* 91, no. 1 (February 1983):70–96.

[13] Reported in James Pesando, Inflation-Indexed Pensions: Investment Policy Implications, *Canadian Investment Review* 1, no. 1 (Fall 1988):35–39. This article also reports that the effects of unanticipated inflation on bonds and equities were less severe when a longer time period, 1929 to 1985 was examined.

**TABLE 11.2**

Sensitivities of Assets to Expected and Unexpected Inflation, Six-Month Holding Periods, July 1959–July 1971.

| Asset | Sensitivity to Expected Inflation $(h_i^e)$ | Sensitivity to Unexpected Inflation $(h_i^u)$ |
|---|---|---|
| 1–2 year US government bonds | 1.08 | −1.15 |
| 2–3 year US government bonds | 1.03 | −1.75 |
| 3–4 year US government bonds | .88 | −2.37 |
| 4–5 year US government bonds | .79 | −2.75 |
| Private residential real estate | 1.27 | 1.14 |
| Common stocks [a] | −4.26 | −2.09 |

[a] Value-weighted average of all stocks listed on New York Stock Exchange.

SOURCE: Eugene F. Fama and G. William Schwert, "Asset Returns and Inflation," *Journal of Financial Economics* 5, no. 2 (November 1977):130–1. By permission of North-Holland Publishing Co., Amsterdam.

Assume that inflation is expected to run at the semiannual rate of 5% (that is, 10% per year) throughout the future. At the beginning of the year, a 10% one-year government bond is priced to return 5% per six months (that is, it is selling for par of $1000, provides $50 coupon payments every six months, and is expected to sell for $1000 at midyear, right after a coupon payment is made). Now, assume that during the first half of the year inflation runs at the semiannual rate of 6% (that is, 12% per year). Investors are likely to revise their estimate of inflation upward for the second half of the year—say from 5% to 5.5%. But, if the one-year bond is to return 5.5% over the second half of the year, its price at midyear must be lower than it would have been if it were to provide a return of 5% over the second half of the year. In particular, its price would have to be $995.26, not the expected $1000. This means that investors who held it during the first half of the year would not obtain a return of 5%, but instead would obtain a lesser return of 4.53%, since they would receive a lower-than-expected selling price at the end of the first six months.

As a result, higher-than-expected inflation (6% > 5%) caused them to obtain a lower-than-expected return (4.53% < 5%). Similarly, lower-than-expected inflation would cause investors to obtain a higher-than-expected return. This means that the six-month return on a one-year government bond would have a negative relationship with unexpected inflation, as was observed in Table 11.2.

Next, consider the price impact on a 10% two-year government bond that is also initially priced to have a semiannual return of 5% (that is, it is selling for par of $1000 and provides $50 coupon payments every six months for the next two years). Again, assume inflation over the first six months turns out to be 6%, whereupon investors revise their expectations of the future semiannual rate of inflation to be 5.5%. Now, if the two-year bond is to have a semiannual return of 5.5% over the remaining 18 months of its life, its price will have to drop by even more than the drop in the price of the one-year bond. In particular, its price would have to drop to $986.50, which is less than the $995.26 price of the one-year bond.

As a result, higher-than-expected inflation (6%) would cause the two-year bonds to have a lower-than-expected six-month return (3.65%). Furthermore, this return is even

A. 10% One-year government bond with semiannual $50 coupon payments:
Assume it is currently priced at $1000 so as to provide the investor with a 5% semiannual return.
Price at the end of six months in order to provide an investor with a return of 5% over the last six months of the bond's life:

$$(\$1050/1.05) = \$1000.$$

Expected return over first six months:

$$[(\$1000 - \$1000) + \$50]/\$1000 = 5\%.$$

Price at the end of six months in order to provide an investor with a return of 5.5% over the last six months of the bond's life:

$$(\$1050/1.055) = \$995.26.$$

Actual return realized over the first six months:

$$[(\$995.26 - \$1000) + \$50]/\$1000 = 4.53\%.$$

B. 10% Two-year government bond with semiannual $50 coupon payments:
Assume it is currently priced at $1000 so as to provide the investor with a 5% semiannual return.
Price at the end of six months in order to provide an investor with a 5% semiannual return over the last 18 months of the bond's life:

$$(\$1050/1.05^3) + (\$50/1.05^2) + (\$50/1.05^1) = \$1000.$$

Expected return over first six months:

$$[(\$1000 - \$1000) + \$50]/\$1000 = 5\%.$$

Price at the end of six months in order to provide an investor with a semiannual return of 5.5% over the last 18 months of the bond's life:

$$(\$1050/1.055^3) + (\$50/1.055^2) + (\$50/1.055^1) = \$986.51.$$

Actual return realized over the first six months:

$$[(\$986.51 - \$1000) + \$50]/\$1000 = 3.65\%.$$

---

lower than the six-month return on the one-year bonds (4.53%). Conversely, lower-than-expected inflation would cause the two-year bonds to have a higher-than-expected six-month return. Furthermore, this return is even higher than the six-month return on the one-year bonds. Consequently, the six-month return on a two-year government bond would have an even more negative relationship with unexpected inflation than the one-year government bond, and indeed this is what was observed in Table 11.2. Also, this analysis implies that the negative relationship between returns and unexpected inflation will, in general, be more negative the longer the life of the government bond. Again, this is what is observed in Table 11.2.

Residential real estate provides a bright spot in an otherwise gloomy record of the relationship between security returns and unexpected inflation. As shown in Table 11.2, it alone had positive estimates with values near one for both $h_i^e$ and $h_i^u$. Thus, it appears that residential real estate has historically served as a hedge against both expected and unexpected inflation.

The record of common stocks as an inflation hedge is depressing, to say the least. With negative values for both $h_i^e$ and $h_i^u$, historically they have not served as hedges against either expected or unexpected inflation.[14] Quite the contrary — stock returns have tended to be lower when the rate of either expected or unexpected inflation is greater.[15] In turn, this implies that stock returns have tended to be lower when the actual rate of inflation is greater.

However, this does not imply that stocks cannot provide returns greater than the rate of inflation. Indeed, there is every reason to expect stocks to provide positive real returns over the long term. After all, in Chapter 1 it was observed that over the time period of 1950 to 1987, the average annual rate of inflation was 4.76%, whereas the average annual return on common stocks was 12.50%. Thus, over this time period, common stocks had a positive real return of approximately $7.74\% = 12.50\% - 4.76\%$.

## 11.10 INFLATION HEDGING AND EXPECTED RETURN

The original capital asset pricing model deals with nominal returns. If the rate of inflation is reasonably predictable, this causes no problem, for inflation will add little to the uncertainty concerning the return of any asset. But if there is considerable uncertainty about the rate of inflation, the situation is different. First, the real return of a default-free investment such as a Treasury bill will not be certain. Second, the risk associated with the real return of the market portfolio may differ considerably from the risk associated with its nominal return. Third, the beta of a security relative to the market portfolio may change when both the security's returns and market portfolio's returns are expressed in real terms instead of nominal returns.

If investors think in terms of real returns, the relationship between risk and return may look like that shown in Figure 11.2. The shaded area in part (a) indicates the "real" capital market line, which represents all available risk-return combinations in terms of real returns (note that there is no risk-free alternative). Point $M$ represents the market portfolio, which is assumed to be an efficient investment. The situation is thus formally equivalent to the *zero-beta* model. As part (b) shows, securities will be priced as if it were possible to borrow or lend without limit at a risk-free rate of ERZ. Thus, all securities and portfolios will plot along a straight line such as that shown in part (b), relating expected real return to "real beta." The equation of this "real" security market line is

$$\text{ERR}_i = \text{ERZ} + (\text{ERR}_M - \text{ERZ})\beta_i^r \qquad (11.11)$$

---

[14] These observations appear to be the result of a positive relationship between stock returns and real activity in the economy, and a negative relationship between real activity, and inflation. See Eugene F. Fama, "Stock Returns, Real Activity, Inflation, and Money," *American Economic Review* 71, no. 4 (September 1981): 545–64; and Stephen A. Buser and Patrick J. Hess, "Stock Returns, Inflation, and Treasury Yields," unpublished paper, University of Minnesota, September, 1988.

[15] A subsequent study of common stocks found that unexpected inflation did not benefit firms with relatively high levels of nominal liabilities (such as accounts payable and long-term debt). This was surprising, since it was thought that these firms would gain from unexpected inflation due to an unexpected decline in the real value of their nominal liabilities (more simply, unexpected inflation should benefit debtors at the expense of creditors). See French, Ruback, and Schwert, "Effects of Nominal Contracting."

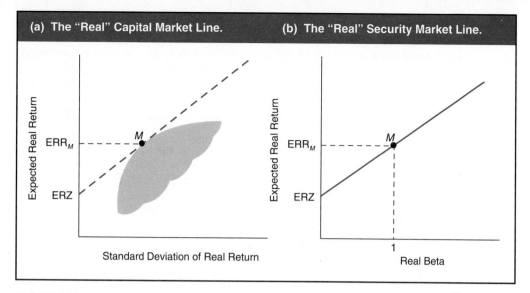

**(a) The "Real" Capital Market Line.**

**(b) The "Real" Security Market Line.**

**FIGURE 11-2**
The capital asset pricing model in real terms.

where:
$ERR_i$ = the expected real return on security $i$,
$ERZ$ = the expected real return of a security or portfolio with a real beta of zero,
$ERR_M$ = the expected real return on the market portfolio, and
$\beta_i^r$ = security $i$'s real beta (that is, $cov(RR_i , RR_M)/var(RR_M)$).

Equation (11.11) provides a succinct statement of the effect of uncertain inflation on security expected returns. But what does it imply about the relationship among expected nominal returns, nominal betas, and sensitivities of nominal returns to inflation? As shown in the appendix, in such a world, securities will also plot on a security market plane with these three attributes on the axes. The equation of such a plane is

$$ENR_i = Z_1 + Z_2 \beta_i^n - Z_3 h_i^u \qquad (11.12)$$

where:
$ENR_i$ = the expected nominal return on security $i$,
$Z_1$ = the expected nominal return on a security or portfolio with both $\beta_i^n$ and $h_i^u$ equal to zero,
$\beta_i^n$ = security $i$'s nominal (that is, traditional) beta (that is, $cov(NR_i, NR_M)/var(NR_M)$),
$h_i^u$ = security $i$'s sensitivity to unexpected inflation ($cov(NR_i, UI)/var(UI)$),
$UI$ = unexpected inflation,
$Z_2$ = a positive constant, and
$Z_3$ = a positive constant.

In a world of uncertain inflation, the third term ($Z_3 h_i^u$) indicates:

Securities will be priced to give lower expected nominal returns, other things equal, the greater their ability to hedge against unexpected inflation.

INFLATION

**297**

The value of $Z_3$ indicates the reduction in expected nominal return per unit increase in inflation sensitivity. Not surprisingly, the greater the uncertainty about inflation, the greater will be the magnitude of this reduction. However, since uncertainty concerning the market portfolio's nominal return is typically much greater than that concerning inflation, the effect of differences in $\beta_i^n$ on $\text{ENR}_i$ — indicated by the magnitude of $Z_2$ — will generally be considerably greater.

Stocks of firms with large net monetary debtor positions should be better hedges against unexpected inflation than those of firms with large net monetary creditor positions. However, differences in inflation sensitivities among stocks may be relatively small and difficult to predict in advance (this is apparently true in the United States; see footnote 14). If so, the inclusion of inflation sensitivity in a security market plane or hyperplane may add only slightly to the explanation of differences in expected returns under normal circumstances. But when uncertainty about inflation is considerable, differences in hedging abilities — especially among different classes of assets — are likely to be accompanied by substantial differences in expected returns.

As is typical in an efficient market, bad news tends to accompany good news. For example, the good news might be that real estate is a good hedge against inflation; the bad news is that its expected return is less than that of assets that entail similar risk in other regards but that are poorer hedges against inflation.

## 11.11    SUMMARY

Like taxes, inflation seems to be continually present in Canada's postwar economy. It is of importance to investors because of its effect on both the pricing of securities and the subsequent level of nominal and real returns. In particular, the expected rate of inflation has an impact on how various securities are priced in the marketplace. For example, Treasury bills appear to be priced so as to reflect the consensus opinion about what inflation will be over their lifetime.

Having purchased a security, the subsequent actual rate of inflation will determine the investor's real return. Real returns are important to the investor because they represent how much an investor's purchasing power has increased (or decreased) and thus indicate how much better (or worse) off the investor is.

In general, when inflation turns out to be greater than expected, borrowers gain and lenders lose. That is, the actual real return paid by borrowers and received by lenders is less than what they initially expected. Conversely, when inflation turns out to be less than expected, borrowers lose and lenders gain. One method of removing such risks from fixed-income securities involves indexation, whereby security payments are adjusted to reflect the rate of inflation that has actually occurred. However, such indexing is rarely seen in Canada.

It makes sense for investors to want to hold securities that provide protection against both expected and unexpected inflation. Unfortunately, with the exception of real estate, the US historical record suggests that most securities do not provide such protection. Fixed-income securities appear to be priced to protect the investor against expected inflation, but provide little protection against unexpected inflation. More surprising is the observation that common stocks do not appear to offer protection against either expected or unexpected inflation. Nevertheless, over the long term, common stocks do appear to have positive real returns of approximately 9%.

# EXPECTED RETURNS, BETAS, AND INFLATION HEDGING

In a world of uncertain inflation where investors are concerned with real returns, security prices could adjust until all securities and portfolios plotted on the "real" security market line given in equation (11.11). To see how this relates to more traditional concepts, equation (11.5) can be used to show that

$$RR_i = NR_i - I \tag{11.13}$$

$$RR_M = NR_M - I \tag{11.14}$$

where $I$ is the rate of inflation and the other terms are as defined earlier in the chapter. Equations (11.13) and (11.14) can be used to show that

$$ERR_i = ENR_i - EI \tag{11.15}$$

$$ERR_M = ENR_M - EI \tag{11.16}$$

where EI is the expected rate of inflation.

Substituting the right-hand sides of equations (11.15) and (11.16) into equation (11.11) results in

$$ENR_i - EI = ERZ + (ENR_M - EI - ERZ)\beta_i^r \tag{11.17}$$

where, by definition:

$$\beta_i^r = \frac{cov(RR_i, RR_M)}{var(RR_M)}. \tag{11.18}$$

Using equations (11.13) and (11.14), equation (11.18) can be rewritten as

$$beta_i^r = \frac{cov(NR_i, NR_M)}{var(RR_M)} - \frac{cov(NR_i, I)}{var(RR_M)} - \frac{cov(NR_M, I)}{var(RR_M)} + \frac{var(I)}{var(RR_M)} \tag{11.19}$$

which can be shown to be equivalent to:

$$\beta_i^r = \frac{var(NR_M)}{var(RR_M)}\beta_i^n - \frac{var(I)}{var(RR_M)}h_i^u + \frac{var(I) - cov(NR_M, I)}{var(RR_M)}. \tag{11.20}$$

Substituting the right-hand side of equation (11.20) for $\beta_i^r$ in equation (11.17) results in:

$$ENR_i = \left\{ EI + ERZ + (ENR_M - EI - ERZ)\left[\frac{var(I) - cov(NR_M, I)}{var(RR_M)}\right]\right\}$$
$$+ \left\{ (ENR_M - EI - ERZ)\left[\frac{var(NR_M)}{var(RR_M)}\right]\right\}\beta_i^n \tag{11.21}$$
$$- \left\{ (ENR_M - EI - ERZ)\left[\frac{var(I)}{var(RR_M)}\right]\right\}h_i^u$$

which reduces to the equation shown earlier in the chapter:

$$ENR_i = Z_1 + Z_2\beta_i^n - Z_3h_i^u. \tag{11.12}$$

In examining equation (11.12), first note that

$$\frac{Z_2}{Z_3} = \frac{var(NR_M)}{var(I)}$$

and, since the variance of $NR_M$ is large (for example, $400 = 20^2$) relative to that of $I$ (for example, $25 = 5^2$), $Z_2$ is likely to be considerably greater than $Z_3$. This means that the effect of $\beta_i^n$ on $ENR_i$ is likely to be considerably greater than the effect of $h_i^u$ on $ENR_i$. Second, note that if var($I$) = 0, then equation (11.12) simplifies to the zero-beta version of the capital asset pricing model.

## QUESTIONS AND PROBLEMS

1. Given the following beginning and ending values for a particular price index, and the respective number of years between the measurement of the two values, calculate the annual compounded (geometric mean) inflation rate.

|    | Price Index Beginning Value | Price Index Ending Value | Years Covered |
|----|------|------|---|
| a. | 100  | 115  | 1 |
| b. | 115  | 170  | 3 |
| c. | 170  | 150  | 2 |

2. Why do cost of living indices frequently overstate the true economic impact of inflation on typical consumers?

3. Distinguish between the nominal and the real rate of return on an investment.

4. Ken Higgins started 1991 with investments valued at $10,500. At the end of 1991 those same investments were worth $12,000. During the same time period the price index rose from 210 to 230. What was Ken's real rate of return during 1991?

5. Why is it reasonable to assume that rational investors will build in an expected inflation premium into the returns they require from their investments?

6. In the late 1970s and early 1980s, a period of unexpectedly high inflation, Harry Fell referred to long-term bonds issued by corporations and the government as "certificates of confiscation." Why would Harry make such a comment?

7. Also in the late 1970s and early 1980s, there was considerable discussion concerning the "quality" of corporate earnings. Straight-line depreciation and the FIFO inventory valuation methods were often cited as the causes of "poor quality" earnings. Further, it was argued that these accounting methods effectively resulted in tax overpayments. Discuss the reasons for both contentions.

8. Why is it often argued that the federal government is the greatest beneficiary of inflation?

9. Many economists contend that during periods of inflation, taxes on investment income reflect, in part, a tax on the return of capital and, hence, are inequitable. Explain the reasoning behind this argument.

10. Explain why the returns on bonds are found to be negatively correlated with unexpected inflation. Why does this relationship become progressively more negative as one considers longer lived bonds?

11. Sherry Magee bought a two-year 12% coupon Canada bond at the beginning of 1989. The bond was bought at its face value of $10,000. Over the first year, inflation ran at a semiannual rate of 8%. Investors' inflation expectations at the end of 1989 rose to a 7% semiannual rate.

   a. At the beginning of 1990, at what price would the bond have to sell at in order to offer investors a 7% semiannual return over the last year of the bond's life?

b.  If the bond were priced at the figure calculated in part (a), what return would Sherry have earned over the year 1989?

12. Common stocks, somewhat surprisingly, do not appear to be effective hedges against either expected or unexpected inflation. Explain why the stocks of some companies might be better hedges against inflation than others.

13. Assume that the current relationship between expected nominal returns, beta values, and inflation sensitivities has been estimated to be:

$$ENR_i = 6.0 + (4.0 * \beta_i) - (.20 * h_i)$$

Stock A has a beta of 1.00 and provides no hedge against inflation. What should be its expected return? Stock B has a beta of 1.10. How sensitive to inflation would its return have to be to make its appropriate expected nominal return equal to that of stock A?

## SUGGESTED READINGS

James E. Hatch and Robert W. White, *Canadian Stocks, Bonds, Bills, and Inflation: 1950–1987* (Charlottesville, Va.: The Research Foundation of The Institute of Chartered Financial Analysts, 1988) shows the historical record of inflation rates and real returns in Canada.

Thomas Beechy, *Accounting for Price Changes* (Toronto, Ont.: Allyn and Bacon, 1989) discusses the difficulties inherent in designing accounting systems that control for inflation.

# Chapter 12

# FIXED-INCOME SECURITIES

This chapter provides a broad survey of the major types of fixed-income securities, with an emphasis on those currently popular in Canada. A security is a contract giving the investor certain rights to the future prospects of the issuer. These rights can differ from one security to another and the future prospects of issuers can also differ substantially, therefore, the number of different types of fixed-income securities is too high to allow a complete survey to be included.

The term *fixed-income* is commonly used to cover the types of securities discussed in this chapter, but it can be misleading. Typically, these securities *promise* the investors that they will receive certain specified cash flows at certain specified times in the future. If a security provides only a single cash flow, it is known as a *pure-discount security*. Alternatively, it may involve multiple cash flows. If all these cash flows (except for the last one) are of the same size, they are generally referred to as *coupon payments*. The specified date beyond which the investor will no longer receive cash flows is known as the *maturity date*. On this date the investor receives the *principal* (also known as the *par value* or *face value*) associated with the security, along with the last coupon payment. All the cash flows promised, however, may not be received. That is, there is some risk, however small, that a promised payment will not be made in full and on time.

## 12.1 SAVINGS DEPOSITS

Perhaps the most familiar type of fixed-income investment is the personal savings account at a chartered bank, trust company, credit union, or caisse populaire. Such an account provides substantial (if not complete) safety of principal, low probability of failure to receive interest, high liquidity, and a relatively low return.

### ☐ 12.1.1 Chartered Banks

Many people maintain a chequing account in a chartered bank. Formally, these accounts are termed *demand deposits*, since money can be withdrawn on demand by the depositors. While the bookkeeping required to keep track of withdrawals and deposits is costly to the bank, the balance in such an account is available to support interest-earning loans made by the bank. Banks offer an array of chequing accounts with different terms and conditions. Figure 12.1 shows the different types of demand deposits offered by

## DEPOSIT PRODUCTS

| Investment Builder™ account [1] | % |
|---|---|
| On portion of daily closing balance of $100,000 or more | 6.44 |
| PLUS On portion of daily closing balance when $60,000 to less than $100,000 | 6.39 |
| PLUS On total daily closing balance when daily closing balance is $25,000 to $59,999 | 5.28 |
| On total daily closing balance when daily closing balance is $10,000 to $24,999 | 4.76 |
| On total daily closing balance when daily closing balance is $5,000 to $9,999 | 4.60 |

(Interest paid monthly. No interest is calculated on those days when the daily balance is below $5,000.)

| Moneybuilder® account | |
|---|---|
| On portion of daily closing balance of $3,000 or more | 4.50 |
| PLUS On total daily closing balance when daily closing balance is $1,000 to $2,999 | 3.25 |

(Interest paid monthly. No interest is calculated on those days when the daily balance is below $1,000.)

| Money Manager® account | |
|---|---|
| On total daily closing balance of $2,000 or more | 3.25 |
| When daily balance falls below $2,000 | 3.00 |

(Interest paid monthly)

| Daily Interest Savings account [1] | |
|---|---|
| On daily closing balance | 3.25 |

(Interest paid monthly)

| My First Account® | % |
|---|---|
| On daily closing balance | 3.25 |

(Interest paid monthly)

| Premium Savings account [2] | |
|---|---|
| On minimum monthly balance | 3.25 |

(Interest paid April 30 and October 31)

| Plan 60 Premium Savings account [2] | |
|---|---|
| On minimum monthly balance | 3.75 |

(Interest paid monthly)

| U.S. Dollar Daily Interest Chequing account [3] | |
|---|---|
| On portion of daily closing balance $25,000 or more | 4.000 |
| PLUS On portion of daily closing balance when $5,000 to $25,000 | 3.875 |
| PLUS On total daily closing balance less than $5,000 | 3.625 |

(Interest paid monthly)

**FIGURE 12-1**

Chartered bank deposit accounts.

*SOURCE:* Toronto-Dominion Bank, *Financial Rate Letter*, (December 2, 1991).

a chartered bank. In general, customers with small balances who write many cheques pay the bank, whereas those with large balances who write few cheques are paid by the bank. This is because the bank pays interest on the customer's deposit (either on the daily closing balance or on the minimum balance maintained in the account over a specified period) and at the same time charges for handling the customer's cheques and for other services. In some cases accounts with larger minimum balances are paid higher interest rates.

An alternative to a chequing account is a savings account. This type of account typically earns a higher rate of interest than a chequing account but offers no chequing privileges. Cash withdrawals may be made at any time. Service charges and interest are determined in the same manner as for a chequing account. Almost any amount may be invested in a savings account. No security is issued; instead, the current balance plus interest earned is posted either to the depositor's passbook or recorded in a monthly statement.

Credit unions offer accounts similar to those described above, and many investment companies (described in Chapter 20) provide at least limited cheque-writing services.

*Time deposits*, also known as *guaranteed investment certificates* (GICs) or *term deposits*, have a stated maturity date (for example, one year after the initial deposit) with interest paid at maturity on short term (less than one year) deposits and either annually or semi-annually on long-term deposits. In practice, such deposits can be withdrawn at any time. A penalty must be paid, however, when this is done prior to maturity. Often, the penalty takes the form of recomputing the interest earned using a lower rate. Most types of time deposits require a minimum investment, for example, $1000 each.

## □ 12.1.2  Trust and Mortgage Loan Companies

In general, trust and mortgage loan companies accept demand and shorter-term deposits (up to five years), then use the money primarily to make longer-term loans, often for home mortgages. Trust companies offer accounts and services that are very similar to those provided by chartered banks and, therefore, are referred to as *near banks*.

The interest rates and maturities on deposits offered by these institutions are generally similar to those offered by the chartered banks. Figure 12–2 shows the current short and medium term retail rates offered by various financial institutions as reported weekly in *The Globe and Mail: Report on Business*.

## □ 12.1.3  Credit Unions

A credit union accepts deposits from members of the credit union (membership is limited to individuals sharing some kind of common bond, often a common employer) and uses them to make loans to other members. Typically, loans are relatively small and relatively short-term (for example, to finance the purchase of an automobile). Excess funds are invested in highly liquid short-term assets.

Each credit union is owned by its members, who elect a board of directors. The interest rates and maturities on deposits are generally similar to those on savings accounts in banks or trust companies, but earn dividends instead of interest. Many credit unions also offer GICs and chequing accounts to their members.

## □ 12.1.4  Other Types of Personal Savings Accounts

A number of institutions similar to those described above also exist. In some countries, the government-run post office accepts savings deposits. In Canada, some provincial governments operate savings banks, such as *The Province of Ontario Savings Office*. Certain kinds of life insurance policies include a savings component — payments often exceed the amount strictly required to pay for the insurance involved. The cash value of such a policy may be obtained by cancelation; alternatively, some or all of it may be borrowed without canceling the policy. The implicit rate of return on the cash value of an insurance policy is typically low, reflecting the extremely low risk to the policyholder and the length of the insurance company's commitment.

# INTEREST RATES

This survey of rates offered by a sample group of companies was prepared by Cannex Financial Exchanges, Apr. 24, 1992, at 5:00 p.m. Savings rates are non-redeemable except where indicated by an 'r'

## SAVINGS RATES

| Company | ($1,000 balance) Savings account | Chequing account | Minimum deposit | (Interest paid at maturity) 30 days | 60 days | 90 days | 120 days | 180 days | 270 days | Minimum deposit | (Interest paid annually) One year | Two years | Three years | Four years | Five years |
|---|---|---|---|---|---|---|---|---|---|---|---|---|---|---|---|
| **BANKS** | | | | | | | | | | | | | | | |
| Banca Comm. Ital. Canada, Toronto | 3.25 | 2.50 | 5,000 | r 6.00 | r 6.05 | r 6.30 | r 6.30 | r 6.30 | r 6.30 | 1,000 | r 6.88 | r 7.50 | r 8.00 | r 8.25 | r 8.50 |
| Bank Leumi Le-Israel, Toronto | 2.75 | - | 100,000 | r 5.50 | r 5.50 | r 5.50 | r 5.75 | r 6.00 | r 6.00 | - | - | - | - | - | - |
| Bank of Montreal. Toronto | 2.50 | 2.75 | 5,000 | 5.75 | 6.00 | 6.00 | 6.00 | 6.25 | 6.25 | 1,000 | 6.75 | 7.50 | 8.00 | 8.25 | 8.50 |
| Bank of Nova Scotia, Toronto | 2.50 | 2.50 | 5,000 | 5.90 | 5.90 | 5.90 | 6.00 | 6.25 | 6.25 | 1,000 | 6.75 | 7.50 | 8.00 | 8.25 | 8.50 |
| CIBC, Toronto | 2.50 | 2.75 | 5,000 | 5.75 | 6.00 | 6.00 | 6.00 | 6.25 | 6.25 | 1,000 | 6.75 | 7.50 | 8.00 | 8.25 | 8.75 |
| Citibank, Toronto | 3.75 | 2.50 | 5,000 | r 6.00 | r 6.00 | r 6.00 | r 6.00 | r 6.25 | r 6.25 | 5,000 | r 6.75 | r 7.50 | r 8.00 | r 8.25 | r 8.50 |
| HongKong Bank, Vancouver | 2.75 | 2.75 | 5,000 | 6.00 | 6.00 | 6.00 | 6.00 | 6.25 | 6.25 | 1,000 | 6.75 | 7.50 | 8.00 | 8.25 | 8.50 |
| Laurentian Bank of Can., Montreal | 2.50 | 2.50 | 5,000 | 6.00 | 6.00 | 6.25 | 6.25 | 6.25 | 6.25 | 1,000 | - | 7.50 | 8.00 | 8.25 | 8.75 |
| National Bank, Montreal | 2.50 | 2.75 | 5,000 | 6.00 | 6.00 | 6.00 | 6.00 | 6.25 | 6.25 | 1,000 | 6.75 | 7.50 | 8.00 | 8.25 | 8.50 |
| Royal Bank of Canada, Montreal | 2.50 | 2.50 | 5,000 | 5.75 | 6.00 | 6.00 | 6.00 | 6.25 | 6.25 | 500 | 6.75 | 7.50 | 8.00 | 8.25 | 8.50 |
| Security Pacific Bank, Vancouver | - | - | 5,000 | 5.50 | 5.50 | 5.50 | 5.50 | 5.50 | 5.50 | 5,000 | 6.50 | 7.00 | 7.50 | 7.75 | 8.00 |
| Toronto-Dominion Bank, Toronto | 2.50 | 2.50 | 5,000 | 6.00 | 6.00 | 6.00 | 6.00 | 6.25 | 6.25 | 1,000 | 6.75 | 7.50 | 8.00 | 8.25 | 8.50 |
| **TRUST COMPANIES** | | | | | | | | | | | | | | | |
| AGF Trust Co., Toronto | - | - | 5,000 | r 5.75 | r 5.75 | r 5.75 | r 5.75 | r 5.75 | r 5.75 | 1,000 | 7.55 | 7.05 | 7.55 | 8.80 | 9.05 |
| Aetna Trust, Vancouver | - | - | 25,000 | - | - | r 6.75 | r 6.75 | r 6.75 | r 6.75 | 5,000 | 7.50 | 8.00 | 8.25 | 8.75 | 9.00 |
| Bayshore Trust, Toronto | - | - | 5,000 | 6.75 | 6.75 | 6.75 | 7.00 | 7.00 | 7.00 | 1,000 | 7.50 | 8.25 | 8.75 | 8.75 | 9.00 |
| Bonaventure Trust, Montreal | - | - | 5,000 | 6.00 | 6.00 | 6.13 | 6.25 | 6.38 | 6.38 | 1,000 | 7.38 | 8.00 | 8.50 | 8.75 | 9.00 |
| Cabot Trust, North York | - | - | 5,000 | r 5.75 | r 5.75 | r 5.75 | r 5.75 | r 5.75 | r 5.75 | 500 | 7.25 | 7.75 | 8.25 | 8.50 | 8.75 |
| Canada Trust, Toronto | - | 2.75 | 5,000 | r 6.00 | r 6.00 | r 6.00 | r 6.00 | r 6.25 | r 6.25 | 1,000 | 6.75 | 7.50 | 8.00 | 8.25 | 8.75 |
| Central Guaranty Trust, Halifax | - | - | 5,000 | r 6.00 | r 6.00 | r 6.25 | r 6.25 | r 6.50 | r 6.50 | 500 | 7.25 | 8.00 | 8.50 | 8.50 | 9.25 |
| Citizens Trust Co., Vancouver | 4.00 | 3.00 | 5,000 | r 6.00 | r 6.00 | r 6.00 | r 6.25 | r 6.25 | r 6.50 | 1,000 | 7.25 | 8.00 | 8.25 | 8.50 | 9.00 |
| Co-Operative Trust. Saskatoon | - | - | 5,000 | 6.00 | 6.00 | 6.00 | 6.00 | 6.25 | 6.25 | 500 | 7.00 | 7.50 | 8.00 | 8.25 | 8.75 |
| Community Trust. Toronto | - | - | 1,000 | r 5.50 | r 5.75 | r 6.00 | r 6.00 | r 6.25 | r 6.25 | 1,000 | 6.50 | 7.00 | 7.25 | 7.50 | 7.75 |
| First Line Trust. Toronto | - | - | 5,000 | 6.88 | 6.88 | 6.88 | 7.00 | 7.00 | 7.00 | 1,000 | 7.13 | 7.88 | 8.38 | 8.63 | 9.00 |
| General Trust, Toronto | 3.00 | 3.25 | 5,000 | 6.25 | 6.25 | 6.50 | 6.50 | 6.75 | 6.75 | 1,000 | 7.25 | 8.00 | 8.50 | 8.75 | 9.00 |
| Household Trust, North York | - | - | 5,000 | 6.75 | 6.75 | 7.00 | 7.00 | 7.25 | 7.25 | 500 | 7.63 | 8.00 | 8.25 | 8.25 | 8.75 |
| Huronia Trust, Orillia | - | - | 25,000 | 6.50 | 6.50 | 6.50 | 6.50 | 6.50 | 6.50 | 500 | 7.25 | 7.75 | 8.25 | 8.50 | 8.75 |
| Income Trust, Hamilton | - | - | 5,000 | 6.75 | 6.88 | 7.25 | 7.35 | 7.45 | 7.55 | 1,000 | 7.63 | 8.00 | 8.50 | 8.75 | 9.00 |
| Inland Trust Co., Winnipeg | - | - | 5,000 | 6.22 | 6.22 | 6.22 | 6.42 | 6.42 | 6.42 | 1,000 | 7.02 | 7.72 | 8.22 | 8.82 | 8.62 |
| Investors Group Trust, Winnipeg | - | - | - | - | - | - | - | - | - | 1,000 | 7.00 | 7.75 | 8.25 | 8.50 | 8.75 |
| London Trust, North York | - | - | 5,000 | 6.50 | 6.50 | 6.75 | 6.75 | 7.00 | 7.25 | 5,000 | 7.25 | 7.75 | 8.25 | 8.50 | 8.75 |
| Mackenzie Trust, Toronto | - | - | 25,000 | 7.00 | 7.00 | 7.00 | 7.00 | 7.00 | 7.00 | 2,500 | 7.50 | 8.00 | 8.63 | 8.75 | 9.00 |
| Metropolitan Trust, Edmonton | - | - | 5,000 | r 6.25 | r 6.25 | r 6.25 | r 6.25 | r 6.50 | r 6.50 | 1,000 | 6.75 | 7.50 | 8.00 | 8.25 | 8.50 |
| Monarch Trust, Toronto | - | - | 25,000 | - | 6.75 | 6.75 | 6.75 | 6.75 | 6.75 | 25,000 | 7.25 | 7.75 | 8.25 | 8.25 | 8.75 |
| Montreal Trust, Montreal | 2.00 | - | 5,000 | r 6.00 | r 6.00 | r 6.00 | r 6.25 | r 6.25 | r 6.25 | 500 | 7.00 | 7.75 | 8.25 | 8.25 | 9.25 |
| Morgan Trust, Toronto | - | - | 5,000 | r 7.13 | r 7.00 | r 7.00 | r 7.00 | r 7.00 | r 7.00 | 500 | 7.25 | 7.88 | 8.63 | 8.63 | 8.88 |
| Municipal Trust, Barrie | 3.25 | 3.25 | 10,000 | r 6.25 | r 6.25 | r 6.25 | r 6.25 | r 6.50 | r 6.50 | 500 | 7.13 | 7.75 | 8.25 | 8.50 | 9.00 |
| Mutual Trust, Toronto | - | - | 5,000 | r 6.25 | r 6.25 | r 6.55 | r 6.55 | r 6.85 | r 6.85 | 5,000 | r 7.25 | r 8.00 | r 8.35 | r 8.80 | r 9.00 |
| National Trust, Toronto | 2.75 | 3.00 | 5,000 | r 6.00 | r 6.00 | r 6.00 | r 6.25 | r 6.25 | r 6.25 | 500 | 7.25 | 8.00 | 8.50 | 8.50 | 9.25 |
| North West Trust, Edmonton | - | - | 5,000 | r 6.50 | r 6.50 | r 6.50 | r 6.50 | r 6.75 | r 6.75 | 500 | 7.50 | 8.00 | 8.50 | 8.75 | 9.00 |
| Peace Hills Trust, Edmonton | 4.50 | 4.25 | 1,000 | 6.00 | 6.00 | 6.00 | 6.00 | 6.25 | 6.25 | 1,000 | 7.00 | 7.50 | 8.00 | 8.25 | 8.75 |
| Peoples Trust, Edmonton | - | - | 5,000 | 6.90 | 6.90 | 6.90 | 6.90 | 7.20 | 7.50 | 5,000 | 7.75 | 8.00 | 8.50 | 8.75 | 9.00 |
| Premier Trust, Toronto | 2.75 | 3.00 | 5,000 | r 6.00 | r 6.00 | r 6.00 | r 6.25 | r 6.25 | r 6.25 | 500 | 7.25 | 8.00 | 8.50 | 8.50 | 9.25 |
| **OTHER INSTITUTIONS** | | | | | | | | | | | | | | | |
| Alberta Treasury Branch, Edmonton | - | - | 1,000 | - | - | - | - | 6.25 | 6.25 | 1,000 | 6.75 | 7.50 | 8.00 | 8.25 | 8.75 |
| Avestel Credit Union, Hamilton | - | - | 5,000 | - | - | r 5.50 | - | r 6.00 | - | 500 | 6.75 | 7.50 | 8.00 | 8.25 | 8.75 |
| Canada Life, Toronto | - | - | 1,000 | r 5.50 | r 5.75 | r 6.25 | r 6.25 | r 6.75 | r 6.75 | - | - | - | - | - | - |
| Capital City Savings, Edmonton | - | - | 1,000 | 5.25 | 5.25 | 5.50 | 5.50 | 5.50 | 5.75 | 1,000 | 7.00 | 7.75 | 8.50 | 8.50 | 9.00 |
| Commercial Union Life, Scarborough | - | - | - | - | - | - | - | - | - | 10,000 | r 6.30 | r 7.00 | r 7.85 | r 7.90 | r 8.05 |
| Empire Life. Kingston | - | - | - | - | - | - | - | - | - | 1,000 | 7.00 | 7.25 | 8.00 | 7.75 | 8.50 |
| Fede Des Caisses De Mtl, Montreal | 2.50 | 1.50 | 2,000 | - | - | - | - | r 5.00 | r 5.00 | 1,000 | 6.75 | 7.88 | 8.50 | 8.50 | 9.00 |
| First Calgary Financial, Calgary | 2.50 | 2.75 | 5,000 | r 3.50 | r 4.25 | r 4.25 | r 4.25 | r 5.00 | r 5.00 | 1,000 | 6.75 | 7.50 | 8.00 | 8.25 | 8.50 |
| Great West Life, Winnipeg | - | - | - | - | - | - | - | - | - | 1,000 | 6.75 | 7.50 | 8.00 | 8.25 | 8.50 |
| Home Savings & Loan. St. Catharines | - | - | 5,000 | 4.00 | 7.00 | 7.00 | 7.00 | 7.25 | 7.25 | 5,000 | 7.50 | 8.00 | 8.50 | 8.50 | 8.75 |
| Industrial Alliance, Sillery | - | - | 100 | - | r 5.50 | r 5.50 | r 5.50 | r 5.50 | r 5.75 | 100 | r 6.50 | r 7.00 | r 7.75 | r 8.00 | r 8.50 |
| Landmark Savings & Loan, Toronto | - | - | 5,000 | 6.50 | 6.50 | 6.50 | 6.75 | 6.75 | 6.75 | 500 | 7.50 | 8.00 | 8.50 | 8.75 | 9.00 |
| London Life, London | - | - | 2,500 | - | - | - | - | - | r 5.84 | 10,000 | 6.75 | 7.50 | 7.75 | 8.00 | 8.50 |
| ManuLife Financial, Waterloo | - | - | - | - | - | - | - | - | - | 1,000 | r 6.75 | r 7.50 | r 8.00 | r 8.25 | r 8.50 |
| Metropolitan Life, Ottawa | - | - | - | - | - | - | - | - | - | 1,000 | 6.75 | 7.50 | 8.00 | 8.30 | 8.75 |
| Mutual Life of Canada, Waterloo | - | - | - | - | - | - | - | - | - | 1,000 | r 6.50 | r 7.15 | r 7.65 | r 7.85 | r 8.30 |
| NN Financial, Don Mills | - | - | - | - | - | - | - | - | - | 10,000 | 7.25 | - | 8.25 | - | 8.75 |
| Prov Ont Savings Office, Oshawa | - | 3.50 | - | - | - | - | - | - | - | 500 | 7.25 | 8.00 | 8.50 | 8.75 | 9.00 |
| Prudential Insurance, Scarborough | - | - | - | - | - | - | - | - | - | - | - | - | - | - | - |
| Royal Lepage Mortgage, London | - | - | - | - | - | - | - | - | - | - | - | - | - | - | - |

## FIGURE 12-2

Short and mid term interest rates offered by various financial institutions.

*SOURCE:* Reprinted by permission of *The Globe and Mail: Report on Business,* Thomson Newspapers Company Limited, (April 27, 1992).

## ☐ 12.1.5  Deposit Insurance

In 1967, the *Canadian Deposit Insurance Corporation* (CDIC) was created by the federal government to guarantee deposits in all federally incorporated chartered banks, and trust and loan companies and all provincially incorporated trust and loan companies, with the exception of those in the Province of Quebec. The Quebec Deposit Insurance Board (QDIB) was established to insure deposits of all deposit accepting institutions in Quebec as well as deposits accepted outside Quebec by institutions incorporated in that province. In 1990, the CDIC had 151 insured member institutions — 116 federally and 35 provincially incorporated.

The CDIC was created to achieve several objectives:

1. protection of small depositors,
2. provision of last resort facilities,
3. improvement in the minimum financial standards of deposit taking institutions across the country, and
4. maintenance of confidence and stability in the financial system.

The deposit insurance system was designed to operate much like a casualty insurance company. The premiums collected from the insured member institutions together with income from investments are used to cover operating expenses and losses, with any excess contributing to an increase in reserves. In a properly functioning deposit insurance system the premium plus investment income should be sufficient to cover expenses, anticipated and expected unanticipated losses.

The insured limit under the *Canada Deposit Insurance Act* on Canadian dollar deposits with an original term to maturity of five years or less was set at $60,000 in 1983 and has remained at that level since. Judicious use of multiple accounts in different financial institutions makes it possible to increase the total amount covered by deposit insurance. Member institutions were originally required to pay an annual insurance premium of 1/30th of 1% of insured deposits, but this was raised to 0.1% in 1988. All member institutions pay the same premium with no risk differential.

Claims were minimal prior to 1983. There was, however, a dramatic increase in claims in the period 1983 to 1986 as several financial institutions became insolvent and were declared bankrupt. The Deposit Insurance Fund's surplus of $253 million at the end of 1982 became a deficit of $1,245 million in 1986 and stood at $643 million at the end of 1991.

---

## 12.2  MONEY MARKET INSTRUMENTS

Certain types of short-term (meaning, arbitrarily, one year or less), highly marketable loans play a major role in the investment and borrowing activities of industrial corporations and financial intermediaries. Individual investors with substantial funds may invest in such *money market instruments* directly but may also do so indirectly via money market accounts at various financial institutions.[1]

---

[1] Short-term obligations and bonds of the Government of Canada and its agencies that mature in less than three years are also considered to be money market instruments. Useful descriptions of the various types of money market instruments are contained in W.T.Hunter, *Canadian Financial Markets*, (Peterborough, Ont.: Broadview Press Ltd.), 1988; and James E. Hatch and Robert W. White, *Canadian Stocks, Bonds, Bills, and*

# MONEY MARKETS

| ADMINISTERED RATES | |
| --- | --- |
| Bank of Canada | 8.04% |
| Canadian prime | 8.50-8.75% |

**MONEY MARKET RATES**
(for transactions
of $1-million or more)

| | |
| --- | --- |
| 3-month treasury bills | 7.790% |
| 6-month treasury bills | 7.503% |
| 1-year treasury bills | 7.464% |
| 2001 Canada bonds | 8.68% |
| 2011 Canada bonds | 9.12% |
| 30-day comm. paper | 8.20% |
| 60-day comm. paper | 8.10% |
| 90-day comm. paper | 8.00% |
| 30-day banker's accept. | 8.13% |
| 60-day banker's accept. | 7.99% |
| 90-day banker's accept. | 7.87% |
| 1-month dollar swaps | 7.86% |
| 2-month dollar swaps | 7.88% |
| 3-month dollar swaps | 7.67% |
| 6-month dollar swaps | 7.51% |
| 1-year dollar swaps | 7.45% |
| Call money | 10.00% |

**UNITED STATES**

NEW YORK (AP) — Money rates for Thursday as reported by Telerate Systems Inc:
Telerate interest rate index: 5.086
Prime Rate: 8.00
Discount Rate: 5.00
Broker call loan rate: 7.00-7.50
Federal funds market rate:
High 5.1875, low 5.0, last 5.125
Dealers commercial paper: 30-180 days: 5.05-5.05
Commercial paper by finance company:
30-270 days: 4.91-5.02
Bankers acceptances dealer indications: 30 days, 5.01; 60 days, 5.10; 90 days, 5.05; 120 days, 5.02; 150 days, 5.00; 180 days, 5.00
Certificates of Deposit Primary: 30 days, 4.60; 90 days,

4.68; 180 days, 4.69
Certificates of Deposit by dealer: 30 days, 5.10; 60 days, 5.25; 90 days, 5.20; 120 days, 5.20; 150 days, 5.20; 180 days, 5.20
Eurodollar rates: Overnight, 5-5.125; 1 month, 5-5.125; 3 months, 5.125-5.25; 6 months, 5.125-5.25; 1 year, 5.25-5.375
London Interbank Offered Rate: 3 months, 5.125; 6 months, 5.125
Treasury Bill auction results: average discount rate: 3-month as of Oct 28: 4.99; 6-month as of Oct 28: 5.04
Treasury Bill, annualized rate on weekly average basis, yield adjusted for constant maturity, 1-year, as of Oct.28 5.39
Treasury Bill market rate, 1-year: 4.83-4.81
Treasury Bond market rate, 30-year: 7.90

**FIGURE 12-3**
Canadian and US money market rates quoted in the financial press.

*SOURCE:* Reprinted by permission of *The Globe and Mail: Report on Business,* Thomson Newspapers Company Limited, (November 11, 1991).

Some money market instruments are negotiable and are traded in active secondary dealer markets; others are not. Some may be purchased by anyone with adequate funds, others only by particular types of institutions. Many are sold on a discount basis, for example, a 91-day Treasury bill with a face value of $100,000 might be sold for $98,000 — where the face value of $100,000 is to be paid to the investor at maturity and the difference of $2000 represents interest income.

Interest rates on such money market instruments are often reported on an *annualized rate basis*. This means that in the example above, the T-bill will be described in the media as providing a rate of 8.19% per year calculated as follows:

$$( \$2000 / \$98,000 ) \times ( 365 / 91 ) \times 100 = 8.19\%$$

Over the 91-day period the investor receives a return of $2000/$98,000 or 2.04%. If, however, the proceeds were reinvested at the same rate four times over the actual return or *annual percentage rate* (APR) would be $1.0204^4 - 1 = 8.41\%$. Both *The Globe and Mail: Report on Business* and *The Financial Post* publish, daily, a list of the current interest rates on a number of Canadian, US and international money market instruments. Figure 12–3 presents samples of these lists. Table 12.1 shows the size of the Canadian money market broken-down by type of instrument. Most of these are described in the next section.

---

*Inflation: 1950–1987,* (Charlottesville, Va.: The Research Foundation of The Institute of Chartered Financial Analysts), 1988.

**TABLE 12.1**

Money Market Instruments Held Outside the Bank of Canada, December, 1991.

| Type of Instrument | | Amount (in Millions) |
|---|---|---|
| Treasury bills: | | |
| Government of Canada | $125,152 | |
| Provincial governments | 13,452 | |
| Municipal governments | 525 | |
| Sub-total Treasury Bills | | $139,129 |
| Short-term paper: | | |
| Bankers' acceptances | $ 44,109 | |
| Finance paper | 9,004 | |
| Commercial paper | 22,432 | |
| Sub-total Short-term Paper | | 75,545 |
| Total Money Market | | $214,674 |

SOURCE: *Bank of Canada Review,* November 1991 issue.

## ☐ 12.2.1 Finance and Commercial Paper

*Finance paper* is an unsecured short-term promissory note issued in either Canadian dollars or other currencies (usually US dollars) by sales finance and consumer loan companies. Commercial and industrial corporations issue *commercial paper* with characteristics similar to that of finance paper but offering slightly higher rates.[2] Finance paper is secured by the pledge of the instalment obligations that the company will receive. Commercial paper is often backed by either a standby line of credit at a bank or a guarantee from a parent company or affiliate to insure that the loan will be paid off when it comes due. The interest rates on finance and commercial paper reflect this low risk, being relatively low in comparison to other corporate fixed-income securities and slightly above Treasury Bills.

Finance and commercial paper is issued in minimum denominations of $50,000, with maturities of 30 to 365 days for the former and one to 365 days for the latter (but typically less than 90 days). The secondary market for both types of paper is limited, therefore, they are usually held to maturity. Commercial paper often has a 24-hour prepayment provision whereby the company can repay the note on one day's notice.

## ☐ 12.2.2 Bankers' Acceptances

In Canada, a *bankers' acceptance* is a pure-discount security that is a substitute for commercial paper as a source of financing. It can be regarded as a negotiable, certified cheque made out to the bearer. The firm seeking financing must write a bill for $100,000 or a multiple thereof payable to itself within 180 days or less for acceptance by its bank. *Acceptance* means that the bank will guarantee payment. Once accepted the company

---

[2] About 22% of all finance and commercial paper outstanding at the end of 1990 was denominated in a foreign currency.

can endorse the bill to bearer and sell it (at a discount) in the money market. At maturity the bank is obliged to redeem the bill and it collects the necessary funds from the issuing company. The effective rate of interest is only slightly higher than that on T-bills reflecting the high credit-worthiness of the company and the bank's guarantee. In addition to the interest the issuing corporation must also pay the bank a fee for accepting the bill.

In the United States banker's acceptances were created to finance goods in transit, but currently they are generally used to finance foreign trade. The buyer of goods imported from abroad makes out a bill payable to itself as described above, then has it accepted by its bank and turns it over to the seller.

The seller of the goods, having received the accepted bill, need not wait until it is due in order to receive payment. It can be sold in the money market at a discount.

## ☐ 12.2.3 Term Deposits Issued by Financial Institutions

### Negotiable deposits

*Bearer Deposit Notes* (BDNs) are the only short term instruments issued by the Canadian chartered banks that are traded in the money market. These are issued in multiples of $100,000 with maturities ranging from 30 to 365 days. They are transferable but not redeemable before maturity and, therefore, marketable. US banks issue similar securities, but these are known as *Certificates of Deposit* (CDs) (or Jumbo CDs when they are in large denominations).

### Non-negotiable deposits

The chartered banks also issue Certificates of Deposit that are similar to BDNs but are neither transferable nor negotiable. These are also called Term Deposit Receipts or Term Notes and are issued in denominations ranging from $5000 to $100,000 with maturities ranging from one day to five years.

Trust and mortgage loan companies issue similar instruments under a variety of names (Deposit Receipts, Guaranteed Trust Certificates, Guaranteed Investment Certificates and Guaranteed Investment Receipts). In general, term deposits have a minimum denomination of $5000 with one day to one year maturities and receipts or certificates have a minimum denomination of $500 with one to five year maturities.

## ☐ 12.2.4 Eurodollars

In the world of international finance, large short-term Certificates of Deposit (CDs) denominated in dollars and issued by banks outside North America (most often in London) are known as *Eurodollar CDs* (or simply Euro CDs). Dollar-denominated time deposits in banks outside North America are known as *Eurodollar deposits*. A key distinction between Euro CDs and Eurodollar deposits is that Euro CDs are negotiable, meaning they can be traded, whereas Eurodollar deposits are nonnegotiable, meaning they cannot be traded.

The demand and supply conditions for such instruments may differ from the conditions for other Canadian and US money market instruments, owing to restrictions imposed (or likely to be imposed) by the Canadian and US governments. Enough commonality exists, however, to keep interest rates from markedly diverging from those available in North America. Euro CDs are not covered by deposit insurance as are deposits issued by Canadian financial institutions.

### ☐ 12.2.5 Repurchase Agreements

Often one investor (often a financial institution) will sell another investor (often another financial institution) a money market instrument and agree to repurchase it for an agreed-upon price at a later date. For example, investor A might sell investor B, for a price of $10 million, a number of Treasury bills that mature in 180 days. Investor A signs a *repurchase agreement* with investor B specifying that after 30 days, investor A will repurchase these Treasury bills for $10.1 million. Thus, investor A will be paying investor B $100,000 in interest for a 30 day loan of $10 million. Investor B is, in essence, purchasing a money market instrument that matures in 30 days.

## 12.3   CANADIAN GOVERNMENT SECURITIES

It should come as no surprise that the Canadian government relies heavily on debt financing. In recent years revenues have seldom covered expenses, and the difference has been financed primarily by issuing debt instruments. Moreover, new debt must be issued in order to raise the necessary funds to pay off old debts that mature, an operation known as *debt refunding*. In addition to issuing its own debt the Canadian government implicitly guarantees the debts of certain federal agencies such as the Export Development Corporation, the Farm Credit Corporation, and the Federal Business Development Bank. The bonds of these agencies are generally regarded as being of high quality but low liquidity. In the past, the government has also unconditionally guaranteed the principal and interest of debt securities of certain Crown Corporations.

Some idea of the magnitude and ownership of Canadian government marketable, term debt (one year or more) can be gained by examining Table 12.2. The federal government, through the Bank of Canada is a moderately large holder, as are provincial and local governments. The vast majority of these bonds, however, are held by the private sector notably by foreign investors and trusteed pension funds. The remainder are fairly uniformly distributed amongst the various Canadian institutions and individuals. Over 97% of these bonds are denominated in Canadian dollars with the remainder issued predominantly in Eurodollars or Japanese yen.

Eighty-seven percent of the total public debt is marketable, meaning it is represented by securities that can be sold at any time by the original purchaser through investment dealers. The major nonmarketable issues are held by individuals in the form of Canada Savings Bonds. Marketable issues include Treasury bills, and bonds of different maturities. Table 12.3 shows the amounts in each category and the maturity structure of the marketable securities in December 1990.

The Bank of Canada has considerable latitude in selecting maturities for new issues and makes a practice of providing bonds of different maturities with each issue — presumably to appeal to investors with different horizons. At the end of 1990 more than

**TABLE 12.2**

Ownership of Outstanding Government of Canada Marketable Term Debt, December 1990. [a]

| Held by | Amount (in millions) | Percent of Total |
|---|---|---|
| Chartered banks | $ 6,383 | 4.4% |
| Thrift institutions | 2,978 | 2.0 |
| Life insurance companies | 11,828 | 8.1 |
| Property and casualty insurance companies | 6,341 | 4.3 |
| Trusteed pension funds | 29,934 | 20.5 |
| Mutual funds | 4,268 | 2.9 |
| Investment dealers | 1,041 | 0.7 |
| Non-financial private corporations | 545 | 0.4 |
| Misc. private financial institutions | 326 | 0.2 |
| Foreign investors | 53,763 | 36.8 |
| Individuals and non-incorporated business | 4,333 | 3.0 |
| Sub-total — privately held federal bonds | $121,740 | 83.3% |
| Non-financial government enterprise | $ 478 | 0.3 |
| Public financial institutions | 1,873 | 1.3 |
| Social security funds | 3,495 | 2.4 |
| Provincial and local governments | 8,719 | 6.0 |
| Bank of Canada | 9,751 | 6.7 |
| Federal government | 102 | – |
| Sub-total publicly held federal bonds | $ 24,418 | 16.7% |
| Total federal marketable bonds | $146,158 | 100.0% |

[a] Excludes Treasury bills but includes federal government guaranteed issues.

SOURCE: Statistics, Canada, *National Balance Sheet Accounts: System of National Accounts*, 1990, Ottawa, April 1991.

55% of the total debt was short-term, maturing in three years or less, and about 63% had a maturity date within five years.[3]

The three principal types of debt issued by the Canadian government as well as two derivative securities are discussed next.

## ☐ 12.3.1 Government of Canada Treasury Bills

Treasury bills are issued on a discount basis, with maturities of up to 52 weeks, in denominations of $5000, $25,000, $100,000, and $1 million (although at times denominations as small as $1000 have been offered). All are issued in *bearer form* only, this means that the buyer's name is neither recorded in the Bank of Canada's books nor on the security itself. The face value is payable at maturity to the current holder of the security. Although Treasury bills are sold at discount, their dollar yield (that is, the

---

[3] The effective maturity of the nonmarketable debt is not easy to determine because Canada Savings Bonds are redeemable by the buyer on demand at any time.

**TABLE 12.3**

Maturity Structure of Marketable Interest-Bearing Government of Canada Debt Held Outside the Bank of Canada, December 1990.

| Type and Maturity | Amount (in millions) | Percent of Total |
|---|---|---|
| Nonmarketable issues: | | |
| Canada Savings Bonds | $ 33,978 | 11.5% |
| Foreign series | 1,122 | 0.4 |
| Other a | 3,493 | 1.0 |
| Total Nonmarketable Debt | $ 38,593 | 13.0% |
| Marketable issues: | | |
| Within 3 years: | | |
| Treasury bills | $125,152 | 42.2% |
| Under 3 years | 38,219 | 12.9 |
| 3-5 years | 25,327 | 8.5 |
| 5-10 years | 29,529 | 10.0 |
| 10 years and over | 39,797 | 13.4 |
| Total Marketable Debt | $258,024 | 87.0% |
| Total Debt | $296,617 | 100.0% |

a All of these are bonds held by the Canada Pension Plan Investment Fund.

SOURCE: *Bank of Canada Review,* November 1991 Issue.

difference between the purchase price and face value if the bill is held to maturity) is treated as interest income for tax purposes.

Offerings of 91-day and 182-day bills are made once each week, 364-day bills are offered most weeks, and occasionally shorter maturities are also offered. All are sold at auction every Thursday at noon (Wednesday if Thursday is a holiday) by the Bank of Canada acting as an agent of the Minister of Finance. The Bank of Canada itself and *primary distributors* (specified chartered banks and investment dealers) are eligible to bid on bills intended for resale, but others may bid on their own account. Bids may be entered on either a competitive or noncompetitive basis. With a competitive bid, the investor states a price he or she is willing to pay. For example, an investor might enter a bid for a stated number of 91-day bills at a price of 98.512. If the bid is accepted, the investor will pay $98,512.00 for each $100,000 of face value, meaning that an investment of $98,512.00 will generate a receipt of $100,000 if held to maturity 91 days later. With a noncompetitive bid, the investor agrees to pay the average price of all bids that will be accepted by the Bank of Canada.

The results of the auction are announced by the Bank of Canada at about 2:00 p.m. on Thursday. Generally bids are received for more bills than are being offered, therefore, some bidders are not successful. All noncompetitive bids are accepted with the balance of the issue allocated between the highest competitive bidders. Every Friday *The Globe and Mail: Report on Business* publishes the results of the auction that took place on the

**Dow Jones Service**

OTTAWA — The average yield at this week's auction of $4-billion of 91-day Government of Canada treasury bills was 7.79 per cent, down from 7.919 per cent last week.

As a result, the Bank of Canada's bank rate falls to 8.04 per cent from 8.17 per cent.

Accepted yields for the 91-day bills ranged from a high of 7.8 per cent for a price equivalent of $98.09244 to a low of 7.77 per cent for a price equivalent of $98.09964. The price equivalent at the average yield was $98.09495.

For an offering of $1.9-billion of 182-day treasury bills, accepted yields ranged from a high of 7.53 per cent for a price equivalent of $96.38119 to a low of 7.47 per cent for a price equivalent of $96.40899.

The average yield of 7.503 per cent provided a price equivalent of $96.39364. Last week's average yield was 7.817 per cent.

For an offering of $1.1-billion of 364-day bills, accepted yields ranged from a high of 7.49 per cent for a price equivalent of $93.04967 to a low of 7.44 per cent for a price equivalent of $93.09287. The average yield of 7.464 per cent provided a price equivalent of $93.07181. Last week's average yield was 7.839 per cent.

All the bills are dated Nov. 1. The 91-day bills mature Jan. 31, the 182-day bills on May 1 and the 364-day bills on Oct. 30, 1992.

On offer next week will be $3.2-billion of 91-day bills, $1.5-billion of 182-day bills and $1-billion of 364-day bills.

**FIGURE 12-4**
Treasury bill auction results for October 31, 1991.

*SOURCE:* Reprinted by permission of *The Globe and Mail: Report on Business,* Thomson Newspapers Limited, (November 1, 1991).

previous day and the amounts to be offered the following week. Figure 12.4 presents the results of the auction that took place on November 1, 1991.

Individuals may purchase Treasury bills indirectly from a bank or investment dealer who offer them at a slightly higher price than that paid at the auction (i.e., at a lower yield). Figure 12.5 shows the yields quoted by a chartered bank to its retail customers for different amounts and maturities of Treasury bills.

There is an active secondary market where institutions may trade Treasury bills with investment dealers. The bid-ask spread on these transactions varies between 1 and 5 basis points (for example, a dealer may quote bid 7.36%, ask 7.32%, meaning that the dealer is willing to pay a price that will earn him an annualized rate of 7.36%) depending on the size of the transaction and the volatility of the market.

## ☐ 12.3.2 Government of Canada Short Term Bonds

These consist of bonds and government guaranteed bonds with a residual maturity of three years or less and may consist of either medium (maturity between three and ten years) or long term bonds that are approaching maturity or newly issued short term bonds. Short term bonds are traded in the money market although the characteristics and marketing of newly issued bonds with a maturity of three years are more like those of medium and long term bonds discussed below.

Prices and yields on short term bonds are quoted in the newspapers along with other Government of Canada bonds. The following is a typical bond quotation reported in *The Financial Post* on November 11, 1991:

**FIGURE 12-5**

Treasury bill quotations.

*SOURCE:* Toronto-Dominion Bank, *Financial Rate Letter,* (December 2, 1991).

| Nov. 8 1991 | Int. Rate % | Maturity Date | Bid $ | Yield |
| --- | --- | --- | --- | --- |
| Canada | 15.000 | Jul 1 92 | 104.40 | 7.69 |

This indicates that this short term bond maturing on July 1, 1992 carries a coupon rate of 15% and could be sold to a dealer for 104.4% of par value or $1044.00 per $1000 of par value. The effective yield-to-maturity at the time, based on the bid price, is approximately 7.69%. A purchaser of this bond could expect to pay the ask price which is generally $0.10 to $0.15 higher than the bid for government bonds.

In practice, the situation facing a potential buyer (or seller) is somewhat more complicated. The buyer is required to pay the seller not only the ask price (say, $104.55) but also any *accrued interest*. For example, on November 8, 130 days have elapsed since the last coupon payment and 54 days remain until the next, therefore, an amount equal to $130/184 = 0.7065$ of the semiannual coupon ($0.7065 \times \$150 = \$105.98$) is added to the stated purchase price to arrive at the settlement price (in this case, $105.98 + $1045.50 = $1151.48). Similarly if an investor were to sell this bond the dealer would pay the stated bid price plus accrued interest ($105.98 + $1044.00 = $1149.98). This procedure is commonly followed with all bonds.

## □ 12.3.3  Government of Canada Medium and Long Term Bonds

Medium term bonds have maturities from three to ten years at the time of issue. Long term bonds are those with initial maturities greater than ten years. Interest or coupon payments are generally made semiannually at a set rate. Bonds may be issued in either *bearer* or *registered* form, commonly in denominations of $1000, $5000, $25,000, $100,000 or $1 million. Bonds issued in bearer form have numbered and dated coupons attached to the *bond certificate* that may be detached and cashed on the due date (but not before). The name of the owner of a *registered bond* is recorded at the Bank of Canada in Ottawa and also appears on the *bond certificate*. Interest is paid by cheque directly to the owner. Transfer of ownership of a registered bond is somewhat more complicated than for a bearer bond although the former provides security in the event of a theft.[4]

Currently two outstanding issues have a *call or redemption feature* that allows them to be "called" on specified notice (thirty days in one case and thirty to sixty in the other). The Bank of Canada has the right to force the investor to sell the bonds back to the government at a pre-determined price (par or slightly above). Both issues provide *call protection* in that the call provision does not come into effect for several years after the date of issue.

For callable issues, the yield-to-maturity is calculated using the stated price. If this price is greater than par, then the calculation of yield-to-maturity is based on an assumption that the bond will be called at the earliest allowable date.

Several issues also include a *purchase fund*, under whose provisions the Government of Canada undertakes to retire a specified fraction of the issue prior to maturity by purchasing the bonds in the open market at prices not exceeding a specified value (usually par or slightly below).

Many Government of Canada bonds trade in an active secondary market. Prices and yields of more heavily traded Government of Canada, Provincial and corporate bonds are quoted daily in *The Globe and Mail: Report on Business* and *The Financial Post*. Figure 12.6 illustrates the typical information provided in the former publication.

## ☐ 12.3.4 Canada Savings Bonds

Once a year, generally for about two weeks ending on November 1, nonmarketable *Canada Savings Bonds* (CSBs) are offered — only to individuals, estates, and specified trusts . No more than a specified amount may be purchased by any one person in a single year, but the amount may vary from year to year (for example, $20,000 in 1987, $75,000 in 1991). Term to maturity varies from issue to issue, in the early 1980s seven year terms prevailed, but the 1991 series had a 12 year term. Term to maturity is not an important feature because the valuable option CSBs provide is the possibility of redemption, at face value plus accrued interest, at any time prior to maturity by presenting the bonds at any financial institution.

Two types of CSBs are available. Simple interest bonds pay interest annually on November 1 each year. Compound interest bonds are essentially pure-discount bonds, meaning that no interest is paid on them prior to maturity at which time a lump sum representing principal plus interest is paid.

All CSBs are floating rate bonds with an annual adjustment period. The interest rate payable is announced for the first year at the time of issue. In subsequent years the interest rate is equal to the rate paid on the newly issued CSBs. In any given year, therefore, all CSB series pay the same interest rate.[5] Both types are fully registered and may be neither transferred nor assigned although some banks will accept CSBs as collateral for loans. These bonds are available in denominations from $100 to $10,000 and may be

---

[4] Some bonds currently in existence are registered as to principal only. These carry coupons like a bearer bond but the owner's name is recorded on the bond certificate. Such bonds are no longer issued.

[5] In times of rapidly rising interest rates the Bank of Canada has been forced to change rates during the year in an effort to stem the flood of redemptions, but has not always been successful. In 1990, redemptions exceeded the new issue by over $8 billion.

# CANADIAN BONDS

Selected quotations, with changes since the previous day, on actively traded bond issues, provided by RBC Dominion Securities. Yields are calculated to full maturity, unless marked C to indicate callable date. Price is the midpoint between final bid and ask quotations Oct. 31, 1991.

| Issuer | Coupon | Maturity | Price | Yield | $ Chg |
|---|---|---|---|---|---|
| **GOVERNMENT OF CANADA** | | | | | |
| CANADA | 10.25 | 5 DEC 92 | 102.750 | 7.549 | NC |
| CANADA | 9.50 | 1 SEP 93 | 103.400 | 7.460 | +0.050 |
| CANADA | 8.75 | 6 SEP 93 | 102.275 | 7.393 | +0.050 |
| CANADA | 9.25 | 1 OCT 94 | 103.900 | 7.721 | +0.050 |
| CANADA | 10.50 | 1 JUN 95 | 107.375 | 8.074 | +0.100 |
| CANADA | 9.25 | 1 OCT 96 | 104.400 | 8.139 | +0.300 |
| CANADA | 8.25 | 1 MAR 97 | 100.500 | 8.128 | +0.250 |
| CANADA | 9.75 | 1 OCT 97 | 106.550 | 8.319 | +0.300 |
| CANADA | 9.50 | 1 OCT 98 | 105.500 | 8.429 | +0.200 |
| CANADA | 9.25 | 1 DEC 99 | 104.150 | 8.526 | +0.250 |
| CANADA | 9.75 | 1 JUN 01 | 106.750 | 8.694 | +0.200 |
| CANADA | 9.50 | 1 OCT 01 | 105.125 | 8.714 | +0.250 |
| CANADA | 9.75 | 1 DEC 01 | 106.900 | 8.705 | +0.200 |
| CANADA | 8.50 | 1 APR 02 | 99.275 | 8.605 | +0.250 |
| CANADA | 10.00 | 1 MAY 02 | 108.375 | 8.762 | +0.250 |
| CANADA | 11.75 | 1 FEB 03 | 118.975 | 9.023 | +0.200 |
| CANADA | 10.25 | 1 FEB 04 | 109.950 | 8.895 | +0.250 |
| CANADA | 10.00 | 1 JUN 08 | 107.800 | 9.079 | +0.350 |
| CANADA | 9.50 | 1 JUN 10 | 104.200 | 9.028 | +0.400 |
| CANADA | 9.00 | 1 MAR 11 | 100.350 | 8.959 | +0.400 |
| CANADA | 10.25 | 15 MAR 14 | 110.100 | 9.177 | +0.400 |
| CANADA | 10.50 | 15 MAR 21 | 112.400 | 9.262 | +0.400 |
| CANADA | 9.75 | 1 JUN 21 | 106.350 | 9.125 | +0.400 |
| **PROVINCIAL** | | | | | |
| ALBERTA | 9.75 | 8 MAY 98 | 104.875 | 8.751 | +0.200 |
| ALBERTA | 10.25 | 22 AUG 01 | 107.300 | 9.103 | +0.200 |
| B C | 9.80 | 12 SEP 94 | 103.875 | 8.042 | +0.100 |
| B C | 10.15 | 29 AUG 01 | 106.025 | 9.200 | +0.200 |
| B C | 10.75 | 21 FEB 11 | 109.525 | 9.649 | +0.350 |
| HYDRO QUEBEC | 9.25 | 2 DEC 96 | 101.875 | 8.781 | +0.100 |
| HYDRO QUEBEC | 10.88 | 25 JUL 01 | 108.575 | 9.499 | +0.150 |
| HYDRO QUEBEC | 11.00 | 15 AUG 20 | 109.375 | 9.999 | +0.100 |
| MANITOBA | 11.25 | 17 OCT 00 | 111.300 | 9.355 | +0.200 |
| MANITOBA | 10.50 | 5 MAR 31 | 106.875 | 9.807 | +0.500 |
| NEW BRUNSWIC | 11.25 | 18 OCT 95 | 108.375 | 8.694 | +0.150 |
| NEW BRUNSWIC | 10.13 | 31 OCT 11 | 102.875 | 9.794 | +0.400 |
| NEWFOUNDLAND | 10.13 | 22 NOV 14 | 99.975 | 10.127 | +0.400 |
| NFLD&LAB HYD | 10.75 | 17 SEP 01 | 106.875 | 9.650 | +0.150 |
| N S POWER | 11.85 | 24 OCT 95 | 110.175 | 8.753 | +0.150 |

| Issuer | Coupon | Maturity | Price | Yield | $ Chg |
|---|---|---|---|---|---|
| N S POWER | 11.00 | 28 FEB 31 | 110.375 | 9.942 | +0.450 |
| ONTARIO HYD | 10.00 | 16 JUN 93 | 103.575 | 7.584 | +0.050 |
| ONTARIO HYD | 10.75 | 19 NOV 95 | 107.425 | 8.533 | +0.150 |
| ONTARIO HYD | 10.88 | 8 JAN 96 | 107.700 | 8.629 | +0.200 |
| ONTARIO HYD | 9.63 | 3 AUG 99 | 103.375 | 9.005 | +0.250 |
| ONTARIO HYD | 10.00 | 19 MAR 01 | 104.925 | 9.201 | +0.200 |
| ONTARIO HYD | 10.75 | 6 AUG 21 | 109.575 | 9.754 | +0.400 |
| ONTARIO HYD | 10.13 | 15 OCT 21 | 103.825 | 9.729 | +0.400 |
| ONTARIO | 8.75 | 16 APR 97 | 100.500 | 8.631 | +0.175 |
| ONTARIO | 10.20 | 27 AUG 98 | 106.400 | 8.920 | +0.200 |
| ONTARIO | 10.50 | 12 DEC 01 | 107.975 | 9.264 | +0.200 |
| P E I | 11.00 | 19 SEP 11 | 108.400 | 10.015 | +0.400 |
| QUEBEC | 10.25 | 7 APR 98 | 105.375 | 9.121 | +0.150 |
| QUEBEC | 10.25 | 15 OCT 01 | 104.850 | 9.484 | +0.150 |
| SASKATCHEWAN | 10.00 | 21 NOV 94 | 104.875 | 8.153 | +0.050 |
| SASKATCHEWAN | 10.13 | 3 JUL 98 | 105.150 | 9.072 | +0.200 |
| SASKATCHEWAN | 10.25 | 10 APR 14 | 103.325 | 9.877 | +0.400 |
| TORONTO -MET | 10.38 | 4 SEP 01 | 106.525 | 9.341 | +0.200 |
| **CORPORATE** | | | | | |
| BELL CANADA | 10.50 | 15 MAY 98 | 107.625 | 8.931 | +0.125 |
| BELL CANADA | 10.35 | 15 DEC 09 | 105.000 | 9.754 | +0.250 |
| BELL CANADA | 11.45 | 15 APR 10 | 113.375 | 9.860 | +0.500 |
| BC TELEPHONE | 10.50 | 12 JUN 00 | 106.750 | 9.337 | +0.125 |
| BC TELEPHONE | 10.65 | 19 JUN 21 | 107.875 | 9.826 | +0.500 |
| BANK OF N S | 10.75 | 26 MAR 01 | 107.375 | 9.540 | +0.125 |
| CONSUMER GAS | 10.80 | 15 APR 11 | 106.500 | 10.032 | +0.375 |
| CDN IMP BANK | 10.38 | 31 JAN 00 | 105.875 | 9.331 | +0.125 |
| CDN IMP BANK | 9.40 | 3 DEC 01/96 | 102.000 | 8.898R | +0.250 |
| CDN PACIFIC | 10.50 | 30 APR 01 | 105.375 | 9.622 | +0.250 |
| CP SECURITIE | 10.50 | 2 AUG 96 | 105.500 | 9.039 | +0.250 |
| CDN UTIL | 11.40 | 15 AUG 10 | 112.625 | 9.902 | +0.500 |
| GAZ METRO | 10.45 | 31 OCT 16 | 102.750 | 10.145 | +0.375 |
| IMPERIAL OIL | 9.88 | 15 DEC 99 | 104.250 | 9.119 | +0.125 |
| NOVA CORP | 10.75 | 14 APR 99 | 104.125 | 9.949 | +0.125 |
| PANCDN PETE | 10.55 | 4 JAN 00 | 106.750 | 9.345 | +0.250 |
| ROYAL BANK | 10.75 | 15 AUG 01 | 108.125 | 9.453 | +0.125 |
| ROYAL BANK | 10.50 | 1 MAR 02 | 107.000 | 9.420 | +0.250 |
| TRANSALTA UT | 11.38 | 1 AUG 00 | 111.500 | 9.409 | +0.250 |
| THOMSON CORP | 10.55 | 10 MAY 01 | 106.875 | 9.438 | +0.125 |

**FIGURE 12-6**

Price quotations for actively traded Canadian Bonds.

*SOURCE:* Reprinted by the permission of *The Globe and Mail: Report on Business,* Thomson Newspapers Limited, (November 1, 1991).

purchased from chartered banks and other financial institutions. Some employers allow their employees to obtain them through payroll savings plans.

Income from CSBs is taxed in the same manner as any other fixed income security — payments from simple interest bonds must be reported in the year in which they are received and accrued interest on compound interest bonds must be reported, despite the fact that no interest has actually been received. Each year the Bank of Canada publishes tables showing the amount of accrued interest that must be reported for compound interest bonds.

## □ 12.3.5 Zero-Coupon or Strip Bonds

A noncallable Government of Canada bond is, in effect, a portfolio of pure-discount or *zero-coupon* bonds. That is, each coupon payment, as well as the principal, can be viewed as a bond in itself; the investor who owns the bond can therefore be viewed as holding a number of individual pure-discount bonds. In 1982, a number of brokerage firms began separating these components, using a process known as *coupon stripping.*

The process is straightforward when dealing with bearer bonds. The numbered and dated coupons (also known as *sentinels*) are simply detached from the bond certificate and sold individually at appropriate discounts. The *bond residue* or *corpus* representing the principal to be repaid at maturity is also sold at a discount. The buyer takes delivery of either the coupon or the naked bond certificate.

With registered bonds the process is slightly more complicated. Bonds of a given issue are purchased and placed in trust with a custodian (for example, a trust company). Sets of *receipts* are then issued, one set for each coupon date. For example, an August 15, 1997 receipt might entitle its holder to receive $1000 on that date (and nothing on any other date). On each coupon date the custodian receives the payments made by the issuer and distributes the funds to the receipt holders.

In addition to issuing a set of receipts corresponding to coupon dates, another set representing the corpus is issued. Holders of the latter receipts, therefore, share in the principal payment.[6]

Strip bonds were first introduced in the US where three early examples were Lehman Brothers' Lehman Investment Opportunity Notes (LIONs), Merrill Lynch's Treasury Investment Growth Receipts (TIGRs), and Salomon Brothers' Certificates of Accrual on Treasury Securities (CATs). Not surprisingly, such securities are known in the trade as "animals."

Noting the favorable market reaction to the offering of these stripped securities, in 1985 the US Treasury Department introduced a program for investors called Separate Trading of Registered Interest and Principal Securities (STRIPS). This program allows purchasers of certain coupon-bearing US Treasury securities to keep whatever cash payments they want and to sell the rest.

Figure 12.7 shows typical market prices for a set of stripped default-free securities, where price is expressed as a percent of maturity value. As the figure shows, the longer the investor has to wait until maturity, the lower the price of the security. In Canada, strip bonds are derived from federal and provincial securities and trade in the OTC market, but prices are not quoted in the business press. Investors wishing to trade these securities may approach the chartered banks or dealers who specialize in them to obtain quotes. Figure 12.8 shows a typical bank quotation for both Government of Canada and provincial stripped coupons.

---

[6] If the underlying bond is callable all coupons payable after the date of first call remain with the corpus.

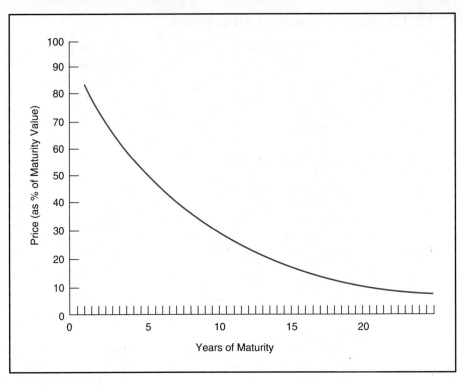

**FIGURE 12-7**
Typical market prices for a set of stripped default-free securities.

| Stripped Coupons | |
| --- | --- |
| Government of Canada Strips | Yield[7] |
| 1 year | 7.150 |
| 3 years | 7.600 |
| 5 years | 8.100 |
| 10 years | 8.700 |
| 20 years | 9.300 |
| | |
| Provincial Strips | |
| 1 year | N/A |
| 3 years | N/A |
| 5 years | 8.200 |
| 10 years | 8.800 |
| 20 years | 9.400 |

**FIGURE 12-8**

Quotations for stripped coupons.

*SOURCE:* Toronto-Dominion Bank, *Financial Rate Letter,* (December 2, 1991).

## ☐ 12.3.6 Real Return Bonds

On December 10, 1991, the Government of Canada issued $700 million of non-callable 4.25% *Real Return Bonds* maturing on December 1, 2021. These were designed to provide a real return of 4.25% over their lifetime and, therefore, are inflation protected, indexed bonds. The indexation procedure is, in principle, straightforward. If the Consumer Price Index corresponding to the date of issue is $CPI_o$ and the CPI at time t is $CPI_t$, then an Index Ratio, IR, is defined as follows:

$$IR_t = CPI_t/CPI_o$$

On each coupon date the cash payment is computed by multiplying the *real* coupon rate by the Index Ratio. The Principal is also adjusted by multiplying the original face value ($1000) by the corresponding Index Ratio.

Complications arise because Statistics Canada reports the CPI monthly, but six weeks in arrears. Appropriate procedures for dealing with this issue and for calculating accrued interest are described in the *Offering Circular* or prospectus issued by the Government of Canada and in pamphlets published by the underwriters

## ☐ 12.3.7 Mortgage Backed Securities

Technically these are not Government of Canada securities but they are guaranteed by the government and are conveniently described here. A *mortgage backed security* (MBS) is a flow-through security that represents an ownership interest in a pool of residential first mortgages with similar terms to maturity (usually five years) and similar interest rates. The mortgages must be individually guaranteed under the National Housing Act (NHA). They are assembled, by a financial institution (such as a bank, trust company, credit union, etc.), into an MBS that is underwritten by the Canada Mortgage and Housing Corporation (CMHC) — a federal government agency — then sub-divided into individual units and sold to the general public in minimum denominations of $5000.

Unlike most bonds, MBSs pay investors, on a monthly basis, an amount that represents a pro rata return of principal as well as interest on the underlying mortgages. For example, a holder of a $25,000 certificate from a $1 million pool would indirectly "own" 2.5% of each mortgage in the pool. Each month the homeowners make mortgage payments that are part principal and part interest. In turn, each month the investor receives 2.5% of the aggregate amount paid by the homeowners, less a small service charge. The mortgages are free from default risk because timely payment to the investor is guaranteed by CMHC, whether or not the issuer receives payment from the homeowner.

Two types of MBS are available — those consisting of nonprepayable mortgages and those consisting of prepayable mortgages.

There is a risk associated with the latter. When interest rates fall, homeowners prepaying or paying off their mortgages reduce the investor's return because both the term to maturity and the interest payments are reduced. MBSs based on prepayable mortgages would, therefore, be expected to sell at lower prices (higher yields) than those based on nonprepayable mortgages. The quoted prices and yields presented in Figure 12.9 show that this is, in fact, the case. The yield differences are, however, quite small suggesting that prepayment risk is not perceived to be high.

## MORTGAGE-BACKED SECURITIES

Mortgage-backed securities are investments in pools of residential mortgages guaranteed by the Canadian government under the National Housing Act. This representative list of actively traded pools is provided by Wood Gundy Inc. and shows the gross bid price for transactions of at least $1-million at Friday's close. The list is divided between open mortgages that are prepayable, and are likely to produce accelerated return of principal, and closed mortgages, on which unscheduled principal payments are not permitted.

### Dec. 20 PREPAYABLE

| Pool | Issuer | Maturity | Coupon | Price | Yield |
|------|--------|----------|--------|-------|-------|
| 96400262 | Central Guar. | Nov.92 | 9.875 | 101.15512 | 8.05 |
| 96400569 | CIBC | Sep.92 | 9.625 | 100.76324 | 7.99 |
| 96401328 | CIBC | Oct.93 | 10.750 | 103.56339 | 8.28 |
| 96401682 | Shoppers | Aug.94 | 10.000 | 103.19000 | 8.42 |
| 96401864 | Shoppers | Aug.94 | 9.375 | 102.06168 | 8.31 |
| 96402045 | Standard | Oct.94 | 9.750 | 102.88118 | 8.39 |
| 96402169 | FirstLine | Jan.95 | 9.875 | 103.49045 | 8.37 |
| 96402300 | Central Guar. | Jan.95 | 10.250 | 104.28262 | 8.43 |
| 96402797 | Shoppers | Jun.95 | 10.250 | 103.42054 | 8.91 |
| 96403639 | FirstLine | May.96 | 10.125 | 104.14630 | 8.81 |

### NONPREPAYABLE

| Pool | Issuer | Maturity | Coupon | Price | Yield |
|------|--------|----------|--------|-------|-------|
| 99000010 | TD | Jul.93 | 10.000 | 102.52631 | 7.95 |
| 99000036 | CIBC | Aug.93 | 10.000 | 102.66973 | 7.95 |
| 99000184 | TD | Nov.93 | 10.500 | 103.91695 | 7.95 |
| 99000614 | Central Guar. | Apr.94 | 10.375 | 104.27384 | 8.07 |
| 99000630 | Central Guar. | Apr.94 | 10.750 | 105.01698 | 8.07 |
| 99001018 | Nat. Trust | Dec.94 | 10.000 | 104.38506 | 8.12 |
| 99001075 | CIBC | Jan.95 | 10.250 | 104.72674 | 8.27 |
| 99001208 | Nat. Trust | Apr.95 | 11.000 | 106.10771 | 8.63 |
| 99001950 | CIBC | Feb.96 | 10.375 | 105.68028 | 8.55 |
| 99002305 | Nat. Trust | May.96 | 9.500 | 103.50566 | 8.40 |

**FIGURE 12-9**

Quoted prices and yields of mortgage backed securities.

*SOURCE:* Reprinted by the permission of *The Globe and Mail: Report on Business,* Thomson Newspapers Limited, (December 23, 1991).

---

## 12.4 PROVINCIAL, TERRITORIAL, AND LOCAL GOVERNMENT SECURITIES

Provincial, territorial, and municipal governments all borrow money to finance their investments and operations. In aggregate the provincial and territorial governments have more term debt outstanding than the federal government. The securities issued by the first two are collectively referred to as *provincial bonds* or "provincials," while those of the third group are called *municipal bonds*, or simply "municipals" (the securities of the Canadian government are referred to as "Canadas"). Table 12.4 shows the distribution of ownership of provincial, territorial, and municipal term debt as of the end of 1990.

### ☐ 12.4.1 Provincial and Territorial Bonds

Provincials are issued to finance public works and, recently, social welfare programs. The payments on these securities are supported by the provincial tax revenues. Many provinces also guarantee the bonds issued by provincial authorities and commissions notably their Hydro-Electric Commissions. As Figure 12.6 indicates, Hydro-Quebec and Ontario Hydro bonds are listed amongst the more actively traded issues. The three principal holders of provincials are the trusteed pension plans, social security funds (notably the Canada Pension Plan) and foreign investors. The provinces have, in general, been more aggressive than the federal government in tapping foreign markets for funds which provide better borrowing rates and conditions. Close to one-third of the outstanding issues are denominated in foreign currencies, notably US dollars (16%), Eurodollars (8%), Swiss francs (3%), and Japanese yen (3%). At the time of issue their coupon rates were significantly below those prevailing in the domestic market. As a result the provinces have assumed a significant degree of foreign exchange risk.

To assist municipalities, the provinces raise funds through government agencies such as the Alberta Municipal Financing Corporation and the Ontario Municipal Improvements Corporation. These agencies float large bond issues (guaranteed by the

**TABLE 12.4**

Ownership of Outstanding Provincial, Territorial and Municipal Term Debt, December 1990 [a].

| | Provincials | | Municipals | |
|---|---|---|---|---|
| Held by | Amount [b] | Percent of Total | Amount [b] | Percent of Total |
| Chartered banks | $    1,005 | 0.5% | $     139 | 0.4% |
| Thrift institutions | 1,894 | 1.0 | 972 | 3.0 |
| Life insurance companies | 6,917 | 3.5 | 2,427 | 7.6 |
| Property and casualty insurance companies | 3,834 | 2.0 | 1,145 | 3.6 |
| Trusteed pension funds | 47,094 | 24.1 | 2,913 | 9.1 |
| Mutual funds | 835 | 0.4 | 47 | 0.2 |
| Investment dealers | 506 | 0.3 | 18 | 0.1 |
| Non-financial private corporations | 197 | 0.1 | 15 | 0.1 |
| Misc. private financial institutions | 11 | – | – | – |
| Foreign investors | 65,007 | 33.2 | 4,211 | 13.2 |
| Individuals and non-incorporated business | 5,750 | 2.9 | 6,685 | 20.9 |
| Sub-total — privately held term debt | $133,054 | 68.0% | $18,572 | 58.1% |
| Non-financial government enterprise | 3,011 | 1.5 | 99 | 0.3 |
| Public financial institutions | 8,271 | 4.2 | 1,232 | 3.9 |
| Social security funds | 33,748 | 17.3 | | |
| Provincial and local governments | 17,538 | 9.0 | 12,067 | 37.7 |
| Federal government | 12 | – | 4 | – |
| Sub-total publicly held term debt | $  62,580 | 32.0% | $13,402 | 41.9% |
| Total term debt | $195,634 | 100.0% | $31,974 | 100.0% |

[a] Excludes Treasury bills but includes provincial government guaranteed issues.

[b] in millions of dollars.

SOURCE: Statistics Canada *National Balance Sheet Accounts: System of National Accounts, 1990,* Ottawa, April 1991.

province) at advantageous rates and then distribute the proceeds to small municipalities that would otherwise have difficulty raising funds. An investor purchasing these bonds is effectively investing in a portfolio of municipal bonds that are guaranteed by the provincial government.

### ☐ 12.4.2 Municipal Bonds

Municipals are usually issued by larger cities as *instalment debentures*, where specified groups of debentures mature in each succeeding year. The largest cities like Montreal, Toronto, and Vancouver may issue *term debentures* (that is, debentures that all mature on the same date) or a mixture of serial and term bonds. These issues are generally underwriten by an investment dealer that specializes in municipals or they are sold through a *private placement*. Table 12.4 indicates that the holders of municipal bonds are more widely varied than those of federal and provincial bonds. It should be noted, however, that no municipals appear in Figure 12.6 where actively traded issues are listed.

In recent years municipalities have, more frequently, been using non-market sources of capital such as the provincial agencies mentioned above, senior levels of government, and the Canada Pension Plan and provincial pension plan funds. Foreign sources, predominantly in the US, have also been used, but these represented only about 8% of the total at the end of 1990.

---

## 12.5　EUROBONDS

Owing in part to government restrictions on investment in foreign securities, a number of borrowers have found it advantageous to sell securities in other countries. The term *Eurobond* is loosely applied to bonds that are offered outside the country of the borrower and usually outside the country in whose currency the securities are denominated. Thus, a bond issued by a Canadian corporation that is denominated in Japanese yen and sold in Germany and Switzerland would be referred to as a Eurobond.[7]

Since the Eurobond market is neither regulated nor taxed, it offers substantial advantages for many issuers and buyers of bonds. For example, a foreign subsidiary of a Canadian corporation may issue a Eurobond in "bearer" form. No tax is withheld by the corporation, and the tax paid by the purchaser (if any) depends on his or her country of residence. Because of these regulatory and tax advantages interest rates on Eurobonds tend to be somewhat lower than those of domestic bonds denominated in the same currency

A recent development has been the appearance of *Global Issues*. These are large issues that appear simultaneously in several countries and are underwritten by investment dealers in those countries. For example, a recent Ontario Hydro issue of $1.5 billion was issued in Canadian dollars and underwritten in, among other markets, the US, the UK, Japan, several European countries and Australia. With world-wide distribution of this kind it is possible to maintain a 24 hour market in these securities and, therefore, enhanced liquidity.

---

[7] In contrast, a *foreign bond* is a bond that is offered outside the country of the borrower and inside the country in whose currency it is denominated. Thus, a bond issued by a US corporation that is denominated in yen and sold in Japan would be referred to as a foreign bond (in this case, a "samurai bond"). For more on international bond markets (as well as Eurocurrency markets), see J. Orlin Grabbe, *International Financial Markets* (New York: Elsevier Science, 1986).

# CORPORATE BONDS

*Corporate bonds* are similar to other kinds of fixed-income securities in that they carry the promise of specified payments at specified times and provide legal remedies in the event of default. Restrictions are often placed on the activities of the issuing corporation in order to provide additional protection for bondholders (for example, there may be restrictions on the amount of additional bonds that can be issued in the future).

From the viewpoint of the issuing corporation, debt differs from equity in two crucial respects. First, principal and interest payments are obligatory. Failure to make any payment in full and on time can expose the issuer to expensive, time-consuming, and potentially disruptive legal actions. Second, unlike dividend payments, interest payments are considered expenses to the corporation, and hence can be deducted from earnings before calculating the corporation's income tax liability. As a result, each dollar paid in interest reduces earnings before taxes by a dollar, thereby reducing corporate taxes by $0.40 for a firm in the 40% marginal tax bracket. This leads to less than a dollar decline in earnings after taxes (in the 40% tax bracket example, the decline in earnings is $0.60).

## ☐ 12.6.1  The Indenture

An issue of bonds is generally covered by a *trust indenture* or *trust deed*, in which the issuing corporation promises a specified *trustee* that it will comply with a number of stated provisions. Chief among these is the timely payment of required coupons and principal on the issue. Other terms are often included to control the sale of pledged property, the issuance of other bonds, and the like.

The trustee for a bond issue, usually a trust company, acts on behalf of the bondholders. Some actions may be required by the indenture, whereas others, such as acting in response to a request from specific bondholders, may be done at the trustee's discretion.

If the corporation defaults on an interest payment, after a relatively short period of time (perhaps one to six months) the entire principal typically becomes due and payable — a procedure designed to enhance the bondholders' status in any forthcoming bankruptcy or related legal proceedings.

## ☐ 12.6.2  Types of Bonds

An exhaustive list of the names used to describe bonds would be intolerably long. Different names are often used for the same type of bond, and occasionally the same name will be used for two quite different bonds. A few major types do predominate, however, with relatively standard nomenclature.

### Mortgage Bonds

Bonds of this type represent debt that is secured by the pledge of specific property. In the event of default, the bondholders are entitled to obtain the property in question and sell it to satisfy their claims on the firm. In addition to the property itself, the holders of mortgage bonds have an unsecured claim or *floating charge* on the all other assets of the corporation.

Mortgage bondholders are usually protected by terms included in the bond indenture. The corporation may be constrained from pledging property for other bonds (or such bonds, if issued, must be "junior," or "second," mortgages, with only a secondary claim on the property). Certain property acquired by the corporation after the bonds were issued may also be pledged to support the bonds.

## Collateral Trust Bonds

These bonds are backed by other securities that are usually held by the trustee. A common situation of this sort arises when the securities of a subsidiary firm are pledged as collateral by the parent firm.

## Equipment Obligations

These securities (also known also as equipment trust certificates) are backed by specific pieces of equipment for example, railroad cars and commercial aircraft. If necessary, the equipment can be readily sold and delivered to a new owner. The legal arrangements used to facilitate the issuance of such bonds can be very complex. The most popular procedure uses the *Philadelphia plan*, in which the trustee initially holds the equipment, issues obligations, and leases the equipment to a corporation. Money received from the lessee is subsequently used to make interest and principal payments to the holders of the obligations; ultimately, if all payments are made on schedule, the leasing corporation takes title to the equipment.

## Debentures

These are general obligations of the issuing corporation and thus represent unsecured credit. To protect the holders of such bonds, the indenture will usually limit the future issuance of secured debt as well as any additional unsecured debt.

## Subordinated Debentures

When more than one issue of debentures is outstanding, a hierarchy may be specified. For example, subordinated debentures are junior to unsubordinated debentures, meaning that in the event of bankruptcy, junior claims are to be considered only after senior claims have been fully satisfied.

## Other Types of Bonds

*Income bonds* are more like preferred shares (described in a later section) than bonds. Payment of interest in full and on schedule is not absolutely required, and failure to do so need not send the corporation into bankruptcy. Since November 17, 1978 interest on such bonds has qualified as a tax deductible expense in Canada for the issuing corporation. Except in reorganizations, this type of bond is rarely used, .

*Guaranteed bonds* are issued by one corporation but backed in some way by another (for example, by a parent firm). *Participation bonds* require stated interest payments and provide additional amounts if earnings exceed some stated level. In *Serial bonds*, different portions of the issue mature at different dates.

*Convertible bonds* may, at the holder's option, be exchanged for other securities, often common shares. Such bonds, which have become very popular in recent years, are discussed in more detail in Chapter 18.

*Extendible bonds* give the bondholder, on a specific date, the option of extending the term to maturity of his or her bond. For example, a five year extendible bond may allow the investor, within six months of maturity, to extend the maturity by five years at the same or slightly higher interest rate.

*Retractable bonds* give the bondholder, on a specified date, the option of reducing the term to maturity of his or her bond.

## ☐ 12.6.3 Call Provisions

Management would like to have the right to pay off the corporation's bonds at par at any time prior to maturity. Reducing debt or altering maturity by refunding provides desirable flexibility. Most important, expensive high-coupon debt issued during a time of high interest rates can be replaced with cheaper low-coupon debt if rates decline.

Not surprisingly, investors hold a different opinion on the matter. The issuer's ability to redeem an issue at par at any time virtually precludes a rise in price over par and robs the holder of potential gains from the price appreciation associated with declining interest rates; moreover, it introduces a new form of uncertainty. A bond with such a feature will almost certainly sell for less than one without it.

Despite the cost of obtaining this sort of flexibility, many corporations include in their bond indentures *call provisions* that give the corporation the option to call some or all of the bonds from their holders at stated prices during specified periods prior to maturity. In a sense, the firm sells a bond and simultaneously buys an option from the holders. The net price of the bond, therefore, is the difference between the value of the bond and the option. (Note that retractable bonds give the investor the option of forcing the issuer to call the security.)

Investors are often given some *call protection*: During the first few years after being issued, a bond may not be callable. An alternative form of call protection is a provision that states that the issue is *non-refundable for financial advantage*. This means that the corporation may not call the bonds in order to replace them with bonds carrying a lower coupon rate but may call them to retire the issue without replacing it.

When a bond is callable, a *call premium* may be specified in the call provision. If the issue is called when a call premium is specified then the issuer must pay the bondholders a *call price* that is a stated amount above par. Generally, the call premium declines as the maturity date approaches.

An entire issue may be called, or only specific bonds that are chosen randomly by the trustee may be called. In either case, *a notice of redemption* will appear in advance in the financial press.

## ☐ 12.6.4 Sinking Funds

A bond indenture will often require the issuing corporation to make annual payments into a *sinking fund*. Each payment covers part of the principal as well as the interest, thereby reducing the amount outstanding at maturity.

Sinking funds operate by having the corporation transfer cash to the trustee who then purchases bonds in the open market. Alternatively, the corporation may obtain the bonds, by either purchase or call, and deposit them with the trustee. Call prices for sinking fund purchases may differ from those specified when the entire issue is to be repaid prior to maturity.

Required contributions to a sinking fund may or may not be the same each year. In some cases, the required amount may depend on earnings or output; in others, the goal is to make the annual payments equal.

## ☐ 12.6.5 Private Placements

Bonds intended for eventual public sale are usually issued in denominations of $1000 each. Both bearer and registered forms may be utilized. Often, however, a single investor (or a small group of investors) will buy an entire issue. Such *private placements* are typically purchased by large financial institutions.

## ☐ 12.6.6 Bankruptcy

When a corporation fails to make a scheduled coupon or principal payment on a bond, the corporation is said to be in default on that obligation. If the payment is not made within a relatively short period, litigation will usually follow.

A corporation unable to meet its obligatory debt payments is said to be technically insolvent (or insolvent in the equity sense). If the value of the firm's assets falls below its liabilities, it is said to be insolvent (or insolvent in the bankruptcy sense).

If voluntary agreements with creditors cannot be obtained, bankruptcy — usually "voluntary" — is filed by the corporation itself. Subsequent developments involve, among others, courts, court-appointed officials, representatives of the firm's creditors, and the management of the firm.

### Liquidation

A question that arises in many bankruptcies is whether or not the firm's assets should be liquidated (that is, sold) and the proceeds divided among the creditors. Such an action is taken only if the court feels the resulting value would exceed that likely to be obtained if the firm continued in operation (perhaps after substantial reorganization).

If the firm's assets are liquidated in a *straight bankruptcy*, secured creditors receive either the property pledged for their loans or the proceeds from the sale of the secured property. If this amount falls short of their claims, the difference is considered an unsecured debt of the firm; on the other hand, any excess is made available for other creditors. Next, assets are used to pay the claims of priority creditors to the extent possible. These include claims for such items as administrative expenses, wages (up to a stated limit per person), uninsured pension claims, taxes, and rents. Anything left over is used to pay unsecured creditors in proportion to their claims on the firm.

### Reorganization in Lieu of Bankruptcy

If the value of a firm's assets, when employed as part of a "going concern," appears to exceed their value in liquidation, a reorganization of the firm and its liabilities may be undertaken. Such proceedings, conducted under the provisions of *The Bankruptcy Act*, may be voluntary (initiated by the firm) or involuntary (initiated by three or more creditors). A number of parties must concur in the proposed reorganization, including the holders of two-thirds of the value in each general class of creditor that is affected by the reorganization.

Among the goals of reorganization are "fair and equitable" treatment of various classes of securities and the elimination of "burdensome" debt obligations. Typically, creditors are given new claims on the reorganized firm, with the amounts of the new claims intended to be at least equal in value to the amounts that the creditors would have received in liquidation. For example, holders of debentures might receive bonds of longer maturity, holders of subordinated debentures might become shareholders, and shareholders might be left without any claims on the firm.

### Some Financial Aspects of Bankruptcy

Although the subject is far too complex for detailed treatment here, two aspects of bankruptcy deserve some discussion. First, the choice between continuation of a firm and liquidation of its assets should be unrelated to reasons for bankruptcy. If an asset can be sold for more than the present value of its future earnings, it should be. Management may have to be taken to court to be forced to do this, but the issue is not one of solvency or lack thereof.

Second, the definition of insolvency is rather vague. Assume, for example, that assets can be adequately valued at either the larger of liquidating or going-concern value. A firm is said to be insolvent if this value is less than that of the firm's liabilities. How should these liabilities be valued? Their current market value will frequently be less than the value of the assets, whereas their book value may be greater than the value of the assets.

## ☐ 12.6.7  Ownership of Corporate Bonds

At the end of 1990, investors held more than $126 billion of corporate and foreign bonds. As can be seen in Table 12.5, the largest investors were life insurance companies, pension funds, and foreign investors. Over 50% of these bonds were issued in foreign currencies, the principal ones being US dollars (15%), Eurodollars (22%), Swiss francs (6%) and Japanese yen (4%).

Some firms use foreign denominated bond issues in order to hedge their foreign exchange exposure in the product market. For example, a Canadian pulp and paper company with substantial US sales, whose product prices are quoted in US dollars, loses revenue when the Canadian dollar rises vis-à-vis the US dollar. If its debt is US dollar denominated then the Canadian dollar value of its interest payments will also fall providing at least a partial off-set.

## ☐ 12.6.8  The Secondary Bond Market

Most trading in corporate bonds takes place through dealers in the over-the-counter market. A small number of debentures are listed on the Alberta, Vancouver, and Toronto Stock Exchanges. About 100 dealers and a few banks and trust companies are active in the OTC market. The major dealers and large institutional clients are electronically linked — bid and offer prices for a wide range of bonds are displayed on video screens located in their offices. Some dealers issue periodic quotation sheets that are reported in the daily business press.

**TABLE 12.5**

Ownership of Outstanding Corporate and Foreign Bonds, December 1990.

| Held by | Amount (in millions) | Percent of Total |
|---|---|---|
| Chartered banks | $ 2,969 | 2.1% |
| Thrift institutions | 7,382 | 5.8 |
| Life insurance companies | 24,640 | 19.5 |
| Property and casualty insurance companies | 4,484 | 3.5 |
| Trusteed pension funds | 14,465 | 11.4 |
| Mutual funds | 1,415 | 1.1 |
| Investment dealers | 298 | 0.2 |
| Non-financial private corporations | 2,148 | 1.7 |
| Misc. private financial institutions | 2,433 | 1.9 |
| Foreign investors | 55,911 | 44.2 |
| Individuals and non-incorporated business | 6,273 | 5.0 |
| Sub-total — privately held corporate bonds | $122,418 | 96.8% |
| Non-financial government enterprise | $ 138 | 0.1 |
| Public financial institutions | 820 | 0.6 |
| Provincial and local governments | 3,028 | 2.4 |
| Federal government | 40 | – |
| Sub-total publicly held bonds | $ 4,026 | 3.2% |
| Total corporate bonds | $126,444 | 100.0% |

SOURCE: Statistics, Canada, *National Balance Sheet Accounts: System of National Accounts, 1990,* Ottawa, April 1991.

## 12.7    TAX TREATMENT OF FIXED INCOME SECURITIES

The tax treatment of coupon-bearing securities is not complicated — the coupon payment must be reported as income in the year that it is received and tax is payable at the regular rate.

Coupon-bearing securities bought at either a discount or a premium in the marketplace, if held to maturity, affect the investor's income tax because the difference between the purchase price and the par value must be treated as either a capital gain or loss at maturity.

Revenue Canada also requires that taxes be paid annually on the accrued interest on zero-coupon or pure discount securities.

For example, a stripped bond that matures in two years for $1000 can be purchased currently for $850. Thus, the investor will earn $150 in interest over two years, realizing it only when the bond matures. Revenue Canada, however, requires that the investor pay taxes on a portion of the $150 each year, but has no specific rules as to how the accrual should be calculated as long as the method used is "reasonable." One simple alternative is to allocate an equal fraction of the implied interest to each year to maturity. The investor would then report $75 ($150/2) per year as interest income. An alternative is to use the *economic accrual method*. In this method the yield is first calculated, which in this case is ($1000/$850)$^{1/2} - 1 = 8.46\%$. This means that the implied value of the bond at the end of the first year is $850 \times 1.0846 = $921.91$; thus, the amount of interest income to be recognized that year is $921.91 − $850 = $71.91$ or $850 \times 0.0846$. The amount of interest income to be recognized in the second year, assuming the bond is held to maturity, will be $1000 − $921.91 = $78.09$ or $921.21 \times 0.0846$ (note that $1000 = $921.91 \times 1.0846$). This method results in a lower reported interest income in the first year and a larger one in the second and, therefore, reduces the present value of the investor's two tax bills.

With zero-coupon bonds the investor has a cash outflow when purchasing the bond and also has to pay tax on the accrued interest every year until it matures. The investor only receives a cash inflow at maturity. As a result, such securities are attractive primarily for tax-exempt or low tax bracket investors (for example, as RRSP investments).

The taxation of Real Return Bonds presents some special features. Adjusted coupon payments must be reported in the year they are received in the normal manner, in addition, the inflationary adjustment to the Principal that accrues during the year must be included in taxable income. Thus, for taxation year, $T$, the amount Principal $\times$ [$IR_T$ − $IR_{T-1}$] must be reported as income. The taxation of these bonds resembles that of strip bonds in that tax must be paid on an amount that has not yet been received, a factor that makes them less attractive to taxed investors.

## 12.8  PREFERRED SHARES

In some respects, *preferred shares* are like perpetual bonds. A given annual dollar amount is promised by the issuer to the investor. This amount may be stated as a percent of the stock's par value (for example, 8% of $100, meaning $8 per year), or directly as a dollar figure (for example, $2.75 per year). Since the security is a stock, such payments are called dividends rather than interest. They do not qualify as a tax-deductible expense for the issuing corporation, but do qualify for the personal dividend tax credit. Furthermore, failure to make such payments does not constitute grounds for bankruptcy proceedings.

A recent innovation is *variable* or *floating rate* preferred (known as adjustable rate preferred stock (ARPS) in the US), where the dividend is reset periodically in terms of an established market rate with an underlying floor (or minimum payment). For example, the annualized "percent of par" for the minimum payment may be set at 8% and the quarterly dividends reset every three months to equal half the prevailing Bank of Canada rate plus 1.5%. Any difference between 8% and the actual dividends paid must be made up in the final quarter.

Related to variable rate preferred are *money market* or *auction preferred shares* (known as *dutch auction rate* preferred stock (DARPS) in the US).[8] The price of these is fixed but the dividend is reset periodically (usually every calendar month) at a level that is determined at an auction between current and potential owners. If the auction is not successful then a minimum dividend rate is triggered. This rate is predetermined in relation to an established market based rate such as the prime rate or the current bankers' acceptance yield.

---

[8] Presumably these are referred to as dutch auction preferred because the lowest bidder is the winner. For a discussion of ARPS and DARPS, see Michael J. Alderson, Keith C. Brown, and Scott L. Lummer, "Dutch Auction Rate Preferred Stock," *Financial Management* 16, no. 2 (Summer 1987):68–73.

Preferred shares are generally "preferred as to dividends." Specified payments must be made on the preferred shares before any dividends may be paid to holders of the firm's common stock. Failure to pay a preferred dividend in full does not constitute default, but unpaid dividends are usually *cumulative*. This means that all previously unpaid preferred share dividends must be paid (but seldom with interest) before any dividends may be paid on the common stock.

No indenture is provided with a preferred share issue. Various provisions protecting the preferred shareholders against potentially harmful actions, however, may be written into the corporation's charter. For example, one provision may limit the dollar amount of senior securities that can be issued in the future. Although preferred shareholders typically do not have voting rights, there may be another provision that gives them voting rights when the corporation is in arrears on its preferred dividends.

Many issues of preferred shares are callable, often at a premium; such stock is sometimes said to be redeemable at a stated redemption price. *Retractable* preferred provide the investor with an option to force the redemption of the issue by the company at a specified date and price. *Participating* preferred shares entitle the holder to receive extra dividends when earnings permit. *Convertible* preferred shares may, at the option of the holder, be converted into another security (usually the firm's common stock) on stated terms. Some firms issue more than one class of preferred shares, with preference accorded the various classes in a specified order.

In the event of a dissolution of the firm, preferred shares takes precedence over common stock in the liquidation of assets. Generally this means that preferred shareholders are entitled to receive the share's par value before any payment is made to common shareholders.

Since preferred shares have many features of a bond without the substantial tax advantage that bonds give to the issuer, they are used less often than debt. In 1990, $0.942 billion of such shares were issued, compared with $8.6 billion of publicly offered corporate debt.[9]

As indicated in Chapter 10, interest income from bonds held by a corporate investor is subject to corporate income tax at an effective rate in excess of 40%, while dividend income is generally tax exempt. For this reason, preferred shares tend to sell at prices that give lower before-tax returns than long-term bonds even though the latter may be considerably lower in risk. As a result, preferred shares are generally unattractive holdings for tax-exempt noncorporate investors.

Many preferred shares are traded on major exchanges in a manner similar to common stocks. Typically, they are assigned to the same market-maker responsible for the firm's common stock. Trading prices are reported in the financial press in the same format as that used for common stocks.

---

[9] *Bank of Canada Review*, November 1991.

# SUMMARY

There are many types of fixed-income securities that are available for purchase by investors in Canada. In general, as their name implies, they promise to make certain cash payments to their owners at certain times in the future. They belong in several categories — savings deposits, money market instruments, Canadian government securities, provincial and municipal government securities, foreign and Eurobonds, corporate bonds, and preferred stock. Most of these securities are bought and sold through dealers in the over-the-counter market. An exception are preferred shares which are generally listed on organized exchanges and are assigned to a market-maker.

## QUESTIONS AND PROBLEMS

1. Consider a 91-day Treasury bill, issued today, which is selling for $9,675.00. (Its face value is $10,000.00.)
   a. What is the annual equivalent yield of the security?
   b. What would be the annual yield if the funds were reinvested for a year at that rate?

2. Government of Canada bonds are issued in both bearer and registered forms. Given the characteristics of bearer and registered bonds, discuss the advantages and disadvantages of each form.

3. Using *The Globe and Mail: Report on Business* as a data source, identify a particular Canada bond. What is its coupon rate? What is its maturity date? What is the latest price? What is the security's yield-to-maturity?

4. Describe the standard practice by which sellers of government and corporate bonds are compensated for accrued interest.

5. Why does Revenue Canada treat the difference between the price of a zero-coupon bond purchased at a discount and its face value as ordinary income to the investor, as opposed to treating it as a capital gain?

6. Bonds issued by federal agencies carry an explicit or implicit promise that the federal government will ensure payment of interest and principal. Why then are these securities usually priced by the market to offer yields above Treasury securities?

7. What is a mortgage backed security? What is the primary risk such securities present to investors?

8. Distinguish between a general obligation municipal bond and a revenue bond.

9. Eurobonds have become very popular forms of financing in recent years. What features of the Eurobond market make Eurobonds attractive to issuers and bondholders?

10. A callable bond is sometimes described as a combination of a noncallable bond and an option. Explain why this description is appropriate. Further, explain how these two features affect the price of a callable bond.

11. Consider a $10,000 Canada bond with a 7.5% coupon interest rate and a 25-year term-to-maturity. The bond has a call provision, effective 15 years from today. The bond has just been sold for $10,020. If the current yield-to-maturity on other such bonds, with the same term-to-maturity and coupon interest rate but callable immediately, is 8%, what dollar value are investors placing on the deferred call provision? Assume that interest payments are made annually.

12. Chris Dolan is considering purchasing one of two bonds: a corporate bond with a 9% coupon interest rate, selling at par, or a preferred share, with a 6% dividend rate. Given that Chris lives in Ontario, is in the 26% federal tax bracket, and assuming that all other relevant factors are the same between the two securities, which should Chris select? (Ignore any surtaxes and use the dividend tax credit factors given in Chapter 10.)

13. Is it true that most corporations which default on their debt eventually enter bankruptcy and see their assets liquidated to repay creditors? Explain.

## SUGGESTED READINGS

*The Canadian Securities Course* (Toronto, Ont.: The Canadian Securities Institute, 1989) Chapters 2, 7, 8 and 11, and

W.T. Hunter, *Canadian Financial Markets* (Peterborough, Ont.: Broadview Press, 1988) Chapters 1 to 5 and 9 provide useful descriptions of the major fixed income markets in Canada and abroad.

The *Bank of Canada Review* periodically analyzes the workings of different segments of security markets in Canada.

# Chapter 13

# BOND ANALYSIS

Consider an investor who believes that the bond market is not semistrong-form efficient. That is, the investor believes that there are situations where public information can be used to identify mispriced bonds. To translate that belief into action about which bonds to buy and sell, an analytical procedure is needed. One procedure involves comparing a bond's yield-to-maturity with a yield-to-maturity that the investor feels is appropriate, based on the characteristics of the bond as well as current market conditions. If the yield-to-maturity is higher than the appropriate yield-to-maturity, then the bond is said to be *underpriced* (or undervalued) and is a candidate for buying. Conversely, if the yield-to-maturity is lower than the appropriate one, then the bond is said to be *overpriced* (or overvalued) and is a candidate for selling (or even short selling).

Alternatively, the investor could estimate the bond's "true," or "intrinsic," value, and compare it with the bond's current market price. Specifically, if the current market price is less than the bond's intrinsic value, then the bond is underpriced, and if it is greater, then the bond is overpriced.

Both procedures for analyzing bonds are based on the capitalization of income method of valuation. The first procedure involving yields is analogous to the internal rate of return method that is discussed in most introductory finance textbooks, whereas the second procedure involving intrinsic value is analogous to the net present value method that also appears in such books. Although the focus in those books is on making an investment decision involving some type of real asset (such as whether or not a new piece of machinery should be purchased), the focus here is on making an investment decision involving a particular type of financial asset — bonds.

## 13.1 APPLYING THE CAPITALIZATION OF INCOME METHOD TO BONDS

An investor who believes the bond market is efficient would question the ability of other investors to identify mispriced situations. However, if an investor believes such situations exist, then an economically sensible and logical approach to valuation is needed to identify them. One such approach is the *capitalization of income method of valuation*.[1]

---

[1] This method is discussed more extensively in Chapter 16.

This method of valuation states that the intrinsic value of any asset is based on the discounted value of the cash flows that the investor expects to receive in the future from owning the asset. As mentioned earlier, one way that this method has been applied to bond valuation is to compare the bond's yield-to-maturity ($y$) with the appropriate one ($y^*$). Specifically, if $y > y^*$, then the bond is underpriced, and if $y < y^*$, then the bond is overpriced. However, if $y = y^*$, then the bond is said to be fairly priced.

Letting $P$ denote the current market price of a bond with a remaining life of $n$ years and promising cash flows to the investor of $C_1$ in year 1, $C_2$ in year 2, and so on, the yield-to-maturity (more specifically, the *promised yield-to-maturity*) of the bond is the value of $y$ that solves the following equation:

$$P = \frac{C_1}{(1+y)^1} + \frac{C_2}{(1+y)^2} + \frac{C_3}{(1+y)^3} + \cdots + \frac{C_n}{(1+y)^n}.$$

Using summation notation, this equation can be rewritten as:

$$P = \sum_{t=1}^{n} \frac{C_t}{(1+y)^t}. \qquad (13.1)$$

For example, consider a bond that is currently selling for $900 and has a remaining life of three years. For ease of exposition, assume it makes annual coupon payments amounting to $60 per year and has a par value of $1000. That is, $C_1 = \$60$, $C_2 = \$60$, and $C_3 = \$1060 = \$1000 + \$60$. Using equation (13.1), the yield-to-maturity on this bond is the value of $y$ that solves the following equation:

$$\$900 = \frac{\$60}{(1+y)^1} + \frac{\$60}{(1+y)^2} + \frac{\$1060}{(1+y)^3}$$

which is $y = 10.02\%$. If subsequent analysis indicates that the yield-to-maturity should be 9.00%, then this bond is underpriced, since $y = 10.02\% > y^* = 9.00\%$.

Alternatively, the intrinsic value of a bond can be calculated using the following formula:

$$V = \frac{C_1}{(1+y^*)^1} + \frac{C_2}{(1+y^*)^2} + \frac{C_3}{(1+y^*)^3} + \cdots + \frac{C_n}{(1+y^*)^n}.$$

or, using summation notation,

$$V = \sum_{t=1}^{n} \frac{C_t}{(1+y^*)^t}. \qquad (13.2)$$

Since the purchase price of the bond is its market price P, the net present value (NPV) to the investor is equal to the difference between the value of the bond and the purchase price:

$$\text{NPV} = V - P \qquad (13.3)$$

$$= \left[ \sum_{t=1}^{n} \frac{C_t}{(1+y^*)^t} \right] - P.$$

The NPV of the bond in the previous example is the solution to the following equation:

$$NPV = \left[ \frac{\$60}{(1+.09)^1} + \frac{\$60}{(1+.09)^2} + \frac{\$1060}{(1+.09)^3} \right] - \$900$$

$$= \$24.06.$$

Since this bond has a positive NPV, it is underpriced. This will always be the case when a bond has a yield-to-maturity that is more than appropriate (earlier, it was shown that this bond's yield-to-maturity was 10.02%, which is more than 9.00%, the appropriate yield-to-maturity). That is, in general, any bond with $y > y^*$ will always have a positive NPV and vice versa, so that under either method it would be underpriced.[2]

Alternatively, if the investor had determined that $y^*$ was equal to 11.00%, then the bond's NPV would have been $-\$22.19$. This would suggest the bond was overpriced, just as would have been noted when the yield-to-maturity of 10.02% was compared with 11.00%. This will always be the case — a bond with $y < y^*$ will always have a negative NPV and vice versa, so that under either method it would be found to be overpriced.

It should also be pointed out that if the investor had determined that $y*$ had a value of approximately the same magnitude as the bond's yield-to-maturity of 10%, then the NPV of the bond would be approximately zero. In such a situation, the bond would be viewed as being fairly priced.

Note that in order to use the capitalization of income method of valuation, the values of $C_t$, $P$, and $y^*$ must be determined. It is generally quite easy to determine the values for $C_t$ and $P$, since they are the bond's promised cash flows and current market price, respectively. However, determining the value of $y^*$ is difficult, since the investor must estimate an appropriate value for the bond. Such a decision will depend on the characteristics of the bond, as well as on current market conditions. Given that the key ingredient in bond analysis is determining the appropriate value of $y^*$, the next section discusses the attributes that should be considered in making such a determination.

## 13.2 BOND ATTRIBUTES

Five primary attributes of a bond are important in bond valuation: (1) length of time until maturity; (2) coupon rate; (3) call provisions; (4) taxation; (5) marketability; and (6) likelihood of default. At any time, the structure of market prices for bonds differing in these dimensions can be examined and described in terms of yields-to-maturity. This underlying structure is sometimes referred to as the *yield structure*. Often, attention is confined to differences along a single dimension, holding the other attributes constant. For example, the set of yields of bonds of different maturities constitutes the *term structure* (discussed in Chapter 4), and the set of yields of bonds of different default risk is referred to as the *risk structure*.

---

[2] A more accurate method of determining a bond's intrinsic value involves the use of spot rates. That is, in determining the NPV of this bond, the investor might have determined that the relevant spot rates for the one-year, two-year, and three-year cash flows are 8.24%, 8.69%, and 9.03%, respectively. Using these values, the bond's intrinsic value would be equal to $[\$60/(1.0824)] + [\$60/(1.0869)^2] + [\$1060/(1.0903)^3] = \$924.06$. Although $V$ is the same in this example when either spot rates or $y^*$ are used in the calculations, this need not always be the case.

Most bond analysts consider the yields-to-maturity for default-free bonds to form the yield structure; "risk differentials" are then added to obtain the relevant yields-to-maturity for bonds of lower quality. While subject to some criticism, this procedure makes it possible to think about a complicated set of relationships sequentially.

The differential between the yields of two bonds is usually called a *yield spread*. Most often, it involves a bond that is under analysis and a comparable default-free bond (that is, a government security of similar maturity and coupon rate). Yield spreads are sometimes measured in *basis points*, where one basis point equals .01%. If the yield-to-maturity for one bond is 8.50% and that of another is 8.90%, the yield spread is 40 basis points.

## 13.2.1 Coupon Rate and the Length of Time Until Maturity

These attributes of a bond are important because they determine the size and timing of the cash flows that are promised to the bondholder by the issuer. Given a bond's current market price, these attributes can be used to determine the bond's yield-to-maturity, which will subsequently be compared with what the investor thinks it should be. More specifically, if the market for Canada bonds is viewed as being efficient, then the yield-to-maturity on a Canada bond that is similar to the bond under evaluation can form a starting point for the analysis.

Consider the previously mentioned bond selling for $900 that has promised cash flows over the next three years of $60, $60, and $1060, respectively. Suppose there is a Canada bond that provides a cash flow over the next three years of $50, $50, and $1050 and is selling for $912.89. The yield-to-maturity on this second security is 8.5%, information that can be used to determine what the yield-to-maturity should be on the $900 bond. In this situation, the yield spread between the bond and the government security is 1.52% = 10.02% - 8.50% and the analyst must then consider whether or not this spread is appropriate.

## 13.2.2 Call Provisions

There are times when, by historical standards, yields-to-maturity are relatively high. Bonds issued during such times may, at first glance, appear to be unusually attractive investments. However, deeper analysis indicates this is not necessarily the case because many corporate bonds have a *call provision* that enables the issuer to redeem the bonds prior to maturity, usually for a price somewhat above par. This price is known as the *call price*, and the difference between it and the par value of the bond is known as the *call premium*. An issuer will often find it financially advantageous to call the existing bonds if yields drop substantially after the bonds were initially sold, since the issuer will be able to replace them with lower yielding securities that are less costly.[3]

---

[3] Many corporate bonds have, in addition to a call provision, a provision for a sinking fund where each year the issuer retires a prespecified portion of the original bond issue. For a further discussion of sinking funds, see James C. Van Horne, *Financial Market Rates and Flows* (Englewood Cliffs, N.J.: Prentice Hall, 1984):215–18. This book also presents a detailed discussion of the other attributes of bonds that are of importance in valuation.

For example, consider a ten-year bond issued at par ($1000) that has a coupon rate of 12% and is callable at $1050 any time after it has been outstanding for five years.[4] If, after five years, yields on similar five-year bonds were 8% the bond would probably be called. This means that an investor who had planned on receiving annual coupon payments of $120 for ten years would instead actually receive the call price of $1050 after five years. At this time, the investor could take the $1050 and reinvest it in the 8% bonds, thereby receiving $84 per year in coupon payments over the last five years (it is assumed here that the investor can purchase a fraction of a bond, so that the full $1050 can be invested in the 8% bonds).

In this example, the investor might have thought that the original bond would remain outstanding for the full ten years, in which case the yield-to-maturity on the initial $1000 investment would have been 12%. However, this apparent yield would not have been earned, since the issuer would have called the bond after five years. In this case, in return for an initial investment of $1000, the investor would receive coupon payments of $120 for each of the first five years, $84 for each of the next five years, and $1050 at the end of the tenth year as a return of principal. Given this pattern of cash flows, the actual yield-to-maturity over the ten years would be 10.96%.

This example suggests that the higher the coupon rate of a callable bond, the greater is the likely divergence between actual and apparent yields. This is borne out by experience. Figure 13.1 plots the coupon rate, set at time of issue, on the horizontal axis. Since most bonds are initially sold at (or very close to) par, the coupon rate is also a measure of the yield-to-maturity that an investor may have thought was obtainable by purchasing one of the newly issued bonds.

The vertical axis in this figure plots the actual yield-to-maturity obtained up to the original maturity date by an investor, assuming that the payments received in the event of a call were reinvested in noncallable bonds with appropriate maturities. The curve is based on experience for a group of callable bonds issued by utility companies during a period of fluctuating interest rates. As can be seen, the coupon rate and actual yield are quite similar in magnitude until the coupon rate approaches 5%. At this point, higher coupon rates are no longer associated with higher actual yields, since these coupon rates were relatively high during the time period examined; as a consequence, most of the bonds with coupon rates above 5% were ultimately called.

The upshot is that bonds with greater likelihood of being called should have a higher yield-to-maturity. That is, the higher the coupon rate or the lower the call premium, the higher the yield-to-maturity should be. Equivalently, bonds with higher coupon rates or lower call premiums will have lower intrinsic values, keeping everything else equal.

## ☐ 13.2.3 Taxation

Taxation affects bond prices and yields in other ways. For example, low-coupon bonds selling at a discount provide returns in two forms: coupon payments and capital gains. In Canada, the former are taxed as ordinary income, and the latter (at a reduced rate) as

---

[4] In this example, the *yield-to-call* (or, to be more specific, the yield-to-first-call) is 12.78%. That is, 12.78% is the discount rate that makes the present value of $120 received after each of the first four years and $1170($1050 + $120) at the end of five years equal to the issue price of the bond, $1000. Note that the yield-to-first-call is greater than the bond's promised yield-to-maturity at the time of issue (12%).

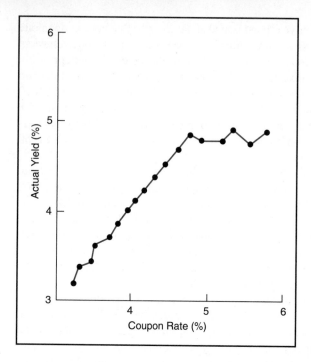

**FIGURE 13-1**
Promised and actual yields of callable Aa
utility bonds, 1956–1964.

*SOURCE:* Frank C. Jen and James E. Wert, "The
Effect of Call Risk on Corporate Bond Yields,"
*Journal of Finance* 22, no. 4 (December 1967):646.

capital gains. Furthermore, taxes on the latter may be deferred until the bond is either
sold or matures. This means that such *deep discount bonds* have a double tax advantage.
Other things being equal they should, therefore, have lower before-tax yields than high-
coupon bonds. That is, low-coupon bonds have a higher intrinsic value than high-coupon
bonds.

## □ 13.2.4 Marketability

*Marketability* (sometimes also referred to as liquidity) refers to the ease with which an
investor can sell an asset quickly without having to make a substantial price concession.
An example of an illiquid asset is a "collectible," such as a piece of artwork. An investor
who owns a Van Gogh painting may have to settle for a relatively low price if he or she
has to sell it within an hour. If the sale can be postponed for a length of time in order to
set up a public auction, a much higher price could probably be obtained. Alternatively,
an investor with $1,000,000 worth of BCE common stock who has to sell these shares
within an hour will probably be able to receive a price close to that previously paid for
them. Furthermore, it is unlikely that waiting would increase the expected selling price
of such securities.

Since most bonds are bought and sold in dealer markets, one measure of a bond's
marketability is the bid-ask spread that the dealers are quoting on the bonds. Bonds that
are actively traded tend to have lower bid-ask spreads than bonds that are inactive. This is
because the dealer is more exposed to risk when making a market in an inactive security
than when making a market in an active security. The source of this risk is the inventory
that the dealer holds and the fact that interest rates in general may move in a way that

causes the dealer to lose money on his or her inventory. Accordingly, bonds that are actively traded should have a lower yield-to-maturity and a higher intrinsic value than bonds that are inactive, keeping everything else equal.

## ☐ 13.2.5  Likelihood of Default

In Canada, two corporations — the Canadian Bond Rating Service (CBRS) and Dominion Bond Rating Service (DBRS) — provide ratings of the creditworthiness of many corporate, municipal, and provincial bonds. In the US, Standard & Poor's Corporation and Moody's Investors Service, Inc. provide similar information. These *bond ratings* are often used by investors as an indication of the likelihood of default by the issuer. Figures 13.2 and 13.3 provide details of the CBRS and DBRS ratings.[5]

A broader categorization is often employed, with bonds classified as being of either investment grade or speculative grade. Typically, *investment grade bonds* are bonds that have been assigned to one of the top four ratings (AAA through BBB by DBRS; A++ through B++ by CBRS). In contrast, *speculative grade bonds* are bonds that have been assigned to one of the lower ratings (BB and below by DBRS; B+ and below by CBRS). Sometimes these low-rated securities are called *junk bonds*.

Certain regulated financial institutions (such as trust companies, insurance companies, and pension plans) are prohibited from purchasing bonds that are not of investment grade. Because an important group of investors is encouraged or forced to purchase them, investment grade bonds are believed to command "superpremium" prices, and hence disproportionately low yields. If this were true, a major disparity in yields would attract many new issuers, thereby increasing the supply of such bonds and causing the prices to fall and yields to rise. For a significant superpremium to persist substantial market segmentation on both the buying and the selling side would be required. Since there is no clear evidence that segmentation exists, it seems likely that the differences in yields between investment grade bonds and speculative grade bonds are roughly proportional to differences in default risk.

Ratings are designed "to provide investors with a readily identifiable measure of the financial strength of a debt issue. In this way its relative level of risk and hence the required return may be compared to other types of securities throughout a diversified portfolio."[6] Moreover:

> Ratings involve judgments about the future on the one hand, and they are used by investors as a means of protection on the other, therefore, an effort is made when assigning ratings to look at the "worst" potential outcomes in the "visible" future, as well as the past record and the present status. Investors using the ratings should not expect to find in them a reflection of statistical factors alone. They are an appraisal of long-term risks, including the recognition of many non-statistical factors.[7]

---

[5] Both rating agencies use finer gradations than those shown in the figures. The ratings may be augmented by the addition of the qualifiers "high" or "low" to indicate both the relative ranking and the trend within a classification.

[6] *The CBRS Method of Rating* (Montreal: Canadian Bond Rating Service, Inc., 1989):6.

[7] *Moody's Bond Record*, (New York: Moody's Investors Service, Inc., January 1988):1.

### Highest Quality A++

This category encompasses bonds of outstanding quality. They possess the highest degree of protection of principal and interest. Companies with debt rated A++ are generally large national and/or multinational corporations whose products or services are essential to the Canadian economy.

These companies are the acknowledged leaders in their respective industries and have clearly demonstrated their ability to best withstand adverse economic or trade conditions either national or international in scope. Characteristically, these companies have had a long and creditable history of superior debt protection, in which the quality of their assets and earnings has been constantly maintained or improved, with strong evidence that this will continue.

### Very Good Quality A+

Bonds rated A+ are similar in characteristics to those rated A++ and can also be considered superior in quality. These companies have demonstrated a long and satisfactory history of growth with above-average protection of principal and interest on their debt securities.

These bonds are generally rated lower in quality because the margin of assets or earnings protection may not be as large or as stable as those rated A++. In both these categories the nature and quality of the asset and earning coverages are more important than the numerical values of the ratios.

### Good Quality A

Bonds rated A are considered to be good quality securities and to have favorable long-term investment characteristics. The main feature that distinguishes them from the higher rated securities is that these companies are more susceptible to adverse trade or economic conditions. Consequently, the protection is lower than for the categories of A++ and A+.

In all cases the A rated companies have maintained a history of adequate asset and earnings protection. There may be certain elements that may impair this protection sometime in the future. Confidence that the current overall financial position will be maintained or improved is slightly lower than for the securities rated above.

### Medium Quality B++

Issues rated B++ are classified as medium or average grade credits and are considered to be investment grade. These companies are generally more susceptible than any of the higher rated companies to swings in economic or trade conditions that would cause a deterioration in protection should the company enter a period of poor operating conditions.

There may be factors present either from within or without the company that may adversely affect the long-term level of protection of the debt. These companies bear closer scrutiny but in all cases both interest and principal are adequately protected at the present time.

### Lower Medium Quality B+

Bonds which are rated B+ are considered to be lower medium grade securities and have limited long-term protective investment characteristics. Assets and earnings coverage may be modest or unstable.

**FIGURE 13-2**
Canadian Bond Rating Service's rating definitions of long-term debt.

A significant deterioration in interest and principal protection may occur during periods of adverse economic or trade conditions. During periods of normal or improving economic conditions, assets and earnings protection are adequate. However, the company's ability to continually improve its financial position and level of debt protection is at present limited.

### Poor Quality B

Securities rated B lack most qualities necessary for the long-term fixed income investment. Companies in this category have a general history of volatile operating conditions, and the assurance has been in doubt that principal and interest protection will be maintained at an adequate level. Current coverages may be below industry standards and there is little assurance that debt protection will significantly improve.

### Speculative Quality C

Securities in this category are clearly speculative. The companies are generally junior in many respects and there is little assurance that the adequate coverage of principal and interest can be maintained uninterruptedly over a period of time.

### Default D

Bonds in this category are in default of some provisions in their trust deed and the companies may or may not be in the process of liquidation.

### Rating Suspended

A company which has its rating currrently suspended is experiencing severe financial or operating problems of which the outcome is uncertain. The company may or may not be in default but at present there is uncertainty as to the company's ability to pay off its debt.

Note: (High) and (Low) designations after a rating indicate an issuer's relative strength within a rating category.

**FIGURE 13-2** (Continued)

*SOURCE: The CBRS Method of Rating: Corporate and Government Securities,* Canadian Bond Rating Service Inc., 1989:16,17.

Despite this disclaimer, the influence of "statistical factors" on the ratings is apparently significant. Several studies have investigated the relationship between historical measures of a firm's performance and the ratings assigned its bonds.[8] Many of the differences in the ratings accorded various bonds can, in fact, be attributed to differences in the issuers' situations, measured in traditional ways. For corporate bonds, better ratings are generally associated with lower financial leverage (that is, debt to total assets); smaller past variation in earnings over time; larger asset base (firm size); more profitable

---

[8] For example, see Thomas F. Pogue and Robert M. Soldofsky, "What's in a Bond Rating?" *Journal of Financial and Quantitative Analysis* 4, no. 2 (June 1969):201–28; R. R. West, "An Alternate Approach to Predicting Corporate Bond Ratings," *Journal of Accounting Research* 8, no. 1 (Spring 1970):118–25; George E. Pinches and Kent A. Mingo, "A Multivariate Analysis of Industrial Bond Ratings," *Journal of Finance* 28, no. 1 (March 1973):1-18, and "The Role of Subordination and Industrial Bond Ratings," *Journal of Finance* 30, no. 1 (March 1975):201–6; Robert S. Kaplan and Gabriel Urwitz, "Statistical Models of Bond Ratings: A Methodological Inquiry," *Journal of Business* 52, no. 2 (April 1979):231–61; Ahmed Belkaoui, *Industrial Bonds and the Rating Process* (Westport, Conn.: Quorum Books, 1983); Tom Barnes and Tom Byng, "The Prediction of Corporate Bond Ratings: The Canadian Case", *Canadian Journal of Administrative Sciences* 5,no. 3 (September 1988):27–33; Halim Bishara, "Determinants of Canadian Corporate Bond Ratings: A Multivariate Analysis", *Proceedings*, Administrative Sciences Association of Canada Conference, Halifax, June 1988:12–21.

### AAA "Near Perfection"

Bonds which are rated AAA are of the highest investment quality. The degree of protection afforded principal and interest is of the highest order. Earnings are relatively stable, the structure of the industry in which the Company operates is very strong, and the outlook for future profitability is extremely favorable. There are few qualifying factors present which would detract from the performance of the Company, and the strength of liquidity ratios is unquestioned for the industry in which the Company operates.

### AA Well Above Average

Bonds rated AA are of superior investment quality, and protection of interest and principal is considered high. In many cases, they differ from bonds rated AAA to a small degree.

### A Up to High Average, Upper Medium Grade

Bonds rated A are upper medium grade securities. Protection of interest and principal is still substantial, but the degree of strength is less than with AA rated companies. Companies in this category may be more susceptible to adverse economic conditions.

### BBB Up to Low Average, Medium Grade

Bonds rated BBB are medium grade securities. Protection of interest and principal is considered adequate, but the Company may be more susceptible to economic cycles, or there may be other adversities present which reduce the strength of these bonds.

### BB Mildly Speculative

Bonds rated BB are lower medium grade obligations, and are considered mildly speculative and below average. The degree of protection afforded interest and principal is uncertain, particularly during periods of economic recession, and the size of the Company may be relatively small.

### B Middle Speculative

Bonds rated B are "middle" speculative. Uncertainty exists as to the ability of the Company to pay interest and principal on a continuing basis in the future, especially in periods of economic recession.

### CCC Highly Speculative

Bonds rated CCC are considered highly speculative and are in danger of default of interest and principal. The degree of adverse elements present is more severe than bonds rated B.

### CC In Default

Bonds rated CC are in default of either interest or principal, and other severe adverse elements are present.

### C Second Tier of Debt of a Company in Default

C is the lowest rating provided. Bonds rated C differ from bonds rated CC with respect to the relative liquidation values.

**FIGURE 13-3**
Dominion Bond Rating Service's bond rating scale.

**FIGURE 13-3** (Continued)

*SOURCE: DBRS,* Dominion Bond Rating Service Limited, 1992:7.

operations; and lack of subordination to other debt issues.[9] The results obtained by Canadian studies are similar to those of US studies. One use of these findings is in the development of models for predicting the initial ratings that will be given to forthcoming bond issues as well as for predicting changes in the ratings of outstanding bonds.

## Default Premiums

Since common stocks do not "promise" any cash flows to the investor, they are not subject to default. To assess the investment prospects for a common stock, all possible holding-period returns might be considered. By multiplying each return by its perceived probability of occurrence and then adding up the products, an estimate of the expected holding period return can be determined.

A similar procedure can be employed with bonds, with the analysis usually focusing on yield-to-maturity. Formally, all possible yields are considered, along with their respective probabilities, and a weighted average is computed to determine the *expected yield-to-maturity*. As long as there is any possibility of default or late payment, the expected yield will fall below the promised yield. In general, the greater the risk of default and the greater the amount of loss in the event of default, the greater will be this disparity.

This is illustrated in Figure 13.4 for a hypothetical risky bond. Its promised yield-to-maturity is 12% but, owing to a high default risk, the expected yield is only 9%. The 3% difference between the promised and expected yields is the *default premium*. Any bond that has some probability of default should offer such a premium, and it should be greater, the greater the probability of default.

Just how large should a bond's default premium be? According to one model, the answer depends on both the probability of default and the likely financial loss to the

---

[9] A summary of previous studies identifying the factors affecting municipal bond ratings (as well as corporate bond ratings) in the US is contained in Chapter 14 of George Foster, *Financial Statement Analysis* (Englewood Cliffs, N.J.: Prentice Hall, 1986). For a description of the rating of municipal bonds, see John E. Petersen, *The Rating Game* (New York: The Twentieth Century Fund, 1974).

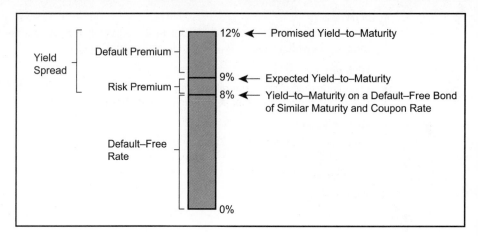

**FIGURE 13-4**
Yield-to-maturity for a risky bond.

bondholder in the event of default.[10] Also important in this model is the level of the bond's expected yield-to-maturity.

Consider a bond that is perceived to be equally likely to default in each year (given it did not default in the previous year), with the probability that it will default in any given year denoted by $p_d$. Assume that if the bond does default, a payment equal to $(1 - \lambda)$ times its market price a year earlier will be made to the owner of each bond. According to this model, a bond will be fairly priced if its promised yield-to-maturity $(y)$ is

$$y = \frac{\bar{y} + \lambda p_d}{1 - p_d} \qquad (13.4)$$

where $\bar{y}$ denotes the bond's expected yield-to-maturity. The difference (d) between a bond's promised yield-to-maturity $(y)$ and its expected yield-to-maturity $(\bar{y})$ was referred to earlier as the bond's default premium. Using equation (13.4), this difference for a fairly priced bond will be equal to

$$d = y - \bar{y}$$
$$= \left[\frac{\bar{y} + \lambda p_d}{1 - p_d}\right] - \bar{y} \qquad (13.5)$$

As an example, consider the bond illustrated in Figure 13.4. Assume that this bond has a 6% annual default probability and that it is estimated that if the bond does default, each bondholder will receive an amount equal to 60% of the bond's market price a year earlier (meaning that $1 - \lambda = .60$, which in turn means that $\lambda = .40$). Using equation (13.5), this bond would be fairly priced if its default premium were equal to

---

[10] The model was developed by Gordon Pye in "Gauging the Default Premium," *Financial Analysts Journal* 30, no. 1 (January/February 1974):49–52.

**TABLE 13.1**

Actual and Realized Bond Yields-to-Maturity, 1900–1943.

### (a) All Large and a Sample of Small Issues

| Composite Rating | Comparable Moody's Rating | Promised Yield-to-Maturity at Issue | Percent Defaulting Prior to Maturity | Actual-Yield-to-Maturity |
|---|---|---|---|---|
| I | Aaa | 4.5% | 5.9% | 5.1% |
| II | Aa | 4.6 | 6.0 | 5.0 |
| III | A | 4.9 | 13.4 | 5.0 |
| IV | Baa | 5.4 | 19.1 | 5.7 |
| V-IX | below Baa | 9.5 | 42.4 | 8.6 |

### (b) All Large Issues

| Composite Rating | Comparable Moody's Rating | Promised Yield-to-Maturity | Actual Yield-to-Maturity | Modified Actual Yield-to-Maturity |
|---|---|---|---|---|
| I | Aaa | 4.5% | 5.1% | 4.3% |
| II | Aa | 4.5 | 5.1 | 4.3 |
| III | A | 4.9 | 5.0 | 4.3 |
| IV | Baa | 5.4 | 5.8 | 4.5 |

SOURCE: (a) W. Braddock Hickman, *Corporate Bond Quality and Investor Experience* (Princeton, N.J.: Princeton University Press, 1953):10. (b) Harold G. Fraine and Robert H. Mills, "The Effect of Defaults and Credit Deterioration on Yields of Corporate Bonds," *Journal of Finance* 16, no. 3 (September 1961):433.

$$d = \left[ \frac{.09 + (.40 \times .06)}{1 - .06} \right] - .09$$

$$= .0313$$

or 3.13%. Since the actual default premium earlier was estimated to be 3%, it can be seen that the two figures are similar. This suggests the actual default premium is appropriate, according to this model.

What sort of default experience might the long-run bond investor anticipate? And, how is this experience likely to be related to the ratings of the bonds held? In a massive US study of all large bond issues and a sample of small bond issues, Hickman attempted to answer these questions.[11] He analyzed investor experience for each bond from 1900 through 1943 to determine the actual yield-to-maturity, measured from the date of issuance to the date on which the bond matured, defaulted, or was called — whichever came first. He then compared this actual yield with the promised yield-to-maturity based on the price at time of issue. Every bond was also classified according to the ratings assigned at time of issue. Part (a) of Table 13.1 shows the major results.

---

[11] W. Braddock Hickman, *Corporate Bond Quality and Investor Experience* (Princeton, N.J.: Princeton University Press, 1958).

As might be expected, Hickman found that, in general, the riskier the bond, the higher the promised yield at time of issue and the higher the percentage of bonds that subsequently defaulted. However, a surprise was uncovered when the actual yields-to-maturity were compared with promised yields-to-maturity. As the last column on the right of the table shows, in four out of five rating classifications, the actual yield was found to *exceed* the promised yield. Fortunately, a convenient explanation exists for this finding — the period studied by Hickman was one where a substantial drop in interest rates occurred. This is important because the drop made it attractive for issuers to call their outstanding bonds, paying the bondholders a call premium in the process and resulting in an actual yield above the promised yield.

To see what might have happened had this not been the case, Fraine and Mills reanalyzed the data for large investment-grade issues.[12] Their results are shown in part (b) of Table 13.1. The initial columns differ from those in part (a) because smaller issues were excluded. The major difference between the parts appears in the right-hand column, where Fraine and Mills substituted a bond's promised yield for its actual yield whenever the latter was larger, thereby removing the effects of most calls. Unlike Hickman, their results suggest that there was little difference in actual yields within the highest rating classifications.

More recently, Altman and Nammacher examined the default experience of corporate bonds over the period of 1970 to 1984.[13] Like Hickman, they also found that bonds with a speculative grade rating at the time of issue subsequently had a much higher default rate than bonds that were initially of investment grade. However, this does not mean that speculative bonds are poor investments. Indeed, after subtracting for losses due to defaults, such low-grade bonds were found to offer attractive returns.

## Risk Premiums

It is useful to compare the expected return of a risky security with the certain return of a default-free security. In an efficient market, the difference in these returns will be related to the relevant risk of the security. Consider common stocks, where the investor has a holding period of one year or less. In this situation, the expected return on a share is typically compared with the yield of a Treasury bill having a maturity date corresponding with the end of the holding period (note that the yield on such a Treasury bill is equal to its holding-period return).

Traditionally, a risky bond's expected yield-to-maturity is compared with that of a default-free bond of similar maturity and coupon rate. The difference between these yields is known as the bond's *risk premium*. In the example shown in Figure 13.4, default-free bonds of similar maturity and coupon rate offer a certain 8% yield-to-maturity. Since the risky bond's expected yield-to-maturity is 9%, its risk premium is 1% (that is, 100 basis points).

Every bond that might default should offer a default premium. But the risk premium is another matter. Any security's expected return should be related only to its contribution to the risk of a well-diversified portfolio; its total risk is not directly relevant.

---

[12] Harold G. Fraine and Robert H. Mills, "The Effect of Defaults and Credit Deterioration on Yields of Corporate Bonds," *Journal of Finance* 16, no. 3 (September 1961):423–34.

[13] Edward I. Altman and Scott A. Nammacher, "The Default Rate Experience on High-Yield Corporate Debt," *Financial Analysts Journal* 41, no. 4 (July-August 1985):25–41.

**FIGURE 13-5**

Default rates 1900–1965.

*SOURCE:* Adapted from Thomas R. Atkinson and Elizabeth T. Simpson, *Trends in Corporate Bond Quality* (Columbia University Press, 1967):5.

For example, if a group of companies all faced the possibility of bankruptcy, but from totally unrelated causes, a portfolio that included all their bonds would subsequently provide an actual return very close to its expected return. This is because the default premiums earned on the bonds that did not default would offset the losses incurred from those bonds that did default. Consequently, there would be little reason for this expected return to differ significantly from that of a default-free bond, since there is little doubt concerning what its actual return will be. Accordingly, each bond should be priced to offer little or no risk premium (but each bond should have a substantial default premium).

However, the risks associated with bonds are not unrelated. Figure 13.5 shows for each year from 1900 to 1965 the ratio of the par value of corporate bonds defaulting during the year to the par value outstanding at the beginning of the year. Not surprisingly, the peaks coincide with periods of economic distress.[14] When business is bad, most firms are affected. The market value of a firm's common stock will decline when an economic downturn is anticipated. If the likelihood of default on its debt also increases, the market value of its outstanding bonds will follow suit. Thus, the holding-period return on a bond may be correlated with the returns of other bonds and with those of stocks. Most important, a risky bond's holding-period return is likely to be correlated, to at least some extent, with the return on a widely diversified "market portfolio" that includes both corporate bonds and stocks. This part of the risk of a bond should command a risk premium in the form of a higher expected return, since it is not diversifiable.

The riskier a bond is, the greater its likelihood of default and, in turn, the greater its potential sensitivity to market declines representing lowered assessments of prospects for the economy as a whole. This is illustrated in Table 13.2, which summarizes the investment performance of three portfolios of US bonds, known as bond funds, in the Keystone group. All values shown in the table are based on annual returns earned

---

[14]A similar observation has been made for municipal bonds. See George H. Hempel, *The Postwar Quality of State and Local Debt* (New York: Columbia University Press, 1971).

over a 20-year period by each portfolio. As might be anticipated, the most risky bond portfolio (fund B4) had the highest average return and highest standard deviation of return, whereas the least risky bond portfolio (fund B1) had the lowest average return and lowest standard deviation.

**TABLE 13.2**
Risk and Return, Keystone Bond Funds, 1968–1987.

|  | Fund B1 | Fund B2 | Fund B4 |
|---|---|---|---|
|  | Conservative Bonds | Investment Grade Bonds | Discount Bonds |
| Average return (% per year) | 7.52 | 8.70 | 9.05 |
| Standard deviation of return (% per year) | 8.69 | 9.53 | 10.96 |
| Beta value, relative to S&P 500 | .27 | .41 | .50 |
| Proportion of variance explained by S&P | .26 | .50 | .55 |

To estimate each portfolio's sensitivity to changes in stock prices, each portfolio's returns were compared with those of Standard & Poor's 500. Specifically, a beta was calculated for each portfolio in order to measure the sensitivity of each portfolio to swings in the stock market. As can be seen in the table, the riskier the portfolio, the higher the estimated beta, indicating that riskier bonds moved more with stocks and thus should have had higher average returns.

The final row in the table shows the proportion of the year-to-year variation in bond portfolio returns that were associated with stock market swings. As indicated, relatively more of the risky portfolio's variation was associated with the stock market than was the case with the less risky portfolio. Thus, for less-risky bonds, interest-rate risk appears to have been more important than stock market risk.[15]

## 13.3 THE RISK STRUCTURE OF INTEREST RATES

The greater a bond's risk of default, the greater its default premium. This alone will cause a bond with a higher default risk to offer a higher promised yield-to-maturity. If it is also true that the greater a bond's risk of default, the greater its risk premium, then the promised yield-to-maturity will have to be even higher. Differences in agency ratings should be associated with differences in yields-to-maturity if the ratings reflect the risk of default.

Figure 13.6(a) shows that this is indeed the case. Each of the curves plots the promised yield-to-maturity for a group of corporate bonds assigned the same ratings.

---

[15] In a study of preferred shares, it was found that the price movements of low-rated preferred shares were related more to the price movements of common stocks than to the price movements of bonds; for high-rated preferred shares, the findings were just the opposite. See John S. Bildersee, "Some Aspects of the Performance of Non-Convertible Preferred Stocks," *Journal of Finance* 28, no. 5 (December 1973):1187–1201.

It is clear that bonds are priced so that higher promised yields are associated with lower ratings. Figure 13.6(b), however, shows that the yield differences between rating categories vary considerably over time, suggesting that agency ratings indicate *relative* levels of risk instead of *absolute* levels of risk.

If an absolute level of risk were indicated by a rating classification, then each classification would be associated with a particular probability of default (or, more accurately, a range of probabilities of default). Consequently, as the economy became more uncertain (for example, an increased probability of a recession), bonds would be reclassified as necessary, with most moving to lower ratings. In this situation, yield spreads between classifications would change only slightly, since each classification would still reflect bonds having the same probability of default. However, Figure 13.6(b) shows that these spreads change considerably over time, an observation that can be interpreted as evidence that the bond market does not believe that the ratings reflect absolute levels of risk.

Rating agencies appear to prefer to avoid making a large number of rating changes as the economy becomes more uncertain. Instead, they prefer to use the classifications to indicate relative levels of risk. This means that an overall increase in economic uncertainty does not result in a significant number of reclassifications. Thus, the probability of default associated with bonds in a given rating classification is greater at such a time. In turn, the yield spreads between classifications of corporate bonds and the yield spreads between corporate and government bonds both increase. Indeed, there is evidence that the spread between the promised yields of bonds of different rating classifications increases when the degree of uncertainty about the economy increases.

Some models have attempted to take advantage of this observation in order to predict the amount of economic uncertainty. In particular, these models use the size of the yield spread between, say, bonds rated AAA and those rated BBB as an indication of the degree of economic uncertainty. For example, if this spread is widening, then that might be taken as an indication that the near-term future of the economy was becoming more uncertain. It should be noted that there are other models that do look not at yield spreads but at differences in the holding-period returns of AAA and BBB bonds.

## 13.4 DETERMINANTS OF YIELD SPREADS

As mentioned previously, when bond analysts refer to a corporate bond's yield spread, they are typically referring to the difference between the corporate bond's promised yield-to-maturity and that of another bond (often a default-free government security) having similar maturity and coupon rate. The greater the risk of default, the greater this spread should be. Moreover, bonds that have more marketability might command an additional "premium" in price and hence offer a lower yield-to-maturity with a corresponding lower spread. Given a large enough sample of bonds, it should be possible to see if these relationships really do exist.

A US study of corporate bond prices did this.[16] Three measures were used to assess the probability of default:

---

[16] Lawrence Fisher, "Determinants of Risk Premiums on Corporate Bonds," *Journal of Political Economy* 67, no. 3 (June 1959):217–37.

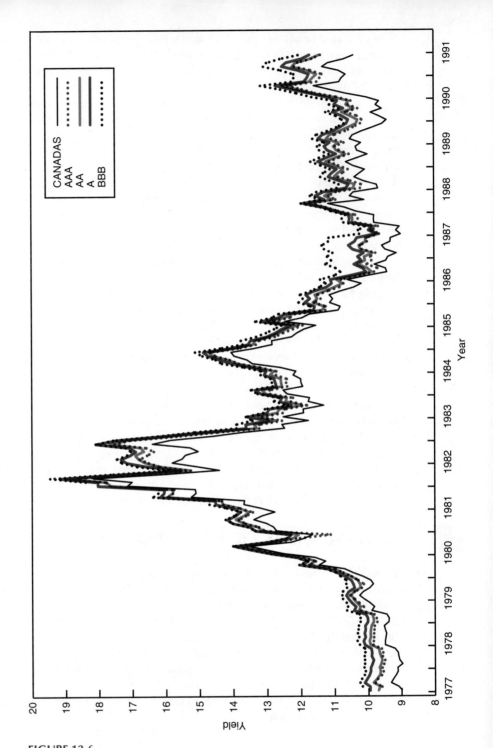

**FIGURE 13-6**

(a) Corporate bond yields by ratings, 1977–1990.

*SOURCE:* Adapted from Melanie Moore, *ScotiaMcLeod's Handbook of Canadian Debt Market Indices,: 1947 –1990,* (ScotiaMcLeod Inc., 1991):40–7.

**FIGURE 13-6**

(b) Yield spreads over time, January 2, 1985 to January 30, 1992.

*SOURCE:* Canada Life Assurance Company.

1. The extent to which the firm's net income had varied over the preceding nine years (measured by the coefficient of variation of earnings — that is, the ratio of standard deviation of earnings to average earnings),
2. The length of time that the firm had operated without forcing any of its creditors to take a loss, and
3. The ratio of the market value of the firm's equity to the par value of its debt.

A fourth measure was used to provide an indication of marketability:

4. The market value of the firm's outstanding debt.

First, these measures were calculated, along with the yield spread, for each one of 366 bonds. Second, the logarithm of every yield spread and measure was calculated. Third, statistical methods were used to analyze the relationship between a bond's yield spread

and these measures. The one that was found to describe this relationship most accurately
was:

$$\text{Yield spread} = .987 + .307(\text{earnings variability})$$
$$- .253(\text{time without default}) \qquad (13.6)$$
$$- .537(\text{equity/debt ratio})$$
$$- .275(\text{market value of debt}).$$

This form of the relationship accounted for roughly 75% of the variation in the bonds'
yield spreads.

The advantage of an equation such as this is that the coefficients can be easily
interpreted. Since all yield spreads and values had been converted to logarithms, the
effect is similar to that of using ratio scales on all axes of a diagram. This means that a
1% increase in a bond's earnings variability can be expected to bring about an increase
of .307% in the bond's yield spread, other things being equal. Similarly, a 1% increase
in a bond's time without default can be expected to cause a decrease of approximately
.253% in the bond's yield spread, and so on. Each coefficient is an elasticity, indicating
the percentage change in a bond's yield spread likely to accompany a 1% change in
the associated measure. Since every measure was found to be related in the expected
direction to the yield spread, the study provides substantial support for the notion that
bonds with higher default risk and less marketability have higher yield spreads.[17]

## 13.5    FINANCIAL RATIOS AS PREDICTORS OF DEFAULT

For years, security analysts have used accounting ratios to indicate the probability
that a firm will fail to meet its financial obligations. Specific procedures have been
developed to predict default with such ratios. Univariate analysis attempts to find the
best single predictor for this purpose, whereas multivariate analysis searches for the
best combination of two or more predictors.

### ☐ 13.5.1   Univariate Methods

Cash inflows can be viewed as contributions to the firm's cash balance, and cash outflows
can be viewed as drains on this balance. When the balance falls below zero, default is
likely to occur. This means that the probability of default will be greater for the firm
when (1) the existing cash balance is smaller; (2) the expected net cash flow (measured
before payments to creditors and shareholders) is smaller; and (3) the net cash flow is
more variable.

In an examination of various measures used to assess these factors, it was found
that the ratio of net cash flow (income before depreciation, depletion, and amortization
charges) to total debt was particularly useful.[18] Figure 13.7(a) shows the mean value of

---

[17] See pp. 510–11 in Foster, *Financial Statement Analysis*, for a discussion of yield spreads of municipal bonds.

[18] William H. Beaver, "Market Prices, Financial Ratios and the Prediction of Failure," *Journal of Accounting Research* 6, no. 2 (Autumn 1968):1979–92. For a more recent study, see James M. Gahlon and Robert L. Vigeland, "Early Warning Signs of Bankruptcy Using Cash Flow Analysis," *Journal of Commercial Bank Lending* 71, no. 4 (December 1988):4–15.

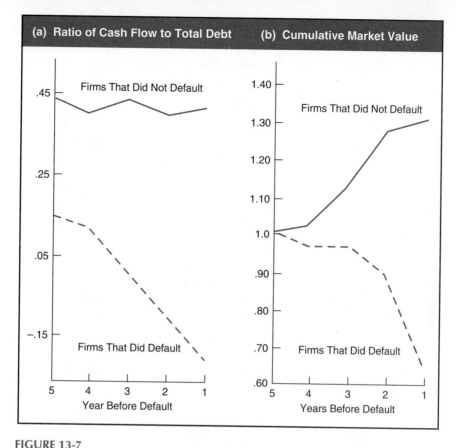

**FIGURE 13-7**

Financial ratios and market prices for firms that defaulted and those that did not.

*SOURCE:* William H. Beaver, "Market Prices, Financial Ratios and the Prediction of Failure," *Journal of Accounting Research* 6, no. 2 (Autumn 1968):182, 185.

this ratio for a group of firms that defaulted on a promised payment and for a companion group that did not. As early as five years before default the two groups' ratios diverged, and the spread widened as the year of default approached.

This changing spread suggests that the probability of default may not be constant through time. Instead, warning signals may indicate an increase in the probability, which should, in turn, cause a fall in the market price of the firm's bonds along with a fall in the market price of its common stock. Figure 13.7(b) shows that such signals are indeed recognized in the marketplace. The median market value of common stock in the firms that did not default went up, while that of the firms that subsequently defaulted went down as the date of default approached.

Canadian stock market data were used to compare the characteristics of a sample of 25 firms that failed with those of a matched sample of firms that did not fail. This showed that impending failure was characterized by: decreasing common stock returns starting about 12 months prior to failure; increasing total risk (increasing variance of returns) also starting about 12 months prior to failure; and a shift from systematic to unsystematic risk as evidenced by a decrease in beta starting about 24 months prior to failure. They concluded that market participants could use their techniques to anticipate failure, on average, 15 months before its occurence.[19]

## ☐ 13.5.2  Multivariate Methods

Combinations of certain financial ratios have been considered as possible predictors of default.[20] Statistical analysis has indicated that the most accurate method of predicting default has been to calculate a firm's *Z score* from some of its financial ratios as follows:

$$Z = 1.2\,X_1 + 1.4\,X_2 + 3.3\,X_3 + .6\,X_4 + .99\,X_5 \qquad (13.7)$$

where the following ratios are calculated from information contained in the firm's most recent income statement and balance sheet:

$X_1$ = (current assets − current liabilities)/total assets
$X_2$ = retained earnings/total assets
$X_3$ = earnings before interest and taxes/total assets
$X_4$ = market value of equity/book value of total debt
$X_5$ = sales/total assets.

Any firm with a $Z$-score below 1.8 is considered a likely candidate for default, and the lower the score, the greater the likelihood.

A corresponding Canadian study found that the following financial ratios were significant:[21]

$X_1$ = sales/total assets
$X_2$ = total debt/total assets
$X_3$ = current assets/current liabilities
$X_4$ = net profits after tax/total debt
$X_5$ = rate of growth of equity − rate of asset growth.

In this case a critical score of −0.33 indicates a significant probability of default.

---

[19] Vijay M. Jog and Allan L. Riding, "Canadian Stock Market Reactions to Impending Corporate Failure," *Proceedings*, Administrative Sciences Association of Canada Conference, Whistler, B.C. (June 1988):226–40.

[20] Edward I. Altman, "Financial Ratios, Discriminant Analysis and the Prediction of Corporate Bankruptcy," *Journal of Finance* 23, no. 4 (September 1968):589–609.

[21] Edward I. Altman and Mario Y. Lavallee, "Business Failure Classification in Canada, *Journal of Business Administration: Capital Markets in Canada*, 12, no. 1 (Fall 1980):147–64. Subsequent refinements to this model have been made, leading to a revised procedure known as *zeta analysis*. See Edward I. Altman, Robert G. Haldeman, and P. Narayanan, "Zeta Analysis: A New Model to Identify Bankruptcy Risk of Corporations," *Journal of Banking and Finance* 1, no. 1 (June 1977):29–54; and J. A. Ohlson, "Financial Ratios and the Probabilistic Prediction of Bankruptcy," *Journal of Accounting Research* 18, no. 1 (Spring 1980):109-31. For a study that suggests the predictive accuracy of both the Z-model and Zeta-model can be improved by adding certain cash flow-based variables, see Abdul Aziz and Gerald H. Lawson, "Cash Flow Reporting and Financial Distress Models: Testing of Hypotheses," *Financial Management* 18, no. 1 (Spring 1989):55–63. A summary of the literature on univariate and multivariate models is contained in Chapter 15 of Foster, *Financial Statement Analysis*.

## ☐ 13.5.3 Investment Implications

The preceding discussion does not mean that securities of firms whose cash-flow-to-total-debt ratio or $Z$-score had declined should be avoided. It should be remembered that the firms represented by the dashed lines in Figure 13.7 were chosen because they eventually defaulted. Had all firms with declining ratios been selected, corresponding decreases in their market price would undoubtedly have been observed, reflecting the increased probability of future default. However, only some of these firms would have ultimately defaulted, whereas the others would have recovered. Consequently, the gains on the firms that recovered might well have offset the losses on the firms that defaulted. In summary, the net result from purchasing a portfolio of stocks that had declining ratios or $Z$-scores is that the investor would have received an average return.

What about purchasing bonds of companies that have just had their ratings increased and selling (or avoiding) bonds of companies that have just had their ratings decreased? After all, such changes in ratings should be related to a change in the default risk of the issuer. In a US study that looked at the behavior of bond prices around the time of ratings changes, some evidence was found that the bond price adjustment to a rating change occurred in the period from 18 to 7 months *before* the rating change.[22] Little or no evidence of a substantive price change was found either during the month of the rating change or in the period from six months before to six months after the rating change. These findings are consistent with the notion that the bond market is semistrong-form efficient, since bond ratings are predictable from publicly available information.

## 13.6 SUMMARY

Bond analysts are concerned with identifying bonds that are mispriced. In doing so, they often estimate an appropriate yield-to-maturity for a given bond, based on the bond's characteristics and current market conditions. Bond attributes that are important in determining an appropriate yield-to-maturity consist of (1) length of time until maturity; (2) coupon rate; (3) call provisions; (4) tax status; (5) marketability; and (6) likelihood of default.

Determining an appropriate yield-to-maturity on a bond can be related to the use of the capitalization of income method of valuation. This method states that the intrinsic value of any financial asset is simply the present value of the expected future cash flows associated with the asset. In the case of bonds, the cash flows typically consist of coupon payments and par value.

Although the intrinsic value of a bond can be calculated and compared to the bond's market price, it is more common for bond analysts to see whether or not the bond's promised yield-to-maturity is appropriate. If the promised yield is more than appropriate, the bond is underpriced; if the promised yield is less than appropriate, the bond is overpriced.

---

[22] Mark I. Weinstein, "The Effect of a Rating Change Announcement on Bond Price," *Journal of Financial Economics* 5, no. 3 (December 1977):329–50.

1. Pierre Tebeau is considering investing in a bond currently selling for $8,785.07. The bond has four years to maturity, a $10,000 face value, and an 8% coupon rate. The next interest payment is due one year from today. The appropriate discount rate for investments of similar risk is 10%.

    a. Calculate the intrinsic value of the bond. Based on this calculation, should Pierre purchase the bond?

    b. Calculate the yield-to-maturity of the bond. Based on this calculation, should Pierre purchase the bond?

2. Consider two bonds that both carry coupon rates of 8% and exhibit similar risk characteristics. However, the first bond has five years to maturity while the second has ten years to maturity. The appropriate discount rate for investments of similar risk is 8%. If the discount rate rises by two percentage points, what will be the respective percentage price changes of the two bonds?

3. Why is it convenient to use Canada bonds as a starting point for analyzing bond yields?

4. Burleigh Grimes purchased at par a bond with a face value of $1000. The bond had five years to maturity and a 10% coupon rate. The bond was called two years later for a price of $1100, after making its second annual interest payment. Burleigh then reinvested the proceeds in a bond selling at its face value of $1000, with three years to maturity and a 7% coupon rate. What was Burleigh's actual yield-to-maturity over the five-year period?

5. Nellie Fox acquired at par a bond for $1000 that offered a 9% coupon rate. At the time of purchase, the bond had four years to maturity. Assuming annual interest payments, calculate Nellie's actual yield-to-maturity if all the interest payments were reinvested in an investment earning 15% per year. What would Nellie's actual yield-to-maturity be if all interest payments were spent immediately upon receipt?

6. Distinguish between yield-to-first-call and yield-to-maturity.

7. Based on the default premium model presented in the text, what is the fair value default premium for a bond with an expected yield-to-maturity of 8.5%, a 10% annual default probability, and an expected loss as a percent of market value of 60%?

8. Corporate default appears to be an event specific to an individual company. Yet despite the apparent diversifiable nature of corporate default (meaning that relatively few bonds would default in a well-diversified portfolio), the bond market systematically adds default premiums when valuing corporate bonds. Explain why.

9. Junk bonds are often viewed by investors as having financial characteristics much more akin to common stocks than to high grade corporate bonds. Why?

10. According to Larry Cross, "agency ratings indicate *relative* levels of risk instead of *absolute* levels of risk." Explain the meaning of Larry's statement.

11. Joe Chin has noted that the spread between the yield-to-maturity on BBB-rated bonds and that on AAA-rated bonds has recently widened considerably. Explain to Joe what this change might indicate.

# SUGGESTED READINGS

*The Canadian Securities Course* (Toronto, Ont.: The Canadian Securities Institute, 1989) Chapters 9 and 10, describes bond analysis.

*DBRS*, (Toronto, Ont.: Dominion Bond Rating Service Limited, undated) and

*The CBRS Method of Rating: Corporate and Government Securities* (Montreal, Que.: Canadian Bond Rating Service, 1989) describe the methods these companies use to rate Commercial Paper and short-term debt, Bonds and long-term debt and Preferred shares.

Edward I. Altman and Mario Y. Lavallee, "Business Failure Classification in Canada," *Journal of Business Administration*, 12, no. 1 (Fall 1980):147–64 develops a bankruptcy prediction model using Canadian data.

# Chapter 14

# BOND PORTFOLIO MANAGEMENT

The methods currently in use for managing bond portfolios can be divided into two general categories — passive and active. Methods in the passive category rest on the basic assumption that bond markets are semistrong-form efficient. That is, current bond prices are viewed as accurately reflecting all publicly available information. Thus, bonds are felt to be priced fairly in the marketplace, providing a return that is commensurate with the risk involved. In addition to believing that individual bonds are not mispriced, passive investors also believe that attempting to predict interest rates is, in general, futile. In summary, passive management rests on the belief that attempts at both security selection (that is, identifying mispriced bonds) and market timing (for example, buying long-term bonds when interest rates are predicted to fall and replacing them with short-term bonds when interest rates are predicted to rise) will be unsuccessful in providing the investor with above-average returns.

Active methods of bond portfolio management are based on the assumption that the bond market is not so efficient, thereby giving some investors the opportunity to earn above-average returns. That is, active management is based on the ability of the portfolio manager either to identify mispriced bonds or to "time" the bond market by accurately predicting interest rates.

This chapter discusses these two general approaches to bond portfolio management. It begins by reviewing some of the findings regarding the efficiency of the bond market.

## 14.1 BOND MARKET EFFICIENCY

In assessing the efficiency of the bond market, a sample of the major US studies and the few Canadian studies available are mentioned. The impression obtained from reading them is that US bond markets appear to be highly, but not perfectly, semistrong-form efficient. That is, bond prices tend to reflect almost all publicly available information. Not surprisingly, this impression is similar to the one obtained from studies of the efficiency of stock markets.

Canadian markets are less active, therefore, some inefficiencies which may not be economically significant appear to exist. These are discussed below.

## □ 14.1.1  Price Behavior of Treasury Bills

An early study of bond market efficiency focused on the price behavior of Treasury bills. In particular, the prices of Treasury bills were analyzed on a weekly basis from October 1946 through December 1964, a total of 796 weeks. The study found that knowledge of how Treasury bill prices changed in the past was of little use in trying to predict how they would change in the future. Consequently, the results from this study are consistent with the notion that the market for Treasury bills is weak-form efficient.[1]

## □ 14.1.2  Experts' Predictions of Interest Rates

Bond market efficiency has also been studied by examining the accuracy of interest rate predictions that have been made by experts. These people use a wide range of techniques and a number of different sources of information. Since it is reasonable to assume their information is publicly available, such studies can be viewed as tests of semistrong-form efficiency.

One way these tests have been conducted involves the building of statistical models that are based on what the experts have said in regard to how interest rates should be predicted. Once these models have been constructed, their predictive accuracy can be evaluated. In one study, six different models were constructed and then their one-month ahead predictions were tested over the two-year period of 1973 to 1974. Consistent with the notion of efficient markets, it was found that a simple model of "no change" was more accurate in predicting interest rates than any of the six statistical models.[2]

Another way these tests have been conducted involves comparing a set of explicit predictions with what subsequently actually occurred. One source of such predictions is the quarterly survey of interest rate expectations that appears in the *Goldsmith-Nagan Bond and Money Market Newsletter*, published by Goldsmith-Nagan, Inc. Specifically, this survey reports the predictions made by a number (roughly 50) of "money market professionals" regarding three-month ahead and six-month ahead levels of 10 different interest rates. In one study, the predictions made from September 1969 through December 1972 (that is, 14 sets of quarterly predictions) were compared with those of a "no-change" model — that is, a model that forecasts no change from the current level of interest rates.[3]

Interestingly, the professionals seemed to forecast better than the no-change model for short-term interest rates (such as forecasting what the three-month Treasury bill rate will be three months in the future) but did worse than the no-change model for longer-term interest rates (such as forecasting what the intermediate-term Treasury note rate will be three months in the future).

---

[1] For details, see Richard Roll, *The Behavior of Interest Rates* (New York: Basic Books, Inc., 1970). Interestingly, this study also produced evidence rejecting the unbiased expectations theory of the term structure of interest rates.

[2] J. Walter Elliott and Jerome R. Baier, "Econometric Models and Current Interest Rates: How Well Do They Predict Future Rates?" *Journal of Finance* 34, no. 4 (September 1979):975–86. It should be noted that the models used by major economic forecasting firms tend to have similar amounts of accuracy. See Stephen K. McNees, "Forecasting Accuracy of Alternative Techniques: A Comparison of US Macroeconomic Forecasts," *Journal of Business & Economic Statistics* 4, no. 1 (January 1986):5–15, particularly Table 6 where 90-day Treasury bill rate forecasts are evaluated.

[3] Michael J. Prell, "How Well Do the Experts Forecast Interest Rates?" Federal Reserve Bank of Kansas City *Monthly Review* (September-October 1973):3–13.

A subsequent study examined the Goldsmith-Nagan predictions of three-month Treasury bill rates six months in the future during the time period from March 1970 through September 1979 (39 predictions).[4] These predictions were compared with those of three "simple" models, the first one being the no-change model. The second simple model was based on the liquidity preference theory of the term structure of interest rates (discussed in Chapter 4). According to this theory, the forward rate implicit in current market rates should be equal to the expected future interest rate plus a liquidity premium. Thus, a forecast of the expected future interest rate can be gotten by subtracting an estimate of the liquidity premium from the forward rate. The third simple model was what statisticians refer to as an autoregressive model. Basically, a forecast of the future Treasury bill rate was formed from the current Treasury bill rate as well as what the Treasury bill rate was one, two, three, and six quarters ago. The study found that the professionals were more accurate than both the no-change model and the liquidity premium model but were less accurate than the autoregressive model.

Another study evaluated the six-month ahead predictions of three-month Treasury bill rates that were made by nine economists and reported semiannually in *The Wall Street Journal*. Evaluating the forecasts published from December 1981 through June 1986, it was found that the no-change model was more accurate.[5]

An extensive Canadian study was triggered by the observation that October 1979 ushered in a regime of high and volatile interest rates that lasted several years. The hypothesis that forecasters might perform "better" in such an environment was tested. The study went on to compare the performance of the simple no-change model with concensus forecasts of short and long term interest rates provided by three institutions (McLeod, Young, Weir and Company [now ScotiaMcLeod Inc.], The Conference Board of Canada and Data Resources Incorporated of Canada) over two time periods, the second quarter of 1975 to the third quarter of 1979 and the fourth quarter of 1979 to the fourth quarter of 1984.[6] These institutions report interest rate forecasts for each of the following two quarters as part of their regular quarterly macroeconomic forecasts. The McLeod, Young, Weir forecasts perform as well or slightly better than the simple model in both time periods, but both the Conference Board and Data Resources forecasts deteriorate noticeably in the second period. A significant observation is the deterioration of the accuracy of all short term interest rate forecasts (including the simple model) in the second period.

In summary, it appears from this evidence that the no-change model sometimes provides the most accurate forecasts of future interest rates while occasionally the experts are more accurate. On balance, a reasonable interpretation of these results is that the bond market is nearly semistrong-form efficient. While the bond market may not be

---

[4] Adrian W. Throop, "Interest Rate Forecasts and Market Efficiency," Federal Reserve Bank of San Francisco *Economic Review* (Spring 1981):29–43. This article contains a useful reference list of other studies concerning the prediction of interest rates.

[5] Forecasts implicit in the futures market (discussed in Chapter 19) for Treasury bills were also found to be more accurate than those of the economists but less accurate than those of the no-change model over this time period. For a longer time period, the futures market and no-change model forecasts were of comparable accuracy. See Michael T. Belognia, "Predicting Interest Rates: A Comparison of Professional and Market-Based Forecasts," Federal Reserve Bank of St. Louis *Review* 69, no. 3 (March 1987):9–15.

[6] James E. Pesando and Andre Plourde, "The October 1979 Change in the US Monetary Regime: Its Impact on the Forecastability of Canadian Interest Rates," *Journal of Finance*, 43, no.1 (March 1988):217–39.

perfectly efficient, the evidence clearly suggests that it is hard to be able to consistently forecast interest rates with greater accuracy than a no-change model.[7]

## ☐ 14.1.3 Price Reaction to Bond Rating Changes

A different type of test of market efficiency concerned the reaction of bond prices to rating changes. If ratings are based on public information, then any rating change would follow the release of such information. This suggests that in a semistrong-form efficient market, a bond's price would react to the release of the public information rather than the subsequent announcement of the rating change. Thus, an announcement of a rating change should not trigger a subsequent adjustment in the associated bond's price.

In a study that examined 100 rating changes that took place during the period of 1962 through 1974, no significant changes in bond prices were detected in the period from six months before through six months after the announcement of the change. However, a significant change was observed in the period from 18 months through 7 months before the announcement. Specifically, ratings increases were preceded by price increases, and rating decreases were preceded by price decreases.[8]

No comparable Canadian study is available but the similarity between the bond rating processes in the two countries suggests that Canadian investors are also likely to anticipate bond rating changes.

## ☐ 14.1.4 Money Supply Announcements

Every week, generally on Thursday, the Federal Reserve Board announces the current size of the money supply in the US economy. Now, it is known that interest rates are related to, among other things, the availability of credit and that the money supply affects this availability. This means that if the money supply figures are surprisingly high or low, then the announcement should trigger adjustments in the levels of various interest rates.[9] Furthermore, such adjustments should take place rapidly in a semistrong-form efficient market. Past studies indicate that such adjustments are indeed rapid, generally taking place within a day after the announcement.[10]

---

[7] The reported accuracy of macroeconomic forecasters in regard to Treasury bill rates (see the Early Quarter results for a two-quarter horizon in Table 6 of McNees, "Forecast Accuracy") can be compared to the reported accuracy of the no-change model (see Table 1 of Belognia, "Predicting Interest Rates"). While such a comparison should be done with caution, it does suggest that the no-change model is of similar, and in some cases, superior, accuracy.

[8] See Mark I. Weinstein, "The Effect of a Rating Change Announcement on Bond Price," *Journal of Financial Economics* 5, no. 3 (December 1977):329–50. A study of the prices of the common stocks associated with bonds that had rating changes reported similar results — share prices tended to change several months prior to the announcement dates of the rating changes. See George E. Pinches and J. Clay Singleton, "The Adjustment of Stock Prices to Bond Rating Changes," *Journal of Finance* 33, no. 1 (March 1978):29–44.

[9] For an explanation of this adjustment process, see Richard G. Sheehan, "Weekly Money Announcements: New Information and Its Effects," Federal Reserve Bank of St. Louis *Review* 67, no. 7 (August/September 1985):25–34.

[10] See, for example, Thomas Urich and Paul Wachtel, "Market Response to Weekly Money Supply Announcements in the 1970s," *Journal of Finance* 36, no. 5 (December 1981):1063–72, and "The Effects of Inflation and Money Supply Announcements on Interest Rates," *Journal of Finance* 39, no. 4 (September 1984):1177–88; and Bradford Cornell, "Money Supply Announcements and Interest Rates: Another View," *Journal of Business* 56, no. 1 (January 1983):1–23.

In October 1979, the US Federal Reserve set monetary growth as one of its principal macroeconomic targets and started controlling the money supply. Given the inter-relationship of the US and Canadian economies, changes in the US money supply should also affect Canadian interest rates. A study by Bailey reports that, since that date, Canadian short term interest rates and bond prices (as well as share prices) respond to unanticipated changes in the level of the US money supply.[11] This result is consistent with semi-strong form efficiency.

## ☐ 14.1.5 A Direct Test of Bond Market Efficiency

A direct test of the efficiency of both the US and Canadian bond markets was carried out by Appelt and Schulman.[12] They calculated zero coupon yield curves for both markets on the same days using the prices of available coupon bonds. Figure 14.1 (a) shows the US term structure for March 31, 1988 and Figure 14.1 (b) shows the Canadian term structure on the same day. Using these data they calculated "revealed spot rates" by following a simple arbitrage procedure that can be applied when there is more than one bond issue with the same maturity but different coupon rates. For example, consider the following two bonds:

|         | Coupon | Maturity | Price    | Principal |
|---------|--------|----------|----------|-----------|
| Bond 1: | 10.5 % | 95.02.15 | $110.78  | $100.00   |
| Bond 2: | 11.25% | 95.02.15 | $114.63  | $100.00   |

Shorting Bond 1 and buying Bond 2 in the correct proportions results in an arbitrage portfolio with a zero net coupon income. This can be achieved by selling $1125 of face value of Bond 1 and buying $1050 of face value of Bond 2 with the following result:

|         | Coupon Stream | Current Investment | Receipt at Maturity |
|---------|---------------|--------------------|---------------------|
| Bond 1: | $−118.125     | $−1246.48          | $−1125.00           |
| Bond 2: | $ 118.125     | $ 1203.62          | $ 1050.00           |
| Net     | $ 0.000       | $ 42.66            | $ −75.00            |

The net result is the same as borrowing $42.66 on March 31, 1988 and repaying $75.00 on February 15, 1995. The implied interest rate is 8.37% (neglecting transaction costs) — about 21 basis points lower than the risk-free spot rate for a 6.88 year bond. By examining all possible such combinations in both markets, the revealed spot rates across the maturity spectrum could be calculated. Figures 14.2 (a) and (b) show these revealed rates for US Treasury securities and Canadas respectively. Figure 14.2 (a) shows that there are some arbitrage opportunities to be exploited in the US market especially at the longer end of the maturity spectrum, but these are relatively small. Figure 14.2 (b) shows that there are substantially larger arbitrage opportunities in the Canadian market. Two factors may explain the differences, first, transactions costs in Canada are higher than those in the US and second, the returns on low coupon bonds receive favorable tax treatment in Canada which they do not in the US. The authors argue that the transactions costs

---

[11] W.Bailey, "The Effect of US Money Supply Announcements on Canadian Stock, Bond, and Currency Prices," *Canadian Journal of Economics* 22, no. 3 (August 1989):607–18.

[12] T.Appelt and E.Schulman, "The Government of Canada Bond Market: Is it Efficiently Priced?" *Canadian Investment Review* I, no.1 (Fall 1988):63–70.

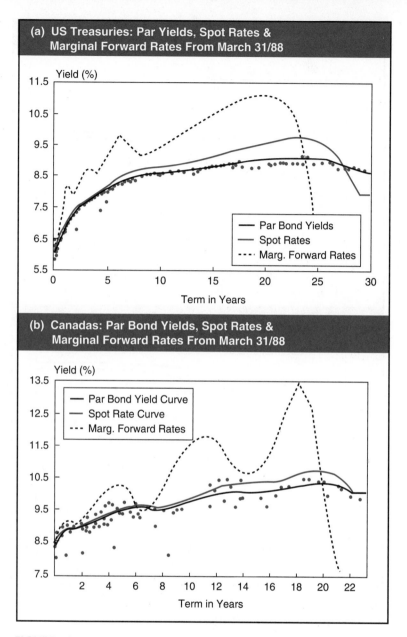

**FIGURE 14-1**

Par yields, spot rates, and marginal forward rates, March 31, 1988.

(a) US Treasuries

(b) Canadas

*SOURCE:* T. Appelt and E. Schulman, "The Government of Canada Bond Market: Is it Efficiently Priced?", *Canadian Investment Review*, I, no. 1 (Fall 1988):63–72.

in Canada would have to be two to three times the levels observed in the US to explain the differences and that taxation alone cannot explain the degree of mispricing of low coupon bonds. They conclude that there are arbitrageable opportunities in both markets

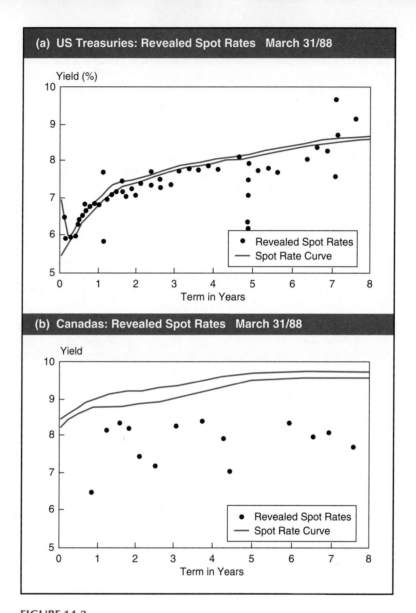

**FIGURE 14-2**
Revealed spot rates, March 31, 1988.
(a) US Treasuries
(b) Canadas

*SOURCE:* T. Appelt and E. Schulman, "The Government of Canada Bond Market: Is it Efficiently Priced?", *Canadian Investment Review* I, no. 1 (Fall 1988):63–72.

but more so in Canada. For these to be exploitable, however, it must be possible to borrow the securities (with margin requirements that are not onerous) that should be sold short.

In summary, the evidence on the efficiency of the bond market is consistent with the notion that it is highly, but not perfectly, semistrong-form efficient. Statistical tests of past prices of Treasury bills suggest it is efficient. It appears that corporate bonds reflect the information leading to a rating change in a timely fashion and that interest rates change rapidly when there is a surprise in the announced size of the money supply, observations that are also consistent with the notion of efficiency.

There is some evidence, however, suggesting that certain professionals are occasionally able to make accurate interest rate forecasts. It also appears that there are some limited arbitrage opportunities available. With this in mind, it is not surprising that some bond managers have opted to follow a passive approach to investing while others have decided to be more active. These two approaches are presented next, beginning with a discussion of some bond pricing theorems. In turn, these theorems will be related to duration, a concept introduced in Chapter 4, which is the basis for one method of passively managing a bond portfolio.

## 14.2 BOND-PRICING THEOREMS

Bond-pricing theorems deal with how bond prices move in response to changes in their yields-to-maturity. Before presenting the theorems, a brief review of some terms associated with bonds is given.

The typical bond is characterized by a promise to pay the investor two types of cash flows. The first involves the payment of a fixed dollar amount periodically (usually every six months), with the last payment being on a stated date. The second type of cash flow involves the payment of a lump sum on this stated date. The periodic payments are known as *coupon payments*, and the lump sum payment is known as the bond's principal (or par value or face value). A bond's *coupon rate* is calculated by dividing the dollar amount of the coupon payments a bondholder would receive over the course of a year by the principal of the bond. Lastly, the amount of time left until the last promised payment is made is known as the bond's *term-to-maturity*, whereas the discount rate that makes the present value of all the cash flows equal to the market price of the bond is known as the bond's *yield-to-maturity* (or, simply, yield).

Note that if a bond has a market price that is equal to its par value, then its yield-to-maturity will be equal to its coupon rate. However, if the market price is less than par value (a situation where the bond is said to be selling at a discount), then the bond will have a yield-to-maturity that is greater than the coupon rate. Conversely, if the market price is greater than par value (a situation where the bond is said to be selling at a premium), then the bond will have a yield-to-maturity that is less than the coupon rate.

With this in mind, five theorems that deal with bond pricing have been derived.[13] For ease of exposition, it is assumed that there is one coupon payment per year (that is, coupon payments are made every 12 months). The theorems are as follows:

---

[13] Burton G. Malkiel, "Expectations, Bond Prices, and the Term Structure of Interest Rates," *Quarterly Journal of Economics* 76, no. 2 (May 1962):197–218. Also see Frank J. Fabozzi and T. Dessa Fabozzi, *Bond Markets, Analysis and Strategies* (Englewood Cliffs, N.J.: Prentice Hall, 1989), particularly Chapter 4.

1. *If a bond's market price increases, then its yield must decrease; conversely, if a bond's market price decreases, then its yield must increase.*

As an example, consider bond A that has a life of five years and a par value of $1000 and pays coupons annually of $80. Its yield is 8%, since it is currently selling for $1000. However, if its price increases to $1100, then its yield will fall to 5.76%. Conversely, if its price falls to $900, then its yield will rise to 10.68%.

2. *If a bond's yield does not change over its life, then the size of its discount or premium will decrease as its life gets shorter.*

As an example, consider bond B that has a life of five years and a par value of $1000 and pays coupons annually of $60. Its current market price is $883.31, indicating it has a yield of 9%. After one year, if it still has a yield of 9%, it will be selling for $902.81. Thus, its discount has decreased from $1000 − $883.31 = $116.69 to $1000 − $902.81 = $97.19, for a change of $116.69 − $97.19 = $19.50.

An equivalent interpretation of this theorem is that if two bonds have the same coupon rate, par value, and yield, then the one with the shorter life will sell for a smaller discount or premium. Consider two bonds, one with a life of five years and the other with a life of four years. Both bonds have a par value of $1000, pay annual coupons of $60, and yield 9%. In this situation, the one with a five-year life has a discount of $116.69, whereas the one with a four-year life has a smaller discount of $97.19.

3. *If a bond's yield does not change over its life, then the size of its discount or premium will decrease at an increasing rate as it approaches maturity.*

As an example, consider bond B again. After two years, if it still has a yield of 9%, it will be selling for $924.06. Thus, its discount has decreased to $1000 − $924.06 = $75.94. Now, the amount of the change in the discount from five years to four years was $116.69 − $97.19 = $19.50, for a percentage change from par of 19.50%. However, the amount of the change from four years to three years is larger, going from $97.19 to $75.94, for a dollar change of $21.25 and a percentage change from par of 21.25%.

4. *A decrease in a bond's yield will raise the bond's price by an amount that is greater in size than the corresponding fall in the bond's price that would occur if there were an equal-sized increase in the bond's yield.*

As an example, consider bond C that has a life of five years and a coupon rate of 7%. Since it is currently selling at its par value of $1000, its yield is 7%. If its yield rises by 1% to 8%, then it will be selling for $960.07, a change of $39.93. Alternatively, if its yield falls by 1% to 6%, then it will be selling for $1042.12, a change of $42.12, which is of greater magnitude than the $39.93 associated with the 1% rise in the bond's yield.

This property is sometimes referred to as *convexity*, since a graph representing a bond's price as a function of its yield will be negatively sloped and convex.

5. *The percentage change in a bond's price due to a change in its yield will be smaller if its coupon rate is higher. (Note: This theorem does not apply to bonds with a life of one year or to bonds that have no maturity date, known as consols, or perpetuities.)*

As an example, compare bond D with bond C. Bond D has a coupon rate of 9%, which is 2% larger than C's. However, bond D has the same life (five years) and yield (7%) as C. Thus, D's current market price is $1082.00. If the yield on both C and D increases to 8%, then their prices will be $960.07 and $1039.93, respectively.

**TABLE 14.1**
Calculation of Duration.

| Time Until Receipt of Cash Flow | Amount of Cash Flow | Present Value Factor | Present Value of Cash Flow | Present Value of Cash Flow × Time |
|---|---|---|---|---|
| 1 | $ 80 | .9091 | $ 72.73 | $ 72.73 |
| 2 | 80 | .8264 | 66.12 | 132.23 |
| 3 | 1,080 | .7513 | 811.40 | 2434.21 |
| | | | $950.25 | $2639.17 |

$$\text{Duration} = \frac{\$2639.17}{\$950.25} = 2.78 \text{ years}$$

This represents a decrease in the price of C equal to $1000 − $960.07 = $39.93, or 3.993% (*note*: 3.993% = $39.93/$1000). For D, the decrease in price is equal to $1082 − $1039.93 = $42.07, or 3.889% (*note*: 3.889% = $42.07/$1082). Since D has the higher coupon rate, it has the smaller percentage change in price.

It is important for a bond analyst to understand thoroughly these properties of bond prices, since they are valuable in forecasting how bond prices will respond to changes in interest rates. In addition, duration is valuable in understanding how the prices of bonds change in response to a change in interest rates. This concept forms the basis for one method of passively managing a bond portfolio and is discussed next.

## 14.3 DURATION

One implication of theorem 5 is that bonds having the same maturity date but different coupon sizes may react to a given change in interest rates in a dissimilar manner. That is, the prices of these bonds may adjust by notably different amounts when there is a given change in interest rates. However, bonds with the same duration will react quite similarly.

## 14.3.1 Calculation

As mentioned in Chapter 4, *duration* is a measure of the "average maturity" of the stream of payments associated with a bond. More specifically, it is a weighted average of the lengths of time until the remaining payments are made. Consider, for example, a bond with annual coupon payments of $80, a remaining life of three years, and a par value of $1000. Since it has a current market price of $950.25, it has a yield-to-maturity of 10.00%. As shown in Table 14.1, its duration is 2.78 years. Note that this is calculated by taking the present value of each cash flow, multiplying each one by the respective amount of time until it is received, summing the resulting figures up, and then dividing this sum ($2639.17) by the market price of the bond ($950.25).

Specifically, the formula for a bond's duration ($D$) is

$$D = \frac{\sum_{t=1}^{T} PV(C_t) \times t}{P_0} \qquad (14.1)$$

where $PV(C_t)$ denotes the present value of the cash flow to be received at time $t$, calculated using a discount rate equal to the bond's yield-to-maturity; $P_0$ denotes the current market price of the bond; and $T$ denotes the bond's remaining life.[14]

Why is duration thought of as the "average maturity of the stream of payments associated with a bond?" This can be seen by realizing that the current market price of the bond, $P_0$, is equal to the sum of the present values of the cash flows, $PV(C_t)$, where the discount rate is the bond's yield-to-maturity:

$$P_0 = \sum_{t=1}^{T} PV(C_t). \qquad (14.2)$$

Thus, there is an equivalent method for calculating a bond's duration that can be seen by rewriting equation (14.1) in a slightly different manner:

$$D = \sum_{t=1}^{T} \left[ \frac{PV(C_t)}{P_0} \times t \right]. \qquad (14.3)$$

First, the present value of each cash flow [$PV(C_t)$] is expressed as a proportion of the market price ($P_0$). Second, these proportions are multiplied by the respective amount of time until the cash flows are received. Third, these figures are added, with the sum being equal to the bond's duration.

In the example shown in Table 14.1, note that $72.73/\$950.25 = .07653$ of the bond's market price is to be received in one year. Similarly, $66.12/\$950.25 = .06958$ is to be received in two years, and $811.40/\$950.25 = .85388$ is to be received in three years. Note how these proportions sum to one, which means that they can be interpreted as weights in calculating a weighted average. Thus, to calculate the average maturity of the payments associated with a bond, each weight needs to be multiplied by the respective amount of time until the corresponding cash flow is to be received, and then the products need to be summed up: $(1 \times .07653) + (2 \times .06958) + (3 \times .85388) = 2.78$ years.

Note how a zero-coupon bond will have a duration equal to its remaining life, $T$, since there is only one cash flow associated with such a bond. That is, since $P_0 =$

[14] There are other methods of calculating a bond's duration. For example, instead of using the bond's yield to calculate $PV(C_t)$, the appropriate current spot rate could be used. The concept of duration was initially developed in 1938 by Frederick R. Macauley, a Canadian actuary, in *Some Theoretical Problems Suggested by the Movements of Interest Rates, Bond Yields, and Stock Prices in the United States Since 1856* (New York: National Bureau of Economic Research). For an interesting article describing the development of the concept of duration (as well as immunization), see Roman L. Weil, "Macaulay's Duration: An Appreciation," *Journal of Business* 46, no. 4 (October 1973):589–92.

PV($C_T$) for such bonds, equation (14.3) reduces to:

$$D = \frac{\text{PV}(C_T)}{P_0} \times T$$
$$= 1 \times T$$
$$= T.$$

For any coupon-bearing bond, its duration will always be less than the amount of time to its maturity date, $T$. Again, examination of equation (14.3) indicates why this is so. Since the largest value that $t$ can have is $T$, and each value of $t$ is multiplied by a weight equal to PV($C_t$)/$P_0$, it follows that $D$ must be less than $T$.

## ☐ 14.3.2 Changes in the Term Structure

As mentioned earlier, when interest rates change, most bond prices also change, but some react more than others. Even bonds with the same maturity date can react quite differently to a given change in interest rates. However, it can be shown that the percentage change in a bond's price is related to its duration in the following fashion:

$$\begin{array}{ccc} \text{Percentage} & & \text{percentage change} \\ \text{change in} & \cong -D \times & \text{in (one plus the} \\ \text{price} & & \text{bond's yield} \end{array} \qquad (14.4)$$

where the symbol $\cong$ means "is approximately equal to." This formula implies that when the yields of two bonds having the same duration change by the same percentage, then the prices of the two bonds will change by approximately equal percentages.

For example, the bond shown in Table 14.1 had a duration of 2.78 and a yield of 10%. If its yield changes to 11%, then the percentage change in (one plus the bond's yield) is $(1.11 - 1.10)/(1.10) = .91\%$. Thus, its price should change by approximately $-2.78 \times .91\% = -2.53\%$. Using a discount rate of 11%, its price can be calculated to equal $926.69, for an actual price change of $950.25 - $926.69 = $23.56 and a percentage change of $23.56/$950.25 = 2.48\%$. Any other bond having a duration of 2.78 years will experience a similar price change if it has a similar percentage change in its yield.

Consider a bond with a maturity of four years that also has a duration of 2.78 years. When there is a shift in interest rates and the yields on the three- and four-year bonds change by the same amount, then their prices will change similarly. For example, if the yield on the four-year bond goes from 10.8% to 11.81% at the same time the yield on the three-year bond is going from 10% to 11%, then the percentage change in the present value of the four-year bond will be approximately $-2.78 \times [(1.1181 - 1.108)/1.108] = -2.78 \times .91\% = 2.53\%$, which is the same as the percentage change for the three-year bond.

What if the percentage change in one plus the bond's yield is different? Perhaps when the three-year bond goes from a yield of 10% to a yield of 11% (a percentage change of $(1.11 - 1.10)/1.10 = .91\%$), the four-year bond will go from a yield of 10.8% to a yield of 11.5% (a percentage change of $(1.115 - 1.108)/1.108 = .63\%$). In this case, the percentage change in price for the four-year bond will be approximately $-2.78 \times [(1.115 - 1.108)/(1.108)] = -1.75\%$, which is a smaller change than the -2.53% associated with the three-year bond. Accordingly, even though the two bonds have the same duration, it does not automatically follow that their prices will react identically to any change in yields, since these yield changes can be different for two bonds having the same duration.

## 14.4    IMMUNIZATION

The introduction of the concept of duration has led to the development of the technique of bond portfolio management known as *immunization*.[15] Specifically, this technique allegedly allows a bond portfolio manager to be relatively certain of being able to meet a given promised stream of cash outflows. Thus, once the portfolio has been formed, it is "immunized" from any adverse effects associated with future changes in interest rates.

## ☐ 14.4.1  How Immunization Is Accomplished

Immunization is accomplished by simply calculating the duration of the promised outflows and then investing in a portfolio of bonds that have an identical duration. In doing so, this technique takes advantage of the observation that the *duration of a portfolio of bonds is equal to the weighted average of the durations of the individual bonds in the portfolio.* For example, if one-third of a portfolio's funds are invested in bonds having a duration of six years and two-thirds of its funds are in bonds having a duration of three years, then the portfolio itself has a duration of $[(1/3) \times 6] + [(2/3) \times 3] = 4$ years.

Consider a simple situation where a portfolio manager has one and only one cash outflow to make from his or her portfolio — an amount equal to $1,000,000 that is to be paid in two years. Since there is only one cash outflow, its duration is simply two years. Now, the bond portfolio manager is considering investing in two different bond issues. The first bond issue is the one shown in Table 14.1, where the bonds have a maturity of three years. The second bond issue involves a set of bonds that mature in one year, providing the holder of each bond with a single payment of $1070 (consisting of a single coupon payment of $70 and a par value of $1000). Since these bonds are currently selling for $972.73, their yield-to-maturity is 10%.

Consider the choices open to the portfolio manager. All the portfolio's funds could be invested in the one-year bonds, with the notion of reinvesting the proceeds from the maturing bonds one year from now in another one-year issue. However, doing so would entail risks. In particular, if interest rates were to decline over the next year, then the funds from the maturing one-year bonds must be reinvested at a lower rate than the currently available 10%. Thus, the portfolio manager faces reinvestment-rate risk due to the possibility that the funds one year from now can only be reinvested at a lower rate.[16]

[15] For the initial development, see F. M. Redington, "Review of the Principles of Life-Office Valuations," *Journal of the Institute of Actuaries* 78, no. 3 (1952):286–315. A useful book that discusses duration-based investment strategies has been written by Gerald O. Bierwag, entitled *Duration Analysis* (Cambridge, Mass: Ballinger Publishing Company, 1987).

[16] If there were two-year coupon-bearing bonds available for investment, then there would be no reinvestment-rate risk associated with the principal. However, the investor would still face reinvestment-rate risk in terms of the coupon payments received after one year. Although such risk appears to be relatively minor in this example, such risk becomes much more substantial in situations involving promised cash outflows that are more than two years into the future.

A second alternative would be for the portfolio manager to invest all the funds in the three-year issue. However, this also entails risks. In particular, the three-year bonds will have to be sold after two years in order to come up with the $1,000,000. The risk is that interest rates will have risen before then, meaning that bond prices, in general, will have fallen and the bonds will not have a selling price that is equal to or greater than $1,000,000. Thus, the portfolio manager faces interest-rate risk with this strategy.

One proposed solution is to invest part of the portfolio's funds in the one-year bonds and the rest in the three-year bonds. How much should be placed in each issue? If immunization is to be used, the solution can be found by solving simultaneously a set of two equations involving two unknowns:

$$W_1 + W_3 = 1 \qquad (14.5)$$
$$(W_1 \times 1) + (W_3 \times 2.78) = 2. \qquad (14.6)$$

Here, $W_1$ and $W_3$ denote the weights (or proportions) of the portfolio's funds that are to be invested in the bonds with maturities of one and three years, respectively. Note how equation (14.5) states that the sum of the weights must equal 1, whereas equation (14.6) states that the weighted average of the durations of the bonds in the portfolio must equal the duration of the cash outflow, which is two years.

The solution to these two equations is easily found. First, equation (14.5) is rewritten as

$$W_1 = 1 - W_3. \qquad (14.7)$$

Then, $1 - W_3$ is substituted for $W_1$ in equation (14.6), resulting in

$$[(1 - W_3) \times 1] + (W_3 \times 2.78) = 2. \qquad (14.8)$$

Since this is one equation with one unknown, $W_3$, it can be easily solved. Doing so results in $W_3 = .5618$. Inserting this value into equation (14.7) indicates that $W_1 = .4382$. Thus, the portfolio manager should put 43.82% of the portfolio's funds in the one-year bonds and 56.18% in the three-year bonds.

In this case, the portfolio manager would need $1,000,000/(1.10^2) = $826,446$ in order to purchase bonds that would create a fully immunized portfolio. With this money, $.4382 \times $826,446 = $362,149$ would be used to buy one-year bonds and $.5618 \times $826,446 = $464,297$ would be used to buy three-year bonds. Since the current market prices of the one-year and three-year bonds are $972.73 and $950.25, respectively, this means that 372 (= $362,149/$972.73) one-year bonds and 489 (= $464,297/$950.25) three-year bonds would be purchased.

What does immunization accomplish? According to theory, if yields rise, then the portfolio's losses due to the selling of the three-year bonds at a discount after two years will be exactly offset by the gains from reinvesting the maturing one-year bonds (and first-year coupons on the three-year bonds) at the higher rate. Alternatively, if yields fall, then the loss from being able to reinvest the maturing one-year bonds (and first-year coupons on the three-year bonds) at a lower rate will be exactly offset by being able to sell the three-year bonds after two years at a premium. Thus, the portfolio is immunized from the effect of any movements in the interest rates in the future.

Table 14.2 shows more explicitly what would happen to the portfolio. The second column shows what the portfolio would be worth at the end of two years if yields remained at 10% over the next two years. As can be seen, the value of the portfolio of one-year and three-year bonds would be approximately equal to the promised cash outflow of $1,000,000. Alternatively, if yields fell to 9% or rose to 11% before one year had passed and remained at the new level, then value of the portfolio would be slightly more than the needed $1,000.000.

**TABLE 14.2**
An Example of an Immunized Portfolio.

| | Yield-to Maturity at the end of One Year | | |
|---|---|---|---|
| | 9% | 10% | 11% |
| Value at $t = 2$ from reinvesting one-year bond proceeds: | | | |
| $[\$1070 \times 372.3 \times (1 + y)] =$ | $ 434,213 | $438,197 | $ 442,181 |
| Value at $t = 2$ of three-year bonds: | | | |
| Value from reinvesting coupons received at $t = 1$: | | | |
| $[\$80 \times 488.6 \times (1 + y)] =$ | 42,606 | 42,997 | 43,388 |
| Coupons received at $t = 2$: | | | |
| $[\$80 \times 488.6] =$ | 39,088 | 39,088 | 39,088 |
| Selling price at $t = 2$: | | | |
| $[\$1080 \times 488.6/(1 + y)] =$ | 484,117 | 479,716 | 475,395 |
| Aggregate portfolio value at $t = 2$ | $1,000,024 | $999,998 | $1,000,052 |

## ☐ 14.4.2  Problems with Immunization

The previous paragraph described what immunization accomplishes in theory. This leaves open the possibility that it might not work quite as well in practice. What can cause it to work less than perfectly? In terms of the example, what can cause the value of the portfolio to be less than $1,000,000 at the end of two years?

### Default and Call Risk

To begin with, immunization is based on the belief that all the bonds' promised cash flows will subsequently be paid in full and on time. This means that immunization is based on the assumption that the bond will not default and will not be called before maturity — that is, the bonds are assumed to be free from both call risk and default risk. Consequently, if a bond in the portfolio either enters into default or is called, the portfolio will not be immunized.[17]

---

[17] For a discussion of how to include nondefault-free callable bonds in an immunized portfolio, see Gordon J. Alexander and Bruce G. Resnick, "Using Linear and Goal Programming to Immunize Bond Portfolios," *Journal of Banking and Finance* 9, no. 1 (March 1985):35–54; and G. O. Bierwag and George G. Kaufman, "Durations of Non-Default-Free Securities," *Financial Analysts Journal* 44, no. 4 (July/August 1988):39–46, 62.

## Multiple Nonparallel Shifts in a Nonhorizontal Yield Curve

Immunization is also based on the assumption that the yield curve is horizontal and that any shifts in it will be parallel and will occur before any payments are received from the bonds that were purchased. In the example, both the one-year and three-year bonds had the same 10% yield-to-maturity at the start, and the shift of 1% in yields was assumed to be the same for both bond issues. Furthermore, this shift was assumed to occur sometime before one year had passed.

In reality, the yield curve will not be horizontal at the start, and shifts in it are not likely to be either parallel or restricted in when they occur. Perhaps the one-year and three-year bonds will have initial yields of 10% and 10.5%, respectively, with the yields on the one-year and three-year bonds falling by 1% and .8%, respectively, after one year. Indeed, there is evidence that there is greater volatility in yields of shorter-term securities.[18] If these kinds of shifts were to occur, then it is possible that the portfolio would not be immunized.

If the bond portfolio manager followed a special kind of immunization known as *cash matching*, then frequent nonparallel shifts in a nonhorizontal yield curve would have no adverse effect on the portfolio. This is because cash matching involves the purchase of bonds so that the cash received each period from the bonds is identical in size to the promised cash outflow for that period.

Such a cash-matching portfolio of bonds is often referred to as a *dedicated portfolio*. Note that there is no need to reinvest any cash inflows in the future with a dedicated portfolio, so there is no reinvestment rate risk. Furthermore, since bonds do not have to be sold prior to maturity, there is no interest rate risk either.[19]

In the simplest situation where there is one promised cash outflow, the dedicated portfolio would consist of zero-coupon bonds, where each bond has a life corresponding to the date of the promised cash outflow. In the previous example where there was a promised cash outflow of $1,000,000 after two years, this would be accomplished by purchasing the requisite number of zero-coupon bonds having a maturity of two years.

However, cash matching is often not so easily accomplished. This is because the promised cash outflows may involve an uneven stream of payments for which no zero-coupon bonds exist. Indeed, it can be difficult (if not impossible) and expensive to match cash inflows exactly with promised outflows.

Another potential way around the problem of having nonhorizontal yield curves that have nonparallel shifts is to use one of a variety of more complicated immunization models. These models involve various other assumptions about the current shape of the yield curve and how it will shift in the future. Consequently, the bond portfolio manager must choose the one that is personally viewed as being most accurate. Interestingly, various studies have found that the best performer was the version of immunization that has been described in this chapter, and not the more complicated models. Thus, some

---

[18] See in George G. Kaufman, G. O. Bierwag, and Alden Toevs, eds., *Innovations in Bond Portfolio Management: Duration Analysis and Immunization* (Greenwich, Conn: JAI Press Inc., 1983) the articles by Jeffrey Nelson and Stephen Schaefer, "The Dynamics of the Term Structure and Alternative Portfolio Immunization Strategies," 61–101, and Jonathan E. Ingersoll, Jr., "Is Immunization Feasible? Evidence from the CRSP Data," 163–82.

[19] For more on dedicated portfolios, see Martin L. Leibowitz, "The Dedicated Bond Portfolio in Pension Funds — Part I: Motivations and Basics," *Financial Analysts Journal* 42, no. 1 (January/February 1986):69–75, and "The Dedicated Bond Portfolio in Pension Funds-Part II: Immunization, Horizon Matching and Contingent Procedures," *Financial Analysts Journal* 42, no. 2 (March/April 1986):47–57.

researchers argue that the portfolio manager interested in immunization would be well advised to use this version.[20]

An implication is that regardless of the model being used, the bond portfolio manager must recognize that there is a risk being incurred — the risk that the yield curve will shift in a way that does not correspond with the way assumed by the model. For example, if the model presented here is used, then the bond portfolio is facing risk in that the yield curve will not shift in a parallel manner. Consequently, some people have argued that none of the immunization models are useful.[21] Others have argued that there are ways to use immunization in the presence of such risk, which has been called *stochastic process risk*.[22]

## Rebalancing

Another problem with the use of immunization is the effect of the passage of time on the duration of the bonds held and on the duration of the promised cash outflows. As time passes and yields change, these durations can change at different rates so that the portfolio is no longer immunized. This means that the portfolio may need to be *rebalanced* fairly often.

Here, rebalancing refers to selling some bonds currently held and replacing them with others so that afterward, the duration of the portfolio matches the duration of the promised cash outflows. However, since rebalancing causes the portfolio manager to incur transaction costs, the manager might not want to rebalance whenever the durations do not match, since the costs might outweigh the perceived gains from rebalancing. Ultimately, the bond portfolio manager will have to decide how frequently to rebalance the portfolio, taking into consideration the risk of being unbalanced along with the transaction costs associated with rebalancing.

## Choosing Among Many Candidates

Lastly, there are usually many portfolios that have a duration of the requisite length. Which one is the bond portfolio manager to choose? In the example, imagine that in addition to the one-year and three-year bonds, there is a zero-coupon bond having a life of four years (thus, its duration is also four years) that the manager is considering. Now the manager faces a choice of which portfolio to hold, since there are many with the requisite duration of two years. In addition to the one previously described that consisted of just one-year and three-year bonds, there is also one where two-thirds and one-third of the portfolio's funds are invested in one-year bonds and four-year bonds, respectively.

---

[20] For a summary and set of references, see G. O. Bierwag, George G. Kaufman, Robert Schweitzer, and Alden Toevs, "The Art of Risk Management in Bond Portfolios," *Journal of Portfolio Management* 7, no. 3 (Spring 1981):27-36; G. O. Bierwag, George G. Kaufman, and Alden Toevs, "Duration: Its Development and Use in Bond Portfolio Management," *Financial Analysts Journal* 39, no. 4 (July-August 1983):15–35; and Stephen M. Schaefer, "Immunization and Duration: A Review of Theory, Performance and Applications," *Midland Corporate Finance Journal* 2, no. 3 (Fall 1984):41–58.

[21] See N. Bulent Gultekin and Richard J. Rogalski, "Alternative Duration Specifications and the Measurement of Basis Risk," *Journal of Business* 57, no. 2 (April 1984):241–64; for a rebuttal, see G. O. Bierwag, George G. Kaufman, Cynthia M. Latta, and Gordon S. Roberts, "Duration: Response to Critics," *Journal of Portfolio Management* 13, no. 2 (Winter 1987):48–52.

[22] G. O. Bierwag, George G. Kaufman, and Alden Toevs, "Bond Portfolio Immunization and Stochastic Process Risk," *Journal of Bank Research* 13 (Winter 1983):282–91.

(Note how the duration of this portfolio is also two years: $(^2/_3 \times 1) + (^1/_3 \times 4) = 2$.) Furthermore, there are many other candidate portfolios.

One possible solution is to choose the portfolio having the highest average yield-to-maturity. Here, the yield of each issue is multiplied by the percentage of the portfolio's funds that are invested in that issue. Another possible solution is to choose the portfolio that most closely resembles a "bullet," or "focused," portfolio, since it has been argued that such a portfolio has less stochastic process risk than any other. Such a portfolio is one where the bonds in it have durations (or, alternatively, term-to-maturities) most closely matching the duration of the promised outflows. In the example, the portfolio consisting of just one-year and three-year bonds is more focused than the one consisting of the one-year and four-year bonds.

Two Canadian studies have found that the simple Macauley measure of duration, despite stochastic process risk, explains about 80% of the variability in Government of Canada bond returns. Furthermore, a simple portfolio construction procedure worked as effectively as the bullet portfolio. The simple procedure consisted in first choosing a bond with a maturity equal to the horizon date and then adding a second bond with a longer duration in the appropriate proportions to make the portfolio duration equal to the horizon.[23]

---

## 14.5    ACTIVE MANAGEMENT

As mentioned earlier, active management of a bond portfolio is based on the belief that the bond market is not perfectly efficient. Such management can involve security selection, where attempts are made at identifying mispriced bonds. Alternatively, it can involve market timing, where attempts are made at forecasting general movements in interest rates. It is also possible for an active portfolio manager to be involved in both security selection and market timing. While there are a large number of methods of actively managing a bond portfolio, some general types of active management can be described.

## ☐ 14.5.1   Horizon Analysis

The return on a bond over any given holding period depends on its price at the beginning of the period and its price at the end of the period, as well as its coupon rate. Thus, the return on a bond over a one-year period will depend on the yield structure at the beginning of the year and the yield structure at the end of the year, since the price of the bond at these two points in time will depend on these structures. It follows that possible subsequent changes to the beginning-of-period yield structure must be analyzed in order to analyze possible bond returns over a given holding period. Bond portfolio managers who believe they (or their staffs) are able to identify such changes will want to translate their beliefs into action.

---

[23] For a discussion of how to select the "best" immunizing portfolio, see Alexander and Resnick, "Using Linear and Goal Programming to Immunize Bond Portfolios."; I.Fooladi and G.Roberts, "How Effective are Duration-based Bond Strategies in Canada?" *Canadian Investment Review*, II, no. 1 (Spring 1989):57–62; G.O.Bierwag, I.Fooladi and G.Roberts, "Designing an Immunized Portfolio: Is M-Squared the Key?" Dalhousie University Working Paper, October 1988.

One way of doing this is known as *horizon analysis*, where a single holding period is selected for analysis and possible yield structures at the end of the period (that is, at the "horizon") are considered.[24] The possible returns for two bonds — one currently held and one candidate to replace it — are then analyzed. In doing so, neither bond is assumed to default up to the horizon date. In the process of the analysis, the sensitivities of the returns to changes in key assumptions regarding yields are estimated, allowing at least a rough assessment of some of the relevant risks.

Horizon analysis can be viewed as another way of implementing the capitalization-of-income method of valuation that was discussed in Chapter 13. By focusing on the estimated end-of-period price of a bond, it seeks to determine if the current market price is relatively high or low. That is, for a given estimated end-of-period price, a bond will have a relatively high expected return if its current price is relatively low. Conversely, a bond will have a relatively low expected return if its current price is relatively high.

Figure 14.3 represents a page from a standard yield book for bonds with a 4% coupon. As indicated, a 4% bond with ten years remaining to maturity that is currently priced at $67.48 (for ease of exposition, a par of $100 is used here) will have a 9% promised annual yield-to-maturity (or 4.5% semiannually). Five years into the future, such a bond's term-to-maturity will have decreased and the relevant promised yield-to-maturity will probably have changed. Thus, as time passes, the bond might follow a path through the table such as that shown by the dashed line. If so, it would end up at a price of $83.78 at the horizon (five years hence), with an 8% promised annual yield-to-maturity (or 4% semiannually).

Over any holding period, a bond's return typically will be affected by both the passage of time and a change in yields. Horizon analysis breaks this into two parts: one due solely to the passage of time, with no change in yields, and the other due solely to a change in yield, with no passage of time. This is illustrated in Figure 14.3. The total price change from $67.48 to $83.78 (or $16.30) is broken into a change from $67.48 to $80.22 (or $12.74), followed by an instantaneous change from $80.22 to $83.78 (or $3.56). The intermediate value is the price the bond would command at the horizon if its promised yield-to-maturity had remained unchanged at its initial level of 9%. The actual price is that which it commands at its actual yield-to-maturity of 8%. In summary, the total price change can be broken into two parts, representing the two effects:

$$\text{Price change} = \text{time effect} + \text{yield change effect}. \qquad (14.9)$$

Thus far, no account has been taken of the coupon payments to be received before the horizon date. In principle, one should consider all possible uses of such cash flows or at least analyze possible alternative yield structures during the period to determine likely reinvestment opportunities. In practice, this is rarely done. Instead, a single reinvestment rate is assumed and the future value of all coupon payments at the horizon date is determined by compounding each one using this rate.[25] This takes care of both interest (coupons) and "interest on interest" (that is, interest earned from reinvesting coupon

---

[24] See Martin L. Leibowitz, "Horizon Analysis for Managed Bond Portfolios," *Journal of Portfolio Management* 1, no. 3 (Spring (1975):23–34, and "An Analytic Approach to the Bond Market," in *Financial Analyst's Handbook*, ed. Sumner N. Levine (Homewood, Ill.: Dow Jones-Irwin, Inc., 1975), 226–77.

[25] The longer the horizon, the greater the importance of the size of the reinvestment rate in determining a bond's return. This means that if the investor's horizon is greater than ten years for example, then alternative reinvestment rates should be considered.

| Yield to Maturity (%) | YEARS TO MATURITY 10 Yrs ... | 9 Yrs ... | 5 Yrs | 1 Yrs | 0 Yrs |
|---|---|---|---|---|---|
| 7.00 | 78.68 | 80.22 | 87.53 | 97.15 | 100.00 |
| 7.50 | 75.68 | 77.39 | 85.63 | 96.69 | 100.00 |
| $Y_H$ (8.00) | 72.82 | 74.68 | (83.78) ← $P_H$ | 96.23 | 100.00 |
| 8.50 | 70.09 | 72.09 | 81.98 | 95.77 | 100.00 |
| | | Actual Price Pattern Over Time | Yield Change Effect | | |
| $Y_O$ (9.00) $P_O$ (67.48) | 69.60 | (83.78) → $P_A$ | | 95.32 | 100.00 |
| | | Time Effect | | | |
| 9.50 | 64.99 | 67.22 | 78.51 | 94.87 | 100.00 |
| 10.00 | 62.61 | 64.92 ... | 76.83 ... | 94.42 | 100.00 |
| 10.50 | 60.34 | 62.74 | 75.21 | 93.98 | 100.00 |
| 11.00 | 58.17 | 60.64 | 73.62 | 93.54 | 100.00 |

**FIGURE 14-3**

The effect of time and yield change on a 4% coupon bond. *Note:* $Y_0$ and $P_0$ denote the bond's yield-to-maturity and price at the beginning of the period; $Y_H$ and $P_H$ denote the bond's yield-to-maturity and price at the horizon (that is, at the end of the period); $P_A$ denotes the bond's price at the horizon if its yield had remained at $Y_0 = 9\%$; yields are compounded semiannually.

SOURCE: William L. Leibowitz, "Horizon Analysis for Managed Bond Portfolios," *Journal of Portfolio Management* 1, no. 3 (Spring 1975):26.

payments), with only the former being accurately predictable at the beginning of the period.

For example, if $2 is received every six months (as in Figure 14.3) with the first payment occurring six months from now and the last one occurring five years from now, and each payment is reinvested at 4.25% per six months, then the value of the end of five years will be approximately $24.29. Of this amount, $20 can be considered interest (coupon payments of $2 for 10 six-month periods) with the remaining $4.29 being interest on interest.

In summary, a bond's overall dollar return has four components — the time effect, the yield change effect, the coupons, and the interest from reinvesting the coupons. In the example, the overall dollar return is:

$$\begin{aligned}
\begin{matrix} \text{Overall} \\ \text{dollar} \\ \text{return} \end{matrix} &= \begin{matrix} \text{time} \\ \text{effect} \end{matrix} + \begin{matrix} \text{yield} \\ \text{change} \\ \text{effect} \end{matrix} + \text{coupons} + \begin{matrix} \text{interest} \\ \text{on} \\ \text{coupons} \end{matrix} \\
&= (\$80.22 - \$67.48) + (\$83.78 - \$80.22) + \$20.00 + \$4.29 \\
&= \$12.74 + \$3.56 + \$20.00 + \$4.29 \\
&= \$40.59.
\end{aligned}$$

This overall dollar return can be converted into an overall rate of return by dividing it by the market price of the bond at the beginning of the period, $67.48. In doing so, it can be seen that a bond's overall rate of return consists of four components:

$$\begin{aligned}
\begin{matrix} \text{Overall} \\ \text{dollar} \\ \text{return} \end{matrix} &= \frac{\$12.74}{\$67.48} + \frac{\$3.56}{\$67.48} + \frac{\$20.00}{\$67.48} + \frac{\$4.29}{\$67.48} \\
&= .1888 + .0528 + .2964 + .0635 \\
&= .6015
\end{aligned}$$

or 60.15%. The first term is the return due to the passage of time, the second term is the return due to yield change, the third term is coupon return, and the fourth term is the return due to the reinvestment of the coupon payments.

Since the second term is uncertain, it is important to analyze it further. In the example, a change in yield from 9.0% to 8.0% will result in a change in the market price from $80.22 to $83.78. Given 8.0% was the expected yield at the horizon, an expected overall rate of return of 60.15% was computed. By using different end-of-period yields, different overall rates of return can be calculated. Then, with estimates of the probabilities of these yields occurring, a feel for the bond's risk can be obtained. Indeed, it can now be seen why bond portfolio managers devote a great deal of attention to making predictions of future yields.

## ☐ 14.5.2 Bond Swaps

Given a set of predictions about future bond yields, holding-period returns over one or more horizons for one or more bonds can be estimated. The goal of *bond swapping* is to manage a portfolio actively by exchanging bonds to take advantage of any superior ability to predict such yields.[26] In making a swap, the portfolio manager believes that an overpriced bond is being exchanged for an underpriced bond. Some swaps are based on the belief that the market will correct for its mispricing in a short period of time, whereas other types of swaps are based on a belief that corrections will either never take place or will take place over a long period of time.

There are a large number of categories for classifying swaps, and the distinctions between the categories are often blurred. Nevertheless, many bond swaps can be placed in one of four general categories:

---

[26] Bond swaps should not be confused with interest rate swaps, where two issuers of debt keep the respective amounts raised but exchange interest payments. See, for example, Stuart M. Turnbull, "Swaps: A Zero Sum Game?" *Financial Management* 16, no. 1 (Spring 1987):15–21.

Ideally, the *substitution swap* is an exchange of a bond for a perfect substitute, or "twin" bond. The motivation here is temporary price advantage, presumably resulting from a momentary imbalance in the relative supply/demand conditions in the marketplace.

The *intermarket spread swap* is a more general movement out of one market component and into another with the intention of exploiting a currently advantageous yield relationship. The idea here is to take advantage of these changing relationships between the two market components. Although such swaps will almost always have some sensitivity to the direction of the overall market, the idealized focus of this type of swap is the spread relationship itself.

The *rate anticipation swap*, on the other hand, is designed to profit from an anticipated movement in overall market rates.

The *pure-yield pickup swap* is oriented toward yield improvements over the long term with little heed being paid to interim price movements in either the respective market components or the market as a whole.[27]

Consider a hypothetical portfolio manager who holds some of a 30-year, AA utility bond issue that has a 7% coupon rate. Since these bonds are currently selling at par, their yield-to-maturity is 7%. Now, imagine that there is another 30-year, AA utility bond issue with a 7% coupon rate that is being made available to the manager at a price so that its yield-to-maturity is 7.10%. An example of a substitution swap is where the manager exchanges a given dollar amount of the currently held bonds for an equivalent dollar amount of the second bond issue, thereby picking up 10 basis points in yield.

Alternatively, the manager might note that there is a 10-year, AA utility bond issue outstanding that carries a 6% coupon and is priced at par; thus, its yield is 6%. In this case, there is a 100-basis-point yield spread between the currently held 30-year bonds and the 10-year bonds. If the manager feels this spread is too low, then an intermarket spread swap might be used where some of the 30-year bonds are exchanged for an equivalent dollar amount of the 10-year bonds. Since the manager expects the spread to increase in the future, the yield on the 10-year bonds is expected to fall. This means the price on these bonds is expected to rise by an abnormal amount, resulting in an abnormally high holding-period return.

Another possibility is that the manager feels that yields in general are going to rise. In such a situation, the manager will recognize that the currently held portfolio is very risky because longer-term bonds generally move downward further in price for a given rise in yields than do shorter-term bonds. Accordingly, the manager might use a rate anticipation swap to exchange a given dollar amount of the 30-year bonds for an equivalent amount of some short-term bonds.

Lastly, the manager might not want to make any predictions about future yields or yield spreads. Instead, it might simply be noted that some 30-year, AA industrial bonds are currently priced to yield 8%. In this case, the manager might want to enter a pure-yield pickup swap, where some of the 7% utility bonds are exchanged for an equivalent dollar amount of the 8% industrial bonds, the motivation being to earn the extra 100 basis points in yield from the industrials.

---

[27] Martin L. Leibowitz, "Horizon Analysis for Managed Bond Portfolios," *Journal of Portfolio Management* 1, no. 3 (Spring 1975):32-33. See also Sidney Homer and Martin L. Leibowitz, *Inside the Yield Book* (Englewood Cliffs, N.J.: Prentice Hall, 1972) and Chapter 16 in Marcia Stigum and Frank J. Fabozzi, *The Dow Jones-Irwin Guide to Bond and Money Market Investments* (Homewood, Ill.: Dow Jones-Irwin, Inc., 1987).

### ☐ 14.5.3  Contingent Immunization

One method of bond portfolio management that has both passive and active elements is *contingent immunization*. In the simplest form of contingent immunization, the portfolio is actively managed as long as favorable results are obtained. However, if unfavorable results occur, then the portfolio is immediately immunized.

As an illustration, consider the earlier example where the portfolio manager had to come up with $1,000,000 at the end of two years, and the current yield curve was horizontal at 10%. In this situation, it was mentioned that the portfolio manager could immunize the portfolio by investing $826,446 in one-year and three-year bonds. However, it may be that the portfolio manager convinces the client that the portfolio should be contingently immunized with $841,680. This means that the portfolio manager must be certain that the portfolio will be worth at least $1,000,000 at the end of the two years, with any excess going to the client and the manager being compensated accordingly. Equivalently, the portfolio manager must earn a minimum average return of 9% (note that $841,680 \times 1.09^2 = \$1,000,000$) over the two years. Here, the client is willing to settle for as low a return as 9% but hopes that the portfolio manager will be able to exceed the 10% return that could have been locked in with an immunized portfolio.

In this situation, the manager would proceed to manage the portfolio actively by attempting to engage either in selectivity or timing (or both). Perhaps the arrangement with the client is that the status of the portfolio will be reviewed weekly, and yields that are currently available will be determined.

Consider how the review would be conducted after one year has elapsed and the yield curve is still horizontal but at 11%. First of all, it is noted that $\$1,000,000/(1.11) = \$900,901$ would be needed to immunize the portfolio at that point. Second, the market value of the current portfolio is determined to be $930,000. Now, in this example, the arrangement between the client and portfolio manager is that the manager can continue to manage the portfolio actively as long as it is worth at least $10,000 more than the amount needed for immunization. Since it is worth $930,000, an amount greater than $900,901 + \$10,000 = \$910,901$, the portfolio manager can continue being active. However, if the portfolio had been worth less than $910,901, then, according to the agreement, the manager would have immediately immunized the portfolio.[28]

### ☐ 14.5.4  Riding the Yield Curve

*Riding the yield curve* is a method of bond portfolio management sometimes used by people who, having liquidity as a primary objective, invest in short-term fixed-income securities. One way of investing is simply to purchase these securities, hold them until

---

[28] For more on contingent immunization, see the articles by Leibowitz cited in footnote 16 along with Martin L. Leibowitz and Alfred Weinberger, "Contingent Immunization — Part I: Risk Control Procedures," *Financial Analysts Journal* 38, no. 6 (November/December 1982):17–31, and "Contingent Immunization — Part II: Problem Areas," *Financial Analysts Journal* 39, no. 1 (January/February 1983):39–50.

they mature, and then reinvest them. An alternative way is to ride the yield curve, provided certain conditions exist.[29]

One condition is that the yield curve be upward-sloping, indicating that longer-term securities have higher yields. Another condition is that the investor believes that the yield curve will remain upward-sloping. Given these two conditions, the investor who is riding the yield curve will purchase securities that have a somewhat longer term-to-maturity than desired and then sell them before they mature, thereby capturing some capital gains.

For example, consider an investor who prefers investing in 91-day Treasury bills. Currently, such bills are selling for $98.25 per $100 of face value, yielding 7.14% (note that $7.14\% = ((\$100 - 98.25)/98.25) \times (100 \times 365/91)$. However, 182-day Treasury bills are currently selling for $96.20, providing a higher yield of 7.92% (note that $7.92\% = ((\$100 - 96.2)/96.2) \times (100 \times 365/182))$. If this investor believes that the yield curve will remain upward-sloping over the next three months, it can be shown that riding the yield curve will result in a higher return than simply buying and holding 91-day Treasury bills.

If the investor buys and holds the 91-day Treasury bills, then the resulting annualized rate of return will be 7.14% (as calculated above)

Alternatively, if the investor buys 182-day Treasury bills and subsequently sells them after 91 days, then the expected selling price will be $98.25 (note that this is the same as the current price of 91-day bills, since it is assumed that the yield curve will not have changed after 90 days have elapsed). This means that the expected return is

$$((\$98.25 - \$96.20)/\$96.00) \times (100 \times 365/91) = 8.55\%$$

The expected return from riding the yield curve, therefore, is higher. This is because the investor expects to benefit from a decline in yield that is due to the shortening of the maturity of the Treasury bills that were initially purchased and not to a shift in the yield curve.

It should be kept in mind that if the yield curve changes adversely, then this strategy can reduce the investor's return.[30] That is, riding the yield curve is riskier than simply buying securities that mature at the appropriate time. Similarly, there are two transactions necessary (buying and then selling the security) when riding the yield curve, whereas a maturity strategy has only one transaction (buying the security). Thus, there will be larger transactions costs associated with riding the yield curve.

---

[29] For more on riding the yield curve, see Stigum and Fabozzi, *The Dow Jones-Irwin Guide to Bond and Money Market Investments*, pp. 270–72; Jerome S. Osteryoung, Gordon S. Roberts, and Daniel E. McCarty, "Ride the Yield Curve When Investing Idle Funds in Treasury Bills?" *Financial Executive* 47, no. 4 (April 1979):10–15; and Edward A. Dyl and Michael D. Joehnk, "Riding the Yield Curve: Does It Work?" *Journal of Portfolio Management* 7, no. 3 (Spring 1981):13–17.

[30] According to the unbiased expectations theory (discussed in Chapter 4), the yield curve would be expected to shift in such a manner that the expected return on both strategies (in the example, buy and hold the 91-day Treasury bills versus buy and sell the 182-day Treasury bills 91 days later) would be the same.

# BONDS VERSUS STOCKS

Bonds and stocks are different kinds of securities, with quite different characteristics. Making an investment decision between them should not be based on some simple one-dimensional comparison. In many cases this decision, known as *asset allocation*, will involve investing in both bonds and stocks.[31]

While historical relationships may not be useful for accurately predicting future relationships, it is instructive to examine the average values, standard deviations, and correlations of past stock and bond returns. These statistics are presented in Table 14.3, based on quarterly excess returns during one time period, 1926–1985, and two subperiods, 1926–1945 and 1946–1985.

**TABLE 14.3**

Historical Relationships Between Bonds and Stocks in the United States and Canada.

|  | *Stocks* | *Bonds* | *Correlation* |
|---|---|---|---|
| **1. US Data** | | | |
| A. 1926-1985: | | | |
| Average quarterly excess return | 2.20% | 0.41% | |
| Standard deviation | 12.39 | 3.98 | |
| Correlation | | | 0.30 |
| B. 1926–1945: | | | |
| Average quarterly excess return | 2.94% | 1.11% | |
| Standard deviation | 18.68 | 1.99 | |
| Correlation | | | 0.45 |
| C. 1946–1985: | | | |
| Average quarterly excess return | 1.83% | 0.06% | |
| Standard deviation | 7.54 | 4.65 | |
| Correlation | | | 0.40 |
| **2. Canadian Data** [a] | | | |
| D. 1950–1989: | | | |
| Average quarterly excess return | 1.52% | −0.05% | |
| Standard deviation | 8.96 | 4.48 | |
| Correlation | | | 0.00 |

[a] Based on annual data.

SOURCES: US data adapted from Meir Statman and Neal L. Ushman, "Bond Versus Stocks: Another Look," *Journal of Portfolio Management* 13, no. 2 (Winter 1987):33–38. Canadian data adapted from Melanie Moore, *ScotiaMcLeod's Handbook of Canadian Debt Market Indices: 1947–1990*, ScotiaMcLeod Inc., February 1991.

---

[31] Chapter 22 presents a discussion of some methods for making the asset allocation decision. For a model on how to measure the interest rate sensitivity of a portfolio consisting of both stocks and bonds, see Martin L. Leibowitz, "Total Portfolio Duration: A New Perspective on Asset Allocation," *Financial Analysts Journal* 42, no. 5 (September/October 1986):18–29.

The similarity in the results obtained in both countries is notable with the exception of the correlation coefficient. Based on average returns, stocks appear to have a substantial advantage for the investor with a reasonably long horizon. However, there is good reason to believe that the average returns on long-term bonds are not representative of investors' expectations for future returns. The returns show the results obtained by purchasing a long-term bond, holding it for a period of time, and then replacing it with another long-term bond. The total returns include both income and capital gains or losses. During this period, in both countries, bond price changes were negative more often than positive, averaging roughly $-1\%$ per year. A better estimate of investors' expectations might be obtained by assuming that the expected price would be as likely to increase as decrease. Expected future returns on bonds might then have been roughly 1% per year (.25% per quarter) greater than shown in the table.

For an investor concerned with month-to-month variation (such as an investor with a possible need for liquidity or with a short horizon), bonds look relatively more attractive than stocks. This can be seen by examining the standard deviation of returns. In this sense, stocks were riskier than bonds during the period and both subperiods. Note that the increased uncertainty concerning the rate of inflation during the postwar subperiod has increased the variability of bond returns.

The correlation between stock and bond returns has been low, and during various periods it has had negative values. This indicates that portfolios combining both stocks and bonds can benefit considerably from the resulting diversification. More recently, however, correlations in the US have been positive, due in part to common reactions to changes in inflationary expectations (a phenomenon that does not appear to have occured in Canada). Consequently, the gains from diversification have recently been reduced. Nevertheless, from the historical record, it seems reasonable to expect that, in the future, bonds will again offer the benefits of diversification.

## 14.7    SUMMARY

This chapter has presented a discussion of bond portfolio management. Various methods exist and can be classified as being either passive or active in nature. Passive methods are based on the assumption that bond markets are efficient, whereas active methods are based on the assumption that bond markets exhibit occasional inefficiencies. There have been many US studies that have attempted to determine the degree of efficiency in the bond market. On balance, these studies indicate that the bond market is highly, but not perfectly, efficient. This means that while it is possible to earn abnormally high returns, it is exceptionally difficult to do so.

The available evidence suggests that the Canadian bond market is less active and probably less efficient than its US counterpart, but that the inefficiencies may be difficult to exploit given the higher transactions costs.

One passive method of managing a bond portfolio is based on the concept of duration and is known as immunization. With this strategy, the portfolio manager is attempting to lock in a given return on a portfolio. That is, the manager is attempting to construct a portfolio that will not be adversely affected by future movements in interest rates. This is accomplished by purchasing bonds so that the weighted average of their durations equals the length of the manager's holding period. Although immunization does not work perfectly in practice, a number of people believe it works better than a maturity strategy, where the manager purchases bonds that mature at the end of the holding period.

A number of methods of active management have been discussed in this chapter. They include horizon analysis, swapping, contingent immunization, and riding the yield curve. All these methods seek to provide the portfolio manager with abnormally high returns. Whether they consistently work or not is an unanswered question.

Lastly, bond returns were compared historically with stock returns. It appears that bond returns have had both lower returns and less risk than stocks. Of particular interest is the fact that the correlation of bond and stock returns has typically been low and even negative during some time periods. This suggests that diversification across both stocks and bonds will be worthwhile in the future.

## QUESTIONS AND PROBLEMS

1. Bonds A and B possess coupon rates of 4% and 12%, respectively. Both bonds have ten years to maturity and pay interest annually. If the discount rate on both bonds A and B rises from 8% to 10%, calculate the expected percentage changes in the bonds' prices. Explain why the bonds differ in terms of their percentage price changes.

2. Bonds C and D both possess coupon rates of 10%. However, bond C has four years to maturity, while bond D has ten years to maturity. Assuming a constant discount rate of 8% for both bonds, and assuming that all other relevant factors remain the same, calculate the expected percentage changes in the bonds' prices one year from today. Explain why the bonds differ in terms of their percentage price changes.

3. Consider a bond selling at its par value of $1000, with three years to maturity and a 6% coupon rate (with annual interest payments). Calculate the bond's duration.

4. Recalculate your answer to question 3 assuming a 10% coupon rate. Why does the bond's duration change?

5. Why must the duration of a coupon-bearing bond always be less than the time to its maturity date?

6. Rank order the following bonds in terms of duration. Explain the rationale behind your rankings. (You do not have to actually calculate the bonds' durations. Simply logical reasoning will suffice.)

| Bond | Term-to-Maturity | Coupon Interest Rate | Yield-to-Maturity |
|------|------------------|----------------------|-------------------|
| 1 | 30 years | 10.0% | 10.0% |
| 2 | 30 | 0.0 | 10.0 |
| 3 | 30 | 10.0 | 7.0 |
| 4 | 5 | 10.0 | 10.0 |

7. What impact would you expect the option features of callable bonds and mortgage backed securities to have on the expected durations of such bonds as opposed to the durations calculated based on the bonds' stated maturity dates?

8. Consider a bond with a 3.5 year duration. If its yield-to-maturity increases from 8.0% to 8.3%, what is the expected percentage change in the price of the bond?

9. Explain why "immunization" permits a bond investor to be confident of meeting a given liability on a predetermined future date.
10. Why can nonparallel shifts in the yield curve cause problems for an investor seeking to construct an immunized bond portfolio?
11. Describe the four components of return on a bond investment over a given holding period.
12. Distinguish between a substitution swap and an intermarket swap.

## SUGGESTED READINGS

Timothy Appelt and Evan Schulman, "The Government of Canada Bond Market: Is It Efficiently Priced?" *Canadian Investment Review* I, no. 1 (Fall 1988):63–72 is a comparative test of Canadian and United States bond market efficiencies.

Frank J. Fabozzi and T. Dessa Fabozzi, *Bond Markets, Analysis and Strategies* (Englewood Cliffs, NJ: Prentice Hall, 1989) describes bond theorems in Chapter 4 plus bond investment strategies in subsequent chapters.

Sidney Homer and Martin L. Liebowitz, *Inside the Yield Book: New Tools for Bond Market Strategies* (Englewood Cliffs, N.J.: Prentice Hall, 1989) developed the taxonomy of active bond portfolio strategies.

Frederick R. Macauley, "Some Theoretical Problems Suggested by the Movements of Interest Rates, Bond Yields, and Stock Prices in the United States Since 1856" (New York, NY.: National Bureau of Economic Research, 1938). Macauley, a Canadian actuary who worked for the Sun Life Assurance Company, developed the concept of duration in this article.

Gerald O. Bierwag, *Duration Analysis* (Cambridge, Mass.: Ballinger Publishing Company, 1987) describes a number of investment strategies based on the use of duration.

Andre Thibeault and Larry Wynant, "Investor Reaction to the Political Environment in Quebec," *Canadian Public Policy* (Spring 1979):236–47 describes the impact of political risk on the pricing of bonds in Canada.

# Chapter 15

# COMMON SHARES

Common shares are easier to describe than fixed-income securities such as bonds but are harder to analyze. Fixed-income securities almost always have a limited life and an upper dollar limit on cash payments to investors. Common shares have neither. Although the basic principles of valuation apply to both, the role of uncertainty is larger for common shares, so much so that it often dominates all other elements in their valuation.

Common shares represent *equity*, or an ownership position, in a corporation. It is a residual claim, in the sense that creditors and preferred shareholders must be paid as scheduled before common shareholders can receive any payments. In bankruptcy, common shareholders are in principle entitled to any value remaining after all other claimants have been satisfied. (However, in practice courts sometimes violate this principle.)

The great advantage of the corporate form of organization is the *limited liability* of its owners. Common shares are generally "full-paid and nonassessable," meaning common shareholders may lose their investment, but no more. That is, common shareholders have no additional liability if the corporation fails to meet its obligations.

## 15.1 THE CORPORATE FORM

A corporation exists only when it has been granted a *charter*, or certificate of incorporation, by the Federal government or a provincial government. This document specifies the rights and obligations of shareholders. It may be amended with the approval of the shareholders, perhaps by a majority or two-thirds vote, where each share of stock generally entitles its owner to one vote. Both the initial terms of the charter and the terms of any amendment must also be approved by the jurisdiction in which the corporation is chartered.

### ☐ 15.1.1 Share Certificates

The ownership of a firm's stock has typically been represented by a single certificate, with the number of shares held by the particular investor noted on it. Such a share certificate is usually registered, with the name, address, and holdings of the investor included on the corporation's books. Dividend payments, voting material, annual and quarterly reports, and other mailings are then sent directly to the investor, taking into account the size of his or her holdings.

Shares of stock held by an investor may be transferred to a new owner with the assistance of either the issuing corporation or, more commonly, its designated *transfer agent*. This agent cancels the old share certificate and issues a new one in its place, made out to the new owner. Frequently a *registrar* will make sure that the cancelation and issuance of certificates has been done properly. Usually banks and trust companies act as transfer agents and registrars. Many shareholders have chosen to avoid these rather cumbersome procedures. Instead, clearing arrangements (discussed in Chapter 2) are used to substitute computerized records for embossed certificates.

## ☐ 15.1.2  Voting

Since an owner of a share of common stock is one of the owners of a corporation, he or she is entitled to vote on matters brought up at the corporation's annual meeting and to vote for the corporation's directors. Any owner may attend and vote in person, but most choose instead to vote by *proxy*. That is, the incumbent directors and senior management typically solicit all the shareholders, asking each one to sign a proxy statement. Such a statement is a power of attorney authorizing the designated party listed on the statement to cast all of the investor's votes on any matter brought up at the meeting. Occasionally, desired positions on specific issues may be solicited on the proxy statement. However, most of the time the positions held by the incumbents are made known with the proxy solicitation. Since the majority of votes are generally controlled by the incumbents via proxy statements, the actual voting turns out to be perfunctory, leaving little if any controversy or excitement.

Once in a while, however, a *proxy fight* develops. Insurgents from outside the corporation solicit proxies to vote against the incumbents, often in order to effect a takeover of some sort. Shareholders are deluged with literature and appeals for their proxies. The incumbents often win, but the possibility of a loss in such a skirmish tends to curb activities clearly not in the shareholders' best interests.

When proposals are to be voted on, the number of votes given an investor equals the number of shares held. Thus, when a yes or no vote is called for, anyone controlling a majority of the shares can ensure that the outcome he or she favors will receive a majority of the votes. When directors are to be elected, however, there are two types of voting systems that can be used, one of which does not give a majority owner complete control of the outcome. This type of voting system is known as a *cumulative voting system*, whereas the type of voting system that does allow a majority owner to control the outcome completely is known as a *majority voting system*.

Under both systems, the winners of the election are those candidates who have received the highest vote totals. Thus, if six candidates were running for the three directorships, the three receiving the largest number of votes would be elected.

With both voting systems, a shareholder receives a total number of votes that is equal to the number of directors to be elected times the number of shares owned. However, with the majority voting system, the shareholder may only give any one candidate, as a maximum, a number of votes equal to the number of shares owned. This means that in a situation where three directors are to be elected, a shareholder with 400 shares would have 1200 votes but could give no more than 400 of these votes to any one candidate.

Note that if there are a total of 1000 shares outstanding and one shareholder owns (or has proxies for) 501 shares, then he or she can give 501 votes to each of the three candidates he or she favors. In doing so, this shareholder will be certain they are elected, regardless of how the remaining 499 shares are voted. The majority shareholder's candidates would each have 501 votes, whereas the *most* any other candidate could receive is 499 votes. Thus, with a majority voting system, a shareholder owning (or controlling with proxies) one share more than 50% can be certain of electing all the candidates he or she favors.

The cumulative voting system differs from the majority voting system in that a shareholder can cast his or her votes in any manner. As a result, a minority shareholder can be certain of having some representation on the board of directors, provided the number of shares owned is sufficiently large. In the previous example, the minority owner of the 400 shares could cast all his or her 1200 votes for one candidate. Imagine that this owner wanted director A to be elected, but the majority owner of 501 shares wanted candidates B, C, and D to be elected. In this situation, the minority shareholder could give all 1200 votes to A and be certain that A would be one of the three directors elected, regardless of what the majority shareholder did. If the majority owner held the remaining 600 shares, he or she would have 1800 votes. There is no way that candidate A, favored by the minority shareholder, can come in lower than second place in the vote totals. This is because A will receive 1200 votes, and there is no way that the 1800 votes of the majority shareholder can be cast to give more than one of his or her favored candidates a vote total in excess of 1200. Thus, the minority shareholder can be certain that A will be elected, whereas the majority shareholder can be certain that only 2 of his or her favorites will be elected.

In general, the formula for determining the minimum number of shares a shareholder must own in order to be able to elect a certain number of candidates under a cumulative voting system is

$$n = \left( \frac{ds}{D + 1} \right) + 1 \tag{15.1}$$

where:

  $n$ = the minimum number of shares that must be owned,
  $d$ = the number of directors the shareholder wants to be certain of electing,
  $s$ = the number of shares outstanding, and
  $D$ = the number of directors to be elected.

Thus, the minimum number of shares a shareholder needs in order to be certain of electing one director when three are to be elected and there are 1000 shares outstanding is $[(1 \times 1000)/(3+1)]+1 = 251$. Since in the example the minority shareholder owned 400 shares, it can be seen from the formula that he or she is certain of being able to elect one director. Note that the minimum number of shares that must be owned in order to be certain of electing two directors is $[(2 \times 1000)/(3+1)] + 1 = 501$. The minimum number owned to be certain of electing all three directors is $[(3 \times 1000)/(3+1)]+1 = 751$.

In summary, the cumulative voting system gives minority shareholders the right to have some representation on the board of directors, provided the number of shares owned is sufficiently large. In contrast, the majority voting system does not give minority shareholders the right to such representation, even if 49.9% of the shares are owned by the minority shareholder.

The voting system that a corporation decides to use depends not only on the desires of the corporate founders but also on the jurisdiction in which the firm is incorporated. Under Alberta, British Columbia, Ontario or federal incorporation, cumulative voting is permitted providing there are specific provisions in the company's articles or bylaws.

## ☐ 15.1.3 Tender Offers

Periodically, a firm or a wealthy individual who is convinced that the management of a corporation is not fully exploiting its opportunities will attempt a *takeover*. This is frequently done with a *tender offer* being made by a *bidder* to a *target* firm.[1] Before this offer is announced, a small number of the target firm's shares are usually acquired by the bidder in the open market through the use of brokers (if the firm's shares are traded in Ontario then once 10% of the stock has been acquired, the bidder becomes an "insider" under the *Ontario Securities Act* and must report all further trades to the Ontario Securities Commission).

Then, in the bidder's quest to acquire a substantial number of the target's shares, the bid is announced to the public. Advertisements to purchase shares are placed in the financial press, and material describing the bid is mailed to the target's shareholders. The bidder generally offers to buy, at a stated price, some or all shares offered ("tendered") by the current shareholders of the target. This buying offer is usually contingent on the tender of a minimum number of shares by the target's shareholders by a fixed date. When the buying offer is first made, the offered price ("tender price") is generally set considerably above the current market price, although the offer itself usually leads to a subsequent price increase.

Management of the target firm frequently responds to tender offers with advertisements, mailings, and the like, urging its shareholders to reject the bidder's offer. Sometimes a *white knight* will be sought, meaning another firm that is favorably inclined towards current management will be invited to make a better offer to the target's shareholders. Another type of response by management is to pay *greenmail* to the bidder, meaning that any shares held by the bidder will be bought by the target firm at an above-market price. Still another type of response is for management of the target firm to issue a tender offer of its own, known as a *repurchase offer*, where the firm offers to buy back some of its own stock. (Occasionally repurchase offers are made by firms that have not received tender offers from outside bidders.)

Other types of corporate defenses include the *Pac-Man defense*, where the initial target turns around and makes a tender offer for the initial acquirer, the *crown jewel defense*, where the target sells its most attractive assets to make the firm less attractive, and the use of *poison pills*, where the target gives its shareholders certain rights that can

---

[1] Another form of a takeover is a *merger*. A merger occurs when two firms combine their operations, the result being that only one firm exists. Mergers usually are negotiated by the management of the two firms. Tender offers differ in that the management of the bidder makes a direct appeal to the shareholders of the target firm for their shares. Tender offers also differ in that afterward both firms will still exist, since most tender offers are not for all the shares of the target. For a discussion of the motivations for mergers and tender offers, see Michael C. Jensen and Richard S. Ruback, "The Market for Corporate Control: The Scientific Evidence," *Journal of Financial Economics* 11, nos. 1–4 (April 1983):5–50, and Richard Roll, "The Hubris Hypothesis of Corporate Takeovers," *Journal of Business* 59, no. 1, pt. 2 (April 1986):197–216. A method for acquirers to use in evaluating potential targets is presented in Chapter 9 of Alfred Rappaport, *Creating Shareholder Value* (New York: The Free Press, 1986).

be exercised only in the event of a subsequent takeover and that, once exercised, will be extremely onerous to the acquirer.

## 15.1.4 Ownership Versus Control

Much has been written about the effects of the separation of ownership and control of the modern corporation.[2] This separation gives rise to what is known as a *principal-agent problem*. In particular, shareholders can be viewed as principals who hire management to act as their agents. The agent is to make decisions that maximize shareholder wealth as reflected in the firm's stock price. No problem would exist if shareholders could *monitor* the managers without cost, since the shareholders would then be capable of determining for certain whether or not management had acted in their best interests. However, monitoring is not costless, and complete monitoring of every decision is, practically speaking, impossible.[3] As a result some, but not complete, monitoring is done. This gives management a certain degree of latitude in making decisions and leaves open the possibility that some decisions will be made that are not in the shareholders' best interests.[4] However, the possibility of a proxy fight or tender offer provides at least some check on such decisions.

To align the interests of management with their own, shareholders frequently offer certain incentives to management. An example is the use of stock options. These options are given to certain high-level managers and allow them to purchase a specified number of shares at a stated price (often above the market price when the options are initially issued) by a stated date. Thus, they motivate these managers to make decisions that will increase the stock price of the firm as much as possible.

## 15.1.5 Shareholders' Equity

### Par Value

When a corporation is first chartered, it is authorized to issue up to a stated number of shares of common stock, each of which will often carry a specified *par value*. Legally, a corporation may be precluded from making payments to common shareholders if doing so would reduce the balance sheet value of shareholders' equity below the amount represented by the par value of outstanding stock. For this reason the par value is typically low relative to the price for which the stock is initially sold. Some corporations issue no-par shares (if so, a stated value must be recorded in place of the par value).

When shares are initially sold for more than their par value, the difference may be carried separately on the corporation's books under shareholders' equity. Frequently,

---

[2] See, for example, Michael C. Jensen and William H. Meckling, "Theory of the Firm: Managerial Behavior, Agency Costs and Ownership Structure," *Journal of Financial Economics* 3, no. 4 (October 1976):305–60; Eugene F. Fama, "Agency Problems and the Theory of the Firm," *Journal of Political Economy* 88, no. 2 (April 1980):288–307; Eugene F. Fama and Michael C. Jensen, "Separation of Ownership and Control," *Journal of Law and Economics* 26, (June 1983):301–25; Eugene F. Fama and Michael C. Jensen, "Agency Problems and Residual Claims," *Journal of Law and Economics* 26, (June 1983):327–49, and the entire issue of vol. 11 (April 1983) of the *Journal of Financial Economics*.

[3] An example of monitoring is having the firm's financial statements independently audited.

[4] For example, management may decide to have lavishly furnished offices and an executive jet when the conduct of business suggests that these are not merited.

the entry is for "capital contributed in excess of par value" or "paid-in capital." The par value of the stock is carried in a separate account, generally simply entitled "common stock," with the amount equal to the number of shares outstanding times the par value per share (for no-par shares, the stated value).

## Book Value

With the passage of time, a corporation will generate income, much of which is paid out to creditors (as interest) and shareholders (as dividends). Any remainder is added to the amount shown as cumulative retained earnings on the corporation's books. The sum of the cumulative retained earnings and other entries (such as "common stock" and "capital contributed in excess of par value") under shareholders' equity is the *book value of the equity*. The *book value per share* is obtained by dividing the book value of the equity by the number of shares outstanding.

## Treasury Shares

Typically, a corporation issues only a part of its authorized stock. Some of the remainder may be specifically reserved for outstanding options, convertible securities, and so on.

When a corporation repurchases some of its own shares, either in the open market through the services of a broker or with a tender offer, the shares may be "held in the treasury." Such *treasury shares* do not carry votes or receive dividends and are equivalent economically (though not legally) to unissued shares.

If a corporation wishes to issue new stock in excess of the amount originally authorized, the charter must be amended. This requires approval by both the chartering jurisdiction and the shareholders.

## Restricted Shares

Some corporations issue two or more classes of common shares, one or more of which may be restricted. Restricted shares are defined under the *Ontario Securities Act* as equity shares that are not common shares. Equity shares, in turn, are defined as shares of a company that carry a residual right to participate to an unlimited degree in the earnings of the issuing corporation and in its assets upon liquidation. The important feature of this definition is the fact that they participate in the earnings and assets. Common shares are those with unrestricted voting rights per share that are are not less than the voting rights of any other outstanding issue.

The *Act* goes on to recognize three types of restricted shares as follows:

i. Restricted voting shares are those that carry a right to vote that is subject to some restriction on the number or percentage of shares that may be voted by the owner.
ii. Subordinate voting shares are those that carry a right to vote, where there is another class of shares outstanding that carry a greater right to vote.
iii. Non-voting shares are those that carry no right to vote (or a right to vote in certain limited circumstances).

Subordinate and non-voting shares frequently have a preferred position over the voting shares in regard to dividends (and sometimes in liquidation). These shares are unlike preferred shares in that they participate in the earnings of the corporation and do not have a prescribed dividend.

At the end of 1989, 189 companies had dual classes of shares listed on the TSE representing 15% of all shares listed and 11.5% of the market value of the TSE 300 index.[5] Ownership of Canadian corporations is closely held so the issuance of restricted or non-voting shares is seen as a means of raising additional equity capital without diluting control. Their existence has raised concerns that concentrated voting power with a low investment in the corporation could lead to abuse of other shareholders by the owners of the control block(s). One area of particular concern has been the distribution of the control premium in the event of a takeover. In the absence of any specific provisions, a potential acquirer need only negotiate with the holders of voting or superior voting shares, ignoring the other shareholders. Following considerable controversy most issuers of restricted voting shares have incorporated *coattail* provisions in their bylaws to allow the holders of restricted voting shares to participate in the takeover premium.

A typical of example subordinate voting shares is Ivaco Inc. that has 12.9 million Class A shares that are entitled to one vote each and 7.0 million Class B shares entitled to 10 votes each. The Class A shares will receive 120% of the dividend declared on Class B shares and are protected against any sub-division or consolidation (but not stock dividends). The coattail provision as described in the 1990 Annual Report reads as follows:

> "In the event an offer is made to holders of Class B shares and a similar offer is not made to Class A shareholders then each Class A share will, for the purposes of such an offer only, be deemed to have been converted to Class B shares in order that the Class A shares will be treated equally with the Class B shares."

In Ivaco's case the Ivanier family plus the company's officers and directors hold over 60% of the votes primarily through holdings of Class B shares. Furthermore, the class B shares may be freely converted into Class A shares on a one-for-one basis.

Absolute control of Ivaco can be secured by owning 4.15 million Class B shares or less than 21% of the total equity.[6]

The valuation of restricted voting shares presents some interesting challenges given the existence of dividend preferences and coattail provisions. Considerable research has been undertaken that indicates that the value of a vote is worth between 1% and 16% of the equity value. The value of a vote is manifested in a premium paid for the voting over the non- or restricted voting shares. This voting premium, however, is sometimes obscured by the effect of the dividend preference. In the case of Ivaco, for example, the Class A shares closed at $3.15 and the Class B at $3.05 on February 20, 1992. On the face of it there appears to be no voting premium. In similar circumstances, Robinson and White estimated that the expected net present value of the dividend difference is larger than the price difference, therefore, the existence of a premium cannot be ruled out.[7]

---

[5] B. Smith and B. Amoako-Adu, "Financing Canadian Corporations with Restricted Voting Shares," NCMRD Working Paper, London, Ont. 1991.

[6] Ivaco is not an extreme example, absolute control of Canadian Tire Corporation can be secured with ownership of about 2.1% of the equity.

[7] C. Robinson and A. White," Empirical Evidence on the Relative Valuation of Voting and Restricted Voting Shares," *Canadian Journal of Administrative Sciences* 7, no. 4 (December 1990):9–18. For a summary of the issues and a comprehensive literature review, see E. Maynes, C. Robinson and A. White, "How Much Is A Share Vote Worth?" *Canadian Investment Review* III, no. 1 (Spring 1990):49–55.

## Stripped Common Shares

These securities are designed to allow investors to separate the dividend portion of a return on a common share from the capital gain. They can be described most easily with an example.

An underwriter floats a new investment corporation and issues two types of securities: preferred shares and capital shares. The proceeds from the sale of these securities are used to purchase the shares of a large and creditworthy company, such as the Bank of Nova Scotia (BNS). The investment corporation is designed to be unwound at the end of a specified period. After the original issue an investor can buy or sell either of these securities through a broker and can find each listed on the Toronto Stock Exchange under the name of the investment corporation. BNS itself has nothing to do with either the creation or subsequent trading of these securities.

The owner of preferred shares is entitled to all cash dividends BNS pays the underwriter and, at the liquidation of the investment corporation, any price appreciation up to a set amount. The owner of an instalment receipt is entitled to all the remaining (if any) price appreciation on BNS. A recent example involving BNS stock was the underlying security is SNT preferred and SNT capital shares. When BNS shares were recently selling for $20.75 the preferred sold for 12.38 and the capital stock for $8.38. The preferred receives all dividends issued by BNS and participates in 25% of any capital gain over $27 on BNS stock at expiry on February 8, 1996. The full capital gain up to $27 plus 75% of any over $27 accrues to the capital shares. The price of the underlying security is divided between the two classes of shares. The preferred receive the full dividend but pay a lower price and, therefore, obtain a higher yield. The capital shares behave rather like a warrant and provide more leverage than owning the underlying shares.

Since the first issue of these securities in 1986 a number of dealers have floated issues of stripped common shares using bank stocks as the underlying securities in most cases. In the US, similar securities are issued by the Americus Shareowner Service Corporation. The preferred shares are referred to as *primes* and the instalment receipts as *scores*.

---

## 15.2    CASH DIVIDENDS

Payments made in cash to shareholders are termed *dividends*. These are typically declared quarterly by the board of directors and paid to the shareholders of record at a date, known as the *date of record*, specified by the board. The dividends may be of almost any size, subject to certain restrictions such as those contained in the charter or in documents given to creditors. Thus, even though this is unusual, dividends may even be larger than the current earnings of the corporation. (If so, they are usually paid out of past earnings.)

Compiling a list of shareholders to receive the dividend is not as simple as it may initially seem, since for many firms the list changes almost constantly as shares are bought and sold. The way of identifying those shareholders who are to receive the dividend is by use of an *ex-dividend date*. Because of the time required to record the transfer of ownership of common stock, major stock exchanges specify an ex-dividend date that is four business days before the date of record. Shares purchased before an ex-dividend date are entitled to receive the dividend in question; those purchased on or after the ex-dividend date are not entitled to the dividend.

For example, a dividend may be declared on April 15 with a date of record of Friday, May 15. In this situation Monday, May 11, is the ex-dividend date. If an investor bought shares on Friday, May 8, he or she would subsequently receive the cash dividend (unless the shares were sold later in the day on the 8th). However, if the shares were bought on Monday, May 11, the investor would not receive the cash dividend. Besides a declaration date (April 15), an ex-dividend date (May 11), and a date-of-record (May 15), there is also a fourth date, the *payment date*. On this date (perhaps May 25) the cheques for the cash dividends are put in the mail.

## 15.3 STOCK DIVIDENDS AND STOCK SPLITS

Occasionally, the board of directors decides to forgo a cash dividend and declares a *stock dividend* instead. For example, if a 5% stock dividend is declared, the owner of 100 shares receives 5 additional shares issued for this occasion. The accounting treatment of a stock dividend is to increase the "common stock" and "capital contributed in excess of par" accounts by an amount equal to the market value of the stock at the time of the dividend times the number of new shares issued (the "common stock" account would increase by an amount equal to the par value times the number of new shares; the remainder of the increase would go into the "capital contributed in excess of par" account). In order to keep the total book value of shareholders' equity the same, the "retained earnings" account is reduced by a equivalent amount.

A *stock split* is similar to a stock dividend in that the shareholder owns more shares afterward. However, it is different in both magnitude and accounting treatment. With a stock split, all the old shares are destroyed and new ones are issued with a new par value; afterward, the number of new shares outstanding is usually larger than the previous number of old shares by 25% or more, with the exact amount depending on the size of the split. In contrast, a stock dividend usually results in an increase of less than 25%. While a stock dividend results in adjustments to the dollar figures in certain shareholders' equity accounts, no adjustments are made for a split. For example, if a stock with par value $1 is split 2-for-1, the holder of 200 old shares will receive 400 new shares with par value $0.50, and none of the dollar figures in shareholders' equity would change.

A *reverse stock split* or *consolidation* reduces the number of shares and increases the par value per share. For example, in a reverse 2-for-1 split, the holder of 200 shares with par value $1 would exchange them for 100 shares with par value $2. Again, there would not be any change in the dollar figures in shareholders' equity.

Stock dividends and splits must be taken into account when following the price of a company's shares. For example, a fall in price per share may be due solely to a large stock dividend. To reduce confusion, most financial services provide data adjusted for at least some of these changes. Thus, if a stock split 2-for-1 on January 30, 1992, prices prior to that date might be divided by 2 to facilitate comparison.

## ☐ 15.3.1 Reasons for Stock Dividends and Splits

Why do corporations issue stock dividends and split their stocks? Nothing of importance would appear to be changed, since such actions do not increase revenues or reduce expenses. All that happens is that there is a change in the size of the units in which ownership may be bought and sold. Moreover, since the process involves administrative effort and costs something to execute, one wonders why it is done.

It is sometimes argued that shareholders respond positively to "tangible" evidence of the growth of their corporation. Another view holds that splits and stock dividends, by decreasing the price per share, may bring the stock's price into a more desirable trading range and hence increase the total value of the amount outstanding.

Figure 15.1 presents the average behavior of stock returns for 219 stock splits that occurred between 1945 and 1965. For each split, the stock's "abnormal" return was determined by relating monthly returns on the stock to the corresponding returns in the stock market. This was done month by month for the 54-month period immediately prior to the split and the 54-month period immediately following it. These abnormal returns were averaged across firms for each month relative to the firm's split and then cumulated across time.

As the figure shows, the stocks tended to have a positive cumulative abnormal return of about 30% during the 54 months prior to splitting. This was probably not due to anticipation of the coming split, since these splits are not announced until roughly two months before the effective date (denoted by 0 in the figure). The causal relationship could well be just the reverse: Stocks split after unusual price increases. That is, unexpected positive developments (such as unexpected large increases in earnings) caused abnormal increases in the stock prices of these firms, after which the firms decided to split their stock. The behavior of the postsplit prices indicates that afterwards investors did not continue to receive positive abnormal returns. In the study shown in Figure 15.1, investors actually lost some ground. Other studies, using different stocks and time periods, found either no abnormal returns or slightly positive abnormal returns after the split.

A comparable Canadian study of 177 stock splits that occured between 1963 and 1975 shows a similar but not identical pattern of abnormal returns. The disturbing feature, however, is the suggestion that the market is inefficient in that the maximum abnormal return is recorded about six months *after* the announcement as shown in Figure 15.2. A further study of 241 stock splits recorded between 1977 and 1985 using weekly data produced results closer to Figure 15.1 with the maximum abnormal return occuring at week minus one.[8] The overall effect of stock splits in Canadian markets is an unresolved issue.

US evidence also suggests that rather than *decreasing* transaction costs, stock splits actually *increased* them. A study of presplit and postsplit behavior showed that after splits, trading volume rose less than proportionately, and both commission costs and bid-ask spreads, expressed as a percentage of value, increased — hardly reactions that

---

[8] See Eugene F. Fama, Lawrence Fisher, Michael C. Jensen, and Richard Roll, "The Adjustment of Stock Prices to New Information," *International Economic Review* 10, no. 1 (February 1969):1–21; and Guy Charest, "Split Information, Stock Returns and Market Efficiency — I," *Journal of Financial Economics* 6, no. 2/3 (June/September 1978):265–96; Guy Charest, "Returns to Splitting Stocks on the Toronto Stock Exchange," *Journal of Business Administration* 12, no. 1 (Fall 1980): 19–37; Halim Bishara, "Stock Splits, Stock Returns and Trading Benefits on Canadian Stock Markets," *Akron Business and Economic Review* 19, no. 3 (Fall 1988):57–65.

**FIGURE 15-1**
Abnormal stock returns before and after stock splits.

*SOURCE:* Sasson Bar-Yosef and Lawrence D. Brown, "A Re-examination of Stock Splits Using Moving Betas," *Journal of Finance* 32, no. 4 (September 1977):1074.

are favorable to shareholders.[9] For example, after a 2-for-1 stock split, there will be twice as many shares outstanding, so it is reasonable to expect the daily number of shares that are traded to double and also to expect the commission for buying 200 shares after the split to be the same as the commission for buying 100 shares before the split. Instead, it was found that after the split the number of shares traded daily was less than twice as large and the commission was larger.

## 15.4    PREEMPTIVE RIGHTS

Under common law (and most provincial laws), a shareholder has an inherent right to maintain his or her proportionate ownership of the corporation. The existence of these *preemptive rights* means that when new shares are to be sold, the current shareholders must be given the right of first refusal in regard to the purchase of the shares.[10] This is accomplished by issuing a certificate to each shareholder that indicates the number of new shares he or she is authorized to purchase. This number will be proportional to the number of existing shares currently owned by the shareholder. Usually, the new shares will be priced below the current market price of the stock, making such *rights* valuable.

---

[9] See Thomas E. Copeland, "Liquidity Changes Following Stock Splits," *Journal of Finance* 34, no. 1 (March 1979):115–41.

[10] Current shareholders may not be given this right if there is a provision in the charter denying it or if it is denied by the shareholders at the annual meeting.

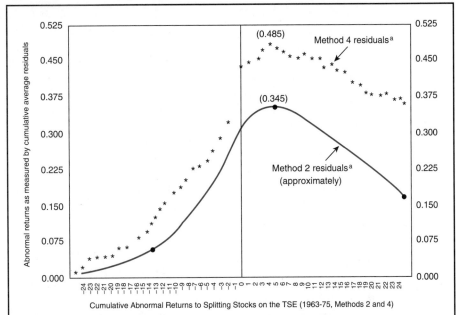

**FIGURE 15-2**

Cumulative abnormal returns to splitting stocks on the Toronto Stock Exchange, 1963–75.

*SOURCE:* G.Charest, "Returns to Splitting Stocks on the Toronto Stock Exchange," *Journal of Business Administration* 12, no. 1 (Fall 1980):28.

The shareholder can exercise the rights by purchasing his or her allotted amount of new shares, thereby maintaining his or her proportional ownership in the firm, but at the cost of providing additional capital. Alternatively, the rights can be sold to someone else.[11]

For example, if a firm needs $10,000,000 for new equipment, it may decide to sell new shares in order to raise the capital. Given that the current market price of the stock is $60 per share, a *rights offering* may be used to raise the capital, in which the *subscription price* is set at $50 per share.[12] Accordingly, $10,000,000/\$50 = 200,000$ new shares are to be sold. Assuming the firm has 4,000,000 shares outstanding, this means that the owner of one share will receive the right to buy $200,000/4,000,000 = \frac{1}{20}$ of a new share. Since the number of rights received is equal to the number of shares owned, it can be seen that 20 shares must be owned in order to be able to buy one new share. Thus, if a shareholder owns 100 shares, he or she will receive 100 rights, allowing him or her

---

[11] The investor could simply let the rights expire, causing that investor's proportion in the corporation to decline as others are given ownership in the expanded firm in return for the provision of new capital. Sometimes there is an *oversubscription privilege* given to the subscribing shareholders. This means that those shareholders who have exercised their rights will be given an opportunity to buy the shares that were not purchased.

[12] The subscription price is usually set at roughly 80% of the current market price of the stock.

to buy $(1/20) \times 100 = 5$ new shares. These rights are valuable because the owner of them can buy stock at $50 a share when the market price is significantly higher. The current owner of 100 shares can either use the 100 rights by coming up with cash equal to $5 \times \$50 = \$250$ or sell the 100 rights to someone else. But this raises a question: What is a fair price for the rights?

Rights are distributed in a manner similar to cash dividends. That is, there is a date of record and, four business days earlier, an *ex-rights date*. Before the ex-rights date, the value of a right can be calculated by using the following equation:

$$C_o - (RN + S) = R \qquad (15.2)$$

where:

$C_o$ is the "rights-on" market price of the stock,
$R$ is the value of a right,
$N$ is the number of rights needed to buy one share, and
$S$ is the subscription price.

The equation can be interpreted in the following manner. If an investor purchases one share before the ex-rights date, by definition he or she pays the market price of $C_o$, shown on the left-hand side of the equation. Alternatively, the investor could purchase the number of rights necessary to buy one share of the new stock at a cost of $RN$ and set aside an amount of money equal to the subscription price $S$. The total cost of doing this is $RN + S$. The only difference between the two alternatives is that the first one gives the investor not only one share of stock but also one right. Thus, the difference in the cost of the two alternatives, $C_o - (RN + S)$, must equal the value of a right, $R$, as shown in equation (15.2).

Equation (15.2) can be rewritten as

$$R = \frac{C_o - S}{N + 1}. \qquad (15.3)$$

Thus, in the previous example, the value of a right when a share is selling for $60 would be equal to approximately $(\$60 - \$50)/(20 + 1) = \$.48$.

On or after the ex-rights date, the value of a right can be calculated by using the following equation:

$$C_e - (RN + S) = 0 \qquad (15.4)$$

where $C_e$ is the ex-rights market price of a share. The reasoning behind this equation is similar to the reasoning behind equation (15.2). That is, an investor can purchase one share by either buying it in the open market at a cost of $C_e$ or by purchasing the requisite number of rights and setting aside the subscription price, for a total cost of $RN + S$. Since the purchase of one share ex-rights means the investor does not receive a right, the two alternatives provide the investor with the same item. Thus, the cost of these two alternatives should be equivalent, so the difference in their cost should be zero.

Equation (15.4) can be rewritten as

$$R = \frac{C_e - S}{N}. \qquad (15.5)$$

In the previous example, if a share is selling for $56 after the ex-rights date, then the value of a right at that time would be approximately $(\$56 - \$50)/20 = \$.30$.

# SHARE PRICE AND VOLUME QUOTATIONS

Figures 15.3 and 15.4 provide examples of quotations summarizing a day's transactions in stocks traded over the counter and on the TSE.

Active stocks, that traded on the previous day, reported by the Canadian Dealing Network, Inc., are shown in the top section of Figure 15.3. After the security's name the trading volume, highest, lowest and closing prices recorded the previous day are shown together with the change in price from the prior trading day. Bid and asked offers for issues that did not trade are shown in the bottom section of Figure 15.3 following the security's name.

Weekly activity in shares traded on the Toronto Stock Exchange, reported on Saturdays, is shown in Figure 15.4. The accompanying instructions in the table entitled *How to Read the Stock Tables* describe the information that is provided. The daily reports present the same information but omit the weekly summary.

# INSIDER TRADING

The Ontario Securities Commission requires the officers and directors of a corporation whose securities are traded on an organized exchange in Ontario to report any transactions they have made in the firm's shares within 10 days after the end of the month in which the transaction(s) occured. Shareholders who own 10% or more of the firm's shares, known as *beneficial owners*, must also report their trading activities. Such shareholders, officers, and directors are often referred to as *insiders*. The information they provide about their trading activity is subsequently reported in the Ontario Securities Commission's weekly *Ontario Securities Commission Bulletin*. [13] Almost two months may elapse before knowledge of these trades becomes widespread. For example, the information about trades made in January must be reported by early February and will appear in the late February issue of the OSC Bulletin. When a person first acquires 10% of a firm's shares he or she is subject to the OSC's *early warning disclosure*. This requires them to make an immediate public announcement and report the transaction to the OSC within one day.

The business press reports information about insider trading obtained from the OSC Bulletin. In addition, some investment dealers use insider trading activity as part of the information employed to develop buy and sell recommendations.

It is illegal for anyone to enter into a security transaction if they have taken advantage of "inside" information about the corporation that is unavailable to other people involved in the transaction. This proscription includes not only insiders but also those to whom they give such secret information (the recipient of such a tip is termed the *tipee*).

---

[13] In some provinces, notably Quebec and Alberta insiders are required to report their activity within 10 days of executing a trade.

# CDN UNLISTED

Prices of unlisted stocks provided at 5 p.m. yesterday by Canadian Dealing Network Inc., in cents unless marked $.

| Stock | Volume | High | Low | Close | Chg. |
|---|---|---|---|---|---|
| Advantex | 57671 | 160 | 125 | 160 | +10 |
| Anglo Sws | 3000 | 11 | 11 | 11 | +1 |
| Ansil Res | 74 | 60 | 60 | 60 | −10 |
| BCI A | 12775 | 240 | 210 | 240 | |
| Batery Tec | 15000 | 110 | 105 | 110 | |
| Belteco Hld | 4500 | 120 | 80 | 80 | |
| Bestquipt S | 6800 | 80 | 80 | 80 | |
| BI Heavn | 500 | 15 | 15 | 15 | |
| Boston B | 500 | 150 | 150 | 150 | +38 |
| Bright R | 500 | 100 | 100 | 100 | −20 |
| Burgess | 440 | 3 | 3 | 3 | −17 |
| Canmine | 15000 | 20 | 18 | 20 | +1 |
| Castle Cap | 10000 | 50 | 50 | 50 | −3 |
| Chocolat A | 1000 | 20 | 20 | 20 | +5 |
| Craibbe | 20000 | 75 | 74 | 74 | +4 |
| Dateland C | 145400 | 29 | 20 | 27 | +7 |
| Denroy M | 1500 | 30 | 30 | 30 | −6 |
| Deprenyl a | 1850 | $10¾ | 10½ | 10½ | |
| Dexus I A | 15 | 375 | 375 | 375 | −25 |
| Dexus I B | 15 | 375 | 375 | 375 | −25 |
| Dasyn Tech | 8000 | 52 | 50 | 50 | +3 |
| Dime Res | 45750 | 115 | 95 | 110 | |
| Docu Fax | 1000 | 40 | 40 | 40 | −50 |
| Euro Dsny | 3070 | $33½ | 33 | 33½ | −¾ |
| Falcon S | 14800 | $5 | 485 | 490 | +10 |
| Fost Brew | 6638 | 150 | 150 | 150 | |
| Geneva L | 1000 | 15 | 15 | 15 | |
| Gracefield | 44100 | 42 | 42 | 42 | |
| Gmit clb A | 249 | 350 | 300 | 350 | +50 |
| Gm Line B | 10000 | 22 | 22 | 22 | |
| Horn Fault | 6000 | 60 | 50 | 50 | +20 |
| Interstar M | 1050 | 95 | 95 | 95 | −6 |
| Is Tel 77 | 200 | $19¾ | 19¾ | 19¾ | −¼ |
| Kirkton Res | 1000 | 25 | 25 | 25 | −25 |
| Laverty I | 1000 | 110 | 110 | 110 | |
| Mad Grant | 650 | 140 | 140 | 140 | +15 |
| McNickel | 1000 | 2 | 2 | 2 | −3 |
| Microbx B | 5000 | 50 | 50 | 50 | +2 |
| Mirror O | 54000 | 110 | 110 | 110 | |
| Mitron Tec | 1000 | 25 | 25 | 25 | |
| Monac Acs | 4000 | 40 | 40 | 40 | |
| Mt Keno | 10000 | 18 | 18 | 18 | −2 |
| Mtn Beavr | 1750 | 30 | 30 | 30 | |
| Mtn Bvr W | 1750 | 1 | 1 | 1 | |
| Ont Queb | | 6 $130 | 130 | 130 | −6 |
| Optimal R | 15575 | 195 | 175 | 195 | +15 |
| Pelango | 5000 | 37 | 37 | 37 | −2 |
| Petrolantc | 55000 | 26 | 23 | 24 | − |
| Portrait I | 19250 | 130 | 100 | 125 | |
| Putco Hld | 97 | 100 | 100 | 100 | −25 |
| Putco H II | 1900 | 125 | 125 | 125 | |
| Rmi Med | 23532 | 235 | 230 | 235 | +5 |
| Rmi Med W | 5000 | 85 | 85 | 85 | |
| Sandy Lk | 83500 | 58 | 33 | 58 | |
| Sandy L W | 2000 | 2 | 2 | 2 | |
| Sheffield | 3500 | 105 | 105 | 105 | +5 |
| Sheldon | 2000 | 25 | 25 | 25 | −2 |
| Strike M | 5000 | 18 | 18 | 18 | −2 |
| Torvalon C | 64120 | 170 | 155 | 170 | |
| Ultracell M | 39900 | 120 | 120 | 120 | |
| Van Ollie | 1000 | 25 | 25 | 25 | +15 |
| Welcm plc | 796 | $22 | 21½ | 21½ | −¾ |
| Wst Troy | 14000 | 95 | 75 | 95 | |
| White Str | 12000 | 63 | 58 | 58 | |
| York Bay | 25000 | 100 | 100 | 100 | −25 |

Total Volume 897.723

## UNLISTED BID AND ASKED

| Unlisted | Bid | Ask |
|---|---|---|
| ATI C | 140 | 160 |
| Abby L | $21 | 24 |
| Abrt F | $10¾ | |
| Adv A | 5 | 30 |
| Agt prt | $10 | |
| Agt P 91 | $10 | |
| Alid nth | 10 | 20 |
| Almrk | 27 | 29 |
| Amrtk | 12 | 15 |
| Amhr I | 200 | |
| Amtel | $7 | 7½ |
| Andr 6 | $5½ | |
| Anglo P | 5 | 8 |
| Arjon | 4 | 6 |
| Asquth | 5 | 15 |
| Augdm | ½ | 10 |
| Aurelin | 10 | 15 |
| Aurict | 25 | 50 |
| Ashrm | $5¼ | 6 |
| Bnd Or | 3 | 8 |
| Beld C B | 55 | 65 |
| B Greg | 5 | 9 |
| Blk Riv | 10 | |

| | Bid | Ask |
|---|---|---|
| Cmstk | 3 | 6 |
| Copr A | 20 | 23 |
| Consl r | 8 | 15 |
| Conqst | 5 | 8 |
| Cons R | 25 | |
| C Stnfrd | 25 | 75 |
| C Tonk | 5 | |
| C Genl | 1 | 10 |
| Cntl Cpr | 14 | 16 |
| Copqst | 18 | 22 |
| Costgn | 20 | 30 |
| Cvngt I | 10 | 20 |
| Cross C | 10 | 15 |
| Cuda C | 10 | 15 |
| Dalhsi | 45 | 55 |
| Dayton | 10 | 40 |
| Denb | 350 | 450 |
| Depr W | $6¾ | 7 |
| Derlak | 30 | 40 |
| Dstrbi | 3 | |
| Dexx | 7 | 9 |
| Dino I | 15 | 50 |
| D Angl | $200 | |
| D Ann | $50 | |

| | Bid | Ask |
|---|---|---|
| Force R | 2 | 8 |
| Fortun | 15 | 20 |
| Foxgr | 1 | 10 |
| Galtc | $50 | |
| Garsn c | 10 | |
| Grwy U | 5 | 15 |
| Geodyn | 7 | 10 |
| Gmge | 2 | 6 |
| Gridtn | 2 | 8 |
| Godrch | $29 | 32 |
| G Carib | 5 | |
| G Cres | 5 | 10 |
| G Harx | 26 | 28 |
| G Hope | 15 | 30 |
| G Shaft | 10 | |
| Gldqst | 12 | 15 |
| Gmd E | 10 | 20 |
| Gmd O | 10 | 25 |
| G Fort | 25 | 50 |
| Gt Nth | 40 | |
| GWst L | $560 | 620 |
| H O Fm | 140 | 250 |
| Hale R | ? | |
| Htn A c | 60 | |

| | Bid | Ask |
|---|---|---|
| Jonpi w | ½ | |
| July R | 15 | 30 |
| Kenn | 1 | 3 |
| Kidstn | 110 | 135 |
| Kingb C | 60 | 80 |
| Kngcrs | 1 | |
| Kinc | 1 | |
| Laird G | 2 | 40 |
| Langis | 5 | 10 |
| Laser E | 70 | 120 |
| Laser F | 10 | 25 |
| Lassie | 23 | 28 |
| Legacy | 10 | |
| Leggo h | 5 | 10 |
| Lenox | 375 | 400 |
| Lobo G | 7 | 13 |
| Lmbrd | 5 | 15 |
| Lond LI | $1480 | 1520 |
| Lndn S | 20 | 30 |
| Lngfrd | 50 | |
| Lngfd p | 245 | |
| Luvcrt | 12 | 15 |
| Lyndx | 5 | 10 |

| | Bid | Ask |
|---|---|---|
| Nik Rm | 2 | 5 |
| N Hawk | 10 | 15 |
| Noea | 3 | 8 |
| NTel A | $11¾ | 12½ |
| NTel B | $11¼ | 12½ |
| NTel C | $11¾ | 12½ |
| NTel D | $11¾ | |
| NTel E | $18¼ | |
| NTel 2a | $10¾ | |
| NTel 2b | $11¼ | |
| Nthfld C | 1 | |
| Nthfl A | 37 | 45 |
| Nthfld P | 15 | 30 |
| Nova | ½ | 5 |
| NS Svg | $12 | |
| Oakvil | 400 | |
| Orym | 1 | |
| Optical | 1 | |
| Orphee | 25 | 50 |
| Otawa S | 40 | |
| PMC p | 400 | |
| Pwa C | $9 | 9½ |
| Paca | 25 | 100 |

| | Bid | Ask |
|---|---|---|
| Ry Crst | 15 | 30 |
| Salk U | 35 | |
| Santa V | $6 | 6¾ |
| Sctre p | $10 | |
| Sedona | 15 | 20 |
| Shling I | 5 | 25 |
| Shrsn | 75 | 100 |
| Slate | 5 | 15 |
| Sby 6¼ | $12¾ | 13¾ |
| Solex | 1 | |
| Sams | 3 | 6 |
| Spnex C | 120 | 130 |
| Stmfrd | ? | |
| Star | 10 | 30 |
| Star G | 30 | |
| Sarat | 1 | 3 |
| So Ind | 55 | 100 |
| Sucr M | 10 | 20 |
| Surry | 10 | |
| Suncor | $17½ | 25 |
| Sungld | 95 | 115 |
| Sucr Sol | 20 | |
| Sucr F | 5 | |

**FIGURE 15-3**

Summary of shares quoted on the CDN network.

SOURCE: Reprinted by permission of *The Globe and Mail: Report on Business*, Thomson Newspapers Company Limited (January 8, 1992).

Legal issues aside, two questions of relevance to outside investors may be posed: (1) Do insiders make unusual profits on transactions in their own stocks? (2) If they do, can others profit by following their example as soon as it becomes public knowledge?

Insiders trade their shares for many reasons. For example, some purchases result from the exercise of options and some sales result from the need for cash. Moreover, it is not unusual to find some insiders purchasing shares during a month in which other insiders are selling . However, when a major piece of inside information suggests that a

## HOW TO READ THE STOCK TABLES

| 52-week | | | | Friday | | | | This week | | | | | Share | P/E |
|---|---|---|---|---|---|---|---|---|---|---|---|---|---|---|
| high | low | Stock | Symbol Div | Hi/bid | Lo/ask | Chg | Vol(h) | High | Low | Close | Chg | Vol(h) Yield | profit | ratio |

### A-B

*(stock table data)*

All securities that were traded in Canada this week are listed in these tables by stock exchange. Most issues that were not traded during the week are shown separately by exchange, with the highest price that has been bid to buy the stock and the lowest price asked by a seller.

Most stocks are listed alphabetically. But on the Toronto Stock Exchange, debentures, non-equity warrants, partly paid shares, partnership and trust units and shares traded in U.S. funds are at the end of the main list. Montreal Exchange trading in junior companies' stock, in partly paid shares, trust units and shares traded in U.S. funds or from international markets are also listed separately.

The tables of U.S. stock trading include securities of special interest to Canadian investors as well as several hundred of yesterday's most active issues on the New York Stock Exchange, the American Stock Exchange and the National Association of Security Dealers Automated Quotations trading system. U.S. trading is quoted in U.S. dollars. New York and American Stock Exchange quotations are composites of prices on those and other U.S. exchanges.

Each stock's name is preceded by its high and low trading price in the past 52 weeks. Some are preceded by a ↑ to indicate a new 52-week high was set on Friday or a ↓ to show a new 52-week low in yesterday's trading.

An s at the beginning of a line shows the 52-week high-low range has been adjusted because the stock has recently split or a stock dividend amounting to 25 per cent or more has been paid. An n means the stock is a new issue. The notation xd indicates the stock is trading ex-dividend and the next dividend payment will be made to the current owner of record; xc means a coming capital gains distribution will be paid to the current owner.

The company's name is followed by the stock's exchange trading symbol, which is used by brokers and many computerized information services. The suffix .PR as part of a symbol indicates a preferred share; WT is a warrant; .UN is a unit.

The following columns show Friday's highest and lowest trading prices and the change in price (if any) from the previous trading day. The volume of trading is shown in hundreds. Thus, 150 would indicate 15,000 shares were traded. A z preceding the volume figure indicates the sales are reported in full. If the volume is shown as nt (no trading), the price under "high" is the highest bid and under "low" is the lowest offer to sell.

The next five columns show the week's high and low trading prices, the last traded price, the change from the previous week's closing price and the week's volume in hundreds.

Toronto, Montreal and U.S. listings also show the annual dividend value, and the yield when there is a dividend. (Yield is expressed as a percentage and is calculated by dividing the dividend by the current market price.) The price/earnings ratio is also shown for common stocks on those lists. (The P/E ratio is the number of times by which the current stock price exceeds the company's latest 12-month earnings.)

Other footnotes: a — in U.S. dollars (on Canadian exchanges). au — in Australian dollars. b — in British pounds or pence. c — in Canadian dollars (on U.S. exchanges). ci — commercial/industrial stock (on the Vancouver Stock Exchange). da — dividend in arrears. dc — dividend paid in Canadian dollars, but stock trades in U.S. funds. in — inactive stock (on the VSE). j — subject to special reporting rules. nl — mutual fund with no front-end load or contingent deferred sales load. nv — non-voting. rc — in bankruptcy or receivership or being reorganized under the Bankruptcy Act, or securities assumed by such companies. rf — redemption fee or contingent deferred sales load may apply. rs — resource stock (VSE). rv — shareholders' voting is restricted. sv — subordinate-voting. y — in Japanese yen.

## FIGURE 15-4

Summary of activity in shares traded on the Toronto Stock Exchange.

*SOURCE:* Reprinted by permission of *The Globe and Mail: Report on Business*, Thomson Newspapers Company Limited (April 25, 1992).

stock's value differs significantly from its current market price, it would be reasonable to expect a preponderance of insider trades on one side of the market (that is, either purchases or sales).

One way to search for such situations is to examine the *OSC Bulletin* and count the number of times during a month that insiders traded their firm's shares (excluding the exercise of options). If the number of purchases exceeds the number of sales, it might be inferred that favorable inside information motivated the insider trades during the month. If the number of sales exceeds the number of purchases this can be regarded as an unfavorable signal.

Different cutoff levels could be used in this process to reflect the intensity of insider trading. A cutoff of 1 would require a simple majority of trades of one type, whereas a cutoff of 5 would require a "supermajority" of trades of one type.

Such a procedure was used in a detailed US study of insider transactions during the 1950s and 1960s.[14] Table 15.1 summarizes the key results. The two columns on the right-hand side of the table indicate the abnormal returns over an eight-month period on securities that exceeded the cutoff level for insider trading. For example, during the 1960s, if an investor purchased every stock in the sample for which there were three or more net purchasers and sold every stock for which there were three or more more net sellers during a month, more or less coincident with the transactions of the insiders themselves, then the investor would have earned, on average, an abnormal return of 5.07% over the subsequent eight months. If the transactions had been made instead at roughly the time the information was published in the SEC's *Official Summary*, an average abnormal return of 4.94% would have been earned over the next eight months.

**TABLE 15.1**

Abnormal Returns Associated with Insider Trading.

| Sample | | | Average Abnormal Return over Eight Months Following | |
|---|---|---|---|---|
| Cut-off (No. of Net Purchasers or Sellers) | No. of Cases | Period | Month of Transaction | Month Information Became Publicly Available |
| 1 | 362 | 1960s | 1.36% | .70% |
| 3 | 861 | 1960s | 5.07 | 4.94 |
| 4 | 293 | 1950s | 5.14 | 4.12 |
| 5 | 157 | 1950s | 4.48 | 4.08 |

SOURCE: Jeffrey F. Jaffe, "Special Information and Insider Trading," *Journal of Business* 47, no. 3 (July 1974):421, 426.

As the first row in the table shows, a bare majority of insider trades does not appear to isolate possible effects of insider information. But a majority of three, four, or five does seem to do so. The figures shown are gross of any transaction costs, but even so it appears that insiders can and do make money from their special knowledge of their companies. This is not surprising, since if anyone can know the true value of a firm, it should be the insiders. Since the information these insiders presumably are using is nonpublic in nature, these findings suggest that markets are not strong-form efficient. (The notion of market efficiency was introduced in Chapter 3.)

---

[14]Jeffrey F. Jaffe, "Special Information and Insider Trading," *Journal of Business* 47, no. 3 (July 1974):410–28. See also Joseph E. Finnerty, "Insiders and Market Efficiency," *Journal of Finance* 31, no. 4 (September 1976):1141–48.

On the other hand, the abnormal returns associated with transactions that could have been made by outsiders, using only publicly available information on insider trading, are quite surprising. Moreover, those associated with cutoffs of three, four, or five pass statistical tests designed to see if they might be simply due to chance. After transaction costs, trades designed to capitalize on such information would still appear to produce abnormal returns (although not highly so), suggesting that markets are not even semistrong-form efficient. However, more recent studies have found that outsiders cannot use the publicly available information about insider trading to make abnormal profits; these studies thus support the notion that markets are semistrong-form efficient.[15] Whether or not insider trading information can be profitably used by outsiders is an open question given the conflicting evidence. It is also possible that the inefficiency has disappeared as a result of the publicity it has received.

The Canadian situation is less contradictory. Figure 15.5 shows the cumulative average residuals, based on monthly data, for both buy and sell signals derived from an examination of some 17,000 insider trades executed between 1967 and 1977. Period 0 on the graph represents the publication date of the OSC Bulletin and, therefore, indicates the time when outsiders would become aware of inside trading activity. The CARs for month minus one (when the insiders traded) indicate that insiders, on average, are able to buy low and sell high, that outsiders can profit from observing the actions of insiders, and that abnormal returns persist for about 12 months after the original signal. None of these conclusions are consistent with semi-strong form market efficiency. These results have been confirmed by a number of other studies. Some of these also find that not all insiders are equal. Directors of firms who are also bank directors appear to have access to better inside information than other insiders.[16]

## 15.7 EX ANTE AND EX POST VALUES

Equilibrium theories such as the capital asset pricing model and arbitrage pricing theory imply that in the opinion of well-informed investors, securities with certain attributes will, other things being equal, have large expected returns, whereas those with other attributes will have small expected returns. Thus, the focus of these theories is on future, or *ex ante*, expected returns. However, only historical, or *ex post*, returns are subsequently observed. These historical returns are undoubtedly different from the expected returns, making it extremely difficult to tell whether security attributes and expected returns do, in fact, go together in the manner implied by either the CAPM or APT. Moreover, such theories are relatively silent concerning simple ways in which

---

[15] See Herbert S. Kerr, "The Battle of Insider Trading and Market Efficiency," *Journal of Portfolio Management* 6, no. 4 (Summer 1980):47–58; and Wayne Y. Lee and Michael E. Solt, "Insider Trading: A Poor Guide to Market Timing," *Journal of Portfolio Management* 12, no. 4 (Summer 1986):65–71.

[16] D.J.Fowler and C.H.Rorke,"Insider Trading Profits on the Toronto Stock Exchange, 1967–1977," *Canadian Journal of Administrative Sciences* 5, no. 1 (March 1988):13–24. This study also found that the abnormal returns were higher for thinner stocks than for those more frequently traded. See also J. Baesel and G.Stein, "The Value of Information: Inferences from the Profitability of Insider Trading," 14 (September 1979):553–69; M.H.Lee and H.Bishara, "Recent Canadian Experiences on the Profitability of Insider Trades," *Financial Review* 24, no. 2 (May 1989):235–49; J-M Suret and E.Cormier, "Insiders and the Stock Market," *Canadian Investment Review* III, no. 2 (Fall 1990):87–90. This study finds that abnormal returns persist after insider trading information has been distributed to a brokerage firm's clients. R. Heinkel and A.Kraus, "The Effect of Insider Trading on Average Rates of Return," *Canadian Journal of Economics* 20, no. 3 (August 1987):588–611 examined insider trades on the Vancouver Stock Exchange and found weak evidence of superior insider profits.

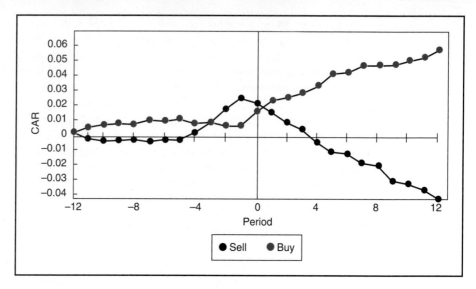

**FIGURE 15-5**

Cumulative abnormal returns to insider trades.

*SOURCE:* D.Fowler and H.Rorke, "Insider Trading Profits on the Toronto Stock Exchange: 1967–1977," *Canadian Journal of Administrative Sciences* 5, no. 1 (March 1988):20.

a security's future, or ex ante, attributes and expected return might be estimated by examining historical, or ex post, returns.

To bridge this gap, a number of investigators have used the average historical return of a security as an estimate of its expected return. This requires an assumption that the expected return did not change over some arbitrary time period and that this time period contains a sufficient number of historical returns to make a reasonably accurate estimate of the expected return. However, an objection may be made in that expectations almost certainly would have changed over the time period needed to obtain a reasonably useful estimate of the expected return for any given security.[17] Despite this objection, it is worthwhile examining historical returns to see how they can be used to come up with meaningful predictions about the future.[18] The next section explores the prediction of a firm's beta. It begins by discussing the estimation of the firm's historical beta by use of the characteristic line.

[17] It has been argued that roughly 300 months (25 years) of historical returns are needed in order for a simple averaging technique to produce reasonably useful estimates of expected returns, provided that the "true" but unobserved expected return is constant during this entire period. See J. D. Jobson and Bob Korkie, "Estimation for Markowitz Efficient Portfolios," *Journal of the American Statistical Association* 75, no. 371 (September 1980):544–54 and "Putting Markowitz Theory to Work," *Journal of Portfolio Management* 7, no. 4 (Summer 1981):70–74.

[18] In doing so, a number of researchers have uncovered certain "empirical regularities" in common stock returns; Appendix A discusses a number of them. For a more detailed summary, see Donald B. Keim, "The CAPM and Equity Return Regularities," *Financial Analysts Journal* 42, no. 3 (May/June 1986):19-34; Douglas K. Pearce, "Challenges to the Concept of Market Efficiency," Federal Reserve Bank of Kansas City *Economic Review* 72, no. 8 (September/October 1987):16-33; and Robert A. Haugen and Josef Lakonishok, *The Incredible January Effect* (Homewood, Ill.: Dow Jones-Irwin, 1988).

# COMMON STOCK BETAS

For purposes of portfolio management, the relevant risk of a security concerns its impact on the risk of a well-diversified portfolio. In the world of the CAPM, such portfolios would be subject primarily to market risk. This suggests the importance of a security's beta, which measures its sensitivity to future market movements. To estimate beta, in principle the possible sources of such movements should be considered. Then, the reaction of the security's price to each of these sources should be estimated, along with the probability of each reaction. In the process, the economics of the relevant industry and firm, the impact of both operating and financial leverage on the firm, and other fundamental factors should be taken into account.

But what about investigating the extent to which the security's price moved with the market in the past? Such an approach ignores the myriad possible differences between the past and the future. However, it is easily done and provides a useful starting point.

As shown in Chapter 8, a security's beta can be regarded as the slope of the security's characteristic line. If this line were constant over time, meaning it was not changing from period to period, then the *historical beta* for a security could be estimated by examining the historical relationship between the excess returns on the security and on the market portfolio. The statistical procedure used for making such estimates of ex post betas is *simple linear regression*, also known as ordinary least squares (OLS).[19]

As an example, consider estimating the ex post beta for Stelco using TSE total return index and the 91-day Treasury bill rate as surrogates for the market portfolio and the risk-free rate respectively. Part (a) of Table 15.2 presents the data necessary to calculate the returns on a quarterly basis over the four-year period from 1982 to 1985 for both Stelco and the TSE 300. Part (b) presents the 91-day Treasury bill rate at the beginning of each quarter, the returns on both Stelco and the TSE 300, and the excess returns on both Stelco and the TSE 300. Part (c) presents the calculations necessary to determine Stelco's ex post beta and alpha as well as certain other statistical parameters. As can be seen, Stelco's beta and alpha were equal to 1.01 and -2.07%, respectively, over this period.[20]

---

[19] For an discussion of regression, see Peter Tryfos, *Business Statistics* (Toronto, Ont.: McGraw-Hill Ryerson, 1989).

[20] Stelco's beta and alpha would have been equal to 1.00 and -2.08%, respectively, if returns had been used in the calculations instead of *excess* returns. Using returns or excess returns (as well as including or ignoring dividends in calculating returns) appears to make little difference to the estimate of beta. However, there is some difference in the estimate of alpha; consequently, it is appropriate to use excess returns when estimating alpha. See William F. Sharpe and Guy M. Cooper, "Risk-Return Classes of New York Stock Exchange Common Stocks, 1931–1967," *Financial Analysts Journal* 28, no. 2 (March/April 1972):46–54.

**TABLE 15.2**

The Ex Post Characteristic Line for Stelco, 1986–1989.

### a. Quarterly Data

| Quarter | | Stelco | | | TSE 300 Total Return | |
|---|---|---|---|---|---|---|
| | | Price at Start | Price at End | Div. | Index at Start | Index at End |
| 1986 | 1 | $22.875 | $26.875 | $0.25 | 4238.78 | 4486.28 |
| | 2 | 26.875 | 25.250 | 0.25 | 4486.28 | 4577.12 |
| | 3 | 25.250 | 21.375 | 0.25 | 4577.12 | 4451.70 |
| | 4 | 21.375 | 19.250 | 0.25 | 4451.70 | 4618.32 |
| 1987 | 1 | 19.250 | 23.625 | 0.25 | 4618.32 | 5666.89 |
| | 2 | 23.625 | 24.375 | 0.25 | 5666.89 | 5705.34 |
| | 3 | 24.375 | 25.250 | 0.25 | 5705.34 | 5987.36 |
| | 4 | 25.250 | 22.000 | 0.25 | 5987.36 | 4889.82 |
| 1988 | 1 | 22.000 | 23.625 | 0.25 | 4889.82 | 5166.26 |
| | 2 | 23.625 | 24.875 | 0.25 | 5166.26 | 5410.06 |
| | 3 | 24.875 | 22.625 | 0.25 | 5410.06 | 5212.87 |
| | 4 | 22.625 | 22.000 | 0.25 | 5212.87 | 5431.68 |
| 1989 | 1 | 22.000 | 23.125 | 0.25 | 5431.68 | 5782.84 |
| | 2 | 23.125 | 22.250 | 0.25 | 5782.84 | 6138.42 |
| | 3 | 22.250 | 22.125 | 0.25 | 6138.42 | 6489.76 |
| | 4 | 22.125 | 21.000 | 0.25 | 6489.76 | 6592.58 |

### b. Returns

| Quarter | | 91–Day Treasury Bill Return | Stelco | | TSE 300 | |
|---|---|---|---|---|---|---|
| | | | Return | Excess Return | Return | Excess Return |
| 1986 | 1 | 2.64 | 18.58 | 15.94 | 5.84 | 3.20 |
| | 2 | 2.20 | −5.12 | −7.32 | 2.02 | −0.18 |
| | 3 | 2.07 | −14.36 | −16.43 | −2.74 | −4.81 |
| | 2 | 2.08 | −8.77 | −10.85 | 3.74 | 1.66 |
| 1987 | 1 | 1.82 | 24.03 | 22.21 | 22.70 | 20.88 |
| | 2 | 2.00 | 4.23 | 2.23 | 0.68 | −1.32 |
| | 3 | 2.26 | 4.62 | 2.36 | 4.94 | 2.68 |
| | 4 | 1.95 | −11.88 | −13.83 | −18.33 | −20.28 |
| 1988 | 1 | 2.09 | 8.52 | 6.43 | 5.65 | 3.56 |
| | 2 | 2.21 | 6.35 | 4.14 | 4.72 | 2.51 |
| | 3 | 2.32 | −8.04 | −10.36 | −3.64 | −5.96 |
| | 4 | 2.60 | −1.66 | −4.26 | 4.20 | 1.60 |
| 1989 | 1 | 2.80 | 6.25 | 3.45 | 6.47 | 3.67 |
| | 2 | 3.09 | −2.70 | −5.79 | 6.15 | 3.06 |
| | 3 | 3.02 | 0.56 | −2.46 | 5.72 | 2.70 |
| | 4 | 3.04 | −3.95 | 6.99 | 1.58 | −1.46 |

## c. Calculations [a]

| Quarter | | Stelco Excess Returns = Y (1) | TSE 300 Excess Returns = X (2) | $Y^2$ (3) | $X^2$ (4) | $X \times Y$ (5) |
|---|---|---|---|---|---|---|
| 1986 | 1 | 15.94 | 3.20 | 254.06 | 10.23 | 50.99 |
| | 2 | −7.32 | −0.18 | 53.53 | 0.03 | 1.28 |
| | 3 | −16.43 | −4.81 | 269.83 | 23.14 | 79.01 |
| | 4 | −10.85 | 1.66 | 117.76 | 2.77 | −18.05 |
| 1987 | 1 | 22.21 | 20.88 | 493.11 | 436.17 | 463.76 |
| | 2 | 2.23 | −1.32 | 4.99 | 1.75 | −2.95 |
| | 3 | 2.36 | 2.68 | 5.55 | 7.20 | 6.32 |
| | 4 | −13.83 | −20.28 | 191.30 | 411.32 | 280.51 |
| 1988 | 1 | 6.43 | 3.56 | 41.38 | 12.70 | 22.92 |
| | 2 | 4.14 | 2.51 | 17.13 | 6.30 | 10.39 |
| | 3 | −10.36 | −5.96 | 107.33 | 35.58 | 61.80 |
| | 4 | −4.26 | 1.60 | 18.13 | 2.55 | −6.80 |
| 1989 | 1 | 3.45 | 3.67 | 11.90 | 13.43 | 12.64 |
| | 2 | −5.79 | 3.06 | 33.56 | 9.36 | −17.72 |
| | 3 | −2.46 | 2.70 | 6.04 | 7.31 | −6.65 |
| | 4 | −6.99 | −1.46 | 48.93 | 2.12 | 10.18 |
| Sum ($\Sigma$) | | −21.53 | 11.52 | 1674.52 | 981.94 | 947.64 |
| | | $= \Sigma Y$ | $= \Sigma X$ | $= \Sigma Y^2$ | $= \Sigma X^2$ | $= \Sigma XY$ |

1. Beta:

$$\frac{(T \times \Sigma XY) - (\Sigma Y \times \Sigma X)}{(T \times \Sigma X^2) - (\Sigma X)^2} = \frac{(16 \times 947.64) - (-21.53 \times 11.52)}{(16 \times 981.94) - (11.52)^2} = 1.01$$

2. Alpha:

$$\left(\frac{\Sigma Y}{T}\right) - \left(beta \times \frac{\Sigma X}{T}\right) = \left(\frac{-21.53}{16}\right) - \left(1.01 \times \frac{11.52}{16}\right) = -2.07\%$$

3. Standard deviation of random error term:

$$\left[\frac{\Sigma Y^2 - (alpha \times \Sigma Y) - (beta \times \Sigma XY)}{T - 2}\right]^{1/2}$$

$$= \left[\frac{1674.52 - (-2.05 \times -21.53) - (1.01 \times 947.64)}{16 - 2}\right]^{1/2} = 7.273\%$$

4. Standard error of beta:

Standard deviation of random error term$/\{\Sigma X^2 - [(\Sigma X)^2/T]\}^{1/2}$

$$= \frac{7.273}{\{981.94 - [(11.52)^2/16]\}^{1/2}} = .233$$

5. Standard error of alpha:

Standard deviation of random error term$/\{T - [(\Sigma X)^2/\Sigma X^2]\}^{1/2}$

$$= \frac{7.273}{\{16 - [(11.52)^2/981.94]\}^{1/2}} = 1.826$$

6. Correlation coefficient:

$$\frac{(T \times \Sigma XY) - (\Sigma Y \times \Sigma X)}{\{[(T \times \Sigma Y^2) - (\Sigma Y)^2] \times [(T \times \Sigma X^2) - (\Sigma X)^2]\}^{1/2}}$$

$$\frac{(16 \times 947.64) - (-21.53 \times 11.52)}{\{[(16 \times 1674.52) - (-21.53)^2] \times [(16 \times 981.94) - (11.52)^2]\}^{1/2}} = .761$$

7. Coefficient of determination:

$$(\text{Correlation coefficient})^2 = (.761)^2 = .579$$

8. Coefficient of nondetermination:

$$1 - \text{coefficient of determination} = 1 - .579 = .421$$

---

[a] All summations are to be carried out over $t$, where $t$ goes from 1 to $T$ (in this example, $t = 1, 2, \ldots, 16$).

Given these values for alpha and beta, the ex post characteristic line for Stelco is:

$$r_{STE} - r_f = -2.07\% + 1.01(r_M - r_f) + \epsilon_{STE} \qquad (15.6)$$

Figure 15.6 presents a scatter diagram of the excess returns on Stelco ($r_{STE} - r_f$) and the TSE 300 ($r_M - r_f$). Also shown in the figure is a graph of the characteristic line, except that the random error term is deleted. That is, the figure has a graph of the following line:

$$r_{STE} - r_f = -2.07\% + 1.01(r_M - r_f). \qquad (15.7)$$

The vertical distance of each point in the scatter diagram from this characteristic line represents an estimate of the size of the random error term for the corresponding quarter. The exact distance can be found by rewriting equation (15.6) as:

$$[r_{STE} - r_f] - [-2.07\% + 1.15(r_M - r_f)] = \epsilon_{STE} \qquad (15.8)$$

For example, looking at part c of Table 15.2, in the third quarter of 1988 the excess returns on Stelco and the TSE 300 were $-10.36\%$ and $-5.96\%$, respectively. The value of $\epsilon_{STE}$ for that quarter can be calculated by using equation (15.8), as follows:

$$[-10.36\%] - [-2.07\% + 1.01(-5.96\%)] = -2.27\%.$$

The values of $\epsilon_{STE}$ can be similarly calculated for the other 15 quarters of the estimation period. The standard deviation of the resulting set of 16 numbers is an estimate of the *standard deviation of the random error term* (or residual standard deviation) and is shown in part c of Table 15.2 to be equal to 7.273%. This number can be viewed as an estimate of the historical unique risk of Stelco.

The characteristic line for Stelco shown in Figure 15.6 corresponds to the regression line for the scatter diagram. Recalling that a straight line is defined by its intercept and slope, it can be shown that there are no other values for alpha and beta that will define a straight line fitting the scatter diagram any better than the regression line. This means that there is no line that could be drawn that would result in a smaller standard deviation of the random error term. Thus, the regression line is often referred to as the line of *best fit*.

Equivalently, the line of best fit is the line that has the smallest sum of squared values of the random error terms. That is, the 16 random error terms associated with the

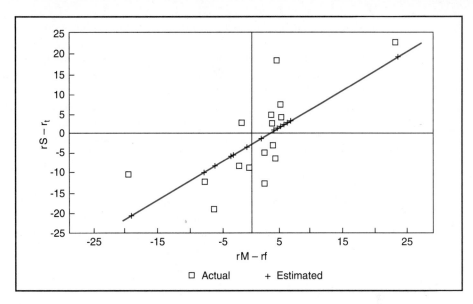

**FIGURE 15-6**
Ex post characteristic line for Stelco.

regression line can each be squared and then summed. This sum (sum of squared errors) is smaller for the line of best fit than the sum associated with any other line.

For example, if alpha were equal to 1.5% and beta equal to .8 in equation (15.8), then the value of the random error term of $\epsilon_{STE}$ could be calculated for each of the 16 quarters. With these 16 values, the standard deviation of the random error term could be calculated by squaring each value, summing up the squared values, and dividing the sum by 14 = (16 - 2); the standard deviation of the random error term would then be the square root of this number. However, it would be larger than 7.273%, which is the standard deviation of the random error term associated with the line of best fit (that is, the line with an alpha of −2.07% and a beta of 1.01).

It should be remembered that a security's "true" historical beta cannot be observed. All that can be done is to estimate its value. Thus, even if a security's true beta remained the same forever, its estimated value, obtained in the manner shown in Table 15.2, would still change from time to time because of errors (known as sampling errors) in estimating it. For example, if the 16 quarters from 1982 to 1985 were examined, the resulting estimated beta for Stelco would almost certainly be different from 1.01, the estimated value for 1986 to 1989. The *standard error of beta* shown in part (c) of Table 15.2 attempts to indicate the extent of such estimation errors. Given a number of necessary assumptions (for example, the true beta did not change during the estimation period of 1986 to 1989), the chances are roughly two out of three that the true beta is within a standard error, plus or minus, of the estimated beta. Thus, Stelco's true beta is likely to be between the values of .777( 1.01 − .233) and 1.243( 1.01 + .233). Similarly, the *standard error of alpha* provides an indication of the magnitude of the possible sampling error that has been made in estimating alpha.

The *correlation coefficient* provides an indication of how closely the excess returns on Stelco were associated with the excess returns on the TSE 300. Since its range is between -1 and +1, the value for Stelco of .761 indicates a strong positive relationship between Stelco and the TSE 300. That is, larger excess returns for Stelco seem to be associated with larger excess returns on the TSE 300.

The *coefficient of determination* represents the proportion of variation in the excess return on Stelco that is related to the variation in the excess return on the TSE 300. That is, it shows how much of the movement in Stelco's excess returns can be explained by movements in the excess returns on the TSE 300. With a value of .579, it can be seen that the majority of the movement in the excess return on Stelco from 1986 to 1989 can be attributed to movement in the excess return on the TSE 300.

Since the *coefficient of nondetermination* is 1 minus the coefficient of determination, it represents the proportion of movement in the excess return on Stelco that is not due to movement in the excess return on the TSE 300. Thus, 42.1% of the movement in Stelco cannot be attributed to movement in the TSE 300.

## ☐ 15.8.1 Adjusting Beta

Without any information at all, it would be reasonable to estimate the beta of a stock to be equal to 1.0, the average size of beta. Given a chance to see how the stock moved relative to the market over some time period, a modification of this prior estimate would seem appropriate. Such a modification would sensibly produce a final estimate of beta that would lie between the value of 1.0 and its estimated value based purely on historical price changes.

Formal procedures for making such modifications have been adopted by most investment firms that estimate betas. The specific adjustments made typically differ from time to time and, in some cases, from stock to stock. For example Merrill Lynch calculates *adjusted beta* values by giving approximately 66% weight to the historical estimate of beta and approximately 34% weight to the prior value of beta of 1.0 for each stock. More generally,

$$\beta_a = (.66 \times \beta_h) + (.34 \times 1.0) \qquad (15.9)$$

where $\beta_a$ and $\beta_h$ are the adjusted and historical betas, respectively.[21] Examination of equation (15.9) indicates that this procedure takes the historical beta for a security and adjusts it by giving it a value closer to 1.0. Thus, historical betas less than 1.0 are made larger but are still less than 1.0, and historical betas greater than 1.0 are made smaller but are still greater than 1.0. The adjustments are in this direction because weights (.66 and .34) are positive and add up to 1.0, indicating the adjustment procedure is an averaging technique.

Table 15.3 shows the extent to which such a procedure anticipates differences between historical and future betas. The second column lists the unadjusted historical betas for eight portfolios of 100 securities each, based on monthly price changes from July 1947 through June 1954 (the portfolios were designed to have significantly different

---

[21] Adjusted betas are also published in the *Value Line Investment Survey* and the *Value Line Investment Survey: Canadian Edition*; their adjusted beta is equal to $(.67 \times \beta_h) + (.35 \times 1.0)$. Thus, the adjustment procedures of Value Line and Merrill Lynch are quite similar. See Meir Statman, "Betas Compared: Merrill Lynch vs. Value Line," *Journal of Portfolio Management* 7, no. 2 (Winter 1981):41–44.

betas during this period). The third column of the table shows the values obtained when an adjustment of the type used by Merrill Lynch was applied. The betas in the fourth column are based on price changes over the subsequent seven years. For a majority of the portfolios, the adjusted betas are closer in magnitude to the subsequent historical betas than are the unadjusted betas. This suggests that the adjusted historical beta is a more accurate estimate of the future beta than the unadjusted historical beta.

The fifth column of Table 15.3 shows the historical betas estimated using data from a third seven-year period. Comparing the unadjusted betas in columns 2, 4, and 5, it can be seen that there is a continuing tendency for betas to shrink toward the mean value of 1.0 over time. Thus, adjustment procedures seem to have some usefulness when it comes to estimating betas for a future time period.

**TABLE 15.3**
Ex Ante and Ex Post Beta Values for Portfolios of 100 Securities Each.

| Portfolio (1) | July 1947-June 1954 | | July 1954-June 1961 (4) | July 1961-June 1968 (5) |
|---|---|---|---|---|
| | Unadjusted (2) | Adjusted (3) | | |
| 1 | .36 | .48 | .57 | .72 |
| 2 | .61 | .68 | .71 | .79 |
| 3 | .78 | .82 | .88 | .88 |
| 4 | .91 | .93 | .96 | .92 |
| 5 | 1.01 | 1.01 | 1.03 | 1.04 |
| 6 | 1.13 | 1.10 | 1.13 | 1.02 |
| 7 | 1.26 | 1.21 | 1.24 | 1.08 |
| 8 | 1.47 | 1.39 | 1.32 | 1.15 |

SOURCE: Marshall E. Blume, "Betas and Their Regression Tendencies," *Journal of Finance* 30, no. 3 (June 1975):792.

It seems plausible that true betas not only vary over time but have a tendency to move back toward average levels, since extreme values are likely to be moderated over time. A firm whose operations or financing make the risk of its equity considerably different from that of other firms is more likely to move back toward the average than away from it. Such changes in betas are due to real economic phenomena, not simply an artifact of overly simple statistical procedures. There is, however, no reason to expect every stock's true beta to move to the same average in the same manner at the same speed. In this regard, some fundamental analysis of the firm may prove more useful than the adoption of more sophisticated statistical methods for processing past price changes in estimating beta.

At the portfolio level, historical betas can provide useful information about future betas, but historical betas for individual securities are subject to great error and should be treated accordingly. Table 15.4 provides another view. Every stock listed on the New York Stock Exchange was assigned to one of ten classes in each year from 1931 through 1967, based on the magnitude of its historical beta calculated using data from the preceding five years. The stocks in the top 10% of each January's ranking were assigned to class 10, the next 10% to class 9, and so on. The table shows the percent of the stocks that were in the same class and within one risk class five years later. Also shown are the entries that would be expected if there were no relationship between such past and future beta classes. Examination of the table reveals that individual security betas have some but not a great deal of predictive value.

**TABLE 15.4**
Movement of Stocks Among Beta Classes.

| Risk Class | Percent of Stocks in the Same Beta Class Five Years Later | | Percent of Stocks in the Same Beta Class or Within One Risk Class Five Years Later | |
|---|---|---|---|---|
| | Actual | Expected if There Were No Relationship | Actual | Expected if There Were No Relationship |
| 10 (highest beta values) | 35.2% | 10% | 69.3% | 20% |
| 9 | 18.4 | 10 | 53.7 | 30 |
| 8 | 16.4 | 10 | 45.3 | 30 |
| 7 | 13.3 | 10 | 40.9 | 30 |
| 6 | 13.9 | 10 | 39.3 | 30 |
| 5 | 13.6 | 10 | 41.7 | 30 |
| 4 | 13.2 | 10 | 40.2 | 30 |
| 3 | 15.9 | 10 | 44.6 | 30 |
| 2 | 21.5 | 10 | 60.9 | 30 |
| 1 (lowest beta values) | 40.5 | 10 | 62.3 | 20 |

SOURCE: William F. Sharpe and Guy M. Cooper, "Risk-Return Classes of New York Stock Exchange Common Stocks, 1931–1967," *Financial Analysts Journal* 28, no. 2 (March/April 1972):53.

Figure 15.7 shows that the predictive ability of historical portfolio betas improves with the amount of diversification in a portfolio. The vertical axis plots the percentage of the differences in (measured) portfolio betas (based on weekly price changes) in one year that can be attributed to differences in their (measured) betas in the prior year. The horizontal axis indicates the number of securities in each portfolio. It can be seen in the figure that the historical betas for portfolios containing roughly 10 to 20 securities or more have a high degree of predictive ability. Thus, individual security betas are worth estimating even though they are rather inaccurate when viewed by themselves. This is because their individual inaccuracies seem to cancel out one another when the beta of a diversified portfolio is calculated, resulting in quite an accurate estimate of the portfolio's beta.

## ☐ 15.8.2 Industry Beta Values

The beta of a firm depends on both the demand for the firm's products and the firm's operating costs. However, most firms have both debt and equity outstanding. This means that the beta of a firm's *equity* (that is, stock) depends on the beta of the firm and the firm's financial leverage. For example, imagine there are two firms that are identical in

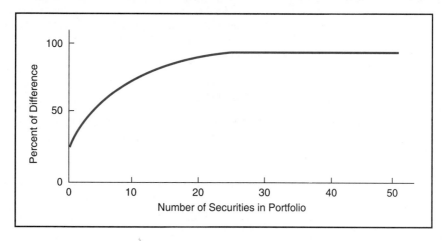

**FIGURE 15-7**
Percent of differences in beta values attributable to differences in prior year's betas.

*SOURCE:* Robert A. Levy, "On the Short-term Stationarity of Beta Coefficients," *Financial Analysis Journal* 27, no. 6 (November/December 1971):57.

every way except that firm A has debt, whereas firm B is free of debt. This means that even though they have the same earnings before interest and taxes (EBIT), they will have different earnings after taxes (EAT) because A, unlike B, has to make interest payments. In this situation, the firm betas for A and B are the same, but the stock beta for A is greater than the stock beta for B. The difference in the debt is the reason for the difference in the stock betas because the debt makes A's earnings available to common shareholders more variable than B's. Thus, the stock beta for A could be viewed as being equal to the stock beta it would have if it had no debt (that is, the beta of B) plus an adjustment for the amount of debt it actually has outstanding.

Firms in industries having highly cyclical demand or large fixed costs might be expected to have higher firm betas than those in industries with more stable demand or greater variable costs, since they will have greater variability in EBIT. Differences in financial leverage could wholly offset such factors, leaving few, if any, differences among the stock betas of firms in different industries. However, this does not seem to be the case. Firms in certain industries do tend to have higher stock betas than those in other industries, and, by and large, the classifications agree with prior expectations.

Figure 15.8 shows the predicted average values of beta for stocks in various industry classifications. Stock prices of firms whose products are termed necessities tend to respond less than the stock prices of most other firms when expectations about the future health of the economy are revised. That is, firms producing necessities (such as utilities or food) tend to have lower betas because they tend to have more stable earnings. On the other hand, stock prices of firms that manufacture luxuries tend to respond more than most others when expectations about the future health of the economy are revised. That is, firms in luxuries (such as travel or electronics) tend to have high betas because they tend to have cyclical earnings. The mining industries also have high betas reflecting the cyclical nature of their earnings.

Information of the type shown in Figure 15.8 can be used to adjust historical betas. For example, the knowledge that a corporation is in the transportion industry suggests that a reasonable prior estimate of the beta of its stock is 1.35. Thus, it makes more sense to adjust its historical beta toward a value of 1.35 than to 1.0, the average for all stocks, as was suggested in equation (15.9).

## □ 15.8.3 Beta Prediction Equations

The procedure used to adjust historical betas involves an implicit prediction equation for future betas. Equation (15.9) can be written more generally as

$$\beta_a = a + b\beta_h \qquad (15.10)$$

where $a$ and $b$ are constants. However, a stock's historical beta ($\beta_h$) is only one of several pieces of information that can be used to predict its future beta ($\beta_a$). For example, firms in the airline industry tend to have higher betas than those in the utility industry. This can be incorporated by including industry effects in the equation:[22]

$$\beta_a = a + b\beta_h + (c_1 \times E_1) + (c_2 \times E_2) + \cdots \qquad (15.11)$$

where $a$, $b$, $c_1$, and $c_2$ are constants. $E_1$ is the percentage of the firm's earnings that are from industry number 1 (perhaps the airline industry); $E_2$ is the percentage of the firm's earnings that are from industry number 2 (perhaps the utility industry); and so on.

Other attributes can also be used. For example, stocks with high dividend yields might have lower betas because more of their value is associated with near-term than with far-term dividends. The equation could thus be augmented to

$$\beta_a = a + b\beta_h + (c_1 \times E_1) + (c_2 \times E_2) + \cdots + (d \times Y) \qquad (15.12)$$

where $d$ is a constant and $Y$ is the dividend yield of the firm's stock.

Table 15.5 shows a beta prediction equation of this form, using historic data from 1928 through 1982.[23] To estimate the beta of a security using this prediction equation, start with a constant based on the industry (referred to as the *sector*) in which the security is classified. Then add to this constant an amount equal to the security's historical beta times .576 (note that this is similar to the adjustment to historical beta shown in equation (15.9)). Finally, add (1) the security's dividend yield times -.019 and (2) the security's "size attribute" times $-.105$.[24] Algebraically, the model is:

$$\beta_a = a_s + (.576 \times \beta_h) + (-.019 \times Y) + (-.105 \times S) \qquad (15.13)$$

where $a_s$ denotes the constant associated with the sector to which the stock belongs, $\beta_h$ is the historical beta, $Y$ is the dividend yield, and $S$ is the size of the firm. With this formula, securities having higher yields are predicted to have lower betas, as are those with larger market values of equity outstanding.

---

[22] For a firm whose earnings are entirely in one industry, this is equivalent to adjusting the historical beta of its stock toward an industry average.

[23] In this model, both historical and adjusted betas are calculated relative to a value-weighted index of the returns on all stocks listed on the New York Stock Exchange. All attributes were calculated using data available a full month prior to the beginning of the month in which stock returns are measured. This avoids statistical problems and provides results that can be used for actual portfolio management.

[24] The dividend yield is measured in percent per year. The *size attribute* is calculated by taking the logarithm (to the base 10) of the total market value of equity outstanding (that is, price per share times shares outstanding), expressed in billions of dollars.

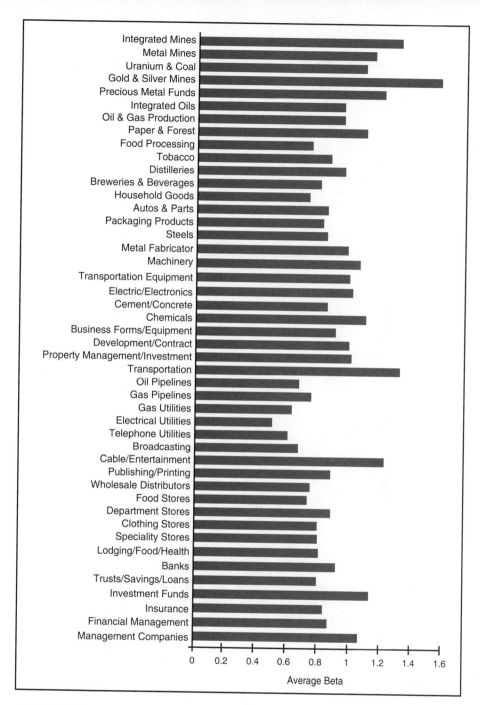

**FIGURE 15-8**
Predicted Beta by Industry.

*SOURCE: The Canadian Equity Model* (Montreal: BARRA International, Ltd.,1990)

**TABLE 15.5**

A Beta Prediction Equation Derived from a Factor Model.

| Constant Term | |
| --- | --- |
| Sector | Value |
| Basic industry | .455 |
| Capital goods | .425 |
| Consumer staple | .307 |
| Consumer cyclical | .443 |
| Credit cyclical | .429 |
| Energy | .394 |
| Finance | .398 |
| Transportation | .255 |
| Utilities | .340 |

| Variable Term | |
| --- | --- |
| Attribute | Coefficient |
| Beta | .576 |
| Yield | −.019 |
| Size | −.105 |

SOURCE: Blake Grossman and William F. Sharpe, "Factors in Security Returns," paper presented at the Center for the Study of Banking and Financial Markets, University of Washington, March 1984.

## An Example

As an example, consider a stock that is classified as belonging to "basic industry." It has a historical beta of 1.2, a dividend yield over the previous 12 months of 4%, and an aggregate market value of $7 billion (that is, the firm has 100 million shares outstanding and the stock is selling for $70 per share). Using equation (15.13), its adjusted beta is

$$\beta_a = .455 + (.576 \times 1.2) + (-.019 \times 4) + [-.105 \times (\log 7)]$$

$$= .455 + .69 - .08 - .09$$

$$= .98.$$

Such prediction equations, based on multifactor models, fit historical data considerably better than those that use only historical betas. One study reported an improvement of 86% over the more simple adjusted beta approach.[25] However, such figures describe only the extent to which the equations fit a given set of data. Since the true test of a prediction equation is its ability to *predict*, only extensive experience with such approaches can, in the final analysis, determine how well various factor models can predict beta values.

---

[25] Barr Rosenberg and Vinay Marathe, "The Prediction of Investment Risk: Systematic and Residual Risk," *Proceedings of the Seminar on the Analysis of Security Prices, University of Chicago,* November 1975. Also see Barr Rosenberg, "Prediction of Common Stock Investment Risk," *Journal of Portfolio Management,* 11, no. 1 (Fall 1984):44–53, and "Prediction of Common Stock Betas," *Journal of Portfolio Management* 11, no. 2 (Winter 1985):5–14.

### ☐ 15.8.4  Beta Services

Services providing betas on a regular basis in published form are available in several countries. Many use only past price changes to form estimates. Some derive their estimates from more general factor models. One service uses weekly data for two years; another, monthly data for five years. One estimates betas for US securities relative to Standard & Poor's 500; another, relative to the New York Stock Exchange Composite Index; and so on. In each case, estimates for individual securities are subject to error. Thus, it is hardly surprising that estimated values for a given security obtained by different services using different procedures are not the same. This does not indicate that some are useless, only that they should be used appropriately and with caution.

In Canada, betas are provided by *The Polymetric Report, The Value Line Investment Survey: Canadian Edition* and the *Beta Book* published by *Barra International, Ltd.*

## 15.9    FACTOR MODELS OF STOCK RETURNS

To operate successfully in the stock market one needs a good model of the relationships among stock returns. Theory provides little guidance concerning the best level of detail for such a model and the specific aspects to be included. The task is thus primarily empirical. Procedures employed for estimating stock factor models typically combine *judgments* concerning important factors with *statistical analysis* of historic data. Both art and science are involved.

### ☐ 15.9.1  A One-Factor Model

Figure 15.9 provides a (hypothetical) example of the relationship between stock returns in a given time period and one attribute. Each point represents one stock, showing its return during the month of January 19XX (on the vertical axis) and its dividend yield (on the horizontal axis). In this case, securities with higher yields tended to do better (have higher returns) than those with lower yields. To quantify the relationship, a straight line has been fitted to the data points using (simple) regression analysis. Since the points represent different securities and one time period, this is an example of *cross-sectional analysis*.

The equation of the line in Figure 15.9 is

$$\text{Return} = 4.0 + (.5 \times \text{yield}).$$

This can be written somewhat more generally as

$$\text{Return} = f_0 + (f_1 \times \text{yield})$$

where:

$f_0$ = the zero factor
$f_1$ = factor 1.

The vertical intercept indicates the return on a typical stock with zero yield. Thus, it is termed the *zero factor*. In Figure 15.9, it is 4%. The slope indicates the additional return per unit increase in yield. Since yield is the first (and only) *attribute* in this example, the slope is termed *factor 1*. In Figure 15.9, the yield factor is 0.5 (= $(7 - 4)/6$).

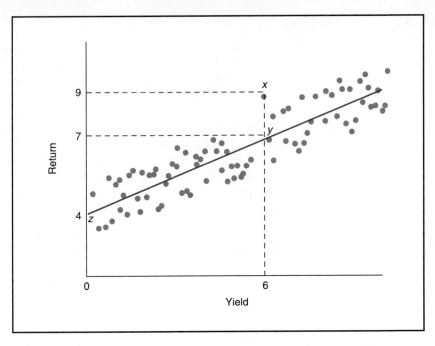

**FIGURE 15-9**
A one-factor model.

The return on any given security may lie above or below the line. A complete description of the relationship can be written as

$$r_{it} = f_{0t} + b_{i1t}f_{1t} + \epsilon_{it} \qquad (15.14)$$

where:

$r_{it}$ = the return on security $i$ in period $t$,
$b_{i1t}$ = security $i$'s sensitivity to factor 1 in period $t$,
$f_{0t}$ = the "zero factor" in period $t$,
$f_{1t}$ = factor 1 in period $t$, and
$\epsilon_{it}$ = security $i$'s *nonfactor return* in period $t$.

Each symbol has been assigned a time-subscript ($t$) to indicate the particular time period (here, January 19XX). The yield *attribute* has been denoted in the conventional manner, since it is assumed to indicate *sensitivity* to the *yield factor*. The final term indicates the *nonfactor* return of the security during the time period. In Figure 15.9, for example, security $x$ had a nonfactor return of +2%, since it returned 9% while the typical stock with the same yield (such as stock $y$) returned only 7%.

Empirically determined factors are closely related to the more fundamental factors of a standard factor model but may differ in certain respects. (Appendix B provides the details.) To emphasize the difference between "empirical factors" and "fundamental factors," the former will be denoted by lowercase letters.

In months such as that shown in Figure 15.9, high-yield securities tend to outperform low-yield securities: the yield factor is *positive*. In other months, high-yield securities tend to underperform low-yield securities. The regression line in the corresponding diagram is downward-sloping and the yield factor is *negative*. In still other months there is no relationship between yield and return. The regression line in the corresponding diagram is flat and the yield factor is *zero*.

## ☐ 15.9.2  A Two-Factor Model

In some months small stocks tend to outperform large stocks. In other months the converse is true. To measure this, one can analyze the relationship between security returns and size. For this purpose, many models use a "size attribute" computed by taking the logarithm of the total market value of equity outstanding (where the latter is computed by multiplying a security's price per share times the number of shares outstanding). Thus, a stock with $1 million of value might be assigned a size attribute of 0, a stock with $10 million a size attribute of 1, a stock with $100 million a size attribute of 2, and so on. This convention is based on the empirical observation that the impact of the "size factor" on a security with a large total value is likely to be twice as great as that on a security with one-tenth the total value. More succinctly: the effect appears to be roughly "linear in the logarithms."

To estimate the "size factor" in a given month, the procedure used in Figure 15.9 to estimate the yield factor could be employed. The size attributes of securities could be plotted on the horizontal axis and their returns plotted (as before) on the vertical axis. The slope of the resultant line would provide an estimate of the size factor for the month.

This procedure has drawbacks, however. Large stocks tend to have high yields. Thus, differences in returns between large and small stocks might be due to some extent to differences in yield, not size. The estimated size factor might be, in part, a reflection of a true yield factor. The problem is, of course, symmetrical. A yield factor estimated as in Figure 15.9 might be, in part, a reflection of a true size factor.

To mitigate this problem, returns can be compared with *both* size and yield attributes, using *multiple* regression. Figure 15.10 provides an illustration. Each security is represented by a point in a three-dimensional graph, with return during the month shown on the vertical axis, its yield attribute shown on one of the bottom axes, and its size attribute shown on the other. Cross-sectional multiple regression analysis is then used to fit a *plane* to the data.

The relationship in Figure 15.10 can be written as

$$r_{it} = f_{0t} + b_{i1t}f_{1t} + b_{i2t}f_{2t} + \epsilon_{it}. \qquad (15.15)$$

In this case, the zero factor indicates the return on a typical stock with zero yield and a zero size attribute (for example, a market value of $1 million). Factor 1 is the yield factor — that is, the slope of the plane in the "yield direction." It indicates the additional return per unit of yield *holding other attributes* (here, size) *constant*. Factor 2 is the size factor: the slope of the plane in the "size direction." It indicates the additional return per unit of size, *holding other attributes* (here, yield) *constant*. The nonfactor return for a security indicates the difference between its return and that typical of securities with the same attributes (here, securities with the same yield and size).

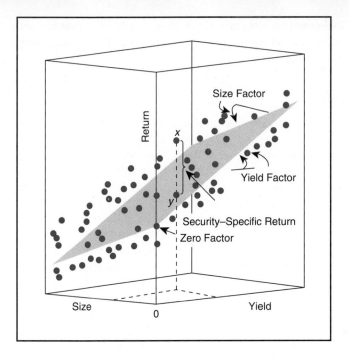

FIGURE 15-10
A two-factor model.

## ☐ 15.9.3 Multifactor Models

The inclusion of both yield and size, and the use of multiple regression analysis, can help sort out the effects of differences in yield and size on differences in security returns. It cannot deal adequately with influences that are not represented at all, nor can it guarantee that the included attributes are not simply serving as "proxies" for other, more fundamental attributes. Statistical tests can indicate the ability of the variables included in the analysis to explain or predict *past* security returns. But judgment and luck are required to identify variables that can help predict *future* security expected returns, risks, and correlations.

Most factor models of stock returns employ more than two factors (and some use a great many more than two). With $M$ attributes, diagrams must be forsaken, since $M + 1$ dimensions would be required. Cross-sectional multiple regression analysis can be used, however, to obtain a relationship of the form

$$r_{it} = f_{0t} + b_{i1t}f_{1t} + b_{i2t}f_{2t} + \cdots + b_{iMt}f_{Mt} + \epsilon_{it}. \qquad (15.16)$$

If a diagram could be drawn, this would plot as a *hyperplane* (the generalization of a plane). In the regression analysis, each security provides one observation, with the return for the month serving as the dependent variable and the selected attributes as the independent variables. The intercept and the slope coefficients from the regression are the factor values, and the residuals' values are the securities' nonfactor returns.

## ☐ 15.9.4 Zero-One Attributes

Attributes such as a security's historic beta, dividend yield, or size are measured with numbers such as .95 or 1.03. But some attributes are represented more simply, with either 0 or 1. For example, consider a "basic industry attribute." Securities of firms in such industries could be assigned an attribute of 1 (indicating that all their activities are classified in this sector), while securities of firms in other industries could be assigned a basic industry attribute of 0 (indicating that none of their activities is classified in this sector). While a more sophisticated analysis might allow firms to be classified in two or more industries, using values between 0 and 1, most factor models have at least some zero-one attributes of this type.

An extreme model uses only such attributes. $M$ sectors are identified, with

$$b_{ijt} = \begin{cases} 1, & \text{if security } i \text{ is in sector } j \\ 0, & \text{if security } i \text{ is not in sector } j \end{cases}$$

$$f_{jt} = \text{the "sector } j \text{ factor" for period } t.$$

Note that when each security is classified as belonging in one (and only one) sector, no zero factor is used.

A more common approach uses some attributes that are of the zero-one type and some that are not. The factor model used to obtain the beta prediction equation in Table 15.5 was of this type.

## 15.10    ESTIMATING RISKS AND CORRELATIONS

After fitting a factor model using data for January 19XX, it is a simple matter to fit the same model using data for February 19XX. February returns are used as the dependent variable and security attributes calculated prior to February as independent variables. The resulting coefficients are the February factor values and the residual values are the securities' nonfactor returns for the month.

After five years of this sort of activity, 60 sets of factor values will have been obtained. *If the future is expected to be like the past*, these results can be used to estimate likely factor values for next month. For example, the *average* value of a factor over the last 60 months could be taken as an estimate of the *expected* value of the factor for next month. The *actual* standard deviation of the factor over the past five years could be taken as an estimate of the *uncertainty* concerning its value next month. The *actual* correlation between two factors over the last 60 months could be taken as an estimate of the relevant correlation estimate for next month's values, and so on.

A similar procedure could be applied to the nonfactor returns. After five years, 60 such values will have been obtained for every security. *If the future is expected to be like the past*, the average nonfactor return for security 1 over the last 60 months could be taken as an estimate of its expected value for next month, and the standard deviation of the values could be taken as an estimate of the uncertainty regarding next month's value (that is, the security's *nonfactor risk* ). While historic nonfactor returns of some securities may have been correlated with those of other securities or factor values, if the model is "well specified," such correlations should be relatively small and could be assumed to be zero in the future.

Analysis of the behavior of factor values and nonmarket returns from period to period constitutes a final phase when estimating a factor model. After many (for example, 60) cross-sectional analyses, a *time-series analysis* is performed. This may be simple (for example, computing averages, standard deviations, and correlations) or complex (searching for time-dependent patterns in the data, and so on). The goal is to find some way to use *historic* data to make predictions about *future* returns and factor values.

Just as historic data are often used to provide simple estimates of future beta values, so, too, historic factor model results are often used to provide estimates of future *risks* (standard deviations, beta values, and so on) and *correlations*. Empirical evidence suggests that historic data are less valuable for predicting *expected* returns. These are usually estimated more directly, using procedures of the type described in Chapter 16.

## 15.11 ESTIMATING SENSITIVITIES TO FACTORS

In some factor models, security attributes that serve as sensitivities to factors are selected on "fundamental" grounds. Zero-one variables are based on standard classifications of securities by industry; historic betas are calculated utilizing a selected number of months of prior data; dividend yields, market values of equity outstanding, and other values are computed in standard ways, and so on.

Statistical tests may be used to assess the relevance of such preselected attributes and factors. But such tests cannot measure the usefulness of factors not considered at all.

Some factor models are estimated with a *multiple-phase* approach. In the first phase, historic data are analyzed to obtain promising security attributes. In the second phase, these attributes are used to estimate factor values for various periods. In the final (third) phase, results from the cross-sectional regressions are analyzed (using time-series methods) to estimate risks, correlations, and so on. Statistical procedures can be used to indicate the extent to which the resulting model "fits the data." More relevant are *out-of-sample tests*, which measure the ability of the model to predict risks, returns, correlations, and so on in periods subsequent to those from which the historic data were taken. Such tests can (and should) be the fourth phase of the analysis.

### ☐ 15.11.1 Homogeneous Security Groups

Most stock returns move together to some extent when expectations of the future of the economy change and "the market" moves accordingly. But *nonmarket* returns of various securities also move together. A *homogeneous group* is composed of securities that tend to move together, even when there is little or no change in the overall level of the stock market.

Some idea of the ways in which such groups can be identified can be gained from the results of a study that was designed to find possible comovement due to neither market nor industry effects. One hundred stocks were selected to cover many different industries in the hope of thwarting any attempt by the computer to group along industry lines. Monthly price changes from 1961 through 1969 were analyzed using a statistical procedure known as *cluster analysis*.

In this case the computer analyzed stock returns and was instructed to stop grouping stocks together when four major clusters remained. With relatively few exceptions, stocks in the first cluster were those considered by most analysts to be *growth stocks*: "companies expected to show an above average rate of secular expansion."[26] The second cluster contained mostly *cyclical stocks*: "those of companies that have an above average exposure to the vagaries of the economic environment."[27] The third group included predominantly *stable stocks*: "those of companies whose earning power is less affected than the average firm by the economic cycle."[28] The final group showed that at least one industry had sufficient homogeneity to stand out despite the attempt to ignore industry effects: during the period studied, the eight oil companies' prices moved together in a manner sufficiently unique to cause the computer to group them in a completely separate cluster.[29]

How much variation in prices could be attributed to these factors? Table 15.6 shows the average values for the stocks in each of the four clusters. Also shown is the size of the market effect (roughly 30%). The results, combined with those of the earlier study, suggest that sector comovement can be as important as industry comovement.

**TABLE 15.6**

Influence of Market and Sector Factors on Security Returns.

| Sector | Average Percent of Variation in Monthly Return From 1961 through 1969 due to: | |
| --- | --- | --- |
| | The Market Factor | The Sector Factor |
| Growth stocks | 31% | 15% |
| Stable stocks | 29 | 12 |
| Cyclical stocks | 33 | 9 |
| Oil stocks | 31 | 31 |

*SOURCE:* James L. Farrell, Jr., "Analyzing Covariation of Returns to Determine Homogeneous Stock Groupings," *Journal of Business* 47, no. 2 (April 1974):201.

Table 15.7 provides a dramatic indication of the possible results from concentration in market sectors. The relative proportions in the four sectors are shown for the portfolio represented by Standard & Poor's 500 and for two mutual funds. The two funds had similar market exposures, as indicated by their estimated beta values. During the 19-month period from December 31, 1972, through July 31, 1974, the "market" fell 29%,

---

[26] James L. Farrell, Jr., "Homogeneous Stock Groupings: Implications for Portfolio Mangement," *Financial Analysts Journal* 31, no. 3 (May/June 1975):50.

[27] Farrell, "Homogeneous Stock Groupings," p. 50.

[28] Farrell, "Homogeneous Stock Groupings," p. 50.

[29] An earlier study found that for the typical stock, approximately 50% of the total price variance from 1927 through 1960 could be attributed to market effects. Roughly an additional 10% could be attributed to industrywide factors. The first figure declined through the period, reaching approximately 30% for the typical stock in the latter part, while the second figure changed little. See Benjamin F. King, "Market and Industry Factors in Stock Price Behavior," *Journal of Business* 39, no. 1 (January 1966):139–70.

suggesting that one might have expected the two funds to fall by roughly 32% (since $1.1 \times 29\% = 31.9\%$).

**TABLE 15.7**
Sector Concentration and Portfolio Return.

| | Percent Invested | | |
| --- | --- | --- | --- |
| Sector | Standard and Poor's 500-Stock Index | Affiliated Fund | T. Rowe Price Fund |
| Growth | 39.8% | 10.5% | 80.2% |
| Cyclical | 24.0 | 57.5 | 8.7 |
| Stable | 20.0 | 18.0 | 4.1 |
| Oil | 16.2 | 14.0 | 7.0 |
| Estimated beta | 1.00 | 1.09 | 1.11 |
| Performance | −29% | -16% | -42% |

SOURCE: James L. Farrell, Jr., "Homogeneous Stock Groupings: Implications for Portfolio Management," *Financial Analysts Journal* 31, no. 3 (May/June 1975):58.

In fact, one fund's shares fell much less than the market, and the other's shares fell much more. The portfolio composition figures show why. This was a period when growth stocks did especially poorly. The first fund was well positioned, concentrating more money in cyclical stocks and less in growth stocks than did the market as a whole. The second was poorly positioned, with a heavy concentration in growth stocks, to its investors' detriment. The results could be reversed in a period in which growth stocks do especially well. The point is not that one fund or investment strategy is better than another — rather, that neither fund was in fact as well diversified as a simple check of the number of stocks might suggest.

## ☐ 15.11.2 Group Factors

Once homogeneous groups have been identified via cluster analysis or some other method, they may be incorporated into a factor model. The simplest procedure is to assign each security entirely to the group with which it "clusters." The corresponding factor model could include a "market sensitivity" attribute (based, for example, on historic beta) and one zero-one attribute for each of the homogeneous groups. The factors from the cross-section analyses would then represent "the market" and the nonmarket returns of each of the homogeneous groups.

An alternative procedure includes an intermediate step. The nonmarket returns of each security over time are compared with those of the homogeneous groups. For each security a time-series regression is performed, and the sensitivities of the security to each of the groups are estimated. These are used as the corresponding attributes in the final phase, instead of zero-one variables.

In a model based on this approach using data from 1968 through 1978 for over 500 stocks, the Boston Company obtained five nonmarket factors, characterized as (1) growth, (2) utility, (3) oil and related, (4) basic industries, and (5) consumer cyclical.[30]

## ☐ 15.11.3 Composite Attributes

Many models use values such as historic betas, yields, and measures of size as attributes. Each can be considered a *simple attribute*, since it is related to either a single aspect of the security or a ratio of two such aspects.

Some models go farther, combining several aspects of a security into one *composite attribute*, several other aspects into a second composite attribute, and so on. Choices of aspects and formulas for combining them are usually based on econometric analyses of historic data. Table 15.8 shows the fundamental attributes used to compute each of ten composite attributes in one model of TSE stock returns. In addition to the factors shown this model also includes 19 industry groups. Figure 15.11 shows a comparison of the explanatory power of this composite model with the classical single factor model (SFM) and a combination of the SFM plus the industry groups. In all time periods the composite model outperformed the other two. The SFM, on average, explained about 21% of the monthly return variance, the combined model explained about 40% and the composite model 45%.

## ☐ 15.11.4 Scenario Approaches

A more fundamental approach is employed by Salomon Brothers — a major institutional brokerage firm:

> The idea ... is simple. We build a simple model of corporate profits, specified in terms of a few revenue variables and a few cost variables. One of these simple models is constructed for each company in our data base (about 1500 companies). These are linked to a macro model of the economy. Then the macro model is estimated in several scenarios, a "base case" and a number of alternatives. Each of the alternatives is constructed by altering a single one of the major governing variables that determine the character of the base case. For each scenario, profit models are built for each of about 400 lines of business, a set that includes all the major businesses pursued by the companies in our data base. Finally, the growth rate of profits of each company is modeled in each of the cases, by putting together the appropriate lines of business in the appropriate proportions. From the data thus obtained, we can estimate the sensitivity of the growth rate of a company's expected profits to each of the variables that was used to determine an alternative scenario. These sensitivities are the essential ingredients in the Fundamental Factor Model.[31]

---

[30] Robert D. Arnott, "Cluster Analysis and Stock Price Comovement," *Financial Analysts Journal* 36, no. 6 (November/December 1980):56-62. For an interesting use of cluster analysis, see Jeffery V. Bailey and Robert D. Arnott, "Cluster Analysis and Manager Selection," *Financial Analysts Journal* 42, no. 6 (November/December 1986):20–28.

[31] Tony Estep, Nick Hanson, Michelle Clayman, Cal Johnson, and Jonathan Singer, "The Fundamental Factor Model of Risk and Return in Common Stocks," Salomon Brothers, July 1981. Also see Tony Estep, Nick Hanson, and Cal Johnson, "Sources of Value and Risk in Common Stocks," *Journal of Portfolio Management* 9, no. 4 (Summer 1983):10.

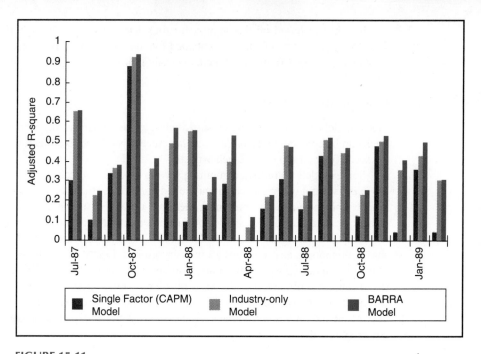

**FIGURE 15-11**
Explanatory power of the BARRA Canadian equity model on a month by month basis.

SOURCE: P.Muller, "Building a Canadian Equities Risk Model," *Canadian Investment Review* II, no. 1 (Spring 1989):41.

The factors used in this model consist of (1) inflation, (2) real economic growth, (3) oil prices, (4) defense spending, and (5) real interest rates. For each security, the procedure provides five attributes, representing the sensitivities of the corporation's profits over the next five years to changes in the corresponding variables.

Figure 15.12 shows the relative performance of five "factor play portfolios" over 17 months. Each was constructed to be sensitive to one of the five factors and relatively insensitive to the other four. Changes in the values of such portfolios can be interpreted as representing changes in *expectations* concerning the associated fundamental economic factors.

## ☐ 15.11.5 Sensitivities to Macroeconomic Variables

The Salomon Brothers approach uses forward-looking projections of a relatively detailed type to estimate the sensitivities of corporate profits to changes in fundamental economic variables. A simpler approach, based on the assumption that history can provide adequate guidance concerning the future, compares changes in security values with estimates of changes in expectations concerning macroeconomic variables.

In such an analysis, it is important that only changes in *expectations* of such variables be used, since security prices change significantly only in response to *unanticipated* changes in prospects for future profits. Unfortunately, it is often difficult to estimate changes in expectations about future values of key economic variables.

## TABLE 15.8
### Risk Indices and Component Descriptors in the Canadian Equity Market.

**Variability in Markets**
Historical Beta
Historical Sigma
Cumulative Range
Recent Price Volatility (12 months)
Recent Price Volatility (3 months)

**Momentum**
Relative Strength
Historical Alpha

**Growth**
Growth in Assets (5 year)
Growth in Revenues (5 year)
Growth in Assets (1 year)
Growth in Revenues (1 year)

**Size**
Log of Market Capitalization
Log of Total Assets

**Liquidity**
Lagged Beta

**Profitability**
Return on Common Equity
Growth in Earnings (5 years)

**Value**
Earnings to Price Ratio
Cash Flow to Price Ratio
Sales to Price Ratio
Book to Price Ratio
Total Coverage of Dividends

**Financial Leverage**
Debt to Equity
Debt to Assets

**Yield**
Current Yield
5 year Average Yield

**US Sensitivity**
Cross-Listing Indicator
S&P500 Sensitivity

SOURCE: P.Muller, "Building a Canadian Equities Risk Model," *Canadian Investment Review* II, no.1 (Spring 1989):40

In a study using this approach, four variables were found to be useful: (1) the growth rate in US industrial production, (2) unanticipated changes in risk premiums, measured by the difference between the return on a portfolio of "under Baa bonds" and that of a portfolio of Aaa bonds, (3) twists in the yield curve, measured by the difference between the return on a portfolio of long-term government bonds and that of Treasury bills, and (4) unanticipated inflation, measured by the difference between actual inflation and a prediction derived from Treasury bill rates. The same four factors plus the value-weighted return on a "market" portfolio consisting of all stocks listed on the TSE were found to systematically affect Canadian stock returns.[32]

Once values for such unanticipated changes in expectations concerning macrovariables have been obtained, the desired sensitivites of security returns can be estimated. For each security a time-series regression is performed, with each time period providing one observation. In the regression, the security's return is the dependent variable, and the changes in expectations of the macrovariables are the independent variables. The resulting coefficients are estimates of the sensitivities of the security to each of the economic factors. These are then used as the security's attributes when estimating the factor model.

---

[32] Nai-fu Chen, Richard Roll, and Stephen A. Ross, "Economic Forces and the Stock Market," *Journal of Business* 59, no. 3 (July 1986):383–403; E.Otuteye, "How Economic Factors Explain Canadian Stock Returns," *Canadian Investment Review* IV, no. 1 (Spring 1991):93–9.

**FIGURE 15-12**
Relative performance of economic factor portfolios.

*SOURCE:* Tony Estep, Nick Hanson, and Cal Johnson, "Sources of Value and Risk in Common Stocks," *Journal of Portfolio Management* 9, no. 4 (Summer 1983):11.

## ☐ 15.11.6 Factor Analysis

Cluster analysis can be used to estimate zero-one security attributes from historic returns. These attributes can then be used in cross-sectional analyses to derive factor values. The resulting factors may be recognizable as, for example, changes in fundamental economic factors, or they may appear to be simply statistical artifacts. With such a mechanical approach, it may be difficult or impossible to incorporate additional (fundamental) information.

This type of procedure assumes that historic returns contain all the information needed to produce useful estimates of future risks and correlations.

*Factor analysis*, a more complex procedure, is similar in spirit.[33] Given returns for many securities over many time periods, a computer is used to (1) determine a reasonable number of attributes, (2) compute the corresponding attributes for each security, and (3) derive the corresponding factors for each time period. An early study employing factor analysis suggested that five factors might suffice to represent the "pervasive" underlying determinants of correlation among security returns. Other studies have found more "significant" factors. Canadian studies have found that one to four significant factors are sufficient to explain the variance of stock returns.[34]

There is more information about securities than that reflected in past returns alone, and it is undoubtedly desirable to take it into account when estimating factor models. Factor analysis can provide useful guidance concerning the appropriate number of factors, useful variables, and so on but should not be used as a "black box" into which returns are placed and out of which come purely mechanical estimates of future prospects, to be used "as is."

## 15.12 SUMMARY

The corporate form of organization is relatively new. One of the features of this form of organization is that of limited liability, meaning that common shareholders may lose their investment, but no more. Another feature is that common shareholders have a residual claim on the earnings of the corporation, since other security holders, such as preferred shareholders and bondholders, have priority. A third feature is that common shareholders may vote on issues brought up at the annual meeting and on who will represent them on the board of directors. In regard to electing directors, there are two types of voting systems currently in use, cumulative and majority. The main difference between the two systems has to do with minority representation on the board.

Common shareholders may receive cash dividends or stock dividends from the corporation. In the case of stock dividends, it has been shown that this type of paper transaction does not make shareholders better off. However, this is not surprising, since stock dividends do not result in the corporation being in a healthier financial position. That is, the issuing of stock dividends does not increase sales nor does it decrease expenses. Similarly, common shareholders may experience a stock split but will not be better off as a result.

The relevant measue of the risk of a share of common stock is the impact that the share will have on the risk of a well-diversified portfolio. According to the CAPM,

---

[33] The term *factor analysis* denotes a general approach; there are, in fact, many alternative statistical procedures for performing such an analysis.

[34] Richard Roll and Stephen A. Ross, "An Empirical Investigation of the Arbitrage Pricing Theory," *Journal of Finance* 35, no. 5 (December 1980):1073–1103;P.Hughes, "A Test of the Arbitrage Pricing Theory, "*Canadian Journal of Administrative Sciences* 1, no. 2 (December 1984):195–214.

this impact is reflected by the stock's beta. Thus, in measuring a stock's risk over the forthcoming holding period, an investor needs to estimate the stock's ex ante beta. One way of doing this is by using past returns to estimate the ex post characteristic line for the stock; one of the results of doing this will be the ex post beta. Having estimated the ex post beta, there are a variety of ways of "adjusting" it to arrive at a more accurate estimate of the ex ante beta.

To operate successfully in the stock market, a good model of the relationships among stock returns is needed. Typically, the procedures employed for estimating stock factor models combine judgment with statistical analysis of historical returns. Thus, both art and science are involved.

## APPENDIX A

## EMPIRICAL REGULARITIES

Recently a number of researchers have uncovered certain *empirical regularities* in common stock returns. That is, certain cross-sectional differences among stock returns have been found to occur with regularity. Some regularities should occur according to certain asset pricing models. For example, the CAPM asserts that different stocks should have different returns because different stocks have different betas. What makes the regularities that are about to be discussed of special interest is that they do not appear to be predicted by any of the asset pricing models. Accordingly, they are sometimes also referred to as *anomalies*.

## A.1 THE SIZE EFFECT

One measure of the size of a firm at a particular time is the aggregate market value of its common stock. That is, the size of a firm can be measured by multiplying the market price of its common stock at a particular time by the number of shares it has outstanding.[35] A simple test for seeing if firms that are of smaller size have had higher returns than firms of larger size was conducted by Ibbotson and Sinquefield.[36] All stocks on the New York Stock Exchange were ranked by market value outstanding on December 31, 1925. A portfolio was then formed using the stocks in the bottom quintile (that is, the smallest 20%). Within the portfolio, stocks were purchased in proportion to

---

[35] Some studies have used other measures of size, such as the price-to-earnings ratio (or its inverse, the earnings-to-price ratio) and the ratio of book value of equity per share to market value per share, with similar findings. See S. Basu, "Investment Performance of Common Stocks in Relation to their Price-Earnings Ratios: A Test of the Efficient Market Hypothesis," *Journal of Finance* 32, no. 3 (June 1977):663–82 and "The Relationship Between Earnings' Yield, Market Value and Return for NYSE Common Stocks: Further Evidence," *Journal of Financial Economics* 12, no. 1 (June 1983):129–56; Barr Rosenberg, Kenneth Reid, and Ronald Lanstein, "Persuasive Evidence of Market Inefficiency," *Journal of Portfolio Management* 11, no. 3 (Spring 1985):9–16; Marc R. Reinganum, "Misspecification of Capital Asset Pricing: Empirical Anomalies Based on Earnings' Yields and Market Values," *Journal of Financial Economics* 9, no. 1 (March 1981):19–46; Rolf W. Banz and William J. Breen, "Sample Dependent Results Using Accounting and Market Data: Some Evidence," *Journal of Finance* 41, no. 4 (September 1986):779–93; Jeffrey Jaffe, Donald B. Kiem, and Randolph Westerfield, "Earnings Yields, Market Values, and Stock Returns, *Journal of Finance* 44, no. 1 (March 1989):135–48.

[36] Roger G. Ibbotson and Rex A. Sinquefield, *Stocks, Bonds, Bills and Inflation: The Past and the Future* (Financial Analysts' Research Foundation, 1982). More elaborate studies of the size effect include Rolf Banz, "The Relationship Between Return and Market Value of Common Stocks," *Journal of Financial Economics* 9, no. 1 (March 1981):3–18; and Marc R. Reinganum, "Misspecification of Capital Asset Pricing."

their market value (that is, the portfolio was value-weighted). This portfolio was "held" for five years. On December 31, 1930, all the stocks on the NYSE were again ranked on size and a new value-weighted portfolio formed from the bottom quintile. This portfolio was "held" for the next five years, when another similar revision was made; such revising continued through 1980.

Returns for the "small-firm portfolio" were then calculated for every month from 1926 through 1983. Table 15.9 contrasts the performance of this portfolio with that of Standard & Poor's 500. Since the S&P 500 consists of stocks with large market capitalizations, this can be viewed as a comparison of small stocks with large ones.

**TABLE 15.9**
Small- and Large-Stock Performance, 1926–1983.

|  | Small Stocks | SP500 | Small Stocks − SP500 |
|---|---|---|---|
| Average annual return | 17.05% | 11.26% | 5.79% |
| Annual standard deviation | 32.35% | 20.62% | 18.34% |
| Number of months with positive values | 406 | 408 | 360 |
| Percent of months with positive values | 58.3% | 58.6% | 51.7% |

*SOURCE:* Based on data in Roger G. Ibbotson, *Stocks, Bonds, Bills and Inflation 1984 Yearbook* (Chicago: R. G. Ibbotson Associates, Inc., 1984).

On the average, the small-firm portfolio outperformed the S&P 500 by 0.48% per month, or approximately 5.79% per year. Although the small-firm portfolio outperformed the S&P 500 only 51.7% of the time, the average difference was positive and statistically significant. This does not imply that a small-firm investment strategy dominated investing in the S&P 500. Table 15.9 indicates that the small-firm portfolio's returns varied much more, having a standard deviation of 32.35%, whereas that of the S&P 500 was 20.62%.

## A.2   SEASONALITY IN STOCK RETURNS

The desire of individuals for liquidity may be thought to change from day to day and from month to month. If so, there may be seasonal patterns in stock returns. One might presume that such patterns would be relatively unimportant. Indeed, according to the notion of efficient markets, such patterns should be quite minor (if they exist at all), since they are not suggested by any asset pricing model. However, the evidence indicates that at least two are significant: the "January effect" and the "day-of-the-week effect."

## ☐ A.2.1    The January Effect

There is no apparent reason to expect stock returns to be higher in certain months than in others. However, in a study that looked at average monthly returns on NYSE-listed common stocks, significant seasonalities were found.[37] In particular, the average return in January was higher than the average return in any other month. Table 15.10 indicates the average stock return in January and the other 11 months for various time periods. Although the difference in returns was minor in the early part of the century, more recently it appears that the average return in January has been approximately 3% higher than the average monthly return in February through December.[38]

**TABLE 15.10**

Seasonality in Stock Returns.

| Time Period | Average Stock Return in January | Average Stock Return in Other Months | Difference in Returns |
|---|---|---|---|
| 1904–1928 | 1.30% | .44% | .86% |
| 1929–1940 | 6.63 | −.60 | 7.23 |
| 1941–1974 | 3.91 | .70 | 3.21 |
| 1904–1974 | 3.48 | .42 | 3.06 |

SOURCE: Michael S. Rozeff and William R. Kinney, Jr. "Capital Market Seasonality: The Case of Stock Returns," *Journal of Financial Economics* 3, no. 4 (October 1976):388.

## ☐ A.2.2    The Day-of-the-Week Effect

It has generally been assumed that the expected daily returns on stocks are the same for all days of the week. That is, the expected return on a given stock is the same for Monday as it is for Tuesday, and so on. However, a number of studies have uncovered evidence that refutes this belief. Two early studies looked at the average daily return on NYSE-listed securities and found that the return on Monday was quite different.[39] In particular, the average return on Monday was found to be much lower than the average return on any other day of the week. Furthermore, the average return on Monday was negative, whereas the other days of the week had positive average returns. Table 15.11 displays these findings.

The return for Monday is calculated using the closing price on Monday and the closing price on Friday. Thus, the change in the price of a stock for Monday actually represents the change in price *over the weekend* as well as during Monday. This

---

[37] Michael S. Rozeff and William R. Kinney, Jr., "Capital Market Seasonality: The Case of Stock Returns," *Journal of Financial Economics* 3, no. 4 (October 1976):379–402. For an argument that the market does not have a January Effect, see Jay R. Ritter and Navin Chopra, "Portfolio Rebalancing and the Turn-of-the-Year Effect," *Journal of Finance* 44, no. 1 (March 1989):149–66.

[38] Interestingly, it appears that returns over the first half of any month are significantly higher than the returns over the second half of the month. See Robert A. Ariel, "A Monthly Effect in Stock Returns," *Journal of Financial Economics* 18, no. 1 (March 1987):161–74.

[39] Kenneth R. French, "Stock Returns and the Weekend Effect," *Journal of Financial Economics* 8, no. 1 (March 1980):55–69; and Michael R. Gibbons and Patrick Hess, "Day of the Week Effects and Asset Returns," *Journal of Business* 54, no. 4 (October 1981):579–96.

observation has caused some people to refer to the "day-of-the-week" effect as the "weekend" effect and has led to further examination of daily returns.

**TABLE 15.11**

Analysis of Daily Returns.

|  | Monday | Tuesday | Wednesday | Thursday | Friday |
|---|---|---|---|---|---|
| A. French study | | | | | |
| January 1953-December 1977 | −.17% | .02% | .10% | .04% | .09% |
| B. Gibbons and Hess study | | | | | |
| July 1962-December 1978 | −.13% | .00% | .10% | .03% | .08% |

SOURCE: Kenneth R. French, "Stock Returns and the Weekend Effect," *Journal of Financial Economics* 8, no. 1 (March 1980):58; and Michael R. Gibbons and Patrick Hess, "Day of the Week Effects and Asset Returns," *Journal of Business* 54, no. 4 (October 1981):582–83.

One method for studying the weekend effect is to divide daily returns into two parts. The first part is the return from the close of the previous day to the open of the current day and is referred to as the nontrading-period return. It uses the price of the last trade of the previous day (the *close*) and the price of the first trade of the current day (the *open*) and calculates the return using these prices as the beginning and ending prices, respectively. The second part is the return from the open of the current day to the close of the current day, which is referred to as the trading-period return. It uses the prices of the first and last trades of the current day (the open and close) as the beginning and ending prices, respectively.

For example, the average stock return for Monday involves the change in a stock's price from Friday's close to Monday's close. This change in price can be divided into the change from Friday's close to Monday's open (the nontrading period for Monday) and from Monday's open to Monday's close (the trading period for Monday). Such a division will indicate if the negative return observed for Monday occurred during the weekend or during trading on Monday.

Table 15.12 displays the results of two studies that divided daily returns in this manner.[40] The study by Rogalski examined the set of 500 stocks in the S&P 500, whereas the study by Harris examined all NYSE-listed stocks (a total of 1616 stocks). As shown in Table 15.12, the negative daily return for Monday was observed in both studies. However, the Rogalski study suggests that this negative return occurred over the nontrading period from Friday's close to Monday's open.[41] Consequently, the weekend effect is really a nontrading-weekend effect.

---

[40] Richard J. Rogalski, "New Findings Regarding Day-of-the-Week Returns Over Trading and Non-trading Periods: A Note," *Journal of Finance* 39, no. 5 (December 1984):1603–14; Lawrence Harris, "How to Profit from Intradaily Stock Returns," *Journal of Portfolio Management* 12, no. 2 (Winter 1986):61–64, and "A Transaction Data Study of Weekly and Intradaily Patterns in Stock Returns," *Journal of Financial Economics* 16, no. 1 (May 1986):99–117.

[41] Rogalski reported similar findings for the set of 30 stocks in the Dow Jones Industrial Average. His DJIA results were confirmed over the 1974–1983 period by Michael Smirlock and Laura Starks, "Day-of-the-Week and Intraday Effects in Stock Returns," *Journal of Financial Economics* 17, no. 1 (September 1986):197–210. Interestingly, stock prices have been found to be more volatile during trading periods than nontrading peiods; see Kenneth R. French and Richard Roll, "Stock Return Variances: The Arrival of Information and the Reaction of Traders," *Journal of Financial Economics* 17, no. 1 (September 1986), 5–26.

The Harris study, involving a larger sample of stocks but a shorter time period, reached a different conclusion. This study found that the negative daily return for Monday was composed of two roughly equal-sized negative returns during the nontrading period and trading period. Statistical tests indicated that the average nontrading-period return for Monday as well as the average trading-period return for Monday were different from the corresponding average returns for the other four days of the week.

These two studies can be reconciled by noting that the Rogalski study involved a sample of large-sized firms, since the S&P 500 consists of such firms, whereas the Harris study involved both small- and large-sized firms. Thus, the behavior of the small firms in the Harris study's sample may have been the source of the discrepancy. With this in mind, Harris looked at the returns of subsamples based on size and indeed found that this was the reason for the discrepancy. That is, the negative average Monday return appears to have occurred during the nontrading period for large-sized firms, whereas for small-sized firms, the negative average Monday return appears to have occurred mostly during the trading period. Since Harris's results in Table 15.12 involved averaging across both large and small firms, it is not surprising that the negative daily return for Monday was composed of two negative returns of roughly equal size during the trading and nontrading periods.

**TABLE 15.12**

Decomposition of Daily Returns.

| | S&P 500 [a] January 1979-April 1984 | | | All NYSE [b] December 1981-January 1983 | | |
|---|---|---|---|---|---|---|
| | Daily | Nontrading | Trading | Daily | Nontrading | Trading |
| Monday | −.12% | −.13% | .01% | −.18% | −.08% | −.09% |
| Tuesday | .09 | .08 | .01 | .10 | −.01 | .11 |
| Wednesday | .13 | .05 | .08 | .15 | .05 | .10 |
| Thursday | .02 | .09 | −.07 | .17 | .02 | .15 |
| Friday | .07 | .03 | .04 | .20 | .06 | 14 |

SOURCE: [a] Richard J. Rogalski, "New Findings Regarding Day-of-the-Week Returns over Trading and Non-trading Periods: A Note," *Journal of Finance* 39, no. 5 (December 1984):1605;

[b] Lawrence Harris, "How to Profit from Intradaily Stock Returns," *Journal of Portfolio Management* 12, no. 2 (Winter 1986):62.

## A.3  INTERRELATIONSHIPS

Given the presence of three regularities (the size, January, and day-of-the-week effects), researchers have attempted to see if there are any interrelationships between them. For example, is the January effect more pronounced for small firms? Is the day-of-the-week effect unrelated to the size effect? Is the day-of-the-week effect more dramatic in January than in the other months of the year? A brief discussion of some of the numerous studies that have examined such questions follows.

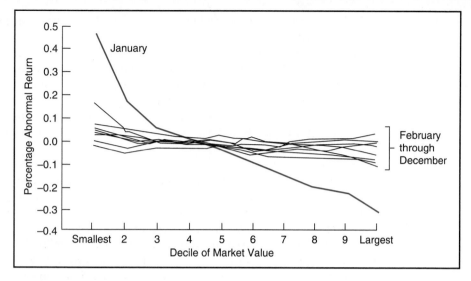

**FIGURE 15-13**
Interrelationship between the size effect and the January effect.

*SOURCE:* Donald B. Keim, "Size-related Anomalies and Stock Return Seasonality: Further Empirical Evidence," *Journal of Financial Economics* 12, no. 1 (June 1983):21.

## ☐ A.3.1  Size and January Effects

Having observed that small firms have higher returns than large firms and that returns in January are higher than in any other month of the year, it is interesting to ponder whether or not these two effects are somehow interrelated. One study that examined this issue found that the two effects were strongly interrelated.[42] All NYSE-listed and AMEX-listed stocks over the 17-year period of 1963 to 1979 were examined in this study. At the end of each year, each firm was ranked by the size of the aggregate market value of its equity (that is, the year-end market price per share times the number of shares outstanding). Ten portfolios were then formed based on size with portfolio number 1 containing the smallest 10% of the firms, portfolio number 2 containing the next smallest 10%, and so on.

Abnormal returns were calculated subsequently for each portfolio on a monthly basis over the 17-year period and averaged for each month. Figure 15.13 displays the results.

It can be seen from this figure that the size effect was most pronounced in January, since the line for this month slopes down sharply from left to right. The other 11 months of the year appear to be quite similar to each other. Generally, each one of these months displays a slight downward slope, indicating that the size effect also existed for these months but only to a minor degree. Also of interest is the observation that large firms had a negative abnormal return in January. Thus, the January effect has been due primarily

---

[42] Donald B. Keim, "Size-related Anomalies and Stock Return Seasonality: Further Empirical Evidence," *Journal of Financial Economics* 12, no. 1 (June 1983):13–32.

to the behavior of small firms, and the size effect has been concentrated mainly in the month of January.

Further examination of this interrelationship between the size effect and the January effect has revealed that it is concentrated in the first five trading days of January.[43] In particular, the difference in returns between the smallest-firm portfolio and the largest-firm portfolio over these five days was 8.0%, whereas over the entire year it was 30.4%. Thus, 26.3% (8.0%/30.4%) of the annual size effect occurred during these five days (if the size effect had been spread evenly over the year, then .4% of it would have been attributed to these five days).

Attempts have been made to explain this interrelationship between the January effect and the size effect. One explanation that appears to have some merit has to do with "tax selling." This explanation begins by arguing that stocks that have declined during the year have downward pressure on their prices near year-end as investors sell them to realize capital losses in order to minimize tax payments. After the end of the year, this pressure is removed and the prices jump back to their "fair" values. Note that this argument flies in the face of the notion of efficient markets (the notion of efficient markets would suggest that this cannot be true because if investors sensed that stocks were becoming undervalued at year-end, they would flood the market with buy orders, thereby preventing any substantive undervaluation from occurring). Nevertheless, it does appear to have some merit in that those stocks that declined during the previous year had the largest appreciation in January.[44] However, this association between January returns and previous years' stock price declines does not appear to be attributable to price pressure caused by tax selling. This is because the biggest "losers" during a year appear subsequently to have abnormally high returns for as long as five Januaries thereafter. This contradicts the tax-selling argument, since according to this argument, the abnormal price rebound should occur in only the first subsequent January.[45]

A second possible explanation is that small stocks may be relatively riskier in January than during the rest of the year. If this is true, then they should have a relatively higher average return in January. A study finding that the betas of small stocks tend to increase at the beginning of the year lends support to this explanation.[46]

---

[43] Rogalski ("New Findings") also finds that the anomalous price behavior of stocks in January mostly occurs in the first five trading days. Roll has observed that the largest daily differences in the returns between small firms and large firms occurs over the last trading day of the year and the first four trading days of the year; furthermore, eight of the subsequent ten trading days also have notably large differences in returns. See Richard Roll, "Vas ist das?" *Journal of Portfolio Management* 9, no. 2 (Winter 1983):18–28.

[44] See Roll, "Vas ist das?"; Edward A. Dyl, "Capital Gains Taxation and Year-End Stock Market Behavior," *Journal of Finance* 32, no. 1 (March 1977):165–75; Ben Branch, "A Tax Loss Trading Rule," *Journal of Business* 50, no. 2 (April 1977):198–207; Marc R. Reinganum, "The Anomalous Stock Market Behavior of Small Firms in January: Empirical Tests for Tax-loss Selling Effects," *Journal of Financial Economics* 12, no. 1 (June 1983):89–104; Josef Lakonishok and Seymour Smidt, "Capital Gain Taxation and Volume of Trading," *Journal of Finance* 41, no. 4 (September 1986):951–74.

[45] See K. C. Chan, "Can Tax-Loss Selling Explain the January Seasonal in Stock Returns?" *Journal of Finance* 41, no. 5 (December 1986):1115-28; and Werner F. M. DeBondt and Richard Thaler, "Does the Stock Market Overreact?" *Journal of Finance* 40, no. 3 (July 1985):793-805, and "Further Evidence on Investor Overreaction and Stock Market Seasonality," *Journal of Finance* 42, no. 3 (July 1987):557–81.

[46] Richard J. Rogalski and Seha M. Tinic, "The January Size Effect: Anomaly or Risk Mismeasurement?" *Financial Analysts Journal* 42, no. 6 (November-December 1986):63–70. See also Avner Arbel, "Generic Stocks: An Old Product in a New Package," *Journal of Portfolio Management* 11, no. 4 (Summer 1985):4–13.

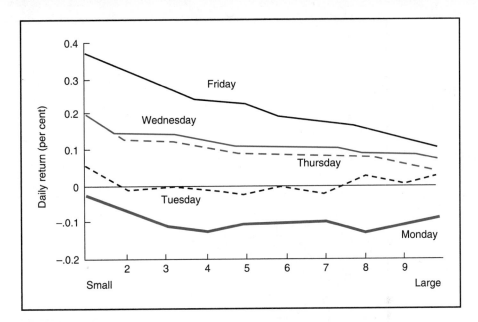

**FIGURE 15-14**
Interrelationship between the size effect and the day-of-the-week effect.

*SOURCE:* Donald B. Keim, "The CAPM and Equity Return Regularities," *Financial Analysts Journal* 42, no. 3 (May/June 1986):24.

## □ A.3.2 Size and Day-of-the-Week Effects

A recent study has extended the previously mentioned studies of the day-of-the-week effect back to 1928.[47] That is, daily data from 1928 through 1982 were examined and negative Monday returns were documented over the 55-year period. Furthermore, a similar day-of-the-week effect was observed in a sample of over-the-counter stocks for the period of 1979 to 1982. Then, using all NYSE-listed and AMEX-listed stocks for the period of 1963 to 1979, ten size-based portfolios were formed. Finally, the average return on each day of the week was calculated for each portfolio. As shown in Figure 15.14, negative Monday returns were observed for all sizes of portfolios, and there did not appear to be a systematic relationship between portfolio size and the size of the Monday return. Thus, it appears that the size effect and the day-of-the-week effect have not been related to each other.[48]

Another study examined all the transactions on the NYSE during the period of December 1, 1981, through January 31, 1983, by calculating the rate of return on each stock over 15-minute intervals during trading hours.[49] Figure 15.15 displays the results

---

[47] Donald B. Keim and Robert F. Stambaugh, "A Further Investigation of the Weekend Effect in Stock Returns," *Journal of Finance* 39, no. 3 (July 1984):819–35.

[48] Interestingly, there did appear to be a relationship between portfolio size and the size of the Friday return. In particular, Friday returns were the largest of the week for all portfolio sizes, and the smaller the portfolio the larger the Friday return. These interrelationships were also documented by Harris, "A Transaction Data Study."

[49] Harris, "A Transaction Data Study" and "How to Profit."

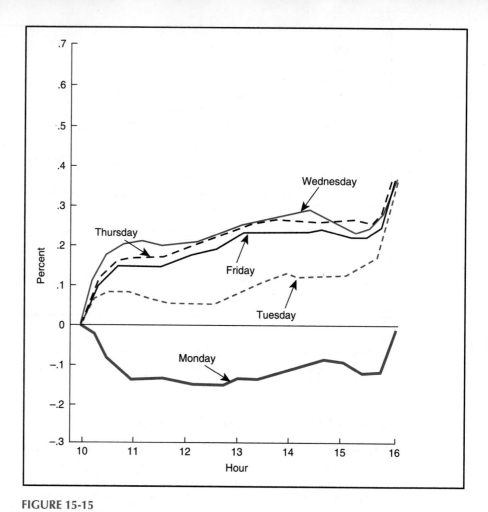

**FIGURE 15-15**
Cumulated fifteen-minute intraday returns.

SOURCE: Lawrence Harris, "How to Profit from Intradaily Stock Returns," *Journal of Portfolio Management* 12, no. 2 (Winter 1986):63.

for all the 1616 stocks listed on the NYSE during this time period. Several interesting observations can be made. First, the negative returns during trading hours on Monday occurred mostly during the first 45 minutes. After these 45 minutes had elapsed, the behavior of stock prices on Mondays was similar to the other days of the week. Second, on Tuesdays through Fridays, there was a notable upward movement in prices during the first 45 minutes of trading. Third, on all days of the week there was a notable upward price movement at the end of trading hours (further analysis indicated that most of this "end-of-the-day effect" occurred from the next to the last transaction to the last transaction). After forming ten portfolios by firm size, these patterns were found to exist for all firm sizes. Thus, both studies that tested to see if there was some relationship between size and the day-of-the-week effect found that none existed.

## January and Day-of-the-Week Effects

The results of a study that examined the daily returns on all NYSE-listed and AMEX-listed stocks for the period of 1963 to 1982 are shown in Table 15.13.[50] It can be seen in this table that there has been a striking difference in the day-of-the-week effect between the month of January and the other 11 months of the year. That is, the negative Monday returns that have been widely documented appear to have occurred in the months of February through December but not in January.

**TABLE 15.13**
The January Effect and the Day-of-the-Week Effect.

|  | Monday | Tuesday | Wednesday | Thursday | Friday |
|---|---|---|---|---|---|
| a. January returns | .28% | .17% | .14% | .43% | .49% |
| b. February-December returns | −.15 | −.02 | .14 | .07 | .19 |

*SOURCE:* Richard J. Rogalski, "New Findings Regarding Day-of-the-Week Returns over Trading and Non-trading Periods: A Note," *Journal of Finance* 39, no. 5 (December 1984):1609–11.

### Size, January, and Day-of-the-Week Effects

Lastly, interrelations between all three empirical regularities have been examined. The preceding study divided the set of NYSE and AMEX stocks into ten portfolios based on size and then examined the returns for each portfolio in a manner similar to Table 15.13. The results for the first, fourth, seventh, and tenth portfolios (that is, the smallest, fourth smallest, seventh smallest, and largest portfolios) are shown in Table 15.14.

**TABLE 15.14**
Size, January, and Day-of-the-Week Effects.

|  | Portfolio | Monday | Tuesday | Wednesday | Thursday | Friday |
|---|---|---|---|---|---|---|
| a. January returns |  |  |  |  |  |  |
| Smallest = | 1 | .82% | .58% | .47% | .73% | .92% |
|  | 4 | .32 | .20 | .16 | .51 | .57 |
|  | 7 | .15 | .09 | .06 | .36 | .36 |
| Largest = | 10 | .02 | −.07 | −.03 | .20 | .19 |
| b. February-December returns |  |  |  |  |  |  |
| Smallest = | 1 | −.07% | −.04% | .15% | .15% | .29% |
|  | 4 | −.18 | −.04 | .14 | .09 | .22 |
|  | 7 | −.16 | .00 | .14 | .06 | .15 |
| Largest = | 10 | −.13 | .04 | .12 | .03 | .09 |

*SOURCE:* Richard J. Rogalski, "New Findings Regarding Day-of-the-Week Returns over Trading and Non-trading Periods: A Note," *Journal of Finance* 39, no. 5 (December 1984):1609–11.

---

[50] Rogalski, "New Findings."

Several observations can be made. First, the average Monday return in January was positive for all portfolio sizes, whereas during the rest of the year it was negative for all portfolio sizes. Second, the average Monday return in January was related to firm size, with smaller firms having larger returns. Furthermore, this was true for any day during January. Third, during the rest of the year there was a clear relationship between the firm size and the day of the week only on Thursday and Friday, where the smaller the firm the larger the return.

## A.4    EMPIRICAL REGULARITIES IN CANADIAN EQUITY MARKETS

The Canadian situation with respect to the study of empirical regularities is similar to that in the US — many observations but little explanation. Given this lack of explanation this section will briefly discuss those anomalies that have been identified in Canada and list references so that interested readers may pursue the subject further.[51]

### ☐ A.4.1    The Size Effect

Data presented by Hatch and White, reproduced in Table 15.15 strongly suggests the existence of a small firm effect.

TABLE 15.15
Small- and Large-Stock Performance, 1950-1987.

|  | Small Stocks | Large Stocks |
| --- | --- | --- |
| *Value Weighted* | | |
| Average monthly return | 1.30% | 0.98% |
| Monthly standard deviation | 5.05% | 4.45% |
| *Equally Weighted* | | |
| Average monthly return | 1.69% | 1.07% |
| Monthly standard deviation | 5.40% | 4.47% |

*SOURCE:* Reprinted, with permission, from J.E.Hatch and R.W.White, *Canadian Stocks, Bonds, Bills and Inflation: 1957–1987.* Copyright 1988, The Research Foundation of The Institute of Chartered Financial Analysts, Charlottesville, Va.

A rigorous study examined this phenomenon in considerable detail that included adjustments for the effects of non-synchronous trading and discovered the existence of a significant size effect. Other studies described below that examine interrelationships between the size effect and other regularities confirm its existence. Mittoo, however, argues that the small firm effect disappeared from both US and Canadian markets after published research documented its existence and institutions started offering small

---

[51] For an excellent summary, marred only by the lack of an adequate bibliography, see V.M.Jog, "Stock Pricing Anomalies: Canadian Experience," *Canadian Investment Review*, I, no.1 (Fall 1988): 55–62.

capitalization investment funds. Table 15.16 shows that the differential returns to small firms effectively disappeared from both US and Canadian markets after May 1982.[52]

**TABLE 15.16**
Change in the Size Effect

| Period | Pre Information July 62-April 82 | Post Information May 82-Sept 87 |
|---|---|---|
| a. US Market | | |
| Annual Size Effect | 9.4% | −3.0% |
| T-statistics | 5.5 | −0.8 |
| | Pre Information Jan 53-April 82 | Post Information May 82-May 90 |
| b. Canadian Market | | |
| Size Effect | 4.5% | −0.8% |
| T-statistics | 3.7 | −0.3 |

SOURCE: U.R.Mittoo, "Do Financial Markets Learn from Academic Research?" *Canadian Investment Review*, IV, no. 1 (Spring 1991):85–5.

## ☐ A.4.2   Seasonality in Stock Returns

Several time-related effects have been identified, the best known of which is the January or turn-of-the-year effect. This empirical regularity has been investigated and documented by several researchers. The results of a typical study are summarized in Table 15.17 and show that there is a pronounced January effect in all stocks, large and small, but smaller stocks earn higher returns in January than other firms. Morgan et al. report that the January return accounts for practically all the annual abnormal return earned by small firms. They conclude that there are no abnormal returns to small firms except in January.

Evidence on the tax loss selling hypothesis, however, is mixed. Canada should provide an excellent testing ground for this hypothesis because the capital gains tax was only introduced in 1972. It would be reasonable to expect, therefore, that there should be no January effect prior to 1972. The results presented in Table 15.17, however, clearly show that this effect predates the introduction of the capital gains tax.[53]

---

[52] I.G.Morgan, A.L.MacBeth and D.J.Novak, "The Relationship Between Equity Value and Abnormal returns in the Canadian Stock Market," Kingston: Queen's University School of Business Working Paper; U.R.Mittoo, "Do Financial Markets Learn from Academic Research?" *Canadian Investment Review*, IV, no. 1 (Spring 1991):83–6.

[53] A.J.Berges, J.J.McConell and G.Schlarbaum, "The Turn-of-the-Year in Canada," *Journal of Finance*, 39, no. 1 (March 1984):185–92;S.M.Tinic, G.Barone-Adessi and R.R.West, "Seasonality in Canadian Stock Prices: A Test of the 'Tax-Loss-Selling' Hypothesis," *Journal of Financial and Quantitative Research*, 22, no.1 (March 1987):51–63.

**TABLE 15.17**

Average Monthly Returns on the TSE 300, on the Market Value-Weighted Laval Index (MVWI), and on the Equally-Weighted Laval Index (EWI).

| | TSE300 | | MVWI | | EWI | |
|---|---|---|---|---|---|---|
| Period | January | Other Months | January | Other Months | January | Other Months |
| 1963–71 | 9.98% | 0.58% | 2.64% | 0.92% | 3.66% | 0.91% |
| 1972–86 | 3.13% | 0.82% | 3.51% | 1.54% | 5.90% | 0.97% |

SOURCE: V.M.Jog, "Stock Pricing Anomalies: Canadian Experience," *Canadian Investment Review*, I, no.1 (Fall 1988):56.

Unlike the US, however, the turn-of-the-year effect in Canada should manifest itself during the last week of December rather than in January. In Canada, share ownership must be transferred from seller to buyer before a capital gain or loss may be reported for tax purposes. This means that a trade must be executed five trading days before year-end in order to qualify. In most years, the cut-off date is December 20 or 21 (in contrast, in the US simple execution is sufficient to qualify). Stock prices should, therefore, "rebound" during the last week in December if tax loss selling is a significant factor. Two studies have found that this is, in fact, the case.[54]

The day-of-the-week effect has also been reported by several researchers as shown in Table 15.18. Returns are significantly negative on Mondays and positive on Fridays with positive but insignificant returns on other days. Despite the existence of these regularities it is probable that transactions costs would eliminate any profit from a trading rule based on these results. Discretionary traders, however, may find it useful to postpone purchases from Monday to Tuesday and to advance sales from Monday to the previous Friday.[55]

---

[54] C.B.Cadsby, "Canadian Calendar Anomalies and the Capital Asset Pricing Model," in *A Reappraisal of the Efficiency of Financial Markets*, eds.R.M.C.Guimarães, B.G.Kingsman and S.J.Taylor, (Berlin: Springer-Verlag; 1989) reports that the turn-of-the-year effect in Canada lasts from December 21 to January 5. M.D.Griffiths, "Systematic Changes in Investor Trading Behavior at the Turn-of-the-Year: An Intraday Study," Milwaukee: University of Wisconsin-Milwaukee School of Business Administration Working Paper, 1991. Griffiths also reports that informed investors not subject to capital gains also engage in year end trading, see M.D.Griffiths, "The Role of Informed Traders in the Canadian Turn-of- the-Year Effect," *Proceedings*, Administrative Sciences Association of Canada, Whistler, B.C., 1990.

[55] T.Chamberlain, C.S.Cheung and C.Kwan, "Day of the Week patterns in Stock Returns: The Canadian Evidence," *Canadian Journal of Administrative Sciences* 5, no.4 (December 1988);H.Bishara, "Stock Returns and the Weekend Effect in Canada," *Akron Business and Economic Review* 20, no. 2 (Summer 1989):62–71;J.F.Jaffe and R.Westerfield, "A Twist on the Monday Effect in Stock Prices: Evidence from the US and Foreign Stock Markets," *Journal of Banking and Finance* 13, no. 4/5 (September 1989):641–50.

**TABLE 15.18**

Average % Returns by Day of the Week.

| Researchers | Index | Period | Mon. | Tues. | Wed. | Thurs. | Fri. |
|---|---|---|---|---|---|---|---|
| **Canada** | | | | | | | |
| Jaffe & Westerfield | TSE300(2) | 1976–83 | −.14 | .02 | .12 | .11 | .14 |
| Chamberlain et al. | TSE300(2) | 1978–85 | −.15 | .07 | .13 | .11 | .14 |
| | TSE300(3) | 1978–85 | −.10 | .05 | .08 | .07 | .11 |
| Bishara | TSE300(2) | 1968–87(4) | −.49 | .01 | .06 | .24 | .21 |
| **International** | | | | | | | |
| Jaffe & Westerfield | US | 1962–83(1) | −.13 | .02 | .11 | .03 | .08 |
| | Japan | 1970–83(1) | −.02 | −.09 | .15 | .03 | .06 |
| | UK | 1950–83(1) | −.14 | .09 | .08 | .05 | .06 |
| | Australia | 1973–83(1) | −.05 | −.13 | .04 | .17 | .13 |

(1) - Close-to-close    (3) - Open-to-close
(2) - Close-to-open    (4) - Only till March 1987

*SOURCE:* V.M.Jog, "Stock Pricing Anomalies: Canadian Experience," *Canadian Investment Review*, I, no.1 (Fall 1988):56.

Jog and Riding have reported a month-end effect similar to that reported in US markets, shown in Table 15.19. They find that abnormally high returns are recorded on the last trading day of the calendar month and the first two trading days of the subsequent month. The returns from these three days of each month account for about 60% of the total returns on the TSE 300 for the period 1976–1984. A subsequent study indicates that a strategy based on this regularity would probably not be profitable because of transactions costs. An international study finds that the turn of the month effects are significant in Canada, the UK, Australia, Switzerland and West Germany, whereas pre-holiday effects (similar to the Friday anomaly) are only found in Canada, Japan, Hong Kong and Australia.[56]

---

[56] V.Jog and A.L.Riding, "The Month-End Effect in Canadian Stock Prices: Some Anomalous Findings," *Canadian Journal of Administrative Sciences* 6, no. 4 (December 1989):7–17; V.Jog and A.L.Riding, "Lunar Cycles in Stock Prices," *Financial Analysts' Journal* 45, no. 2 (March/April 1989):63–8; C.B.Cadsby and M.Ratner, "Turn-of-the-month and Pre-holiday Effects on Stock Returns: Some International Evidence," *Journal of Banking and Finance* 16, forthcoming as of June 1992.

**TABLE 15.19**

Average Wealth Relatives and Tests of Deviations from the Mean.

| Day in Trading Month | Average Daily Wealth Relative | T Test Statistic† |
|:---:|:---:|:---:|
| −9 | 0.075% | 0.68 |
| −8 | 0.019% | −0.65 |
| −7 | 0.026% | −0.41 |
| −6 | 0.084% | 0.33 |
| −5 | 0.022% | −0.51 |
| −4 | 0.006% | −1.88 |
| −3 | 0.033% | −0.36 |
| −2 | 0.040% | −0.23 |
| −1 | 0.041% | −0.19 |
| 1 | 0.160% | 1.70* |
| 2 | 0.159% | 1.27 |
| 3 | 0.230% | 2.16* |
| 4 | 0.012% | −0.70 |
| 5 | 0.015% | −0.56 |
| 6 | 0.000% | −1.02 |
| 7 | 0.014% | −0.58 |
| 8 | 0.061% | 0.01 |
| 9 | 0.110% | 1.77 |

†Test:  $H_0$:  Average return for trading day = overall average daily return, against
     $H_1$:  Average return for trading day < overall average daily return.
*Statistically significant at the 5% level.

*SOURCE:* V.Jog and A.L.Riding, "The Month-End Effect in Canadian Stock Prices: Some Anomalous Findings," *Canadian Journal of Administrative Sciences*, 6, no. 4 (December 1989):7–17.

---

**A.5**

# SUMMARY OF EMPIRICAL REGULARITIES

On balance, what do these regularities suggest the investor should do? First, investors who want to buy stocks should avoid doing so early on Monday. During the other days of the week they should do so as early as possible. Second, investors who want to sell stocks should try to sell late on Friday. If this is not possible, they should wait until at least 45 minutes after the opening except on Monday, when they should try to sell at the opening. Third, if small firms are to be purchased, they should be purchased in late December or somewhat earlier; if small firms are to be sold, they should be sold in mid-January or somewhat later. Fourth, if large firms are to be purchased, they should be purchased in early February or somewhat later; if large firms are to be sold, they should be sold in late December or somewhat earlier.

Several words of caution are in order here. First, it should be noted that there is some question whether or not the first two recommendations are useful during the month of January. Second, none of these empirical regularities is of a sufficient magnitude to suggest that riches are to be made by exploiting them. Indeed, transactions costs would devour most, if not all, of any profits that may be made. All that they suggest is that if, for whatever reason, a buy or sell order is to be placed, there are some times when it may be more advantageous to do so. Third, while these regularities have been found to exist in the past — and in some instances for long periods of time — there is no guarantee that they will continue to exist in the future. It may be the case that as more investors become aware of them and time their trades accordingly, these regularities will cease to exist.

## APPENDIX B

## EMPIRICAL AND FUNDAMENTAL FACTORS

As indicated in the text, factors determined empirically may differ from fundamental factors. This will be the case even if the relevant attributes are selected and measured without error.

Assume that the underlying factor model is:

$$r_i = a_i + b_{i1} F_1 + \cdots + b_{iM} F_M + e_i. \tag{15.17}$$

From the assumption that the final term has an expected value of zero:

$$\bar{r}_i = a_i + b_{i1} \overline{F}_1 + \cdots + b_{iM} \overline{F}_M \tag{15.18}$$

where:

$$\bar{r}_i = \text{the expected return on security } i$$
$$\overline{F}_1, \ldots, \overline{F}_M = \text{the expected values of factors } 1, \ldots, M. \text{ |medskip The Arbitrage}$$

Pricing Theory implies that:

$$\bar{r}_i = r_f + b_{i1} \lambda_1 + \cdots + b_{iM} \lambda_M \tag{15.19}$$

where:

$$r_f = \text{the riskless rate of interest}$$
$$\lambda_1, \ldots, \lambda_m = \text{the expected return premiums for factors } 1, \ldots, M. \text{ |medskip Since}$$

both equations indicate the expected return on the security, the two right-hand sides must equal. This implies that

$$a_i = r_f + b_{i1} (\lambda_1 - \overline{F}_1) + \cdots + b_{iM} (\lambda_M - \overline{F}_M). \tag{15.20}$$

Substituting this value into the equation of the underlying factor model gives

$$r_i = r_f + b_{i1} (\lambda_1 + F_1 - \overline{F}_1) + \cdots + b_{iM} (\lambda_M + F_M - \overline{F}_M) + e_i. \tag{15.21}$$

When security returns are regressed on the relevant attributes, the "empirical factors" obtained will equal the parenthesized expressions. Using the notation from the chapter:

$$f_1 = \lambda_1 + (F_1 - \overline{F}_1)$$

$$\vdots$$

$$f_M = \lambda_M + (F_M - \overline{F}_M)$$

where:
$$f_1, \ldots, f_M = \text{empirical factors } 1, \ldots, M.$$

Thus each empirical factor will equal the expected return premium for the corresponding fundamental factor plus the deviation of the fundamental factor from its expected value.

If all relevant attributes are included, the intercept in the cross-section regression should equal the riskless rate of interest. And if historic results are adequate proxies for unchanging expectations, the average values of the empirical factors should equal the expected return premiums. As indicated in the chapter, these are stringent requirements, unlikely to be totally fulfilled in practice.

# APPENDIX C

## BETA ESTIMATION IN THINLY TRADED MARKETS

The majority of the shares listed on the TSE are relatively thinly traded. A study that examined trading frequencies found that only 6% of stocks had a recorded trade on the last trading day of each month over the ten year period 1970 to 1979. A further 52% had a recorded trade each month, but not necessarily on the last day. The remaining stocks had one or more months when no trades were executed.[57] There is unpublished evidence that trading frequencies have improved in later years, nevertheless thin trading remains a pervasive problem on the TSE. This section will deal non-rigorously with the problems associated with beta estimation in thinly traded markets and will discuss the solutions that have been proposed.

Defining a frequently traded stock as one that has a recorded trade on the last trading day of each month then the return is calculated using prices recorded at time $t$ and time $t-1$ and is represented by $R_{k,t}$ in Figure 15.16. Thin security $j$, on the other hand, trades less frequently and less consistently such that the last trade occurs at time $t^*$ and the observed return is measured using prices recorded at $t^*$ and $t-1^*$ and is represented by $R_{jt}^*$ in Figure 15.16. It is clear from Figure 15.16 that the overlap between the two returns is less than perfect. The magnitude of the covariance of the returns between the two securities depends on the size of the overlap. The measured covariance between $R_{jt}^*$ and $R_{kt}$ will, therefore, be downward biased when compared with the covariance between two frequently traded securities because there is a less than complete overlap.

A broad index of security returns represents a variety of stocks listed on the exchange and will, therefore, include both frequently traded and thin securities. The observed return on such an index is represented by $R_{It}^*$ that can be compared with an index consisting of only frequently traded stocks represented by $R_{It}$ in Figure 15.17. As discussed in Chapter 8 the variance of the return on an index consists of the sum of the variances of the individual stocks plus twice the covariances. Because there is only an incomplete overlap between the returns on the stocks that make up the index the covariances are almost all downward biased and, therefore, the measured variance of the index will in turn be downward biased when compared with an index consisting of frequently traded stocks.

Recalling that the beta of security, $j$, is calculated as follows:

$$\beta_j = \text{Cov}(R_{jt}^*, R_{It}^*)/\text{Var}(R_{It}^*) \qquad (15.22)$$

will itself be biased because both the numerator and denominator are themselves downward biased. If security, $j$, trades either much more or much less frequently than the average security in the index then the bias in the numerator will be larger than the bias in the denominator and the estimated beta will be downward biased. If security, $j$, trades only slightly more or less than the representative security in the index then the

---

[57] D. Fowler and H. Rorke, "Thin Trading and Beta Estimation Problems On the Toronto Stock Exchange," *Journal of Business Administration* 12, no. 1 (Fall 1980); 77–90.

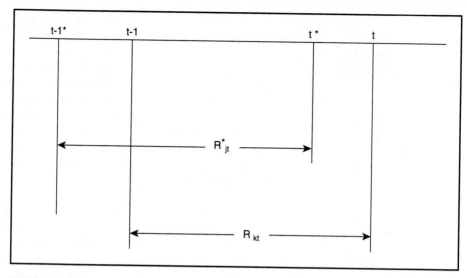

**FIGURE 15-16**
Relationship between the observed returns on thin security, $j$, and frequently traded security, $k$.

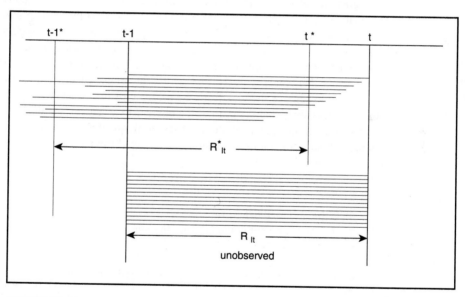

**FIGURE 15-17**
Relationship between the observed and true but unobserved index returns.

bias in the denominator will be larger than that of the numerator and the estimated beta will be upward biased. In a few cases the biases will approximately cancel out and the beta estimate will only be slightly biased.

There is another interesting and useful property of indices containing thin securities that was reported by Fisher. Because the frequently traded securities in the index trade later in the period than the thin ones the former incorporate the most up-to-date information in their prices and, therefore, in the index. The thin securities, however, only reflect this news in the next period. The return on the thin securities, therefore, only "catch up" one period later. If the new information is the result of good news then some of the stocks in the index will reflect it this period and the remainder in the next. The index returns will, therefore, be positively serially correlated when thin stocks are present even if the returns on the underlying securities are serially uncorrelated. Working has shown theoretically that an index containing a wide variety of securities that trade every period but at different times within the period will have a serial correlation coefficient that approaches 0.25.[58]

The serial correlation coefficient of the index returns can, therefore, be used as a rough guide to the degree of "thinness" of the index. An index consisting of only frequently traded securities will have a serial correlation coefficient close to zero whereas one with many thin stocks will approach 0.25.

A number of different approaches have been suggested for obtaining unbiased beta estimates in thinly traded markets, but the technique developed by Scholes and Williams has probably gained the greatest acceptance because of its elegance and simplicity.[59] This is a four step procedure that requires three regressions. First, the stock's return is regressed against the concurrent index return ($R_{jt}$ vs. $R_{It}$, the conventional beta estimator), second, the stock's return is regressed against the leading index return ($R_{jt}$ vs. $R_{It+1}$), and third, the stock's return is regressed against the lagging index return ($R_{jt}$ vs. $R_{It-1}$). The nonsynchronous regression coefficients capture the portion of the covariance that is missing in the concurrent regression. The sum of these three coefficients then deals with the bias in the numerator of the beta estimator. All that remains is to remove the bias from the estimate of the variance of the index. Scholes and Williams show that the ratio of the observed variance of the thinly traded index to the variance of an equivalent, but unobserved frequently traded index is $(1 + 2\rho_I)$. An unbiased beta estimator can, therefore, be obtained from the following expression:

$$\beta_j^u = (\beta_j^+ + \beta_j^\circ + \beta_j^-)/(1 + 2\rho_I) \tag{15.23}$$

where

$\beta_j^u$ is the unbiased beta estimator,
$\beta_j^+$ is the coefficient obtained from the regression of $R_{jt}$ vs. $R_{It+1}$,

---

[58] L.Fisher,"Some New Stock Market Indexes," *Journal of Business* 39, Suppl. (January 1966):191–225; H. Working, "Note on the Correlation of First Differences of Averages in a Random Chain," *Econometrica* 28, (October 1960):916–8.

[59] M.Scholes and J.Williams, "Estimating Betas from Nonsynchronous Data," *Journal of Financial Economics* 5, no. 3 (December 1977):309–29. Other techniques that produce unbiased estimators have been proposed. The method developed by E.Dimson, "Risk Measurement when Shares are Subject to Infrequent Trading," *Journal of Financial Economics* 7, no. 2 (June 1979):197–226 when modified as described by D.Fowler and H.Rorke, "Risk Measurement when Shares are Subject to Infrequent Trading: Commemt," *Journal of Financial Economics* 12, no. 2 (August 1983):279–283 produces an estimator equivalent to that of Scholes and Williams. See also D.Fowler, H.Rorke and V.Jog, "A Bias-correcting Procedure for Beta Estimation in the Presence of Thin Trading," *Journal of Financial Research* 12, no. 1 (Spring 1989):23–32; K.Cohen, G.Hawawini, S.Maier, R.Schwartz and D.Whitcomb, "Friction in the Trading Process and the Estimation of Systematic Risk," *Journal of Financial Economics* 12, no. 2 (August 1983):263–78, and P.Marsh, "Equity Rights Issues and the Efficiency of the UK Stock Market," *Journal of Finance* 34, no. 4 (September 1979):839–62.

$\beta_j{}^o$ is the coefficient obtained from the regression of $R_{jt}$ vs. $R_{It}$,

$\beta_j{}^-$ is the coefficient obtained from the regression of $R_{jt}$ vs. $R_{It-1}$,

and $\rho_I$ is the index's serial correlation coefficient obtained by regressing $R_{It}$ vs. $R_{It-1}$.

Table 15.20 shows the betas estimated by both the conventional method and the Scholes-Williams technique (together with the non-synchronous coefficients) for an index of relatively frequently traded stocks (the TSE 300) and a thinner index. The latter includes more stocks than the former and, in addition, places more weight on the smaller capitalization stocks that generally trade less frequently. As expected, the serial correlation coefficient of the TSE 300, 0.0596, is substantially smaller than that of the other index, 0.1621.

**TABLE 15.20**

Demonstration of the Scholes-Williams Estimation Technique using Monthly Data.

| Index Stock | TSE 300 Total Return | | | |
|---|---|---|---|---|
| | $\beta_j^+$ | $\beta_j^0$ | $\beta_j^-$ | $\beta_j^u$ |
| Andres Wines | 0.1103 | 0.8535 | 0.5231 | 1.3286 |
| BCE | 0.1158 | 0.3698 | 0.0957 | 0.5194 |
| Canadian Tire | 0.4137 | 0.5723 | 0.2158 | 1.0739 |
| Goldmark | 0.2744 | 0.5362 | 0.0052 | 0.7290 |
| Imperial Oil | −0.0362 | 0.8850 | 0.1528 | 0.8949 |
| Royal Bank of Canada | 0.0911 | 0.7594 | −0.1222 | 0.6507 |
| STELCO | 0.0151 | 1.1987 | 0.2335 | 1.2931 |
| Union Carbide | −0.0220 | 0.9577 | 0.0422 | 0.8738 |
| $\rho_I$ | 0.0596 | | | |
| Index Stock | Equally Weighted Laval Stocks | | | |
| | $\beta_j^+$ | $\beta_j^0$ | $\beta_j^-$ | $\beta_j^u$ |
| Andres Wines | 0.1684 | 0.8765 | 0.3613 | 1.0620 |
| BCE | 0.1528 | 0.2971 | 0.2971 | 0.3870 |
| Canadian Tire | 0.3884 | 0.8478 | 0.0642 | 0.9821 |
| Goldmark | 0.2395 | 0.9285 | −0.0041 | 0.8790 |
| Imperial Oil | 0.0696 | 0.8515 | 0.2235 | 0.8644 |
| Royal Bank of Canada | 0.0719 | 0.5133 | −0.1214 | 0.3503 |
| STELCO | 0.2464 | 0.9553 | 0.0875 | 0.9736 |
| Union Carbide | 0.1377 | 0.8613 | 0.0841 | 0.8179 |
| $\rho_I$ | 0.1621 | | | |

Table 15.20 also shows that the significance of the nonsynchronous coefficients depends on the "thinness" of the index. Despite its simplicity, the Scholes-Williams technique produces unbiased, but imprecise beta estimates because the estimator has a large variance as a result of being the sum of three separate regression coefficients. The estimation problems become much more severe when there are months with missing prices. The Scholes-Williams technique can be adapted to meet this situation but the

precision of the estimator suffers even more. No completely satisfactory solution to the problem of estimating betas in thinly traded markets has been proposed.

## QUESTIONS AND PROBLEMS

1. Tadoussac Company is conducting the annual election for its five-member board of directors. The firm has 1,600,000 shares of voting common stock outstanding.
   a. Under a majority voting system, how many shares must a shareholder own to ensure being able to elect his or her choices to each of the five director seats?
   b. Under a cumulative voting system, how many shares must a shareholder own to ensure being able to elect his or her choices to two of the director seats?
   c. Art Latham holds 20% of Tadoussac's outstanding shares. How many directors can Art elect under a cumulative voting system?

2. As takeover and merger activity has increased in recent years, the issue of corporate ownership versus control has become more controversial. Discuss the principal-agent problem as it relates to shareholder-management relations. Specifically, why is there a potential conflict between the two groups? What steps can be taken to mitigate this problem?

3. Why might a corporation wish to issue more than one class of common shares?

4. With respect to the payment of corporate dividends, distinguish between declaration date, ex-dividend date, and date-of-record.

5. Theoretical arguments and empirical research support the case that stock dividends and splits do not enhance shareholder wealth. However, corporations continue to declare stock dividends and splits. Summarize the arguments for and against stock dividends and splits from the perspective of the shareholder.

6. St. Boniface Ltd. is planning to raise $28,000,000 through the sale of new common stock under a rights offering. The subscription price is $70 per share while the stock currently sells for $80 per share, rights-on. Total outstanding shares equal 10,000,000. Of this amount, Annie Jones owns 100,000 shares.
   a. How many shares of stock will each right permit its owner to purchase?
   b. What will be the total value of Annie's rights a day before the ex-rights date, assuming the market price of St. Boniface shares remains at $80 per share?
   c. After the ex-rights date, if the market value of each St. Boniface Ltd. right equals $.20, what must be the ex-rights market price of St. Boniface's shares?

7. From the perspective of efficient market proponents, why is it surprising that trades based on insider trading data found in the *Ontario Securities Commission Bulletin* appear to produce significant abnormal profits?

8. Shown here are ten quarters of excess return data for Labrador Associates stock, as well as excess return data over the same period for a broad stock market index. Using this information, calculate the following statistics for Labrador Associates stock.
   a. Beta
   b. Alpha
   c. Standard deviation of random error term
   d. Coefficient of determination

| Quarter | Labrador Excess Return | Market Excess Return |
|---------|------------------------|----------------------|
| 1 | 3.8% | 2.7% |
| 2 | 5.3 | 3.1 |
| 3 | −7.2 | −4.9 |
| 4 | 10.1 | 9.9 |
| 5 | 1.0 | 2.7 |
| 6 | 2.5 | 1.2 |
| 7 | 6.4 | 3.8 |
| 8 | 4.8 | 4.0 |
| 9 | 6.0 | 5.5 |
| 10 | 2.2 | 2.0 |

9. Explain the primary differences between multiple-factor models of beta and historical models of beta. In particular, why might you expect that the multiple-factor models would do a better job of forecasting betas than do the historical models?

10. Generally, stocks with a relatively low price per share (roughly $5 per share or less) have higher betas than stocks with a higher price per share. What attributes of low-price stocks might you expect to be correlated with higher beta values?

11. Graham Dean owns a portfolio of 50 securities. Having read research that indicates that a well-diversified portfolio can be achieved with 10-20 randomly-selected securities, Graham believes almost all nonmarket risk has been eliminated in the 50-security portfolio. Is Graham's portfolio truly well diversified if many of its securities happen to be contained in a single homogeneous security group? Explain.

12. (Appendix Question) The empirical regularities cited in this chapter have potentially troubling implications for the Capital Asset Pricing Model and/or the concept of highly efficient markets. Discuss some of these implications.

## SUGGESTED READINGS

*The Canadian Securities Course* (Toronto, Ont.: The Canadian Securities Institute, 1989). Chapter 12 describes the properties of common shares and the rights of shareholders.

E. F. Fama, L. Fisher, M. Jensen and R. Roll, "The Adjustment of Stock Prices to New Information," *International Economic Review* (February 1969) was the first of the semi-strong form of market efficiency and developed residual analysis as a suitable methodology.

Nejat Seyhun, "Insider's Profits, Costs of Trading and Market Efficiency," *Journal of Financial Economics* 16, no. 2, (June 1986) and

David J. Fowler and C. Harvey Rorke, "Insider Trading Profits on the Toronto Stock Exchange, 1967–1977," *Canadian Journal of Administrative Sciences* 5, no. 1 (March 1988):13–25 provide additional evidence about the profitability of insider trading in the United States and Canada.

Barr Rosenberg and J. Guy, "Predictions of Beta from Investment Fundamentals," *Financial Analyst Journal* 32 (May-June 1976),

James L. Farrell, Jr., *A Guide to Portfolio Management*, and *The Canadian Equity Model* (Montreal, Que.: BARRA International, Ltd., 1990) deal with applications of one or other version of the CAPM to practical investment strategies.

Elroy Dimson, *Stock Market Anomalies* (Cambridge, UK: Cambridge University Press, 1988) and

Vijay M. Jog, "Stock Pricing Anomalies: Canadian Experience," *Canadian Investment Review* I, no. 1 (Fall 1988):55–62 provide many examples of stock price anomalies, the latter in a Canadian setting.

Elizabeth Maynes, Chris Robinson and Alan White, "How Much is a Share Vote Worth?" *Canadian Investment Review* III, no. 1 (Spring 1990):49–56 deals with the problem of valuing non-voting shares.

# Chapter 16

# THE VALUATION OF COMMON SHARES

In Chapter 15, it was noted that one purpose of financial analysis is to identify mispriced securities. Fundamental analysis was mentioned as one approach for conducting a search for such securities. With this approach, the security analyst makes estimates of such things as the firm's future earnings and dividends. If these estimates are substantially different from the average estimates of other analysts but are viewed as being more accurate, then a mispriced security will have been identified. If it is also felt that the market price of the security will adjust to reflect these more accurate estimates, then the analyst will issue either a buy or sell recommendation, depending upon the direction of the anticipated price adjustment. Based upon the capitalization of income method of valuation, dividend discount models have been frequently used by fundamental analysts as a means of identifying mispriced common stocks.

## 16.1 CAPITALIZATION OF INCOME METHOD OF VALUATION

There are many ways to implement the fundamental analysis approach to identifying mispriced securities. A number of them are either directly or indirectly related to what is sometimes referred to as the *capitalization of income method of valuation*.[1] This method states that the true, or intrinsic, value of any asset is based on the cash flows that the investor expects to receive in the future from owning the asset. Since these cash flows are expected in the future, they are discounted to reflect the time value of money, with the *discount rate* reflecting not only the time value of money but also the riskiness of the cash flows.

---

[1] The appendix describes a model used by some fundamental analysts for identifying mispriced common stocks that is not directly related to the capitalization of income method of valuation. For a description of the typical financial characteristics of a stock market "winner," see Marc R. Reinganum, "The Anatomy of a Stock Market Winner," *Financial Analysts Journal* 44, no. 2 (March/April 1988):16–28.

Algebraically, the intrinsic value of the asset $(V)$ is equal to the sum of the present values of the expected cash flows:

$$V = \frac{C_1}{(1+k)^1} + \frac{C_2}{(1+k)^2} + \frac{C_3}{(1+k)^3} + \cdots = \sum_{t=1}^{\infty} \frac{C_t}{(1+k)^t} \qquad (16.1)$$

where $C_t$ denotes the expected cash flow associated with the asset at time $t$ and $k$ is the appropriate discount rate for cash flows of this degree risk. In this equation, the discount rate is assumed to be the same for all periods. Since the symbol $\infty$ above the summation sign in the equation denotes infinity, all expected cash flows, from immediately after making the investment until infinity, are discounted at the same rate in determining $V$.[2]

## ☐ 16.1.1  Net Present Value

For the sake of convenience, let the current moment in time be denoted by zero, or $t = 0$. If the cost of purchasing an asset at $t = 0$ is $P$, then its *net present value* (NPV) is equal to the difference between its intrinsic value and cost, or

$$\text{NPV} = V - P = \left[ \sum_{t=1}^{\infty} \frac{C_t}{(1+k)^t} \right] - P. \qquad (16.2)$$

The net present value calculation shown here is conceptually the same as the net present value calculation made for capital budgeting decisions that has long been advocated in introductory finance textbooks. Capital budgeting decisions involve deciding whether or not a given investment project should be undertaken (for example, should a new machine be purchased?). In making this decision, the focal point is the NPV of the project. Specifically, an investment project would be viewed favorably if the NPV is positive and unfavorably if its NPV is negative. For a simple project involving a cash outflow now (at $t = 0$) and expected cash inflows in the future, a positive NPV means that the present value of all the expected cash inflows is greater than cost of making the investment. Conversely, a negative NPV means that the present value of all the expected cash inflows is less than the cost of making the investment.

The same views about NPV apply when financial assets (such as a share of common stock), instead of real assets (such as a new machine), are being considered for purchase. That is, a financial asset is viewed favorably and said to be underpriced, or undervalued, if $\text{NPV} > 0$. Conversely, a financial asset is viewed unfavorably and said to be overpriced, or overvalued, if $\text{NPV} < 0$. From equation (16.2), this is equivalent to stating that a financial asset is underpriced if $V > P$:

$$\sum_{t=1}^{\infty} \frac{C_t}{(1+k)^t} > P. \qquad (16.3)$$

---

[2] Sometimes the expected cash flows after some time period will be equal to zero, meaning that the summation only needs to be carried out to that point. Even if they are never equal to zero, in many cases the denominator in equation (15.1) will become so large as $t$ gets large (for example, if $t$ is 40 or more for a discount rate of 15%) that the present value of all expected cash flows past an arbitrary time in the future will be roughly zero and can be safely ignored.

Conversely, the asset is overvalued if $V < P$:

$$\sum_{t=1}^{\infty} \frac{C_t}{(1+k)^t} < P. \tag{16.4}$$

## ☐ 16.1.2 Internal Rate of Return

Another way of making capital budgeting decisions in a manner that is similar to NPV involves calculating the *internal rate of return* (IRR) associated with the investment project. With IRR, NPV in equation (16.2) is set equal to zero and the discount rate becomes the unknown that must be calculated. That is, the IRR for a given investment is the discount rate that makes the net present value of the investment equal to zero. Algebraically, the procedure involves solving the following equation for the internal rate of return, denoted by $k^*$:

$$0 = \sum_{t=1}^{\infty} \frac{C_t}{(1+k^*)^t} - P \tag{16.5}$$

where $k^*$ is the IRR of the investment. Equivalently, equation (16.5) can be rewritten as

$$P = \sum_{t=1}^{\infty} \frac{C_t}{(1+k^*)^t}. \tag{16.6}$$

The decision rule for IRR involves comparing the project's IRR, denoted by $k^*$, with the required rate of return for an investment of similar risk, denoted by k. Specifically, the investment would be viewed favorably if $k^* > k$ and unfavorably if $k^* < k$. As with NPV, the same decision rule applies if either a real asset or financial asset is being considered for possible investment.

## ☐ 16.1.3 An Application to Common Shares

This chapter is concerned with using the capitalization of income method to determine the intrinsic value of common shares.[3] Since the cash flows associated with an investment in any particular common stock are the dividends that are expected to be paid throughout the future on the shares purchased, the models suggested by this method of valuation are often known as *dividend discount models* (DDMs).[4] Accordingly, $D_t$ will be used instead of $C_t$ to denote the expected cash flow in period $t$ associated with

---

[3] Chapter 13 discussed how to use this method to value bonds.

[4] Since the focus of DDMs is on predicting dividends, there is a particular situation where using DDMs to value common shares is exceptionally difficult. This is the situation where the firm has not paid dividends on its shares in the recent past, which results in a complete lack of a historical record on which to base a prediction of dividends. Examples include valuing the shares of a firm being sold to the public for the first time (known as an initial public offering, or ipo) and valuing the shares of a firm that has not paid dividends recently (perhaps the firm has never paid dividends, or perhaps it has suspended paying them). A more extensive discussion of DDMs is contained in the entire November–December 1985 issue of the *Financial Analysts Journal*. For an article that describes some of the current applications of DDMs, see Barbara Donnelly, "The Dividend Discount Model Comes into Its Own," *Institutional Investor* 19, no. 3 (March 1985):77–82.

a particular share of common stock, resulting in the following restatement of equation (16.1):

$$V = \frac{D_1}{(1+k)^1} + \frac{D_2}{(1+k)^2} + \frac{D_3}{(1+k)^3} + \cdots$$

$$= \sum_{t=1}^{\infty} \frac{D_t}{(1+k)^t}. \tag{16.7}$$

Usually the focus of DDMs is on determining the true, or intrinsic, value of *one* share of a particular company's common stock, even if larger-size purchases are being contemplated. This is because it is usually believed that larger-size purchases can be made at a cost that is a simple multiple of the cost of one share (for example, the cost of 1000 shares is usually assumed to be 1000 times the cost of one share). Thus, the numerator in DDMs is the cash dividends *per share* that are expected in the future.

However, there is a complication in using equation (16.7) to determine the intrinsic value of a share of common stock. In particular, in order to use this equation the investor must forecast *all* future dividends. Since common shares do not have a fixed lifetime, this suggests that an infinitely long stream of dividends must be forecast. While this may seem to be an impossible task, with the addition of certain assumptions, the equation can be made tractable (that is, usable).

These assumptions center around *dividend growth rates*. That is, the dividend per share at any time $t$ can be viewed as being equal to the dividend per share at time $t-1$ times a dividend growth rate of $g_t$ :

$$D_t = D_{t-1}(1+g_t) \tag{16.8}$$

or, equivalently,

$$\frac{D_t - D_{t-1}}{D_{t-1}} = g_t. \tag{16.9}$$

For example, if the dividend per share expected at $t=2$ is \$4 and the dividend per share expected at $t=3$ is \$4.20, then $g_3 = (\$4.20 - \$4)/\$4 = 5\%$. The different types of tractable DDMs reflect different sets of assumptions about dividend growth rates and are presented next. The discussion begins with the simplest case, the zero-growth model.

## 16.2    THE ZERO-GROWTH MODEL

One assumption that could be made about future dividends is that they will remain at a fixed dollar amount. That is, the dollar amount of dividends per share that were paid over the past year ($D_0$) will also be paid over the next year ($D_1$), the year after that ($D_2$), the year after that ($D_3$), and so on. That is,

$$D_0 = D_1 = D_2 = D_3 = \cdots$$

This is equivalent to assuming that all the dividend growth rates are zero, since if $g_t = 0$, then $D_t = D_{t-1}$ in equation (16.8). Accordingly, this model is often referred to as the *zero-growth* (or no-growth) *model*.

The impact of this assumption on equation (16.7) can be analyzed by noting what happens when $D_t$ is replaced by $D_0$ in the numerator:

$$V = \sum_{t=1}^{\infty} \frac{D_0}{(1+k)^t}.$$ (16.10)

Fortunately, equation (16.10) can be simplified by noting that $D_0$ is a fixed dollar amount, which means it can be written outside the summation sign:

$$V = D_0 \left[ \sum_{t=1}^{\infty} \frac{1}{(1+k)^t} \right].$$ (16.11)

The next step involves using a property of infinite series from mathematics. If $k > 0$, then it can be shown that

$$\sum_{t=1}^{\infty} \frac{1}{(1+k)^t} = \frac{1}{k}.$$ (16.12)

Applying this property to equation (16.11) results in the following formula for the zero-growth model:

$$V = \frac{D_0}{k_0}$$ (16.13)

Since $D_0 = D_1$, equation (16.13) is sometimes written as

$$V = \frac{D_1}{k}.$$ (16.14)

As an example of how this DDM can be used, assume that the Zinc Company is expected to pay cash dividends amounting to $8 per share into the indefinite future and has a required rate of return of 10%. Using either equation (16.13) or equation (16.14), it can be seen that the value of a share of Zinc stock is equal to $8/.10 = $80$. With a current stock price of $65 per share, equation (16.2) would suggest that the NPV per share is $80 - $65 = $15$. Equivalently, since $V = $80 > P = $65$, the stock is underpriced by $15 per share and would be a candidate for purchase.

## ☐ 16.2.1  Internal Rate of Return

Equation (16.13) can be reformulated to solve for the internal rate of return on an investment in a zero growth security. First, the current price of the security is substituted for $V$; second, $k^*$ is substituted for $k$. Doing so results in

$$P = \frac{D_0}{k^*}$$

which can be rewritten as

$$k^* = \frac{D_0}{P} \quad (16.15\,a)$$

$$= \frac{D_1}{P}. \quad (16.15\,b)$$

Applying this formula to the stock of Zinc indicates that $k^* = \$8/\$65 = 12.3\%$. Since the IRR from an investment in Zinc exceeds the required rate of return on Zinc ($12.3\% > 10\%$), this method also indicates that Zinc is underpriced.[5]

## ☐ 16.2.2 An Application

The zero-growth model may seem quite restrictive. After all, it does not seem reasonable to assume a given stock will pay a fixed dollar-size dividend forever. While such a criticism has validity for common stock valuation, there is one particular situation where this model is quite useful. Specifically, whenever the intrinsic value of a share of preferred stock is to be determined, this DDM is often appropriate. It is appropriate because most preferred shares are *nonparticipating*, meaning they pay a fixed dollar-size dividend that will not be changed as earnings per share changes. Furthermore, it can be expected to be paid forever, since preferred shares do not have a fixed lifetime.

## 16.3    THE CONSTANT-GROWTH MODEL

The next type of DDM to be considered is one that assumes dividends grow from period to period at the same rate forever, which is therefore known as the *constant-growth model*. Specifically, the dividends per share that were paid over the previous year ($D_0$) are expected to grow at a given rate $g$, so that the dividends expected over the next year ($D_1$) are expected to be equal to $D_0(1 + g)$. Dividends the year after that are again expected to grow by the rate $g$, meaning that $D_2 = D_1(1 + g)$. Since $D_1 = D_0(1 + g)$, this is equivalent to assuming that $D_2 = D_0(1 + g)^2$ and, in general,

$$D_t = D_{t-1}(1 + g) \qquad (16.16a)$$
$$= D_0(1 + g)^t. \qquad (16.16b)$$

The impact of this assumption on equation (16.7) can be analyzed by noting what happens when $D_t$ is replaced by $D_0(1 + g)^t$ in the numerator:

$$V = \sum_{t=1}^{\infty} \frac{D_0(1 + g)^t}{(1 + k)^t}. \qquad (16.17)$$

Fortunately, equation (16.17) can be simplified by noting that $D_0$ is a given dollar amount, which means it can be written outside the summation sign:

$$V = D_0 \left[ \sum_{t=1}^{\infty} \frac{(1 + g)^t}{(1 + k)^t} \right]. \qquad (16.18)$$

The next step involves using a property of infinite series from mathematics. If $k > g$, then it can be shown that

$$\sum_{t=1}^{\infty} \frac{(1 + g)^t}{(1 + k)^t} = \frac{1 + g}{k - g}. \qquad (16.19)$$

---

[5] A share of common stock has a positive NPV if and only if it has an IRR greater than its required rate of return. Thus, there can never be inconsistent signals given by the two approaches. That is, there will never be a situation where one approach indicates a share is underpriced and the other approach indicates it is overpriced. This is true not only for the zero-growth model but for all DDMs.

Substituting equation (16.19) into equation (16.18) results in the valuation formula for the constant growth model:

$$V = D_0 \left[ \frac{1+g}{k-g} \right].$$ (16.20)

Sometimes equation (16.20) is rewritten as

$$V = \frac{D_1}{k-g}$$ (16.21)

since $D_1 = D_0(1+g)$.

As an example of how this DDM can be used, assume that during the past year the Copper Company paid dividends amounting to $1.80 per share. The forecast is that dividends on Copper shares will increase by 5% per year into the indefinite future. Thus, dividends over the next year are expected to equal $1.80(1 + .05) = $1.89. Using equation (16.20) and assuming the required rate of return of 11%, it can be seen that the value of a share of Copper stock is equal to $1.80[(1 + .05)/(.11 − .05)] = $1.89/(.11 − .05) = $31.50. With a current stock price of $40 per share, equation (16.2) would suggest that the NPV per share is $31.50 − $40 = −$8.50. Equivalently, since $V = $31.50 < P = $40$, the stock is overpriced by $8.50 per share and would be a candidate for sale if currently owned.

## ☐ 16.3.1 Internal Rate of Return

Equation (16.20) can be reformulated to solve for the internal rate of return on an investment in a constant growth security. First, the current price of the security is substituted for $V$ and then $k^*$ is substituted for k. Doing so results in

$$P = D_0 \left[ \frac{1+g}{k^* - g} \right]$$ (16.22)

which can be rewritten as

$$k^* = \frac{D_0(1+g)}{P} + g$$ (16.23a)

$$= \frac{D_1}{P} + g.$$ (16.23b)

Applying this formula to the shares of Copper indicates that $k^* = [$1.80(1 + .05)/$40] + .05 = [$1.89/$40] + .05 = 9.725\%$. Since the required rate of return on Copper exceeds the IRR from an investment in Copper (11% > 9.725%), this method also indicates that Copper is overpriced.

## ☐ 16.3.2 Relationship to the Zero-Growth Model

The zero-growth model of the previous section can be shown to be a special case of the constant-growth model. In particular, if the growth rate $g$ is assumed to be 0, then dividends will be a fixed dollar amount forever, which is the same as saying that there will be zero growth. Letting $g = 0$ in equations (16.20) and (16.23a) results in two equations that are identical to (16.13) and (16.15a), respectively.

While assuming constant growth may seem less restrictive than assuming no growth, it may still be viewed as unrealistic in many cases. However, as will be shown

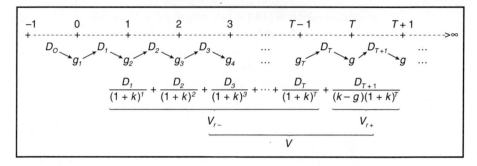

**FIGURE 16-1**
Time line for multiple growth model.

next, the constant-growth model is important because it is embedded in the multiple-growth model.

# THE MULTIPLE-GROWTH MODEL

The most general DDM for valuing common stocks is the *multiple-growth model*. With this model, the focus is on a time in the future after which dividends are expected to grow at a constant rate $g$. Although the investor is still concerned with forecasting dividends, these dividends do not need to have any specific pattern until this time, after which they will be assumed to have the specific pattern of constant growth. If this time is denoted by $T$, then dividends $D_1, D_2, D_3, ..., D_T$ will be forecast separately by the investor (the investor also forecasts when this time $T$ will occur). Thereafter, dividends are assumed to grow by a constant rate $g$ that the investor must also forecast, meaning that

$$D_{T+1} = D_T(1 + g)$$
$$D_{T+2} = D_{T+1}(1 + g) = D_T(1 + g)^2$$
$$D_{T+3} = D_{T+2}(1 + g) = D_T(1 + g)^3$$

and so on. Figure 16.1 presents a time line of dividends and growth rates associated with the multiple-growth model.

In determining the value of a share of common stock with the multiple growth model, the present value of the forecasted stream of dividends must be determined. This can be done by dividing the stream into two parts, finding the present value of each part, and then adding these two present values together.

The first part consists of finding the present value of all the forecasted dividends up to and including $T$. Denoting this present value by $V_{T-}$, it is equal to

$$V_{T-} = \sum_{t=1}^{T} \frac{D_t}{(1 + k)^t}. \tag{16.24}$$

The second part consists of finding the present value of all the forecasted dividends after $T$ and involves the application of the constant growth model. The application begins by imagining that the investor is not at time zero ($t = 0$) but is at time $T$ ($t = T$) and has not changed his or her forecast of dividends for the shares. This means that next period's dividend, $D_{T+1}$, and all those thereafter are expected to grow at the rate $g$. Thus, the investor would be viewing the stock as having a constant growth rate, and its value *at time T* ($V_T$) could be determined with the constant-growth model of equation (16.21):

$$V_T = D_{T+1} \left[ \frac{1}{k-g} \right].$$  (16.25)

One way to view $V_T$ is that it represents a lump sum that is just as desirable as the stream of dividends after $T$. That is, an investor would find a lump sum of cash equal to $V_T$, to be received at $T$, to be equally desirable to the stream of dividends $D_{T+1}$, $D_{T+2}$, $D_{T+3}$, and so on. Now, given that the investor is at time zero ($t = 0$), not at $T$, the present value at $t = 0$ of the lump sum $V_T$ must be determined. This is done simply by discounting it for $T$ periods at the rate $k$, resulting in the following formula for finding the present value at time zero for all dividends after $T$, denoted by $V_{T+}$:

$$V_{T+} = V_T \left[ \frac{1}{(1+k)^T} \right]$$

$$= \frac{D_{T+1}}{(k-g)(1+k)^T}.$$  (16.26)

Having found the present value of all dividends up to and including $T$ with equation (16.24) and the present value of all dividends after $T$ with equation (16.26), the value of a share can be determined by summing these two amounts:

$$V = V_{T-} + V_{T+}$$

$$= \sum_{t=1}^{T} \frac{D_t}{(1+k)^t} + \frac{D_{T+1}}{(k-g)(1+k)^T}.$$  (16.27)

Figure 16.1 illustrates the valuation procedure for the multiple growth DDM that is given in equation (16.27).

## An Example

As an example of how this DDM can be used, assume that during the past year the Magnesium Company paid dividends amounting to $.75 per share. Over the next year Magnesium is expected to pay dividends of $2 per share. Thus, $g_1 = (D_1 - D_0)/D_0 = ($2 - $.75)/$.75 = 167\%$. The year after that dividends are expected to amount to $3 per share, indicating that $g_2 = (D_2 - D_1)/D_1 = ($3 - $2)/$2 = 50\%$. At this time, the forecast is that dividends will grow by 10% per year into the indefinite future, indicating that $T = 2$ and $g = 10\%$. Consequently, $D_{T+1} = D_3 = $3(1+.10) = $3.30$.

Given a required rate of return on Magnesium shares of 15%, the value of $V_{T-}$ and $V_{T+}$ can be calculated, respectively, as follows:

$$V_{T-} = \frac{$2}{(1+.15)^1} + \frac{$3}{(1+.15)^2}$$

$$= $4.01$$

$$V_{T+} = \frac{$3.30}{(.15 - .10)(1+.15)^2}$$

$$= $49.91$$

Summing $V_{T-}$ and $V_{T+}$ results in a value for $V$ of $\$4.01 + \$49.91 = \$53.92$. With a current stock price of $55 per share, Magnesium appears to be fairly priced. That is, since $V$ and $P$ are nearly of equal size, Magnesium is not mispriced.

## ☐ 16.4.1 Internal Rate of Return

The zero-growth and constant-growth models had equations for $V$ that could be reformulated in order to solve for the internal rate of return on an investment in a share. Unfortunately, a convenient expression similar to equations (16.15a), (16.15b), (16.23a), and (16.23b) is not available for the multiple-growth model. This can be seen by noting that the expression for IRR is derived by substituting $P$ for $V$ and $k^*$ for $k$ in equation (16.27):

$$P = \sum_{t=1}^{T} \frac{D_t}{(1 + k^*)^t} + \frac{D_{T+1}}{(k^* - g)(1 + k^*)^T}. \qquad (16.28)$$

This equation cannot be rewritten with $k^*$ isolated on the left-hand side, meaning that a closed-form expression for IRR does not exist for the multiple growth model.

However, all is not lost. It is still possible to calculate the IRR for an investment in a share conforming to the multiple growth model by using an "educated" trial-and-error method. That is, after setting up equation (16.28), an estimate for $k^*$ can be tried. If the resulting value on the right-hand side is larger than $P$, then a larger $k^*$ can be tried. Conversely, if the resulting value is smaller than $P$, then a smaller $k^*$ can be tried. Continuing this search process, the investor could hone in on the value of $k^*$.[6]

Applying equation (16.28) to the Magnesium Company results in

$$\$55 = \frac{\$2}{(1 + k^*)^1} + \frac{\$3}{(1 + k^*)^2} + \frac{\$3.30}{(k^* - .10)(1 + k^*)^2}. \qquad (16.29)$$

Initially a rate of 14% may be used in attempting to solve this equation for $k^*$. Inserting 14% for $k^*$ in the right-hand side of equation (16.29) results in a value of $67.54. Earlier 15% was used in determining $V$ and resulted in a value of $53.92. This means that $k^*$ must have a value between 14% and 15%, since $55 is between $67.54 and $53.92. If 14.5% is tried next, the resulting value is $59.97, suggesting a higher rate should be tried. If 14.8% and 14.9% are subsequently tried, the respective resulting values are $56.18 and $55.03. Since $55.03 is the closest to $P$, the IRR associated with an investment in Magnesium is 14.9%. Given a required return of 15% and an IRR of approximately that amount, the stock of Magnesium appears to be fairly priced.

---

[6] It would be a relatively simple matter to program a computer to conduct the search for $k^*$ in equation (16.28).

## ☐ 16.4.2 Relationship to the Constant-Growth Model

The constant-growth model can be shown to be a special case of the multiple-growth model. In particular, if the time when constant growth is assumed to begin is set equal to zero, then

$$V_{T-} = \sum_{t=1}^{T} \frac{D_t}{(1+k)^t} = 0$$

and

$$V_{T+} = \frac{D_{T+1}}{(k-g)(1+k)^T} = \frac{D_1}{k-g}$$

since $T = 0$ and $(1+k)^0 = 1$. Given that the multiple-growth model states that $V = V_{T-} + V_{T+}$, it can be seen that setting $T = 0$ results in $V = D_1/(k-g)$, a formula tha is equivalent to the formula for the constant growth model.

## ☐ 16.4.3 Two-Phase and Three-Phase Models

Two dividend discount models that are sometimes used are the two-phase and the three-phase models.[7] The two-phase model assumes a constant growth rate $(g_1)$ exists only until some time $T$, when a different growth rate $(g_2)$ is assumed to begin and continue thereafter. The three-phase model assumes a constant growth rate $(g_1)$ exists only until some time $T_1$, when a second growth rate is assumed to begin and last until a later time $T_2$, when a third growth rate is assumed to begin and last thereafter. By letting $V_{T+}$ denote the present value of all dividends after the last growth rate has begun and $V_{T-}$ denote the present value of all the preceding dividends, it can be seen that these models are just special cases of the multiple growth models.

In applying the capitalization of income method of valuation to common shares, it might seem appropriate to assume that they will be sold at some point in the future. In this case, the expected cash flows would consist of the dividends up to that point as well as the expected selling price. Since dividends after the selling date would be ignored, the use of a dividend discount model may seem to be improper. However, as is shown next, this is not so.

---

## 16.5    VALUATION BASED ON A FINITE HOLDING PERIOD

The capitalization of income method of valuation involves discounting all dividends that are expected throughout the future. Since the simplified models of zero growth, constant growth, and multiple growth are based on this method, they too involve a future stream of dividends. Upon reflection, it may seem that such models are relevant only for an investor who plans to hold a stock forever, since such an investor would expect to receive this stream of future dividends.

---

[7] For a discussion of these models, see Russell J. Fuller and Chi-Cheng Hsia, "A Simplified Common Stock Valuation Model," *Financial Analysts Journal* 40, no. 5 (September/October 1984):49–56; and Eric H. Sorensen and David A. Williamson, "Some Evidence on the Value of Dividend Discount Models," *Financial Analysts Journal* 41, no. 6 (November/December 1985):60–69.

But what about an investor who plans to sell the stock in a year?[8] In such a situation, the cash flows that the investor expects to receive from purchasing a share of the stock are equal to the dividend expected one year from now (for ease of exposition, it is assumed that common shares pay dividends annually) and the expected selling price of the shares. Thus, it would seem appropriate to determine the intrinsic value of the shares to the investor by discounting these two cash flows at the required rate of return as follows:

$$V = \frac{D_1 + P_1}{(1 + k)}$$

$$= \frac{D_1}{1 + k} + \frac{P_1}{1 + k}$$

(16.30)

where $D_1$ and $P_1$ are the expected dividend and selling price at $t = 1$, respectively.

In order to use equation (16.30), the expected price of the stock at $t = 1$ must be estimated. The simplest approach assumes that the selling price will be based on the dividends that are expected to be paid after the selling date, $t = 1$. Thus, the expected selling price at $t = 1$ is

$$P_1 = \frac{D_2}{(1 + k)^1} + \frac{D_3}{(1 + k)^2} + \frac{D_4}{(1 + k)^3} + \cdots$$

$$= \sum_{t=2}^{\infty} \frac{D_t}{(1 + k)_{t-1}}.$$

(16.31)

Substituting equation (16.31) for $P_1$ in the right-hand side of equation (16.30) results in

$$V = \frac{D_1}{1 + k} + \left[ \frac{D_2}{(1 + k)^1} + \frac{D_3}{(1 + k)^2} + \frac{D_4}{(1 + k)^3} + \cdots \right] \left[ \frac{1}{1 + k} \right]$$

$$= \frac{D_1}{(1 + k)^1} + \frac{D_2}{(1 + k)^2} + \frac{D_3}{(1 + k)^3} + \frac{D_4}{(1 + k)^4} + \cdots$$

$$= \sum_{t=1}^{\infty} \frac{D_t}{(1 + k)^t}$$

which is exactly the same as equation (16.7). Thus, valuing a share of common stock by discounting its dividends up to some point in the future and its expected selling price at that time is equivalent to valuing a share by discounting all future dividends. Simply stated, the two are equivalent because the expected selling price is itself based on dividends to be paid after the selling date. Thus, equation (16.7) — as well as the zero-growth, constant-growth, and multiple-growth models that are based on it — is appropriate for determining the intrinsic value of a share of common stock regardless of the length of the investor's planned holding period.

## An Example

As an example, reconsider the common shares of the Copper Company. Over the past year it was noted that Copper paid dividends of $1.80 per share, with the forecast that the dividends would grow by 5% per year forever. This means that dividends over

---

[8] The analysis is similar if it is assumed that the investor plans to sell the stock after some other length of time, such as six months or two years.

the next two years ($D_1$ and $D_2$) are forecast to be $\$1.80(1 + .05) = \$1.89$ and $\$1.89(1 + .05) = \$1.985$, respectively. If the investor plans to sell the shares after one year, the selling price can be estimated by noting that at $t = 1$, the forecast of dividends for the forthcoming year would be $D_2$, or $\$1.985$. Thus, the anticipated selling price at $t = 1$, denoted by $P_1$, would be equal to $\$1.985/(.11 - .05) = \$33.08$. Accordingly, the intrinsic value of Copper to such an investor would be equal to the present value of the expected cash flows, which are $D_1 = \$1.89$ and $P_1 = \$33.08$. Using equation (16.30) and assuming a required rate of 11%, this value is equal to $(\$1.89 + \$33.08)/(1 + .11) = \$31.50$. Note that this is the same amount that was calculated earlier when all the dividends from now to infinity were discounted using the constant growth model: $V = D_1/(k - g) = \$1.89/(.11 - .05) = \$31.50$.

---

16.6    ## MODELS BASED ON PRICE-EARNINGS RATIOS

Despite the inherent sensibility of dividend discount models, many security analysts use a much simpler procedure to value common shares. First, a stock's earnings per share over the forthcoming year ($E_1$) will be estimated and then the analyst (or someone else) will estimate a "normal" *price-earnings ratio* for the stock. The product of these two numbers gives the estimated future price ($P_1$). Together with estimated dividends to be paid during the period ($D_1$) and current price ($P$), the estimated return on the stock over the period can be determined:

$$\text{Expected return} = \frac{(P_1 - P) + D_1}{P}. \tag{16.32}$$

Some security analysts expand this procedure, estimating earnings per share and price-earnings ratios for optimistic, most likely, and pessimistic scenarios to produce a rudimentary probability distribution of a security's return. Other analysts determine whether a share is underpriced or overpriced by comparing its actual price-earnings ratio with its normal price-earnings ratio, as is shown next.[9]

In order to make this comparison, equation (16.7) must be rearranged and some new variables must be introduced. To begin, it should be noted that earnings per share ($E_t$) are related to dividends per share ($D_t$) by the firm's *payout ratio* ($p_t$):

$$D_t = p_t E_t. \tag{16.33}$$

Note that if an analyst has forecast earnings per share and payout ratios, then he or she has implicitly forecast dividends.

Equation (16.33) can be used to restate the various DDMs where the focus is on estimating what the share's price-earnings ratio should be instead of on estimating its intrinsic value. In order to do so, $p_t E_t$ is substituted for $D_t$ in the right-hand side of equation (16.7), resulting in a general formula for determining a stock's intrinsic value that involves discounting earnings:

---

[9] Alternatively, some analysts focus on the *earnings-price ratio*, which is the reciprocal of the price-earnings ratio. Accordingly, the formulas for a share's normal earnings-price ratio can be found by simply taking the reciprocal of the forthcoming formulas for determining its normal price-earnings ratio.

$$V = \frac{D_1}{(1+k)^1} + \frac{D_2}{(1+k)^2} + \frac{D_3}{(1+k)^3} + \cdots$$

$$= \frac{p_1 E_1}{(1+k)^1} + \frac{p_2 E_2}{(1+k)^2} + \frac{p_3 E_3}{(1+k)^3} + \cdots \tag{16.34}$$

$$= \sum_{t=1}^{\infty} \frac{p_t E_t}{(1+k)^t}.$$

Earlier, it was noted that dividends in adjacent time periods could be viewed as being "linked" to each other by a dividend growth rate, $g_t$. Similarly, earnings per share in any year $t$ can be linked to earnings per share in the previous year $t-1$ by a growth rate in earnings per share, $g_{et}$:

$$E_t = E_{t-1}(1 + g_{et}). \tag{16.35}$$

This implies that

$$E_1 = E_0(1 + g_{e1})$$
$$E_2 = E_1(1 + g_{e2}) = E_0(1 + g_{e1})(1 + g_{e2})$$
$$E_3 = E_2(1 + g_{e3}) = E_0(1 + g_{e1})(1 + g_{e2})(1 + g_{e3})$$

and so on, where $E_0$ is the actual level of earnings per share over the past year, $E_1$ is the expected level of earnings per share over the forthcoming year, $E_2$ is the expected level of earnings per share for the year after $E_1$, and $E_3$ is the expected level of earnings per share for the year after $E_2$.

These equations relating expected future earnings per share to $E_0$ can be substituted into equation (16.34), resulting in

$$V = \frac{p_1[E_0(1 + g_{e1})]}{(1+k)^1} + \frac{p_2[E_0(1 + g_{e1})(1 + g_{e2})]}{(1+k)^2} \tag{16.36}$$
$$+ \frac{p_3[E_0(1 + g_{e1})(1 + g_{e2})(1 + g_{e3})]}{(1+k)^3} + \cdots$$

Since $V$ is the intrinsic value of a share of stock, it represents what the share should be selling for if it were fairly priced. It follows that $V/E_0$ represents what the price-earnings ratio should be for the share if it were fairly priced; it is sometimes referred to as the share's *normal* price-earnings ratio. Dividing both sides of equation (16.36) by $E_0$ and simplifying results in the formula for determining the normal price-earnings ratio:

$$\frac{V}{E_o} = \frac{p_1[(1 + g_{e1})]}{(1+k)^1} + \frac{p_2[(1 + g_{e1})(1 + g_{e2})]}{(1+k)^2} \tag{16.37}$$
$$+ \frac{p_3[(1 + g_{e1})(1 + g_{e2})(1 + g_{e3})]}{(1+k)^3} + \cdots$$

This shows that, other things being equal, a share's normal price-earnings ratio will be *higher*:

The *greater* the expected payout ratios ($p_1, p_2, p_3, \ldots$),
The *greater* the expected growth rates in earnings per share ($g_{e1}, g_{e2}, g_{e3}, \ldots$), and

The *smaller* the required rate of return ($k$).

The qualifying phrase "other things being equal" should not be overlooked. For example, a firm cannot increase the value of its shares by simply planning on having greater payouts. This will increase $p_1$, $p_2$, $p_3$, ...but will decrease the expected growth rates in earnings per share $g_{e1}$, $g_{e2}$, $g_{e3}$, .... Assuming the firm's investment policy is not altered, the effects of the reduced growth in earnings per share will just offset the effects of the increased payouts, leaving value per share unchanged.

Earlier, it was noted that a share was viewed as being underpriced if $V > P$ and overpriced if $V < P$. Since dividing both sides of an inequality by a positive constant will not change the direction of the inequality, such a division can be done here to the two inequalities involving $V$ and $P$, where the positive constant is $E_0$. The result is that a share can be viewed as being underpriced if $V/E_0 > P/E_0$ and overpriced if $V/E_0 < P/E_0$. Thus, a share will be underpriced if its normal price-earnings ratio is greater than its actual price-earnings ratio and overpriced if its normal price-earnings ratio is less than its actual price-earnings ratio.

Unfortunately, equation (16.37) is intractable, meaning it cannot be used to estimate the normal price-earnings ratio for any share. However, simplifying assumptions can be made that result in tractable formulas for estimating normal price-earnings ratios. These assumptions, along with the formulas, parallel those made previously regarding dividends and, with one exception, are discussed next.[10]

## ☐ 16.6.1 The Zero-Growth Model

The zero-growth model assumed that dividends per share remained at a fixed dollar amount forever. This is equivalent to assuming that earnings per share remain at a fixed dollar amount forever, with the firm maintaining a 100% payout ratio. It is assumed to be 100% because if a lesser amount were assumed to be paid out, it would mean that the firm was retaining part of its earnings. These retained earnings would be put to some use and would thus be expected to increase future earnings per share. However, future earnings per share have been assumed to be constant, so it would be inconsistent to assume constant earnings and a payout ratio of less than 100%.

Accordingly, the zero-growth model assumes $p_t = 1$ for all time periods and $E_0 = E_1 = E_2 = E_3$ and so on. This means that $D_0 = E_0 = D_1 = E_1 = D_2 = E_2$ and so on, allowing valuation equation (16.13) to be restated as

$$V = \frac{E_0}{k}.$$
(16.38)

Dividing equation (16.38) by $E_0$ results in the formula for the normal price-earnings ratio for a stock having zero growth:

$$\frac{V}{E_0} = \frac{1}{k}.$$
(16.39)

---

[10] The exception is the multiple-growth case, which is discussed in Appendix B.

## An Example

Earlier, it was assumed that the Zinc Company was a zero-growth firm paying dividends of $8 per share, selling for $65 a share, and having a required rate of return of 10%. Since Zinc is a zero growth company, this means that it has a 100% payout ratio, which, in turn, means that $E_0 = \$8$. At this point, equation (16.38) can be used to note that a normal price-earnings ratio for Zinc is $1/.10 = 10$. Since Zinc has an actual price-earnings ratio of $\$65/\$8 = 8.1$ and since $V/E_0 = 10 > P/E_0 = 8.1$, it can be seen that Zinc shares are underpriced.

## ☐ 16.6.2 The Constant Growth Model

Earlier, it was noted that dividends in adjacent time periods could be viewed as being connected to each other by a dividend growth rate, $g_t$. Similarly, it was noted that earnings per share can be connected by an earnings growth rate, $g_{et}$. The constant growth model assumes that the growth rate in dividends per share will be the same throughout the future. An equivalent assumption is that earnings per share will grow at a constant rate $(g_e)$ throughout the future, with the payout ratio remaining at a constant level $(p)$. This means that

$$E_1 = E_0(1 + g_e)$$
$$E_2 = E_1(1 + g_e) = E_0(1 + g_e)(1 + g_e)$$
$$E_3 = E_2(1 + g_e) = E_0(1 + g_e)(1 + g_e)(1 + g_e)$$

and so on. In general, earnings in year $t$ can be connected to $E_0$ as follows:

$$E_t = E_0(1 + g_e)^t. \tag{16.40}$$

Substituting equation (16.40) into the numerator of equation (16.34) and recognizing that $p_t = p$ results in the following:

$$V = \sum_{t=1}^{\infty} \frac{pE_0(1 + g_e)^t}{(1 + k)^t}$$

$$= pE_0 \left[ \sum_{t=1}^{\infty} \frac{(1 + g_e)^t}{(1 + k)^t} \right]. \tag{16.41}$$

The same mathematical property of infinite series given in equation (16.19) can be applied to equation (16.41), resulting in

$$V = pE_0 \left[ \frac{1 + g_e}{k - g_e} \right]. \tag{16.42}$$

It can be noted that the earnings-based constant growth model has a numerator identical to the numerator of the dividend-based constant growth model, since $pE_0 = D_0$. Furthermore, the denominators of the two models are identical if the growth rates in earnings and dividends are the same (that is, if $g_e = g$). Examination of the assumptions of the models reveals that these growth rates must be equal. This can be seen by recalling that constant earnings growth means

$$E_t = E_{t-1}(1 + g_e).$$

When both sides of this equation are multiplied by the constant payout ratio, the result is

$$pE_t = pE_{t-1}(1 + g_e).$$

Since $pE_t = D_t$ and $pE_{T-1} = D_{T-1}$, this equation reduces to:

$$D_t = D_{t-1}(1 + g_e)$$

which indicates that dividends in any period $t - 1$ will grow by the earnings growth rate, $g_e$. Since the dividend-based constant growth model assumed dividends in any period $t - 1$ would grow by the dividend growth rate $g$, it can be seen that the two growth rates must be equal for the two models to be equivalent.

Equation (16.42) can be restated by dividing each side by $E_0$, resulting in the following formula for determining the normal price-earnings ratio for a stock with constant growth:

$$\frac{V}{E_0} = p\left[\frac{1 + g_e}{k - g_e}\right]. \qquad (16.43)$$

## An Example

Earlier, it was assumed that the Copper Company had paid dividends of $1.80 per share over the past year, with a forecast that dividends would grow by 5% per year forever. Furthermore, it was assumed that the required rate of return on Copper was 11%, and the current stock price was $40 per share. Now, assuming $E_0$ was $2.70, it can be seen that the payout ratio was equal to $1.80/$2.70 = $66^2/_3\%$. This means that the normal price-earnings ratio for Copper, according to equation (16.43), is equal to .6667[(1 + .05)/(.11 − .05)] = 11.67. Since this is less than Copper's actual price-earnings ratio of $40/$2.70 = 14.81, it follows that the shares of Copper Company are overpriced.

## 16.7 SOURCES OF EARNINGS GROWTH

So far, no explanation has been given as to why earnings or dividends can be expected to grow in the future. One way of providing such an explanation utilizes the constant-growth model. Assuming that no new capital is obtained externally and no shares are repurchased (meaning the number of shares outstanding does not increase or decrease), the portion of earnings not paid to shareholders as dividends will be used to pay for the firm's new investments. Given that $p_t$ denotes the payout ratio in year $t$, then $(1 - p_t)$ is equal to the portion of earnings not paid out, known as the *retention ratio*. Furthermore, the firm's new investments, stated on a per-share basis and denoted by $I_t$, will be

$$I_t = (1 - p_t)E_t. \qquad (16.44)$$

If these new investments have an average return on equity of $r_t$ in period $t$ and every year thereafter, they will add $r_t I_t$ to earnings per share in year $t + 1$ and every year thereafter. If all previous investments also produce perpetual earnings at a constant rate of return, next year's earnings will equal this year's earnings plus the new earnings resulting from this year's new investments:

$$E_{t+1} = E_t + r_t I_t$$
$$= E_t + r_t(1 - p_t) E_t$$
$$= E_t[1 + r_t(1 - p_t)]. \tag{16.45}$$

Since the growth rate in earnings per share, as defined earlier, is

$$E_{t+1} = E_t(1 + g_{et+1}) \tag{16.46}$$

a comparison of equations (16.45) and (16.46) indicates that

$$g_{et+1} = r_t(1 - p_t). \tag{16.47}$$

If the growth rate in earnings per share ($g_{et+1}$) is to be constant over time, then the average return on equity for new investments ($r_t$) and payout ratio ($p_t$) must also be constant over time. In this situation, equation (16.47) can be simplified by removing the time subscripts:

$$g_e = r(1 - p). \tag{16.48a}$$

Since the growth rate in dividends per share ($g$) is equal to the growth rate in earnings per share ($g_e$), this equation can be rewritten as

$$g = r(1 - p). \tag{16.48b}$$

From this equation it can be seen that the growth rate $g$ depends on (1) the proportion of earnings that is retained ($1 - p$) and (2) the average return on equity for the earnings that are retained ($r$).

The constant-growth valuation formula given in equation (16.20) can be modified by replacing $g$ with the expression on the right-hand side of equation (16.48b), resulting in

$$V = D_0 \left( \frac{1 + g}{k - g} \right)$$
$$= D_0 \left[ \frac{1 + r(1 - p)}{k - r(1 - p)} \right] \tag{16.49}$$

In terms of price-earnings ratios, the formula in equation (16.43) becomes:

$$\frac{V}{E_0} = p \left( \frac{1 + g_e}{k - g_e} \right)$$
$$= p \left[ \frac{1 + r(1 - p)}{k - r(1 - p)} \right] \tag{16.50}$$

Under these assumptions, a share's price-earnings ratio should be greater, the greater its average return on equity for new investments, other things being equal.

```
-1                      0                        1                        2
+---------------------- + ---------------------- + ---------------------- + ----->∞
     E₀ = $2.70                      $2.700                     $2.700        ...
                          $.90 × .15 =   .135                    .135         ...
                                 E₁ = $2.835      $.945 × .15 =   .142        ...
                                                        E₂ = $2.977           ...

     I₀ = $ .90                 I₁ = $ .945              I₂ = $ .992          ...
     D₀ =  1.80                 D₁ =  1.890              D₂ =  1.985          ...
     E₀ = $2.70                 E₁ = $2.835              E₂ = $2.977          ...
```

**FIGURE 16-2**

Growth in earnings for Copper Company.

## ☐ 16.7.1  An Example

Continuing with the Copper Company, recall that $E_0$ = $2.70 and $p$ = 66 $\frac{2}{3}$%. This means that 33 $\frac{1}{3}$% of earnings per share over the past year were retained and reinvested, an amount equal to .3333 × $2.70 = $.90. The earnings per share in the forthcoming year ($E_1$) are expected to be $2.70(1 + .05) = $2.835, since the growth rate ($g$) for Copper is 5%. The source of the increase in earnings per share of $2.835 − $2.70 = $.135 is the $.90 per share that was reinvested at $t$ = 0. The average return on equity for new investments ($r$) is 15%, since $.135/$.90 = 15%. That is, the reinvested earnings of $.90 per share can be viewed as having generated an annual increase in earnings per share of $.135. This increase will occur not only at $t$ = 1 but also at $t$ = 2, $t$ = 3, and so on. Equivalently, a $.90 investment at $t$ = 0 will generate a perpetual annual cash inflow of $.135 beginning at $t$ = 1.

Expected dividends at $t$ = 1 can be calculated by multiplying the expected payout ratio ($p$) of 66$\frac{2}{3}$% times the expected earnings per share ($E_1$) of $2.835, or .6667 × $2.835 = $1.89. It can also be calculated by multiplying 1 plus the growth rate ($g$) of 5% times the past amount of dividends per share ($D_0$) of $1.80, or 1.05 × $1.80 = $1.89. It can be seen that the growth rate in dividends per share of 5% is equal to the product of the retention rate (33 $\frac{1}{3}$%) and the average return on equity for new investments (15%), an amount equal to .3333 × .15 = 5%.

Two years from now ($t$ = 2), earnings per share are anticipated to be $2.835 × (1 + .05) = $2.977, a further increase of $2.977 − $2.835 = $.142 that is due to the retention and reinvestment of .3333 × $2.835 = $.945 per share at $t$ = 1. This expected increase in earnings per share of $.142 is the result of earning 15% on the reinvested $.945, since .15 × $.945 = $.142. In summary, the expected earnings per share at $t$ = 2 have three components. The first is the earnings attributable to the assets held at $t$ = 0, an amount equal to $2.70. The second is the earnings attributable to the reinvestment of $.90 at $t$ = 0, earning $.135. The third is the earnings attributable to the reinvestment of $.945 at $t$ = 1, earning $.142. These three components, when summed, equal $E_2$ = $2.70 + $.135 + $.142 = $2.977. Dividends at $t$ = 2 are expected to be 5% larger than at $t$ = 1, or 1.05 × $1.89 = $1.985 per share. This amount corresponds to the amount calculated by multiplying the payout ratio times the expected earnings per share at $t$ = 2, or .6667 × $2.977 = $1.985. Figure 16.2 summarizes the example.

# A COMMONLY USED APPROACH

There are many ways that DDMs have been used in the investment community. One commonly used approach is based on the multiple-growth model and a view that companies typically evolve through three stages during their lifetime.[11] These stages are as follows.

### Growth Stage

The growth stage is characterized by rapidly expanding sales, high profit margins, and abnormally high growth in earnings per share. Because the expected profitability of new investment opportunities is high, the payout ratio is generally low. The unusually high earnings enjoyed in this stage attracts competitors, leading to a gradual decline in the growth rate.

### Transition Stage

In the later years of a company's life, increased product saturation begins to reduce its growth rate, and its profit margin comes under pressure. Since there are fewer new investment opportunities, the company begins to pay out a larger percentage of earnings.

### Maturity Stage (or Steady-State Stage)

Eventually, the company reaches a position where its new investment opportunities offer, on average, slightly attractive returns on equity. At that time, its earnings growth rate, payout ratio, and average return on equity stabilize for the remaining life of the company.[12]

Figure 16.3 portrays the stages. Note that the vertical scale is logarithmic, so that a straight line represents a constant rate of growth.

In applying the multiple-growth DDM, a security analyst must estimate a number of variables for each stock being evaluated. One method involves estimating values for the following variables:

1. Expected earnings and dividends for the next five years.
2. The growth rate of earnings and the payout ratio for the start of the transition stage, which is assumed to be in year six.
3. The duration of the transition stage — that is, the number of years until the company reaches the maturity stage.
4. Growth patterns for earnings per share and the payout ratio during the transition stage.
5. The combination of an earnings growth rate and payout ratio that produces the desired average return on equity for new investments during the maturity stage.[13]

---

[11] This approach is based on the work of Nicholas Molodovsky in "Common Stock Valuation," *Financial Analysts Journal* 20, no. 1 (March/April 1965):104–23. The specific version presented here is based on one that has been used by Merrill Lynch and is described in Carmine J. Grigoli, "Demystifying Dividend Discount Models," Merrill Lynch Quantitative Research, April 1982.

[12] Adapted from Grigoli, "Demystifying Dividend Discount Models."

[13] Adapted from Grigoli, "Demystifying Dividend Discount Models."

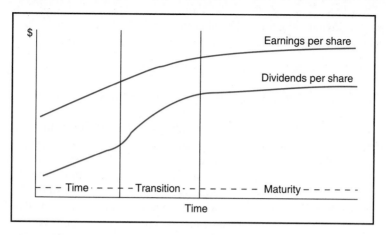

**FIGURE 16-3**

The three stages of the multiple-growth model.

*SOURCE:* Adapted from Carmine J. Grigoli, "Demystifying Dividend Discount Models," Merrill Lynch Quantitative Research, April 1982.

The following example shows just how the estimated values for these variables can be used to determine the intrinsic value of a share of stock.

## ☐ 16.8.1 An Example

Consider using this approach in analyzing the ABC Company on April 30, 1988. Over the past year, ABC has had earnings per share of $1.67 and dividends per share of $.40. After carefully studying ABC, the security analyst has made the following forecasts of earnings per share and dividends per share for the next five years;

| | | | | |
|---|---|---|---|---|
| $E_1 = \$2.67$ | $E_2 = \$4.00$ | $E_3 = \$6.00$ | $E_4 = \$8.00$ | $E_5 = \$10.00$ |
| $D_1 = \$.60$ | $D_2 = \$1.60$ | $D_3 = \$2.40$ | $D_4 = \$3.20$ | $D_5 = \$5.00$ |

These forecasts imply the following payout ratios and earnings-per-share growth rates:

| | | | | |
|---|---|---|---|---|
| $p_1 = 22\%$ | $p_2 = 40\%$ | $p_3 = 40\%$ | $p_4 = 40\%$ | $p_5 = 50\%$ |
| $g_{e1} = 60\%$ | $g_{e2} = 50\%$ | $g_{e3} = 50\%$ | $g_{e4} = 33\%$ | $g_{e5} = 25\%$ |

Furthermore, the analyst believes that ABC will enter the transition stage at the end of the fifth year (that is, the sixth year will be the first year of the transition stage) and that the transition stage will last three years. Earnings per share and the payout ratio for year 6 are forecast to be $E_6 = \$11.90$ and $p_6 = 55\%$ (thus, $g_{e6} = (\$11.90 - \$10.00)/\$10.00 = 19\%$ and $D_6 = .55 \times \$11.90 = \$6.55$).

The maturity stage is forecast to have an earnings per share growth rate of 4% and a payout ratio of 70%. It was shown in equation (16.48b) that with the constant growth model, $g = r(1 - p)$, where $r$ is the average return on equity for new investments and

$p$ is the payout ratio. Since the maturity stage has constant growth, this equation can be reformulated and used to determine $r$:

$$r = \frac{g}{1-p}. \tag{16.51}$$

Thus, $r$ for ABC has an implied value of $4\%/(100\% - 70\%) = 13.33\%$ which is assumed to be satisfactory.

At this point, there is only one missing piece of information that is needed to determine the value of ABC—the earnings per share growth rates and the payout ratios for the transition stage. Taking earnings per share first, it has been forecast that $g_{e6} = 19\%$ and that $g_{e9} = 4\%$. One method of determining how 19% will "decay" to 4% is to note that there are three years between the sixth and ninth years and that $19\% - 4\% = 15\%$. A linear decay rate can be determined by noting that $15\%/(3\text{ years}) = 5\%$ per year. This rate of 5% is deducted from 19% to get $g_{e7}$, resulting in $19\% - 5\% = 14\%$. Then, it is deducted from 14% to get $g_{e8}$, resulting in $14\% - 5\% = 9\%$. Lastly, as a check, it can be noted that $9\% - 5\% = 4\%$, the value that was forecast for $g_{e9}$.

A similar procedure can be used to determine how the payout ratio of 55% in year 6 will grow to 70% in year 9. The linear growth rate is $(70\% - 55\%)/(3\text{ years}) = 15\%/(3\text{ years}) = 5\%$ per year, indicating $p_7 = 55\% + 5\% = 60\%$ and $p_8 = 60\% + 5\% = 65\%$. Again, a check indicates that $65\% + 5\% = 70\%$, the value that was forecast for $p_9$.

With these forecasts of earnings per share growth rates and payout ratios in hand, forecasts of dividends per share can now be made:

$$
\begin{aligned}
D_7 &= p_7 E_7 \\
&= p_7 E_6 (1 + g_{e7}) \\
&= .60 \times \$11.90 \times (1 + .14) \\
&= .60 \times \$13.57 \\
&= \$8.14 \\
D_8 &= p_8 E_8 \\
&= p_8 E_6 (1 + g_{e7})(1 + g_{e8}) \\
&= .65 \times \$11.90 \times (1 + .14) \times (1 + .09) \\
&= .65 \times \$14.79 \\
&= \$9.61 \\
D_9 &= p_9 E_9 \\
&= p_9 E_6 (1 + g_{e7})(1 + g_{e8})(1 + g_{e9}) \\
&= .70 \times \$11.90 \times (1 + .14) \times (1 + .09) \times (1 + .04) \\
&= .70 \times \$15.38 \\
&= \$10.76.
\end{aligned}
$$

Given a required rate of return on ABC of 12.3%, it can be seen that all the necessary inputs for the multiple growth model have been determined. To begin, it can be seen that $T = 8$, indicating that $V_{T-}$ involves determining the present value of $D_1$ through $D_8$:

$$V_{T-} = \frac{\$.60}{(1+.123)^1} + \frac{\$1.60}{(1+.123)^2} + \frac{\$2.40}{(1+.123)^3} + \frac{\$3.20}{(1+.123)^4}$$
$$+ \frac{\$5.00}{(1+.123)^5} + \frac{\$6.55}{(1+.123)^6} + \frac{\$8.14}{(1+.123)^7} + \frac{\$9.61}{(1+.123)^8}$$
$$= \$18.99.$$

Then, $V_{T+}$ can be determined using $D_9$:

$$V_{T+} = \frac{\$10.76}{(.123 - .04)(1+.123)^8}$$
$$= \$51.25.$$

Combining $V_{T-}$ and $V_{T+}$ results in the intrinsic value of ABC:

$$V = V_{T-} + V_{T+}$$
$$= \$18.99 + \$51.25$$
$$= \$70.24.$$

Given a current market price for ABC of $50, it can be seen that its stock is underpriced by $70.24 - $50 = $20.24 per share. Equivalently, it can be noted that the actual price-earnings ratio for ABC is $50/$1.67 = 29.9 but that a normal price-earnings ratio would be higher, equal to $70.24/$1.67 = 42.1, again indicating that ABC is underpriced.

## ☐ 16.8.2 Implied Returns

As shown with the previous example, once the analyst has made certain forecasts, it is relatively straightforward to determine a company's expected dividends for each year up through the first year of the maturity stage. Then, the present value of these predicted dividends can be calculated for a given required rate of return. However, many investment firms use a computerized trial-and-error search procedure to determine the discount rate that equates the present value of the share's expected dividends with its current price. Sometimes this long-run internal rate of return is referred to as the security's *implied return*. In the case of ABC, its implied return at the end of April 1988 is 14.8%.

## ☐ 16.8.3 The Security Market Line

After implied returns have been estimated for a number of stocks, the associated beta for each stock can be estimated. Then, for all the stocks analyzed, this information can be plotted on a graph that has implied returns on the vertical axis and betas on the horizontal axis.

At this point, there are two methods for estimating the security market line (SML).[14] One method involves determining a line of best fit for this graph by using a statistical

---

[14] There are numerous methods besides those described here. Some of them are based on more complicated versions of the CAPM, whereas others are based on APT (discussed in Chapter 9).

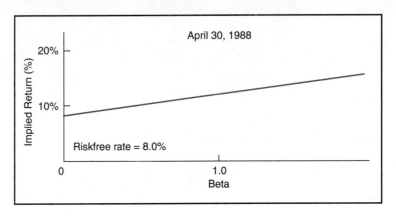

**FIGURE 16-4**
A security market line estimated from implied returns.

procedure known as simple regression. That is, the values of an intercept term and a slope term are determined from the data, thereby indicating the location of the straight line that best describes the relationship between implied returns and betas.

Figure 16.4 provides an example of the estimated SML at the end of April, 1988. In this case, the SML has been determined to have an intercept of 8% and a slope of 4%, indicating that, in general, securities with higher betas are expected to have higher implied returns in the forthcoming period. Depending on the sizes of the implied returns, such lines can have steeper or flatter slopes or even negative slopes.

The second method of estimating the SML involves calculating the implied return for a portfolio of common stocks. This is done by taking a value-weighted average of the implied returns of the stocks in the portfolio, with the resulting return being an estimate of the implied return on the market portfolio. Given this return and a beta of 1, the market portfolio can be plotted on a graph having implied returns on the vertical axis and betas on the horizontal axis. Next, the risk-free rate, having a beta of 0, can be plotted on the same graph. Finally, the SML is determined by simply connecting these two points with a straight line.

Either of these SMLs can be used to determine the required return on a stock. However, they will probably result in different numbers, since the two lines will probably have different intercepts and slopes. For example, note that the first method does not force the SML to go through the risk-free rate, whereas the second method does. Which one is more accurate can ultimately be determined only by the performance obtained when decisions are based on one method versus that achievable with the other.

## ☐ 16.8.4 Required Returns and Alphas

Once a security's beta has been estimated, its required return can be determined from the estimated SML. For example, the equation for the SML on April 30, 1988 (shown in Figure 16.4), is:

$$k_i = 8 + 4\beta_i.$$

Thus, if ABC has an estimated beta of 1.1 at the end of April 1988, then it would have a required return equal to $8 + (4 \times 1.1) = 12.4\%$.

Once the required return on a stock has been determined, the difference between its implied return (from the dividend discount model) and this required return can be calculated. This difference can then be viewed as an estimate of the stock's *alpha* and represents "...the degree to which a stock is mispriced. Positive alphas indicate undervalued securities and negative alphas indicate overvalued securities."[15] In the case of ABC, its implied and required returns at the end of April 1988 were 14.8% and 12.4%, respectively. Thus, its estimated alpha is $14.8\% - 12.4\% = 2.4\%$. Since this is a positive number, ABC can be viewed as being underpriced.

## ☐ 16.8.5  The Implied Return on the Stock Market

Another product of this analysis is that the implied return for the portfolio of stocks can be compared with expected returns on bonds. Specifically, the difference between the stock and bond returns can be used as an input for recommendations concerning asset allocation between stocks and bonds. That is, it can be used to form recommendations regarding what percentage of an investor's money should go into stocks and what percentage should go into bonds. Typically, the greater the implied return on stocks relative to bonds, the larger the percentage of the investor's money that should be placed in common stocks.

## 16.9  DIVIDEND DISCOUNT MODELS AND EXPECTED RETURNS

The procedures described here are similar to those employed by a number of brokerage firms and portfolio managers.[16] A security's implied return, obtained from a dividend discount model, is often treated as an expected return, which in turn can be divided into two components — the security's required return and alpha. However, the expected return on a stock over a given holding period may differ from its DDM-based implied rate, $k^*$. A simple set of examples will indicate why this difference can exist.

Assume that a security analyst predicts that a stock will pay a dividend of $1.10 per share per year forever. On the other hand, the consensus opinion of "the market" (most other investors) is that the dividend will equal $1.00 per year forever. This suggests that the analyst's prediction is a deviant, or nonconsensus, prediction.

Assume that both the analyst and other investors agree that the required rate of return for a stock of this type is 10%. Using the formula for the zero-growth model, the value of a share is $D_1/.10 = 10 D_1$, meaning that a share should sell for ten times its expected dividend. Since other investors expect to receive $1.00 per year, the stock has a current price ($P$) of $10 per share. The analyst feels the stock has a value of $1.10/.10 = $11$ and thus feels it is underpriced by $11 - $10 = $1$ per share.

---

[15] Carmine J. Grigoli, "Common Stock Valuation," Merrill Lynch Quantitative Analysis, May/June 1984. A subsequent procedure divides the estimated alpha by an estimate of the security's unique risk (that is, nonmarket or unsystematic risk) to obtain a *standardized alpha*. Then, based on the magnitude of the standardized alpha, the security is classified into one of ten *standardized alpha deciles*.

[16] An example of a similar procedure that has been used by Wells Fargo Investment Advisors is described by George Foster in *Financial Statement Analysis* (Englewood Cliffs, N.J.: Prentice Hall, 1986):428–30.

In this situation, the implied return according to the analyst is $1.10/$10 = 11\%$. If the analyst buys a share now with a plan to sell it a year later, the rate of return the analyst might expect to earn depends on what assumptions are made regarding (1) the *accuracy of the prediction* and (2) the *rate of convergence of investors' predictions*.

**TABLE 16.1**

Predictive Accuracy and Convergence of Predictions.

| | A | B | C | D |
|---|---|---|---|---|
| *Predictive Accuracy* | *100%* | *100%* | *50%* | *50%* |
| *Expected Amount of Convergence* | *0%* | *100%* | *0%* | *100%* |
| Actual dividend $D_1$ | $ 1.10 | $ 1.10 | $ 1.05 | $ 1.05 |
| Dividend predictions $D_2$ | | | | |
|   Consensus of other investors | 1.00 | 1.10 | 1.00 | 1.05 |
|   Analyst | 1.10 | 1.10 | 1.05 | 1.05 |
| Share price $P_1$ [a] | 10.00 | 11.00 | 10.00 | 10.50 |
| Performance: | | | | |
|   Dividend yield $D_1/P$ | 11% | 11% | 10.5% | 10.5% |
|   Capital gain $(P_1 - P)/P$ | 0 | 10 | 0.0 | 5.0 |
|   Total actual return | 11% | 21% | 10.5% | 15.5% |
|   Less required return | 10 | 10 | 10.0 | 10.0 |
|   Actual alpha | 1% | 11% | 0.5% | 5.5% |

[a] $P_1$ is equal to the consensus dividend prediction at $t = 1$ divided by the required return of 10%. The example assumes the current share price $P$ is $10, and dividends are forecast by the consensus at $t = 0$ to remain constant at $1.00 per share, whereas the analyst forecasts the dividends at $t = 0$ to remain constant at $1.10 per share.

The cases shown in Columns A and B of Table 16.1 assume that the analyst's prediction is correct—at the end of the year the stock does in fact pay the predicted dividend of $1.10 per share. However, in column A, it is assumed that the other investors will regard the higher dividend as a fluke and steadfastly refuse to alter their projections of subsequent dividends from their initial estimate of $1.00. As a result, the security's price at $t = 1$ can be expected to remain at $10( $1.00 / .10)$. In this case, the analyst's total return is expected to be 11%( $1.10/$10)$, which is attributed entirely to dividends, since no capital gains are expected.

The 11% expected return can also be viewed as consisting of the required return of 10% plus an alpha of 1% that is equal to the portion of the dividend unanticipated by the other investors, $.10/$10. Accordingly, if it is assumed that the analyst's prediction is perfect but there will be no convergence of predictions, then expected return would be set at the implied rate, 11%, and the alpha would be set at 1%.

Column B shows a very different situation. Here, it is assumed that the other investors will see the error of their ways and completely revise their predictions. At the end of the year, it is expected that they too will predict future dividends of $1.10 per year thereafter; thus, the stock is expected to be selling for $11 per share ($1.10/.10)$ at $t = 1$. Under these conditions, the analyst can expect to achieve a total return of 21% by selling the shares at the end of the year for $11, obtaining 11% ( $1.10/$10)$ in dividend yield and 10% ( $1/$10)$ in capital gain.

The 10% expected capital gains result directly from the expected repricing of the security due to the complete convergence of predictions. In this case, the fruits of the analyst's superior prediction are expected to be obtained all in one year. Instead of 1% extra per year forever, as in column A, the analyst expects to obtain 1% ($.10/$10) in extra dividend yield plus 10% ($1/$10) in capital gains this year. By continuing to hold the shares in subsequent years, the analyst would expect to earn only the required return of 10% over those years. Accordingly, if it is assumed that the analyst's prediction is perfect and there is complete convergence of predictions, the expected return would be set at 21% and the alpha would be set at 11%.

Unlike the cases in columns A and B, the cases in columns C and D do not assume that the analyst's prediction is perfect. Specifically, it is assumed that actual dividends exceed the consensus forecast of $1.00 by only $.05 instead of by $.10, the amount predicted by the analyst.

In the case shown in Column C, it is assumed that the other investors will regard the first year's dividend of $1.05 as a fluke and refuse to alter their predictions for subsequent years. As a result, the stock price at $t = 1$ will remain at $10, limiting the total actual return to 10.5%. Due to an overly optimistic deviant prediction, the alpha (0.5%) is less than the amount in column A (1%). Accordingly, if it is assumed that the analyst's deviant predictions are halfway accurate but there is no convergence of predictions, the expected return and the alpha would be set at 10.5% and .5%, respectively.

The case in Column D assumes that at year-end, both the analyst and other investors regard the actual dividend of $1.05 as permanent and revise their predictions for subsequent dividends accordingly. Here the two effects operate in different directions. Due to the overly optimistic prediction, the dividend yield will be 10.5%, which is less than the predicted 11%. But since the prediction was in the right direction, capital gains will be realized, as other investors revise their predictions in consideration of the actual results. In this case, the capital gains will more than offset the less-than-expected yield, providing a total return of 15.5% and an alpha of 5.5% that are substantially above the required return and expected alpha of 10% and 1%, respectively. Accordingly, if it is assumed that the analyst's predictions are halfway accurate and there will be complete convergence of predictions, the expected return and alpha would be set at 15.5% and 5.5%, respectively.

In other cases of this sort, the expected return could be more or less than the implied rate. Other things being equal, the expected return will be larger, the greater the assumed degree of predictive accuracy and the faster the assumed rate of convergence of predictions.[17]

Many investors use the implied rate (that is, the internal rate of return, $k^*$) as a surrogate for a relatively short-term (for example, one-year) expected return, as in column A. This could reflect an assumption of perfect predictive accuracy and no convergence of predictions. More likely, it reflects beliefs that (1) deviant predictions are less than perfectly accurate and (2) other investors will revise their predictions in

---

[17] In a perfectly efficient market (in the semistrong-form sense), the expected degree of predictive accuracy for any analyst using public information would be zero. That is, these analysts would sometimes be right and sometimes be wrong, so that on balance their predictions would be of no value and the average actual alpha would be zero. In such a situation, the expected return for any security would be set at its required return and the expected alpha would be set at zero.

the corresponding direction by a large-enough amount to provide capital gains that will offset any shortfall from the predicted dividend yield.

An alternative approach does not simply use outputs from a dividend discount model as is but adjusts them, based on relationships between previous predictions and actual outcomes. Parts (a) and (b) of Figure 16.5 provide examples.

Each point in Figure 16.5(a) plots a predicted return on the stock market (on the horizontal axis) and the subsequent actual return for that period (on the vertical axis). The line of best fit (determined by simple regression) through the points indicates the general relationship between prediction and outcome. If the current prediction is 14%, history suggests that an estimate of 15% would be superior.

Each point in Figure 16.5(b) plots a predicted alpha value for a security (on the horizontal axis) and the subsequent abnormal return for that period (on the vertical axis). Such a diagram can be made for all the securities about which a particular analyst makes predictions, or for all the securities about which the investment firm makes predictions. Again, a line of best fit can be drawn through the points. In this case, if the current prediction of a security's alpha is +1%, this relationship suggests that an adjusted estimate of +2.5% would be superior.

An important byproduct of this type of analysis is the measure of correlation between predicted and actual outcomes, indicating the nearness of the points to the line. This can serve as a measure of predictive accuracy. If the correlation is too small to be significantly different from zero in a statistical sense, the value of the predictions is subject to considerable question.[18]

## 16.10    SUMMARY

One approach for conducting a search for mispriced securities involves the use of fundamental analysis. In its most basic form, fundamental analysis involves the use of a dividend discount model, where the security analyst forecasts the future stream of dividends on a given stock. After discounting these dividends to get their present value, the analyst is in a position to determine if the stock is mispriced. Specifically, if the current market price of the stock is less than the present value of its forecasted dividends, then the stock is underpriced; if it is more, then the stock is overpriced.

Alternatively, the analyst could determine the discount rate that makes the present value of the forecasted dividends equal to the current market price of the stock. If this rate is more than what is required for stocks of similar risk, then the stock is underpriced; if it is less, then the stock is overpriced.

If these discount rates are taken to be the expected returns on the stocks that have been analyzed, then an equation for the security market line can be estimated. In this situation, the estimated SML is an example of a cross-sectional valuation equation.

---

[18] The correlation coefficient is sometimes referred to as an *information coefficient* (IC). It has been argued that a value of .15 is indicative of good performance with regard to stock forecasting and that several different forecasters have recorded ICs of this magnitude (a value of zero would be expected in a perfectly efficient market). See Keith P. Ambachtsheer, "Profit Potential in an 'Almost Efficient' Market," *Journal of Portfolio Management* 1, no. 1 (Fall 1974):84–87 and "Where Are the Customers' Alphas?" *Journal of Portfolio Management* 4, no. 1 (Fall 1977):52–56; Keith P. Ambachtsheer and James L. Farrell, Jr., "Can Active Management Add Value?" *Financial Analysts Journal* 35, no. 6 (November-December 1979):39–47; and S. D. Hodges and R. A. Brealey, "Portfolio Selection in a Dynamic and Uncertain World," *Financial Analysts Journal* 29, no. 2 (March-April 1973):50–65.

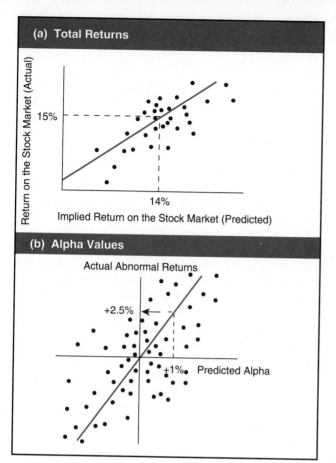

**FIGURE 16-5**
Adjusting predictions.

The use of deviations of individual securities' expected returns from such an equation to identify mispriced securities assumes that deviant predictions have some accuracy. Unfortunately, deviations often persist, indicating that they may be due more to errors in dividend projections or to ignoring relevant factors in the valuation equation than to temporary mispricing. Perhaps more vexing is the fact that both the SML and the betas are likely to change over time. Consequently, the analyst must attempt to shoot at a moving target. That is, the analyst must estimate when and by how much the SML and individual betas will shift, a nearly impossible task.

This does not imply that "bottom-up" analysis of the type described here is useless. Quite the contrary. It provides estimates of the manner in which the market currently values securities, and this is essential information. Even if the deviations of the expected returns of individual securities from the forecasted SML reflect only predictive errors and are thus of no significance, the SML itself could be a good estimate of the current relationship between expected returns and betas and could justify the effort. And if the deviations indicate likely mispricing rather than errors in security analysis, the procedure could be even more valuable.

# THE GRAHAM-REA MODEL

In 1934, a book that was to become the cornerstone of fundamental analysis was published by Benjamin Graham and David L. Dodd. This book, entitled *Security Analysis*, argued that the *future earnings power* of the firm was the most important determinant of it's share's value.[19] However, in 1974 Graham himself repudiated the book and the principles contained in it.[20] Instead of following his old approach, Graham, along with James Rea, developed a new approach to identifying underpriced common stocks.[21] The reason for his change in attitude was his belief that the stock market was becoming more and more efficient and that only smaller and smaller pockets of inefficiencies were in existence. Since Graham and Rea believed these inefficiencies tended to be present in the stocks of certain identifiable firms, they developed a set of criteria to spot such stocks.

The Graham-Rea approach can be applied mechanically, since it involves examining the current financial statements of the firm under consideration and relating certain items from these statements to the firm's current stock price and the current yield on triple-A bonds. Ten questions that can be answered with a simple yes or no are involved. Table 16.2 lists them, indicating that the first five questions deal with "rewards" and second five questions deal with "risks." The idea behind these questions is to identify stocks that have the highest reward-to-risk ratio. In order for a stock to be recommended for purchase by Graham and Rea, it need not provide a yes answer to all of the questions.

The simplest way to use the questions is to first remove all stocks that do not provide a yes answer to question 6. Then, of the remaining stocks, remove those that do not provide a yes answer to either question 1, question 3, or question 5. The stocks that are left are candidates for purchase.

---

[19] Graham and Dodd also argued that each dollar of dividends is worth four times as much as each dollar of retained earnings. Subsequent examination of market data indicates that argument has no support. See J. Ronald Hoffmeister and Edward A. Dyl, "Dividends and Share Value: Graham and Dodd Revisited," *Financial Analysts Journal* 41, no. 3 (May/June 1985):77-78; and Lewis D. Johnson, "Dividends and Share Value: Graham and Dodd Revisited, Again," *Financial Analysts Journal* 41, no. 5 (September/October 1985):79–80. For the most recent edition of the book, see Sidney Cottle, Roger F. Murray, and Frank E. Block, *Graham and Dodd's Security Analysis*, 5th ed. (New York: McGraw-Hill, Inc., 1988). For a brief discussion of their approach to investing, see Roger F. Murray, "Graham and Dodd: A Durable Discipline," *Financial Analysts Journal* 40, no. 5 (September/October 1984):18–23.

[20] See "A Conversation with Benjamin Graham," *Financial Analysts Journal* 32, no. 5 (September/October 1976):20–23.

[21] For a description of this approach, see Paul Blustein, "Ben Graham's Last Will and Testament," *Forbes* 1 August 1977, 43–45; and James B. Rea, "Remembering Benjamin Graham—Teacher and Friend," *Journal of Portfolio Management* 3, no. 4 (Summer 1977):66–72.

**TABLE 16.2**

Graham-Rea Stock Selection Questions.

A. Rewards:

    1. Is the price-earnings ratio less than one-half the reciprocal of the triple-A bond yield? (For example, if the current triple-A rate is 12%, then the reciprocal is $8\frac{1}{3}$, and half of that is $4\frac{1}{6}$. Thus, for a stock to provide a yes answer to this question, its price-earnings ratio must be less than $4\frac{1}{6}$.)

    2. Is the price-earnings ratio less than 40% of the highest average price-earnings ratio of the last five years? (Here, the average price-earnings for a stock for a given year is the average stock price for the year divided by the earnings per share for that year.)

    3. Is the dividend yield at least two-thirds the triple-A bond yield?

    4. Is the stock price below two-thirds of the tangible book value per share? (Here tangible book value per share is simply total assets less total debt, with the difference divided by the number of shares outstanding.)

    5. Is the stock price below $\frac{2}{3}$ of the net current asset value per share? (Here net current asset value per share is current assets less total debt, with the difference divided by the number of shares outstanding.)

B. Risks:

    6. Is the debt-to-equity ratio less than one? (Here the debt-to-equity ratio is simple total debt divided by total equity as shown on the balance sheet.)

    7. Is the current ratio greater than two? (Here the current ratio is current assets divided by current liabilities.)

    8. Is total debt less than twice the net current asset value? (Here net current asset value is current assets less total debt.)

    9. Has the earnings per share growth rate of the last 10 years averaged at least 7% per year? (If the earnings per share over the last year is denoted by $E_0$ and the earnings per share over the year ending ten years ago is denoted by $E_{10}$, then the growth rate is the value of $g$ that solves the equation $E_0 = E_{10}(1 + g)^{10}$. To provide a yes answer to this question, $g$ must be least 7%.)

    10. Over the time period examined in question 9, have eight or more of the annual growth rates in earnings per share been equal to $-5\%$ or more? (Here the ten annual growth rates in earnings per share would be calculated and then examined to see that no more than two of them were less than $-5\%$.)

SOURCE: Adapted from Paul Blustein, "Ben Graham's Last Will and Testament," *Forbes* 1 August 1977, 43–45, and James B. Rea, "Remembering Benjamin Graham—Teacher and Friend," *Journal of Portfolio Management* 3, no. 4 (Summer 1977):66-72.

In determining when to sell, the Graham-Rea approach says that the investor should sell as soon as the stock has risen 50% or two years have passed since the stock was purchased, whichever occurs first. However, if neither of these two sell signals has occurred and the stock either stops paying dividends or no longer generates the appropriate yes answers to the questions, then it should be sold immediately.

How well has the Graham-Rea approach to investing worked? In a recent study of this approach that focused on New York Stock Exchange and American Stock Exchange securities, three observations were particularly interesting.[22] First, since the approach was publicized it was found that the number of stocks that provided the appropriate yes answers declined dramatically (for example, by 1980 yes answers to questions 1 and 6 occurred for only five securities). Second, the historical record suggests that positive

---

[22] Henry R. Oppenheimer, "A Test of Ben Graham's Stock Selection Criteria," *Financial Analysts Journal* 40, no. 5 (September/October 1984):68–74.

abnormal returns would have been earned had this approach been used subsequent to its publication. Third, since many of the firms recommended for purchase were small firms, it is possible that all that this approach does is capture the size effect (that is, the small-firm effect that was discussed in the appendix to Chapter 15). However, the study found that even after adjusting for the size effect, the approach would still have earned positive abnormal returns since its publication.[23]

In closing, it should be noted that a number of professional portfolio managers currently follow the Graham-Rea approach to investing in the United States. Examples include the Rea-Graham Fund, LMH Fund, Sequoia Fund, and Pacific Partners Fund.

# THE MULTIPLE-GROWTH MODEL AND THE PRICE-EARNINGS MODEL

Earlier, it was noted that the most general dividend discount model was the multiple-growth model, where dividends were allowed to grow at varying rates until some point in time denoted $T$, after which they were assumed to grow at a constant rate. In this situation, the present value of all the dividends was found by adding the present value of all dividends up to and including $T$, denoted by $V_{T-}$, and the present value of all dividends after $T$, denoted by $V_{T+}$. Specifically, equation (16.27) stated that

$$V = V_{T-} + V_{T+}$$

$$= \sum_{t=1}^{T} \frac{D_t}{(1+k)^t} + \frac{D_{T+1}}{(k-g)(1+k)^T}.$$

In general, earnings per share in any period $t$ can be expressed as being equal to $E_0$ times the product of all the growth rates from the time zero to time $t$:

$$E_t = E_0(1+g_{e1})(1+g_{e2})\cdots(1+g_{et}). \qquad (16.52)$$

Since the dividends per share in any period $t$ are equal to the payout ratio times the earnings per share, it follows from equation (16.52) that

$$D_t = p_t E_t$$
$$= p_t E_0(1+g_{e1})(1+g_{e2})\cdots(1+g_{et}). \qquad (16.53)$$

This allows the following expression for $V_{T-}$:

$$V_{T-} = \frac{p_1 E_0(1+g_{e1})}{(1+k)^1} + \frac{p_2 E_0(1+g_{e1})(1+g_{e2})}{(1+k)^2} + \cdots$$
$$+ \frac{p_T E_0(1+g_{e1})(1+g_{e2})\cdots(1+g_{eT})}{(1+k)^T}. \qquad (16.54)$$

---

[23] A subsequent study focused on only one of the ten Graham-Rea questions, number 5 in Table 16.2. It found that portfolios consisting of securities that had yes answers to this question would have earned above-market returns. See Henry R. Oppenheimer, "Ben Graham's Net Current Asset Values: A Performance Update," *Financial Analysts Journal* 42, no. 6 (November/December 1986):40–47.

Similarly, the expression for $V_{T+}$ is

$$V_{T+} = \frac{pE_0(1 + g_{e1})(1 + g_{e2}) \cdots (1 + g_{eT})(1 + g)}{(k - g)(1 + k)^T}. \quad (16.55)$$

Adding $V_{T-}$ and $V_{T+}$ together and then dividing by $E_0$ gives the following formula for determining a share's normal price-earnings ratio with the multiple-growth model:

$$\frac{V}{E_0} = \frac{p_1(1 + g_{e1})}{(1 + k)^1} + \frac{p_2(1 + g_{e1})(1 + g_{e2})}{(1 + k)^2} + \cdots$$

$$+ \frac{p_T(1 + g_{e1})(1 + g_{e2}) \cdots (1 + g_{eT})}{(1 + k)^T}. \quad (16.56)$$

$$+ \frac{p(1 + g_{e1})(1 + g_{e2}) \cdots (1 + g_{eT})(1 + g)}{(k - g)(1 + k)^T}.$$

As an example, consider the Magnesium Company again. Its share price is currently $55, and over the past year, earnings per share and dividends per share were $3 and $.75, respectively. For the next two years, forecasted earnings and dividends, along with the earnings growth rates and payout ratios, are as follows:

$D_1 = \$2.00$  $E_1 = \$5.00$  $g_{e1} = 67\%$  $p_1 = 40\%$
$D_2 = \$3.00$  $E_2 = \$6.00$  $g_{e2} = 20\%$  $p_2 = 50\%$.

Constant growth in dividends and earnings of 10% is forecast to begin at $T = 2$, meaning that $D_3 = \$3.30$, $E_3 = \$6.60$, $g = 10\%$, and $p = 50\%$.

Given a required return is 15%, equation (16.56) can be used to calculate the normal price-earnings ratio for Magnesium as follows:

$$\frac{V}{E_0} = \frac{.40(1 + .67)}{(1 + .15)^1} + \frac{.50(1 + .67)(1 + .20)}{(1 + .15)^2} + \frac{.50(1 + .67)(1 + .20)(1 + .10)}{(.15 - .10)(1 + .15)^2}$$

$$= .58 + .76 + 16.63$$

$$= 17.97.$$

Since the actual price-earnings ratio of $55/\$3 = 18.33$ is close to the normal price-earnings ratio of 17.97, the stock of the Magnesium Company can be viewed as fairly valued.[24]

_____

[24] Earlier, it was noted that the intrinsic value of Magnesium was $53.92. Since $E_0$ for Magnesium was $3, it can be verified that the normal price-earnings ratio is 17.97 by noting that $\$53.92/\$3 = 17.97$.

1. Surrey Products currently pays a dividend of $3.00 per share on its common stock.
   a. If Surrey Products plans to increase its dividend at a rate of 5% per year indefinitely, what will be the dividend per share in 10 years?
   b. If Surrey Products' dividend per share is expected to be $4.20 per share at the end of five years, at what annual rate is the dividend expected to grow?

2. Jackson Information Services currently pays a dividend of $5.00 per share on its common stock. The dividend is expected to grow at 4% per year forever. Stocks with similar risk currently are priced to provide a 12% expected return. What is the intrinsic value of Jackson stock?

3. Select a stock whose name begins with the first letter of your last name. From the *Value Line Investment Survey: Canadian Edition* find the average annual compounded growth rate in its share's dividend over the last five years. Assume that this growth rate will continue indefinitely. From the same source find the beta of the stock. Assuming a riskfree rate of return of 7% and a market expected return of 15%, calculate the SML and the required return on the stock. Finally, using the dividend growth rate and required return, calculate the intrinsic value of the stock. (*Note*: If the data for your stock is incompatible with the constant growth DDM, select another stock.) Compare this intrinsic value to the latest closing price for the stock. Is the stock underpriced or overpriced? What potential problems are involved with this approach to making investment decisions?

4. The constant growth model is an overly simplistic means of valuing most corporations' stocks. However, a number of market analysts believe it is a useful means of estimating a fair value for the stock market as a whole. Why might the constant growth DDM be a more reasonable valuation tool for the market in aggregate as opposed to individual stocks?

5. Stratford Air Cleaners Ltd. currently pays a dividend on its stock of $6 per share. Next year the dividend is expected to remain constant and then increase to $7 the year after. From that point on, the dividend is expected to grow at $3 per year indefinitely. Stocks with similar risk are currently priced to provide a 10% expected return. What is the intrinsic value of Stratford's stock?

6. Chief Medical Inc. is a little known producer of heart pacemakers. The earnings and dividend growth prospects of the company are disputed by analysts. Albert Bender is forecasting 5% growth in dividends indefinitely. However, his brother John is predicting a 20% growth in dividends, but only for the next three years, after which the growth rate is expected to decline to 4% for the indefinite future. Chief dividends per share are currently $3.00. Stocks with similar risk are currently priced to provide a 14% expected return.
   a. What is the intrinsic value of Chief's shares according to Albert?
   b. What is the intrinsic value of Chief's shares according to John?
   c. Assume that Chief's stock now sells for $39 3/4 per share. If the stock is fairly priced at the present time, what is the implied perpetual dividend growth rate? What is the implied P/E (price-earnings ratio) on next year's earnings, based on this perpetual dividend growth assumption and assuming a 25% payout ratio?

7. Lansing Technologies, a publicly held venture capital investment firm, is currently paying a dividend of $2 per share on earnings of $4 per share. Its stock is selling

for $200 per share. Stocks of similar risk are priced to return 15%. What kind of return on equity could explain investors' willingness to pay a price equal to 50 times earnings on this stock?

8. Olympia Corp. is expected to pay out 40% of its earnings and to earn an average of 15% per year on its incremental reinvested earnings forever. Stocks with similar risk are currently priced to provide a 12% expected return. By what percentage can Olympia's earnings be expected to grow each year? What is an appropriate price-earnings multiple for the stock? What portion of the return on Olympia stock is expected to come from capital gains? From dividend yield?

9. A three-stage DDM has become a very popular common stock valuation model. It is used by a number of institutional investors and brokerage firms. What advantages does it offer relative to a simple constant growth DDM? Despite its increased sophistication compared to the constant growth DDM, what disadvantages does it still retain?

10. Fay Thomas, a financial analyst, once remarked: "Even if your dividend estimates and discount rate assumption are correct, dividend discount models identify stocks that will produce positive alphas only if other investors eventually come to agree with the DDM's valuation conclusions." Is this statement correct? Why or why not?

11. Some people assert that a "true" growth company is one whose dividends grow at a rate greater than its required rate of return. Why is the constant growth DDM incapable of valuing such a "true" growth stock?

12. What explanations can you offer for the fact that the Security Market Line shown in Figure 16.4 is so flat?

## SUGGESTED READINGS

M.J. Gordon, "The Savings, Investment and Valuation of a Corporation," *Review of Economics and Statistics* 44 (February 1962):37–51. This article first systematized the development of the DDM.

Carmine J. Grigoli, "Demystifying Dividend Discount Models," *Merrill Lynch Quantitative Research* (April 1982) and

James L. Farrell, Jr., *A Guide to Portfolio Management*, both discuss the implementation of the DDM in some detail. The latter also provides a discussion of the application of Information Coefficients to security selection.

B. Graham, D.L. Dodd and S. Cottle, *Security Analysis: Principles and Technique* (New York, NY: McGraw-Hill, 1962) is the most recent version of this classic work.

# Chapter 17

---

# EARNINGS

---

Chapter 16 discussed how the intrinsic value of a share of common stock could be determined by discounting expected dividends per share at a rate of return that was appropriate for a security of similar risk. Alternatively, the implied return on a share of common stock could be determined by finding the discount rate that makes the present value of all the expected dividends equal to the current market price of the stock. In either case, a forecast of dividends per share is necessary. Since dividends per share are equal to earnings per share times a payout ratio, dividends can be forecast by forecasting earnings per share and payout ratios.

Currently, there are numerous methods used by security analysts for forecasting either earnings or dividends. This chapter presents a discussion of some of the important features of dividends and earnings of which the analyst should be aware in making such forecasts. The chapter begins with a discussion of the relationship between earnings, dividends, and investment.

## 17.1 SHARE VALUATION BASED ON EARNINGS

A continual controversy in the investment community concerns the relevance of dividends versus earnings as the underlying source of value of a share of common stock. Clearly, earnings are important to shareholders because earnings provide the cash flow necessary for paying dividends. However, dividends are also important because dividends are what shareholders actually receive from the firm and are the focus of the dividend discount models discussed in Chapter 16. Indeed, it would seem that if management increased the proportion of earnings per share paid out as dividends, they could make their shareholders wealthier, suggesting that the *dividend decision* (deciding on the amount of dividends to pay) is a very important one.

Ultimately, this controversy was resolved in 1961 when Merton Miller and Franco Modigliani published a seminal paper showing that the underlying source of value of a share of common stock was earnings, not dividends.[1] An implication is that the dividend decision is relatively unimportant to the shareholders, since it will not affect the value of their investment in the firm.

---

[1] Merton H. Miller and Franco Modigliani, "Dividend Policy, Growth, and the Valuation of Shares," *Journal of Business* 34, no. 4 (October 1961):411–33.

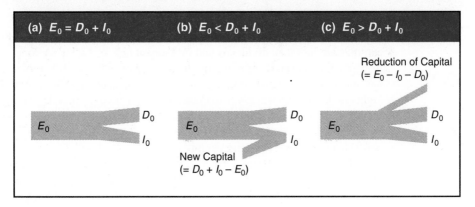

**FIGURE 17-1**
Earnings, dividends, and investment.

In the course of a year, a firm generates revenues and incurs costs. With cash accounting, the difference between revenues and costs is called cash flow. With accrual accounting, used by almost all firms, both revenues and costs are likely to include estimates made by accountants of the values of noncash items. Items such as depreciation charges are deducted from cash flow to obtain earnings. Moreover, each year some amount is invested in the business. Of the total (gross) investment, a portion is equal in value to the estimated depreciation of various real assets (like machines and buildings); the rest is new (net) investment.

The dollar amount of new investment each year should be based on the investment opportunities available to the firm and should be unaffected by the dollar amount of dividends that has been paid out. In particular, any investment opportunity whose net present value (NPV) is positive should be undertaken. This means that the future prospects of the firm can be described by a stream of expected earnings ($E_1$, $E_2$, $E_3$, ...) and the expected net investment required to produce such earnings ($I_1$, $I_2$, $I_3$, ...). Taking these two streams as given, it can be shown that management can set the total dollar amount of current dividends ($D_0$) at any level without making the current shareholders either better or worse off.[2] This is done next, with the focus on earnings and how they can be used to pay for new investments and dividends.

## ☐ 17.1.1 Earnings, Dividends, and Investment

Figure 17.1(a) shows one way that the firm can use total earnings for the current year ($E_0$). In this situation, new investment ($I_0$) is financed out of earnings, and the firm uses the remainder of the earnings to pay dividends ($D_0$) to its shareholders. For example, if the Plum Company has just earned $5000 and has new investments it would like to make that cost $3000, then Plum could pay for these investments out of earnings and declare a dividend of $2000.

---

[2] Here, the quantities of earnings ($E_t$), new investment ($I_t$), and dividends ($D_t$) are measured for the firm on an aggregate basis, not a per-share basis. Note that dividends cannot be set at an arbitrary high value relative to earnings (for example, earnings of $10 million and dividends of $100 million), since the firm would then be unable to get the necessary funds to pay the dividends.

Although earnings are exactly equal to dividends and investment ($E_0 = D_0 + I_0$), as in Figure 17.1(a), this need not be the case. In the situation shown in Figure 17.1(b), earnings are less than dividends and investment ($E_0 < D_0 + I_0$). Since the amount of investment has been determined by the number of positive NPV projects that the firm has, this inequality occurs because the firm has decided to pay its current shareholders a higher dividend than was given in Figure 17.1(a). However, in order for higher dividends to be paid, additional funds must be obtained from outside the firm. This is accomplished by a new sale of common stock (it is assumed that the flotation costs associated with a new sale of common stock are negligible).

The funds are obtained through a new sale of common stock instead of through a new sale of debt because of a desire to avoid the confounding effects of a change in the firm's debt-equity ratio. That is, if debt financing is to be allowed, then two things would be changing at the same time — the amount of the dividend and the debt-equity ratio for the firm. As a result, if shareholders appear to be made better off by a change in the amount of the dividend, their betterment may actually be due to a change in the debt-equity ratio. By prohibiting debt financing, the debt-equity ratio will remain constant and only the amount of the dividend will be allowed to change. Thus, if shareholders appear to be better off, it has to be due to the change in the amount of the dividend, since everything else (specifically, the amount of investment and the debt-equity ratio) has remained fixed.

Note that if investment is financed out of earnings, as in Figure 17.1(a), then it has been financed with equity, obtained internally. In Figure 17.1(b), investment has also been financed with equity, but here the equity has been obtained externally. As a result, the debt-equity ratio for the firm is the same in both situations.

In the case of Plum, instead of paying dividends amounting to $2000, the firm could decide to pay dividends amounting to $3000. Since investment is equal to $3000, Plum will have a cash outflow of $3000 + $3000 = $6000 with earnings amounting to only $5000. This means that Plum will have to sell $6000 − $5000 = $1000 of new common stock.

In Figure 17.1(c), the situation is reversed from 17.1(b), since earnings are now greater than dividends and investment ($E_0 > D_0 + I_0$). Given that the amount of investment has been determined by the number of positive NPV projects that the firm has, this inequality occurs because the firm has decided to pay its shareholders a lower dividend than was given in Figure 17.1(a). In paying this smaller dividend, the firm will be left with excess cash. It is assumed that the firm will use this cash to repurchase some of its outstanding shares in the marketplace (and that the transactions costs associated with such repurchases are negligible).

This last assumption is made due to the desire to keep the situation comparable to the two earlier ones. Allowing the firm to keep the excess cash would be tantamount to letting the firm invest the cash, an investment decision that was not made in the two earlier cases and, therefore, does not have a positive NPV (remember that $I_0$ consists of all positive NPV projects). Allowing the firm to keep the excess cash would also mean that the firm has made a decision to lower its debt-equity ratio because retention of the excess cash would increase the amount of equity for the firm, thereby decreasing the amount of debt outstanding relative to the amount of equity.

Continuing with the Plum Company, dividends could be set at $1000 instead of $2000 or $3000. In this case, the firm would have a cash outflow for dividends and investment amounting to $1000 + $3000 = $4000$. With earnings of $5000, this means that there will be $5000 − $4000 = $1000$ of cash left for the firm to use to repurchase its own shares.

Thus, the firm has a decision to make regarding the size of its current dividends. The amount of current earnings $E_0$ and the amount of new investment $I_0$ have been determined. What is left to be decided is the amount of dividends, $D_0$. They can be set equal to earnings less investment (as in Figure 17.1(a)), greater than this amount (as in Figure 17.1(b)), or less than this amount (as in Figure 17.1(c)). The question that remains to be answered is, Will one of these three levels of dividends make the current shareholders better off than the other two? That is, which level of dividends — $1000, $2000, or $3000 — will make the current shareholders better off?

The simplest way to answer this question is to consider a shareholder who presently holds 1% of the common stock of the firm and is determined to maintain this percentage ownership in the future.[3] If the firm follows a dividend policy as shown in Figure 17.1(a), the shareholder's current dividends will equal $.01 D_0$, or, equivalently, $.01(E_0 − I_0)$. Similarly, the shareholder's future dividends will equal $.01 D_t$, or $.01(E_t − I_t)$.

If the firm follows a dividend policy as shown in Figure 17.1(b), however, the shareholder must invest additional funds in the firm's common stock in order to avoid a diminished proportional ownership position in the firm. This investment is necessary because in this situation the firm must raise funds by selling additional shares in order to pay for the larger cash dividends. Since $E_0 < D_0 + I_0$, the total amount of funds that the firm needs to raise is the amount $F_0$, such that

$$E_0 + F_0 = D_0 + I_0 \qquad (17.1)$$

or

$$F_0 = D_0 + I_0 − E_0. \qquad (17.2)$$

The amount of the additional investment that the shareholder needs to make in order to maintain a 1% position in the firm is $.01 F_0$, which from equation (17.2) is equal to $.01(D_0 + I_0 − E_0)$. Since the shareholder receives 1% of the dividends, the net amount the shareholder receives at time zero is equal to $.01 D_0 − .01 F_0$, or

$$.01 D_0 − .01(D_0 + I_0 − E_0) = .01 E_0 − .01 I_0. \qquad (17.3)$$

Interestingly, the net amount the shareholder receives, $.01 E_0 − .01 I_0$, is the same as in the first situation. This is because the amount of the extra cash dividend received is exactly offset by the amount the shareholder needs to spend to maintain his or her position of ownership in the firm.

If the firm follows a dividend policy as shown in Figure 17.1(c), then the firm will be repurchasing shares. Accordingly, the shareholder must sell some shares back to the firm in order to avoid having an increased ownership position in the firm. Since $E_0 > D_0 + I_0$, the total amount of funds that the firm will spend on repurchasing its own shares is the amount $R_0$, such that

$$E_0 = D_0 + I_0 + R_0 \qquad (17.4)$$

---

[3] The use of such a shareholder is for ease of exposition; the same answer would be obtained if other types of shareholders (such as those who are not interested in maintaining a proportional ownership position in the firm in the future) are considered.

or

$$R_0 = E_0 - D_0 - I_0.$$ (17.5)

The amount of stock that the shareholder needs to sell back to the firm to maintain a 1% position in the firm is $.01 R_0$, which from equation (17.5) is equal to $.01( E_0 - D_0 - I_0)$. Since the shareholder receives 1% of the dividends, the total amount the shareholder receives at time zero is equal to $.01 D_0 + .01 R_0$, or

$$.01 D_0 + .01( E_0 - D_0 - I_0) = .01 E_0 - .01 I_0.$$ (17.6)

Again, this amount, $.01 E_0 - .01 I_0$, is the same as in the first situation. That is, in the third situation, the smaller amount of the cash dividend received by the shareholder is exactly made up for by the amount of cash received from the repurchase of shares by the firm.

Thus, no matter what the firm's dividend policy, a shareholder choosing to maintain a constant proportional ownership will be able to spend the same amount of money on consumption at time zero. This amount will be equal to the proportion times the quantity $E_0 - I_0$. Furthermore, this will also be true in the future. That is, in any year $t$ the shareholder will be able to spend on consumption an amount that is equal to the proportion times the quantity $E_t - I_t$.

## ☐ 17.1.2 Earnings Determine Market Value

In determining the value of 1% of the current shares outstanding, remember that the firm is about to declare and pay current dividends. Regardless of the magnitude of these dividends, the shareholder will be able to spend on consumption an amount equal to only $.01( E_0 - I_0)$. Furthermore, the shareholder will be able to spend on consumption an amount equal to $.01( E_t - I_t)$ in any future year $t$. Discounting these expected amounts by a (constant) rate $k$ reveals that the value of 1% of the current shares outstanding will be

$$.01 V = \frac{.01( E_0 - I_0)}{(1 + k)^0} + \frac{.01( E_1 - I_1)}{(1 + k)^1} + \frac{.01( E_2 - I_2)}{(1 + k)^2} + \cdots.$$

Multiplying both sides of this equation by 100 results in the following expression for the total market value of all shares outstanding:

$$V = \frac{(E_0 - I_0)}{(1 + k)^0} + \frac{(E_1 - I_1)}{(1 + k)^1} + \frac{(E_2 - I_2)}{(1 + k)^2} + \cdots.$$ (17.7)

Equation (17.7) shows that the aggregate market value of equity is equal to the present value of expected earnings net of required investment. Note how the size of the dividends does not enter into the formula. This indicates that the market value of the stock is independent of the dividend decision made by the firm. Instead, the market value of the firm is related to the earnings prospects of the firm, along with the required amounts of new investment needed to produce those earnings.[4]

---

[4] It has been argued that if the tax rate on dividends is greater than the tax rate on capital gains, then shareholders will earn more on an after-tax basis if the firm has a relatively low payout ratio. An additional benefit to shareholders if the firm has a low payout ratio is that capital gains taxes are paid only when the stock is sold and can therefore be deferred. Thus, it appears that shareholders are better off if the firm has a relatively
*(continued)*

There is nothing inconsistent between the dividend discount models presented in Chapter 16 and the irrelevance of the dividend decision. The dividend discount models indicated that the value of one share of common stock was equal to the present value of all the dividends expected in the future. The dividend irrelevance argument suggests that if the firm decides to increase its current dividend, then new shares will need to be sold. This, in turn, suggests that future dividends will be smaller, since the aggregate amount of dividends will have to be divided among an increased number of shares outstanding. Ultimately, the current shareholders will be neither better nor worse off, since the increased current dividend will be exactly offset by the decreased future dividends. Conversely, if the firm decides to decrease its current dividend, then shares will be repurchased and future dividends will be increased due to the fewer shares outstanding. Ultimately, the decreased current dividend will be exactly offset by the increased future dividends, again leaving current shareholders neither better nor worse off.

All this can be illustrated with the earlier example of the Plum Company. Since Plum currently has reported earnings of $5000 and investments totaling $3000, if dividends amounting to $2000 were paid, then the shareholder owning 1% of the firm would receive cash amounting to $.01 \times \$2000 = \$200$.

Alternatively, if dividends amounting to $3000 were paid, then Plum would have to raise $1000 from the sale of new common stock. The shareholder would receive $.01 \times \$3000 = \$300$ in dividends but would have to pay $.01 \times \$1000 = \$100$ to purchase 1% of the new stock, thereby maintaining his or her 1% position of ownership. Consequently, the net cash flow to the shareholder would be $\$300 - \$100 = \$200$, the same amount as in the previous situation.

Lastly, if dividends amounting to $1000 were paid, then Plum would have cash amounting to $1000 to use to repurchase common stock. The shareholder, desirous of maintaining a 1% position, would thus sell shares amounting to $.01 \times \$1000 = \$100$. As a result, the shareholder would have a cash inflow totaling $\$100 + \$100 = \$200$, again the same amount as in the two previous situations.

Under all three situations, the 1% shareholder would receive the same cash flow at the present time ($200) and have the same claim on the future earnings of Plum. That is, in all three cases, the shareholder would still own 1% of Plum and would therefore receive the same amount of dividends in the future. Accordingly, the 1% shareholder (and all the others) will be neither better nor worse off if Plum pays a dividend amounting to $1000, $2000, or $3000. In summary, the dividend decision is a nonevent — whatever the level of dividends, current shareholders will be neither better nor worse off.

---

low payout ratio. However, with the *Tax Reform Act* of 1986 in the US, the tax rate on dividends is equal to the tax rate on capital gains, making it largely academic whether or not such an argument is valid. For a more detailed discussion of the issue, along with the relevant citations, see pp. 128–35 of Gordon J. Alexander and Jack Clark Francis, *Portfolio Analysis* (Englewood Cliffs, N.J.: Prentice Hall, 1986). The situation in Canada is rather different in that the dividend tax credit alters the relationship between the tax rates on dividends and capital gains. In general, the only real tax advantage to capital gains in Canada is the realization provision which allows the investor to choose when to incur the tax liabilility.

# DETERMINANTS OF DIVIDENDS

Few firms attempt to maintain a constant ratio of dividends to current earnings, since doing so would result in a fluctuating dollar amount of dividends. Dividends would fluctuate because earnings on a year-to-year basis are likely to be quite variable. Instead, firms attempt to maintain a desired ratio of dividends to earnings over some relatively long period, meaning that there is a target payout ratio of dividends to long-run, or sustainable, earnings. As a result, dividends are usually kept at a constant dollar amount and are increased only when management is confident it will be relatively easy to keep paying this increased amount in the future.[5] Nonetheless, larger earnings are likely to be accompanied by some sort of increase in dividends, as Table 17.1 shows.

**TABLE 17.1**

Dividend and Earnings Changes for 392 Major Industrial Firms, 1946–1964.

| Earnings Changes | | | Percent of Cases in Which Firms | | |
|---|---|---|---|---|---|
| Current Year | Previous Year | Percent of Cases | Increased Dividends | Did Not Change Dividends | Decreased Dividends |
| + | | 59.3% | 65.8% | 13.9% | 20.3% |
| − | | 40.7 | 42.8 | 17.9 | 39.5 |
| + | + | 33.4 | 74.8 | 11.4 | 13.8 |
| + | − | 25.9 | 54.1 | 17.2 | 28.7 |
| − | + | 24.7 | 49.7 | 16.9 | 33.4 |
| − | − | 16.0 | 31.8 | 19.4 | 48.8 |

SOURCE: Eugene F. Fama and Harvey Babiak, "Dividend Policy: An Empirical Analysis," *Journal of the American Statistical Association* 63, no. 324 (December 1969):1134.

The first two lines of this table indicate that of the firms examined, 59.3% of the time their earnings rose and the remainder of the time (40.7% = 100% − 59.3%) their earnings fell. The majority of the time when current earnings rose, firms increased their current dividends. However, whenever current earnings fell, firms would increase their current dividends as frequently as they would decrease their current dividends (note that, roughly speaking, 42.8% ≈ 39.5%).

The next two lines of the table suggest that firms are more likely to increase current dividends if they have had two consecutive years of rising earnings than if they have had falling and then rising earnings (74.8% > 54.1%). The last two lines of the table suggest that firms are more likely to decrease current dividends if they have had two consecutive years of falling earnings than if they have had rising and then falling earnings (48.8% > 33.4%). Overall, the table shows that firms in general are more likely to increase dividends than to decrease them.

---

[5] In addition to a regular dividend, sometimes a firm will declare a "special," or "extra," dividend, usually at year-end. By calling it a special dividend, the firm is conveying a message to its shareholders that such a dividend is a one-time event.

A formal representation of the kind of behavior implied by a constant long-run target payout ratio begins by assuming that the goal of the firm is to pay out $p^*$ (for example, $p^* = 60\%$) of long-run earnings.[6] If this target ratio were maintained every year, total dividends paid in year $t$ would be

$$D_t^* = p^* E_t \qquad (17.8)$$

where $D_t^*$ denotes the target amount for dividends to be paid in year $t$ and $E_t$ is the amount of earnings in year $t$. The difference between target dividends in year $t$ and the previous year's actual dividends is determined by subtracting $D_{t-1}^*$ from both sides of equation (17.8), resulting in

$$D_t^* - D_{t-1} = p^* E_t - D_{t-1}. \qquad (17.9)$$

Although firms would like to change their dividends from $D_{t-1}$ to $D_t^*$, few (if any) firms would actually change their dividends by this amount. Instead, the actual change in dividends is a proportion of the desired change:

$$D_t - D_{t-1} = a(D_t^* - D_{t-1}) \qquad (17.10)$$

where $a$ is a "speed of adjustment" coefficient, a number between 0 and 1.

For example, if a firm has just earned $5 million ($E_t$ = $5 million) and has a target payout ratio of 60%, then it would like to pay dividends amounting to $.6 \times$ $5 million = $3 million. Assuming it paid dividends of $2 million dollars last year, this represents an increase of $3 million $-$ $2 million = $1 million. However, if $a$ = 50%, then the firm will actually increase the dividends by $.5 \times$ $1 million = $500,000. Thus, actual dividends will be equal to $2.5 million = $2 million + $500,000, an amount equal to last year's dividends plus the change in dividends from last year to this year.

This model can be summarized by substituting $p^* E_t$ for $D_t^*$ in equation (17.10) and then solving the resulting expression for $D_t$:

$$D_t = ap^* E_t + (1 - a) D_{t-1}. \qquad (17.11)$$

Equation (17.11) indicates that the amount of current dividends is based on the amount of current earnings and the amount of the previous year's dividends.[7] In the previous example, $a$ = 50%, $p^*$ = 60%, $E_t$ = $5 million, and $D_{t-1}$ = $2 million. Thus, actual dividends $D_t$ would be equal to $(.5 \times .6 \times$ $5 million$) + [(1 - .5) \times$ $2 million$] = $2.5 million.

---

[6] See John Lintner, "Distribution of Incomes of Corporations Among Dividends, Retained Earnings, and Taxes," *American Economic Review* 46, no. 2 (May 1956):97–113. A similar model that used lagged share prices instead of contemporaneous accounting earnings was able to perform on a par with Lintner's earnings model. See Terry A. Marsh and Robert C. Merton, "Dividend Behavior for the Aggregate Stock Market," *Journal of Business* 60, no. 1 (January 1987): 1–40.

[7] Looking backward in time, it can be shown that current dividends $D_t$ are a linear function of past earnings $E_{t-1}, E_{t-2}, E_{t-3}$, and so on. More specifically, it can be shown that:

$$D_t = ap^* [(1 - a)^0 E_t + (1 - a)^1 E_{t-1} + (1 - a)^2 E_{t-2} + (1 - a)^3 E_{t-3} + \cdots].$$

Since the quantity $(1 - a)$ is a positive fraction (for example, $1/3$), when it is raised to a power it becomes smaller in value, with larger powers resulting in values closer to zero. Thus, current dividends depend more on recent past earnings than on distant past earnings, and the equation can be approximated by using an arbitrary number of past earnings (the accuracy of the approximation depends on the number used.)

By subtracting $D_{t-1}$ from both sides of equation (17.11), it can be seen that the change in dividends is equal to:

$$D_t - D_{t-1} = ap^*E_t - aD_{t-1}. \qquad (17.12)$$

When written in this form, the model suggests that the size of the change in dividends will be positively related to the current amount of earnings (since $ap^*$ is a positive number) and negatively related to the amount of the previous period's dividends (since $-aD_{t-1}$ is a negative number). Thus, the larger the current earnings are, the larger the change in dividends, but the larger the previous period's dividends, the smaller the change in dividends.

Statistical analysis has been used to see how well this model describes the way a sample of firms set the amount of their dividends. Table 17.2 summarizes some of the values obtained in one such study. The average firm had a target payout ratio of 59.1% and adjusted dividends by 26.9% of the way toward its target each year. However, most firms' dividends varied substantially from the pattern implied by their targets and adjustment factors. Somewhat less than half (42%) of the annual variance in the typical firm's dividends could be explained in this manner. This means that the model, while having explained a portion of the changes in dividends that have occurred, has left a substantial portion unexplained.

**TABLE 17.2**

Target Payout Ratios and Speed of Dividend Adjustment Factors for 298 US Firms, 1946–1968.

| | Speed of Adjustment Coefficient | | Target Payout Ratio | | Percent of Variance Explained | |
|---|---|---|---|---|---|---|
| Value | Percent of Firms with Smaller Value | Value | Percent of Firms with Smaller Value | Value | Percent of Firms with Smaller Value |
| .104 | 10% | .401 | 10% | 11% | 10% |
| .182 | 30 | .525 | 30 | 32 | 30 |
| .251 | 50 | .584 | 50 | 42 | 50 |
| .339 | 70 | .660 | 70 | 54 | 70 |
| .470 | 90 | .779 | 90 | 72 | 90 |
| average .269 | | average .591 | | average 42 | |

SOURCE: Eugene F. Fama, "The Empirical Relationship Between the Dividend and Investment Decisions of Firms," *American Economic Review* 64, no. 3 (June 1974):310.

The results from a comparable Canadian study of 40 companies in the manufacturing sector from 1947 to 1970 are shown in Table 17.3. In this case, however, current dividends were regressed against cash flow (rather than earnings) and the dividend paid in the prior period. The average target payout ratio and speed of adjustment coefficient were 0.316 and 0.379 respectively. The cash flow model used here appears to describe the firms' dividend behavior better than the earnings model used in the US in that it explains about 77% of the variance of the typical firm's dividend compared with 42%. The behavior of a few Canadian firms, however, does not conform well to this model in that these firms have low speed of adjustment coefficients, implying that they make little or no adjustment to their dividends in response to changes in cash flow.

**TABLE 17.3**

Target Payout Ratios and Speed of Dividend Adjustment Factors for 40 Canadian Firms, 1947–1970.

| Speed of Adjustment Coefficient | | Target Payout Ratio | | Percent of Variance Explained | |
|---|---|---|---|---|---|
| Value | Percent of Firms with Smaller Value | Value | Percent of Firms with Smaller Value | Value | Percent of Firms with Smaller Value |
| .204 | 25% | .244 | 25% | 72% | 25% |
| .324 | 50 | .313 | 50 | 85 | 50 |
| .506 | 75 | .374 | 75 | 93 | 75 |
| average .379 | | average .316 | | average 77 | |

SOURCE: J-P.D.Chateau, "La Politique de distribution de dividends des sociétés: une étude mi-croéconométrique," *Canadian Journal of Economics* 9, no. 2 (1976):255–77.

## 17.3 THE INFORMATION CONTENT OF DIVIDENDS

It is reasonable to believe that management has more information about the future earnings of the firm than does the public (which includes its own shareholders). This situation of *asymmetric information* suggests that management will seek to convey their information to the public if they have an incentive to do so. Assuming they have such an incentive, one way of doing so is by announcing a change in the amount of the firm's dividends. When used in this manner, dividend announcements are said to be a *signaling device* that can be used by management to convey information to the public.[8]

A relatively simple view of dividend changes is that an announced increase in dividends is a signal that management has increased its assessment of the future earnings for the firm. The announced increase in dividends is therefore "good news" and will, in turn, cause investors to raise their expectations regarding the future earnings of the firm. Conversely, an announced decrease in dividends is a signal that management has decreased its assessment of the future earnings for the firm. The announced

---

[8] Other signaling devices include changes in the firm's capital structure (for example, announcing an issuance of debt with the proceeds being used to repurchase shares). It has been argued that in order for the signal to be useful to the public, (1) management must have an incentive to send a truthful signal; (2) the signal cannot be imitated by competitors in different financial positions; and (3) there cannot be a cheaper means of conveying the same information. See Stephen A. Ross, "The Determination of Financial Structure: The Incentive-Signalling Approach," *Bell Journal of Economics* 8, no. 1 (Spring 1977):23–40. A summary and list of other important papers in this area is in J. Fred Weston and Thomas E. Copeland, *Managerial Finance* (Chicago: Dryden Press, 1986):661–664.

decrease in dividends is therefore "bad news" and will, in turn, cause investors to lower their expectations regarding the future earnings of the firm. An implication is that an announced increase in dividends will cause the firm's share price to rise, and an announced decrease will cause it to fall.

This simple model of dividend changes can be thought of as a special case of the model given in equation (17.12), where the speed of adjustment $a$ is zero. With this model, the expected change in dividends, $D_t - D_{t-1}$, is zero, suggesting that a simple increase in dividends will be viewed as good news. Conversely, a simple decrease in dividends will be viewed as bad news.

One way of testing to see if dividend changes do indeed convey information to the public is to see how share prices react to announcements of changes in dividends. However, care must be exercised in conducting such a study, because the firm's announcement of dividends is often made at the same time that the firm announces its earnings. Thus, if such announcements are made at the same time, any price change in the firm's common shares may be attributable to either (or both) announcements. One study attempted to avoid this problem of contamination by looking only at cases where the announcement of earnings was at least 11 trading days apart from the announcement of dividends.[9] Figure 17.2 provides an illustration of the average abnormal return associated with a firm's dividend announcement for those firms that announced their dividends 11 or more days after they announced their earnings (similar results were obtained when the authors examined those cases where dividend announcements preceded earnings announcements).

In those cases where firms announced an increase in their dividends, there is a significant positive reaction in their share prices. Conversely, in those cases where firms announced a decrease in their dividends, there is a significant negative reaction in their share prices. These findings strongly support the *information content of dividends hypothesis*, where dividend announcements are asserted to contain inside information about the firm's future prospects.

A study by Charest, that was not free of possible contamination by earnings announcements, found that dividend changes in Canada are anticipated by the market several months in advance of the announcement as shown in Figure 17.3.[10] Here also dividend increases (decreases) are accompanied by positive (negative) reactions in the stock prices. These findings are also consistent with the information content of dividends hypothesis.

It should be noted that there is nothing inconsistent with dividends being used as a signal and with the dividend irrelevance argument of Miller and Modigliani that was made earlier. In particular, shareholders will be neither better nor worse off if the level of dividends, relative to earnings, is high or low. Changes in dividends, however, may

---

[9] Joseph Aharony and Itzhak Swary, "Quarterly Dividend and Earnings Announcements and Stockholders' Returns: An Empirical Analysis," *Journal of Finance* 35, no. 1 (March 1980):1-12. Similar results are reported in Clarence C. Y. Kwan, "Efficient Market Tests of the Informational Content of Dividend Announcements: Critique and Extension," *Journal of Financial and Quantitative Analysis* 16, no. 2 (June 1981):193-206. For a study on the timing of dividend announcements, as well as a listing of studies concerning dividend announcements, see Avner Kalay and Uri Loewenstein, "The Informational Content of the Timing of Dividend Announcements," *Journal of Financial Economics* 16, no. 3 (July 1986):373–88.

[10] G. Charest, "Returns to Dividend Changing Stocks on the Toronto Stock Exchange," *Journal of Business Administration* 12, no. 1 (Fall 1980):1–18.

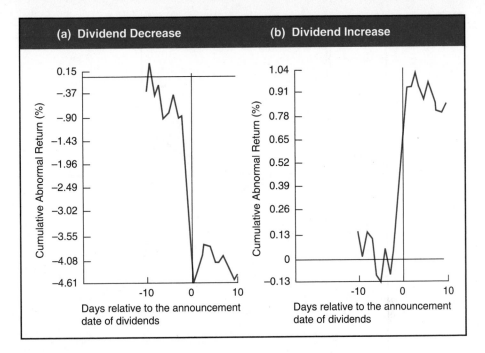

**(a) Dividend Decrease**

**(b) Dividend Increase**

Days relative to the announcement date of dividends

Days relative to the announcement date of dividends

**FIGURE 17-2**
Cumulative abnormal returns starting ten days before a dividend announcement.

*SOURCE:* Joseph Aharony and Itzhak Swary, "Quarterly Dividend and Earnings Announcements and Stockholders' Returns: An Empirical Analysis," *Journal of Finance* 35, no. 1 (March 1980):8.

be important because they convey information to the public about the future earnings prospects for the firm.

## 17.4 ACCOUNTING EARNINGS VERSUS ECONOMIC EARNINGS

Since the prediction of earnings is of critical importance in security analysis and investment research, a review of what is known about earnings and the relationship between earnings and prices is essential. At a fundamental level, consideration of the concept of *earnings* itself is needed. Specifically, just what is meant by earnings to those who produce the figures, and how does this meaning affect the valuation process?

### ☐ 17.4.1 Accounting Earnings

A firm's accountants operate under constraints and guidelines imposed by regulatory authorities and professional organizations such as the Ontario Securities Commission (OSC) and the Canadian Institute of Chartered Accountants (CICA). In cooperation with management, the accountants produce, on a quarterly basis, a set of financial statements for the firm that ends with a figure for the firm's *accounting earnings* (also known as the firm's reported earnings). In a broad sense, such earnings represent the difference

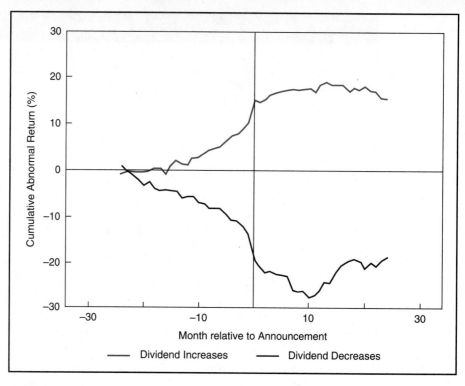

**FIGURE 17-3**
Cumulative abnormal returns starting twenty-four months before a dividend announcement.

SOURCE: Adapted from G. Charest, "Returns to Dividend Changing Stocks on the Toronto Stock Exchange," *Journal of Business Administration* 12, no. 1 (Fall 1980):7–8.

between revenues and costs, including the costs associated with nonequity sources of funds (such as debt). This difference, the total earnings available for common stock, is divided by the number of shares outstanding to calculate *earnings per share* (EPS). It may also be divided by the book value per share to calculate the *return on equity* (ROE).

A basic principle of accounting makes the book value of a firm's equity at the end of a period (such as a quarter or year) equal to (1) its value at the end of the previous period plus (2) the portion of accounting earnings for the period that is retained by the firm (here it assumed that there has been no change in the number of shares outstanding during the period). Letting $B_t$ denote the book value of the equity of the firm at the end of period $t$, $E_t^a$ denote the accounting earnings for period $t$, and $D_t$ denote the dividends paid during period $t$, this relationship can be expressed algebraically as

$$B_t = B_{t-1} + E_t^a - D_t \qquad (17.13)$$

From equation (17.13), it can be seen that accounting earnings equals the change in book value of equity plus dividends paid:

$$E_t^a = B_t - B_{t-1} + D_t. \qquad (17.14)$$

## □ 17.4.2 Economic Earnings

*Economic earnings* $(E_t^e)$ may be defined as the amount that would be obtained in equation (17.14) if the change in the book value of the firm equaled the change in the *economic value of the firm*:

$$E_t^e = V_t - V_{t-1} + D_t. \tag{17.15}$$

Here the change in the economic value of the firm during period $t$, $V_t - V_{t-1}$, is defined as the change in the market value of the firm's common stock (assuming there is no change in the market value of the other securities of the firm).[11]

It is easy to show that reported book values and market values (that is, economic values) of stocks are often considerably different. Figure 17.4 shows the ratio of (1) the year-end market price per share for Standard & Poor's Industrial Stock Index to (2) the corresponding year-end book value per share. It can be seen that the ratio is typically greater than 1.0 and has fluctuated considerably from year to year.

Figure 17.5 plots book values (horizontal axis) and market values (vertical axis) for the stocks in the Dow Jones Industrial Average. If investors viewed market and book values as nearly equivalent, the points would plot along a 45° line (that is, a line with a slope of one) that emanates from the origin. However, as the extensive scatter of the points indicates, market values diverge from book values by different amounts for different stocks.

Both Figure 17.4 and Figure 17.5 indicate that there can be sizable differences between market and book values. Since equations (17.14) and (17.15) show that accounting and economic earnings will be equal only if market and book values are equal, the evidence thus suggests that accounting and economic earnings differ by varying amounts for different firms.

The trouble with accounting earnings is the belief held by certain accountants that investors consider current and recent accounting earnings when estimating the value of a security.[12] This tempts management to try to "manage" such earnings in order to make a firm appear more valuable than it is, thereby fooling investors, at least temporarily. This is permissible since the *generally accepted accounting principles* (GAAP) set by the regulatory authorities (such as the CICA) allow a large amount of discretion in how certain items are accounted for (examples include methods for depreciation and inventory valuation). As a result, management may pressure accountants to use those principles that maximize the level of reported earnings, result in a high growth rate of reported earnings, or "smooth" earnings by reducing the year-to-year variability of earnings around a growth rate.[13] Some of these activities can be continued only for a limited number of years; others can go on indefinitely.

---

[11] Sir John R. Hicks, winner of the 1972 Nobel Award in Economics, has defined the weekly economic income of an individual as "the maximum value which he can consume during a week and still be as well off at the end of the week as he was at the beginning" (*Value and Capital*, London: Oxford University Press, 1946, p. 172). The definition of the economic earnings of a firm that is given in equation (17.15) can be viewed as an extension of Hicks' definition for an individual.

[12] Two assertions that have been made in regard to what investors look at when valuing stocks are known as the mechanistic hypothesis and the myopic hypothesis. The former asserts that investors look only at reported earnings and the latter asserts that investors look only at the short-term future. Both these assertions seem to be invalid when data are analyzed. For an in-depth discussion, see George Foster, *Financial Statement Analysis* (Englewood Cliffs, N.J.: Prentice Hall, 1986):443–45.

[13] For a discussion of a number of related issues, see Ross Watts, "Does It Pay to Manipulate EPS?" in *Issues in Corporate Finance* (New York: Stern Stewart Putnam & Macklis, Ltd., 1983).

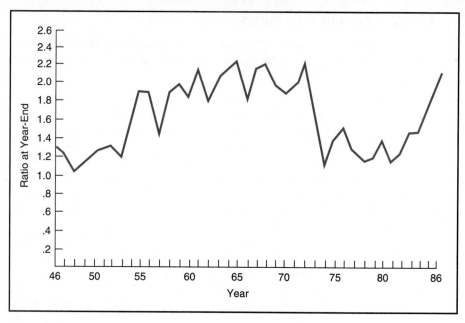

**FIGURE 17-4**

Ratio of price to book value: Standard & Poor's Industrial Stock Index, 1946–1986.

*SOURCE:* Standard & Poor's *Statistical Service,* various issues.

To obtain a truly independent estimate of value, analysts must dissect reported earnings. In doing so, they should not be fooled by any accounting illusions, meaning they should not be fooled by any manipulations that may have been made by the accountants at management's request. Anyone who estimates value by applying a formula (no matter how complex) to reported earnings is not producing an estimate that is completely free from all possible manipulations by management. This is not to say that reported earnings are irrelevant for security valuation. Instead, they should be viewed as one source of information about the future prospects of a firm.

## 17.5    PRICE-EARNINGS RATIOS

Chapter 16 discussed how dividend discount models could be used to determine if stocks were either underpriced or overpriced. One means of making this determination is to compare the actual price-earnings ratio for a firm with what the security analyst had determined it should be. In view of this use of price-earnings ratios, some evidence on the behavior of overall earnings, prices, and price-earnings ratios is now presented.

Part (a) of Figure 17.6 presents a plot of the year-end price-earnings ratios for Standard & Poor's 500. It can be seen from this that the variation in the ratio on a year-to-year basis is considerable, suggesting that investors do not simply apply a standard multiple to earnings in order to determine an appropriate value.

Part (b) of Figure 17.6 presents a similar plot of price-earnings ratios for the TSE 300. This also shows a wide variation from year to year, particularly early in 1992 when

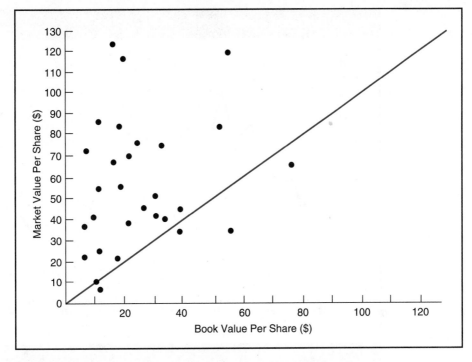

**FIGURE 17-5**
Market and book values, stocks in Dow Jones Industrial Average, year-end 1986 (except Navistar, which had a negative book value).

the ratio rises sharply. The commentary included with the graph suggests one possible explanation for the variability. The large extraordinary writedowns reflect an adjustment of the accounts to reflect the fact that that firms paid too much for assets in the 1980s or did not exercise due diligence in the control of operations. These high P/E ratios are, therefore, transitory. The average P/E of those firms with positive earnings is 15, a figure that is in line with the historical record.

An alternative explanation is that the method of calculation is faulty. Price-earnings ratios are calculated by dividing the current price by the most recently reported earnings. The current price is generally believed to reflect the companies' future prospects while the reported earnings are a retrospective look at the companies' performance and, therefore, the two are not directly related. For example, at the start of a recession reported earnings are high, but prices (based on pessimistic expectations) are low, therefore, the P/E ratios tend to be low. Near the end of a recession earnings are still low but prices are high (reflecting an imminent recovery) so the resultant P/E ratios are high. It would be more consistent, therefore, to calculate the ratio of current price to expected earnings rather than current earnings in order to reduce the effect of the business cycle.

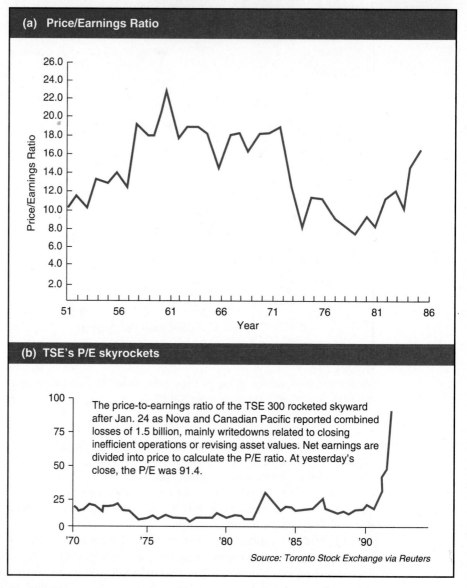

**(a) Price/Earnings Ratio**

Price/Earnings Ratio

Year

**(b) TSE's P/E skyrockets**

The price-to-earnings ratio of the TSE 300 rocketed skyward after Jan. 24 as Nova and Canadian Pacific reported combined losses of 1.5 billion, mainly writedowns related to closing inefficient operations or revising asset values. Net earnings are divided into price to calculate the P/E ratio. At yesterday's close, the P/E was 91.4.

*Source: Toronto Stock Exchange via Reuters*

**FIGURE 17-6**
Price-earnings ratios, US and Canada.
(a) Standard & Poor's 500, year-end, 1951–1986.
(b) TSE 300, 1970-1992.

SOURCE: (a) Standard & Poor's *Statistical Service*, various issues. (b) *The Globe and Mail: Report on Business*, Thomson Newspapers Limited, February 7, 1992.

## ☐ 17.5.1  Permanent and Temporary Components of Earnings

When individual common stocks are analyzed, they too show considerable variation in their price-earnings ratios over time. Furthermore, their ratios are quite different from each other at any time. One possible explanation notes that reported earnings can be viewed as having two components. The *permanent* component is the component that is likely to be repeated in the future, whereas the *transitory* component is not likely to be repeated.

Earlier, it was argued that the intrinsic value of a share depends on the firm's future earnings prospects. This suggests that changes in a share's intrinsic value and, in turn, its price, will be correlated with changes in the permanent component of its earnings but not with changes in the transitory component. If the transitory component is positive, then the price-earnings ratio will be relatively low due to a relatively large number in the denominator. Conversely, if the transitory component is negative, then the price-earnings ratio will be relatively high due to a relatively small number in the denominator.

As an example, consider a firm whose current stock price is $30 per share. Its permanent component of earnings per share over the past year is $4, and its transitory component is $1, resulting in reported earnings of $4 + $1 = $5 and a price-earnings ratio of $30 /$5 = 6. Remember that this share's current price is based on its future prospects, which, in turn, are based on the permanent component of earnings per share over the past year. Thus, if the firm had the same permanent component of $4 but had a transitory component of −$1 instead of $1, the stock would still have a current price of $30 per share. However, its reported earnings would have been $4 − $1 = $3 and its price-earnings ratio would have been $30 /$3 = 10.

The permanent component of earnings will change over time, causing investors to revise their forecasts. This will lead to a change in a firm's stock price and, in turn, its price-earnings ratio. However, changes in the transitory component will have an even greater effect on the price-earnings ratio because this component will sometimes be positive and sometimes be negative. As a result, a firm's price-earnings ratio will be variable over time, as was shown in Figure 17.6(a) for the S&P 500. This also means that at any point in time, the transitory component of earnings for a group of firms will have varying sizes, some being positive and some being negative. As a result, at any point in time, firms will have a range of different price-earnings ratios.

If this was a complete explanation for the considerable variation in price-earnings ratios over time and across firms, then most of the variation in a firm's price-earnings ratio would itself be transitory. That is, the ratio would vary over time around some average value. However, the evidence suggests this is not the case. Figure 17.7 shows the behavior over time of such ratios for two groups of stocks. The first group includes stocks with high price-earnings ratios at the beginning of the period (that is, during a portfolio-formation period). The other includes stocks with low price-earnings ratios at the beginning of the period.

Over time, the price-earnings ratios tend to revert to an average ratio for the market as a whole. The changes are substantial in the first two years, owing undoubtedly to the influence of transitory components of earnings. That is, those stocks in the high price-earnings ratio group apparently had, on the average, a negative transitory component in their earnings in the portfolio formation period. (Remember that such a component would tend to give a stock a high ratio.) Conversely, those stocks in the low price-earnings ratio group apparently had, on average, a positive transitory component. (Remember that such a component would tend to give a stock a low ratio.) Over future periods, each group of stocks would tend to have an equal number of stocks with positive

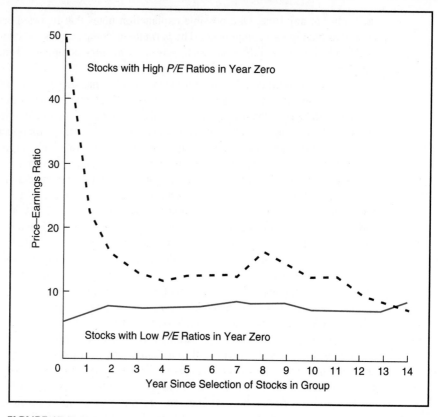

**FIGURE 17-7**

Price-earnings ratios over time for two groups of stocks.

*SOURCE:* William Beaver and Dale Morse, "What Determines Price-Earnings Ratios?" *Financial Analysts Journal* 34, no. 4 (July-August 1978):68.

and negative transitory components, resulting in an average transitory component for each group of roughly zero.

However, Figure 17.7 also shows that the two groups of stocks have different price-earnings ratios for many years after the portfolio formation period. Two explanations can be offered for this persistent difference. First, appropriate discount rates (that is, required returns) differ because of differences in security attributes. This means that there is no reason to expect different firms to have the same ratio. Second, there may be permanent differences between economic and reported earnings due to the use of different accounting methods. As mentioned earlier, there is evidence that the market sees through such differences in reported earnings. Thus, it is not surprising that the price-earnings ratios of stocks differ and that some of the differences are long lasting.[14]

---

[14] For a more thorough discussion of permanent and transitory components of earnings and their relationship to price-earnings ratios, see Chapters 4 and 5 of William H. Beaver, *Financial Reporting: An Accounting Revolution* (Englewood Cliffs, N.J.: Prentice Hall, 1981); William Beaver and Dale Morse, "What Determines Price-Earnings Ratios?" *Financial Analysts Journal* 34, no. 4 (July-August 1978):65–76; and Foster, *Financial Statement Analysis*, 437–42.

**TABLE 17.4**
Earnings Growth Rates, 610 Firms, 1950–1964.

| Length of Run | Actual Number of Good Runs | Actual Number of Bad Runs | Number of Good or Bad Runs Expected if the Odds Each Year were 50–50, Regardless of Past Performance |
|---|---|---|---|
| 1 | 1,152 | 1,102 | 1,068 |
| 2 | 562 | 590 | 534 |
| 3 | 266 | 300 | 267 |
| 4 | 114 | 120 | 133 |
| 5 | 55 | 63 | 67 |
| 6 | 24 | 20 | 33 |
| 7 | 23 | 12 | 17 |
| 8 | 5 | 6 | 8 |
| 9 | 3 | 3 | 4 |
| 10 | 6 | 0 | 2 |
| 11 | 2 | 0 | 1 |
| 12 | 1 | 0 | 1 |
| 13 | 0 | 0 | 0 |
| 14 | 0 | 1 | 0 |

*SOURCE:* Richard A. Brealey, *An Introduction to Risk and Return from Common Stocks* (Cambridge, Mass.: The MIT Press, 1983):89.

## 17.6 RELATIVE GROWTH RATES OF FIRMS' EARNINGS

Since security analysis typically involves forecasting earnings per share, it is useful to examine the historical record to see how earnings per share have changed over time. An interesting question about growth rates in firm earnings over time focuses on *growth stocks*. The very idea of a growth stock suggests that growth in some firms' earnings will exceed the average growth of all firms' earnings in most years, whereas other firms' earnings will grow less than the average.

The results of a study of the earnings' growth rates for 610 industrial companies from 1950 through 1964 are shown in Table 17.4. In every year, each firm's earnings were compared with its earnings in the previous year and the percentage change calculated. The year was counted as "good" for the firm if its percentage change was in the top half of the changes for all firms that year and "bad" if it was in the bottom half. If some firms tend to consistently experience above-average earnings growth rates, then fairly long runs of consistently good years should occur for these firms. Conversely, if some firms tend to consistently experience below-average earnings growth rates, then they should have fairly long runs of consistently bad years.

The middle two columns of Table 17.4 indicate the actual number of runs of various lengths. The right-hand column shows the number that would be expected if there was a 50-50 chance of either a good year or a bad year. The three columns are remarkably similar. Above-average earnings growth in the past does not appear to indicate above-average growth in the future, and below-average growth in the past does not appear to indicate below-average growth in the future. Flipping a coin seems to be as reliable a predictor of future growth as looking at past growth rates.

A study using longer time periods for measuring growth reached generally similar conclusions.[15] For each of 323 companies with positive earnings in each year from 1946 through 1965, average growth rates were computed for (1) the period from 1946 through 1955 and (2) the period from 1956 through 1965. Differences among firms' earnings growth rates in the first period accounted for less than 1% of the variation in the differences among their earnings growth rates in the second period.

## ☐ 17.6.1 Annual Earnings

The results of these studies, as well as certain other studies, suggest that *annual* reported earnings follow what is known in statistics as a *random walk model*.[16] That is, annual earnings for the forthcoming year ($E_t$) can be thought of as being equal to annual earnings over the past year ($E_{t-1}$) plus a random error term. (Remember that a random error term can be thought of as a roulette wheel where the numbers on the wheel are distributed around zero.) Thus,

$$E_t = E_{t-1} + \epsilon_t \qquad (17.16)$$

where $\epsilon_t$ is the random error term. With this model, the estimate of next year's earnings is simply the past year's earnings, $E_{t-1}$. Another way of viewing a random walk model for earnings is that the change in earnings is independent and identically distributed:

$$E_t - E_{t-1} = \epsilon_t. \qquad (17.17)$$

This means that the change in earnings, $E_t - E_{t-1}$, is unrelated to past changes in earnings and can be thought of as a spin from a roulette wheel that is perhaps unique to the firm but, more importantly, is used year after year. Since the expected outcome from a spin of the roulette wheel is zero, the expected change in earnings is zero. This implies that the expected level of earnings is equal to the past year's earnings, as was suggested earlier.

## ☐ 17.6.2 Quarterly Earnings

In terms of *quarterly* earnings, consideration must be given to the fact that there is typically a seasonal component to a firm's earnings (for example, many firms have high earnings during the quarter that includes Christmas). As a result, a slightly different model appears to be best for forecasting purposes. This model forecasts the growth in earnings for the forthcoming quarter relative to the same quarter one year ago, a quantity denoted by $QE_t - QE_{t-4}$. It does so by relating this growth to the growth during the most recent quarter relative to the comparable quarter one year before it,

---

[15] John Lintner and Robert Glauber, "Higgledy Piggledy Growth in America," in James Lorie and Richard Brealey, eds., *Modern Developments in Investment Management* (Hinsdale, Ill.: The Dryden Press, 1978).

[16] For a discussion of these studies, see Chapter 6 of Ross L. Watts and Jerold L. Zimmerman, *Positive Accounting Theory* (Englewood Cliffs, N.J.: Prentice Hall, 1986); and Foster, *Financial Statement Analysis*, Chapter 7 (particularly pp. 238–42).

$QE_{t-1} - QE_{t-5}$. Formally, the model for the "seasonally differenced series" of quarterly earnings is known as an *autoregressive model of order 1* and is as follows:

$$QE_t - QE_{t-4} = a(QE_{t-1} - QE_{t-5}) + b + e_t \qquad (17.18)$$

where $a$ and $b$ are constants and $e_t$ is a random error term.

Alternatively, the model can be rewritten by moving the term $QE_{t-4}$ to the right-hand side:

$$QE_t = QE_{t-4} + a(QE_{t-1} - QE_{t-5}) + b + e_t. \qquad (17.19)$$

By estimating the constants $a$ and $b$, this model can be used for forecasting quarterly earnings.[17]

For example, assuming estimates for $a$ and $b$ of .4 and .05, respectively, the forecast of a firm's earnings for the next quarter would be equal to $QE_{t-4} + .4(QE_{t-4} - QE_{t-5}) + .05$. Thus, if a firm had earnings per share for the last quarter $(t - 1)$ of \$3, for four quarters before now $(t - 4)$ of \$2, and for five quarters before now $(t - 5)$ of \$2.60, then its forecasted earnings for the forthcoming quarter would be equal to \$2 + .4(\$3 − \$2.60) + \$.05 = \$2.21. Note how the forecast consists of three components — a component equal to last quarter's earnings (\$2), a component that considers the year-to-year quarterly growth in earnings (.4(\$3 − \$2.60) = \$.16), and a component that is a constant (\$.05).[18]

---

## 17.7 COMOVEMENT OF EARNINGS

Past changes in security prices are of limited value for the prediction of future changes. And past changes in the overall level of the market are of limited help in the prediction of future market moves. However, security price changes are related to concurrent changes in the prices of the market portfolio and, to a lesser extent, an "industry" portfolio.[19] Although the strength of these relationships differs among securities, historical data can generally be utilized to help estimate the relative future strengths of the relationships for different securities. For example, the relationship between a security's returns and market returns has been referred to as the security's beta and can be estimated by examining historical returns. Similarly, the industry that a security belongs to can be determined

---

[17] For a discussion of this model, see George Foster, "Quarterly Accounting Data: Time-Series Properties and Predictive-Ability Results," *Accounting Review* 52, no. 1 (January 1977):1–21. This model can also be used to forecast annual earnings by working forward one quarter at a time and then adding up the forecasts for the forthcoming four quarters. Doing so would result in a forecast of annual earnings $(E_t)$ equal to $E_{t-1} + c(QE_{t-1} - QE_{t-5}) + 4b$, where $c = a^1 + a^2 + a^3 + a^4$. Note that the random walk model is a special case where $a$ and $b$ are equal to zero. See Watts and Zimmerman, *Positive Accounting Theory*, pp. 152–53, for a discussion of this model and a study that estimated values for $a$ and $b$. Also see Foster, *Financial Statement Analysis*, 230–45.

[18] It has been argued recently that a slight improvement can be made in this model by replacing the constant term component with what is known as a "moving average" component, which is based on the size of the random error term that occurred four quarters before now $(e_{t-4})$. See Lawrence D. Brown and Michael S. Rozeff, "Univariate Time-Series Models of Quarterly Accounting Earnings per Share: A Proposed Model," *Journal of Accounting Research* 17, no. 1 (Spring 1979):179–89; and Allen W. Bathke, Jr. and Kenneth S. Lorek, "The Relationship Between Time Series Models and the Security Market's Expectations of Quarterly Earnings," *Accounting Review* 59, no. 2 (April 1984):163–76.

[19] Although the definition of what constitutes an industry differs from one study to another, various authors have found that security price movements can be attributed not only to market price movements but also to industry price movements. See Alexander and Francis, *Portfolio Analysis*, 195–96, for a description of these studies and the relevant citations.

and a portfolio of stocks in that industry constructed. Then the historical returns on the security can be compared to this portfolio and an industry beta can be estimated.

It has been argued that security prices are determined by economic earnings and that security price movements are related to movements in market and industry prices. Thus, an interesting issue is whether or not movements in the economic earnings of a firm are related to movements in the economic earnings of the market and industry portfolios. Such an issue has been explored by looking at accounting earnings and assuming they are correlated with economic earnings.

Table 17.5 shows that such relationships do exist, at least to some extent. Earnings reported by 217 corporations from 1948 through 1966 were compared first with the earnings for Standard & Poor's 425-stock index (which served as a surrogate for marketwide earnings) and then with the average earnings of all firms in the same industry. The proportion of the variation of each firm's earnings that could be attributed to each of these factors was determined. The results shown in the table are the average proportions for all the firms in each industry.

**TABLE 17.5**

The Proportion of the Variation of a Firm's Earnings Attributable to Marketwide and Industry Earnings Changes.

| | Proportion Attributable to: | |
| --- | --- | --- |
| Industry | Marketwide Earnings Changes | Additional Influence of Changes in Industry Earnings |
| Aircraft | 11% | 5% |
| Autos | 48 | 11 |
| Beer | 11 | 7 |
| Cement | 6 | 32 |
| Chemicals | 41 | 8 |
| Cosmetics | 5 | 6 |
| Department stores | 30 | 37 |
| Drugs | 14 | 7 |
| Electricals | 24 | 8 |
| Food | 10 | 10 |
| Machinery | 19 | 16 |
| Nonferrous metals | 26 | 25 |
| Office machinery | 14 | 6 |
| Oil | 13 | 49 |
| Paper | 27 | 28 |
| Rubber | 26 | 48 |
| Steel | 32 | 21 |
| Supermarkets | 6 | 33 |
| Textiles and clothing | 25 | 29 |
| Tobacco | 8 | 19 |
| All firms | 21 | 21 |

SOURCE: Richard Brealey, "Some Implications of the Comovement of American Company Earnings," Applied Economics 3, no. 3 (September 1971):187.

The results differ notably from one industry to another, with the marketwide factor ranging between 5% and 48% and the industry factor ranging from 5% to 49%. The bottom row of the table shows the values obtained by averaging over all 217 corporations. Changes in marketwide earnings accounted for 21% of the variation in the earnings of the typical firm, and changes in the earnings of firms in its industry accounted for another 21%.

Earlier, it was mentioned that a security's beta (sometimes known as its *market beta*) is a measure of how the price of the security will covary with the price of the market portfolio. Similarly, a security's *accounting beta* is a measure of how the accounting earnings of the security will covary with the accounting earnings of the market portfolio. If security prices are related to earnings, then it seems reasonable to expect market betas to be related to accounting betas. Studies that have examined this issue have found that market and accounting betas are significantly correlated, with accounting betas explaining between 20% and 40% of the variation that is observed in market betas.[20]

## 17.8 EARNINGS ANNOUNCEMENTS AND PRICE CHANGES

A number of studies have shown substantial price changes for stocks of companies that report earnings that differ substantially from consensus expectations. One study looked at three groups of 50 stocks.[21] The first group consisted of the 50 stocks listed on the NYSE that experienced the greatest price rise during 1970. The second group consisted of 50 stocks chosen randomly from all those listed on the NYSE during 1970. The third group consisted of the 50 stocks listed on the NYSE that experienced the greatest price decline during 1970. As shown in Figure 17.8, the median changes in the prices of the stocks in the top, random, and bottom groups were 48.4%, −3.2%, and −56.7%, respectively.

Next, the study looked at the actual change in earnings per share from 1969 to 1970 for each stock in each group. As shown in Figure 17.8, the median changes in earnings per share for the top, random, and bottom groups were 21.4%, −10.5%, and −83.0%, respectively.

Lastly, the study determined the forecasted change in earnings per share at the beginning of 1970 for each stock in each group. This was done by using the predictions contained in Standard & Poor's *Earnings Forecaster*, where estimates made by a number of investment research organizations are reported. The median forecasted changes in earnings per share for the top, random, and bottom groups are shown in Figure 17.8 to be 7.7%, 5.8%, and 15.3%, respectively.

Interestingly, the forecasts of earnings per share hardly correspond to the price movements of the stocks. In fact, the stocks in the bottom group were expected to increase earnings by more than that in the top group (15.3%, compared with +7.7%).

---

[20] See, for example, Ray Ball and Philip Brown, "Portfolio Theory and Accounting," *Journal of Accounting Research* 7, no. 2 (Autumn 1969):300–23; and William Beaver and James Manegold, "The Association Between Market-Determined and Accounting-Determined Measures of Systematic Risk: Some Further Evidence," *Journal of Financial and Quantitative Analysis* 10, no. 2 (June 1975):231–84.

[21] Victor Niederhoffer and Patrick J. Regan, "Earnings Changes, Analysts' Forecasts, and Stock Prices," *Financial Analysts Journal* 28, no. 3 (May-June 1972):65–71.

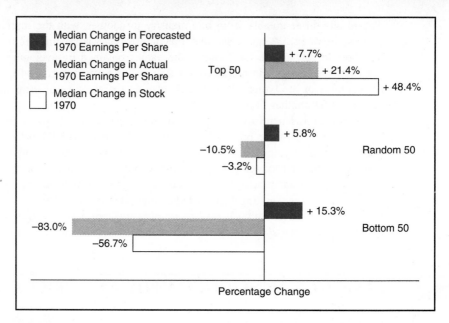

**FIGURE 17-8**
Earnings and price changes: selected stocks listed on the New York Stock Exchange during 1970.

*SOURCE:* Victor Niederhoffer and Patrick J. Regan, "Earnings Changes, Analysts' Forecasts, and Stock Prices," *Financial Analysts Journal* 28, no. 3 (May-June 1972):67.

However, the prediction for the bottom group was disastrously wrong, with a median earnings per share decline of 83.0%. And, as Figure 17.8 shows, prices definitely followed suit. Overall, it appears that unexpected changes in earnings do indeed affect security prices.

But do earnings surprises affect prices before or after their announcement? In a completely efficient market, such information would be reflected in prices as soon as it had been disseminated to a few major market participants. The reaction of security prices around the time of earnings announcements has been examined by a number of authors and is discussed next.

## ☐ 17.8.1 Deviations from Time-Series Models of Earnings

A comprehensive study involving 2053 firms from 1974 through 1981 provided evidence concerning the speed of response of security prices to earnings announcements.[22] For each company, an expected earnings figure was computed for each quarter, using the model of the time-series behavior of earnings shown in equation (17.19). With this model, the expected earnings for a firm during period $t$ was equal to $QE_{t-4} + a(QE_{t-1} - $

---

[22] George Foster, Chris Olsen, and Terry Shevlin, "Earnings Releases, Anomalies and the Behavior of Security Returns," *Accounting Review* 59, no. 4 (October 1984):574–603. For a related paper, see Roger Kormendi and Robert Lipe, "Earnings Innovations, Earnings Persistence, and Stock Returns," *Journal of Business* 60, no. 3 (July 1987):323–45.

$QE_{t-5}) + b$. For example, the earnings expected for the firm in the second quarter of 1988 equaled (1) the firm's earnings in the second quarter of 1987 plus (2) the change in earnings from the first quarter of 1987 to the first quarter of 1988 times the parameter $a$ plus (3) the parameter $b$. The values of $a$ and $b$ were determined by analysis of the behavior of earnings prior to the second quarter of 1988.

Given actual earnings and an estimate of expected earnings, a forecast error ($FE_t$) can be computed for the firm:

$$FE_t = QE_t - \overrightarrow{QE_t} \qquad (17.20)$$

where $QE_t$ is the actual earnings for quarter $t$ and $\overrightarrow{QE_t}$ is the expected earnings for quarter $t$, forecast at time $t-1$. Simply stated, equation (17.20) indicates that the forecast error for a quarter is the difference between actual earnings for that quarter and the expected earnings.

The forecast error provides a measure of the "surprise" in the quarterly earnings announcement, but it fails to differentiate between stocks for which large forecast errors are routine and those for which they are rare. The important surprises are those associated with forecast errors that are large by historical standards. To account for this, a forecast error can be related to previous errors to obtain a measure of *standardized unexpected earnings* (SUE):

$$\text{SUE}_t = \frac{FE_t}{\sigma_{FEt}} \qquad (17.21)$$

where $\sigma_{FEt}$ is the standard deviation of forecast errors for the 20 quarterly earnings of the firm prior to t. (That is, forecast errors were determined for 20 quarters before t, then the standard deviation for this set of 20 errors was estimated.)

For example, a firm with a forecast of earnings per share of $3 that subsequently reports actual earnings of $5 will have a forecast error of $5 − $3 = $2. That is, the earnings announcement will surprise people by $2. If the standard deviation of past errors is $.80, this surprise will be notable, since SUE = $2 /$ .80 = 2.50. However, if the standard deviation is $4, then this surprise is minor, since SUE = $2 /$4 = .50. Thus, a large positive value for SUE would indicate that the earnings announcement contained significant good news, whereas a large negative SUE would indicate that the earnings announcement contained significant bad news.

In the study, the SUEs associated with all the earnings announcements for all the firms were ranked from smallest to largest. Then they were divided into ten equal-sized groups based on the ranking. Group 1 consisted of those announcements resulting in the most-negative SUEs, and group 10 consisted of those with the most-positive SUEs. After forming these ten groups, the stock returns for each firm in each group were measured for the period from 60 days before its earnings announcement through 60 days after its announcement. Figure 17.9 shows the *abnormal return* for the average firm in each of the ten groups for three different time periods.

Part (a) shows the average abnormal return for the period from 60 days before the earnings announcement through the day the announcement appeared in the *Wall Street Journal*. This period is denoted by (−60, 0).

Part (b) shows the average abnormal return for the two-day period consisting of the day before the announcement appeared in the *Wall Street Journal* and the day the announcement appeared, a period that is denoted by (−1, 0). Since day 0 is the day the announcement appeared in the *Wall Street Journal*, day −1 is the day the announcement was made to the public. If this announcement was made after trading hours on day $-1$, investors would not have been able to buy or sell the shares until the next day, day 0. If the announcement was made during trading hours on day $-1$, then investors could have acted on that day. Due to the inability to pinpoint the hour of the announcement, the return over the two-day period was examined to see the immediate impact of the announcement on the price of the security.

Part (c) shows the average abnormal return for the period from the day after the announcement through 60 days after the announcement, a period that is denoted by (1, 60).

Part (a) shows that prices of firms that announced unexpected high earnings (such as SUE group 10) tended to increase *prior* to the announcement (date 0), suggesting that information relevant to the earnings announcement was becoming available to the market prior to the actual announcement. Conversely, prices of firms that announced unexpectedly low earnings (such as SUE group 1) tended to decrease prior to the announcement, undoubtedly for the same reason. In general, there seems to be a strong positive correspondence between the size of the unexpected earnings and the size of the abnormal return. Note that if an investor knew what the earnings were going to be 60 days before the announcement, then this information could be exploited by either buying the shares if the firm was going to announce unexpected large earnings, or short selling the shares if the firm was going to announce unexpected low earnings. However, since investors generally do not have prior access to earnings, such exploitation is generally impossible. Thus, the existence of abnormal returns prior to the announcement date does not necessarily indicate some sort of market inefficiency.

Part (b) shows that the larger the size of the unexpected earnings, the larger the price movement during the two-day period surrounding the announcement. For example, firms in SUE group 1 had an abnormal return of $-1.34\%$, whereas those in SUE group 10 had an abnormal return of $1.26\%$. As in part (a), there is a positive relationship between the size of the unexpected earnings and the abnormal stock return.[23] Thus, it appears that the market reacted in a predictable fashion, pushing up the stock prices of those firms announcing good news and pushing down the stock prices of those firms announcing bad news.

As shown in part (c), the changes in stock prices after the announcement dates are quite remarkable in that they appear to suggest an inefficiency exists in the market. Prices of stocks of firms announcing unexpectedly high earnings tended to increase for many days *after* the announcement (the average abnormal return over the 60-day period after the announcement was $3.23\%$ for SUE group 10). Conversely, the prices of firms announcing unexpectedly low earnings tended to decrease for many days after the announcement (the average abnormal return over the 60-day period subsequent to the announcement was $-3.08\%$ for SUE group 1).

As was noted, in the two previous parts there seems to be a strong positive correspondence between the size of the unexpected earnings and the size of the abnormal

---

[23] Studies have shown that earnings announcements containing good news are often made earlier than expected, whereas those containing bad news are often made later than expected. These studies also show that the *timeliness* (defined as the difference between the actual announcement date and the expected announcement date) affects the size of the abnormal return. Interestingly, around the time of earnings announcements there appears to be both increased trading volume and increased variability in security returns. See Foster, *Financial Statement Analysis*, 377–86; and V. V. Chari, Ravi Jagannathan, and Aharon Ofer, "Seasonalities in Security Returns: The Case of Earnings Announcements," *Journal of Financial Economics* 20, no. 1 (May 1988):101–21.

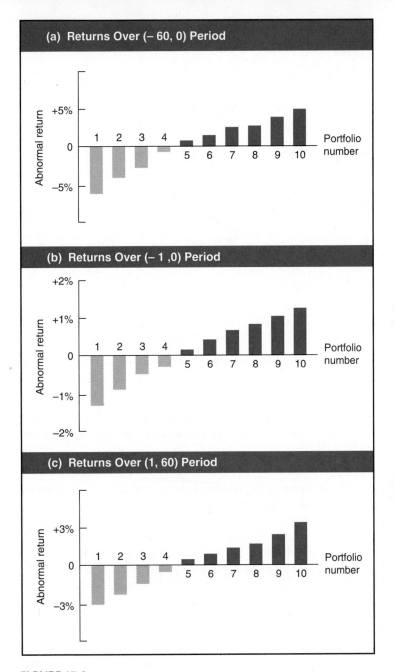

**FIGURE 17-9**
Security returns in period surrounding earnings announcements, US results.

*SOURCE:* George Foster, Chris Olsen, and Terry Shevlin, "Earnings Releases, Anomalies, and the Behavior of Security Returns," *Accounting Review* 59, no. 4 (October 1984):587.

**FIGURE 17-10**

Security returns in period surrounding earnings announcements, Canadian results.

*SOURCE:* Adapted from J.Desrochers, "Bénéfice annuel et réaction boursière au Canada," *Finéco* 1, no. 1 (automne 1991):72.

return. This observation suggests that an investor could make abnormal returns by simply looking at quarterly earnings announcements and, based on the magnitude and sign of the unexpected component, act appropriately. That is, if the firm announced earnings that were notably above expectations, the investor should subsequently purchase some of the firm's stock. In contrast, if the announced earnings were notably below expectations, the investor should subsequently sell any holdings and perhaps even short sell the firm's shares. Announcements of earnings that were reasonably close to expectations would not motivate either a buy or sell order.

Figure 17.10 shows the TSE's reaction to earnings announcements for 400 earnings increases and 300 earnings decreases over the 1980–84 period.[24] A simple no-change forecasting model was used to determine the magnitude of the earnings' "surprises." Positive (negative) and significant forecast errors were observed following earnings increases (decreases). The upward drift following the announcement of the increases suggests that some inefficiencies may exist in the Canadian market. Whether or not these can be profitably exploited remains a moot question.

---

[24]J. Desrochers,"Bénéfice annuel et réaction boursière au Canada," Finéco, 1, no. 1 (automne 1991):61–80.

# ☐ 17.8.2 Security Analysts' Estimates of Future Earnings

In using only the historical record of past earnings to forecast future earnings, it was mentioned earlier that an autoregressive model of order 1, as shown in equation (17.19), seemed to work about as well as any other model. However, security analysts do not restrict themselves just to past earnings when developing their forecasts. Instead, they look at many different pieces of information. This raises several interesting questions. How well can analysts forecast earnings? And do their forecasts incorporate information other than that contained in past earnings? The results of one study that provides some answers to these questions are shown in Table 17.6[25]

**TABLE 17.6**
Accuracy of Mechanical and Judgmental Earnings Forecasts.

| Earnings Forecast Error as a Percent of Actual Earnings | Percent of Forecasts With a Smaller Error | |
| --- | --- | --- |
| | Mechanical Model | Analysts' Forecasts |
| 5% | 15.0% | 18.0% |
| 10 | 26.5 | 32.0 |
| 25 | 54.5 | 63.5 |
| 50 | 81.0 | 86.5 |
| 75 | 87.5 | 90.5 |
| 100 | 89.5 | 92.0 |

SOURCE: Lawrence D. Brown and Michael S. Rozeff, "The Superiority of Analyst Forecasts as Measures of Expectations: Evidence from Earnings," *Journal of Finance* 33, no. 1 (March 1978):7–8.

In this study, two sets of forecasts were examined for the quarterly earnings of 50 firms over the period from 1971 through 1975. The first set was obtained by applying sophisticated mechanical models to each firm's previous earnings history (such as the autoregressive model of equation (17.19)). The second set was obtained from the earnings forecasts of security analysts as reported in the *Value Line Investment Survey*.[26] The results suggest that the analysts outperformed the mechanical model.[27] For example,

---

[25] Lawrence D. Brown and Michael S. Rozeff, "The Superiority of Analyst Forecasts as Measures of Expectations: Evidence from Earnings," *Journal of Finance* 33, no. 1 (March 1978):1–16. Also see Lawrence D. Brown and Michael S. Rozeff, "Analysts Can Forecast Accurately!" *Journal of Portfolio Management* 6, no. 3 (Spring 1980):31–34; Lawrence D. Brown, Robert L. Hagerman, Paul A. Griffin, and Mark E. Zmijewski, "Security Analyst Superiority Relative to Univariate Time-Series Models in Forecasting Quarterly Earnings," *Journal of Accounting and Economics* 9, no. 1 (April 1987):40–47; and Dan Givoly and Josef Lakonishok, "The Quality of Analysts' Forecasts of Earnings," *Financial Analysts Journal* 40, no. 5 (September-October 1984):40–47. The citations in the last two papers provide a useful set of references for the reader who is interested in this topic.

[26] Value Line also ranks stocks in terms of their relative attractiveness as investments. For a discussion of the usefulness of the Value Line rankings, see the appendix.

[27] A similar observation was made in a study that examined the forecasts made during the period of 1961 to 1969 by a sample of security analysts working for banks, mutual funds, brokerage houses, investment advisory firms, and pension funds. However, the forecasts were not found to be useful in identifying stocks that subsequently had positive abnormal returns. See John G. Cragg and Burton G. Malkiel, *Expectations and the Structure of Share Prices* (Chicago: The University of Chicago Press, 1982):85–86 and 165.

63.5% of the analysts' forecasts were within 25% of the actual earnings values, whereas only 54.4% of the forecasts made via mechanical models came as close. Analysts appear to base their forecasts on both past earnings and other information, and the latter appears to help.

Often, management itself will make a forecast of next year's earnings for the firm. Generally, the forecasts of security analysts are not as accurate as the forecasts of management when both sets of forecasts are made at about the same time. Since management has private information about the firm, this observation is not surprising.[28]

## ☐ 17.8.3  Revisions in Security Analysts' Forecasts

When new news about a company becomes available, professional security analysts revise their forecasts of the firm's earnings. As investors respond to such revisions by buying or selling the firm's stock, its price will, in turn, adjust. This raises some interesting questions regarding such revisions. Will this process from revision to stock price adjustment be rapid or somewhat slow? Is the information that caused analysts to revise their earnings estimates valuable to only those who get it early? Should an investor favor stocks whose earnings estimates have been revised upward in the last month? Conversely, should an investor avoid stocks whose earnings estimates have been revised downward?

One study that sought answers to these questions used the earnings forecasts for 2700 companies that are provided to institutional investors by Lynch, Jones and Ryan through their *Institutional Brokers Estimate System* (IBES) database.[29] This study noted that 77.2% of the earnings-per-share forecasts made one year in advance (FY1) were not revised each month and that this percentage increased as the year to be forecast became more distant. Possible explanations are that the security analysts are too busy to revise all their forecasts each month or that only a small number of stocks have new information each month. The study also found that the closer the year whose earnings were being forecast, the more accurate the forecast, an observation that is probably due to the information being of higher quality and quantity as the year gets closer.

To continue, this study also calculated a consensus forecast for a firm's earnings in a particular year by determining the average of the forecasts. Firms were then categorized into those for which these forecasts subsequently were (1) increased or (2) decreased. Returns for securities in each category over the period starting one month after the date of the forecast revision and continuing for 11 more months were determined and averaged. Table 17.7 shows some of the results.

---

[28] See Foster, *Financial Statement Analysis*, 280–85, for a discussion of the properties of management forecasts.

[29] The forecasts are made by analysts at over 80 brokerage firms. See Philip Brown, George Foster, and Eric Noreen, *Security Analyst Multi-Year Earnings Forecasts and the Capital Market* (Sarasota, Fl.: American Accounting Association, 1985). See also Gary A. Benesh and Pamela P. Peterson, "On the Relation Between Earnings Changes, Analysts' Forecasts and Stock Price Fluctuations," *Financial Analysts Journal* 42, no. 6 (November/December 1986):29–39, 55, along with their list of citations. Another database similar to IBES is *The Icarus Service* provided by Zachs Investment Research, Inc., which provides summaries of forecasts for 2400 companies from 50 US brokerage firms.

**TABLE 17.7**

Forecast Revisions and Abnormal Returns, 1976–1980.

| Revision of Consensus Forecast for: | | Average Cumulative Abnormal Return for |
|---|---|---|
| Earnings One Year Ahead | Earnings Two Years Ahead | Months +1 through +12 After Date of Revision |
| Increased | | + .04% |
| Decreased | | −3.80 |
| Increased | Increased | + .60 |
| Decreased | Decreased | −4.57 |

SOURCE: Philip Brown, George Foster, and Eric Noreen, *Security Analyst Multi-Year Earnings Forecasts and the Capital Market* (Sarasota, Fl.: American Accounting Association, 1985):71, 104.

Stocks whose initial earnings forecasts for one year ahead were subsequently increased did not experience significantly abnormal returns — the abnormal return over the 12-month period was +0 .04%. On the other hand, stocks whose initial earnings forecasts were subsequently decreased did have significant abnormal returns of −3 .80%.

Stocks whose earnings forecasts for both one year ahead and two years ahead changed in the same direction experienced even greater abnormal returns. This finding suggests that capital markets look at more than just current earnings in valuing securities. Furthermore, the results suggest that an inefficiency exists in the stock market in that apparently investors can avoid abnormally poor returns by immediately selling a stock if the stock's forecasted earnings have been revised downwards.

Hennessey used the IBES database for Canadian stocks to perform a comparable study of one year ahead forecast revisions for three types of revision — positive, no revision, and negative.[30] The results are presented in Figure 17.11 and show that the market anticipates positive and negative revisions starting about 12 months prior to the revision. The surprising feature, however, is that an investor could apparently earn excess returns by purchasing stocks with positive revisions at the time the revision is reported. These excess returns persist for about 12 months following the revision. There is no comparable continued negative reaction following downward revisions. Once again this reveals another situation where Canadian stock prices react to new information with some delay.

## ☐ 17.8.4 Sources of Errors in Forecasting

Since security analysts' forecasts are not perfect, it is interesting to consider the major source of their errors. One study examined the IBES database and attempted to break down the forecast errors into three components: (1) errors that could be traced to misjudgments about the economy; (2) errors that could be traced to misjudgments about

---

[30] S. Hennessey, "Earnings Forecast Revisions and Security Returns: Canadian Evidence," School of Business, University of Prince Edward Island Working Paper, October 1991.

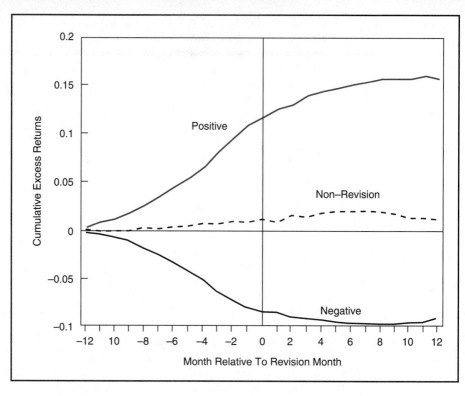

**FIGURE 17-11**
Forecast revisions and abnormal returns, Canadian results, 1979–1988.

*SOURCE:* S. Hennessey, "Earnings Forecast Revisions and Security Returns: Canadian Evidence," School of Business, University of Prince Edward Island Working Paper (October 1991), Figure 1.

the firm's particular industry; and (3) errors that were purely due to misjudgments about the firm.[31]

The results indicated the following: Less than 3% of the typical error was due to a misjudgment about the economy; roughly 30% of the typical error was due to a misjudgment about the industry; and more than 65% of the typical error was due to a misjudgment about the firm.

## ☐ 17.8.5 Unexpected Earnings and Abnormal Returns

One plausible explanation for these results concerns the cost of information transfer. New news must reach a large number of investors before the appropriate new equilibrium price can be completely established. Although large institutional investors can obtain news quickly, it may take some time before it reaches smaller institutional investors and individuals. Thus, after an earnings announcement or forecast revision,

---

[31] Edwin J. Elton, Martin J. Gruber, and Mustafa N. Gultekin, "Professional Expectations: Accuracy and Diagnosis of Errors," *Journal of Financial and Quantitative Analysis* 19, no. 4 (December 1984):351–63.

there can be a period of abnormal price movement that is related in sign and magnitude to the nature of the announcement.

Alternatively, perhaps the measurement of abnormal returns has been in error. In making such a measurement, a determination of what is a normal return must be made. Such a determination is not straightforward; instead it is fraught with difficulty. This means that the estimated abnormal returns could actually be due to measurement errors, leaving open the possibility that a more accurate measure of normal return would have resulted in no significant abnormal returns.

Nevertheless, there appear to be striking differences in subsequent stock returns for firms with different SUEs and different revisions in earnings forecasts. Such differences cannot be explained wholly by different levels of beta. While the magnitudes of the return differences may be too small to warrant extensive trading, they do suggest the consideration of such things as SUE values and forecast revisions when money must be invested or a portion of an existing portfolio liquidated.

## 17.9 SUMMARY

This chapter has presented some of the important features of dividends and earnings of which a security analyst should be aware when preparing forecasts and making investment recommendations. First of all, it was shown that there is no conflict regarding the underlying source of value for a share of stock. In particular, earnings were shown to be the source of value, not dividends.

Second, a model for explaining the amount of dividends was presented. In this model, the amount of dividends is based on current earnings and the amount of dividends paid in the previous year. However, this model does not work perfectly in explaining dividends. One reason for this failure is that dividends are sometimes used as a signaling device by management to convey information to the public. Consistent with this notion is the observation that an announcement of an unexpected increase in dividends typically results in an upward movement in the firm's stock price, whereas an unexpected decrease results in a downward movement.

Third, it was shown that security analysts should not be fooled by accounting illusions. That is, when analysts are determining the true economic value and earnings of the firm, they should recognize the discretion that accountants have in preparing financial statements. Indeed, the evidence suggests that analysts do see through the veil of accounting illusions, since they appear to be able to estimate earnings more accurately than mechanical models that are based on accounting earnings. In terms of mechanical models, a random walk model seems to be reasonable for describing annual earnings; an autoregressive model of order one is reasonable for describing quarterly earnings.

Fourth, it was shown that one way of explaining why firms have different price-earnings ratios is to recognize that earnings have a permanent and a temporary component. Since prices typically reflect just the permanent component, whereas price-earnings ratios are based on both components, these ratios vary widely.

Fifth, it was shown that there is a positive relationship between accounting betas and market betas. That is, firms whose earnings covary more with marketwide earnings are likely to have higher market betas.

Sixth, it appears that stocks with the highest returns typically have earnings per share that are substantially greater than expected, whereas those with the lowest returns have earnings per share that are substantially less than expected. Two observations are consistent with this: (1) the greater the amount of unexpected earnings, the greater the stock return before, during, and after the announcement date; and (2) revisions in analysts' forecasts tend to be reflected in stock prices. In summary, the enormous amount of effort devoted to forecasting earnings seems to be justified in that superior ability can result in abnormally high returns.

## APPENDIX A

## VALUE LINE RANKINGS

It has been observed that investors can use the information contained in either a quarterly earnings announcement or a revision of an earnings forecast by security analysts to make abnormal returns. Another source of information that may be useful to investors is the *Value Line Investment Survey* (published by Value Line, Inc., New York, for $495 per year, which is reputed to be the largest investment advisory service in the United States).

Each week, every one of approximately 1700 stocks is assigned one of five possible ranks by Value Line. By design, the categories include the same number of stocks each week, as follows:

| Rank | Number of Stocks |
| --- | --- |
| 1 (highest) | 100 |
| 2 (above average) | 300 |
| 3 (average) | 900 |
| 4 (below average) | 300 |
| 5 (lowest) | 100 |

Many factors go into the ranking procedure. Not surprisingly, the exact details have not been revealed. However, the key elements are all based on publicly available information: [32]

1. The most recent year's earnings and average stock price, relative to the comparable values for the previous ten years, and the stock's average price over the preceding 10 weeks relative to that of the preceding 52 weeks.
2. A price momentum element that is based on the stock's current price-earnings ratio relative to that of the market, compared with the average of the corresponding figures over the last five years.
3. An earnings momentum element that is based on the most recent quarter's earnings relative to the amount reported four quarters earlier.

---

[32] For details, see Arnold Bernhard, *Investing in Common Stocks with the Aid of the Value Line Rankings and other Criteria of Stock Value* (New York: Arnold Bernhard and Co., Inc., 1975). Late in 1991 Value Line introduced a similar service for Canadian investors. A complete description of the information provided is contained in *How to Use the Value Line Investment Survey, Canadian Edition: A Subscriber's Guide, A Practical Guide to Better Investing* (New York: Value Line Publishing, Inc., 1991). The Canadian quarterly reports and weekly updates cover 70 Canadian and 30 foreign stocks.

4. An earnings surprise element, where the most recent quarter's earnings are compared with the amount forecast by Value Line's security analysts.

A test of the resulting rankings showed them to be of some value.[33] Beginning in November 26, 1965, five portfolios were formed (on paper). The first included all stocks ranked 1 at that time, in equal dollar values; the second included all stocks ranked 2, and so on. After six months each portfolio was altered as necessary to again include equal dollar values of all stocks with the appropriate ranks at that time. The procedure was continued until February 3, 1978, when the last set of portfolios was formed. Then, each portfolio's actual rate of return was measured and adjustments for risk were made to determine abnormal returns. The results, shown in Table 17.8, indicate that both the actual and abnormal returns are perfectly ordered with the rankings of the securities in the portfolios. More in-depth analysis indicated that most of the abnormal returns occurred in the 13-week period subsequent to the formation date. Interestingly, this study shows that the only notable abnormal return is for the securities with a ranking of 5. This suggests that an investor should sell (or even short sell) any securities that have such a ranking.

**TABLE 17.8**
Performance of Portfolios Formed on the Basis of Value Line Rankings.

| | Ranking | | | | |
| --- | --- | --- | --- | --- | --- |
| | 1 | 2 | 3 | 4 | 5 |
| Actual return over subsequent 26 weeks | 7.38% | 6.51% | 4.10% | 2.70% | .37% |
| Abnormal return over subsequent 26 weeks | .33% | .35% | −.57% | −1.12% | −3.05% |

SOURCE: Thomas E. Copeland and David Mayers, "The Value Line Enigma (1965-1978): A Case Study of Performance Evaluation Issues," *Journal of Financial Economics* 10, no. 3 (November 1982):298, 301.

This study also looked at those securities whose rank had been changed by Value Line. Roughly 70 to 80 securities change ranks each week, evenly split between those being upgraded and those being downgraded. Almost all the changes are of one rank (seldom does a security jump two ranks, for example from 1 to 3, or vice versa). Focusing the analysis around the time of the change in rank, it was determined that, on the average, securities whose rank had been upgraded earned an abnormal return of .77% in the subsequent 13 weeks. Conversely, those securities whose rank had been downgraded earned an abnormal return of -1.42% in the subsequent 13 weeks. Overall, most of the

---

[33] Thomas E. Copeland and David Mayers, "The Value Line Enigma (1965–1978): A Case Study of Performance Evaluation Issues," *Journal of Financial Economics* 10, no. 3 (November 1982):289–321.

adjustment in the stock prices of these securities was found to be concentrated in the two-week period subsequent to the publication of the change in rank.[34]

These results do not suggest that Value Line provides a guaranteed formula for outstanding portfolio performance. No transactions costs were charged in the calculations, and turnover was high.[35] But the results do suggest that in choosing among stocks, Value Line rankings may prove useful.[36] It can be conjectured that Value Line rankings "work" primarily because they use quarterly earnings in both the earnings momentum and surprise elements that go into the Value Line ranking procedure.[37] After all, it has been noted that there are abnormal price movements subsequent to the announcement of quarterly earnings.

To summarize, the results suggest there is a two-part puzzle associated with Value Line ranks. First, Value Line appears to have superior forcasting ability that is based on public information. Second, the market takes time to adjust to the Value Line rankings. Both these observations are puzzling because they are inconsistent with the notion of efficient markets.

## QUESTIONS AND PROBLEMS

1. For a given level of earnings $(E)$, net new investment $(I)$, and dividends $(D)$, explain why a firm must issue new stock if $E < D + I$ and it desires to maintain a constant debt-equity ratio. Similarly, why must it repurchase shares if $E > D + I$ and it desires to maintain a constant debt-equity ratio?

2. Why is an individual shareholder indifferent between the firm retaining $1 of earnings or paying out the $1 of earnings as a dividend, assuming that the shareholder maintains constant proportional ownership in the firm and the firm maintains a constant debt-equity ratio?

3. If the dividend decision is truly irrelevant to the economic value of a corporation, are dividend discount models of any use in estimating the fair price of a corporation's stock? Explain.

4. How are dividends used as a signaling device by corporate management? To the extent that dividends are a signaling device, how are dividend changes related to stock prices?

---

[34] A later study found that most of the adjustment actually was in the three-day period after the change. The most notable price movement was associated with those stocks being upgraded from 2 to 1. Other notable but less sizable price movements were associated with upgrades from 3 to 2 and downgrades from 1 to 2 and 2 to 3. See Scott E. Stickel, "The Effect of Value Line Investment Survey Rank Changes on Common Stock Prices," *Journal of Financial Economics* 14, no. 1 (March 1985):121–43.

[35] A discussion of transactions costs is contained in Copeland and Mayers, "The Value Line Enigma," 319–20; and Clark Holloway, "A Note on Testing an Aggressive Investment Strategy Using Value Line Ranks," *Journal of Finance* 36, no. 3 (June 1981):711–19.

[36] Value Line also provides a measure of the risk of individual securities (known as Safety Rank). Interestingly, this rank measure was found to be more highly correlated with subsequent returns than either beta or standard deviation, suggesting it is a useful measure of a security's risk. See Russell J. Fuller and G. Wenchi Wong, "Traditional versus Theoretical Risk Measures," *Financial Analysts Journal* 44, no. 2 (March/April 1988):52–57, 67.

[37] One speculation is that the rankings are simply capturing the size effect by giving higher ranks to smaller firms (the size effect is discussed in Appendix A to Chapter 15). However, tests suggest this is not true. See Gur Huberman and Shmuel Kandel, "Value Line Rank and Firm Size," *Journal of Business* 60, no. 4 (October 1987):577–89.

5. Discuss why there generally does not exist a one-to-one relationship between corporations' book values and their market values.
6. The price per share of Loon Lake Company is less than its book value. Does this indicate that those who now hold the firm's shares have lost money in the past? Does it indicate that they are likely to lose money in the future? Does it indicate that Loon Lake Company should not undertake any further capital investment? Explain your answers.
7. Why might a steady trend in a firm's reported earnings from year to year suggest that the figures do not represent the firm's economic earnings?
8. Reported earnings typically differ, sometimes considerably, from economic earnings. Nevertheless, it is often argued that reported earnings are intended simply to provide a "source of information" to investors about the value of the firm. If so, might there not be many alternative accounting procedures of equal use to investors? How might one go about evaluating the usefulness of such procedures?
9. Price-earnings ratios for individual companies vary over time and across firms. Discuss some of the possible reasons for this variability.
10. Harry Clift once wrote in a market newsletter that, "I focus my research on consensus earnings forecasts. Those companies that the consensus believes will produce the largest earnings increases next year are most likely to produce the best returns." Is Harry's opinion consistent with empirical evidence? Explain why or why not.
11. Why might the price of a stock react only partially to an "earnings surprise" on the first day or two after the earnings announcement?
12. (Appendix Question) The Value Line ranking system has long shown a consistent ability to produce positive risk-adjusted returns. These results have been particularly disconcerting for efficient markets proponents. Why?

## SUGGESTED READINGS

*The Canadian Securities Course* (Toronto, Ont.: The Canadian Securities Institute, 1989). Chapters 5 and 6 provide a discussion of financial statement analysis.

# Chapter 18

# OPTIONS

In the world of investments, an *option* is a type of contract between two parties where one party grants the other the right to buy a specific asset at a specific price within a specific time period. Alternatively, the contract may grant the other person the right to sell a specific asset at a specific price within a specific time period. The person who has received the right and thus has a decision to make is known as the option buyer, since he or she must pay for this right. The person who has sold the right to the buyer and thus must respond to the buyer's decision is known as the option writer.

The variety of contracts containing an option feature is enormous. Even within the domain of publicly traded securities, many types can be found. Traditionally, only certain instruments are referred to as options; the others, though similar in nature, are designated in other ways. This chapter presents an introduction to the institutional features of such contracts, along with some basics regarding how they are valued in the marketplace.

## 18.1    TYPES OF OPTION CONTRACTS

### ☐ 18.1.1   Call Options

The commonest type of option contract is the *call option* for shares of common stock. It gives the buyer the right to buy ("call away") a specific number of shares of a specific company from the option writer at a specific purchase price at any time up to and including a specific date. The contract specifies four items:

1. The company whose shares can be bought
2. The number of shares that can be bought (usually 100)
3. The purchase price for those shares, known as the *exercise price* (or *strike price*)
4. The date when the right to buy expires, known as the *expiration date*

**Trading Call Options**

Before 1973, the year options started trading on an organized exchange in the US, a call option buyer had to search for a call option writer before a contract could be executed.[1] In addition, contracts were not yet standardized so that the number of shares, the strike price and the expiration date all had to be agreeable to both parties.

---

[1] Prior to 1973 in the US and 1975 in Canada, options were traded over the counter through the efforts of dealers and brokers. These dealers and brokers brought buyers and writers together, arranged terms, helped with the paperwork, and charged fees for their efforts.

An example will be used to illustrate some of the trading of call options. Suppose that Widget Corporation's stock is currently selling for $45 per share. Investor B is optimistic about Widget's prospects and is interested in buying a call option contract that allows him or her to acquire 100 shares of Widget stock at $50 per share at any time over the next six months. At the same time investor W is pessimistic about Widget's prospects and does not expect the stock price to rise above $50 per share over the next six months. After some search they find one another (with no assistance from a broker) and enter into a contract.

If, at any time during the next six months, the share price rises above $50, to say $55, investor B can exercise the option and require W to buy the stock (if W does not already own it) and sell it at $50. Investor B, thus, gains $5 per share and investor W loses $5 per share. If, however, the share price remains unchanged for six months at $45 investor B allows the option to expire unexercised and neither gains or loses. It is clear then that if the share price rises above $50 B gains and W loses whereas if the share price does not rise above $50 neither party gains or loses. B must, therefore, provide W with an incentive to write such a contract. The price per share that B pays W for the contract is known as the *premium*. If, for example, B pays W $3 per share for the call option then B gains when the option is exercised when the stock price is above $53 per share and W gains as long as the stock price remains below $53 per share.

One of the attractions of buying call options is the high degree of leverage they provide as shown in the following example. If B buys the call option and the share price rises from $45 to $55 the percentage gain is $(55 - 50 - 3)/3 = 0.667$ or 66.7%, where $3 is the cost of buying the option. If B buys the shares instead the percentage gain is only $(55 - 45)/45 = 0.222$ or 22.2%.

To be released from the contract before the expiration date B or W can either sell the contract back to the other at a mutually agreeable price or find a third party willing to assume the contract. The third party would buy from B or be paid by W. In these circumstances both the original parties, B and W, are said to have *closed out* their positions. The responsibilty for either negotiating the repurchase/resale of the contract or for finding a third party willing to assume the contract rests solely with the original buyer or writer. Trading in options before 1973, therefore, was a laborious and risky process.

Currently in Canada and the United States there are standardized contracts and organized exchanges for trading listed options. *Trans Canada Options Inc.* (TCO), a company that is jointly owned by the Montreal Exchange and the Toronto and Vancouver Stock Exchanges, greatly facilitates trading by maintaining a computer system that records the position of each investor in each listed option. The Options Clearing Corporation (OCC) performs the same function in the United States.

Although the mechanics are rather complex, the principles are simple. As soon as a buyer and a writer agree on a particular option contract and the buyer pays the agreed-upon premium, the TCO steps in, becoming the effective writer as far as the buyer is concerned and the effective buyer as far as the writer is concerned. Thus, all direct links between the original buyer and writer are severed. If a buyer chooses to exercise an option, the TCO will randomly choose a writer who has not closed his or her position and assign the exercise notice accordingly. The TCO also guarantees delivery if the writer is unable to deliver the shares.

The TCO makes it possible for buyers and writers to close out (or unwind) their positions at any time. If a buyer subsequently becomes a writer of the same contract, meaning that the buyer later sells the contract to someone else, the TCO computer will note the offsetting positions in this investor's account and will simply cancel both entries. Thus, an investor who buys a contract on Monday and sells it on Tuesday will be treated as if a contract had been bought on Monday and an identical contract written on Tuesday. The computer will note that the investor's net position is zero and will remove both entries. The second trade is a *closing sale*, since it serves to close out the investor's position from the earlier trade. Closing sales thus allow buyers to sell options rather than exercise them.

A similar procedure allows a writer to pay to be relieved of the potential obligation to deliver stock. Consider an investor who writes a contract on Wednesday and buys an identical one on Thursday. The latter is a *closing purchase* and, analogous to a closing sale, serves to close out the investor's position from the earlier trade.

Call options are *protected* against stock splits and stock dividends on the underlying stock. In the example where the option was on 100 shares of Widget stock with an exercise price of $50, a 2-for-1 stock split would cause the contract to be altered so that it became one for 200 shares at $25 per share. Stock splits and stock dividends cause the share price to fall below what it otherwise would have been, thereby working to the disadvantage of the call option buyer and to the advantage of the call option writer.

There is no protection for listed call options against cash dividends, in that, the exercise price and number of shares are unaffected by the payment of cash dividends.[2] For example, the terms of the Widget call option would remain the same if Widget declared a $4 per share cash dividend.

## ☐ 18.1.2  Put Options

A second type of option contract for common stocks is the *put option*. It gives the buyer the right to sell ("put away") a specific number of shares of a specific company to the option writer at a specific selling price at any time up to and including a specific date. The contract specifies four items that are analagous to those for call options:

1. The company whose shares can be sold
2. The number of shares that can be sold
3. The selling price for those shares, known as the *exercise price* (or *strike price*)
4. The date when the right to sell expires, known as the *expiration date*

### Trading Put Options

The trading of put options is analogous to that of call options. Suppose that XYZ Company's stock is currently selling for $30 per share. Investor B is pessimistic about XYZ's prospects and is interested in buying a call option contract that allows him or her to sell 100 shares of Widget stock at $30 per share at any time over the next six months. At the same time, investor W is optimistic about Widget's prospects and does not expect

---

[2] However, there is protection for any cash dividend that is formally designated a *return of capital*. Furthermore, options that are traded over the counter typically are protected from any type of cash dividend. In both cases, the protection is in the form of a reduction in the exercise price.

the share price to fall below $30 over the next six months. After some search they find one another (with no assistance from a broker) and enter into a contract.

If, at any time during the next six months, the share price falls below $30, to say $25, investor B can exercise the option and require W to buy the stock at $30 per share (when it is only worth $25). Investor B, thus, gains $5 per share and investor W loses $5 per share. If, however, the share price remains unchanged for six months at $35 investor B allows the option to expire unexercised and neither gains or loses. It is clear then that if the share price falls below $30 B gains and W loses whereas if the share price does not fall below $30 neither party gains or loses. B must, therefore, provide W with an incentive to write such a contract. The price per share that B pays W for the contract is known as the *premium*.

As with call options, the buyer and writer may close out (or unwind) their positions at any time by simply entering an offsetting transaction. This is easily done for listed put options in Canada and the United States, since these contracts are standardized and the TCO records the position of each investor in each listed put option.

As soon as a buyer and a writer agree to trade a particular put option contract and the buyer pays the premium, the TCO steps in, becoming the effective writer as far as the buyer is concerned and the effective buyer as far as the writer is concerned. If a buyer chooses to exercise an option, the TCO randomly chooses a writer who has not closed his or her position and assigns the exercise notice accordingly. The TCO also guarantees delivery of the exercise price if the writer is unable to pay the necessary cash.

Puts are protected against stock splits and stock dividends on the underlying stock. In the example where the option was on 100 shares of XYZ stock with an exercise price of $30, a 2-for-1 stock split would cause the contract to be altered so that it was for 200 shares at $15 per share. Listed puts are not protected against cash dividends.

## 18.2    OPTION TRADING IN CANADA

Before January 1992, TSE traded options were introduced on a nine month cycle as is done in US markets. Beginning in January 1992, a new set of options on a given stock begin trading on the TSE every month. Figure 18.1 shows the available expiry dates listed by cycle and by month. Each underlying stock is assigned to a given cycle and options are introduced according to the schedule shown. For example, in January, options on Canadian Pacific (a cycle 5(2) stock) will be introduced with an August expiry such that contracts with January, February, May, and August expiries will be available. In February, contracts expiring in March will be introduced to replace the January options that expired and so on. The object is to maintain contracts with expiry in the two near months and two more distant months in existence at all times. The maximum term to expiry is eight months. The exercise prices of the new options are determined using the schedule shown in Table 18.1 and the proviso that their prices should bracket the current market price.

## OPTION EXPIRIES AVAILABLE – LISTED BY CYCLE AND BY MONTH

**CYCLE 5(1)**

| JAN | FEB | MAR | APR | MAY | JUN | JUL | AUG | SEP | OCT | NOV | DEC |
|---|---|---|---|---|---|---|---|---|---|---|---|
| JAN | FEB | MAR | APR | MAY | JUN | JUL | AUG | SEP | OCT | NOV | DEC |
| FEB | MAR | APR | MAY | JUN | JUL | AUG | SEP | OCT | NOV | DEC | JAN |
| APR | APR | JUL | JUL | JUL | OCT | OCT | OCT | JAN | JAN | JAN | APR |
| JUL | JUL | OCT | OCT | OCT | JAN | JAN | JAN | APR | APR | APR | JUL |

**CYCLE 5(2)**

| JAN | FEB | MAR | APR | MAY | JUN | JUL | AUG | SEP | OCT | NOV | DEC |
|---|---|---|---|---|---|---|---|---|---|---|---|
| JAN | FEB | MAR | APR | MAY | JUN | JUL | AUG | SEP | OCT | NOV | DEC |
| FEB | MAR | APR | MAY | JUN | JUL | AUG | SEP | OCT | NOV | DEC | JAN |
| MAY | MAY | MAY | AUG | AUG | AUG | NOV | NOV | NOV | FEB | FEB | FEB |
| AUG | AUG | AUG | NOV | NOV | NOV | FEB | FEB | FEB | MAY | MAY | MAY |

**CYCLE 5(3)**

| JAN | FEB | MAR | APR | MAY | JUN | JUL | AUG | SEP | OCT | NOV | DEC |
|---|---|---|---|---|---|---|---|---|---|---|---|
| JAN | FEB | MAR | APR | MAY | JUN | JUL | AUG | SEP | OCT | NOV | DEC |
| FEB | MAR | APR | MAY | JUN | JUL | AUG | SEP | OCT | NOV | DEC | JAN |
| MAR | JUN | JUN | JUN | SEP | SEP | SEP | DEC | DEC | DEC | MAR | MAR |
| JUN | SEP | SEP | SEP | DEC | DEC | DEC | MAR | MAR | MAR | JUN | JUN |

**HOW TO USE THIS CHART:** Look up the cycle and the month, e.g. Canadian Pacific is a Cycle 5(2). In March the options available are March, April, May and August. After the March expiry, move to the April column, March has been deleted, and November added on.

The
Toronto Futures
Exchange

*The Exchange*

**FIGURE 18-1**

Options expiry cycles.

*SOURCE:* Reprinted by permission of *The Toronto Stock Exchange, Derivative Markets Division.*

**TABLE 18.1**

Exercise Price Price Intervals for New Options for Different Prices of the Underlying Stock.

| Stock Price | Exercise Price Interval |
|---|---|
| Less than $20 | $1.00 |
| $20 to $30 | $1.00 or $2.50 (optional) |
| $30 to $75 | $2.50 |
| Over $75 | $5.00 |

*SOURCE:* Information provided by Derivatives Markets, Marketing, Toronto Stock Exchange, January 1992.

For example, if in January Canadian Pacific is selling for $18.50, then the two August call options introduced have exercise prices of $18 and $19; similarly, the two August put options have exercise prices of $18 and $19. Exchange officials acting in conjunction with the market makers have some latitude in setting the price and introduction date of additional options on a volatile stock.

An option remains listed until its expiry date. Listed options on common stocks generally expire on the Saturday after the third Friday of the specified month. Index options (to be discussed later) expire on the third Friday of the month. Trading ends on the last business day prior to the expiry date.

In the US option trading activity is rather more extensive than in Canada with common stock options traded on the Chicago Board Options Exchange (CBOE) and on the American, Pacific, Philadelphia, and New York Stock Exchanges.[3]

Figure 18.2 shows a portion of the daily listing of the trading activity of Trans Canada Options. The first row for each company shows the name of the company, the closing price of its shares and the option volume (Opt Vol). The option volume is the total number of contracts of all series of options on that stock which traded during the previous trading day. Indented below the name are the expiry month and exercise price (P for put, otherwise call) for each series followed by the bid and ask prices for each series, the last recorded premium, the number of contracts traded and the open interest. The open interest is the number of contracts outstanding in that series. For example, on April 24, 1992 Alcan Aluminum common stock closed at $25 \frac{1}{8}$. The prices for the last trades of Alcan June and August call options (with an exercise price of $25 per share) were $1.00 and $1.50, respectively. Similarly, the prices for the last trades of Alcan November put options (with an exercise price of $25) that stop trading on the third Friday of November were $1.75. The bid and ask prices were $1.65 and $1.80 respectively. If on a particular day some options are not traded there will be no record.

The last entries show the total volume (the number of contracts traded) and total open interest (the number of contracts outstanding) for calls and puts. The first entries of Figure 18.2 indicate the five "most active" options.

Investors may place the same kinds of orders for options as for stocks — market, limit, stop, and stop-limit orders (these were discussed in Chapter 2). However, the way the orders for options are executed on the exchanges is, in some ways, different from the way that orders for stocks are executed.

As mentioned in Chapter 2, trading on stock exchanges centers around market-makers. On the options trading floor of the TSE there are are also market-makers known as *specialists*. They serve two functions, acting as both dealers and brokers. As dealers, they set the bid and asked prices and keep an inventory of the options (and the underlying stocks) that are assigned to them. They buy into and sell from that inventory as required to maintain a market. As brokers, they keep the limit order book and execute the orders in it as market prices move up and down. There are also *competitive option traders* (COTs), who trade solely for their own account, hoping to buy low and sell high, and *floor traders*, who handle orders from the public.

Orders may be executed either by means of an auction at the trading post with "open outcry," (meaning that the auction is conducted orally) or entered electronically through the *Market Order System of Trading* (MOST). Option trading is, therefore, a hybrid system in the process of evolving towards full automation. The MOST system guarantees a complete fill at the current bid or offer price for every market and tradeable limit order

---

[3] For a detailed description of how options are created and traded in the US, see Chapter 3 of John C. Cox and Mark Rubinstein, *Options Markets* (Englewood Cliffs, N.J.: Prentice Hall, 1985).

# TRANS CANADA OPTIONS

Trans Canada Options combine Montreal, Toronto and Vancouver option trading. P is a put.

**Five most active TCO option classes**

| | Volume | Op Int |
|---|---|---|
| TSE 35 Index | 1310 | 9322 |
| Biochem Pharma | 707 | 43967 |
| Bombardier B | 583 | 5061 |
| Northern Tel | 437 | 3057 |
| Cdn Impl Bk | 397 | 3041 |

| Series | Bid | Ask | Last | Vol | Op Int |
|---|---|---|---|---|---|
| Air Canada | C $5¾ | | Opt Vol | | 22 |
| JY $6 | 35 | 45 | 35 | 11 | 26 |
| $6 P | 35 | 45 | 45 | 11 | 26 |
| Alcan Alumin. | C $25¼ | | Opt Vol | | 222 |
| MY $22½ | 260 | 280 | 255 | 30 | 520 |
| $22½ P | 5 | 20 | 10 | 20 | 1048 |
| $25 | 55 | 60 | 45 | 10 | 2482 |
| $25 P | 65 | 80 | 70 | 14 | 301 |
| JN $25 | 105 | 120 | 100 | 35 | 105 |
| AG $25 | 155 | 165 | 150 | 45 | 1057 |
| $25 P | 145 | 160 | 150 | 10 | 294 |
| $27½ | 55 | 60 | 60 | 5 | 1287 |
| NV $22½ | 370 | 395 | 395 | 20 | 31 |
| $25 | 205 | 220 | 205 | 8 | 316 |
| $25 P | 165 | 180 | 175 | 5 | 100 |
| $27½ | 90 | 105 | 85 | 20 | 20 |
| Amer Barrick | C $27¾ | | Opt Vol | | 88 |
| MY $32½ P | 495 | 5¼ | 500 | 2 | 9 |
| JN $27½ P | 115 | 140 | 130 | 10 | 40 |
| JY $27½ P | 140 | 165 | 145 | 10 | 282 |
| $30 | 90 | 105 | 90 | 10 | 253 |
| $32½ P | 495 | 5¼ | 5¼ | 5 | 55 |
| OC $27½ | 280 | 305 | 280 | 3 | 41 |
| $32½ P | 5⅛ | 5½ | 5¼ | 5 | 27 |
| $35 | 60 | 85 | 85 | 43 | 100 |
| Biochem Pharm | C $32¾ | | Opt Vol | | 707 |
| MY $28 P | 15 | 40 | 20 | 40 | 247 |
| $32 | 180 | 205 | 205 | 40 | 2241 |
| $32 P | 125 | 150 | 110 | 10 | 1181 |
| $34 | 90 | 115 | 90 | 20 | 1192 |
| $36 | 25 | 50 | 50 | 10 | 944 |
| JN $20 P | 15 | 40 | 25 | 17 | 871 |
| $24 P | 35 | 60 | 55 | 14 | 491 |
| $26 P | 70 | 95 | 95 | 10 | 258 |
| $28 | 6⅛ | 6½ | 6⅛ | 30 | 2246 |
| $28 P | 105 | 130 | 105 | 20 | 528 |
| $30 | 485 | 5¼ | 5¼ | 9 | 2360 |
| $30 P | 190 | 215 | 190 | 6 | 327 |
| $34 | 250 | 275 | 260 | 9 | 1401 |
| $36 | 185 | 210 | 215 | 252 | 7149 |
| JY $32 | 460 | 485 | 465 | 4 | 70 |
| $32 P | 340 | 365 | 340 | 4 | 14 |
| $36 | 275 | 300 | 300 | 9 | 251 |
| SP $30 | $7 | 7¾ | 7¾ | 40 | 38 |
| $32 | $6 | 6⅜ | 6½ | 3 | 617 |
| $36 | 420 | 445 | 420 | 160 | 1286 |
| Biomira Inc. | C $15¾ | | Opt Vol | | 272 |
| MY $15 P | 70 | 95 | 90 | 60 | 55 |
| $17 | 45 | 70 | 75 | 5 | 28 |
| $18 | 25 | 50 | 50 | 75 | 119 |
| $19 | 5 | 30 | 30 | 7 | 42 |
| JN $18 | 80 | 105 | 80 | 10 | 186 |
| $20 P | 475 | 500 | 470 | 10 | 23 |
| $22 | 15 | 40 | 45 | 7 | 109 |
| $22 P | 6½ | 6¾ | $7 | 5 | 120 |
| $23 P | 7½ | 7¼ | $8 | 8 | 37 |
| SP $15 P | 210 | 235 | 205 | 5 | 25 |
| $18 P | 195 | 220 | 200 | 30 | 271 |

| Series | Bid | Ask | Last | Vol | Op Int |
|---|---|---|---|---|---|
| $30 | 25 | 50 | 30 | 10 | 206 |
| DC $15 | 395 | 420 | 430 | 20 | 130 |
| $15 P | 270 | 295 | 270 | 2 | 2 |
| $19 | 255 | 280 | 250 | 5 | 20 |
| $19 P | 5⅛ | 5½ | 5½ | 13 | 13 |
| Bk of Montreal | C $43¾ | | Opt Vol | | 36 |
| JY $43 | 185 | 210 | 195 | 10 | 122 |
| $44 | 135 | 160 | 140 | 13 | 271 |
| $46 P | 250 | 275 | 245 | 10 | 32 |
| OC $42 P | 100 | 125 | 130 | 3 | 20 |
| Bk. of Nova Scot | C $19¾ | | Opt Vol | | 23 |
| SP $19 | 190 | 215 | 195 | 10 | 73 |
| $20 P | 110 | 135 | 115 | 3 | 80 |
| DC $20 | 180 | 205 | 195 | 10 | 10 |
| Bombardier B | C $14¼ | | Opt Vol | | 583 |
| JY $12½ P | 10 | 35 | 20 | 5 | 126 |
| $13 | 165 | 190 | 190 | 70 | 282 |
| $14 | 100 | 125 | 120 | 20 | 173 |
| $14 P | 50 | 75 | 55 | 10 | 17 |
| $14½ | 75 | 100 | 95 | 5 | 39 |
| $16 | 35 | 50 | 50 | 5 | 353 |
| $17 | 15 | 40 | 30 | 10 | 454 |
| OC $15 | 95 | 120 | 115 | 10 | 256 |
| $15½ | 75 | 100 | 85 | 200 | 202 |
| $16 | 60 | 85 | 80 | 10 | 232 |
| $17 P | 295 | 320 | 300 | 5 | 92 |
| JA $15 | 160 | 165 | 170 | 210 | 216 |
| $15 P | 165 | 190 | 160 | 23 | 33 |
| BCE Inc | C $43¾ | | Opt Vol | | 320 |
| JN $42½ P | 70 | 95 | 60 | 20 | 22 |
| $45 | 55 | 80 | 50 | 77 | 97 |
| $45 P | 200 | 225 | 165 | 10 | 10 |
| AG $45 P | 205 | 230 | 170 | 23 | 45 |
| $50 | 50 | 75 | 55 | 10 | 17 |
| $50 P | 6¾ | $7 | 5¼ | 2 | 33 |
| NV $42½ | 230 | 255 | 305 | 23 | 28 |
| $42½ P | 110 | 135 | 95 | 20 | 25 |
| $45 | 110 | 135 | 160 | 20 | 30 |
| $47½ | 50 | 65 | 75 | 100 | 185 |
| Canadian Pacific | C $17 | | Opt Vol | | 29 |
| MY $19 P | 185 | 210 | 175 | 10 | 39 |
| AG $19 P | 185 | 210 | 210 | 10 | 89 |
| Cascades Inc | C $7¾ | | Opt Vol | | 38 |
| DC $8 | 80 | 95 | 80 | 38 | 188 |
| Cdn Impl Bk | C $27 | | Opt Vol | | 397 |
| JN $30 P | 300 | 325 | 260 | 20 | 122 |
| $32 | 5 | 25 | 25 | 26 | 27 |
| $33 | 1 | 20 | 15 | 200 | 108 |
| SP $28 | 135 | 160 | 155 | 30 | 145 |
| $33 P | 5¾ | 6¼ | 5¾ | 5 | |
| DC $27 | 230 | 255 | 230 | 51 | 35 |
| $27 P | 150 | 175 | 130 | 20 | 56 |
| $28 | 185 | 210 | 220 | 45 | 170 |
| Corel Systems | C $20¼ | | Opt Vol | | 105 |
| MY $22½ | 35 | 60 | 50 | 20 | 40 |
| JN $20 | 175 | 200 | 200 | 10 | 20 |
| JY $15 | 5½ | $6 | 5¾ | 40 | 45 |
| $15 P | 20 | 45 | 25 | 10 | 60 |
| $22½ | 115 | 140 | 125 | 10 | 30 |
| OC $22½ | 215 | 250 | 215 | 10 | 28 |
| $25 P | 5¾ | 5¼ | 5¼ | 10 | 10 |
| CDA Jun 2021 9.7 | C 103¼ | | Opt Vol | | 20 |
| MY $100 | 295 | 320 | 295 | 20 | |
| CDA Mar 2011 9 | C $97¼ | | Opt Vol | | 12 |
| JN $98 | 85 | 110 | 80 | 10 | 76 |
| SP $100 | 85 | 100 | 90 | 2 | 17 |
| CDA Oct 2001 9.5 | C 102¾ | | Opt Vol | | 15 |

| Series | Bid | Ask | Last | Vol | Op Int |
|---|---|---|---|---|---|
| SP $102 | 170 | 195 | 185 | 10 | 34 |
| $103 | 130 | 155 | 145 | 5 | 9 |
| Deprenyl Res. | C $12¾ | | Opt Vol | | 147 |
| MY $14 | 40 | 50 | 50 | 67 | 89 |
| $16 | 5 | 30 | 20 | 10 | 61 |
| JN $13 | 130 | 155 | 155 | 6 | 6 |
| $14 | 85 | 110 | 95 | 10 | 10 |
| JY $15 | 90 | 115 | 110 | 10 | 150 |
| $16 | 65 | 90 | 75 | 30 | 132 |
| $18 | 40 | 65 | 50 | 4 | 164 |
| OC $20 | 60 | 85 | 75 | 10 | 208 |
| Domtar Inc | C $6¾ | | Opt Vol | | 10 |
| AG $9 P | 245 | 270 | 250 | 10 | 20 |
| Echo Bay Mines | C $6¾ | | Opt Vol | | 9 |
| JY $9 | 5 | 20 | 20 | 5 | 119 |
| OC $8 | 40 | 60 | 60 | 4 | 112 |
| Gulf Canada Res | C $7½ | | Opt Vol | | 98 |
| AG $8 | 65 | 90 | 75 | 98 | 170 |
| Hees Intl | C $15 | | Opt Vol | | 7 |
| MY $16 P | 85 | 110 | 85 | 7 | 10 |
| Imperial Oil Ltd | C $39¾ | | Opt Vol | | 195 |
| MY $40 | 65 | 80 | 75 | 10 | 382 |
| $45 | 1 | 20 | 15 | 125 | 209 |
| AG $42½ | 100 | 120 | 120 | 10 | 309 |
| NV $37½ P | 100 | 125 | 100 | 50 | 121 |
| Inco Ltd | C $34¼ | | Opt Vol | | 270 |
| MY $35 | 50 | 60 | 60 | 30 | 745 |
| $37½ | 10 | 20 | 10 | 10 | 618 |
| $37½ P | 350 | 375 | 360 | 20 | 491 |
| JN $35 | 110 | 125 | 115 | 30 | 100 |
| AG $37½ | 100 | 115 | 105 | 40 | 646 |
| NV $35 P | 270 | 295 | 275 | 80 | 150 |
| $37½ | 150 | 165 | 150 | 40 | 195 |
| $37½ P | 415 | 440 | 410 | 20 | 230 |
| Intl Corona Corp | C 425 | | Opt Vol | | 10 |
| NV $5 | 35 | 55 | 50 | 40 | 132 |
| John Labatt Ltd | C $24¾ | | Opt Vol | | 19 |
| NV $25 | 175 | 200 | 210 | 10 | 20 |
| Lac Minerals | C $7¼ | | Opt Vol | | 120 |
| JN $7 | 55 | 80 | 60 | 20 | 100 |
| SP $8 | 40 | 60 | 40 | 100 | 141 |
| Laidlaw Inc B | C $11¼ | | Opt Vol | | 22 |
| JN $11 | 65 | 70 | 70 | 7 | 1458 |
| $12 | 30 | 35 | 25 | 10 | 9284 |
| $13 P | 185 | 210 | 185 | 5 | 189 |
| Loewen Group | C $18½ | | Opt Vol | | 2 |
| JN $18 | 110 | 135 | 135 | 2 | 66 |
| Magne Intl Cl A | C $29¼ | | Opt Vol | | 15 |
| NV $29 P | 350 | 375 | 345 | 5 | 5 |
| Moore Corp Ltd | C $24¾ | | Opt Vol | | 15 |
| AG $25 | 130 | 150 | 140 | 10 | 140 |
| NV $25 | 185 | 210 | 190 | 5 | 5 |
| National Bank | C $8¾ | | Opt Vol | | 110 |
| AG $10 | 25 | 35 | 40 | 20 | 302 |
| NV $8 | 145 | 165 | 155 | 10 | 162 |
| $9 | 75 | 100 | 100 | 50 | 534 |
| $9 P | 55 | 80 | 60 | 10 | 339 |
| $10 | 35 | 60 | 50 | 20 | 536 |
| Noranda Inc. | C $16¾ | | Opt Vol | | 125 |
| NV $17 | 100 | 125 | 120 | 125 | 145 |
| Northern Tel | C $50¾ | | Opt Vol | | 125 |
| MY $50 P | 75 | 95 | 85 | 20 | 146 |
| $52½ P | 195 | 215 | 130 | 50 | 278 |
| $55 | 20 | 35 | 35 | 3 | 501 |
| JY $47½ P | 75 | 100 | 80 | 10 | 24 |
| $50 P | 160 | 180 | 125 | 40 | 184 |
| $52½ | 190 | 210 | 210 | 7 | 222 |

| Series | Bid | Ask | Last | Vol | Op Int |
|---|---|---|---|---|---|
| $52¾ P | 285 | 305 | 245 | 12 | 149 |
| $55 | 105 | 125 | 120 | 283 | 249 |
| OC $50 P | 230 | 250 | 190 | 10 | 30 |
| $55 | 240 | 260 | 250 | 7 | 197 |
| Nova Alta Corp | C $7¾ | | Opt Vol | | 30 |
| MY $8 | 10 | 15 | 15 | 20 | 3765 |
| AG $8 | 35 | 45 | 35 | 10 | 1401 |
| Petro-Canada | C $8¾ | | Opt Vol | | 12 |
| JN $11 P | 235 | 260 | 250 | 2 | 2 |
| DC $10 | 30 | 50 | 30 | 10 | 62 |
| Placer Dome | C $12 | | Opt Vol | | 93 |
| JN $12 P | 45 | 60 | 50 | 20 | 1643 |
| $13 | 20 | 35 | 25 | 20 | 1066 |
| SP $12 P | 75 | 95 | 95 | 5 | 208 |
| DC $13 | 90 | 105 | 90 | 48 | 68 |
| Potash Corp. | C $23¾ | | Opt Vol | | 5 |
| DC $25 P | 135 | 150 | 165 | 5 | 10 |
| Quadra Logic | C $8¾ | | Opt Vol | | 20 |
| OC $9 | 113 | 125 | 120 | 20 | 24 |
| Rogers Comm.B | C $13 | | Opt Vol | | 5 |
| JY $15 | 15 | 40 | 20 | 5 | 259 |
| Royal Bk Cda | C $23½ | | Opt Vol | | 15 |
| JY $26 | 35 | 50 | 30 | 10 | 794 |
| OC $25 | 95 | 115 | 125 | 5 | 116 |
| Royal Trustco | C $7¾ | | Opt Vol | | 46 |
| MY $8 P | 40 | 60 | 55 | 12 | 559 |
| $9 P | 135 | 155 | 145 | 8 | 90 |
| NV $8 P | 90 | 110 | 90 | 8 | 143 |
| $9 P | 160 | 180 | 160 | 18 | 138 |
| Seagram Co. | C $42¼ | | Opt Vol | | 114 |
| MY $145 | 155 | 180 | 150 | 100 | 125 |
| JN $140 | 5¼ | 6¼ | 6¼ | 5 | 13 |
| JY $145 | 455 | 500 | 450 | 9 | 513 |
| Shl Systemhouse | C $15¾ | | Opt Vol | | 10 |
| JN $17 P | 185 | 205 | 175 | 10 | |
| Telus Corp. | C $14¼ | | Opt Vol | | 15 |
| SP $16 | 10 | 20 | 10 | 15 | 225 |
| Transalta Utiliti | C $12¾ | | Opt Vol | | 20 |
| DC $13 | 35 | 50 | 45 | 20 | 40 |
| TransCda Pipe | C $16¾ | | Opt Vol | | 50 |
| NV $18 | 20 | 35 | 25 | 50 | 50 |
| TD Bank | C $16¾ | | Opt Vol | | 41 |
| MY $18 P | 115 | 140 | 100 | 6 | |
| JN $17 | 55 | 65 | 60 | 30 | 1051 |
| SP $18 | 45 | 65 | 60 | 5 | 850 |
| TSE 35 Index | C181.93 | | Opt Vol | | 1310 |
| MY $180 | 270 | 300 | 300 | 85 | 166 |
| $180 P | 145 | 175 | 145 | 115 | 506 |
| $182 | 140 | 160 | 160 | 140 | 124 |
| $182 P | 230 | 250 | 230 | 70 | 130 |
| $185 | 80 | 90 | 85 | 285 | 416 |
| $185 P | 390 | 420 | 390 | 200 | 317 |
| $187 | 35 | 55 | 50 | 65 | 194 |
| $187 P | 5⅛ | 6¾ | 5⅛ | 30 | 40 |
| $190 | 10 | 35 | 25 | 8 | 573 |
| JN $175 P | 115 | 135 | 120 | 20 | 193 |
| $180 | 265 | 285 | 225 | 31 | 549 |
| $185 | 205 | 235 | 240 | 45 | 151 |
| $185 P | 5⅛ | 5¼ | 430 | 7 | 844 |
| $190 | 110 | 130 | 115 | 150 | 895 |
| SP $175 P | 265 | 285 | 215 | 10 | 490 |
| $200 | 100 | 120 | 150 | 9 | 136 |
| TSE 35 Tips | C$18.30 | | Opt Vol | | 10 |
| SP $18¼ | 60 | 95 | 100 | 10 | 71 |
| Total contract volume | | | | | 6298 |
| Total open interest | | | | | 259638 |

**FIGURE 18-2**

Listed options quotations.

*SOURCE:* Reprinted by permission of *The Globe and Mail: Report on Business,* Thomson Newspapers Company Limited (April 25, 1992).

for 10 contracts or less, and provides immediate price confirmation electronically. In addition, MOST orders are transmitted to the floor. If a price that is better than the current bid or ask is available from a trader on the floor then a delayed, but improved fill will be confirmed.

More than one specialist may be assigned to the options on a given stock (a few have as many as seven). The specialists have the choice of maintaining either an open or a closed limit order book that, unlike the stock exchange limit order book, has manual entries. The information in an open book is available to all market participants, whereas that in a closed book is known only to the specialists. Specialists must provide a minimum guaranteed fill (MGF) that is generally ten contracts but some offer an MGF as large as 25 contracts. In addition they must ensure that the maximum spread between the bid and ask prices of options on a particular stock is not exceeded. A typical schedule is shown below in Table 18.2.

**TABLE 18.2**

Maximum Spread Between Bid and Ask Prices for Option Contracts.

| Option Price | Maximum Spread |
|---|---|
| below $1.00 | $0.10 |
| $1.00 to $2.00 | $0.15 |
| $2.00 to $5.00 | $0.25 |
| $5.00 to $10.00 | $0.375 |
| over $10.00 | $0.50 |

In North America all options are traded in continuous markets, meaning that orders can be executed any time the exchanges are open. Trading in options, however, is frequently far from continuous. In the financial press, it is not unusual to find prices for various options that appear to be out of line with one another or with the price of the underlying stock. It should be remembered that each listed price is that of the last trade recorded in the day and that these trades may have taken place at different times. Observed price disparities may simply reflect trading that occurred before and after major news, rather than concurrent values at which arbitrage trades could have been made.

Although a commission must be paid to a stockbroker whenever an option is either written, bought, or sold, the size of the commission has been reduced substantially since the 1970s when options began to be traded on organized exchanges. Furthermore, this commission is typically smaller than the commission paid if the underlying stock is purchased instead of the option. However, the investor should be aware that exercising an option typically results in both the writer and buyer having to pay commissions equivalent to those that would be incurred if the stock itself were being traded.

## 18.3  MARGIN

In contrast to a stock buyer, a call or put buyer is not allowed to use margin. The option buyer is required to pay 100% of the option's purchase price. The buyer of an option, however, would like some assurance that the writer can deliver as required if the option is exercised. Specifically, the buyer of a call option would like some guarantee that the writer is capable of delivering the requisite shares, and the buyer of a put option would like some guarantee that the writer is capable of delivering the necessary cash. Since all option contracts are with Trans Canada Options, Inc., the TCO is also concerned about the ability of the writer to fulfill the terms of the contract.

To relieve the TCO of this concern, writer's margin requirements have been set by the exchanges where the options are traded. However, brokerage firms, since they are ultimately liable to the TCO for the actions of their clients, are allowed to impose stricter requirements if they so desire.

If a call is exercised, shares are delivered by the writer in exchange for the exercise price. If a put is exercised, cash is delivered in exchange for shares. In either case, the cost to the option writer is the difference between the exercise price and the stock's market value at the time of exercise. Since the TCO is at risk if the writer is unable to bear this cost, it is not surprising that the TCO has a system in place that protects itself. This system is known as *margin*, and it is similar in some ways to the notion of margin associated with short sales of stocks (discussed in Chapter 2).

Before proceeding further some terminology must be defined. A call option is said to be *at the money* if the underlying stock has a market price roughly equal to the call's exercise price. If the stock's market price is below the exercise price, the call is said to be *out of the money*, and if the market price is above the exercise price, the call is said to be *in the money*. Occasionally finer gradations are invoked, and one hears of "near the money," "deep in the money," "far out of the money," and so on.

In a situation known as *covered call writing*, where the writer of a call owns the underlying stock, the writer does not need to provide any cash margin. If the option is out of the money, then the premium paid by the buyer is given to the writer but the writer's shares are kept in escrow by the brokerage firm.[4] Thus, if the buyer chooses to exercise the option, the requisite shares are at hand for delivery. If the option expires or if the writer enters a closing purchase, then the writer will have access to the shares. If, however, the share price moves up so that the option goes into the money the writer will be required to add the difference between the share and exercise prices to the margin account.

In situations known as *naked call writing*, where the writer of the option does not own the underlying stock, the margin requirements are slightly more complicated. Specifically, the amount that must be maintained in the margin account is the sum of three components: first, the option premium, second, 25% of the market value of the underlying stock, third, an amount equal to the share price less the exercise price. If the option is out of the money then the third figure will be negative. At no time, however, must the margin fall below the option premium plus 5% of the value of the stock. The amount required is the larger of these two calculations.

As an example of the margin required for naked call writing, consider an investor who writes a February $42 \frac{1}{2}$ call contract and receives, through his broker, a premium of $0.20 per share. If the underlying stock is selling for $39 \frac{1}{2}$, then the margin is calculated as follows:

Margin:

Option premium = $0.20 × 100 shares =     $ 20.00
25% of market value of stock =
   .25 × $39.5 × 100 shares =     $987.50

---

[4] The option writer may have purchased the shares on margin and, therefore, have borrowed 70% of the value of the stock from the broker.

Stock price less exercise price =
$$(39.5 - 42.5) \times 100 = \qquad -\$300.00$$
$$\text{Sum} = \$20 + 987.50 - 300 = \qquad \underline{\$707.50}$$
Check:

option premium plus 5% of value of stock = $217.50

therefore the amount required is $707.50.

Another investor, however, may have written a February 35 call on the same stock receiving a premium of $4.45. This writer will have to provide the following margin:

Actual Margin:

Option premium = $4.45 × 100 shares =      $445.00

25% of market value of stock =

    .25 × $39.5 × 100 shares =      $987.50

Stock price less exercise price =

$$(39.5 - 35) \times 100 = \qquad \underline{\$450.00}$$
$$\text{Sum} = \$445 + 987.50 + 450 = \qquad \underline{\$1{,}882.50}$$

Check:

option premium plus 5% of value of stock =   $642.50

therefore the amount required is $1,882.50.

In the first case, the writer need only add $687.50 to the margin account as the premium received is part of the total. In the second case, however, the writer must provide $1,437.50 of new money and can expect a margin call if the share price rises further. The minimum margin will only apply to options that are "deep out of the money."

For puts, the margin requirements are similar. If the brokerage account of the writer of a put contains cash (or other securities) amounting to the exercise price of the put, then no margin is required. Furthermore, the writer can remove from the account an amount of cash that is equal to the premium received. The reason for this is that the account will still have collateral that is equal in value to the exercise price.

If, however, the brokerage account of a put writer does not contain cash (or securities), then the process is known as *naked put writing*. The amount of margin required for such a writer is calculated in a manner similar to that for the writer of a naked call option. That is, the put writer must provide margin equal to the option premium plus 25% of the market value of the underlying stock plus the difference between the exercise price and the share price. For out of the money puts the third amount will be negative and will reduce the margin requirement. The minimum margin will again be equal to the sum of the option premium and 5% of the market price of the underlying security.

It should be noted that these are minimum maintenance margin requirements and that any adverse movement in the share price will result in a margin call. Furthermore, the calculation of margin requirements becomes much more complex when the individual is engaged in various investment activities (such as simultaneously buying and writing different put and call options as well as buying some common stocks on margin while short selling others).

# TAXATION OF OPTION PROFITS AND LOSSES

Revenue Canada's rules regarding the reporting of gains and losses incurred through options trading are not crystal clear, especially when dealing with naked option writing. As indicated in Chapter 10, the investor has the option of declaring that his or her investment gains or losses should be treated as either income or capital gains or losses as long as this is done consistently through time. Interpretation Bulletin 479R section 25 states that gains or losses incurred from either holding (buying) options or writing covered calls should be reported on the same account as the investor's transactions in shares. Writing naked calls, however, is different. Section 25 (c) states "the gain or loss realized by the writer of naked options is normally on income account. However, the Department will accept reporting of gains and losses on capital account provided the practice is followed consistently from year to year." Commissions paid are added to purchase prices and subtracted from selling prices in determining the amount of the capital gains or losses. Any frequent trader in options is subject to the risk of being deemed to be a "sophisticated or professional investor" and, therefore, required to report gains and losses as income (see section 11).

## Example 1

Consider a call option buyer. If the call is exercised, the buyer is considered to have bought the shares for a total cost equal to the exercise price plus the premium paid for the option itself (plus commissions). When the stock is subsequently sold, the difference between this cost and the selling price (less commissions) is the buyer's capital gain or loss. If the option expires out of the money (i.e., without being either closed out or exercised) then the cost of the option is treated as either a deduction from income or a capital loss depending on the investor's normal practice. If the call buyer later sells the option instead of exercising it, the gain or loss is the difference between the buying and selling prices (less commissions).

## Example 2

Consider the writer of a call option. If the call is exercised, the writer is considered to have sold the shares for a total value equal to the exercise price plus the premium received for the option (less commissions). The difference between this value and the price paid when the stock was purchased (plus commissions) is the amount of the gain or loss incurred by the writer. If the call writer later buys the option, thereby closing out his or her position, the difference between the premium that was received when the option was written and the premium that was paid to close out the position (less commissions) is the amount of the gain or loss. However, if the option expires unexercised, then the writer will have a gain equal to the amount of the premium received (less commissions).

## Example 3

The treatment of puts is similar. If the put expires unexercised, then the buyer has a loss and the writer has a gain equal to the premium on the put (adjusted for commissions). If a closing transaction is entered, then the difference between the buying and selling prices (adjusted for commissions) is the amount of the gain or loss. If the put is exercised, then the buyer has a gain equal to the exercise price less the amount paid for both the stock and the put (less commissions). The writer who receives the stock is treated as having made

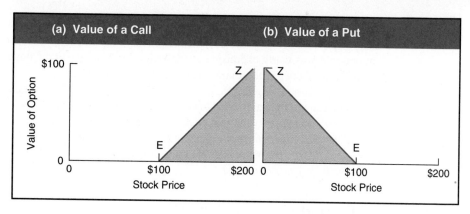

**FIGURE 18-3**
Values of options at expiration.

a stock purchase for an amount equal to the exercise price less the premium received on the put (less commissions).

These and other rules give rise to a number of strategies that take tax consequences into account. For example, consider an investor who owns a stock whose market price has risen dramatically. If the investor now sells it, a capital gain is incurred. However, if instead, the investor buys a January put and holds off selling the stock until the turn of the year, the capital gain is not realized until the following year, so no taxes need be paid in the current year. The gain on the stock will have been protected by the use of the put. In January, the investor can decide to either exercise the put or sell the stock, realizing the gain at that time, thus deferring tax payments for a year.

# 18.5 VALUATION OF OPTIONS

## ☐ 18.5.1 Valuation at Expiration

The value of an option is related to the value of the underlying security in a manner that is most easily seen just prior to expiration (which, for simplicity, will be referred to as *at expiration*). Figure 18.3(a) relates the value of a call option with an exercise price of $100 to the price of the underlying stock at expiration. If the share price is below $100, the option will be worthless when it expires. If the price is above $100, the option can be exercised for $100 to obtain a security with a greater value, resulting in a net gain to the option buyer that will equal the difference between the security's market price and the exercise price. However, there is no need for the option buyer actually to exercise the option. Instead, the option writer can simply pay the buyer the difference between the security price and the exercise price, thereby allowing both parties to avoid the inconvenience of exercise. This is commonly done for listed options (by using the services of the TCO), although a minority of investors choose to exercise their options, possibly for tax purposes.

Figure 18.3(b) shows the value at expiration of a put option with an exercise price of $100. If the stock price is above $100, the option will be worthless when it expires. If the price is below $100, the option can be exercised to obtain $100 for stock having a lower value, resulting in a net gain to the option buyer that will equal the difference between the exercise price and the stock's market price. As with a call option, neither the put option buyer or writer need actually deal in the stock. Instead, the writer of any put option that is worth exercising at expiration can simply pay the buyer of the option the difference between the share price and the exercise price.

In both parts of Figure 18.3, the lines indicating the value of a call and a put at expiration can also be interpreted to be the value of a call or put *at the moment the option is exercised*, no matter when that occurs during the life of the option. In particular, for calls the angled line connecting points $O$, $E$, and $Z$ is known as the *intrinsic value of the call*. Similarly, for puts the angled line connecting points $Z$, $E$, and \$200 is known as the *intrinsic value of the put*.

## ☐ 18.5.2 Profits and Losses at Expiration

Figure 18.3 shows the values of call and put options at expiration. However, in order to determine profits and losses from buying or writing these options, the premiums involved must be taken into consideration.[5] Figure 18.4 does this for investors who engage in simple option strategies as well as for investors who engage in some of the more complicated option strategies. Each strategy assumes the underlying stock is selling for \$100 at the time an option is initially bought or written. It is also assumed that closing transactions are made just prior to the expiration date for the option being considered. Outcomes are shown for each of five strategies. Since the profit obtained by a buyer is the writer's loss, and vice versa, each diagram in the figure has a corresponding mirror image.

Figure 18.4(a) and (b) show the profits and losses associated with buying and writing a call, respectively. Similarly, parts (c) and (d) show the profits and losses associated with buying and writing a put, respectively. It can be seen that parts (a) and (c) in Figure 18.4, other than reflecting the premiums paid, are identical to parts (a) and (b) in Figure 18.3.

Parts (e) and (f) in Figure 18.4 illustrate a more complicated options strategy known as a *straddle*. This strategy involves buying (or writing) both a call and a put on the same stock, with the options having the same exercise price and expiration date.[6] Note how part (e) can be obtained by adding the profits and losses shown in parts (a) and (c), where part (f) can be obtained by adding the profits and losses shown in parts (b) and (d). It can also be seen that parts (e) and (f) are mirror images of each other, again reflecting the fact that the profits to buyers equal the losses to writers, and vice versa.

Part (g) of Figure 18.4 shows the profit or loss made by an investor who avoids options entirely but buys a share of the underlying stock (at \$100) at the same time that others buy or write options and sells the stock when the options expire. Assuming

---

[5] Since the premium is paid by the buyer to the writer at the time the option is created, it should be compounded to an equivalent value at expiration using an appropriate rate of interest when calculating profits and losses.

[6] *Strips* and *straps* are options strategies similar to a straddle; the former involves combining two puts with one call and the latter involves combining two calls with one put. Another kind of strategy is known as a *spread*, where one call is bought while another is written on the same underlying security. Specifically, a price spread involves two calls having the same expiration date but different exercise prices; a time spread involves two calls having the same exercise price but different expiration dates.

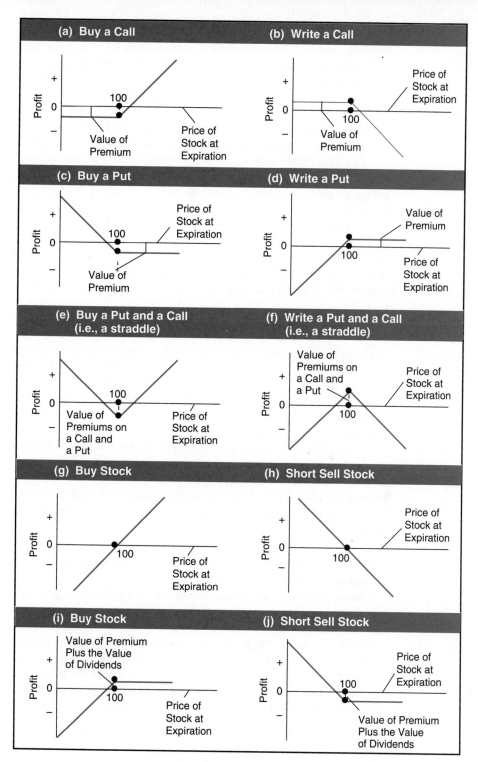

**FIGURE 18-4**
Profits and losses from various strategies.

no dividends are paid in the interim, the relationship is that shown by the solid line.[7] Similarly, part (h) shows the profit or loss obtained by an investor who short sells the stock at the initial date and then buys it back at the expiration date.

Part (i) of Figure 18.4 shows the results obtained by an investor who buys one share of stock and simultaneously writes a call on it; these results can be obtained by adding the profits and losses shown in parts (b) and (g). As mentioned earlier, such an investor is said to have written a fully covered option. In contrast, the writer who does not hold the underlying stock, depicted in part (b), is said to have written a naked option.

Part (j) of Figure 18.4 shows the results obtained by an investor who short sells one share of stock and simultaneously buys a call option; these results can be obtained by adding the profits and losses in parts (a) and (h). Note that this part is the mirror image of part (i).

Comparison of the diagrams in Figure 18.4 suggests that similar results can be obtained via alternative strategies. Parts (c) and (j) are similar, as are (d) and (i). Neither the premiums involved nor the initial investments required need be equal in every case. Nonetheless, the similarity of the results obtained with different packages of securities suggests that the total market values of the packages will be similar.

## ☐ 18.5.3 Limits on the Value of a Call Option

Consider three investments. The first is a call option having an exercise price of $E$ and an expiration date, measured in years, of .50 (that is, the expiration date is in six months); the second is the stock on which the option is written; and the third is a riskless investment. With regard to the riskless investment, it is assumed for simplicity that funds can be deposited in a bank at any time during the life of the option and thereafter will earn a fixed periodic risk-free rate.

What is the *most* an investor should pay for this call option? Remembering that the buyer of a call option has the right to purchase a share of stock, it is not sensible for an investor to pay more for the right to purchase a share of common stock than the current price of the share itself. That is, investors should be unwilling to pay more for a call option than for the price of the underlying share. This provides an upper limit on the value of the call:

$$P_c \leq P_s \tag{18.1}$$

where $P_c$ denotes the current market price of the call option and $P_s$ denotes the current market price of the underlying stock.

What is the *least* an investor should pay for a call option? Consider the position of an investor who buys one call option and deposits an amount of money into the bank account that pays the risk-free rate. The size of this deposit is equal to the present value of the exercise price, $PV(E)$. It is assumed for simplicity that no dividends will be paid on the common stock at any time up to the expiration date of the option.

Compare this position with a position consisting of the purchase of one share of the underlying common stock. At the expiration of the option, the underlying stock will be selling at a price either above or below the exercise price. If it is above the exercise

---

[7] If there are dividends, they should be expressed as a compounded value at the expiration date associated with the options (since they would have been previously received) and added to the line, thereby shifting it upwards.

price, then the investor should use the funds in the bank account to exercise the call option (remember, the deposit of PV($E$) will have earned the risk-free rate so that it will now be worth $E$). Doing so will deplete the bank account while providing the investor with one share of common stock. Thus, if the price of the shares at expiration is above the exercise price, both positions result in the investor owning a share of common stock and are thus of equivalent values.

However, the position of buying a call and making a bank deposit is of superior value if the common stock is selling for a price that is below the exercise price at expiration. In this situation the option is worthless, but the bank account will have a balance equal to the exercise price, $E$. Thus, part of $E$ can be used to purchase a share of common stock in the secondary market. The remaining balance in the account will represent the amount by which this position ended up being superior.

Since the investor who buys a call and makes the requisite bank deposit ends being better off in some cases and equally well off in other cases, it is logical that the initial cost of taking this position should be greater than the initial cost of buying a share of common stock. Thus, the following inequality should hold:

$$P_c + \text{PV}(E) \geq P_s \qquad (18.2)$$

where the left-hand side shows the cost of buying a call and making the requisite bank deposit and the right-hand side is simply the cost of purchasing a share of the underlying common stock. This inequality can be rearranged, resulting in the following lower limit on the price of a call option:

$$P_c \geq P_s - \text{PV}(E). \qquad (18.3)$$

As an example, consider a call option that has an exercise price of $100 and an expiration date that is nine months in the future. If the risk-free rate is 8% per year, the present value of the exercise price can be calculated as:

$$\text{PV}(\$100) = \frac{\$100}{(1 + .08)^{.75}}$$
$$= \$94.39$$

since nine months $= .75$ of a year. Thus, an investor could buy one call for a price equal to $P_c$, deposit $94.39 in a bank account that earns 8%, and have a position that is superior to buying one share of common stock at the current price of $P_s$. The reason for this superiority can be seen by examining the possible market values of the two positions at the expiration date of the call option.

On this date the bank deposit will have grown so that its balance is $100. If a share at that time is selling for more than $100, the call will be exercised using the entire bank balance. In this case the investor who bought the call and made the bank deposit is no better or worse off than if the stock had been purchased instead. However, if a share is selling at expiration for less than $100 — say, $80 — then the call option is worthless but the bank account has $100 in it. Thus, a share of stock could be bought for $80, leaving $20 in the bank account and resulting in the investor being better off than if a share of stock had been initially bought. Accordingly, the cost of buying the call and making the bank deposit must be greater than the cost of buying a share of the underlying stock, as indicated by inequality (18.2).

In addition to inequality (18.2), there is another lower limit to the price of a call option. Specifically, a call option cannot have a negative price. Here a negative price implies that a writer would pay a buyer to take a call option and hold onto it. This is not sensible because the buyer is not under any obligation to exercise the call option. Thus, a writer who pays a buyer to take and hold the option would simply be giving money away. Since this will not happen, there is a second lower limit on the price of a call:

$$P_c \geq 0. \tag{18.4}$$

These three inequalities — (18.1), (18.3), and (18.4) — provide a set of limits on the value of a call option (a set of three limits on the value of a put option is discussed shortly). If the market price of the call were to move outside one of these limits, there would be an opportunity for investors to make abnormal profits via arbitrage. Although transaction costs and taxes might make it unprofitable for some investors to take advantage of such situations, a substantial departure would certainly lead others to act, thereby setting in motion forces that would quickly bring the price of the call back within the limits.

In the example, imagine the option had a price of $7.00 when the stock was selling for $110 per share and there were nine months until expiration, so that PV($100) = $94.39. In this situation, inequality (18.3) does not hold, since the left-hand side is equal to $7.00, whereas the right-hand side is larger, being equal to $15.61 = $110 − $94.39. Consequently, an investor should immediately buy the call and make the requisite bank deposit, while simultaneously short selling the common stock. The cost of doing so would be $101.39 ($7.00 + $94.39), assuming that the bank deposit can be used to meet the initial margin requirement on the short sale. Once these transactions have been made, the investor will be certain of making more than the risk-free rate of return.

If at the end of nine months the stock is selling for more than $100 per share, the investor will exercise each call by using the $100 bank balance and then cover the short sale, getting back the short sale proceeds of $110. Thus, the investor's rate of return on the initial investment of $101.39 ($7.00 + $94.39) will be equal to ($110 − $101.39)/$101.39 = 8.49%.

If the stock price is less than $100 per share at expiration, then each call will be worthless when it expires, and part of the bank balance can be used to cover the short sale. Assuming the stock is selling for $90 per share at expiration, the bank account will have a $10 ($100 − $90) balance after the short sale is covered. Since the investor will then receive the short sale proceeds of $110, the rate of return on the $101.39 initial investment will be equal to ($10 + $110 − $101.39)/$101.39 = 18.39%. Furthermore, the lower the price, the greater the return.[8] Thus, it can be seen that if inequality (18.3) were violated, there would be an opportunity for investors to be certain of making at least 8.49% over nine months, which when annualized is notably greater than the 8% annual risk-free rate of return.

However, the ensuing large number of call purchases will cause the price of the calls ($7) to rise. Conversely, the large amount of short selling will cause the price of the underlying stock ($110) to fall. These prices will quickly adjust (perhaps to $12 and $104, respectively) until inequality (18.3) does hold.

---

[8] If the stock is at $100 per share on the expiration date, then the investor's rate of return will be ($0 + $110 − $101.39)/$101.39 = 8.49%. Share prices between $100 and $90 will provide the investor with a return between 8.49% and 18.39%.

In Figure 18.5 these limits are expressed as equalities. Specifically, inequalities (18.1), (18.3), and (18.4) are given by, respectively,

$$P_c = P_s \tag{18.5}$$

$$P_c = P_s - \text{PV}(E) \tag{18.6}$$

$$P_c = 0. \tag{18.7}$$

Each of these equations represents a straight line that is shown in the figure. These lines serve as boundaries of the shaded region, which indicates where the call option must be priced so that none of the limits are violated.

Figure 18.5 also shows the way the limits change as time passes and the expiration date becomes nearer. Note that the boundary corresponding to equation (18.6) moves to the right as the expiration date approaches, causing the shaded region to become larger. This occurs because the present value of the exercise price rises as the expiration date becomes nearer. That is, $\text{PV}(E)$ rises because the length of time $E$ is discounted is smaller. For example, if $E = \$100$, then discounting $\$100$ over four months will result in a larger figure than discounting $\$100$ over eight months. Ultimately, just prior to expiration the effect of discounting will be so negligible that $\text{PV}(E) = E$ and the boundary shown by equation (18.6) will simply be

$$P_c = P_s - E. \tag{18.8}$$

Note how this equation corresponds to the value of a call option moments before it expires, as indicated in Figure 18.3(a).

## ☐ 18.5.4 Valuation with Simple Price Changes

To make concrete some further principles of option valuation, it will prove helpful to deal with a rather simple kind of stock.[9] Figure 18.6(a) shows the general nature of its behavior. In any given period its price will either rise to ($P_{s,t+1}^+$) or fall to ($P_{s,t+1}^-$).

Looking ahead from time $t$ to time $t+1$, there are two possible states of the world — up (+) and down (−). Associated with each state is a known stock price; and a known probability ($p^+$ and $p^-$) that either will occur.

For every time and stock value there will be some corresponding value for a call option on the stock. These amounts are also indicated in Figure 18.6(a).

The final item in Figure 18.6(a) represents the results obtained by investing some amount of money, $X$, in the bank. It will grow to $(1 + R)$ times its initial value by the end of the period, and this return is certain. Equivalently, the risk-free rate of interest is fixed at $R$ per period.

All assumptions used previously will be retained. The option under study has an exercise price of $\$100$ and the stock will pay no dividends prior to expiration.

Figure 18.6(b) shows specific numeric values that will be used henceforth. The stock price is assumed to have a 60% chance of increasing 5% each period and a 40% chance

---

[9] This "binomial" approach to option valuation was initially presented by William F. Sharpe in the first edition of *Investments* (Englewood Cliffs, N.J.: Prentice Hall, 1978) and has been expanded upon by John C. Cox, Stephen A. Ross, and Mark Rubinstein, "Option Pricing: A Simplified Approach," *Journal of Financial Economics* 7, no. 3 (September 1979):229–63; and Richard J. Rendleman, Jr. and Brit J. Bartter, "Two-State Option Pricing," *Journal of Finance* 34, no. 5 (December 1979):1093–1110.

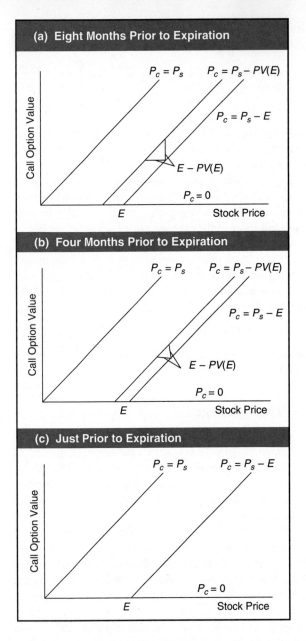

**FIGURE 18-5**
Limits on the values of a call option.

of decreasing 5%; its expected return thus equals $(.6 \times +5) + (.4 \times -5)$, or 1% per period. The risk-free interest rate is half this, .5% per period (that is, $R = .005$).

Figure 18.6(c) fills in some more values. It covers the situation when the stock price is \$100 per share one period prior to expiration. The time of expiration is denoted by T, one period prior to expiration, $T - 1$, two periods prior, $T - 2$, and so on.

There is a good reason for starting with the period prior to expiration. At expiration, the option value associated with every possible stock price is known: It is $(P_{s,T} - E)$

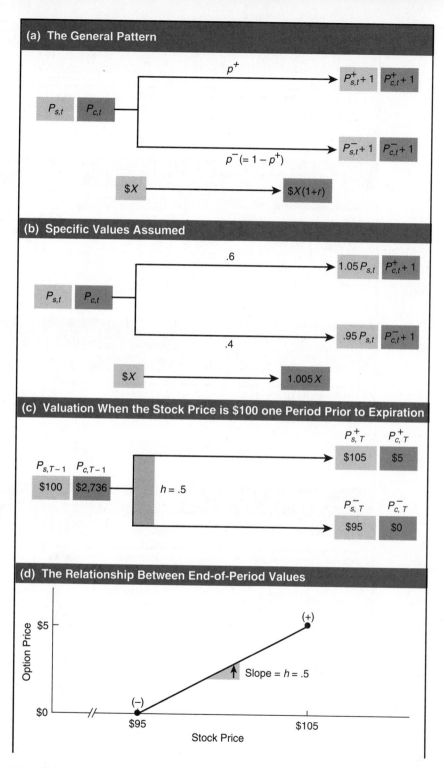

**FIGURE 18-6**
Stock and option prices.

**(e) Balance Sheets for a Hedged Position**

| Time: $T-1$ | | Time: $T$ | | | |
|---|---|---|---|---|---|
| | | State: + | | State: − | |
| 1/2 Share of Stock $50 | 1 Option: $P_{c,T-1}$ Net Worth: $50 - P_{c,e-1}$ | 1/2 Share of Stock $52.50 | 1 Option: $5 Net Worth: $47.50 | 1/2 Share of Stock $47.50 | 1 Option: $0 Net Worth: $47.50 |

**(f) Balance Sheets for a Hedged Position When the Option is Correctly Priced**

| Time: $T-1$ | | Time: $T$ | | | |
|---|---|---|---|---|---|
| | | State: + | | State: − | |
| 1/2 Share of Stock $50 | 1 Option: $2.736 Net Worth: 47.264 | 1/2 Share of Stock $52.50 | 1 Option: $5 Net Worth: $47.50 | 1/2 Share of Stock $47.50 | 1 Option: $0 Net Worth: $47.50 |

$$\text{Return} = \frac{\$47.50 - \$47.264}{\$47.264} = .005 = .5\%$$

**(g) Balance Sheets for a Hedged Position When the Option is Overpriced**

| Time: $T-1$ | | Time: $T$ | | | |
|---|---|---|---|---|---|
| | | State: + | | State: − | |
| 1/2 Share of Stock $50 | 1 Option: $2.80 Net Worth: 47.20 | 1/2 Share of Stock $52.50 | 1 Option: $5 Net Worth: $47.50 | 1/2 Share of Stock $47.50 | 1 Option: $0 Net Worth: $47.50 |

$$\text{Return} = \frac{\$47.50 - \$47.20}{\$47.20} = .006 = .6\%$$

**(h) Balance Sheets for a Reverse Hedge When the Option is Underpriced**

| Time: $T-1$ | | Time: $T$ | | | |
|---|---|---|---|---|---|
| | | State: + | | State: − | |
| 1 Option: $2.60 Bank Account: $50 | 1/2 Share of Stock: $50 Net Worth: $2.60 | 1 Option: $5 Bank Account: $50.25 | 1/2 Share of Stock: $50.25 Net Worth: $2.75 | 1 Option: $0 Bank Account: $50.25 | 1/2 Share of Stock: $47.50 Net Worth: $2.75 |

$$\text{Return} = \frac{\$2.75 - \$2.60}{\$2.60} = .058 = 5.8\%$$

**FIGURE 18-6**
*(Continued)*

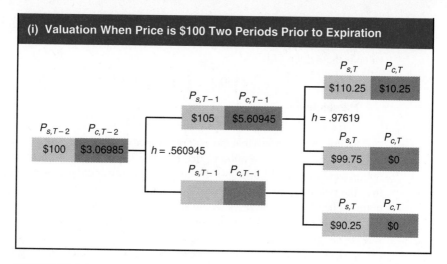

**(i) Valuation When Price is $100 Two Periods Prior to Expiration**

|  | $P_{s,T-2}$ | $P_{c,T-2}$ |
|  | $100 | $3.06985 |

$h = .560945$

| $P_{s,T-1}$ | $P_{c,T-1}$ |
| $105 | $5.60945 |

$h = .97619$

| $P_{s,T-1}$ | $P_{c,T-1}$ |

| $P_{s,T}$ | $P_{c,T}$ |
| $110.25 | $10.25 |

| $P_{s,T}$ | $P_{c,T}$ |
| $99.75 | $0 |

| $P_{s,T}$ | $P_{c,T}$ |
| $90.25 | $0 |

**FIGURE 18-6**
*(Continued)*

or zero, whichever is larger. In the situation shown in Figure 18.6(c), the end-of-period option value will be either $5 or $0.

What does this imply for the price of the option at the beginning of the period — that is, how was the box for $P_{c,T-1}$ in Figure 18.6(c) filled in? Not surprisingly, by analogy, as is shown next.

Figure 18.6(d) plots the end-of-period values for the stock and the option. Since there are only two possibilities, all (two) of the points lie on a straight line. The securities' returns are perfectly positively correlated. Whenever this is the case, it is possible to *hedge* one against the other and eliminate all risk.

The difference between the share prices in the two states is $10; the difference between the option prices is $5. It is possible to hold stock and write a call option and to arrange the proportions so that the differences in payoffs in the two positions are exactly equal. The investor's end-of-period net worth will then be the same in either event. In this case, the appropriate *hedge ratio* is .5; for every option written (sold), one-half a share of stock should be purchased. More generally, the appropriate hedge ratio, denoted by $h$, is simply the difference between the end-of-period option values, divided by the difference between the end-of-period stock values:

$$h = \frac{P_{c,t+1}^+ - P_{c,t+1}^-}{P_{s,t+1}^+ - P_{s,t+1}^-}. \tag{18.9}$$

Figure 18.6(e) shows how this can be employed. An investor buys half a share of stock and sells one call option. The initial investment required is $50 minus the (yet-to-be-determined) price received for writing the option. The value of the "portfolio" at the end of the period will be $47.50, *no matter which state occurs*. The investor has set up a *risk-free hedge* by using the appropriate hedge ratio indicated by equation (18.9).

Now for the analogy where $t + 1 = T$. The rate of interest on a risk-free investment also returns .5% per period. Since the ending value will be $47.50, the required option value is that which satisfies

$$(\$50 - P_{c,T-1})1.005 = \$47.50.$$

The solution is

$$P_{c,T-1} = \$2.736.$$

Figure 18.6(f) shows that the hedging strategy will in fact give a certain return equal to the risk-free rate if the option price equals $2.736. Figure 18.6(g) shows that if the option were overpriced, at $2.80, the hedging strategy could give a certain return greater than the risk-free rate. Such a situation would attract attention, bringing out would-be option sellers whose activities would shortly drive the price back down.

What if the option were underpriced, say at $2.60? Then clever investors could *reverse hedge*, buying options and selling stock. Figure 18.6(h) shows a case in which the stock is sold short and the proceeds placed in an interest-earning bank account.[10] A certain 5.8% per period is returned on invested funds. Such a situation would attract would-be option buyers, driving the price back up.

Figure 18.6(f) thus portrays the likely situation and an option pricing formula. The option price at time $t$ must satisfy:

$$(hP_{s,t} - P_{c,t})(1 + R) = \begin{Bmatrix} [hP^+_{s,t+1} - P^+_{c,t+1}] \\ [hP^-_{s,t+1} - P^-_{c,t+1}] \end{Bmatrix} \qquad (18.10)$$

where $h$ is the hedge ratio required to give a risk-free return. The first expression in parentheses on the left represents the funds invested at the beginning of the period. The brackets on the right indicate that either of the two included expressions can be used, for they are both equal to the certain end-of-period value. The formula simply requires the option to be priced so that a portfolio hedged to remove all risk will return the risk-free rate on the funds invested.

Having established the principles summarized in equations (18.9) and (18.10), it is possible to determine the option value for any time and stock price. Figure 18.6(i) does this for the case in which the stock price is $100 per share two periods prior to expiration. The option price boxes are filled in from right to left. Option values at expiration are simply $(P_s - 100)$ or zero, whichever is larger. This takes care of the option values at time $T$.

Turning to time $T - 1$, note that if a situation will lead to a worthless option no matter what, the option is already worthless. Thus if the stock price is $95 per share one period prior to expiration, the option will definitely expire worthless, and the option value is zero. This takes care of another box.

Turning to the situation in which the stock price is $105 per share one period prior to expiration, equation (18.9) is used to determine the hedge ratio (.97619) and then equation (18.10) applied to determine the option price ($5.60945).

---

[10] This is generally not possible in practice, lowering or eliminating the profit from such a hedge and raising the possibility that the option could sell at any price within a band limited by the prices at which hedging or reverse hedging would become profitable.

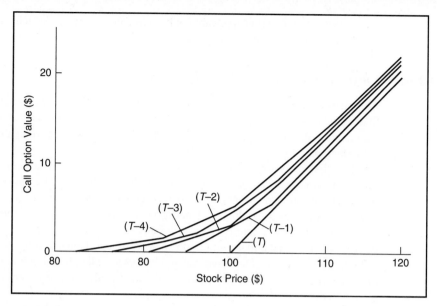

**FIGURE 18-7**
Option values at various times prior to expiration (based on the numeric example in Figure 18.6).

To find the remaining hedge ratio (.560945) and option price ($3.06985), equations (18.9) and (18.10) are applied again using the relevant share values ($105 and $95) and the previously computed associated option values ($5.60945 and $0).

Figure 18.7 shows some values obtained with this kind of *recursive* calculation. Each curve plots option values associated with various stock prices at a specific time prior to expiration.

One characteristic of the curves in Figure 18.7 is quite general:

> If two call options are otherwise identical but one has a longer time remaining before expiration, the longer one will be worth at least as much as the shorter one and generally will be worth more.

## 18.6 THE BLACK-SCHOLES MODEL FOR CALL OPTIONS

In a world with neither taxes nor transactions costs, an investor could adjust hedge positions continously. The effective length of a period would thus be very small. The smaller the length of each period, the closer the value of a call option calculated in the manner described in the previous section would be to that given by an option valuation formula developed by Black and Scholes.[11] This model can be used to determine the fair (or true) value of a call and was initially developed for call options on stocks that will not pay any dividends between the time the option is written and the time it expires.

---

[11] Fischer Black and Myron Scholes, "The Pricing of Options and Corporate Liabilities," *Journal of Political Economy* 81, no. 3 (May/June 1973):637–54.

Furthermore, the model is applicable only to *European options*, which are options that can be exercised only on their expiration dates.

## ☐ 18.6.1 Limitations on the Model's Use

At first, this model might seem to have limited use, since almost all options in the United States are known as *American options*, meaning they can be exercised at any time up to their expiration date. Furthermore, most of the common stocks on which they are written do, in fact, pay dividends.

The first drawback of the Black-Scholes model — that it is only applicable to European options — can be dispensed with rather easily when the option is a call and the underlying stock does not pay dividends. This is because it has been shown that it is unwise for an investor holding an American call option on a non-dividend-paying stock to exercise it prior to maturity.[12] Since there is no reason for exercising such an option prior to maturity, the opportunity to do so is worthless. Consequently, there will be no difference in the value of an American and European call option. In turn, this means that the Black-Scholes model can be used to estimate the fair value of American call options on non-dividend-paying stocks.

Figure 18.8 shows why the Black-Scholes model can be used. As mentioned earlier, the value of an option if it were exercised immediately is known as its intrinsic value. This value is equal to zero if the option is out of the money. However, it is equal to the difference between the share price and exercise price if the option is in the money. The excess of the price of the option over its intrinsic value is the option's *time value* (or time premium). As shown in Figure 18.3(a) for call options, at expiration the time value is zero. However, before then the time value is positive. Note that a call option's premium is simply the sum of its intrinsic and time values.

An investor considering exercising a call option on a non-dividend-paying stock prior to its expiration date will always find it cheaper to sell the call option and purchase the stock in the marketplace. This is because exercising the call will result in the investor losing the time value of the option (hence the expression that call options are "worth more alive than dead").

For example, consider a stock that has a current price of $110 per share. If this stock has a call option with an exercise price of $100 that is selling for $14, then the intrinsic and time values of this option are $10 ($110 − $100) and $4 ($14 − $10), respectively. An investor who owns one of these calls could exercise it by spending an additional $100. However, it would be cheaper for the investor to get the share of stock by selling the call option and buying the share of stock in the marketplace, since the additional cost would only be $96 ($110 − $14).

The second drawback of the Black-Scholes model — that it is only applicable to non-dividend-paying stocks — cannot be easily dismissed, since many call options are written on stocks that will pay dividends during the life of the option. In this situation, some procedures have been suggested on how this formula can be amended in order to value call options on such stocks. One of these procedures is presented later.

---

[12] See Robert C. Merton, "Theory of Rational Option Pricing," *Bell Journal of Economics and Management Science* 4, no. 1 (Spring 1973):141–83.

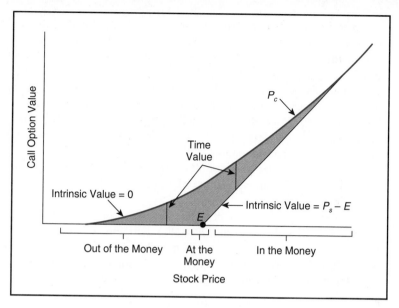

**FIGURE 18-8**
Option terminology for calls.

## 18.6.2 The Formula

In the absence of taxes and transactions costs, the fair value of a call option can be estimated by using the formula developed by Black and Scholes. It has been widely used by those who trade options to search for situations where the market price of an option differs substantially from its fair value. A call option that is found to be selling for substantially less than its Black-Scholes value is a candidate for purchase, whereas one that is found to be selling for substantially more is a candidate for writing. The Black-Scholes formula for estimating the fair value of a call option ($V_c$) is

$$V_c = P_s N(d_1) - \frac{E}{e^{RT}} N(d_2)$$  (18.11)

where:

$$d_1 = \frac{\ln(P_s/E) + (R + .5\sigma^2)T}{\sigma\sqrt{T}}$$  (18.12)

$$d_2 = \frac{\ln(P_s/E) + (R + .5\sigma^2)T}{\sigma\sqrt{T}}$$  (18.13a)

$$= d_1 - \sigma\sqrt{T}$$  (18.13b)

and where:
$P_s$ is the current market price of the underlying stock
$E$ is the exercise price of the option
$R$ is the continuously compounded risk-free rate of return expressed on an annual basis
$T$ is time remaining before expiration expressed as a fraction of a year

$\sigma$ is the risk of the underlying common stock, measured by the standard deviation of the continuously compounded annual rate of return on the stock.

Mathematically, $e$ is the base of natural logarithms and is approximately equal to 2.71828. This means that $E/e^{RT}$ is the present value of the exercise price when a continuous discount rate is used (it is analagous to $E/(1+R)^T$, the present value of the exercise price using a discrete discount rate). The quantity $\ln(P_s/E)$ is the natural logarithm of $P_s/E$. Lastly, $N(d_1)$ and $N(d_2)$ denote the probabilities that deviations of less than $d_1$ and $d_2$, respectively, will occur in a normal distribution that has a mean of 0 and a standard deviation of 1.

Table 18.3 provides values of $N(d)$ for various levels of $d$.[13] This table and a pocket calculator are all that are needed in order to use the Black-Scholes formula for valuing a call option.

For example, consider a call option that expires in three months and has an exercise price of \$40 (thus, $T = .25$ and $E = 40$). Furthermore, the current price and risk of the underlying common stock are \$36 and 50%, respectively, whereas the risk-free rate is 5% (thus, $P_s = 36$, $R = .05$, and $\sigma = .50$). Solving equations (18.12) and (18.13b) provides the following values for $d_1$ and $d_2$:

$$d_1 = \frac{\ln(36/40) + [.05 + .5(.50)^2].25}{.50\sqrt{.25}} = -.25$$

$$d_2 = -.25 - .50\sqrt{.25} = -.50.$$

Table 18.3 can be used to find the corresponding values of $N(d_1)$ and $N(d_2)$:

$$N(d_1) = N(-.25) = .4013$$
$$N(d_2) = N(-.50) = .3085.$$

Finally, equation (18.11) can be used to estimate the fair value of this call option:

$$V_c = (36 \times .4013) - \left(\frac{40}{e^{.05 \times .25}} \times .3085\right) = \$2.26.$$

If this call option is currently selling for \$5, the investor should consider writing some of them. This is because they are overpriced (according to the Black-Scholes model), suggesting that their price will fall in the near future. Thus, the writer would receive a premium of \$5 and would expect to be able to enter a closing buy order later for a lower price, making a profit on the difference. Conversely, if the call option were selling for \$1, the investor should consider buying some of them. This is because they are underpriced and can be expected to rise in value in the future.

---

[13] Table 18.3 is an abbreviated version of a standard cumulative normal distribution table. More detailed versions can be found in most statistics textbooks.

**TABLE 18.3**
Values of $N(d)$ for Selected Values of $d$.

| $d$ | $N(d)$ | $d$ | $N(d)$ | $d$ | $N(d)$ |
|---|---|---|---|---|---|
| | | −1.00 | .1587 | 1.00 | .8413 |
| −2.95 | .0016 | −.95 | .1711 | 1.05 | .8531 |
| −2.90 | .0019 | −.90 | .1841 | 1.10 | .8643 |
| −2.85 | .0022 | −.85 | .1977 | 1.15 | .8749 |
| −2.80 | .0026 | −.80 | .2119 | 1.20 | .8849 |
| −2.75 | .0030 | −.75 | .2266 | 1.25 | .8944 |
| −2.70 | .0035 | −.70 | .2420 | 1.30 | .9032 |
| −2.65 | .0040 | −.65 | .2578 | 1.35 | .9115 |
| −2.60 | .0047 | −.60 | .2743 | 1.40 | .9192 |
| −2.55 | .0054 | −.55 | .2912 | 1.45 | .9265 |
| −2.50 | .0062 | −.50 | .3085 | 1.50 | .9332 |
| −2.45 | .0071 | −.45 | .3264 | 1.55 | .9394 |
| −2.40 | .0082 | −.40 | .3446 | 1.60 | .9452 |
| −2.35 | .0094 | −.35 | .3632 | 1.65 | .9505 |
| −2.30 | .0107 | −.30 | .3821 | 1.70 | .9554 |
| −2.25 | .0122 | −.25 | .4013 | 1.75 | .9599 |
| −2.20 | .0139 | −.20 | .4207 | 1.80 | .9641 |
| −2.15 | .0158 | −.15 | .4404 | 1.85 | .9678 |
| −2.10 | .0179 | −.10 | .4602 | 1.90 | .9713 |
| −2.05 | .0202 | −.05 | .4801 | 1.95 | .9744 |
| −2.00 | .0228 | .00 | .5000 | 2.00 | .9773 |
| −1.95 | .0256 | .05 | .5199 | 2.05 | .9798 |
| −1.90 | .0287 | .10 | .5398 | 2.10 | .9821 |
| −1.85 | .0322 | .15 | .5596 | 2.15 | .9842 |
| −1.80 | .0359 | .20 | .5793 | 2.20 | .9861 |
| −1.75 | .0401 | .25 | .5987 | 2.25 | .9878 |
| −1.70 | .0446 | .30 | .6179 | 2.30 | .9893 |
| −1.65 | .0495 | .35 | .6368 | 2.35 | .9906 |
| −1.60 | .0548 | .40 | .6554 | 2.40 | .9918 |
| −1.55 | .0606 | .45 | .6736 | 2.45 | .9929 |
| −1.50 | .0668 | .50 | .6915 | 2.50 | .9938 |
| −1.45 | .0735 | .55 | .7088 | 2.55 | .9946 |
| −1.40 | .0808 | .60 | .7257 | 2.60 | .9953 |
| −1.35 | .0885 | .65 | .7422 | 2.65 | .9960 |
| −1.30 | .0968 | .70 | .7580 | 2.70 | .9965 |
| −1.25 | .1057 | .75 | .7734 | 2.75 | .9970 |
| −1.20 | .1151 | .80 | .7881 | 2.80 | .9974 |
| −1.15 | .1251 | .85 | .8023 | 2.85 | .9978 |
| −1.10 | .1357 | .90 | .8159 | 2.90 | .9981 |
| −1.05 | .1469 | .95 | .8289 | 2.95 | .9984 |

## ☐ 18.6.3 Static Analysis

Close scrutiny of the Black-Scholes formula reveals some interesting features of European call option pricing. In particular, it can be noticed that the fair value of a call option is dependent on five inputs — the market price of the common stock ($P_s$), the exercise price of the option ($E$), the length of time until the expiration date ($T$), the risk-free rate ($R$), and the risk of the common stock ($\sigma$). What happens to the fair value of a call option when one of these inputs is changed while the other four remain the same?

1. The higher the price of the underlying stock ($P_s$), the higher the value of the call option.
2. The higher the exercise price ($E$), the lower the value of the call option.
3. The longer the time to the expiration date ($T$), the higher the value of the call option.
4. The higher the risk-free rate ($R$), the higher the value of the call option.
5. The greater the risk ($\sigma$) of the common stock, the higher the value of the call option.

Of these five factors, the first three ($P_s$, $E$, and $T$) are readily determined. The fourth factor, the risk-free rate, is often estimated by using the yield-to-maturity on a Treasury bill having a maturity date close to the expiration date of the option. The fifth factor, the risk of the underlying stock, is not readily observed; consequently, various methods for estimating it have been proposed. Two of these methods are presented next.

## ☐ 18.6.4 Estimating a Stock's Risk from Historical Prices

One method for estimating the risk of the underlying common stock associated with a call option involves analyzing historical prices of the shares. Initially, a set of $n + 1$ market prices on the underlying shares must be obtained from either financial publications like *The Globe and Mail: Report on Business* or a computer database. These prices are then used to calculate a set of $n$ continuously compounded returns as follows:

$$r_t = \ln\left(\frac{P_{st}}{P_{st-1}}\right) \qquad (18.14)$$

where $P_{st}$ and $P_{st-1}$ denote the market price of the underlying shares at times $t$ and $t - 1$, respectively. Here, ln denotes the natural logarithm of the quantity $P_{st}/P_{st-1}$, which gives a continuously compounded return.

For example, the set of market prices for the shares might consist of the closing price at the end of each of 53 weeks. If the price at the end of one week were $105 and the price at the end of the next week were $107, then the return $r_t$ would be equal to $\ln(107/105) = 1.886\%$. Similar calculations will result in a set of 52 returns.

Having calculated a set of $n$ returns on the stock, the next step involves using them to estimate the stock's average return:

$$ar = \frac{1}{n}\sum_{t=1}^{n} r_t. \qquad (18.15)$$

The average return is then used in estimating the per-period variance (that is, the square of the per-period standard deviation):

$$s^2 = \frac{1}{n-1}\sum_{t=1}^{n}(r_t - ar)^2. \qquad (18.16)$$

This is called the per-period variance because its size is dependent on the length of time over which each return is measured. In the example, weekly returns were calculated and would lead to the estimation of a weekly variance. Alternatively, daily returns could have been used, leading to a daily variance that would be of smaller magnitude than the weekly variance. However, what is needed is not either a weekly or daily variance but an annual variance. This is obtained by multiplying the per-period variance by the number of periods in a year. Thus, an estimated weekly variance would be multiplied by 52 in order to estimate the annual variance, $\sigma^2$ (that is, $\sigma^2 = 52\,s^2$). Alternatively, subjective estimates of the probabilities of possible future prices can be made and then used to estimate the total risk of the stock. Lastly, it is possible to combine these two methods to arrive at an estimate.

For any estimate of future uncertainty, historical data are helpful but not definitive. And since recent data may prove more meaningful than older data, some analysts study daily price changes over the most recent 6 to 12 months, sometimes giving more weight to later days than to earlier ones. Others take into account the price histories of related stocks and the possibility that a stock whose price has recently decreased may be more risky in the future than it was in the past. Still others make explicit subjective estimates of the future, taking into account changes in uncertainty concerning the economy in general as well as uncertainty in specific industries and in stocks.

In some cases, an analyst's estimate of a stock's risk over the next three months may differ from that for the following three months, leading to the use of different values of $\sigma$ for call options on the same stock when these options have different expiration dates.

## ☐ 18.6.5 The Market Consensus of a Stock's Risk

Another way to estimate a stock's risk is based on the assumption that a currently outstanding call option is fairly priced in the marketplace. Since this means that $P_c = V_c$, the current market price of the call ($P_c$) can be entered in place of the fair value of the call ($V_c$) on the left-hand side of equation (18.11). Next, all the other factors except for $\sigma$ are entered on the right-hand side, and the resulting equation is solved for $\sigma$, the only unknown variable. The solution for $\sigma$ can be interpreted as representing a consensus opinion in the marketplace on the size of the stock's risk and is known as the stock's *implicit volatility*.

For example, assume that the risk-free rate is 6% and that a six-month option with an exercise price of $40 sells for $4 when the price of the underlying stock is $36 per share. Different estimates of $\sigma$ can be substituted into the right-hand side of equation (18.11) until a value of $4 for this side of the equation is obtained. In this example, an estimated value of .40 (that is, 40%) for $\sigma$ will result in a number for the right-hand side of equation (18.11) that is equal to $4, which is the current market price of the option that is on the left-hand side.

The procedure can be modified by applying it to several call options on the same stock. For example, $\sigma$ can be estimated for each of several call options on the same stock that have different exercise prices but the same expiration date. Then, the resulting estimates for $\sigma$ can be averaged and, in turn, used to determine the fair value of another call option on the same stock having yet another exercise price but a similar expiration date.

In the example, $\sigma$ can be estimated not only for a six-month option having an exercise price of $40 but also for six-month options having exercise prices of $35 and $45. Then, the three estimates of $\sigma$ can be averaged to produce a "best estimate" of $\sigma$, which is used to value a six-month $50 option on the same stock.

Alternatively, the procedure can be modified by averaging the estimates for $\sigma$ associated with each of several expiration dates. In the example, $\sigma$ can be estimated not only for a six-month option having an exercise price of $40 but also for three-month and nine-month options that have an exercise price of $40. The three estimates of $\sigma$ can be averaged to produce a best estimate of $\sigma$, which is subsequently used to determine the fair value of a one-month $40 option on the same stock.

There are other ways of using a set of estimates of $\sigma$ that correspond to different call options on the same stock. Perhaps $\sigma$ will be estimated for a set of calls having different expiration prices and different exercise prices and then averaged. Perhaps $\sigma$ will be estimated from historical returns using equation (18.14), with the resulting figure averaged with one or more estimates of the stock's implicit volatility. While it is still too early to tell, it appears that methods based on calculating implicit volatilities are better than methods based on historical returns.[14]

## □ 18.6.6 Hedge Ratios

The curve in Figure 18.8 shows the relationship between the Black-Scholes value of a call option and the price of the underlying stock. The slope of this curve at any point represents the expected change in the value of the option per dollar change in the price of the underlying common stock. This amount is known as the *hedge ratio* (or delta) of the call option and is equal to $N(d_1)$ in equation (18.11). As can be seen in Figure 18.8 (assuming the market price of the call is equal to its Black-Scholes value), the slope (that is, the hedge ratio) of the curve is always positive. Furthermore, if the stock has a relatively low market price the slope will be near 0; for higher stock prices the slope increases and ultimately approaches a value of 1 for relatively high stock prices.

Because the hedge ratio is typically less than 1, a $1 increase in the share price will typically result in an increase in a call option's value of less than $1. However, the percentage change in the value of the call option will generally be greater than the percentage change in the price of the share. It is this relationship that leads people to say that options offer high leverage.

The reason for referring to the slope of the Black-Scholes value curve as the hedge ratio is that a "hedge" portfolio, meaning a nearly risk-free portfolio, can be formed by simultaneously writing one call option and purchasing a number of shares equal to the hedge ratio, $N(d_1)$. For example, assume the hedge ratio is .5, indicating that the hedge portfolio consists of writing one call and buying .5 shares of stock. Now, if the stock price rises by $1 per share, the value of the call option will rise by approximately $.50. This means that the hedge portfolio would lose approximately $.50 on the written call option but gain $.50 from the rise in the stock's price. Conversely, a $1 decrease in the stock's price would result in a $.50 gain on the written call option but a loss of $.50 on

---

[14] For a further discussion of these methods, see Chapter 6 of Cox and Rubinstein, *Options Markets*; Chapter 9 of Robert A. Jarrow and Andrew Rudd, *Option Pricing* (Homewood, Ill.: Richard D. Irwin, Inc., 1983); and Chapter 10 of Peter Ritchken, *Options* (Glenview, Ill.: Scott, Foresman and Company, 1987).

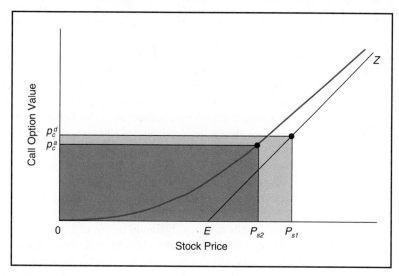

**FIGURE 18-9**
Option values before and after an ex-dividend date.

the share of stock. Overall, it can be seen that the hedge portfolio will neither gain nor lose value when the price of the underlying common stock changes by a relatively small amount.

Even if the Black-Scholes model is valid and all the inputs have been correctly specified, it should be noted that risk is not permanently eliminated in the hedge portfolio when the portfolio is first formed (or, for that matter, at any time). This is because the hedge ratio will change as the stock price changes and as the life of the option decreases with the passage of time. In order to eliminate risk from the hedge portfolio, the investor will continuously have to alter its composition. Altering it less often will reduce but not completely eliminate risk.

## ☐ 18.6.7 Adjustments for Dividends

Thus far, the issue of dividend payments on the underlying stock during the life of an option has been avoided. Other things being equal, the greater the amount of the dividends to be paid during the life of a call option, the lower the value of the call option. This is because the greater the dividend a firm declares, the lower will be its share price. Since options are not "dividend protected," this lower share price will result in a lower value for the call option.

Moreover, it may pay to exercise an American call option just prior to an ex-dividend date. Earlier, it was mentioned that in the absence of dividends, an American call option would be worth at least as much "alive" (not exercised) as "dead" (exercised). When dividends are involved, however, the situation may be different. This is shown in Figure 18.9.

The call option's value if exercised immediately, referred to in Figure 18.8 as the option's *intrinsic value*, lies along the lower boundary OEZ. If allowed to live, the option's value will lie along the higher Black-Scholes curve as shown in the figure.

Imagine that the stock is currently priced at $P_{s1}$ per share and is about to go ex-dividend for the last time prior to the option's expiration. Afterward, it can be expected to sell for a lower price, $P_{s2}$. The Black-Scholes formula can be used to estimate the option's value if it remains alive just after the ex-dividend date. In Figure 18.9, this alive value is $P_c^a$. If instead the option is exercised just before the ex-dividend date, while the stock price is still $P_{s1}$ per share, the investor will obtain the dead value (that is, the intrinsic value) of $P_c^d$. If $P_c^d$ is greater than $P_c^a$ (as is the case in this figure), the option should be exercised now, just before the ex-dividend date; if $P_c^d$ is less than $P_c^a$, the option should not be exercised.

For a call option on a dividend-paying stock, the possibility of early exercise must be taken into consideration. A number of models have been recommended for doing this, one of which is presented here.[15] This model is known as the *pseudo-American model* and assumes that the dividends to be paid on the common stock over the life of the call option can be predicted with certainty. It should be pointed out that this assumption is not unreasonable, since firms are generally predictable in terms of the timing and size of their quarterly dividends over the next nine months, the maximum life of an option. For ease of exposition, it will be assumed that only one dividend has yet to be paid on the stock and that its ex-dividend date and payment date are the same.

The procedure for using the pseudo-American model for estimating the value of a call option begins by subtracting the present value of the future dividend from the current market price of the common stock. If the dividend, denoted by $D$, is to be paid at time $t$, then the dividend-adjusted stock price $P_s^*$ per share is

$$P_s^* = P_s - \frac{D}{e^{Rt}} \qquad (18.17)$$

where $R$ is the risk-free rate. Then, this dividend-adjusted price is used in place of $P_s$ while all the other inputs $(E, R, \sigma, T)$ in the Black-Scholes formula given in equation (18.11) are unchanged. Solving the formula for $V_c$ provides an estimate of the value for the call option that is based on the assumption it will be held until expiration. In the next step, an estimate of the value of the call option is determined based on the assumption that it will be exercised just before the ex-dividend date. As before, the dividend-adjusted price $P_s^*$ is used instead of $P_s$. However, two additional changes must be made to the inputs. Specifically, the time to the ex-dividend date $t$ is to be used instead of the time to expiration $T$, and a dividend-adjusted exercise price equal to $E - D$ is to be used instead of the actual exercise price $E$. The exercise price is adjusted in this manner because the investor will receive the dividend by exercising the option just before the ex-dividend date and thus must come up only with cash equal to $E - D$ in order to exercise the option at that time. The value for $V_c$ that is obtained when $P_s^*$, $t$, and $E - D$ (as well as $R$ and $\sigma$) are used in the Black-Scholes formula is the value of the call associated with early exercise.

The final estimate of the value for the call option will be the larger of the two estimates for $V_c$ that correspond to holding the option to expiration and exercising it just

---

[15] For a more detailed explanation of this model, see pp. 124–32 of Jarrow and Rudd, *Option Pricing*; and pp. 168–69 of Ritchken, *Options*. For a description of other models, see Chapters 9 and 10 of Jarrow and Rudd, *Option Pricing*; pp. 200–203 of Ritchken, *Options*; and Chapters 5 and 6 of Cox and Rubinstein, *Options Markets*.

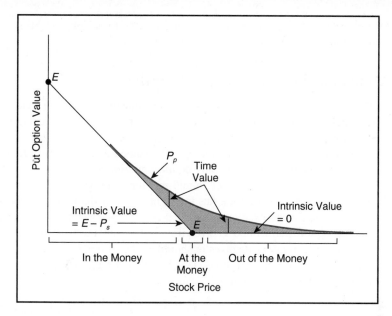

**FIGURE 18-10**
Option terminology for puts.

before the ex-dividend date. Although this method is not exact, it is probably sufficient for many options.[16]

## 18.7 THE VALUATION OF PUT OPTIONS

As with a call option, a put option is said to be *at the money* if the underlying stock has a market price roughly equal to the put's exercise price. However, the terms *out of the money* and *in the money* have, in one sense, opposite meanings for puts and calls. In particular, a put option is out of the money if the underlying stock has a market price above the exercise price and is in the money if the market price is below the exercise price. Figure 18.10 provides an illustration of how these terms apply to a put option.

As mentioned earlier, the value of either a call or put, if it were exercised immediately, is known as its intrinsic value. This value is equal to zero if the option is out of the money and is equal to the difference between the stock price and exercise price if the stock is in the money. Thus, in another sense, the terms out of the money and in the money have similar meanings for puts and calls.

The excess of the price of a call or put over this intrinsic value is the option's time value (or time premium). As shown for calls and puts in parts (a) and (b) of Figure 18.3, respectively, the time value is zero at expiration. However, Figures 18.8 and 18.10 show

---

[16] For a comparison of various techniques, see Robert Geske and Kuldeep Shastri, "Valuation by Approximation: A Comparison of Alternative Option Valuation Techniques," *Journal of Financial and Quantitative Analysis* 20, no. 1 (March 1985):45–71; and Chapters 1–4 of Stuart M. Turnbull, *Option Valuation* (Holt, Rinehart & Winston of Canada, Limited, 1987). Turnbull's book comes with floppy disks that contain many computer programs for valuing options.

that the time value is generally positive before expiration. Note that an option's premium is simply the sum of its intrinsic value and time value.

## ☐ 18.7.1 Limits on the Value of a Put Option

Earlier, one upper and two lower limits on the value of a call option were presented. Not surprisingly, put options also have limits on their values. In discussing these limits, it will be assumed that the underlying common stock will not pay any dividends during the life of the put option. Furthermore, it is assumed that the put is a European option, meaning that it can be exercised only on its expiration date.

What is the *most* an investor should pay for a put option? Remembering that the buyer of a European put option has the right to sell a share of common stock on the expiration date for the exercise price $E$, it is not sensible for an investor to pay more for the put option than will be received if it is exercised. Furthermore, since it cannot be exercised until expiration, an investor should not be willing to pay more than the present value of the exercise price, $PV(E)$. This means that there will be the following upper limit on the value of a put option:

$$P_p \leq PV(E) \tag{18.18}$$

where $P_p$ denotes the current market price of the put option.

There are two lower limits to the value of a put. In order to understand the first one, consider an investor who deposits an amount of cash equal to the present value of the exercise price in the bank. At the expiration date the investor's deposit will have grown to be equal to the exercise price, $E$.

Compare this position with a position of buying a put option and one share of the underlying common stock for a total cost of $P_p + P_s$. At the expiration date of the option, the underlying stock will be selling at a price either above or below the exercise price. If it is below the exercise price, then the investor would exercise the put by giving up the share of stock and receiving cash equal to the exercise price $E$ in return. Thus, if the price of the stock at expiration is below the exercise price, both positions result in the investor having cash equal to $E$.

However, the position of buying a put and a share is of greater value if the common stock is selling for a price that is above the exercise price at expiration. Although the put will be worthless in this situation, the share of common stock with which the investor is left has a value greater than $E$. Since the investor who buys a put and a share ends up being better off in some cases and equally well off in other cases, it is logical that the initial cost of taking this position should be greater than the initial cost of making the bank deposit. Thus, the following inequality should hold:

$$P_p + P_s \geq PV(E) \tag{18.19}$$

where the left-hand side shows the cost of buying a put and a share and the right-hand side shows the cost of making the bank deposit. This inequality can be rearranged, resulting in the following lower limit on the price of a put:

$$P_p \geq PV(E) - P_s. \tag{18.20}$$

As an example, consider a put option that has an exercise price of $100 and an expiration date that is six months in the future. If the risk-free rate is 10% per year, the present value of the exercise price can be calculated as

$$PV(\$100) = \frac{\$100}{(1 + .10)^{.50}}$$

$$= \$95.35$$

since six months = .50 year. Thus, an investor could deposit $95.35 in a bank account that earns 10% and have a position that is inferior to buying one put option and one share of the underlying stock for a combined price of $P_p + P_s$. The reason for this inferiority can be seen by examining the possible market values of the two positions at the expiration date of the put option.

On this date the bank deposit will have grown so that its balance is $100. If the stock at that time is selling for less than $100 per share, the put will be exercised, giving the investor an amount of cash equal to the bank balance. In this case the investor who bought the put and share is not better or worse off than if the bank deposit had been made instead. However, if the stock is selling at expiration for more than $100 — say, $120 per share — then the put option is worthless but the stock is worth more than the $100 bank balance. Thus, the investor will be better off if a put and a share of stock had been purchased initially. Accordingly, the cost of buying the put and share must be greater than the cost of making the bank deposit, as indicated by inequality (18.19).

In addition to inequality (18.20), there is another lower limit to the price of a put option. Specifically, a put option cannot have a negative price. Here a negative price would imply that a writer would pay a buyer to take and hold onto a put option. This is not sensible because the buyer is not under any obligation to exercise the put option. Thus, a writer who pays a buyer to take and hold onto the option would simply be giving money away. Since this will not happen, there is a second lower limit on the price of a put:

$$P_p \geq 0. \tag{18.21}$$

These three inequalities — (18.18), (18.20), and (18.21) — provide a set of limits on the value of a put option. If the market price of the put were to move outside one of these limits, there would be an opportunity for investors to make abnormal profits via arbitrage. Although transaction costs and taxes might make it unprofitable for some investors to take advantage of such situations, a substantial departure would certainly lead others to act, thereby setting in motion forces that would quickly bring the price of the put back within the limits.

In the example, suppose the option had a price of $3.00 when the stock was selling for $80 per share and there were six months until expiration, so that PV($100) = $95.35. In this situation inequality (18.20) does not hold, since the left-hand side is equal to $3.00, whereas the right-hand side is larger, equal to $15.35 = $95.35 − $80.00. Consequently, an investor should immediately buy a put and a share of the stock for a cost of $83($3 + $80). In doing so the investor can be certain of making more than the risk-free rate of return.[17]

---

[17] If the investor could borrow money, the rate of return from buying puts and the stock would exceed the risk-free return by an even greater amount.

If at the end of six months the stock is selling for less than $100 per share, the investor will exercise each put by delivering the shares of stock, getting back the exercise price of $100. Thus, the investor's rate of return on the initial investment of $83($3 + $80) will be equal to ($100 − $83)/$83 = 20.48%.

If the stock price is greater than $100 per share at expiration, then each put will be worthless when it expires, and the investor will be left with just the stock. Assuming the stock is selling for $110 per share at expiration, the rate of return on the $83 initial investment will be equal to ($110 − $83)/$83 = 32.53%. Furthermore, the higher the stock price, the greater the return. Thus, it can be seen that if inequality (18.20) was violated, there would be an opportunity for investors to be certain of making at least 20.48% over six months, which when annualized is notably greater than the 10% annual risk-free rate of return.

However, the ensuing large number of put and stock purchases will cause their prices ($3 and $80, respectively) to rise. These prices will quickly adjust (perhaps to $10 and $90, respectively) until inequality (18.20) does hold.

In Figure 18.11 these limits are expressed as equalities. Specifically, inequalities (18.18), (18.20), and (18.21) are given by, respectively,

$$P_p = \text{PV}(E) \tag{18.22}$$

$$P_p = \text{PV}(E) - P_s \tag{18.23}$$

$$P_p = 0. \tag{18.24}$$

Each one of these equations represents a straight line shown in the figure. These lines serve as boundaries of the shaded region, which indicates where the put option must be priced so that none of the limits are violated.

Figure 18.11 also shows the way the limits change as time passes and the expiration date becomes nearer. Note that the boundary corresponding to equation (18.22) moves up, whereas the boundary corresponding to equation (18.23) moves to the right as the expiration date approaches. This change occurs because the present value of the exercise price rises as the expiration date becomes nearer. That is, $\text{PV}(E)$ rises because the length of time $E$ is discounted is smaller. For example, if $E = \$100$, then discounting $100 over three months will result in a larger figure than discounting $100 over six months. Ultimately, just prior to expiration the effect of discounting will be so negligible that $\text{PV}(E) = E$ and the boundary shown by equation (18.23) will simply be

$$P_p = E - P_s. \tag{18.25}$$

Note how this equation corresponds to the value of a put option moments before it expires as indicated earlier in Figure 18.3(b).

## ☐ 18.7.2 Put-Call Parity

Black and Scholes have shown that the market prices of a put and a call on the same underlying stock with the same exercise price and expiration date are related. This relationship is known as *put-call parity*. However, it should be noted that their analysis applies to European options on stocks that pay no dividends.

Assume that a call option with an exercise price of $E$ sells for $P_c$ and a put option on the same stock with the same exercise price and expiration date sells for $P_p$. Furthermore, assume that it is possible to make a bank deposit today for an amount that is equal to

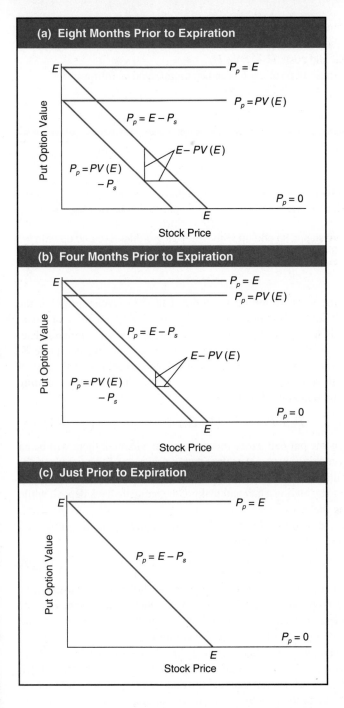

**(a) Eight Months Prior to Expiration**

$P_p = E$

$P_p = PV(E)$

$P_p = E - P_s$

$E - PV(E)$

$P_p = PV(E) - P_s$

$P_p = 0$

Put Option Value

$E$

Stock Price

**(b) Four Months Prior to Expiration**

$P_p = E$

$P_p = PV(E)$

$P_p = E - P_s$

$E - PV(E)$

$P_p = PV(E) - P_s$

$P_p = 0$

Put Option Value

$E$

Stock Price

**(c) Just Prior to Expiration**

$P_p = E$

$P_p = E - P_s$

$P_p = 0$

Put Option Value

$E$

Stock Price

**FIGURE 18-11**
Limits on the value of a put option.

the present value of the exercise price, PV($E$), so that when the options expire the bank balance will be equal to the exercise price $E$. Lastly, denote the current market price of the underlying stock as $P_s$.

Consider the following two investment strategies. The first one involves buying a put and a share of stock and costs $P_p + P_s$. The second involves buying a call and making the requisite bank deposit and costs $P_c + PV(E)$.

The outcomes from these two strategies can be summarized as follows:

| | Strategy 1 | Strategy 2 |
|---|---|---|
| Cost: | $P_p + P_s$ | $P_c + PV(E)$ |
| **Value at Expiration:** | | |
| Stock price > $E$ | Put worthless, so end up owning a share of stock | Bank balance of $E$ used to exercise call, so end up owning a share of stock |
| Stock price < $E$ | Exercise put, so end up with cash equal to $E$ | Call worthless, so end up with bank balance of $E$ |

As this table shows, if the stock is selling for more than the exercise price on the expiration date, then both strategies end up with the investor owning a share of stock. Alternatively, if the stock is selling for less than the exercise price on the expiration date, then both strategies end up with the investor owning cash equal to the exercise price $E$. Thus, regardless of the ending stock price, the investor will end up being exactly as well off with strategy 1 as with strategy 2. Since the two strategies have the same ending value, they should have the same initial cost:

$$P_p + P_s = P_c + PV(E). \qquad (18.26)$$

This equation is known as the put-call parity theorem; if it is violated, there will be an opportunity for risklessly making abnormal profits (that is, arbitrage). For example, if the left-hand side is greater than the right-hand side, investors would be certain of making more than the risk-free rate by buying a call and making the requisite bank deposit while writing a put and shorting the stock.

Equation (18.26) can be rearranged in the following manner so that it can be used to estimate the value of European put options:

$$P_p = P_c + PV(E) - P_s. \qquad (18.27)$$

Thus, the value of a put can be estimated by using the Black-Scholes formula to estimate the value of a matching call option, then adding an amount equal to the present value of the exercise price to this estimate, and finally subtracting from this sum an amount that is equal to the current market price of the underlying common stock.

For example, consider a put option that expires in three months and has an exercise price of $40, while the current market price and risk of the underlying common stock are $36 per share and 50%, respectively. Assuming the risk-free rate is 5%, it was shown earlier that the Black-Scholes estimate of the value for a matching call option was $2.26. Since the 5% risk-free rate is a continuously compounded rate, the present value of the exercise price is equal to $40/(e^{.05 \times .25}) = \$39.50$. At this point, having determined that $P_c = \$2.26$, $PV(E) = \$39.50$ and $P_s = \$36$, equation (18.27) can be used to estimate the value of the put option as being equal to $5.76 = \$2.26 + \$39.50 - \$36$.

Alternatively, the Black-Scholes formula for estimating the value of a call given in equation (18.11) can be substituted for $P_c$ in equation (18.27). After doing so and simplifying, an equation that can be used directly for estimating the value of a put is obtained:

$$P_p = \frac{E}{e^{RT}} N(-d_2) - P_s N(-d_1) \qquad (18.28)$$

where $d_1$ and $d_2$ are given in equations (18.12) and (18.13a), respectively.

In the previous example, $d_1 = -.25$ and $d_2 = -.50$; thus $N(-d_1) = N(.25) = .5987$ and $N(-d_2) = N(.50) = .6915$. Applying equation (18.28), the value of this put can be estimated directly:

$$P_p = \left( \frac{40}{e^{.05 \times .25}} \times .6915 \right) - (36 \times .5987) = \$5.76,$$

which is the same estimated value as indicated earlier when equation (18.27) was used.

## ☐ 18.7.3 Static Analysis

Close scrutiny of the put-call parity equation reveals some interesting features of European put option pricing. In particular, it can be noticed that the value of a put option is dependent on the values of the same five inputs used for call valuation—the market price of the common stock ($P_s$), the exercise price of the option ($E$), the length of time until the expiration date ($T$), the risk-free rate ($R$), and the risk of the common stock ($\sigma$). What happens to the value of a put option when one of these inputs is changed while the other four remain the same?

1. The higher the price of the underlying stock ($P_s$), the lower the value of the put option.
2. The higher the exercise price ($E$), the higher the value of the put option.
3. Generally, the longer the time to the expiration date ($T$), the higher the value of the put option.
4. The higher the risk-free rate ($R$), the lower the value of the put option.
5. The greater the risk ($\sigma$) of the common stock, the higher the value of the put option.

The relationships for the underlying stock price ($P$), exercise price ($E$), and risk-free rate ($R$) are in the opposite direction from those shown earlier for call options, whereas the relationships for the time to the expiration date ($T$) and risk ($\sigma$) are in the same direction. It should be noted that exceptions can occur with $T$ when the put is deep in the money. In such a situation, a longer time to expiration could actually decrease the value of the put.

## ☐ 18.7.4 Early Exercise and Dividends

Equations (18.27) and (18.28) apply to a European put on a stock that will not pay dividends prior to the option's expiration. As with call options, complications arise when it is recognized that most put options are American, meaning they can be exercised before expiration, and that often dividends on the underlying common stock are paid before the expiration date.

Consider first the ability to exercise a put option at any time up to its expiration date. Earlier, it was shown that if there were no dividends on the underlying stock, then a call option was worth more alive than dead, meaning call options should not be exercised prior to expiration. Such an argument does *not* hold for put options.

Specifically, if a put option is in the money, meaning the market price of the stock is less than the exercise price, then the investor may want to exercise the put option. In doing so, the investor will receive an additional amount of cash equal to $E - P_s$. In turn, this cash can be invested at the risk-free rate to earn money over the remaining life of the option. Since these earnings would not be received by the investor if the put option were held, it would be advantageous in some cases to exercise the put early and thereby receive the earnings.

The possibility of early exercise affects the boundary conditions given in equations (18.18) and (18.20). Specifically, the present value of the exercise price, PV($E$), that appears in these two inequalities should be replaced by the exercise price, $E$. Thus, the set of boundary conditions for an American put option will be:

$$P_p \leq E \tag{18.29}$$
$$P_p \geq E - P_s \tag{18.30}$$
$$P_p \geq 0. \tag{18.31}$$

Consider next the impact of dividends on put valuation. Previously, it was shown that the owner of a call may find it optimal to exercise just *before* an ex-dividend date, since doing so allowed the investor to receive the forthcoming dividends on the stock. With respect to a put, the owner may find it optimal to exercise just *after* the ex-dividend date, since the corresponding drop in the stock price will cause the value of the put to rise.[18]

One approach to valuing an American put on a dividend-paying stock is to use the *pseudo-American model*. As with calls, it is assumed that the size and timing of dividends to be paid on the stock during the life of the put are known with certainty. Consider valuing a put on a stock that will pay one dividend of size $D$ at time $t$ before the expiration date $T$.

First, the current market price of the underlying stock is reduced by the present value of the dividend as shown earlier in equation (18.17). Second, the put is valued using this dividend-adjusted stock price, along with the other inputs ($E$, $R$, $\sigma$, $T$), in equation (18.28); the result will be an estimate of the value of the put, assuming that it will not be exercised until expiration.

Third, the value of the put is estimated by assuming it will be exercised just after the ex-dividend date. This is done by using the time to the ex-dividend date $t$ instead of the time to the expiration date $T$, along with the dividend-adjusted stock price and the other inputs ($E$, $R$, $\sigma$) in equation (18.28).

Finally, the estimated value of the put is the higher of the two estimates — that is, the estimate based on the assumption that the put will be held to expiration and the estimate based on the assumption that the put will be exercised just after the ex-dividend date. It can be argued that the intrinsic value of the put (that is, the exercise price less the

---

[18] See Robert Geske and Kuldeep Shastri, "The Early Exercise of American Puts," *Journal of Banking and Finance* 9, no. 2 (June 1985):207–19.

unadjusted stock price) should also be compared with these estimated values, with the highest of the three of them being used as an estimate of the put's fair value.[19]

## 18.8    OPTIONS ON OTHER KINDS OF ASSETS

Not all options are written on individual issues of common stock. In recent years, many new and somewhat exotic options have been created that have as an underlying asset something other than the stock of a particular company. Some of them are discussed here; the appendix discusses others, and the next chapter discusses what are known as futures options.

### ☐ 18.8.1   Index Options

A call option on Inco stock is a relatively simple instrument. Upon exercise, the call buyer "calls away" 100 shares of Inco stock. The call writer is required to deliver the actual shares. In practice, both the buyer and writer may find it advantageous to close their positions in order to avoid the costs associated with the physical transfer of shares. In this event, the buyer may expect a gain (and the seller a loss) approximately equal to the difference between the current market price of the security and the option's exercise price.

It would be entirely feasible to specify that upon expiration, only a "cash settlement" procedure could be used. Here, the writer would be required to pay the buyer an amount equal to the difference between the current price of the security and the call option's exercise price (provided the current price is larger than the exercise price). Similarly, for puts, the writer could be required to pay the buyer an amount equal to the difference between the option's exercise price and the current market price (provided the exercise price is larger than the current price).

While listed options on individual securities retain the obligation to "deliver," the realization that cash settlement can serve as a subsitute has allowed the creation of index options.

An index option is based on a stock price index level. Some indices are designed to reflect movements in the stock market, broadly construed. Other specialized indices are intended to capture changes in the fortunes of particular industries or sectors. Figure 18.12 shows the major indices on which options have been offered in the United States, along with their quotations. Some of the indices are highly specialized, consisting of only a few stocks. Others are representative of major portions of the stock market. The AMEX Market Value Index covers all the stocks on the American Stock Exchange, and the NYSE Composite Index covers all the stocks on the New York Stock Exchange. The Standard & Poor's 500 Stock Index covers 500 large exchange-listed stocks.

In Canada the only index options traded are those based on the Toronto 35 Index that was designed by the TSE in 1987 specifically for trading derivative securities (i.e., predominantly options and futures). These are European options that can only be exercised on the expiry date — the third Friday of the expiry month. The companies

---

[19] For more exact approaches to valuing American puts, see Chapter 15 in Jarrow and Rudd, *Option Pricing*; Chapters 4 and 5 of Cox and Rubinstein, *Options Markets*; and pp. 169–70 and 203–5 of Ritchken, *Options*.

included in this index are among the largest listed firms with the most heavily traded issues on the TSE. Trading details for these options, identified as TSE 35 Index, are included with other Trans Canada Options in Figure 18.2.

Contracts for index options are not stated in terms of numbers of shares. Instead, the size of a contract is determined as the product of the level of the index and a multiplier specified by the exchange on which the option is traded. The premium (price) of an index option times the applicable multiplier indicates the total amount paid.

For example, on November 8, 1991 the call option on the TSE 35 Index with an exercise price of $205 (when the index was at $195^{3}/_{4}$) that expires in March has an indicated premium of $2.45. Since the multiplier for TSE 35 option contracts is 100, an investor has to pay $245.00 (2.45 × 100) (plus a commission) for this contract.

After purchasing this contract, the investor could later sell it or exercise it for its cash settlement value. Perhaps in January the TSE 35 will be at 210. In this case, the investor could exercise the call, receiving its intrinsic value of $500 ((210 − 205) × 100) less a commission) for doing so. Alternatively, the investor could simply sell the call on the exchange; in which case, the amount received might be $550 (less a commission), since its price would have risen to $5^{1/2}$ an amount equal to the sum of its intrinsic and time values (see Figure 18.8).

A related contract is the *Toronto 35 Index Participation Option* (TIP Options). TIPs, (described in Chapter 15) are in effect units of a fund, managed by the TSE, that mimics the TSE 35 Index. These units and their related options are traded on the exchange. The price of a TIP unit is approximately $^{1}/_{10}$ of the value of the index. These options are treated in the same way as ordinary stock options and their trading details are shown in Figure 18.2 under TSE 35 Tips.

## ☐ 18.8.2 Interest Rate Options

Call and put options are also traded on two long Canada benchmark bond issues — the 9% March 2011 and the 9.5% October 2001 — with a given dollar amount of face value ($25,000) to be delivered upon exercise. Figure 18.2 shows the trading details for these two options.

For example, a CDA Mar 2011 9 contract with December expiry and a striking price of 98 last traded at 400. This contract gives the buyer the right to purchase $100 of face value for $98.00 on or before the expiry date. As the bonds are currently selling for $100.625 this is an in the money contract. The quoted last price of 400 means that the buyer had to pay $4.00 per $100 of face value, therefore, the total cost of the contract was $1,000 ($4 × 250) (plus commissions).

A wider range of interest rate options, such as US Treasury Bill, Treasury Note, and Treasury Bond options, are available on US exchanges. Typical quotations from the Chicago Board Options Exchange are shown in Figure 18.13.

Valuation models that are used to price interest rate options are significantly different from equity option models, such as Black-Scholes. The latter are not used because they assume a constant interest rate and do not incorporate the term structure.

# INDEX TRADING

OPTIONS

Wednesday, May 6, 1992

## CHICAGO BOARD

### S&P 100 INDEX-$100 times index

| Strike Price | Calls–Last May | Jun | Jul | Puts–Last May | Jun | Jul |
|---|---|---|---|---|---|---|
| 350 | 42¼ | .... | .... | ⅛ | ⅞ | 1 13/16 |
| 355 | 37¼ | .... | .... | 3/16 | 1⅛ | 2 1/16 |
| 360 | .... | .... | .... | ¼ | 1 7/16 | 2½ |
| 365 | 26⅞ | .... | .... | ⅜ | 1⅞ | 3¼ |
| 370 | 21¾ | 24 | 26 | ½ | 2 7/16 | 4⅛ |
| 375 | 16½ | 19⅞ | .... | ¾ | 3¼ | 4⅞ |
| 380 | 11¼ | 14¾ | 17 | 1⅛ | 4⅛ | 6¼ |
| 385 | 7 | 10⅞ | 14 | 1⅞ | 5⅝ | 8 |
| 390 | 3½ | 7¾ | 10¾ | 3½ | 7⅞ | 9¼ |
| 395 | 1 7/16 | 5¼ | 7¾ | 6⅞ | 10¼ | 12 |
| 400 | ½ | 3¾ | 5⅜ | 10½ | 13½ | 14½ |
| 405 | 3/16 | 1⅞ | 3½ | 15 | 16¾ | 18½ |
| 410 | 1/16 | 1 1/16 | 2 9/16 | 18¾ | 20 | 21½ |

Total call volume 90,189   Total call open int. 354,853
Total put volume 99,289   Total put open int. 445,019
The index: High 392.78; Low 390.45; Close 390.51, –1.10

### S&P 500 INDEX-$100 times index

| Strike Price | Calls–Last May | Jun | Jul | Puts–Last May | Jun | Jul |
|---|---|---|---|---|---|---|
| 325 | .... | 92½ | .... | .... | ⅛ | ¼ |
| 350 | .... | .... | .... | .... | ⅜ | .... |
| 375 | .... | .... | .... | .... | 1⅛ | .... |
| 380 | 37⅛ | .... | 40⅜ | ⅛ | 1⅛ | 2¼ |
| 385 | .... | .... | .... | 3/16 | .... | .... |
| 390 | .... | .... | .... | ⅜ | .... | 3½ |
| 395 | 22 | 24½ | .... | ½ | 2⅝ | .... |
| 400 | 17¾ | 20 | 23⅛ | ¾ | 3⅛ | 5 |
| 405 | 13 | 15⅞ | .... | 1⅛ | 4¼ | .... |
| 410 | 8¼ | 12¾ | .... | 1⅞ | 5¾ | 8 |
| 415 | 4¾ | 9⅜ | .... | 3⅜ | 7½ | 9¼ |
| 420 | 2½ | 6⅝ | .... | 5⅞ | 9½ | 11¼ |
| 425 | 2½ | 6⅝ | .... | 5⅞ | 9½ | 11¼ |
| 430 | ⅞ | 4 | .... | 8¾ | 12¾ | .... |
| 435 | 3/16 | 2⅝ | 4¾ | 13¾ | 15¼ | .... |
| 440 | ⅛ | 1½ | .... | 18¾ | .... | 20⅛ |
| 445 | .... | 1 | .... | 23 | .... | .... |
| 450 | .... | 3/16 | .... | .... | .... | .... |

Total call volume 20,557   Total call open int. 335,502
Total put volume 11,443   Total put open int. 538,060
The index: High 418.48; Low 416.40; Close 416.79, –0.05

### LEAPS-S&P 100 INDEX

| Strike Price | Calls–Last Dec 92 | Dec 93 | Puts–Last Dec 92 | Dec 93 |
|---|---|---|---|---|
| 27½ | .... | .... | 1/16 | 9/16¼ |
| 30 | .... | .... | ¼ | .... |
| 32½ | .... | .... | ½ | .... |
| 35 | 5 | .... | 13/16 | 1⅞ |
| 37½ | 3⅛ | .... | 1½ | .... |
| 40 | .... | .... | 2 7/16 | 3⅜ |

Total call volume 13   Total call open int. 33,028
Total put volume 253   Total put open int. 145,402
The index: High 39.28; Low 39.05; Close 39.05, +0.11

### LEAPS-S&P 500 INDEX

| Strike Price | Calls–Last Dec 92 | Dec 93 | Puts–Last Dec 92 | Dec 93 |
|---|---|---|---|---|
| 40 | .... | .... | .... | 2¼ |
| 42½ | .... | 3½ | .... | 3⅜ |

Total call volume 10   Total call open int. 30,902
Total put volume 869   Total put open int. 114,921
The index: High 41.85; Low 41.64; Close 41.68, unch.

### CAPS-S&P 100 INDEX

| Strike Price | Calls–Last Jun 92 | Aug 92 | Puts–Last Jun 92 | Aug 92 |
|---|---|---|---|---|
| 380 | .... | .... | .... | 7¼ |

Total call volume 0   Total call open int. 242
Total put volume 2   Total put open int. 3,104
The index: High 392.78; Low 390.45; Close 390.51, –1.10

### CAPS-S&P 500 INDEX

| Strike Price | Calls–Last Jun 92 | Sep 92 | Puts–Last Jun 92 | Sep 92 |
|---|---|---|---|---|
| 410 | 12¼ | .... | .... | .... |

Total call volume 3   Total call open int. 492
Total put volume 0   Total put open int. 4,635
The index: High 418.48; Low 416.40; Close 416.79, –0.05

## AMERICAN

### S&P MIDCAP INDEX

| Strike Price | Calls–Last May | Jun | Jul | Puts–Last May | Jun | Jul |
|---|---|---|---|---|---|---|
| 140 | 5¼ | 6⅞ | .... | ⅜ | 1¾ | .... |
| 142½ | 3½ | .... | .... | ¾ | 2⅜ | .... |
| 145 | 1⅜ | 3½ | .... | 1⅜ | 3 | .... |
| 147½ | ⅝ | .... | .... | 3 | 4 | .... |
| 150 | ¼ | .... | .... | 4¾ | .... | .... |
| 155 | ¼ | .... | .... | .... | .... | .... |

Total call volume 862   Total call open int. 30,160
Total put volume 1,722   Total put open int. 44,550
The index: High 145.65; Low 144.91; Close 145.29, +0.36

### MAJOR MARKET INDEX

| Strike Price | Calls–Last May | Jun | Jul | Puts–Last May | Jun | Jul |
|---|---|---|---|---|---|---|
| 275 | .... | .... | 1 9/16 | .... | .... | .... |
| 300 | .... | .... | .... | 5/16 | .... | .... |
| 305 | .... | .... | .... | ⅜ | .... | .... |
| 310 | .... | .... | .... | 1/16 | .... | .... |
| 320 | .... | .... | .... | .... | .... | 1⅜ |
| 325 | .... | .... | .... | 1/16 | .... | .... |
| 330 | 25⅛ | .... | .... | .... | .... | .... |
| 335 | .... | .... | .... | 5/16 | .... | .... |
| 340 | .... | .... | .... | ½ | 2¼ | .... |
| 345 | 10½ | .... | .... | 1 | 3¾ | .... |
| 350 | 6¾ | .... | .... | 1⅝ | 4¾ | .... |
| 355 | 3 | 7⅝ | .... | 3⅜ | 6⅞ | 8⅝ |
| 360 | 1⅛ | 4⅜ | 6¼ | 6¾ | 9⅛ | .... |
| 365 | 5/16 | .... | .... | 10½ | .... | .... |
| 370 | ⅛ | 1 7/16 | .... | .... | .... | .... |
| 375 | .... | 11/16 | .... | .... | .... | .... |

Total call volume 2,044   Total call open int. 56,851
Total put volume 2,715   Total put open int. 75,709
The index: High 356.55; Low 354.74; Close 354.89, –0.43

## LEAPS-MAJOR MARKET INDEX

| Strike Price | Calls–Last Dec 92 | Dec 93 | Dec 94 | Puts–Last Dec 92 | Dec 93 | Dec 94 |
|---|---|---|---|---|---|---|
| 30 | .... | .... | .... | .... | ⅜ | .... |
| 32½ | .... | .... | .... | ⅜ | .... | .... |
| 35 | 2 1/16 | .... | .... | .... | .... | 1 15/16 |
| 37½ | .... | .... | .... | .... | .... | 3½ |

Total call volume 19   Total call open int. 94,629
Total put volume 315   Total put open int. 188,849
The index: High 35.66; Low 35.47; Close 35.49, –0.04

### INSTITUTIONAL INDEX

| Strike Price | Calls–Last May | Jun | Jul | Puts–Last May | Jun | Jul |
|---|---|---|---|---|---|---|
| 400 | .... | .... | .... | 5/16 | .... | .... |
| 410 | .... | .... | .... | ½ | .... | .... |
| 415 | .... | .... | .... | ¾ | .... | .... |
| 420 | 11½ | .... | .... | 1½ | .... | .... |
| 425 | 7½ | 10⅞ | .... | 2⅛ | 6 | .... |
| 430 | 4⅛ | .... | .... | 3¾ | .... | .... |
| 435 | 1 13/16 | .... | .... | .... | .... | .... |
| 440 | 13/16 | .... | .... | .... | .... | .... |

Total call volume 233   Total call open int. 53,470
Total put volume 245   Total put open int. 70,441
The index: High 431.68; Low 429.00; Close 429.17, –0.80

### JAPAN INDEX

| Strike Price | Calls–Last May | Jun | Jul | Puts–Last May | Jun | Jul |
|---|---|---|---|---|---|---|
| 160 | 19¾ | .... | .... | .... | .... | .... |
| 165 | 15¼ | .... | .... | .... | .... | 2¼ |
| 170 | 10¾ | 13⅞ | .... | ¾ | 2¼ | .... |
| 175 | 6⅝ | 10 | .... | 15/16 | 3¼ | .... |
| 180 | 3⅜ | 7 | 9¼ | 2 | 4¼ | 6 |
| 185 | 1 13/16 | 4¾ | .... | 3¾ | 6 | 8 |
| 190 | ⅝ | 2⅞ | .... | 5⅝ | 8½ | .... |
| 195 | 1 9/16 | .... | .... | 10½ | 11¼ | .... |
| 200 | .... | .... | .... | ¾ | 20 | .... |
| 210 | ¼ | .... | .... | .... | .... | .... |
| 225 | .... | .... | .... | .... | 44¼ | .... |

Total call volume 1,084   Total call open int. 17,878
Total put volume 669   Total put open int. 24,418
The index: Close 180.03, +5.60

## PHILADELPHIA

### GOLD/SILVER INDEX

| Strike Price | Calls–Last May | Jun | Jul | Puts–Last May | Jun | Jul |
|---|---|---|---|---|---|---|
| 65 | 8⅜ | .... | .... | .... | ⅜ | .... |
| 70 | 3¼ | 5 | .... | .... | 1 9/16 | .... |
| 75 | ⅞ | 2⅝ | 3⅞ | 2 3/16 | 3⅞ | .... |
| 80 | .... | 13/16 | .... | .... | .... | .... |
| | .... | 2 | .... | .... | .... | .... |

Total call volume 235   Total call open int. 3,481
Total put volume 83   Total put open int. 1,137
The index: High 74.34; Low 73.03; Close 73.53, +0.43

### VALUE LINE INDEX OPTIONS

| Strike Price | Calls–Last May | Jun | Jul | Puts–Last May | Jun | Jul |
|---|---|---|---|---|---|---|
| 340 | .... | .... | .... | .... | 2 | .... |
| 345 | .... | .... | .... | ½ | .... | .... |
| 350 | .... | 11⅛ | .... | .... | 4¼ | 6 |
| 355 | .... | .... | .... | .... | .... | .... |
| 360 | 3⅜ | .... | .... | 5¼ | .... | .... |

Total call volume 47   Total call open int. 4,604
Total put volume 24   Total put open int. 2,258
The index: High 355.95; Low 354.57; Close 355.67, +1.13

### UTILITIES INDEX

| Strike Price | Calls–Last May | Jun | Jul | Puts–Last May | Jun | Jul |
|---|---|---|---|---|---|---|
| 250 | .... | 6 | .... | .... | .... | .... |
| 260 | ⅞ | .... | .... | .... | .... | .... |

Total call volume 14   Total call open int. 955
Total put volume 0   Total put open int. 261
The index: High 256.21; Low 254.84; Close 255.32, –0.15

## PACIFIC

### FINANCIAL NEWS COMPOSITE INDEX

| Strike Price | Calls–Last May | Jun | Sep | Puts–Last May | Jun | Sep |
|---|---|---|---|---|---|---|
| 245 | .... | 43¼ | .... | .... | .... | .... |
| 275 | 13¾ | 15 | .... | .... | .... | .... |
| 280 | 9⅛ | .... | .... | .... | .... | .... |
| 285 | .... | 7¼ | .... | .... | .... | .... |
| 290 | 1⅞ | 4⅞ | .... | 3⅜ | .... | .... |
| 295 | 9/16 | 2¾ | .... | .... | .... | .... |
| 300 | .... | .... | .... | 12⅛ | .... | .... |

Total call volume 160   Total call open int. 2,284
Total put volume 51   Total put open int. 941
The index: High 289.60; Low 288.22; Close 288.30, –0.07

## NEW YORK

### NYSE INDEX OPTIONS

| Strike Price | Calls–Last May | Jun | Jul | Puts–Last May | Jun | Jul |
|---|---|---|---|---|---|---|
| 225 | .... | .... | .... | 11/16 | 2 15/16 | .... |
| 230 | 1 11/16 | 4¼ | .... | .... | .... | 5⅞ |

Total call volume 22   Total call open int. 146
Total put volume 16   Total put open int. 1,163
The index: High 230.33; Low 229.42; Close 229.56, +0.06

**FIGURE 18-12**
Index options quotations.

*SOURCE:* Reprinted by permission of *The Wall Street Journal,* (C) Dow Jones & Company, Inc. (May 6, 1992):C15.

OPTIONS

569

**FIGURE 18-13**

Interest rate options quotations.

*SOURCE:* Reprinted by permission of *The Wall Street Journal,* (C) Dow Jones & Company, Inc. (May 6, 1992):C13.

☐ **18.8.3 Foreign Currency Options**

No foreign currency options are traded on Canadian exchanges. But call and put options on foreign currencies such as Swiss francs are traded in the US. These are similar to stock options — when exercised, the underlying asset must be delivered. Since each option involves units of a foreign (non-United States) currency, delivery is made in a bank account in the country of origin of the currency in question (typically, brokers can readily assist an investor in arranging for this to be done). Figure 18.14 shows some of these options that have been offered along with their quotations.

For example, the Philadelphia Exchange (PHLX) maintains an option market in foreign currencies, one of which is Swiss francs. Specifically, these options involve the delivery of 62,500 Swiss francs. In December 1988, one of the call options on this currency had an exercise price of 70 and an expiration date of March 1989. That is, the dollar amount involved in the exercise of this option was $43,750 (= 62,500 × $.70). The market price (that is, the premium) for this call was 1.17 on December 8, 1988, meaning the cost of purchasing the call was $731.25 ($.0117 × 62,500). Since the exchange rate on that date (68.23, or $.6823 per Swiss franc) was less than the exercise price of this call ($.70), the option was out of the money.

**18.9**    **PORTFOLIO INSURANCE**

One use of options is in creating *portfolio insurance*. Consider an investor who holds a highly diversified portfolio. This investor would like to be able to benefit from any upward movements that may subsequently occur in the stock market but would also like to be protected from any downward movements.[20] As described below there are, in principle, three ways this can be accomplished.

---

[20] In an efficient market, investors with "average" attitudes toward risk should not purchase portfolio insurance. Those who are especially averse to "downside risk" (relative to "upside potential") may find it useful to buy insurance. The key is the nature of the investor's attitudes toward risk and return. See Hayne E. Leland, "Who Should Buy Portfolio Insurance?" *Journal of Finance* 35, no. 2 (May 1980):581–94.

# OPTIONS
## PHILADELPHIA

Wednesday, May 6, 1992

| Option & Underlying | Strike Price | Calls—Last May | Jun | Sep | Puts—Last May | Jun | Sep |
|---|---|---|---|---|---|---|---|
| 50,000 Australian Dollars-cents per unit. | | | | | | | |
| ADollr..... | 75 | r | 0.86 | r | r | r | r |
| 75.82 .... | 76 | 0.14 | r | r | r | r | r |
| 31,250 British Pounds-European Style. | | | | | | | |
| BPound .. | 177½ | 1.50 | 2.15 | r | r | r | r |
| 178.56 .. | 180 | 0.79 | 1.52 | r | r | r | r |
| 31,250 British Pounds-cents per unit. | | | | | | | |
| BPound .. | 170 | r | r | 9.15 | r | 0.22 | r |
| 178.56 .. | 172½ | 5.85 | 5.95 | r | r | r | r |
| 178.56 .. | 175 | 4.42 | 4.60 | r | 0.13 | 0.95 | r |
| 178.56 .. | 177½ | 2.15 | 2.45 | r | 0.60 | 2.38 | r |
| 178.56 .. | 180 | r | r | r | 2.12 | r | r |
| 178.56 .. | 182½ | 0.25 | r | r | r | r | r |
| 50,000 Canadian Dollars-European Style. | | | | | | | |
| CDollar.... | 83 | r | 0.78 | r | r | r | r |
| 50,000 Canadian Dollars-cents per unit. | | | | | | | |
| CDollr..... | 83½ | 0.27 | r | r | 0.28 | r | r |
| 83.89 .... | 88 | r | r | r | r | r | 5.12 |
| 250,000 French Francs-10ths of a cent per unit. | | | | | | | |
| FFranc.... | 16½ | r | r | r | r | 0.06 | r |
| 181.21 ... | 18 | r | 2.66 | r | r | r | r |
| 181.21 ... | 18½ | r | 0.80 | r | r | r | r |
| 1,000,000 GermanMark-JapaneseYen cross. | | | | | | | |
| GMk-JYn . | 81 | 0.44 | 0.71 | r | 0.41 | 1.08 | r |
| 62,500 German Marks-European Style. | | | | | | | |
| DMark .... | 51 | r | 0.29 | r | r | r | r |
| 61.07 .... | 58½ | r | r | r | s | r | 0.13 | s |
| 61.07 .... | 60 | 1.14 | r | r | r | 0.45 | r |
| 61.07 .... | 60½ | 0.75 | r | r | s | r | s |
| 61.07 .... | 61 | r | r | 1.16 | r | r | r |
| 61.07 .... | 61½ | 0.21 | 0.53 | s | r | r | s |
| 61.07 .... | 62½ | r | 0.26 | s | r | r | s |
| 61.07 .... | 63 | r | r | 0.54 | r | r | r |
| 62,500 German Marks-cents per unit. | | | | | | | |
| DMark .... | 55 | r | r | r | r | r | 0.19 |
| 61.07 .... | 57 | r | 4.38 | r | r | 0.03 | r |
| 61.07 .... | 58 | r | r | 3.19 | r | 0.08 | r |
| 61.07 .... | 58½ | r | r | s | r | 0.13 | s |
| 61.07 .... | 59 | r | r | r | r | 0.22 | 1.08 |
| 61.07 .... | 59½ | 1.75 | r | s | 0.04 | 0.28 | s |
| 61.07 .... | 60 | 1.21 | 1.37 | r | 0.09 | 0.44 | 1.50 |
| 61.07 .... | 60½ | 1.02 | 1.02 | s | 0.16 | r | s |
| 61.07 .... | 61 | 0.65 | 0.81 | 1.20 | 0.32 | 0.82 | 2.00 |
| 61.07 .... | 61½ | 0.33 | 0.65 | s | r | 1.08 | s |
| 61.07 .... | 62 | 0.17 | 0.36 | r | r | r | r |
| 61.07 .... | 62½ | r | 0.27 | s | r | 1.90 | s |
| 61.07 .... | 64 | r | 0.06 | r | r | r | r |
| 6,250,000 Japanese Yen-100ths of a cent per unit. | | | | | | | |
| JYen...... | 74 | 1.58 | r | r | r | 0.30 | r |
| 75.14 .... | 74½ | r | r | s | r | 0.43 | s |
| 75.14 .... | 75 | 0.81 | 0.99 | 1.69 | r | r | 1.48 |
| 75.14 .... | 75½ | 0.41 | 0.74 | s | r | 0.88 | s |
| 75.14 .... | 76 | 0.24 | 0.53 | r | 0.67 | r | r |
| 75.14 .... | 77 | r | 0.30 | r | r | r | r |
| 75.14 .... | 78½ | r | 0.09 | s | r | r | s |
| 6,250,000 Japanese Yen-European Style. | | | | | | | |
| JYen...... | 73 | r | r | r | r | 0.11 | r |
| 75.14 .... | 75½ | r | 0.83 | s | r | r | s |
| 75.14 .... | 77 | r | 0.31 | r | r | r | r |
| 62,500 Swiss Francs-European Style. | | | | | | | |
| SFranc.... | 65 | r | r | r | 0.07 | 0.46 | r |
| 66.42 .... | 65½ | r | r | s | 0.15 | r | s |
| 66.42 .... | 66 | r | r | r | 0.31 | 0.86 | r |
| 66.42 .... | 67 | r | 0.45 | r | r | r | r |
| 66.42 .... | 67½ | 0.09 | r | s | r | r | s |
| 66.42 .... | 68½ | r | 0.15 | s | r | r | s |
| 66.42 .... | 69 | 0.02 | r | r | r | r | r |
| 62,500 Swiss Francs-cents per unit. | | | | | | | |
| SFranc.... | 64 | r | r | r | r | 0.22 | r |
| 66.42 .... | 65 | r | r | r | 0.05 | 0.52 | 1.48 |
| 66.42 .... | 65½ | r | r | s | 0.12 | r | s |
| 66.42 .... | 66 | r | r | r | 0.38 | r | s |
| 66.42 .... | 66½ | 0.53 | r | s | r | r | s |
| 66.42 .... | 67 | 0.16 | 0.60 | r | r | r | r |
| 66.42 .... | 68 | r | 0.38 | 0.79 | r | r | r |
| Total Call Vol | 20,547 | | | Call Open Int | 308,335 | | |
| Total Put Vol | 13,154 | | | Put Open Int | 509,943 | | |

**FIGURE 18-14**

Foreign currency options quotations.

*SOURCE:* Reprinted by permission of *The Wall Street Journal,* (C) Dow Jones & Company, Inc. (May 6, 1992):C13.

## ☐ 18.9.1 Purchasing an Insurance Policy

One alternative would be to sign a contract with an insurance company. For example, assume that a portfolio is currently worth $100,000. The insurance company might agree to cover any loss in value over some specified period, such as over the forthcoming year. At the end of the year, if the portfolio value were $95,000, the insurance company would pay the investor $5000. On the other hand, if the value were $105,000, the insurance company would pay nothing.

Figure 18.15(a) illustrates this situation. The horizontal axis measures the value of the portfolio at year-end. The 45° line *OBC* shows the value of the uninsured portfolio, whereas curve *ABC* shows the value of the insured portfolio. As the figure shows, if the portfolio value at the end of the year is more than $100,000, then the insured portfolio will be worth the same amount as the uninsured portfolio. However, if the portfolio value is less than $100,000, then the insured portfolio is worth more, with the difference between the *OB* and *AB* representing the size of the payment made to the investor by the insurance company.

Unfortunately, insurance companies rarely sign contracts of this sort. However, this is not the only alternative. Instead of dealing with an insurance company, the investor could consider purchasing a put option.

## ☐ 18.9.2 Purchasing a Protective Put

Assume that a put option is available on a stock market index that closely resembles the investor's portfolio. Curve *ADE* in Figure 18.15(b) shows the value to a buyer of such a put at the expiration date, where the put has an exercise price of $100,000 (note how it corresponds to Figure 18.3(b)). Curve *OBC* is the value of the portfolio on the expiration date, assuming the put was not purchased.

What would happen to an investor who (1) held the portfolio and (2) purchased this put? Figure 18.15(c) shows the answer. The value of the portfolio (*ABC*) is simply the combination of the values shown in Figure 18.15(b). Not surprisingly, it is precisely the same as curve ABC in Figure 18.15(a).

In this case, the purchase of a put provides protection against declines in portfolio value. In this role, it is termed a protective put. In practice, stock indices may not closely correspond with an investor's portfolio. Thus, purchase of a put on a stock index may provide only imperfect insurance. In a graph such as that shown in Figure 18.15(c), the resulting curve would be somewhat fuzzy due to the possible divergence of values of the portfolio and index. For example, the portfolio may decline in value by $25,000, while the index is declining by only $10,000. In this case, the portfolio would be insured for only 40% of its decline in value ($40\% = \$10,000/\$25,000$).

What if neither explicit insurance nor an appropriate put were available? Can something still be done to insure the portfolio's value against market declines? Yes, if the allocation of funds between the portfolio and a riskless security can be altered frequently enough (and at reasonable cost). This type of portfolio insurance involves the creation of a *synthetic put*, and its application involves the use of a dynamic strategy for asset allocation, which is discussed next.

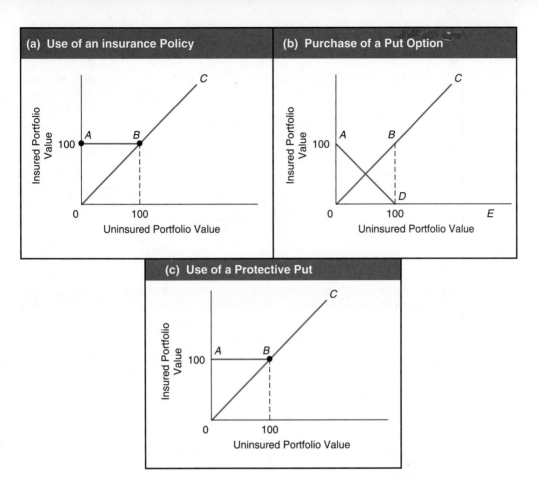

**FIGURE 18-15**
Portfolio insurance.

### ☐ 18.9.3 Creating a Synthetic Put

Insuring a portfolio by creating a synthetic put can most easily be described with an example.[21] Assume that an individual is considering investing $100,000 in a portfolio of common stocks whose returns follow a binomial process such that the market value of this portfolio will either increase to $120,000 or decrease to $80,000 in six months. If it increases to $120,000, then it will be worth either $140,000 or $100,000 after another six months. Alternatively, if it decreases to $80,000, then it will ultimately be worth either

---

[21] For an exposition, see Mark Rubinstein and Hayne E. Leland, "Replicating Options with Positions in Stock and Cash," *Financial Analysts Journal* 37, no. 4 (July/August 1981):63–72; Mark Rubinstein, "Alternative Paths to Portfolio Insurance," *Financial Analysts Journal* 41, no. 4 (July/August 1985):42–52; Robert Ferguson, "How To Beat the S&P 500 (without losing sleep)," *Financial Analysts Journal* 42, no. 2 (March/April 1986):37–46; and Thomas J. O'Brien, *How Option Replicating Portfolio Insurance Works: Expanded Details*, Monograph Series in Finance and Economics 1988–4, Salomon Brothers Center for the Study of Financial Institutions, Stern School of Business, New York University.

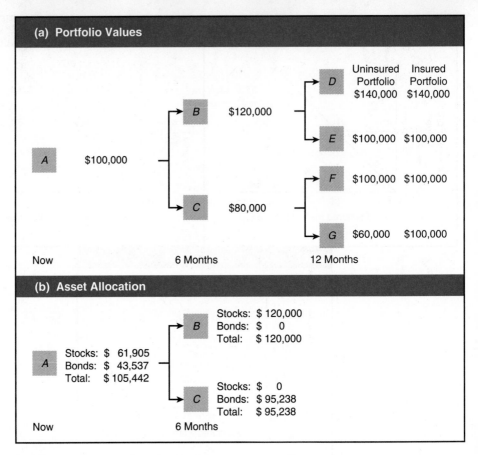

**FIGURE 18-16**
Creation of a synthetic put.

$100,000 or $60,000. Each of these possible "states of the world" is indicated by a letter in Figure 18.16(a), with the current state being denoted by A.

Figure 18.16(a) also shows two sets of terminal portfolio values (that is, portfolio values after 12 months) for this common stock portfolio. The first set gives the values of the uninsured portfolio. The second shows the desired portfolio values — that is, the values of an insured portfolio assuming that the investor wants to be certain that the terminal value of the portfolio is at least $100,000, while not foregoing any upside potential associated with state D.[22]

What should the investor do initially in order to achieve this? Clearly, the investor cannot simply purchase the portfolio of stocks, since then the portfolio will be worth only

---

[22] In this example, portfolio insurance is sought for a one-year horizon with a floor of 0% (meaning the investor does not want to lose any of the initial investment over the next 12 months). Other horizons and floors, such as a two-year horizon with a floor of -5% (meaning the investor does not want to lose more than 5% of the initial investment over the next 24 months), are possible.

$60,000 if state $G$ occurs. However, the investor could purchase portfolio insurance — that is, create a synthetic put — by investing in both the stock portfolio and risk-free bonds.

For example, suppose that six months from now state $B$ has occurred. How might one be certain to have $140,000 if the final state is $D$ and $100,000 if the state is $E$? The answer is simple — make sure that the portfolio at that point is worth $120,000. Thus, an initial investment strategy is required that will provide $120,000 if state $B$ occurs six months from now.

Alternatively, suppose that after six months state $C$ occurs. In this situation, how might one be certain to have $100,000 regardless of the final state (F or G)? If risk-free bonds return 5% per six months, then the investor should purchase $95,238 ($100,000/1.05) of these bonds. This means that an initial investment strategy is required that will provide $95,238 if state $C$ occurs.

Figure 18.16(b) shows the investments and the amounts required in situations $B$ and $C$. It remains only to determine an appropriate initial investment (at point $A$).

An amount of $1 invested in the common stock portfolio at $A$ will grow to $1.20 after six months if the state $B$ occurs. More generally, $s$ invested in the common stock portfolio at $A$ will grow to $1.2\,s$ if $B$ occurs. Similarly, $b$ invested in bonds at $A$ will grow to $1.05b$ after six months. Thus, a set of initial investments that will provide $120,000 if state $B$ occurs can be found by solving the following equation for $s$ and $b$:

$$1.2\,s + 1.05\,b = \$120,000. \qquad (18.32)$$

If state $C$ occurs, then $s$ invested in the common stock portfolio will be worth $.8\,s$, whereas $b$ invested in bonds will be worth $1.05\,b$. Thus, a set of initial investments that will provide $95,238 if state $C$ occurs can be found by solving the following equation for $s$ and $b$:

$$.8\,s + 1.05\,b = \$95,238. \qquad (18.33)$$

The solutions for $s$ and $b$, shown in Figure 18.16(b), show that the investor should initially invest $61,905 in common stocks and $43,537 in bonds (that is, $s = \$61,905$ and $b = \$43,537$), for a total initial investment of $105,442.

This is equivalent to investing $100,000 in the common stock portfolio and buying a protective put option (or an insurance policy) for $5442. Indeed, this analysis provides the appropriate price for such an option or insurance policy. In this case, the investor created a synthetic put where the stock portfolio is the underlying asset.

By design, this initial investment will provide precisely the desired ending values, but only if the asset mix is altered as the different states are revealed. A dynamic strategy is used in which investments are bought and sold at intermediate points, depending on the returns on the underlying assets. The objective of the dynamic strategy is to minimize the cost of the hedge.

In the example, if state $B$ occurs, the stocks will be worth $74,286 ($\$61,905 \times 1.2$) and the bonds will be worth $45,714 ($\$43,537 \times 1.05$, for an aggregate value of $120,000. The bonds would then be sold and the proceeds invested in the common stock portfolio such that the investor is entirely invested in common stocks for the last six months.

However, if state $C$ occurs, the stocks will be worth $49,524 ($\$61,905 \times .8$) and the bonds will be worth $45,714 ($\$43,537 \times 1.05$), for an aggregate value of $95,238.

The stocks would then be sold and the proceeds invested in the risk-free bonds for the last six months.

Thus, if the initial portfolio rises in value, bonds are sold and the proceeds invested in common stocks. If the initial portfolio falls in value, the stock portfolio is sold and the proceeds invested in bonds. In this example, the percentage invested in stocks is initially 58.71%. ($61,905/$105,442) and subsequently goes to either 100% (if stocks go up) or 0% (if stocks go down).

More realistic applications may involve more time intervals within a one-year period, with smaller stock price movements in each interval. Consequently, there would be more changes in the mix of stocks and bonds after each interval, but the changes would be of smaller magnitude. Nevertheless, the essential nature of the strategy is the same:

> When stock prices rise, sell some bonds and buy more stocks.
> When stock prices fall, sell some stocks and buy more bonds.

Computers are used to monitor stock price movements for investors who have obtained portfolio insurance in this manner. When these movements are large enough, the computer places the requisite buy and sell orders electronically. Since much of this monitoring and ordering is programmed into a computer, portfolio insurance is often referred to as *program trading*.[23]

If there are only two states of the world in each interval and there are no transaction costs, then a "perfectly insured portfolio" can be achieved with a dynamic strategy. In practice, however, the results are likely to be only approximate for two reasons. First, there are transaction costs associated with buying and selling securities for the dynamic strategy.[24] Second, if an interval is defined as the length of time over which only two alternative states may occur, then the length of an interval may be so short that the number of transactions required becomes impossibly large.

In practice, arbitrary rules are applied to avoid frequent revisions and the associated high level of transaction costs, while being reasonably certain of providing the desired level of insurance.[25] Unfortunately, these arbitrary rules did not perform well on Black Monday and Terrible Tuesday (October 19-20, 1987). During these two days, stock prices moved downward so fast that reallocation could not be carried out in a timely fashion and portfolio insurance could not provide the anticipated protection. As a result,

---

[23] The next chapter discusses another form of program trading that is known as index arbitrage.

[24] There is another dynamic strategy for insuring the portfolio that is often preferred because it has smaller transaction costs. Instead of combining stocks with a risk-free bond, it involves combining stocks with a short position in index futures, a type of financial contract that is discussed in the next chapter.

[25] For a discussion of transactions costs, see Hayne E. Leland, "Option Pricing and Replication with Transactions Costs," *Journal of Finance* 40, no. 5 (December 1985):1283–1301. For tests of some commonly used arbitrary rules, see Ethan S. Etzioni, "Rebalance Disciplines for Portfolio Insurance," *Journal of Portfolio Management* 13, no. 1 (Fall 1986):59–62; C. B. Garcia and F. J. Gould, "An Empirical Study of Portfolio Insurance," *Financial Analysts Journal* 43, no. 4 (July/August 1987):44–54; and Robert Ferguson, "A Comparison of the Mean-Variance and Long-Term Return Characteristics of 3 Investment Strategies," *Financial Analysts Journal* 43, no. 4 (July/August 1987):55–66.

some people believe that dynamic strategies will be used less frequently in the future and that puts will be used more often.[26]

## 18.10 SUMMARY

This chapter introduced the two main types of option contracts that currently are in existence. Call options allow one person (known as the buyer) to purchase from another person (known as the writer) a specific asset at a specific price at any time up until a stated expiration date. Put options allow one person (known as the buyer) to sell another person (known as the writer) a specific asset at a specific price at any time up until a stated expiration date. Calls and puts typically involve 100 shares of a specific company's stock and have an expiration date of nine months or less.

An investor interested in options can be either a buyer or a writer of an option. However, once a position in an option is assumed, it need not be held for the life of the option. Instead, an offsetting transaction can be made, meaning a buyer can subsequently sell the contract to someone else and a writer can subsequently buy the contract back from someone else. What makes all this possible and relatively easy to do is the fact that the terms of these contracts are standardized, thereby allowing them to be traded on certain organized exchanges at market-determined prices. Thus, a writer who wishes to buy the contract back does not need to deal with the specific investor who bought the contract in the first place. All that is necessary is for the writer to buy any contract that has the same terms as the one that was originally written.

The value of an option is bounded by certain market conditions. That is, it can be shown that options have one upper bound and two lower bounds on their values. Should an option have a market price that is outside these bounds, then an opportunity exists for investors to engage in arbitrage, meaning investors would be able to make abnormal returns with certainty.

Within these bounds, an estimate of the true value of an option can be determined by using a formula developed by Black and Scholes. This formula shows that the value of an option is determined by five factors — the market price of the underlying stock, the exercise price, the life of the option, the risk-free rate, and the risk of the common stock. It can also be shown that a call and put option on the same stock have values that are linked to each other by what is known as the put-call parity theorem, provided the options have the same exercise price and expiration date.

Unfortunately, the Black-Scholes formula and put-call parity theorem are applicable only to European options on stocks that do not pay cash dividends over the life of the option. Adjustments can be made, however, so that reasonably accurate estimates of the value of American options on dividend-paying stocks can be obtained.

In addition to put and call options on individual common stocks, options on other kinds of assets exist. Examples include stock indices, debt instruments, and foreign currency. Furthermore, synthetic options can be created by holding the underlying asset and a bond in relative amounts that vary with the market price of the underlying asset.

---

[26] See Mark Rubinstein, "Portfolio Insurance and the Market Crash," *Financial Analysts Journal* 44, no. 1 (January/February 1988):38–47. For a discussion of various types of dynamic strategies, see Andre F. Perold and William F. Sharpe, "Dynamic Strategies for Asset Allocation," *Financial Analysts Journal* 44, no. 1 (January/February 1988):16–27.

Portfolio insurance, where an investor establishes a floor on the portfolio's return over some specified horizon, involves the creation of a synthetic put.

## APPENDIX A

## SECURITIES WITH OPTION-LIKE FEATURES

Many securities have features that are similar to stock options, particularly call options. In some cases, the option-like features are explicit. In other cases, more subtle option-like features are involved. This appendix discusses some of these securities.

### A.1 WARRANTS

A *warrant* (or more precisely, *warrant for purchase of common shares*) is a call option issued by the firm whose common shares serve as the underlying security. At the time of issue, a warrant usually has a longer time to expiration (for example, five or more years) than a typical call option. Some perpetual warrants, with no expiration date, have also been issued. Generally, warrants may be exercised before expiration — that is, they are American call options — but some require an initial waiting period.

The exercise price may be fixed or it may change during the life of the warrant, usually increasing in steps. The initial exercise price is typically set to exceed the market price of the underlying security at the time the warrant is issued, often by a substantial amount.

At the time of issue, one warrant typically entitles the holder to purchase one share of stock for the appropriate exercise price. However, most warrants are protected against stock splits and stock dividends. This means that any warrant with such protection will enable the investor to buy more or less than one share at an altered exercise price if a stock dividend or stock split is declared. For example, a two-for-one stock split would allow the warrantholder to purchase two shares at one-half the original exercise price, whereas a one-for-two reverse stock split would allow the warrantholder to purchase one-half share at twice the original exercise price.

Warrants may be distributed to shareholders in lieu of a stock or cash dividend or sold directly as a new security issue. Alternatively, warrants may be issued in order to "sweeten" an offering of some other kind of security. For example, a bond may be sold by the firm with warrants attached to it. In some cases, the warrants are nondetachable, except upon exercise. This means that if an investor wants to sell one of the bonds, the warrants must either be exercised or sold with the bond. In other cases, the warrants are detachable, meaning that after the initial sale of the bonds an investor may sell either the bonds or the warrants (or both).

Terms associated with a warrant are contained in a warrant agreement, which serves the same function as an indenture for a bond issue. In this agreement, the scope of the warrantholder's protection is defined (for example, the treatment of warrants in the event of a merger); it may also specify certain restrictions on corporate behavior.

Some warrants that are issued with bonds have an additional attribute. Although they may be detached and exercised by paying cash to the corporation, an alternative method of payment is provided. This alternative allows bonds from the initial issue to be used in lieu of cash to pay the exercise price, with the bonds being valued at par for this purpose.

One difference between warrants and call options is the limitation on the amount of warrants that are outstanding. A specific number of warrants of a particular type will be issued; the total cannot easily be increased and typically is reduced as the warrants are exercised. In contrast, a call option can be created whenever two people wish to create one; thus, the number outstanding is not fixed. Exercise of a call option on its stock has no more effect on a corporation than a transaction in its stock on the secondary market. However, the exercise of a warrant does have an effect. In particular, it leaves the corporation with more cash, fewer warrants outstanding, and more shares outstanding.

Warrants are traded on major stock exchanges and on the over-the-counter market. Quotations for those with active markets are provided in the financial press in the sections devoted to stocks.

---

## A.2    RIGHTS

A right is similar to a warrant in that it also is a call option issued by the firm whose shares serve as the underlying security.[27] Rights are issued to give existing shareholders a preemptive right to subscribe to a new issue of common shares before the general public is given an opportunity. Each share of stock receives one right. A stated number of rights plus cash equal to a specified subscription price are required in order to obtain one new share. To insure the sale of the new shares, the subscription price is usually set below the stock's market price at the time the rights are issued. This does not mean that new subscribers get a bargain, since they must pay old shareholders for the required number of rights, which become valuable as a result.

Rights generally have short lives (from two to ten weeks) and may be freely traded prior to exercise. Up to a specified date, old shares of the stock trade *cum rights*, meaning the buyer of the shares is entitled to receive the rights when issued. Afterward, the shares trades *ex rights* at a correspondingly lower price. Rights for popular issues of stock are sometimes traded on exchanges; others are available in the over-the-counter market. Often trading begins prior to actual availability, with the rights sold for delivery on a *when-issued* basis.

A right is, in effect, a warrant, although one with a rather short time before expiration. It also differs with regard to exercise price, which is typically set above the stock's market price at issuance for a warrant and below it for a right. Because of their short lives, rights need not be protected against stock splits and stock dividends. Otherwise, they have all the attributes of a warrant and should be valued accordingly.

---

[27] Rights are also discussed in Chapter 15.

# BOND CALL PROVISIONS

Most corporate bonds have call provisions that allow the firm to repurchase the bonds before maturity, usually at a price above par value.[28] This amounts to the sale of a straight bond and the simultaneous purchase by the corporation of a call option sold by the purchaser of the bond. The premium is paid by the corporation in the form of a relatively lower selling price for the bond. The writer of the option is the bond purchaser.

Bond call provisions usually can be exercised only after some specified date (for example, five years after issue). Moreover, the exercise price, known as the call premium, may be different for different exercise dates (typically shrinking in size the longer the bond is outstanding). The implicit call option associated with such a bond is thus both longer-lived and more complex than those traded on the listed options markets.

# CONVERTIBLE SECURITIES

A particularly popular financial instrument is a security that can be converted into a different security of the same firm under certain conditions. The typical case involves bonds or preferred shares convertible into shares of the firm's common stock, with a stated number of shares received for each bond. Usually, no cash is involved: The old security is simply traded in, and the appropriate number of new securities are issued in return. Convertible preferred shares are issued from time to time, but tax effects make them, like other preferred shares, attractive primarily to corporate investors. For other investors, many issues of convertible bonds are available.

If a $1000 par value bond can be converted into 20 shares of common stock, the conversion ratio is 20. Alternatively, the conversion price may be said to be $50 ($1000/20), since $50 of the bond's par value must be given up to obtain one common share. Neither the conversion ratio nor the conversion price is affected by changes in a bond's market value.

Conversion ratios are typically set so that conversion will not prove attractive unless the stock price increases substantially from its value at the time the convertible security was first issued. This is similar to the general practice used in setting exercise prices for warrants.

A convertible bond's conversion value, obtained by multiplying the conversion ratio by the stock's current market price, is the value that would be obtained by conversion; it is the bond's current "value as stock." The conversion premium is the amount by which the bond's current market price exceeds its conversion value, expressed as a percent of the latter. A related amount is the convertible's investment value. This value is an estimate, based on the convertible's maturity date, coupon rate, and rating, of the amount for which the bond might sell if it were not convertible. Equivalently, it is the convertible's "value as a straight bond."

Consider a $1000 par value bond convertible into 20 shares of stock. If the market price of the stock is $60 per share, then the conversion value of the bond is $1200 ($60 × 20). If the current market price of the convertible bond is $1300, then its conversion premium is $100 (= $1300 − $1200). Its investment value may be estimated

---

[28] Bond call provisions are also discussed in Chapters 12 and 13.

to be $950, meaning that the bond would sell for this much if it did not provide the investor with the option of convertibility. Figure 18.17 shows the details of some actively traded convertible securities offered by a well-known investment dealer.

Convertible securities of great complexity can be found. Some may be converted only after an initial waiting period. Some may be converted up to the bond's maturity date; others only for a stated, shorter period. Some have different conversion ratios for different years. A few can be converted into packages of two or more different securities; others require the additional payment of cash upon conversion.

Convertible bonds are usually protected against stock splits and stock dividends via adjustment in the conversion ratio. For example, a bond with an initial conversion ratio of 20 could be adjusted to have a ratio of 22 following a 10% stock dividend. Protection against cash dividends is not generally provided, but some indentures require that the holders of convertible bonds be notified prior to payment of cash dividends so they may convert before the resultant fall in the stock's market price.

Convertible securities often contain a call provision, which may be used by the corporation to force conversion when the stock's market price is sufficiently high to make the value of the stock obtained on conversion exceed the call price of the bond. For example, if the conversion value of the bond is $1200 (the bond is convertible into 20 shares of stock that are currently selling for $60 per share) and the call price is $1100, the firm can force conversion by calling the bond. This is because a bondholder faces two choices when the call is received — either convert and receive 20 shares collectively worth $1200 or receive cash of $1100 — and should choose the shares since they have the higher value.

A convertible bond is, for practical purposes, a bond with nondetachable warrants plus the restriction that *only* the bond is usable (at par) to pay the exercise price. If the bond were not callable, the value of this package would equal the value of a straight noncallable bond (that is, the estimated investment value) plus that of the warrants. However, most convertible bonds are callable and thus involve a double option: The holder has an option to convert the bond to stock, and the issuing corporation has an option to buy the bond back from the investors.

## QUESTIONS AND PROBLEMS

1. Why have organized options exchanges been so important to the growth in options trading?
2. Peter McPhee has just written a call option on Jasper Computer Services stock. Specifically, Peter sold four June 50 contracts at a premium of $3 per share. Jasper stock currently sells for $48 per share. How much margin was required?
3. Elizabeth Stroud has only a few hours left to decide whether to exercise a call option on Caledonia Company stock. The call option has an exercise price of $54. Elizabeth originally purchased the call six months ago for $400 (or $4 per share).
   a. For what range of stock prices should Elizabeth exercise the call on the last day of the call's life?
   b. For what range of stock prices would Elizabeth realize a net loss (including the premium paid for the call)?
   c. If Elizabeth had purchased a put instead of a call, how would your answers to parts (a) and (b) change?

# CONVERTIBLE DEBENTURES

Selected quotations on actively traded debentures, provided by Wood Gundy Inc.

Bond price is the final bid quotation and share price is the bid price at the close of trading /Dec. 20, 1991. Yields are calculated to full maturity. Conversion rate is the number of shares for each $100 of bonds. Premium is the amount paid in excess of immediate conversion into shares, expressed as a percentage.

| Issuer | Coupon | Maturity | Bond price | Yield | Conv. rate | Share price | Premium |
|---|---|---|---|---|---|---|---|
| AGF Management | 7 | 30 Jun 2002 | 73.00 | 11.49 | 5.00 | 7.25 | 106.90 |
| Alberta Energy | 6.75 | 30 Jun 2002 | 77.00 | 10.40 | 4.28 | 11.75 | 57.16 |
| Alberta Energy | 7.25 | 30 Sep 2003 | 79.00 | 10.38 | 3.92 | 11.75 | 75.77 |
| Amoco (U.S.$) | 7.375 | 1 Sep 2013 | 106.00 | 6.84 | 1.90 | 48.13 | 16.71 |
| BF Realty Holdings | 8 | 30 Jun 1998 | 4.00 | 0.00 | 20.83 | 0.09 | 295.36 |
| BF Realty Holdings | 10.75 | 31 Jan 2001 | 4.00 | 0.00 | 6.67 | 0.09 | 1135.23 |
| Cambridge Shopping | 8 | 1 Mar 2003 | 94.00 | 8.85 | 3.69 | 20.00 | 32.90 |
| Cambridge Shopping | 7.5 | 1 Jun 2004 | 80.00 | 10.40 | 2.70 | 20.00 | 49.85 |
| Campeau | 7.5 | 30 Sep 1997 | 11.00 | 80.62 | 3.17 | 0.52 | 687.40 |
| Canada Helicopter | 8 | 31 Aug 2007 | 64.00 | 13.61 | 8.33 | 5.25 | 55.43 |
| Canam Manac Group | 8.5 | 30 Sep 1998 | 57.00 | 20.55 | 10.25 | 2.85 | 112.24 |
| Consolidated Enfield | 8 | 31 Mar 2002 | 40.00 | 23.90 | 1.48 | 1.20 | 2713.41 |
| Consumers Packaging | 8 | 1 May 2003 | 42.00 | 22.14 | 4.08 | 3.00 | 324.84 |
| Conwest Exploration | 7.25 | 14 Jun 2002 | 75.00 | 11.40 | 5.56 | 8.88 | 58.18 |
| Czar Resources | 8.75 | 15 Jun 1995 | 72.00 | 20.44 | 58.82 | 0.51 | 156.66 |
| Devtek | 8 | 30 Apr 1998 | 71.00 | 15.31 | 8.33 | 4.75 | 87.02 |
| Dickenson Mines | 8.5 | 30 Sep 1995 | 91.00 | 11.52 | 12.50 | 3.40 | 121.18 |
| Emco | 8 | 31 Dec 2000 | 61.00 | 16.46 | 6.67 | 4.80 | 99.99 |
| Emco | 7.25 | 30 Apr 2002 | 55.00 | 16.44 | 5.71 | 4.80 | 111.47 |
| Encor Energy | 8.5 | 1 Dec 2000 | 47.00 | 22.52 | 35.70 | 0.28 | 390.17 |
| Federal Industries | 9 | 31 Oct 1999 | 77.00 | 13.91 | 5.41 | 7.38 | 100.69 |
| Federal Industries | 8 | 15 Jun 2006 | 62.00 | 14.28 | 5.41 | 7.38 | 63.06 |
| Hees International | 3.170 | 31 May 2088 | 44.00 | 7.21 | 14.00 | 8.49 |  |
| Hollinger (adj. rate) | 7.625 | 30 Sep 2008 | 92.00 | 8.53 | 6.72 | 11.75 | 18.99 |
| Irwin Toy Ltd. | 14.5 | 15 Aug 1992 | 100.00 | 13.95 | 9.76 | 5.38 | 94.51 |
| Ivaco | 7.5 | 15 Apr 2010 | 56.00 | 14.36 | 3.13 | 15.50 | 21.81 |
| Kaufel Group | 7.75 | 28 Jul 1998 | 80.00 | 12.27 | 8.33 | 6.25 | 59.42 |
| Labatt (adj. rate) | 6 | 28 Feb 2006 | 142.00 | 2.47 | 5.59 | 25.13 | 4.59 |
| Labatt (adj. rate) | 5 | 1 Apr 2007 | 94.00 | 5.59 | 3.70 | 25.13 | 3.16 |
| Maclean Hunter | 8.25 | 1 May 2004 | 212.00 | 0.00 | 19.75 | 11.00 | 0.00 |
| MacMillan Bloedel (adj.rate) | 5 | 1 May 2007 | 67.00 | 9.01 | 3.49 | 17.00 | 16.30 |
| Malette | 8.5 | 27 Nov 1996 | 100.00 | 8.50 | 12.12 | 7.50 | 15.50 |
| Mark Resources | 7 | 15 Apr 2002 | 68.00 | 12.64 | 7.41 | 5.88 | 65.46 |
| Mark Resources | 8 | 30 Nov 2004 | 74.00 | 12.01 | 8.00 | 5.88 | 61.70 |
| Metall Mining | 7.5 | 25 Jul 1999 | 93.00 | 8.78 | 7.27 | 10.25 | 31.46 |
| Midland Walwyn | 7.5 | 30 Sep 1997 | 78.00 | 13.06 | 2.86 | 4.85 | 499.00 |
| Minnova (adj. rate) | 5 | 30 Sep 2007 | 58.00 | 10.51 | 2.92 | 16.00 | 30.57 |
| Newfoundland Capital | 8 | 31 Mar 1993 | 70.00 | 41.06 | 9.09 | 2.35 | 251.06 |
| Noranda (adj. rate) | 5 | 30 Apr 2007 | 57.00 | 10.80 | 2.86 | 16.88 | 22.38 |
| Norcen (adj. rate) | 6 | 15 Dec 2006 | 148.00 | 2.21 | 6.45 | 22.75 | 4.24 |
| Norcen (adj. rate) | 5 | 30 Mar 2007 | 92.00 | 5.80 | 4.00 | 22.75 | 3.30 |
| Numac Oil & Gas | 7 | 15 Apr 2002 | 69.00 | 12.41 | 7.41 | 5.63 | 77.61 |
| Poco Petroleums | 7.5 | 16 Feb 1997 | 76.00 | 14.25 | 6.56 | 5.38 | 121.32 |
| Potash Corp. of Sask. | 10.75 | 1 Dec 1992 | 116.00 | 0.00 | 0.00 | 20.25 | 4.88 |
| PWA | 7.875 | 30 Dec 1996 | 58.00 | 22.21 | 4.17 | 5.38 | 167.89 |
| Rogers Communications | 7.5 | 1 Sep 1999 | 86.00 | 10.17 | 4.83 | 13.13 | 38.87 |
| Sceptre Resource | 8.75 | 31 May 1995 | 74.00 | 19.54 | 11.77 | 1.71 | 282.74 |
| Sceptre Resources | 7 | 31 Mar 2002 | 59.00 | 14.93 | 22.22 | 1.71 | 89.48 |
| Sceptre Resources | 8 | 30 Sep 2002 | 56.00 | 17.06 | 16.67 | 1.71 | 114.03 |
| Silcorp | 8 | 30 Jun 2006 | 25.00 | 33.17 | 4.82 | 1.75 | 315.02 |
| Stelco | 7.75 | 31 Aug 1998 | 65.00 | 16.63 | 3.51 | 5.75 | 232.07 |
| Teleglobe Inc. | 7.75 | 15 Apr 1994 | 97.00 | 9.23 | 8.00 | 10.75 | 16.28 |
| Thornmark Equities | 8 | 31 Jan 1998 | 76.00 | 13.99 | 3.45 | 15.50 | 44.08 |
| Tridel | 9 | 15 Dec 2006 | 70.00 | 13.79 | 6.67 | 8.50 | 32.35 |
| Ultramar Capital | 9.5 | 30 Apr 2001 | 95.00 | 10.34 | 12.66 | 5.50 | 37.89 |
| Vencap Equities | 12 | 2 Jul 1998 | 117.00 | 8.54 | 40.00 | 3.25 | 0.00 |
| Videotron Ltee | 7.5 | 31 Mar 2002 | 89.00 | 9.18 | 4.55 | 14.88 | 34.60 |
| Woodward's | 10 | 1 Nov 2004 | 104.00 | 9.45 | 46.95 | 1.65 | 48.46 |

**FIGURE 18-17**

Convertible debenture quotations.

*SOURCE:* Reprinted by permission of *The Globe and Mail: Report on Business,* Thomson Newspapers Company Limited (November 11, 1991).

4. On November 18, 1991, three call options on Richmond Associates stock, all expiring in December 1991, sold for the following prices:

| Exercise Price | Option Price |
|---|---|
| $50 | $7 1/2 |
| 60 | 3 |
| 70 | 1 1/2 |

Fred Marberry is considering a "butterfly spread" that involves the following positions:

Buy 1 call at $50 exercise price
Sell (write) 2 calls at $60 exercise price
Buy 1 call at $70 exercise price

   a. What would be the values at expiration of Fred's spread if Richmond Associates' stock price is below $50 per share? Between $50 and $60? Between $60 and $70? Above $70?
   b. What dollar investment would be required of Fred to establish the spread?
5. What is the time value of an option? Why does an option's time value decline as the option approaches expiration?
6. Explain why call options on nondividend-paying stocks are "worth more alive than dead."
7. List the variables needed to estimate the value of a call option. Describe how a change in the value of these variables affects the value of a call option.
8. Given the information below, calculate the three-month call option price that is consistent with the Black-Scholes model.
$$P_s = \$47, E = \$45, R = .05, \sigma = .40$$
9. If the premium on a call option has recently declined, does this indicate that the option is a better buy than it was previously? Why or why not?
10. A six-month call option with an exercise price of $40 is selling for $5. The current price of the stock is $41.25 per share. The hedge ratio of the option is .65.
   a. What percentage change in the option's price is likely to accompany a 1% change in the stock's price?
   b. If the beta of the stock is 1.10, what is the beta of the option? (*Hint*: Recall what the beta of a stock implies about the relationship between the stock's price to that of the market.)
11. In February 1988, George Gardner sold a September 55 call on Concord Corp. stock for $4.375 per share and simultaneously bought a September 55 put on the same stock for $6 per share. At the time, Treasury bills coming due in September were priced to yield 12.6% and Concord stock sold for $53 per share.
   a. What value would put-call parity suggest was appropriate for the Concord put?
   b. Concord was expected to make three dividend payments between February and September. Could that account for the discrepancy between your answer to part (a) and the actual price of the put? Why or why not?
   c. If Concord stock were to fall to a very low value before September, might it pay for George to exercise the put? Why or why not?

12. Distinguish between portfolio insurance implemented through a protective put and through dynamic asset allocation.
13. (Appendix Question) What is the primary advantage to an investor of a warrant compared to a call option?
14. (Appendix Question) Waverley Inc. has a 10% subordinated convertible debenture outstanding, maturing in 8 years. The bond's face value is $1,000. It currently sells for 99 of par. The bond is convertible into 15 shares of common stock. The company's common stock currently sells for $50 per share.
   a. What is the bond's conversion value?
   b. What is the bond's conversion premium?
   c. What is the bond's investment value?

# SUGGESTED READINGS

The Toronto Stock Exchange publishes a number of informative pamphlets designed to encourage investors to trade options. See, for example, *Canadian Put and Call Options, Writing Covered Calls*, and *Toronto 35 Index Options*.

John C. Cox and Mark Rubinstein, *Options Markets* (Englewood Cliffs, NJ: Prentice Hall, 1985) and

John Hull, *Options, Futures and other Derivative Securities* (Englewood Cliffs, NJ: Prentice Hall, 1989) are two books (among several) that provide coverage of options, their trading and valuation.

P.P. Boyle, "A Lattice Framework for Options Pricing when there are Two State Variables," *Journal of Financial and Quantitative Analysis* 23, no. 1 (March 1988):1–12 and

P.P. Boyle, "Option Valuation Using a Three Jump Process," *International Options Journal*, 3, no. 1 (1986):7–12 show the versatility of the the binomial (and trinomial) approach to valuing options.

Fischer Black and Myron Scholes, "The Pricing of Options and Corporate Liabilities," *Journal of Political Economy* 81, no. 3 (May/June 1973):637–54 is the classical article on option valuation.

Hayne E. Leland, "Who Should Buy Portfolio Insurance?", *Journal of Finance*, no. 2 (May 1980):581–94 and

Mark Rubinstein and Hayne E. Leland, "Replicating Options with Positions in Stocks and Cash," *Financial Analyst Journal* 41, no. 4 (July/August 1985):42–52 deal with the essentials of portfolio insurance.

# Chapter 19

# FUTURES

Consider a contract that involves the delivery of some specific asset by a seller to a buyer at an agreed-upon future date. Although such a contract also specifies the purchase price, the asset is not to be paid for until the delivery date. However, the buyer and the seller are both requested to make a security deposit at the time the contract is signed. The reason for this deposit is to protect each person from experiencing any losses, should the other person renege on the contract.

These contracts are often referred to as *futures* (short for futures contract), and in the United States they involve assets such as agricultural goods (for example, wheat), natural resources (for example, copper), foreign currencies (for example, Swiss francs), fixed-income securities (for example, Treasury bonds), and market indices (for example, the Standard & Poor's 500).[1] As with options, standardization of the terms in these contracts makes it relatively easy for anyone to create and subsequently trade the contracts.

Futures contracts are available on exchanges in Canada on agricultural products (cereals), bankers' acceptances, long Canada Bonds and the Toronto 35 index. Canadian investors can readily trade futures contracts on other commodities on US exchanges. The Canadian business press provides price quotations for contracts traded in both countries.

There are two types of people who deal in futures — speculators and hedgers. *Speculators* buy and sell futures for the sole purpose of making a profit by selling them at a price that is higher (they hope) than their buying price; such people neither produce nor use the asset in the ordinary course of business. In contrast, *hedgers* buy and sell futures to offset an otherwise risky position in the spot market; in the ordinary course of business, they either produce or use the asset.

For example, consider wheat futures. A farmer might note today that the market price for a wheat futures contract with delivery around harvest time is $105 per tonne. The farmer has two alternatives: he could either sell wheat futures today, or he could wait until harvest and sell the wheat in the spot market at that time.[2] Waiting until harvest, however, entails risk because the spot price of wheat could fall by then, perhaps to $85 per tonne, which could bring him personal ruin. Selling wheat futures today would allow the farmer to lock in the $105-per-tonne selling price, thereby removing an element of

---

[1] The term *commodity futures* is often used to refer to futures on agricultural goods and natural resources.

[2] The *spot market* involves the immediate exchange of an asset for cash; the purchase price of the asset is known as its *spot price*.

risk from his primary business, growing wheat. Thus, a farmer who sells futures is known as a hedger or, more specifically, a *short hedger*.

Perhaps the buyer of the farmer's futures contract is a baker who uses wheat in making bread. Currently, the baker has enough wheat in inventory to last until harvest season. In anticipation of the need to replenish the inventory at that time, the baker could buy a wheat futures contract today at $105 per tonne or simply wait until the inventory runs low and then buy wheat in the spot market. However, there is a chance that, in the latter case, the spot price will be $125 per tonne. Should this happen, the baker would have to raise the selling price of bread and perhaps lose sales in doing so. Alternatively, by purchasing wheat futures, the baker can lock in a $105-per-tonne purchase price, thereby removing an element of risk from the bread business. Thus, a baker who buys futures is also known as a hedger or, more specifically, a *long hedger*.

The farmer and baker can be compared with a speculator — a person who buys and sells wheat futures, based on the forecast price of wheat, in the pursuit of relatively short-term profits. As mentioned earlier, such a person neither produces nor uses the asset in the ordinary course of business.

A speculator who thinks the price of wheat is going to rise substantially will buy wheat futures. Later, this person will enter a *reversing trade* by selling wheat futures; if the forecast was accurate, a profit is made on an increase in the wheat futures price.

For example, consider a speculator expecting at least a $20 per tonne rise in the spot price of wheat. While this person could buy wheat, store it, and later hope to sell it at the anticipated higher price, it would be easier and more profitable to buy a wheat futures contract today at $105 per tonne. Later, assuming the spot price of wheat rises by $20, the speculator would enter a reversing trade by selling the wheat futures contract for perhaps $125 per tonne (a $20 rise in the spot price of wheat will cause the futures price to rise by about $20). Thus, the speculator will make a profit of $20 per tonne, or $400 in total, since these contracts are for 20 tonnes.[3] As will be shown later, the speculator might need to make a security deposit of $100 at the time the wheat futures contract was bought. Since this is returned when the reversing trade is made, the speculator's rate of return is quite high (400%) relative to the percentage rise in the price of wheat (19%).

Alternatively, if a speculator forecasts a substantial price decline, then initially wheat futures would be sold. Later, the person would enter a reversing trade by purchasing wheat futures; assuming the forecast was accurate, a profit is made on the decrease in the wheat futures price.

---

## 19.1   THE FUTURES CONTRACT

Futures contracts are standardized in terms of delivery as well as to the type of asset that is permissible for delivery. For example, *The Winnipeg Commodity Exchange* (WCE) specifies the following requirements for its wheat contracts:

1. The seller agrees to deliver 20 tonnes of No. 3 CWRS wheat at the agreed-upon price. Alternatively, three other grades can be delivered at $5.00 per tonne

---

[3] Prices quoted in the business press refer to 20 tonne contracts (a *job lot*) although a board lot is generally 100 tonnes.

discounts from the agreed-upon price. In any case, the seller is allowed to decide which grade shall be delivered.

2. The grain will be delivered by registered warehouse receipts issued by approved warehouses in Thunder Bay, Ontario.

3. Delivery will take place during the contract month, with the seller allowed to decide the actual date. Delivery must be completed by the last business day of the contract month. Alternative delivery points are permitted for some cereals, but delivery at these must be completed by the eighth business day before the end of the contract month.

4. Upon delivery of the warehouse receipt from the seller to the buyer, the latter will pay the former the agreed-upon price in cash.

After an organized exchange has set all the terms of a futures contract except for its price, the exchange will authorize trading in the contract.[4] Buyers and sellers (or their representatives) meet at a specific place on the floor of the exchange and try to agree on a price at which to trade. If they succeed, one or more contracts will be created, with all the standard terms plus an additional one — the price involved. Prices are normally stated on a per-unit basis. Thus, if a buyer and seller agree to a price of $105 per tonne for a contract of 20 tonnes of wheat, the amount of money involved is $2,100.

Figure 19.1 shows a set of daily quotations of the prices at which commodity futures contracts were traded on The Winnipeg Exchange and the total volume of sales for each type of contract. Such listings of active futures markets are published regularly in the financial press, with each item for delivery having a heading that indicates the number of units per contract (e.g. 20 metric tons for oats) and the terms on which prices are stated (dollars per ton).

Below the heading for the asset are certain details for each type of contract. In Figure 19.1, for example, there are five different futures contracts for wheat, having different delivery dates that are shown in the third column. The first two columns show the *seasonal high (SeaHi)* and the *seasonal low (SeaLow)* that are the highest and lowest prices recorded during the lifetime of the contract. In the fourth, fifth, sixth, and seventh columns are the *open*, denoting the price at which the first transaction was made; the *high* and *low*, representing the highest and lowest prices recorded during the preceeding trading day; and the *settle*, a price (for example, the average of the high and low prices) that is representative of trades executed during the "closing period" designated by the exchange (for example, the last two minutes of trading). The eighth and ninth columns show the *change* from the previous day's settlement price and the *open interest* (the number of outstanding contracts) on the previous day.

For each futures contract, information is summarized below the figures for the last delivery date and indicates the estimated and previous sales (that is, the number of contracts traded on that day and on the previous trading day) as well as the total open interest in those contracts on the previous day and the change in total open interest from the previous day (in the case of canola, these summary figures are below the December 1992 delivery date figures).

---

[4] For a relatively complete description of the terms for many exchange-traded futures contracts, see the *Commodity Trading Manual* (Chicago Board of Trade, 1985); Robert W. Kolb, *Understanding Futures Markets* (Glenview, Ill.: Scott, Foresman and Company, 1988); and the extensive literature published by The Winnipeg Commodity Exchange. The first two of these books also contain descriptions of various futures exchanges.

# WINNIPEG COMMODITY EXCHANGE

| SeaHi | SeaLow | Mth. | Open | High | Low | Settle | Chg. | Opint |
|---|---|---|---|---|---|---|---|---|
| **WHEAT** 20 metric tons- can $ per ton | | | | | | | | |
| 106.00 | 89.80 | Mar | 101.50 | 101.70 | 101.20 | 101.40 | —.10 | 4,996 |
| 103.90 | 95.00 | May | 102.50 | 102.50 | 102.00 | 102.10 | ... | 3,331 |
| 104.50 | 96.00 | Jul | 103.30 | 103.50 | 103.30 | 103.40 | +.10 | 977 |
| 106.50 | 102.30 | Oct | 104.00 | 104.00 | 104.00 | 104.10 | +.10 | 262 |
| 105.00 | 104.00 | Dec | 105.00 | 105.00 | 105.00 | 105.00 | ... | |
| Est Sales | | Prv Sales | | Prv Open Int | | | | Chg. |
| | | 366 | | 9,566 | | | | —156 |
| **OATS** 20 metric tons- can $ per ton | | | | | | | | |
| 107.60 | 89.50 | Mar | 104.50 | 104.50 | 104.50 | 104.50 | ... | 551 |
| 106.00 | 92.00 | May | | | | 105.90 | ... | 101 |
| 111.00 | 100.00 | Jul | | | | 106.20 | ... | 5 |
| 115.00 | 107.70 | Oct | | | | 108.40 | ... | 28 |
| | | Dec | | | | 108.50 | ... | 16 |
| Est Sales | | Prv Sales | | Prv Open Int | | | | Chg. |
| | | 37 | | 701 | | | | —22 |
| **RYE** 20 metric tons- can $ per ton | | | | | | | | |
| 106.00 | 87.50 | Mar | 98.60 | 98.60 | 98.60 | 98.60 | ... | 858 |
| 108.20 | 89.50 | May | 101.60 | 101.60 | 101.60 | 101.60 | +.10 | 208 |
| 105.50 | 101.00 | Jul | | | | 105.00 | ... | 5 |
| 106.00 | 103.00 | Oct | 106.00 | 106.00 | 106.00 | 106.00 | ... | |
| Est Sales | | Prv Sales | | Prv Open Int | | | | Chg. |
| | | 155 | | 798 | | | | —289 |
| **BARLEY** 20 metric tons- can $ per ton | | | | | | | | |
| 98.50 | 81.00 | Mar | 89.00 | 89.00 | 88.70 | 88.70 | ... | 3,927 |
| 94.80 | 84.50 | May | 90.50 | 90.50 | 90.40 | 90.20 | +.10 | 1,082 |

| SeaHi | SeaLow | Mth. | Open | High | Low | Settle | Chg. | Opint |
|---|---|---|---|---|---|---|---|---|
| 97.00 | 90.00 | Jul | | | | 92.00 | +.20 | 286 |
| 97.00 | 89.80 | Oct | | | | 93.40 | +.10 | 228 |
| 91.00 | 91.00 | Dec | 91.00 | 91.00 | 91.00 | 91.00 | ... | |
| Est Sales | | Prv Sales | | Prv Open Int | | | | Chg. |
| | | 305 | | 5,523 | | | | —93 |
| **CANOLA** 20 metric tons- can $ per ton | | | | | | | | |
| 317.50 | 255.00 | Jan | 262.00 | 262.50 | 261.00 | 262.50 | +.30 | 1,832 |
| 319.80 | 261.30 | Mar | 264.80 | 265.60 | 263.60 | 265.10 | +.10 | 10,027 |
| 321.00 | 267.00 | Jun | 270.50 | 271.00 | 269.10 | 270.20 | —.30 | 5,446 |
| 300.00 | 275.70 | Sep | 276.00 | 276.20 | 276.00 | 276.20 | —.80 | 112 |
| 291.70 | 280.00 | Nov | | | | 280.50 | —.60 | 448 |
| Est Sales | | Prv Sales | | Prv Open Int | | | | Chg. |
| | | 2,730 | | 17,865 | | | | —100 |
| **FLAXSEED** 20 metric tons- can $ per ton | | | | | | | | |
| 233.50 | 186.40 | Mar | 192.90 | 194.20 | 192.40 | 193.10 | +.20 | 2,086 |
| 232.00 | 189.70 | May | 198.00 | 198.70 | 197.00 | 197.90 | +.20 | 1,312 |
| 219.80 | 195.10 | Jul | 202.00 | 202.00 | 202.00 | 201.50 | —.60 | 1,486 |
| 216.50 | 202.20 | Oct | 209.00 | 210.00 | 208.80 | 209.00 | —.50 | 271 |
| 214.00 | 210.70 | Dec | 213.00 | 213.00 | 213.00 | 213.00 | —1.00 | |
| Est Sales | | Prv Sales | | Prv Open Int | | | | Chg. |
| | | 401 | | 5,155 | | | | +224 |
| **WESTERN BARLEY** 20 metric tons- can $ per ton | | | | | | | | |
| 98.50 | 80.00 | Feb | | | | 86.20 | +.90 | 576 |
| 94.80 | 83.50 | May | 89.90 | 90.50 | 89.90 | 90.50 | +.60 | 454 |
| 94.00 | 91.00 | Aug | | | | 93.80 | ... | 18 |
| 95.00 | 91.00 | Nov | 95.00 | 95.00 | 95.00 | 95.00 | ... | |
| Est Sales | | Prv Sales | | Prv Open Int | | | | Chg. |
| | | 26 | | 1,048 | | | | —7 |

**FIGURE 19-1**

Quotations for commodity future prices.

*SOURCE:* Reprinted by permission of *The Globe and Mail: Report on Business,* Thomson Newspapers Company Limited, (January 8, 1992).

## ☐ 19.1.1 Futures Markets

The futures contracts shown in Figure 19.1 were traded on The Winnipeg Commodity Exchange, the only one of its kind in Canada.

In the United States, futures contracts are traded on various organized exchanges, notably the Chicago Board of Trade (CBT), currently the largest futures exchange in the world.

The method of trading futures on organized exchanges is similar in some ways and different in other ways from the way that stocks and options are traded. Like stocks and options, customers can place market, limit, and stop orders. Furthermore, once an order is transmitted to an exchange floor, it must be taken to a designated spot for execution by a member of the exchange, just as is done for stocks and options. This spot is known as a "pit" because of its shape, which is circular with a set of interior descending steps on which members stand. What transpires in the pit is what distinguishes trading in futures from trading in stocks and options.

First of all, there are no specialists or market-makers on futures exchanges. Trading is carried out by floor brokers, who may trade for their own personal account in an attempt to make profits by buying low and selling high, or for the firm they work for, or they may execute customers' orders. In doing so, they (or their phone clerks) each keep a file of any stop or limit orders that cannot be immediately executed. All orders are treated equally on the floor regardless of where they originate. Floor brokers are in some ways similar to market-makers, since a floor broker may have an inventory of futures contracts and may act as a dealer. However, unlike a market-maker, a floor broker is not required to do so.

Second, all futures orders must be announced by "open outcry," meaning that any member wishing to buy or sell any futures contract must verbally announce the order and a price at which the member is willing to trade. By doing so, the order is exposed to everyone in the pit, thereby enabling an auction to take place that will lead to the order being filled at the best possible price.

## ☐ 19.1.2 The Clearinghouse

Each futures exchange has an associated clearinghouse that becomes the "seller's buyer" and the "buyer's seller" as soon as a trade is concluded. The procedure is similar to that used for options, which is not surprising, since the first market in listed options was set up by people associated with a futures exchange (specifically, the Chicago Board Options Exchange was set up by the Chicago Board of Trade). In Winnipeg the clearing house is Winnipeg Commodity Clearing Ltd.

In order to understand how a clearinghouse operates, consider the futures market for wheat. Assume that on the first day of trading in July wheat, buyer B agrees to purchase 20 tonnes (one contract) from seller S for $105 per tonne (actually, what happens is that a floor broker working for B's brokerage firm and a floor broker working for S's brokerage firm meet in the wheat pit and agree on a price). In this situation, B believes that the price of wheat is going to rise, whereas S believes it is going to fall.

After B and S reach their agreement, the clearinghouse will immediately step in and break the transaction apart. That is, B and S no longer deal directly with each other. Now it is the obligation of the clearinghouse to deliver the wheat to B and to accept delivery from S. At this point, there is an open interest of one contract (20 tonnes) in July wheat, since only one contract exists at this time (technically, there are two, since the clearinghouse has separate contracts with B and S).

It is important to realize that if nothing else is done at this point, the clearinghouse is in a potentially risky position. For example, if the price of wheat rises to $125 per tonne by July, what happens if S does not deliver the wheat? The clearinghouse would have to buy the wheat on the spot market for $2500 (20 × $125) and then deliver it to B. Because the clearinghouse will receive the selling price of $2100 (20 × $105) from B in return, it will have lost $400. Although the clearinghouse has a claim on S for the $400, it faces protracted legal battles in trying to recover this amount and may end up with little or nothing from S.

Alternatively, if the price of wheat falls to $85 per tonne by July, then B will be paying $2100 for delivery of wheat that is only worth $1700 (10 × $85) on the spot market. What happens if B refuses to make payment? In this case, the clearinghouse will not deliver the wheat that it received from S. Instead, it will have to sell the wheat for $1700 on the spot market. Since the clearinghouse paid $2100 for the wheat, it has lost $400. Again, although the clearinghouse has a claim on B for the $400, it may end up with little or nothing from B.

The procedures that protect the clearinghouse from such potential losses involve having brokers (1) impose initial margin requirements on both buyers and sellers; (2) mark to market the accounts of buyers and sellers every day; and (3) impose daily maintenance margin requirements on both buyers and sellers.

## Initial Margin

In order to buy and sell futures, an investor must open a commodity account with a brokerage firm. This type of account must be kept separate from other accounts (such as a cash account or a margin account) that the investor might have. Whenever a futures contract is signed, both the buyer and seller are required to post initial margin. That is, both the buyer and seller are required to make security deposits that are intended to guarantee that they will in fact be able to fulfill their obligations; accordingly, initial margin is often referred to as *performance margin*. The amount of this margin is roughly 5% to 15% of the total purchase price of the futures contract. In Winnipeg, however, it is stated as a given dollar amount regardless of the purchase price, $100 for speculators and $70 for hedgers per 20 tonne contract.[5]

For example, a July wheat futures contract for 20 tonnes at $105 per bushel would have a total purchase price of $2100 ($20 \times \$105$). With a 5% initial margin requirement, buyer B and seller S (both speculators) would each have to make a deposit of $100 (approximately $.05 \times \$21,000$). This deposit can be made in the form of cash, cash equivalents (such as Treasury bills), or a bank line of credit and forms the equity in the account on the first day.

Although initial margin provides some protection to the clearinghouse, it does not provide complete protection. As indicated earlier, if the price of wheat rises to $125 per tonne by July, the clearinghouse faces a potential loss of $400, only $100 of which can be quickly recovered due to the margin deposit. This is where the use of marking to market, coupled with a maintenance margin requirement, provides the requisite amount of additional protection.

## Marking to Market

In order to understand marking to market, the previous example, where B and S were, respectively, a buyer and a seller of a 20-tonne wheat futures contract at $105 per tonne, is continued. Assume now that on the second day of trading the settle price of July wheat is $106 per tonne. In this situation, S has "lost" $20 due to the rise in the price of wheat from $105 to $106 per tonne, whereas B has "made" $20. Thus, the equity in the account of S is reduced by $20 and the equity in the account of B is increased by $20. Since the initial equity was equal to the initial margin requirement of $100, this means that S has equity of $80, and B has equity of $120. This process of adjusting the equity in an investor's commodity account in order to reflect the change in the settle price of the futures contract is known as *marking to market*. It should also be noted that each day, as part of the marking-to-market process, the clearinghouse replaces each existing futures contract with a new one that has the settle price as reported in the financial press as the purchase price in the new contract.

In general, the equity in either a buyer or seller's commodity account is the sum of (1) the initial margin deposit and (2) the sum of all daily gains, less losses, on open positions in futures. Since the amount of the gains (less losses) changes every day, the amount of equity changes every day.

---

[5] Since Black Monday and Terrible Tuesday (October 19–20, 1987), a number of people have advocated an increase in the size of the performance margin deposit for certain futures contracts (particularly stock index futures, which are discussed later). The level of performance (and maintenance) margin is set by each exchange, with brokers being allowed to set it higher.

In the example, if the settle price of the July wheat futures contract had fallen to $103.5 per tonne the day after rising to $106, then B would have lost $50 (20 × ($106 − $103.50)), whereas S would have made $50 on that day. When their accounts are marked to market at the end of the day, the equity in B's account would have dropped from $120 to $70, and S's equity would have risen from $80 to $130.

## Maintenance Margin

Another key concept is the requirement of maintenance margin. According to this requirement, the investor must keep the commodity account's equity equal to or greater than a certain percentage of the amount deposited as initial margin. In Winnipeg this percentage is 70% for speculators and 100% for hedgers, therefore, the speculator must have equity equal to or greater than 70% of the initial margin. If this requirement is not met, the investor will receive a margin call from his or her broker. This call is a request for an additional deposit of cash (nothing else can be deposited for this purpose) to bring the equity up to the initial margin level. If the investor does not (or cannot) respond, then the broker will close out the investor's position by entering a reversing trade in the investor's account.

For example, reconsider investors B and S who had, respectively, bought and sold a July wheat futures contract at $105 per tonne; each investor had made a deposit of $100 in order to meet the initial margin requirement. The next day, the price of the wheat futures contract rose to $107 per tonne, or $2140. Thus, B's equity had increased to $140, whereas S's equity had decreased to $60. With the maintenance margin requirement set at 70% of initial margin, both B and S are required to have equity of at least $70 (.70 × $100) in their accounts every day. Since the actual level of equity for B clearly exceeds this amount, B does not need to do anything. Indeed, B may withdraw an amount of cash equal to the amount by which the equity exceeds the initial margin; in this example, B can withdraw cash of $40.

However, S is undermargined and will be asked to make a cash deposit of at least $40, since this would increase the equity from $60 to $100, the level of the initial margin. In the event that S refuses to make this deposit, the broker will enter a reversing trade for S by purchasing a July wheat futures contract. The result is that S will simply receive an amount of money approximately equal to the account's equity, $60, and the account will be closed. Since S initially deposited $100, this represents a personal loss of $40.

## Reversing Trades

Suppose that on the next day, B finds that people are paying $108 per tonne for July wheat. This represents an additional profit to B of $1.00 per tonne, since the price was $107 the previous day. If B believes that the price of July wheat will not go any higher, then B might sell a July wheat futures contract for $108 to someone else. In this situation, B has made a reversing trade, since B now has offsetting positions with respect to July wheat (equivalently, B is said to have unwound, or closed out, his or her position in July wheat).

At this point, the benefit to B of having a clearinghouse involved can be seen. Nominally, B is obligated to deliver 20 tonnes of wheat to the clearinghouse in July, which is in turn obligated to deliver it back to B. This situation occurs because B is involved in two July wheat contracts, one as a seller and one as a buyer. However, the clearinghouse will note that B has offsetting positions in July wheat and will immediately cancel both of them. Furthermore, once the reversing trade had been made, B will be able to withdraw the initial margin of $100 as well as the $60 $(20 \times (\$108 - \$105))$ profit that has been made.

In effect, a futures contract is replaced every day by (1) adjusting the equity in the investor's commodity account and (2) drawing up a new contract that has a purchase price equal to the current settle price. This daily marking-to-market procedure, coupled with margin requirements, results in the clearinghouse always having a security deposit of sufficient size to protect it from losses due to the actions of the individual investors.[6]

These rather complex arrangements make it possible for futures traders to think in very simple terms. In the example, B bought a contract of July wheat at $105 and sold it two days later for $108, making a profit of $3 per tonne. If S, having initially sold a contract of July wheat at $105, later made a reversing trade for $107, then S's position can also be thought of in simple terms — specifically, S sold July wheat for $105 and later bought it back for $107, suffering a loss of $2 per tonne in the process.

## ☐ 19.1.3 Futures Positions

In the previous example, B was the person who initially bought a July wheat futures contract. Accordingly, B now has a long position and is said to be long one contract of July wheat. In contrast, S, having initially sold a July wheat futures contract, has a short position and is said to be short one contract of July wheat.

The process of marking to market every day means that changes in the settle price are realized as soon as they occur. When the settle price *rises*, those with long positions realize *profits* equal to the change and those who are short realize *losses*. When the settle price *falls*, those with long positions realize *losses*, whereas those with short positions realize *profits*. In either event, total profits always equal total losses.

## ☐ 19.1.4 Taxation

Earlier, it was mentioned that there are two types of people who deal in futures — speculators and hedgers. These two types of investors are treated differently by Revenue Canada.

A speculator in futures (whether long or short) is considered to have a capital asset for tax purposes. When the position is closed out, the resultant profit or loss is treated as a capital gain or loss, and is taxed accordingly. That is, net gains are taxed at 75% of the individual's ordinary income tax rate, and net losses are carried back to previous years as described in Chapter 10.

In contrast, as a hedger deals in futures as part of a normal business activity, the resulting profits or losses are viewed as ordinary income or losses for the business, and taxed accordingly.

---

[6] Actually, only brokerage firms belong to a clearinghouse, and it is *their* accounts that are settled by the clearinghouse at the end of every day. Each brokerage firm acts in turn as a clearinghouse for its own clients. For more information on clearing procedures, see Chapter 4 of the *Commodity Trading Manual*.

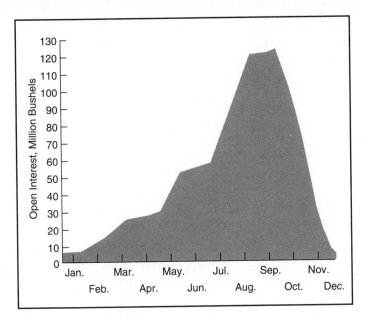

**FIGURE 19-2**
Open interest, December 1978, Chicago Board of Trade Wheat Contract: January 3, 1978 through December 28, 1978.

## □ 19.1.5  Open Interest

When trading is first allowed in a contract, there is no open interest, since no contracts are outstanding. Subsequently, as people begin to make transactions, the open interest grows. At any time, open interest equals the amount that those with short positions (the sellers) are currently obligated to deliver. It also equals the amount that those with long positions (the buyers) are obligated to receive.

Open interest figures are typically shown with futures prices in the financial press. For example, Figure 19.1 indicates that on January 8, 1992, a total of 4,996 contracts in March 1992 wheat were outstanding on The Winnipeg Commodity Exchange. Note the substantial differences in the open interest figures for the other wheat contracts on the (WCE) that day. This is quite typical of agricultural commodities around the world. Figure 19.2 shows why. Open interest in a wheat contract on the Chicago Board of Trade is shown for every month from the preceding January until the contract expired at the end of the delivery month, December. From January until the end of September, more trades were generally made to open new positions than to reverse old ones, and open interest continued to increase. As the delivery month came closer, reversing trades began to outnumber those intended to open new positions, and the open interest began to decline. The amount remaining at the beginning of December was the maximum number of bushels of wheat that could have been delivered against futures contracts at that time, but most of these contracts were also settled by reversing trades instead of delivery.

Relatively few futures positions — less than 3% of the total — end in actual delivery of the asset involved.[7] However, the fact that delivery is a possibility makes a contract's value in the delivery month differ only slightly, if at all, from the spot price (that is, the current market price) of the asset.

If not reversed, most futures contracts require delivery of the corresponding asset. Notable exceptions are market index futures, since they do not require delivery of the set of securities comprising the corresponding index. Instead, an amount proportional to the difference between the level of the index and the purchase price is to be paid *in cash* on the delivery date. Nevertheless, as with other types of futures, most positions in market index futures are closed out with reversing trades prior to the date at which delivery (in cash) is required.

## ☐ 19.1.6 Price Limits

The by-laws of the WCE place dollar limits on the extent to which futures prices are allowed to vary from day to day. These price limits on futures are imposed so that traders who might overreact to major news are protected from voluntarily entering into agreements under such conditions. For example, if July wheat contracts had closed at $105 on the previous day and the daily price limit was $5, then only contracts for July wheat at prices in the range from $100 to $110 would be allowed. If news during the day led traders to consider $115 a reasonable price for the contract, they would have to (1) trade privately, foregoing the advantages offered by the exchange; or (2) trade on the exchange at the limit price of $110; or (3) wait until the next day, when the range of acceptable prices would be from $105 to $115.

One negative result of this "limit move" up to $110 or down to $100 is that all traders may choose option 3 and, therefore, no July wheat contracts will be traded on that day. This is because nobody will want to sell these wheat contracts for a below-market price of $110, preferring to wait until the next day when the range of acceptable prices is raised. Indeed, if the news is important enough (such as hail storms in Saskatchewan, that destroy the wheat crop and dramatically increase the price of wheat futures), the daily limit moves could prevent trading from taking place for several days. In an attempt to avoid this situation the WCE has ruled that when two of the three nearest contracts close at the normal limit (up or down) then the daily price limit is immediately expanded by 50% and remains there for the next three days. If after three days trading at the expanded limit continues then the expanded limit remains in force until two of the three nearest contracts close within the expanded limit.

Interestingly, initial margins are usually set at an amount that is roughly equal to the price limit times the size of the contract. In the case of wheat having a $5 price limit and a contract for 20 tonnes, the initial margin is $100 ($5 × 20). Thus, if the price of wheat moves the limit against the investor, no more than the initial margin of $100 will be lost on the day of the adverse limit move. In a sense, the price limit protects the investor from losing more than $100 on that day. However, it is possible that the investor cannot enter a reversing trade after prices have reached the limit, meaning that much larger losses could be incurred later.

---

[7] Merrill Lynch, Pierce, Fenner & Smith, Inc., *Speculating on Inflation: Futures Trading in Interest Rates, Foreign Currencies and Precious Metals*, July 1979.

## BASIS

The difference between the current spot price on an asset (that is, the price of the asset for immediate delivery) and the futures price (that is, the purchase price stated in the futures contract) is known as the *basis* for the futures:

$$\text{Basis} = \text{current spot price} - \text{futures price.} \qquad (19.1)$$

A person with a short position in a futures contract and a long position in the corresponding asset (meaning he or she owns the asset) will profit if the basis is positive and widens (or is negative and narrows). This is because the futures price will be falling or the spot price will be rising (or both); falling futures prices benefit those who are short, and rising spot prices benefit those who own the asset. Using the same type of reasoning, it can be shown that this person will lose if the basis is positive and narrows (or is negative and widens).

Conversely, a person with a long position in a futures contract and a short position in the corresponding asset (meaning he or she has borrowed the asset and sold it and now has an obligation to buy the asset in order to repay the loan) will profit if the basis is positive and narrows (or is negative and widens). However, a loss would be incurred if a positive basis widens (or a negative basis narrows).

The risk of the basis narrowing or widening, causing gains or losses to these people, is known as *basis risk*. The only type of uncertainty they face is about the difference between the spot price of the specific asset and the price of the futures contract. Such a person is said to be *speculating on the basis*.[8]

## SPREADS

It is quite possible to take a long position in a futures contract and a short position in another futures contract in the same asset but with a different delivery date. The person who does this is speculating on changes in the difference between the prices of the two contracts, a difference that constitutes the basis for this particular hedge.

Others attempt to profit from temporary imbalances among the prices of futures contracts on different but related assets. For example, one might take a long position in soybeans along with a short position in an item produced from soybeans, such as soybean meal. Another possibility involves a position in wheat with an offsetting position in corn, which serves as a substitute for wheat in many applications.

These people are known as *spreaders* and, like those who speculate on the basis, they reduce or eliminate the risk associated with general price moves. Instead, they take on the risk associated with changes in price differences in the hope that their alleged superior knowledge and ability will enable them to make profits consistently from such changes.

---

[8] For more on the relationship between spot and futures prices as reflected in the basis, see the *Commodity Trading Manual*, pp. 64–83. It should be noted that sometimes basis is defined as the futures price less the current spot price — the reverse of what is shown in equation (19.1).

**SPOT PRICES**

Most futures exchanges dealing in agricultural commodities provide areas in which buyers and sellers can negotiate cash (or spot) sales. No attempt is made to standardize such agreements; everything, including grade, location, and delivery, is negotiable. For this reason there is no such thing as a standardized spot price. Instead, the price of the futures contract that is closest to delivery is often used as a surrogate for the spot price. In fact, deals in the spot market may even be made in terms of the price of the nearest futures contract — for example, two parties might agree to trade at $0.75 per tonne more than the relevant futures price. In essence, such spot trades are conducted in terms of the basis.

The price of any asset is determined by demand and supply. It is in the realm of supply that agricultural commodities such as wheat differ from automobiles, for example. Wheat is a seasonal commodity, generally harvested in Canada from July through September (although in other countries harvests occur at other times). Seasonality has important implications for price determination for such commodities.

*Carrying costs* are a key concept. These include all costs associated with holding an inventory of the commodity. The major components are foregone interest on the money invested in the inventory and the cost of storage for the inventory.

If everyone knew that the spot price of a commodity was certain to rise by an amount exceeding its carrying cost, people would start to purchase and store the current supply in order to make a profit from selling it at a later date. As a result, its current spot price would rise, until the predicted future spot price was equal to the current spot price and carrying costs.

For example, if three-month carrying costs amount to $2 per tonne of wheat, then in a world of certainty the current spot price would, in equilibrium, have to rise by $2 over the next three months. Consider what anyone would do if the spot price was going to rise by more than this amount. Given a current spot price of $105 and a predicted three-month ahead spot price of $109, the investor could buy wheat now at $105 and store it for $2, while selling a three-month futures contract for $109. In doing so, the investor would, without risk, make a profit of $2[$109 − ($105 + $2)] per tonne. However, others would also do the same thing until the difference between the current spot price and three-month futures price settled at $2 per tonne.

In contrast, if everyone knew the spot price of a commodity was certain to rise by an amount less than its carrying cost, people would refrain from purchasing and storing the commodity. That is, the only people buying the wheat would be those who had a current use for it. Consequently, the current spot price would fall until the predicted future spot price was equal to the current spot price and carrying costs.

In practice there is considerable uncertainty about the future price of any commodity. However, the costs associated with storing inventories lead to a typical pattern in which prices of seasonal commodities tend to increase after the main harvest season and fall as each new harvest comes in. Figure 19.3 shows a possible pattern for spot prices over three years when the harvests are of equal size each year. While uncertainty brings relatively random price changes, a pattern roughly similar to this can often be seen in the movements of spot prices.

For natural resources that have futures contracts, such as copper, gold, and silver, there is no "harvest season." Thus, for those items there is no seasonal pattern in spot

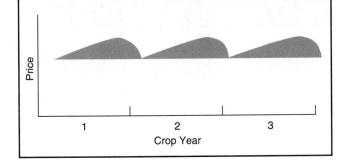

**FIGURE 19-3**
Spot prices for a seasonal commodity.

prices similar to Figure 19.3. Instead, the spot prices are simply a horizontal line. This is also true for foreign currencies, fixed-income securities, foreign exchange and market indices.

**FUTURES PRICES**

☐ **19.5.1 Certainty**

If all spot prices could be predicted with certainty, there would be no reason for anyone to be either a buyer or seller of futures contracts. To understand why, imagine what a futures contract would look like in a world of certainty. First of all, the purchase price in the future contract would simply equal the (perfectly predictable) expected spot price on the delivery date. This means that neither buyers nor sellers would be able to make profits from the existence of futures. Second of all, the purchase price would not change as the delivery date got closer. Lastly, no margin would be necessary because there would not be any unexpected "adverse" price movements.

Figure 19.4(a) shows the relationship between the current spot price and the prices of three futures contracts for a seasonal commodity harvested each year in June. The curved line reflects the spot price of the commodity over time. It can be seen that the pattern of the spot price corresponds to the pattern shown in Figure 19.3, rising to a high about May and then declining quickly to a low about October. Three futures contracts are assumed to be traded at any time, offering delivery on the last day of March, July, and September, respectively. Each contract is traded during the 364 days prior to the specified delivery date. Since no uncertainty is involved, there will not be any adverse price movements. Thus, no margin need be posted by either the buyer or seller of the futures contract. Furthermore, the futures price will not change as time elapses. Consequently, the price of the March futures will always be the same, corresponding to a horizontal line in the figure. Similarly, the prices of the July and September futures contracts will remain the same, although at different levels. However, as time passes, the spot price changes, following the cyclical path shown by the curved line in Figure 19.4(a).

Note that during the life of the futures contract the spot price is sometimes above and sometimes below the futures price. Note also that at some times "distant" futures contracts sell for more than "near" ones, and at other times the situation is reversed. This is shown in parts (b) and (c) of Figure 19.4, respectively, which plot the prices of various contracts versus their remaining lives at two times of the year. In this case, if contracts

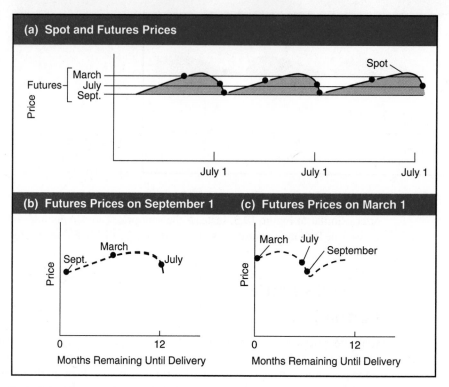

**FIGURE 19-4**
Commodity prices in a world of certainty.

were available for every possible delivery date, their prices would plot along the dashed curves, which reflect the (known) future pattern of spot rates.

## ☐ 19.5.2 Uncertainty

As a starting point, it is useful to know something about the way in which futures prices and spot prices are related to each other in a world of certainty where forecasting is done with complete accuracy. However, what happens when uncertainty is introduced? Exactly how are futures prices related to expected spot prices? Although there are several possible explanations, no definitive answer has been provided.

### Expectations Hypothesis

One possible explanation of the result of uncertainty is given by the *expectations hypothesis*: The current purchase price of a futures contract equals the market consensus expectation of the spot price on the delivery date. In symbols,

$$P_f = \bar{P}_s$$

where $P_f$ is the current purchase price of the futures contract and $\bar{P}_s$ is the expected spot price of the asset on the delivery date. Thus, if a July wheat futures contract is currently

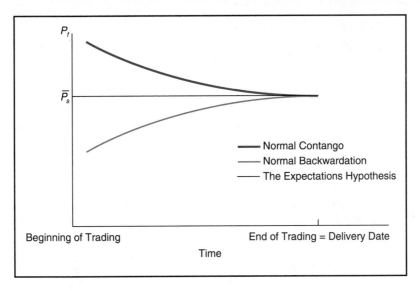

**FIGURE 19-5**
Price of futures contract through time when the spot price expected at the time of delivery does not change.

selling for $105 per tonne, then it can be inferred that the consensus opinion is that in July the spot price of wheat will be $105.

If the expectations hypothesis is correct, a speculator should not expect either to win or lose from a position in the futures market, be it long or short. Neglecting margin requirements, a speculator who takes a long position in futures agrees to pay $P_f$ at the delivery date for an asset that is expected to be worth $\bar{P}_s$ at that time. Thus, the long speculator's expected profit is equal to $\bar{P}_s - P_f$, which is zero. Conversely, a speculator with a short position will have sold an asset at a price of $P_f$ and will expect to enter a reversing trade at $\bar{P}_s$ on the delivery date. Thus, the short speculator's expected profit is equal to $P_f - \bar{P}_s$, which is zero.

The expectations hypothesis is often defended on the grounds that speculators are indifferent to risk and are thus happy to accommodate hedgers without any compensation in the form of a risk premium. The reason for their indifference has to do with the belief that the impact of a specific futures position on the risk of a diversified portfolio that includes many types of assets will be very small. Thus, speculators holding diversified portfolios may be willing to take over some risk from hedgers with little (if any) compensation in the form of a risk premium.

Figure 19.5 shows the pattern of futures prices implied by the expectations hypothesis, given the expected spot price $\bar{P}_s$ does not change during the life of the contract.

## Normal Backwardation

John Maynard Keynes felt that the expectations hypothesis did not correctly explain futures prices.[9] He argued that, on balance, hedgers will want to be short in futures, and therefore they will have to entice the speculators to be long in futures. Since there are risks associated with being long, Keynes hypothesized that the hedgers would have to entice the speculators by making the expected return from a long position greater than the risk-free rate. This requires the futures price to be less than the expected spot price:

$$P_f < \bar{P}_s.$$

Thus, a speculator who bought a futures contract at a price of $P_f$ would expect to be able to sell it on (or near) the delivery date at a higher price, $\bar{P}_s$. This relationship between the futures and expected spot price has been referred to as *normal backwardation* and implies that the price of a futures contract can be expected to rise during its life, as shown in Figure 19.5.

## Normal Contango

A contrary hypothesis holds that, on balance, hedgers will want to be long in futures, and therefore they will have to entice speculators to be short in futures. Since there are risks associated with being short, it can be hypothesized that the hedgers will have to entice the speculators by making the expected return from a short position greater than the risk-free rate. This requires the futures price to be greater than the expected spot price:

$$P_f > \bar{P}_s.$$

Thus, a speculator who short sold a futures contract at a price of $P_f$ would expect to be able to buy it back on (or near) the delivery date at a lower price, $\bar{P}_s$. This relationship between the futures and expected spot price has been referred to as *normal contango* and implies that the price of a futures contract can be expected to fall during its life, as shown in Figure 19.5.[10]

## 19.6    RETURNS ON FUTURES

A US study shows that, during the period from 1950 through 1976, a portfolio made up of unlevered positions in 23 different futures contracts was compared with a diversified portfolio of common stocks.[11] The average rate of return and risk level of the two portfolios were found to be of similar magnitude:

---

[9] J. M. Keynes, *Treatise on Money*, vol. 2 (London: Macmillan, 1930):142–44.

[10] There are other hypotheses regarding the relationship between futures prices and expected spot prices. See, for example, Paul H. Cootner, "Speculation and Hedging," Stanford University, *Food Research Institute Studies*, Supplement, 1967.

[11] The futures contracts consisted of agricultural goods and natural resources; see Zvi Bodie and Victor Rosansky, "Risk and Return in Commodity Futures," *Financial Analysts Journal* 36, no. 3 (May/June 1980):27–39. Similar conclusions were reached when the period 1978 to 1981 was examined. See Cheng F. Lee, Raymond M. Leuthold, and Jean E. Cordier, "The Stock Market and the Commodity Futures Market: Diversification and Arbitrage Potential," *Financial Analysts Journal* 41, no. 4 (July/August 1985):53–60.

| Portfolio | Average Annual Return | Standard Deviation |
|---|---|---|
| Futures | 13.83% | 22.43% |
| Common stocks | 13.05 | 18.95 |

Given these results, an investor might view the two alternatives as equally desirable. However, during the period 1950 to 1976, a combination of the two portfolios was found to be more desirable than either portfolio by itself. This was due to the fact that the returns of futures and stock portfolios were negatively correlated, suggesting that the return on a combined portfolio would have had considerably less variation than either one separately. Specifically, the correlation coefficient was found to be equal to -.24, resulting in the following standard deviations for portfolios with different combinations:

| Percent in Stocks | Percent in Futures | Standard Deviation | Average Annual Return |
|---|---|---|---|
| 0% | 100% | 22.43% | 13.83% |
| 20 | 80 | 17.43 | 13.67 |
| 40 | 60 | 13.77 | 13.52 |
| 60 | 40 | 12.68 | 13.36 |
| 80 | 20 | 14.74 | 13.21 |
| 100 | 0 | 18.95 | 13.05 |

Although there was little difference in the level of the average return for the various portfolios, there was a noticeable change in the level of risk. In particular, the portfolio with 60% in stocks and 40% in futures seems to have had much less risk than the others.

Also of interest was the observation that futures have been found to be at least a partial hedge against inflation. During the period 1950 to 1976, the returns on the portfolio of 23 futures were positively correlated with changes in the Consumer Price Index, having a correlation coefficient of .58. In contrast, the returns on the portfolio of common stocks were negatively correlated with changes in the Consumer Price Index, having a correlation coefficient of -.43.

## 19.7    FINANCIAL FUTURES

Futures contracts were limited to those on agricultural goods and natural resources until the 1970s. Since then, financial futures, based on foreign currencies, fixed-income securities, and market indices, have been introduced on major exchanges around the world. Indeed, in terms of trading volume, they are now more important than the traditional futures contracts and the underlying securities. Unlike other types of futures that permit delivery anytime during a given month, most financial futures (the exceptions involve some fixed-income futures) have a specific delivery date.

# ☐ 19.7.1 Foreign Currency Futures

Anyone who has crossed a national border knows that there is an active spot market for foreign currency and that the rate at which one currency can be exchanged for another varies over time. At any particular point in time, however, all such rates must be in conformance or else a riskless profit-making situation would arise. For example, it is possible to exchange Canadian dollars for British pounds, then exchange the British pounds for French francs, and finally, to exchange the French francs for dollars. If all three exchange rates are not in line, an investor might end up with more dollars at the end of this chain of transactions than at the beginning. Such an opportunity would attract large amounts of money, placing pressure on exchange rates and rapidly restoring balance. While transactions costs and certain exchange restrictions might limit the ability of people to exploit such imbalances among exchange rates, they would nevertheless force the rates into being closely lined up.

The familiar market in foreign currency, operated by banks, travel agents, and others, is in effect a spot market, since both the agreement on terms and the actual exchange of currencies occur at the same time. There are also markets for agreements involving the future delivery of foreign currency.

The largest such market is operated by banks and specialized brokers, who maintain close communications with each other throughout the world. Corporations, institutions, and some individuals deal in this market via large banks. Substantial amounts of money are involved, and every agreement is negotiated separately. Typical rates are quoted daily in the financial press, as shown in Figure 19.6. This network of large institutions is generally termed the *market for forward exchange*, since there is no marking to market. Furthermore, since the contracts are not standardized, no organized secondary market for them exists.

However, there is a market that deals in standardized futures contracts for foreign currency.[12] Procedures are similar to those used for commodity futures. For example, one of the currency futures contracts traded on the International Monetary Market (IMM) of the Chicago Mercantile Exchange requires the seller to deliver 12,500,000 Japanese yen to the buyer on a specific date for a number of US dollars agreed upon in advance. Only the price of the transaction (expressed in both dollars per yen and yen per dollar) is negotiated by the parties involved; all other terms are standard. Clearing procedures allow positions to be covered by reversing trades, and few contracts result in the actual delivery of foreign currency. As shown in Figure 19.7, prices and volumes for such contracts are quoted daily in the financial press along with those for other futures.

Markets for foreign currency futures attract both hedgers and speculators. Hedgers wish to reduce or possibly eliminate the risk associated with planned future transfers of funds from one country to another.

---

[12] The prices of foreign currency forward and futures contracts appear to be quite similar. See Bradford Cornell and Marc Reinganum, "Forward and Futures Prices: Evidence from the Foreign Exchange Market," *Journal of Finance* 36, no. 5 (December 1981):1035–45. For an introductory discussion of the pricing relationships between spot, forward, and futures contracts, see Kenneth R. French, "Pricing Financial Futures Contracts: An Introduction," *Journal of Applied Corporate Finance* 2 (1989):59–66; and Darrell Duffie, *Futures Markets* (Englewood Cliffs, N.J.: Prentice Hall, 1989):152–57.

# FOREIGN EXCHANGE

Mid-market rates in Toronto at noon, Jan. 6, 1992. Prepared by the Bank of Montreal Treasury Group.

| | | $1 U.S. in Cdn.$ = | $1 Cdn. in U.S.$ = |
|---|---|---|---|
| U.S./Canada spot | | 1.1429 | 0.8750 |
| 1 month forward | | 1.1460 | 0.8726 |
| 2 months forward | | 1.1490 | 0.8703 |
| 3 months forward | | 1.1516 | 0.8684 |
| 6 months forward | | 1.1584 | 0.8633 |
| 12 months forward | | 1.1712 | 0.8538 |
| 3 years forward | | 1.2194 | 0.8201 |
| 5 years forward | | 1.2404 | 0.8062 |
| 7 years forward | | 1.2654 | 0.7903 |
| 10 years forward | | 1.2879 | 0.7765 |
| Canadian dollar | High | 1.1530 | 0.8673 |
| in 1992: | Low | 1.1420 | 0.8757 |
| | Average | 1.1471 | 0.8718 |

| Country | Currency | Cdn. $ per unit | U.S. $ per unit |
|---|---|---|---|
| Britain | Pound | 2.1452 | 1.8770 |
| 1 month forward | | 2.1389 | 1.8664 |
| 2 months forward | | 2.1339 | 1.8572 |
| 3 months forward | | 2.1277 | 1.8476 |
| 6 months forward | | 2.1071 | 1.8190 |
| 12 months forward | | 2.0718 | 1.7690 |
| Germany | Mark | 0.7524 | 0.6583 |
| 1 month forward | | 0.7507 | 0.6550 |
| 3 months forward | | 0.7478 | 0.6493 |
| 6 months forward | | 0.7422 | 0.6407 |
| 12 months forward | | 0.7332 | 0.6260 |
| Japan | Yen | 0.009213 | 0.008061 |
| 1 month forward | | 0.009228 | 0.008053 |
| 3 months forward | | 0.009258 | 0.008039 |
| 6 months forward | | 0.009294 | 0.008023 |
| 12 months forward | | 0.009383 | 0.008011 |
| Algeria | Dinar | 0.0538 | 0.0471 |
| Antigua, Grenada and St. Lucia | E.C.Dollar | 0.4241 | 0.3711 |
| Argentina | Peso | 1.17800 | 1.03072 |
| Australia | Dollar | 0.8731 | 0.7639 |
| Austria | Schilling | 0.10651 | 0.09320 |
| Bahamas | Dollar | 1.1429 | 1.0000 |
| Barbados | Dollar | 0.5663 | 0.4955 |
| Belgium | Franc | 0.03648 | 0.03192 |
| Bermuda | Dollar | 1.1429 | 1.0000 |
| Brazil | Cruzeiro | 0.00112 | 0.00098 |
| Bulgaria | Lev | 0.0662 | 0.0579 |
| Chile | Peso | 0.0031 | 0.0027 |
| China | Renminbi | 0.2100 | 0.1837 |
| Cyprus | Pound | 2.6064 | 2.2805 |
| Czechoslovakia | Koruna | 0.0409 | 0.0358 |
| Denmark | Krone | 0.1935 | 0.1693 |
| Egypt | Pound | 0.3556 | 0.3111 |

| Country | Currency | Cdn. $ per unit | U.S. $ per unit |
|---|---|---|---|
| Fiji | Dollar | 0.7760 | 0.6790 |
| Finland | Markka | 0.2764 | 0.2418 |
| France | Franc | 0.2204 | 0.1928 |
| Greece | Drachma | 0.00651 | 0.00570 |
| Hong Kong | Dollar | 0.1474 | 0.1289 |
| Hungary | Forint | 0.01499 | 0.01312 |
| Iceland | Krona | 0.02045 | 0.01789 |
| India | Rupee | 0.04469 | 0.03910 |
| Indonesia | Rupiah | 0.00057 | 0.00050 |
| Ireland | Punt | 1.9909 | 1.7420 |
| Israel | N. Shekel | 0.50061 | 0.43802 |
| Italy | Lira | 0.000996 | 0.000871 |
| Jamaica | Dollar | 0.05953 | 0.05208 |
| Jordan | Dinar | 1.7290 | 1.5129 |
| Lebanon | Pound | 0.00130 | 0.00114 |
| Luxembourg | Franc | 0.03648 | 0.03192 |
| Malaysia | Ringgit | 0.4218 | 0.3691 |
| Mexico | Peso | 0.00037 | 0.00033 |
| Netherlands | Guilder | 0.6680 | 0.5845 |
| New Zealand | Dollar | 0.6243 | 0.5462 |
| Norway | Krone | 0.1912 | 0.1673 |
| Pakistan | Rupee | 0.04646 | 0.04065 |
| Philippines | Peso | 0.04354 | 0.03810 |
| Poland | Zloty | 0.00011 | 0.00010 |
| Portugal | Escudo | 0.00862 | 0.00754 |
| Romania | Leu | 0.0060 | 0.0053 |
| Russia | Ruble | 2.0182 | 1.7658 |
| Saudi Arabia | Riyal | 0.3048 | 0.2667 |
| Singapore | Dollar | 0.7040 | 0.6160 |
| South Africa | Rand | 0.4170 | 0.3649 |
| South Korea | Won | 0.001506 | 0.001318 |
| Spain | Peseta | 0.01182 | 0.01034 |
| Sudan | Pound | 0.0759 | 0.0664 |
| Sweden | Krona | 0.2065 | 0.1807 |
| Switzerland | Franc | 0.8475 | 0.7415 |
| Taiwan | Dollar | 0.0452 | 0.0395 |
| Thailand | Baht | 0.0455 | 0.0398 |
| Trinidad, Tobago | Dollar | 0.2692 | 0.2356 |
| Venezuela | Bolivar | 0.01937 | 0.01695 |
| Yugoslavia | Dinar | 0.049691 | 0.043478 |
| Zambia | Kwacha | 0.0130 | 0.0113 |
| European Currency Unit | | 1.5261 | 1.3353 |
| Special Drawing Right | | 1.6284 | 1.4248 |

The U.S. dollar closed at $1.1426 in terms of Canadian funds, down $0.0038 from Friday. The pound sterling closed at $2.1513, up $0.0316.

In New York, the Canadian dollar closed up $0.0029 at $0.8752 in terms of U.S. funds. The pound sterling was up $0.0338 to $1.8828.

**FIGURE 19-6**

Quotations for foreign exchange.

SOURCE: Reprinted by permission of *The Globe and Mail: Report on Business*, Thomson Newspapers Company Limited, (January 7, 1992).

## An Example

For example, a US importer might know on November 8, 1991, that he or she will have to make a payment of 50 million yen to a Japanese exporter in May 1992. The current exchange rate is $.007578 per yen (or, equivalently, 131.96 yen per dollar),

# FUTURES PRICES

Quotations for Friday, November 8, 1991

| Season | | | | | | Net | Prev |
| High | Low | Month | Open | High | Low | Settle | Chge | Op.Int |

## CURRENCIES

**BRITISH POUND (IMM)** £62,500
US$ per £; 0.0002 = $12.50 per contract
Est. Vol. 10,001, Prev. Vol. 11,303, Prev. Open Int. 30,998

| 1.8008 | 1.5670 | Dec91 | 1.7515 | 1.7630 | 1.7510 | 1.7592 | − .0016 | 28,136 |
| 1.7570 | 1.5560 | Mar92 | 1.7290 | 1.7420 | 1.7290 | 1.7382 | − .0012 | 2,835 |

**CANADIAN DOLLAR (IMM)** $100,000
US$ per C$; 0.0001 = $10 per contract
Est. Vol. 16,127, Prev. Vol. 4,827, Prev. Open Int. 30,145

| .8906 | .8153 | Dec91 | .8870 | .8872 | .8803 | .8811 | − .0075 | 25,054 |
| .8857 | .8233 | Mar92 | .8825 | .8825 | .8757 | .8765 | − .0078 | 4,216 |
| .8820 | .8330 | Jun92 | .8786 | .8787 | .8715 | .8725 | − .0081 | 726 |

**DEUTSCHEMARK (IMM)** 125,000 marks
US$ per mark; 0.0001 = $12.50 per contract
Est. Vol. 48,215, Prev. Vol. 59,772, Prev. Open Int. 78,287

| .6781 | .5365 | Dec91 | .6035 | .6079 | .6034 | .6056 | − .0012 | 72,445 |
| .6065 | .5346 | Mar92 | .5976 | .6009 | .5970 | .5993 | − .0010 | 5,352 |
| .5985 | .5322 | Jun92 | .5945 | .5945 | .5930 | .5933 | − .0008 | 485 |

**JAPANESE YEN (IMM)** 12.5 million yen
US$ per yen (scaled .00); 0.0001 = $12.50 per contract
Est. Vol. 13,693, Prev. Vol. 13,764, Prev. Open Int. 77,532

| .7781 | .6997 | Dec91 | .7668 | .7681 | .7651 | .7667 | − .0025 | 71,750 |
| .7784 | .7000 | Mar92 | .7650 | .7664 | .7635 | .7651 | − .0024 | 3,071 |
| .7730 | .7020 | Jun92 | .7640 | .7640 | .7640 | .7640 | − .0027 | 837 |
| .7711 | .7179 | Sep92 | .7641 | .7641 | .7641 | .7641 | − .0026 | 599 |
| .7720 | .7392 | Dec92 | .7642 | .7642 | .7642 | .7642 | − .0029 | 1,275 |

**SWISS FRANC (IMM)** 125,000 francs
US$ per franc; 0.0001 = $12.50 per contract
Est. Vol. 18,331, Prev. Vol. 20,486, Prev. Open Int. 31,744

| .8090 | .6235 | Dec91 | .6849 | .6893 | .6847 | .6871 | − .0015 | 29,430 |
| .6995 | .6233 | Mar92 | .6798 | .6842 | .6795 | .6823 | − .0010 | 2,103 |
| .6860 | .1430 | Jun92 | .6760 | .6785 | .6755 | .6777 | − .0007 | 211 |

**AUSTRALIAN DOLLAR (IMM)** A$100,000
US$ per A$; 0.0001 = $10 per contract
Est. Vol. 110, Prev. Vol. 189, Prev. Open Int. 1,475

| .7960 | .7360 | Dec91 | .7825 | .7835 | .7812 | .7822 | + .0006 | 1,458 |

**FIGURE 19-7**

Quotations for foreign exchange future contracts.

*SOURCE:* Reprinted by permission of *The Financial Post,* Southam Publications Limited, (November 11, 1991).

so the anticipated dollar size of the payment is $378,900 ($ .007578 × 50,000,000). The risk the importer faces by simply waiting until May to make this payment is that the exchange rate will change in an unfavorable manner — perhaps rising to $.0080 per yen, in which case the dollar cost to the importer will have risen to $400,000 ($ .0080 × 50,000,000). The importer can hedge this risk by purchasing a May futures contract for yen. Figure 19.7(b) indicates that the settle price on November 8, 1991, for a contract was $.007651, meaning that the dollar cost of the contract is $382,550 ($ .007651 × 50,000,000). Thus, for a cost of $3,650 ($382,550 − $378,900), the importer can remove the risk of the yen appreciating against the dollar before the payment date.

Speculators are attracted to the foreign currency futures market when they believe the current price of the futures contract is substantially different from what they expect the spot rate to be on the delivery date.

For example, a speculator might believe the price of the March futures contract for Japanese yen is too high. Perhaps a speculator might believe that when March comes around, the exchange rate will be $.0075 per yen (or, equivalently, 133.33 yen per dollar). By selling (that is, shorting) a March futures contract for yen, the speculator will be selling yen for $.007651, the settle price on November 8, 1991. At the time delivery has to be made, the speculator believes yen can be bought on the spot market for $.0075, thereby allowing a profit to be made on the difference between the selling and buying prices.[13] Specifically, the speculator expects to be able to make a profit of $1887.50 (($.007651 − $.0075) × 12,500,000) per futures contract.

## ☐ 19.7.2 Interest Rate Futures

Futures involving fixed-income securities are often referred to as interest rate futures, because their prices are greatly influenced by current and expected future interest rates. More specifically, their pricing can be related to the term structure of interest rates, which in turn is related to the concept of forward rates.[14]

### An Example

Just how the pricing of interest rate futures is related to the concept of forward rates can be illustrated with an example. Consider the futures market for US 90-day Treasury bills. As Figure 19.8 indicates, on November 8, 1991, a purchaser of a futures contract calling for delivery in June 1992 of $1,000,000 face value of US 90-day Treasury bills (maturing in September 1992) would have paid a settle price of 95.35. More precisely, in June 1992 the seller of the contract will be obliged to deliver Treasury bills to the buyer for an amount that would make the interest rate on the T-bills, stated on a discount basis, equal to 4.65% per year. Thus, on November 8, 1991, the forward rate on 90-day Treasury bills to be delivered in June 1992 was 4.65%.

As with commodity futures, neither the buyers nor the sellers of such contracts are required to maintain their positions until the delivery date. Reversing trades can be made at any time, and relatively few contracts result in actual delivery.

Figure 19.8 shows that on November 8, 1991, the structure of 90-day forward rates was nearly flat, interest rates ranged from 4.61% for December 1991 delivery to 5.37% for December 1992 delivery. Under the unbiased expectations hypothesis (discussed in Chapter 13), these forward rates represent what investors, on average, think spot rates will be in the future. Specifically, the 4.65% forward rate on 90-day Treasury bills to be delivered in June 1992 can be taken to indicate that on November 8, 1991, investors, on average, expect the interest rate on 90-day Treasury bills to be equal to 4.65% in June 1992. Since the interest rate that is available on November 8, 1991, on 90-day Treasury bills for immediate delivery is 4.62%, it can be seen that investors, on average, expect the interest rate to remain nearly stable.

Actively traded US interest rate futures involve underlying securities ranging from short term (such as 90-day Treasury bills) to intermediate term (such as 10-year Treasury notes) to long term (such as 15-year Treasury bonds). Prices are generally stated in

---

[13] Actually, the typical speculator will plan to realize this profit by entering a reversing trade instead of buying yen on the spot market and then making delivery. Similarly, the previously mentioned hedging importer will typically plan to enter a reversing trade.

[14] See Chapter 13 for a discussion of term structure and forward rates. For a discussion of how interest rate futures are related to yield curves, see Chapter 4 of Robert W. Kolb, *Interest Rate Futures* (Richmond, Va.: Robert F. Dame, Inc., 1982); Chapter 5 of Edward W. Schwarz, Joanne M. Hill, and Thomas Schneeweis, *Financial Futures* (Homewood, Ill.: Richard D. Irwin, Inc., 1986); and Martin L. Leibowitz, *The Analysis of Value and Volatility in Financial Futures*, Monograph Series in Finance and Economics 1981–3, Salomon Brothers Center for the Study of Financial Institutions, Graduate School of Business Administration, New York University.

# FUTURES PRICES

Quotations for Friday, November 8, 1991

| Season High | Low | Month | Open | High | Low | Settle | Net Chge | Prev Op.Int |
|---|---|---|---|---|---|---|---|---|

## FINANCIALS

**CDN. GOVT. BONDS 9% (ME) $100,000**
points of 100%; 0.01 = $10 per contract
Est. Vol. 3,061, Prev. Vol. 2,378, Prev. Open Int. 7,080

| 102.48 | 92.23 | Dec91 | 101.70 | 102.48 | 101.25 | 101.29 | - .09 | 6,996 |

**U.S. TREASURY BONDS 8% (CBOT) US$100,000**
points and 32nds of 100%; 1/32nd = $31.25 per contract
Est. Vol. 340,000, Prev. Vol. 355,967, Prev. Open Int. 319,570

| 100-24 | 85-19 | Dec91 | 100 | 100-24 | 99-31 | 100- 9 | + 0-13 | 278,846 |
| 99-27 | 85-14 | Mar92 | 99- 3 | 99-27 | 99- 2 | 99-13 | + 0-14 | 24,847 |
| 98-28 | 85- 3 | Jun92 | 98- 5 | 98-28 | 98- 5 | 98-16 | + 0-15 | 8,917 |
| 98- 3 | 84-31 | Sep92 | 97-20 | 97-30 | 97-20 | 97-21 | + 0-17 | 2,286 |
| 97-13 | 84-23 | Dec92 | 96-26 | 97- 2 | 96-26 | 96-26 | + 0-18 | 4,147 |
| 96-31 | 89-30 | Mar93 | 96 | 96-10 | 96 | 96- 2 | + 0-19 | 495 |

**U.S. TREASURY NOTES 8% (CBOT) US$100,000**
points and 32nds of 100%; 1/32nd = $31.25 per contract
Est. Vol. 23,000, Prev. Vol. 25,895, Prev. Open Int. 91,885

| 103-18 | 95-15 | Dec91 | 103-10 | 103-18 | 103- 1 | 103- 9 | + 0- 1 | 83,369 |
| 102-24 | 95- 8 | Mar92 | 102-15 | 102-24 | 102- 9 | 102-15 | ...... | 8,211 |
| 101-23 | 98- 5 | Jun92 | 101-23 | 101-23 | 101-18 | 101-21 | + 0- 1 | 304 |

**LONG GILT 9% (LIFFE) £50,000 notional value**
points and 32nds of 100%; 1/32nd = £15.625 per contract
Est. Vol. 38,518, Prev. Vol. 27,004, Prev. Open Int. 46,068

| 97- 8 | 89-10 | Dec91 | 94-30 | 95-27 | 94-30 | 95-20 | + 0-24 | 43,494 |
| 96-24 | 90- 7 | Mar92 | 95- 9 | 95-26 | 95- 9 | 95-20 | + 0-21 | 2,574 |

**GERMAN GOVT. BONDS 6% (LIFFE) DM250,000 notional value**
points of 100%; 0.01 pt. = DM25 per contract
Est. Vol. 64,438, Prev. Vol. 46,644, Prev. Open Int. 78,818

| 86.73 | 83.73 | Dec91 | 86.04 | 86.30 | 85.95 | 86.22 | + .39 | 73,515 |
| 86.75 | 83.86 | Mar92 | 86.32 | 86.59 | 86.32 | 86.55 | + .37 | 5,303 |

**U.S. TREASURY BILLS 3 MONTH (IMM) US$1,000,000**
points of 100%; 0.01 = $25 per contract
Est. Vol. 3,802, Prev. Vol. 5,555, Prev. Open Int. 55,326

| 95.43 | 92.24 | Dec91 | 95.41 | 95.42 | 95.38 | 95.39 | - .01 | 23,151 |
| 95.56 | 93.42 | Mar92 | 95.55 | 95.56 | 95.50 | 95.52 | - .02 | 28,114 |
| 95.38 | 93.15 | Jun92 | 95.36 | 95.38 | 95.33 | 95.35 | + .01 | 3,578 |
| 95.11 | 93.05 | Sep92 | 95.11 | 95.11 | 95.09 | 95.09 | ...... | 350 |
| 94.66 | 93.60 | Dec92 | 94.63 | 94.66 | 94.63 | 94.63 | ...... | 133 |

**STERLING 3 MONTH (LIFFE) £500,000**
points of 100%; 0.01 pt. = £12.50 per contract
Est. Vol. 39,516, Prev. Vol. 24,738, Prev. Open Int. 154,894

| 90.35 | 86.52 | Dec91 | 89.86 | 89.93 | 89.86 | 89.89 | + .02 | 51,664 |
| 90.49 | 86.68 | Mar92 | 90.29 | 90.36 | 90.29 | 90.35 | + .06 | 42,772 |
| 90.46 | 87.45 | Jun92 | 90.40 | 90.44 | 90.39 | 90.42 | + .04 | 33,931 |
| 90.41 | 87.44 | Sep92 | 90.36 | 90.41 | 90.36 | 90.39 | + .04 | 10,131 |
| 90.32 | 87.44 | Dec92 | 90.30 | 90.30 | 90.28 | 90.29 | + .03 | 6,650 |
| 90.16 | 87.45 | Mar93 | 90.13 | 90.14 | 90.11 | 90.13 | + .04 | 4,360 |
| 90.09 | 87.47 | Jun93 | 90.01 | 90.01 | 89.99 | 89.99 | + .02 | 2,032 |
| 90.08 | 87.98 | Sep93 | 89.93 | 89.97 | 89.93 | 89.96 | + .04 | 1,713 |
| 90.02 | 88.93 | Dec93 | 89.90 | 89.91 | 89.90 | 89.90 | + .03 | 1,641 |

**U.S. DOLLAR INDEX (FINEX) 500 x index**
points and US cents; 0.01 = $5 per contract
Est. Vol. 3,000, Prev. Vol. 3,390, Prev. Open Int. 6,227

| 98.96 | 88.47 | Dec91 | 89.53 | 89.54 | 89.04 | 89.34 | + .20 | 5,163 |
| 99.67 | 89.60 | Mar92 | 90.61 | 90.61 | 90.25 | 90.40 | + .21 | 1,035 |

**BANKERS ACCEPTANCES (ME) $1,000,000**
points of 100%; 0.01 = $25 per contract
Est. Vol. 2,273, Prev. Vol. 2,041, Prev. Open Int. 19,564

| 92.92 | 86.50 | Dec91 | 92.86 | 92.86 | 92.60 | 92.60 | - .27 | 4,850 |
| 93.31 | 88.18 | Mar92 | 93.21 | 93.23 | 92.86 | 92.86 | - .39 | 4,717 |
| 93.27 | 87.97 | Jun92 | 93.17 | 93.19 | 92.94 | 92.94 | - .27 | 4,259 |
| 93.05 | 87.90 | Sep92 | 93.00 | 93.00 | 92.85 | 92.85 | - .20 | 1,876 |
| 92.80 | 87.80 | Dec92 | 92.73 | 92.73 | 92.40 | 92.40 | - .40 | 1,843 |
| 92.47 | 89.19 | Mar93 | 92.30 | 92.35 | 92.15 | 92.15 | - .32 | 918 |
| 92.23 | 88.95 | Jun93 | 92.10 | 92.14 | 91.85 | 91.95 | - .28 | 821 |
| 91.90 | 89.94 | Sep93 | 91.80 | 91.80 | 91.60 | 91.60 | - .30 | 280 |

**EURODOLLARS (IMM) US$1,000,000**
points of 100%; 0.01 = $25 per contract
Est. Vol. 176,570, Prev. Vol. 141,963, Prev. Open Int. 1,026,332

| 94.94 | 90.04 | Dec91 | 94.92 | 94.94 | 94.87 | 94.88 | - .03 | 246,808 |
| 95.06 | 90.34 | Mar92 | 95.04 | 95.06 | 94.98 | 94.99 | - .03 | 235,707 |
| 94.83 | 90.35 | Jun92 | 94.82 | 94.83 | 94.77 | 94.78 | ...... | 142,354 |
| 94.53 | 90.32 | Sep92 | 94.52 | 94.53 | 94.47 | 94.48 | - .01 | 96,147 |
| 94.02 | 90.24 | Dec92 | 94.01 | 94.02 | 93.95 | 93.95 | - .02 | 69,091 |
| 93.80 | 90.28 | Mar93 | 93.80 | 93.80 | 93.73 | 93.74 | - .02 | 54,758 |
| 93.45 | 90.63 | Jun93 | 93.43 | 93.45 | 93.38 | 93.39 | - .02 | 43,007 |
| 93.15 | 90.58 | Sep93 | 93.15 | 93.15 | 93.08 | 93.10 | - .02 | 30,918 |
| 92.75 | 90.98 | Dec93 | 92.74 | 92.75 | 92.71 | 92.71 | ...... | 20,993 |
| 92.71 | 91.00 | Mar94 | 92.71 | 92.71 | 92.67 | 92.67 | ...... | 27,172 |
| 92.44 | 90.92 | Jun94 | 92.44 | 92.44 | 92.40 | 92.41 | ...... | 17,707 |
| 92.21 | 91.85 | Sep94 | 92.21 | 92.21 | 92.17 | 92.18 | + .01 | 11,800 |
| 91.89 | 91.56 | Dec94 | 91.89 | 91.89 | 91.86 | 91.87 | + .01 | 9,898 |
| 91.88 | 91.55 | Mar95 | 91.88 | 91.88 | 91.85 | 91.86 | + .01 | 6,991 |
| 91.76 | 91.44 | Jun95 | 91.73 | 91.76 | 91.73 | 91.74 | + .01 | 6,623 |
| 91.69 | 91.31 | Sep95 | 91.60 | 91.60 | 91.58 | 91.59 | + .01 | 6,358 |

**EURODOLLARS (LIFFE) US$1,000,000**
points of 100%; 0.01 pt. = $25 per contract
Est. Vol. 3,252, Prev. Vol. 1,406, Prev. Open Int. 36,008

| 94.95 | 90.32 | Dec91 | 94.93 | 94.94 | 94.91 | 94.92 | ...... | 17,696 |
| 95.06 | 90.35 | Mar92 | 95.06 | 95.06 | 95.01 | 95.03 | + .02 | 9,359 |
| 94.83 | 90.93 | Jun92 | 94.82 | 94.83 | 94.79 | 94.81 | + .06 | 5,080 |
| 95.10 | 90.97 | Sep92 | 94.52 | 94.53 | 94.49 | 94.50 | + .06 | 2,348 |
| 93.99 | 90.84 | Dec92 | 93.99 | 93.99 | 93.99 | 93.99 | + .07 | 580 |
| 93.79 | 91.18 | Mar93 | 93.79 | 93.79 | 93.76 | 93.77 | + .07 | 441 |
| 93.42 | 91.47 | Jun93 | 93.42 | 93.42 | 93.42 | 93.42 | + .07 | 370 |
| 93.13 | 92.42 | Sep93 | 93.13 | 93.13 | 93.13 | 93.13 | + .08 | 134 |

**FIGURE 19-8**

Interest rate (financial) future contracts.

*SOURCE:* Reprinted by permission of *The Financial Post,* Southam Publications Limited, (November 11, 1991).

# FUTURES PRICES

Quotations for Friday, November 8, 1991

| Season High | Low | Month | Open | High | Low | Settle | Net Chge | Prev Op.Int |
|---|---|---|---|---|---|---|---|---|

## INDEXES

**S+P 500 COMPOSITE INDEX (CME)** 500 x index
points; 0.05 pt. = $25 per contract
Est. Vol. 44,709, Prev. Vol. 45,569, Prev. Open Int. 146,783

| 401.50 | 318.50 | Dec91 | 396.35 | 397.75 | 393.20 | 393.45 | − .85 | 139,086 |
| 404.00 | 374.70 | Mar92 | 398.15 | 399.70 | 395.30 | 395.50 | − .85 | 6,569 |
| 407.00 | 380.50 | Jun92 | 400.55 | 401.50 | 396.90 | 397.30 | − .85 | 1,096 |

**NYSE COMPOSITE INDEX (NYFE)** 500 x index
points; 0.05 pt. = $25 per contract
Est. Vol. 5,229, Prev. Vol. 6,254, Prev. Open Int. 5,919

| 219.70 | 174.85 | Dec91 | 218.65 | 219.35 | 216.90 | 217.05 | − .60 | 4,870 |
| 220.35 | 205.90 | Mar92 | 219.60 | 219.75 | 218.00 | 218.00 | − .60 | 760 |
| 221.40 | 208.45 | Jun92 | 219.05 | 219.05 | 219.05 | 219.05 | − .60 | 167 |
| 220.75 | 211.85 | Sep92 | 220.10 | 220.10 | 220.10 | 220.10 | − .60 | 122 |

**VALUE LINE COMPOSITE INDEX (KBOT)** 500 x index
points; 0.05 pt. = $25 per contract
Est. Vol. N.A., Prev. Vol. 276, Prev. Open Int. 1,746

| 327.60 | 237.45 | Dec91 | 325.97 | 327.60 | 323.10 | 323.30 | − 1.35 | 1,561 |
| 329.50 | 303.00 | Mar92 | 328.70 | 329.50 | 325.70 | 325.70 | − 1.40 | 183 |

**MAJOR MARKET INDEX (CBOT)** US$250 x index
points; 0.05 pt. = $12.50 per contract
Est. Vol. 2,000, Prev. Vol. 2,093, Prev. Open Int. 3,415

| 326.20 | 307.25 | Nov91 | 325.50 | 326.20 | 322.00 | 322.10 | − 1.65 | 2,965 |
| 326.90 | 311.25 | Dec91 | 325.80 | 326.50 | 322.50 | 322.50 | − 1.50 | 431 |

**COMMODITY RESEARCH BUREAU (NYFE)** 250 x index
points; 0.05 pt. = $12.50 per contract
Est. Vol. 250, Prev. Vol. 208, Prev. Open Int. 1,228

| 222.00 | 205.90 | Dec91 | 214.50 | 216.00 | 214.45 | 215.45 | + .30 | 800 |
| 220.80 | 206.90 | Mar92 | 214.90 | 216.50 | 214.85 | 216.10 | + .50 | 210 |
| 221.15 | 207.30 | May92 | 215.40 | 216.50 | 215.30 | 216.50 | + .45 | 113 |
| 221.65 | 214.00 | Jul92 | 217.00 | 217.00 | 217.00 | 217.00 | + .50 | 105 |

**TORONTO 35 (TFE)** 500 x index
points; 0.02 pt. = $10 per contract
Est. Vol. 336, Prev. Vol. 236, Prev. Open Int. 1,944

| 196.90 | 184.10 | Nov91 | 196.00 | 196.90 | 195.88 | 195.90 | + 1.10 | 754 |
| 197.76 | 184.78 | Dec91 | 197.30 | 197.30 | 196.30 | 196.30 | + 1.10 | 1,190 |

**FIGURE 19-9**
Index futures.

*SOURCE:* Reprinted by permission of *The Financial Post*, Southam Publications Limited, (November 11, 1991).

terms of percentages of par values for the corresponding securities; yields-to-maturity (or discounts) associated with the settle prices are also shown.[15]

## ☐ 19.7.3 Market Index Futures

Figure 19.9 shows a set of quotations for futures contracts on a variety of market indices. Each of these contracts involves the payment of *cash* on the delivery date of an amount equal to a *multiplier* times the difference between (1) the value of the index at the close of the last trading day of the contract and (2) the purchase price of the futures contract. If the index is above the futures price, those with short positions pay those with long positions. If the index is below the futures price, those with long positions pay those with short positions.

---

[15] For Treasury bills, the discounts and associated prices are annualized. For some interest rate futures, there is flexibility in just what the seller has to deliver, known as the *quality option*. Sometimes there is also some flexibility regarding when an intention to deliver must be announced, known as the *wild card option*. See, for example, Chapter 3 of Kolb, *Interest Rate Futures*; and Chapters 2 (Appendix) and 14 of Schwarz, Hill, and Schneeweis, *Financial Futures*; and Chapter 9 of Duffie, *Futures Markets*. In Canada interest rate futures on Canadian government bonds and bankers' acceptances are available on the Montreal Exchange as shown in Figure 19.8. Figure 19.8 also shows quotations for Eurodollar, sterling and German government bonds traded on the London futures exchange (LIFFE).

In practice, a clearinghouse is used, and all contracts are marked to market every day. In a sense, the delivery day differs from other days in only one respect—all open positions are marked to market for the last time and then closed.

Cash settlement provides results similar to those associated with delivery of all the securities in the index. It avoids the effort and transaction costs associated with (1) the purchase of securities by people who have taken short futures positions; (2) the delivery of these securities to people who have taken long futures positions; and (3) the subsequent sale of the securities by those who receive them.

## Major Contracts

Shown in Figure 19.9 are the six market index futures contracts. Five of these futures involved stock indices, with the most popular one in terms of both trading volume and open interest being based on the Standard & Poor's 500. This contract is traded on the Index and Option Market Division of the Chicago Mercantile Exchange (CME), whereas the next most popular one, based on the New York Stock Exchange Composite Stock Index, is traded at the New York Futures Exchange (NYFE).[16] Three other stock index futures involve the Major Market Index (this index, when multiplied by five, closely resembles the Dow Jones Industrial Average; it is traded on the Chicago Board of Trade); the Value Line Average Stock Index (traded on the Kansas City Board of Trade); and the Toronto 35 Index (traded on the *Toronto Futures Exchange*, TFE, a subsidiary of the TSE). Also shown in Figure 19.9 is the CRB Index Futures contract. This contract, traded on the NYFE, is based on an index that is computed daily from the settlement prices on a number of commodity futures contracts.

For all contracts but the Major Market Index Futures, the multiplier is $500; for the Major Market Index, it is $250. This means that the purchase of an S&P 500 contract when the index is 150 costs $75,000 ($500 × 150); a subsequent sale of this contract when the index is 155 would result in proceeds of $77,500 and a profit of $2500.

## Trading Volume

The volume of trading in futures contracts in the US is very large. To assess its relative size, the number of contracts can be multiplied by the total dollar value represented by one contract. As shown in Figure 19.9, the estimated volume on November 8, 1991, for S&P 500 futures was 44,709 contracts. At a value of 393.45 for the lowest-priced S&P 500 contract, the total dollar value is in excess of $44,709 \times 393.45 \times \$500 = \$8.8$ billion! On many days, the dollar value involved in trades of S&P 500 futures exceeds that of trades of individual stocks.

The situation is quite different on the TFE as interest in index futures has not developed in Canada to the extent that it has in the US On November 8, 1991 about 336 index futures traded representing a total dollar volume of $32.9 million or about 0.4% of the US trading value and 7.7% of the total value of TSE equity trades on that day.

---

[16] The NYFE is a subsidiary of the New York Stock Exchange.

## Hedging

What accounts for the popularity of stock index futures in general and the S&P 500 in particular in the US? Simply stated, they provide relatively inexpensive and highly liquid positions similar to those obtained with diversified stock portfolios.

For example, instead of purchasing 500 stocks in anticipation of a market advance, one can invest an equivalent amount of money in Treasury bills and take a long position in S&P 500 futures. Alternatively, instead of trying to take short positions in 500 stocks in anticipation of a market decline, one can take a short position in S&P 500 futures, using Treasury bills as margin.

Another important use of market index futures involves allowing broker-dealers to hedge market risk that is associated with temporary positions they often take in the course of their business.[17] This hedging ultimately benefits investors by providing them with greater liquidity than they would otherwise have.

For example, consider an investor who wants to sell a large block of shares. In this situation, a broker-dealer might agree to purchase the shares immediately at an agreed-upon price and then spend time lining up buyers. In the interim, however, economic news might cause the market to fall, and with it the price of the shares. This would cause the broker-dealer to experience a loss, since the broker-dealer owns the shares during the period between purchasing it from the investor and lining up the ultimate buyers. One traditional way that broker-dealers protect themselves (at least partially) from this risk is to pay the investor a relatively low price for the shares. However, the broker-dealer can now hedge this risk (at least partially) by shorting index futures at the time the shares are bought from the investor and reversing this position when the ultimate buyers are found.

Conversely, when an investor wants to buy a large block of shares, a broker-dealer might agree to provide it at a certain price and then go about the task of lining up sellers. In the interim, however, economic news might cause the market to rise, and with it the price of the shares. This would cause the broker-dealer to experience a loss, since the price that will have to be paid to the sellers might end up being greater than the price agreed to with the investor. Traditionally, broker-dealers protect themselves from such risk by charging the investor a relatively high price for the shares. However, a broker-dealer can now hedge this risk (at least partially) by going long in index futures at the time the investor agrees to buy the shares and then reversing this position when the shares are ultimately bought.

Given competition among broker-dealers, the existence of index futures will lead broker-dealers to provide higher bid prices and lower asked prices. This reduced bid-ask spread means that the advent of index futures has provided the associated spot market for stocks (that is, an organized stock exchange) with greater liquidity.

It should be pointed out that the use of index futures in such situations does not remove all risk from the position of the broker-dealer. All it removes is market risk, since these futures contracts involve a broad market index, not an individual stock. Thus, it is possible for the broker-dealer to experience a loss even if an appropriate position has been taken in futures. Specifically, the shares with which the broker-dealer is involved

---

[17] Similarly, interest rate futures are often used by financial institutions to hedge interest rate risk that they may be exposed to. That is, when a large movement in interest rates would cause a large loss, these institutions will seek protection by either buying or selling interest rate futures.

may move up or down in price while the index remains stable, or the index may move up or down while the shares remain stable. In either case, the broker-dealer who has hedged with index futures may still experience a loss. The possibility of this happening will be substantial when the broker-dealer has little diversification, with the greatest possibility associated with a one-stock portfolio.

## Index Arbitrage

When stock index futures were first proposed, a number of people predicted that at long last there would be an indicator of investor's expectations about the future course of the stock market. It was said that the market price of such a futures contract would indicate the consensus opinion of investors concerning the future level of the associated index. In times of optimism, the futures price might be much higher than the current level of the market, while in times of pessimism, the futures price might be much lower.

Such predictions have since been found to be quite off the mark. This is because the price of a futures contract on an asset will not diverge too much from the spot price of the asset. Should a relatively large divergence occur, clever investors known as "arbitrageurs" can be expected to make trades designed to capture riskless (that is, "arbitrage") profits.

The presence of these arbitrageurs does have an effect on the pricing of stock index futures. Their actions will force the price of a stock index futures contract to stay close to an "appropriate" relationship with the current level of the associated index. To find out just what is meant by appropriate, consider a hypothetical example where today is a day in June when the TSE 35 is at 200 and a December TSE 35 futures contract is selling for 210. The following investment strategies can be compared:

1. Purchase the stocks in the TSE 35, hold them until December and then sell them on the delivery date of the December TSE 35 contract.
2. Purchase a December TSE 35 futures contract along with Treasury bills that mature in December. Hold the futures contract until the delivery date in December.

Strategy 1 would cost $200 (in "index terms") at the outset. In return, it would provide the investor with (1) an amount of money equal to the value of the TSE 35 on the delivery date and (2) dividends on those stocks that went ex-dividend prior to the delivery date. That is, by denoting the level the TSE 35 will have on the delivery date as $P_d$ and assuming the dividend yield over the six-month time period from June to December is 3%, the investor following strategy 1 will receive in December an amount that is equal to $P_d + \$6$ (that is, $P_d + (.03 \times \$200)$).

Assume that $200 is invested in Treasury bills in strategy 2. Since Treasury bills can be used as margin on futures, the total cost of strategy 2 is $200, which is the same as the cost of strategy 1. In return, strategy 2 would provide the investor with (1) an amount of money equal to the difference between the value of the TSE 35 and $210 on the delivery date and (2) the face value of the Treasury bills on the delivery date. That is, assuming that the yield on the Treasury bills is 5%, the investor following strategy 2 will receive in December an amount that is equal to $P_d$ (that is, $(P_d - \$210) + (1.05 \times \$200)$).

By design, both strategies require the same initial outlay. Furthermore, both strategies are subject to precisely the same uncertainty, the unknown level of the TSE 35 on the future delivery date, denoted by $P_d$. However, the inflows are not equal, indicating that an opportunity exists for *index arbitrage*.[18]

In this example, index arbitrage would cause an investor to go long on strategy 1 and short on strategy 2 because strategy 1 has a higher payoff than strategy 2 (note that $P_d + \$6 > P_d - \$10$). Going long on strategy 1 means that the investor is to do exactly what was indicated earlier — purchase the stocks in the TSE 35 and hold them until the December delivery date. Going short on strategy 2 means doing exactly the opposite. The investor shorts (that is, sells) a December TSE 35 futures contract and sells Treasury bills that mature in December. The net cash outflow of going long on strategy 1 and short on strategy 2 is zero — the $200 spent buying the stocks in going long on strategy 1, was obtained by selling $200 worth of December Treasury bills when going short on strategy 2. The margin necessary for being short on the future contract is met by having purchased the underlying stocks. Thus, no additional cash needs to be committed in order to engage in index arbitrage — owning Treasury bills that mature in December is sufficient.

Having gone long on strategy 1 and short on strategy 2, what is the investor's position on the delivery date in December? First, the investor bought the individual stocks in the TSE 35 at $200 and assured himself of a selling price of $210 by being short the TSE 35 futures contract. Thus, the investor has made $10 from being long on the individual stocks and short on the futures on the index. Second, the investor has received dividends totaling $6 ($.03 \times \$200$) from owning the stocks from June to December. Third, by selling, in June, $200 of December Treasury bills the investor has foregone the $10 ($.05 \times \$200$) on them. Overall, the investor has increased the dollar return by $6 ($10 + \$6 - \$10$). Furthermore, this increase is certain, meaning it will be received regardless of what happens to the level of the TSE 35. Thus, by going long on strategy 1 and short on strategy 2, the investor will not have increased the risk of his or her portfolio but will have increased the dollar return.

Earlier, it was mentioned that an investor going long on strategy 1 would receive cash of $P_d + \$6$ in December, whereas an investor going long on strategy 2 would receive cash of $P_d$. From these figures it can be seen that going long on strategy 1 and short on strategy 2 will provide a net dollar return of $6 (that is, $(P_d + \$6) - P_d$). However, if enough investors do this, the opportunity for making the $6 riskless profit will disappear. This is because (1) going long on the individual stocks will push the prices of these stocks up, thereby raising the level of the TSE 35 above 200; and (2) going short on the TSE 35 futures will reduce the price of the futures below 210. These two adjustments will continue until it is no longer profitable to go long on strategy 1 and short on strategy 2.

What if the price of the TSE 35 December futures contract were $190 instead of $210? The dollar return from being long on strategy 1 is still equal to $P_d + \$6$. However, the dollar return from being long on strategy 2 will be different. Purchasing Treasury bills and the futures contract will provide the investor with a dollar return in December of $P_d + \$20$ (that is, $(P_d - \$190) + (1.05 \times \$200)$). Since these two inflows are not equal, again there is an opportunity for index arbitrage. However, it would involve the investor going short on strategy 1 and long on strategy 2. This is because strategy 1 now

---

[18] Index arbitrage is one of two forms of *program trading*; the other form, known as *portfolio insurance*, was discussed in Chapter 18. For a discussion and example of how futures can be used to procure portfolio insurance, see Stephen R. King and Eli M. Remolona, "The Pricing and Hedging of Market Index Deposits," Federal Reserve Bank of New York *Quarterly Review* 12, no. 2 (Summer 1987):9–20.

has a lower payoff than strategy 2 (note that $P_d + \$6 < P_d + \$20$). By doing this, the investor will, without risk, earn \$14 (that is, $(P_d + \$20) - (P_d + \$6)$). Furthermore, being short the individual stocks and long the futures will reduce the level of the TSE 35 below 200 and raise the price of the futures above 190.

In equilibrium, since these two strategies cost the same to implement, prices will adjust so that their dollar returns are equal. Letting $y$ denote the dividend yield on the stocks in the index, $P_f$ denote the current price of the futures contract on the index, and $P_c$ denote the current level of the index, the dollar return from strategy 1 is

$$P_d + yP_c.$$

Letting $i$ denote the interest rate on Treasury bills, the dollar return from strategy 2 is

$$(P_d - P_f) + [(1 + i) \times P_c].$$

Setting these two dollar returns equal to each other results in

$$P_d + yP_c = (P_d - P_f) + [(1 + i) \times P_c]. \tag{19.2}$$

Simplifying this equation results in

$$P_f - P_c = (i - y)P_c. \tag{19.3}$$

Equation (19.3) indicates that the difference between the price of the futures contract and the current level of the index should depend only on (1) the current level of the index, $P_c$, and (2) the difference between the interest rate on Treasury bills and the dividend yield on the index, $(i - y)$. As the delivery date nears, the difference between the interest rate and dividend yield diminishes, converging to zero on the delivery date. Thus, as the delivery date approaches, the futures price $(P_f)$ should converge to the current price $(P_c)$.

In the example the interest rate was 5%, the dividend yield was 3%, and the current level of the TSE 35 was 200. This means that the difference between the TSE 35 December futures contract and the current level of the TSE 35 should be $(.05 - .03) \times 200 = 4$. Equivalently, the equilibrium price of the futures contract when the TSE 35 is 200 would be 204. Note that when three of the six months have passed, the interest rate and dividend yield will be 2.5% (5%/2) and 1.5% (3%/2), respectively. Thus, the difference should be about $(.025 - .015) \times 200 = 2$, assuming the TSE 35 is still at 200 at that time.

In practice, the situation is not this simple for a number of reasons. Positions in futures, stocks, and Treasury bills involve transactions costs.[19] This means that arbitrage will not take place unless the difference diverges far enough from the amount shown in equation (19.3) to warrant incurring such costs. The futures price, and hence the difference, can be expected to move within a range around the "theoretical value," with the width of the band determined by the costs of those who can engage in transactions most efficiently.

To add to the complexity, both the dividend yield and relevant interest rate on the Treasury bills are subject to some uncertainty. Neither the amounts of dividends to be

---

[19] People involved in index arbitrage need to be able quickly to make a large number of transactions in individual stocks. In order to do this, they often have their computers send in their orders through the MOST system discussed in Chapter 2.

declared nor their timing can be specified completely in advance. And, since futures positions must be marked to market daily, the amount of cash required for strategy 2 may have to be varied via additional borrowing (if short on this strategy) or lending (if long on this strategy). Furthermore, on occasion market prices may be reported with a substantial time lag, making the current level and futures price of the index appear to be out of line when they actually are not. Thus, an investor may enter into the transactions necessary for index arbitrage when actual prices are in equilibrium, thereby resulting in a useless incurring of transaction costs.

Stock index futures are used extensively by professional money managers. As a result, prices of such contracts are likely to track their underlying indices very closely, taking into account both dividends and current interest rates. It is unlikely that a private investor will be able to exploit "mispricing" of such a contract by engaging in index arbitrage. Nevertheless, stock index futures can provide inexpensive ways to take positions in the stock market or to hedge portions of the risk associated with other positions. Furthermore, their use can lower transactions costs by reducing the size of the bid-ask spread for investors who may never take direct positions in such contracts.

The 35 underlying stocks in the TSE 35, a "mutual" fund consisting of these stocks in the form of TIPs, TSE 35 options and TSE 35 futures contracts can all be traded and it is possible to arbitrage freely between all four of these securities. One therefore expects these four securities to be fairly priced at most times.

The existence of index arbitrage permits the use of stock index futures as a substitute for holding the underlying stocks. The substitution of a futures position for a stock portfolio has led to the development of synthetic index funds. These allow a foreign investor to gain access to Canadian equity markets, without hiring either research and portfolio management services or an investment counsellor, by creating a synthetic Toronto 35 index fund using futures contracts. The earlier example illustrated the equivalence of a TSE 35 stock position and a combination of TSE 35 futures contracts and Treasury bills, therefore, the investor can replicate the return on the index with minimal transactions costs and management fees.

## 19.8   FUTURES VERSUS CALL OPTIONS

People occasionally make the mistake of confusing a futures contract with an options contract.[20] With an options contract, there is the possibility that both of the parties involved will have nothing to do at the end of the life of the contract. In particular, if the option is "out of the money" on the expiration date, then the options contract will be worthless and can be thrown away. However, with a futures contract, both parties involved will have something to do at the end of the life of the contract. In particular, the parties are obligated to complete the transaction, either by a reversing trade or by actual delivery.

Figure 19.10 contrasts the situation faced by the buyer and seller of a call option with the situation faced by the buyer and seller of a futures contract. Specifically, terminal

---

[20] Adding to the confusion is the existence of a contract known as a *futures option*, which is an option that has a futures contract instead of a stock as its underlying asset. Futures options are discussed in more detail in the appendix to this chapter.

**FIGURE 19-10**
Terminal values of positions in calls and futures.

values for buyers and sellers are shown at the last possible moment — the expiration date for the option, and the delivery date for the futures contract.

As shown in part (a) of Figure 19.10, no matter what the price of the underlying stock, an option buyer cannot lose and an option seller cannot gain on the expiration date. Option buyers compensate sellers for putting themselves in this position by paying them a premium when the contract is signed.

The situation is quite different with a futures contract. As shown in part (b), the buyer may gain or lose, depending on the price of the asset in the delivery month. Whatever the buyer gains or loses, an exactly offsetting loss or gain will be registered by the seller. The higher the contract price (that is, the price of the futures contract when the buyer purchased it from the seller), the greater the likelihood that the buyer will lose and the seller will gain. The lower the contract price, the greater the likelihood that the seller will lose and the buyer will gain.

## 19.9 SYNTHETIC FUTURES

For some assets, futures contracts are unavailable but both put and call options are available. In such cases, an investor can create a *synthetic futures contract.*

The clearest example involves European options on common stocks. As shown in the previous chapter, the purchase of a European call option and the sale of a European put option at the same exercise price and with the same expiration date will provide a value at expiration that will be related, dollar for dollar, to the stock price at that time. This is shown in Figure 19.11.

Part (a) shows the payoffs associated with the purchase of a call at an exercise price of E, whereas part (b) shows the payoff associated with the sale of a put at the same exercise price. The results obtained by taking *both* positions are those shown by the solid line in part (c).

Depending on the prices (that is, premiums) of the call and put, this strategy may initially require either a net outflow of cash or provide a net inflow. For comparability

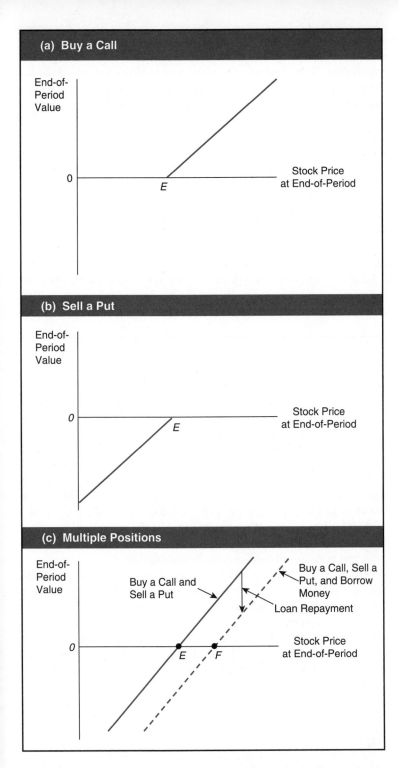

**(a) Buy a Call**

End-of-Period Value

0

E

Stock Price at End-of-Period

**(b) Sell a Put**

End-of-Period Value

0

E

Stock Price at End-of-Period

**(c) Multiple Positions**

End-of-Period Value

Buy a Call and Sell a Put

Buy a Call, Sell a Put, and Borrow Money

Loan Repayment

0

E   F

Stock Price at End-of-Period

**FIGURE 19-11**
Creating a synthetic futures contract.

with the purchase of a futures contract, this cash flow may be offset with borrowing or lending as required to bring the net investment to zero. The dashed line in part (c) shows a case in which the call option costs more than is provided by the sale of the put option. The difference is borrowed, requiring the loan repayment shown in the figure. The dashed line thus indicates the net end-of-period payoffs for a strategy requiring no initial outlay. Since these payoffs are equivalent to the payoffs from a futures contract with a contract price equal to $F$, a "synthetic" futures contract has been created.

In practice, the equivalence is not perfect. Listed options are American, not European, raising the possibility that the buyer of the put will exercise it prior to maturity. Moreover, the synthetic future is not marked to market on a daily basis. Despite these differences, the existence of well-functioning markets for call and put options will enable investors to create synthetic futures on the underlying asset.

TSE 35 options, because they are European contracts, can be used to create synthetic futures positions. For example, the simultaneous sale of five puts and purchase of five calls with the same exercise price and expiration date is equivalent to being long one futures contract. Arbitrage opportunities will exist if the synthetic price differs from the futures price. The arbitrage transactions, known as conversions and reconversions, require the simultaneous execution of both option and futures trades.

## 19.10 SUMMARY

A futures contract involves the delivery of a specific type of asset at a specific location at a given future point in time. These contracts can be bought and sold at market-based prices on certain organized exchanges due to the fact that the terms of the contract are standardized. In particular, the type of asset, time of delivery, and place of delivery are standardized. Futures contracts currently in existence involve such assets as agricultural goods, natural resources, foreign currencies, fixed-income securities, and market indices.

People who buy and sell such contracts can be classified as either hedgers or speculators. Hedgers are people whose primary motive for buying or selling such contracts is to reduce risk, since these people either produce or use the asset in the ordinary course of their business. Speculators, on the other hand, buy and sell futures in the pursuit of relatively short-term profits. That is, they seek to buy futures contracts at relatively low prices, and hope to sell them at notably higher prices.[21]

Although futures contracts involve the future delivery of an asset, the purchase price of the asset is established when the contract is sold on an exchange. Thus, the purchase price is a market-based one and is related to the anticipated spot price of the asset on the delivery date. Since the anticipated spot price of the asset is, in turn, related to the current spot price of the asset, it is not surprising that the purchase price of the futures contract is related to the current spot price of the asset. Just how these prices are related depends on the asset to be delivered, since some of them are much more costly to store for future delivery than others. Nevertheless, should the price of the futures contract get too far removed from the current spot price of the asset, certain investors, known as

---

[21] Interestingly, in the US there has been rapid growth in the number of *commodity funds* since 1979. These are investment companies that speculate in futures, their performance, however, has not been attractive. See Edwin J. Elton, Martin J. Gruber, and Joel C. Rentzler, "Professionally Managed, Publicly Traded Commodity Funds," *Journal of Business* 60, no. 2 (April 1987):175–99.

arbitrageurs, will immediately enter a larger number of orders in order to make a riskless profit from the perceived price discrepancy. Their actions will cause prices to adjust until the opportunity to make such profits disappears. One prominent example involves index arbitrage, where the futures contract has a stock market index as its asset.

In the previous chapter, it was mentioned that an investor could synthetically create either a put or call option on a stock. Interestingly, futures contracts can also be created synthetically. However, in order to do so, an investor must deal in both puts and calls on the asset.

Given sufficient interest, almost anything can be the subject of futures trading, either directly or synthetically. Where there is risk, there will be a demand for ways to reduce it. Futures markets accommodate this demand and facilitate speculation as well. Looking ahead, new futures markets will open and old ones will close, as dictated by the interests of hedgers and speculators.

## APPENDIX A

# FUTURES OPTIONS

The previous chapter described options, while this chapter has described futures. Interestingly, there are contracts currently in existence that are known as *futures options* (or options on futures). As might be expected, these contracts are, in a sense, combinations of futures and options contracts. In particular, a futures option is an option where the underlying asset is a specific futures contract, with the expiration date on the option being the same as the delivery date on the futures contract.[22] Figure 19.12 provides quotations on some of the more frequently traded ones in the US. As the figure shows, there are both put and call options on futures. Thus, an investor can be either a buyer or a writer of either a put or a call option on a futures contract.[23] Two futures options contracts are available on Canadian exchanges — a contract on canola traded on the WCE (not quoted in the financial press) and a bond futures contract traded on the Montreal Exchange.

---

[22] The near-simultaneous quarterly expiration of (1) options on individual stocks and market indices, (2) futures on market indices, and (3) options on market index futures has been referred to as the *triple witching hour*. When it occurs, the stock market is allegedly roiled, particularly in the latter part of the day. See Hans R. Stoll and Robert E. Whaley, "Program Trading and Expiration Day Effects," *Financial Analysts Journal* 43, no. 2 (March/April 1987):16–28; Arnold Kling, "How the Stock Market Can Learn to Live with Index Futures and Options," *Financial Analysts Journal* :43, no. 5 (September/October 1987):33–39; and G. J. Santoni, "Has Programmed Trading Made Stock Prices More Volatile?" Federal Reserve Bank of St. Louis *Review* 69, no. 5 (May 1987):18–29.

[23] For more on futures options, see Chapter 12 of Kolb, *Understanding Futures Markets*; Chapter 17 of Schwarz, Hill, and Schneeweis, *Financial Futures*; Chapters 29 and 34 of Lawrence G. McMillan, *Options as a Strategic Investment* (New York: NYIF Corp., 1986); Chapter 11 of Peter Ritchken, *Options* (Glenview, Ill.: Scott, Foresman and Company, 1987); and Chapter 7 of John C. Cox and Mark Rubinstein, *Options Markets* (Englewood Cliffs, N.J.: Prentice Hall, 1985). For a computer program that can be used to determine the "true" value of these complex contracts, see Chapter 8 of Stuart M. Turnbull, *Option Valuation* (Holt, Rinehart & Winston of Canada, Limited, 1987).

# FUTURES OPTIONS PRICES

Wednesday, May 6, 1992.

## AGRICULTURAL

**CORN (CBT)**
5,000 bu.; cents per bu.

| Strike Price | Calls–Settle Jly | Sep | Dec | Puts–Settle Jly | Sep | Dec |
|---|---|---|---|---|---|---|
| 240 | 21¼ | 24½ | 27¼ | 1¼ | 6 | 8½ |
| 250 | 13½ | 18¼ | 21½ | 3½ | 10 | 12¾ |
| 260 | 8 | 13½ | 18 | 8¼ | 14½ | 18½ |
| 270 | 4¾ | 11½ | 14¾ | 14¾ | 22 | 24¼ |
| 280 | 2¾ | 9 | 12 | 22¾ | 29 | 31½ |
| 290 | 1½ | 6½ | 9¾ | 31½ | 37 | 39 |

Est. vol. 7,500;
Tues vol. 5,799 calls; 1,752 puts
Op. int. Tues 101,404 calls; 53,857 puts

**SOYBEANS (CBT)**
5,000 bu.; cents per bu.

| Strike Price | Calls–Settle Jly | Sep | Dec | Puts–Settle Jly | Sep | Dec |
|---|---|---|---|---|---|---|
| 550 | 45 | 51¼ | 57¼ | 1¾ | 4¼ | 7¾ |
| 575 | 25½ | 34½ | 42 | 6¾ | 13 | 16 |
| 600 | 12¾ | 25 | 31 | 19 | 27 | 30 |
| 625 | 6⅞ | 17 | 24½ | 38 | 43¼ | 47 |
| 650 | 4 | 12⅜ | 19¼ | 60 | 63½ | .... |
| 675 | 2½ | 9½ | 15 | 83½ | .... | .... |

Est. vol. 6,500;
Tues vol. 4,888 calls; 1,616 puts
Op. int. Tues 86,347 calls; 26,083 puts

## OIL

**CRUDE OIL (NYM)**
1,000 bbls.; $ per bbl.

| Strike Price | Calls–Settle Jun | Jly | Aug | Puts–Settle Jun | Jly | Aug |
|---|---|---|---|---|---|---|
| 19 | 1.78 | 1.93 | 2.00 | .01 | .09 | .14 |
| 20 | .79 | 1.09 | 1.19 | .02 | .24 | .33 |
| 21 | .08 | .46 | .59 | .31 | .61 | .72 |
| 22 | .01 | .16 | .26 | 1.24 | 1.30 | 1.38 |
| 23 | .01 | .05 | .11 | .... | 2.19 | 2.23 |
| 24 | .01 | .02 | .05 | .... | .... | .... |

Est. vol. 27,969;
Tues vol. 16,438 calls; 10,148 puts
Op. int. Tues 175,013 calls; 138,777 puts

**HEATING OIL No.2 (NYM)**
42,000 gal.; $ per gal.

| Strike Price | Calls–Settle Jun | Jly | Aug | Puts–Settle Jun | Jly | Aug |
|---|---|---|---|---|---|---|
| 54 | .0309 | .0320 | .0392 | .0002 | .0045 | .0055 |
| 56 | .0117 | .0176 | .0254 | .0010 | .0100 | .0115 |
| 58 | .0011 | .0085 | .0150 | .... | .0208 | .0210 |
| 60 | .0003 | .0035 | .0080 | .... | .... | .... |
| 62 | .0001 | .0015 | .0045 | .... | .... | .... |
| 64 | .0001 | .0010 | .... | .... | .... | .... |

Est. vol. 4,788;
Fri vol. 858 calls; 1,543 puts
Op. int. Fri 19,987 calls; 19,202 puts

## LIVESTOCK

**CATTLE-FEEDER (CME)**
44,000 lbs.; cents per lb.

| Strike Price | Calls–Settle May | Aug | Sep | Puts–Settle May | Aug | Sep |
|---|---|---|---|---|---|---|
| 74 | 4.52 | 2.62 | .... | 0.05 | 1.15 | 1.60 |
| 76 | 2.55 | 1.37 | 1.30 | 0.07 | 1.95 | 2.50 |
| 78 | 0.72 | 0.60 | 0.60 | 0.25 | 3.12 | .... |
| 80 | 0.05 | 0.20 | 0.17 | 1.57 | .... | .... |
| 82 | 0.02 | 0.05 | 0.10 | 3.55 | 6.52 | .... |
| 84 | 0.02 | 0.02 | 0.02 | 5.55 | 8.52 | .... |

Est. vol. 330;
Tues vol. 57 calls; 139 puts
Op. int. Tues 2,526 calls; 4,687 puts

**CATTLE-LIVE (CME)**
40,000 lbs.; cents per lb.

| Strike Price | Calls–Settle Jun | Aug | Oct | Puts–Settle Jun | Aug | Oct |
|---|---|---|---|---|---|---|
| 70 | 4.10 | 2.10 | 2.07 | 0.12 | 1.20 | 1.90 |
| 72 | 2.32 | 1.02 | 1.07 | 0.35 | 2.10 | 2.87 |
| 74 | 0.95 | 0.45 | 0.45 | 0.97 | 3.52 | .... |
| 76 | 0.25 | 0.17 | 0.20 | 2.27 | .... | .... |
| 78 | 0.05 | 0.05 | 0.10 | 4.07 | .... | .... |
| 80 | 0.00 | .... | .... | .... | .... | .... |

Est. vol. 3,536;
Tues vol. 1,045 calls; 1,118 puts
Op. int. Tues 14,616 calls; 30,566 puts

## METALS

**COPPER (CMX)**
25,000 lbs.; cents per lb.

| Strike Price | Calls–Settle Jly | Sep | Dec | Puts–Settle Jly | Sep | Dec |
|---|---|---|---|---|---|---|
| 96 | 4.85 | 5.50 | 6.65 | 0.40 | 0.90 | 1.70 |
| 98 | 3.10 | 4.05 | 5.20 | 0.65 | 1.30 | 2.25 |
| 100 | 1.80 | 2.70 | 4.00 | 1.35 | 1.95 | 3.05 |
| 102 | 1.00 | 1.90 | 3.10 | 2.55 | 3.15 | 4.10 |
| 104 | 0.40 | 1.25 | 2.35 | 3.95 | 4.40 | 5.40 |
| 105 | 0.30 | .... | 4.85 | .... | .... | .... |

Est. vol. 150;
Tues vol. 34 calls; 19 puts
Op. int. Tues 4,871 calls; 2,992 puts

**GOLD (CMX)**
100 troy ounces; $ per troy ounce

| Strike Price | Calls–Settle Jun | Jly | Aug | Puts–Settle Jun | Jly | Aug |
|---|---|---|---|---|---|---|
| 320 | 17.50 | 19.70 | 20.00 | 0.10 | 0.40 | 0.80 |
| 330 | 7.70 | 10.40 | 11.40 | 0.20 | 1.10 | 2.20 |
| 340 | 0.40 | 3.50 | 5.10 | 2.90 | 4.10 | 5.80 |
| 350 | 0.10 | 1.00 | 2.00 | 12.60 | 11.60 | 12.70 |
| 360 | 0.10 | 0.40 | 0.90 | 22.50 | 20.90 | 21.60 |
| 370 | 0.10 | 0.20 | 0.50 | 32.50 | 30.70 | 31.20 |

Est. vol. 3,000;
Tues vol. 2,974 calls; 644 puts
Op. int. Tues 87,702 calls; 26,659 puts

## CURRENCY

**JAPANESE YEN (IMM)**
12,500,000 yen; cents per 100 yen

| Strike Price | Calls–Settle May | Jun | Jly | Puts–Settle May | Jun | Jly |
|---|---|---|---|---|---|---|
| 7450 | 1.13 | 1.42 | 1.59 | 0.04 | 0.33 | 0.63 |
| 7500 | 0.67 | 1.07 | 1.29 | 0.08 | 0.48 | 0.82 |
| 7550 | 0.32 | 0.79 | 1.07 | 0.23 | 0.70 | .... |
| 7600 | 0.14 | 0.57 | 0.80 | 0.55 | 0.98 | .... |
| 7650 | 0.05 | 0.40 | 0.62 | 0.96 | 1.31 | .... |
| 7700 | 0.03 | 0.28 | 0.47 | 1.44 | 1.69 | .... |

Est. vol. 9,193;
Tues vol. 1,594 calls; 2,761 puts
Op. int. Tues 45,526 calls; 49,249 puts

**DEUTSCHEMARK (IMM)**
125,000 marks; cents per mark

| Strike Price | Calls–Settle May | Jun | Jly | Puts–Settle May | Jun | Jly |
|---|---|---|---|---|---|---|
| 6000 | 1.10 | 1.37 | 1.12 | 0.05 | 0.33 | 0.93 |
| 6050 | 0.66 | 1.04 | 0.88 | 0.11 | 0.49 | 1.19 |
| 6100 | 0.32 | 0.76 | 0.69 | 0.27 | 0.71 | .... |
| 6150 | 0.13 | 0.53 | 0.53 | 0.58 | 0.98 | .... |
| 6200 | 0.06 | 0.36 | 0.40 | 1.01 | 1.31 | .... |
| 6250 | 0.02 | 0.24 | .... | 1.68 | .... | .... |

Est. vol. 25,041;
Tues vol. 11,197 calls; 6,326 puts
Op. int. Tues 94,539 calls; 117,630 puts

**CANADIAN DOLLAR (IMM)**
100,000 Can.$; cents per Can.$

| Strike Price | Calls–Settle May | Jun | Jly | Puts–Settle May | Jun | Jly |
|---|---|---|---|---|---|---|
| 8250 | .... | 1.03 | .... | 0.01 | 0.17 | .... |
| 8300 | 0.42 | 0.67 | 0.54 | 0.05 | 0.30 | 0.72 |
| 8350 | 0.10 | 0.41 | 0.35 | 0.23 | 0.54 | .... |
| 8400 | 0.02 | 0.21 | 0.22 | 0.65 | 0.84 | 1.39 |
| 8450 | .0000 | 0.10 | .... | 1.13 | 1.23 | .... |
| 8500 | .0000 | 0.05 | 0.08 | .... | 1.67 | .... |

Est. vol. 2,107;
Tues vol. 479 calls; 115 puts
Op. int. Tues 11,747 calls; 13,959 puts

**BRITISH POUND (IMM)**
62,500 pounds; cents per pound

| Strike Price | Calls–Settle May | Jun | Jly | Puts–Settle May | Jun | Jly |
|---|---|---|---|---|---|---|
| 1725 | 6.12 | 6.42 | 4.98 | 0.004 | 0.36 | 1.46 |
| 1750 | 3.68 | 4.38 | 3.44 | 0.06 | 0.78 | 2.40 |
| 1775 | 1.46 | 2.72 | 2.24 | 0.36 | 1.60 | .... |
| 1800 | 0.30 | 1.46 | 1.38 | 1.70 | 2.86 | .... |
| 1825 | 0.06 | 0.74 | .... | 3.94 | 4.62 | .... |
| 1850 | 0.004 | 0.34 | 0.46 | .... | 6.70 | .... |

Est. vol. 3,835;
Tues vol. 734 calls; 1,372 puts
Op. int. Tues 14,495 calls; 15,444 puts

**SWISS FRANC (IMM)**
125,000 francs; cents per franc

| Strike Price | Calls–Settle May | Jun | Jly | Puts–Settle May | Jun | Jly |
|---|---|---|---|---|---|---|
| 6550 | 0.99 | 1.35 | 1.18 | 0.07 | 0.43 | 1.01 |
| 6600 | 0.57 | 1.03 | 0.96 | 0.15 | 0.61 | .... |
| 6650 | 0.27 | 0.77 | 0.76 | 0.35 | 0.85 | .... |
| 6700 | 0.12 | 0.56 | 0.59 | 0.70 | 1.14 | .... |
| 6750 | 0.06 | 0.40 | 0.46 | 1.14 | 1.48 | .... |
| 6800 | 0.01 | 0.27 | 0.35 | 1.59 | 1.84 | .... |

Est. vol. 3,161;
Tues vol. 1,878 calls; 730 puts
Op. int. Tues 18,514 calls; 17,787 puts

**MARK/YEN CROSS RATE (IMM)**
125,000 marks; yen per mark

| Strike Price | Calls–Settle May | Jun | Puts–Settle May | Jun |
|---|---|---|---|---|
| 8000 | 0.81 | 1.24 | 0.06 | 0.48 |
| 8050 | 0.41 | 0.93 | 0.18 | 0.68 |
| 8100 | 0.15 | 0.69 | 0.41 | 0.94 |
| 8150 | 0.07 | .... | 0.81 | .... |
| 8200 | 0.03 | 0.34 | 1.28 | 1.59 |
| 8250 | 0.01 | .... | .... | .... |

Est. vol. 1,810;
Tues vol. 80 calls; 0 puts
Op. int. Tues 3,561 calls; 2,912 puts

**U.S. DOLLAR INDEX (FINEX)**
500 times index

| Strike Price | Calls–Settle May | Jun | Jly | Puts–Settle May | Jun | Jly |
|---|---|---|---|---|---|---|
| 87 | .... | 2.47 | .... | 0.01 | 0.21 | .... |
| 88 | 1.32 | 1.71 | .... | 0.05 | 0.44 | .... |
| 89 | 0.55 | 1.09 | .... | 0.28 | 0.82 | .... |
| 90 | 0.14 | 0.64 | 1.63 | 0.87 | 1.36 | 1.06 |
| 91 | 0.01 | 0.34 | 1.13 | 1.75 | 2.06 | 1.56 |
| 92 | 0.01 | 0.16 | 0.75 | 2.73 | 2.88 | .... |

Est. vol. 9,415;
Tues vol. 1,103 calls; 640 puts
Op. int. Tues 20,430 calls; 17,667 puts

## INDEX

**S&P 500 STOCK INDEX (CME)**
$500 times premium

| Strike Price | Calls–Settle May | Jun | Jly | Puts–Settle May | Jun | Jly |
|---|---|---|---|---|---|---|
| 405 | 12.55 | 15.70 | 18.85 | 0.95 | 4.15 | 6.10 |
| 410 | 8.25 | 12.00 | 15.30 | 1.65 | 5.45 | 7.50 |
| 415 | 4.65 | 8.80 | 12.05 | 3.05 | 7.20 | 9.25 |
| 420 | 2.10 | 6.10 | .... | 5.50 | 9.50 | .... |
| 425 | 0.75 | 4.00 | 6.75 | 9.15 | 12.35 | .... |
| 430 | 0.25 | 2.40 | 4.75 | 13.60 | 15.70 | .... |

Est. vol. 4,846;
Tues vol. 2,122 calls; 5,024 puts
Op. int. Tues 30,781 calls; 70,537 puts

## INTEREST RATE

**T-BONDS (CBT)**
$100,000; points and 64ths of 100%

| Strike Price | Calls–Settle Jun | Sep | Dec | Puts–Settle Jun | Sep | Dec |
|---|---|---|---|---|---|---|
| 94 | 5-10 | 4-37 | .... | 0-01 | 0-40 | 1-30 |
| 96 | 3-12 | 3-10 | 3-08 | 0-02 | 1-10 | 2-13 |
| 98 | 1-25 | 1-63 | 2-09 | 0-14 | 1-60 | 3-11 |
| 100 | 0-18 | 1-07 | 1-25 | 1-08 | 3-03 | 4-24 |
| 102 | 0-02 | 0-36 | 0-53 | 2-56 | 4-30 | .... |
| 104 | 0-01 | 0-17 | 0-32 | 4-54 | 6-11 | 7-26 |

Est. vol. 55,000;
Tues vol. 18,469 calls; 16,260 puts
Op. int. Tues 383,979 calls; 241,603 puts

**T-NOTES (CBT)**
$100,000; points and 64ths of 100%

| Strike Price | Calls–Settle Jun | Sep | Dec | Puts–Settle Jun | Sep | Dec |
|---|---|---|---|---|---|---|
| 100 | 2-43 | 2-27 | 2-16 | 0-02 | 0-60 | 1-56 |
| 101 | 1-47 | 1-52 | .... | 0-05 | 1-21 | .... |
| 102 | 0-59 | 1-20 | .... | 0-17 | 1-52 | .... |
| 103 | 0-21 | 0-57 | .... | 0-43 | 2-25 | .... |
| 104 | 0-05 | 0-38 | .... | 1-27 | .... | .... |
| 105 | 0-01 | 0-24 | .... | 2-23 | .... | .... |

Est. vol. 3,600;
Tues vol. 2,088 calls; 2,253 puts
Op. int. Tues 54,496 calls; 50,680 puts

**MUNICIPAL BOND INDEX (CBT)**
$100,000; pts. & 64ths of 100%

| Strike Price | Calls–Settle Jun | Sep | Dec | Puts–Settle Jun | Sep | Dec |
|---|---|---|---|---|---|---|
| 92 | .... | .... | 2-10 | 0-05 | .... | 0-60 |
| 93 | 1-53 | .... | 1-38 | 0-08 | .... | 1-22 |
| 94 | .... | .... | 1-10 | 0-24 | .... | 1-54 |
| 95 | 0-31 | .... | 0-51 | 0-50 | .... | 2-29 |
| 96 | 0-13 | .... | 0-38 | 1-32 | .... | 3-15 |
| 97 | 0-05 | .... | .... | .... | .... | .... |

Est. vol. 25;
Tues vol. 5 calls; 4 puts
Op. int. Tues 5,908 calls; 6,733 puts

**5 YR TREAS NOTES (CBT)**
$100,000; points and 64ths of 100%

| Strike Price | Calls–Settle Jun | Sep | Dec | Puts–Settle Jun | Sep | Dec |
|---|---|---|---|---|---|---|
| 10350 | 1-13 | 1-06 | .... | 0-05 | 1-06 | .... |
| 10400 | 0-50 | 0-53 | .... | 0-10 | .... | .... |
| 10450 | 0-26 | .... | .... | 0-19 | .... | .... |
| 10500 | 0-14 | 0-33 | .... | 0-38 | .... | .... |
| 10550 | 0-06 | 0-25 | .... | .... | .... | .... |
| 10600 | 0-02 | 0-19 | .... | .... | .... | .... |

Est. vol. 2,200;
Tues vol. 352 calls; 551 puts
Op. int. Tues 11,719 calls; 9,781 puts

**EURODOLLAR (IMM)**
$ million; pts. of 100%

| Strike Price | Calls–Settle Jun | Sep | Dec | Puts–Settle Jun | Sep | Dec |
|---|---|---|---|---|---|---|
| 9550 | 0.49 | 0.36 | 0.18 | 0.01 | 0.18 | 0.66 |
| 9575 | 0.26 | 0.22 | 0.12 | 0.03 | 0.29 | 0.85 |
| 9600 | 0.08 | 0.12 | 0.07 | 0.10 | 0.44 | 1.04 |
| 9625 | 0.02 | 0.06 | .... | 0.29 | 0.63 | .... |
| 9650 | .0004 | 0.03 | .... | 0.52 | .... | .... |
| 9675 | .... | .... | .... | .... | .... | .... |

Est. vol. 59,449;
Tues vol. 38,319 calls; 21,497 puts
Op. int. Tues 387,839 calls; 431,556 puts

**LIBOR – 1 Mo. (IMM)**
$3 million; pts. of 100%

| Strike Price | Calls–Settle May | Jun | Jly | Puts–Settle May | Jun | Jly |
|---|---|---|---|---|---|---|
| 9550 | 0.60 | 0.57 | 0.55 | .0004 | .0004 | 0.02 |
| 9575 | 0.36 | 0.33 | 0.32 | 0.01 | 0.01 | 0.04 |
| 9600 | 0.12 | 0.13 | 0.15 | 0.02 | 0.06 | 0.12 |
| 9625 | 0.01 | 0.03 | 0.05 | 0.16 | .... | 0.27 |
| 9650 | .... | .... | .... | .... | .... | .... |
| 9675 | .... | .... | .... | .... | .... | .... |

Est. vol. 20;
Tues vol. 65 calls; 150 puts
Op. int. Tues 3,908 calls; 2,564 puts

**TREASURY BILLS (IMM)**
$1 million; pts. of 100%

| Strike Price | Calls–Settle Jun | Sep | Dec | Puts–Settle Jun | Sep | Dec |
|---|---|---|---|---|---|---|
| 9575 | 0.57 | 0.40 | .... | .0004 | 0.06 | .... |
| 9600 | 0.32 | 0.23 | .... | .0004 | 0.15 | .... |
| 9625 | 0.10 | 0.11 | .... | 0.03 | 0.27 | .... |
| 9650 | .0004 | .... | .... | 0.18 | .... | .... |
| 9675 | .... | .... | .... | .... | .... | .... |
| 9700 | .... | .... | .... | .... | .... | .... |

Est. vol. 102;
Tues vol. 2,648 calls; 2,371 puts

**EURODOLLAR (LIFFE)**
$1 million; pts. of 100%

| Strike Price | Calls–Settle Jun | Sep | Dec | Puts–Settle Jun | Sep | Dec |
|---|---|---|---|---|---|---|
| 9525 | 0.75 | 0.54 | 0.28 | 0.01 | 0.11 | 0.54 |
| 9550 | 0.51 | 0.37 | 0.18 | 0.02 | 0.19 | 0.69 |
| 9575 | 0.27 | 0.23 | 0.11 | 0.03 | 0.30 | 0.87 |
| 9600 | 0.10 | 0.13 | 0.06 | 0.11 | 0.45 | 1.07 |
| 9625 | 0.03 | 0.06 | 0.03 | 0.29 | 0.61 | 1.29 |
| 9650 | 0.02 | 0.02 | 0.01 | 0.52 | 0.84 | 1.52 |

Est. vol. Wed, 350; 50 puts
Tues vol. 2,350 calls; 7,453 puts

**LONG GILT (LIFFE)**
£50,000; 64ths of 100%

| Strike Price | Calls–Settle Jun | Sep | Puts–Settle Jun | Sep |
|---|---|---|---|---|
| 96 | 2-45 | 3-16 | 0-01 | 0-24 |
| 97 | 1-49 | 2-30 | 0-05 | 0-38 |
| 99 | 0-59 | 1-51 | .... | 0-58 |
| 100 | 0-23 | 1-16 | 0-43 | 1-24 |
| 101 | 0-07 | 0-53 | 1-27 | 1-61 |
| 102 | 0-02 | 0-53 | 2-22 | 2-41 |

Est. vol. Wed, 3,204 calls; 4,733 puts
Op. int. Tues. 68,383 calls; 90,828 puts

**FIGURE 19-12**
Quotations for futures options.

SOURCE: Reprinted by permission of *The Wall Street Journal,* (C) Dow Jones & Company, Inc. (May 7, 1992):C14–C16.

# CALL OPTIONS ON FUTURES CONTRACTS

If a call option on a futures contract is exercised, then the writer must deliver the appropriate futures contract to the buyer. For example, consider the buyer of a call option on December corn where the exercise price is 260 (that is, $2.60) per bushel. Since the futures contract is for 5000 bushels, the total exercise price is $13,000 (5000 × $2.60). If the buyer purchased this option at the settle price on May 7, 1992 that is given in Figure 19.12, then the buyer would have paid the writer a premium of 18 (that is, $.18) per bushel or $900 (5000 × $.18) in total.

If the buyer subsequently decides to exercise this option, then the writer of this option must deliver a December corn futures contract to the buyer. Furthermore, this futures contract will be fully marked to market at the time it is delivered. In the example, assume that the option is exercised in August when December corn futures are selling for $3.00 per bushel. What happens in August is that the call writer must provide the call buyer with a December corn futures contract that has a delivery price of $2.60 that has been marked to market. This can be accomplished in two steps. First, the writer must purchase a December corn futures contract and deliver it to the call buyer. Even though the cost of the futures will be $3.00 per bushel (the current market price of December corn futures), this is costless to the call writer. Second, the futures contract that has been delivered must be marked to market, which is done by having the call writer pay the call buyer an amount of cash equal to $.40 ($3.00 − $2.60) per bushel or $2000 (5000 × $.40) in aggregate. Thus, the call writer has lost $1100 ($2000 − $900), whereas the call buyer has made an equivalent amount.

This example has shown what happens when the call is exercised, but it should be noted that most futures options are not exercised. Instead, just as with most options and futures, buyers and writers of futures options typically make reversing trades before the expiration date.

# PUT OPTIONS ON FUTURES CONTRACTS

If a put option on a futures contract is exercised, then the writer must accept delivery of the appropriate futures contract from the buyer. For example, consider the buyer of a put option on December corn where the exercise price is 260, meaning $2.60 per bushel, or $13,000 in total, since the futures contract is for 5000 bushels. If the buyer purchased this put at the settle price on May 7, 1992, that is given in Figure 19.12, then the buyer would have paid the writer a premium of 18½ per bushel, or $925 (5000 × $.185) in total.

If the buyer subsequently decides to exercise this option, then the writer of this option must accept delivery of a December corn futures contract from the buyer. Furthermore, this futures contract must be fully marked to market at the time it is delivered. In the example, assume that the option is exercised in August when December corn futures are selling for $2.20 per bushel. What happens in August is that the put buyer will become the seller of a December corn futures contract where the purchase price is $2.20 per bushel. Even though this is the current market price of December corn futures, this is costless to the put buyer. However, when this futures contract is marked to market, the put writer must pay the put buyer an amount of cash equal to $.40 ($2.60 − $2.20) per bushel or $2000 (5000 $\times$ $ .40 ) in aggregate. Thus, the put writer has lost $1075 ($2000 $-$ $925), whereas the put buyer has made an equivalent amount.

Again, it should be kept in mind that most put options on futures are not exercised. Instead, these option buyers and writers typically enter reversing trades sometime before the expiration date.

## A.3 COMPARISON WITH FUTURES AND OPTIONS

At this point, it is worthwhile thinking about the distinctions between futures and futures options. In doing so, consider an investor who is contemplating *buying* a futures contract. If this contract is purchased, the investor can potentially make or lose a great deal of money. In particular, if the price of the asset rises substantially, then so will the price of the futures, and the investor will have made a sizable profit. In contrast, if the price of the asset drops substantially, then the investor will have lost a sizable amount of money.

In comparison, if the investor had bought a futures call option on the asset, then the investor would also make a sizable profit if the price of the asset rose substantially. Unlike futures, however, if the price of the asset dropped, then the investor need not worry about incurring a sizable loss. Instead, only the premium (the price paid to buy the futures option) would be lost. This does not mean that purchasing a futures call option is better than purchasing a futures contract because the protection on the downside that an investor gets from buying a futures call option is paid for in the form of the premium. This premium would not be present if the investor had bought a futures contract instead.

Consider next an investor who is contemplating *selling* a futures contract. In doing so, the investor can potentially make a great deal of money if the price of the asset declines substantially. However, if the price of the asset rises substantially, then the investor can lose a sizable amount of money.

In comparison, the investor can buy a futures put option on the asset. If this is done, the investor can make a sizable profit if the price of the asset declined substantially. Unlike futures, however, if the price of the asset rose, then the investor need not worry about incurring a sizable loss. Instead, only the premium is lost. Again, this does not mean that purchasing a futures put option is better than selling a futures contract.

## QUESTIONS AND PROBLEMS

1. Distinguish between a speculator and a hedger. Give an example of a short hedger and a long hedger.
2. Rejean LaFlamme has just bought four October 20-tonne barley futures contracts at $91.20 per tonne. The initial margin requirement is 5%. The maintenance margin requirement is 70% of the initial margin requirement.
   a. How many dollars in initial margin must Rejean put up?
   b. If the October price of barley rises to $96.40, how much equity is in Rejean's commodity account?
   c. If the October price of barley falls to $83.40, how much equity is in Rejean's commodity account? Will Rejean receive a margin call?
3. How does a futures contract differ from a forward contract?
4. Do exchange-imposed price limits protect futures traders from losses that would result in the absence of such limits? Explain.

5. A publication used by farmers such as Mike Brown provides diagrams of the typical annual patterns of "cash prices" for a number of seasonal commodities. Should Mike expect that the price of a futures contract will follow the same pattern? Why or why not?

6. In the market for a particular agricultural or natural resource commodity, what kind of market forces might lead to normal backwardation or normal contango?

7. Esther Crabtree believes that the spread between long-term and short-term interest rates is going to narrow in the next few months, but does not know which direction interest rates in general will move. What financial futures position would permit Esther to profit from this forecast if it is correct?

8. Why does hedging a common stock portfolio using stock index futures work best if the portfolio being hedged is very similar to the underlying stock index of the futures contract?

9. Assume that the TSE 35 currently has a value of 200 (in "index" terms). The dividend yield on the underlying stocks in the index is expected to be 4% over the next six months. New issue six-month Treasury bills now sell for a six-month yield of 6%.
   a. What is the theoretical value of a six-month futures contract on the TSE 35?
   b. What potential problems are inherent in this calculation?

10. In December 1989, Debbie Hamner bought a January 1990 gold futures contract on the New York Commodity Exchange for $487.50 per ounce. Simultaneously, Debbie sold an October 1991 contract for $614.80. At the time, yields on Treasury notes with 1.75 years to maturity were 10.50%. Will this transaction be profitable for Debbie? What factors are relevant to making this calculation?

11. In each of the following situations, discuss how Harry Yuen might use stock index futures to protect a well-diversified stock portfolio:
   a. Harry expects to receive a sizable bonus check next month and would like to invest in stocks, believing that current stock market prices are extremely attractive (but realizing they may not remain so for long).
   b. Harry expects the stock market to decline dramatically very soon and realizes that quickly selling a stock portfolio would result in a significant transactions costs.
   c. Harry has a large, unrealized gain and for tax purposes would like to defer the gain until the next tax year, which is several weeks away.

12. (Appendix Question) Distinguish between futures contracts and options on futures contracts.

---

# SUGGESTED READINGS

The Winnipeg Commodity Exchange publishes a variety of informative pamphlets describing the contracts offered and their trading.

C.A. Carter and R.M.A. Lyons, "Hedging Canadian Grains and Oilseeds," (Winnipeg, Man.: The Winnipeg Commodity Exchange, 1991) describes hedging procedures in considerable detail.

Gerald D. Gay, *Interest Rate Futures: Concepts and Issues* (Richmond, Va.: Robert F. Dane Inc., 1982),

Robert W. Kolb, *Understanding Futures Markets* (Glenview, Ill.: Scott, Foresman and Company, 1988) and

Darrell Duffie, *Futures Markets* (Englewood Cliffs, NJ: Prentice Hall, 1989) all provide useful information on the design, trading and valuation of futures contracts.

# Chapter 20

# INVESTMENT COMPANIES

*Investment companies* are a type of financial intermediary. They obtain money from investors and use it to purchase financial assets such as stocks and bonds. In return, the investors receive certain rights regarding the financial assets the company has bought and any earnings that it may make. In the simplest and most common situation, the investment company has only one type of investor — shareholders. These shareholders directly own the investment company and thus indirectly own the financial assets that the company itself owns.

For an individual, there are two advantages to investing in such companies instead of investing directly in the financial assets these companies own. Specifically, the advantages arise from (1) economies of scale and (2) professional management. In describing these benefits, consider an individual with moderate financial resources who wishes to invest in the stock market.

In terms of economies of scale, the individual could buy stocks in odd lots and thus have a diversified portfolio. However, the brokerage commissions on odd-lot transactions are relatively high. Alternatively, the individual could purchase round lots but would only be able to afford a few different securities. Unfortunately, the individual would then be giving up the benefits of owning a well-diversified portfolio, in which declines in some securities would more likely be offset by gains in others. In order to receive the benefits of diversification and substantially reduced brokerage commissions, the individual could invest in the shares of an investment company. That is, economies of scale make it possible for an investment company to provide diversification at a lower cost per dollar of investment than would be incurred by a small individual investor.

In terms of professional management, the individual investing directly in the stock market would have to go through all the details of investing, including such things as making all buying and selling decisions as well as keeping records of all transactions for tax purposes. In doing so, the individual would have to be continually on the lookout for mispriced securities in an attempt to find undervalued ones for purchase, while selling any that were found to be overvalued. Simultaneously, the individual would have to keep track of the overall risk level of the portfolio so that it did not deviate from some desired level. However, by purchasing shares of an investment company, the individual can turn over all of these details to a professional money manager.

Many of these managers hope to identify areas of mispricing in the market, exploit them, and share the resultant abnormal gains with investors by charging them for a portion of the gains. However, it appears that they typically cannot find enough mispriced situations so as to recoup more than the additional costs they have incurred, costs that take the form of increased management fees and transaction costs due to the continual buying and selling of securities. Nevertheless, other potential advantages to be gained from investing in an investment company may still outweigh any disadvantages.

Investment companies differ in many ways, and classification is difficult. Common practice is followed here; the term is restricted to those financial intermediaries that do not obtain money from depositors. Thus, the traditional operations of trust companies and banks, for example, are excluded. However, the process of deregulation is rapidly breaking down previous barriers so that the future may very well bring even more competition for traditional investment companies.

## 20.1 NET ASSET VALUE

An important concept in understanding how investment companies operate is *net asset value* (NAV). Given that an investment company has assets consisting of various marketable securities, it is generally quite easy to determine the market value of all the assets held by the investment company at the end of each business day. For example, an investment company holding various common stocks traded on the Toronto Stock Exchange could easily find out what the closing prices were at the end of the day and then simply multiply these prices by the number of shares they own. After adding up these figures, any liabilities the investment company had outstanding would be subtracted to give the NAV. Dividing the NAV by the number of outstanding shares of the investment company produces the NAVPS for the investment company.

Equivalently, an investment company's NAVPS at the end of day $t$ ($\text{NAVPS}_t$) can be determined by using the following equation:

$$\text{NAVPS}_t = \frac{\text{MVA}_t - \text{LIAB}_t}{\text{NSO}_t} \qquad (20.1)$$

where $\text{MVA}_t$, $\text{LIAB}_t$, and $\text{NSO}_t$ denote the market value of the investment company's assets, the dollar amount of the investment company's liabilities, and the number of shares the investment company has outstanding, respectively, as of the end of day $t$. Thus, an investment company with 4,000,000 shares outstanding whose assets consisted of common stocks with an aggregate market value of $102,000,000 and whose liabilities amounted to $2,000,000 as of November 15, 1988, would report a net asset value on that date of ($102,000,000 - $2,000,000)/4,000,000 = $25 per share.

It should be noted that an investment company's NAVPS changes each and every day, since the values of either $\text{MVA}_t$, $\text{LIAB}_t$, or $\text{NSO}_t$ (or all three) change.

## 20.2 MAJOR TYPES OF INVESTMENT COMPANIES

The *Investment Funds Institute of Canada* classifies *managed investment companies* as follows:

Closed-end investment companies
Open-end investment companies, or investment funds.

Managed investment companies, whether incorporated or unincorporated, have a board of directors that is elected by its shareholders to oversee the operation of the company. The board commonly hires a firm — the "investment manager" — to manage the company's assets for an annual fee that is typically based (at least in part) on the total market value of the assets. These management companies may be independent firms, investment advisers, firms associated with brokerage firms, or insurance companies. Often the management company is the business entity (for example, a subsidiary of a brokerage firm) that started and promoted the investment company. One management company may have contracts to manage a number of investment companies, each of which is a separate entity with its own board of directors.

Annual management fees average about 2% (they range from 0.25% to 2.8%) of the market value of the investment company's total assets, with the percentage decreasing as the assets increase. Some funds provide "incentive compensation," where the better the fund's investment performance, the higher the fee paid to the management company.

In addition to the fee paid by an investment company to its management company, there are administrative and custodial expenses. These services are usually arranged by the investment manager, but the costs are charged to the investment company. For the typical investment company, such annual expenses are roughly 0.50% of the market value of its total assets. The term management fees tends to be used rather loosely; it includes administrative and custodial expenses in some cases and not in others. In order to compare costs on a uniform basis the industry has defined the management expense ratio to be the total costs divided by the average net monthly assets for the year. The total costs include all fees paid by the fund (to the investment company and any third parties) except brokerage fees and taxes.

## ☐ 20.2.1 Closed-End Investment Companies

*Closed-end investment companies* (or closed-end funds) are a dying breed in Canada. These companies issue a specific number of shares at their inception. The number remains unchanged until such time as additional shares are issued. Their shares are traded either on an organized exchange or in the over-the-counter market. Thus, an investor who wants to buy or sell shares of a closed-end fund simply places an order with a broker, just as if he or she wanted to buy or sell shares of BCE.

Most closed-end funds have unlimited lives. Dividends and interest received and any net capital gains realized by a closed-end fund are paid out to its shareholders. However, most funds allow (and encourage) the reinvestment of such payments. The fund keeps the money and sends the investor additional shares based on the net asset value per share at that time. For example, consider a closed-end fund that has just declared a dividend of $1 per share. If its net asset value were $15 per share, a holder of 30 shares would have a choice of receiving either $30 ( $30 \times \$1$ ) or 2 shares ( $\$30 / \$15$ ).

Being a corporation, closed-end funds can issue new shares not only through reinvestment plans but also with public stock offerings. However, this is done infrequently, and the fund's capital structure is closed most of the time.

Although it is seldom done, most closed-end funds can repurchase their own shares in the open market. If a fund's market price falls substantially below net asset value, a repurchase will increase the fund's net asset value per share. For example, if net asset value were $20 per share at a time when the fund's shares could be purchased in the open market (say, on the Toronto Stock Exchange) for $16 per share, the managers of the fund could sell $20 worth of securities from the fund's portfolio, buy back one of the

## CLOSED END FUNDS

| | Net asset value † $ per unit | Market value $ per unit | Discount (–) premium (+) |
|---|---|---|---|
| BGR Precious Metals | 8.16 | 7³/₈ | –10.2% |
| Canada Income Plus | 9.82 | 9 | –8.4% |
| Canada Trust Income Invest. ‡ | 9.25 | 9 | –2.7% |
| Canadian General Investments ‡ | 66.99 | 44 | –34.3% |
| Central Fund of Canada | 4.87 | 4.40 | –9.7% |
| Economic Investment Trust * | 67.53 | 42 | –37.8% |
| Equity Investments | 0.59 | 0.60 | +1.7% |
| Equity Preservation | 0.94 | 1.30 | +38.3% |
| Equity Reserve | 0.73 | 0.71 | –2.7% |
| First Australia Prime Income | 12.23 | 12 | –1.9% |
| First Mercantile Currency | 8.00 | 7⁵/₈ | –4.7% |
| Germany Fund of Canada | 10.56 | 8³/₄ | –17.1% |
| Global Government Plus | 8.89 | 8³/₄ | –2.7% |
| Goldcorp Investments | 5.73 | 3.45 | –39.8% |
| Growth Investment | 23.62 | 22¹/₄ | –5.8% |
| MPG Investment ‡ | 12.67 | 8⁷/₈ | –30.0% |
| Quebec Growth | 6.05 | 4.60 | –24.0% |
| Third Canadian Investments ‡ | 51.29 | 46 | –10.3% |
| United Corporations ‡ | 41.74 | 27⁵/₈ | –33.8% |

Discount (–), premium (+) based on market to NAV. † Funds valued weekly on Nov. 7. ‡ Valuation at end Sept.; end Oct. for CTII. * Valuation quarterly. Market value based on TSE closing or bid prices on Nov. 7; ME for Que. Gth.

**FIGURE 20-1**

Listing of closed-end funds.

*SOURCE:* Reprinted by permission of *The Financial Post,* The Financial Post Company (November 8, 1991)

fund's outstanding shares, and have $4 left over. If the $4 were used to buy securities for the fund, the net asset value per share would increase, with the size of the increase depending on, in addition to the number of shares repurchased and their repurchase price, the number of remaining shares.

Provided that the closed-end funds are listed on an exchange or traded actively in the over-the-counter market their market prices are published daily in the financial press. However, their net asset values are only published weekly, based on closing market prices for securities in their portfolios as of the previous Friday. Figure 20.1 provides an example. Both the net asset value and the market value based on either the closing or bid price at which the fund's shares traded on the day in question are shown. The final column indicates the percentage difference between each fund's share price and its net asset value. If this difference is positive (meaning the share price is greater than the NAVPS), the fund's shares are said to be selling at a premium. Conversely, if this difference is negative (meaning the share price is less than the NAVPS), the fund's shares are said to be selling at a discount. For example, Figure 20.1 indicates that the Germany Fund of Canada was selling at a discount while the Equity Preservation Fund was selling for a premium. The first of these two investment companies, specializing in German equities, is known as a "country fund."

## ☐ 20.2.2 Open-End Investment Companies

An investment company that stands ready at all times to purchase its own shares at or near their net asset value is termed an *open-end investment company* (or investment trust or open-end fund). These include both incorporated companies or unincorporated trusts.[1]

Most of these companies, commonly known as *mutual funds*, also offer new shares to the public for a price at or near their net asset values on demand.

Some open-end companies, known as *no-load funds*, sell their shares at a price equal to net asset value. Others, known as *load funds*, offer shares through brokers or other selling organizations, thereby adding a percentage *load charge* to the net asset value. The percentage charged is usually larger, the smaller the amount invested, and rarely exceeds 9%. For example, a selling organization receiving $1000 to be invested in a fund might retain as much as $90, leaving $910 to be used to purchase the fund's shares at the current net asset value per share. While this is usually described as a load charge of 9%, it is equal to $9.9\% = \$90/\$910$ of the amount ultimately invested. Load charges of this magnitude are levied by many funds for small purchases.[2]

When mutual fund shareholders want to sell their shares, they usually receive an amount equal to the fund's net asset value times the number of shares sold. However, a few funds charge a *redemption fee* (also known as a back-end load, or exit fee, or contingent deferred sales charge), which varies from 1 to 5% but may run as high as 7% of the fund's net asset value.[3] Typically, the funds that charge such a fee will lower the percentage payable if the shareholder has owned the shares over a long period. Thus, investors selling their shares within six months of purchase might have to pay a 5% fee, whereas investors selling their shares after owning them for five or more years might not have to pay any fee; for periods between six months and five years, a sliding-scale fee may be applicable.

Not surprisingly, the performance of non-load funds as a whole does not differ in any notable way from that of load funds. The load charge, which goes to the selling organization, represents the cost of education and persuasion. No load funds do not employ sales people and are generally purchased directly from the financial institution that manages them.

Figure 20.2 shows a portion of the quotations for mutual funds provided in the financial press daily.[4] Following the name is a brief description of the loading fees charged, the eligibility for RRSP investment, the method of distributing (i.e. selling) the fund and the net asset value, based on closing prices for the fund's securities on the day in question. The final column indicates the difference (in dollars) between the day's net asset value per share and that computed at the close of the previous trading day.

Figure 20.3 shows the weekly quotations that appear for a special type of mutual fund known as a money market fund. Such funds invest in short-term, fixed-income securities such as Treasury bills, commercial paper, and bank term deposits. Next to the name of such a fund is shown a brief description of the way the fund is sold, the current annualized yield, and the compounded annual yield known as the effective yield, with the final column showing the change in the yield from the previous day. Not shown, but

---

[1] For practical purposes, except for some tax considerations that will be discussed subsequently, the differences between the two are negligible.

[2] Funds that have a load charge of 3.5% or less are often referred to as *low-load funds*.

[3] Most funds with a load charge apply either a front-end or a back-end fee, however, a few apply both and a very few offer an option of either fee.

[4] Funds are listed under a name in boldface type. This is the name of the common investment management company that is associated with those funds.

# CANADIAN MUTUAL FUNDS

Recent prices of investment funds supplied by Fundata Canada at 5:30 p.m. April 24. Prices reported by funds are the net asset value per share or unit last calculated and are for information purposes only. Confirmation of price should be obtained from the fund. Chg—change from last valuation: D—distributed by fund sponsor; G—redemption charge; I—distributed by independent dealers; L—sales charge; M—minimum purchase of $150,000; N—no sales charge; O—optional front—end or redemption charge; R—eligible for RRSPs; S—stock split; U—U.S. currency; X—ex—dividend; Y—delayed NAVPS; Z—not available for purchase.

## MEMBERS

| Fund | Load | RSP | Dist | Value | Chg |
|---|---|---|---|---|---|
| **ABC FUNDS** | | | | | |
| ymFully-Mgd | N | RD | | 5.60 | -11 |
| ymFund-Value | N | RD | | 5.65 | -08 |
| **ADMAX INV.** | | | | | |
| uAme PerfSUS | O | D | | 4.56 | -03 |
| Ame Perform | O | D | | 5.41 | -03 |
| Canadian Inc | O | RD | | 5.14 | -03 |
| Cdn Perform | O | RD | | 4.81 | -02 |
| Polyvmetric | O | RI | | 4.80 | -02 |
| US Poly | O | I | | 5.17 | -03 |
| uUS Poly $US | O | I | | 4.36 | -03 |
| **AGF GROUP** | | | | | |
| AGF Asian | O | I | | 6.78 | -04 |
| Amer Grth | O | I | | 8.80 | +01 |
| Cdn Bond | O | RI | | 4.72 | +02 |
| Cdn Equ | O | RI | | 8.60 | -01 |
| Cdn Res | O | RI | | 6.91 | -06 |
| Conv Inc | O | RI | | 8.82 | -02 |
| Corp Inv | L | RI | | 11.94 | +02 |
| Crp Inv Stk | L | RI | | 6.29 | +01 |
| Global | O | I | | 9.74 | +02 |
| Grth Equ | O | RI | | 11.38 | — |
| Hincome | O | I | | 9.57 | — |
| Japan | O | I | | 3.88 | +01 |
| Special | O | I | | 7.24 | -05 |
| **ALL-CANADIAN** | | | | | |
| Compound | L | RZ | | 12.94 | -02 |
| Dividend | L | RI | | 9.39 | -02 |
| Natural Res | L | RI | | 2.43 | -01 |
| Revenue Gth | L | RI | | 3.33 | +01 |
| **ALLIED CAPITAL** | | | | | |
| Canadian | N | RD | | 4.89 | -01 |
| Dividend | N | RD | | 3.92 | — |
| Income | N | RD | | 5.66 | +02 |
| Internt'l Cdn | N | D | | 4.95 | +01 |
| uInternt'l US | N | D | | 4.18 | +01 |
| **ALTAMIRA** | | | | | |
| AltaFund | N | RI | | 10.61 | -04 |
| Balanced | N | RD | | 9.90 | -01 |
| Bond | N | RD | | 11.12 | +01 |
| Capital Gwth | N | RD | | 10.03 | -04 |
| yDiversifd | N | D | | 8.98 | +01 |
| Equity | N | RD | | 22.29 | -10 |
| Global Money | N | RI | | 10.51 | +02 |
| Gro + Inc | N | RD | | 6.03 | -01 |
| Income | N | RD | | 6.83 | +02 |
| Resource | N | RD | | 7.37 | -01 |
| Select Amer | N | I | | 12.47 | -06 |
| Special Gro | N | RD | | 10.84 | +03 |
| **ASSOCIATE INV** | | | | | |
| Assor.Inv | G | RD | | 6.90 | -02 |
| **BANK OF MONTREAL** | | | | | |
| F.C.Balanced | N | RD | | 10.15 | -01 |
| F.C.Bond | N | RD | | 10.54 | +03 |
| F.C.Eqty Ind | N | RD | | 9.85 | -06 |
| F.C.Mortgage | N | RD | | 11.95 | +00 |
| **BEUTEL GOODMAN** | | | | | |
| yAM + Int'l | N | I | | 5.61 | -04 |
| yBalanced | N | RI | | 10.48 | -06 |
| yCDN Equity | N | RI | | 9.68 | -10 |
| yIncome | N | RI | | 10.44 | -04 |
| **BNP (CDA) FONDS** | | | | | |
| yActions | N | RD | | 25.08 | — |
| yObligations | N | RD | | 10.17 | +03 |
| **BOLTON TREMBLAY** | | | | | |
| xBond | L | RI | | 5.31 | -03 |
| Cda Cum | L | RI | | 14.01 | -03 |
| xIncome | L | RI | | 9.05 | -03 |
| Intern'l | L | I | | 7.74 | — |
| Ldmk Ame | G | I | | 5.61 | — |
| Ldmk Bal | N | RI | | 4.76 | — |
| xLdmk Bond | G | RI | | 5.29 | -01 |
| Ldmk Can | G | RI | | 5.23 | -01 |
| Ldmk Intl | G | I | | 6.18 | — |
| Ldmk SmCp | L | RI | | 5.08 | +02 |
| Optimi Cdn | L | RI | | 6.72 | — |
| Pld.Rsces | L | RI | | 11.53 | +06 |
| Taurus | L | I | | 5.14 | -01 |
| **BPI CAPITAL** | | | | | |
| Am.Eq.Gwth | O | I | | 10.87 | -02 |
| Cdn.Bond | O | RI | | 10.16 | +03 |
| Cdn.Equity | O | I | | 9.06 | -08 |
| Global Bal. | O | I | | 9.20 | +03 |
| Global Eq. | O | I | | 13.40 | +04 |
| One DecisnFd | O | I | | 10.49 | -02 |
| **BULLOCK GROUP** | | | | | |
| American C$ | O | I | | 17.40 | -07 |
| uAmerican US$ | L | I | | 14.68 | -06 |
| Balanced | O | I | | 9.95 | -01 |
| CIF | O | RI | | 6.09 | -05 |
| Growth | O | RI | | 2.43 | +01 |
| **CALDWELL SECURITIES** | | | | | |
| yAssociate | G | RD | | 5.22 | -07 |
| yInternational | G | D | | 5.29 | -09 |
| **CANADA TRUST** | | | | | |
| yCTIF Equity | N | RD | | 56.97 | +68 |
| yCTIF Income | N | RD | | 9.96 | -03 |
| Ev Balanced | N | RD | | 11.62 | — |
| Ev Bond | N | RD | | 10.86 | +05 |
| Ev Int'l | N | D | | 15.09 | +04 |
| Ev Nor Ame | N | D | | 26.82 | -10 |
| yEv RSP Mtg | N | RD | | 56.83 | -46 |
| Ev Spec Eq | N | RD | | 13.45 | +01 |
| Ev Stock | N | RD | | 10.72 | -05 |
| Ev US Bond | N | D | | 9.77 | +01 |
| Ev US Equity | N | I | | 11.94 | -03 |
| yRSP Equity | N | RD | | 124.82 | -4.52 |
| yRSP Income | N | RD | | 62.28 | -1.29 |
| **CENTRAL GUARANTY** | | | | | |
| yFut Cd Gth | N | RD | | 11.71 | +11 |
| yFut Gov Bd. | N | RD | | 10.22 | -04 |
| yFut Income | N | RD | | 11.05 | +06 |
| yFut Mortgage | N | RD | | 10.57 | +03 |
| yFut Select | N | RD | | 10.73 | +05 |
| **CENTRAL GUARANTY** | | | | | |
| yInv Equity | N | D | | 6.66 | +06 |
| yInv Income | N | D | | 4.74 | -10 |
| **CENTURY** | | | | | |
| yDJ | | I | | 10.68 | +02 |
| **CHOU ASSOC MGT** | | | | | |
| Associates | L | I | | 22.94 | -09 |
| RRSP | L | RI | | 9.93 | -16 |
| **CHURCH STREET** | | | | | |
| Balanced | N | RD | | 10.66 | -09 |
| Equity | N | RD | | 10.02 | -15 |
| Income | N | RD | | 10.07 | -04 |
| **CIBC FUNDS** | | | | | |
| Balanced | N | RD | | 10.74 | +00 |
| CIBC Cap App | N | I | | 11.57 | +10 |
| CIBC Eqy Inc | N | RD | | 9.85 | -04 |
| Cdn Bon | N | RD | | 10.46 | +04 |
| Cdn Equity | N | RD | | 9.55 | -06 |
| Global | N | D | | 11.51 | +06 |
| Hyp Asian | O | D | | 10.81 | +07 |
| Hyp Euro | O | D | | 9.80 | +06 |
| Hyp Fixed | O | RD | | 10.76 | +04 |
| Hyp Mngd | O | RD | | 10.69 | +00 |
| Hyp SMM Cdn | O | D | | 9.98 | -00 |
| uHyp ST MMT | O | D | | 9.83 | +01 |
| Hyp Val Line | L | I | | 11.21 | -06 |
| Mortgage | N | RD | | 11.72 | +11 |
| US Equity | N | D | | 11.18 | +05 |
| **CLEAN ENVIRONMENT** | | | | | |
| Balanced | O | I | | 4.98 | +01 |
| Equity | O | I | | 4.96 | +01 |
| **CONFED GROUP** | | | | | |
| Growth | L | RD | | 6.92 | -05 |
| Mortgage | L | RD | | 5.15 | +01 |
| **COOPERANTS GROUP** | | | | | |
| yuAmer.Eqty. | L | D | | 9.54 | — |
| yBalanced | L | RD | | 9.79 | +01 |
| yCdn.Equ. | L | RD | | 8.76 | -02 |
| yEquity | L | RD | | 10.43 | +03 |
| yReal Estate | L | RD | | 51.48 | -92 |
| **COUNSEL GROUP** | | | | | |
| yReal Estate | G | RD | | 22.38 | +16 |
| **CUNDILL GROUP** | | | | | |
| Security | L | RI | | 10.52 | +10 |
| Value | L | I | | 10.66 | +07 |
| **DYNAMIC GROUP** | | | | | |
| Dyn Am CDN | O | I | | 8.15 | — |
| uDyn Am US | O | I | | 6.87 | -01 |
| Dyn Cdn | O | RI | | 12.90 | -02 |
| Dyn Div | O | RI | | 4.91 | — |
| Dyn Glo Bond | O | RI | | 4.96 | -01 |
| Dyn Green | O | I | | 4.75 | +01 |
| Dyn Income | O | RI | | 5.49 | +02 |
| Dyn Mgd Port | O | RI | | 6.29 | +01 |
| Dyn Partners | O | RI | | 5.36 | — |
| Dyn Prec Met | O | RI | | .95 | -01 |
| Dyn Str Bon | O | I | | 9.80 | +06 |
| Europe 92 | O | I | | 8.68 | +04 |
| **ELLIOTT + PAGE** | | | | | |
| EP Bal | O | RD | | 26.78 | -08 |
| EP Bond | O | RD | | 26.19 | +09 |
| EP Equ | O | RD | | 29.43 | -16 |
| **ETHICAL GWTH** | | | | | |
| yEthical Gwth | O | RD | | 5.92 | -08 |
| **EXTRO GROUP** | | | | | |
| yExtro Korea | O | I | | 10.74 | -01 |
| yExtro Tiger | O | RI | | 9.51 | +01 |
| yInternt'l | L | RI | | 4.71 | +01 |
| **FIDELITY INV.** | | | | | |
| Cap Buildr | O | RI | | 13.26 | +05 |
| yFar East CD | O | I | | 12.19 | +13 |
| yFar East US | O | I | | 10.28 | +11 |
| Gov't Bond | O | RI | | 10.75 | +02 |
| Gr + Inc | O | RI | | 11.52 | -02 |
| Gr America CD | O | I | | 15.54 | -05 |
| uGr America US | O | I | | 13.11 | -04 |
| yIntP'tolio CD | O | I | | 12.09 | +02 |
| yuIntP'tolio US | O | I | | 10.20 | +02 |
| **FINSCO FUNDS** | | | | | |
| JF Bal | L | RI | | 8.96 | — |
| JF Bond | L | RI | | 9.10 | +03 |
| JF Cdn Equ | L | RI | | 10.23 | -03 |
| JFAmEq C$ | L | I | | 13.01 | -03 |
| uJFAmEq US$ | L | I | | 10.97 | -03 |
| **FIRST CITY FUNDS** | | | | | |
| Growth | N | RD | | 5.02 | -03 |
| Income | N | RD | | 5.12 | +02 |
| yRealFund | G | RI | | 5.98 | — |
| **FONDS DESJARDINS** | | | | | |
| yActions | N | RD | | 17.44 | +19 |
| yEnviro | N | RD | | 10.61 | +08 |
| yEquilibre | N | RD | | 10.38 | +05 |
| yHypo | N | RD | | 4.49 | +01 |
| yIntern'tl | N | D | | 19.91 | +42 |
| yOblig | N | RD | | 4.65 | -01 |
| **FONDS FICADRE** | | | | | |
| yActions | G | RD | | 11.26 | -13 |
| yEquilibre | G | RD | | 10.95 | -07 |
| yObligations | G | RD | | 10.82 | -01 |
| **FONDS SNF** | | | | | |
| yActions | G | RD | | 6.24 | -11 |
| yEquilibree | G | RD | | 9.62 | -07 |
| yObligations | G | RD | | 10.11 | +00 |
| **GUARANTY REALTY** | | | | | |
| yProp Fund | O | RI | | 8.57 | — |
| **GBC FUNDS** | | | | | |
| yBond | N | RD | | 10.66 | -06 |
| yCanada | N | RD | | 8.46 | -07 |
| yNor Ame | N | D | | 3.84 | -11 |
| **GLOBAL STRATEGY** | | | | | |
| Americas | O | RI | | 11.22 | -01 |
| Canadian | O | RI | | 9.20 | -01 |
| Europe | O | I | | 9.65 | +06 |
| Far East | O | I | | 11.26 | +03 |
| Global Fund | O | I | | 15.71 | +04 |
| Income Fund | O | RI | | 10.54 | +03 |
| Real Estate | O | I | | 7.63 | +05 |
| World Bond | O | I | | 9.87 | +02 |
| World Money | O | I | | 10.17 | +02 |
| **GUARDIAN GROUP** | | | | | |
| American Eq. | O | I | | 24.96 | -05 |
| Balanced | O | RI | | 14.58 | +03 |
| CIPF86 | G | RZ | | 9.40 | — |
| Canada Bond | O | RI | | 9.80 | — |
| Canadian Eq. | O | RI | | 4.63 | — |
| Diversified | O | RI | | 5.09 | — |
| Enterprise | O | RI | | 9.43 | +03 |
| yGlobal Eq. | O | I | | 3.91 | +02 |
| Growth Equ | O | I | | 5.89 | -02 |
| yttl. Income | O | RI | | 8.15 | -01 |
| North Amer | N | Z | | 6.25 | -01 |
| uPac.Rim | N | Z | | 13.01 | +13 |
| Ptd.Div | O | I | | 8.47 | -02 |
| Vantage Bon | G | RZ | | 5.15 | — |
| yVantage Int'l | G | Z | | 4.03 | +02 |
| Vantage U.S. | G | Z | | 4.62 | -01 |
| **HONGKONG BANK CAN.** | | | | | |
| yBalanced | N | RD | | 10.14 | -12 |
| yEqu Index | N | RD | | 9.94 | -09 |
| **INDUSTRIAL GR.** | | | | | |
| uIndust Am $US | O | I | | 7.64 | +00 |
| Indust AmSCdn | O | I | | 9.05 | +00 |
| Indust Bal | O | RI | | 5.04 | -00 |
| Indust Bond | O | RI | | 10.77 | +03 |
| Indust Div | O | RI | | 7.46 | +01 |
| Indust Eq | O | RI | | 12.15 | +05 |
| Indust Future | O | RI | | 4.85 | -01 |
| Indust Global | O | I | | 5.50 | -03 |
| Indust Gwth | O | RI | | 12.47 | -01 |
| Indust Hor | O | RI | | 5.20 | -03 |
| Indust Inc | O | RI | | 8.84 | +02 |
| Indust Pens | O | RI | | 3.89 | +01 |
| Indust SCP | O | RI | | 10.00 | — |
| Indust USEG | O | I | | 4.37 | -04 |
| Mack Eq | O | RI | | 1.74 | -00 |
| Mack Income | O | RI | | 1.19 | +00 |
| **INVESNAT** | | | | | |
| Act-Eqty | N | RD | | 5.19 | -03 |
| Equ-Bal | N | RD | | 5.19 | -00 |
| xHypo-Mort | N | RD | | 10.28 | -05 |
| Oblig-Bond | N | RD | | 5.30 | — |
| **INVESTORS GROUP** | | | | | |
| yBond | G | RD | | 4.45 | -00 |
| uCdn Equity | L | RD | | 6.57 | +01 |
| yDividend | L | D | | 9.96 | +03 |
| yEuropean Fund | L | D | | 5.53 | +02 |
| yGlobal | L | D | | 6.37 | +05 |
| yGro P'folio | L | D | | 5.55 | +00 |
| yGroPlus P'fol | L | D | | 5.35 | — |
| yInc P'folio | L | RD | | 5.25 | +02 |
| yIncPlus P'fol | L | RD | | 5.29 | +03 |
| yJapan | L | D | | 10.87 | +11 |
| yMtge | G | RD | | 5.05 | +00 |
| yMutual | L | D | | 8.02 | +00 |
| yN.A. Growth | L | D | | 10.43 | +01 |
| yPacificFund | L | D | | 6.47 | +03 |
| yReal Prop | L | RD | | 5.16 | +01 |
| yRetGro P'fol | L | RD | | 5.28 | +02 |
| yRetPlus P'fol | L | RD | | 5.31 | +02 |
| yRetiremnt | L | RD | | 9.34 | -00 |
| ySpecial | L | D | | 12.51 | -02 |
| ySumma | L | RD | | 5.07 | +01 |
| yU.S. Growth | L | D | | 14.55 | +10 |
| **J. HEWARD GROUP** | | | | | |
| JH Amer Cdn | O | I | | 9.57 | -05 |
| uJH Amer Us | O | I | | 8.07 | -04 |
| JH Balanced | O | RI | | 11.57 | -01 |
| JH Bond | O | RI | | 10.15 | +03 |
| JH FdLtd | O | RI | | 8.60 | -02 |
| **LAURENTIAN** | | | | | |
| Endur Bal | G | RD | | 5.55 | — |
| Endur Bond | G | RD | | 5.42 | — |
| Endur Cdn | G | RD | | 4.90 | -02 |
| Endur Global | G | D | | 5.14 | — |
| Viking Cdn | L | RD | | 5.73 | -03 |
| Viking Com | L | D | | 6.46 | — |
| Viking Div | L | RD | | 7.55 | -03 |
| Viking Gth | L | D | | 7.20 | -03 |
| Viking Inc | L | RD | | 4.18 | +01 |
| Viking Int'l | L | D | | 8.01 | — |
| **M. K. WONG GROUP** | | | | | |
| yLotus Fund | N | RD | | 11.26 | -09 |
| **MD MGMT** | | | | | |
| yMD Bond | N | RD | | 13.41 | +04 |
| yMD Equity | N | RD | | 7.93 | +07 |
| yMD Grth | N | D | | 4.89 | +07 |
| yMD Money | N | RD | | 52.32 | +07 |
| yMDR.A | N | RD | | 16.81 | +09 |
| yMDR.B | N | D | | 16.00 | +08 |
| yPer G | N | Z | | 2.15 | -01 |
| yPer G II | N | Z | | 2.02 | -01 |
| yPer G.III | N | Z | | 1.89 | -01 |
| yPer G.IV | N | Z | | 2.14 | -01 |
| yPer G.V | N | Z | | 1.71 | +01 |
| yPer G.VI | N | Z | | 1.58 | +01 |
| yPer G.VII | N | Z | | 2.52 | +01 |
| yPer G.VIII | N | Z | | 2.11 | — |
| **METFIN** | | | | | |
| yReal Estate | G | RI | | 10.19 | — |
| **METROPOLITAN GR.** | | | | | |
| vBal Growth | L | RD | | 5.96 | +01 |
| yBond | L | RD | | 2.79 | — |
| yCanadian | L | RD | | 5.42 | — |
| yCollective | L | D | | 19.61 | +11 |
| yProtection | L | RD | | 10.02 | -00 |
| ySpeculators | L | D | | 8.28 | +03 |
| yVenture | L | D | | 10.86 | -06 |
| **MOF GROUP** | | | | | |
| yMult. Opp. Fd. | L | RD | | 2.29 | -03 |
| ySpec. Opp. Fd | L | RD | | 1.14 | +03 |
| **MONTREAL TRUST GR.** | | | | | |
| yBalanced | N | RD | | 10.54 | -03 |
| yDividend | N | D | | 6.96 | -03 |
| yEquity | N | D | | 23.81 | -18 |
| yIncome | N | D | | 8.67 | -03 |
| yInternat'l | N | D | | 27.77 | -25 |
| yMtge | N | D | | 10.24 | -04 |
| yTot Return | N | D | | 10.44 | -04 |
| **MUTUAL GROUP** | | | | | |
| Amerilund | L | D | | 11.41 | -08 |
| Bond Fund | L | RD | | 10.74 | +03 |
| CIF | L | RD | | 8.47 | -08 |
| Sect Pac | O | I | | 6.49 | +02 |
| Sect Res | O | I | | 3.64 | +04 |
| **WALTAINE FUNDS** | | | | | |
| Balanced | N | RD | | 9.99 | -03 |
| Div. Growth | N | RD | | 7.76 | -05 |
| Income | N | RD | | 9.16 | -03 |

## NON-MEMBERS

| Fund | Load | RSP | Dist | Value | Chg |
|---|---|---|---|---|---|
| **AIC GROUP** | | | | | |
| Advntage | O | RD | | 14.06 | -04 |
| Value | O | D | | 11.34 | -09 |
| **CMP FUNDS** | | | | | |
| ADF VI | N | RZ | | 1.05 | — |
| ADF VII | L | RZ | | 1.37 | — |
| ADF VIII | N | RZ | | 2.34 | — |
| ADF IX | N | RZ | | 2.01 | — |
| ADF X | N | RZ | | .80 | — |
| ADF XI | N | RZ | | .35 | — |
| ADF XII | N | RZ | | .75 | — |
| ADF XIV | N | RZ | | .26 | +01 |
| ADF XV | N | RZ | | 1.12 | -01 |
| Chevron II | N | RZ | | 2.49 | -01 |
| **CALPA** | | | | | |
| Gyro Bond | N | RD | | 10.81 | +04 |
| Gyro Equity | N | RD | | 9.82 | -04 |
| **C-ANAES** | | | | | |
| yC-Anaes | N | RD | | 9.11 | +09 |
| **CAN NAT RES** | | | | | |
| yCan Nat Res | L | RI | | 3.70 | -03 |
| **CAPITAL CITY** | | | | | |
| vi-Plan Bal | N | RD | | 10.15 | -01 |
| **CAPSTONE GROUP** | | | | | |
| Internt'l C$ | N | D | | 5.98 | -00 |
| uInternt'l US$ | N | D | | 5.64 | +00 |
| Investment | N | RD | | 5.95 | +01 |
| **CDN BAR MGMT** | | | | | |
| yCiB Global | N | D | | 10.76 | +13 |
| **CO-OP TRUST GR.** | | | | | |
| yGrowth | N | RD | | 14.21 | +15 |
| yIncome | N | RD | | 9.45 | -15 |
| **CONCORDE** | | | | | |
| yCroissance | O | RD | | 4.85 | +02 |
| yHypotheques | L | RI | | 10.29 | +00 |
| yRevenu | O | RD | | 10.00 | +02 |
| **CSA MGMT LTD.** | | | | | |
| Goldfund | L | I | | 3.76 | -04 |
| Goldtrust | L | RI | | 4.08 | -01 |
| **DOMINION EQUITY** | | | | | |
| yDomequity | N | RD | | 4.99 | — |
| **DUNEDIN** | | | | | |
| yIntern'l I | L | I | | 91.70 | +92 |
| **F.I. EXAR** | | | | | |
| yImmobilier | L | RI | | 12.13 | +47 |
| **FONDS EUROPEEN** | | | | | |
| F Euro PL&P | G | RI | | 12.19 | +05 |
| **FRIEDBERG COM. MGMT** | | | | | |
| yDouble Gold | L | I | | 1.268 | +01 |
| yProc.Metals | L | Z | | 7.40 | -06 |
| **INTEGRA CAP** | | | | | |
| Balanced | L | RI | | 10.78 | -01 |
| **MAR EQUITY** | | | | | |
| yMar Equity | N | D | | 6.31 | -03 |
| **MARLBORO** | | | | | |
| yMarlboro | L | RI | | 8.07 | +13 |
| **MIDDLEFIELD GR.** | | | | | |
| yTRF Mutual | L | RZ | | 9.58 | -03 |
| **MTC GROUP** | | | | | |
| yGrowth | L | RZ | | 7.87 | +05 |
| **NORAM** | | | | | |
| yCanadian | L | RI | | 7.60 | -09 |
| yInternat'l | L | I | | 9.49 | -19 |
| **NORTHERN GROUP** | | | | | |
| E.uro | G | I | | 7.22 | +00 |
| **NW GROUP** | | | | | |
| yCanadian | L | RD | | 9.79 | -01 |
| yEquity | L | Z | | 16.88 | -13 |
| **O.I.Q. FERIQUE** | | | | | |
| yActions | N | RD | | 23.15 | +41 |
| yEquilibre | N | RD | | 32.31 | +34 |
| yMM | N | RD | | 31.03 | +03 |
| yObligations | N | RD | | 30.50 | +04 |
| **ORBIT GROUP** | | | | | |
| yWorld | L | I | | 5.26 | +01 |
| **PRENOR TRUST** | | | | | |
| yTeach.sp'rd | N | RZ | | 109.78 | -3.13 |
| **PRET ET REVENU** | | | | | |
| yAmerican | N | D | | 38.37 | +27 |
| yCanadienne | N | RD | | 9.45 | +08 |
| yFonds H | N | RD | | 5.27 | -08 |
| yOblig | N | RD | | 10.23 | -02 |
| yRetra't | N | RD | | 28.34 | +10 |

**FIGURE 20-2**

Listing of mutual funds.

*SOURCE:* Reprinted by permission of *The Globe and Mail: Report on Business*, Thomson Newspapers Company Limited (April 25, 1992).

an important factor in deciding in which money market fund to invest, is the degree of safety (that is, default risk) associated with the assets held by each fund.

A number of institutions similar to investment companies exist. The next section describes some of the more important types of securities they offer.

## 20.3 SIMILAR TYPES OF INVESTMENTS

### ☐ 20.3.1 Fixed and Deferred Annuities

A *fixed annuity* is a contract in which a life insurance company promises to pay the investor a fixed dollar amount on a regular (generally monthly) basis.[5] The size and number of these payments will depend on how much money the investor gives the insurance company and the size of an up-front fee (if any) that is charged. Also important are the investor's age and the annuity option that the investor chooses.

One option the investor may choose is a life annuity, where fixed dollar payments are provided regularly until the investor's death. Another option is a joint and last survivor annuity, where fixed dollar payments of a lesser amount continue on a regular basis until both the investor and spouse have died. A third option is a period certain annuity (or fixed period annuity), where fixed dollar payments are made on a regular basis for a prespecified number of years (perhaps 5, 10, 15, or 20); if the investor dies before then, subsequent payments are made to the investor's beneficiary. A fourth option, known as a life annuity with a period certain, is a combination of the first and third options. With this option, the investor receives regular fixed dollar payments until death. However, if death should occur before some prespecified number of years have elapsed, then payments will continue until that number of years has elapsed.

The previous discussion described an immediate annuity, where the investor purchases a fixed annuity with a single payment. However, the investor also has the option of making a single payment and acquiring a *deferred annuity* that starts making periodic payments on a specified future date based on the principal and accumulated investment returns. A variant on this is a *guaranteed investment annuity* that gives the investor the option of receiving either periodic payments or a lump sum at maturity.

### ☐ 20.3.2 Pooled Funds

Trust and insurance companies invest money for individuals and organizations. Trust companies manage personal trust funds; both trust and insurance companies manage individual retirement funds. Any such fund can be invested on an individual basis, with specific securities selected and held in a separate account. This is often done for large accounts. To capture economies of scale, small accounts are often pooled, allowing joint participation in one or more large pools of securities.

The vehicle utilized in this process is the *pooled fund*. In form (but not in law), it is similar to an open-end mutual fund. The securities in the fund are valued periodically, and total value divided by current number of units determines net asset value per unit. On any valuation date, money from an account may be used to purchase units at this

---

[5] Although not offered in Canada *variable annuities* are available in the US. With this kind of annuity, the regular payments are not of a prespecified size but instead are dependent directly on the performance of a portfolio managed by the insurance company.

**MEMBERS**

| Fund | Dist | Cur | Eff | Chg |
|---|---|---|---|---|
| **AGF GROUP** | | | | |
| MMF | I | 6.68 | 6.90 | +.02 |
| uUS MMF | I | 3.31 | 3.36 | -.09 |
| **ALLIED CAPITAL** | | | | |
| MMF | D | 6.02 | 6.20 | — |
| **BANK OF MONTREAL** | | | | |
| F.C.MMF | D | 6.26 | 6.46 | +.01 |
| **BEUTEL GOODMAN** | | | | |
| yMMF | I | 8.60 | 8.97 | — |
| **BNP (CDA) FONDS** | | | | |
| yuMM SUS | D | 3.18 | 3.23 | -.05 |
| yMM Cdn | D | 5.42 | 5.57 | -.79 |
| **BOLTON TREMBLAY** | | | | |
| Ldmk S/T Int. | I | 6.17 | 6.36 | +.01 |
| Mny Fd | I | 6.67 | 6.89 | +.01 |
| **BPI CAPITAL** | | | | |
| MMF | I | 6.00 | 6.18 | — |
| **CANADA TRUST** | | | | |
| Ev MMF | D | 6.48 | 6.69 | — |
| **CENTRAL GUARANTY** | | | | |
| Fut MMF | D | 7.52 | 7.80 | +.02 |
| **CHURCH STREET** | | | | |
| MMF | D | 6.66 | 6.88 | -.16 |
| **CIBC FUNDS** | | | | |
| CdnTBill | D | 5.87 | 6.04 | — |
| MMF | D | 6.12 | 6.31 | — |
| mPrem MMF | D | 6.91 | 7.15 | — |
| mPremTBill | D | 6.63 | 6.85 | -.01 |
| uUS MMF | D | 3.22 | 3.27 | — |
| **CLEAN ENVIRONMENT** | | | | |
| MMF | I | 7.13 | 7.39 | — |
| **DYNAMIC GROUP** | | | | |
| Dyn MMF | I | 7.27 | 7.54 | +.02 |
| **ELLIOTT + PAGE** | | | | |
| EP Mon | D | 6.92 | 7.16 | -.01 |
| **FIDELITY INV.** | | | | |
| S Asset | I | 6.61 | 6.83 | -.03 |
| **FINSCO FUNDS** | | | | |
| MMF | I | 6.40 | 6.61 | — |
| T-Bill | I | 5.85 | 6.02 | — |
| uUS MMF | I | 3.05 | 3.10 | — |
| **FIRST CITY FUNDS** | | | | |
| Govt M | D | 6.42 | 6.62 | +.00 |
| **FONDS DESJARDINS** | | | | |
| yMM | D | 6.66 | 6.88 | -.61 |
| **FONDS FICADRE** | | | | |
| yMM | D | 6.50 | 6.71 | -.38 |
| **FONDS SNF** | | | | |
| yMM | D | 6.60 | 6.81 | -.34 |
| **GBC FUNDS** | | | | |
| yMMF | D | 6.89 | 7.13 | +.35 |
| **GLOBAL STRATEGY** | | | | |
| T-Bill | I | 6.76 | 6.99 | +.01 |
| uUS $ | I | 3.32 | 3.37 | +.02 |
| **GUARDIAN GROUP** | | | | |
| S T Mny | I | 6.49 | 6.70 | -.03 |
| uUS MMF | I | 3.35 | 3.41 | — |
| **HONGKONG BANK CAN.** | | | | |
| yMMF | D | 5.53 | 5.68 | -.20 |
| **INDUSTRIAL GR.** | | | | |
| CS Mgt | I | 6.94 | 7.18 | +.10 |
| Sh. Term | I | 5.25 | 5.39 | — |
| **INVESNAT** | | | | |
| MMF | D | 6.36 | 6.56 | -.03 |
| T-Bill | D | 6.41 | 6.62 | -.10 |
| uUS MMF | D | 3.07 | 3.12 | -.01 |
| **INVESTORS GROUP** | | | | |
| yMMF | D | 5.98 | 6.16 | -.01 |
| **LAURENTIAN** | | | | |
| V MMF | D | 6.09 | 6.28 | |
| **M. K. WONG GROUP** | | | | |
| yMKW | | | | |
| Income | D | 6.63 | 6.85 | -.03 |
| **MONTREAL TRUST GR.** | | | | |
| yMMF | D | 6.50 | 6.71 | -.10 |
| **MUTUAL GROUP** | | | | |
| MMF | D | 6.14 | 6.33 | — |
| **NATIONAL TRUST** | | | | |
| yMMF | D | 6.07 | 6.25 | -.13 |
| **ONT. TEACHERS GR.** | | | | |
| yFixVal | D | 6.86 | 7.10 | -.09 |
| **PHN GROUP** | | | | |
| MMF | D | 6.92 | 7.16 | -.03 |
| uUS MMF | D | 3.70 | 3.77 | -.03 |
| **PRUDENTIAL GROUP** | | | | |
| MMF | D | 7.39 | 7.66 | |
| **PURSUIT GR** | | | | |
| yMMF | I | 7.46 | 7.74 | -.21 |
| **ROYAL TRUST GR.** | | | | |
| ySCDN MMF | D | 6.10 | 6.29 | -.15 |
| yuSUS MMF | D | 2.76 | 2.80 | -.99 |
| yCdn T-Bill | D | 4.64 | 4.75 | -.89 |
| **ROYFUND GROUP** | | | | |
| Cdn.T-Bill | D | 6.67 | 6.90 | -.00 |
| MMF | D | 6.68 | 6.90 | -.00 |
| uMMF US | D | 3.08 | 3.13 | +.00 |
| **SAGIT GROUP** | | | | |
| TC MMF | I | 6.40 | 6.61 | |
| **SCEPTRE FUNDS** | | | | |
| MMF | D | 6.63 | 6.85 | +.04 |
| **SCOTIA FUNDS** | | | | |
| GoCT-B | D | 6.25 | 6.45 | -.00 |
| MMF | D | 6.39 | 6.60 | -.00 |
| **SENTINEL** | | | | |
| MMF | I | 6.96 | 7.20 | +.03 |
| **SPECTRUM** | | | | |
| Cash | I | 6.34 | 6.54 | -.03 |
| Saving | I | 6.45 | 6.66 | -.04 |
| **STRATA FUNDS** | | | | |
| MMF | D | 6.04 | 6.22 | -.04 |
| **TD GREEN LINE** | | | | |
| Cdn MMF | D | 7.26 | 7.53 | -.03 |
| Cdn T-Bill | D | 6.54 | 6.75 | -.00 |
| uUS MMF | D | 3.10 | 3.15 | -.01 |
| **TALVEST FUNDS** | | | | |
| MMF | I | 6.18 | 6.37 | -.03 |
| **TEMPLETON GR** | | | | |
| yT-Bill | I | 6.49 | 6.70 | -.02 |
| **TRIMARK GROUP** | | | | |
| Interest | I | 6.71 | 6.94 | — |
| **20-20 GROUP FIN** | | | | |
| MMF | I | 6.83 | 7.06 | -.00 |
| **UNITED GROUP** | | | | |
| MMF Cdn | I | 7.16 | 7.42 | +.01 |
| uMMF US | I | 1.40 | 1.41 | +.02 |
| **UNIVERSAL GROUP** | | | | |
| MMF | I | 6.79 | 7.02 | +.01 |
| **WALTAINE FUNDS** | | | | |
| Instant MMF | D | 6.74 | 6.96 | |

**NON-MEMBERS**

| Fund | Dist | Cur | Eff | Chg |
|---|---|---|---|---|
| **CAPSTONE GROUP** | | | | |
| CS Mgt | D | 6.52 | 6.74 | +.13 |
| **CO-OP TRUST GR.** | | | | |
| yInt Fund | D | | .00 | |
| **CONCORDE** | | | | |
| yMM | | 5.13 | 5.26 | +.08 |
| **PRET ET REVENU** | | | | |
| yMM | D | 6.41 | 6.62 | |

**FIGURE 20-3**

Listing of money market mutual funds.

*SOURCE:* Reprinted by permission of *The Globe and Mail: Report on Business,* Thomson Newspapers Company Limited (April 25, 1992).

value. Alternatively, units purchased at an earlier date may be redeemed at the current net asset value.

A trust or insurance company may offer several pooled funds. One fund may hold only short-term money market instruments, whereas another holds long-term bonds and yet another holds common stocks. A pooled fund investing in mortgages may also be offered, as may one investing in real property.[6] When a menu of this sort is available, money from a given trust or retirement account can be invested in two or more pooled funds.

## ☐ 20.3.3 Real Estate Investment Trusts

*Real estate investment trusts* (REITs) are available in the US, but not in Canada. These are a useful vehicle for the individual investor to use to invest in real estate. Although not classified as investment companies for legal purposes, REITs are similar to closed-end funds in that they serve as a conduit for earnings on certain types of investments, passing them on to their shareholders and avoiding corporate taxation.

REITs must invest primarily in real estate or loans secured by real estate. They can obtain funds by issuing shares, bonds, and even warrants. They can also borrow from banks, issue mortgages on some or all of their property, and issue commercial paper. The shares of many REITs are listed on major exchanges, and thus price and volume quotations on them are given regularly in the financial press.

Like managed investment companies, REITs hire a management firm for a fee — typically about 1% of the value of assets per year. Most trusts are affiliated with banks, life insurance companies, or mortgage firms, which create them and then serve as their investment managers.

There are two major types of REITs. *Mortgage trusts* invest primarily in mortgages as well as construction and development loans. The latter, which constitute the bulk of the assets of many trusts, are loans made to the builder or developer of a project, with the property serving as collateral. The loans, generally fairly short term, are made on the premise that the property will be finished on time and sold for an amount sufficient to allow the developer to pay off the loan on schedule. *Equity trusts* invest directly in real estate; in effect, they serve as landlords. The property may be financed in part by issuing mortgages. A few firms, termed mixed or hybrid trusts, are neither predominantly mortgage nor equity trusts, but combinations of the two types.

Most REITs are highly leveraged. A typical trust might have debt amounting to 70% of its total assets. Consequently, any decline in the value of the property held by such a trust will generally cause a greater percentage decline in the market value of its common stock. Furthermore, adverse changes in the relationship between the interest paid on a trust's short-term debt and that earned on the trust's assets will also result in declines in the market value of the trust's common stock.

In the recession of 1973 to 1974, there were a large number of defaults on construction and development loans and on some long-term mortgages. Many REITs

---

[6] Pooled funds are referred to as commingled funds in the US. Due to the illiquidity of the assets, the sponsor of real property commingled funds may reserve the right to limit the redemption of units, either temporarily or until sale of the underlying property. For an analysis of the performance of such funds, see Mike Miles and Arthur Esty, "How Well Do Commingled Real Estate Funds Perform?" *Journal of Portfolio Management* 8, no. 2 (Winter 1982):62–68.

were left with partially finished buildings. Moreover, the short-term interest rates that REITs had to pay on much of their debt were higher than the long-term interest rates that they were receiving on the mortgages they owned. From October 25, 1973, to August 19, 1974, the average stock prices of industrial firms fell by 27%, whereas the average equity and mortgage REIT fell more than 50% and 70%, respectively.[7] Many trusts went bankrupt, including some associated with extremely well-known financial institutions.

The experience of the early 1970s undoubtedly diminished the enthusiasm of those who invested heavily in REITs (especially those who failed to appreciate the fact that leverage increases risk as well as expected return).[8] Nevertheless, REITs are a desirable investment for many individuals due to their unique investment policies and typically high leverage. However, only a portion of an individual's portfolio should usually consist of such securities.[9]

## 20.4    TAXATION OF INVESTMENT FUNDS

Investment funds can be either incorporated or unincorporated. The former are regulated by either the federal or provincial *Corporations Act*, depending on the jurisdiction in which it is chartered. The latter are subject to the appropriate provincial *Securities Act* and national policies agreed to by all provinces. They are taxed differently.

### ☐ 20.4.1   Incorporated Investment Funds

Incorporated funds are taxed as Canadian corporations at a 25% tax rate if they meet certain conditions. In order to qualify for this rate, 85% of their gross revenues must be derived from Canadian sources; interest may only account for 25% of their gross income; *and* at least 85% of taxable income must be distributed to shareholders as dividends. Failure to meet these three conditions results in tax being assessed at a regular corporate tax rate of about 45%. Dividends received by unit holders are treated as bona fide dividends from Canadian corporations and, therefore, eligible for the dividend tax credit even though the fund's income may have been derived from interest income or dividends from foreign corporations. Furthermore, dividends received by the fund from tax-paying Canadian corporations are not subject to tax.

A fund that meets the necessary conditions and is largely invested in equities should not face a significant tax bill.

---

[7] "Real Estate Investment Trusts: A Background Analysis and Recent Industry Developments, 1961–1974," Economic Staff Paper 75, no. 1, Office of Economic Research, US Securities and Exchange Commission (1975).

[8] REITs were offered in Canada in the early 1970s but did not survive the debacle described above. There are now a few mutual funds specializing in real estate investment.

[9] For empirical evidence, see William L. Burns and Donald R. Epley, "The Performance of Portfolios of REITS+Stocks," *Journal of Portfolio Management* 8, no. 3 (Spring 1982):37–42.

## □ 20.4.2 Unincorporated Investment Funds

These funds are not subject to tax. The fund's income, net of expenses, is flowed through to the individual unit holder and taxed in his or her hands. Thus, unit holders have to pay taxes on their proportionate share of the interest income, dividends, and realized capital gains received by the fund. Dividends from taxable Canadian corporations qualify for the dividend tax credit and capital gains are taxed at 75% of the regular rate (assuming that the investor's lifetime capital gains tax exemption has been exhausted). The fund's expenses are also flowed through to the investor and may be allocated to income in the most advantageous way. In general, expenses will first be allocated to foreign income, followed by interest income, then either dividends or capital gains depending on the investor's situation.

The total tax payable on income derived from an incorporated fund is very similar to that from an unincorporated fund. Incorporation is perhaps slightly advantageous in that it allows the fund a small measure of flexibility because it can retain for reinvestment up to 15% of its income.

## 20.5    REGULATION AND INVESTMENT POLICIES

Investment funds are subject to provincial regulation under the appropriate *Securities Act* augmented by a number of national policies that have been agreed to by all provinces, but particularly National Policy No. 39, Mutual Funds.

Mutual funds can only be sold with a prospectus that describes (among other items) the fund's investment policies, discloses the fees and expenses, and particularly any incentive fees payable to the investment managers. Management expense ratios and financial statements for five prior years must also be included.

The regulations can influence a mutual fund's investment policy. For example, a mutual fund that wishes to become a qualified investment for registered retirement savings plans must limit the proportion of its funds that it invests in foreign securities. It is important, therefore, to understand the constraints imposed by legislation.

## □ 20.5.1 Regulation of Mutual Funds

National Policy No. 39 imposes certain restrictions on both the investments that a mutual fund may undertake and the practices that it follows. Table 20.1 gives the list of investment restrictions imposed by this policy.

TABLE 20.1
Investment Restrictions under National Policy No. 39.

---

SECTION 2.04 - INVESTMENT RESTRICTIONS
    A mutual fund shall not without the prior approval of the securities authorities:
(1) purchase the securities of any issuer (other than securities issued or guaranteed as to principal and interest by the Government of Canada or an agency thereof or by the Government of any Province of Canada or an agency thereof or by the Government of the United States of America or an agency thereof) if, as a result thereof:

(a) more than 10% of the net assets of the mutual fund (taken at market value at the time of such purchase) would be invested in the securities of such issuer; or

(b) the mutual fund would hold more than 10% of any class or series of a class of securities of such issuer, provided that for the purpose of making this determination, all debt obligations of an issuer maturing in less than one year shall be regarded as a single series of a class of securities;

(2) purchase real estate;

(3) purchase mortgages other than permitted mortgages;

(4) purchase permitted mortgages if following such purchase more than 10% of the total assets of the mutual fund (taken at market value at the time of such purchase) would consist of permitted mortgages;

(5) purchase restricted securities if following such purchase more than 10% of the total assets of the mutual fund (taken at market value at the time of purchase) would consist of illiquid investments;

(6) write any option other than a covered clearing corporation call option;

(7) purchase clearing corporation options (other than to close out covered clearing corporation call options previously written) or warrants or rights if, after giving effect to such purchase, more than 10% of the net assets of the mutual fund (taken at market value at the time of such purchase) would consist of such options, warrants or rights, provided that nothing herein contained will prevent:

(a) the acquisition of securities that have attached thereto warrants or rights, or

(b) the acquisition of securities that are offered in units consisting in part of warrants or rights, or

(c) the acquisition of warrants or rights that are issued to the mutual fund as a holder of any security;

(8) purchase securities for the purpose of exercising control or management of the issuer of such securities;

(9) purchase gold or gold certificates if following such purchase more than 10% of the total assets of the mutual fund (taken at market value at the time of such purchase) would consist of gold and gold certificates, provided that any purchase of gold certificates shall be restricted to gold certificates issued by an issuer approved by the Canadian securities authorities;

(10) purchase or sell commodities or commodity futures contracts or commodity futures options, provided that the restriction herein contained on the purchase or sale of commodities will not restrict the mutual fund from holding cash or cash deposits or from purchasing gold or gold certificates to the extent that such purchase if not otherwise restricted by this Section 2.04;

(11) invest in securities of any other mutual fund, provided that nothing herein contained will prevent a mutual fund from investing in securities of any other mutual fund where:

(a) adequate provisions are made to address any conflicts which result in the mutual funds by reason of such investment and such provisions are described in the prospectus of the mutual fund; and

(b) the arrangement between or in respect of the mutual funds is such so as to avoid the duplication of management fees and sales charges and such arrangement is described in the prospectus of the mutual fund; and

(c) either such other mutual fund is qualified for sale pursuant to a prospectus which has been filed and accepted in the Provinces or Territories of Canada where the securities of the mutual fund are qualified for sale pursuant to a prospectus which has been filed and accepted in such Provinces or Territories of Canada; or

(d) the only way that the mutual fund may invest in a foreign country is through a mutual fund established with the approval of the Government of such foreign country and there is disclosure in the prospectus of the mutual fund of the risk factors which may be associated with the investment in foreign countries such as the imposition of foreign investment and exchange control laws and the fact that financial and other reporting and auditing standards and practices and disclosure may be less extensive than comparable requirements in Canada and the United States.

*SOURCE:* Investment Funds Institute of Canada, *The Canadian Investment Funds Course* (Toronto, 1990):C-6–C-7.

Section 2.04(3) and (4) do not apply to mutual funds that specialize in mortgage investment as their primary aim. Section 2.04(1) clearly aims at insuring that the mutual fund will be adequately diversified. Investments that involve a conflict of interest (for example, the purchase of newly issued securities when the investment managers and the underwriters belong to the same firm) are prohibited. The US has similar rules governing the investment policies of mutual funds, if perhaps not quite so detailed.

Table 20.2 lists the investment practices that must be cleared with the regulatory authorities before being implemented.

**TABLE 20.2**
Restricted Investment Practices under National Policy No. 39.

SECTION 2.05 - INVESTMENT PRACTICES
   A mutual fund shall not without the prior approval of the securities authorities:
(1) borrow money or mortgage or pledge any of its assets except as a temporary measure for the purpose of accommodating requests for the redemption of securities issued by the mutual fund while effecting an orderly liquidation of portfolio securities, provided that after giving effect to such borrowing the outstanding amount of all such borrowings does not exceed 5% of the net assets of the mutual fund taken at market value at the time of such borrowing;
(2) invest more than 10% of its net assets (taken at market value at the time of investment) in illiquid investments;
(3) purchase securities on margin;
(4) sell securities short;
(5) purchase any security which may by its terms require the mutual fund to make a contribution in addition to the payment of the purchase price, provided that this restriction shall not apply so as to prevent the purchase or sale of clearing corporation options or the purchase of warrants or rights otherwise permitted to be purchased or sold or the purchase of securities which are paid for on an instalment basis where the total purchase price and the amount of all such instalments is fixed at the time the first instalment is paid;
(6) engage in the business of underwriting securities or marketing to the public securities of any other issuer;
(7) lend money, provided that this restriction shall not apply so as to prevent the purchase of debt obligations;
(8) lend portfolio securities;
(9) guarantee the securities or obligations of any other person or corporation;
(10) purchase securities other than through normal market facilities unless the purchase price approximates the prevailing market price or is negotiated on an arm's length basis;

(11) contract with the manager or the portfolio adviser or the trustee of the mutual fund or with any director or officer of the mutual fund or of the manager or of the portfolio adviser or of the trustee of the mutual fund or with any of their respective associates or affiliates or with any entity having fewer than 100 participants of record of which any director or officer of the mutual fund or of the manager or of the portfolio adviser or of the trustee of the mutual fund may be a director, officer or participant as principals in making purchases or sales of portfolio securities.

---

SOURCE: Investment Funds Institute of Canada, *The Canadian Investment Funds Course* (Toronto, 1990):C-8.

An illiquid investment in Section 2.05(2) is defined as one that cannot be readily disposed of in its customary marketplace or where regular quotations are not regularly published. Examples of illiquid investments are limited partnership interests not traded on an exchange and securities of private companies. The use of currency forward and futures contracts is permitted providing that these are used to hedge the portfolio against adverse foreign currency fluctuations.

# ☐ 20.5.2  Investment Policies

Different investment companies follow different investment policies. Some companies are designed as substitutes for their shareholders' entire portfolio; others expect their shareholders to own other securities. Some restrict their domain or selection methods severely; others give their managers wide latitude. Many engage in highly active management, with substantial portfolio changes designed to exploit perceived superior investment predictions. However, others are more passive, concentrating instead on tailoring a portfolio to serve the interests of a particular clientele.

The Investment Funds Institute of Canada identifies five generic types of funds that are distinguished by broad differences in their investment policies. These are:

Fixed Income Funds (Bond Funds)
Balanced Funds
Common Stock or Growth Funds
Specialty Funds
Fixed Trusts[10]

Most funds fall into one of the first three categories, however, funds in the fourth category have become significant. Specialty funds include mortgage funds, money market funds, dividend funds, option income funds, real estate funds, and global funds.

Categorization of a specific fund can be difficult, but broad classes can be identified. As mentioned earlier, money market funds hold short-term (typically less than one year) fixed-income instruments such as bank certificates of deposit, commercial paper, and Treasury bills. These open-end funds make it possible for small investors to move in and out of the short-term market. The fund manager will charge an annual fee for this

---

[10] All the capital of a fixed trust is invested in specific securities on a long-term basis. As new capital is introduced it is invested in the same securities in the same proportions. This policy minimizes transaction and management costs but reduces flexibility. Fixed trusts have been declining in number as a larger variety of funds have been introduced.

service, usually between 0.25% and 1% of the average value of total assets. There are usually no load charges, and investors may add money to, or remove money from, their accounts at almost any time.

Bond funds invest in fixed-income securities. Some go farther, specifying that particular types will be emphasized. There are corporate bond funds, government bond funds (Canadian and/or US), global bond funds, and so on. A few funds concentrate on holding preferred shares or both bonds and preferred shares in their portfolios. These funds aim to provide the investor with price stability and income.

Many funds consider themselves managers for the bulk of the investment assets of their clients. Those that hold both equity and fixed-income securities particularly fit this description and are referred to as balanced funds. These funds seek to "combine capital growth (gains) with income and price stability."[11] Some of these funds hold relatively constant mixes of bonds, preferred shares, convertible bonds, and equities; others alter the proportions periodically in attempts to "time the market." Option-income funds are a type of balanced fund that invests primarily in high-dividend-paying common stocks, while controlling risk by writing call options on these stocks. (Call options are discussed in Chapter 18.)

The largest group of investment funds are common stock or growth funds, of which a large variety exist. A diversified common stock fund invests most of its assets in common stocks, although some short-term money market instruments are often held to accommodate irregular cash flows or to engage in market timing. The majority of common stock funds have as their objective either growth; or combined long-term growth and income.[12] Two factors appear to be involved in these objectives: the relative importance of dividend income versus capital gains and the overall level of risk to be taken. Since high-dividend portfolios are generally less risky than those with low dividends, relatively few major conflicts arise.

Some specialized investment companies concentrate on the securities of firms in a particular *industry* or *sector*. For example, there are resource funds, real estate funds, small capitalization stock funds, and gold funds. Others provide a convenient means for holding the securities of firms in a particular *country* or *region*, such as the Extro Korea or Dynamic Europe 1992 funds. There are also investment companies that invest even more widely internationally, purchasing stocks from a variety of different countries. International funds are those investing in non-Canadian securities, while global funds invest in both Canadian and non-Canadian securities.

An index fund attempts to provide results similar or identical to those computed for a specified market index. For example, the *Green Line Canadian Equity Fund*, a no-load open-end investment fund, provides a vehicle for small investors who wish to obtain results similar to those of TSE 300-stock index.

---

[11] The Investment Funds Institute of Canada, *The Canadian Investment Funds Course*, Toronto, 1991.

[12] The statement of a fund's objectives can be obtained from its prospectus that must be available to all prospective buyers. Sometimes picturesque terminology, such as "maximum capital gain" or "aggressive growth," is used to describe the objectives making the official statement of investment objectives less than lucid.

# MUTUAL FUND ACCOUNTS

## ☐ 20.6.1 Accumulation Plans

Although an investor can purchase shares in a fund and receive all distributions in cash, this is only one of many possible arrangements. Mutual funds offer plans of several types to satisfy investors' desires for different patterns of contributions and withdrawals over time. Accumulation plans are designed for those who do not want to receive any income or capital gains distributions over some period of time. The simplest procedure involves automatic reinvestment of these distributions, where the shareholder elects to receive additional shares in the fund instead of cash. As with other plans, this often involves fractional shares, but since most accounts are maintained via computerized records, this poses no problem.

Voluntary accumulation plans allow an investor to add to an account as desired, subject only to some minimum amount that must be invested each time. Alternatively, a fixed dollar amount may be invested at periodic intervals — in some cases via automatic bank transfers.

Contractual accumulation plans call for a fixed amount to be contributed at regular intervals (usually monthly) over a relatively long period (often five or more years). Sales charges may or may not be lower than those applicable to a voluntary accumulation plan. The investor is not legally bound to make all the payments, but since a large proportion of early contributions typically goes toward sales charges, commitment to a contractual plan should not be considered if cancelation is at all likely.

National Policy No. 39 places limits on the load charges for contractual plans. Specifically, no more than 50% of the first year's contribution may be allocated to sales charges (that is, at least half must be invested in fund shares). Moreover, if a 50% "front-end" load charge is assessed in the first year, then the sales charges in subsequent years must be such that the total sales charges over the life of the plan do not exceed 12% of the total contributions. A few funds offer insurance with their contractual accumulation plans. This insurance provides the remaining contributions if the investor dies or is disabled before all the contracted payments have been made. The premium for such insurance is, in effect, added to the sales charge.

## ☐ 20.6.2 Registered Retirement Savings Plans

Accumulation of untaxed funds for retirement may be accomplished via a Registered Retirement Savings Plan (RRSP). These were discussed in some detail in Chapter 10. Mutual funds that hold more than 10% of their assets in foreign securities are not eligible for inclusion in RRSP accounts. RRSP accounts are trusteed and maintained by a financial institution such as a bank or trust company. The simplest procedure is to invest the funds in either demand or term deposits or in eligible mutual funds managed by the institution. An alternative is to establish a *self-directed* RRSP that allows the contributor to invest in a wider variety of eligible securities and mutual funds. Institutions generally charge a modest annual fee (typically $100) for providing custodial and book-keeping services for self-directed plans.

It is increasingly common to find several investment companies operating as a "family of funds." An investor may purchase shares in more than one of the funds under common management and also may switch money from one fund to another. (Sales charges for switching between funds in the same company are typically lower than those applicable to switching between different companies and in some cases transfers between a family of funds managed by the same company may be made without charge.) A single account is usually maintained, with all contributions, withdrawals, and tax information included in one statement. The investor then has the opportunity to make timing decisions (for example, switching money from one fund to another when the latter is believed to be underpriced).

Many mutual funds offer voluntary withdrawal plans. The investor instructs the fund to pay out periodically (for example, monthly) either a fixed amount or a specified percentage of the account's value, thereby decreasing the number of shares that the investor owns.

---

## 20.7    MUTUAL FUND PERFORMANCE

Mutual funds need to compute and publicize their net asset values daily. Since their income and capital gain distributions are also publicized, they are ideal candidates for studies of the performance of professionally managed portfolios. Thus, it is hardly surprising that mutual funds have frequently been the subject of extensive study in the US. Ironically, despite the importance of mutual funds in RRSP investments, only a limited number of Canadian studies (to be discussed in a later section) have been undertaken. In all these studies, the rate of return on a mutual fund for period $t$ is calculated by adding the change in net asset value to the amount of income and capital gains distributions made during the period, denoted $I_t$ and $G_t$, respectively, and dividing this total by the net asset value at the beginning of the period:

$$r_t = \frac{(NAV_t - NAV_{t-1}) + I_t + G_t}{NAV_{t-1}} \tag{20.2}$$

For example, a mutual fund that had a net asset value of $10 at the beginning of month $t$ and made income and capital gain distributions of, respectively, $.05 and $.04 per share during the month, and then ended the month with a net asset value of $10.03 would have a monthly return of

$$r_t = \frac{(\$10.03 - \$10.00) + \$.05 + \$.04}{\$10.00}$$

$$= 1.20\%.$$

It should be noted that returns calculated in this manner can be used to evaluate the performance of the portfolio manager of a mutual fund, since it indicates the results of the manager's investment decisions. However, it does not necessarily indicate the return earned by the shareholders in the fund, since there may have been a load charge involved. In the example, perhaps the investor paid $10.50 at the beginning of the month for one share of this fund, with $.50 being a front-end load. If this were the case, the investor's return for this month could be calculated using equation (20.2), where $NAV_{t-1}$ would be $10.50, not $10.00:

$$r_t = \frac{(\$10.03 - \$10.50) + \$.05 + \$.04}{\$10.50}$$

$$= -3.62\%.$$

Thus, the return for the investor who bought one share at the beginning of the month and paid a $.50 per share load charge at that time would be $-3.62\%$. However, the portfolio manager was only given $10.00 per share to invest, since the load charge was given to those people that were responsible for getting the investor to buy the share. Accordingly, the portfolio manager should be evaluated on the basis of the return provided on the $10.00, which in this example was 1.20%.

Recently, data on professionally managed pension funds and bank commingled funds have become available. The performance of the managers of such funds appears to be similar to that of mutual fund managers: They do reasonably well tailoring portfolios to meet clients' objectives, but few seem to be able to consistently "beat the market." Although the following sections deal only with US mutual funds, many of the results apply to other investment companies, both in the United States and in other countries.[13]

## □ 20.7.1 Risk Control

One of the functions that a mutual fund can perform for its investors is the maintenance of a particular risk posture. Formal statements of objectives provide some idea of a fund's intended posture, but often the wording is vague. Nevertheless, there appears to be a general relationship between portfolio risk and stated objectives.

Figure 20.4 summarizes information on the standard deviations of monthly excess returns over a ten-year period for funds with similar objectives, using classifications assigned by Wiesenberger Investment Companies Service's annual *Investment Companies* at the beginning of the period. In particular, the monthly returns for each one of 123 mutual funds were calculated using equation (20.2). Then, using these 120 monthly returns, the standard deviation was calculated for each one of the funds. Each bar in the figure plots the range of values of the standard deviations for funds having the same objective, with the average standard deviation being shown by a square near the middle of the bar. It can be seen that generally, the lower the amount of promised risk, the lower the amount of actual risk (a similar looking figure resulted when beta was used). However, the overlapping of some of the bars indicates that some

---

[13] For evidence on funds outside the United States see, for example, Jess H. Chua and Richard S. Woodward, "Gains from Market Timing," Monograph Series in Finance and Economics 1986-2, Salomon Brothers Center for the Study of Financial Institutions, Graduate School of Business Administration, New York University; Andre L. Farber, "Performance of Internationally Diversified Mutual Funds," in *International Capital Markets*, eds. Edwin J. Elton and Martin J. Gruber (Amsterdam: North-Holland Publishing Company, 1975):298–309; Michael A. Firth, "The Investment Performance of Unit Trusts in the Period 1965–75," *Journal of Money, Credit and Banking* 9, no. 4 (November 1977):597–604; James R. F. Guy, "The Performance of the British Investment Trust Industry," *Journal of Finance* 33, no. 2 (May 1978):443–55, and "An Examination of the Effects of International Diversification from the British Viewpoint on Both Hypothetical and Real Portfolios," *Journal of Finance* 33, no. 5 (December 1978):1425–38; John G. McDonald, "French Mutual Fund Performance: Evaluation of Internationally Diversified Portfolios," *Journal of Finance* 28, no. 5 (December 1973):1161–80; Juan A. Palacios, "The Stock Market in Spain: Tests of Efficiency and Capital Market Theory," in *International Capital Markets*, eds. Edwin J. Elton and Martin J. Gruber (Amsterdam: North-Holland Publishing Company, 1975):114–49; and R. S. Woodward, "The Performance of U.K. Investment Trusts as Internationally Diversified Portfolios Over the Period 1968 to 1977," *Journal of Banking and Finance* 7, no. 3 (September 1983):417–26.

**FIGURE 20-4**

Risk versus fund objectives: 123 mutual funds, 1960–1969.

*SOURCE:* John G. McDonald, "Objectives and Performance of Mutual Funds, 1960-1969," *Journal of Financial and Quantitative Analysis* 9, no. 3 (June 1974): 316.

funds with conservative objectives took on more risk than others with less conservative objectives.

It is quite possible that past risk exposure may be a better guide to future risk exposure than the rather general statements found in a fund's prospectus. Figure 20.5 shows that this is often the case. Each point plots the beta for a fund in two different periods (based on daily returns). Even though the points do not plot neatly along a 45° line from the origin that represents equal betas in both periods, there is a clear relationship between "past beta" and "future beta." This suggests that the typical mutual fund keeps it at roughly the same value over time.

## □ 20.7.2 Diversification

An important task for any investment manager is the provision of an appropriate degree of portfolio diversification. The correct amount depends on the proportion of client's funds managed and on the likelihood that superior abnormal returns can be obtained by sacrificing diversification. Since most mutual funds are intended to be a major component of a shareholder's portfolio, it is reasonable to expect them to be substantially diversified.

Figure 20.6 shows that many are. Quarterly excess returns over a five-year period were computed for 100 funds and compared with corresponding values for Standard & Poor's 500-stock index. For each fund a value of $R^2$, the coefficient of determination, was computed. This indicates the proportion of the variation in a fund's excess returns that can be attributed to variations in excess returns on the index. As the figure shows, approximately 90% of the quarter-by-quarter variation in a typical fund's excess return was associated with swings in the value of the S&P 500 during this period, with values ranging from 66% to 98%.

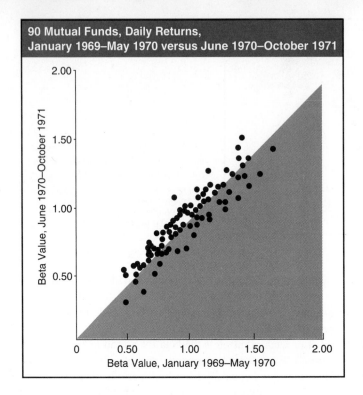

**FIGURE 20-5**

Past versus future beta values: 90 mutual funds, January 1969-May 1970 versus June 1970-October 1971.

*SOURCE:* Gerald A. Pogue and Walter Conway, "On the Stability of Mutual Fund Beta Values" (unpublished working paper, MIT Sloan School of Management, June 1972).

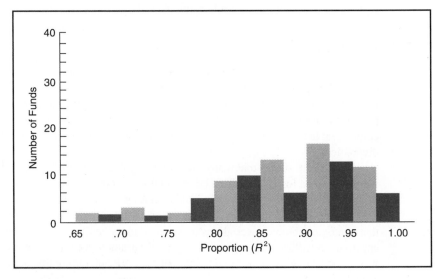

**FIGURE 20-6**

Proportion of variation in quarterly returns attributable to market fluctuations: 100 mutual funds, 1970–1974.

*SOURCE:* Merrill Lynch, Pierce, Fenner & Smith, Inc., *Investment Performance Analysis, Comparative Survey, 1970–1974.*

# □ 20.7.3 Average Return

One way to evaluate the general performance of mutual funds is to compare their average return with that of a suitable market index of comparable securities. This is done every quarter by the *Financial Times* in their *Funds Survey*; Figure 20.7 is an example. Similar data also appear monthly in *The Globe and Mail: Report on Business*. Funds are grouped according to the type of securities they predominantly invest in and to their eligibility for RRSP investment. As well as reporting one month, three month and one year changes in Net Asset Values these tables provide three, five and ten year compound rates of return, the variability of the one month rate of return and a variability ranking against other funds in the same table. For comparison purposes similar data are also provided for a 91-Day (Total Return) T-Bill index, the CPI, the ScotiaMcLeod Universe Bond Index and both the S&P 500 and TSE 300 stock indices.

Many US studies have compared the performance of investment companies that invest primarily in common stocks with the performance of a *benchmark portfolio* that consisted of a combination of (1) a market index, such as Standard & Poor's 500-stock index, and (2) a risk-free asset, such as Treasury bills.[14] Each particular combination was chosen so that the benchmark portfolio had a risk level that was equal to that of the investment company. Thus, an investment company that had a beta of 0.80 would be compared with a benchmark portfolio that had 80% invested in the market index and 20% invested in the risk-free asset.[15]

One way of determining whether or not a mutual fund has beaten the market is to subtract the average return on the benchmark portfolio from the average return of the mutual fund. This amount, when risk is measured by beta, is the fund's ex post alpha. Figure 20.8(a) shows the distribution of ex post alpha values for 70 mutual funds, based on monthly returns beginning in 1955 and going through 1964. The average value was .09% per year, suggesting that the typical fund provided approximately the same return as a market-based passive fund with a constant beta equal to the fund's average beta. Of the 70 funds, 40 had positive ex post alphas and 30 had negative ex post alphas.

Different time periods give slightly different results. Figure 20.8(b) shows the distribution of ex post alphas based on monthly returns for 125 funds beginning in 1960 and going through 1969. The average alpha was .05% per month, or about .60% per year. During this period, the typical fund outperformed a passive fund of similar risk by slightly more than .50% per year, and slightly more than half (53%) of the funds had positive ex post alphas.

Figure 20.8(c) provides a third example. It shows returns for 100 funds based on quarterly returns beginning in 1970 and going through 1974. The average ex post alpha

---

[14] Another useful benchmark portfolio is the relevant Lipper mutual fund index published weekly in *Barron's*. Performance evaluation for common stock portfolios is discussed in detail in Chapter 23. For a more in-depth summary, see Chapter 13 of Gordon J. Alexander and Jack Clark Francis, *Portfolio Analysis* (Englewood Cliffs, N. J.: Prentice Hall, 1986).

[15] Alternatively, the benchmark portfolio may be based on the investment company's standard deviation relative to that of a market index, such as the S&P 500. For example, if the investment company's standard deviation has been 60% of the index's standard deviation, then the mix should consist of 60% invested in the market index and 40% invested in the risk-free asset. The results from evaluating mutual fund performance when using beta as the measure of risk seems to be very similar to the results when standard deviation is used. See, for example, Hany A. Shawky, "An Update on Mutual Funds: Better Grades," *Journal of Portfolio Management* 8, no. 2 (Winter 1982):29–34.

**FIGURE 20-7**
Mutual fund performance.

*SOURCE:* Reprinted by permission of *Southam Information and Technology Group,* appearing in *The Financial Times* (April 20, 1992).

was −.50% per quarter, or approximately −2.00% per year, and only 20 of the funds had positive alphas.

# Equity Funds — RRSP-Eligible

| Southam variability ranking | Max. sales fee % | Codes | Total assets $ mil. | % fgn | Dividend $ | Net asset value $ | Mutual Fund | 1 mo. | 3 mo. | 1 yr. | 3 yr. | 5 yr. | 10 yr. |
|---|---|---|---|---|---|---|---|---|---|---|---|---|---|
| N/A | | R | 469 | 5 | | 3.85 | 20/20 Cdn Asset Allocation | -3.0 | -1.3 | 7.4 | | | |
| N/A | | R | 40 | 3 | | 12.68 | 20/20 Cdn Growth Fund | -4.4 | -1.2 | 4.9 | | | |
| N/A | | R | 34 | 4 | | 11.51 | 20/20 RSP Growth Fund | -4.5 | -1.5 | 5.0 | | | |
| 14 | 1.95 | NLP | 9 | 3 | 0.047 | 5.59 | ABC Fully Managed Fund | -1.2 | 1.7 | 5.4 | 11.5 | | |
| 50 | 3.35 | NLP | 3 | 6 | | 5.65 | ABC Fundamental Value Fund | -1.4 | 4.8 | 8.6 | 13.9 | | |
| 65 | 4.10 | 9.00 | 384 | 6 | | 8.76 | AGF Canadian Equity Fund | -2.7 | 1.4 | 1.9 | -1.4 | -1.7 | 11.3 |
| 96 | 5.07 | 9.00 | 27 | 3 | | 7.08 | AGF Cdn Resources Fund | -4.0 | -4.8 | -14.1 | -2.2 | -4.6 | 3.1 |
| 33 | 2.50 | 9.00 | 17 | 10 | | 8.86 | AGF Convertible Income Fund | -1.4 | 5.3 | 18.8 | 4.4 | | |
| 95 | 5.04 | 9.00 | 96 | | | 11.60 | AGF Growth Equity Fund | -1.6 | 10.2 | 16.7 | 6.6 | -1.0 | 10.9 |
| 99 | 5.83 | 9.00 | 24 | 8 | | 14.72 | AIC Advantage Fund | -3.2 | 9.7 | 26.8 | 13.3 | 5.8 | |
| N/A | | R | 7 | | | 4.87 | Admax Canadian Performance | -3.7 | -1.7 | 2.2 | | | |
| 35 | 2.57 | 8.00 | 12 | | | 12.98 | All-Canadian Compound Fund | -1.6 | -1.1 | 1.6 | 2.7 | 0.6 | 8.5 |
| 35 | 2.59 | 8.00 | 13 | | | 9.42 | All-Canadian Dividend Fund | -1.7 | -1.5 | 1.5 | 2.6 | 0.6 | 8.2 |
| 97 | 5.19 | NL | ! | 17 | | 5.07 | Allied Canadian Fund | -7.0 | 10.0 | 15.0 | 7.5 | -3.0 | |
| N/A | | | 64 | 3 | | 10.66 | AltaFund | -1.9 | 5.6 | | | | |
| 53 | 3.59 | NL | 25 | | | 9.88 | Altamira Balanced Fund | -2.5 | 0.9 | 2.2 | 0.7 | -2.3 | |
| 57 | 3.87 | NLP | 11 | | 0.010 | 9.97 | Altamira Capital Growth Fund | -2.2 | 6.0 | 16.1 | 10.9 | 4.9 | 11.3 |
| 54 | 3.65 | NLP | 290 | | | 22.11 | Altamira Equity Fund | -0.3 | 16.3 | 40.9 | 26.2 | | |
| 13 | 1.95 | NLP | 57 | 9 | 0.070 | 5.99 | Altamira Growth & Income Fund | -0.7 | 2.4 | 15.3 | 11.7 | 10.7 | |
| N/A | | | 15 | | | 7.37 | Altamira Resource | 4.5 | 23.7 | 40.9 | | | |
| 82 | 4.59 | NL | 31 | 3 | | 11.13 | Altamira Special Growth Fund | 2.1 | 19.2 | 35.9 | 17.7 | 6.6 | |
| 48 | 3.22 | 1.00 R | 8 | | 0.090 | 6.94 | Associate Investors | -3.7 | -3.6 | 1.9 | 3.2 | 4.2 | 13.4 |
| 56 | 3.80 | R | 2 | | | 9.42 | BPI Cdn Equity Fund | -4.5 | -1.4 | -1.8 | -1.5 | | |
| 40 | 2.87 | R | 17 | 12 | | 10.61 | BPI One Decision Fund | -3.8 | -3.5 | -3.7 | 5.6 | 2.6 | |
| 39 | 2.82 | | 5 | 10 | | 12.04 | Batirente-Section Action | -3.9 | -2.3 | -4.2 | -0.7 | | |
| 8 | 1.69 | | 17 | 3 | | 14.01 | Batirente-Section Diversifiee | -2.6 | -2.1 | 7.4 | 8.3 | | |
| N/A | | | 44 | 9 | 0.076 | 10.51 | Beutel Goodman Balanced | -2.3 | -3.8 | 5.6 | | | |
| N/A | | | 8 | | 0.044 | 9.76 | Beutel Goodman Cdn Equity | -3.3 | -4.1 | -4.5 | | | |
| 78 | 4.53 | NL | 2 | 18 | | 16.22 | Bissett Canadian Equity | -2.9 | -0.6 | 5.3 | 6.7 | 3.2 | |
| N/A | | | ! | 12 | | 10.07 | Bissett Retirement | -2.1 | -0.8 | | | | |
| 67 | 4.13 | 9.00 | 58 | 15 | | 14.53 | Bolton Tremblay Cda Cum Fund | -3.9 | 0.4 | 1.0 | 1.5 | 0.6 | 8.7 |
| 50 | 3.28 | 9.00 | 5 | | | 5.17 | Bolton Tremblay Discovery | -1.7 | 4.2 | 14.2 | 4.6 | | |
| 22 | 2.11 | R | 17 | 6 | 0.100 | 4.80 | Bolton Tremblay LDMK Bal | -1.2 | 0.0 | 7.3 | 7.6 | | |
| N/A | | R | 62 | 16 | | 5.40 | Bolton Tremblay LDMK Cdn | -3.9 | 2.1 | 7.4 | | | |
| 65 | 4.10 | | 5 | 13 | | 7.01 | Bolton Tremblay Optimal Cdn | -3.7 | 3.9 | 3.4 | 3.1 | 1.8 | |
| 98 | 5.72 | 9.00 | 17 | 3 | | 11.81 | Bolton Tremblay Planned Res | -4.8 | 3.5 | 11.9 | 4.2 | 0.9 | 7.6 |
| 8 | 1.69 | 9.00 P | 2 | 8 | | 10.00 | Bullock Balanced Fund | -2.7 | -2.3 | 3.7 | 4.3 | | |
| 83 | 4.63 | 9.00 | 17 | 17 | | 2.47 | Bullock Growth Fund | -2.8 | 4.7 | 10.0 | 3.3 | 0.5 | 7.4 |
| 23 | 2.13 | X | 15 | | | 34.63 | CDA RSP Balanced | -2.4 | -1.9 | 8.1 | 8.5 | 6.3 | 12.1 |
| 62 | 4.01 | X | 40 | 14 | | 17.46 | CDA RSP Common Stock | -3.7 | -2.8 | 3.0 | 4.5 | 3.5 | 13.7 |
| 12 | 1.92 | NL | 164 | 6 | 0.056 | 10.85 | CIBC Bal Income & Growth Fund | -3.1 | -2.8 | 4.6 | 7.6 | | |
| 35 | 2.56 | NL | 62 | | | 9.70 | CIBC Canadian Equity Fund | -4.2 | -3.9 | -5.5 | 1.8 | | |
| 26 | 2.21 | | 21 | 5 | | 24.15 | Caisse de Sec du Spectacle | -2.3 | -1.1 | 9.4 | 9.5 | 6.0 | 11.7 |
| N/A | | R | 7 | 16 | | 5.14 | Caldwell Securities Associate | -5.2 | -3.1 | 3.0 | | | |
| 5 | 1.40 | R | 13 | | | 6.89 | Cambridge Balanced Fund | 0.3 | 2.4 | 13.5 | 9.1 | 7.6 | 12.8 |
| 47 | 3.20 | R | 45 | 3 | | 7.73 | Cambridge Growth Fund | 1.0 | 5.0 | 12.2 | 8.4 | 7.2 | 16.3 |
| 97 | 5.39 | R | 2 | 6 | | 1.80 | Cambridge Resource Fund | -0.6 | 12.5 | -10.7 | -10.5 | -6.5 | 5.0 |
| 98 | 5.57 | R | 3 | 2 | | 7.07 | Cambridge Special Equity | -2.9 | 9.8 | -5.6 | -7.2 | | |
| 72 | 4.36 | 9.00 P | 59 | 12 | | 6.23 | Canadian Investment Fund | -4.9 | -4.0 | -3.0 | 1.3 | 0.1 | 9.6 |
| 1 | 0.76 | R | 2 | | | 10.32 | Canadian Protected Fund | -0.2 | 0.0 | 4.3 | 6.3 | 6.6 | |
| 43 | 3.02 | NL | 6 | 16 | 0.040 | 5.99 | Capstone Investment Trust | -2.4 | -1.3 | 0.0 | 7.6 | 2.7 | 10.2 |
| 20 | 2.05 | | 6 | 9 | 0.119 | 6.56 | Cassels Blaikie Canadian | -1.8 | -1.6 | 8.4 | 9.2 | 6.7 | |
| 80 | 4.55 | 7.00 R | 34 | 10 | | 195.79 | Cda Life Bal Eqty Income E-2 | -2.7 | 1.2 | 7.9 | 3.1 | 3.4 | 13.6 |
| 71 | 4.28 | PR | 236 | 11 | | 88.60 | Cda Life Cdn & Intl Equity S-9 | -2.5 | 1.6 | 7.4 | 2.1 | 3.3 | 12.7 |
| 31 | 2.43 | R | 386 | 11 | | 22.56 | Cda Life Managed Fund S-35 | -1.6 | 0.4 | 9.3 | 6.5 | 5.7 | |
| 86 | 4.68 | NL | 27 | | 0.117 | 56.85 | Cda Trust Inv Fund Equity | -3.6 | -0.1 | -2.2 | 3.2 | 0.4 | 9.9 |
| 88 | 4.79 | | 304 | | | 124.82 | Cda Trust RRSP Equity | -3.5 | -1.3 | -1.0 | 3.5 | 0.8 | 9.8 |

**FIGURE 20-7**
(Continued)

These results suggest that the average mutual fund has not significantly outperformed an equal-risk passive alternative over any extended period. This is not too surprising. After all, the market's performance is itself an average of the performance of all investors. If, on the average, mutual funds had beaten the market, then some other group of investors would have lost to the market. With the substantial amount of professional management in today's stock market, it is difficult to think of a likely group of victims.

| Southam variability ranking | Max. sales fee % | Codes | Total assets $ mil. | % fgn | Dividend $ | Net asset value $ | Mutual Fund | 1 mo | 3 mo | 1 yr | 3 yr | 5 yr | 10 yr |
|---|---|---|---|---|---|---|---|---|---|---|---|---|---|

# Preferred Dividend Funds

| Southam variability ranking | Max. sales fee % | Codes | Total assets $ mil. | % fgn | Dividend $ | Net asset value $ | Mutual Fund | 1 mo | 3 mo | 1 yr | 3 yr | 5 yr | 10 yr |
|---|---|---|---|---|---|---|---|---|---|---|---|---|---|
| N/A | 2.66 | R | 27 | | 0.128 | 9.97 | 20/20 Dividend Fund | -2.6 | -0.8 | 5.4 | 6.9 | 6.7 | |
| N/A | | R | 136 | | 0.066 | 9.49 | AGF High Income Fund | -0.7 | 0.2 | 8.9 | | | |
| N/A | 1.51 | NL | ! | | 0.030 | 3.93 | Allied Dividend Fund | 0.0 | -0.9 | 7.5 | 3.8 | 3.2 | |
| N/A | 1.49 | 5.00 | 31 | | 0.049 | 9.19 | Bolton Tremblay Income Fund | -2.5 | -0.8 | 4.6 | 6.1 | 5.4 | 9.1 |
| N/A | 1.24 | R | 13 | | 0.030 | 4.92 | Dynamic Dividend Fund | -0.6 | -0.3 | 9.6 | 7.1 | 6.9 | |
| N/A | 2.42 | NLP | 9 | | 0.217 | 11.06 | FuturLink Income Fund | 0.1 | 0.5 | 14.2 | 11.1 | | |
| N/A | 1.21 | 4.00 | 8 | | 0.050 | 8.51 | Guardian Pref Dividend Fund | -0.8 | -0.1 | 9.9 | 6.1 | 5.7 | |
| N/A | 1.88 | R | 1550 | | | 9.95 | Investors Dividend Fund | -2.4 | -2.6 | 9.1 | 9.3 | 7.5 | 12.5 |
| N/A | 2.04 | NL | 8 | | 0.144 | 9.08 | Montreal Trust Dividend Fund | -1.6 | 0.1 | 9.0 | 7.5 | 5.3 | |
| N/A | 3.21 | NL | 23 | | 0.120 | 15.04 | PH&N Dividend Income Fund | -2.8 | -2.4 | 4.6 | 7.0 | 6.3 | 12.8 |
| N/A | 2.61 | NL | 3 | | 0.049 | 3.95 | Prudential Dividend Fund | -1.4 | 5.1 | 6.3 | 0.0 | 3.0 | |
| N/A | 1.83 | NL | 13 | | 0.088 | 8.66 | Royal Trust Growth & Income | -2.5 | 0.2 | 3.6 | 4.0 | 3.9 | |
| N/A | 1.73 | NL | 37 | | 0.051 | 10.29 | Spectrum Dividend Fund | -2.8 | -2.2 | 3.3 | 6.3 | | |
| N/A | 2.30 | 3.50 R | 173 | | 0.102 | 7.65 | Viking Dividend Fund Ltd | -1.7 | -1.0 | 7.3 | 7.7 | 6.8 | 13.4 |
| | | | | | | | HIGHEST IN GROUP | 0.1 | 5.1 | 14.2 | 11.1 | 7.5 | 13.4 |
| | | | | | | | LOWEST IN GROUP | -2.8 | -2.6 | 3.3 | 0.0 | 3.0 | 9.1 |
| | | | | | | | AVERAGE IN GROUP | -1.6 | -0.4 | 7.4 | 6.4 | 5.5 | 12.0 |

# Money Market Funds

| Southam variability ranking | Max. sales fee % | Codes | Total assets $ mil. | % fgn | Dividend $ | Net asset value $ | Mutual Fund | 1 mo | 3 mo | 1 yr | 3 yr | 5 yr | 10 yr |
|---|---|---|---|---|---|---|---|---|---|---|---|---|---|
| N/A | | R | 66 | | 0.063 | 10.00 | 20/20 Money Market | 0.6 | 1.8 | 8.7 | | | |
| N/A | 0.15 | R | 189 | | 0.055 | 10.00 | AGF Money Market Account | 0.5 | 1.6 | 8.1 | 10.7 | 10.0 | 10.1 |
| N/A | | | 6 | | 0.038 | 10.00 | AGF U.S. Money Market* | 0.4 | 1.1 | 5.2 | | | |
| N/A | 0.15 | NL | ! | | 0.027 | 5.00 | Allied Money Fund | 0.5 | 1.5 | 7.5 | 9.8 | 9.2 | |
| N/A | 0.18 | NL | 5 | | 0.045 | 10.00 | BPI Money Market Fund | 0.5 | 1.5 | 7.4 | 10.3 | | |
| N/A | 0.36 | | 1 | | | 14.69 | Batirente-Section MMK | -0.5 | 0.5 | 7.6 | 10.5 | | |
| N/A | | | 103 | | 0.073 | 10.00 | Beutel Goodman Money Market | 0.7 | 2.2 | 9.3 | | | |
| N/A | | R | 14 | | 0.053 | 10.00 | Bolton Tremblay LDMK ST Int | 0.5 | 1.5 | 6.8 | | | |
| N/A | 0.15 | 2.00 | 124 | | 0.057 | 10.00 | Bolton-Tremblay Money Fund | 0.6 | 1.7 | 8.3 | 10.9 | 10.1 | 10.2 |
| N/A | 0.22 | X | 27 | | | 59.90 | CDA RSP Money Market | 0.5 | 1.6 | 8.4 | 11.0 | 10.0 | 10.1 |
| N/A | | | 44 | | 0.028 | 10.00 | CIBC $U.S. Money Market* | 0.3 | 0.8 | | | | |
| N/A | | | 237 | | 0.052 | 10.00 | CIBC Canadian T-Bill | 0.5 | 1.5 | 7.4 | | | |
| N/A | 0.17 | NL | 1534 | | 0.054 | 10.00 | CIBC Money Market Fund | 0.5 | 1.6 | 7.9 | 10.8 | | |
| N/A | | | 581 | | 0.057 | 10.00 | CIBC Premium T-Bill | 0.6 | 1.6 | 8.0 | | | |
| N/A | 0.23 | | 4 | | 0.049 | 10.00 | Capstone Cash Management | 0.5 | 1.6 | 8.6 | 11.1 | | |
| N/A | 0.22 | R | 115 | | | 51.10 | Cda Life Money Market S-29 | 0.4 | 1.4 | 7.9 | 10.5 | 9.3 | 9.4 |
| N/A | 0.13 | | 2 | | 0.057 | 10.00 | Church Street Money Market | 0.6 | 1.7 | 8.8 | 10.6 | | |
| N/A | | | ! | | 0.060 | 10.00 | Clean Environment MMK | 0.6 | | | | | |
| N/A | 0.22 | LP | 31 | | | 302.93 | Crown Life Pen Short Term | 0.6 | 1.6 | 8.2 | 10.8 | 10.0 | 10.1 |
| N/A | 0.17 | R | 67 | | 0.055 | 10.00 | Dynamic Money Market Fund | 0.6 | 1.7 | 8.4 | 10.7 | 9.7 | |
| N/A | 0.21 | NL | 312 | | 0.005 | 1.00 | Elliott & Page Money Fund | 0.5 | 1.4 | 8.7 | 11.5 | 10.5 | |
| N/A | 0.23 | 0.25 | 7 | | | 13.50 | Empire Money Market | 0.5 | 1.4 | 7.9 | 10.1 | | |
| N/A | 0.21 | | 377 | | 0.057 | 10.00 | Everest Money Market Fund | 0.6 | 1.7 | 8.3 | 11.2 | 10.3 | |
| N/A | 0.20 | 2.00 | 30 | | 0.058 | 10.00 | Talvest Money Fund | 0.6 | 1.9 | 8.8 | 11.1 | 10.2 | |
| N/A | 0.16 | | 15 | | 0.057 | 10.00 | Templeton Treasury Bill | 0.6 | 1.7 | 8.2 | 10.8 | | |
| N/A | 0.34 | R | 3 | | 0.060 | 10.00 | Trans-Cda Money Market Fd | 0.6 | 1.8 | 8.1 | 8.7 | 7.0 | |
| N/A | 0.17 | 2.00 | 78 | | 0.057 | 10.00 | Trimark Interest Fund | 0.6 | 1.7 | 7.9 | 10.8 | 10.0 | |
| N/A | 0.41 | NLP | 23 | | 0.052 | 10.08 | Trust General Money Market | 0.5 | 1.4 | 8.4 | 10.7 | 10.0 | |
| N/A | | | 10 | | 0.048 | 10.00 | Trust Pret Revenu Money Mkt | 0.5 | 1.6 | 7.9 | | | |
| N/A | 0.14 | 2.00 | 80 | | 0.062 | 10.00 | United Cdn Money Market Fund | 0.6 | 1.8 | 9.1 | 11.4 | | |
| N/A | 0.22 | 2.00 | ! | | 0.016 | 5.00 | United US$ Money Market* | 0.3 | 0.5 | 3.0 | 5.1 | | |
| N/A | | R | 30 | | 0.059 | 10.00 | Universal Money Market | 0.6 | 1.8 | 8.3 | | | |
| N/A | 0.26 | 9.00 | 2 | | | 6.36 | Universal Sector Currency* | 0.3 | 1.3 | 4.8 | 6.3 | | |
| N/A | 0.16 | L | 50 | | 0.053 | 10.00 | Viking Money Market Fund | 0.5 | 1.5 | 7.7 | 10.5 | 9.9 | |
| N/A | 0.15 | | 13 | | 0.059 | 10.00 | Waltaine Instant MMF | 0.6 | 1.7 | 8.4 | 10.8 | | |
| | | | | | | | HIGHEST IN GROUP | 1.0 | 2.5 | 17.5 | 11.5 | 10.5 | 10.5 |
| | | | | | | | LOWEST IN GROUP | -0.6 | 0.1 | 3.0 | 5.1 | 7.0 | 9.4 |
| | | | | | | | AVERAGE IN GROUP | 0.5 | 1.5 | 7.9 | 10.1 | 9.7 | 9.9 |

# Market Indexes

| Southam variability ranking | Mutual Fund | 1 mo | 3 mo | 1 yr | 3 yr | 5 yr | 10 yr |
|---|---|---|---|---|---|---|---|
| 0.15 | 91 Day Canada T Bill | 0.6 | 1.8 | 8.0 | 10.8 | 10.3 | 10.2 |
| 0.57 | Consumer Price Index | 0.1 | 0.1 | 1.7 | 4.4 | 4.4 | 4.7 |
| 1.94 | ScotiaMcLeod Universe Bond Ind | -1.5 | -1.4 | 14.4 | 13.0 | 9.8 | 14.7 |
| 5.07 | Standard & Poor's 500 Index | -1.7 | -0.3 | 10.6 | 11.5 | 6.5 | 16.8 |
| 4.56 | TSE Total Return Index | -4.3 | -2.1 | 1.3 | 2.1 | 1.7 | 11.9 |

**FIGURE 20-7**
(Continued)

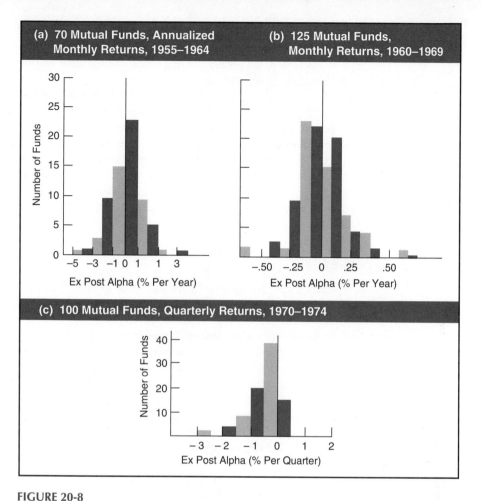

**FIGURE 20-8**
Mutual fund performance: ex post alpha values.

*SOURCE:* (a) adapted from Norman E. Mains, "Risk, the Pricing of Capital Assets, and the Evaluation of Investment Portfolios: Comment," *Journal of Business* 50, no. 3 (July 1977):378–80; (b) United States Securities and Exchange Commission, *Institutional Investor Study Report*, March 10, 1971 (Washington DC: US Governmental Printing Office); (c) Merrill Lynch, Pierce, Fenner & Smith, Inc., *Investment Performance Analysis, Comparative Survey, 1970–1974.*

## ☐ 20.7.4 Consistency of Performance

Despite the rather negative results described thus far, there remains the possibility that a few funds may consistently beat the market due to superior management. Consider identifying for further analysis those funds that had a run of $Y$ years of superior performance (perhaps $Y$ = 5 years). Some (perhaps all) of these funds may simply have had a string of good luck, whereas others may have been managed in a consistently superior fashion. The lucky ones have a 50% chance of above-average performance in the next year (that is, in year $Y + 1$), whereas the skilled ones have better than a 50% chance. This means that if all the managers have simply been lucky, then roughly 50% of the funds will have superior performance in the next year (that is, in year

$Y + 1$). However, if some of the managers are indeed skilled, then more than 50% of the managers will have superior performance in the next year. Furthermore, the greater the number that are skilled, the greater the proportion of funds that will turn in an above-average performance in the next year.

One major study in the US examined annual differential returns for 115 funds from 1955 through 1964 and found that of those portfolios that outperformed the market over a three-year period, only 53.4% did so again in the fourth year.[16] Since similar percentages were reported for one-, two-, four-, and five-year periods, it appears that there is little support for the notion that a significant number of mutual fund managers are skilled enough to consistently outperform a passive portfolio that has equal risk. One possible explanation is that there are skilled mutual fund managers, but they either extract an amount equal to their superior returns in salaries or move from fund to fund often enough to make it difficult to verify their existence.

## ☐ 20.7.5 Expenses

Funds typically incur two kinds of expenses. Management fees and administrative expenses are direct and generally reported. Transaction costs are only partly measurable in that brokerage commissions are reported, but implicit costs such as bid-ask spreads and the price impacts of trading are usually not even estimated.

By adding management and administrative expenses and explicit transactions costs to a fund's rate of return, it is possible to obtain an estimate of its gross performance (that is, its performance based on the assumption that such expenses were nonexistent). This is done by adding to the numerator of equation (20.2) the per-share values of such expenses. In the example shown earlier, perhaps the fund had paid expenses of this nature totaling $.02 per share during month $t$. In such a situation, the net return of $ .12 / $10.00 = 1.20% corresponds to a gross return of ($ .12 + $ .02) / $10.00 = 1.40%.

Figure 20.9 shows the distribution of ex post alphas based on this measure of gross performance for the funds covered in the analysis previously summarized in Figure 20.8(a). While ex post alphas based on *net* performance averaged .09% per year, the ex post alphas based on *gross* performance averaged 1.07% per year. Moreover, 50 of the 70 funds had positive ex post alphas based on gross performance. This suggests portfolio managers have some skill, but not enough to recoup the transaction costs that are incurred in hiring them and carrying out their buy and sell orders.

A study by the Securities and Exchange Commission in the US attempted to estimate the relationship between several factors and portfolio performance.[17] Ex post alphas were computed and analyzed for 132 mutual funds using monthly returns from 1965 through 1969. The following observations were made:

> Larger funds performed no better, other things being equal, than smaller funds, where size is measured by the fund's total assets.

---

[16] Michael C. Jensen, "Risk, the Pricing of Capital Assets, and the Evaluation of Investment Portfolios," *Journal of Business* 42, no. 2 (April 1969):167-247. Similar results have been reported for bond portfolios; see Mark Kritzman, "Can Bond Managers Perform Consistently?" *Journal of Portfolio Management* 9, no. 4 (Summer 1983):54–56.

[17] *Institutional Investor Study Report of the Securities and Exchange Commission* (Washington, DC: US Government Printing Office, 1971): vol. 2, pp. 328–32.

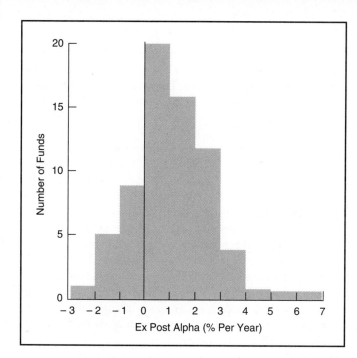

**FIGURE 20-9**
Mutual fund performance: ex post alpha values based on gross returns.

*SOURCE:* Adapted from Norman E. Mains, "Risk, the Pricing of Capital Assets, and the Evaluation of Investment Portfolios: Comment," *Journal of Business* 50, no. 3 (July 1977):378–80.

Funds with load charges performed no better, other things being equal, than those with no load charges (consequently, investors in load funds did worse than those in no-load funds).

Funds associated with management companies having larger amounts of assets under their control performed no better, other things being equal, than those with smaller amounts under their control.

However, fund performance was found to be *negatively* related to *portfolio turnover*, which is a periodic measure of how much buying and selling of securities was incurred (technically, it is the ratio of the smaller of purchases or sales during a time period divided by the average total asset value during the period). This suggests that, on the average, the more frequently a mutual fund's portfolio was revised, the lower its subsequent performance.

One possible explanation for this observation is that in an efficient market, more frequent revisions will cause a fund to incur more transaction costs, but without being able to consistently receive gains from the purchase of underpriced securities as an offset. Sometimes revisions in a fund's portfolio may be desirable in order to maintain a desired risk level or dividend yield, but revisions intended to exploit supposed market inefficiencies generally prove undesirable due to the associated transaction costs.

## ☐ 20.7.6 Market Timing

To achieve superior portfolio performance, an investor must either select securities that outperform others of comparable risk or switch from risk class to risk class at appropriate times. The latter strategy is often called *market timing*. The idea is to hold a high-beta portfolio prior to market rises and a low-beta portfolio prior to market declines. An all-equity fund can change its beta by switching among stocks that have different betas. That is, a high-beta portfolio can be achieved by holding high-beta securities, and a low-beta portfolio can be achieved by holding low-beta securities. Although a balanced fund can also do this, it can change its beta in another manner — namely, by altering the relative proportions it has invested in stocks and bonds. Typically, the more a balanced fund has invested in stocks, the higher its beta.

Successful market timing will eventually be reflected in a positive ex post alpha that is based on long-term performance. Overall performance may also be separated into one part attributed to security selection and another part attributed to market timing.

In a US study of the performance of 57 mutual funds over the period from 1953 through 1962, only one was found with a record suggesting any significant ability to time the market.[18] A later study of the performance of 116 funds from February 1968 through June 1980 found that only three funds had significant timing ability over the entire period, with only one fund having a record indicating significant market timing ability in both the first and the second half of the period.[19]

Such results are not surprising. If many funds were consistently successful at market timing, they would have shown up in the previously mentioned tests for superior overall performance unless they were consistently engaging in inferior security selection that offset their superior timing ability. However, such a situation seems highly improbable. More likely, investment managers find it as difficult to time the market as to select underpriced securities. Such is the lot of an investor in a highly efficient market.

## ☐ 20.7.7 Performance of Canadian Mutual Funds

Canadian studies of mutual fund performance are not plentiful. An early study, using Jensen's methodology, examined the performance of 19 Canadian mutual funds over the period 1960 to 1974.[20] The average beta for these funds was only 0.79 with a maximum of 0.99 and a minimum of 0.54, indicating that these funds are quite conservatively managed. The average R-squared was only 0.52 with a maximum of 0.69 and a minimum of 0.24 that suggests that these funds were not well diversified and had significant levels of unsystematic risk. None of the funds showed superior performance and, even

---

[18] Jack L. Treynor and Kay Mazuy, "Can Mutual Funds Outguess the Market?" *Harvard Business Review* 44, no. 4 (July-August 1966):131–36.

[19] Roy D. Henriksson, "Market Timing and Mutual Fund Performance: An Empirical Investigation," *Journal of Business* 57, no. 1, pt. 1 (January 1984):73–96. Similar results suggesting that mutual fund managers have no special ability to time the market is provided by Stanley J. Kon, "The Market-Timing Performance of Mutual Fund Managers," *Journal of Business* 56, no. 3 (July 1983):323–47; Eric C. Chang and Wilbur G. Lewellen, "Market Timing and Mutual Fund Investment Performance," *Journal of Business* 57, no. 1, pt. 1 (January 1984):57–72; and Chua and Woodward, "Gains from Stock Market Timing." op. cit.

[20] D.Grant, "Investment Performance of Canadian Mutual Funds: 1960–1974," *Journal of Business Administration* 8, no. 1 (Fall 1976):1–9.

after allowing for management and administration costs, underperformed the TSE index which was used as a benchmark portfolio .

Dhingra attempted to determine whether ex post systematic risk levels of mutual funds were consistent with their stated investment objectives. Data on 88 mutual funds whose stated objectives could be identified were collected for the period 1966 to 1975. These funds fell into two categories — growth funds or income funds. In general, growth funds generated higher returns and exhibited higher betas than income funds suggesting that the funds are generally managed in a style consistent with their stated objectives. This conclusion is borne out by a later study of 71 mutual funds over the 1980 to 1989 time period which found that performance was not consistent from year to year but that management style was.[21]

Do mutual funds provide protection against inflation? was the question addressed by Calvet and Lefoll. Using Jensen's measure of performance on a sample of 17 mutual funds from 1966 to 1979 they concluded that Canadian funds perform no better than the market after risk adjustment and provide no better inflation protection. The fund alphas and betas were remarkably similar in both real and nominal terms.[22]

Two studies examine the potential gains from market timing in Canada.[23] The first uses simulations to obtain estimates of the gains to be obtained from less than perfect forecasts of future market conditions. With perfect hindsight, after including modest transactions costs, a fund manager who switches between common stocks and T-Bills can expect a return of about 4% more and a standard deviation of about 5% less than buying and holding a market index . With less than perfect foresight the manager must achieve an accuracy of 80% in forecasting both bull and bear markets in order to outperform a buy and hold strategy. This is probably beyond the reach of most managers.

The second compares two different approaches to market timing. One, referred to as a *swing fund* (SW) approach, requires the manager to shift funds between asset classes in response to new forecasts about economic conditions. The other approach, referred to as *tactical asset allocation* (TAA), relies on the derivative securities market to implement shifts between asset classes. A comparison of eight TAA simulation models with six SF managers showed that six of the TAA models and three SF managers showed statistically significant market timing ability. On average the TAA "managers" outperformed the SF managers in market timing ability, although both added value to the portfolios.

---

[21] H.L.Dhingra, "Portfolio Volatility Adjustment by Canadian Mutual Funds, *Journal of Business Finance and Accounting* 5, no.4 (Winter 1978):305–33. J.McLaughlin and N.Bossen, "The Historical Performance of Canadian Investment Managers: Predictors of Future Performance?" *Canadian Investment Review* III, no.1 (Spring 1990):87–91.

[22] A.L.Calvet and J.Lefoll, "Performance and Systematic Risk Stability Canadian Mutual Funds under Inflation," *Journal of Business Finance and Accounting* 8, no.2 (Summer 1981):279–89.

[23] J.H.Chua, R.S.Woodward and E.C.To, "Potential Gains from Stock Market Timing in Canada," *Financial Analysts Journal* 43 (September-October 1987):50–6;E.J.Weigel and J.H.Ilkiw, "Market Timing Skills in Canada: An Assessment," *Canadian Investment Review* IV, no.1 (Spring 1991):19–28.

Several studies have shown that the performance of diversified closed-end investment company managers in the United States is similar to that of open-end investment company managers.[24] When returns are measured by changes in net asset values (plus all distributions), closed-end investment companies appear to be neither better nor worse than open-end ones. Again, there is little evidence that portfolio managers can either select underpriced securities or time the market successfully.

However, there is more to be said about closed-end funds. An investor can purchase an open-end fund's shares for their net asset value (plus any required load charge) and sell them later at the subsequent net asset value. Except for any load charges, the performance of the *management* of such a fund, based on net asset values, corresponds exactly to the returns provided to the *shareholders*. This is not the case for closed-end investment companies, since investors buy and sell shares of investment companies at prices determined on the open (secondary) market. Although some companies have share prices that are above their net asset values (such shares are said to sell at a premium), many have share prices below their net asset values (such shares are said to sell at a discount). Canadian closed-end mutual funds exhibit the same divergence between net asset value and share price as shown in Figure 20.1.

The fact that the price of a closed-end investment company differs from its net asset value, with the magnitude of the difference varying from time to time, introduces an added source of risk and potential return to investors. By purchasing shares at a discount, an investor may be able to earn more than just the change in the company's net asset value. Even if the company's discount remains constant, the effective dividend yield will be greater than that of an otherwise similar no-load, open-end investment company, since the purchase price will be less. If the discount is substantial when the shares are purchased, it may subsequently narrow, and the return will be even greater.[25] On the other hand, if the discount increases, the investor's overall return may be less than that of an otherwise comparable open-end investment company.

Some of the risk associated with varying discounts can be reduced by holding a portfolio of shares in several closed-end investment companies. Discounts on different companies move together, but not perfectly. For example, past data suggest that the standard deviation of the percentage change in the ratio of market price to net asset value for a portfolio of 10 to 12 closed-end investment companies is likely to be approximately half that of a typical investment in the shares of a single closed-end investment company.[26]

---

[24] See, for example, William F. Sharpe and Howard B. Sosin, "Closed-End Investment Companies in the United States: Risk and Return," *Proceedings*, 1974 Meeting of the European Finance Association, ed. B. Jacquillat (Amsterdam: North-Holland Publishing Co., 1975); Antonio Vives, "Analysis of Forecasting Ability of Closed-End Fund's Management," (working paper, Carnegie-Mellon University, September 1975) and "Discounts and Premiums on Closed-End Funds: A Theoretical and Empirical Analysis," (Ph.D. diss., Carnegie-Mellon University, 1975).

[25] There is some evidence that discounts narrow during "down markets" and widen during "up markets." See R. Malcolm Richards, Donald R. Fraser, and John C. Groth, "Premiums, Discounts, and the Volatility of Closed-End Mutual Funds," *Financial Review* (Fall 1979):26–33, and "The Attractions of Closed-End Bond Funds," *Journal of Portfolio Management* 8, no. 2 (Winter 1982):56–61.

[26] Sharpe and Sosin, "Closed-End Investment Companies in the United States."

Explaining the behavior of prices of closed-end investment companies is a challenge for anyone believing that capital markets are perfectly efficient. For anyone not firmly committed to such a view, the purchase of shares of closed-end investment companies at prices sufficiently below net asset values may provide an opportunity for superior returns.[27] One way of realizing superior returns is for the closed-end investment company to convert to an open-end one.[28] By doing so, the discount on the shares would have to disappear, since conversion would result in the investment company offering its shareholders the right to redeem their shares for net asset value.

## 20.9  SUMMARY

This chapter has described various types of investment companies, along with the advantages associated with investing in them. Unit investment trusts typically make a set of initial investments in fixed-income securities and then hold onto these securities until they mature. Investors in such a trust periodically receive their portion of the interest that the trust itself receives from the securities. Furthermore, the investors receive their portion of the principal on the securities as they mature. Usually, the sponsor of such a trust maintains a secondary market in the certificates that represent ownership in the trust.

Alternatively, investors can decide to purchase shares of managed investment companies, which are continually involved in buying and selling certain kinds of securities. There are two types of managed investment companies — closed-end funds and open-end funds (the latter are more commonly known as mutual funds).

An investor who buys and sells shares of closed-end funds will typically do so by using a broker. The shares of such funds are traded just like the shares of an industrial corporation, with a price determined in the marketplace. Thus, the number of shares outstanding for a closed-end fund is fixed.

In contrast, an investor interested in buying or selling shares of an open-end fund generally deals directly with the fund. The price paid to buy shares is based on the fund's net asset value on the date of purchase, a figure that represents the market value of the assets held by the company on a per share basis. Some open-end funds make the investor pay a commission, known as a load charge, when buying the shares. Others, known as no-load funds, do not impose such a commission. In either case, when an investor subsequently decides to sell shares that were previously purchased, the selling price is based on net asset value at that time.

There are a variety of other types of investments that are similar in nature to the shares of investment companies. Fixed and deferred annuities can be purchased by investors, providing them with periodic payments of a fixed dollar amount either immediately or at some future specified time. Individuals can direct institutions to

---

[27] Burton G. Malkiel advocated such an investment strategy in the 1973, 1975, and 1981 editions of *A Random Walk Down Wall Street* (New York: W. W. Norton & Company, Inc.), but not in the 1985 edition. The basis for his initial advocacy can be found in two studies: Burton Malkiel, "The Valuation of Closed-End Investment Company Shares," *Journal of Finance* 32, no. 3 (June 1977):847–59; and Rex Thompson, "The Information Content of Discounts and Premiums on Closed-End Fund Shares," *Journal of Financial Economics* 6, no. 2/3 (June/September 1978):151–86.

[28] For an analysis of the "open-ending" of closed-end investment companies, see Greggory A. Brauer, " 'Open-Ending' Closed-End Funds," *Journal of Financial Economics* 13, no. 4 (December 1984):491–507.

invest their money in any one of a number of pooled funds that specialize in making investments in, for example, corporate bonds or common stocks. Individuals can invest indirectly in real estate by either having a bank place their money in a pooled fund that specializes in such investments or in the US by purchasing shares of a real estate investment trust.

Due to data availability, mutual funds have been the subject of many studies of portfolio performance in the US. The results show that, on average, those mutual funds that indicated they would pursue more risky investment strategies do indeed provide their investors with returns that had higher standard deviations and betas. However, the typical fund was not able to provide its investors with superior rates of return. Furthermore, those few that had been able to provide such returns were generally unable to do so consistently.

More detailed studies indicated that the average fund was not able to engage in selectivity or timing activities in a manner that provided its investors with superior returns. Since fund managers use publicly available information in making their investment decisions, these findings are consistent with the notion of semistrong-form market efficiency. However, this should not be interpreted to mean that individuals should steer clear of mutual funds. Instead, individuals can still look for such funds to provide them with low-cost diversification that could be achieved by selecting a no-load index fund. Furthermore, such funds will simplify and reduce the amount of the individual's time that is spent on keeping records and investing.

## QUESTIONS AND PROBLEMS

1. Distinguish between closed-end and open-end investment companies.
2. Based on the evidence presented in the text, how much importance should Lou Pike attach to the past performance of mutual funds if Lou is attempting to select a superior performing fund?
3. What factors should you consider in selecting a mutual fund?
4. Why do some mutual funds have load charges while others do not? Why are investors willing to pay load charges?
5. Why do the stated percentage load charges of mutual funds not fully reflect the percentage costs of these sales fees?
6. Distinguish between a common stock fund and a balanced fund. In particular, compare their expected return and risk characteristics.
7. If most investment managers appear unable to "beat the market" on a risk-adjusted basis, should an investor still consider investing in investment companies? Why or why not?
8. Discuss the advantages and disadvantages of closed end compared to open end investment companies.
9. Marie Lajoie was attempting to calculate the performance of an investment in the Mercury Fund, an open-end investment company, over the calendar year 1991. Marie took the 1991 year-end net asset value (NAV) of the fund, subtracted the 1990 year-end NAV, and divided by the 1990 year-end NAV. Was Marie's performance measurement formula correct? Explain.
10. Assuming that certain conditions are satisfied, the income earned by incorporated investment companies is taxed at a lower rate than other financial institutions. Why?

11. Why do the market prices of closed-end investment company shares represent a "mystery" to proponents of market efficiency?

## SUGGESTED READINGS

*The Canadian Securities Course* (Toronto, Ont.: The Canadian Securities Institute, 1989). Chapter 19 describes mutual funds as well as a number of other special types of securities covered in other chapters of this book.

*The Canadian Investments Funds Course* (Toronto, Ont.: The Investment Funds Institute of Canada, 1991) provides exhaustive coverage of mutual funds in Canada.

Gordon J. Alexander and Jack Clark Francis, *Portfolio Analysis* (Englewood Cliffs, NJ: Prentice Hall, 1986). Chapter 13 gives a summary of mutual fund performance in the United States.

# Chapter 21

# FINANCIAL ANALYSIS

In a broad sense, financial analysis involves determining the levels of risk and expected return of individual financial assets as well as groups of financial assets. For example, financial analysis involves both individual common stocks, such as Stelco; groups of common stocks, such as the steel industry; or, on an even larger basis, the stock market itself. In this case, financial analysis would result in a decision of how to split the investor's money between the stock and bond markets as well as a decision of whether to buy or sell steel stocks in general and Stelco in particular.

An alternative definition of financial analysis is more pragmatic: Financial analysis is what financial analysts do. *The Financial Analyst's Handbook* [1] defines the term *financial analyst* as synonymous with security analyst or investment analyst — "one who analyzes securities and makes recommendations thereon." [2] Using this definition, financial analysis can be viewed as the activity of providing inputs to the portfolio management process. This chapter takes such a view in discussing financial analysis.

## 21.1 PROFESSIONAL ORGANIZATIONS

In Canada and the United States, those who belong to a local society of financial analysts automatically belong to an umbrella organization known as the Financial Analysts Federation. Among other things, membership brings with it a subscription to the *Financial Analysts Journal*, a major source of information on basic research done by other analysts and by members of the academic community. In 1986, there were about 15,000 members in the 56 local societies of the Federation.

In 1962, The Institute of Chartered Financial Analysts was formed by the Financial Analysts Federation to award the professional designation of Chartered Financial Analyst (CFA). Since then more than 10,000 analysts have received the CFA designation. To become a CFA, one must have several years of practical experience and pass a series of three examinations. [3] Figure 21.1, which shows the subjects covered

---

[1] Sumner N. Levine, ed., *Financial Analyst's Handbook I* (Homewood, Ill.: Dow Jones-Irwin, 1975).

[2] William C. Norby, "Overview of Financial Analysis," in Levine, *Financial Analyst's Handbook I*, 3.

[3] To obtain more information about becoming a CFA, contact the Toronto Society of Financial Analysts, 390 Bay Street, Toronto, Ontario, M5H 9Z9, the telephone number is (416) 366–5755. A useful annual publication of the Institute is *The CFA Candidate Study and Examination Program Review*.

in each of the examinations, provides a good summary of the types of knowledge the successful financial analyst needs.

Societies of financial analysts have been formed around the world. For example, the European Federation of Financial Analysts draws its membership from ten European countries. Other societies are located in countries such as Australia, Japan, and Brazil.

## 21.2    REASONS FOR FINANCIAL ANALYSIS

There are two primary reasons for engaging in financial analysis. The first reason is to try to determine certain characteristics of securities; the second reason is to attempt to identify mispriced securities. These reasons are discussed next.

### ☐ 21.2.1   Determining Security Characteristics

According to modern portfolio theory, a financial analyst will want to estimate a security's future beta and unique risk, since these are needed to determine the risk (measured by standard deviation) of a portfolio. Perhaps the analyst may also want to estimate the dividend yield of a security over the next year in order to determine its suitability for portfolios in which dividend yield is relevant (owing to, for instance, legal restrictions). Careful analysis of such things as a company's dividend policy and likely future cash flows may lead to better estimates than can be obtained by simply extrapolating last year's dividend yield.

In many cases it may be desirable to know something about the sources of a security's risk and return. If a portfolio is being managed for a person who is in the oil business, one might want to minimize the sensitivity of the portfolio's return to changes in oil prices. This is because it is likely that if oil prices are in a decline, then the person's income from the oil business will also be in a decline. If the portfolio were sensitive to oil prices (which would be the case if it contained a substantial investment in oil stocks), then it too would be in a decline in value, thereby reinforcing the deterioration of the person's financial position.[4]

### ☐ 21.2.2   Attempting to Identify Mispriced Securities

A search for a mispriced security typically involves the use of *fundamental analysis*. In essence, this entails searching for a security in which the financial analyst's estimates of such things as the firm's future earnings and dividends:

1. Differ substantially from consensus (that is, average) estimates of others,
2. Are viewed as being closer to the correct values than the consensus estimates, and
3. Are not currently reflected in the security's market price but eventually will be reflected in its market price.

---

[4] For a discussion regarding portfolio selection by an investor who has earned income (for example, from wages or from running a business), see Edward M. Miller, "Portfolio Selection in a Fluctuating Economy," *Financial Analysts Journal* 34, no. 3 (May/June 1978):77–83.

**General Topic Outline**
**CFA Candidate Study**
**and Examination Program**

Candidate
Level

I  II  III

**Ethical and Professional Standards,**
**Securities Law and Regulations**

**Applicable Laws and Regulations**
Nature and applicability of fiduciary standards
Pertinent laws and regulations
Organization and purpose of governing regulatory bodies

**Professional Code and Standards**
Code of Ethics
Standards of Professional Conduct
ICFA Bylaws, Article IX
AIMR Bylaws, Article X
AIMR Rules of Procedure

**Ethical Standards and Professional Obligations**
Relationships with:
(a) clients, customers, public;
(b) corporate managements;
(c) employers, associates, other analysts
Insider information
Supervisory responsibilities
Research reports and investment recommendations
Compensation
Conflicts of interest
Fiduciary duties
Professional misconduct
Investment suitability

**Identification of Issues and Administration of**
**Ethical Conduct**
Fiduciary responsibility
Insider trading
Corporate governance and the institutional investor
The Prudent Man Rule
Competency and proper care
Conflicts of interest in setting and receiving compensation
General business ethical values and obligations
Ethical organization cultures

I  II  III

**Financial Accounting**

**Role and Function of Basic Accounting Statements**
Income statement
Balance sheet
Statement of cash flows

**Using and Interpreting Accounting Statements**
Revenue recognition
Inventory costing
Depreciation methods
Investments in marketable securities
Off-balance sheet financing
Troubled debt restructuring
Leases
Postemployment benefits
Income taxes
Prior period adjustments
Earnings per share
Analysis of liquidity cash flow
Foreign currency translation
Intercorporate investments
Business combinations

**Special Topics**
Goals of financial statement analysis
Implications of efficient market hypothesis
The setting of accounting standards
Adjustments to financial statements
International accounting
Price level adjustments
Current accounting issues

**Quantitative Analysis**

I  II  III

Introduction to quantitative methods
Mathematics of compound interest, present and future values
Basic statistics and regression analysis
Measures of risk
Introduction of derivative securities
Advanced regression analysis
Basic options and futures pricing
Advanced options and futures pricing

**Economics**

I  II  III

**Focus on Macroeconomics**
Concept and measurement of GNP
Business fluctuations and economic forecasting
Inflationary process
Aggregate supply and demand
Macro schools of thought

**International Economics**
Comparative advantage
International payments
Foreign exchange

**Focus on Microeconomics and Analysis**
Consumer behavior and business decision making
Costs and supply of goods
Product life cycle
Business structure and regulation

**Economic Forecasting**
Forecasting tools
Relative success
Determinants of interest rates

**Applications to Security Analysis and**
**Portfolio Management**
Economic factor returns
Currency hedging

**Current Economic Issues**
U.S.
Global

**Techniques of Analysis—Fixed Income Securities**

I  II  III

**Introduction**
Features of fixed income securities
International fixed income market

**Mathematical Properties**
Price/yield relationship
Duration and convexity

**Credit Evaluation**
Bond ratings
Earnings and cash flow analysis
Asset protection
Contractual covenants

**Market Analysis**
Yield curves
Forecasting interest rates
International
Derivative securities

**Portfolio Strategies**
Active
Passive
Index
Immunization / dedication

**FIGURE 21-1**

General topic outline, CFA Candidate Study and Examination Program.

| Techniques of Analysis—Equity Securities | Objective of Analysis — Portfolio Management |
|---|---|
| I  II  III | I  II  III |

**Techniques of Analysis—Equity Securities**

**Introduction**
Investment environment
Securities markets
Mechanics of securities transactions
History of stock market — rate of return comparisons
Global investing

**Financial Analysis**
Ratios
Decomposition of ROE
Analysis of financial statements
Capital structure

**Valuation Approaches**
Earnings
Dividend discount
Cash flow
Asset valuations
Technical analysis
Other
Anomalies

**Company Analysis and Evaluation**
Fundamental analysis
Industry and economy context
Outline for analysis
Competitive environment
Corporate strategy
Example of research report

**Investment Strategies**
Trends
Market inefficiencies
Psychological influences

**Corporate Restructuring**
Leveraged buyouts
Takeovers

**Venture Capital and Closely Held Companies**
Analysis
Valuation

**Objective of Analysis — Portfolio Management**

**Principles of Financial Asset Management**
Definition of portfolio management, basic concepts—return, risk, diversification, portfolio efficiency
Evolution of portfolio management—traditional and recent developments

**Investor Objectives, Constraints and Policies**
Liquidity requirement
Return requirement
Risk tolerance
Time horizon
Tax considerations
Regulatory and legal considerations
Unique needs, circumstances and preferences
Determination of portfolio policies

**Asset Allocation**
Expected return and risk
Estimation issues
The optimal portfolio
Dynamic strategies

**Derivative Security Analysis**
Boundaries and basic properties of option values
Arbitrage and option valuation
Option pricing models
Empirical analysis of options
Option pricing theory applied to other assets
Financial futures

**Expectational Factors**
Social, political and economic
Capital markets
Individual financial assets

**Integration of Portfolio Policies and Expectational Factors**
Portfolio construction—asset allocation, active / passive strategies
Monitoring portfolio and responding to change—objectives, constraints and policies, expectational factors
Execution—timing, commission costs, price effects

**Portfolio Performance Appraisal**
Performance criteria—absolute performance, relative to portfolio objectives and risk level, relative to other portfolios with similar objectives
Measurement of performance—valuation of assets, accounting for income, rates of return and volatility
Evaluation of results—relationship to performance criteria, sources or results
Universe comparisons
Risk adjustment
Benchmark error
Ambiguity between skill and chance
Performance attribution
Normal portfolio
Non-parametric performance measurement
Incentive fees
Gaming performance measurement

**FIGURE 21-1** *(Continued)*

*SOURCE: The CFA Candidate Study and Examination Program Review* (Charlottesville, VA: The Institute of Chartered Financial Analysts, 1991):3–4.

Two rather different approaches may be taken in the search for mispriced securities using fundamental analysis. The first approach involves valuation, where an attempt is made to determine the appropriate "intrinsic" or "true" value for a security. After making this determination, the intrinsic value is compared with the security's current market price. If the market price is substantially greater than the intrinsic value, the security is said to be overpriced, or overvalued. If the market price is substantially less than the intrinsic value, the security is said to be underpriced, or undervalued. Instead of comparing price with value, the analyst sometimes estimates a security's expected return over a specified period, given its current market price and intrinsic value. This estimate is then compared with the "appropriate" return for securities with similar attributes.[5]

Determining a security's intrinsic value may be done in great detail, using estimates of all major factors (for example, gross national product of the economy, industry sales, firm sales and expenses, and capitalization rates). Alternatively, a shortcut may be taken where, for example, an estimate of earnings per share may be multiplied by a "justified," or "normal," price-earnings ratio to determine the intrinsic value of a share of common stock.[6]

A second approach has the analyst estimate only one or two financial variables and then compare these estimates directly with consensus estimates. For example, next year's earnings per share for a stock may be estimated. If the analyst's estimate substantially exceeds the consensus of other analysts' estimates, the stock may be considered an attractive investment. This is because the analyst expects the actual earnings to provide a happy surprise for the market when announced. In turn, there will be an increase in the share's price at that time, resulting in the investor receiving a greater-than-normal return. Conversely, when an analyst's estimate of earnings per share is substantially below that of the other analysts, then the analyst expects the market will receive an unhappy surprise. The resulting decrease in the share's price will lead to a smaller-than-normal return.

At an aggregate level, an analyst may be more optimistic about the economy than the consensus of other analysts. This would suggest that a larger-than-normal investment in stocks be taken, offset perhaps by a smaller-than-normal investment in fixed-income securities. Conversely, a relatively pessimistic view would suggest a smaller-than-normal investment in stocks, offset perhaps by a larger-than-normal investment in fixed-income securities.

Alternatively, the analyst might agree with the consensus view on both the economy and the individual characteristics of specific securities but feel that the consensus view of the prospects for a certain group of securities in a particular industry is in error. In such a case, a larger-than-normal investment may be made in stocks from an industry having prospects about which the analyst feels relatively optimistic. Conversely, a smaller-than-normal investment would be made in stocks from an industry about which the analyst feels relatively pessimistic.

Fundamental analysis of common stocks is discussed in more detail later in this chapter. At that time the method of technical analysis is introduced and compared with fundamental analysis.

## ☐ 21.2.3 Beating the Market

Many books and articles have been written that allegedly show how financial analysis can be used to beat the market, meaning they purport to show how to make abnormally high returns by investing in the stock market. In order to evaluate such systems, an understanding of what "the market" is and how to measure its performance is in order.

---

[5] The capitalization of income method of valuation is often used in the search for mispriced securities. This method was discussed in Chapters 13 and 16, where it was applied to bonds and stocks, respectively.

[6] To avoid complications arising when seeking the intrinsic value of a share that has negative earnings per share, some analysts estimate sales per share and multiply this figure by a "normal" price-sales ratio.

## North American Indexes

### Toronto Stock Exchange

| 52 Week High | 52 Week Low | Index | High | Low | Close | Net Chge | % Chge |
|---|---|---|---|---|---|---|---|
| 3672.58 | 3315.91 | TSE 300 Composite | 3571.97 | 3551.18 | 3551.18 | -19.63 | -0.5 |
| 3324.89 | 2679.50 | Metals & Minerals | 3174.10 | 3135.69 | 3138.01 | -9.13 | -0.3 |
| 3584.61 | 2862.97 | Integrated Mines | 3409.14 | 3364.03 | 3367.58 | -8.58 | -0.3 |
| 1996.09 | 1591.29 | Metal Mines | 1793.41 | 1758.78 | 1769.99 | +1.44 | +0.1 |
| 1405.52 | 1110.41 | Non-Base Metals | 1359.81 | 1351.00 | 1351.00 | -11.92 | -0.9 |
| 5632.72 | 4468.45 | Gold & Silver | 4969.14 | 4915.98 | 4969.14 | -31.77 | -0.6 |
| 5671.22 | 4493.07 | Gold & Silver Mines | 4999.82 | 4945.91 | 4999.82 | -32.48 | -0.6 |
| 673.37 | 553.49 | Precious Metal Funds | 608.13 | 602.81 | 605.67 | +0.41 | +0.1 |
| 4062.75 | 3054.58 | Oil & Gas | 3229.02 | 3205.55 | 3209.48 | -34.91 | -1.1 |
| 4887.91 | 3304.30 | Integrated Oils | 3710.41 | 3672.95 | 3674.84 | -40.56 | -1.1 |
| 3763.61 | 2968.67 | Oil & Gas Producers | 3071.82 | 3039.40 | 3044.89 | -32.86 | -1.1 |
| 3879.61 | 2947.89 | Paper & Forest Products | 3341.35 | 3311.88 | 3323.55 | -12.83 | -0.4 |
| 6539.43 | 4811.20 | Consumer Products | 6471.37 | 6403.13 | 6418.71 | -37.69 | -0.6 |
| 6944.89 | 5179.81 | Food Processing | 6691.03 | 6600.89 | 6621.35 | -92.53 | -1.4 |
| 10164.28 | 6975.29 | Tobacco | 9888.50 | 9763.86 | 9795.02 | -93.48 | -0.9 |
| 9087.58 | 6560.29 | Distilleries | 8798.39 | 8687.59 | 8721.47 | -46.15 | -0.5 |
| 6194.71 | 4951.54 | Breweries & Beverages | 6103.96 | 6067.10 | 6078.86 | -2.39 | -0.1 |
| 1296.02 | 958.35 | Household Goods | 1291.94 | 1268.90 | 1284.01 | +0.54 | nil |
| 4804.04 | 1617.22 | Autos & Parts | 4804.04 | 4690.17 | 4706.93 | -43.16 | -0.9 |
| 2500.04 | 2053.68 | Packaging Products | 2182.10 | 2169.50 | 2169.50 | +16.42 | +0.8 |
| 1066.77 | 965.11 | Biotech & Pharma | 995.99 | 976.65 | 976.65 | -10.08 | -1.0 |
| 1165.19 | 1817.16 | Industrial Products | 2184.34 | 2164.27 | 2168.03 | -11.96 | -0.5 |
| 1165.19 | 861.31 | Steel | 957.01 | 949.52 | 950.94 | -6.07 | -0.6 |
| 2954.22 | 2252.22 | Fab & Engineering | 2925.22 | 2900.35 | 2900.35 | -13.63 | -0.5 |
| 15916.26 | 8111.50 | Transportation Equip | 15266.36 | 15264.06 | 15264.06 | +102.30 | +0.7 |
| 6171.33 | 3755.74 | Technology | 6151.75 | 6064.10 | 6088.68 | -58.64 | -1.0 |
| 5434.74 | 4055.13 | Cement & Concrete | 4810.68 | 4715.73 | 4780.41 | +64.68 | +1.4 |
| 2864.10 | 2229.53 | Chemicals | 2840.49 | 2803.21 | 2805.85 | +0.85 | nil |
| 1884.80 | 1285.39 | Business Services | 1363.22 | 1349.41 | 1349.41 | -19.72 | -1.4 |
| 9954.77 | 6482.00 | Real Estate & Construction | 6917.21 | 6832.46 | 6832.46 | -67.62 | -1.0 |
| 8974.53 | 4042.78 | Transportation & Environment | 4912.22 | 4841.02 | 4841.02 | -50.45 | -1.0 |
| 4068.07 | 3445.06 | Pipelines | 3542.98 | 3508.39 | 3532.20 | -10.78 | -0.3 |
| 3474.35 | 2866.59 | Utilities | 3322.18 | 3301.31 | 3303.77 | -9.29 | -0.3 |
| 3366.68 | 2713.40 | Telephone Utilities | 3223.82 | 3203.02 | 3203.02 | -11.72 | -0.4 |
| 3514.76 | 3292.77 | Gas & Electrical Utilities | 3333.91 | 3292.77 | 3313.15 | +4.82 | +0.1 |
| 7677.56 | 6185.06 | Communications & Media | 7421.01 | 7334.83 | 7335.61 | -41.52 | -0.6 |
| 4369.20 | 3434.86 | Broadcasting | 4265.90 | 4255.39 | 4265.90 | +7.74 | +0.2 |
| 17041.87 | 10655.34 | Cable & Entertainment | 16209.93 | 16121.66 | 16131.00 | -96.62 | -0.6 |
| 7754.72 | 6219.93 | Publishing & Printing | 7411.72 | 7314.68 | 7314.68 | -46.08 | -0.6 |
| 4558.24 | 3920.42 | Merchandising | 4090.20 | 4066.62 | 4066.62 | -22.44 | -0.5 |
| 4188.05 | 3359.47 | Wholesale Distributors | 3846.37 | 3797.28 | 3802.10 | -44.27 | -1.2 |
| 8343.92 | 5901.98 | Food Stores | 6074.11 | 6024.09 | 6024.09 | -20.19 | -0.3 |
| 2020.46 | 1389.35 | Department Stores | 1429.53 | 1410.22 | 1421.87 | -3.67 | -0.3 |
| 5244.42 | 1673.78 | Clothing Stores | 2189.20 | 2143.22 | 2189.20 | +15.33 | +0.7 |
| 2921.96 | 2288.86 | Specialty Stores | 2333.06 | 2309.60 | 2312.58 | -24.79 | -1.1 |
| 39154.37 | 23288.42 | Hospitality | 37547.27 | 37494.92 | 37494.92 | -77.49 | -0.1 |
| 3105.19 | 2560.84 | Financial Services | 2798.48 | 2770.34 | 2770.30 | -17.00 | -0.6 |
| 3491.28 | 2742.19 | Banks | 3101.24 | 3065.83 | 3065.83 | -20.72 | -0.7 |
| 2960.99 | 1714.91 | Trust, Savings & Loans | 2072.37 | 2045.68 | 2045.68 | unch | unch |

### (Toronto Stock Exchange, continued)

| 52 Week High | 52 Week Low | Index | High | Low | Close | Net Chge | % Chge |
|---|---|---|---|---|---|---|---|
| 5085.61 | 3870.04 | Investment Cos | 4935.87 | 4880.45 | 4880.45 | -51.35 | -1.0 |
| 1814.33 | 1561.52 | Insurance | 1765.35 | 1751.44 | 1763.54 | +3.34 | +0.2 |
| 1274.70 | 903.37 | Financial Mgt. Cos | 976.53 | 966.80 | 971.61 | -0.22 | nil |
| 4901.71 | 3816.92 | Conglomerates | 4112.21 | 4071.47 | 4078.70 | -16.34 | -0.4 |
| 1417.40 | 821.31 | High Technology | 1411.80 | 1392.90 | 1396.91 | -13.22 | -0.9 |
| 27.22 | 14.52 | Computer Industry | 27.22 | 26.89 | 27.00 | +0.34 | +1.3 |
| 26.51 | 15.47 | Systems & Software | 26.51 | 26.17 | 26.27 | +0.37 | +1.4 |
| 27.46 | 9.95 | Manufacturers | 27.12 | 26.75 | 27.09 | nil | -0.1 |
| 9.79 | 6.33 | Distributors | 9.25 | 9.25 | 9.25 | unch | unch |
| 1782.14 | 1224.23 | Electronics | 1703.16 | 1677.84 | 1699.30 | +19.75 | +1.2 |
| 61.09 | 31.62 | Component Mfgs | 61.00 | 60.48 | 60.48 | -0.18 | -0.3 |
| 1884.92 | 1296.06 | System Manufacturers | 1775.09 | 1747.01 | 1772.21 | +23.23 | +1.3 |
| 1538.75 | 902.83 | Communications | 1529.17 | 1505.43 | 1508.60 | -23.75 | -1.5 |
| 1610.02 | 940.53 | Telecommunications | 1599.93 | 1573.79 | 1577.44 | -25.84 | -1.6 |
| 26.29 | 9.17 | Data Communications | 18.34 | 16.20 | 17.73 | +1.53 | +9.4 |
| 918.08 | 235.58 | Biotech & Pharma | 852.71 | 831.45 | 831.45 | -7.55 | -0.9 |
| 201.53 | 182.09 | TSE 35 | 193.73 | 191.65 | 191.85 | -1.59 | -0.8 |

### Montreal Exchange

| 52 Week High | 52 Week Low | Index | High | Low | Close | Net Chge | % Chge |
|---|---|---|---|---|---|---|---|
| 1942.25 | 1757.29 | Market Portfolio | 1870.13 | 1854.62 | 1855.78 | -15.90 | -0.8 |
| 2157.52 | 1578.42 | Banking | 2157.52 | 2134.21 | 2134.21 | -14.35 | -0.7 |
| 2763.13 | 2104.18 | Forest Products | 2354.36 | 2327.55 | 2336.49 | -2.23 | -0.1 |
| 1780.77 | 1367.58 | Industrial Products | 1776.83 | 1758.41 | 1762.36 | -17.10 | -1.0 |
| 2005.26 | 1578.42 | Mining & Minerals | 1873.43 | 1861.82 | 1865.30 | -8.13 | -0.4 |
| 1586.85 | 1154.22 | Oil & Gas | 1227.81 | 1210.41 | 1214.40 | -19.57 | -1.6 |
| 1887.13 | 1648.52 | Utilities | 1811.64 | 1798.85 | 1801.41 | -3.84 | -0.2 |

### Vancouver Stock Exchange

| 52 Week High | 52 Week Low | Index | High | Low | Close | Net Chge | % Chge |
|---|---|---|---|---|---|---|---|
| 670.16 | 518.81 | Composite | 670.16 | 663.22 | 665.05 | -2.62 | -0.4 |
| 1161.86 | 637.51 | Commercial & Industrial | 1161.86 | 1146.35 | 1150.35 | -8.37 | -0.7 |
| 596.40 | 439.85 | Resource | 532.31 | 519.19 | 523.53 | -4.97 | -0.9 |
| 581.13 | 433.18 | Venture | 581.13 | 575.21 | 576.98 | -0.76 | -0.1 |

### Dow Jones

| 52 Week High | 52 Week Low | Index | High | Low | Close | Net Chge | % Chge |
|---|---|---|---|---|---|---|---|
| 3313.95 | 2822.52 | Industrials | 3268.56 | 3219.14 | 3224.73 | -21.24 | -0.7 |
| 1465.25 | 1066.64 | Transportation | 1430.86 | 1405.45 | 1420.03 | +13.83 | +1.0 |
| 226.52 | 194.54 | Utilities | 208.00 | 205.43 | 206.00 | -1.81 | -0.9 |
| 1199.62 | 1002.59 | Composite | 1180.97 | 1166.93 | 1168.82 | -2.31 | -0.2 |

### Standard & Poor's

| 52 Week High | 52 Week Low | Index | High | Low | Close | Net Chge | % Chge |
|---|---|---|---|---|---|---|---|
| 421.18 | 359.32 | 500 Composite | 413.28 | 406.34 | 407.38 | -5.10 | -1.2 |
| 499.89 | 423.79 | 400 Industrials | 491.53 | 482.59 | 483.91 | -7.09 | -1.4 |
| 358.54 | 259.06 | Transportation | 353.06 | 347.12 | 350.93 | +3.97 | +1.1 |
| 35.16 | 27.26 | Financial | 34.35 | 33.89 | 33.93 | -0.16 | -0.5 |
| 155.76 | 133.40 | Utilities | 143.85 | 141.99 | 142.43 | -1.13 | -0.8 |
| 392.85 | 339.68 | 100 Stocks | 385.35 | 378.15 | 379.76 | -4.51 | -1.2 |

### New York Stock Exchange

| 52 Week High | 52 Week Low | Index | High | Low | Close | Net Chge | % Chge |
|---|---|---|---|---|---|---|---|
| 232.13 | 196.06 | Composite | 228.60 | 225.22 | 225.65 | -2.51 | -1.1 |
| 290.46 | 244.27 | Industrials | 286.53 | 281.73 | 282.35 | -3.89 | -1.4 |
| 211.79 | 157.93 | Transportation | 207.21 | 204.34 | 206.16 | +1.75 | +0.9 |
| 102.28 | 87.68 | Utilities | 96.73 | 95.72 | 95.92 | -0.52 | -0.5 |
| 177.85 | 139.66 | Financial | 174.31 | 172.65 | 172.73 | -0.75 | -0.4 |
| 342.02 | 277.76 | Value Line Average | 362.02 | 358.65 | 358.73 | -2.17 | -0.6 |

### American Stock Exchange

| 52 Week High | 52 Week Low | Index | High | Low | Close | Net Chge | % Chge |
|---|---|---|---|---|---|---|---|
| 417.42 | 336.88 | AMEX Average | 414.28 | 409.02 | 409.20 | -5.07 | -1.2 |
| 354.47 | 295.90 | AMEX Major Market Index | 349.06 | 342.57 | 343.30 | -4.01 | -1.2 |

### Nasdaq

| 52 Week High | 52 Week Low | Index | High | Low | Close | Net Chge | % Chge |
|---|---|---|---|---|---|---|---|
| 640.81 | 436.77 | Composite | 637.28 | 626.37 | 626.41 | -10.02 | -1.6 |
| 740.69 | 483.45 | Industrials | 731.85 | 714.54 | 714.54 | -15.85 | -2.2 |
| 633.41 | 505.73 | Insurance | 633.41 | 626.44 | 626.98 | -2.19 | -0.3 |
| 389.64 | 289.83 | Banks | 389.64 | 385.70 | 386.31 | -2.86 | -0.7 |
| 611.23 | 405.10 | Financial | 611.23 | 607.12 | 607.20 | -1.14 | -0.2 |
| 627.56 | 470.96 | Transportation | 627.56 | 618.77 | 619.86 | -2.53 | -0.4 |
| 675.81 | 534.81 | Utilities | 660.07 | 653.07 | 655.54 | -1.21 | -0.2 |
| 283.34 | 193.66 | National Market Composite | 281.45 | 276.73 | 276.73 | -4.46 | -1.6 |
| 296.00 | 193.99 | National Market Industrials | 292.16 | 285.18 | 285.18 | -6.37 | -2.2 |

## Hourly Markets

| Time | S & P 500 | DJ Inds | DJ Util | DJ Trans | TSE 300 | TSE 35 |
|---|---|---|---|---|---|---|
| 9:45 | 411.80 | 3245.08 | 207.37 | 1406.39 | 3571.67 | 193.45 |
| 10:00 | 412.16 | 3250.00 | 207.56 | 1420.21 | 3569.61 | 193.26 |
| 11:00 | 412.03 | 3252.23 | 207.06 | 1426.94 | 3569.13 | 192.44 |
| 12:00 | 412.28 | 3256.48 | 207.19 | 1427.87 | 3569.25 | 193.14 |
| 1:00 | 412.06 | 3261.63 | 207.06 | 1426.94 | 3569.38 | 192.68 |
| 2:00 | 410.84 | 3253.13 | 207.00 | 1425.45 | 3564.11 | 192.70 |
| 3:00 | 409.23 | 3240.83 | 206.62 | 1425.26 | 3563.41 | 192.75 |
| Close | 407.38 | 3224.73 | 206.00 | 1420.03 | 3551.18 | 191.85 |
| Previous day | 412.48 | 3245.97 | 207.81 | 1406.20 | 3570.81 | 193.44 |
| Week ago | 413.76 | 3251.57 | 208.69 | 1390.32 | 3597.85 | 195.00 |
| Month ago | 412.64 | 3223.39 | 212.19 | 1391.07 | 3620.44 | 197.75 |
| Year ago | 369.39 | 2932.18 | 216.11 | 1118.83 | 3530.94 | 195.03 |

**FIGURE 21-2**

North American stock market indices published daily in *The Financial Post*.

SOURCE: *The Financial Post*, The Financial Post Company (February 19, 1992):36.

## Market Indices

What did the market do yesterday? How much would an unmanaged common stock portfolio have returned last year? Such questions are often answered by examining the performance of a *market index*. Figure 21.2 displays many indices that are commonly discussed. These indices differ from one another with respect to (1) the securities included in the index and (2) the method employed in calculating the value of the index.

In order to understand how some of the most popular indices are computed, consider a simple example where the market index is based on two stocks, referred to as A and B. At the end of day $t$, their closing prices are, respectively, $10 and $20 per share. Furthermore, at this time A has 1500 shares outstanding and B has 2000 shares outstanding.

There are three weighting methods that are often used in computing a market index. The first method, involving *price weighting*, begins by summing the prices of the shares that are included in the index and ends by dividing this sum by a constant (the divisor). If the index includes only stocks A and B and was started on day $t$, the divisor would be equal to the number of stocks in the average, 2. Thus, on day $t$ the index would have a value of $(10 + 20)/2 = 15$. The divisor is adjusted thereafter whenever there is a stock split in order to avoid giving misleading indications of the market's direction.[7]

For example, assume that on day $t + 1$, B splits 2-for-1 and closes at $11 per share, while A closes at $13. In this situation, it is clear that the market has risen, since both stocks have a higher price than on day $t$ after adjusting B for the split. If nothing were done in computing the index, its value on day $t + 1$ would be $(13 + 11)/2 = 12$, a drop of $20\% = (12 - 15)/15$ from day $t$ that falsely suggests the market went down on day $t + 1$. In reality, the market went up to $[13 + (11 \times 2)]/2 = 17.5$, a gain of $16.67\% = (17.5 - 15)/15$.

A stock split is accounted for in a price-weighted index by adjusting the divisor whenever a split takes place. In the example, the divisor is adjusted by examining the index on day $t + 1$, the day of the split.

More specifically, the following equation would be solved for the unknown divisor $d$:

$$\frac{13 + 11}{d} = 17.5. \qquad (21.1)$$

The value of $d$ that solves this equation is 1.37. The new divisor will continue in use after day $t + 1$ until there is another split, when it will again be recalculated.

The Dow Jones Industrial Average, one of the most widely followed indices, is calculated in this manner; it involves the prices of 30 stocks that generally represent large-sized firms. Two other Dow Jones averages, one of which uses 20 transportation stocks, the other of which uses 15 utility stocks, are similarly calculated. Levels of these Dow Jones averages are reported in almost every daily newspaper. Historical data on the averages, including quarterly dividends and earnings figures, are published from time to time in *Barron's* and other periodicals.[8]

A second weighting method is known as *value weighting* (or capitalization weighting). With this method, the prices of the shares of the stocks in the index are multiplied by their respective numbers of shares outstanding and then added up in order to arrive at a figure equal to the aggregate market value for that day. This figure is then divided by the corresponding figure for the day the index was started, with the resulting value being multiplied by an arbitrarily set beginning index value.

Continuing with the example, assume that the start-up day for the index is day $t$ and that the index is assigned a beginning value of 100. First, note that the aggregate market value on day $t$ is equal to $(\$10 \times 1500) + (\$20 \times 2000) = \$55,000$. Next, note that the aggregate market value on day $t+1$ is equal to $(\$13 \times 1500) + (\$11 \times 4000) = \$63,500$. Dividing $63,500 by $55,000 and then multiplying the result by 100 gives the index

---

[7] The divisor is also adjusted whenever the composition of the stocks in the index changes (meaning whenever one stock is substituted for another).

[8] The Montreal Exchange index is calculated in this manner. The Montreal *Market Portfolio Index* consists of 25 of the largest publicly held corporations in Canada.

value for day $t + 1$ of ($\$63,500/\$55,000) \times 100 = 115.45$. Thus, the market would be reported as having risen by $15.45\% = (115.45 - 100)/100$ from day $t$ to day $t + 1$.

The Standard & Poor's 500, widely used by institutional investors, is a value-weighted average of 500 large-sized stocks. Standard & Poor's also computes value-weighted indices for industrial, transportation, utility, and financial stocks. Furthermore, a variety of industry indices are also calculated. Values for all indices, along with quarterly data on dividends, earnings, and sales, may be found in Standard & Poor's *Analysts' Handbook* (annual), *Trade and Securities Statistics* (annual), and *Analysts' Handbook Supplement* (monthly). The Vancouver Stock Exchange index is a value-weighted index of those companies that trade at least 50% of their volume on the VSE.

More comprehensive value-weighted indices for US stocks are also computed. The New York Stock Exchange publishes a composite index of all stocks listed on that exchange, as well as four subindices (industrials, utilities, transportation, and finance). The American Stock Exchange computes an index of its stocks. The National Association of Securities Dealers (NASD), using its automated quotation service (NASDAQ), computes indices based on the market value of approximately 5000 over-the-counter stocks; in addition to a composite index, NASD calculates indices for six categories representing industrials, banks, insurance, other finance, transportation, and utilities. NASD also publishes four indices that are based on just those stocks in their National Market System (the previously mentioned NASD indices are based on both NMS and non-NMS stocks).

The TSE 300 is a modified value-weighted index. The number of shares in all control blocks (representing more than 20% of outstanding shares) is subtracted from the number of shares outstanding to determine an adjusted market value. The following are the criteria for inclusion in the TSE 300: an adjusted market value of greater than $3 million, an annual trading volume of at least 25,000 shares, and trading value greater than $1 million per year. The 300 stocks with the largest adjusted market value that meet the above criteria are included in the index. The TSE 35 is also a modified value-weighted index that includes 35 of Canada's larger publicly listed corporations that are among the more heavily traded issues on the TSE. In order to prevent one stock from dominating this index the maximum weight assigned to any stock is 10%.

The values of the TSE 300 (and its associated sub-indices), the TSE 35, the Montreal Exchange, Vancouver Stock Exchange and various US indices are published daily in *The Financial Post* as shown in Figure 21.2.

Both the TSE 300 and the TSE 35 are calculated in two forms — a price index and a total return index. The former follows the procedure described above and represents aggregate price movements. The total return index includes dividend payments on each of the stocks as well as capital gains.[9]

The third method of weighting is known as *equal weighting*. With this method, equal dollar-size investments are made in the securities in the index. In the case of stocks A and B, on day $t$ the equal-weighted index would involve one share of A and one-half

---

[9]The broadest value-weighted index is calculated by Wilshire Associates. Their index, known as the Wilshire 5000 Equity Index, is based on all stocks listed on the New York and American Stock exchanges plus those "actively traded over-the-counter." The Russell 1000, 2000, and 3000 are also broad value-weighted indices, covering roughly the largest 1000 stocks; the next 2000; and the sum of the two. In terms of international indices, *Morgan Stanley Capital International Perspective* publishes value-weighted indices using various combinations of 1371 stocks from 19 different countries, resulting in a "world market index." These and other international indices are discussed in Chapter 24 (see Figure 24.2).

share of B, resulting in a value of $(10 \times 1) + [20 \times (1/2)] = 20$. On day $t + 1$, the index would adjust for the split of B by multiplying its price by 1 (instead of 1/2, as was previously done), resulting in an index value of $(13 \times 1) + (11 \times 1) = 24$, an increase of $20\% = (24 - 20)/20$. An example is the index calculated by the *Indicator Digest*, involving common stocks listed on the New York Stock Exchange.

One popular index that does not involve price weighting, value weighting, or equal weighting is the *Value Line Composite Average*. This index is computed daily by multiplying the previous day's index by the geometric mean of the daily *price relatives* (today's price divided by yesterday's price) of the relevant stocks in the index. For example, the value of the index consisting of stocks A and B on day $t + 1$ would be calculated by first determining the price relatives to be equal to $(13/10) = 1.3$ for A and $(11 \times 2)/20 = 1.1$ for B. Then the geometric mean would be calculated as[10]

$$(1.3 \times 1.1)^{1/2} = 1.1958.$$

If the value of the index on day $t$ was 120, then the value on day $t + 1$ would be reported as $120 \times 1.1958 = 143.496$, an increase of $1.1958 - 1 = 19.58\%$. In the case of the Value Line index, the initial value was set at 100 on June 30, 1961, and has been updated ever since then in this manner.[11]

In summary, four types of indices have been presented; various people use these indices when they refer to how the market has done. However, the indices can give notably different answers. In the example shown here, the market was calculated to have risen by either 16.67%, 15.45%, 20%, or 19.58%, depending on the index used. In practice, most professional money managers use either the TSE 300 or the S&P 500 as the barometer (depending on the market in which they are trading) since they have a fairly wide base and weight larger companies more heavily than smaller companies.

## Conveying Advice on Beating the Market

It is interesting to ponder whether or not advice on how to beat the market will remain useful after becoming public. It seems logical that any such prescription that has been in print for long is not likely to allow the investor to beat the market without fail. Even if an approach has worked in the past (just because someone asserts it has worked does not mean that it, in fact, has worked), as more and more investors apply it, prices will be driven to levels at which the approach will not work in the future. Any system designed to beat the market, once known to more than a few people, carries the seeds of its own destruction.

There are two reasons for not including advice on "guaranteed" ways to beat the market in this book. First, to do so would make a successful system public and hence unsuccessful. Second, the authors know of no such system. Some apparent anomalies and possible inefficiencies have been described previously. But any book that purports to open the door to the *certainty* of making abnormally high returns for those who follow its advice should be regarded with the greatest skepticism.

---

[10] In order to determine the geometric mean for $N$ stocks, multiply their price relatives and then take the $N$th root of the resulting product.

[11] Value Line also has indices for industrials, rails, and utilities that are similarly computed and updated. Before March 1986 the Montreal Exchange index was also a geometric index.

This does not mean that financial analysis is useless. Although individuals should be skeptical when others tell them how to use financial analysis to beat the market, individuals can try to understand the market with the use of financial analysis.

## ☐ 21.2.4 Financial Analysis and Market Efficiency

The concept of an efficient market (discussed in Chapter 3) may appear to be based on a paradox. Financial analysts carefully analyze the prospects for companies, industries, and the economy in the search for mispriced securities. If an undervalued security is found, for example, then it will be purchased. However, the act of purchasing the security will tend to push its price upward toward its intrinsic value, thereby making it no longer undervalued. That is, financial analysis tends to result in security prices that reflect intrinsic values, which is equivalent to saying that financial analysis tends to make markets efficient. But if this is the case, why would anyone perform financial analysis in an attempt to identify mispriced securities?

There are two responses to this question. First, there are costs associated with performing financial analysis. This means that financial analysis may not be conducted on all securities all the time. As a result, the prices of all securities will not reflect intrinsic values all the time. Pockets of opportunity may arise from time to time, thereby opening the possibility for added benefits from financial analysis. This suggests that people should engage in financial analysis only to the point at which the added benefits cover the added costs.[12] Ultimately, in a highly competitive market, prices would be close enough to intrinsic values to make it worthwhile for only the most skillful analysts to search for mispriced securities. Thus, the market would be nearly, but not perfectly, efficient.[13]

The other response to the question focuses on the first reason given earlier for engaging in financial analysis: to determine certain characteristics of securities. This reason is appropriate even in a perfectly efficient market. Since investors differ in their circumstances (consider the person in the oil business, discussed earlier), portfolios should be "tailored" to accommodate such differences. Successful performance of this task generally requires estimation of certain characteristics of securities, thereby justifying the use of financial analysis.

## ☐ 21.2.5 Needed Skills

To understand and estimate the risk and return of individual securities as well as groups of securities (such as industries), financial markets and the principles of valuation must be understood. Much of the material required for such an understanding can be found in this book. But, as Figure 21.1 indicates, even more is required. Future prospects must be estimated and interrelationships assessed. This requires the skills of an economist and

---

[12] If the added benefits exceeded the added costs, then it would be profitable to perform more financial analysis because the incremental benefits from doing so would cover the associated costs. If, on the other hand, the added costs exceeded the added benefits, then it would be profitable to cut back on the amount of financial analysis because costs would be reduced by an amount greater than benefits.

[13] For an interesting argument on why the existence of trading costs results in some investors performing financial analysis in an efficient market, see Bradford Cornell and Richard Roll, "Strategies for Pairwise Competitions in Markets and Organizations," *Bell Journal of Economics* 12, no. 1 (Spring 1981):201–13.

an understanding of industrial organization. To process relevant historical data, some command of quantitative methods is needed, along with an understanding of the nuances of accounting.

This book cannot provide all the material one needs to become a successful financial analyst. Books on accounting, economics, industrial organization, and quantitative methods are required. Instead, some techniques used by financial analysts are discussed, along with some of the pitfalls involved. In addition, sources of investment information are presented.

## 21.3 EVALUATING INVESTMENT SYSTEMS

Many statements have been made in the past asserting that some mechanical investment system, using only available historical data and a set of objective analytical procedures, can provide results superior to those obtained with a *passive investment system*. (A passive investment system involves simply buying and holding a well-diversified portfolio of stocks over a performance evaluation period; the return on a market index is often used as a substitute for such a portfolio.) Some mechanical systems simply provide predictions of how the market will behave; others prescribe a complete set of instructions for investing in individual securities. All of them present impressive statistics based on tests using data from some past evaluation period.

Consider as examples the following four statements:

> "...switch from bonds to stocks after the growth rate of the money supply has risen for two months; switch from stocks to bonds after the growth rate of the money supply has been below its most recent peak for 15 months. Historically, such a policy would have produced over twice the return obtained by simply holding stocks."
>
> "...this simple formula predicted over 95% of the quarterly variation in Standard & Poor's 500-stock index over the period studied."
>
> "...A portfolio of the 25 stocks with the greatest historical relative strength would have outperformed a portfolio of the 25 stocks with the smallest relative strength in 8 months out of 12."
>
> "...This completely objective stock selection procedure, which can be performed without error on a microcomputer, would have outperformed 80% of the professionally managed portfolios during the period in question."

Statements such as these four have been made in the past and will undoubtedly continue to be made in the future. Advocates of such mechanical investment systems may sincerely believe they have found the path to instant affluence. However, their proofs often rest on shaky ground. When evaluating any system, it is imperative that several possible errors be avoided.

## ☐ 21.3.1 Failure to Adjust for Risk

According to the capital asset pricing model, any investment system that results in the selection of high-beta stocks is likely to produce above-average returns in bull markets and below-average returns in bear markets. Since the stock market over the long term has trended upward, on balance such a system will tend to produce above-average returns over the long run. However, an evaluation of the performance of any investment system should involve not only measuring the resulting average return but also determining the amount of risk incurred. Then the average return from a passive investment system of similar risk can be computed for comparison. Techniques for making such comparisons are presented in Chapter 23.

## 21.3.2 Failure to Consider Transaction Costs

Systems that rely on constant trading may produce gross returns that exceed those of a passive investment strategy of comparable risk. But this is not an accurate evaluation of a system's performance because transactions costs should be considered in measuring returns. Net returns are calculated by adding transaction costs to the purchase price of an investment and deducting them from the investment's selling price.

For example, if 100 shares of a stock are purchased at $19 per share with a transaction cost of $100, then the cost of the investment is ( $100 \times \$19$) + $100 = \$2000$. If the stock is subsequently sold for $23 per share, with another $100 transaction cost, then the proceeds from the sale are ( $100 \times \$23$) $- \$100 = \$2200$. As a result, the net return is ( $\$2200 - \$2000)/\$2000 = 10\%$, whereas the gross return is ( $\$2300 - \$1900)/\$1900 = 21.05\%$, a substantial difference.

## 21.3.3 Failure to Consider Dividends

When the performance of a mechanical system is compared with that of a passive investment system, dividends (and interest payments) are often ignored. This may seriously bias the results. For example, a system may be advocated that, in effect, selects low-yield stocks. The prices of such stocks should increase at a faster rate than those of high-yield stocks with the same amount of risk. This is because a stock's return consists of both dividends and capital appreciation. If two stocks have the same risk, they should have the same return, meaning that the stock with a smaller yield will have a larger capital appreciation. Thus, if just capital appreciation is examined, a system that selects low-yield stocks would tend to show a more rapid rate of capital appreciation than a passive investment strategy involving a well-diversified portfolio consisting of both low-yield and high-yield stocks. Consequently, when yields of systems differ significantly from average yields, it is important to examine returns, not the rate of capital appreciation.

## 21.3.4 Nonoperational Systems

Although obvious, it still must be mentioned: To be useful, a system must not require information about the future. For example, many systems require action after some time series of values (such as a stock's price per share) has reached a peak or trough. But it is rarely apparent until well afterwards that in fact a peak or trough has been reached.

A similar situation arises when an equation is estimated from a set of data. For example, a system might assume that there is a relationship between the money supply at time $t - 1$ and share prices at time $t$. The general relationship might be

$$\bar{I}_t = a + bM_{t-1} \tag{21.2}$$

where $\bar{I}_t$ is the predicted level of the TSE 300 at time $t$, $M_{t-1}$ is the level of the money supply at time $t$ - 1, and $a$ and $b$ are constants. In this system, the level of the TSE 300 one period from now can be predicted from the current level of the money supply.

To make such a system operational, specific numerical values for $a$ and $b$ are needed. These numbers might be estimated by examining monthly data over a ten-year period from 1978 through 1987, which means that these numbers would be known only after 1987. However, some people might test the predictive ability of the equation over the same ten-year period of 1978 to 1987 using these numbers. In doing so, they fail to realize that the system would not have been operational with these numbers for this test period, since the numbers were determined after the test period. A true test of the predictive ability of this or any system must involve an estimation period that is earlier than the test period. That is, the test period must use *out-of-sample data*, as is discussed shortly.

## ☐ 21.3.5 Spurious Fits

Using a set of data from a past period, it is not too difficult to discover a system that works quite well when tested on the same data. In spite of the previously mentioned criticism that such a system would not have been operational during the test period, some investors might still be tempted to use it in the future if it worked well enough in retrospect. However, there is another criticism that can be made about such a system.

Imagine that equation (21.2) did not appear to work well. If so, then the following equation could be tried:

$$\bar{I}_t = a + bM_{t-1} + cM_{t-2} \tag{21.3}$$

where $M_{t-2}$ is the level of the money supply at time $t - 2$ and $c$ is a constant. If equation (21.3) does not seem to work well, more variables and constants could be tried. Ultimately an equation could be found that appears to work quite well. However, this does not mean that it would be useful to the investor. If 100 seemingly irrelevant systems are tried with a set of data, due to the laws of probability one of them is likely to give results that are "statistically significant at the 1% level." This should not cause undue excitement, since it would not have any notable predictive power in the future.

For example, share prices in the United States have been shown to be correlated with both sunspot activity and with the length of skirts. Few would associate causal relationships in these instances. Instead, these correlations are likely to have been *spurious*, meaning they probably were coincidental. Without solid reasons to believe that a relationship is due to underlying forces, it would be unwise to predict its continuation in the future.

## ☐ 21.3.6 Comparisons with Easily Beaten Systems

Often an investment system is said to explain a large part of the variation in some stock index. Figure 21.3 shows the quarterly level of the S&P 500 over a ten-year period (the solid curve) and the levels predicted by a system based on historic levels of the money supply (the dotted curve). The two sets of values appear to be quite similar.

This is actually not very impressive. An extremely simple set of predictions, shown by the dashed curve in Figure 21.3, is even better. This procedure predicts that each quarter's index will equal that of the preceding quarter:

$$\overline{SP}_t = \overline{SP}_{t-1}. \tag{21.4}$$

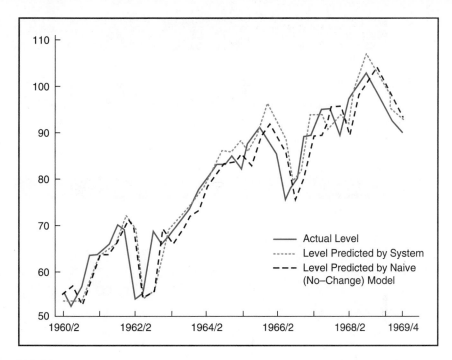

**FIGURE 21-3**
Actual and predicted levels, Standard & Poor's 500-Stock Index, Second Quarter 1960 through Fourth Quarter 1969.

*SOURCE:* Kenneth E. Homa and Dwight M. Jaffee, "The Supply of Money and Common Stock Prices," *Journal of Finance* 26, no. 5 (December 1971):1052.

Any system that is purported to be able to beat the market must predict percentage price changes (or returns), not price levels, because such changes (or returns) determine profits and losses. Thus, a good test is the extent to which predicted changes conform to actual changes. Figure 21.4 shows the percentage price change predicted by the system analyzed in Figure 21.3, along with the corresponding actual change for each quarter. The relationship is, at best, tenuous.

## ☐ 21.3.7 Reliance on Misleading Visual Comparisons

Occasionally the proponent of a system will produce a graph that plots both the level of an indicator intended to predict market moves and the levels of the market itself. Visual comparison of the two curves may suggest that the indicator does indeed predict changes in the market. However, the eye cannot easily differentiate between a situation in which changes in a market "predictor" *lead* the market and one in which the changes *lag* behind the market. This is a crucial distinction because only a leading indicator can bring superior investment performance.

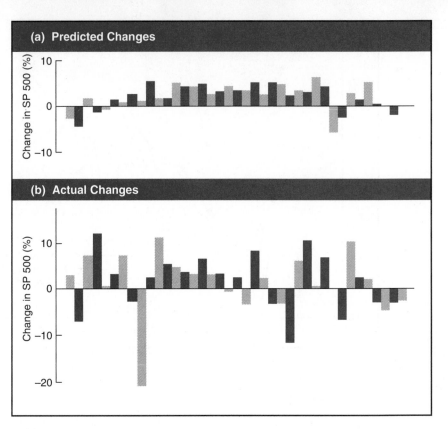

**FIGURE 21-4**
Predicted and actual quarterly percentage changes, Standard & Poor's 500-Stock Index, Second Quarter 1960 through Fourth Quarter 1969.

*SOURCE:* Kenneth E. Homa and Dwight M. Jaffee, "The Supply of Money and Common Stock Prices," *Journal of Finance* 26, no. 5 (December 1971):1052.

## ☐ 21.3.8 Ex Post Selection Bias

Many studies describe a stock-selection system that outperformed standard stock market indices. Some of these systems avoid the errors considered thus far, but another error may be involved. To facilitate computer-based analysis, a standard set of data might have been employed. For example, an investigator might use a database prepared in 1991 with share price data relating to the period from 1980 through 1990. The stocks included in the database might have been chosen because they existed and were important in 1991 (for example, they might have been considered important because they were listed on the TSE in 1991). Discovering a superior investment system from analysis of this database is subject to the criticism of involving *ex post selection bias*. That is, the system discovered in 1991 was based on an analysis of those stocks that were certain to be alive, well, and important in 1990. Accordingly, it should have done well over the period from 1980 to 1990. Studies of this type implicitly commit an error described earlier — they use information not available in advance. In particular, they assume that it was known in 1980 which stocks would be still listed in 1990.

## ☐ 21.3.9  Failure to Use Out-of-Sample Data

Can any evidence concerning a system's ability to beat the market be persuasive? Probably not to those who believe absolutely in market efficiency. But there are appropriate tests that can be undertaken.

The search for a system should be conducted using one set of data, and the test of the system's predictive ability should be performed using an entirely different set of data. The latter set of data is sometimes known as *out-of-sample data* (or a holdout sample). To be complete, such a test should involve the (simulated) management of a portfolio and be designed so that each investment decision is based solely on information available at the time the decision is made. Finally, the performance of the system should be measured in the way one would measure the performance of any investment manager (discussed in Chapter 23). This involves, among other things, attempting to determine the probability that the investment results were due to chance rather than skill.

Figure 21.5 shows the performance of one system using out-of-sample data. Values forecast by three predictive systems for quarterly percentage changes in the S&P 500 are shown, along with the subsequent actual changes. Each of the predictive systems worked extremely well with past data. The same cannot be said for their predictions using out-of-sample data.

## 21.4    FUNDAMENTAL VERSUS TECHNICAL ANALYSIS

One of the major divisions in the ranks of financial analysts is between those using fundamental analysis (known as fundamental analysts, or fundamentalists) and those using *technical analysis* (known as technical analysts, or technicians). The fundamentalist tends to look forward; the technician, backward. The fundamentalist is concerned with such things as future earnings and dividends, whereas the technician thinks little (if at all) about such things.

> Technical analysis is the study of the internal stock exchange information as such. The word "technical" implies a study of the market itself and not of those external factors which are reflected in the market …[A]ll the relevant factors, whatever they may be, can be reduced to the volume of the stock exchange transactions and the level of share prices; or more generally, to the sum of the statistical information produced by the market.[14]

The technician usually attempts to predict short-term price movements and thus makes recommendations concerning the *timing* of purchases and sales of either specific stocks or of groups of stocks (such as industries) or of stocks in general. It is sometimes said that fundamental analysis is designed to answer the question What? and technical analysis to answer the question When?

The concept of technical analysis is completely at odds with the notion of efficient markets:

> …the methodology of technical analysis …rests upon the assumption that history tends to repeat itself in the stock exchange. If a certain pattern of activity has in the past

---

[14] Felix Rosenfeld, ed., *The Evaluation of Ordinary Shares*, a summary of the proceedings of the Eighth Congress of the European Federation of Financial Analysts Societies (Paris: Dunod, 1975):297.

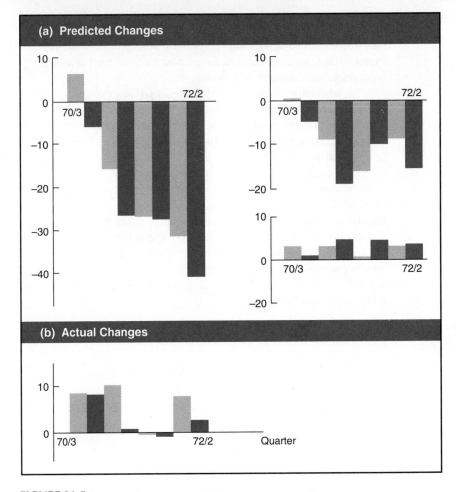

**FIGURE 21-5**
Predicted and actual quarterly percentage changes, Standard & Poor's 500-Stock Index,
Third Quarter 1970 through Second Quarter 1972.

*SOURCE:* James E. Pesando, "The Supply of Money and Common Stock Prices: Further Observations on
the Econometric Evidence," *Journal of Finance* 29, no. 3 (June 1974):916.

produced certain results nine times out of ten, one can assume a strong likelihood of the
same outcome whenever this pattern appears in the future. *It should be emphasized,
however, that a large part of the methodology of technical analysis lacks a strictly
logical explanation.*[15] [Italics added.]

Thus, technicians assert that the study of past patterns of things such as prices and
volumes allows the investor to identify accurately times when certain specific stocks
(or groups of stocks, or the market in general) are either overpriced or underpriced.

---

[15] Rosenfeld, *The Evaluation of Ordinary Shares*:297–98.

> Like a medical thermometer, [technical analysis] is a signalling device; sometimes a false indication is given when there is no cause for alarm, but when there is cause for alarm, the signal will almost invariably be flashed.[16]

The rest of this chapter is concerned with the principles of fundamental analysis, since such analysis is more prevalent than technical analysis and is essential if capital markets are to be efficient. Technical analysis is discussed briefly in the first appendix to this chapter, since there is little evidence showing it to be useful in enabling investors to beat the market.[17] Many "proofs" of the ability of technical analysis to beat the market have been offered, but most have committed at least one of the errors described earlier.

## ☐ 21.4.1 Top-Down versus Bottom-Up Forecasting

Fundamental analysts forecast, among other things, future levels of the economy's gross national product, future sales and earnings for a number of industries, and future sales and earnings for an even larger number of firms. Eventually such forecasts are converted to estimates of expected returns of specific stocks and, perhaps, certain industries and the stock market itself. In some cases the conversion is made explicitly. For example, an estimate of next year's earnings per share for a firm may be multiplied by a projected price-earnings ratio in order to estimate the expected price of the firm's shares a year hence, thereby allowing a forecast of the expected return to be made. In other cases the conversion is implicit. For example, stocks with projected earnings exceeding consensus estimates may be placed on an "approved" list.

Some investment organizations that employ financial analysts follow a sequential *top-down approach* to forecasting. With this approach, the financial analysts are first involved in making forecasts for the economy, then for industries, and finally for companies. The industry forecasts are based on the forecasts for the economy and, in turn, the company forecasts are based on the forecasts for both its industry and the economy.

Other investment organizations begin with estimates of the prospects for companies and then build to estimates of the prospects for industries and ultimately the economy. Such a *bottom-up approach* may unknowingly involve inconsistent assumptions. For example, one analyst may use one forecast of foreign exchange rates in projecting the foreign sales of company A, whereas another analyst may use a different forecast in projecting the foreign sales of company B. Top-down systems are less susceptible to this danger, since all the analysts in the organization would use the same forecast of exchange rates.

In practice, a combination of the two approaches is often employed. For example, forecasts are made for the economy in a top-down manner. These forecasts then provide a setting within which financial analysts make bottom-up forecasts for individual companies. The sum of the individual forecasts should be consistent with the original

---

[16] Robin J. Russo, *Compare—A Technical Timing System* (New York: Dean Witter & Co. Inc., 1976).

[17] See, for example, Robert A. Levy, "The Predictive Significance of Five-Point Chart Patterns," *Journal of Business* 44, no. 3 (July 1971):316–23; and Eugene F. Fama, "Efficient Capital Markets: A Review of Theory and Empirical Work," *Journal of Finance* 25, no. 2 (May 1970):383–417.

economywide forecast.[18] If not, the process is repeated (perhaps with additional controls) to ensure consistency.

## ☐ 21.4.2  Probabilistic Forecasting

Explicit probabilistic forecasting often focuses on economywide forecasts, since uncertainty at this level is of the greatest importance in determining the risk and expected return of a well-diversified portfolio. A few alternative economic scenarios may be forecast, along with their respective probability of occurrence. Then accompanying projections are made of the prospects for industries, companies, and share prices. Such an exercise provides an idea of the likely sensitivities of different stocks to surprises concerning the economy. By assigning probabilities to the different scenarios, risks may also be estimated.

## ☐ 21.4.3  Econometric Models

An *econometric model* is a statistical model that provides a means of forecasting the levels of certain variables, known as *endogenous variables*. In order to make these forecasts, the model relies on assumptions that have been made in regard to the levels of certain other variables, known as *exogenous variables*. The model may be extremely complex or it may be a simple formula that can be used with a desk calculator. In any event, it should involve a blend of economics and statistics, where economics is used to suggest the forms of relevant relationships and statistical procedures are applied to historical data to estimate the exact nature of the relationships involved.

Some investment organizations utilize large-scale econometric models to translate predictions about such factors as the federal budget, expected consumer spending, and planned business investment into predictions of future levels of gross national product, inflation, and unemployment. Several firms and nonprofit organizations maintain such models, selling either the forecasts or the computer program itself to investment organizations, corporate planners, public agencies, and others.

The developers of large-scale models usually provide several "standard" predictions, based on different sets of assumptions about the exogenous variables; some also assign probabilities to the alternative predictions. In some cases, users can substitute their own sets of assumptions and subsequently examine the resulting predictions.

Large-scale econometric models of this type employ many equations that describe many important relationships. Although estimates of the magnitudes of such relationships are obtained from historical data, these estimates may or may not enable the model to work well in the future. When predictions turn out to be poor, it is sometimes said that there have been *structural changes* in the underlying economic relationships. However, the failure may be due to the influence of factors omitted from the model. In any event, such a situation necessitates changes in either the size of the estimates or the basic form of the econometric model or even both. Rare indeed is the user who does not fine-tune

---

[18] Input-output analysis is sometimes used to ensure consistency between various industries and the economy in aggregate. This type of analysis is based on the notion that the output of certain industries (for example, the steel industry) is the input for certain other industries (for example, the household appliance industry).

(or completely overhaul) such a model from time to time as further experience is accumulated.

## ☐ 21.4.4 Financial Statement Analysis

For some, the image of a typical financial analyst is that of a gnome, fully equipped with green eyeshade, poring over financial statements in a back room. Though the physical description is rarely accurate, it is true that many analysts do study financial statements in an attempt to predict the future.

A company's financial statements can be regarded as the output of a model of the firm — a model designed by management, the company's accountants, and (indirectly) the tax authorities. Different companies use different models, meaning they treat similar events in different ways. One reason this is possible is because generally accepted accounting principles (GAAP), as established by the Canadian Institute of Chartered Accountants (CICA), allow a certain degree of latitude in how to account for various events. Examples include the method of depreciating assets (straight-line or accelerated) and the method of valuing inventory.

To understand a company fully and to compare it with others that use different accounting procedures, the financial analyst must be a financial detective, looking for clues in footnotes and the accompanying text that discuss how the financial statements were prepared. Those who take bottom-line figures such as earnings per share on faith may be more surprised by future developments than those who try to look behind the accounting veil.

The ultimate goal of the fundamental analyst is to determine the values of the outstanding claims on a firm's income (claimants include the firm's bondholders and shareholders). The firm's income must first be projected; then the possible distributions of that income among the claimants must be considered, with relevant probabilities assessed.

In practice, shortcut procedures are often used. Many analysts focus on reported accounting figures, even though such numbers may not adequately reflect true economic values. In addition, simple measures are often used to assess complex relationships. For example, some analysts attempt to estimate the probability that short-term creditors will be paid in full and on time by examining the ratio of liquid assets to the amount of short-term debt. Similarly, the probability that interest will be paid to bondholders in a timely fashion is often estimated by examining the ratio of earnings before interest and taxes to the periodic amount of such interest payments. Often the prospects for a firm's common stock are estimated by examining the ratio of earnings after taxes to the book value of equity.

The use of ratios such as these to facilitate predicting the future is widespread. Some ratios use items from the same financial statement (either a particular balance sheet or income statement), whereas others use items from two different statements. Still other ratios use items from two or more statements of the same type but of different years (for example, this year's balance sheet and last year's balance sheet), or incorporate data on market values.

Ratios may be used in several ways. Some analysts apply absolute standards, on the grounds that a substandard ratio indicates a potential weakness that merits further analysis. Other analysts compare a company's ratios to those of the "average" firm in the same industry in order to detect differences that may need further consideration. Yet others analyze trends in a company's ratios over time, hoping it will help them predict future changes. Still others combine ratios with technical analysis in order to arrive at investment decisions.

One example of how ratios can be used for investing involves the use of price-earnings ratios. This method is partly technical in nature, since it is based on the notion of *contrary opinion*. Specifically, it is based on a belief that stocks with low price-earnings ratios are out of favor in the investment community.[19] Accordingly, this contrarian investment strategy involves simply finding stocks with low price-earnings ratios and then investing in them. Stocks with high price-earnings ratios would be shunned with this strategy, since they would generally represent stocks that are viewed favorably in the investment community. Small firms typically have had higher returns than large firms, even after adjusting for differences in risk; given that small firms typically have had low price-earnings ratios, it is not surprising that such a strategy has been successful in the past.[20] Whether the success will continue in the future is another matter.

Another use of ratios is illustrated in Figure 21.6. In this figure, each ratio is equal to the product of the two ratios on its right-hand side, with one exception. The exception is the turnover ratio (sales/assets), whose reciprocal (assets/sales) equals the sum of the reciprocals of the four ratios on its right-hand side. Given the interrelationships among the ratios, it can be seen that once the future values of these ratios are forecast, then an implied forecast for the price of the firm's shares can be computed. The difficulty with such an approach, however, is in accurately predicting the future values of the ratios.

Ratio analysis can be very sophisticated, but it can also be overly simplistic. Routine extrapolation of a present ratio (or its recent trend) may produce a poor estimate of its future value. (For example, there is no reason for a firm to maintain a constant ratio of inventory to sales). Moreover, a series of simple projections may produce inconsistent financial statements. For example, projections of ratios imply predictions of the levels of various balance sheet items. However, it may be that when these levels are looked at altogether, the resulting balance sheet does not balance.

To project future financial statements, one should build a model that includes the relationships among the items on such statements and outside factors. Traditional ratio analysis does this, but somewhat crudely. A much better procedure uses microcomputers and a type of software known as spreadsheets.[21]

Basically, a spreadsheet is an arrangement of information in rows and columns. Each cell on a traditional (paper) spreadsheet typically contains a number or a label. Some of the numbers (for example, sales) are entered directly; others (for example, earnings before interest and taxes) are computed from the numbers in other cells.

An electronic spreadsheet simulates a traditional spreadsheet on a computer screen. There are, however, notable differences. Most importantly, cells can contain formulas. For example, the cell for earnings before interest and taxes (EBIT) could contain the formula for calculating the value as well as the value produced by the formula. Normally,

---

[19] David Dremen, *Contrarian Investment Strategy* (New York: Random House, Inc., 1979).

[20] The observation that small firms typically have had abnormally high returns is an empirical regularity known as the size effect; it is discussed in the appendix to Chapter 15.

[21] Lotus Development Corporation has been one of the leading developers of such software. The products Lotus 1-2-3 and Symphony have been top sellers.

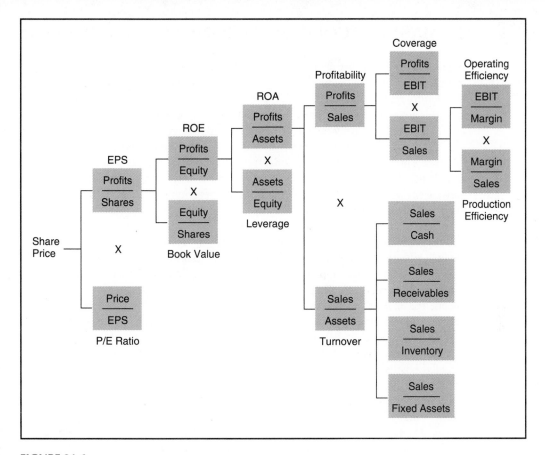

**FIGURE 21-6**
The use of predicted ratios to compute predicted price.

*SOURCE:* Samuel E. Stewart, Jr., "Corporate Forecasting," in Sumner N. Levine, ed., *Financial Analyst's Handbook I* (Homewood Il: Dow Jones & Company, Inc., 1975):912.

only the value would be displayed, giving an outward appearance similar to that of a traditional spreadsheet. However, any change in the number in the cell for sales would immediately change the value of EBIT, since the formula for EBIT would contain the value for sales as an input. This feature of electronic spreadsheets allows the user to rapidly explore the implications of changes in key assumptions (such as prices, quantities, and costs) on various balance sheet and income statement items. Accordingly, exploration of this sort is often known as sensitivity analysis, or what-if analysis.

In summary, financial statement analysis can help an analyst understand what a company is, where it may be going, what factors affect it, and how these factors affect it. If others are doing such analysis and doing it well, it will be difficult to find mispriced securities in this manner. But it should be possible to more accurately identify firms likely to go bankrupt, firms with higher or lower betas, firms with greater or lesser sensitivities to major factors, and so forth. Increased understanding of such aspects may well provide ample reward for the effort entailed.

When a security analyst decides that a stock is mispriced and informs certain clients of this, some of the clients may act on the information. As they do so, the price of the security may be afffected. As news of the analyst's recommendation spreads, more investors may act, and the price may react even more. At some point, the analyst's information will be "fully reflected" in the security's price.

If the analyst decides a stock is underpriced and clients subsequently purchase it, the share's price will tend to rise. Conversely, if the analyst decides a stock is overpriced and clients subsequently sell it, the share's price will tend to decline. If the analyst's views were well founded, no subsequent counterreaction in the share's price would be expected. Otherwise, the price is likely to return to its prerecommendation level at some later time.

An interesting example of the impact of analysts' recommendations is provided by the behavior of prices of stocks mentioned in the "Heard on the Street" column of the *Wall Street Journal*, which periodically summarizes recent stock recommendations. An analyst's opinion is typically published in "Heard on the Street" after it is first given to clients. The analyst's view is thus "somewhat public" for several days before publication, but when the column appears the opinion becomes "very public," since it then reaches a substantially larger audience.

Part (a) of Figure 21.7 summarizes the price reactions of about 597 stocks that received positive opinions in "Heard on the Street" during 1970 and 1971. Part (b) summarizes the reactions of about 188 stocks that received negative opinions during the same time period. In each panel, the vertical axis plots the average cumulative abnormal return — that is, the average return, adjusted for normal reactions to overall market moves. The horizontal axes indicate trading days relative to the date of publication of the recommendation, going from 20 days before to 20 days after publication.

As shown in the two parts, the publication of such a recommendation does typically affect a share's price.[22] After adjusting for market moves, on the publication date the price of the shares recommended for purchase rose .923%, whereas that of the shares recommended for sale fell 2.374%. Furthermore, after making such adjustments, 70% of the 597 stocks recommended for purchase rose on the date of publication, and 90% of the 188 stocks recommended for sale fell on the date of publication.

The roughly horizontal lines after day 0 in both parts show that both types of recommendations appeared to contain information. This is because the horizontal lines indicate that there was no significant counterreaction in the 20 days after either a buy or sell recommendation was made.

The upward moves in part (a) prior to day 0 suggest prior purchases of the stocks have been made by clients of the analysts. An alternative explanation is that analysts simply recommended purchases of stocks that had recently risen in price. Note, however, that part (b) is quite different: There is no distinct pattern prior to the date of publication

---

[22] Similar observations have been made in regard to the recommendations made by a major brokerage house. See John C. Groth, Wilbur G. Lewellen, Gary G. Schlarbaum, and Ronald C. Lease, "An Analysis of Brokerage House Securities Recommendations," *Financial Analysts Journal* 35, no. 1 (January/February 1979):32–40. For a comment on this study, see the letter to the editor in the May/June 1980 issue by Clinton M. Bidwell, with a responding letter to the editor in the July/August 1980 issue by Wilbur G. Lewellen. Also see the first footnote in Chapter 22.

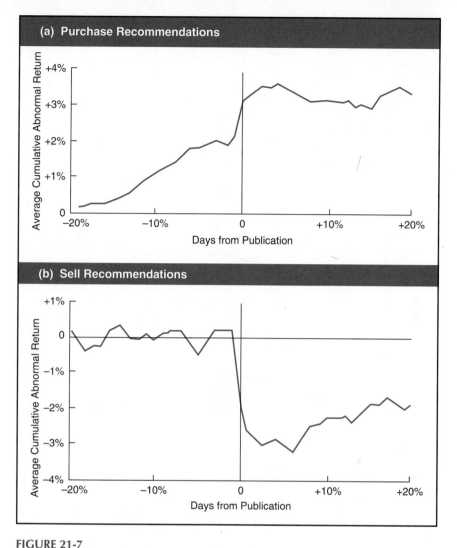

**FIGURE 21-7**

Effect on stock prices of stock recommendations in "Heard on the Street": 1970 and 1971.

*SOURCE:* Peter Lloyd Davies and Michael Canes, "Stock Prices and the Publication of Second-Hand Information," *Journal of Business* 51, no. 1 (January 1978):52.

of a sell recommendation. This suggests that the analysts did not tend to recommend the sale of securities that had recently fallen in price.

A study of the recommendations made by a regional Canadian investment service company obtained similar results.[23] This company published lists of *recommended,*

---

[23] J.Bjerring, J.Lakonishok and T.Vermaelen, "Stock Prices and Analysts' Recommendations," *Journal of Finance* 38, no. 1 (March 1983):187–204. A similar study over a later time period (March 1983 through December 1985) found that following Canadian analysts' recommendations provided substantial gains, see L.Brown, G.Richardson and C.Trzcinka, "Strong-Form Efficiency on the Toronto Stock Exchange: An

**FIGURE 21-8**
Cumulative abnormal returns from a broker's recommended list compared with the representative list, US and Canadian stocks.

*SOURCE:* J.Bjerring, J.Lakonishok and T.Vermaelen, "Stock Prices and Financial Analysts' Recommendations," *Journal of Finance* 38, no. 1 (March 1983):198.

*speculative*, and *representative* stocks. The recommended lists consisted of stocks the firm's investment committee recommended for purchase, the speculative list contained stocks regarded as risky and the representative list consisted of stocks that either had been recently dropped from the recommended list or had been evaluated by a new analyst for the first time. The stocks on the representative list were interpreted to be those an investor should hold if it was already owned, but was not encouraged to buy. The firm provided these lists for both Canadian and US stocks. Figure 21.8 presents a comparison of the cumulative abnormal returns for the combined Canadian and US stocks on the recommended and representative lists over the period September 1977 through February 1981 and covered 221 recommendations. This shows that substantial returns could be achieved by following the buy recommendations. The firm was successful in both outperforming the TSE 300 in a bull market with their Canadian recommendations and the S&P 500 with their US recommendations. Stocks on the speculative list showed negative, but not statistically significant, abnormal returns. Representative stocks showed no abnormal returns.

Examination of Analyst Price Forecasts," *Contemporary Accounting Research* 7, no. 2 (Spring 1991):323–46.

# SOURCES OF INVESTMENT INFORMATION

Since information affects the values of investments, the serious financial analyst must be well informed. There is a staggering array of such investment information, some of it published on paper (hard copy) and some of it appearing in computer-readable form.

## ☐ 21.6.1 Publications

Space precludes a detailed listing of publications relating to investing, however, Appendix B to this chapter presents a selected bibliography of general sources of investment information. Nothing can substitute for a careful perusal of these (and other) publications, and no attempt is made here to describe each one. Instead, some of the more essential sources of information for a Canadian investor are discussed below.

A serious investor should, at the very least, read *The Globe and Mail: Report on Business* and/or *The Financial Post* plus the *Wall Street Journal* and *The Financial Times* (London). These provide extensive statistical data, financial news, analysis, and even a bit of humor. Other daily newspapers contain financial information, but much less than those listed above. A weekly publication with a wealth of interesting commentary on the local scene is the *Financial Times* (Toronto).

A useful source of daily stock price and volume figures is the *Toronto Stock Exchange Daily Record*. Historical data and analyses for 70 Canadian and 30 foreign stocks can be found in the *Value Line Investment Survey: Canadian Edition*. Adjusted betas are also shown for the individual stocks in the *Survey*.[24] *The Toronto Stock Exchange Monthly Review* also contains a wealth of historical information.

In addition to providing bond quality ratings the bond rating service companies produce other useful information. For example, *Canadian Bond Rating Service* provides ratings, on a quarterly basis, for bonds and debentures, commercial paper, asset-backed securities, mortgage-backed securities, provincial and municipal government bonds, crown corporations, eurobonds, preferred shares and investment funds as well as industry and individual company financial analyses.

Publications of major security analysts' societies include the *Financial Analysts Journal*, (US); *Analyse Financière* (France); and *The Investment Analyst* (United Kingdom). Academic journals that emphasize various aspects of investing include the *Journal of Business*, the *Journal of Finance*, the *Journal of Financial and Quantitative Analysis*, the *Journal of Financial Economics,* the *Review of Financial Studies*, the *Canadian Journal of Administrative Sciences, Finéco*, and the proceedings of the *Administrative Sciences Association of Canada: Finance Division*.

Anyone interested in the management of money for institutional or corporate investors (especially pension funds) should read the *Canadian Investment Review* and the *Journal of Portfolio Management*, which publish the views of both practitioners and academicians. Periodicals aimed at institutional investors and money managers are *Benefits Canada, Canadian Business* and the *Investor's Digest*.

---

[24] These estimates for common stocks appear to be useful in helping the US investor beat the market. See the appendix to Chapter 17.

A company's annual report provides useful information, which can be supplemented by information filed with the *Ontario Securities Commission* and published in their weekly *Bulletin*.

Sources of macroeconomic data such as monetary aggregates (like the money supply) and other monetary items are the monthly *Bank of Canada Review* and the *Bank of Canada Weekly Financial Statistics*. The C.D.Howe Institute and the Economic Council of Canada provide analysis of economic conditions and forecasts on a periodic basis.

The Conference Board of Canada and Data Resources of Canada publish quarterly macroeconomic forecasts based on economic indicators. *Leading indicators* have been found to signal future changes in the economy, whereas *lagging indicators* change after the economy has done so; *coincident indicators* change simultaneously with the economy. Data on national income and production along with industry information is published regularly by the Statistics Canada.

## ☐ 21.6.2  Computer-Readable Data

The rapid increase in the use of microcomputers by those who invest money for others as well as by those who invest for themselves has led to a major expansion in the availability of computer-readable investment data.

Large amounts of financial and economic data, such as common stock prices and financial statements, are provided on magnetic tapes that are made available to investors for a fee by Standard & Poor's Canadian Compustat Services, Infoglobe, *The Financial Post* Corporate Database, Micromedia and Value Line, Inc. These databases are also available on a dial-up basis via time-shared computer services and on disks for use in microcomputers.

Dial-up services are also provided by *Telerate, Bloomberg, Interactive Data Corporation*, and others. Each service is designed so that users of microcomputers can download prices and other data into their own machines easily and inexpensively. Often the data are in spreadsheet format, readily available for analysis using, for example, Lotus 1-2-3.

Databases containing prices, fundamental information, and predictions made by brokerage houses and others are provided on compact disks by Standard and Poor's Corporation.

## 21.7  SUMMARY

Financial analysts are people who evaluate securities and then make investment recommendations. These recommendations may be used by professional money managers known as portfolio managers or by certain clients of the analyst. Typically, the financial analyst is trying to determine certain characteristics of securities and to identify mispriced securities. Most methods of performing financial analysis can be categorized as being either fundamental or technical in nature.

Fundamentalists typically forecast future sales, expenses, and earnings for firms. With these forecasts, projections of either future stock prices or returns are made. In contrast, technicians typically focus on charts of stock prices and trading volumes, looking for patterns that are in the early stages of unfolding. Once the beginning of a pattern is identified, then the future can be predicted, since it should turn out to be the ending part of the pattern.

Some financial analysts claim to have some kind of an investment system that will enable them to accurately identify mispriced securities. Furthermore, they often claim their systems have been successful in the past and produce evidence that allegedly supports their assertion. However, just because these analysts claim to have a successful system does not mean that it really has worked in the past and will continue to work in the future. Investors must carefully scrutinize any test results that may be offered, as there often is some kind of error made in assessing the track record of such systems.

## APPENDIX A

# TECHNICAL ANALYSIS

Most (but not all) technical analysts rely on charts of share prices and trading volumes. Virtually all employ colorful, and sometimes even mystical, terminology. For example, a significant price rise on relatively large trading volume might be described as an accumulation, where the stock is allegedly moving from "weak hands" to "strong hands." This is because a rising share price on large trading volume is viewed as a situation where demand is stronger than supply. In contrast, a significant price decline on relatively large trading volume may be described as a distribution, where the stock is allegedly moving from strong hands to weak hands. This is because a declining share price on large trading volume is viewed as a situation where supply is stronger than demand. In both situations, relatively large trading volume might be considered a sign of a sustainable change in the share's price, whereas relatively small trading volume indicates a transitory change.

What if there is a period when a share's price does not move significantly? If the share's price movements are within a narrow band, the stock is said to be in a consolidation phase. A price level above which a stock has difficulty rising is known as a resistance level, and a price level below which a stock does not seem to fall is known as a support level.

Such statements may sound meaningful, but they fail to pass the tests of simple logic. First of all, changes in a share's price occur when the consensus opinion concerning its value changes. This means that large volume associated with a price change reflects only a substantial difference of opinion concerning the impact of new information on the stock's value; small volume reflects smaller differences of opinion. Second, if price or volume data could be used to predict future short-term price moves, investors would rush to exploit such information, moving prices rapidly enough to make the information useless.

# CHARTS

*Chartists* (technicians who rely on chart formations) nonetheless believe that certain patterns carry great significance, although they often disagree among themselves on the significance of a pattern or even on the existence of a pattern. Before displaying some hypothetical examples of patterns, it should be noted that there are three basic types of charts used. They are known as bar charts, line charts, and point and figure charts.

For a *bar chart* the horizontal axis is a time line, with the vertical axis measuring a particular share's price. More specifically, corresponding to a given day on the horizontal axis will be a vertical line, the top and bottom of which represent the high and low price for that stock on that day. Somewhere on this vertical line will be a small horizontal line representing the closing price for the day. As an example, consider the following hypothetical stock, whose trading background over the last five days is as follows:

| Day | High Price | Low Price | Closing Price | Volume |
|-----|------------|-----------|---------------|--------|
| $t-5$ | 11 | 9 | 10 | 200 |
| $t-4$ | 12 | 9 | 11 | 300 |
| $t-3$ | 13 | 12 | 12 | 400 |
| $t-2$ | 11 | 10 | 11 | 200 |
| $t-1$ | 14 | 11 | 12 | 500 |

Part (a) of Figure 21.9 presents a bar chart for this stock, whereas part (b) indicates how such a bar chart of prices can be augmented by adding trading volume at the bottom.

Figure 21.10(a) shows a type of bar chart that is known as "head and shoulders." As time passed, the share's price initially rose, hit a peak at $A$, and then fell to a bottom at $B$. Recovering from this fall, it went up to an even higher peak at $C$ but then fell again to a bottom at $D$. Next, it rose to a peak at $E$ that was not as high as the previous peak, $C$, and then started to fall. As soon as the price went down past its previous low, $D$, immediately a forecast was made that the stock was going to plunge much lower (if the stock had not reached a level equal to $D$, no such forecast would have been made). Figure 21.10(b) shows a type of bar chart know as "inverted head and shoulders," which results in a forecast that the stock is going to rise quickly by a substantial amount.[25]

For a *line chart*, the axes are the same as with a bar chart. However, only closing prices are presented, and they are connected to each other successively with straight lines, as illustrated in part (c) of Figure 21.9. While not shown, line charts are also frequently augmented with volume data in a manner identical to bar charts.

Details of construction of *point and figure charts* vary, but the idea is to plot closing prices that form a trend in a single column, moving to the next column only when the trend is reversed. For example, closing prices might be rounded to the nearest dollar and

---

[25] For details on many kinds of patterns, see Alan R. Shaw, "Technical Analysis," in Sumner N. Levine, ed., *Financial Analyst's Handbook I* (Homewood, Ill.: Dow Jones-Irwin, Inc., 1975): 944-88; and Chapter 8 in Jerome B. Cohen, Edward D. Zinbarg, and Arthur Zeikel, *Investment Analysis and Portfolio Management* (Homewood, Ill.: Richard D. Irwin, Inc., 1987).

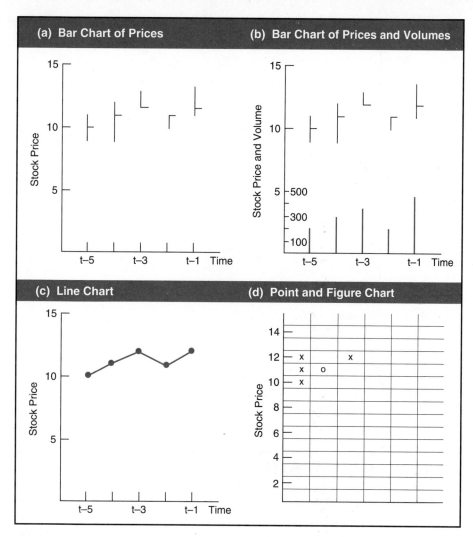

**FIGURE 21-9**
Types of charts.

the chart begun by plotting a beginning rounded price on a certain day. As long as the (rounded) price does not change, nothing is done. When a different price is recorded, it is plotted on the chart. A price higher than the initial price is indicated with an $X$, with any gaps between the prices also marked with an $X$. A price below the initial price is marked with an $O$ in a similar fashion. Then when a price that is different from the last one is recorded, it is plotted in the same column if it is in the same direction.

For example, if the first different price is above the beginning price, this price is plotted above the original. Then, if a price is recorded that is above the second one, it is plotted in the same column, but if it is below the second one, then it is plotted in a new column to the right of the first column. Continuing, as long as new prices are in the same direction, they are plotted in the same column. Whenever there is a reversal, a new

**FIGURE 21-10**
Bar chart patterns.

column is started. Part (d) of Figure 21.9 presents a point and figure chart for the same hypothetical stock used in the other panels.

Point and figure enthusiasts look for all sorts of patterns in their charts. As with all chartist techniques, the idea is to recognize a pattern early enough to profit from one's ability to foresee the future course of prices — a neat trick, if one can do it.

## A.2   MOVING AVERAGES

Many other procedures are used by technicians. Some construct moving averages to try to detect "intermediate" and long-term" trends. Here a set number of the most recent closing prices on a security are averaged each day. (For example, daily closing prices over the previous 200 days may be used.) This means that each day, the oldest price is replaced with the most recent price in the set of closing prices that will be averaged. Frequently a line chart of these moving averages is plotted along with a line chart of daily closing prices. Each day the charts are updated and then examined for trends to see if there is a buy or sell signal present somewhere.

Alternatively, a long-term moving average may be compared with a short-term moving average (the distinction between the two averages is that the long-term average uses a substantially larger set of closing prices in its calculations than the short-term average). When the short-term average crosses the long-term average, a "signal" is said to have been given. The action recommended will depend on such things as whether the averages have been rising or falling, as well as the direction from which the short-term average crossed the long-term average (it may have been below and now is above, or it may have been above and now is below).

**FIGURE 21-11**
Moving average price chart for 90 day Euro-dollar charts March '92 futures.
*SOURCE:* The Canada Life Assurance Company, January 1992.

**A.3**  **RELATIVE STRENGTH MEASURES**

Another procedure used by technicians involves measuring what they call relative strength. For example, a share's price may be divided by a price index of its industry each day to indicate the stock's movement relative to its industry. Similarly, an industry index may be divided by a market index to indicate the industry's movement relative to the market, or a share's price may be divided by a market index to indicate a stock's movement relative to the market. The idea here is to examine changes in these relative strength measures with the hope of finding a pattern that can be used to accurately predict the future.

Some procedures of technical analysts focus on relationships among different indexes. For example, the Dow theory requires that a pattern in the Dow Jones Industrial Average be "confirmed" by a certain movement in the Dow Jones Railroad (now Transportation) Average before action be taken. Another example involves computing the difference between the number of issues advancing and the number declining each day. A chart of the differences cumulated over time, known as the advance-decline line, may then be compared with a market index such as the Dow Jones Industrial Average.

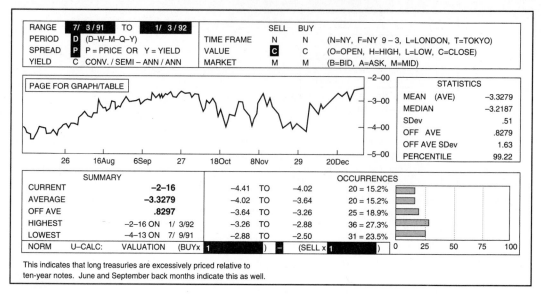

**FIGURE 21-12**
Historical price spread between US Treasury bonds and notes.

*SOURCE:* The Canada Life Assurance Company, January 1992.

## A.4 CONTRARY OPINION

A large number of technical procedures are based on the idea of contrary opinion. The idea here is to determine what the losers are doing and then do the opposite. For example, one might see whether the "odd-lotters" (those who buy and sell in lots of less than 100 shares each) are buying and then sell any holdings of these stocks. If "the little investor is usually wrong," this will be a procedure that is usually right. However, the basic premise about the little investor has yet to be established.

The widespread availability of personal computers and "dial-up" services with data on share prices and volumes has made it possible for individual investors to engage in technical analysis in the privacy of their own homes. Producers of software have been quick to provide programs to perform such analysis, complete with multicolored graphs. Nevertheless, the number of individual investors that use fundamental analysis is much larger than the number using technical analysis. Furthermore, fundamental analysis is also the dominant method among those who manage money for a living, the professional money managers.

The use of charts to forecast the future and to find undervalued securities is not confined to the stock market. Figures 21.11 to 21.12 show two charts prepared for an institutional fixed income investor and include the analyst's interpretation of the trends that are presented. The chart in Figure 21.11 could be used (together with other information) in the preparation of an interest rate forecast, while Figure 21.12 identifies a pricing imbalance between US Treasury bonds (maturities over 10 years) and US Treasury Notes (maturities from one to ten years).

## APPENDIX B

# SOURCES OF INVESTMENT INFORMATION

I. General Information on Business and Financial Developments
- A. Economic and Financial Data
  1. *Bank of Canada Review*
  2. *Bank of England Quarterly Bulletin*
  3. *Federal Reserve Bank Reviews* (US)
  4. Statistics Canada Publications
     - a. *Canada Year Book* (bienniel)
     - b. *Canadian Statistical Review* (monthly)
     - c. *Canadian Economic Observer* (monthly)
     - d. *Canadian Economic Observer: Historical Statistical Supplement* (annual)
     - e. *National Income and Expenditure Accounts* (quarterly)
     - f. *Financial Flow Accounts* (quarterly)
     - g. *Financial Flow and National Balance Sheet Accounts* (annual)
- B. Daily Newspapers
  1. *The Globe and Mail: Report on Business*
  2. *The Financial Post*
  3. *The Wall Street Journal* (US)
  4. *Financial Times* (UK)
  5. *Journal of Commerce* (US)
- C. Weekly Publications
  1. *Financial Times*
  2. *The Economist* (UK)
  3. *Barron's* (US)
  4. *Business Week* (US)
  5. *Newsweek* (US)
  6. *Time* (US)
  7. *US News and World Report*
- D. Magazines
  1. *Canadian Business*

    2. *Canadian Shareowner*

    3. *Benefits Canada*

    4. *Alberta Business*

    5. *Metropolitan Toronto Business Journal*

    6. *Enterprise*

    7. *Profit: The Magazine for Entrepreneurs*

    8. *Forbes* (US)

    9. *Fortune* (US)

    10. *Financial Executive* (US)

E. Practitioner Journals

    1. *Canadian Investment Review*

    2. *Business Quarterly*

    3. *Mergers and Acquisitions*

    4. *Financial Analysts Journal* (US)

    5. *Journal of Portfolio Management* (US)

    6. *Harvard Business Review* (US)

    7. *Mergers and Acquisitions* (US)

    8. *Institutional Investor* (US)

F. Academic Journals

    1. *Canadian Journal of Administrative Sciences*

    2. *Canadian Journal of Economics*

    3. *Journal of Business Administration*

    4. *Canadian Journal of World Business*

    5. *Journal of Business*

    6. *Journal of Finance*

    7. *Journal of Financial and Quantitative Analysis*

    8. *Journal of Banking and Finance*

    9. *Journal of Money, Credit and Banking*

    10. *Review of Financial Studies*

II. Industry Information

A. Statistics Canada Publications

    a. *Gross Domestic Product by Industry* (monthly)

    b. *Monthly Survey of Manufacturing*

    c. *Manufacturing Industries of Canada, National and Provincial Areas* (annual)

    d. *Quarterly Financial Statistics for Enterprises*

    e. *Corporation Financial Statistics* (annual)

    f. *Corporation Taxation Statistics* (annual)

    g. Individual Industry Reports classified by two and three digit SIC code

B. Reports by Investment Services

    1. *Canadian Credit Review*

    2. *Canadian Bond Rating Service Industry Studies*

    3. *The Polymetric Report* (TSE Edition)

    4. Globe Information Services

5. *The Financial Post* Publications
   a. *Survey of Industrials*
   b. *Survey of Mines and Energy Resources*
   c. *Survey of Predecessor and Defunct Companies*
6. Reports and Brochures published by Brockerage and Banking Firms

III. Company Information

A. Corporate Reports
   1. Annual reports to Shareholders
   2. *The Financial Post* Card Service
   3. Company prospectuses
   4. *Ontario Securities Commission Weekly Report*

B. Publications by Financial Service Companies
   1. *The Financial Post*
      a. *Corporate Earnings Record*
      b. *Annual Dividend Record*
      c. *Record of New Issues*
      d. *Corporate Actions*
      e. *International Data Service: Company Evaluations*
      f. *Corporate Bond Prices*
      g. *Corporate Bond Record*
      h. *Preferred Shares and Warrants*
      i. *Survey of Funds*
      j. *Mutual Fund Fundamentals*
   2. Globe Information Services: Financial and Investment Databases
      a. *Marketscan Plus*
      b. *Corporate Canada On-line*
      c. *The Report on Business Corporate Database*
      d. *Canadian Financial Database*
      e. *Mutual Funds*
   3. *The Polymetric Report*
   4. *The Value Line Investment Survey: Canadian Edition*
   5. Canadian Bond Rating Service
      a. *Credit Analysis*
      b. *Corporate Reports*
      c. *Corporate Analyst*
      d. *Mutual Fund Ratings*
      e. *Corporate Debt Security Ratings*
      f. *Preferred Share Ratings*
      g. *Commercial Paper Ratings*
   6. Dominion Bond Rating Service
      a. *Commercial and Short Term Security Ratings*
      b. *Bond and Long Term Security Ratings*
      c. *Preferred Share Ratings*
   7. Toronto Stock Exchange
      a. *Company Manual*
      b. *Listing Statement*

## QUESTIONS AND PROBLEMS

1. It is often argued that the TSE 300 is a better indicator than the TSE 35 of the performance of the entire Canadian stock market. Explain the reasoning behind this contention.

2. Consider three stocks, X, Y, and Z, with the following closing prices per share on two particular dates:

| Stock | Date 1 | Date 2 |
|-------|--------|--------|
| X | $16 | $24 |
| Y | 5 | 4 |
| Z | 24 | 32 |

On date 1 there are 100 shares of stock X, 200 shares of stock Y, and 100 shares of stock Z outstanding.

    a. Construct a price-weighted market index using the three stocks, X, Y, and Z. What is the index's value on date 1?

    b. What is the price-weighted index's value on date 2?

    c. Assume that on date 2, stock X splits 4-for-1. What is the price-weighted index's value on that date?

    d. Construct a value-weighted index using the three stocks. Assign the value-weighted index a value of 100 on date 1. What is the index's value on date 2?

3. According to Frank Fain, "The success of a stock market index depends on its ability to measure the performance of stocks not included in the index." Explain what Frank means.

4. Compare the price reaction to the purchase of stocks that have been identified with a system that previously has been able to "beat the market" with the reactions to (a) the accurate prediction of rainfall, and (b) the accurate prediction of the locations of enemy submarines.

5. If security markets are highly efficient, what role is there for financial analysts?

6. Listed below are several test results from studies of mechanical investment systems. For each test result, identify the primary research error committed and comment as to why the error is applicable to the study.

    a. A portfolio managed using a filter rule (that is, buying a stock after it has appreciated in price by x%, holding the stock until its price has depreciated by x%, then selling the stock) outperforms a broad market index when the filter is very small (that is, when x is small).

    b. An investment system estimated over the 1970 to 1980 time period indicates that the system outperformed a broad market index in the latter half of that period.

    c. A portfolio composed of stocks of highly cyclical industrial companies outperforms a broad market index.

    d. Buying and selling Canadian stocks based on a measure of liberal and conservative voting patterns in Great Britain produces returns that outperform a broad Canadian market index.

    e. The price performance of a portfolio of ipo (that is, initial public offering) high-technology stocks outperforms a broad market index.

7. Ben Falk, a portfolio manager for a large pension fund, is fond of saying "Buy low, sell high." Why is Ben's suggested system not operational?

8. Distinguish between "top-down" and "bottom-up" approaches to financial forecasting. What are the primary advantages and disadvantages of each approach?

9. Is it true that when comparing the reported earnings of corporations, "a dollar is a dollar"?

10. (Appendix Question) Technical analysis is predicated on share prices moving in repetitive patterns. What would one have to believe about the timing of the receipt of information by financial markets participants in order to believe in the existence of such patterns?

11. (Appendix Question) The closing, high, and low prices for Canada Packers stock over a ten-day interval are shown below. Construct a bar chart for Canada Packers stock over this period of time.

| Canada Packers | | | |
|---|---|---|---|
| Day | Closing Price | High | Low |
| 1 | 20 | 21 | 19 |
| 2 | $20\frac{1}{4}$ | $20\frac{1}{4}$ | 18 |
| 3 | 21 | 22 | $20\frac{1}{2}$ |
| 4 | $21\frac{1}{8}$ | $22\frac{7}{8}$ | $21\frac{1}{8}$ |
| 5 | 21 | $23\frac{1}{4}$ | 20 |
| 6 | $21\frac{3}{4}$ | 22 | $20\frac{3}{4}$ |
| 7 | 22 | $23\frac{1}{2}$ | $20\frac{1}{8}$ |
| 8 | $20\frac{1}{8}$ | 22 | $19\frac{1}{4}$ |
| 9 | $19\frac{1}{8}$ | $21\frac{1}{2}$ | 19 |
| 10 | $18\frac{1}{4}$ | $21\frac{7}{8}$ | $17\frac{1}{8}$ |

12. (Appendix Question) Calculate the relative strength of Canada Packers stock versus the TSE 300 over the ten-day period referred to in problem 11, given the following closing prices for the TSE 300:

| | | | | | Day | | | | | |
|---|---|---|---|---|---|---|---|---|---|---|
| | 1 | 2 | 3 | 4 | 5 | 6 | 7 | 8 | 9 | 10 |
| TSE 300 Closing Price | 300 | 302 | 306 | 310 | 320 | 315 | 330 | 325 | 325 | 330 |

## SUGGESTED READINGS

The Toronto Stock Exchange provides information on the structure and level of its indices in publications such as the *Index Monthly Report covering the TSE 300 Composite Index and Toronto 35 Index: A Measure of Opportunity.*

*The Canadian Securities Course* (Toronto, Ont.: The Canadian Securities Institute, 1989). Chapter 13 describes the fundamental and technical factors affecting security prices.

Jack L. Treynor and Fischer Black, "How to Use Security Analysis to Improve Portfolio Selection," *Journal of Business* 46, no. 1 (January 1973):66–86 demonstrates how to use the results of security analysis to improve performance.

# Chapter 22

# INVESTMENT MANAGEMENT

Investment management, also known as portfolio management, is the process by which money is managed. It may be active or passive, may use explicit or implicit procedures, and may be relatively controlled or uncontrolled. The trend is toward highly controlled operations consistent with the notion that capital markets are relatively efficient. However, approaches vary, and many different investment styles can be found. This chapter discusses investment management and in doing so presents various types of investment styles.

## 22.1 TRADITIONAL INVESTMENT MANAGEMENT ORGANIZATIONS

Few like to be called "traditional." However, many investment management organizations follow procedures that have changed little from those that were popular decades ago and thus deserve the title. Figure 22.1 shows the major characteristics of a typical organization of this type.

Projections concerning the economy, security and money markets, and so on are made (often qualitatively) by economists, technicians, fundamentalists or other market experts within or outside the organization. The projected economic environment is communicated via briefings, reports, and so on — usually in a rather implicit and qualitative manner — to the organization's *security analysts*. Each analyst is responsible for a group of securities, often those in one or more industries (in some organizations, analysts are called industry specialists). Often a group of analysts report to a senior analyst responsible for a sector of the economy or market.

The analysts, often drawing heavily on reports of others (for example, "street analysts" in brokerage houses), make predictions about the securities for which they are responsible. In a sense, such predictions are conditional on the assumed economic and market environments, although the relationship is typically quite loose.

Analysts' predictions seldom specify an expected rate of return or the time over which predicted performance will take place. Instead, an analyst's feelings about a security are often summarized by assigning it one of five codes, where a 1 represents a buy and a 5 represents a sell, as indicated in Figure 22.1. (Some organizations reverse the numbers, so that a 5 is a buy and a 1 is a sell; some European organizations favor

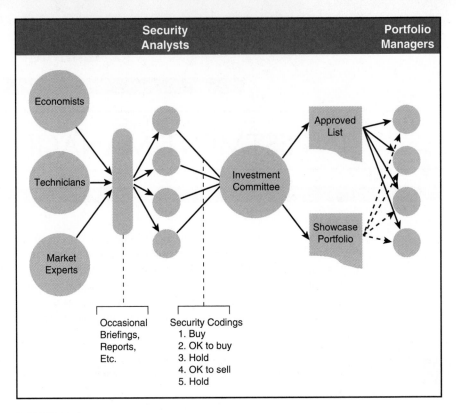

Economists

Technicians

Market
Experts

Investment
Committee

Approved
List

Showcase
Portfolio

Occasional
Briefings,
Reports,
Etc.

Security Codings
1. Buy
2. OK to buy
3. Hold
4. OK to sell
5. Hold

**FIGURE 22-1**
A traditional investment management organization.

five codes that are denoted by $+$, $0+$, $0$, $0-$, and $-$; some organizations have long-term lists as well as short-term lists.)[1]

These security codings constitute the information formally transmitted to an *investment committee*, which typically includes the senior management of the organization. In addition, analysts occasionally brief the investment committee on their feelings about various securities. The investment commitee's major formal output is often an *approved* (or authorized) *list*, which consists of the securities deemed worthy of accumulation in a given portfolio. The rules of the organization typically specify that any security on the list may be bought, while those not on the list should be either held or sold, barring special circumstances.

The presence or absence of a security on the approved list constitutes the major information transmitted explicitly from the investment committee to a *portfolio manager* (or, for example, a trust officer in a bank). In some organizations, senior management supervises a "showcase portfolio" (for example, a bank's major commingled equity

---

[1] One study found that a firm's share price tended to move upward when analysts upgraded its coding and downward when analysts downgraded its coding. See Edwin J. Elton, Martin J. Gruber, and Seth Grossman, "Discrete Expectational Data and Portfolio Performance," *Journal of Finance* 41, no. 3 (July 1986):699–713; also see footnote 22 in Chapter 21.

fund), the composition of which indicates to portfolio managers the relative intensity of senior management's feelings regarding different securities.

In many ways, this description is a caricature of an investment organization — even one run along traditional lines. But many of these attributes can be observed in practice. Traditional organizations may deal with uncertainty only obliquely, and they may utilize inconsistent estimates. Furthermore, they may fail to fully take into account the relative efficiency of modern capital markets.

## 22.2 INVESTMENT MANAGEMENT FUNCTIONS

In Chapter 1, a five-step procedure was outlined for making investment decisions. These steps can all be viewed as functions of investment management, and must be undertaken for each client whose money is being managed. They are as follows:

1. *Set investment policy* — determine how much investable wealth the client has, as well as pinpointing his or her investment objectives.
2. *Perform security analysis* — scrutinize individual securities or groups of securities in order to identify mispriced situations.
3. *Construct a portfolio* — identify specific securities to invest in, along with the proportion of investable wealth to be put in each security.
4. *Revise the portfolio* — determine which securities in the current portfolio are to be sold and which securities are to be purchased to replace them.
5. *Evaluate the performance of the portfolio* — determine the actual performance of a portfolio in terms of risk and return, and compare the performance with that of an appropriate "benchmark" portfolio.

The remainder of this chapter deals with how an investment management organization would perform the first four functions; the next chapter deals with the fifth function.

## 22.3 SETTING INVESTMENT POLICY

One of the key characteristics that differentiates clients from one another concerns their investment objectives. According to modern portfolio theory, these objectives are reflected in the client's attitude toward risk and expected return. As mentioned in Chapter 6, indifference curves are one method of describing these objectives. However, determining a client's indifference curves is not a simple task. In practice, it is often done in an indirect and approximate fashion by estimating the client's level of *risk tolerance*, denoted by $\tau$.[2]

---

[2] The following analysis is discussed in more detail in William F. Sharpe, *Asset Allocation Tools* (Redwood City, Calif.: The Scientific Press, 1987):34–39; and William F. Sharpe, "Integrated Asset Allocation," *Financial Analysts Journal* 43, no. 5 (September/October 1987):25–32.

## ☐ 22.3.1  Estimating Risk Tolerance

The starting point in making an estimation of risk tolerance is to provide the client with a set of estimates of the risks and expected returns for different combinations of two hypothetical portfolios. For example, imagine the client is told that the expected return on a stock portfolio is 12%, whereas the return on a risk-free portfolio consisting of Treasury bills is 7.5% (that is, $\bar{r}_S = 12\%$ and $r_F = 7.5\%$). Similarly, the client is told that the standard deviation on the stock portfolio is 15%, whereas the standard deviation on the risk-free portfolio is, by definition, 0.0% (that is, $\sigma_S = 15\%$ and $\sigma_F = 0.0\%$). Additionally, the client is told that all combinations of these two portfolios lie on a straight line that connects them (this is because the covariance between these two portfolios is 0.0, meaning that $\sigma_{SF} = 0.0$). Some combinations of these two portfolios are shown in Table 22.1.

TABLE 22.1

Combinations of Stock and Risk-Free Treasury Bill Portfolios.

| Proportion in | | Expected Return | Standard Deviation | Implied Level of Risk Tolerance |
|---|---|---|---|---|
| Stocks | Bonds | | | |
| 100% | 0% | 12.00% | 15.0% | 100% |
| 90 | 10 | 11.55 | 13.5 | 90 |
| 80 | 20 | 11.10 | 12.0 | 80 |
| 70 | 30 | 10.65 | 10.5 | 70 |
| 60 | 40 | 10.20 | 9.0 | 60 |
| 50 | 50 | 9.75 | 7.5 | 50 |
| 40 | 60 | 9.30 | 6.0 | 40 |
| 30 | 70 | 8.85 | 4.5 | 30 |
| 20 | 80 | 8.40 | 3.0 | 20 |
| 10 | 90 | 7.95 | 1.5 | 10 |
| 0 | 100 | 7.50 | 0.0 | 00 |

Note that the investor is being presented with the efficient set that arises given a set of stocks and risk-free borrowing and lending rates. As shown in Chapter 7, this efficient set is linear, meaning it is a straight line that emanates at the risk-free rate and goes through a tangency portfolio that consists of a certain combination of common stocks.

At this point, the client is asked to identify the combination that appears to be most desirable, in terms of expected return and standard deviation. Note that asking the investor to identify the most desirable combination is equivalent to asking the investor to locate where his or her indifference curves are tangent to the linear efficient set, since this point will represent the most desirable portfolio.[3]

---

[3] If such a decision is made on behalf of the client (for example, by a trustee for one or more beneficiaries), the task is much more difficult, but a decision is still required.

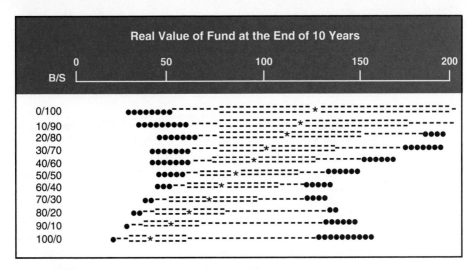

**FIGURE 22-2**
Effect of the bond/stock mix on the real value of an endowment fund.

## □ 22.3.2 The Trade-off Between Risk and Expected Return

Investment managers and advisory organizations have developed various procedures for helping clients understand the trade-off between risk and expected return so that they can make reasonable decisions in this regard. Figure 22.2 illustrates one of these methods.

### An Example

Figure 22.2 is based on a study done for a college. At the time of the study, an amount equal to 6% of the market value of the college's endowment fund was being spent each year. The study assumed that the amount spent in future years would be the same in real dollars. Given this assumption, what might be the real dollar value of the fund at the end of ten years, and how might this be affected by the proportions invested in stocks and bonds?

To answer the question, historical real returns from representative portfolios of bonds and stocks were used. For example, to construct the bar graph at the top of Figure 22.2, a mix of 0% in bonds and 100% in stocks was assumed. The value of the fund was assumed to equal 100 at the beginning of 1926, and year-by-year results were computed for the ten-year period from 1926 through 1935, using the assumed 6% spending rule and the actual real returns in each year. The real value of the fund at the end of 1935 was then determined. The procedure was repeated using returns from 1927 through 1936, 1928 through 1937, and so on, ending with the ten-year period of 1975 through 1984. Thus, 50 periods of ten years each were examined.

The bar graph summarizes the frequency distribution of the resulting 50 end-of-period real values, as follows:

```
Percent of      ....  ------------- * ------------------ ....
Cases Below   ᴀ    ᴀ        ᴀ              ᴀ              ᴀ      ᴀ  ᴀ
Plotted
Value         5   15       25             50             75    85 95
```

Note that the asterisk indicates the *median* real dollar value of the fund at the end of ten years for various mixes of stocks and bonds. For the 0/100 mix, the median value of the fund at the end of ten years was approximately 125, or 25% higher than at the start. As can be seen, the lower the proportion in stocks, the lower the median value.

However, attention should also be given to the dispersion of ending values. This can be done by looking at the distance between the left-most and right-most dots. For example, looking at the 60/40 mix, it can be seen that 5% of the time the fund had a value at the end of ten years that was equal to or less than 40 (the left-most dot), and that 5% of the time it had an ending value equal to or greater than 130 (the right-most dot). Thus, 90% of the time (that is, for 45 of the 50 ten-year periods) the ending value was between 40 and 130. In general, it can be seen that the dispersion of possible ending values decreases with a decrease in the proportion invested in stocks until the mix is roughly 60/40, and then the dispersion starts to increase as the proportion in stocks drops further.

In summary, this kind of information is useful in helping the client understand the implications of a portfolio having a higher level of expected return as well as a higher standard deviation. With such information, the client can more easily decide on the stock/bond mix felt to be best.

After the client has selected the best stock/bond mix, what can be said about his or her risk tolerance? One would, of course, like to identify all the indifference curves that represent a client's attitude toward risk and expected return. However, in practice a more modest goal is usually adopted—to obtain a reasonable representation of the shape of such curves in the likely region of risk and expected return within which the client's optimal choices will most likely fall.

The points in Figure 22.3 plot the alternative mixes presented to the client that were given in Table 22.1. Curve *FCS* shows the risk-return characteristics of all possible mixes and point *C* identifies the attributes of the mix chosen by the client. Note that in this figure, expected return is measured on the vertical axis and variance on the horizontal axis. Although the combinations available to the client plot on a straight line when standard deviation is measured on the horizontal axis, the combinations plot on a concave curve when variance is used (as in this figure).

Assuming that all the possible mixes had been presented to the client and point *C* had been chosen, it could be inferred that the slope of the client's indifference curve going through *C* is precisely equal to that of curve *FCS* at this point. As mentioned earlier, this follows from the observation that the portfolio on the efficient set that a client identifies as being the best one corresponds to the one where the client's indifference curves are just tangent to the efficient set.

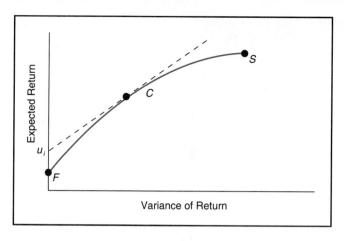

Variance of Return

**FIGURE 22-3**
Inferring client risk tolerance.

### □ 22.3.3 Constant Risk Tolerance

In principle, the choice of a mix provides information about the slope of an indifference curve at only one point. To go beyond this, an assumption must be made about the general shape of the client's indifference curves. An assumption commonly made is that the client has constant risk tolerance over a range of alternative portfolios in the neighborhood of the point originally chosen. Figure 22.4 shows the nature of this assumption. As indicated in part (a), indifference curves in a diagram with variance on the horizontal axis are *linear* when it is assumed that the client has constant risk tolerance. This means that the equation for an indifference curve of such an investor is equivalent to the equation for a straight line, where the variable on the horizontal axis is variance ($\sigma_p^2$) and the variable on the vertical axis is expected return ($\bar{r}_p$). Given that the equation of a straight line takes the form of $Y = a + bX$, where $a$ is the vertical intercept and $b$ is the slope, the equation for an indifference curve can be written as

$$\bar{r}_p = a + b\sigma_p^2$$

or

$$\bar{r}_p = u_i + \frac{1}{\tau}\sigma_p^2 \qquad (22.1)$$

where $u_i$ is the vertical intercept for indifference curve $i$ and the slope of the indifference curve is $1/\tau$. Note how any two indifference curves for a client differ from one another by the value of the vertical intercept. This is because the indifference curves are parallel, meaning they have the same slope, $1/\tau$.

Figure 22.4(b) plots the same indifference curves in a more familiar manner — with *standard deviation* on the horizontal axis. Note that the curves have the conventional shape — they indicate that the investor requires more return to compensate for an additional unit of standard deviation as the risk of the portfolio increases. That is, the curves are *convex* when standard deviation is measured on the horizontal axis.

In order to estimate the client's level of risk tolerance, $\tau$, it was mentioned that the slope of the indifference curves, $1/\tau$, would be set equal to the slope of the efficient

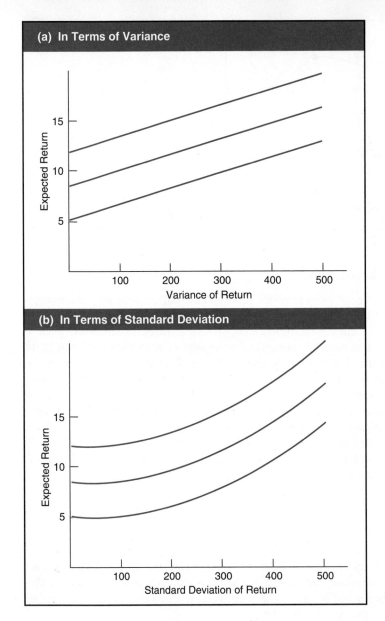

**(a) In Terms of Variance**

Expected Return

Variance of Return

**(b) In Terms of Standard Deviation**

Expected Return

Standard Deviation of Return

**FIGURE 22-4**
Constant risk tolerance.

set at the location of the portfolio that was selected, denoted by portfolio $C$. Doing so results in the following formula for estimating $\tau$:

$$\tau = \frac{2[(\bar{r}_C - r_F)\sigma_S^2]}{(\bar{r}_S - r_F)^2} \tag{22.2}$$

where $\bar{r}_C$ denotes the expected return of the portfolio that the client selected, $\bar{r}_S$ and $r_F$ denote the expected return of the stock portfolio and risk-free rate, respectively, and $\sigma_S^2$

denotes the variance of the stock portfolios. (A detailed presentation of how this formula was derived is presented in the appendix to this chapter.)

In the example, the client was given a choice between $S$, $F$, and various combinations of $S$ and $F$, where $\bar{r}_S = 12\%$, $r_F = 7.5\%$, and $\sigma_S^2 = (15)^2 = 225$. By using equation (22.2), the level of risk tolerance $\tau$ inferred from the choice of portfolio $C$ can be determined to be equal to

$$\tau = \frac{2[(\bar{r}_C - 7.5)225]}{(12 - 7.5)^2}$$
$$= 22.22\bar{r}_C - 166.67. \qquad (22.3)$$

Assuming the choice of a portfolio consisting of a 50% investment in stocks and a 50% investment in risk-free Treasury bills, the client in this example has chosen a portfolio $C$ with an expected return of 9.75%. Accordingly, equation (22.3) can be used to determine the value of $\tau$ for this client, resulting in an estimated level of risk tolerance $\tau$ equal to $50 = (22.22 \times 9.75) - 166.67$. Thus, the client's indifference curves are estimated to have the form of

$$\bar{r}_p = u_i + \frac{1}{50}\sigma_p^2. \qquad (22.4)$$

Table 22.1 shows the inferred level of risk tolerance $\tau$ if a different portfolio had been chosen by the client (these levels were determined by substituting the appropriate values for $\bar{r}_C$ into the right-hand side of equation (22.3) and then solving for $\tau$). First, note that the level of risk tolerance is the same as the percentage invested in the stock portfolio associated with $C$. That is, equation (22.3) can be rewritten as $\tau = 100X_S$, where $X_S$ is the proportion invested in the stock portfolio associated with $C$. It can be shown that this will always be the case when $\bar{r}_S - r_F = 4.5\%$ and $\sigma_S = 15\%$, figures that correspond very roughly to the postwar experience in Canada and the United States.

Second, note how the level of risk tolerance is lower if the selected portfolio is more conservative (that is, when the level of expected return and standard deviation is lower). Thus, more conservative risk-averse clients will have lower levels of risk tolerance than less conservative risk-averse clients.

Having estimated the client's indifference curves, recall from Chapter 6 that the objective of investment management is to identify the portfolio that lies on the indifference curve furthest to the northwest, because such a portfolio will offer the investor the level of expected return and risk that is preferable to all the other portfolios. This is equivalent to identifying the portfolio that lies on the indifference curve that has the highest vertical intercept, $u_i$. This can be seen graphically in Figure 22.4(a) and (b), where the indifference curves have been extended to the vertical axis.

## ☐ 22.3.4 Certainty Equivalent Return

The term $u_i$ can be thought of as the *certainty equivalent return* for any portfolio that lies on indifference curve $i$.[4] Thus, portfolio $C$ in Figure 22.3 is as desirable for this particular client as a portfolio with an expected return of $u_i$ and no risk — that is, one providing a

---

[4] The term $u_i$ is also known as the expected utility of indifference curve i; it represents the level of satisfaction associated with all portfolios plotting on indifference curve i.

return of $u_i$ with certainty. When viewed in this manner, the job of the portfolio manager is to identify the portfolio with the highest certainty equivalent return.

Equation (22.1) can be rewritten so that the certainty equivalent return $u_i$ appears on the left-hand side. Doing so results in

$$u_i = \bar{r}_p - \frac{1}{\tau}\sigma_p^2. \tag{22.5}$$

This equation shows that the certainty equivalent return can be thought of as a risk-adjusted expected return, since a risk penalty that depends on the portfolio's variance and the client's risk tolerance is subtracted from the portfolio's expected return in determining $u_i$.

In the example, the investor selected the portfolio with $\bar{r}_p = 9.75\%$ and $\sigma_p^2 = 7.5^2 = 56.25$. Thus, the certainty equivalent return for this portfolio is $9.75 - (56.25/50) = 8.625\%$. Equivalently, the risk penalty for the portfolio that was selected was $56.25/50 = 1.125\%$. If the certainty equivalent return for any other portfolio shown in Table 22.1 is calculated, it will have a lower value (for example, the 80/20 portfolio has a certainty equivalent return of $11.1 - (144/50) = 8.22\%$). Thus, the goal of investment management can be thought of as identifying the portfolio that has the maximum value of $\bar{r}_p - (\sigma_p^2/\tau)$, since it will provide the client with the maximum certainty equivalent return.

## 22.4  SECURITY ANALYSIS AND PORTFOLIO CONSTRUCTION

### ☐ 22.4.1  Passive and Active Management

Within the investment industry, a distinction is often made between *passive management* — holding securities for relatively long periods with small and infrequent changes — and *active management*. Passive managers generally act as if the security markets are relatively efficient. Put somewhat differently, their decisions are consistent with the acceptance of consensus estimates of risk and return. The portfolios they hold may be surrogates for the market portfolios that are known as *index funds*, or they may be portfolios that are tailored to suit clients with characteristics that differ from those of the average investor.[5] In either case, passive portfolio managers do not try to beat the market.

For example, a passive manager might only have to choose the appropriate mixture of Treasury bills and an index fund that is a surrogate for the market portfolio. The best mixture would depend on the shape and location of the client's indifference curves. Figure 22.5 provides an illustration.

Point $F$ plots the risk-free return offered by Treasury bills, and point $M$ plots the risk and expected return of the surrogate market portfolio, using consensus estimates. Mixtures of the two investments plot along line $FM$. The client's attitude toward risk and return is shown by the set of indifference curves, and the optimal mixture lies at the point $O^*$, where an indifference curve is tangent to line $FM$. In this example, the best

---

[5] An example of a tailored portfolio would be one consisting of stocks with high dividend yields. Such a portfolio might be purchased for a corporate investor, since in Canada all dividends received by corporations are exempt from corporate income tax. See Chapter 10.

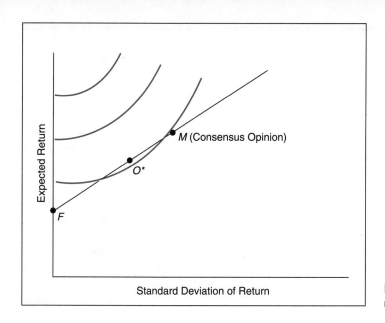

**FIGURE 22-5**
Passive investment management.

mixture uses both Treasury bills and the surrogate market portfolio. In other situations, the surrogate market portfolio might be "levered up" by borrowing (that is, money might be borrowed and added to the client's own investable funds, with the total being used to purchase the surrogate market portfolio).

When management is passive, the overall mixture is altered only when (1) the client's preferences change or (2) the consensus opinion about the risk and return of the surrogate market portfolio changes. The manager must continue to assess the latter and keep in touch with the client concerning the former. But no additional activity is required.

Active managers believe that from time to time there are mispriced securities or groups of securities. They do not act as if they believe that security markets are efficient. Put somewhat differently, they use deviant predictions; that is, their estimates of risks and expected returns differ from consensus opinions. While some managers may be more bullish than average about a security, other managers may be more bearish. The former will hold "more-than-normal" proportions of the security, whereas the latter will hold "less-than-normal" proportions.

Assuming there is no tailoring, it is useful to think of a portfolio as having two components: (1) a market portfolio (actually, a surrogate for it) and (2) deviations designed to take advantage of security mispricing. For example, a portfolio can be broken down as follows:

| Name of Security (Col. 1) | Proportion in Actual Portfolio (Col. 2) | Proportion in Market Portfolio (Col. 3) | Active Position (Col. 4) |
|---|---|---|---|
| $S_1$ | .30 | .45 | −.15 |
| $S_2$ | .20 | .25 | −.05 |
| $S_3$ | .50 | .30 | +.20 |
| | 1.00 | 1.00 | .00 |

The second column shows the actual proportions in the actively managed portfolio. The third column indicates the percentages in a hypothetical surrogate market portfolio — the holdings that might be best for an average client in a perfectly efficient market. The active positions can be represented by the differences between the proportions in the actual and market portfolios. Such differences arise because active managers disagree with the consensus about expected returns or risks. When expressed as differences of this sort, the actual portfolio can be viewed as an investment in the market portfolio with a series of *bets* being placed on certain securities (such as $S_3$) and against certain other securities (such as $S_1$ and $S_2$).

## ☐ 22.4.2 Security Selection, Asset Allocation, and Market Timing

### Security Selection

In principle, the investment manager should make predictions of expected returns, standard deviations, and covariances for all available securities. This will allow an efficient set to be generated, upon which the indifference curves of the client can be plotted. Having done this, the investment manager should invest in those securities that form the optimal portfolio (that is, the portfolio indicated by the point where the indifference curves are tangent to the efficient set) for the client in question. Such a one-stage *security-selection* process is illustrated in Figure 22.6(a).

In practice, this is rarely (if ever) done. Excessive costs would be incurred to obtain detailed predictions of the expected returns, standard deviations, and covariances for all the individual securities under consideration. Instead, the decision of which securities to purchase is made in two or more stages.

Figure 22.6(b) illustrates a two-stage procedure where the investment manager has decided to consider investing in a number of common stocks and corporate bonds for a client. In this case, the expected returns, standard deviations, and covariances are estimated for all common stocks under consideration. Then, based on just these common stocks, the efficient set is formed and the optimal stock portfolio is identified. Next, the same analysis is performed for all corporate bonds under consideration, resulting in the identification of the optimal bond portfolio. The security selection process used in each of these two *asset classes* can be described as being myopic. That is, covariances between the individual common stocks and corporate bonds have not been considered in the identification of the two optimal portfolios.

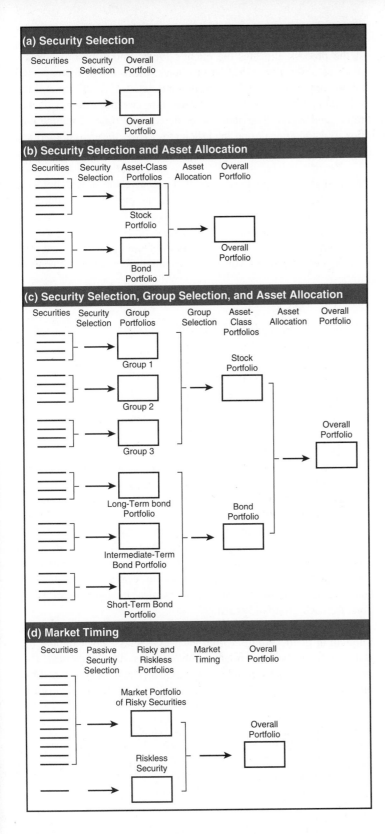

**FIGURE 22-6**
Investment styles.

## Asset Allocation

The second stage of the process allocates the client's funds among two asset class portfolios and is known as *asset allocation*.[6] In this stage, estimates of the expected return and standard deviation are needed for both the optimal stock portfolio and the optimal bond portfolio, along with the covariance between the two portfolios. This will allow the expected return and standard deviation to be determined for all combinations of these two portfolios. Finally, after noting the efficient set from these combinations, the indifference curves of the client can be used to determine which portfolio should be chosen.

For example, the first stage might have indicated the investor should hold the proportions of stocks $S_1$, $S_2$, and $S_3$ given earlier (that is, the optimal stock portfolio has proportions of .30, .20, and .50, respectively). Similarly, the first stage might have indicated that the investor should hold a proportion of .35 in bond $B_1$ and .65 in bond $B_2$. Then the second stage might indicate that the client's funds should be split so that 60% goes into stocks and 40% goes into bonds. This translates into individual investments of the following magnitudes:

*Stocks:*

$S_1$  .60 × .30 =  .18

$S_2$  .60 × .20 =  .12

$S_3$  .60 × .50 =  .30

*Bonds:*

$B_1$  .40 × .35 =  .14

$B_2$  .40 × .65 =  .26

1.00

The two-stage process just discussed can be extended by introducing groups. Figure 22.6(c) illustrates a three-stage process. In the first stage, known as security selection, the investment manager exercises discretion in identifying groups of securities in each asset class. Then, having identified a group, the investment manager determines the optimal portfolio associated with it. For example, within the asset class of common stocks, it could be that the investment manager has identified all industrial stocks as the first group, all utility stocks as the second group, and all transportation stocks as the third group. Within the asset class of bonds, groups of long-term, intermediate-term, and short-term bonds have been identified. Then, the investment manager identifies six optimal portfolios, one for each group of securities.

In the second stage, known as *group selection*, the investment manager determines the appropriate combination of the groups within each asset class. For example, the manager may have decided that the appropriate combination is 70% industrials, 10% utilities, and 20% transportation stocks. Similarly, the manager may have decided that the appropriate combination of bonds is 100% in long-term bonds, with nothing in either

---

[6] For more details, see Sharpe, "Integrated Asset Allocation." For evidence suggesting that asset allocation is the most important decision an investor has to make, see Gary P. Brinson, L. Randolph Hood, and Gilbert L. Beebower, "Determinants of Portfolio Performance," *Financial Analysts Journal* 42, no. 4 (July/August 1986):39–44. For an excellent description of the asset allocation process see R.Auger and D.Parisien, "Understanding Asset Allocation," *Canadian Investment Review* IV, no. 1 (Spring 1991):37–44.

intermediate-term or short-term bonds. Thus, at this stage the manager will determine the composition of an optimal stock portfolio and an optimal bond portfolio but will not know how much to allocate to each one.

The third and final stage makes this allocation and is thus referred to as *asset allocation*. It is performed in a manner that is identical to the second stage of the two-stage procedure illustrated in Figure 22.6(b).

Active or passive management may be used in any stage. For example, "active bets" might be placed on individual securities, with funds allocated across security classes based on consensus expected returns for such classes. That is, the investment manager may decide to start every period with 75% in stocks and 25% in bonds. However, the choice of which individual stocks and bonds to invest in will change with time, based on the manager's forecasts.

Alternatively, passive portfolios of individual securities might be constructed, with deviant predictions of asset classes used to allocate funds actively among the classes. For example, the investment manager may decide always to hold common stocks in the same relative proportions they have in the S&P 500, which is often used as a surrogate for the market portfolio. However, the proportion of funds invested in the S&P 500 will change at the start of every period, based on the prognosis for the stock and bond markets. Thus, during one period the manager may have as much as 100% of the client's funds in stocks, on the strong belief that the stock market is going to rise rapidly in the near future. Conversely, during another period the manager may have as much as 100% of the client's funds in bonds, on the strong belief that the stock market will soon crash dramatically.

## Market Timing

Figure 22.6(d) portrays a manager following a form of investment style that is known as *market timing*. The only active decision concerns the appropriate allocation of funds between a surrogate market portfolio and a risk-free asset such as Treasury bills. An investment organization following this style changes its mixture of risky and risk-free assets based on its own predictions of the risk and expected return of the market relative to the risk-free rate, even if there is no change in consensus predictions or the client's attitude toward risk and return.

Investment organizations that engage in the type of management where "active bets" are placed on individual securities are said to have a *security-selection style*. Those that engage in the type of management where active bets are placed on asset classes are said to have an *asset-allocation style*, with market timing being one specific example. Lastly, investment organizations that place active bets on certain groups of securities are said to employ a *group rotation style*. Some organizations use relatively pure *investment styles*, meaning they use basically just one of the three styles previously mentioned. However, others employ various combinations, making it difficult to classify them into neat categories.

Although these styles have been described in terms of modern portfolio theory, it should be pointed out that other procedures could be used to implement them. For example, with modern portfolio theory, an "optimal stock portfolio" (as in Figure 22.6(b)) is to be identified by use of expected returns, standard deviations, and covariances in conjunction with indifference curves. Once the portfolio is identified, the portfolio manager will have determined the appropriate relative investments in individual common stocks. However, such an identification could be made using some other procedure. Often it is done on a much less formal and quantitative basis.

## 22.5 PORTFOLIO REVISION

With the passage of time, a previously purchased portfolio that is currently held will often be viewed as suboptimal by the investment manager, meaning the portfolio is no longer viewed as the best one for the client. This is because either the client's attitude toward risk and return is thought to have changed or, more likely, the manager's forecasts have changed. In response, the manager could identify a new optimal portfolio and then hope to be able to make the necessary revisions to the current portfolio so that subsequently the new optimal portfolio will be held. However, this is not as straightforward as it might seem at first because transaction costs will have to be paid when any revisions are made.

Such costs were discussed in Chapter 2; they include brokerage commissions and bid-ask spreads. Because of these costs, a security would have to increase in value by a certain amount just to pay these costs and leave the investor neither better nor worse off. This necessary increase in value may exceed 1% for many securities and can range as high as 5% to 10% or more for others.

The existence of transactions costs greatly complicates the life of any investment manager, and the more active the manager, the greater the complications. The hoped-for advantage of any revision must be weighed against the cost of making that revision. That is, a revision can be viewed as bringing certain kinds of benefits — it will either increase the expected return of the portfolio, reduce the standard deviation of the portfolio, or do both. To be weighed against these benefits are the transactions costs that will be incurred if the revision is made. As a result, some of the revisions in the holdings of individual securities that the manager may initially want to make will be dropped from consideration because of the transaction costs involved. The goal of the manager is to identify the set of individual revisions that collectively maximize the improvement, after transactions costs, in the risk-return characteristics of the current portfolio.

In order to identify the set of individual revisions, sophisticated procedures (for example, quadratic programming) are required to compare the relevant costs and benefits.[7] Fortunately, improvements in procedures and dramatic decreases in computing costs have made such approaches economically feasible for many investment managers. Asset allocation programs capable of analyzing dozens of asset classes within a minute on an inexpensive microcomputer are widely available within the professional investment community.

---

[7] For a description of portfolio revision procedures, see pp. 221–28 of Gordon J. Alexander and Jack Clark Francis, *Portfolio Analysis* (Englewood Cliffs, N.J.: Prentice Hall, 1986); and pp. 65–68 of Sharpe, *Asset Allocation Tools*.

The larger the amount of money managed, the more communication there is likely to be between investment manager and client. Not surprisingly, corporate, union, and government officials responsible for pension funds spend a great deal of time with those who manage their money. Such officials also concern themselves with a number of prior questions: Who should manage the money, how should it be managed, and how should the managers be instructed and constrained?

Many of the aspects of manager-client relations can be characterized as responses to a difference of opinion concerning the manager's abilities to make "good bets." Often, clients will divide their funds among two or more managers. This type of *split-funding* is used by most pension funds. Two reasons are given. First, it allows the employment of managers with different skills or different styles. Second, the impact of erroneous "bets" can be reduced by diversifying across different managers, since the managers are the bettors. However, as more investment managers are used, the overall portfolio is likely to appear more like the market portfolio. Thus, extensive use of split-funding can give results similar to those obtained with an explicit passive fund, but at considerably greater cost to the client, owing to the expenses associated with transactions costs and fees charged by the investment managers.

Whether or not split-funding is used, a client who feels that a manager is betting too much would simply like to reduce the size of the bets. For example, the client might ask a manager to diverge only half as much as he or she normally would from passive proportions of individual securities. Thus, if the manager decides that the optimal proportion in stock $S_1$ is 30% and the market proportion is 45%, this would mean that the manager would ultimately only invest a proportion equal to $(30\% + 45\%)/2 = 37.5\%$. However, there is no simple way to monitor compliance. In the example, the manager could buy 45% of $S_1$ and state that he or she originally wanted to invest 60% in it but settled for 45%, even though truthfully he or she originally wanted 45%. Instead, another approach is often employed: Limits are placed on the holdings in any single security.[8]

Institutional investors (for example, pension and endowment funds) typically use more than one investment manager and provide each with a set of objectives and a set of constraints on allowed divergences from such normal positions.[9] Individual investors who employ investment managers tend to give such instructions implicitly, if at all. This may reflect less sophistication, a less formal relationship with the manager, or the fact that the management fee for a small account is not large enough to cover the cost of dealing with a series of objectives and constraints.

---

[8] There are other kinds of limits frequently imposed on the manager, such as limits on the holdings of bonds versus stocks or on the amount invested in a single industry.

[9] Sometimes the objectives are stated in terms of target or normal positions.

# SUMMARY

This chapter discussed a five-step procedure for making investment decisions. The steps are (1) set investment policy, (2) perform security analysis, (3) construct a portfolio, (4) revise the portfolio, and (5) evaluate the performance of the portfolio.

With respect to setting investment policy, a procedure was presented for estimating an investor's indifference curves. This procedure involves asking the investor to identify the most desirable portfolio in a set of portfolios. Once such an identification has been made, the shape of the investor's indifference curves can be determined in a straightforward manner.

In terms of security analysis and portfolio construction, a distinction was made between passive and active management. Passive management rests on a belief that markets are efficient and typically involves investing in an index fund. Active management, on the other hand, involves a belief that mispriced situations occur and can be identified with a reasonable degree of accuracy. There are many forms of active management. They can involve security selection, where individual mispriced securities are sought out, and market timing, where the stock market in aggregate is evaluated to see if it is, in general, mispriced. Variations include looking at various groups of securities in the attempt to identify mispriced ones.

Portfolio revision involves realizing that the currently held portfolio is not optimal. That is, there is another portfolio that the investor would prefer to hold instead of the current one. However, whereas the desired portfolio has superior risk-return characteristics, altering the current portfolio so that it will correspond to the desired one will entail transactions costs. Thus, the investor must balance costs with benefits in making revisions to the currently held portfolio.

The last step, evaluating the performance of a portfolio, was not discussed in this chapter. Due to its importance and complexity, it is the subject of the next chapter.

# APPENDIX A

## DETERMINING THE RISK TOLERANCE OF AN INVESTOR

The purpose of this appendix is to derive in some detail the formula for determining the risk tolerance $\tau$ of an investor. As mentioned earlier, the equation for an indifference curve of an investor having constant risk tolerance is of the form

$$\bar{r}_p = u_i + \frac{1}{\tau}\sigma_p^2 \qquad (22.6)$$

where $u_i$ and $1/\tau$ are the vertical intercept and slope for indifference curve $i$, where variance is measured on the horizontal axis. As the equation shows, an indifference curve will be a straight line, since $u_i$ and $1/\tau$ are constants (thus, the equation is of the general form $Y = a + bX$ and is a straight line). Furthermore, any two indifference curves for an investor will have the same slope ($1/\tau$) but will have different vertical intercepts ($u_i$).

In order to estimate the investor's level of risk tolerance $\tau$, it was mentioned that the slope of the indifference curve, $1/\tau$, would be set equal to the slope of the efficient set at the location of the portfolio that was selected, denoted by portfolio $C$. This is because the indifference curve is tangent to the efficient set at this point, so the two must have the same slope. Thus, the slope of the efficient set at point $C$ must be determined in order to estimate $\tau$.

Let $X_S$ denote the proportion invested in the stock portfolio $S$ and $(1 - X_S)$ denote the proportion invested in a risk-free Treasury bill portfolio $F$. Now the expected return of any portfolio consisting of $S$ and $F$ is simply

$$\bar{r}_p = X_S \bar{r}_S + (1 - X_S) r_F \tag{22.7}$$

where $\bar{r}_S$ and $r_F$ are the expected returns of the stock portfolio and the risk-free rate, respectively. This equation can be solved for $X_S$, resulting in

$$X_S = \frac{\bar{r}_p - r_F}{\bar{r}_S - r_F}. \tag{22.8}$$

The equation for the variance of portfolio $p$ is equal to:

$$\sigma_p^2 = X_S^2 \sigma_S^2 + (1 - X_S)^2 \sigma_F^2 + 2 X_S (1 - X_S) \sigma_{SF} \tag{22.9}$$

where $\sigma_S^2$ and $\sigma_F^2$ are the variances of the stock and risk-free portfolios, respectively, and $\sigma_{SF}$ is the covariance between these two portfolios. However, since $F$ is the risk-free portfolio, by definition $\sigma_F^2$ and $\sigma_{SF}$ are equal to zero. Thus, equation (22.9) reduces to

$$\sigma_p^2 = X_S^2 \sigma_S^2. \tag{22.10}$$

Next, the right-hand side of equation (22.8) can be substituted for $X_S$ in equation (22.10), resulting in

$$\sigma_p^2 = \frac{(\bar{r}_p - r_F)^2}{(\bar{r}_S - r_F)^2} \sigma_S^2. \tag{22.11}$$

This equation can be viewed as describing the functional relationship between the expected return and variance of any portfolio $p$ that can be formed by combining the stock portfolio $S$ and the risk-free portfolio $F$. That is, for a particular $S$ and $F$, it gives the variance for a portfolio consisting of $S$ and $F$ with expected return $\bar{r}_p$. Equivalently, it represents the slope of the curved line in Figure 22.3 that connects $S$ and $F$.

Using calculus, the slope of this line can be shown to be equal to[10]

$$\text{Slope} = \frac{(\bar{r}_S - r_F)^2}{2[(\bar{r}_p - r_F) \sigma_S^2]}. \tag{22.12}$$

The next step in estimating the slope of the client's indifference curves is to note that the portfolio on the curve connecting $S$ and $F$ that is of concern is the tangency portfolio $C$. Thus, the slope of the curve at $C$ is determined by substituting $\bar{r}_C$ for $\bar{r}_p$ in equation (22.12) and equating this value with the slope of the indifference curves, $1/\tau$. Doing this results in the following equation:

$$\frac{1}{\tau} = \frac{(\bar{r}_S - r_F)^2}{2[(\bar{r}_C - r_F) \sigma_S^2]}. \tag{22.13}$$

---

[10] Note that the slope of this line, $d\bar{r}_p / d\sigma_p^2$, is equal to $1/[d\sigma_p^2 / d\bar{r}_p]$. Thus, the slope can be determined by taking the derivative of $\sigma_p^2$ with respect to $\bar{r}_p$ in equation (22.10) and then inverting the resulting expression.

Finally, equation (22.13) can be solved for $\tau$:

$$\tau = \frac{2[(\bar{r}_C - r_F)\sigma_S^2]}{(\bar{r}_S - r_F)^2}. \qquad (22.14)$$

Note that this is the same formula that was given earlier in equation (22.2) for estimating $\tau$, given the client's choice of portfolio $C$.[11]

At point $C$ equation (22.7) can be rewritten as

$$(\bar{r}_S - r_F)X_S = \bar{r}_C - r_F. \qquad (22.15)$$

Thus, $(\bar{r}_S - r_F)X_S$ can be substituted for $\bar{r}_C - r_F$ in the numerator of equation (22.14). Doing so and simplifying results in

$$\tau = \frac{2(X_S\sigma_S^2)}{\bar{r}_S - r_F}. \qquad (22.16)$$

In the example given earlier in the chapter, $\sigma_S = 15\%$ and $\bar{r}_S - r_F = 4.5\%$. Substituting these values into equation (22.16) and simplifying results in

$$\tau = \frac{2[X_S \times 15^2]}{4.5}$$
$$= 100\,X_S \qquad (22.17)$$

as was previously mentioned and illustrated in Table 22.1.

## QUESTIONS AND PROBLEMS

1. Technological changes have decreased the cost and increased the speed of information dissemination in security markets. Why might one suspect that firms following a "traditional" approach to investment management would find it increasingly difficult to generate "positive alphas" (that is, to identify underpriced securities) in this environment?

2. Why is it difficult to specify the risk-return preferences of investment management clients? Why are these problems particularly acute in the case of institutional clients (for example, pension and endowment funds)?

3. Explain the meaning of the slope of an investor's indifference curve at any particular point. For a "typical" risk-averse investor, describe how the investor's risk-return trade-off changes at different points along one of his or her indifference curves.

4. Beth Arlett, a portfolio manager for an investment management firm, has estimated the following risk-return characteristics for the stock and bond markets.

| | Expected Return | Standard Deviation |
| --- | --- | --- |
| Stocks | 18.0% | 22.0% |
| Bonds | 10.0 | 5.0 |

---

[11] Risk tolerance, along with a computer program for estimating the value of $\tau$, is presented in Sharpe, *Asset Allocation Tools*:33–39.

Using these estimates, Beth ran a number of simulations, tracing out the implications of different bond/stock mixes for the financial situation of Zoe Beck, a client. After much thought, Zoe indicated that of the mixes considered, the most desirable was the allocation of 60% to stocks and 40% to bonds. Given this information, calculate Zoe's risk tolerance. [*Hint*: To solve this problem algebraically, write Eq. (22.5) using the 60/40 stock/bond allocation. Do the same for a 61/39 allocation. Finally, set these two formulas equal to each other and solve for the risk tolerance.] Is this answer likely to represent Zoe's risk tolerance over all possible stock/bond allocations?

5. Should an "overpriced" stock definitely be excluded from an investor's portfolio? Why or why not?

6. Studies that simulate the value of an investment portfolio under alternative mixes of stocks and bonds invariably demonstrate that higher stock allocations produce higher returns, particularly as the holding period increases. If you as an investor have a time horizon that is reasonably long, say over ten years, and you have no current income needs, how could you justify holding any bonds in your portfolio?

7. The portfolio manager's job can be defined as identifying the portfolio with the highest certainty equivalent return. Explain.

8. Despite its obvious simplicity and potential benefits, common stock passive management is a relatively "new" investment tool. Yet in the last twenty years, assets under passive management have grown from essentially zero to over $100 billion. What are several possible reasons for the tremendous growth in passive management?

9. It is often argued (especially by active managers) that passive management implies settling for "mediocre" performance. Is this statement necessarily true? Why or why not?

10. Why is the "one-stage" approach to security selection theoretically superior to the "two-stage" approach? Why is the "two-stage" approach preferred by most investment managers?

11. A typical money management firm, particularly one specializing in stocks or bonds, invests in essentially the same portfolio for all of its clients, regardless of the clients' individual risk-return preferences. Speculate as to why money managers often operate in this manner. What can clients do to ensure that their portfolios reflect their own specific risk-return preferences?

12. Many investment management clients split their assets among a number of managers. The rationale for this approach has been described as "diversification of judgment" and "diversification of style." Explain the meaning of these two terms.

## SUGGESTED READINGS

*The Canadian Securities Course* (Toronto, Ont.: The Canadian Securities Institute, 1989). Chapter 20 covers both portfolio construction from a traditional viewpoint as well as portfolio management.

Robert Auger and Denis Parisien, "Understanding Asset Allocation," *Canadian Investment Review* IV, no. 1 (Spring 1991):37–46 and

Kathleen A. Condon, "Portfolio Construction: Asset allocation," in eds. John L. Maginn and Donald L. Tuttle, *Managing Investment Portfolios* (Boston, Mass.: Warren, Gorham & Lamont, 1983) cover the important issues involved in deciding how to distribute funds between asset classes.

James A. Knowles and William R. Waters, "Professional Portfolio Management: Is 'Style' Substance?" *Canadian Investment Review* II, no. 2 (Fall 1989):87–94 conclude that a manager's 'style' may be an important factor in the selection process.

Paul Potvin, "Passive Management, the TSE 300 and the Toronto 35 Stock Indexes," *Canadian Investment Review* V, no. 1 (Spring 1992):61–66 points out the importance of selecting the appropriate index to mimic when undertaking passive management.

# Chapter 23

# PORTFOLIO PERFORMANCE EVALUATION

An investor who has been paying someone actively to manage his or her portfolio has every right to insist on knowing what sort of performance was obtained. Such information can be used to alter either the constraints placed on the manager, the investment objectives given to the manager, or the amount of money allocated to the manager. Perhaps more importantly, by evaluating performance in specified ways, a client can forcefully communicate his or her interests to the investment manager and, in all likelihood, affect the way in which his or her portfolio is managed. Moreover, an investment manager, by evaluating his or her own performance, can identify sources of strength or weakness. Thus, although the previous chapter indicated portfolio performance evaluation was the last stage of the investment management process, it can also be viewed as simply part of a continuing operation.

Superior performance in the past may have been due to good luck, in which case such performance should not be expected to continue in the future. On the other hand, superior performance in the past may have been due to the actions of a highly skilled investment manager (and support staff ). Conversely, inferior performance in the past may have been the result of bad luck, but it may also have been due to excessive turnover, high management fees, or other costs associated with an unskilled investment manager. This suggests that the first task in performance evaluation is to try to determine whether past performance was superior or inferior. Once this task is done, the second task is to try to determine whether such performance was due to skill or luck. Unfortunately, there are difficulties associated with carrying out both of these tasks. Accordingly, this chapter presents not only certain methods that have been advocated and used for evaluating portfolio performance but also a discussion of the difficulties encountered with their use.

# MEASURES OF RETURN

Frequently portfolio performance is evaluated over a time interval of at least four years, with returns measured for a number of periods within the interval—typically monthly or quarterly. This provides a fairly adequate sample size for statistical evaluation (for example, if returns are measured quarterly for four years, there will be 16 observations). Sometimes, however, a shorter time interval must be used in order to avoid examining returns earned under a different investment manager (or the support staff).

In the simplest situation, where the client neither deposits nor withdraws money from the portfolio during a time period, calculation of the portfolio's return is straightforward. All that is required is that the market value of the portfolio be known at two points in time — the beginning and the end of the period.

In general, the market value of a portfolio at a point in time is determined by adding the market values of all the securities held at that particular time. For example, the value of a common stock portfolio at the beginning of a period is calculated by (1) noting the market price per share of each stock held in the portfolio at that time, (2) multiplying each of these share prices by the corresponding number of shares held, and (3) adding the resulting products. This sum will equal the market value of the portfolio at the beginning of the period.

With the beginning and ending portfolio values in hand, the return on the portfolio can be calculated by subtracting the beginning value ($V_b$) from the ending value ($V_e$) and then dividing the difference by the beginning value:

$$r_p = \frac{V_e - V_b}{V_b.}$$

(23.1)

For example, if a portfolio has a market value of $40 million at the beginning of a quarter and a market value of $46 million at the end of the quarter, then the return on this portfolio for the quarter is ($46 million − $40 million)/$40 million = 15%.

Measurement of portfolio returns is complicated by the fact that the client may either add or withdraw money from the portfolio. This means that the percentage change in the market value of the portfolio during a period may not be an accurate measurement of the portfolio's return during that period.

For example, consider a portfolio that at the beginning of a quarter has a market value of $100 million. Just before the end of the quarter the client deposits $5 million with the investment manager, and, subsequently, at the end of the quarter the market value of the portfolio is $103 million. If the quarterly return was measured without consideration of the $5 million deposit, the reported return would be ($103 million − $100 million)/$100 million = 3%. However, this would be incorrect, since $5 million of the ending $103 million market value was not due to the investment actions of the manager. Consideration of the deposit would suggest that a more accurate measure of the quarterly return would be [($103 million − $5 million) − $100 million]/$100 million = −2%.

Identification of exactly *when* any deposits or withdrawals occur is important in accurately measuring portfolio returns. If a deposit or withdrawal occurs just *before* the end of the period, then the return on the portfolio should be calculated by adjusting the ending market value of the portfolio. In the case of a deposit, the ending value should be reduced by the dollar amount (as was done in the previous example); in the case of a withdrawal, the ending value should be increased by the dollar amount.

If a deposit or withdrawal occurs just *after* the start of the period, then the return on the portfolio should be calculated by adjusting the beginning market value of the portfolio. In the case of a deposit, the beginning value should be increased by the dollar amount; in the case of a withdrawal, the beginning value should be decreased by the dollar amount. For example, if the $5 million deposit in the earlier example had been received just after the start of the quarter, the return for the quarter should be calculated as [$103 million − ($100 million + $5 million)]/($100 million + $5 million) = −1.90%.

## 23.1.1 Dollar-Weighted Returns

Difficulties are encountered when deposits or withdrawals occur sometime *between* the beginning and end of the period. One method that has been used for calculating a portfolio's return in this situation results in the portfolio's *dollar-weighted return* (or internal rate of return).

For example, if the $5 million deposit in the earlier example was made in the middle of the quarter, the dollar-weighted return would be calculated by solving the following equation for $r$:

$$\$100 \text{ million} = \frac{-\$5 \text{ million}}{(1+r)} + \frac{\$103 \text{ million}}{(1+r)^2}. \tag{23.2}$$

The solution to this equation, $r = -.98\%$, is a semiquarterly rate of return. It can be converted into a quarterly rate of return by adding 1 to it, squaring this value, and then subtracting 1 from the square, resulting in a quarterly return of $[1 + (-.0098)]^2 - 1 = -1.95\%$.[1]

## 23.1.2 Time-Weighted Returns

Alternatively, the *time-weighted return* on a portfolio can be calculated when there are cash flows occurring between the beginning and end of the period. This method involves using the market value of the portfolio just before each cash flow occurs. In the earlier example, assume that in the middle of the quarter the portfolio had a market value of $96 million, so that right after the $5 million deposit the market value was $96 million + $5 million = $101 million. In this case, the return for the first half of the quarter would be ($96 million − $100 million)/$100 million = −4%; the return for the second half of the quarter would be ($103 million − $101 million)/$101 million = 1.98%.

Next, these two semiquarterly returns can be combined to give a quarterly return by adding 1 to each return, multiplying the sums, and then subtracting 1 from the product. In the example, this procedure results in a quarterly return of $[(1 - .04)(1 + .0198)] - 1 = -2.1\%$.

---

[1] This procedure provides a quarterly return with "quarterly compounding." Alternatively, the semiquarterly return could be doubled, resulting in a quarterly return with "semiquarterly compounding" of $-.98\% \times 2 = -1.96\%$.

## 23.1.3 Comparing Dollar-Weighted and Time-Weighted Returns

Which method is preferable for calculating the return on a portfolio? In the example given here, the dollar-weighted return was $-1.95\%$, whereas the time-weighted return was $-2.1\%$, suggesting the difference between the two methods may not be very important. Although this may be true in certain situations, examples can be given to show that such differences can be quite large and that the time-weighted return method is preferable.

Consider a hypothetical portfolio that starts a quarter with a market value of $50 million. In the middle of the quarter, it has fallen to a market value of $25 million, at which point the client deposits $25 million with the investment manager. At the end of the quarter the portfolio has a market value of $100 million. The semiquarterly dollar-weighted return for this portfolio is equal to the value of $r$ in the following equation:

$$\$50 \text{ million} = \frac{-\$25 \text{ million}}{(1+r)} + \frac{\$100 \text{ million}}{(1+r)^2}.$$

Solving this equation for $r$ results in a value of 18.6%, which in turn equals a quarterly dollar-weighted return of $(1.186)^2 - 1 = 40.66\%$. However, its quarterly time-weighted return is 0%, since its return for the first half of the quarter was $-50\%$ and its return for the second half of the quarter was 100% (note that $(1-.5)(1+1)-1 = 0\%$).

Comparing these two returns — 40.66% and 0% — indicates a sizable difference exists. However, the time-weighted return figure of 0% is more meaningful for performance evaluation than the dollar-weighted return figure of 40.66%. The reason for this can be seen by considering the return over the entire quarter on each dollar that was in the portfolio at the start of the quarter. Each dollar lost half of its value over the first half of the quarter, but then the remaining half-dollar doubled its value over the second half. Consequently, a dollar at the beginning was worth a dollar at the end, suggesting a return of 0% on the portfolio is a more accurate measure of the investment manager's performance than the 40.66% figure.

In general, the dollar-weighted return method of measuring a portfolio's return for purposes of evaluation is regarded as inappropriate. The reason behind this view is that the return is strongly influenced by the size and timing of the cash flows (namely, deposits and withdrawals) over which the investment manager has no control. In the example, the dollar-weighted return was 40.66% because the client fortuitously made a big deposit just before the portfolio appreciated rapidly in value. Thus, the 40.66% return figure is due at least partly to the actions of the client, not the manager.

## 23.1.4 Annualizing Returns

The previous discussion has focused on calculating quarterly returns. Such returns may be added or multiplied to obtain an annual measure of return. For example, if the return in the first, second, third, and fourth quarters of a given year are denoted by $r_1, r_2, r_3$, and $r_4$, respectively, then the annual return could be calculated by adding the four figures:

$$\text{Annual return} = r_1 + r_2 + r_3 + r_4. \tag{23.3}$$

Alternatively, the annual return could be calculated by adding 1 to each quarterly return, then multiplying the four figures, and finally subtracting 1 from the resulting product:

$$\text{Annual return} = [(1 + r_1)(1 + r_2)(1 + r_3)(1 + r_4)] - 1. \qquad (23.4)$$

This return is more accurate because it reflects the value that $1 would have at the end of the year if it were invested at the beginning of the year and grew *with compounding* at the rate of $r_1$ for the first quarter, $r_2$ for the second quarter, $r_3$ for the third quarter, and $r_4$ for the fourth quarter. That is, it assumes reinvestment of both the dollar and any earnings at the end of each quarter.

## 23.2 MAKING RELEVANT COMPARISONS

The essential idea behind performance evaluation is to compare the returns obtained by the investment manager through active management with the returns that could have been obtained for the client if one or more appropriate alternative portfolios had been chosen for investment. The reason for this comparison is straightforward — performance should be evaluated on a relative basis, not on an absolute basis.

As an example, consider a client who is told that his or her portfolio, invested in common stocks and of average risk, had a return of 20% last year. Does this suggest superior or inferior performance? If the stock market went up by 10% last year, then it suggests superior performance and is good news. However, if the stock market went up by 30% last year, then it suggests inferior performance and is bad news. In order to infer whether the manager's performance is superior or inferior, the returns on similar portfolios that are either actively or passively managed are needed for comparison.

Such comparison portfolios are often referred to as *benchmark portfolios*. In selecting them, the client should be certain they are relevant and feasible, meaning they should represent alternative portfolios that could have been chosen for investment instead of the portfolio being evaluated. *Return* is a key aspect of performance, of course, but some way must be found to account for the portfolio's exposure to *risk*. The choice of benchmark portfolios may be restricted to portfolios perceived to have similar levels of risk, thereby permitting a direct comparison of returns.

Figure 23.1 illustrates such a comparison for a hypothetical common stock (or "equity") portfolio referred to as Fund 07632. In this figure, Fund 07632's performance for each year is represented by a diamond. The hypothetical comparison portfolios are a set of other common stock portfolios that are represented by the box surrounding the diamond. The top and bottom lines of the box indicate the returns of the 5th and 95th percentile comparison portfolios, respectively. Similarly, the top and bottom dashed lines represent the 25th and 75th percentiles. The solid line in the middle represents the median (50th percentile) portfolio.

Alternatively, risk may be explicitly measured so that a single measure of performance taking both return and risk into account can be employed. This will allow benchmark portfolios of varying degrees of risk to be compared with the portfolio being evaluated.

The following discussion of risk-adjusted measures of performance concerns equity (common stock) portfolios; bond portfolios are presented later in the chapter.

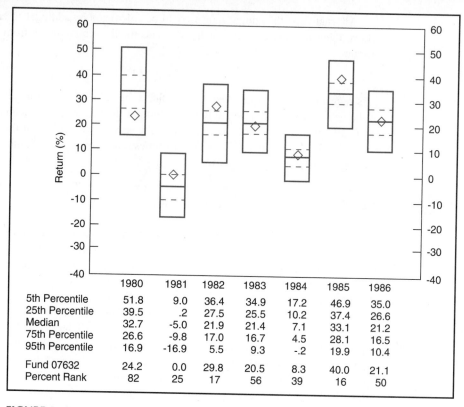

| | 1980 | 1981 | 1982 | 1983 | 1984 | 1985 | 1986 |
|---|---|---|---|---|---|---|---|
| 5th Percentile | 51.8 | 9.0 | 36.4 | 34.9 | 17.2 | 46.9 | 35.0 |
| 25th Percentile | 39.5 | .2 | 27.5 | 25.5 | 10.2 | 37.4 | 26.6 |
| Median | 32.7 | -5.0 | 21.9 | 21.4 | 7.1 | 33.1 | 21.2 |
| 75th Percentile | 26.6 | -9.8 | 17.0 | 16.7 | 4.5 | 28.1 | 16.5 |
| 95th Percentile | 16.9 | -16.9 | 5.5 | 9.3 | -.2 | 19.9 | 10.4 |
| Fund 07632 | 24.2 | 0.0 | 29.8 | 20.5 | 8.3 | 40.0 | 21.1 |
| Percent Rank | 82 | 25 | 17 | 56 | 39 | 16 | 50 |

**FIGURE 23-1**

Comparing returns of equity portfolios.

*SOURCE:* Adapted from SEI, *Funds Evaluation Service.*

## 23.3 RISK-ADJUSTED MEASURES OF PERFORMANCE FOR EQUITY PORTFOLIOS

Having measured the periodic returns for a portfolio during an evaluation interval (for example, quarterly returns for a four-year evaluation interval), the next step is to determine if these returns represent superior or inferior performance. In order to do this, an estimate of the portfolio's risk level during the evaluation interval is needed. For equity portfolios, two kinds of risk can be estimated—the portfolio's market (or systematic) risk, measured by its beta, and the portfolio's total risk, measured by its standard deviation.

It is important to analyze risk appropriately. The key issue here is determining the impact of the portfolio on the client's overall level of risk. If the client has many other assets, then the market risk of the portfolio provides the relevant measure of the portfolio's impact on the client's overall level of risk. If, however, the portfolio provides the client's sole support, then its total risk is the relevant measure of risk. Risk-adjusted performance evaluation is generally based on one of these two viewpoints, taking either market risk or total risk into consideration.

Assume there are $T$ time periods in the evaluation interval (for example, $T = 16$ when there are four years of quarterly data) and let $r_{pt}$ denote the return on the portfolio during period $t$. The *average return* on the portfolio, denoted by $ar_p$, is simply:

$$ar_p = \frac{\sum\limits_{t=1}^{T} r_{pt}}{T}. \tag{23.5}$$

Having calculated $ar_p$, the *ex post standard deviation* can be calculated as

$$\sigma_p = \left[ \frac{\sum\limits_{t=1}^{T} (r_{pt} - ar_p)^2}{T - 1} \right]^{1/2} \tag{23.6}$$

This estimate of the portfolio's standard deviation can be used as an indication of the amount of total risk that the portfolio had during the evaluation interval.[2] It can be compared directly with the standard deviations of other portfolios, as illustrated in Figure 23.2. (This figure is to be interpreted in the same manner as Figure 23.1.)

The returns of a portfolio may also be compared with those of a substitute for the market portfolio, such as the TSE 300, in order to determine the portfolio's *ex post beta* during the evaluation interval. Denoting the excess return on the portfolio during period $t$ by $er_{pt} = r_{pt} - r_{ft}$, the return on the TSE 300 (or some other market substitute) during period $t$ by $r_{Mt}$, and the excess return on the TSE 300 during period $t$ by $er_{Mt} = r_{Mt} - r_{ft}$, this beta can be estimated as follows:

$$\beta_p = \frac{\left( \sum\limits_{t=1}^{T} er_{Mt} er_{pt} \right) - \left( \sum\limits_{t=1}^{T} er_{pt} \sum\limits_{t=1}^{T} er_{Mt} \right)}{\left( T \sum\limits_{t=1}^{T} er_{Mt}^2 \right) - \left( \sum\limits_{t=1}^{T} er_{Mt} \right)^2}. \tag{23.7}$$

This estimate of the portfolio's beta can be used as an indication of the amount of market risk that the portfolio had during the evaluation interval.[3] It can be compared directly with the betas of other portfolios, as illustrated in Figure 23.3.

Although a portfolio's return and a measure of its risk can be compared individually with those of other portfolios, as in Figures 23.1 through 23.3, it is often not clear how the portfolio performed on a risk-adjusted basis relative to these other portfolios. For the fund shown in the figures, the average percent rank for the portfolio's return over the five years ending in 1986 is $(17 + 56 + 39 + 16 + 50)/5 = 36\%$. Over the same period, its standard deviation put it in the 78th percent rank.

---

[2] Sometimes the excess return for a portfolio, which is equal to its return minus the risk-free rate $(r_{pt} - r_{ft})$, is used instead of $r_{pt}$ in equation (23.5) to determine the average excess return (denoted by $aer_p$). Then, the summation in the numerator of equation (23.6) is carried out using $[(r_{pt} - r_{ft}) - aer_p]^2$ instead of $(r_{pt} - ar_p)^2$. The resulting number is the standard deviation of excess returns, which is sometimes used as an estimate of the total risk of the portfolio. Typically, the two standard deviations are quite similar in numerical value.

[3] Equation (23.7) corresponds to the formula for estimating the slope term in a simple regression model where the independent variable is $er_{Mt}$ and the dependent variable is $er_{pt}$. Sometimes returns are used in equation (23.7), where $er_{Mt}$ is replaced by $r_{Mt}$ and $er_{pt}$ is replaced by $r_{pt}$. In this situation, the beta corresponds to the slope term in the *market model* for the portfolio. Typically, the two betas are quite similar in numerical value.

**FIGURE 23-2**

Comparing standard deviations of equity portfolios.

*SOURCE:* Adapted from SEI, *Funds Evaluation Service.*

Assuming the client is concerned with total risk, how does he or she interpret these percent ranks? In the case of the return, the portfolio was slightly above average; in terms of standard deviation, it was less risky than approximately three-fourths of the other portfolios. Overall, this suggests that the portfolio did better on a risk-adjusted basis than the others, but it does not give the client a clear and precise sense of how much better.

Such a sense can be conveyed by certain CAPM-based measures of portfolio performance. Each one of these measures provides an estimate of a portfolio's risk-adjusted performance, thereby allowing the client to see how the portfolio performed relative to other portfolios as well as the market. They are presented next.

**FIGURE 23-3**
Comparing betas of equity portfolios.

*SOURCE:* Adapted from SEI, *Funds Evaluation Service.*

## ☐ 23.3.1 *Ex Post* Characteristic Lines

Over an evaluation interval, an *ex post security market line* (SML) can be estimated by determining the average risk-free rate and market return:

$$ar_f = \frac{\sum_{t=1}^{T} r_{ft}}{T} \tag{23.8}$$

$$ar_M = \frac{\sum_{t=1}^{T} r_{Mt}}{T} \tag{23.9}$$

Once these averages have been calculated, the ex post SML is simply the equation of the line going through the points $(0, ar_f)$ and $(1, ar_M)$:

$$ar_p^e = ar_f + (ar_M - ar_f)\beta_p. \tag{23.10}$$

Equivalently, the equilibrium average return during this interval of time for a portfolio with a beta of $\beta_p$ would simply be equal to $ar_f + (ar_M - ar_f)\beta_p$. Accordingly, $ar_p^e$ can be used as the benchmark return for a portfolio with a beta of $\beta_p$.

Part A of Table 23.1 presents an example by using the quarterly returns for the TSE 300 over the interval 1986 to 1989, along with corresponding returns on 91-day Treasury bills. Using equations (23.8) and (23.9), the average risk-free return and market return

**TABLE 23.1**

The *Ex Post* Characteristic Line for the First Fund, 1986–1989.

### a. Return Data

| Quarter | | Treasury Bill Return | First Fund Return | First Fund Excess Return | TSE 300 Return | TSE 300 Excess Return |
|---------|---|---------|--------|---------|--------|--------|
| 1986 | 1 | 2.64% | 3.94% | 1.30% | 5.84% | 3.20% |
| | 2 | 2.20 | 1.27 | − 0.93 | 2.02 | −0.18 |
| | 3 | 2.07 | −4.89 | −6.96 | −2.74 | −4.81 |
| | 4 | 2.08 | 7.01 | 4.93 | 3.74 | 1.66 |
| 1987 | 1 | 1.82 | 16.59 | 14.77 | 22.70 | 20.88 |
| | 2 | 2.00 | −0.57 | −2.57 | 0.68 | −1.32 |
| | 3 | 2.26 | 8.78 | 6.52 | 4.94 | 2.68 |
| | 4 | 1.95 | −29.44 | −31.39 | −18.33 | −20.28 |
| 1988 | 1 | 2.09 | 10.13 | 8.04 | 5.65 | 3.56 |
| | 2 | 2.21 | 1.50 | −0.71 | 4.72 | 2.51 |
| | 3 | 2.32 | −3.91 | 6.23 | −3.64 | −5.96 |
| | 4 | 2.60 | 7.90 | 5.30 | 4.20 | 1.60 |
| 1989 | 1 | 2.80 | 12.03 | 9.23 | 6.47 | 3.67 |
| | 2 | 3.09 | 3.53 | 0.44 | 6.15 | 3.06 |
| | 3 | 3.02 | 10.80 | 7.78 | 5.72 | 2.70 |
| | 4 | 3.04 | 1.89 | −1.15 | 1.58 | −1.46 |

### b. Calculations[a]

| Quarter | | First Fund Excess Returns = Y (1) | TSE 300 Excess Returns = X (2) | $Y^2$ (3) | $X^2$ (4) | $Y \times X$ (5) |
|---------|---|--------|--------|---------|----------|---------|
| 1986 | 1 | 1.30 | 3.2 | 10.24 | 1.695204 | 4.1664 |
| | 2 | −0.93 | −0.18 | 0.0324 | 0.871235 | 0.168012 |
| | 3 | −6.96 | −4.81 | 23.1361 | 48.40402 | 33.46461 |
| | 4 | 4.93 | 1.66 | 2.7556 | 24.30292 | 8.183468 |
| 1987 | 1 | 14.77 | 20.88 | 435.9744 | 218.1056 | 308.3641 |
| | 2 | −2.57 | −1.32 | 1.7424 | 6.623416 | 3.397152 |
| | 3 | 6.52 | 2.68 | 7.1824 | 42.54170 | 17.48003 |
| | 4 | −31.39 | −20.28 | 411.2784 | 985.3572 | 636.5973 |
| 1988 | 1 | 8.04 | 3.56 | 12.6736 | 64.71880 | 28.63948 |
| | 2 | −0.71 | 2.51 | 6.3001 | 0.503674 | −1.78134 |
| | 3 | −6.23 | −5.96 | 35.5216 | 38.84779 | 37.14748 |
| | 4 | 5.30 | 1.6 | 2.56 | 28.11120 | 8.4832 |
| 1989 | 1 | 9.23 | 3.67 | 13.4689 | 85.10247 | 33.85611 |
| | 2 | 0.44 | 3.06 | 9.3636 | 0.193424 | 1.345788 |
| | 3 | 7.78 | 2.7 | 7.29 | 60.48172 | 20.9979 |
| | 4 | −1.15 | −1.46 | 2.1316 | 1.317444 | 1.675788 |

$\Sigma Y = 8.37$  $\Sigma X = 11.51$  $\Sigma Y^2 = 981.65$  $\Sigma X^2 = 1607.2$  $\Sigma XY = 1142.2$

*(Continued)*

1. Beta:

$$\frac{(T \times \Sigma XY) - (\Sigma Y \times \Sigma X)}{(T \times \Sigma X^2) - (\Sigma X)^2} = \frac{(16 \times 1142.19) - (11.51 \times 8.37)}{(16 \times 981.65) - (11.51)^2} = 1.16$$

2. Alpha:

$$\frac{\Sigma Y}{T} - \left( \text{Beta} \times \frac{\Sigma X}{T} \right) = \frac{8.37}{16} - \left( 1.16 \times \frac{11.51}{16} \right) = -0.31\%$$

3. Standard deviation of random error term:

$$\left[ \frac{\Sigma Y^2 - (\text{alpha} \times \Sigma Y) - (\text{Beta} \times \Sigma XY)}{T - 2} \right]^{1/2}$$

$$= \left[ \frac{1607.18 - (-0.31 \times 8.37) - (1.16 \times 1142.19)}{16 - 2} \right]^{1/2} = 4.49\%$$

4. Standard error of beta:

$$\frac{\text{Standard deviation of random error term}}{[\Sigma X^2 - (\Sigma X)^2/T]^{1/2}} = \frac{4.49}{[981.65 - (11.51)^2/16]^{1/2}} = .14$$

5. Standard error of alpha:

$$\frac{\text{Standard deviation of random error term}}{[T - (\Sigma X)^2/\Sigma X^2]^{1/2}} = \frac{4.49}{[16 - (11.51)^2/981.65]^{1/2}} = 1.12$$

6. Correlation coefficient:

$$\frac{(T \times \Sigma XY) - (\Sigma Y \times \Sigma X)}{[(T \times \Sigma Y^2) - (\Sigma Y)^2] \times [(T \times \Sigma X^2) - (\Sigma X)^2]^{1/2}}$$

$$= \frac{(16 \times 1142.19) - (11.51 \times 8.37)}{[(16 \times 1607.18) - (8.37)^2] \times [(16 \times 981.65) - (11.51)^2]^{1/2}} = .91$$

7. Coefficient of determination:

$$(\text{Correlation coefficient})^2 = (.91)^2 = .83$$

8. Coefficient of nondetermination:

$$1 - \text{coefficient of determination} = 1 - .83 = .17$$

---

[a] All summations are to be carried out over $t$, where $t$ goes from 1 to $T$ (in this example, $t = 1, \ldots, 16$).

were, respectively, 2.39% and 3.05%. Inserting these values into equation (23.10), the ex post SML for this time interval was:

$$ar_p^e = 2.39\% + (3.05\% - 2.39\%)\beta_p$$

$$= 2.39\% + 0.66\%\,\beta_p. \tag{23.11}$$

**FIGURE 23-4**
Performance evaluation using the ex post SML.

Thus, after estimating a portfolio's ex post beta and entering this value on the right-hand side of equation (23.11), a benchmark return for the portfolio can be determined. For example, a portfolio with a beta of .8 during 1986 to 1989 would have a benchmark return of $2.39\% + (0.66\% \times .8) = 2.92\%$. Figure 23.4 presents a graph of the ex post SML given by equation (23.11).

If the average return on a portfolio was $ar_p$, calculated as shown in equation (23.5), then one measure of its risk-adjusted performance would be the difference between its average return and its corresponding equilibrium or benchmark return. This difference is generally referred to as the portfolio's *ex post alpha* (or differential return) and is denoted by $\alpha_p$:

$$\alpha_p = ar_p - ar_p^e. \tag{23.12}$$

A positive value of $\alpha_p$ for a portfolio would indicate that the portfolio had an average return greater than the benchmark return, suggesting its performance was superior. On the other hand, a negative value of $\alpha_p$ would indicate that the portfolio had an average return less than the benchmark return, suggesting its performance was inferior.[4]

----

[4] This measure of performance is sometimes known as the *Jensen coefficient* because it was developed by Michael C. Jensen in "The Performance of Mutual Funds in the Period 1945-1964," *Journal of Finance* 23, no. 2 (May 1968):389–416.

By substituting the right-hand side of equation (23.10) for $ar_p^e$ in equation (23.12), it can be seen that a portfolio's ex post alpha is equal to

$$\alpha_p = ar_p - [ar_f + (ar_M - ar_f)\beta_p]. \qquad (23.13)$$

After determining the values for $\alpha_p$ and $\beta_p$ for a portfolio, the *ex post characteristic line* for the portfolio can be written as

$$r_p - r_f = \alpha_p + \beta_p(r_M - r_f). \qquad (23.14)$$

Graphically, this is the equation of a straight line, where $r_M - r_f$ is measured on the horizontal axis and $r_p - r_f$ is measured on the vertical axis. Furthermore, the line has a vertical intercept of $\alpha_p$ and a slope of $\beta_p$.

As an example, consider the performance of the hypothetical portfolio "First Fund," indicated in part A of Table 23.1 for the evaluation interval of 1986 to 1989. During this interval, the First Fund had an average quarterly return of 2.85%. Using equation (23.7), it can be shown that First Fund had a beta of 1.16. Having an average beta over the 16 quarters that is greater than the market portfolio's beta of 1 indicates that First Fund was aggressive (if it were less than 1, it would have been defensive).

Given these values for its beta and average return, the location of First Fund in Figure 23.4 is represented by the point having coordinates of (1.16, 2.85%), denoted by *FF*. The exact vertical distance from *FF* to the ex post SML can be calculated by using equation (23.13):

$$\begin{aligned}
\alpha_p &= ar_p - [ar_f + (ar_M - ar_f)\beta_p] \\
&= 2.85\% - [2.39\% + (3.05\% - 2.39\%)1.16] \\
&= -0.31\%.
\end{aligned}$$

Since *FF* lies below the ex post SML, its ex post alpha is negative, and its performance would be viewed as inferior.[5] Using equation (23.14), the *ex post* characteristic line for First Fund would be

$$r_p - r_f = -0.31\% + 1.16(r_M - r_f).$$

Figure 23.4 provides an illustration of this line.[6]

The method for determining a portfolio's ex post alpha, beta, and characteristic line suggests the use of a four-step procedure. First, having gathered the necessary return data, the average market return and risk-free rate can be determined with equations (23.8) and (23.9). Second, the portfolio's ex post beta can be determined by using the formula given in equation (23.7). Third, the portfolio's ex post alpha can be determined by using the formula given in equation (23.13). Fourth, these values for alpha and beta can be inserted in equation (23.14) in order to determine the portfolio's ex post characteristic

---

[5] Alternatively, if *FF*'s average return had been 4%, then its coordinates would have been (1.16, 4.00%), placing it above the ex post SML. In this situation, *FF*'s ex post alpha would have been 0.84%, and its performance would have been viewed as superior.

[6] An alternative measure of performance involves dividing the *ex post* alpha by an estimate of the ex post unique (or unsystematic) risk of the portfolio. This measure, known as the *appraisal ratio*, would be equal to $-0.31\%/4.48\% = -0.07$ for First Fund. Comparisons can be made with the value of the appraisal ratio for the market portfolio (its value is defined to be 0) and other portfolios. Note that a positive value indicates superior performance and that the larger the value, the better the performance. See Jack L. Treynor and Fischer Black, "How to Use Security Analysis to Improve Portfolio Selection," *Journal of Business* 46, no. 1 (January 1973):66–86.

line. However, there is a simpler method for determining a portfolio's *ex post* alpha, beta, and characteristic line that also provides a number of other pieces of information relating to the portfolio's performance. This method involves the use of simple linear regression and corresponds to the method presented in Chapter 15 for estimating the ex post characteristic line for an individual security.

With this method, the excess return on portfolio $p$ in a given period $t$ is viewed as having three components. The first component is the portfolio's alpha, the second component is a risk premium equal to the excess return on the market times the portfolio's beta, and the third component is a random error term.[7] These three components can be seen on the right-hand side of the following equation:

$$r_{pt} - r_{ft} = \alpha_p + \beta_p(r_{Mt} - r_{ft}) + \epsilon_{pt}. \qquad (23.15)$$

Since $\alpha_p$ and $\beta_p$ are assumed to be constant during the evaluation interval, equation (23.15) can be viewed as a regression equation. Accordingly, there are certain standard formulas for estimating $\alpha_p$, $\beta_p$, and a number of other statistical parameters associated with the regression equation.

Part (b) of Table 23.1 presents these formulas, with First Fund being used as an example. As can be seen, the formulas indicate that First Fund's ex post alpha and beta were equal to $-0.31\%$ and 1.16, respectively, over the time interval 1986 to 1989. These values are the same as those arising when equations (23.7) and (23.13) were used earlier. Indeed, they will always result in the same values.

Figure 23.5 presents a scatter diagram of the excess returns on First Fund and the TSE 300. Based on equation (23.15), the regression equation for First Fund is

$$r_{FF} - r_f = -0.31\% + 1.16(r_M - r_f) + \epsilon_{FF} \qquad (23.16)$$

where $-0.31\%$ and 1.16 are the estimated *ex post* alpha and beta for First Fund over the 1986 to 1989 time interval. As mentioned earlier, also shown in the figure is the ex post characteristic line for First Fund, a line that is derived by the use of simple linear regression:

$$r_{FF} - r_f = -0.31\% + 1.16(r_M - r_f). \qquad (23.17)$$

The vertical distance between each point in the scatter diagram and the regression line represents an estimate of the size of the random error term for the corresponding quarter. The exact distance can be found by rewriting equation (23.16) as

$$\epsilon_{FF} = (r_{FF} - r_f) - [-0.31\% + 1.16(r_M - r_f)]. \qquad (23.18)$$

For example, in the fourth quarter of 1988 the excess return on First Fund and the TSE 300 were 5.17% and 1.48%, respectively. The value of $\epsilon_{FF}$ for that quarter can be calculated by using equation (23.18) as follows:

$$\epsilon_{FF} = (5.17\%) - [-0.31\% + 1.16(1.48\%)]$$
$$= 3.76\%.$$

The values of $\epsilon_{FF}$ can be calculated similarly for the other 15 quarters of the evaluation interval. The standard deviation of the resulting set of 16 numbers is an

---

[7] The random error term can be viewed as a number that arises from a spin of a roulette wheel, where the numbers on the wheel are symmetrically distributed around zero. That is, the expected outcome from a spin of the roulette wheel is zero; the standard deviation associated with the wheel is denoted by $\sigma_{\epsilon p}$.

**FIGURE 23-5**
Ex post characteristic line for First Fund.

estimate of the standard deviation of the random error term (also known as the residual standard deviation), and is shown in part (b) of Table 23.1 to be equal to 4.48%. This number can be viewed as an estimate of the *ex post unique* (or unsystematic or nonmarket) *risk* of First Fund.

The regression line for First Fund that is shown in Figure 23.5 is the line of best fit for the scatter diagram. Given that a straight line is defined by its intercept and slope, there are no other values for alpha and beta that will define a straight line that fits the scatter diagram any better than this one. In simple regression, *best fit* means that there is no line that could be drawn such that the resulting standard deviation of the random error term is smaller than the one of best fit.

It should be pointed out that a portfolio's "true" ex post beta cannot be observed. All that can be done is to estimate its value. Thus, even if a portfolio's true beta remained the same forever, its estimated value, obtained in the manner illustrated in Table 23.1 and Figure 23.5, would still change from time to time because of errors (known as sampling errors) in estimating it. For example, if the 16 quarters for 1987 to 1990 were examined, the resulting estimated beta for First Fund would almost certainly be different from 1.16, the estimated value for 1986 to 1989.

The *standard error of beta* shown in Table 23.1 attempts to indicate the extent of such estimation errors. Given a number of necessary assumptions (for example, the true beta did not change during the estimation period of 1986 to 1989), the chances are roughly two out of three that the true beta is within one standard error, plus or minus, of the estimated beta. Thus, First Fund's true beta is likely to be between the values of $1.16 - 0.14 = 1.02$ and $1.16 + 0.14 = 1.30$. Similarly, the value for *standard error of alpha* provides an indication of the magnitude of the possible sampling error that has been made in estimating it.

The value for the *correlation coefficient* provides an indication of how closely the excess returns on First Fund were associated with the excess returns on the TSE 300. Since its range is between $-1$ and $+1$, the value for First Fund of 0.91 indicates a strong positive relationship between First Fund and the TSE 300. That is, larger excess returns for First Fund seem to have been closely associated with larger excess returns on the TSE 300.

The *coefficient of determination* represents the proportion of variation in the excess return on First Fund that is related to the variation in the excess return on the TSE 300. That is, it shows how much of the movement in First Fund's excess returns can be explained by movements in the excess returns on the TSE 300. With a value of 0.83, it can be seen that 83% of the movement in the excess return on First Fund over 1986 to 1989 can be attributed to movement in the excess return on the TSE 300.

Since the *coefficient of nondetermination* is 1 minus the coefficient of determination, it represents the proportion of movement in the excess return on First Fund that is not due to movement in the excess return on the TSE 300. Thus, 17% of the movement in First Fund cannot be attributed to movement in the TSE 300.

Although Table 23.1 shows the formulas for calculating all these values, it should be pointed out that there are many different software packages that can carry out all these calculations in a fraction of a second. The only substantive effort involves gathering all the return data shown in part (a) of Table 23.1 and then entering the information into a computer.

## ☐ 23.3.2  The Reward-to-Volatility Ratio

Closely related to the differential return measure of portfolio performance is a measure known as the *reward-to-volatility ratio*.[8] This measure, denoted by $\text{RVOL}_p$, also uses the ex post security market line to form a benchmark for performance evaluation. The calculation of the reward-to-volatility ratio for a portfolio involves dividing its average excess return by its market risk:

$$\text{RVOL}_p = \frac{ar_p - ar_f}{\beta_p}. \tag{23.19}$$

Here, the beta of the portfolio can be determined using the formula in equation (23.7).

Continuing with the example of First Fund, it was noted earlier that its average return for the evaluation interval of 1986 to 1989 was 1.85%. Furthermore, it had been noted that the average Treasury bill rate was 2.39%. Thus, the average excess return for First Fund was $2.85\% - 2.39\% = 0.46\%$ and, given a beta of 1.16, its reward-to-volatility ratio was $0.46\%/1.16 = 0.40\%$.

The reward-to-volatility ratio corresponds to the slope of a line originating at the average risk-free rate and going through the point $(\beta_p, ar_p)$. This can be seen by noting that the slope of a line is easily determined if two points on the line are known—it is simply the vertical distance between the two points (rise) divided by the horizontal distance between the two points (run). In this case, the vertical distance is $ar_p - ar_f$ and the horizontal distance is $\beta_p - 0 = \beta_p$, so the slope is $(ar_p - ar_f)/\beta_p$; this corresponds

---

[8] This measure of performance is sometimes known as the *Treynor ratio* because it was developed by Jack L. Treynor in "How to Rate Management of Investment Funds," *Harvard Business Review* 43, no. 1 (January–February 1965):63–75.

to the formula for $RVOL_p$ given in equation (23.19). Note that the value being measured on the horizontal axis is $\beta_p$ and the value being measured on the vertical axis is $ar_p$, suggesting that the line can be drawn on the same diagram as the ex post SML.

In the First Fund example, remember that the ex post SML for 1986 to 1989 was shown by the solid line in Figure 23.4. Also appearing in this figure was the point denoted by $FF$, corresponding to $(\beta_p, ar_p) = (1.16, 2.85\%)$ for First Fund. The line in this figure with dots and dashes originates from the point $(0, ar_f) = (0, 2.39\%)$, goes through $FF$, and has a slope of $(2.85\% - 2.39\%)/1.16 = 0.40\%$, which corresponds to the value noted earlier for $RVOL_p$.

The benchmark for comparison with this measure of performance is the slope of the ex post SML. Since this line goes through the points $(0, ar_f)$ and $(1, ar_M)$, its slope is simply $(ar_M - ar_f)/(1 - 0) = (ar_M - ar_f)$. If $RVOL_p$ is greater than this value, the portfolio lies above the ex post SML, indicating it has outperformed the market. Alternatively, if $RVOL_p$ is less than this value, the portfolio lies below the ex post SML, indicating it has not performed as well as the market.

In the case of First Fund, the benchmark is $(ar_M - ar_f) = (3.05\% - 2.39\%) = 0.66\%$. Since $RVOL_p$ for First Fund is less than the benchmark $(0.40\% < 0.66\%)$, according to this measure of portfolio performance, First Fund did not perform as well as the market.

In comparing the two measures of performance that are based on the ex post SML, $\alpha_p$ and $RVOL_p$, it should be noted that they *always* give the same assessment of a portfolio's performance relative to the market portfolio. That is, if one measure indicates the portfolio outperformed the market, so will the other. Similarly, if one measure indicates the portfolio did not perform as well as the market, the other measure will show the same thing. This can be seen by noting that any portfolio with a positive ex post alpha (an indication of superior performance) lies *above* the ex post SML and thus must have a slope *greater* than the slope of the ex post SML (also an indication of superior performance). Similarly, any portfolio with a negative ex post alpha (an indication of inferior performance) lies *below* the ex post SML and thus must have a slope *less* than the slope of the ex post SML (also an indication of inferior performance).

However, it should be noted that it is possible for the two measures to rank portfolios differently on the basis of performance simply because the calculations are different. For example, if Second Fund had a beta of 1.5 and an average return of 3.00%, its ex post alpha would be $3.00\% - [2.39\% + (3.05\% - 2.39\%)1.5] = -0.38\%$. Thus, its performance appears to be worse than First Fund, since it has a smaller ex post alpha $(-0.38\% < -0.31\%)$. However, its reward-to-volatility ratio of $0.41\% = (3.00\% - 2.39\%)/1.5$ is larger than the reward-to-volatility of 0.40% for First Fund, suggesting its performance was better than the First Fund.

## ☐ 23.3.3  The Reward-to-Variability Ratio

Both measures of risk-adjusted performance described so far, ex post alpha (that is, differential return) and the reward-to-volatility ratio, use benchmarks that are based on the ex post SML. Accordingly, they measure returns relative to the market risk of the portfolio. In contrast, the *reward-to-variability ratio* is a measure of risk-adjusted performance that uses a benchmark based on the ex post *capital market line* (CML).[9]

This means that it measures returns relative to the total risk of the portfolio, where total risk is the standard deviation of portfolio returns.

In order to use the reward-to-variability ratio ($\text{RVAR}_p$), the location of the ex post CML must be determined. This line goes through two points on a graph where average return is measured on the vertical axis and standard deviation is measured on the horizontal axis. The first point is the vertical intercept of the line and corresponds to the average risk-free rate during the evaluation interval. The second point corresponds to the location of the market portfolio, meaning its coordinates are the average return and standard deviation of return for the market portfolio during the evaluation interval, or $(\sum_M, ar_M)$. Since the ex post CML goes through these two points, its slope can readily be calculated as the vertical distance between the two points divided by the horizontal distance between the two points, or $(ar_M - ar_f)/(\sum_M - 0) = (ar_M - ar_f)/\sum_M$. Given a vertical intercept of $ar_f$, the equation of this line is

$$ar_p^e = \frac{ar_f + ar_M - ar_f}{\sigma_M}\sigma_p. \qquad (23.20)$$

In the example shown in Table 23.1, the average return and standard deviation for the TSE 300, calculated using equations (23.5) and (23.6), were 3.05% and 7.83%, respectively. Since the average return on Treasury bills was 2.39%, the ex post CML for 1986 to 1989 was

$$ar_p^e = 2.39\% + \frac{3.05\% - 2.39\%}{7.83\%}\sigma_p$$
$$= 2.23\% + 0.084\,\sigma_p. \qquad (23.21)$$

Figure 23.6 presents a graph of this line.

Having determined the location of the ex post CML, the average return and standard deviation of the portfolio being evaluated can be determined next by using equations (23.5) and (23.6). With these values in hand, the portfolio can be located on the same graph as the ex post CML. In the case of First Fund, its average return and standard deviation were 2.85% and 10.10%, respectively. Thus, in Figure 23.6 its location corresponds to the point having coordinates (10.1%, 2.85%), which is denoted by $FF$.

The calculation of the reward-to-variability ratio ($\text{RVAR}_p$) is analogous to the calculation of the reward-to-volatility ratio ($\text{RVOL}_p$) described earlier. Specifically, $\text{RVOL}_p$ involves dividing the portfolio's average excess return by its beta, whereas $\text{RVAR}_p$ involves dividing the portfolio's average excess return by its standard deviation:

$$\text{RVAR}_p = \frac{ar_p - ar_f}{\sigma_p}. \qquad (23.22)$$

Note that $\text{RVAR}_p$ corresponds to the slope of a line originating at the average risk-free rate and going through a point having coordinates of $(\sigma_p, ar_p)$. This can be seen by noting that the slope of this line is simply the vertical distance between the two points divided by the horizontal distance between the two points, or $(ar_p - ar_f)/(\sigma_p - 0) = (ar_p - ar_f)/\sigma_p$, which corresponds to the formula for $\text{RVAR}_p$ given in equation (23.22). Since the value being measured on the horizontal axis is $\sigma_p$ and the value being measured on the vertical axis is $ar_p$, the line can be drawn on the same diagram as the ex post CML.

---

[9] This measure of performance is sometimes known as the *Sharpe ratio* because it was developed by William F. Sharpe in "Mutual Fund Performance," *Journal of Business* 39, no. 1 (January 1966):119–38.

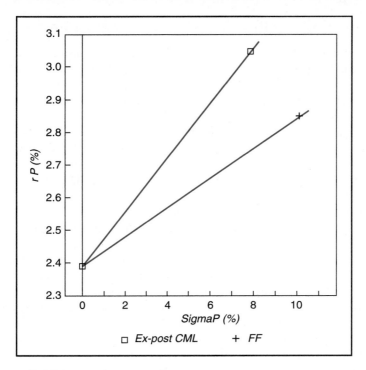

**FIGURE 23-6**
Performance evaluation using the ex post CML.

In the First Fund example, recall that the ex post CML for 1986 to 1989 was shown by the upper line in Figure 23.6. Also appearing in this figure was the point denoted by $FF$, corresponding to $(\sigma_p, ar_p) = (10.1\%, 2.85\%)$ for First Fund. The bottom line in this figure originates from the point $(0, ar_f) = (0, 2.39\%)$ and goes through $FF$; the slope of this line is simply $(2.85\% - 2.39\%)/10.1\% = 0.046$.

Since the ex post CML represents various combinations of risk-free lending or borrowing with investing in the market portfolio, it can be used to provide a benchmark for the reward-to-variability ratio in a manner similar to the SML-based benchmark for the reward-to-volatility ratio. As noted earlier, the slope of the ex post CML is $(ar_M - ar_f)/\sigma_M$. If $RVAR_p$ is greater than this value, the portfolio lies above the ex post CML, indicating it has outperformed the market. Alternatively, if $RVAR_p$ is less than this value, the portfolio lies below the ex post CML, indicating it has not performed as well as the market.[10]

In the case of First Fund, the benchmark is $(3.05\% - 2.39\%)/7.83\% = 0.084$. Since $RVAR_p$ is less than the benchmark $(0.046 < 0.084)$, First Fund did not perform as well as the market, according to this risk-adjusted measure of portfolio performance.

---

[10] There is a second measure of portfolio performance that is based on the ex post CML. This measure, called the *ex post total risk alpha*, is simply the vertical distance the portfolio lies above or below the ex post CML. It is similar to the measure referred to earlier as ex post alpha (or differential return), except that it is based on a different risk measure (total risk instead of market risk) and uses a different benchmark (the ex post CML instead of the ex post SML).

# ☐ 23.3.4 Comparing the Risk-Adjusted Measures of Performance

The measures of performance that are based on the ex post SML, $\alpha_p$ and $RVOL_p$, can be compared with the measure of performance that is based on the ex post CML, $RVAR_p$. Focusing on $RVOL_p$ (the comparison also applies to $\alpha_p$), it should be noted that in certain situations, $RVOL_p$ and $RVAR_p$ can give different assessments of a portfolio's performance relative to the market portfolio.

In particular, if $RVOL_p$ indicates the portfolio outperformed the market, it is possible for $RVAR_p$ to indicate the portfolio did not perform as well as the market. The reason for this is that the portfolio may have a relatively large amount of *unique* risk. Such risk would not be a factor in determining the value of $RVOL_p$ for the portfolio, since only *market risk* is in the denominator. However, such risk would be included in the denominator of $RVAR_p$ for the portfolio, since this measure is based on *total risk* (that is, both market and unique risk). Thus, a portfolio with a low amount of market risk could have a high amount of total risk, resulting in a relatively high $RVOL_p$ (due to the low amount of market risk) and a low $RVAR_p$ (due to the high amount of total risk). Accordingly, $RVOL_p$ could indicate the portfolio outperformed the market, while at the same time $RVAR_p$ indicates it did not perform as well as the market.[11]

As an example, consider Third Fund, which had an average return of 3.0%, a beta of .8, and a standard deviation of 18%. Accordingly, $RVOL_{TF} = (3.0\% - 2.39\%)/.8 = 0.76\%$, indicating that Third Fund outperformed the market portfolio, since the benchmark is $(3.05\% - 2.39\%)/1.0 = 0.66\%$. However, $RVAR_{TF} = (3.0\% - 2.39\%)/18\% = 0.034$, indicating that Third Fund did not perform as well as the market portfolio, since the benchmark is $(3.05\% - 2.39\%)/7.83\% = 0.084$. The reason for the difference can be seen by noting Third Fund's low beta relative to the market $(.8 < 1.0)$ but high standard deviation relative to the market $(18\% > 7.39\%)$. This suggests that Third Fund had a relatively high level of unique risk.

It also follows that it is possible for $RVOL_p$ and $RVAR_p$ to rank two or more portfolios differently on the basis of their performance. This is because these two measures of risk-adjusted performance utilize different types of risk.

Continuing the example, First Fund had an average return of 1.85%, a beta of 1.16, and a standard deviation of 10.1%. Thus, $RVOL_{FF} = (2.85\% - 2.39\%)/1.16 = 0.40\%$, which is less than $RVOL_{TF} = (3.0\% - 2.39\%)/0.8 = 0.76\%$, thereby indicating that First Fund ranked lower than Third Fund. However, $RVAR_{FF} = (2.85\% - 2.39\%)/10.1\% = 0.046$, which is greater than $RVAR_{TF} = 0.034$, thereby indicating that First Fund ranked higher than Third Fund.

Did Third Fund do better or worse than the market on a risk-adjusted basis? And did the Third Fund perform better or worse than First Fund? The answer to these two questions lies in identifying the appropriate measure of risk for the client. If the client has many other assets, then beta is the relevant measure of risk, and performance should be based on $RVOL_p$. To such a client, Third Fund should be viewed as a superior performer relative to both the market and First Fund. However, if the client has few other assets, then standard deviation is the relevant measure of risk, and performance should be based

---

[11] Since the market portfolio does not have any unique risk, it can be shown that if $RVOL_p$ indicates a portfolio did not perform as well as the market, then $RVAR_p$ must also indicate that the portfolio did not perform as well as the market. This is because a portfolio with a relatively high amount of market risk will also have a relatively high amount of total risk.

on RVAR$_p$. To such a client, Third Fund should be viewed as an inferior performer relative to both the market and First Fund.

## 23.4     MARKET TIMING

A successful market timer positions a portfolio to have a relatively high beta during a market rise and a relatively low beta during a market decline. This is because, as noted earlier, the expected return on a portfolio is a linear function of its beta:

$$\bar{r}_p = \alpha_p + r_f + (\bar{r}_M - r_f)\beta_p. \tag{23.23}$$

This means that a high beta portfolio will have a relatively high expected return if a market rise (that is, if $\bar{r}_M > r_f$) is anticipated. Similarly, a low beta portfolio will have a relatively high expected return if a market decline (that is, $\bar{r}_M < r_f$) is anticipated. Accordingly, the portfolio of a successful timer will outperform a benchmark portfolio that has a constant beta equal to the average beta of the timer's portfolio.

For example, if the market timer successfully set the portfolio beta at 0 when $\bar{r}_M < r_f$ and at 2 when $\bar{r}_M > r_f$, the return on the portfolio would be higher than the return on a portfolio having a beta constantly equal to 1. Unfortunately, if the market timer alters the portfolio's beta in ways unrelated to subsequent market moves (for example, sometimes setting the beta equal to zero when $\bar{r}_M > r_f$ and equal to two when $\bar{r}_M < r_f$), then the timer's portfolio will not perform as well as a constant beta portfolio.

To "time the market," either the average beta of the stocks held in the portfolio can be changed or the relative amounts invested in the risk-free asset and stocks can be altered. For example, to increase the beta of a portfolio, low-beta stocks could be sold, with the proceeds used to purchase high-beta stocks. Alternatively, Treasury bills in the portfolio could be sold (or the amount of borrowing increased), with the resulting proceeds invested in stocks.

In Figure 23.7, the excess returns of two hypothetical portfolios are measured on the vertical axis, while those of a market index are on the horizontal axis. Straight lines, fit via standard regression methods, reveal positive ex post alpha values in each case. However, the reasons for this differ. The scatter diagram for the portfolio shown in part (a) seems to indicate that the relationship between the portfolio's excess returns and the market's excess returns was linear, since the points cluster close to the regression line. This suggests that the portfolio consisted of securities in a manner such that the beta of the portfolio was roughly the same at all times. Since the ex post alpha was positive, it appears that the investment manager successfully identified and invested in some underpriced securities.

The scatter diagram for the portfolio shown in part (b) seems to indicate the relationship between this portfolio's excess returns and the market's excess returns was not linear, since the points in the middle lie below the regression line and those at the ends lie above the regression line. This suggests that the portfolio consisted of high-beta securities during periods when the market return was high and low-beta securities during periods when the market return was low. Upon examination, it appears that the portfolio has a positive ex post alpha due to successful market timing by the investment manager.

**FIGURE 23-7**
Superior fund performance.

## ☐ 23.4.1 Quadratic Regression

To measure the ability of an investment manager to time the market successfully, something more complex than a straight line can be fit to scatter diagrams such as those shown in Figure 23.7. One procedure fits a curve, where statistical methods are used to estimate the parameters $a$, $b$, and $c$ in the following quadratic regression equation:

$$r_{pt} - r_{ft} = a + b(r_{Mt} - r_{ft}) + c[(r_{Mt} - r_{ft})^2] + \epsilon_{pt} \qquad (23.24)$$

where $\epsilon_{pt}$ is the random error term.

The *ex post characteristic curve* shown in Figure 23.8(a) is simply the following quadratic function, where the values of $a$, $b$, and $c$ for the portfolio have been estimated by standard regression methods:

$$r_{pt} - r_{ft} = a + b(r_{Mt} - r_{ft}) + c[(r_{Mt} - r_{ft})^2]. \qquad (23.25)$$

If the estimated value of $c$ is positive [as it is for the portfolio depicted in Figure 23.8(a)], the curve would become less steep as one moves to the left. This would indicate that the portfolio manager successfully timed the market.[12] Note that this equation corresponds to the equation for the ex post characteristic line if $c$ is equal to zero; in such a situation, $a$ and $b$ would correspond to the portfolio's ex post alpha and beta, respectively.

---

[12] For details of the method, see Jack L. Treynor and Kay K. Mazuy, "Can Mutual Funds Outguess the Market?", *Harvard Business Review* 44, no. 4 (July-August 1966):131–36; and Anat R. Admati, Sudipto Bhattacharya, Paul Pfleiderer, and Stephen A. Ross, "On Timing and Selectivity," *Journal of Finance* 41, no. 3 (July 1986):715–30.

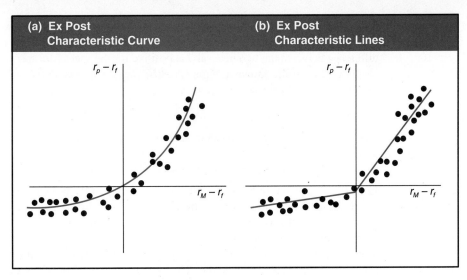

**FIGURE 23-8**
Ex post characteristic curve and lines.

## □ 23.4.2 Dummy Variable Regression

An alternative procedure fits two ex post characteristic lines to the scatter diagram, as shown in Figure 23.8(b). Periods when risky securities outperform risk-free securities (that is, when $r_{Mt} > r_{ft}$) can be termed *up markets*. Periods when risky securities do not perform as well as risk-free securities (that is, when $r_{Mt} < r_{ft}$) can be termed *down markets*. A successful market timer would select a high up-market beta and a low down-market beta. Graphically, the slope of the ex post characteristic line for positive excess market returns is greater than the slope of the ex post characteristic line for negative excess market returns.

To estimate such a relationship, standard regression methods can be used to estimate the parameters $a$, $b$, and $c$ in the following dummy variable regression equation:

$$r_{pt} - r_{ft} = a + b(r_{Mt} - r_{ft}) + c[D_t(r_{Mt} - r_{ft})] + \epsilon_{pt}. \qquad (23.26)$$

Here, $\epsilon_{pt}$ is the random error term and $D_t$ is a dummy variable that is assigned a value of 0 for any time period $t$ when $r_{Mt} > r_{ft}$ and a value of $-1$ for any time period $t$ when $r_{Mt} < r_{ft}$. To see how this works, consider the effective equations for different values of $r_{Mt} - r_{ft}$:

| Value of $r_{Mt} - r_{ft}$ | Equation |
|---|---|
| $> 0$ | $r_{pt} - r_{ft} = a + b(r_{Mt} - r_{ft}) + \epsilon_{pt}$ |
| $= 0$ | $r_{pt} - r_{ft} = a + \epsilon_{pt}$ |
| $< 0$ | $r_{pt} - r_{ft} = a + (b - c)(r_{Mt} - r_{ft}) + \epsilon_{pt}$ |

Note that the parameter $b$ corresponds to the portfolio's up-market beta, whereas $(b-c)$ corresponds to the portfolio's down-market beta. Thus, the parameter $c$ indicates the difference between the two betas and is positive for the successful market timer.

For the portfolio shown in Figure 23.8(b), the ex post characteristic line on the right side of the graph corresponds to the equation

$$r_{pt} - r_{ft} = a + b(r_{Mt} - r_{ft}) \qquad (23.27\,a)$$

whereas the ex post characteristic line shown on the left side of the graph corresponds to the equation

$$r_{pt} - r_{ft} = a + (b-c)(r_{Mt} - r_{ft}). \qquad (23.27\,b)$$

In this example, the investment manager has successfully engaged in market timing, since the slope of the line on the right side (that is, $b$) is greater than the slope of the line on the left side (that is, $b - c$).[13]

In either regression equation (23.24) or (23.26), the value of the parameter $a$ provides an estimate of the investment manager's ability to identify mispriced securities (that is, security selection), and the value of the parameter $c$ provides an estimate of the manager's ability at market timing. The difference between the two equations is that the quadratic equation indicates the portfolio's beta fluctuated over many values, depending on the size of the market's excess returns. This can be seen graphically by noting that the slope of the quadratic curve is continually increasing when moving from left to right in Figure 23.8(a). On the other hand, the dummy variable equation indicates the portfolio's beta fluctuates between just two values, depending on whether $r_M$ is less or greater than $r_f$. This can be seen graphically by noting that the slope of the equation increases from one value (that is, $b - c$) to a second value (that is, $b$) when moving from left to right in Figure 23.8(b).

## TABLE 23.2
Market Timing Test Results for First Fund.

| Parameter Being Estimated [a] | Ex Post Characteristic Line | Quadratic Equation | Dummy Variable Equation |
|---|---|---|---|
| $a$ | -0.31% | 1.10% | 2.20% |
| | (1.13) | (0.82) | (1.01) |
| $b$ | 1.16 | 1.16 | 1.66 |
| | (.14) | (0.096) | (0.16) |
| $c$ | — | -0.02 | -1.01 |
| | — | (.005) | (0.26) |
| Correlation[b] | 0.91 | 0.96 | 0.95 |

[a] Standard errors are shown in parentheses below the respective parameters.

[b] The correlation coefficient for the quadratic and dummy variable equations has been adjusted for the number of independent variables.

---

[13] For details, see Roy D. Henriksson and Robert C. Merton, "On Market Timing and Investment Performance. II. Statistical Procedures for Evaluating Forecasting Skills," *Journal of Business* 54, no. 4 (October 1981):513–33. Other authors have introduced related methods for distinguishing timing from selectivity; for a brief discussion of them, see pp. 254 -59 of Gordon J. Alexander and Jack Clark Francis, *Portfolio Analysis* (Englewood Cliffs, N.J.: Prentice Hall, 1986).

As an example, consider again the First Fund. Table 23.2 presents the results from applying regression equations (23.24) and (23.26) to this portfolio for the 16 quarters in the interval of 1986 to 1989 along with the ex post characteristic line results. The results in the table provide evidence of some positive selectivity, but negative market timing ability by the portfolio manager. This can be seen by noting that the parameter $a$ is negative in the simple regression but becomes positive when the effect of market timing is taken into account. The parameter $c$, however, is negative in both cases indicating that the manager tends to increase beta in down-markets and decrease it in up-markets.[14] The correlation is higher for both multiple regressions than for the ex post characteristic line. This is further evidence that negative market timing ability is present. Care should be taken in drawing conclusions from these regressions. An examination of Figure 23.5 suggests that two large outliers may be producing the results obtained.

## ☐ 23.4.3  Predictions of Market Direction

There is another approach to measuring the market timing ability of an investment manager. Unlike the quadratic and dummy variable regression approaches, this one is based on the market return predictions made by the manager. Rather than examining the returns on the portfolio, this approach examines the predicted market returns by comparing them with actual market returns. Accordingly, it assumes that the investment manager alters the composition of the portfolio based on the prediction that has been made.

Consider an investment manager who, prior to each period, makes a prediction about the market's return. Table 23.3 shows four relevant classifications in each part. These classifications are based on (1) the manager's prediction and (2) the corresponding actual outcome. Results from 100 periods are shown, where in 58 of the periods the market was actually up (that is, in 58 of the periods, $r_M > r_f$) and in 42 of the periods the market was actually down (that is, in 42 of the periods, $r_M < r_f$).[15]

---

[14] The size of parameter $c$ (as well as the parameters $a$ and $b$) should be judged relative to its standard error. In both equations shown here, it is quite large relative to the corresponding standard error. Most standard statistical textbooks have an introductory discussion of the regression procedures that are utilized here. See, for example, Peter Tryfos, *Business Statistics* (Toronto, Ont.: McGraw-Hill Ryerson, 1989).

[15] This conforms to actual experience from 1950 through 1987 when the TSE 300 outperformed Treasury bills 63% of the time.

**TABLE 23.3**

Predictions of Market Direction.

### a. Market Timer A

|  | | Actual | | |
|---|---|:---:|:---:|:---:|
|  | | Up | Down | Total |
| Prediction: | Up | 43 | 26 | 69 |
|  | Down | 18 | 11 | 31 |
|  | Total | 58 | 42 | 100 |
| Percentage right | | | | 52% |
| Predictive accuracy | | 68% | 30% | 98% |

### b. An Eternal Optimist

|  | | Actual | | |
|---|---|:---:|:---:|:---:|
|  | | Up | Down | Total |
| Prediction: | Up | 63 | 37 | 100 |
|  | Down | 0 | 0 | 0 |
|  | Total | 63 | 37 | 100 |
| Percentage right | | | | 63% |
| Predictive accuracy | | 100% | 00% | 100% |

### c. Market Timer B

|  | | Actual | | |
|---|---|:---:|:---:|:---:|
|  | | Up | Down | Total |
| Prediction: | Up | 37 | 17 | 54 |
|  | Down | 26 | 20 | 46 |
|  | Total | 63 | 37 | 100 |
| Percentage right | | | | 57% |
| Predictive accuracy | | 59% | 54% | 113% |

Part (a) shows the results for an investment manager referred to here as Market Timer A. In 52 of the 100 periods, the prediction of Market Timer A was correct — 40 "up" predictions were followed by actual up markets and 12 "down" predictions were followed by actual down markets.

Although it is tempting to consider this record successful, this particular type of analysis does not provide a very useful measure of the predictive ability of the investment manager. The reason can be seen by examining part (b). This part shows the record of the Eternal Optimist, an investment manager who always predicts that stocks will do well. Such a prediction will generally be right more than half the time, since historically there have been more up markets than down markets. In the example shown here, the Eternal Optimist was right 63% of the time. No predictive ability was required to achieve such a record. Instead, the investment manager just had to assume that $r_M$ would be greater than $r_f$ for each period.

The preceding result suggests a measure of the ability of a manager to time the market. As shown in part (a), Market Timer A predicted 43 of the 63 up-market periods correctly. Thus, A's predictive accuracy in up markets equaled 68% (43/63). On the other hand, A predicted only 11 of 37 down markets correctly, for a predictive accuracy of 30% (11/37). As shown in part (b), the Eternal Optimist is perfectly correct (100% = 63/63) in up markets and perfectly incorrect (0% = 0/37) in down markets. A summary measure should take into account the manager's ability to predict accurately both kinds of markets.

One such measure simply adds the two predictive acccuracies. Anyone can achieve a value of 100% for this score by always predicting just one outcome (for example, the Eternal Optimist, who always predicted an up market). A perfect market timer will make a score of 200%, since he or she will be correct 100% of the time in up markets as well as in down markets. Imperfect but valuable market timers will obtain scores between 100% and 200%. The greater the score, the higher the timing ability of the manager.

In the example shown in part (a), Market Timer A fell short of the mark, with an overall score of 98% = 68% + 30%. Part (c) shows the results of a different investment manager, referred to as Market Timer B. This manager was more successful, being right 59% (37/63) of the time in up markets and 54% (20/37) of the time in down markets, for an overall score of 113%. If this reflects skill rather than luck, then B can be expected to enhance the portfolio's rate of return in the future.

## 23.5 | CRITICISMS OF THESE RISK-ADJUSTED PERFORMANCE MEASURES

The previously mentioned risk-adjusted measures of portfolio performance have been criticized on several grounds. Some of the major criticisms are described in this section.

### ☐ 23.5.1 Use of a Market Surrogate

All the measures other than the reward-to-variability ratio require the identification of a market portfolio. This means that whatever surrogate is used, it can be criticized as being inadequate. Indeed, it has been shown that by making slight changes in the surrogate, the performance rankings of a set of portfolios can be completely reversed (that is, the top-ranked portfolio with one surrogate could be the bottom-ranked portfolio if a slightly different surrogate was used). However, it has been noted that when commonly used NYSE-based surrogates are involved, such as the Dow Jones Industrial Average, the S&P 500, and an index comparable to the New York Stock Exchange Composite, the performance rankings of common stock portfolios appear to be quite similar.[16]

---

[16] See Richard Roll, "Ambiguity When Performance Is Measured by the Security Market Line," *Journal of Finance* 33, no. 4 (September 1978):1051–69; and David Peterson and Michael L. Rice, "A Note on Ambiguity in Portfolio Performance Measures," *Journal of Finance* 35, no. 5 (December 1980):1251–56.

## 23.5.2 Distinguishing Skill from Luck

A very long evaluation interval is needed in order to be able to obtain a measure of performance that can distinguish skill from luck on the part of the investment manager. That is, it would be useful to know if an apparently successful manager was skilled or just lucky, since skill can be expected to have a favorable impact on the portfolio's performance in the future, whereas luck cannot be expected to continue. Unfortunately, too many years' worth of experience is generally needed to make such a determination.[17]

## 23.5.3 Measuring the Risk-Free Rate

The use of Treasury bills for measuring the risk-free rate in determining benchmark portfolios based on either the ex post SML or CML can be criticized. Consider a benchmark portfolio that involves an investment in both Treasury bills and the market portfolio. Such a benchmark portfolio can be criticized for having too low a rate of return, making it easy for a portfolio to show superior performance. This is because Treasury bills may provide excessively low returns to compensate for their high degree of liquidity. If a higher risk-free rate (such as the commercial paper rate) is used, then any benchmark portfolio that lies between this risk-free rate and the market portfolio on either the ex post SML or CML will have a higher rate of return and thus represent a higher but more appropriate standard.

Next, consider a benchmark portfolio that involves levering a positive investment in the market portfolio by borrowing at the risk-free rate. Use of the Treasury bill rate can be criticized because realistic borrowing alternatives typically involve a higher rate and are thus less attractive. Accordingly, benchmarks that involve borrowing at the Treasury bill rate have too high a rate of return, making it difficult for a portfolio to show superior performance. If a higher risk-free borrowing rate (such as the call money rate plus a small premium) is used, then any benchmark portfolio involving risk-free borrowing will have a lower rate of return and thus represent a lower but more appropriate standard.

In summary, measures of portfolio performance based on either the ex post SML or CML and utilizing Treasury bills to determine the risk-free rate are alleged to discriminate in favor of conservative portfolios and against aggressive ones.[18]

---

[17] See Dan W. French and Glenn V. Henderson, Jr., "How Well Does Performance Evaluation Perform?" *Journal of Portfolio Management* 11, no. 2 (Winter 1985):15–18.

[18] Some people argue that the use of a market surrogate like the TSE 300 will also result in an unfair standard, since investing in a market surrogate is not as simple as it may seem. With the existence of index funds and index futures, this criticism does not appear to have much force.

### ☐ 23.5.4 Validity of the CAPM

The measures of portfolio performance that involve beta (namely, the ex post alpha and reward-to-volatility measures) are based on the CAPM, yet the CAPM may not be the correct asset pricing model. That is, perhaps assets are priced according to some other model. If so, the use of beta-based performance measures will be inappropriate.

Interestingly, a measure analogous to ex post alpha has been shown to be a meaningful guage of performance if the arbitrage pricing theory's (APT) model of asset pricing is believed to be more appropriate.[19] Furthermore, the reward-to-variability ratio is immune to this criticism, since it uses standard deviation as a measure of risk and does not rely on the validity of the CAPM or the identification of a market portfolio.

### ☐ 23.5.5 Performance Attribution

The previously mentioned risk-adjusted measures of performance concentrate on the question of *how* a portfolio did relative to both a benchmark and a set of other portfolios. The use of quadratic and dummy variable regression is an attempt to evaluate separately the manager's ability at selectivity and timing. However, the client might want to know more about *why* the portfolio had a certain return over a particular time period.[20] *Performance attribution* using a "factor model" is one method that has been used to try to make such a determination; an example is presented in the appendix.

## 23.6 BOND PORTFOLIO PERFORMANCE EVALUATION

The performance of portfolios consisting of bonds (and other types of fixed-income securities) is often evaluated by comparing their total returns (consisting of coupon payments plus capital gains or losses) with those of an index representing a comparable class of securities over some evaluation interval.

### ☐ 23.6.1 Bond Indices

Bond indices typically represent either the average yield-to-maturity or the average price on a portfolio of bonds that have certain similar characteristics. Figure 23.9 presents various bond indices that are published monthly by *ScotiaMcLeod Inc.* Average yield as well as price and total return indices are reported. This bulletin also includes information (not shown) about residential mortgages, money market instruments and Euro-Canadian

---

[19] Under APT (discussed in Chapter 9), there is another measure of portfolio performance that has even more theoretical justification than the APT-based ex post alpha. This measure is analogous to the CAPM-based "appraisal ratio" mentioned in footnote 6 and involves dividing the APT-based ex post alpha by the ex post standard deviation of the APT-based random error term. For details, see Gregory Connor and Robert A. Korajczyk, "Performance Measurement with the Arbitrage Pricing Theory: A New Framework for Analysis," *Journal of Financial Economics* 15, no. 3 (March 1986):373–94; and Bruce N. Lehmann and David M. Modest, "Mutual Fund Performance Evaluation: A Comparison of Benchmarks and Benchmark Comparisons," *Journal of Finance* 42, no. 2 (June 1987):233–65.

[20] For a study that used the CAPM framework to do this, see Eugene F. Fama, "Components of Investment Performance," *Journal of Finance* 27, no. 3 (June 1972):551–67.

# CANADIAN BOND MARKET SECTOR PERFORMANCE

| December 31, 1991 | Avg. Yield | Price Index | Total Return Index | Total Returns Percentage Change Last Month | Last 3 Months | Last 6 Months | Year to Date | Last 1 Year | Sector Weight | Dur- ation* | Avg. Coupon | Avg. Term | Con- vexity |
|---|---|---|---|---|---|---|---|---|---|---|---|---|---|
| **SHORT TERM BOND INDEX** | | | | | | | | | | | | | |
| Canadas | 7.49 | 99.05 | 184.38 | 1.44 | 4.55 | 9.92 | 17.42 | 17.42 | 62.4 | 2.42 | 10.28 | 2.8 | 0.079 |
| Provincials | 8.06 | 102.37 | 188.71 | 1.56 | 4.64 | 10.67 | 19.25 | 19.25 | 28.5 | 2.74 | 10.86 | 3.2 | 0.109 |
| Municipals | 8.19 | 101.27 | 194.07 | 1.64 | 4.76 | 11.07 | 20.50 | 20.50 | 1.8 | 2.68 | 11.08 | 3.2 | 0.095 |
| All Governments | 7.68 | 99.97 | 185.76 | 1.48 | 4.58 | 10.15 | 17.95 | 17.95 | 92.7 | 2.52 | 10.48 | 2.9 | 0.089 |
| AAA | 8.37 | 106.36 | 185.56 | 0.75 | 3.01 | 8.24 | 16.74 | 16.74 | 0.7 | 2.30 | 9.19 | 2.6 | 0.069 |
| AA | 9.06 | 103.77 | 184.01 | 1.00 | 3.74 | 8.79 | 16.98 | 16.98 | 2.0 | 2.85 | 10.40 | 3.5 | 0.104 |
| A | 9.17 | 104.73 | 187.43 | 1.12 | 4.11 | 9.21 | 18.01 | 18.01 | 3.1 | 2.77 | 10.61 | 3.3 | 0.101 |
| BBB | 10.21 | 105.18 | 190.89 | 0.31 | 3.19 | 8.22 | 16.05 | 16.05 | 1.5 | 2.26 | 10.43 | 2.6 | 0.068 |
| All Corporates | 9.28 | 104.59 | 186.90 | 0.89 | 3.70 | 8.79 | 17.15 | 17.15 | 7.3 | 2.64 | 10.38 | 3.2 | 0.092 |
| Overall | 7.80 | 100.26 | 185.82 | 1.44 | 4.51 | 10.04 | 17.89 | 17.89 | 100.0 | 2.53 | 10.47 | 2.9 | 0.089 |
| **MID TERM BOND INDEX\*\*** | | | | | | | | | | | | | |
| Canadas | 8.15 | 106.74 | 193.18 | 2.75 | 7.30 | 16.13 | 23.11 | 23.11 | 52.4 | 5.59 | 10.23 | 7.9 | 0.390 |
| Provincials | 8.77 | 106.30 | 194.52 | 2.64 | 6.65 | 15.73 | 24.45 | 24.45 | 32.1 | 5.16 | 10.25 | 7.7 | 0.341 |
| Municipals | 8.95 | 105.68 | 199.90 | 2.81 | 7.01 | 16.53 | 24.91 | 24.91 | 2.8 | 5.58 | 11.01 | 8.3 | 0.392 |
| All Governments | 8.40 | 106.55 | 193.93 | 2.71 | 7.03 | 15.98 | 23.68 | 23.68 | 87.3 | 5.43 | 10.27 | 7.9 | 0.372 |
| AAA | 8.82 | 108.42 | 190.98 | 2.08 | 6.32 | 15.54 | 23.62 | 23.62 | 1.1 | 5.34 | 10.08 | 7.4 | 0.348 |
| AA | 9.09 | 105.56 | 193.21 | 2.46 | 6.14 | 15.25 | 23.65 | 23.65 | 5.6 | 5.48 | 10.51 | 7.9 | 0.371 |
| A | 9.50 | 105.43 | 194.28 | 1.83 | 5.77 | 14.89 | 23.31 | 23.31 | 4.5 | 5.32 | 10.58 | 7.9 | 0.358 |
| BBB | 10.05 | 103.62 | 192.12 | 1.17 | 5.38 | 14.09 | 21.46 | 21.46 | 1.6 | 4.79 | 10.67 | 6.7 | 0.281 |
| All Corporates | 9.33 | 105.64 | 193.45 | 2.05 | 5.94 | 15.02 | 23.25 | 23.25 | 12.7 | 5.32 | 10.52 | 7.7 | 0.353 |
| Overall | 8.52 | 106.44 | 194.04 | 2.62 | 6.88 | 15.86 | 23.63 | 23.63 | 100.0 | 5.42 | 10.30 | 7.8 | 0.370 |
| **LONG TERM BOND INDEX\*\*** | | | | | | | | | | | | | |
| Canadas | 8.80 | 108.93 | 199.80 | 2.96 | 7.58 | 18.06 | 24.52 | 24.52 | 58.0 | 8.42 | 10.74 | 17.6 | 1.046 |
| Provincials | 9.50 | 105.43 | 200.43 | 2.74 | 6.86 | 17.95 | 26.45 | 26.45 | 31.5 | 7.64 | 10.89 | 18.6 | 0.908 |
| Municipals | 9.68 | 106.16 | 205.51 | 2.81 | 7.30 | 18.70 | 27.15 | 27.15 | 1.5 | 7.91 | 11.21 | 16.0 | 0.889 |
| All Governments | 9.05 | 107.73 | 200.08 | 2.88 | 7.33 | 18.02 | 25.14 | 25.14 | 91.0 | 8.14 | 10.80 | 18.0 | 0.996 |
| AAA | 9.57 | 105.34 | 194.03 | 2.79 | 6.71 | 17.72 | 26.85 | 26.85 | 2.0 | 8.10 | 10.27 | 16.4 | 0.937 |
| AA | 9.68 | 106.63 | 198.97 | 2.80 | 7.07 | 17.59 | 26.51 | 26.51 | 2.3 | 8.41 | 10.89 | 18.9 | 1.048 |
| A | 9.97 | 107.22 | 200.80 | 2.61 | 6.53 | 17.45 | 27.56 | 27.56 | 3.1 | 8.33 | 11.06 | 19.1 | 1.034 |
| BBB | 11.27 | 97.56 | 189.14 | -1.71 | 1.86 | 12.87 | 22.03 | 22.03 | 1.5 | 7.73 | 11.48 | 18.0 | 0.885 |
| All Corporates | 10.03 | 104.94 | 196.59 | 1.95 | 5.89 | 16.76 | 26.16 | 26.16 | 9.0 | 8.20 | 10.91 | 18.2 | 0.991 |
| Overall | 9.14 | 107.55 | 199.86 | 2.79 | 7.19 | 17.90 | 25.30 | 25.30 | 100.0 | 8.15 | 10.81 | 18.0 | 0.995 |

\* All Duration Figures are Macaulay Duration

\*\* ScotiaMcLeod will make available to interested parties two series of unrevised monthly mid and long figures in a new supplementary report titled "Unrevised Mid and Long Term Bond Total Return Indices". Please contact Melanie Moore (416) 862-3031 for further information.
   ScotiaMcLeod Short, Mid and Long Bond Indices measure the returns of 1-5 year, 5-10 year and greater than 10 year bonds respectively.

**FIGURE 23-9**
Bond indices published monthly by ScotiaMcLeod Inc.

*SOURCE:* Melanie Moore, *Debt Market Indices*, ScotiaMcLeod Inc., (December 31, 1991):1.

issues. Historical information is provided in *ScotiaMcLeod's Handbook of Canadian Debt Market Indices* published annually.

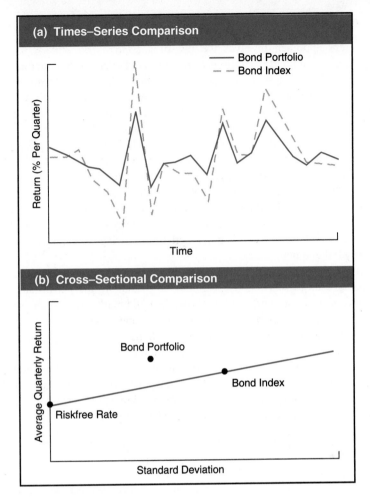

**FIGURE 23-10**
Bond portfolio performance evaluation.

## ☐ 23.6.2 Time Series and Cross-Sectional Comparisons

Figure 23.10 illustrates two ways of comparing the returns on a bond portfolio with those on a bond index over an evaluation interval. In part (a), a time-series comparison is made, where the bond portfolio's quarterly returns over time during the evaluation interval are graphed along with those of the bond index. In part (b), a cross-sectional comparison is made in a manner similar to the equity performance measures that were based on the ex post CML. Here the bond portfolio's average return and standard deviation are graphed and compared with a line that goes through the average risk-free rate and the average return and standard deviation of the bond index (instead of an equity index), based on quarterly returns during the evaluation interval.

## ☐ 23.6.3 Bond Market Line

A different approach involves the use of a *bond market line*.[21] Assume that the performance of a bond portfolio is to be evaluated over a given quarter (or year, since this approach can be used for a longer period). First, the quarterly return for the portfolio is calculated, along with the portfolio's average duration for the quarter (this could be calculated by averaging the portfolio's duration at the beginning and end of the quarter). The portfolio is then plotted on a graph that measures return on the vertical axis and duration on the horizontal axis. Second, the return and average duration for a broadly representative bond index such as the Salomon Brothers' High-Grade Long-Term Corporate Bond Index are calculated for the same quarter, and plotted on the same graph. Third, the 90-day Treasury bill rate at the beginning of the quarter can also be determined and then plotted on the graph (since the Treasury bill is a pure discount security, its duration is the same as its term-to-maturity — 90 days, or roughly .25 years). Lastly, the bond market line is constructed by drawing a straight line connecting the Treasury bill and bond index.

The performance of the bond portfolio can now be evaluated with the bond market line being used to serve as a benchmark in evaluating the performance of the bond portfolio. If the bond portfolio lies above the bond market line, such as the one shown in Figure 23.11, it outperformed the benchmark and its performance would be viewed as superior. Conversely, if it lies below the bond market line, it underperformed the benchmark and its performance is viewed as inferior.[22]

Other bond portfolios and indices can also be shown on the graph to give more information on the relative performance of the portfolio being evaluated. In Figure 23.11, one federal government and three corporate bond indices are shown, in addition to the overall corporate bond index published by Merrill Lynch.

## 23.7 SUMMARY

This chapter has discussed how a portfolio's performance can be evaluated. Doing so is important regardless of whether or not the owner of the portfolio is the one who has been managing the portfolio. If the owner has been the manager, then good performance can be an incentive to continue with existing investment procedures, whereas poor performance can result in changes to these procedures. If the investment manager is someone other than the owner, then good performance can be rewarded, whereas poor performance can result in changing either the constraints placed on the manager, the investment objectives given to the manager, or the size of the portfolio for which the manager is responsible.

In evaluating performance, there are two major tasks. First, it is important to try to determine whether the performance is superior or inferior. This is often done by

---

[21] See Wayne H. Wagner and Dennis A Tito, "Definitive New Measures of Bond Performance and Risk," *Pension World* 13, no. 5 (May 1977):10–12, and "Is Your Bond Manager Skillful?" *Pension World* 13, no. 6 (June 1977):9–13. Bond portfolio performance is also discussed in Peter O. Dietz and Jeannette R. Kirschman, "Evaluating Portfolio Performance," Chapter 14 in *Managing Investment Portfolios*, eds. John L. Maginn and Donald L. Tuttle (Boston, Mass.: Warren, Gorham & Lamont, Inc., 1983).

[22] Using the bond market line as a benchmark in this manner is similar to using the SML as a benchmark in evaluating the performance of equity portfolios.

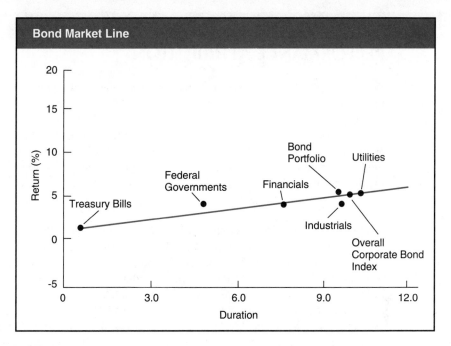

**FIGURE 23-11**
Bond market line.

*SOURCE:* Adapted from Wayne H. Wagner and Dennis A. Tito, "Definitive New Measures of Bond Performance and Risk," *Pension World* 13, no. 5 (May 1977):12.

comparing the performance of the portfolio with the performance of some benchmark portfolio and other actual portfolios. Second, it is also important to try to determine if a portfolio's performance has been the result of skill or luck. After all, if superior performance was due to skill, then such performance can be expected to continue in the future. Unfortunately, neither of these tasks can be done easily and precisely.

Evaluating performance involves determining the average return and risk of the portfolio over some time interval. For equity portfolios, two measures of risk are often used — beta and standard deviation. Sometimes the average return and risk are looked at separately, and sometimes they are combined into a single risk-adjusted measure of performance. Three such risk-adjusted measures were discussed — ex post alpha, reward-to-volatility ratio, and reward-to-variability ratio. More recently developed measures attempt to see if the investment manager has successfully timed the market.

Performance evaluation of bond portfolio managers also involves calculating the periodic returns on the portfolio over some evaluation interval. Then these periodic returns are compared with those on one or more bond indices. This can be accomplished by either graphing the periodic returns over time, or by comparing the average return and standard deviation (or duration) of the portfolio with those of the bond index.

While these performance measures have been subject to various criticisms, it should be kept in mind that risk should not be ignored in portfolio performance measurement. Instead, such measures should be interpreted with caution, and opinions should be formed with extreme care.

## PERFORMANCE ATTRIBUTION

With performance attribution, an attempt is made to ascertain why an equity portfolio had a given return over a particular time period. One procedure for making such a determination involves assuming security returns are related to a number of prespecified factors as well as to sector-factors.[23] For example, there may be a beta factor, a size factor, and two sector-factors that indicate whether or not a stock is an industrial. With such a model, the returns for a set of stocks during a given time period are related to these factors and sector-factors in the following manner:

$$r_i = \beta_i F_1 + s_i F_2 + c_{i1} SF_1 + c_{i2} SF_2 + \epsilon_i. \tag{23.28}$$

Here each stock has four attributes — $\beta_i$, $s_i$, $c_{i1}$, and $c_{i2}$. The attributes $\beta_i$ and $s_i$ are, respectively, the beta and firm size of stock $i$ in a given time period, and $c_{i1}$ and $c_{i2}$ are sector-factor attributes that have values of 1 and 0, respectively, if stock $i$ is an industrial firm and values of 0 and 1 if stock $i$ is not an industrial firm. (For example, it may be a utility or transportation company such as Canadian Utilities or PWA.)

The factors and sector-factors $F_1$, $F_2$, $SF_1$, and $SF_2$ are parameters that can be estimated using a statistical technique known as multiple regression. For example, the returns for 500 firms for 1991 could be calculated. Then, the betas for each stock could be estimated using 16 quarters of returns ending with the last quarter of 1990 (by using the characteristic line equation given earlier). The firm size for each stock could be measured by taking the market price per share as of December 31, 1990, multiplying it by the number of shares outstanding at that time, and then taking the logarithm of the product (expressed in billions). Lastly, each firm can be classified as either an industrial or nonindustrial, resulting in a value of 0 or 1 assigned to $c_{i1}$ and $c_{i2}$. This will give four columns of 500 numbers representing security attributes — one column with the betas for each stock, one column for the firm sizes of each stock, and two columns of 0s and 1s corresponding to whether the firms are industrials or nonindustrials — upon which will be "regressed" the column of returns for the 500 stocks during 1991.

Suppose the resulting regression resulted in estimated values for $F_1$, $F_2$, $SF_1$, and $SF_2$ of 1.20, $-.40$, 10.00, and 9.00, respectively. Then, equation (23.28) for 1991 would be

$$r_i = 1.20\,\beta_i - .40\,s_i + 10.00\,c_{i1} + 9.00\,c_{i2} + \epsilon_i. \tag{23.29}$$

Since the estimated value of $F_1$ (1.20) is positive, the year of 1991 was one where high beta stocks tended to outperform low beta stocks. Furthermore, since the estimated value of $F_2$ ($-.40$) is negative, the year 1991 was one where the stocks of small firms tended to outperform the stocks of large firms. With an estimated value for $SF_1$ that is greater than the estimated value for $SF_2$ ($10.00 > 9.00$), 1991 also appears to have been a year when industrials tended to outperform nonindustrials.

Equation (23.29) can be used to analyze the 1991 return on a stock. Consider, for example, a hypothetical industrial stock that had a return of 12.13%, a beta of .8, and size of 4.00 (its market value was $54.6 billion, so $s_i$ = natural logarithm of 54.6 = ln(54.6) = 4.00). According to equation (23.29), the "normal" return on such a stock is

---

[23] Factor models are discussed in Chapter 9.

$( 1.20 \times .8) - ( .40 \times 4.00) + ( 10.00 \times 1) + ( 9.00 \times 0) = 9.36\%$. Thus, for this stock, its "nonfactor return" ($\epsilon_i$) for 1991 was $12.13\% - 9.36\% = 2.77\%$, suggesting this particular stock did relatively well in comparison with other stocks having comparable attributes.

Similar analysis can be conducted on a portfolio's return for 1991. Consider a hypothetical portfolio that had a return of 10.03% in 1991. Upon close examination, it has been determined that this portfolio had an average beta of 1.3 and an average size of 3.2 (that is, the average value of $s_i$ for all the stocks held was 3.2). Furthermore, 67% of the stocks in the portfolio were industrials and 33% were nonindustrials. According to equation (23.29), the normal return on such a portfolio is $( 1.20 \times 1.30) - ( .40 \times 3.20) + ( 10.00 \times .67) + ( 9.00 \times .33) = 9.95\%$. Since the nonfactor return on this portfolio was $10.03\% - 9.95\% = .08\%$, this portfolio shows little evidence of successful security selection.

Such absolute performance evaluation with a factor model is interesting, but in many cases comparative performance is more relevant. A manager may do poorly in a bad market. But if he or she provides a higher return than would have been obtained otherwise, the client is clearly better off. With comparative performance, the overall return of a portfolio is compared with that of one or more other portfolios or market indices in order to determine the *differences* in the returns. Then the sources of the differences can be determined with *comparative performance attribution*.

Assume that the $i$ in equation (23.28) refers to the portfolio under evaluation. Letting $j$ refer to the return on a portfolio (or market index) to which it is to be compared, the difference in their returns is simply $r_i - r_j$. Using equation (23.28), this difference can be expressed as

$$r_i - r_j = ( \beta_i F_1 + s_i F_2 + c_{i1} SF_1 + c_{i2} SF_2 + \epsilon_i )$$
$$- ( \beta_j F_1 + s_j F_2 + c_{j1} SF_1 + c_{j2} SF_2 + \epsilon_j ). \qquad (23.30)$$

Gathering similar terms, this equation can be rewritten as

$$r_i - r_j = F_1 ( \beta_i - \beta_j ) + F_2 ( s_i - s_j )$$
$$+ SF_1 ( c_{i1} - c_{j1} ) + SF_2 ( c_{i2} - c_{j2} ) + ( \epsilon_i - \epsilon_j ). \qquad (23.31)$$

Each of the first four terms represents a differential effect equal to the product of (1) the difference in the attributes of the two portfolios and (2) the actual value of the related factor. The last term in the equation indicates the difference in the nonfactor returns of the two portfolios.

Table 23.4 provides an example where portfolio $i$ is the one mentioned earlier that had a return in 1987 of 10.03%. It is being compared with a portfolio that had a return in 1987 of 11.21%. This comparison portfolio had a beta of 1.50, and the average size of the firms whose stocks it held was 1.40. Furthermore, 80% of the portfolio's funds were invested in industrials, with the remaining 20% being invested in nonindustrials. Using equation (23.29), the normal return on such a portfolio in 1987 was $( 1.20 \times 1.50) - ( .40 \times 1.40) + ( 10.00 \times .80) + ( 9.00 \times .20) = 11.04\%$, indicating the portfolio had a nonfactor return of $11.21\% - 11.04\% = .17\%$.

**TABLE 23.4**
Comparative Performance Attribution.

|  | Attribute | | | | Differential Effect |
|---|---|---|---|---|---|
|  | Portfolio $i$ (a) | Portfolio $j$ (b) | Difference (c) = (a) − (b) | Factor (d) | (e) = (c) × (d) |
| a. Factors: | | | | | |
| Common factors | | | | | |
| Beta | 1.30 | 1.50 | −.20 | 1.20 | − .24% |
| Size | 3.20 | 1.40 | 1.80 | −.40 | − .72% |
| Sector-factors | | | | | |
| Industrials | .67 | .80 | −.13 | 10.00 | −1.30% |
| Nonindustrials | .33 | .20 | .13 | 9.00 | 1.17% |
|  | | | | | −1.09% |

|  | Returns | | |
|---|---|---|---|
|  | Portfolio $i$ (a) | Portfolio $j$ (b) | Difference (c) = (a) − (b) |
| b. Returns: | | | |
| Factor return | 9.95% | 11.04% | −1.09% |
| Nonfactor return | .08% | .17% | − .09% |
| Total return | 10.03% | 11.21% | −1.18% |

A direct comparison of the two portfolios reveals a difference in returns of $r_i - r_j = 10.03\% - 11.21\% = -1.18\%$. That is, portfolio $i$ performed worse than portfolio $j$ by 1.18%. Security selection played a small role, since the nonfactor returns were both quite low (.08% for portfolio $i$ and .17% for portfolio $j$). On balance, sector selection lowered returns for portfolio $i$ relative to portfolio $j$ slightly — the sum of the values in the last column for the two sector-factors was −0.13%. In portfolio $i$, industrials were underweighted relative to portfolio $j$, while nonindustrials were overweighted. A successful "sector picker" would have placed bets on (that is, overweighted) the sector with a relatively high factor value (industrials) and placed bets against (that is, underweighted) the sector with a relatively low factor value (nonindustrials), leading to a net positive *sector bet effect*. In 1987, the investment manager for portfolio $i$ was not as successful a sector picker as the investment manager for portfolio $j$.

The major sources of the relatively lower performance of portfolio $i$ were those associated with common factors. The manager had lower-beta stocks than those in comparison portfolio $j$ during a period when high-beta stocks tended to do better than low-beta stocks. That is, the manager placed a bet against high-beta stocks in favor of low-beta stocks and lost. He or she also had invested in stocks that were larger than those in portfolio $j$ during a period when larger stocks tended to do poorly. That is, the manager placed a bet against smaller firms in favor of larger firms and lost. Both differences lowered returns relative to the comparison portfolio, with the size bet being more detrimental than the beta bet.

1. Why do cash inflows and outflows between the beginning and end of a performance evaluation period complicate the measurement of portfolio returns?
2. Ginger Beaumont began the year 1991 with a portfolio valued at $10,000 and made a contribution to and a withdrawal from this portfolio over the next three months. Information regarding amounts and dates of these cash flows and the portfolio's market value at various dates is shown below.

| Date | Contribution(+) or Withdrawal(−) | Portfolio Value |
|---|---|---|
| 12/31/90 | $ 0 | $10,000 |
| 1/31/91 | +956 | 9,000 |
| 2/28/91 | −659 | 12,000 |
| 3/31/91 | 0 | 13,000 |

   a. Calculate the dollar-weighted return for the three-month period. (*Hint*: Unless you have a suitable calculator, you will have to use trial and error to find the dollar-weighted return. To begin, the monthly dollar-weighted return is less than 10%.)
   b. Calculate the time-weighted return for the three-month period.
   c. Why is the time-weighted return for the quarter less than the dollar-weighted return in this particular problem?
3. Why does performance evaluation require an appropriate benchmark in order to be meaningful? How would you define the term "appropriate" in this context?
4. It is common practice for performance evaluation services to compare the returns on a common stock portfolio to a distribution of returns obtained from a large sample of other common stock portfolios. What potential problems are involved in this sort of analysis?
5. The performance of the Venus Fund, a common stock mutual fund, compared with that of the TSE 300 over a ten-year period, is as follows:

| | Venus Fund | TSE 300 |
|---|---|---|
| Average quarterly excess return | 0.6% | 0.5% |
| Standard deviation of quarterly excess returns | 9.9% | 6.6% |
| Beta | 1.10 | 1.00 |

Donald Vance is considering investing in either the Venus Fund or another mutual fund whose objective is to track the performance of the TSE 300. Which fund would you recommend that Donald select, assuming that your decision is based solely on past performance? Justify your answer using various measures of risk-adjusted performance.

6. Why is the reward-to-variability ratio a more appropriate measure of performance than the ex post alpha if the portfolio being assessed represents the entire wealth of the portfolio's owner?

7. Can the ex post alpha, the reward-to-volatility ratio, and the reward-to-variability ratio give conflicting answers to the question of whether a particular portfolio has outperformed the market portfolio on a risk-adjusted basis? If so, which of these measures can conflict with the others, and why can this conflict occur?

8. Does a portfolio's ex post alpha measure gains and losses due to security selection, market timing, or both? Explain.

9. Assume that broad stock market indices, such as the TSE 300, are not good surrogates for the "true" market portfolio. What potential problems does this cause for performance evaluation using the ex post alpha measure?

10. You are given the following historical performance information on the capital markets and the Jupiter Fund, a common stock mutual fund.

| Year | Jupiter Fund Beta | Return on Jupiter Fund | Return on TSE 300 | Return on Treasury Bills |
|------|------|------|------|------|
| 1969 | 0.90 | − 2.99% | − 8.50% | 6.58% |
| 1970 | 0.95 | 0.63 | 4.01 | 6.53 |
| 1971 | 0.95 | 22.01 | 14.31 | 4.39 |
| 1972 | 1.00 | 24.08 | 18.98 | 3.84 |
| 1973 | 1.00 | −22.46 | −14.66 | 6.93 |
| 1974 | 0.90 | −25.12 | −26.47 | 8.00 |
| 1975 | 0.80 | 29.72 | 37.20 | 5.80 |
| 1976 | 0.75 | 22.15 | 23.84 | 5.08 |
| 1977 | 0.80 | 0.48 | −7.18 | 5.12 |
| 1978 | 0.85 | 6.85 | 6.56 | 7.18 |

a. Compute the Jupiter Fund's average beta over the ten-year period. What investment percentages in the TSE 300 and Treasury bills are required in order to produce a beta equal to the fund's average beta?

b. Compute the year-by-year returns that would have been earned on a portfolio invested in the TSE 300 and Treasury bills in the proportions calculated in part (a).

c. Compute the year-by-year returns that would have been earned on a portfolio invested in the TSE 300 and Treasury bills in the proportions needed to match Jupiter's beta year by year. (*Note*: These proportions will change yearly as the fund's beta changes yearly.)

d. One measure of a fund's *market timing ability* is the average difference between (1) what the fund would have earned annually by investing in the TSE 300 and Treasury bills so that the year-by-year beta equals the fund's actual year-by-year beta, and (2) what the fund would have earned annually by investing in the TSE 300 and Treasury bills so that the year-by-year beta equals the fund's average beta. Given your previous calculations, evaluate Jupiter's market timing ability.

e. One measure of a fund's *security selection ability* is the average difference between (1) the fund's annual return and, (2) what the fund would have earned annually by investing in the TSE 300 and Treasury bills so that the year-by-year beta equals the fund's actual year-by-year beta. Calculate Jupiter's average return and then, using your previous calculations, evaluate Jupiter's security selection ability.

11. Discuss the potential drawbacks of evaluating bond portfolio performance by using a bond market line.

12. (Appendix Question) What is the purpose of performance attribution? What types of problems can hinder performance attribution?

13. (Appendix Question) Assume that security returns are explained by a sector-factor model. Henri Stephens has been asked to develop a performance attribution report analyzing the returns on Portfolio A versus those of the market portfolio for the year 1988, and has collected the following information:

|  | Portfolio A | Market Portfolio | Sector/Factor Values |
|---|---|---|---|
| 1988 Return | 12.50% | 5.50% | — |
| Beta | 1.10 | 1.00 | −0.50 |
| Size | 1.30 | 6.00 | −0.60 |
| % Industrial | 40% | 80% | 8.00 |
| % Nonindustrial | 60% | 20% | 16.00 |

Unfortunately, Henri is confused by the subject of performance attribution. Carry out the analysis for him.

## SUGGESTED READINGS

Jack L. Treynor, "How to Rate Management of Investment Funds," *Harvard Business Review* 43, no. 1 (January-February 1965):63–75,

William F. Sharpe, "Mutual Fund Performance," *Journal of Business* 39, no. 1 (January 1966):119–38, and

Michael C. Jensen, "The Performance of Mutual Funds in the Period 1945–1964," *Journal of Finance* 23, no. 2 (May 1968):389–416 are the three classic articles on the subject. Each of the authors has a measure of performance named after him.

Eugene F. Fama, "Components of Investment Performance," *Journal of Finance* 27, no. 3 (June 1972):551–67 uses the CAPM as framework for performance evaluation.

Richard Roll, "Ambiguity When Performance is Measured by the Security Market Line," *Journal of Finance* 33, no. 4 (September 1978):1051–68 points the pitfalls involved in using the CAPM as a benchmark for measuring performance.

Gregory Connor and Robert A. Korajczyk, "Performance Measurement with the Arbitrage Pricing Theory: A New Framework for Analysis," *Journal of Financial Economics* 15, no. 3 (March 1986):373–94 advocates the use of the APT to measure performance.

John McLaughlin and Nathan Bossen, "The Historical Performance of Canadian Investment Managers: Predictor of Future Performance," *Canadian Investment Review*

III, no. 1 (Spring 1990):86–91 ask an important question related to the selection of an investment manager.

Timothy Appelt, "Active Management: What is the Right Performance Benchmark?", *Canadian Investment Review* V, no. 1 (Spring 1992):67–74 asks another important question related to performance evaluation of professional managers.

# Chapter 24

EXTENDED DIVERSIFICATION

One of the major themes of modern portfolio theory concerns the merits of diversification: In an efficient capital market, sensible investment strategies will include holdings of many different assets. Previous chapters have considered traditional securities, such as stocks and bonds, and some less traditional ones, such as options and futures. However, an investor should also consider holding foreign securities and tangible assets.

This chapter discusses these two aspects of diversification and then turns to a less lofty subject: betting on sporting events. As indicated in previous chapters, active investment management can be considered a form of betting. This rather subtle form of wagering that is handled by security brokers and dealers is compared and contrasted with the more explicit form handled by people at racetracks and by bookmakers.

## 24.1 INTERNATIONAL INVESTMENT

If the world were under one political jurisdiction, with one currency and complete freedom of trade, then the market portfolio could be thought of as including all securities in the world, each in proportion to its market value. In such a situation, limiting one's investments to securities representing firms located in only one part of the world would most likely result in a relatively low rate of return per unit of risk. After all, few people would advocate that Albertans own only securities issued by Albertan firms. And in a world without political boundaries, few people would advocate that Canadians own only securities issued by Canadian firms.

Unfortunately, there are political boundaries, different currencies, and restrictions on trade and currency exchange. Such unpleasantries diminish, but do not destroy, the advantages to be gained from international investment.

### ☐ 24.1.1 The World Market Wealth Portfolio

Figure 24.1 provides a 1984 year-end estimate of the world market wealth portfolio, defined to include those "capital market securities that are most marketable and most

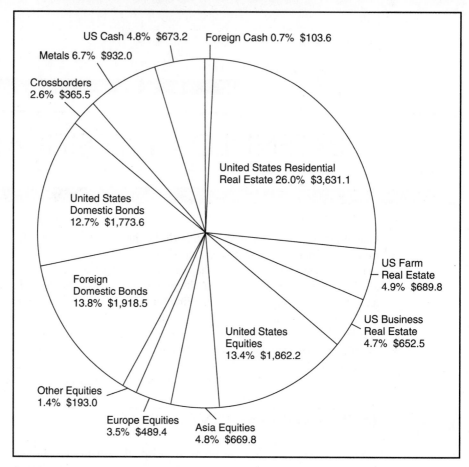

**FIGURE 24-1**

The World Market Wealth Portfolio, year end 1984.

*SOURCE:* Roger G. Ibbotson, Laurence B. Siegel, and Kathryn S. Love, "World Wealth: Market Values and Returns," *Journal of Portfolio Management* 12, no. 1 (Fall 1985):6.

identifiable. These are the securities that make up the opportunity set faced by most investors."[1]

Many problems are encountered in the construction of a world market wealth portfolio. It is almost impossible to represent adequately *all* security markets, as indicated by the authors of the paper from which Figure 24.1 is taken:

> We have excluded huge categories of assets from the portfolio, while at the same time we have included categories that are not wealth at all.
>
> …the most important omission is human capital, which is probably the largest single component of world wealth. We have also excluded …foreign real estate … proprietorships and partnerships …many small corporations …[and] personal holdings

---

[1] Roger G. Ibbotson, Laurence B. Siegel, and Kathryn S. Love, "World Wealth: Market Values and Returns," *Journal of Portfolio Management* 12, no. 1 (Fall 1985):5.

such as automobiles, cash balances, and various consumer capital goods. We have not only omitted a large proportion of wealth, but we also have little idea as to how large the omitted proportion is.

Our inclusions may misrepresent the market even more than our omissions. We have included US and foreign government debt that is almost certainly not backed dollar-for-dollar by government-owned assets such as parks and bridges. More likely, it is backed by claims on a future tax base. Other inclusions in our portfolio also misrepresent wealth. For example, some corporations own parts of other corporations, causing double counting.[2]

Table 24.1 provides a breakdown of the values of equities and bonds that are shown in Figure 24.1.[3] As shown in part (a) of the table, US bonds and stocks made up \$3635.8 billion (= \$1862.2 + \$1773.6) of the \$7272.0 billion world equity and bond value at the end of 1984. In percentage terms, this is about half the value of the world total. Part (b) indicates that most of the US equity total is attributable to the equities listed on the New York Stock Exchange, while most of the foreign equity total is attributable to Asian equities.[4] Part (c) indicates that government debt is larger than corporate debt both inside and outside the United States.

## ☐ 24.1.2 International Equity Indices

In most countries, there are indices of overall stock values and of the values of stocks within various industry or economic sectors. Such indices can be used for assessing "market moves" within the country and, more importantly, for comparative performance measurement. Important indices from countries outside North America include the Financial Times-Stock Exchange 100 Index (often referred to as FT-SE, or the "footsie") for the London Stock Exchange; the Nikkei 225 Index for the Tokyo Stock Exchange; the Paris Bourse's CAC Gen and the DAX Index for the Frankfurt Stock Exchange.[5] As shown in Figure 24.2(a), these and other indices are published daily in *The Financial Post*. With the advent of 24 hour trading across different exchanges worldwide and greater international brokerage representation for investors the financial press also reports quotations for individual companies in different overseas markets. These are also shown in Figure 24.2(a).

On the international level, the indices produced by *Morgan Stanley Capital International Perspective* are also widely used for such purposes. Monthly values are calculated for the levels of 6 international indices, 19 national indices, and 38 international industry indices. Each index represents the value of a market-weighted

---

[2] Ibbotson, Siegel, and Love, "World Wealth: Market Values and Returns," 5.

[3] In this table, preferred shares are arbitrarily listed under corporate debt. Also, a bond is considered to be "crossborder" if the currency of the bond is not the currency of the borrower's home country or the bond is primarily bought by investors outside the borrower's home country.

[4] Since Japanese equities are included in the Asian total, it appears that as of the end of 1984, US equities were of greater market value than Japanese equities. However, data contained in *Morgan Stanley Capital International Perspective*, October 1987 (New York: Morgan Stanley) suggest that Japanese equities have surpassed United States equities in total market value.

[5] Chapter 21 discussed major Canadian and US stock market indices (see Figure 21.2). For a discussion of European stock markets, see Gabriel Hawawini, *European Equity Markets: Price Behavior and Efficiency*, Monograph Series in Finance and Economics 1984–4/5, Salomon Brothers Center for the Study of Financial Institutions, Graduate School of Business Administration, New York University.

**TABLE 24.1**
World Equity and Bond Values, Year-End 1984 (in billions of US dollars).

| A. Summary | | |
|---|---|---|
| United States Equities | $1862.2 | |
| Foreign Equities | 1352.4 | |
| Total Equities | | $3214.4 |
| United States Bonds | $1773.6 | |
| Foreign Bonds | 2284.0 | |
| Total Bonds | | $4057.6 |
| Total Equities and Bonds | | $7272.0 |

| B. Market Values of Equities | | |
|---|---|---|
| United States: | | |
| New York Stock Exchange | $1587.0 | |
| American Stock Exchange | 68.2 | |
| Over-the-Counter | 207.0 | |
| Total United States | | $1862.2 |
| Foreign: | | |
| Europe | $ 489.4 | |
| Asia | 669.8 | |
| Other | 193.0 | |
| Total Foreign | | $1352.4 |
| Total Equities | | $3214.4 |

| C. Market Values of Bonds | | |
|---|---|---|
| United States: | | |
| Government | | |
| Notes | $ 720.0 | |
| Bonds | 164.8 | |
| Agencies | 525.9 | |
| Total Government | | $1410.7 |
| Corporate | | |
| Medium-Term | $ 164.5 | |
| Long-Term | 152.9 | |
| Preferred Shares | 45.5 | |
| Total Corporate | | $ 362.9 |
| Total United States | | $1773.6 |
| Foreign: | | |
| Domestic | | |
| Government | $1288.2 | |
| Corporate | 630.3 | |
| Total Domestic | | $1918.5 |
| Crossborders | | 365.5 |
| Total Foreign | | $2284.0 |
| Total Bonds | | $4057.6 |

SOURCE: Adapted from Roger G. Ibbotson, Laurence B. Siegel, and Kathryn S. Love, "World Wealth: Market Values and Returns," *Journal of Portfolio Management* 12, no. 1 (Fall 1985):7–9.

portfolio of stocks (using total shares outstanding). Values for each of the 19 national indices are given in both the local currency and in US dollars based on exchange rates at the time. Values of the other indices are stated only in US dollars. At last count, 1371 stocks were included, representing approximately 60% of the aggregate market value listed on the 19 covered stock exchanges.[6]

All 1371 stocks are used to compute the "World" index. The "Europe" index includes 526 companies representing 12 European countries. The "Europe, Australia, Far East" (EAFE) index, representing a portfolio of 911 stocks from 17 countries, is widely used by investors as a benchmark when evaluating the performance of international portfolio managers. These indices are published weekly in the *The Globe and Mail: Report on Business*, as shown in Figure 24.2(b); the EAFE, World and Emerging Market indices appear at the bottom of the table.

## ☐ 24.1.3 Risk and Return from Foreign Investing

Investing in a foreign security involves all the risks associated with investing in a domestic security, plus additional risks that are encountered because the investor expects to receive cash flows in the future from the foreign security. However, these cash flows will be in a foreign currency and thus will be of relatively little use to the investor if they cannot be converted into the investor's domestic currency. The additional risks associated with foreign investing are due to uncertainties associated with converting these foreign cash flows into domestic currency. They are known as *political risk* and *exchange* (or currency) *risk*.[7]

Political risk refers to uncertainty about the *ability* of an investor to convert the foreign currency into domestic currency. Specifically, a foreign government might restrict, tax, or completely prohibit the exchange of one currency for another. Since such policies change from time to time, the ability of an investor to repatriate foreign cash flows may be subject to some uncertainty. There may even be a possibility of complete expropriation, making political risk very large.

Exchange risk refers to uncertainty about the *rate* at which a foreign currency can be exchanged for the investor's domestic currency in the future. That is, at the time a foreign security is bought, the rate at which future foreign cash flows can be converted into domestic currency is uncertain, and it is this uncertainty that is known as exchange risk.

### Hedging Exchange Risk

To an extent, exchange risk can be reduced by hedging in the forward (or futures) market for foreign currency. In the case of default-free fixed-income securities, it may be possible to completely eliminate such risk in this way. For example, assume that a one-year pure discount bond paying 1000 British pounds at maturity can be purchased for 925 British pounds. Furthermore, assume that a forward contract can be signed

---

[6] *Morgan Stanley Capital International Perspective*, October 1987 (New York: Morgan Stanley). For more on these and other indices, see Chapter 5 in Bruno Solnik, *International Investments* (Reading, Mass.: Addison-Wesley Publishing Company, Inc., 1986).

[7] The effect these types of risk have on asset pricing has been considered by a number of people. For a discussion and list of references, see Chapters 1 and 5 in Solnik, *International Investments*.

**FIGURE 24-2**

(a) International stock market quotations and equity indices.

*SOURCE:* Reprinted by permission of *The Financial Post,* The Financial Post Company (February 19, 1992).

# THE WEEK IN NUMBERS

## THE MARKETS

|  | This week | Last week | Change |
|---|---|---|---|
| TSE 300 | 3349.69 | 3415.09 | −1.9% |
| Toronto 35 | 181.93 | 186.32 | −2.4% |
| Best group: Mines & minerals | 2990.12 | 2953.02 | −1.3% |
| Worst group: Real estate & const. | 5534.30 | 5869.45 | −5.7% |
| Dow Jones industrial average | 3324.46 | 3366.5 | −1.2% |
| Morgan Stanley World Index | 490.6 | 491.9 | −0.3% |
| −World ex U.S. and Canada (EAFE) | 758.4 | 753.7 | −0.6% |
| −Emerging Markets | 347.5 | 348.2 | −0.2% |

**FIGURE 24-2**

(b) Benchmark international equity indices.

*SOURCE:* Reprinted by permission of *The Globe and Mail: Report on Business,* Thomson Newspapers Company Limited (April 25, 1992).

where the investor will receive $2110.50 for delivering 1000 British pounds a year from now. In this situation, the rate of return *in British pounds* on this security is 8.11% $((1000 - 925)/925))$.

If the current (that is, spot) exchange rate were $2.1673 per pound, then the cost of this bond to a Canadian investor would be $2004.75 $(925 \times \$2.1673)$. Thus, the rate of return *in Canadian dollars* on this British security would be: $((\$2110.50 - \$2004.75)/\$2004.75) = 5.27\%$

Except for political risk, this is a certain return, since exchange risk has been completely removed by hedging with a forward contract.

Unfortunately, it is not possible to hedge completely the exchange risk associated with risky investments. Forward contracts can be made to cover expected cash flows, but if the actual cash flows are larger or smaller than expected, then some of the foreign currency may have to be exchanged at the spot rate prevailing at the time that the cash is received. Since future spot rates usually cannot be predicted with complete certainty, this will affect overall risk. As a practical matter, this "unhedgeable" risk is likely to be small. Nevertheless, the cost of hedging foreign investments may exceed the benefit — perhaps by a large amount.

## Foreign and Domestic Returns

Changes in exchange rates can cause major differences between the returns obtained by domestic investors and the returns obtained by unhedged foreign investors.

Consider a Canadian investor and a Swiss investor, both of whom purchase shares of a Swiss company whose stock is traded only in Switzerland. Let the price of the shares in Swiss francs be $P_0$ at the beginning of a period and $P_1$ at the end of the period. The *domestic return,* denoted by $r_d$, is

$$r_d = \frac{P_1 - P_0}{P_0}. \tag{24.1}$$

For example, if $P_0 = 10$ Swiss francs and $P_1 = 12$ Swiss francs, then $r_d = (12 - 10)/10 = 20\%$.

For the Swiss investor, $r_d$ is the stock's return. Not so for the Canadian investor. Assume that at the beginning of the period the price (in dollars) of one Swiss franc is $0.8481. Denoting this exchange rate (that is, the exchange rate at the beginning of the period) by $X_0$, the cost of a share to the Canadian investor will be $X_0 P_0$. In the example, this cost will be $0.8481 \times 10 = \$8.48$.

Now, assume that the exchange rate rises to $0.8905 per Swiss franc at the end of the period. Denoting this by $X_1$, the ending value of a share for the Canadian investor will be $X_1 P_1$. In the example, this value will be $\$.8905 \times 12 = \$10.69$.

The *foreign return* (that is, the return to a foreign investor), denoted by $r_f$, is:

$$r_f = \frac{X_1 P_1 - X_0 P_0}{X_0 P_0}. \tag{24.2}$$

In the example, the foreign investor (a Canadian) would have earned a return of $r_f = (\$10.69 - \$8.48)/\$8.48 = 26\%$ on an investment in the Swiss firm's stock.

In effect, the Canadian has made *two* investments: (1) an investment in a Swiss stock and (2) an investment in the Swiss franc. Accordingly, the overall return to the Canadian can be decomposed into a return on the investment in the Swiss stock and a return on an investment in the Swiss franc. This can be illustrated by considering a Canadian who had purchased a Swiss franc at the beginning of the period. If the Canadian subsequently sold the franc at the end of the period, the return on foreign currency, denoted by $r_c$, would be

$$r_c = \frac{X_1 - X_0}{X_0}. \tag{24.3}$$

In the example, $r_c = (\$0.8905 - \$0.8481)/\$0.8481 = 5\%$.

From equations (24.1), (24.2), and (24.3), it can be shown that

$$1 + r_f = (1 + r_d)(1 + r_c) \tag{24.4}$$

which can be rewritten as

$$r_f = r_d + r_c + r_d r_c. \tag{24.5}$$

In the example, equation (24.5) reveals that $r_f = .20 + .05 + (.20 \times .05)$, which is equal to 26%.

The last term in this equation $(r_d r_c)$ will generally be smaller than the two preceding ones, since it equals their product and both are generally less than 1.0. Thus, equation (24.5) can be restated as an approximation

$$r_f \approx r_d + r_c. \tag{24.6}$$

It can now be seen that the return on a foreign security $(r_f)$ can be decomposed into two parts, representing the domestic return on the security $(r_d)$ and the return on foreign currency $(r_c)$. In the example, the precise value for $r_f$ was shown earlier to be 26%; use of the approximation indicates its value to be equal to .20 + .05, or 25%. Thus, the approximation is in error by 1%, a relatively small amount.

## Expected Returns

Equation (24.6) leads directly to the proposition that the expected return on a foreign security will approximately equal the expected domestic return plus the expected return on foreign currency:

$$\bar{r}_f \approx \bar{r}_d + \bar{r}_c. \qquad (24.7)$$

It might be tempting for an investor to purchase a foreign security that has a high expected return in its host country, $\bar{r}_d$ , on the belief that this means the security will have a high expected return to the investor, $\bar{r}_f$ . However, equation (24.7) reveals this type of logic to be flawed. Just because a foreign security has a high value for $\bar{r}_d$ does not mean that it has a high value for $\bar{r}_f$ , since $\bar{r}_c$ can be negative. This can be shown by considering the case of bonds.

The expected domestic returns of bonds in countries with high expected inflation rates will typically be high. However, a foreign investor in a country with a lower expected inflation rate should expect a *negative* return on foreign currency, as his or her currency can be expected to *appreciate* relative to that of the country with the higher expected inflation rate. In evaluating the expected return on the foreign security, there is thus good news (a high expected domestic return, $\bar{r}_d$ ) and bad news (a negative expected return on foreign currency, $\bar{r}_c$). On balance, the expected foreign return $\bar{r}_f$ might not be as exceptional as first thought when just $\bar{r}_d$ was considered. Indeed, if markets were completely integrated, it would be reasonable to expect the values of $\bar{r}_d$ and $\bar{r}_c$ to sum to an amount $\bar{r}_f$ that is equal to the expected return on an equivalent bond in the investor's own country.

## Foreign and Domestic Risks

Having seen in equation (24.7) that the expected return on a foreign security consists of two components, it is appropriate that the risk of the foreign security be evaluated next. As before, consider a Canadian investor and a Swiss investor who have purchased shares of a Swiss company. The domestic variance, denoted by $\sigma_d^2$, is the risk that the Swiss investor faces with respect to the Swiss stock. Correspondingly, the foreign variance, denoted by $\sigma_f^2$, is the risk that the Canadian investor faces with respect to the Swiss stock. Based on equation (24.6), it can be shown that the foreign variance consists of three components:

$$\sigma_f^2 = \sigma_d^2 + \sigma_c^2 + 2\rho_{dc}\sigma_d\sigma_c \qquad (24.8)$$

where $\sigma_c^2$ is the variance associated with the currency return to a Canadian from investing in Swiss francs and later exchanging them for Canadian dollars, and $\rho_{dc}$ is the correlation coefficient between the returns on the Swiss stock and the return on Swiss francs.

For example, assume that the domestic variance is 225 (meaning that the domestic standard deviation, $\sigma_d$, is $\sqrt{225} = 15\%$) and the currency variance is 25 (meaning the currency standard deviation, $\sigma_c$, is $\sqrt{25} = 5\%$). If $\rho_{dc} = 0$, then equation (24.8) indicates that the foreign variance is $225 + 25 = 250$. Accordingly, the foreign standard deviation is $\sqrt{250} = 15.8\%$, which is only slightly greater than the domestic standard deviation of 15%.

Equation (24.8) reveals that the smaller the correlation between returns on a foreign currency and returns on a foreign investment, the smaller will be the foreign variance. One study that used data from 17 countries over the period from January 1971 through

December 1980 found an average correlation of .034, which is effectively, zero.[8] Thus, it appears that the correlation is sufficiently small that the foreign variance typically will be near, but not less than, the sum of the domestic and currency variances.[9]

Table 24.2 provides evidence on the relative magnitudes of the three types of risk. Standard deviations of monthly values over the period from December 1970 through December 1980 are shown for domestic risk (corresponding to $\sigma_d$), currency risk (corresponding to $\sigma_c$), and foreign risk (corresponding to $\sigma_f$), where the latter two types of risk have been measured from the perspective of a US investor. The last column represents the ratio of foreign risk to domestic risk. Thus, a ratio greater than 1 can be taken as an indication that the risk to a US investor is greater than the risk to a domestic investor. Indeed, with the exception of Hong Kong stocks, all the ratios are greater than 1, suggesting that fluctuations in currency exchange rates increased the risk a US investor would have faced in buying foreign securities.

The importance of currency risk can easily be exaggerated. Calculations such as those in Table 24.2 assume that investors purchase only domestic goods and services and thus convert all proceeds from foreign investments into their own currency before engaging in any spending for consumption purposes. But most people buy foreign goods and many buy foreign services as well (for example, as tourists). The cheaper another country's currency relative to one's own, the more attractive purchases of its goods and services will be. Other things being equal, it may make sense to invest more in countries whose products and scenery are admired, for the effective currency risk is likely to be smaller there than elsewhere. Furthermore, the riskiness of real returns may be less than that of nominal returns if the exchange rate movements are related to inflation differentials.

## ☐ 24.1.4 The Implications for Canadian Investors

In a global perspective, Canadian markets are small (the equity market represents about 2.5% of global equity capitalization) and heavily concentrated in cyclical resource industries. International investment, therefore, offers Canadian investors an opportunity to increase return and reduce risk through extended diversification. A revealing study demonstrates the advantages of global diversification by examining the effects of adding foreign stocks to a diversified Canadian portfolio.[10] The S&P 500 and EAFE indices were used as proxies for two different kinds of diversified foreign portfolios. The study looked at the addition of these foreign portfolios (both hedged and unhedged) to a domestic portfolio. Hedging was accomplished by buying the appropriate forward contracts. Table 24.3 shows the correlation coefficients between the foreign portfolios (hedged and unhedged) and three classes of Canadian securities.

---

[8] Bruno Solnik and Eric Nemeth, "Asset Returns and Currency Fluctuations: A Time Series Analysis," paper presented at the second tagung, Geld Banken und Versicherungen, Universitat Karlsruhe, December 1982.

[9] Since standard deviation is the square root of variance, this means that the foreign standard deviation will typically be substantially less than the sum of the domestic and currency standard deviations.

[10] Robert Auger and Denis Parisien, "The Risks and Rewards of Global Investing", *Canadian Investment Review* II, no.1 (Spring 1989):25–30.

**TABLE 24.2**

Risks for Domestic and US Investors Based on Historic Values, December 1970-December 1980.

| | (1) Domestic Risk | (2) Currency Risk | (3) Foreign Risk | (4) Foreign Domestic Risk |
|---|---|---|---|---|
| *Stocks* | | | | |
| Australia | 24.62% | 9.15% | 27.15% | 1.10 |
| Belgium | 13.28 | 11.02 | 18.76 | 1.41 |
| Canada | 18.92 | 4.16 | 20.29 | 1.07 |
| Denmark | 15.41 | 10.28 | 17.65 | 1.15 |
| France | 22.00 | 10.24 | 25.81 | 1.17 |
| Germany | 13.87 | 11.87 | 18.39 | 1.33 |
| Hong Kong | 47.95 | 5.63 | 45.80 | .96 |
| Italy | 24.21 | 8.58 | 26.15 | 1.08 |
| Japan | 16.39 | 10.42 | 19.55 | 1.19 |
| Netherlands | 16.37 | 10.97 | 18.91 | 1.16 |
| Norway | 28.61 | 8.89 | 29.92 | 1.05 |
| Singapore | 35.82 | 6.52 | 36.03 | 1.01 |
| Spain | 16.71 | 9.10 | 20.26 | 1.21 |
| Sweden | 15.05 | 8.89 | 18.06 | 1.20 |
| Switzerland | 16.80 | 14.67 | 21.40 | 1.27 |
| United Kingdom | 28.94 | 8.84 | 31.61 | 1.09 |
| United States | 16.00 | .00 | 16.00 | 1.00 |
| *Bonds* | | | | |
| Canada | 6.16 | 4.16 | 7.93 | 1.29 |
| France | 4.39 | 10.24 | 11.80 | 2.69 |
| Germany | 6.91 | 11.87 | 14.35 | 2.08 |
| Japan | 6.53 | 10.42 | 14.36 | 2.20 |
| Netherlands | 7.16 | 10.97 | 13.61 | 1.90 |
| Switzerland | 4.33 | 14.67 | 15.33 | 3.54 |
| United Kingdom | 12.30 | 8.84 | 16.29 | 1.32 |
| United States | 8.96 | .00 | 8.96 | 1.00 |

*SOURCE:* Adapted from Bruno Solnik and Bernard Noetzlin, "Optimal International Asset Allocation," *Journal of Portfolio Management* 9, no. 1 (Fall 1982):13.

## TABLE 24.3

Correlation Coefficients for Domestic and Foreign Returns, 1973–1987.

| | TSE 300 | Cdn. Paper | Cdn. Bonds | Hedged S&P500 | Unhedged S&P500 | Hedged EAFE | Unhedged EAFE |
|---|---|---|---|---|---|---|---|
| TSE300 | 1.0 | −0.2 | 0.2 | 0.7 | 0.7 | 0.5 | 0.4 |
| Cdn. Paper | | 1.0 | 0.0 | 0.0 | 0.0 | −0.1 | −0.3 |
| Cdn. Bonds | | | 1.0 | 0.5 | 0.5 | 0.3 | 0.3 |
| Hedged S&P500 | | | | 1.0 | 1.0 | 0.8 | 0.6 |
| Unhedged S&P500 | | | | | 1.0 | 0.8 | 0.6 |
| Hedged EAFE | | | | | | 1.0 | 0.8 |
| Unhedged EAFE | | | | | | | 1.0 |

*SOURCE:* Robert Auger and Denis Parisien, "The Risks and Rewards of Global Investing", *Canadian Investment Review* II, no.1 (Spring 1989):27.

The correlations between the EAFE portfolios and the Canadian securities are much lower than the correlations between the S&P 500 and the Canadian securities indicating that the EAFE provides useful diversification opportunities. Table 24.4 shows the risk and return relationships for all the investments considered.

## TABLE 24.4

Domestic and Foreign Investments: Annualized Average Returns and Standard Deviations, 1973–1987.

| Period | TSE 300 | Unhedged EAFE | Local EAFE | Hedged EAFE | Unhedged S&P500 | Local S&P500 | Hedged S&P500 | Cdn. Paper | Cdn. Bonds |
|---|---|---|---|---|---|---|---|---|---|
| **1973–1987** | | | | | | | | | |
| Return | 11.0 | 17.7 | 12.0 | 16.0 | 11.8 | 9.8 | 10.7 | 10.8 | 9.7 |
| Standard deviation | 22.2 | 27.2 | 17.3 | 19.3 | 17.8 | 18.0 | 18.5 | 1.2 | 14.5 |
| **1973–1987** | | | | | | | | | |
| Return | 1.6 | 4.6 | −0.2 | 0.2 | 1.7 | −0.2 | 0.8 | 8.6 | 7.2 |
| Standard deviation | 12.4 | 21.6 | 18.0 | 19.5 | 18.8 | 18.2 | 19.2 | 1.7 | 8.5 |
| **1978–1982** | | | | | | | | | |
| Return | 18.3 | 14.5 | 13.8 | 20.8 | 16.8 | 14.0 | 14.5 | 14.0 | 8.1 |
| Standard deviation | 26.1 | 18.6 | 7.9 | 7.6 | 12.4 | 12.8 | 12.3 | 4.1 | 13.9 |
| **1983–1987** | | | | | | | | | |
| Return | 13.8 | 36.2 | 23.7 | 29.0 | 17.5 | 16.4 | 17.7 | 9.9 | 13.9 |
| Standard deviation | 20.4 | 27.1 | 11.6 | 12.4 | 14.4 | 15.5 | 16.0 | 1.5 | 14.9 |

*SOURCE:* Robert Auger and Denis Parisien, "The Risks and Rewards of Global Investing", Canadian Investment Review II, no.1 (Spring 1989):26.

**TABLE 24.5**

Optimal Investment Strategies, 1973–1987.

| Level of risk tolerance: | Lower | ⟶ | Higher |
|---|---|---|---|
| Portfolio weightings (%): | | | |
| Canadian paper | 15 | 15 | 5 |
| Bonds | 45 | 35 | 35 |
| TSE 300 | 25 | 25 | 25 |
| Hedged S&P500 | 0 | 0 | 0 |
| Unhedged S&P500 | 0 | 0 | 0 |
| Hedged EAFE | 15 | 25 | 18 |
| Unhedged EAFE | 0 | 0 | 17 |
| Average Rate of return (%) | 11.2 | 11.8 | 12.6 |
| Standard deviation | 11.2 | 11.6 | 13.9 |

*SOURCE:* Robert Auger and Denis Parisien, "The Risks and Rewards of Global Investing", Canadian Investment Review II, no.1 (Spring 1989):28.

The differences between the columns listed as unhedged and local in this table provide an indication of the degree of foreign exchange risk present. As can be seen, foreign exchange risk varies significantly in different time periods. The hedged EAFE portfolio provides the most attractive risk-return combination of any investment considered. Table 24.5 shows the results of implementing three optimal investment strategies based different on levels of risk tolerance.

All three of these portfolios outperform a portfolio consisting of 100% Canadian stocks. These optimal portfolios exclude US stocks as these do not provide as attractive diversification as does the EAFE index. A prospective investment strategy was also investigated in which an expected return was assigned to each asset class and the optimal portfolios reconstructed. The results were similar to those shown in Table 24.5. The authors report that, for a large institutional investor, hedging can be accomplished at a cost of 0.1 to 0.15% per annum of the value of the portfolio . They conclude that "Foreign investments have a natural place in Canadian investment portfolios, even in conservative ones. They permit an increase in stock exposure without any increase in risk."

Auger and Parisien's results suggest that there is a substantial degree of integration of Canadian and US stock markets. The empirical evidence is mixed. Jorion and Schwartz using data from 1968 to 1982 concluded that there were sufficient rigidities in the financial system that the two markets were effectively segmented, even for interlisted stocks. A more recent study finds that the two markets show evidence of segmentation in the five year period 1977 to 1982, but that there is strong evidence of integration in a later period, 1982 to 1986.[11]

---

[11] P.Jorion and E.S.Schwartz, "Integration versus Segmentation in the Canadian Stock Market," *Journal of Finance* 41, no. 4 (Sept 1988):897–914; U.R.Mittoo, "Additional Evidence on the Integration of the Canadian and US Stock Markets," Department of Accounting and Finance Working Paper, University of Manitoba, October 1991. Further evidence of the benefits of international diversification for Canadian investors is provided in Harry S. Marmer, "International Investing: A New Canadian Perspective," *Canadian Investment Review* IV, no.1 (Spring 1991):47–53.

**TABLE 24.6**

Proportions of Returns on Stocks on Multinational Firms Explained by Stock Market Indices.

| Headquarters Country of Multinational Firms | Proportion of Variance in Returns Explained by | |
| --- | --- | --- |
| | Domestic Market Index | Domestic and Other Market Indices |
| Belgium | 45% | 58% |
| France | 45 | 62 |
| Germany | 65 | 74 |
| Italy | 47 | 51 |
| Netherlands | 50 | 63 |
| Sweden | 42 | 50 |
| Switzerland | 52 | 75 |
| United Kingdom | 44 | 49 |
| United States | 29 | 31 |

SOURCE: Adapted from Bertrand Jacquillat and Bruno Solnik, "Multinationals Are Poor Tools for Diversification," *Journal of Portfolio Management* 4, no. 2 (Winter 1978):10.

## ☐ 24.1.5 Multinational Firms

Firms operating in many countries provide international diversification at the corporate level. One might expect that investment in the stocks of such *multinational firms* could serve as a good substitute for investment in stocks of foreign ("national") firms.

A number of studies have shown that this may not be the case. In one, returns on portfolios of stocks of multinational firms headquartered in each of nine countries were calculated for the period from April 1966 through June 1974. Then each portfolio's returns were compared with the returns on the market index for the country of its headquarters. The middle column in Table 24.6 shows the proportion of each portfolio's variance that can be attributed to movements in its corresponding "domestic" market index. Finally, each portfolio's returns were compared with the returns on market indices in all nine countries. The final column in Table 24.6 shows the proportion of each portfolio's variance that can be attributed to movements in its domestic market index as well as the foreign market indices.

Yalawar examined the diversification efficiency of Canadian multinationals and concluded that those firms whose operations were predominantly outside the US provided some limited diversification opportunities.[12] His sample, however, consisted of only 32 firms with operations outside the US, of which 10 were predominantly in the UK, a market also significantly correlated with Canada's.

During the period covered in Table 24.6, the returns on multinational firms based in the United States had only 2% ( 31% − 29%) of their variance that could be attributed

---

[12] Firms with predominantly US operations provided little diversification. See Y.Yalawar, "Are Common Stocks of Canadian Multinationals Good Tools for International Diversification?" Proceedings, Administrative Sciences Association of Canada Conference, Saskatoon, 1979.

to foreign market indices. This suggests that US-headquartered multinationals were a poor substitute for direct investment in foreign stocks by US investors. The situation was somewhat better for non-US multinationals, since the differences in the percentages shown in the two columns were greater than 2%. One possible explanation for this is that non-US multinationals have more extensive foreign operations than US multinationals.

## ☐ 24.1.6 International Listings

The common stocks of many firms are traded not only on the major stock exchange in their home country but also on an exchange in a foreign country. By doing so, foreign investors no longer have to engage in foreign currency transactions when buying and selling the firm's stock. It is also possible that foreign investors can escape certain taxes and regulations to which the investors would be subject if the security were to be bought in the firm's home country.

As of December 31, 1991 there were 126 Canadian issues representing 119 companies interlisted on US exchanges reported in the *TSE Monthly Review*. Of these 26 were listed on the NYSE, 39 on the ASE, 55 on NASDAQ, and six on unidentified exchanges. These stocks provide US investors with a direct and easy means of participating in the Canadian market thereby achieving a degree of additional diversification. There are also 55 foreign firms listed on the TSE. These are mainly US corporations and a handful of British companies. Access to international diversification through interlisted companies is, therefore, limited for Canadian investors. A number of Canadian brokers, however, are represented on foreign exchanges and can trade there on their customers' behalf. For smaller investors a number of country, international and global funds are available from various financial institutions (see Chapter 20).

In addition to interlisting, foreign securities can be traded in the United States through *American depository receipts* (ADRs). ADRs are financial assets that are issued by US banks and represent indirect ownership of a certain number of shares of a specific foreign firm that are held on deposit in a bank in the firm's home country. The advantage of ADRs over direct ownership is that the investor need not worry about the delivery of the share certificates or converting dividend payments from a foreign currency into US dollars. The depository bank automatically does the convertion for the investor and also forwards all financial reports from the firm; the investor pays the bank a relatively small fee for these services. At the end of 1987, the common stocks of 34 foreign firms were traded as ADRs on the New York Stock Exchange, whereas the stocks of 97 foreign firms were traded as ADRs on the NASDAQ system.[13]

One study examined the diversification implications of investing in ADRs and found that such securities were of notable benefit to US investors.[14]

---

[13] The London Stock Exchange began trading simultaneously many of these ADRs in August 1987, with prices being quoted in US dollars. See National Association of Security Dealers *NASDAQ 1988 Fact Book*, 30–32; New York Stock Exchange *Fact Book 1988*, 25–26.

[14] Dennis T. Officer and J. Ronald Hoffmeister, "ADRs: A Substitute for the Real Thing?" *Journal of Portfolio Management* 13, no. 2 (Winter 1987):61–65. See also Leonard Rosenthal, "An Empirical Test of the Efficiency of the ADR Market," *Journal of Banking and Finance* 7, no. 1 (March 1983):17–29.

**TABLE 24.7**

Correlations of Annual US Dollar-Adjusted Total Equity Returns with World Total Equities, 1960–1980.

| Country | Correlation |
| --- | --- |
| Australia | .753 |
| Austria | −.042 |
| Belgium | .483 |
| Canada | .716 |
| Denmark | .358 |
| France | .384 |
| Germany | .322 |
| Hong Kong | .848 |
| Italy | .281 |
| Japan | .385 |
| Netherlands | .804 |
| Norway | −.045 |
| Singapore | .700 |
| Spain | −.015 |
| Sweden | .470 |
| Switzerland | .557 |
| United Kingdom | .703 |
| United States | .967 |

SOURCE: Adapted from Roger G. Ibbotson, Richard C. Carr, and Anthony W. Robinson, "International Equity and Bond Returns," *Financial Analysts Journal* 38, no. 4 (July/August 1982):71.

## ☐ 24.1.7 Correlations Between Equity Markets

If all economies were tied together completely, stock markets in different countries would move together, and little advantage could be gained through international diversification. But this is not the case. Table 24.7 shows the correlations of returns on diversified "market" portfolios of equities in various national stock markets with the returns on an index of equities in all the included countries (that is, the "world" portfolio). The value for the United States is large, owing primarily to the importance of the United States in the world index. The high Canadian correlation shown is probably due to the high correlation between US and Canadian indices. However, the striking feature is that many of the figures are very small (and some are even negative), even though each of the national indices represents a well-diversified domestic equity portfolio. These low correlations suggest that there are sizable potential advantages, in terms of risk reduction, from international diversification.[15]

---

[15] Another study of 349 stocks in 11 countries revealed an average intercountry correlation coefficient of .234 for the period from January 1973 to December 1983. See D. Chinhyung Cho, Cheol S. Eun, and Lemma W. Senbet, "International Arbitrage Pricing Theory: An Empirical Investigation," *Journal of Finance* 41, no. 2 (June 1986):313–29. For a multiperiod approach that indicates the benefits from international diversification, particularly for highly risk-averse investors, see Robert R. Grauer and Nils H. Hakansson, "Gains From International Diversification: 1968–85 Returns on Portfolios of Stocks and Bonds," *Journal of Finance* 42, no. 3 (July 1987):721–39.

**TABLE 24.8**

Co-Movement of TSE Sub-Indexes and Foreign Markets. (R-Squared between returns, all in CDN$.)

| | United Kingdom | Hong Kong | West Germany | Japan | France |
|---|---|---|---|---|---|
| Metals | 0.25 | 0.13 | 0.00 | 0.11 | 0.23 |
| Golds | 0.19 | 0.14 | 0.01 | 0.08 | 0.09 |
| Oils | 0.18 | 0.19 | 0.00 | 0.02 | 0.03 |
| Forest Products | 0.51 | 0.10 | 0.01 | 0.28 | 0.42 |
| Consumer | 0.51 | 0.12 | 0.14 | 0.15 | 0.44 |
| Steel | 0.36 | 0.04 | 0.00 | 0.11 | 0.16 |
| Real Estate | 0.14 | 0.05 | 0.03 | 0.19 | 0.20 |
| Transportation | 0.28 | 0.17 | 0.00 | 0.12 | 0.16 |
| Pipelines | 0.01 | 0.07 | 0.05 | 0.04 | 0.00 |
| Utilities | 0.04 | 0.03 | 0.01 | 0.00 | 0.02 |
| Communications | 0.22 | 0.05 | 0.08 | 0.09 | 0.36 |
| Retail | 0.30 | 0.03 | 0.18 | 0.05 | 0.28 |
| Banks | 0.01 | 0.07 | 0.12 | 0.07 | 0.13 |
| Financial | 0.07 | 0.08 | 0.14 | 0.01 | 0.19 |
| Management | 0.20 | 0.19 | 0.04 | 0.20 | 0.32 |
| TSE300 | 0.44 | 0.20 | 0.05 | 0.08 | 0.28 |

*SOURCE:* Evan Schulman, "The 'Global Village' Securities Market: Will Canada be a Participant.... or a Bystander?" *Canadian Investment Review* II, no.2 (Fall 1989):63.

The data presented in Table 24.8 shows the correlation between the TSE 300 index and its major sub-indices with five important international equity markets.

With the possible exception of the UK, all countries' correlations are extremely low, showing that international investment provides significant opportunities for diversification.

---

## 24.2   TANGIBLE ASSETS

In the first half of the 1970s, marketable securities such as stocks and bonds provided returns that were relatively disappointing, especially after adjusting for inflation. And, as shown in Chapter 11, neither bonds nor stocks have served as good hedges against unanticipated inflation in recent years. Overall, tangible assets have been better hedges against inflation. One example, real estate, was shown in Chapter 6 to have been an attractive inflation hedge in recent years.[16] Other examples, such as collectible assets and precious metals (like gold and silver), provide various degrees of protection against inflation.

---

[16] While not a tangible asset, commodity futures were shown in Chapter 19 to have also been an attractive inflation hedge.

**Collectible Assets**

Not surprisingly, disenchantment with returns on marketable securities has led some investors to examine a host of tangible assets that are normally considered only by collectors. Table 24.9 shows the average returns over three five-year periods for several different kinds of collectible assets (often simply referred to as *collectibles*).

**TABLE 24.9**
Annual Returns on Collectible Assets, Five-Year Periods Ending June 1.

|                  | 1969–1974 | 1974–1979 | 1979–1984 |
| ---------------- | --------- | --------- | --------- |
| Chinese ceramics | 31.1%     | −3.1%     | 15.7%     |
| Coins            | 9.5       | 32.4      | 11.3      |
| Diamonds         | 11.6      | 13.6      | 6.1       |
| Old masters      | 7.3       | 17.3      | 1.5       |
| US stamps        | 14.1      | 24.9      | 9.8       |

SOURCE: Based on data in R. S. Salomon, Jr., and Mallory J. Lennox, "Financial Assets — A Temporary Setback," *Stock Research Investment Policy,* Salomon Brothers, Inc., June 8, 1984.

Some of the returns shown in the table are quite high. However, none of the collectible assets provided *consistently* high results over all three periods. This is not surprising because if one (or more) had provided consistently high returns, many investors would have been attracted to it and bid its price up to a level where high returns would no longer have been possible.

In a sense, a collectible asset often provides income to the owner in the form of consumption. For example, an investor can admire a Rembrandt, sit on a Chippendale, play a Stradivarius, and drive a Morgan. Value received in this manner is not subject to income taxation and is thus likely to be especially attractive for those in high tax brackets. However, the value of such consumption depends strongly on one's preferences.

If markets are efficient, collectible assets will be priced so those who enjoy them most will find it desirable to hold them in greater-than-market-value proportions, whereas those who enjoy them least will find it desirable to hold them in less-than-market-value proportions (and, in many cases, not at all).

Institutional funds and investment pools have been organized to hold paintings, stamps, coins, and other collectible assets. Such arrangements are subject to serious question if they involve locking such objects in vaults where they cannot be seen by those who derive pleasure from this sort of consumption. On the other hand, if the items are rented to others, the only loss may be that associated with the transfer of a portion of the consumption value to the government in the form of a tax on income.

Investors in collectibles should be aware of two types of risk that are especially notable. The first is that the bid-ask spread is often very large. Thus, an investor must see a large price increase just to recoup the spread and break even. The second is that collectibles are subject to fads. For example, Chinese ceramics may be actively sought by many investors today, leading to high prices and big returns for earlier purchasers. However, they may fall out of favor later on and plunge in value. Unlike financial assets, there is no such thing as "fair" value for collectibles that can act as a kind of anchor for the market price.

## ☐ 24.2.2 Gold

In the United States, private holdings of gold bullion were illegal before the 1970s. There have been no Canadian restrictions on private holdings of gold since the end of World War II. In other countries, investment in gold has long been a tradition. According to one estimate, at the end of 1984 gold represented over 6% of the world market wealth portfolio.[17]

Table 24.10 contrasts a US investor's returns from gold with the returns from US equities over the period from 1960 through 1984. Gold is clearly a risky investment, but in this period, at least, it also provided high average returns.

**TABLE 24.10**

Characteristics of Gold and US Equity Returns, 1960–1984.

|  | Average Annual Return | Standard Deviation of Annual Return |
|---|---|---|
| US equities | 10.20% | 16.89% |
| Gold | 12.62 | 29.87 |
| Correlation: Gold and US equities | −.09 | |
| Gold and inflation | .63 | |

SOURCE: Adapted from Roger G. Ibbotson, Laurence B. Siegel, and Kathryn S. Love, "World Wealth: Market Values and Returns," *Journal of Portfolio Management* 12, no. 1 (Fall 1985):17, 21.

For any single investment, risk and return are only parts of the story: Correlations of an asset's return with the returns on other assets are also relevant. In the period covered in Table 24.10, gold price changes were slightly negatively correlated with stock returns. Similar results have been obtained for other periods. Gold thus appears to be an effective diversifying asset for an equity investor. Table 24.10 also shows that gold prices were highly correlated with the rate of inflation in the United States as measured by changes in the Consumer Price Index. This is consistent with gold's traditional role as a hedge against inflation, since higher inflation generally brings higher gold prices. It should be noted, however, that an international study that examined the inflation hedging properties of gold for investors in six countries — Canada, Germany, Japan, Switzerland, UK, and US — demonstrated that only for US investors was it an effective vehicle.[18]

Investors interested in gold need not restrict themselves to bullion. Other possibilities range from stocks of gold mining companies to gold futures to gold coins and commemoratives. Furthermore, there are other types of precious metals, such as silver and platinum, that investors may want to consider.

---

[17] Ibbotson, Siegel, and Love, "World Wealth: Market Values and Returns," 9.

[18] J.Chua and R.S.Woodward, "Gold as an Inflation Hedge: A Comparative Study of Six Major Industrial Countries," *Journal of Business Finance and Accounting* 9, no.2 (March 1982):191–7.

Throughout the world, large amounts of money are wagered on the outcomes of sporting events. In the United States, betting on horse races is conducted legally at race tracks in many states and via legal off-track betting establishments in some states. In addition, illegal bookmakers in every state accept bets on horse races. Bets on other events — most notably professional football games — are made legally in Nevada and illegally with bookmakers almost everywhere including Canada.

There are some interesting parallels between betting and investing in securities. Both involve an initial outlay of cash and an outcome that, being uncertain, can be thought of as a random variable. For both betting and investing, an individual must have some sort of strategy in deciding where to put his or her money — after all, there are a large number of sporting events as well as securities that are available. Furthermore, these strategies can be thought of as being either fundamental or technical in nature. In the case of fundamental strategies, an investor or bettor looks at the underlying strength of the firm or team or horse that is being evaluated, whereas in the case of a technical strategy, only past performance is of concern. Both of these strategies are typically based on publicly available information; thus, the historical performance of investors and bettors can be examined in order to see if the respective financial markets and "sports markets" are semistrong-form efficient. To begin the discussion, a parallel will be made between a security dealer and a bookmaker.

A security dealer typically wishes to operate with, on average, a small inventory of securities so as to have relatively little exposure to loss through security price fluctuations. To do this, the dealer usually sets a bid price and an asked price that will bring roughly an equal number of orders for purchases and sales in a given time period (say, a week's time). The bid-ask spread represents the dealer's profit margin and part of the investor's transactions costs.

Similarly, in sports betting the bookmaker acts as dealer and wishes to have relatively little "inventory" (exposure to loss). Two major methods are employed to achieve this: *spread betting* and *odds betting*. The former is used for bets on games such as football and baseball and the latter for bets on contests such as horse races and presidential elections.

## ☐ 24.3.1 Spread Betting

In order to understand spread betting, consider a hypothetical professional football game between the San Francisco 49ers and the Minnesota Vikings. It is widely felt that the 49ers are likely to win. Thus, the bookmaker establishes a spread, perhaps deciding that the 49ers are "favored by 7 points." This means that the final score will, in effect, be modified by subtracting 7 points from the 49ers score and then paying those who bet on the "winner" using that adjusted score. People who bet on San Francisco believe that the team will "cover the spread"; those who bet on Minnesota believe that Minnesota will "beat the spread." If the final score is 28 -20 in favor of San Francisco, then after adjusting for the spread the score is 21-20 in favor of San Francisco, and those betting on San Francisco will have won. However, if the final score is 24–20 in favor of San

Francisco, then the adjusted score will be 17–20 in favor of Minnesota, and those betting on Minnesota's beating the spread will have won.[19]

The point spread serves as an equilibrating mechanism. Other things being equal, the greater the spread, the smaller will be the amount bet on San Francisco and the larger the amount bet on Minnesota. At some level the "books will be balanced," meaning an equal amount has been bet on both teams. Given local prejudices, this may be accomplished by San Francisco bookmakers "laying off " excess money bet on the 49ers with Minnesota bookmakers who have excess money bet on the Vikings.

The bookmaker makes a living with a range that corresponds to the security dealer's bid-ask spread. Typically, the bettor puts up $11 for a $10 bet, meaning a winner will receive $10 (plus his or her initial $11 bet, if paid in advance), whereas a loser is out the initial $11 bet. If the books are balanced, the bookmaker will pay out $21 for every $22 taken in. For example, if there is one $11 bet on San Francisco and one $11 bet on Minnesota, the books are balanced. Then, whichever team wins, the bookmaker will pay out $21 of the $22 that has been bet.

While bookmakers generally set point spreads to balance their books, in an efficient market such spreads would provide good estimates of the expected differences in points scored (and, by and large, the evidence is consistent with market efficiency).

# ☐ 24.3.2 Odds Betting

A goal of many "dealers" in bets is to be reasonably certain that after the contest is over, less money will be paid out than is received. To do this, terms must be set so that bets on underdogs are attractive. Spreads are one way; odds are another.

An example from horse racing illustrates the procedure. Assume that Black Socks is favored to win the sixth race at Golden Gate Fields, while the other seven horses are considered inferior but of roughly equal speed. If the payoff per dollar bet were the same for all eight horses, most of the bets would be placed on the favorite. To spread the betting over the contenders, a larger amount must be paid per dollar bet if a long shot is bet on and subsequently wins.

Assume that the odds are set at 7-to-1 for each of the seven slow horses. This means that if $1 is bet on one of them and the horse wins, the bettor will receive $8 (the original $1 that was bet plus $7 in winnings). Assume also that the odds on Black Socks are set at 5-to-3, so that every $3 bet on the favorite will return $8 (the original $3 that was bet plus $5 in winnings) if the horse wins. Now imagine that the amounts bet, given these odds, are as shown in Table 24.11. The total pool, or *handle* (that is, the total amount bet), is $1000, but no matter which horse wins the race, only $800 will be paid out. The remaining $200 is for the track, the government, and the bookmaker and is known as the *take*.

---

[19] In the event of a tie in the adjusted score, the money that was bet is returned to both sides.

TABLE 24.11

Odds, Amounts Bet, and Payouts for a Horse Race.

| Horse | Amount Bet | Odds | Amount Paid Out If Horse Wins |
|---|---|---|---|
| # 1 (favorite) | $ 300 | 5-to-3 | $800 |
| 2 | 100 | 7-to-1 | 800 |
| 3 | 100 | 7-to-1 | 800 |
| 4 | 100 | 7-to-1 | 800 |
| 5 | 100 | 7-to-1 | 800 |
| 6 | 100 | 7-to-1 | 800 |
| 7 | 100 | 7-to-1 | 800 |
| 8 | 100 | 7-to-1 | 800 |
| Total amount bet = | $1000 | | |

The numbers in Table 24.11 may seem contrived, but they represent the kind of situation achieved automatically by parimutuel betting. In this form of wagering (used at most horse racetracks), the actual odds for a horse are determined *after all betting has finished* by subtracting the take (typically about 20%) and the amount bet on the horse from the handle and then dividing this amount by the amount bet on that horse.[20] For example, in the case of Black Socks (horse number 1), the odds are ( $1000 − $200 − $300)/$300 = $500/$300 = 5/3, as shown in the table. It should be noted that the dealer is always assured of receiving a fixed percentage (20%) for transaction costs with this procedure.

Betting on horses is a negative-sum game: Owing to transaction costs, the amount paid out is less than the amount paid in. Consequently, the expected return on the average bet will be negative. Since it is difficult to justify such activity on the basis of hedging, a bettor either (1) erroneously believes that he or she is a superior predictor, (2) is willing to pay in this manner for entertainment, or (3) prefers risk. Undoubtedly, all three aspects play a role in the sports betting market. One attribute that makes betting on sports entertaining is the suspension of the bettor's usual mind-set and the taking of risks with relatively small amounts of money. In such an environment and with limited exposure, even a conservative investor may take pleasure in acting like a riverboat gambler.

Evidence consistent with risk preference of this sort has been found in many analyses of the expected returns from bets on horses with different probabilities of winning races. Figure 24.3 summarizes a number of such studies. The horizontal axis indicates closing odds (on a logarithmic scale). Favorites plot at the left end of the scale and extreme long shots at the right end. The vertical axis indicates average returns. All are negative, but the returns on favorites are considerably better than those on long shots. "Investors" at the track are apparently willing to give up some expected return to get more risk — in this domain they appear to prefer risk.

---

[20] This applies only to bets that a horse will win the race. More complex procedures are used for place (second or better) and show (third or better) bets. In addition, the actual payoff is usually rounded down to the nearest multiple of $.10 per $2 bet, for instance.

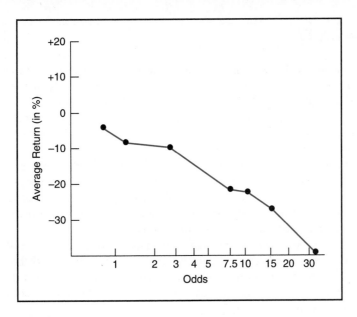

**FIGURE 24-3**
Average return versus odds in horse race betting.

*SOURCE:* Wayne W. Snyder, "Horse Racing: Testing the Efficient Markets Model," *Journal of Finance* 33, no. 4 (September 1978): 1113.

## ☐ 24.3.3 The Efficiency of Horse Race Betting

Investors in stocks can avail themselves of the results of financial analysis, both fundamental and technical. However, the high degree of efficiency of the stock market diminishes the value of such information for a single investor, since much of it is already reflected in security prices.

A similar situation prevails in the market for horse race betting. Fundamental analyses of such factors as the abilities of horses and trainers and the effects of weather abound, as do technical analyses of trends, reversals, and other changes in "form." If the market is efficient, public information provided by such analysts ("handicappers") will be reflected in prices ("closing odds").

In one test that examined the bets placed at Belmont Race Track in New York State, the odds at the track appeared to reflect the information contained in published "picks" by 14 handicappers. However, this did not seem to be the case in the less "professional" (and higher-transaction-cost) off-track betting market—a fact that may give some solace to those who invest in small and little-followed stocks.[21]

---

[21] Stephen Figlewski, "Subjective Information and Market Efficiency in a Betting Market," *Journal of Political Economy* 87, no. 1 (February 1979):75–88. It should be noted that there is some evidence that information is better reflected in the win pool than in the show and place pools. For details of a "system" designed to exploit such discrepancies, see Donald B. Hausch, William T. Ziemba, and Mark Rubenstein, "Efficiency of the Market for Racetrack Betting," *Management Science* 27, no. 12 (December 1981):1435–52; and Peter Asch, Burton G. Malkiel, and Richard E. Quandt, "Market Efficiency in Racetrack Betting," *Journal of Business* 57, no. 2 (April 1984):165–75 and "Market Efficiency in Racetrack Betting: Further Evidence and a Correction," *Journal of Business* 59, no. 1 (January 1986):157–60.

# SUMMARY

As mentioned at the beginning of this chapter, one of the major themes of modern portfolio theory concerns the merits of diversification. Specifically, in an efficient capital market, it is quite sensible for an investor to hold more than one type of asset, since doing so will increase the investor's expected return per unit of risk. Investing in foreign securities and in tangible assets are two methods of diversifying a common stock portfolio that appear to offer such benefits.

Betting on sporting events was discussed because there are some interesting parallels between such betting and investing in securities. For example, both betting and investing involve some form of strategy that can be thought of as being either fundamental or technical in nature. Fundamental strategies would involve examining various types of past data, while technical strategies would involve simply examining past outcomes. After performing such examinations, the investor as well as the bettor would put money on what was perceived to be the favorite, be it a stock, horse, or football team. However, if markets are semi-strong form efficient, then neither the investor nor the bettor that uses publicly available information should be able to consistently "beat the market" or "beat the track."

It is appropriate that this chapter and book be ended on this note. For the financial economist, the relatively efficient nature of security and sports betting markets that has been observed is heartwarming, for it shows once more the effectiveness of competition. For the investor or bettor, such efficiency provides a challenge, to say the least. Accordingly, the next time you place an order with a stockbroker, keep this in mind.

## QUESTIONS AND PROBLEMS

1. What types of political risks are relevant only for foreign investors? What types are relevant for both foreign and domestic investors? To what extent and in what manner would you expect the current prices of securities in a particular country to reflect these types of political risk?

2. Why would an investor wish to hedge the currency risk in a portfolio of foreign securities? What considerations are relevant to making the decision whether to hedge?

3. How might a Canadian citizen or company use currency futures to hedge against exchange-rate risk?

4. Jim Bradley bought a Japanese stock one year ago when it sold for 280 yen per share and the exchange rate was $0.008 per yen. The shares now sell for 350 yen and the exchange rate is $0.010 per yen. The stock paid no dividends over the year. What was Jim's rate of return on this stock? What would be the rate of return on the stock to a Japanese investor?

5. Why is international diversification attractive to an investor like Jane Sinclair who already has a well-diversified domestic portfolio?

6. When a Canadian like Sam Jackson is attempting to estimate the expected return and standard deviation of return for a foreign security, what factors, in addition to those recognized in domestic security analysis, should be considered?

7. Eva Lange is a US citizen who wants the diversification benefits of international investments, but does not want to own foreign securities directly. Would investing

in domestically headquartered multinational corporations and ADRs be effective substitutes for Eva? Explain.

8. Is a low correlation between the price movements of two countries' market indices a sufficient condition to ensure that a portfolio containing securities of both countries dominates a portfolio containing only domestic securities?

9. Hal Chase, a neophyte sports gambler, was heard to remark, "The bookmakers took a terrible beating this week because 80% of the underdogs beat the point spread." Does this seem plausible? Why or why not?

10. Picks of handicappers such as Derek Lubovski generally do not add directly to the information reflected in the odds given at the track. Does this mean that Derek and the other handicappers cannot pick winners? Does this mean that their picks are of no value? What aspects of security markets are comparable to the position of track handicappers?

## SUGGESTED READINGS

Bruno Solnik, *International Investing* (Reading, Mass.: Addison-Wesley Publishing, Co., Inc., 1988) and

Orlin J. Grabbe, *International Financial Markets* (New York, N.Y.: Elsevier Science Publishers, 1986) provide comprehensive coverage of international investing.

Harry Marmer, "International Investing: A New Canadian Perspective," *Canadian Investment Review* IV, no. 1 (Spring 1991):47–55 and

Robert Auger and Denis Parisien, "The Risks and Rewards of Global Investing," *Canadian Investment Review* II, no. 1 (Spring 1989):25–30 cover international investing from a Canadian investor's viewpoint.

# GLOSSARY

**Abnormal Return**   The return earned on a financial asset in excess of that required to compensate for the risk of the asset.

**Account Executive**   A representative of a brokerage firm whose primary responsibility is servicing the accounts of individual investors.

**Accounting Beta**   A relative measure of the sensitivity of a firm's accounting earnings to changes in the accounting earnings of the market portfolio.

**Accounting Earnings**   (Alternatively, Reported Earnings.) A firm's revenues less its expenses. Equivalently, the change in the firm's book value of the equity plus dividends paid to shareholders.

**Accrued Interest**   Interest earned, but not yet paid.

**Active Management**   A form of investment management which involves buying and selling financial assets with the objective of earning positive risk-adjusted returns.

**Active Position**   The difference between the percentage of an investor's portfolio invested in a particular financial asset and the percentage of a benchmark portfolio invested in that same asset.

**Actual Margin**   The equity in an investor's margin account expressed as a percentage of the account's total market value (for margin purchases) or total debt (for short sales).

**Adjusted Beta**   An estimate of a security's future beta, derived initially from historical data, but modified by the assumption that the security's "true" beta has a tendency over time to move toward the market average of 1.0.

**Alpha**   The difference between a security's expected return and its equilibrium expected return.

**Alternative Minimum Tax**   A Revenue Canada requirement that taxpayers with substantial tax-deductible items add back many of the deductions to their regular taxable income. A tax rate of 17% is applied to this adjusted taxable income. If the resulting tax is higher than the individual's normally-calculated tax, then the alternative tax must be paid.

**American Depository Receipts (ADRs)**   Financial assets issued by US banks that represent indirect ownership of a certain number of shares of a non-US firm. ADRs are held on deposit in a bank in the firm's home country.

**American Option**   An option that can be exercised any time through its expiration date.

**Amortization**   A means of depreciating certain intangible assets for corporate income tax purposes.

**Annual Percentage Rate (APR)**   With respect to a loan, the APR is the yield-to-maturity of the loan computed using the most frequent time between payments as the compounding interval.

**Anomaly**   An empirical regularity that is not predicted by any known asset pricing model.

**Approved List**   A list of securities that an investment organization deems worthy of inclusion in a given portfolio.

**Arbitrage**   The simultaneous purchase and sale of the same, or essentially similar, security in two different markets for advantageously different prices.

**Arbitrage Pricing Theory**   An equilibrium model of asset pricing which states that the expected return on a security is a linear function of the security's sensitivity to various common factors.

**Arbitrageur**   A person who engages in arbitrage.

**Ask (or Asked) Price**   The price at which a market-maker is willing to sell a specified quantity of a particular security.

**Asset Allocation** The process of determining the optimal division of an investor's portfolio among available asset classes.

**Asset Class** A broadly defined generic group of financial assets, such as stocks or bonds.

**Asymmetric Information** A situation in which one party has more information than another party.

**At the Money Option** An option whose exercise price is roughly equal to the market price of its underlying asset.

**Attribute** See Factor Loading.

**Average Cost Method** A method of valuing inventories that assumes that equal numbers of old and new goods are sold.

**Average Return on Investment** The total income earned from an investment in an asset, expressed as a percentage of the total investment in the asset.

**Average Tax Rate** The amount of taxes paid expressed as a percentage of the total income subject to tax.

**Back-End Load** See Redemption Fee.

**Bank Discount Basis** A method of calculating the interest rate on a fixed-income security that uses the principal of the security as the security's cost.

**Bankers' Acceptance** A type of money market instrument. It is a promissory note issued by a corporation, with a stated maturity date, that is endorsed by a bank. The bank, by endorsing the note, assumes the obligation that may subsequently be traded.

**Basis** The difference between the spot price of an asset and the futures price of the same asset.

**Basis Point** 1/100th of 1%.

**Basis Risk** The risk to a futures investor of the basis widening or narrowing.

**Bearer Bond** A bond with attached coupons that represent the right to receive interest payments. The owner submits each coupon on its specified date to receive payment. Ownership is transferred by the seller endorsing the bond over to the buyer.

**Benchmark Portfolio** A portfolio, of equivalent risk, against which the performance of an investor's holdings can be compared.

**Best-Efforts Underwriting** A security underwriting in which the members of the investment banking group serve as agents instead of dealers, agreeing only to obtain for the issuer the best price that the market will pay for the security.

**Beta Coefficient** (Alternatively, Market Beta.) A relative measure of the sensitivity of an asset's return to changes in the return on the market portfolio. Mathematically, the beta coefficient of a security is the security's covariance with the market portfolio divided by the variance of the market portfolio.

**Bid-Ask Spread** The difference between the price that a market-maker is willing to pay for a security and the price at which the market-maker is willing to sell the same security.

**Bidder** In the context of a corporate takeover, the firm making a tender offer to the target firm.

**Bid Price** The price at which a market-maker is willing to purchase a specified quantity of a particular security.

**Block House** A brokerage firm with the financial capacity and the trading expertise to deal in block trades.

**Block Trade** A large order (usually 10,000 shares or more) to buy or sell a security.

**Bond Ratings** An indicator of the creditworthiness of specific bond issues. These ratings provide an indication of a bond issuer's likelihood of default.

**Bond Swap** A form of active bond management which entails the replacement of bonds in a portfolio with other bonds so as to enhance the yield of the portfolio.

**Book Value of the Equity** The sum of the cumulative retained earnings and other balance sheet entries classified under shareholders' equity such as common stock and capital contributed in excess of par value.

**Book Value Per Share** A corporation's book value of the equity divided by the number of its common shares outstanding.

**Bottom-Up Forecasting** A sequential approach to security analysis which entails first making forecasts for individual companies, then for industries, and finally for the economy. Each level of forecasts is conditional on the previous level of forecasts made.

**Broker**  An agent, or middleman, who facilitates the buying and selling of securities for investors.

**Call Market**  A security market in which trading is allowed only at certain specified times. At those times, persons interested in trading a particular security are physically brought together and a market clearing price is established.

**Call Money Rate**  The interest rate paid by brokerage firms to banks on loans used to finance margin purchases by the brokerage firm's customers.

**Call Option**  A contract that gives the buyer the right to buy a specific number of shares of a company from the option writer at a specific purchase price during a specific time period.

**Call Premium**  The difference between the call price of a bond and the par value of the bond.

**Call Price**  The price that an issuer must pay bondholders when an issue is retired prior to its stated maturity date.

**Call Provision**  A provision in some bond indentures that permits an issuer to retire some or all of the bonds in a particular bond issue prior to the bonds' stated maturity date.

**Canadian Investor Protection Fund**  An industry maintained fund that insures investors' accounts against loss due to the failure of a brokerage firm.

**Capital Asset Pricing Model (CAPM)**  An equilibrium model of asset pricing which states that the expected return in a security is a positive linear function of the security's sensitivity to changes in the market portfolio's return.

**Capital Cost Allowance**  A procedure, laid down by Revenue Canada, for computing the amount of depreciation that may be claimed as a deduction against income for tax purposes.

**Capital Gain (or Loss)**  The difference between the current market value of an asset and the original cost of the asset, with the cost adjusted for any improvement or depreciation in the asset.

**Capital Market Line**  The set of portfolios obtainable by combining the market portfolio with riskfree borrowing or lending. Assuming homogeneous expectations and perfect markets, the Capital Market Line represents the efficient set.

**Capital Markets**  Financial markets in which financial assets with a term-to-maturity of typically more than one year are traded.

**Capitalization of Income Method Valuation**  An approach to valuing financial assets. It is based on the concept that the "true" or intrinsic value of a financial asset is equal to the discounted value of future cash flows generated by that asset.

**Capitalization-Weighted Market Index**  See Value-Weighted Market Index.

**Cash Account**  An account maintained by an investor with a brokerage firm in which deposits (cash and the proceeds from security sales) must fully cover withdrawals (cash and the costs of security purchases).

**Cash Matching**  A form of immunization which involves the purchase of bonds that generate a stream of cash inflows identical in amount and timing to a set of expected cash outflows over a given period of time.

**Certainty Equivalent Return**  For a particular risky investment, the return on a riskfree investment which makes the investor indifferent between the risky and riskfree investments.

**Certificate of Deposit**  A form of time deposit issued by banks and other financial institutions.

**Certificate of Incorporation**  See Charter.

**Characteristic Line**  (Alternatively, Market Model.) A simple linear regression model expressing the relationship between the excess return on a security and the excess return on the market portfolio.

**Charter**  (Alternatively, Certificate of Incorporation.) A document issued by a state to a corporation that specifies the rights and obligations of the corporation's stockholders.

**Chartist**  A technical analyst who primarily relies on stock price and volume charts when evaluating securities.

**Clearing Corporations**  A cooperative venture between banks, brokerage firms, and other financial intermediaries, which maintains records of transactions made by member firms during a trading day. At the end of the trading day, the clearing corporation calculates net amounts of securities and cash to be delivered among the members, permitting each member to settle once with the clearing corporation.

**Close** See Closing price.

**Closed-End Investment Company** A managed investment company, with an unlimited life, that does not stand ready to purchase its own shares from its owners and rarely issues new shares beyond its initial offering.

**Closing Price** (Alternatively, Close.) The price at which the last trade of the day took place in a particular stock.

**Closing Purchase** The purchase of an option contract by an investor that is designed to offset, and thereby cancel, the previous sale of the same option contract by the investor.

**Closing Sale** The sale of an option contract by an investor that is designed to offset, and thereby cancel, the previous purchase of the same option contract by the investor.

**Coefficient of Determination** (Alternatively, R-squared.) In the context of a simple linear regression, the proportion of the variation in the dependent variable that is related to variation in (that is, "explained by") the independent variable.

**Coefficient of Nondetermination** In the context of a simple linear regression, the proportion of the variation in the dependent variable that is not related to variation in (that is, not "explained by") the independent variable. Equivalently, one minus the coefficient of determination.

**Coincident Indicators** Economic variables which have been found to change at the same time that the economy is changing.

**Collateral Trust Bond** A bond that is backed by other financial assets.

**Commercial Paper** A type of money instrument. It represents unsecured promissory notes of large, financially sound corporations.

**Commingled Fund** An investment fund, offered by a bank or insurance company, which is similar to a mutual fund in that investors are permitted to purchase and redeem units that represent ownership in a pool of securities.

**Commission** The fee an investor pays to a brokerage firm for services rendered in the trading of securities.

**Commodity Fund** An investment company that speculates in futures.

**Common Factor** A factor which affects the return on virtually all securities to a certain extent.

**Common Shares** Legal representation of an equity (or ownership) position in a corporation.

**Comparative Performance Attribution** Comparing the performance of a portfolio with that of one or more other portfolios (or market indices) in order to determine the sources of the differences in their returns.

**Competitive Bidding** With respect to selecting an underwriter, the process of an issuer soliciting bids on the underwriting and choosing the underwriter offering the best overall terms.

**Compounding** The payment of interest on interest.

**Constant Growth Model** A type of dividend discount model in which dividends are assumed to exhibit a constant growth rate.

**Consumer Price Index** A cost-of-living index which is representative of the goods and services purchased by Canadian consumers.

**Contingent Deferred Sales Charge** See Redemption Fee.

**Contingent Immunization** A form of bond management that entails both passive and active elements. Under contingent immunization, as long as "favorable" results are obtained, the bond portfolio is actively managed. However, if "unfavorable" results occur, then the portfolio is immediately immunized.

**Continuous Market** A security market in which trades may occur at any time during business hours.

**Convertible Bond** A bond which may, at the holder's option, be exchanged for other securities, often common stock.

**Corner Portfolio** An efficient portfolio possessing the property that, if combined with any adjacent corner portfolio, the combination will produce another efficient portfolio.

**Correlation Coefficient** A statistical measure similar to covariance, in that it measures the degree of mutual variation between two random variables. The correlation coefficient rescales covariance to facilitate comparison among pairs of random variables. The correlation coefficient is bounded by the values $-1$ and $+1$.

**Cost-of-Living Index** See Consumer Price Index.

**Coupon Payments** The periodic payment of interest on a bond.

**Coupon Rate** The annual dollar amount of coupon payments made by a bond expressed as a percentage of the bond's par value.

**Coupon Stripping** The process of separating and selling the individual cash flows of Treasury notes or bonds.

**Covariance** A statistical measure of the relationship between two random variables. It measures the extent of mutual variation between two random variables.

**Covered Call Writing** The process of writing a call option on an asset owned by the option writer.

**Crown Jewel Defense** A strategy used by corporations to ward off hostile takeovers. The strategy entails the target company selling off its most attractive assets to make itself less attractive to the acquiring firm.

**Cumulative Dividends** A common feature of preferred stock which requires that the issuing corporation pay all previously unpaid preferred stock dividends before any common stock dividends may be paid.

**Cumulative Voting System** In the context of a corporation, a method of voting in which a stockholder is permitted to give any one candidate for the board of directors a maximum number of votes equal to the number of shares owned by that shareholder times the number of directors being elected.

**Currency Risk** See Exchange Risk.

**Current Yield** The annual dollar amount of coupon payments made by a bond expressed as a percentage of the bond's current market price.

**Date of Record** The date, established quarterly by a corporation's board of directors, on which the shareholders of record are determined for the purpose of paying a cash or stock dividend.

**Day-of-the-Week Effect** (Alternatively, Weekend Effect.) An empirical regularity whereby stock returns appear to be lower on Mondays as opposed to other days of the week.

**Day Order** A trading order for which the broker will attempt to fill the order only during the day in which it was entered.

**Dealer** A person who trades in financial assets for his or her own account and maintains an inventory of particular securities. The dealer buys for and sells from this inventory, profiting from the difference in the buying and selling prices.

**Dealer's Spread** The bid-asked spread quoted by a security dealer.

**Debenture** A bond that is not secured by specific property.

**Debit Balance** The dollar amount borrowed from a broker as the result of a margin purchase.

**Debt Refunding** The issuance of new debt for the purpose of paying off currently maturing debt.

**Dedicated Portfolio** A portfolio of bonds that provides its owner with cash inflows that are matched against a specific stream of cash outflows.

**Deep Discount Bond** A bond whose coupon interest rate is considerably below those of other bonds which otherwise possess similar attributes. Hence, these bonds sell at prices significantly below the other bonds.

**Default Premium** The difference between the promised and expected yield-to-maturity on a bond arising from the possibility that the bond issuer might default on the bond.

**Delisting** The process of removing a security's eligibility for trading on an organized security exchange.

**Delta** See Hedge Ratio.

**Demand Deposit** A chequing account at a financial institution.

**Demand for Capital** (Alternatively, Marginal Efficiency of Capital.) The quantity of capital desired by an investor at varying interest-rate levels.

**Demand-to-Buy Schedule** A description of the quantities of a security that an investor is prepared to purchase at alternative prices.

**Demand-to-Hold Schedule** A description of the quantities of a security an investor desires to maintain in his or her portfolio at alternative prices.

**Depletion**  A means of depreciating certain natural resource assets for corporate income tax purposes.

**Depreciation**  An accounting procedure that allocates the cost of a fixed asset over the estimated useful life of the asset.

**Designated Market-Maker**  (Also known as a Registered Trader with responsibilty for a stock.) A dealer who continuously provides bid and ask prices at which he or she is willing to trade a specified number of shares any time an order is entered for which no other counter-party is available.

**Differential Return**  See Ex Post Alpha.

**Discount Broker**  An organization that offers a limited range of brokerage services and charges fees substantially below those of brokerage firms that provide a full range of services.

**Discount Factor**  The present value of one dollar to be received from a security in specified number of years.

**Discount Rate**  The interest rate used in calculating the present value of future cash flows. The discount rate reflects not only the time value of money, but also the riskiness of the cash flows.

**Discounting**  The process of calculating the present value of a given stream of cash flows.

**Discretionary Order**  A trading order that permits the broker to set the specifications for the order.

**Diversification**  The process of adding securities to a portfolio in order to reduce the portfolio's unique risk and, thereby, the portfolio's total risk.

**Dividend Decision**  The process of determining the amount of dividends that a corporation will pay its shareholders.

**Dividend Discount Model**  The term used for the capitalization of income method of valuation as applied to common shares. All variants of dividend discount models assume that the intrinsic value of a share of common stock is equal to the discounted value of the dividends forecast to be paid on the shares.

**Dividend Tax Credit**  A credit applicable to the tax payable on dividend income that lowers the effective tax rate.

**Dividend Yield**  The current annualized dividend paid on a share of common stock, expressed as a percentage of the current market price of the corporation's common stock.

**Dividends**  Cash payments made to shareholders by the corporation.

**Dollar-Weighted Return**  A method of measuring the performance of a portfolio over a particular period of time. It is the discount rate which makes the present value of cash flows into and out of the portfolio, as well as the portfolio's ending value, equal to the portfolio's beginning value.

**Domestic Return**  The return on an investment in a foreign financial asset, excluding the impact of exchange rate changes.

**Double Auction**  Bidding among both buyers and sellers for a security that may occur when the market-maker's bid-ask spread is large enough to permit sales at one or more prices within the spread.

**Duration**  A measure of the average maturity of the stream of payments generated by a financial asset. Mathematically, duration is the weighted average of the lengths of time until the asset's remaining payments are made. The weights in this calculation are the proportion of the asset's total present value of the respective cash flows.

**Earnings Per Share**  A corporation's accounting earnings divided by the number of its common shares outstanding.

**Earnings-Price Ratio**  The reciprocal of the price-earnings ratio.

**Econometric Model**  A statistical model designed to explain and forecast certain economic phenomena.

**Economic Earnings**  The change in the economic value of the firm plus dividends paid to shareholders.

**Economic Value of the Firm**  The aggregate market value of all securities issued by the firm.

**Efficient Market**  A market for securities in which every security's price equals its investment value at all times, implying that a set of information is fully and immediately reflected in market prices.

**Efficient Portfolio**  A portfolio within the feasible set which offers investors both maximum expected return for varying levels of risk and minimum risk for varying levels of expected return.

**Efficient Set (Frontier)**   The set of efficient portfolios.

**Efficient Set Theorem**   The proposition that investors will choose their portfolios only from the set of efficient portfolios.

**Electronic Book**   See Limit Order Book.

**Empirical Regularities**   Differences in returns on securities that occur with regularity from period to period. Of particular interest are empirical regularities not consistent with the Capital Asset Pricing Model.

**Endogenous Variable**   In the context of an econometric model, an economic variable which represents the economic phenomena explained by the model.

**Equal-Weighted Market Index**   A market index in which all the component securities contribute equally to the value of the index, regardless of the various attributes of those securities.

**Equilibrium Expected Return**   The expected return on a security assuming that the security is correctly priced by the market. This "fair" return is determined by an appropriate asset pricing model.

**Equipment Obligation**   (Alternatively, Equipment Trust Certificate.) A bond which is backed by specific pieces of equipment that, if necessary, can be readily sold and delivered to a new owner.

**Equipment Trust Certificate**   See Equipment Obligation.

**Equivalent Yield**   The annualized yield-to-maturity on a fixed-income security sold on a discount basis.

**Estimated Useful Life**   The period over which a fixed asset is expected to contribute to the company's revenue.

**Eurobond**   A bond that is offered outside of the country of the borrower and usually outside of the country in whose currency the security is denominated.

**Eurodollar Certificate of Deposit**   A certificate of deposit denominated in US dollars and issued by banks domiciled outside North America.

**Eurodollar Deposit**   A US dollar-denominated time deposit held in a bank domiciled outside North America.

**European Option**   An option that can only be exercised on its expiration date.

**Ex Ante**   Before the fact; future.

**Ex-Dividend Date**   The date on which ownership of stock is determined for purposes of paying dividends. Owners purchasing shares before the ex-dividend date receive the dividend in question. Owners purchasing shares on or after the ex-dividend date are not entitled to the dividend.

**Ex Post**   After the fact; historical.

**Ex Post Alpha**   (Alternatively, Differential Return.) A portfolio's alpha calculated on an *ex post* basis. Mathematically, over an evaluation interval, it is the difference between the average return on the portfolio and the equilibrium average return on a portfolio of equal market risk.

**Ex Post Selection Bias**   In the context of constructing a security valuation model, the use of securities that have performed well and the avoidance of securities that have performed poorly, thus making the model appear more effective than it truly is.

**Ex-Rights Date**   The date on which ownership of stock is determined for purposes of granting rights to purchase new stock in a rights offering. Owners purchasing shares before the ex-rights date receive the rights in question. Owners purchasing shares on or after the ex-rights date are not entitled to the rights.

**Excess Return**   The difference between the return on a security and the return on a riskfree asset.

**Exchange Risk**   (Alternatively, Currency Risk.) The uncertainty in the return on a foreign financial asset due to unpredictability regarding the rate at which the foreign currency can be exchanged into the investor's own currency.

**Exercise Price**   (Alternatively, Striking Price.) In the case of a call option, the price at which an option buyer may purchase the underlying asset from the option writer. In the case of a put option, the price at which an option buyer may sell the underlying asset to the option writer.

**Exit Fee**   See Redemption Fee.

**Exogenous Variables**   In the context of an econometric model, an economic variable taken as given and used in the model to explain the model's endogenous variables.

**Expectations Hypothesis**  A hypothesis that the futures price of an asset is equal to the expected spot price of the asset on the delivery date of the futures contract.

**Expected Rate of Inflation**  That portion of inflation experienced over a given period of time that was anticipated by investors.

**Expected Return**  The return on a security (or portfolio) over a holding period that an investor anticipates receiving.

**Expected Return Vector**  A column of numbers that correspond to the expected returns for a set of securities.

**Expected Value**  A measure of central tendency of the probability distribution of a random variable. Equivalently, the mean of the random variable.

**Expected Yield-to-Maturity**  The yield-to-maturity on a bond calculated as a weighted average of all possible yields that the bond might produce under different scenarios of default or late payments, where the weights are the probabilities of each scenario occurring.

**Expiration Date**  The date on which the right to buy or sell a security under an option contract ceases.

**Face Value**  See Principal.

**Factor**  (Alternatively, Index.) An aspect of the investment environment which influences the returns of financial assets. To the extent that a factor influences a significant number of financial assets, it is termed common or pervasive.

**Factor Beta**  A relative measure of the mutual variation of a particular common factor with the return on the market portfolio. Mathematically, a factor beta is the covariance of the factor with the market portfolio, divided by the variance of the market portfolio.

**Factor Loading**  (Alternatively, Attribute or Sensitivity.) A measure of the responsiveness of a security's returns to a particular common factor.

**Factor Model**  (Alternatively, Index Model.) A return generating process which attributes the return on a security to the security's sensitivity to the movements of various common factors.

**Factor Risk**  That part of a security's total risk which is related to moves in various common factors and, hence, cannot be diversified away.

**Fail to Deliver**  A situation in which a seller's broker is unable to deliver the traded security to the buyer's broker on or before the required settlement date.

**Feasible Set**  (Alternatively, Opportunity Set.) The set of all portfolios that can be formed from the group of securities being considered by an investor.

**Fill-or-Kill Order**  A trading order which is cancelled if the broker is unable to execute it immediately.

**Financial Analyst**  (Alternatively, Security Analyst or Investment Analyst.) An individual who analyzes financial assets in order to determine the investment characteristics of those assets and to identify mispricings among those assets.

**Financial Asset**  See Security.

**Financial Institution**  See Financial Intermediary.

**Financial Intermediary**  (Alternatively, Financial Institution.) An organization that issues financial claims against itself and uses the proceeds of the issuance primarily to purchase financial assets issued by corporations, government entities, and other financial intermediaries.

**Financial Investment**  An investment in financial assets.

**Financial Leverage**  The use of debt to fund a portion of an investment.

**Financial Market**  (Alternatively, Security Market.) A mechanism designed to facilitate the exchange of financial assets by bringing buyers and sellers of securities together.

**Firm Commitment**  An arrangement between underwriters and a security issuer whereby the underwriters agree to purchase, at the offering price, all of the issue not bought by the public.

**First-in-First-out Method (FIFO)**  A method of valuing inventories that assumes that the company's inventory is sold in direct order of accumulation.

**Fixed Annuity**  A series of payments of a fixed and equal amount.

**Floating Rate**  (Alternatively, Variable Rate.) A rate of interest on a financial asset that may vary over the life of the asset, depending on changes in a specified indicator of current market interest rates.

**Floor Trader** An employee of a member firm who may execute trades on the floor of an exchange. See also Order Trader and Registered Trader.

**Foreign Return** The return on an investment in a foreign financial asset, including the impact of exchange rate changes.

**Forward Rate** The interest rate that links the current spot interest rate over one holding period to the current spot interest rate over a long holding period. Equivalently, the interest rate agreed to at a point in time where the loan will be made at a future date.

**Fourth Market** A US secondary security market in which investors (typically, financial institutions) trade securities directly with each other, bypassing the brokers and dealers on organized security exchanges and the over-the-counter market.

**Fundamental Analysis** A form of security analysis which seeks to determine the intrinsic value of securities based on underlying economic factors. These intrinsic values are compared to current market prices to estimate current levels of mispricing.

**Futures (Future Contract)** An agreement between two people under which the seller promises to deliver a specific asset on a specific future date to the buyer for a predetermined price to be paid on the delivery date.

**Future Option** (Alternatively, Options on Futures.) An option contract for which the deliverable asset is a specific futures contract.

**Generally Accepted Accounting Principles (GAAP)** Accounting rules established by recognized authorities, such as the Canadian Institute of Chartered Accountants (CICA).

**Geometric Mean Return** The compounded per-period average rate of return on a financial asset over a specified time interval.

**Good-Till-Canceled Order** See Open Order.

**Greenmail** An offer by the management of a corporation that is the target of a hostile takeover to repurchase its shares from the hostile bidder at an above-market price.

**Group** In the context of a specific asset class, a collection of financial assets that have common distinguishing financial characteristics.

**Group Selection** A component of the security selection process involving the identification of desirable combinations of groups within an asset class.

**Guaranteed Bond** A bond issued by one corporation but backed by another corporation.

**Hedge Ratio** (Alternatively, Delta.) The expected change in the value of an option per dollar change in the market price of the underlying asset.

**Hedger** An investor in futures contracts whose primary objective is to offset an otherwise risky position.

**Historical Beta** An estimate of a security's beta, derived solely from historical returns. Equivalently, the slope of the ex post characteristic line.

**Holding Period** The length of time over which an investor is assumed to invest a given sum of money.

**Holdout Sample** See Out-of-Sample Data.

**Homogeneous Expectations** A situation in which all investors possess the same perceptions with regard to the expected returns, standard deviations, and covariances of securities.

**Horizon Analysis** A form of active bond management where a single holding period is selected for analysis and possible yield structures at the end of the period are considered. Bonds with the most attractive expected returns under the alternative yield structures are selected for the portfolio.

**Hypothecation Agreement** A legal arrangement between a brokerage firm and an investor that permits the brokerage firm to pledge the investor's securities as collateral for bank loans, provided the securities were purchased through the investor's margin account.

**Idiosyncratic Risk** See Nonfactor Risk.

**Immunization** A bond portfolio management technique that permits an investor to meet a promised stream of cash outflows with a high degree of certainty.

**Implied Volatility** The risk of an asset derived from an options valuation model, assuming that an option on the asset is fairly priced by the market.

**Implied Return**  See Internal Rate of Return.

**In the Money Option**  In the case of a call (put) option, an option whose exercise price is less than (greater than) the market price of its underlying asset.

**Income Bond**  A bond for which the size of the interest payments varies, based on the income of the issuer.

**Indenture**  A legal document formally describing the terms of the legal relationship between a bond issuer and bondholders.

**Index**  See Factor.

**Index Arbitrage**  An investment strategy that involves buying a stock index futures contract and selling the individual stocks in the index or vice versa. The strategy is designed to take advantage of a mispricing between the stock index futures contract and the underlying stocks.

**Index Fund**  A passively managed investment in a diversified portfolio of financial assets designed to mimic the investment performance of a specific market index.

**Index Model**  See Factor Model.

**Indifference Curve**  All combinations of portfolios, considered in terms of expected returns and risk, that provide an investor with an equal amount of satisfaction.

**Inefficient Portfolio**  A portfolio that does not satisfy the criteria of an efficient portfolio and, hence, does not lie on the efficient set.

**Inflation**  The rate of change in a price index over a certain period of time. Equivalently, the percentage change in the purchasing power of a unit of currency over a certain period of time.

**Inflation Hedge**  An asset which preserves the value of its purchasing power over time despite changes in the price level.

**Information Content of Dividends Hypothesis** The proposition that dividend announcements contain inside information about a corporation's future prospects.

**Initial Margin Requirement**  The minimum percentage of a margin purchase (or short sale) price that must come from the investor's own funds.

**Initial Public Offering (IPO)**  (Alternatively, Unseasoned Offering.) The first offering of the shares of a company to the public.

**Initial Wealth**  The value of an investor's portfolio at the beginning of a holding period.

**Insider**  Narrowly defined, shareholders, officers, and directors of a corporation who own a "significant" proportion of a corporation's stock. More broadly defined, anyone who has access to information that is both "materially" related to the value of a corporation's securities and is unavailable to the general public.

**Interest Rate Risk**  The uncertainty in the return on a fixed-income security caused by unanticipated fluctuations in value of the asset due to changes in interest rates.

**Intermarket Spread Swap**  A type of bond swap where an investor moves out of one market segment and into another because the investor believes that one segment is significantly underpriced relative to the other.

**Internal Rate of Return**  (Alternatively, Implied Return.) The discount rate that equates the present value of future cash flows expected to be received from a particular investment to the cost of that investment.

**Intrinsic Value of an Option**  The value of an option if it were exercised immediately. Equivalently, the market price of the asset upon which a call option is written less the exercise price of the option (or the exercise price less the market price of the asset in the case of a put option).

**Investment**  The sacrifice of certain present value for (possibly uncertain) future value.

**Investment Advisor**  An individual or organization that provides investment advice to investors.

**Investment Analyst**  See Financial Analyst.

**Investment Banker**  (Alternatively, Underwriter.) An organization that acts as an intermediary between issuers and the ultimate purchasers of securities in the primary security market.

**Investment Banking**  The process of analyzing and selecting a means of procuring financing on behalf of an issuer of securities.

**Investment Committee**  Within a traditional investment organization, a group of senior management responsible for establishing the organization's broad investment strategy.

**Investment Company** A type of financial intermediary which obtains money from investors and uses that money to purchase financial assets. In return, the investors receive shares in the investment company, and thus indirectly own a proportion of the financial assets that the company itself owns.

**Investment Environment** The financial structure in which investors operate, consisting of the kinds of marketable securities available for purchase or sale and the process by which these securities are bought and sold.

**Investment Grade Bonds** Bonds which possess bond ratings that permit them to be purchased by the vast majority of institutional investors, particularly regulated financial institutions. Usually, investment grade bonds have a BBB (Dominion Bond Rating Service), B++ (Canadian Bond Rating Service) or higher bond rating.

**Investment Policy** A component of the investment process that involves determining an investor's objectives and amount of the funds available to invest.

**Investment Process** The set of procedures by which an investor decides what marketable securities to invest in, how extensive those investments should be, and when the investments should be made.

**Investment Style** The method an investor uses to take active positions in certain types of securities.

**Investment Value** The present value of a security's future prospects as estimated by well-informed market participants.

**January Effect** An empirical regularity whereby stock returns appear to be higher in January as opposed to other months of the year.

**Junk Bonds** See Speculative Grade Bonds.

**Lagging Indicators** Economic variables which have been found to follow movements in the economy.

**Lambda** The expected return premium (above the riskfree rate of interest) per unit of sensitivity to a particular common factor.

**Last-in-First-out Method (LIFO)** A method of valuing inventories that assumes that the company's inventory is sold in inverse order of accumulation.

**Leading Indicators** Economic variables which have been found to signal future changes in the economy.

**Limit Order** A trading order which specifies a limit price at which the broker is to execute the order. The trade will be executed only if the broker can meet or better the limit price.

**Limit Order Book** (Alternatively, Electronic Book.) The records kept by the exchange identifying the limit, stop, and stop limit orders that brokers have entered for execution in a particular security. On the TSE the information in the electronic book is available to all participants.

**Limit Price** The price specified when a limit order is placed with a broker, defining the maximum purchase price or minimum selling price at which the order can be executed.

**Limit Stop Order** A trading order that specifies both a stop price and a limit price. If the security's price reaches or passes the stop price, then a limit order is created at the limit price.

**Limited Liability** An aspect of the corporate form of organization that prevents common shareholders from losing more than their investment if the corporation should default on its obligation.

**Liquidity** (Alternatively, Marketability.) The ability of investors to convert securities to cash at a price similar to the price of the previous trade in the security, assuming no significant new information has arrived since the previous trade. Equivalently, the ability to sell an asset quickly without having to make a substantial price concession.

**Liquidity Preference (Premium) Theory** An explanation of the term structure of interest rates. It holds that the term structure is a result of the preference of investors for short-term securities. Investors can only be induced to hold longer-term securities if they expect to receive a higher return.

**Liquidity Premium** The expected incremental return of longer-term securities over shorter-term securities that compensates investors for the greater interest rate risk entailed in holding longer-term securities.

**Listed Security**  A security that is traded on an organized security exchange.

**Load Charge**  A sales charge levied by a mutual fund when an investor buys its shares.

**Load Fund**  A mutual fund that has a load charge.

**Long Hedger**  A hedger who offsets risk by buying futures contracts.

**Low-Load Fund**  A mutual fund that has a small load charge, usually 3.5% or less.

**Maintenance Margin Requirement**  The minimum actual margin that a brokerage firm will permit commodity futures investors to keep in their margin accounts.

**Majority Voting System**  (Alternatively, Straight Voting System.) In the context of a corporation, a method of voting in which a shareholder is permitted to give any one candidate for the board of directors a maximum number of votes equal to the number of shares owned by that shareholder.

**Managed Investment Company**  An investment company with a portfolio that may be altered at the discretion of the company's portfolio manager.

**Margin Account**  An account maintained by an investor with a brokerage firm in which securities may be purchased by borrowing a portion of the purchase price from the brokerage firm, or may be sold short by borrowing the securities from the brokerage firm.

**Margin Call**  A demand upon an investor by a brokerage firm to increase the equity in the investor's margin account. The margin call is initiated when the investor's actual margin falls below the margin requirement.

**Margin Purchase**  The purchase of securities financed by borrowing a portion of the purchase price from a brokerage firm.

**Marginal Efficiency of Capital**  See Demand for Capital.

**Marginal Return on Investment**  The additional income, expressed as a percentage, earned on each additional dollar invested in an asset.

**Marginal Tax Rate**  The amount of taxes, expressed as a percentage, paid on each additional dollar of taxable income received.

**Markdown**  The difference in prices between what an investor's broker receives and what the investor receives for a security sold in the over-the-counter market.

**Marked (Marking) to the Market**  The process of calculating, on a daily basis, the actual margin in an investor's account. Equivalently, the daily process of adjusting the equity in an investor's account to reflect the daily changes in the market value of the account's assets and liabilities.

**Market Beta**  See Beta Coefficient.

**Market Capitalization**  The aggregate market value of a security, equal to the market price per unit of the security multiplied by the total number of outstanding units of the security.

**Market Discount Function**  The set of discount factors on all default-free bonds across the spectrum of terms-to-maturity.

**Market Index**  A collection of securities whose prices are averaged to reflect the overall investment performance of a particular market for financial assets.

**Market-Maker**  See Designated Market-Maker.

**Market Model**  See Characteristic Line.

**Market Order**  A trading order which instructs the broker to buy or sell a security immediately at the best obtainable price.

**Market Portfolio**  A portfolio consisting of an investment in all securities. The proportion invested in each security equals the percentage of the total market capitalization represented by the security.

**Market Risk**  (Alternatively, Systematic Risk.) A part of a security's total risk that is related to moves in the market portfolio and, hence, cannot be diversified away.

**Market Segmentation Theory**  An explanation of the term structure of interest rates. It holds that various investors and borrowers are restricted by law, preference, or custom to certain maturity ranges. Spot rates in each market segment are determined by supply and demand conditions there.

**Market Timing**  A form of active management that entails shifting an investor's funds between a surrogate market portfolio and a riskfree asset, depending on the investor's perception of their near-term prospects.

**Marketability** See Liquidity.

**Markup** The difference in prices between what an investor pays and what the investor's broker pays for a security purchased in the over- the-counter market.

**Maturity Date** The date upon which a bond issuer repays investors the principal of the bond.

**Member Corporation** See Member Firm.

**Member Firm** (Alternatively, Member Corporation or Member Organization.) A brokerage firm with one or more memberships in an organized security exchange.

**Member Organization** See Member Firm.

**Merger** A form of corporate takeover in which two firms combine their operations and become one firm. Mergers are usually negotiated by the management of the two merging corporations.

**Mispriced Security** A security that is trading at a price substantially different than its intrinsic value.

**Money Market Deposit** A short-term fixed income security.

**Money Markets** Financial markets in which financial assets with a term-to-maturity of typically one year or less are traded.

**Mortgage Bond** A bond which is secured by the pledge of specific property. In the event of default, bondholders are entitled to obtain the property in question and sell it to satisfy their claims on the issuer.

**Multinational Firm** A company whose business operations and financial investments extend across a number of countries.

**Multiple Growth Model** A type of dividend discount model in which dividends are assumed to grow at different rates over specifically defined time periods.

**Municipal Bond** A bond issued by a state or local unit of government.

**Mutual Fund** See Open-end Investment Company.

**Naked Call Writing** The process of writing a call option on a stock that the option writer does not own.

**Naked Put Writing** The process of writing a put option on a stock when the writer does not have the sufficient cash (or securities) in his or her brokerage account to purchase the stock.

**National Association of Securities Dealers Automated Quotations (NASDAQ)** An automated nationwide communications network operated by the National Association of Securities Dealers which connects dealers and brokers in the US over-the-counter market. NASDAQ provides current market-maker bid-ask price quotes to market participants.

**Net Asset Value** The market value of an investment company's assets, less any liabilities, divided by the number of shares outstanding.

**Net Present Value** The present value of future cash flows expected to be received from a particular investment less the cost of that investment.

**No Growth Model** See Zero Growth Model.

**No-Load Fund** A mutual fund that does not have a load charge.

**Nominal Return** The percentage change in the value of an investment in a financial asset, where the beginning and ending values of the asset are not adjusted for inflation over the time of the investment.

**Nonfactor Risk** (Alternatively, Idiosyncratic Risk or Security Specific Risk.) That part of a security's total risk which is not related to moves in various common factors and, hence, can be diversified away.

**Nonmarket Risk** See Unique Risk.

**Nonsatiation** A condition whereby investors are assumed to always prefer higher levels of terminal wealth to lower levels of terminal wealth.

**Normal Backwardation** An expected relationship between the futures price of an asset and the expected spot price of the asset on the delivery date of the contract. Normal backwardation states that the futures price will be less than the expected spot price.

**Normal Contango** An expected relationship between the futures price of an asset and the expected spot price of the asset on the delivery date of the contract. Normal contango states that the futures price will be greater than the expected spot price.

**Normal Probability Distribution** A symmetrical bell-shaped probability distribution, completely described by its mean and standard deviation.

**Normative Economics** A form of economic analysis which is prescriptive in nature, dealing with what "ought to be."

**Odd Lot** An amount of stock, generally from 1 to 99 shares.

**Open** See Opening Price.

**Open-End Investment Company** (Alternatively, Mutual Fund.) A managed investment company, with an unlimited life, that stands ready at all times to purchase its shares from its owners and usually will continuously offer new shares to the public.

**Open Interest** The number of a particular futures contract outstanding at a particular point in time.

**Open Order** (Alternatively, Good-Till-Canceled Order.) A trading order which remains in effect until it is either filled or canceled by the investor.

**Opening Price** (Alternatively, Open.) The price at which the first trade of the day took place in a particular stock.

**Opportunity Set** See Feasible Set.

**Optimal Portfolio** The feasible portfolio that offers an investor the maximum level of satisfaction. This portfolio represents the tangency between the efficient set and an indifference curve of the investor.

**Option** A contract between two investors in which one investor grants the other the right to buy (or sell) a specific asset at a specific price within a specific time period.

**Options on Futures** See Futures Option.

**Order Specification** The investor's instructions to a broker regarding the particular characteristics of a trading order, including the name of the security's issuing firm, whether to buy or sell, order size, maximum time the order is to be outstanding, and the type of order to be used.

**Order Trader** A floor trader who may only trade client orders on the floor of an exchange.

**Ordinary Least Squares** See Simple Linear Regression.

**Organized Exchange** A central physical location where trading of securities is done under a set of rules and regulations.

**Original Issue Discount Security** A security which is issued with a coupon interest rate below prevailing market interest rates on similar securities and, thus, is originally sold at a discount from par value.

**Out of the Money Option** In the case of a call (put) option, an option whose exercise price is greater than (less than) the market price of its underlying asset.

**Out-of-Sample Data** (Alternatively, Holdout Sample.) In the context of constructing a security valuation model, information which is obtained from periods different than those used to estimate the valuation model.

**Overmargined Account** (Alternatively, Unrestricted Account.) A margin account in which the actual margin has risen above the initial margin requirement.

**Overpriced Security** (Alternatively, Overvalued Security.) A security whose expected return is less than its equilibrium expected return. Equivalently, a security with a negative alpha.

**Oversubscription Privilege** The opportunity given shareholders who have exercised their rights in a rights offering to buy shares that were not purchased in the offering.

**Over-the-Counter Market (OTC Market)** A secondary market for securities distinct from an organized security exchange.

**Overvalued Security** See Overpriced Security.

**Pac-Man Defense** A strategy used by corporations to ward off hostile takeovers. The targeted company reverses the takeover effort and seeks to acquire the firm making the initial takeover attempt.

**Par Value of Bond** See Principal.

**Par Value of Common Stock** The nominal value of shares of common stock as legally carried on the books of a corporation.

**Participating Bond** A bond that promises to pay a stated rate of interest to its owner, but may also pay additional interest if the issuer's earnings exceed a specified level.

**Participating Certificate** A bond which represents an ownership interest in a pool of fixed-income securities. The holders of the certificates receive the interest and principal payments on the pooled securities in proportion to their ownership of the pool.

**Passive Investment System**   (Alternatively, Passive Management.) The process of buying and holding a well-diversified portfolio.

**Passive Management**   See Passive Investment System.

**Payout Ratio**   The percentage of a firm's earnings paid to shareholders in the form of cash dividends.

**Pegging**   The process by which investment bankers attempt to stabilize the price of an underwritten security in the secondary market for a period of time after the initial offering date.

**Perfect Markets**   Security markets in which no impediments to investing exist. These impediments include such things as finite divisibility of securities, taxes, transactions costs, and costly information.

**Performance Attribution**   The identification of sources of returns for a portfolio or security over a particular evaluation interval of time.

**Performance Margin**   The initial margin that must be posted by a futures buyer or seller.

**Poison Pill Defense**   A strategy used by corporations to ward off hostile takeovers. The targeted company gives its shareholders certain rights that can be exercised only in the event of a hostile takeover, and that, once exercised, will be extremely onerous to the acquirer.

**Political Risk**   The uncertainty in the return on a foreign financial asset due to the possibility that the foreign government might take actions that are detrimental to the investor's financial interests.

**Portfolio Construction**   (Alternatively, Security Selection.) A component of the investment process that involves identifying which assets to invest in and determining the proportion of funds to invest in each of the assets.

**Portfolio Insurance**   An investment strategy designed to guarantee a minimum rate of return while allowing the investor to benefit substantially from the positive returns generated by an investment in a risky portfolio.

**Portfolio Manager**   An individual who utilizes the information provided by financial analysts to construct a portfolio of financial assets.

**Portfolio Performance Evaluation**   A component of the investment process involving periodic analysis of how a portfolio performed in terms of both returns earned and risk incurred.

**Portfolio Revision**   A component of the investment process, involving periodically repeating the processes of setting investment policy, conducting security analysis, and constructing a portfolio.

**Portfolio Turnover**   A measure of how much buying and selling occurs in a portfolio over a given period of time.

**Positive Economics**   A form of economic analysis that is descriptive in nature, dealing with "what is."

**Preemptive Rights**   When a corporation plans an issuance of new common shares, the right of existing shareholders to purchase the new shares in proportion to the numbers of shares that they currently own.

**Preferred Shares**   A hybrid form of security that has characteristics of both common shares and bonds.

**Premium**   The price of an option contract.

**Price-Earnings Ratio**   A corporation's current stock price divided by its earnings per share.

**Price Impact**   The effect on the price of a security resulting from a trade in that security. Price impact is the result of several factors: size of the trade, demand for immediate liquidity, and presumed information of the individual or organization placing the order.

**Price Relative**   The price of a security in one period divided by the price of that same security in a previous period.

**Price-Weighted Market Index**   A market index in which the contribution of a security to the value of the index is a function of the security's current market price.

**Primary Security Market**   The market in which securities are sold at the time of their initial issuance.

**Principal**   (Alternatively, Face Value or Par Value of Bond.) The nominal value of a bond which is repaid to bondholders at the maturity date.

**Principle of Diminishing Returns**   The proposition that additional investments in a particular asset produce increasingly smaller additional returns.

**Private Placement**   The direct sale of a newly issued security to one or a small number of large institutional investors.

**Probabilistic Forecasting**   A form of security analysis which begins with a series of economic scenarios, along with their respective probabilities of occurrence. Under each of these scenarios, accompanying projections are made as to the prospects for various industries, companies, and stock prices.

**Probability Distribution**   A model describing the relative frequency of possible values that a random variable can assume.

**Professional Money Manager**   An individual or organization that invests funds on behalf of others.

**Program Trading**   The purchase or sale of a collection of securities as if the collection were one security. Program trades are predominently employed in portfolio insurance and index arbitrage strategies.

**Promised Yield-to-Maturity**   The yield-to-maturity on a bond calculated assuming that all promised cash flows are received on a full and timely basis.

**Prospectus**   The official selling circular that must be given to purchasers of new securities registered with the provincial regulator. The prospectus provides information about the issuer's business, its financial condition, and the nature of the security being offered.

**Proxy**   A power of attorney that authorizes a designated party to cast all of a shareholder's votes on any matter brought up at the corporation's annual meeting.

**Proxy Fight**   An attempt by dissident shareholders to solicit proxies to vote against corporate incumbents.

**Pseudo-American Model**   A model for valuing options on stocks that pay dividends over the life of the option. Values for an option are determined by assuming the option is either exercised early (just before each ex-dividend date

for calls; just after each ex-dividend date for puts) or at expiration. The highest value obtained is the value of the option.

**Purchase Group**   See Syndicate.

**Purchasing-Power Risk**   The risk experienced by investors in financial assets due to uncertainty concerning the impact of inflation on the real returns produced by those financial assets.

**Pure-Discount Security**   A fixed-income security that promises to make only one payment to its owner.

**Pure Factor Play**   A portfolio which possesses a unit sensitivity to one factor, no sensitivity to any other factor, and has zero nonfactor risk.

**Pure Yield Pickup Swap**   A type of bond swap where an investor exchanges one bond for another to obtain a higher yield over the long term, with little attention paid to the near-term outlook for the bonds' respective market segments or the market as a whole.

**Put-Call Parity**   The relationship between the market price on a put and a call that have the same exercise price, expiration date, and underlying stock.

**Put Option**   A contract that gives the buyer the right to sell a specific number of shares of a company to the writer at a specific price within a specific time.

**R-Squared**   See Coefficient of Determination.

**Random Error Term**   The difference between the actual value of a random variable and the predicted value based on some model. For a security, the difference between its actual excess return and the excess return calculated from the security's characteristic line.

**Random Variable**   A variable that takes on alternative values according to chance.

**Random Walk (or Random Walk Model)**   In general, it refers to a situation in which changes in the value of a random variable are independent and identically distributed. When applied to common shares, it refers to a situation in which security price changes are independent and identically distributed, meaning that the size of a security's price change from one period to the next can be viewed as being determined by the spin of a roulette wheel.

**Rate Anticipation Swap**   A type of bond swap where an investor exchanges bonds that are expected to perform relatively poorly for those that are expected to perform relatively well, given an anticipated movement in interest rates.

**Rate of Return** The percentage change in the value of an investment in a financial asset (or portfolio of financial assets) over a specified time period.

**Real Estate Investment Trust (REIT)** An investment fund, similar to an investment company, whose investment objective is to hold primarily real-estate-related assets, either through mortgages, construction and development loans, or equity interests.

**Real Investment** An investment involving some kind of tangible asset, such a land, equipment, or buildings.

**Real Return** The percentage change in the value of an investment in a financial asset, where the beginning and ending values of the asset are adjusted for inflation over the time of the investment.

**Real Return Bond** A Government of Canada bond whose coupon payments and face value are indexed to the Consumer Price Index, thereby providing investors with a known real return if held to maturity.

**Realized Capital Gain (or Loss)** A capital gain (or loss) on an asset that is recognized, for tax purposes, through the sale or exchange of the asset.

**Red Herring** A preliminary prospectus that provides much of the information in the final prospectus, but is not an offer to sell the security, nor does it display an actual offering price.

**Redemption Fee** (Alternatively, Back-End Load or Contingent Deferred Sales Charge or Exit Fee.) A fee levied by an investment company when an investor sells shares back to the investment company.

**Regional Brokerage Firm** An organization offering brokerage services that specializes in trading the securities of companies located in a particular region of the country.

**Regional Exchange** An organized exchange which specializes in trading the securities of companies located in a particular region of the country.

**Registered Bond** A bond for which the owner is registered with the issuer. The bondholder receives coupon payments directly from the issuer. Ownership changes require notification of the issuer.

**Registered Representative** See Account Executive.

**Registered Trader** A floor trader who may execute both client and the firm's orders on the floor of an exchange.

**Registrar** A designated agent of a corporation responsible for canceling and issuing shares of stock in the corporation as these shares are issued or traded.

**Registration** A procedure, usually involving the filing of a prospectus with the relevant provincial regulator, that must be completed prior to initiating a public security offering.

**Reinvestment-Rate Risk** The uncertainty in the return on a fixed-income asset caused by unanticipated changes in the interest rate at which cash flows from the asset can be reinvested.

**Replacement Cost Accounting** The use of estimated replacement costs instead of historical book-value costs when calculating corporate earnings.

**Reported Earnings** See Accounting Earnings.

**Repurchase Agreement** A type of money market instrument. It involves the sale of a financial asset from one investor to another. The investor selling the asset simultaneously agrees to repurchase it from the purchaser on a stated future date at a predetermined price, which is higher than the original transaction price.

**Repurchase Offer** An offer by the management of a corporation to buy back some of its own stock.

**Residual Standard Deviation** See Standard Deviation of the Random Error Term.

**Restricted Stock** Equity shares whose voting rights are in some way diminished or curtailed. Restricted voting shares each carry the requisite number of votes per share but the shareholder is not permitted to vote the full number of shares he or she owns. Subordinate voting shares are those with fewer votes per share than regular common shares and non-voting shares are those with no voting rights.

**Retention Ratio** The percentage of a firm's earnings that are not paid to shareholders, but instead are retained by the firm. Equivalently, one minus the payout ratio.

**Return Generating Process**  A statistical model which describes how the returns on a security are produced.

**Return on Equity**  The earnings per share of a firm divided by the firm's book value per share.

**Reverse Stock Split**  A form of stock split whereby the number of shares is reduced and the par value per share is increased.

**Reversing Trade**  The purchase or sale of a futures (or options) contract designed to offset, and thereby cancel, the previous sale or purchase of the same contract.

**Reward-to-Variability Ratio**  An ex post risk-adjusted measure of portfolio performance where risk is defined as the standard deviation of the portfolio's returns. Mathematically, over an evaluation interval, it is the excess return of a portfolio divided by the standard deviation of the portfolio's returns.

**Reward-to-Volatility Ratio**  An ex post risk-adjusted measure of portfolio performance where risk is defined as the market risk of the portfolio. Mathematically, over an evaluation interval it is the excess return of portfolio divided by the beta of the portfolio.

**Right**  An option issued to existing shareholders that permits them to buy a specified number of new shares at a designated subscription price. For each shareholder, this number is proportional to the number of existing shares currently owned by each shareholder.

**Rights Offering**  The sale of new stock conducted by first offering the stock to existing shareholders in proportion to the number of shares owned by each shareholder.

**Risk**  The uncertainty associated with the end-of-period value of an investment in an asset or portfolio of assets.

**Risk-Adjusted Return**  The return on an asset or portfolio, modified to explicitly account for the risk to which the asset or portfolio is exposed.

**Risk-Averse Investor**  An investor who prefers an investment with less risk over one with more risk, assuming that both investments offer the same expected return.

**Risk-free Asset**  An asset whose return over a given holding period is certain and known at the beginning of the holding period.

**Risk-free Borrowing**  The act of borrowing funds that are to be repaid with a known rate of interest.

**Risk-free Lending (Investing)**  The act of investing in a risk-free asset.

**Risk-Neutral Investor**  An investor who has no preference between investments with varying levels of risk, assuming that the investments offer the same expected return.

**Risk Premium**  The difference between the expected yield-to-maturity of a risky bond and the expected yield-to-maturity of a similar default-free bond.

**Risk-Seeking Investor**  An investor who prefers an investment with more risk over one with less risk, assuming that both investments offer the same expected return.

**Risk Structure**  The set of yields-to-maturity across bonds that possess different degrees of default risk, but are similar with respect to other attributes.

**Risk Tolerance**  The trade-off between risk and expected return demanded by a particular investor.

**Round Lot**  An amount of stock generally equal to 100 shares or a multiple of 100 shares.

**Savings**  Foregone consumption. The difference between current income and current consumption.

**Seat**  The designation of membership in an organized exchange. By holding a seat, the member has the privilege of being able to execute trades using the facilities provided by the exchange.

**Secondary Distribution**  A means of selling a block of stock where the shares are sold away from an organized exchange after the close of trading in a manner similar to the sale of new issues of common stock.

**Secondary Security Market**  The market in which securities are traded that have been issued at some previous point in time.

**Sector Factor**  A factor which affects the return on securities within a particular economic sector.

**Securities and Exchange Commission (SEC)**
A US federal agency established by the *Securities Exchange Act* of 1934 that regulates the issuance of securities in the primary market and the trading of securities in the secondary market.

**Security** (Alternatively, Financial Asset.) A legal representation of the right to receive prospective future benefits under stated conditions.

**Security Analysis** A component of the investment process that involves determining the prospective future benefits of a security, the conditions under which such benefits will be received, and the likelihood of such conditions occurring.

**Security Analyst** See Financial Analyst.

**Security Market** See Financial Market.

**Security Market Line** Derived from the CAPM, a linear relationship between the expected returns on securities and the risk of those securities, with risk expressed as the security's beta (or equivalently, the security's covariance with the market portfolio).

**Security Selection** See Portfolio Construction.

**Self-Regulation** A method of governmental regulation where the rules and standards of conduct in security markets are set by firms that operate in these markets, subject to the oversight of various federal agencies as the SEC and CFTC.

**Selling Group** A group of investment banking organizations who, as part of a security underwriting are responsible for selling the security.

**Semistrong-Form Market Efficiency** A level of market efficiency in which all relevant publicly available information is fully and immediately reflected in security prices.

**Sensitivity** See Factor Loading.

**Separation Theorem** A feature of the Capital Asset Pricing Model which states that the optimal combination of risky assets for an investor can be determined without any knowledge about the investor's preferences towards risk and return.

**Serial Bond** A bond issue with different portions of the issue maturing at different dates.

**Settle Price** The representative price for a futures contract determined during the closing period of the futures exchange.

**Settlement Date** The date after a security has been traded, on which the buyer must deliver cash to the seller and the seller must deliver the security to the buyer.

**Shelf Registration** Under National Policy 44, issuers may register securities in advance of their issuance and sell these securities up to two years later.

**Short Hedger** A hedger who offsets risk by selling futures contracts.

**Short Interest Position** The number of shares of a given company that have been sold short and, as of a given date, the loans remain outstanding.

**Short Sale** The sale of a security that is not owned by an investor, but rather is borrowed from a broker. The investor eventually repays the broker in kind by purchasing the same security in a subsequent transaction.

**Simple Linear Regression** (Alternatively, Ordinary Least Squares.) A statistical model of the relationship between two random variables in which one variable is hypothesized to be linearly related to the other. This relationship is depicted by a regression line which is a straight line, "fitted" to pairs of values of the two variables, so that the sum of the squared random error terms is minimized.

**Sinking Fund** Periodic payments made by a bond issuer to reduce, in an orderly manner, the amount of outstanding principal on a bond issue over the life of the bond.

**Size Effect** (Alternatively, Small Firm Effect.) An empirical regularity whereby stock returns appear to differ consistently across the spectrum of market capitalization. Over extended periods of time, smaller capitalization stocks have outperformed larger capitalization stocks on a risk-adjusted basis.

**Small Firm Effect** See Size Effect.

**Soft Dollars** Brokerage commissions ostensibly paid for having a brokerage firm execute a trade and indirectly designated, in part, as payment for non-trade-related services rendered.

**Special Offering** A trade involving a large block of stock on an organized security exchange whereby a number of brokerage firms attempt to execute the order by soliciting offsetting orders from their customers.

**Speculative Grade Bonds** (Also known in the US as Junk Bonds.) Bonds which are not investment grade bonds. Usually, speculative bonds have a BB (Dominion Bond Rating Service) or B+ (Canadian Bond Rating Service) or lower rating.

**Speculator** An investor in future contracts whose primary objective is to make a profit from buying and selling these contracts.

**Split-Funding** A situation in which an institutional investor divides its funds among two or more professional money managers.

**Spot Market** The market for an asset which involves the immediate exchange of the asset for cash.

**Spot Price** The purchase price of an asset in the spot market.

**Spot Rate** The annual yield-to-maturity on a pure-discount security.

**Standard Deviation** A measure of the dispersion of possible outcomes around the expected outcome of a random variable.

**Standard Deviation of the Random Error Term** (Alternatively, Residual Standard Deviation.) In the context of simple linear regression, a measure of the dispersion of possible outcomes of the random error term.

**Standard Error of Alpha** The standard deviation of a security's estimated alpha, as derived from the ex post characteristic line.

**Standard Error of Beta** The standard deviation of a security's estimated beta, as derived from the ex post characteristic line.

**Standardized Unexpected Earnings** The difference between a firm's actual earnings over a given period less an estimate of the firm's expected earnings, with this quantity divided by the standard deviation of the firm's previous earnings forecast errors.

**Standby Agreement** An arrangement between a security issuer and an underwriter as part of a rights offering. The underwriter agrees to purchase at a fixed price all securities not purchased by current stockholders.

**Stochastic Process Risk** In the context of immunization, the risk that the yield curve will shift in a way that prevents an immunized bond portfolio from producing its expected cash inflows.

**Stock Dividend** An accounting transaction that distributes stock to existing shareholders in proportion to the number of shares currently owned by the shareholders. A stock dividend entails a transfer from retained earnings to the capital stock account of a dollar amount that is equal to the market value of the distributed stock.

**Stock Split** Similar to a stock dividend, an accounting transaction that increases the amount of stock held by existing shareholders in proportion to the number of shares currently owned by shareholders. A stock split entails a reduction in the par value of the corporation's stock and the simultaneous exchange of a multiple number of new shares for each existing share.

**Stop Loss Order** See Stop Order.

**Stop Order** (Alternatively, Stop Loss Order.) A trading order that specifies a stop price. If the security's price reaches or passes the stop price, then a market order is created.

**Stop Price** The price specified by an investor when a stop order or a stop limit order is placed that defines the price at which the market order or limit order for the security is to become effective.

**Straddle** An options strategy which involves buying (or writing) both a call and a put on the same asset, with the options having the same exercise price and expiration date.

**Straight Line Method** A method of calculating depreciation that allocates the cost of a fixed asset equally over the estimated useful life of the asset.

**Straight Voting System** See Majority Voting System.

**Street Name** An arrangement between an investor and a brokerage firm where the investor maintains an account in which the investor's securities are registered in the name of the brokerage firm.

**Striking Price** See Exercise Price.

**Strong-Form Market Efficiency** A level of market efficiency in which all relevant information, both public and private, is fully and immediately reflected in security prices.

**Subordinated Debenture** A debenture whose claims, in the event of bankruptcy, are junior to other bonds issued by the firm.

**Subscription Price**   The price at which holders of rights are permitted to purchase shares of stock in a rights offering.

**Substitution Swap**   A type of bond swap where an investor exchanges one bond with a lower yield for another with a higher yield, yet both bonds have essentially the same financial characteristics.

**Supply of Capital**   The quantity of capital offered by investors at varying interest rate levels.

**Supply-to-Sell Schedule**   A description of the quantities of a security that an investor is prepared to sell at alternative prices.

**Sustainable Earnings**   The amount of earnings that a firm could pay out each year, with the result that the firm's future earnings neither increase nor decrease.

**Syndicate**   (Alternatively, Purchase Group.) A group of investment banking organizations that, as part of a security underwriting, are responsible for purchasing the security from the issuer and reselling it to the public.

**Synthetic Futures (Synthetic Futures Contract)**   The creation of a position equivalent to either the purchase of a futures contract by buying a call option and writing a put option on the asset or to the sale of a futures contract by buying a put option and writing a call option on the asset.

**Synthetic Put**   A form of portfolio insurance that emulates the investment outcomes of a put option through the use of a dynamic asset allocation strategy.

**Systematic Risk**   See Market Risk.

**Takeover**   An action by an individual or firm to acquire controlling interest in a corporation.

**Target Firm**   A firm that is the subject of a takeover attempt.

**Technical Analysis**   A form of security analysis which attempts to forecast the movement in the prices of securities based primarily on historical price and volume trends in those securities.

**Tender Offer**   A form of corporate takeover in which a firm or individual offers to buy some or all of the shares of a target firm at a stated price. This offer is publicly advertised and material describing the bid is mailed to the target's stockholders.

**Term Bond**   A bond issued where all of the bonds mature on the same date.

**Term Structure**   The set of yields-to-maturity across bonds that possess different terms-to-maturity, but are similar with respect to other attributes.

**Term-to-Maturity**   The time remaining until a bond's maturity date.

**Terminal Wealth**   The value of an investor's portfolio at the end of a holding period. Equivalently, the investor's initial wealth multiplied times one plus the rate of return earned on the investor's portfolio over the holding period.

**Third Market**   A secondary security market where exchange-listed securities are traded over the counter.

**Time Deposit**   A savings account at a financial institution.

**Time Value (Premium)**   The excess of the market price of an option over its intrinsic value.

**Time-Weighted Return**   A method of measuring the performance of a portfolio over a particular period of time. It is the cumulative compounded rate of return of the portfolio, calculated on each date that a cash flow moves into or out of the portfolio over the performance measurement period.

**Timing**   An aspect of security analysis which entails forecasting the price movements of asset classes relative to one another.

**Top-Down Forecasting**   A sequential approach to security analysis which entails first making forecasts for the economy, then for industries, and finally for individual companies. Each level of forecasts is conditional on the previous level of forecasts made.

**Total Risk**   The standard deviation of the return on a security or a portfolio.

**Trading Halt**   A temporary suspension in the trading of a security on an organized exchange.

**Trading Post**   The physical location on the floor of an organized exchange where a specialist in a particular stock is located and where all orders involving the stock must be taken for execution.

**Transfer Agent**   A designated agent of a corporation, usually a bank, which administers the transfer of shares of a corporation's stock between old and new owners.

**Treasury Bill**   A security issued by the US Treasury with a maximum term-to-maturity of one year. Interest and principal are paid only at maturity.

**Treasury Stock**   Common stock which has been issued by a corporation and then later purchased by the corporation in the open market or through a tender offer. This stock does not include voting rights or rights to receive dividends and is equivalent economically to unissued stock.

**Triple Witching Hour**   The date when options on individual stocks and market indices, futures on market indices, and options on market index futures expire simultaneously.

**Trustee**   An organization, usually a bank, which serves as the representative of bondholders. The trustee acts to protect the interests of bondholders and facilitates communication between them and the issuer.

**Unbiased Expectations Theory**   An explanation of the term structure of interest rates. It holds that a forward rate represents the average opinion of the expected future spot rate for the time period in question.

**Underpriced Security**   (Alternatively, Undervalued Security.) A security whose expected return is greater than its equilibrium expected return. Equivalently, a security with a positive alpha.

**Undervalued Security**   See Underpriced Security.

**Underwriter**   See Investment Banker.

**Unexpected Rate of Inflation**   That portion of inflation experienced over a given period of time that was not anticipated by investors.

**Unique Risk**   (Alternatively, Unsystematic Risk.) That part of a security's total risk which is not related to moves in the market portfolio and, hence, can be diversified away.

**Unit Investment Trust**   An unmanaged investment company with a finite life that raises an initial sum of capital from investors and uses the proceeds to purchase a fixed portfolio of securities (typically bonds).

**Unrealized Capital Gain (or Loss)**   A capital gain (or loss) on an asset that has not yet been recognized for tax purposes through the sale or exchange of the asset.

**Unrestricted Account**   See Overmargined Account.

**Unseasoned Offering**   See Initial Public Offering.

**Unsystematic Risk**   See Unique Risk.

**Up-Tick**   A trade in a security made at a price higher than the price of the previous trade in that same security.

**Value-Weighted Market Index**   (Alternatively, Capitalization-Weighted Market Index.) A market index in which the contribution of a security to the value of the index is a function of the security's market capitalization.

**Variable Rate**   See Floating Rate.

**Variance**   The squared value of the standard deviation.

**Variance-Covariance Matrix**   A table which symmetrically arrays the covariances between a number of random variables. Variances of the random variables lie on the diagonal of the matrix, while covariances between the random variables lie above and below the diagonal.

**Wash Sale**   The sale and subsequent purchase of a "substantially identical" security solely for the purpose of generating a tax deductible capital loss.

**Weak-Form Market Efficiency**   A level of market efficiency in which all previous security price data is fully and immediately reflected in current security prices.

**Weekend Effect**   See Day-of-the-Week Effect.

**White Knight**   Another firm, favorably inclined toward a target firm's current management, which during the process of a hostile takeover of that corporation, agrees to make a better offer to the corporation's shareholders.

**Yield**   The yield-to-maturity of a bond.

**Yield Curve**   A visual representation of the term structure of interest rates.

**Yield Spread**   The difference in the promised yields-to-maturity of two bonds.

**Yield Structure**   The set of yields-to-maturity across bonds differing in terms of a number of attributes. These attributes include term- to-maturity, coupon rate, call provisions, tax status, marketability, and likelihood of default.

**Yield-to-Call**  The yield-to-maturity of a callable bond calculated assuming that the bond is called at the earliest possible time.

**Yield-to-Maturity**  For a particular fixed-income security, the single interest rate (with interest compounded at some specified interval) that, if paid by a bank on the amount invested in the security, would enable the investor to obtain all the payments made by that security. Equivalently, the discount rate that equates the present value of future cash flows from the security to the current market price of the security.

**Zero Coupon Bond**  See Pure-Discount Security.

**Zero Growth Model**  (Alternatively, No Growth Model.) A type of dividend discount model in which dividends are assumed to maintain a constant value in perpetuity.

**Zero-Plus Tick**  A trade in a security made at a price equal to that of the previous trade in that security but higher than that of the last trade made in the security at a different price.

# INDEX

# C

Call loan rate, 22
Call markets, 30
Call options, 526–528, 577
Call premium, 325
Call price, 325
Call provisions:
  corporate bonds, 325
  Government of Canada bonds 315
Canada Savings Bonds, 315–316
*Canadian Bond Rating Service* (CBRS), 339
*Canadian Business*, 681
*Canadian Dealing Network, Inc.* (CDN), 39, 56
Canadian Deposit Insurance Act, 306
*Canadian Deposit Insurance Corporation* (CDIC), 306
Canadian government securities, 310–320
  bonds, 313–319, 585
  Canadian Savings Bonds (CSBs), 315–316
  Real Return Bonds, 318–319
  Treasury bills, 311–313
  zero-coupon bonds, 317–318
*Canadian Investment Review*, 681
*Canadian Investor Protection Fund* (CIPF), 44
Canadian Institute of Chartered Accountants, 290, 675
  *Handbook Section* 4510, 290
Capital asset pricing model (CAPM), 183–224
  assumptions, 184–185
  capital market line, 185–190
  disequilibrium, 208–212
  diversification, 203–208
  equilibrium expected returns, 198
  expected versus actual values, 197–198
  extended versions of, 217–223
    heterogeneous expectations, 219–220
    investment policies when borrowing is restricted/expensive, 217–218

liquidity, 220–223
market and unique risk, 196–197
return-generating processes, 199–203, 210–211
security market line, 190–196
  derivation of, 223–224
synthesis of arbitrage pricing theory (APT) and, 240–243
tests of, 244–251
  historical beta factor, 247–248
  risk-return classes, 245–247
  zero-beta CAPM, 248–249
validity of, 745
Capital cost allowance (CCA), 258–261
Capital gains/losses, personal income taxes, 270–273
  capital account, 272–273
  cumulative net investment losses, 273
  income account, 272–273
  lifetime capital gains exemption, 272
Capital market line (CML), 185–190, 217–218, 729–731, 733–736, 747
  efficient set, 189–190
  market portfolio, 186–187
  separation theorem, 185–186
Capital markets, 9
Capitalization of income method of valuation, 333, 453–456
  dividend discount models (DDMs), 455–456
  internal rate of return, 455
  net present value (NPV), 454–455
Carrying costs, 596
Cash accounts, 21
Cash dividends, common shares, 393–394
Cash-matching portfolio of bonds, 373
Central tendency, 113
Certainty equivalent return, 703–704
Certificates of Accrual on Treasury Securities (CATs), 317

Certificates of deposit (CDs), 309
  Eurodollar CDs, 309
Characteristic lines, 199–200, 210
  graphing of, 211–212
Chartered Financial Analysts (CFAs), 656–660
  candidate study and examination program, general topic outline, 658–659
Charter, 386
Chartered banks:
  certificates of deposit (CDs), 309
  demand deposits, 302–303
  savings deposits, 302–306
  time deposits, 304
Charts, 684–686
  bar charts, 684–686
  line charts, 684–685
  point and figure charts, 684–686
Chicago Board Options Exchange (CBOE), 531, 589
Chicago Board of Trade (CBT), 588, 589, 593
Chicago Mercantile Exchange, 603, 606
Churning, 17
Clearing corporations:
  equities:
    *Canadian Depository for Securities Limited* (CDS), 43
    *West Canada Clearing Corporation* (WCCC), 43
    *West Canada Depository Trust Company* (WCDTC), 43
  options:
    *Trans Canada Options Inc.* (TCO), 39, 527–529, 531, 534, 537
Clearinghouses, futures contracts, 589–592
  *Winnipeg Commodity Clearing Ltd.*, 589
Clearing procedures, 43
Closed-end funds:
  example listing, 626

Investment Dealers Association, 56
Investment environment, 1–9
  securities, 2–9
*Investment Funds Institute of Canada* (IFIC), 624
Investment grade bonds, 339
Investment industry, 14
Investment information:
  sources of, 681–682, 689–692
    computer-readable data, 682
    publications, 681–682
Investment management, 695–714
  asset allocation, 708–709
  functions, 697
  manager-client relations, 711
  market timing, 709
  portfolio revision, 710
  security analysis and portfolio construction, 704–710
  security selection, 706–708
  setting investment policy, 697–704
  traditional investment management organizations, 695–697
Investment process, 1
Investments:
  asset ownership, 12–13
  investment industry, 13–15
  investment process, 9–12
    investment policy, 10
    portfolio construction, 11
    portfolio performance evaluation, 11
    portfolio revision, 11–12
    security analysis, 10–11
Investment system evaluation, 666–671
  easily beaten systems, comparisons of, 668–669
  ex post selection bias, 670
  failure to adjust for risk, 666–667
  failure to consider dividends, 667
  failure to consider transaction costs, 667
  failure to use out-of-sample data, 671

  nonoperational systems, 667–668
  reliance on misleading visual comparisons, 669
  spurious fits, 668
Investment value, *See* Market value
Investment value, of securities, 73

**J**

January effect, 432, 441–442
  and day-of-the-week effect, 439–440
  and size effect, 435–437
*Journal of Portfolio Management*, 681
Junk bonds, 339

**K**

Keynes, John Maynard, 599

**L**

Lagging indicators, 682
Last-in, last-out (LIFO) method, 261–262
Lending indicators, 682
Lehman Investment Opportunity Notes (LIONs), 317
Leverage, 24
  real estate investment trusts (REITs), 631–632
Life insurance policies, savings deposits and, 305
Lifetime capital gains exemption, 272
Limited liability, 386
Limit orders, 19, 531
  limit order book 35, 533
  placement of, 35–36
  price, 19
  TSE, 35–36
Limit Order Trading System (LOTS), 36
Limit-stop orders, 20, 531
Line of best fit, 408
Line charts, 684–685
Liquidations, corporate bonds and, 326
Liquidity, 33, 220–223
  bonds, 339

Liquidity-motivated traders, 41
Liquidity preference theory, 95–97
Liquidity premium, 96
Listed securities, 33
LMH Fund, 484
Load funds, 627
Local government securities, *See* Provincial, Territorial and local government securities
Long hedgers, 586
Long-term bonds, 6
  *See* corporate bonds; Government of Canada bonds

**M**

Macroforecasting, 11
Maintenance margin, futures contracts, 591
Majority voting system, 387
Managed investment companies, 623–629
  closed-end companies, 625–626
  open-end companies, 626–269
Manager-client relations, 711
Margin:
  definition of, 21–24, 533
  options, 533–535
  performance margin, 590
Margin accounts, 21–24
  purchases, 22–24
    actual margin, 23, 28
    agreement, 21
    maintenance margin, futures contracts, 591
    minimum margin requirement, 22–23
  short sales, 25–29
Margin call, 24, 28
Marginal efficiency of capital, 79
Marginal tax rate, 256, 266
Markdown, 39
Marked to the market account, 24
Market capitalization, 47
Market discount function, 84
Market efficiency, 72–73